BEST BOOKS FOR CHILDREN

BEST BOOKS
FOR CHILDREN

Preschool Through
the Middle Grades

EDITED BY John T. Gillespie
AND Christine B. Gilbert

THIRD EDITION

R. R. Bowker Company / New York & London, 1985

Published by R. R. Bowker Company,
  a division of Reed Publishing USA
245 West 17th Street, New York, NY 10011
Copyright © 1985 by Reed Publishing USA,
  a division of Reed Holdings, Inc.
All rights reserved
Printed and bound in the United States of America

Second printing

Library of Congress Cataloging-in-Publication Data

Gillespie, John Thomas, 1928–
  Best books for children, preschool through the
middle grades.

  Includes indexes.
  1. Bibliography—Best books—Children's literature.
2. Children's literature—Bibliography.   3. School
libraries—Book lists.   I. Gilbert, Christine Bell,
1909–   .   II. Title.
Z1037.G48   1985   [PN1009.A1]   011'.62   85-17417
ISBN 0-8352-2131-8

Contents

Preface

This is the third edition of *Best Books for Children*, the first being published in 1978 and the second in 1981. As with the earlier editions, the primary aim of this work is to provide a list of books, gathered from a number of sources, that are highly recommended to satisfy both a child's recreational reading needs and the demands of a typical school curriculum. For greatest depth, coverage has been limited to the age group including preschool children through advanced readers in the sixth grade. Although many of the listed titles indicate use with junior high school students, it is not the intent to give complete coverage for this group.

Of the approximately 11,000 titles included in this book, about 9,240 are individual entries, and over half of these titles are new to this edition. The remainder are related titles covering similar material; they are mentioned in the annotations and can be used with the main entry. When the author of both the main entry and additional title(s) is the same, the author's name is not repeated in the annotation. Instances of similar coverage but differing grade suitability are noted. In fiction areas, multiple listings within the annotations are used primarily for books in a series or sequels. These titles are listed by publication date, the earliest publication date first, not by recommendation or alphabetical sequence. However, in some cases with a large number of titles in a series, an additional entry sometimes has been used. On the other hand, some series are so extensive that, due to space limitations, only representative titles could be included.

For a title to be considered for listing, the basic requirement was multiple recommendations (usually three) in the sources consulted. However, because many of these sources give scant coverage to books that are primarily curriculum-oriented, the number of necessary recommendations for nonfiction titles was sometimes lowered. Beyond this, additional criteria included such obvious considerations as availability, up-to-dateness, accuracy, usefulness, and relevance.

Several sources were used to compile this annotated bibliography. At the outset there was a thorough perusal and evaluation of the entries in the 1981 edition of *Best Books for Children*. All out-of-print titles were dropped, as well as those that were considered no longer relevant or suitable. The other sources consulted were numerous and varied. A review was made of such retrospective sources as *Children's Catalog* (H. W. Wilson) and *The Elementary School Library Collection* (Bro-Dart), but the major tools were current periodicals and annual bibliographies, including *Children's Books* (Library of Congress), *Notable Children's Books* (Association for Library Service to Children), and *Children's Books* (New York Public Library), as well as semiannual roundups in *School Library Journal* and yearly subject listings such as "Outstanding Science Trade Books for Children" (*Science and Children*) and "Notable Children's Trade Books in the Field of Social Studies" (*Social Education*). Many special subject bibliographies also were used. Current book reviewing periodicals were consulted—specifically those issues from June

1980 through December 1984 of four periodicals: *Booklist, Bulletin of Center for Children's Books, Horn Book,* and *School Library Journal.*

It is our hope that this bibliography will be used in four different ways: (1) as a tool to evaluate the adequacy of existing collections, (2) as a book selection instrument for beginning and expanding collections, (3) as an aid for giving reading guidance to children, and (4) as a tool for the preparation of bibliographies and reading lists. To increase the book's usefulness, particularly in the two latter areas, it was decided to arrange the chosen titles under broad interest areas or, as in the case of nonfiction works, by curriculum-oriented subjects rather than by using the Dewey Decimal Classification System for nonfiction and an alphabetical-by-author entry for fiction. In this way, analogous titles that otherwise would have been separated are brought together and can be seen in relation to other important books on the same broad topic. In this regard some arbitrary decisions had to be made. Some examples: all materials on holidays, regardless of their scope (e.g., books on holiday crafts or holiday poetry), were grouped together under the individual holiday (e.g., Christmas); books of mathematical puzzles are placed in the mathematical section and books of science experiments and projects, though often dealing with a particular branch of science, are all grouped under Science—Experiments. There are also a few new subject headings in this edition, including a large section on computers and automation. Such mass market series as *Nancy Drew* and *The Hardy Boys* books have not been included, though individual libraries might wish to purchase them.

Users of previous editions will note that, because of changing emphases in the publishing world, coverage patterns are different in the third edition. There are more recommended fiction titles, more paperback editions, and more ephemeral material like sports biographies and books on curiosities than previously. On the other hand, coverage in such areas as history, geography, and the social sciences has often been decimated through allowing many standard titles to go out-of-print and not replacing them with recommendable substitutes.

A typical entry in the main section contains the following information: (1) author, (2) title, (3) suitable grade levels, (4) indication of illustrations, or illustrator's name where appropriate, (5) date of publication, (6) publisher, (7) price and editions where applicable—LB=library binding, paper=paperback, and (8) annotation. Bibliographical information and prices were verified in *Children's Books in Print,* 1983–1984 (R. R. Bowker Co.) and some publishers' catalogs.

Titles in the main section of this book are given an entry number. To facilitate quick reference, all listings in the indexes refer the user to the entry number, not the page number. *Best Books for Children* includes four indexes—an index of authors/illustrators; one of book titles; one of biographical subjects (individual biographies in the main section are arranged alphabetically under the name of the person who is the subject of the biography); and a subject index. The author index includes the book title(s) as well as the entry number(s). Joint authors' names do not include the book title(s), but are easily identifiable by (jt. auth.) and the entry number(s). Illustrators are listed with entry number(s) only.

Dozens of people were involved in the preparation of this bibliography—specifically we would like to mention the contributions of Bette Vander Werf, and our many helpers at Bowker. To all of you many thanks. We hope that our collected efforts have produced a book of value and use.

Alphabet, Counting, and Concept Books

Alphabet Books

1. Alda, Arlene. *Arlene Alda's ABC* (1–3). 1981, Celestial Arts paper $8.95. Letters are shown in patterns revealed in photographs.

2. Alexander, Anne. *ABC of Cars and Trucks* (PS–1). 1971, Doubleday $8.95; paper $1.95. All sorts of cars are described in pictures and verse.

3. Anglund, Joan Walsh. *In a Pumpkin Shell* (PS–2). Illus. by author. 1960, Harcourt $8.95; paper $2.95. A Mother Goose ABC book.

4. Anno, Mitsumasa. *Anno's Alphabet: An Adventure in Imagination* (PS–2). 1975, Harper $10.53; LB $10.89. A most unusual and distinctive alphabet book that shows the letters as pieces of rough-grained wood and, on the opposite pages, objects beginning with that letter. An excellent introduction to art as well.

5. Arnosky, Jim. *Mouse Writing* (K–2). Illus. by author. 1983, Harcourt LB $10.95. Two skating mice make capital letters.

6. Azarian, Mary. *A Farmer's Alphabet* (PS–2). Illus. by author. 1981, Godine $14.95; paper $7.95. A beautifully illustrated book with two-color woodcuts.

7. Balian, Lorna. *Humbug Potion: An A B Cipher* (1–2). Illus. 1984, Abingdon $12.95. Each letter is given a number (1 to 26) in this unusual alphabet book.

8. Baskin, Leonard, illus. *Hosie's Alphabet* (PS–1). Words by Hosea Tobias and Lisa Baskin. 1972, Viking $10.00. A highly sophisticated dazzling picture book, which is more of an art experience than an alphabet book.

9. Bayer, Jane. *A, My Name Is Alice* (K–3). Illus. by Steven Kellogg. 1984, Dutton $10.63; LB $10.89. Through the alphabet with jump rope rhymes.

10. Beller, Janet. *A-B-Cing: An Action Alphabet* (PS–2). Illus. 1984, Crown $8.95. The ABCs illustrated through various actions.

11. Berger, Terry, and Kandell, Alice S. *Ben's ABC Day* (PS). Illus. 1982, Lothrop $11.25; LB $11.88. The alphabet is introduced by everyday activities.

12. Bourke, Linda. *Handmade ABC: A Manual Alphabet* (2–4). 1981, Addison LB $7.95; paper $3.95. Illustrations show a printed alphabet and a manual one.

13. Boynton, Sandra. *A Is for Angry* (PS–K). Illus. 1983, Workman $9.95. Adjectives are used in this alphabet book.

14. Broomfield, Robert. *The Baby Animal ABC* (PS–1). 1968, Penguin paper $2.95. Pictures of animals and their young are used in this ABC book.

15. Brown, Marcia. *All Butterflies: An ABC* (PS–K). Illus. by author. 1972, Scribners $9.95; paper $2.95. Handsome woodcuts show a variety of creatures in various settings in this delightful alphabet book.

16. Bruna, Dick. *B Is for Bear* (PS–K). Illus. 1977, Methuen $5.50. A simple ABC book with a 2-page spread devoted to each letter and a pictured object.

17. Burton, Marilee Robin. *Aaron Awoke* (PS–1). Illus. by author. 1982, Harper $9.13; LB $8.89. An alphabet book that tells a story about Aaron.

18. Chess, Victoria. *Alfred's Alphabet Walk* (PS–1). Illus. by author. 1979, Greenwillow $10.95; LB $10.51. Alliteration is used to highlight a boy's walk through the ABCs.

19. Crews, Donald. *We Read: A to Z* (PS–1). 1984, Greenwillow $11.00; LB $10.51. A reissue of the 1967 alphabet book.

20. Crowther, Robert. *The Most Amazing Hide-and-Seek Book* (PS–1). 1978, Viking $11.95. Hidden animals are revealed when the reader uses this push/pull alphabet book.

21. De Brunhoff, Laurent. *Babar's ABC* (PS–1). Illus. by author. 1983, Random $5.95; LB $6.99. The beloved elephant now has his own alphabet book.

22. Duke, Kate. *The Guinea Pig ABC* (PS–1). Illus. by author. 1983, Dutton $9.66. An alphabet book featuring lively guinea pigs.

23. Duvoisin, Roger. *A for the Ark* (K–2). Illus. by author. 1952, Lothrop $11.64. A new kind of alphabet book woven around the Old Testament story of the Flood.

24. Eichenberg, Fritz. *Ape in a Cape: An Alphabet of Odd Animals* (PS–1). Illus. by author. 1952, Harcourt paper $3.95. Each letter of the alphabet is represented by a full-page color picture of an animal with a brief nonsense rhyme explaining it.

25. Emberley, Ed. *Ed Emberley's A B C* (PS–1). Illus. by author. 1978, Little $6.95. Each letter is related to an animal in this amusing, often zany treatment.

26. Falls, C. B. *A B C Book* (PS–1). Illus. by author. 1957, Doubleday $8.95; paper $1.95. A lovely alphabet book first published in 1922.

27. Farber, Norma. *As I Was Crossing Boston Common* (K–3). Illus. by Arnold Lobel. 1982, Creative Arts paper $3.95. An alphabetical parade of unusual animals crosses Boston Common at a slow stately pace in this humorous, imaginative picture book.

28. Feelings, Muriel. *Jambo Means Hello: Swahili Alphabet Book* (K–3). Illus. by Tom Feelings. 1981, Dial paper $3.50. An alphabet book that concentrates on the positive, beautiful aspects of African-Swahili life.

29. Gag, Wanda. *The A B C Bunny* (PS–1). Illus. by author. 1933, Putnam $8.95; paper $2.95. Bunny scampers through the alphabet in this classic ABC book.

30. Hague, Kathleen. *Alphabears: An ABC Book* (PS–K). Illus. by Michael Hague. 1984, Holt $10.45. Twenty-six different lovable bears are introduced, one for each letter.

31. Harrison, Ted. *A Northern Alphabet: A Is for Arctic* (K–2). Illus. 1982, Tundra $12.95. Scenes, people, and objects associated with the Far North are used in this alphabet book.

32. Hoban, Tana. *A, B, See!* (PS). Illus. 1982, Greenwillow $10.00; LB $10.88. A type of silhouette is used to illustrate the ABCs.

33. Hyman, Trina S. *A Little Alphabet* (K–2). Illus. by author. 1980, Little $4.95. An alphabet book that also supplies puzzles.

34. Isadora, Rachel. *City Seen from A to Z* (PS–2). Illus. by author. 1983, Greenwillow $8.00; LB $7.63. Everyday objects in the city are used in this alphabet book.

35. Johnson, Crockett. *Harold's ABC* (PS–1). Illus. by author. 1981, Harper paper $1.95. With his magic purple crayon, Harold journeys from A to Z.

36. Kitchen, Bert. *Animal Alphabet* (PS–2). Illus. by author. 1984, Dial $11.60. A stylistic ABC book using both familiar and unfamiliar animals.

37. Lalicki, Barbara, comp. *If There Were Dreams to Sell* (PS–2). Illus. by Margot Tomes. 1984, Lothrop $11.50; LB $11.04. Each letter of the alphabet is represented by a poem.

38. Lear, Edward. *An Edward Lear Alphabet* (K–3). Illus. by Carol Newsom. 1983, Lothrop $9.50; LB $9.12. An alphabet book with accompanying nonsense verses.

39. Lobel, Arnold. *On Market Street* (PS–1). Illus. by Anita Lobel. 1981, Greenwillow $11.25; LB $10.80. A merry alphabet book with objects from apples to zippers.

40. Matthiesen, Thomas. *ABC: An Alphabet Book* (PS). Illus. 1981, Grosset $3.95; LB $3.09. An alphabet book using photos of familiar objects.

41. Merriam, Eve. *Good Night to Annie* (PS–1). Illus. by John Wallner. 1980, Four Winds $8.95. A bedtime alphabet book that shows how animals rest.

42. Miles, Miska. *Apricot ABC* (K–3). Illus. by Peter Parnall. 1969, Little $8.95. An ABC in which fauna and flora are interspersed with the rhymes about what happens to an apricot.

43. Miller, Jane. *Farm Alphabet Book* (PS–K). Illus. 1984, Prentice $7.95. Photographs of farm life make an unusual ABC book.

44. Milne, A. A. *Pooh's Alphabet Book* (1–3). Illus. by Ernest H. Shepard. 1975, Dutton $4.95. A delightful collection of quotations from Milne's works arranged in alphabet-book format.

45. Munari, Bruno. *Bruno Munari's ABC* (PS–1). Illus. by author. 1960, Putnam paper $5.95. An ABC book with characteristic, vibrant illustrations.

46. Nedobeck, Don. *Nedobeck's Alphabet Book* (PS–K). Illus. by author. 1981, Childrens Pr. LB $10.60; Ideals paper $3.95. Large, clear illustrations enliven this alphabet book.

47. Newberry, Clare Turlay. *Kittens ABC* (PS–1). Illus. by author. 1965, Harper $12.95. The lifelike illustrations of kittens are bound to enchant children as they learn the alphabet.

48. Niland, Deborah. *ABC of Monsters* (PS–K). Illus. by author. 1978, McGraw $4.95. Monsters perform antics that represent each letter of the alphabet.

49. Obligado, Lilian. *Faint Frogs Feeling Feverish and Other Terrifically Tantalizing Tongue Twisters* (K–3). Illus. by author. 1983, Viking $12.05. The alphabet is explained through tongue twisters.

50. Oxenbury, Helen. *Helen Oxenbury's ABC of Things* (PS–K). Illus. by author. 1983, Delacorte $12.95; LB $13.95. Groups of unlikely animals and objects are pictured together in this imaginative and humorous alphabet book.

51. Provensen, Alice, and Provensen, Martin, illus. *A Peaceable Kingdom: The Abecedarius* (PS–K). 1978, Viking $9.95; Penguin paper $3.95. A newly illustrated version of Shaker's "Animal Rhymes" first published in 1882.

52. Rey, H. A. *Curious George Learns the Alphabet* (K–2). Illus. by author. 1963, Houghton paper $3.50. George makes learning the alphabet a wonderful and amusing game.

53. Rockwell, Anne. *Albert B. Cub and Zebra: An Alphabet Storybook* (K–2). Illus. 1977, Harper $11.49; LB $11.89. An interesting alphabet book in which readers are supposed to identify objects beginning with a specific letter.

54. Seuss, Dr. *Dr. Seuss' ABC* (K–2). Illus. by author. 1963, Random $4.95; LB $5.99. A master author creates a strikingly popular alphabet book.

55. Stevenson, James. *Grandpa's Great City Tour: An Alphabet Book* (1–3). Illus. by author. 1983, Greenwillow LB $10.88. Grandpa tours the city from A to Z.

56. Tudor, Tasha. *A Is for Annabelle* (PS–1). Illus. by author. 1954, Walck paper $3.95. Two little girls play with an elegant old-fashioned doll in this alphabet book.

57. Watson, Clyde. *Applebet: An ABC* (PS–2). Illus. by Wendy Watson. 1982, Farrar $10.95. An alphabet book in which apples and a country fair provide the links from letter to letter.

58. Weil, Lisl. *Owl and Other Scrambles* (PS–3). Illus. by author. 1980, Dutton $8.95. A puzzle book that deals with letters and simple words.

59. Yolen, Jane. *All in the Woodland Early: An ABC Book* (PS). Music and lyrics by author. Illus. by Jane Breskin Zalben. 1979, Collins $8.95; LB $8.91; Putnam paper $5.95. An ABC book in rhyme that uses animals to bring the letters to life.

Counting Books

60. Anno, Mitsumasa. *Anno's Counting Book: An Adventure in Imagination* (PS–K). 1977, Harper $10.53; LB $10.89. An appealing book on numbers in which the same landscapes are used throughout; houses, birds, trees, and people are added as the seasons progress.

61. Anno, Mitsumasa. *Anno's Counting House* (1–3). Illus. by author. 1982, Putnam $12.95. A way for adults to teach counting.

62. Baker, Jeannie. *One Hungry Spider* (K–3). Illus. by author. 1983, Dutton $9.95. The activities of spiders are used in this counting book.

63. Bang, Molly. *Ten, Nine, Eight* (PS–1). Illus. by author. 1983, Greenwillow $9.55. A counting-down book (from 10 to 1) involving a black child going to bed.

64. Becker, John. *Seven Little Rabbits* (K–2). Illus. by Barbara Cooney. 1973, Walker LB $5.85. A counting book in reverse with charming colored sketches.

65. Boynton, Sandra. *Hippos Go Berserk* (PS–K). Illus. by author. 1979, Little $7.95; paper $3.95. A counting book in rhymes about several hippos.

66. Bruna, Dick. *I Know about Numbers* (PS). Illus. 1981, Methuen $2.95. A very simple 1 to 10 counting book.

67. Burningham, John. *Count Up: Learning Sets* (PS–K). Illus. 1983, Viking $4.95. A preschool mathematics concept book. Others in this series are: *Five Down: Numbers as Signs; Just Cats: Learning Groups; Pigs Plus: Learning Addition; Read One: Numbers as Words; Ride Off: Learning Subtraction* (all 1983, $4.95).

68. Cleveland, David. *The April Rabbits* (PS–1). Illus. by Nurit Karlin. 1978, Putnam $7.95. The days of the month and a group of rabbits are used in this counting book.

69. Crowther, Robert. *The Most Amazing Hide-and Seek Counting Book* (PS–1). 1981, Viking $11.95. A toy book with all sorts of hidden animals.

70. Cushman, Doug. *The Pudgy Fingers Counting Book* (PS). Illus. by author. 1983, Grosset $2.95. A counting book for the very young.

71. Eichenberg, Fritz. *Dancing in the Moon* (PS). Illus. by author. 1955, Harcourt $12.95; paper $1.85. Simple animal nonsense rhymes that use each number from 1 to 20.

72. Feelings, Muriel. *Moja Means One: Swahili Counting Book* (K–3). Illus. by Tom Feelings. 1971, Dial $10.95; paper $2.50. The sights and sounds of East Africa come alive in this charming counting book.

73. Friskey, Margaret. *Chicken Little, Count to Ten* (PS–1). Illus. by Katherine Evans. 1946, Childrens Pr. $9.25. Not one of the 10 animals questioned can tell Chicken Little how to drink. Also use: *One to Ten, Count Again* by Elaine Livermore (1973, Houghton $7.95).

74. Gerstein, Mordicai. *Roll Over!* (PS–K). Illus. 1984, Crown $5.95. A counting rhyme that starts with 10 in a bed until someone says "Roll over."

75. Ginsburg, Mirra. *Kitten from One to Ten* (PS–K). Illus. by Giulio Maestro. 1980, Crown LB $7.95. A kitten finds various objects in this simple counting book.

76. Hawkins, Colin. *Adding Animals* (PS–2). 1983, Putnam $9.95. Simple addition problems are posed in this pop-up book.

77. Hawkins, Colin. *Take Away Monsters* (PS–2). 1984, Putnam $9.95. Subtraction is taught through monsters in the book that uses tabs to change the pictures.

78. Hoban, Tana. *Count and See* (PS–K). Illus. 1972, Macmillan $10.95; paper $2.25. Beginning with numbers 1 to 15, then going to 100; clear photographs of familiar objects are easily recognized and fun to count.

79. Hutchins, Pat. *One Hunter* (PS–2). Illus. by author. 1982, Greenwillow $10.25; LB $10.88. A counting book with a hunter and hidden African animals.

80. Kredenser, Gail. *One Dancing Drum* (PS–1). Illus. by Stan Mack. 1971, Phillips $10.95. Colorful book in which musicians march across the pages in increasing numbers.

81. Langstaff, John. *Over in the Meadow* (PS–1). Illus. by Feodor Rojankovsky. 1957, Harcourt $8.95; paper $2.25. Based on an old animal counting song.

82. Le Sieg, Theo. *Wacky Wednesday* (PS–1). Illus. by George Booth. 1974, Random $4.95. In this counting book, every page has a number of things out of place.

83. Lewin, Betsy. *Cat Count* (PS–3). Illus. by author. 1981, Dodd LB $6.95. A humorous counting book involving cats.

84. Mack, Stan. *Ten Bears in My Bed: A Goodnight Countdown* (PS–K). Illus. 1974, Pantheon LB $7.99. In this children's favorite, based on a counting song, when the "little one" says "Roll over, Roll over," one by one the bears leave the bed.

85. McLeod, Emilie W. *One Snail and Me: A Book of Numbers and Animals and a Bathtub* (K–2). Illus. by Walter Lorraine. 1961, Little $9.95; paper $4.95. Counting is easy when you start with one little girl in a bathtub and add up the animals bathing with her.

86. Marshall, Ray, and Paul, Korky. *Pop-Up Numbers: #1 Addition* (K–2). 1984, Dutton $3.85. A pop-up book that illustrates very simple addition problems. Others in this series are: *Pop-Up Numbers: #2 Subtraction; Pop-Up Numbers: #3 Multiplication; Pop-Up Numbers: #4 Division* (all 1984, $3.95).

87. Mathews, Louise. *Cluck One* (PS–1). Illus. by Jeni Bassett. 1982, Dodd LB $9.95. Every night Weasel adds another egg to Mrs. Cluck's nest.

88. Miller, Jane. *Farm Counting Book* (PS–1). Illus. 1983, Prentice $6.95. A counting book using photographs of farm animals.

89. Milne, A. A. *Pooh's Counting Book* (PS). Illus. by Ernest H. Shepard. 1982, Dutton $4.95. Quotes from the Pooh books are used as the basis of a counting book.

90. Nedobeck, Don. *Nedobeck's Numbers Book* (PS–K). Illus. by author. 1981, Childrens Pr. LB $10.60; Ideals paper $3.95. Big, simple pictures are used to illustrate each of the numbers.

91. Noll, Sally. *Off and Counting* (PS–K). Illus. by author. 1984, Greenwillow $10.00; LB $9.55. A frog counts the animals pictured on each page.

92. Oxenbury, Helen. *Numbers of Things* (PS–2). Illus. by author. 1968, Delacorte $9.95. An imaginative and intriguing tall counting book with handsome, humorous illustrations.

93. Pavey, Peter. *One Dragon's Dream* (PS–1). Illus. by author. 1979, Bradbury $9.95. A counting book plus the masochistic reveries of a dragon.

94. Peek, Merle. *Roll Over! A Counting Song* (PS). Illus. by author. 1981, Houghton $8.95. A counting book from 10 to 1 about animals in a bed.

95. Peppe, Rodney. *Little Numbers* (PS). Illus. 1984, Viking $2.95. A board book that introduces numbers to toddlers.

96. Peppe, Rodney. *Odd One Out* (K–2). Illus. by author. 1974, Viking LB $9.95; Penguin paper $2.95. Several everyday activities are pictured, but each illustration contains some element that is out of place.

97. Pomerantz, Charlotte. *One Duck, Another Duck* (PS). Illus. by Jose Aruego and Ariane Dewey. 1984, Greenwillow $10.00; LB $9.55. Danny tries to count ducks but has problems.

98. Reiss, John J. *Numbers* (PS–1). Illus. by author. 1971, Bradbury $10.95. A number recognition book.

99. Russell, Sandra Joanne. *A Farmer's Dozen* (PS–1). Illus. by author. 1982, Harper $9.57; LB $8.89. A farmer adds to his household in this counting book that goes to 12.

100. Scarry, Richard. *Richard Scarry's Best Counting Book Ever* (PS–3). Illus. by author. 1975, Random $6.95; LB $6.99. Willy Bunny counts everything he sees in this counting book that goes to 100.

101. Sendak, Maurice. *Seven Little Monsters* (K–2). Illus. by author. 1977, Harper $8.61; LB $8.89; paper $1.95. A counting book involving monsters that townspeople try to eliminate.

102. Stobbs, Joanna, and Stobbs, William. *One Sun, Two Eyes, and a Million Stars* (PS–K). Illus. by author. 1983, Oxford $7.95. A counting book that goes from 1 to 20.

103. Testa, Fulvio. *If You Take a Pencil* (2–6). Illus. by author. 1982, Dial $10.95. A handsome collection of pictures is used in this counting book.

104. Thompson, Susan L. *One More Thing, Dad* (PS–2). Illus. by Dora Leder. 1980, Whitman LB $8.75. A simple counting book involving a boy going out of the house.

105. Tudor, Tasha. *1 Is One* (K–2). Illus. by author. 1956, Rand McNally paper $3.95. Original verses with delicate pastel illustrations.

106. Warren, Cathy. *The Ten-Alarm Camp-Out* (PS–2). Illus. by Steven Kellogg. 1983, Lothrop $9.50; LB $9.12. A counting book about Mama Armadillo and her 9 children.

107. Wells, Rosemary. *Max's Toys: A Counting Book* (K–1). Illus. by author. 1979, Dial $3.50. A highly original book that uses toys to introduce numbers 1 through 10.

108. Yolen, Jane. *An Invitation to the Butterfly Ball* (PS). Illus. by Jane Breskin Zalben. 1983, Putnam $5.95. A counting rhyme book that has been a favorite.

109. Youldon, Gillian. *Counting* (PS–1). Illus. by James Hodgson. 1980, Watts $2.95; LB $5.90. A 1 to 10 counting book involving animals.

110. Youldon, Gillian. *Numbers* (PS–K). Illus. 1979, Watts LB $5.90. Outdoor scenes and split pages point up the values of various numbers.

111. Zaslavsky, Claudia. *Count on Your Fingers African Style* (K–3). Illus. by Jerry Pinkney. 1980, Harper $9.57; LB $9.89. A survey on how African tribes use their fingers to count.

Concept Books

General

112. Aliki. *Feelings* (K–2). 1984, Greenwillow $10.00. An introduction to various emotions.

113. Barrett, Judith. *What's Left?* (PS). Illus. by author. 1983, Atheneum $10.95. A series of questions and answers involving everyday occurrences.

114. Berenstain, Stanley. *Inside, Outside, Upside Down* (PS–1). Illus. by author. 1968, Random $4.99; LB $5.99. A bear has a brief trip that explains various concepts.

115. Bester, Roger. *Guess What?* (PS). Illus. 1980, Crown $7.95. A guessing game featuring common animals.

116. Burningham, John. *Sniff Shout* (PS). 1984, Viking $4.95. A preschool vocabulary book. Two others in the series are: *Skip Trip* (1984, $4.95); *Wobble Pop* (1984, $5.95).

117. Cendrars, Blaise. *Shadow* (K–3). Trans. and illus. by Marcia Brown. 1982, Scribners $12.95. The Caldecott Medal winner that explores the mysterious world of shadows.

118. Crews, Donald. *Light* (PS–1). Illus. by author. 1981, Greenwillow $10.25; LB $9.84. Light in various situations is explored in this book.

119. Di Fiori, Lawrence. *My First Word Book* (PS). Illus. 1983, Macmillan $2.95. A few familiar items are captioned and pictured.

120. Duke, Kate. *Guinea Pigs Far and Near* (PS–1). 1984, Dutton $9.66. Concepts such as "far" and "near" are introduced by a group of guinea pigs.

121. Gillham, Bill. *The Early Words Picture Book* (PS). Illus. by Sam Grainger. 1983, Putnam $7.95. Color photos of familiar objects and illustrations of children relating to them.

122. Gillham, Bill. *The First Words Picture Book* (PS). Illus. 1982, Putnam $7.95. A book of pictures and text that shows words that children first speak.

123. Goor, Ron, and Goor, Nancy. *Shadows: Here, There, and Everywhere* (PS–3). Illus. 1981, Harper $9.57; LB $9.89. A simple book that explains what shadows are and how to make them.

124. Hazen, Barbara S. *The Me I See* (1–2). Illus. by Ati Forberg. 1978, Abingdon $6.95. About how each person is different.

125. Hoban, Tana. *More Than One* (K–2). Illus. by author. 1981, Greenwillow $11.25; LB $11.88. A group of photographs illustrate collective nouns.

126. Hoban, Tana. *Push, Pull, Empty, Full: A Book of Opposites* (PS). Illus. by author. 1972, Macmillan $9.95. Clear photographs show pictures that illustrate opposites and help young children learn the principle of comparison.

127. Hoberman, Mary Ann. *A House Is a House for Me* (K–2). Illus. by Betty Fraser. 1978, Viking $7.95; Penguin paper $3.95. This picture book explores the idea that various objects can serve as houses.

128. Holzenthaler, Jean. *My Hands Can* (PS). Illus. by Nancy Tafuri. 1978, Dutton $7.95. All sorts of things that hands can do, such as button buttons.

129. Klein, Leonore. *Old, Older, Oldest* (1–3). Illus. by Leonard Kessler. 1983, Hastings $9.95. The concepts of age and life spans are introduced.

130. Krauss, Ruth. *A Hole Is to Dig* (PS). Illus. by Maurice Sendak. 1952, Harper $7.64; LB $8.89. Child-perceived definitions, such as "the world is so you have something to stand on," complemented by whimsical drawings.

131. Lewis, Steven. *Zoo City* (K–3). Illus. by author. 1976, Greenwillow $11.25. Commonplace articles are matched with look-alike animals.

132. Lionni, Leo. *When?* (PS). Illus. by author. 1983, Pantheon $3.95. The 4 seasons plus night and day are introduced in this wordless book. Others in the series are: *What?; Where?; Who?* (all 1983, $3.95).

133. McMillan, Bruce. *Here a Chick, There a Chick* (PS–1). Illus. 1983, Lothrop $10.18. Synonyms and antonyms are explained through the actions of a chick.

134. McNaughton, Colin. *At Home* (PS). Illus. by author. 1982, Putnam $3.95. A group of opposites involving a chubby hero. Others in the series are: *At Playschool; At the Park; At the Party; At the Stores* (all 1982, $3.95).

135. Maestro, Betsy, and Maestro, Giulio. *Around the Clock with Harriet: A Book about Telling Time* (PS–2). Illus. by Giulio Maestro. 1984, Crown $10.95. An elephant goes through the day's activities in this book to help tell time.

136. Maestro, Betsy, and Maestro, Giulio. *Traffic: A Book of Opposites* (PS–2). Illus. by Giulio Maestro. 1981, Crown $8.95. Various forms of opposites are explored in this concept book.

137. Mathews, Louise. *The Great Take-Away* (K–2). Illus. by Jeni Bassett. 1980, Dodd LB $7.95. A concept book dealing with subtraction.

138. Matthias, Catherine. *Over-Under* (PS–1). Illus. by Gene Sharp. 1984, Childrens Pr. $6.50. Spatial concepts are explained in an easy-to-read format.

139. Olney, Ross R., and Olney, Patricia. *How Long? To Go, to Grow, to Know* (2–3). Illus. by R. W. Alley. 1984, Morrow $9.50; LB $9.12. Changes are explored in this concept book.

140. Parish, Peggy. *I Can—Can You? Level 1* (PS). Illus. by Marylin Hafner. 1984, Greenwillow $2.70. A series of activity concept board books that continues at levels 2, 3, and 4, all for preschoolers.

141. Raynor, Dorka. *My Friends Live in Many Places* (K–5). Illus. 1980, Whitman $8.75. Emotions and feelings displayed in 45 photographs of children from 23 countries.

142. Scarry, Richard. *Richard Scarry's Best Word Book Ever* (PS–2). Illus. by author. 1963, Western $6.95. A diverse, unorthodox picture dictionary for children who like lots of little pictures.

143. Scarry, Richard. *Richard Scarry's Lowly Worm Word Book* (PS). Illus. by author. 1981, Random $2.50. A tiny book showing familiar objects belonging to Lowly Worm.

144. Schwerin, Doris. *The Tomorrow Book* (PS). Illus. by Karen Gundersheimer. 1984, Pantheon $10.95; LB $10.99. A book that introduces the concept of time.

145. Sendak, Maurice. *The Nutshell Library* (PS–3). Illus. by author. 1962, Harper $8.95. Miniature volumes include: an alphabet book, *Alligators All Around,* and a counting book, *One Was Johnny* (both 1962, $9.89).

146. Spier, Peter. *Fast-Slow, High-Low: A Book of Opposites* (K–2). Illus. by author. 1972, Doubleday $9.95; paper $2.95. Delightful pictures in pairs that represent qualities—some very subtle—that are opposites. No text except headings.

147. Tafuri, Nancy. *All Year Long* (PS–1). Illus. by author. 1983, Greenwillow $10.00; LB $10.88. A journey through the months of the year and days of the week.

148. Wheeler, Cindy. *A Good Day, a Good Night* (PS). 1980, Harper LB $9.89. The concepts of night and day are explored in experiences of a cat and a robin.

149. Youldon, Gillian. *Time* (K–1). 1980, Watts $5.90. A split-page book that takes a child hour by hour through a single day.

150. Zolotow, Charlotte. *Some Things Go Together* (PS–2). Illus. by Karen Gundersheimer. 1983, Harper $8.61; LB $9.89. A rhyming picture book of things associated together.

151. Zolotow, Charlotte. *Someone New* (K–3). Illus. by Erik Blegvad. 1978, Harper LB $8.89. In a first-person narrative, a young boy realizes he is changing and growing up.

Colors

152. De Brunhoff, Laurent. *Babar's Book of Colors* (PS–1). 1984, Random $6.95; LB $7.99. Babar's children learn from him about colors.

153. Haskins, Ilma. *Color Seems* (PS–3). Illus. by author. 1974, Vanguard $9.95. An introduction to the world of color.

154. Hoban, Tana. *Is It Red? Is It Yellow? Is It Blue? An Adventure in Color* (PS). Illus. 1978, Morrow $10.95; Scholastic paper $1.95. Without words, this picture book explains the concept of color.

155. Kilroy, Sally. *Baby Colors* (PS–3). Illus. by author. 1983, Four Winds $4.95. A basic exploration of colors.

156. Kumin, Maxine. *What Color Is Caesar?* (K–3). Illus. by Evaline Ness. 1978, McGraw $8.95. A book about colors and how to distinguish them.

157. Lionni, Leo. *Little Blue and Little Yellow* (PS–1). Illus. by author. 1959, Astor-Honor $8.95. All the characters are blobs of color; an ingenious story intended to give the young child an awareness of color.

158. McGovern, Ann. *Black Is Beautiful* (PS–2). Illus. by Hope Warmfeld. 1969, Scholastic paper $1.50. A series of photographs show various objects and natural phenomena stressing the fact that black is beautiful.

159. Pienkowski, Jan. *Colors* (K–1). Illus. by author. 1981, Simon & Schuster $3.95. Ten objects are used as examples of colors.

160. Reiss, John J. *Colors* (PS–1). Illus. by author. 1969, Bradbury $10.95. Boldly designed to attract the youngest, the various hues of the primary and secondary colors, plus white (day) and black (night), are displayed in familiar forms and clearly labeled.

161. Testa, Fulvio. *If You Take a Paintbrush: A Book of Colors* (PS). Illus. by author. 1983, Dial $10.95. An explanation of colors and their uses.

Perception

162. Ahlberg, Janet, and Ahlberg, Allan. *Peek-a-Boo!* (PS). 1980, Viking $10.95; Penguin paper $3.95. Scenes are visible through a peep hole in each page.

163. Aruego, Jose, and Dewey, Ariane. *We Hide, You Seek* (PS). Illus. by author. 1979, Greenwillow $10.95; LB $10.58. An almost wordless picture book in which a rhinoceros sets out to find his friends who are playing hide-and-seek with him.

164. Baylor, Byrd. *The Other Way to Listen* (K–3). Illus. by Peter Parnall. 1978, Scribners $7.95. An old man teaches a young boy how to listen.

165. Brown, Marcia. *Touch Will Tell* (1–4). Illus. 1979, Watts LB $8.90. A concept book that explores a sense of touch and increases one's awareness.

166. Brown, Marcia. *Walk with Your Eyes* (1–4). Illus. 1979, Watts LB $8.90. A reader's powers of observation are highlighted through a nature walk.

167. Daughtry, Duanne. *What's Inside?* (PS–K). Illus. 1984, Knopf $7.95; LB $8.99. A wordless book about what is inside common objects like a pea pod.

168. Domanska, Janina. *What Do You See?* (PS–1). Illus. by author. 1974, Macmillan $9.95. The frog, the fly, the fern, and the bat each see the world from a different point of view in this vibrantly illustrated book.

169. Gardner, Beau. *The Look Again . . . and Again, and Again, and Again Book* (K–4). Illus. by author. 1984, Lothrop $10.50; LB $10.08. A successful turnaround book that uses the reader's powers of observation.

170. Gardner, Beau. *The Turn About, Think About, Look About Book* (K–4). Illus. by author. 1980, Lothrop $10.00; LB $10.88. This book, when turned around, reveals many new shapes and figures.

171. Goor, Ron, and Goor, Nancy. *Signs* (PS–2). Illus. 1983, Harper $9.57; LB $9.89. An introduction to over 50 different signs.

172. Hoban, Tana. *I Read Signs* (PS–2). Illus. by author. 1983, Greenwillow $10.00; LB $10.88. An introduction to some common signs and their meaning. Also use: *I Read Symbols* (1983, Greenwillow $10.00; LB $10.88).

173. Hoban, Tana. *I Walk and Read* (PS–2). Illus. by author. 1984, Greenwillow $10.00; LB $9.55. Common signs are encountered in various colored photographs.

174. Hoban, Tana. *Is It Rough? Is It Smooth? Is It Shiny?* (PS). Illus. by author. 1984, Greenwillow $10.25; LB $9.55. Textures are explored in a series of photographs.

175. Hoban, Tana. *Look Again!* (PS–2). Illus. by author. 1971, Macmillan $8.95. A concept book in which photographs of objects appear in part, as a whole, and then as a part within a composition.

176. Hoban, Tana. *Take Another Look* (PS–1). Illus. by author. 1981, Greenwillow $10.25; LB $9.84. A book that enables readers to guess what each picture really is.

177. Kilroy, Sally. *Noisy Homes* (PS–3). Illus. by author. 1984, Four Winds $2.95. A book that features common household sounds. Also use: *Animal Noises* (1983, Four Winds $2.95); *Babies' Bodies* (1984, Four Winds $2.95).

178. Kuskin, Karla. *Roar and More* (PS–1). Illus. by author. 1977, Harper paper $1.95. Poems and pictures portray the sounds that animals make.

179. Livermore, Elaine. *Find the Cat* (PS–2). Illus. by author. 1973, Houghton LB $10.95; paper $1.95. A puzzle book with a cat skillfully hidden in a series of pictures.

180. Maestro, Betsy, and Maestro, Giulio. *Harriet Reads Signs and More Signs* (PS–K). Illus. by author. 1981, Crown LB $8.95. An elephant learns how to read signs.

181. Morris, Neil, and Morris, Ting. *Find the Canary* (2–4). Illus. by Anna Clarke. 1983, Little $5.70. The reader is invited to find objects hidden in the pictures. Also use: *Hide and Seek; Search for Sam; Where's My Hat?* (all 1983, Little $5.70).

182. Newth, Philip. *Roly Goes Exploring* (K–2). 1981, Putnam $12.95. Subtitle: "A book for blind and sighted children, in Braille and standard type, with pictures to feel as well as to see."

183. Rey, H. A. *See the Circus* (K–3). 1956, Houghton paper $1.75. Under the flap on each page is a secret.

184. Shaw, Charles G. *It Looked Like Spilt Milk* (K–2). Illus. by author. 1947, Harper $10.89. White material appears on each page, but its identity is not revealed until the end.

185. Showers, Paul. *Find Out by Touching* (PS–3). Illus. by Robert Galster. 1961, Harper LB $10.89. The sense of touch explored in words and pictures. Also use: *Listening Walk* (1961, Harper $10.89).

186. Spier, Peter. *Crash! Bang! Boom!* (PS–1). Illus. by author. 1972, Doubleday $9.95; paper $2.95. The author captures the visual essence of a variety of sounds that come from inanimate objects.

187. Spier, Peter. *Gobble, Growl, Grunt* (PS–1). Illus. by author. 1971, Doubleday $10.95; paper $2.95. Over 600 colorful animals march across the pages, with text consisting of the sounds each makes.

188. Zacharias, Thomas, and Zacharias, Wanda. *But Where Is the Green Parrot?* (K–3). Illus. by author. 1968, Delacorte paper $2.75. A puzzle book in which a green parrot is artfully hidden in each of the 9 double-page illustrations.

Size and Shape

189. Brown, Marcia. *Listen to a Shape* (2–4). Illus. by author. 1979, Watts LB $8.90. A variety of shapes are explored in simple text and colored photographs.

190. Charlip, Remy, and Joyner, Jerry. *Thirteen* (1–3). Illus. by author. 1975, Parents $7.95; LB $8.59. A wordless concept book consisting of 13 picture sequences in which shapes evolve into new forms.

191. Emberley, Ed. *Ed Emberley's Amazing Look Through Book* (PS–1). Illus. by author. 1979, Little $4.95. A puzzle book in which youngsters must identify shapes.

192. Emberley, Ed. *The Wing on a Flea: A Book about Shapes* (PS–2). Illus. by author. 1961, Little $7.95. Through rhymes and colorful drawings, children are shown how to identify shapes in everyday objects around them.

193. Fisher, Leonard Everett. *Boxes! Boxes!* (PS–1). Illus. by author. 1984, Viking $9.95. An introduction to boxes of all sizes and shapes.

194. Hoban, Tana. *Circles, Triangles, and Squares* (PS–2). Illus. by author. 1974, Macmillan $10.95. A series of 5 photographs show the 3 most familiar geometric forms.

195. Hoban, Tana. *Over, Under and Through and Other Spacial Concepts* (K–2). Illus. by author. 1973, Macmillan $10.95. Spacial concepts are conveyed through brief text and photographs.

196. Hoban, Tana. *Round and Round and Round* (PS–1). Illus. 1983, Greenwillow $9.00; LB $8.59. A picture book of photographs of round objects.

197. Hoban, Tana. *Shapes and Things* (K–1). 1970, Macmillan $9.95. A recognition book that is a collection of photographs.

198. Jonas, Ann. *Holes and Peeks* (PS–K). Illus. by author. 1984, Greenwillow $10.00; LB $9.55. A young black child explains the difference between scary holes and pleasant objects to peek through.

199. Kalan, Robert. *Blue Sea* (K–3). Illus. by Donald Crews. 1979, Greenwillow $10.50. Big fish and little fish in the sea convey the idea of size.

200. Kohn, Bernice. *Everything Has a Shape and Everything Has a Size* (PS–1). Illus. by Aliki. 1966, Prentice paper $1.50. An introduction to the shapes and sizes of everyday things.

201. Kuskin, Karla. *Herbert Hated Being Small* (K–2). 1979, Houghton LB $6.95. A short boy and tall girl decide to run away.

202. Mathews, Louise. *Gator Pie* (1–3). Illus. by Jeni Bassett. 1979, Dodd $7.95. Fractions are taught when 2 alligators decide to cut up a pie for their friends.

203. Myller, Rolf. *How Big Is a Foot?* (K–2). Illus. by author. 1972, Atheneum paper $0.95. The problem of relative sizes, humorously and imaginatively described.

204. Rahn, Joan Elma. *Holes* (1–3). Illus. 1984, Houghton $9.95. An introduction to the concept of holes and their uses.

205. Reiss, John J. *Shapes* (PS–1). Illus. by author. 1974, Bradbury $10.95. Shapes, such as oval, circle, triangle, rectangle, and square, are presented to young children in vivid primary colors.

206. Satchwell, John. *Big and Little* (PS–K). 1984, Random $1.95. A beginning concept book. Others in this series are: *Counting; Odd One Out; Shapes* (all 1984, $1.95).

207. Schlein, Miriam. *Heavy Is a Hippopotamus* (K–2). 1984, Childrens Pr. $6.95. A concept book about weight.

208. Srivastava, Jane Jonas. *Spaces, Shapes and Sizes* (PS–2). Illus. by Loretta Lustig. 1980, Harper $10.53; LB $10.89. An easily read account that explains the concept of volume.

209. Testa, Fulvio. *If You Look around You* (PS–2). Illus. by author. 1983, Dial $10.63. Shapes and images are discussed in this picture book.

210. Wildsmith, Brian. *What the Moon Saw* (PS–1). Illus. by author. 1978, Oxford $9.95. The Sun shows the Moon many things that involve such basic concepts as numbers and weight.

Nursery Rhymes and Bedtime Books

Nursery Rhymes

211. Alderson, Brian, ed. *Cakes and Custard: Children's Rhymes* (K–4). Illus. by Helen Oxenbury. 1975, Morrow $11.28. A large, bounteous collection that extends from traditional nursery rhymes to the work of contemporary writers.

212. Bayley, Nicola, illus. *Nicola Bayley's Book of Nursery Rhymes* (PS–K). 1977, Knopf $7.95; LB $7.99. A luxuriously illustrated collection of well-known nursery rhymes.

213. Blake, Quentin. *Quentin Blake's Nursery Rhyme Book* (PS–K). Illus. by author. 1984, Harper $7.64; LB $8.89. Sixteen unusual rhymes charmingly illustrated.

214. Blegvad, Lenore, ed. *The Parrot in the Garret and Other Rhymes about Dwellings* (K–3). Illus. by Erik Blegvad. 1982, Atheneum LB $8.95. Each little rhyme is about a different kind of home and its inhabitant.

215. Blegvad, Lenore, ed. *This Little Pig-a-Wig and Other Rhymes about Pigs* (K–2). Illus. by Erik Blegvad. 1978, Atheneum $7.95. Twenty-two rhymes involved with the doings of pigs.

216. Bodecker, N. M., ed. and illus. *It's Raining Said John Twaining: Danish Nursery Rhymes* (PS–K). 1973, Atheneum $6.95; paper $1.95. Comic, detailed drawings illustrate this fresh collection of nursery rhymes that are Danish in origin but universal in appeal.

217. Briggs, Raymond, ed. and illus. *The Mother Goose Treasury* (PS–2). 1966, Putnam $16.95. Bold, humorous drawings bring fresh vitality to this collection of 408 rhymes.

218. Brooke, Leslie, illus. *Ring O'Roses* (PS–2). 1977, Warne $7.95. An action-filled series of pictures gaily illustrate these classic Mother Goose rhymes.

219. Caldecott, Randolph. *Randolph Caldecott's John Gilpin and Other Stories* (K–3). Illus. by author. 1977, Warne LB $9.95. Subtitle: "Containing: The diverting History of John Gilpin; The House that Jack Built; The Frog He Would a-Wooing Go; The Milkmaid."

220. Cauley, Lorinda Bryan. *The Three Little Kittens* (PS). Illus. by author. 1982, Putnam $7.95; paper $3.95. The familiar nursery rhyme charmingly illustrated.

221. Chorao, Kay, illus. *The Baby's Lap Book* (PS–K). 1977, Dutton $9.95. Soft pencil drawings illustrate such familiar Mother Goose rhymes as "Jack Be Nimble" and "Old King Cole."

222. De Angeli, Marguerite, illus. *Book of Nursery and Mother Goose Rhymes* (PS–2). 1954, Doubleday $14.95; paper $5.95. A collection of 376 rhymes illustrated in soft watercolors.

223. Domanska, Janina, illus. *I Saw a Ship A-Sailing* (PS–K). 1972, Macmillan $8.95. Geometric, stylized, bold colorful designs illustrate this well-known rhyme.

224. Fujikawa, Gyo, illus. *Mother Goose* (PS–1). 1968, Grosset $5.95; paper $2.95. An oversize book that contains 300 rhymes.

225. Galdone, Paul, illus. *Old Mother Hubbard and Her Dog* (PS–1). 1960, McGraw $9.95. Lively humorous illustrations accompany this favorite Mother Goose rhyme.

226. Galdone, Paul, illus. *The Old Woman and Her Pig* (K–2). 1960, McGraw $9.95. Delightful, quaint illustrations tell the cumulative story of the old woman who has difficulty getting her pig over the stile and safely home from market.

227. Hague, Michael, sel. *Mother Goose: A Collection of Classic Nursery Rhymes* (PS–K). Illus. by sel. 1984, Holt $12.45. Forty-five nursery rhymes delicately illustrated.

228. Hale, Sara Josepha. *Mary Had a Little Lamb* (PS–1). Illus. by Tomie de Paola. 1984, Holiday $13.95; paper $5.95. A nicely illustrated version of this nursery rhyme.

229. Harrop, Beatrice, sel. *Sing Hey Diddle Diddle: Sixty-Six Nursery Rhymes with Their Traditional Tunes* (PS–3). Illus. by Frank Francis and Bernard Cheese. 1983, Global Library $9.95. A spiral-bound songbook from England.

230. Ivimey, John W. *Complete Version of Ye Three Mice* (PS–2). Illus. by Walton Courbould. 1979, Warne $6.95. The traditional English nursery rhyme in an edition first published in 1904.

231. Jeffers, Susan, ed. and illus. *If Wishes Were Horses: Mother Goose Rhymes* (K–1). 1979, Dutton

11

$9.95. Eight Mother Goose rhymes involving horses.

232. Jeffers, Susan, ed. and illus. *Three Jovial Huntsmen* (K–2). 1973, Bradbury $10.95. All sorts of animals are well hidden in the forest picture as 3 hunters forage for their dinner.

233. Lewis, Bobby. *Home before Midnight: A Traditional Verse* (PS–1). Illus. by author. 1984, Lothrop $11.00; LB $10.51. In a variation on the old story, a woman can't get her pig through a subway turnstile.

234. Lines, Kathleen, comp. *Lavender's Blue: A Book of Nursery Rhymes* (PS–2). Illus. by Harold Jones. 1982, Merrimack $12.95. A standard collection now back in print.

235. Lobel, Arnold, illus. *Gregory Griggs and Other Nursery Rhyme People* (PS–1). 1978, Greenwillow LB $10.51. Out-of-the-ordinary nursery rhymes are included in this refreshingly different collection.

236. Marshall, James. *James Marshall's Mother Goose* (PS–1). Illus. by author. 1979, Farrar $7.95. An ebullient, breezy treatment of traditional material.

237. Martin, Sarah Catherine. *The Comic Adventures of Old Mother Hubbard and Her Dog* (PS–3). Illus. by Tomie de Paola. 1981, Harcourt $11.95; paper $5.95. A handsome version of the classic nursery rhyme.

238. Miller, Mitchell, ed. and illus. *One Misty Moisty Morning: Rhymes from Mother Goose* (PS–1). 1970, Farrar $3.95. Twenty-one little-known Mother Goose rhymes with full-page, storytelling pictures.

239. Moorat, Joseph, ed. *Thirty Old-Time Nursery Songs* (PS–3). Illus. by Paul Woodroffe. 1980, Norton $9.95. A reissue of a 1912 collection of Mother Goose rhymes.

240. Mulherin, Jennifer, ed. *Popular Nursery Rhymes* (K–Up). Illus. 1983, Grosset $8.95. A collection of 104 very popular rhymes.

241. Opie, Iona, and Opie, Peter. *A Nursery Companion* (PS–Up). Illus. 1980, Oxford $25.00. Over 20 tiny books, like *Old Mother Hubbard*, originally printed in the nineteenth century, reprinted in one volume.

242. Opie, Iona, and Opie, Peter, eds. *The Oxford Nursery Rhyme Book* (K–3). Illus. by Joan Hassall. 1955, Oxford $25.00. The most complete Mother Goose collection, with 800 rhymes for reading aloud. Also use: *The Opies Oxford Dictionary of Nursery Rhymes* (1951, Oxford $45.00).

243. Ormerod, Jan. *Rhymes around the Day* (PS). 1983, Lothrop $9.00; LB $8.59. Nursery rhymes are used to illustrate everyday happenings.

244. Patz, Nancy, retel. *Moses Supposes His Toeses Are Roses: And Seven Other Silly Old Rhymes* (K–3). Illus. by retel. 1983, Harcourt $12.95. Eight wonderful nonsense rhymes are well illustrated.

245. Peppe, Rodney, ed. and illus. *Hey Riddle Diddle!* (PS–3). 1979, Penguin paper $2.95. Forty-five Mother Goose rhymes surrounded with detailed collages that will offer surprises long after the riddles themselves have been solved.

246. Petersham, Maud, and Petersham, Miska, illus. *The Rooster Crows: A Book of American Rhymes and Jingles* (K–2). 1969, Macmillan $11.95. Rope skipping, counting, and other game rhymes form the bulk of this jaunty collection.

247. Provensen, Alice, and Provensen, Martin, illus. *The Mother Goose Book* (PS–K). 1976, Random $7.99. The familiar old favorites in eighteenth-century dress.

248. Provensen, Alice, and Provensen, Martin. *Old Mother Hubbard* (PS). Illus. by author. 1983, Random $4.95; paper $1.95. The Mother Goose rhyme charmingly illustrated.

249. Roche, P. K, sel. *Jump All the Morning: A Child's Day in Verse* (PS–1). Illus. by sel. 1984, Viking $9.95. Nursery rhymes show a child's everyday activities.

250. Rockwell, Anne. *Gray Goose and Gander and Other Mother Goose Rhymes* (PS–3). Illus. by author. 1980, Harper $9.95; LB $10.89. A fine collection of 56 of these traditional rhymes.

251. Roffey, Maureen. *The Grand Old Duke of York* (PS–K). Illus. by author. 1978, Bodley Head $6.95. A traditional rhyme illustrated with verve and daring.

252. Rojankovsky, Feodor, illus. *The Tall Book of Mother Goose* (PS). 1942, Harper $6.68; LB $7.89. These 100 old favorites are presented in an unusual format with bold illustrations.

253. Sendak, Maurice, illus. *Hector Protector, and As I Went over the Water* (K–1). 1965, Harper $11.49; LB $11.89. Two brief Mother Goose rhymes expanded with many drawings that make them both humorous and appealing.

254. Stobbs, William. *The House That Jack Built* (PS–K). Illus. 1983, Oxford $7.95. A fine rendering of the favorite nursery rhyme.

255. Stobbs, William. *This Little Piggy* (PS–K). Illus. by author. 1982, Bodley Head $8.95. A nicely illustrated version of this counting rhyme.

256. Tripp, Wallace, comp. *Granfa' Grig Had a Pig and Other Rhymes without Reason* (PS–2). Illus. by comp. 1976, Little $14.45; paper $8.70. A group of both familiar and unfamiliar nursery rhymes.

257. Tudor, Tasha, illus. *Mother Goose* (PS–2). 1944, McKay $8.95. A collection of 77 nursery rhymes with colored illustrations.

258. Weil, Lisl. *Mother Goose Picture Riddles: A Book of Rebuses* (PS–1). Illus. by author. 1981, Holiday LB $8.95. Rebuses on 21 familiar Mother Goose rhymes.

259. Wildsmith, Brian, illus. *Mother Goose* (PS–2). 1982, Oxford $11.95. Original artistic conceptions of the old rhymes with wonderful action in brilliantly colored animal and human figures.

260. Wright, Blanche Fisher, illus. *Real Mother Goose* (PS–3). 1916, Rand McNally $8.95; LB $5.97. Golden anniversary edition with introduction by May Hill Arbuthnot.

Bedtime Books

261. Alexander, Martha. *Maggie's Moon* (PS–1). Illus. by author. 1982, Dial $7.95; LB $7.89. A little girl tries to capture the moon.

262. Asch, Frank. *Goodnight Horsey* (PS–1). Illus. by author. 1981, Prentice $8.95; paper $4.95. A bedtime book that is brief and gentle.

263. Aylesworth, Jim. *Tonight's the Night* (K–2). Illus. by John Wallner. 1981, Whitman LB $8.75. Nocturnal sounds lead Daniel into a dream.

264. Barrett, Judith. *I Hate to Go to Bed* (K–3). Illus. by Ray Cruz. 1977, Scholastic $6.95. Various excuses for not going to sleep are exposed in a humorous text with detailed illustrations.

265. Brown, Margaret Wise. *A Child's Good Night Book* (PS–K). Illus. by Jean Charlot. 1950, Addison $8.95. Animals and children prepare for bed in this rhythmically told story.

266. Brown, Margaret Wise. *Goodnight Moon* (PS). Illus. by Clement Hurd. 1947, Harper $6.68; LB $7.89; paper $2.95. A soothing go-to-sleep story. A pop-up book version is: *The Goodnight Moon Room: A Pop-Up Book* (1984, Harper $8.61).

267. Burningham, John. *The Blanket* (PS–1). Illus. by author. 1976, Harper $3.95; LB $7.89. One night a young child can't find his blanket.

268. Chorao, Kay, sel. *The Baby's Bedtime Book* (PS–K). Illus. by sel. 1984, Dutton $11.60. Twenty-seven verses suitable for bedtime reading.

269. Christelow, Eileen. *Henry and the Dragon* (PS–K). Illus. by author. 1984, Houghton $10.95. Henry thinks he sees a dragon in his bedroom at bedtime.

270. Erskine, Jim. *Bedtime Story* (PS). Illus. by Ann Schweninger. 1982, Crown LB $8.95. A little boy goes to sleep as do many animal friends.

271. Gackenbach, Dick. *Poppy the Panda* (PS–K). Illus. by author. 1984, Houghton LB $11.95. Poppy the Panda doesn't want to go to bed, he hasn't anything nice to wear.

272. Ginsburg, Mirra, adapt. *The Sun's Asleep behind the Hill* (PS–1). Illus. by Paul O. Zelinsky. 1982, Greenwillow $11.25; LB $11.88. At the end of the day all life prepares for rest.

273. Goffstein, M. B. *Sleepy People* (PS–1). Illus. 1979, Farrar $6.95. A nighttime book bound to induce sleep.

274. Highwater, Jamake. *Moonsong Lullaby* (K–3). Illus. 1981, Lothrop $11.25; LB $11.88. A gentle night poem involving animals, plants, and Native Indian culture.

275. Hoberman, Mary Ann. *The Cozy Book* (PS–3). Illus. by Tony Chen. 1982, Viking $12.95. Several forms of coziness are explored, including finally going to bed.

276. Hopkins, Lee Bennett, sel. *And God Bless Me: Prayers, Lullabies and Dream-Poems* (K–3). Illus. by Patricia Henderson Lincoln. 1982, Knopf $8.95; LB $8.99. Simple prayers and other poems associated with bedtime.

277. Keller, Holly. *Ten Sleepy Sheep* (PS–2). Illus. by author. 1983, Greenwillow $9.00; LB $8.59. Lewis begins counting sheep to go to sleep.

278. Larrick, Nancy, comp. *When the Dark Comes Dancing: A Bedtime Poetry Book* (PS–2). Illus. by John Wallner. 1983, Putnam $15.95. Forty-five poems and lullabies designed for bedtime reading.

279. Lesser, Carolyn. *The Goodnight Circle* (PS–2). Illus. by Lorinda Bryan Cauley. 1984, Harcourt $13.95. What animals do between night and morning.

280. Maris, Ron. *My Book* (PS–K). Illus. 1984, Watts $8.95. A peek-a-boo book that leads a cat to bed.

281. Marzollo, Jean. *Close Your Eyes* (PS–2). Illus. by Susan Jeffers. 1978, Dial $9.95; LB $9.89; paper $3.95. A sleep book that tells 2 stories at the same time.

282. Mayer, Mercer. *There's a Nightmare in My Closet* (K–3). Illus. by author. 1968, Dial $10.95; LB $10.89; paper $3.50. A boy brings a creature out of the closet into a more friendly atmosphere.

283. Newfield, Marcia. *Where Did You Put Your Sleep?* (PS–1). Illus. by Andrea Da Rif. 1983, Atheneum $10.95. A little girl who can't go to sleep plays a game with her father.

284. Peterson, Jeanne Whitehouse. *While the Moon Shines Bright: A Bedtime Chant* (PS–2). Illus. by Margot Apple. 1981, Harper LB $9.89. The story of a boy's preparation for bed.

285. Pomerantz, Charlotte. *All Asleep* (PS–1). Illus. by Nancy Tafuri. 1984, Greenwillow $10.00; LB $9.55. A series of poems that are about sleep.

286. Pomerantz, Charlotte. *Posy* (K–3). Illus. by Catherine Stock. 1983, Greenwillow $10.00; LB $10.88. Posy's father tells her 4 bedtime stories about herself.

287. Rice, Eve. *Goodnight, Goodnight* (PS–1). Illus. by author. 1980, Greenwillow $10.00; LB $10.88; Penguin paper $3.50. Except for a playful kitten, a variety of people settle down for a night's rest.

288. Rukeyser, Muriel. *More Night* (PS–2). Illus. by Symeon Shimin. 1981, Harper LB $9.89. All kinds of activities associated with animals and night are described.

289. Scarry, Patsy. *Patsy Scarry's Big Bedtime Storybook* (PS–1). Illus. by Cyndy Szekeres. 1980, Random $5.95; LB $6.99. Sixteen stories featuring Little Richard, a rabbit, and his friends.

290. Segal, Joyce. *It's Time to Go to Bed* (PS–1). Illus. by Robin Eaton. 1979, Doubleday $7.95. A bedtime story for those who don't want to go to bed.

291. Sharmat, Marjorie W. *Goodnight, Andrew, Goodnight, Craig* (PS–3). Illus. by Mary Chalmers. 1969, Harper $9.89. Two brothers in bunk beds can't get to sleep.

292. Skofield, James. *Nightdances* (PS–3). Illus. by Karen Gundersheimer. 1981, Harper $9.13; LB $9.89. A young boy and his family dance before bedtime in this fantasy.

293. Stevenson, James. *We Can't Sleep* (PS–2). Illus. by author. 1982, Greenwillow $10.25; LB $10.88. Grandpa tells his grandchildren of the time when he couldn't sleep.

294. Stevenson, James. *What's Under My Bed?* (1–3). Illus. by author. 1983, Greenwillow $10.00; LB $10.88. A grandfather helps reduce his grandchildren's fears. A sequel is: *Worse Than Willy!* (1984, $10.50; LB $9.55).

295. Stevenson, Robert Louis. *The Moon* (K–2). Illus. by Denise Saldutti. 1984, Harper $10.50; LB $10.89. A short poem on the creatures who value the moonlight.

296. Stoddard, Sandol. *Bedtime Mouse* (PS). Illus. by Lynn Munsinger. 1981, Houghton LB $8.95. Several animals create a fuss before a child can get to sleep.

297. Ward, Andrew. *Baby Bear and the Long Sleep* (PS–2). Illus. by John Walsh. 1980, Little $11.45. A young bear has difficulty going to sleep in the winter.

298. Wells, Rosemary. *Good Night, Fred* (K–2). Illus. by author. 1981, Dial $8.50; LB $8.44; paper $3.95. An older brother gets Fred ready for bed.

299. Whiteside, Karen. *Lullaby of the Wind* (PS–K). Illus. by Kazue Mizumura. 1984, Harper $9.57; LB $9.89. A child prepares for bed and falls asleep.

300. Willoughby, Elaine Macmann. *Boris and the Monsters* (PS–1). Illus. by Lynn Munsinger. 1980, Houghton LB $7.95. Boris makes up many excuses because he is afraid to go to bed.

301. Yolen, Jane. *Dragon Night and Other Lullabies* (1–4). Illus. by Demi. 1980, Methuen $8.95. Lullabies that might be sung by a variety of different creatures.

302. Zolotow, Charlotte. *Flocks of Birds* (PS–3). Illus. by Ruth Bornstein. 1981, Harper $8.61; LB $8.89. Unable to sleep, a little girl thinks about flocks of birds.

303. Zolotow, Charlotte. *I Have a Horse of My Own* (PS–K). Illus. by Yoko Mitsuhashi. 1980, Harper $8.95. At night a little girl and her horse share magical adventures.

304. Zolotow, Charlotte. *The Summer Night* (PS–K). Illus. by Ben Shecter. 1974, Harper $9.57; LB $9.89. A comfortable and comforting story about a little girl who goes to her father when she can't sleep, and they enjoy the night's sights and sounds together until she is ready for bed.

Stories without Words

305. Alexander, Martha. *Bobo's Dream* (PS–2). Illus. by author. 1970, Dial $7.95; LB $7.89; paper $1.75. A small dachshund's dream becomes reality as the outstanding illustrations unfold the tale.

306. Alexander, Martha. *Out, Out, Out!* (PS–1). Illus. by author. 1968, Dial $6.95; LB $6.46. A pigeon enters through the open window, and the clever, unruffled child—unlike the adults in this amusing situation—lures it out of the house; a pantomime for preschoolers with simple lilac and gray wash drawings.

307. Anno, Mitsumasa. *Anno's Flea Market* (K–3). Illus. by author. 1984, Putnam $11.95. A couple tour the marvels and wonders of a flea market.

308. Anno, Mitsumasa. *Anno's Journey* (1–3). Illus. by author. 1978, Collins $10.95; paper $5.95. A journey through town and country with many visual delights.

309. Anno, Mitsumasa. *Topsy-Turvies: Pictures to Stretch the Imagination* (PS–2). Illus. by author. 1970, Weatherhill $6.50. A picture book full of visual tricks and puzzles. See also the sequel: *Upside-Downers: More Pictures to Stretch the Imagination* (1971, $6.50).

310. Aruego, Jose. *Look What I Can Do* (K–2). Illus. by author. 1971, Scribners $6.95; paper $2.95. Almost wordless picture book about the antics that result when one carabao challenges another.

311. Briggs, Raymond. *The Snowman* (K–3). Illus. by author. 1978, Random $7.95. A small boy has adventures with the snowman he has made.

312. Burton, Marilee Robin. *The Elephant's Nest: Four Wordless Stories* (K–2). Illus. by author. 1979, Harper $9.89. A series of fantasies that will appeal to imaginative youngsters.

313. Carle, Eric. *Do You Want to Be My Friend?* (PS–K). Illus. by author. 1971, Harper $11.49; LB $11.89. The end of an animal's tail appears on each page, and the child must guess the animal before turning the page to see the front end.

314. Corbett, Grahame. *Who Is Next?* (PS). Illus. by author. 1982, Dial $3.50. A book of toy figures revealed page by page.

315. Crews, Donald, illus. *Truck* (1–3). 1980, Greenwillow $10.95; LB $10.51. The picture book that traces a truck trip from loading dock to its San Francisco destination.

316. Cristini, Ermanno, and Puricelli, Luigi. *In My Garden* (PS–2). Illus. by author. 1981, Alphabet Pr. $9.95. A journey across a garden where a variety of plants, animals, and insects live.

317. Cristini, Ermanno, and Puricelli, Luigi. *In the Pond* (PS–K). Illus. by author. 1984, Picture Book Studio USA $9.95. A gentle introduction to the forms of life found in a pond.

318. de Paola, Tomie. *The Hunter and the Animals: A Wordless Picture Book* (K–3). Illus. by author. 1981, Holiday LB $11.95; paper $5.95. A hunter lost in the forest is helped by the animals.

319. Felix, Monique. *The Further Adventures of the Little Mouse Trapped in a Book* (PS–K). Illus. by author. 1984, Green Tiger $6.95. A mouse has adventures in the pages of a book in this continuation of *The Story of a Little Mouse Trapped in a Book* (1980, Green Tiger $6.95).

320. Freeman, Don. *The Chalk Box Story* (PS–2). Illus. by author. 1976, Harper $7.95. Eight sticks of chalk create a series of pictures that tell a story.

321. Goodall, John S. *The Adventures of Paddy Pork* (PS–1). Illus. by author. 1968, Harcourt $5.95. A cleverly designed book that shows what befalls a young pig after he runs away to join a traveling circus. Its sequel is: *The Ballooning Adventures of Paddy Pork* (1969, $5.95). See also these other sequels, published by Atheneum: *Paddy's Evening Out* (1973, $6.95); *Paddy Pork's Holiday* (1976, $6.95); *Paddy's New Hat* (1980, $6.95); *Paddy Goes Traveling* (1982, $6.95); *Paddy Pork: Odd Jobs* (1983, $6.95); *Paddy Under Water* (1984, $6.95).

322. Goodall, John S. *Creepy Castle* (PS–K). Illus. by author. 1975, Atheneum $6.95. Depicted in a medieval setting, this concerns the adventures of 2 mice who get locked in a castle, are rescued, and foil the villain.

323. Goodall, John S. *An Edwardian Summer* (K–2). Illus. by author. 1976, Atheneum $6.95. Brother and sister have leisurely experiences on their way to and from school.

324. Goodall, John S. *Jacko* (PS–K). Illus. by author. 1972, Harcourt $9.95; paper $3.95. Jacko, an organ-grinder's monkey, escapes from his master and inadvertently stows away on a sailing ship, hidden in a sea chest. When pirates attack the ship, Jacko escapes and returns once more to his jungle home.

325. Goodall, John S. *The Midnight Adventures of Kelly, Dot, and Esmeralda* (PS–2). Illus. by author. 1973, Atheneum $6.95. A koala bear, a rag doll, and a mouse journey into a magic land.

326. Goodall, John S. *Naughty Nancy* (PS–K). Illus. by author. 1975, Atheneum $6.95. Nancy, a mouse, is the flower girl at her sister's wedding, with disastrous, although humorous, results.

327. Goodall, John S. *The Surprise Picnic* (PS–K). Illus. by author. 1977, Atheneum $6.95. A cat and 2 kittens set off on a picnic and run into many complications. Lots of fun and adventure in this easy-to-follow plot.

328. Greeley, Valerie. *Farm Animals* (PS). Illus. 1984, Harper $2.70. For toddlers, here is a board book without words on farm animals. Also use: *Field Animals; Pets; Zoo Animals* (all 1984, Harper $2.70).

329. Hartelius, Margaret A. *The Chicken's Child* (K–1). 1975, Doubleday $7.95. A hen hatches an alligator's egg.

330. Hauptmann, Tatjana. *Day in the Life of Petronella Pig* (1–3). Illus. by author. 1980, Holt $12.45. The adventures of a mother pig and her mischievous son.

331. Hoban, Tana. *Big Ones, Little Ones* (PS). Illus. by author. 1976, Greenwillow $9.55. A photographic wordless book that shows adult and young animals, some tame and some wild.

332. Hoban, Tana. *Where Is It?* (PS). Illus. by author. 1974, Macmillan $8.95. Large photographs show a rabbit searching for food—where will he find it?

333. Hutchins, Pat. *Changes, Changes* (PS–1). Illus. by author. 1971, Macmillan $10.95; paper $0.95. A wooden doll couple rearrange a set of building blocks to suit different situations.

334. Keats, Ezra Jack. *Clementina's Cactus* (PS–2). Illus. by author. 1982, Viking $11.95. A young girl is curious about a cactus plant she sees.

335. Kessler, Ethel, and Kessler, Leonard. *Big Red Bus* (K–2). Illus. by author. 1957, Doubleday $8.95. Pictures recount all of the many sights on a bus ride.

336. Krahn, Fernando. *Arthur's Adventure in the Abandoned House* (1–3). Illus. by author. 1981, Dutton $8.25. A young backpacker decides to explore an empty house.

337. Krahn, Fernando. *Catch That Cat!* (4–6). Illus. 1978, Dutton $6.95. A boy chases a cat and has an adventure at sea.

338. Krahn, Fernando. *A Funny Friend from Heaven* (1–3). Illus. by author. 1977, Harper $8.95. An angel and a hobo are changed into clowns. Also use: *April Fools* (1974, Dutton $8.95).

339. Krahn, Fernando. *Here Comes Alex Pumpernickel!* (PS–1). 1981, Atlantic/Little $6.95. A day in the life of an enterprising youngster. A sequel is: *Sleep Tight, Alex Pumpernickel* (1982, $7.95).

340. Krahn, Fernando. *The Mystery of the Giant's Footprints* (PS–1). Illus. by author. 1977, Dutton $6.95. A family tracks down the origins of giant footsteps in the snow. Also use: *Self-Made Snowman* (1974, Harper $9.89).

341. Krahn, Fernando. *Robot-Bot-Bot* (1–3). Illus. 1979, Dutton $6.95. A little girl decides to rewire a robot who has been doing housework.

342. Krahn, Fernando. *The Secret in the Dungeon* (PS–1). Illus. by author. 1983, Houghton $9.95. A child's adventures visiting a medieval castle.

343. Krahn, Fernando. *Who's Seen the Scissors?* (PS–1). Illus. by author. 1975, Dutton $6.95. A self-propelled pair of scissors causes havoc in town.

344. McCully, Emily, illus. *Picnic* (PS–2). 1984, Harper $10.53; LB $10.89. An eventful picnic for the mouse family.

345. McKenna, Terry. *The Fox and the Circus Bear* (K–2). Illus. by author. 1982, Gollancz $9.95. A bear is helped by a fox to escape from a circus.

346. Mayer, Mercer. *Ah-Choo* (K–2). Illus. by author. 1976, Dial $4.95; LB $4.58; paper $2.50. A humorous tale told in imaginative pictures.

347. Mayer, Mercer. *A Boy, a Dog and a Frog* (PS–1). Illus. by author. 1967, Dial $8.95; LB $8.89; paper $2.50. Engaging pen-and-ink drawings will delight youngsters into supplying the story line for the boy and his dog on their frog hunt. Sequel: *Frog, Where Are You?* (1969, $6.95; LB $6.89; paper $1.75). Also from the same author and publisher: *A Boy, a Dog, a Frog and a Friend* (1971, $6.95; LB $6.89; paper $2.50); *Frog on His Own* (1973, $6.95; LB $6.89; paper $1.95); *Frog Goes to Dinner* (1974, $6.96; LB $6.89; paper $2.50); *One Frog Too Many* by Mercer Mayer and Marianna Mayer (1975, $4.95; LB $6.89; paper $1.95).

348. Mayer, Mercer. *The Great Cat Chase: A Wordless Book* (PS–K). 1975, Four Winds $4.95; Scholastic paper $1.25. A cat, who rebels against being dressed up and taken for a ride in a baby carriage, leads 3 children on a wild chase as he tries to make his escape.

349. Mayer, Mercer. *Hiccup* (PS–1). Illus. by author. 1976, Dial $6.95; LB $6.89; paper $3.95. A female hippo with a severe case of hiccups is helped by her male companion in this wordless tale.

350. Mayer, Mercer. *Oops* (PS–1). Illus. by author. 1977, Dial $7.95; LB $7.89; paper $1.75. A particularly uncoordinated hippo turns a town topsy-turvy in this wordless book.

351. Mayer, Mercer. *Two Moral Tales* (K–2). Illus. by author. 1974, Four Winds $3.95. Two fables illustrated with humor and style. Also use: *Two More Moral Tales* (1974, Four Winds $3.95).

352. Morris, Terry Nell. *Good Night, Dear Monster!* (PS–2). Illus. by author. 1980, Knopf LB $4.99. Homelessness is the theme of this wordless book.

353. Oakley, Graham. *Graham Oakley's Magical Changes* (K–6). Illus. 1980, Atheneum $12.95. Split pages create a multitude of new objects and shapes.

354. Ormerod, Jan. *Moonlight* (PS–1). Illus. by author. 1982, Lothrop $10.00; LB $10.88; Penguin paper $2.95. The going to bed ritual of a little girl is described in this wordless book.

355. Ormerod, Jan. *Sunshine* (PS–1). Illus. by author. 1981, Lothrop $11.25; LB $11.88; Penguin paper $2.95. A wordless picture book depicting children in the sunshine.

356. Oxenbury, Helen. *Dressing* (PS). Illus. by author. 1981, Simon & Schuster paper $3.50. For 1 and 2 year olds, wordless books that show common objects. Also part of this series are: *Playing; Working* (both 1981, Simon & Schuster paper $3.50).

357. Park, W. B. *Charlie-Bob's Fan* (K–3). Illus. 1981, Harcourt $6.95. A dog tries to turn on a fan to relieve the terrible summer heat.

358. Sasaki, Isao. *Snow* (K–3). Illus. by author. 1982, Viking $9.95. A snowy day at a railway station.

359. Spier, Peter. *Peter Spier's Rain* (PS–1). Illus. by author. 1982, Doubleday $10.95; LB $11.95. A brother and sister experience a rainstorm.

360. Tafuri, Nancy. *Early Morning in the Barn* (PS). Illus. by author. 1983, Greenwillow $11.00; LB $10.51. Only the sounds of farm animals are heard in the pages of this book.

361. Tanaka, Hideyuki. *The Happy Dog* (PS–2). Illus. by author. 1983, Atheneum $6.95. In 3 stories, a shaggy dog gets into mischief.

362. Turkle, Brinton. *Deep in the Forest* (PS–1). Illus. by author. 1976, Dutton $9.95. In a reversal of the Goldilocks story, a mischievous bear tries the porridge, chairs, and beds.

363. Ueno, Noriko. *Elephant Buttons* (PS). Illus. by author. 1973, Harper LB $9.89. An amusing book that shows all elephants with numerous buttons. As the buttons pop open, they reveal another animal and so on until finally a little mouse's buttons pop open, and an elephant balloons out!

364. Van Allsburg, Chris. *The Mysteries of Harris Burdick* (1–Up). Illus. by author. 1984, Houghton $14.95. A group of pictures are presented and youngsters are asked to supply the stories.

365. Van Soelen, Philip. *Cricket in the Grass, and Other Stories* (K–3). Illus. by author. 1979, Scribners $9.95. The food chain told in 5 picture stories.

366. Ward, Lynd. *The Silver Pony: A Story in Pictures* (2–4). Illus. by author. 1973, Houghton $12.95. Handsome pictures grace this story about a farm boy's imaginative adventures on a magnificent winged horse.

367. Wezel, Peter. *The Good Bird* (PS–1). Illus. by author. 1966, Harper $10.89. A picture story of a friendly pink bird who shares a worm with a goldfish.

368. Winter, Paula. *The Bear and the Fly: A Story* (PS). Illus. by author. 1981, Crown $4.95; Scholastic paper $1.95. The havoc caused when a fly interrupts the Bear family's dinner.

369. Winter, Paula. *Sir Andrew* (K–3). Illus. by author. 1980, Crown LB $7.95. The humorous adventures of a donkey named Sir Andrew.

370. Young, Ed, illus. *The Other Bone* (PS–3). 1984, Harper $9.57; LB $9.89. A picture version of the Aesop story of a boy, his dog, and the reflection he sees in the water.

371. Young, Ed. *Up a Tree* (PS–3). Illus. by author. 1983, Harper $8.61; LB $8.89. A cat is chased up a tree by a fierce dog.

Picture Books

Imaginative Stories

Imaginary Animals

372. Adler, David A. *Bunny Rabbit Rebus* (1–3). Illus. by Madelaine Gill Linden. 1983, Harper $7.64; LB $7.89. Mother Rabbit and Little Rabbit set out to get food in this combination story and puzzle.

373. Agee, Jon. *Ellsworth* (K–2). Illus. by author. 1983, Pantheon $10.95; LB $10.99. Ellsworth, a dog who is also an economics professor, faces unemployment.

374. Alexander, Martha. *Blackboard Bear* (PS–1). Illus. by author. 1969, Dial $7.95; LB $7.89; paper $2.50. Spurred on by the older children, a small boy draws a picture of a big bear on his blackboard. The bear steps right down and becomes his playmate. Three sequels are: *And My Mean Old Mother Will Be Sorry, Blackboard Bear* (1972, $9.95; LB $6.46; paper $2.25); *I Sure Am Glad to See You, Blackboard Bear* (1976, $7.95; LB $7.89; paper $1.75); *We're in Big Trouble, Blackboard Bear* (1980, $6.95; LB $6.89; paper $2.50).

375. Alexander, Sue. *World Famous Muriel* (1–3). Illus. by Chris L. Demarest. 1984, Little $11.45. Muriel, a tightrope walker, solves the mystery of the stolen paper lanterns.

376. Aliki. *Keep Your Mouth Closed, Dear* (K–2). Illus. by author. 1966, Dial $9.95; paper $2.50. Charlie, an alligator, puts everything he sees into his mouth. A sequel is: *Use Your Head, Dear* (1983, Greenwillow $10.00; LB $10.88).

377. Allard, Harry. *Bumps in the Night* (K–3). Illus. by James Marshall. 1979, Doubleday LB $7.95. Dudley the Stork thinks his house is haunted.

378. Allard, Harry. *I Will Not Go to Market Today* (PS–1). Illus. by James Marshall. 1979, Dial $8.95; LB $8.89; paper $2.75. A chicken, whose first name is Fenimore, seems destined not to get to market.

379. Allard, Harry. *It's So Nice to Have a Wolf around the House* (PS–2). Illus. by James Marshall. 1977, Doubleday $8.95; paper $2.95. When an elderly man and his pets decide they need a fresh face about the place, a wolf who is a former bank robber pretends to be a dog and applies for the post.

380. Allen, Jeffrey. *Mary Alice, Operator Number Nine* (1–3). Illus. by James Marshall. 1978, Little $7.95; Penguin paper $2.95. Who could take the place of Mary Alice, the time service operator?

381. Allen, Pamela. *Bertie and the Bear* (PS–K). Illus. 1984, Putnam $10.95; paper $4.95. A picture book frolic of a boy and a not-so-fearsome bear.

382. Allen, Pamela. *Mr. Archimedes' Bath* (PS–2). Illus. 1980, Lothrop $11.95; LB $11.47. Every time he and his animal friends take a bath together, the tub overflows.

383. Allen, Pamela. *Who Sank the Boat?* (PS–2). Illus. 1983, Putnam $10.95. One of 5 animal friends is guilty of sinking the boat.

384. Ambrus, Victor G. *Grandma, Felix, and Mustapha Biscuit* (PS–2). Illus. by author. 1982, Morrow $10.75; LB $9.84. Felix the cat has hungry eyes for a hamster named Mustapha Biscuit.

385. Annett, Cora. *The Dog Who Thought He Was a Boy* (K–3). Illus. by Walter Lorraine. 1965, Houghton $8.95. A puppy thinks he is his owner's little brother in a fun-filled story.

386. Asch, Frank. *Happy Birthday, Moon* (PS–1). Illus. by author. 1982, Prentice $9.95. A little bear wants to give the moon a birthday present. Two sequels are: *Mooncake* (1983, $9.95); *Moongame* (1984, $10.95).

387. Asch, Frank. *Just Like Daddy* (PS–1). Illus. by author. 1981, Prentice $10.95; paper $4.95. Fatherhood is explained by a bear and his dad in this warm, humorous book. Two other Bear stories are: *Bread and Honey: A Frank Asch Bear Story* (1982, Dutton $5.50; LB $5.95); *Milk and Cookies* (1982, Dutton $5.50; LB $5.95; paper $1.95).

388. Asch, Frank. *Macgooses' Grocery* (PS–1). Illus. by James Marshall. 1978, Dial $6.95; LB $6.46; paper $1.95. A family decides to give up their duties and let an unhatched chick fend for itself.

389. Asch, Frank. *Moon Bear* (PS–K). Illus. by author. 1978, Scribners $8.95. A bear learns about the phases of the moon.

390. Asch, Frank. *Sand Cake* (K–2). Illus. by author. 1979, Parents $5.50. On the beach, Papa Bear makes a sand cake.

391. Asch, Frank. *Turtle Tale* (PS–2). Illus. by author. 1978, Dial $6.95; LB $6.46; paper $2.75. Whether his head is in or out of his shell, the important thing is that the turtle has a choice.

392. Bach, Alice. *Millicent the Magnificent* (1–3). Illus. 1978, Harper LB $9.57; Dell paper $1.25. Ronald considers himself superior to twin brother Oliver until a young circus bear, Millicent, intervenes.

393. Bach, Alice. *The Most Delicious Camping Trip Ever* (K–2). Illus. by Steven Kellogg. 1976, Harper $8.61; LB $8.89. Two bear cubs and Aunt Bear prepare for a camping trip, which turns out to be more fun than they had expected.

394. Bach, Alice. *The Smartest Bear and His Brother Oliver* (2–4). Illus. by Steven Kellogg. 1975, Harper LB $9.89; Dell paper $0.95. Ronald learns the contents of a whole encyclopedia to be smarter than his brother.

395. Baker, Alan. *Benjamin's Book* (PS–1). Illus. by author. 1983, Lothrop $8.50. Benjamin, a hamster, makes a mess of a page in a book.

396. Baker, Alan. *Benjamin's Dreadful Dream* (1–3). Illus. by author. 1980, Harper LB $7.89. A bespectacled mouse has a series of strange adventures but finally gets back to his own bed.

397. Baker, Betty. *Danby and George* (2–4). Illus. by Adrianne Lobel. 1981, Greenwillow $10.25; LB $9.84. Danby, a deer mouse, and George, a wood rat, share some lighthearted adventures.

398. Barklem, Jill. *The Secret Staircase* (K–3). Illus. by author. 1983, Putnam $8.95. A group of mice enjoy a midwinter frolic.

399. Bate, Lucy. *Little Rabbit's Loose Tooth* (PS–K). Illus. by Diane deGroat. 1975, Crown $8.95; Scholastic paper $3.95. Little Rabbit loses her first tooth and makes the most of it in this beguiling story.

400. Baum, Louis. *Juju and the Pirate* (PS–2). Illus. by Philippe Matter. 1984, Harper $9.95. Juju wants to have a pirate master as her great-great grandfather did.

401. Benchley, Nathaniel. *Walter, the Homing Pigeon* (1–3). Illus. by Whitney Darrow, Jr. 1981, Harper $9.57; LB $9.89. Walter, a homing pigeon, begins dawdling during his first race.

402. Berenstain, Stan, and Berenstain, Jan. *The Berenstain Bears in the Dark* (PS–2). Illus. by author. 1982, Random $4.99; paper $1.50. Brother and Sister Bear in one of a very large series of books.

403. Berson, Harold. *Henry Possum* (K–2). Illus. by author. 1973, Crown LB $5.95. Henry Possum is always too busy watching butterflies and humming birds to pay attention to the safety lessons his mother is trying to teach him.

404. Berson, Harold. *A Moose Is Not a Mouse* (K–2). 1975, Crown $6.95. To this young mouse, a moose is just an oversize mouse, and so Victor grows in daring and attacks the cat, with almost disastrous results.

405. Berson, Harold. *Truffles for Lunch* (K–3). Illus. by author. 1980, Macmillan $9.95. A pig gets his wish and is transformed into a lion.

406. Bond, Felicia. *Poinsettia and Her Family* (PS–3). Illus. by author. 1981, Harper $9.57; LB $9.89. Poinsettia, a pig, resents her large family but misses them when they leave temporarily. Also use: *Poinsettia and the Firefighters* (1984, $10.10; LB $9.89).

407. Bornstein, Ruth. *Little Gorilla* (PS). Illus. by author. 1976, Houghton $9.95. Even though Little Gorilla grows into a big gorilla, everyone still loves him.

408. Boynton, Sandra. *Hester in the Wild* (PS–2). Illus. by author. 1979, Harper $10.10; LB $10.89. Hester, the pig, has bad luck when she tries camping and canoeing.

409. Boynton, Sandra. *If at First . . .* (1–3). Illus. 1980, Little $8.95; paper $3.95. A little brown mouse must get an elephant up a hill.

410. Brandenberg, Franz. *Nice New Neighbors* (K–2). Illus. by Aliki. 1977, Greenwillow LB $7.92. A family of mice children generously include their neighbors, who formerly spurned them, when they decide to give a play—*The Three Blind Mice*.

411. Brett, Jan. *Fritz and the Beautiful Horses* (K–3). Illus. by author. 1981, Houghton $10.95. The pony Fritz is ostracized from the other horses and leads a lonely life.

412. Brewster, Patience. *Ellsworth and the Cats from Mars* (PS–4). Illus. by author. 1981, Houghton $9.95. Ellsworth, a fat yellow cat, zooms into space.

413. Bridwell, Norman. *Clifford's Good Deeds* (PS–1). Illus. by author. 1976, Scholastic paper $3.95. Clifford is a large shaggy dog whose efforts to be helpful result in comic mishaps. Also use: *Clifford Takes a Trip* (1969); *Clifford, the Big Red Dog* (1969); *Clifford's Tricks* (1971); *Clifford, the Small Red Puppy* (1973); *Clifford at the Circus* (1977); *Clifford Goes to Hollywood* (1981) (all paper $1.25).

414. Brock, Betty. *No Flying in the House* (2–4). Illus. by Wallace Tripp. 1970, Harper $10.89; Avon paper $2.84. A small dog seeks shelter for herself and her human friends.

415. Brown, Marc. *Arthur's Eyes* (K–3). 1976, Little $10.45; Avon paper $2.25. Some of aardvark Arthur's problems are solved when he gets glasses, but new problems are created. Two sequels are: *Arthur's Nose* (1976, Little $8.95; Avon paper $2.25); *Arthur Goes to Camp* (1982, Little $12.45; Avon paper $3.70).

416. Brown, Marc, and Brown, Laurene Krasny. *The Bionic Bunny Show* (2–3). Illus. by Marc Brown. 1984, Atlantic/Little $13.95. An ordinary rabbit becomes a super TV star thanks to makeup magic.

417. Brown, Marc, and Krensky, Stephen. *Perfect Pigs: An Introduction to Manners* (K–2). Illus. 1983, Little $12.45; paper $5.95. Pig people show the basics of good manners.

418. Brown, Margaret Wise. *Little Chicken* (PS). Illus. by Leonard Weisgard. 1982, Harper $8.64; LB $8.89. The story of a newly hatched chicken and her search for friends.

419. Brown, Margaret Wise. *Once upon a Time in a Pigpen: And Three Other Stories* (K–3). Illus. by Ann Strugnell. 1980, Addison LB $10.95. Four animals stories—one in verse—by a master storyteller.

420. Brown, Margaret Wise. *The Runaway Bunny* (PS–K). Illus. by Clement Hurd. 1972, Harper $7.89; LB $7.89; paper $2.95. With 9 colorful illustrations, this new edition of an old favorite is a charming story of mother bunny's love for her restless youngster, who keeps trying to escape but is always found.

421. Brown, Ruth. *A Dark Dark Tale* (PS–2). Illus. by author. 1981, Dial $10.95; LB $10.89; paper $3.95. An atmospheric tale about a black cat in a dark, dark house.

422. Browne, Anthony. *Bear Hunt* (PS–K). Illus. 1980, Atheneum $8.95. A white bear draws pictures to get himself out of tight scrapes.

423. Burningham, John. *The Shopping Basket* (PS–2). Illus. by author. 1980, Harper $9.95; LB $10.89. Steven must challenge several animals to retain the contents of his shopping basket.

424. Burningham, John. *Would You Rather . . .* (PS–2). 1978, Harper $9.57; LB $10.89. Riding a bull into a supermarket is one of the imaginative situations described in this humorous book.

425. Byars, Betsy. *The Lace Snail* (K–2). Illus. by author. 1975, Viking $7.95. How does a snail make lace? Snail doesn't know, but she is glad to give some to each animal that asks, as long as it lasts.

426. Calhoun, Mary. *Audubon Cat* (PS–3). Illus. by Susan Bonners. 1981, Morrow $10.25; LB $9.84. When some animals steal her food, a young cat sets out to catch a dinner.

427. Calhoun, Mary. *Cross-Country Cat* (K–2). Illus. by Erick Ingraham. 1979, Morrow $9.25; LB $8.88. A Siamese named Henry sets out on a cross-country skiing adventure.

428. Calhoun, Mary. *Hot-Air Henry* (PS–4). Illus. by Erick Ingraham. 1981, Morrow $10.75; LB $9.84; paper $3.95. Siamese cat Henry sneaks into the basket of a hot air balloon and soon is afloat.

429. Cameron, John. *If Mice Could Fly* (PS–1). Illus. 1979, Atheneum $8.95. This amusing picture book explores the possible consequences if mice became as powerful as cats.

430. Carle, Eric. *The Grouchy Ladybug* (PS–K). Illus. by author. 1977, Harper $9.57; LB $10.89. A grouchy ladybug, who is looking for a fight, challenges every insect and animal she meets regardless of size. Brilliantly illustrated in collage, the pages vary in size with the size of the animal.

431. Carle, Eric. *The Mixed-Up Chameleon* (PS–2). 1984, Harper $12.08; LB $11.89. A new edition of the story of a chameleon who finally decides to be himself.

432. Carlson, Nancy. *Harriet and the Garden* (PS–1). Illus. by author. 1982, Carolrhoda LB $7.95. Harriet, a childlike dog, has several simple adventures. Others in the series are: *Harriet and the Roller Coaster* (1982); *Harriet and Walt* (1982) (both LB $7.95; Penguin paper $3.95); *Harriet's Recital* (1982, LB $7.95).

433. Carlson, Nancy. *Loudmouth George and the Cornet* (PS–2). Illus. by author. 1983, Carolrhoda $6.95. George, a rabbit, gets dismissed from the school band. Others in the series are: *Loudmouth George and the Big Race; Loudmouth George and the Fishing Trip; Loudmouth George and the New Neighbors; Loudmouth George and the Sixth-Grade Bully* (all 1983, $6.95).

434. Carlson, Natalie Savage. *Marie Louise and Christopher at the Carnival* (K–3). Illus. by Jose Aruego and Ariane Dewey. 1981, Scribners $11.95. A snake and mongoose go to a carnival in disguise. Another series title is: *Marie Louise's Heyday* (1975, $6.95; paper $2.95).

435. Cazet, Denys. *Big Shoe, Little Shoe* (PS–1). Illus. 1984, Bradbury $12.95. Louis, a young bunny, plays games with a grandfather.

436. Cazet, Denys. *The Duck with Squeaky Feet* (K–2). Illus. by author. 1980, Bradbury $8.95. A stage show features a cast of humorous animals.

437. Cazet, Denys. *Lucky Me* (PS–2). Illus. by author. 1983, Bradbury $10.95. A cumulative animal story in which an ant colony saves the day for a plump chicken.

438. Chalmers, Mary. *Take a Nap, Harry* (PS–2). 1981, Harper paper $1.50. The adventures of a lovable, small cat. Also in this series: *Be Good, Harry*

(1982, paper $1.50); *Come to the Doctor, Harry* (1982, $7.64; LB $8.89); *Throw a Kiss, Harry* (1982, paper $1.50).

439.   Chorao, Kay. *Kate's Box* (PS–K). Illus. by author. 1982, Dutton $3.95. A brief story about a little elephant called Kate. Others in this series are: *Kate's Car; Kate's Quilt; Kate's Snowman* (all 1982, Dutton $3.95).

440.   Christelow, Eileen. *Henry and the Red Stripes* (PS–1). Illus. by author. 1982, Houghton $10.50. Henry Rabbit paints red stripes on himself and finds he no longer has a natural camouflage.

441.   Christelow, Eileen. *Mr. Murphy's Marvelous Invention* (K–3). Illus. by author. 1983, Houghton $9.95. A pig makes a machine to do housework but it does it all wrong.

442.   Clymer, Eleanor. *Horatio* (K–3). Illus. by Robert Quackenbush. 1974, Atheneum paper $1.25. The adventures of a most sophisticated cat. Four sequels are: *Leave Horatio Alone* (1974, $6.95); *Horatio's Birthday* (1976, $6.95); *Horatio Goes to the Country* (1978, $7.95); *Horatio Solves a Mystery* (1980, $9.95).

443.   Clymer, Ted, and Miles, Miska. *Horse and the Bad Morning* (1–3). Illus. by Leslie Morrill. 1982, Dutton $8.95. Barney and animals try to cheer up Horse.

444.   Cole, Brock. *No More Baths* (PS–1). Illus. by author. 1980, Doubleday $10.95. Jessie thinks she would rather live with animals than take baths.

445.   Conford, Ellen. *Eugene the Brave* (1–3). Illus. by John Larrecq. 1978, Little $8.95. Possum Geraldine pokes fun at her brother's fear of the dark but appreciates his help when she falls in a hole.

446.   Conford, Ellen. *Impossible Possum* (1–3). Illus. by Rosemary Wells. 1971, Little $7.95. Tale of a young possum who has an impossible time learning to hang by his tail.

447.   Conford, Ellen. *Just the Thing for Geraldine* (K–2). Illus. by John Larrecq. 1974, Little $7.95. "Do your own thing" is the message. Poor Geraldine didn't seem to have any artistic accomplishments until her family found out that she excelled as a juggler.

448.   Coombs, Patricia. *Tilabel* (1–3). Illus. by author. 1978, Lothrop $10.25; LB $9.84. A takeoff on the Rumpelstiltskin story.

449.   Cooper, Jacqueline. *Angus and the Mona Lisa* (1–4). Illus. by author. 1981, Lothrop $12.50; LB $12.88. Angus the cat foils a plan to steal the Mona Lisa.

450.   Craft, Ruth. *The Winter Bear* (PS–1). Illus. by Erik Blegvad. 1975, Atheneum $9.95; paper $2.50.

Three children on a wintry day come upon a toy bear, which they take home and lovingly wash, dry, and dress.

451.   Cressey, James. *Fourteen Rats and a Rat-Catcher* (1–3). Illus. by Tamasin Cole. 1978, Prentice LB $6.95. A rat catcher resolves a difference between an old lady and her rats.

452.   Crowe, Robert L. *Tyler Toad and the Thunder* (PS–2). Illus. by Kay Chorao. 1980, Dutton $9.95. Tyler Toad finds that he is not the only animal afraid of thunder.

453.   Cunningham, Julia. *A Mouse Called Junction* (2–4). Illus. by Michael Hague. 1980, Pantheon $7.95; LB $7.99. A small, overprotected mouse sets out in search of adventure.

454.   Dahl, Roald. *The Enormous Crocodile* (K–3). Illus. by Quentin Blake. 1978, Knopf $6.99; LB $4.95. Animals band together to save a group of children from becoming a crocodile's lunch.

455.   Daugherty, James. *Andy and the Lion* (1–4). Illus. by author. 1938, Viking $12.95. A popular, modern version of the story of Androcles and the lion.

456.   Davis, Douglas F. *There's an Elephant in the Garage* (K–2). Illus. by Steven Kellogg. 1979, Dutton $7.95. April, her cat Zelda, and 2 bears hunt elephants.

457.   Davis, Maggie S. *The Best Way to Ripton* (PS–2). Illus. by Stephen Gammell. 1982, Holiday LB $8.95. An old man seeking directions is told all the ways not to get to Ripton.

458.   De Brunhoff, Jean. *The Story of Babar, the Little Elephant* (PS). Illus. by author. 1933, Random $5.95; LB $5.99. A time-tested reading favorite about the little French elephant. Also use: *The Travels of Babar* (1937, $5.95; LB 5.99); *Babar and Father Christmas* (1949, $5.95; LB $5.99).

459.   De Brunhoff, Jean, and De Brunhoff, Laurent. *Babar's Anniversary Album: Six Favorite Stories* (K–1). Illus. by author. 1981, Random $13.95. A collection of 6 of the most popular Babar adventures.

460.   De Brunhoff, Laurent. *Babar's Mystery* (PS–1). Illus. by author. 1978, Random $4.95; LB $6.99. Babar helps capture a robber in this more recent addition to the vast Babar series. Four others in the series are: *Meet Babar and His Family* (1973, paper $1.50); *Babar and the Wully-Wully* (1975, LB $5.99); *Babar Learns to Cook* (1979, LB $4.99; paper $1.50); *Babar and the Ghost* (1981, $4.95; LB $6.99).

461.   Degen, Bruce. *Jamberry* (PS–1). Illus. by author. 1983, Harper $7.64; LB $8.89. A boy and a bear collect berries for jam.

462. Delton, Judy. *Brimhall Turns to Magic* (1–3). Illus. by Bruce Degen. 1979, Lothrop $10.00; LB $10.88. Brimhall has trouble at magic classes even when Bear helps.

463. Delton, Judy. *Duck Goes Fishing* (PS–2). Illus. by Lynn Munsinger. 1983, Whitman $8.25. Duck is a pest on a fishing trip with Owl and Fox.

464. Delton, Judy. *On a Picnic* (K–2). Illus. by Mamoru Funai. 1979, Doubleday LB $6.95. A goose and a gorilla realize their imperfections but end by accepting themselves.

465. Dennis, Wesley. *Flip* (K–2). Illus. by author. 1941, Penguin paper $3.95. A young horse achieves his desire to jump across a brook in his pasture. A sequel is: *Flip and the Morning* (1977, Penguin paper $3.95).

466. de Paola, Tomie. *The Knight and the Dragon* (1–3). Illus. by author. 1980, Putnam $9.95; paper $4.95. An inexperienced knight and an inexperienced dragon prepare themselves to do battle.

467. Dillon, Barbara. *The Beast in the Bed* (K–2). Illus. by Chris Conover. 1981, Morrow $8.95; LB $8.59. A monster befriends Marcia and they share happy moments.

468. Dillon, Barbara. *Who Needs a Bear?* (1–3). Illus. by Diane de Groat. 1981, Morrow $9.25; LB $8.88. Three toys leave their attic home to find someone who will care for them.

469. Dinan, Carolyn. *The Lunch Box Monster* (K–2). Illus. by author. 1983, Faber paper $6.95. A little boy carries around his pet monster in a lunch box.

470. Dubanevich, Arlene. *Pigs in Hiding* (PS–K). Illus. by author. 1983, Scholastic $10.95. In a game of hide-and-seek, 99 porkers hide.

471. du Bois, William Pene. *Lion* (1–3). Illus. by author. 1956, Viking $12.95; Penguin paper $3.95. Brilliant picture book about a designer of animals who had great difficulty in making the word *lion* and the animal lion match.

472. Duran, Bonte. *The Adventures of Arthur and Edmund: A Tale of Two Seals* (K–2). Illus. by author. 1984, Atheneum $10.95. Two seals share some adventures with a human child named Lucy.

473. Duvoisin, Roger. *The Crocodile in the Tree* (K–3). Illus. by author. 1973, Knopf LB $6.99. Farm animals band together to protect a friendly crocodile.

474. Duvoisin, Roger. *Crocus* (PS–1). Illus. by author. 1977, Knopf $5.95; LB $6.99. Vain Crocus Crocodile has his teeth pulled but is assuaged by receiving beautiful false ones. A sequel is: *The Importance of Crocus* (1981, $9.95; LB $9.99).

475. Duvoisin, Roger. *Jasmine* (PS–K). Illus. by author. 1984, Knopf LB $6.99. Jasmine, a captivating plump, pink cow, finds an old flower-bedecked bonnet, which she promptly wears. This upsets the other barnyard animals, who can't adjust to a cow that wants to be different.

476. Duvoisin, Roger. *Petunia* (K–2). Illus. by author. 1950, Knopf LB $7.99. Petunia, the silly goose, finds a book and carries it around believing this will make her wise, until her own foolishness proves her wrong.

477. Duvoisin, Roger. *Snowy and Woody* (3–5). Illus. by author. 1979, Knopf LB $6.99. A polar bear moves south to a warmer climate but quarrels with a resident, Woody, the brown bear.

478. Duvoisin, Roger. *Veronica* (K–3). Illus. by author. 1961, Knopf LB $7.99. Picture story of a rugged individualist hippopotamus.

479. Ellis, Anne Leo. *Dabble Duck* (K–1). Illus. by Sue Truesdell. 1984, Harper $11.05; LB $10.89. A lonely duck befriends a dog.

480. Erickson, Russell E. *A Toad for Tuesday* (K–2). Illus. by Lawrence Di Fiori. 1974, Lothrop $9.36; Dell paper $0.95. Warton, a toad, is captured by Owl, who considers Warton perfect for his birthday dinner—on Tuesday. Warton escapes but finds that after all, Owl has become his friend. Four sequels are: *Warton and Morton* (1976, Lothrop $4.95; Dell paper $0.95); *Warton and the King of the Skies* (1978, Lothrop LB $8.88); *Warton and the Traders* (1979, Lothrop $9.50; LB $9.12); *Warton and the Castaways* (1982, Lothrop $11.25; LB $11.88).

481. Ernst, Kathryn F. *Owl's New Cards* (K–2). Illus. by Diane deGroat. 1977, Crown $5.95. Owl tests his new set of playing cards on Beaver and Weasel with disastrous but amusing results.

482. Ets, Marie Hall. *Elephant in a Well* (PS–K). Illus. by author. 1972, Viking $11.50. A cumulative tale about the efforts of a horse, cow, goat, pig, lamb, dog, and finally a mouse to rescue an elephant who has fallen into the well.

483. Ets, Marie Hall. *In the Forest* (PS). Illus. by author. 1944, Viking LB $10.95; Penguin paper $3.95. A small boy's adventures with his forest friends.

484. Farber, Norma. *How the Left-Behind Beasts Built Ararat* (1–3). Illus. by Antonio Frasconi. 1978, Walker LB $7.45. The story of those animals left behind by Noah.

485. Fatio, Louise. *The Happy Lion* (PS–1). Illus. by Roger Duvoisin. 1964, McGraw $10.95. When his cage is left open, a lion roams the countryside. Also use: *The Happy Lion Roars* (1957, McGraw $7.95).

486. Flack, Marjorie. *Ask Mr. Bear* (PS–1). Illus. by author. 1958, Macmillan $9.95; paper $3.95. To find a present for his mother's birthday, Danny asks a variety of animals for suggestions, with little success until he meets Mr. Bear.

487. Flora, James. *Stewed Goose* (K–3). Illus. by author. 1973, Atheneum $9.95. A zany story of the ways Benjamin B. Bear tries to trap Wacker, a silly goose.

488. Flory, Jane. *The Bear on the Doorstep* (PS–1). Illus. by Carolyn Croll. 1980, Houghton $6.95. A baby bear is adopted by a rabbit family, but he soon grows too large for their household.

489. Forrester, Victoria. *The Magnificent Moo* (PS–1). Illus. by author. 1983, Atheneum $8.95. A cow is frightened by her own "moo" and tries to get rid of it.

490. Freeman, Don. *Beady Bear* (K–2). Illus. by author. 1954, Viking $9.95; Penguin paper $2.95. A toy bear is unhappy living in a cave like other bears and becomes happy when his young owner finds him.

491. Freeman, Don. *Bearymore* (K–3). Illus. by author. 1976, Viking LB $12.50; Penguin paper $2.95. A circus bear must build a new act, but he hibernates instead.

492. Freeman, Don. *Corduroy* (PS–1). Illus. by author. 1968, Viking $9.95; Penguin paper $3.50. The amusing story of a toy bear whose one missing button from his green corduroy overalls almost costs him the opportunity of belonging to someone. A sequel is: *A Pocket for Corduroy* (1978, Viking $9.95; Penguin paper $3.50).

493. Freeman, Don. *Dandelion* (K–2). Illus. by author. 1964, Viking LB $10.95; Penguin paper $3.50. A vain lion goes to a barber shop before a party and makes himself unrecognizable to his friends.

494. Freeman, Don. *The Guard Mouse* (PS–2). Illus. by author. 1982, Viking $12.95. Clyde is a member of the Grenadier Guards at Buckingham Palace.

495. Freeman, Don. *Norman the Doorman* (PS–2). Illus. by author. 1959, Viking $11.50; Penguin paper $3.50. Norman is the doorman at the basement of the art museum and enjoys showing his rodent friends through its treasures.

496. Freeman, Don. *Penguins, of All People* (1–3). Illus. by author. 1971, Viking LB $12.50. Ambassador Peary Byrd Penguin is called to the UN from Antarctica to help solve the problems of the world, but the mission turns into rollicking fun when a penguin delegation arrives to support the ambassador.

497. Freeman, Don. *Will's Quill* (K–2). Illus. by author. 1975, Viking $12.50; Penguin paper $2.95.

Willoughby Waddle, a country goose, goes to Elizabethan London and there meets and helps Shakespeare write his new play with one of Willoughby's own quills.

498. Freschet, Berniece. *Bear Mouse* (K–2). Illus. by Donald Carrick. 1973, Scribners $6.95. The efforts of a bear, or meadow, mouse to sustain herself and her young family in winter are described, as well as her need to ward off predators who are also in search of food.

499. Freschet, Berniece. *Bernard of Scotland Yard* (K–3). Illus. by Gina Freschet. 1978, Scribners $7.95. Bernard, the mouse, is on the trail of some English jewel thieves. A sequel is: *Bernard and the Catnip Caper* (1981, Scribners $9.95).

500. Freschet, Berniece. *The Happy Dromedary* (1–3). Illus. by Glen Rounds. 1977, Scribners $6.95. An original story about how the dromedary got his characteristic appearance.

501. Freschet, Berniece. *Little Black Bear Goes for a Walk* (1–2). Illus. by Glen Rounds. 1977, Scribners $5.95. Little bear takes his first trip alone and encounters many predicaments, but returns home to be comforted by mother—having learned a measure of independence.

502. Friskey, Margaret. *Seven Diving Ducks* (1–3). Illus. by Jean Morey. 1965, Childrens Pr. $9.25. A frightened little duck conquers his fear of the water.

503. Gackenbach, Dick. *The Dog and the Deep Dark Woods* (1–3). Illus. by author. 1984, Harper $9.57; LB $9.89. A story of why the dog left the other animals to come and live with man.

504. Gackenbach, Dick. *Hound and Bear* (PS–3). Illus. by author. 1976, Houghton $7.95. Hound finally agrees to stop playing tricks on long suffering Bear.

505. Gackenbach, Dick. *Little Bug* (PS–2). Illus. by author. 1981, Houghton $9.95. A fearful little bug ventures out into the world.

506. Gackenbach, Dick. *Pepper and All the Legs* (PS–2). Illus. by author. 1978, Houghton $7.95; paper $3.45. The dachshund who appeared in *Claude the Dog* (1974) and *Claude and Pepper* (1976) (both Houghton $7.95) explores his leg's-eye view of people. Another related title is: *What's Claude Doing?* (1984, Houghton $10.95).

507. Gackenbach, Dick. *The Perfect Mouse* (PS–2). Illus. by author. 1984, Macmillan $10.95. Two social-climbing mice want their daughter to marry the Sun.

508. Gackenbach, Dick. *The Pig Who Saw Everything* (K–3). 1978, Houghton $7.95. Henry, a curious pig, explores the world outside the barnyard.

509. Gage, Wilson. *Cully Cully and the Bear* (PS–2). Illus. by James Stevenson. 1983, Greenwillow $9.00; LB $8.59. A woodsman decides he needs a bear rug and goes out hunting to find one.

510. Gantos, Jack. *Rotten Ralph* (K–3). Illus. by author. 1976, Houghton $8.95; paper $4.50. Ralph is truly a nasty cat—mean and disruptive—until he is reformed under unusual circumstances. A sequel is: *Worse Than Rotten, Ralph* (1978, $6.95).

511. Geisert, Arthur. *Pa's Balloon and Other Pig Tales* (2–3). Illus. by author. 1984, Houghton $12.95. Three stories about a pig family and their adventures in a balloon.

512. Gerstein, Mordicai. *Follow Me!* (PS–2). Illus. by author. 1983, Morrow $9.00; LB $8.59. A group of lost ducks finally find home.

513. Getz, Arthur. *Humphrey, the Dancing Pig* (K–2). Illus. by author. 1980, Dial $9.95; LB $9.89; paper $2.75. An overweight pig tries to dance his pounds away.

514. Ginsburg, Mirra. *Across the Stream* (PS–2). Illus. by Nancy Tafuri. 1982, Greenwillow $10.25; LB $10.88. Mother hen saves her 3 chicks from the fox.

515. Ginsburg, Mirra. *The Chick and the Duckling* (PS–K). Trans. and adapted from the Russian by V. Suteyev. Illus. by Jose Aruego and Ariane Dewey. 1972, Macmillan $9.95. A duck and a chick who hatch at the same time become constant companions.

516. Glass, Andrew. *Jackson Makes His Move* (1–3). Illus. by author. 1982, Warne $9.95. Jackson, a raccoon, tries his hand at abstract art.

517. Godden, Rumer. *A Kindle of Kittens* (K–2). Illus. by Lynne Byrnes. 1979, Viking $8.95. A mother cat must find homes for her kittens.

518. Goodspead, Peter. *A Rhinoceros Wakes Me Up in the Morning: A Bedtime Tale* (PS–K). Illus. by Dennis Panek. 1982, Bradbury $10.95. A young boy recounts how various animals help him every day.

519. Gordon, Margaret. *Wilberforce Goes on a Picnic* (PS). Illus. by author. 1982, Morrow $10.75. A little bear goes on a picnic with his grandparents.

520. Graham, Margaret B. *Be Nice to Spiders* (PS–2). Illus. by author. 1967, Harper LB $10.89. Helen, Billy's pet spider, makes all the animals at the zoo happy when she spins webs and catches flies for them.

521. Graham, Margaret B. *Benjy and the Barking Bird* (PS–1). Illus. by author. 1971, Harper $10.89. Tilly the parrot can bark like a dog, and Benjy, a small sensitive dog, is very jealous and takes revenge.

522. Gretz, Susanna. *The Bears Who Went to the Seaside* (K–2). Illus. by author. 1984, Penguin paper $2.95. Five bears and Fred, their dalmatian friend, have fun at the beach.

523. Gretz, Susanna. *Teddy Bears' Moving Day* (PS–1). Illus. by author. 1981, Four Winds $9.95. Robert creates havoc on moving day with his ineptitude. Also use: *Teddy Bears Go Shopping* (1982, Four Winds $9.95).

524. Guzzo, Sandra E. *Fox and Heggie* (PS–3). Illus. by Kathy Parkinson. 1983, Whitman $8.25. Fox wants to buy a Greek fisherman's hat but hasn't the money.

525. Haas, Irene. *The Little Moon Theater* (1–3). Illus. 1981, Atheneum LB $12.95. A dog, a cat, and a girl travel the countryside as a theatrical group.

526. Hall, Malcolm. *Forecast* (1–3). Illus. by Bruce Degen. 1977, Putnam $6.99. Caroline Porcupine of the *Claws n' Paws* newspaper staff takes over the job of weather forecasting with amusing results.

527. Harris, Robin. *Hello Kitty Sleeps Over* (PS). Illus. by J. M. Gray. 1982, Random $3.50. A kitten sleeps at her grandmother's house.

528. Harris, Robin. *My Melody's New Bike* (PS). Illus. by Carolyn Bracken. 1982, Random paper $3.50. A little rabbit gets a tricycle as a birthday present.

529. Hayes, Geoffrey. *Patrick Comes to Puttyville* (K–3). Illus. by author. 1978, Harper $5.95; LB $5.79. Five adventures of the stuffed bear who also appeared in the author's *Bear by Himself* (1976, Harper $6.95; paper $3.79). A further sequel is: *Patrick and Ted* (1984, Four Winds $5.95).

530. Heine, Helme. *Friends* (PS–3). Illus. by author. 1982, Atheneum $12.95. A rooster, mouse, and pig share an outing on a bicycle.

531. Heine, Helme. *The Most Wonderful Egg in the World* (PS–2). Illus. by author. 1983, Atheneum $10.95. Three quarrelsome chickens compete to see who will lay the most beautiful egg.

532. Heine, Helme. *The Pigs' Wedding* (PS–3). Illus. by author. 1979, Atheneum $7.95. Curlytail and Porker say "I do."

533. Himmelman, John. *Talester the Lizard* (PS–2). Illus. by author. 1982, Dial $8.95; LB $8.89. Talester makes a friend of his reflection in a pond.

534. Hoban, Lillian. *Harry's Song* (1–3). Illus. by author. 1980, Greenwillow $10.95; LB $10.51. Harry makes an unusual contribution to the rabbits' winter provisions.

535. Hoban, Lillian. *No, No Sammy Grow* (PS–2). 1981, Greenwillow $10.25; LB $9.84. Sammy refuses to grow up.

536. Hoban, Russell. *Dinner at Alberta's* (K–2). Illus. by James Marshall. 1975, Harper LB $9.89. Arthur, a really sloppy crocodile, valiantly practices his table manners in preparation for dinner at Alberta's, with whom he is smitten.

537. Hoban, Russell. *The Little Brute Family* (K–3). Illus. by Lillian Hoban. 1969, Macmillan $8.95; paper $2.25. The Brute family and their equally disagreeable home are transformed by the actions of Baby Brute.

538. Hofstrand, Mary. *Albion Pig* (PS–K). Illus. by author. 1984, Knopf $10.95; LB $10.99. A pampered pig falls on his head and can't remember who he is.

539. Hogrogian, Nonny. *Carrot Cake* (PS–3). Illus. by author. 1977, Greenwillow LB $10.51. Two married rabbits have marital problems in this humorous story.

540. Holabird, Katharine. *Angelina Ballerina* (PS–2). Illus. by Helen Craig. 1983, Crown $5.95. Angelina Mouseling enrolls in a ballet class.

541. Holl, Adelaide. *The Remarkable Egg* (K–2). Illus. by Roger Duvoisin. 1968, Lothrop $10.80. A series of birds are asked if they own the mysterious egg that has been placed in a nest.

542. Howe, Deborah, and Howe, James. *Teddy Bear's Scrapbook* (2–3). Illus. by David S. Rose. 1980, Atheneum $8.95; Avon paper $1.95. A teddy bear describes the pictures in his scrapbook to a little girl.

543. Howe, James. *The Day the Teacher Went Bananas* (K–3). Illus. by Lillian Hoban. 1984, Dutton $9.66. The new teacher turns out to be a gorilla.

544. Hurd, Thacher. *Axle the Freeway Cat* (K–2). Illus. by author. 1981, Harper LB $9.89. Axle helps a cat in a stalled car that is causing a traffic jam.

545. Hurd, Thacher. *Mama Don't Allow: Starring Miles and the Swamp Band* (PS–1). Illus. 1984, Harper $11.49; LB $11.89. The Swamp Band finds that the only audience that likes them is the alligator.

546. Hurd, Thacher. *Mystery on the Docks* (1–3). Illus. by author. 1983, Harper $9.57; LB $9.89; paper $2.95. Ralph, an opera-lover, rescues his favorite singer from rat-kidnappers.

547. Hutchins, Pat. *Good-Night, Owl* (PS–K). Illus. by author. 1972, Macmillan $10.95. Owl is kept awake by different animal noises, as various animals perch on a branch of his tree; but when darkness falls, owl has his turn and wakes everyone with his screeches.

548. Hutchins, Pat. *Rosie's Walk* (K–2). Illus. by author. 1968, Macmillan $9.95; paper $3.95. Rosie, the hen, miraculously escapes capture by a fox.

549. Isenberg, Barbara, and Wolf, Susan. *The Adventures of Albert, the Running Bear* (PS–2). Illus. by Dick Gackenbach. 1982, Houghton $11.50; paper $4.95. Albert, an overweight bear, accidently wins the Annual City Marathon. Also use: *Albert the Running Bear's Exercise Book* by Barbara Isenberg and Marjorie Jaffe (1984, Houghton $13.95; paper $4.95).

550. Iwamura, Kazuo. *Ton and Pon: Big and Little* (PS–2). Illus. by author. 1984, Bradbury $8.95. The story of 2 dogs and their adventures. A sequel is: *Ton and Pon: Two Good Friends* (1984, $8.95).

551. Jarrell, Randall. *The Gingerbread Rabbit* (PS–2). Illus. by Garth Williams. 1972, Macmillan paper $2.95. A gingerbread rabbit escapes baking but is almost eaten by a fox.

552. Jeschke, Susan. *Perfect the Pig* (K–2). Illus. by author. 1981, Holt $10.00; Scholastic paper $1.95. The adventures of a winged pig named Perfect.

553. Jeschke, Susan. *Sidney* (K–3). Illus. by author. 1975, Holt paper $2.95. A chicken named Sidney pretends to be a fox and actually turns into one.

554. Joerns, Consuelo. *The Foggy Rescue* (K–3). Illus. by author. 1980, Four Winds $7.95. An adventure featuring the mouse family, a shipwreck, and a strange island.

555. Joerns, Consuelo. *Oliver's Escape* (K–2). Illus. by author. 1984, Four Winds $9.95. A dog escapes from a pet shop to find a new home.

556. Johnston, Tony. *Five Little Foxes and the Snow* (PS–K). Illus. by Cyndy Szekeres. 1977, Putnam paper $4.95. Gramma knits mittens for her young foxes so they can enjoy themselves in the snow.

557. Kalan, Robert. *Jump, Frog, Jump!* (PS–2). Illus. by Byron Barton. 1981, Greenwillow $11.25; LB $11.88. A rhyming cumulative tale that ends "jump, frog, jump."

558. Keller, Holly. *Geraldine's Blanket* (PS–2). Illus. 1984, Greenwillow $9.00; LB $8.59. A little pig named Geraldine becomes extremely attached to a blanket her aunt gave her.

559. Keller, Holly. *Will It Rain?* (PS–2). 1984, Greenwillow $10.51. A story of a rainstorm as seen through the eyes of different animals.

560. Kelley, True. *A Valentine for Fuzzboom* (K–2). Illus. by author. 1981, Houghton $5.95; paper $1.95. Lima Bean, a rabbit, has a crush on egotistical Fuzzboom.

561. Kellogg, Steven. *Island of the Skog* (1–3). Illus. by author. 1973, Dial $10.95; LB $8.89; paper $2.25. A new danger is found by mice who have sailed to a distant island to find safety.

562. Kellogg, Steven. *The Mysterious Tadpole* (K–3). Illus. by author. 1977, Dial $11.95; LB $11.89; paper $3.95. When a tadpole grows at an alarming rate, Louis discovers his new pet is really a baby Loch Ness Monster.

563. Kent, Jack. *The Caterpillar and the Polliwog* (K–2). Illus. by author. 1982, Prentice $10.95. The caterpillar and the polliwog become a butterfly and a frog.

564. Kent, Jack. *Joey* (PS–2). Illus. by author. 1984, Prentice $10.95. Joey, a young kangaroo, is not allowed out of his mother's pouch, so he invites his friends in.

565. Kent, Jack. *Little Peep* (PS–2). Illus. by author. 1981, Prentice $9.95; paper $4.95. A chick wants to crow like a rooster.

566. Kent, Jack. *Round Robin* (PS–2). 1982, Prentice $10.95; paper $4.95. The bird clan and their locales are explored in this outlandishly silly saga.

567. Kessler, Leonard. *The Big Mile Race* (1–3). Illus. by author. 1983, Greenwillow $8.50. A group of animals engage in a marathon.

568. Koide, Tan. *May We Sleep Here Tonight?* (PS–2). Illus. by Yasuko Koide. 1983, Atheneum $6.95. Mr. Bear takes in lost animals.

569. Korschunow, Irina. *The Foundling Fox: How the Little Fox Got a Mother* (1–3). Illus. by Reinhard Michl. 1984, Harper $12.02; LB $11.89. An orphaned fox meets a vixen who helps him.

570. Kraus, Robert. *Herman the Helper* (PS–K). Illus. by Jose Aruego and Ariane Dewey. 1974, Windmill paper $3.95. Herman, a green octopus, with his many arms is especially helpful to family and friends and learns to help himself as well.

571. Kraus, Robert. *Leo the Late Bloomer* (PS–K). Illus. by Jose Aruego. 1973, Harper $10.89. Leo, a lion, is just a late bloomer, as Mother tells Father, but Father is worried. But finally Leo blooms—he can read, write, and eat neatly. A beguiling, humorous story.

572. Kraus, Robert. *Owliver* (PS–1). Illus. by Jose Aruego and Ariane Dewey. 1974, Windmill paper $3.95. A fresh, funny, and engaging story of a small owl who imitates and play-acts whatever his mother or father wants him to be—a doctor, lawyer, or actor—and then makes his own decision.

573. Kraus, Robert. *Whose Mouse Are You?* (PS–1). Illus. by Jose Aruego. 1970, Macmillan $9.50; paper $3.95. A young mouse is asked 8 questions by his family—which should delight young chil-

dren who are asked similar questions by their families.

574. Krensky, Stephen. *A Troll in Passing* (3–5). 1980, Atheneum $8.95. Morgan, an adventurous troll, saves his troll colony.

575. Kroll, Steven. *Loose Tooth* (K–2). Illus. by Tricia Tusa. 1984, Holiday $10.95. A boy bat looses his first tooth and his twin bat brother is jealous.

576. Lauber, Patricia. *Home at Last: A Young Cat's Tale* (2–4). Illus. by Mary Chalmers. 1980, Putnam $6.95. Two kittens decide to leave their comfortable home and face life.

577. Lazard, Naomi. *What Amanda Saw* (K–3). Illus. by Paul O. Zelinsky. 1981, Greenwillow $10.25; LB $9.84. Amanda's cat is given a farewell party before leaving for the summer.

578. Leaf, Munro. *Noodle* (K–2). Illus. by Ludwig Bemelmans. 1969, Scholastic paper $1.95. Noodle, the dachshund, tries to find a shape that is better for digging than his own.

579. Leaf, Munro. *The Story of Ferdinand* (K–4). Illus. by Robert Lawson. 1936, Viking $10.95; Penguin paper $3.50. The classic story of the bull who wants only to sit and smell flowers.

580. Le-Tan, Pierre. *Happy Birthday Oliver!* (K–2). Illus. by author. 1979, Random LB $4.99. Oliver is convinced that everyone has forgotten his birthday.

581. Levitin, Sonia. *Nobody Stole the Pie* (K–3). Illus. by Fernando Krahn. 1980, Harcourt $9.95; paper $3.50. Slowly a number of animals pick away at a pie intended for a special celebration until there is only one piece left.

582. Lindgren, Barbro. *The Wild Baby* (PS–K). Illus. by Eva Eriksson. 1981, Greenwillow $11.25; LB $11.84. Baby Ben gets into all sorts of trouble but his mother still loves him. A sequel is: *The Wild Baby Goes to Sea* (1983, $9.00; LB $8.59).

583. Lionni, Leo. *Alexander and the Wind-Up Mouse* (K–2). Illus. by author. 1969, Pantheon $7.99. Alexander, a real mouse, envies Willy, a toy, windup mouse, who is loved and cuddled.

584. Lionni, Leo. *The Biggest House in the World* (PS–2). Illus. by author. 1968, Pantheon LB $9.99; paper $1.45. A young snail, desiring a larger shell, receives fatherly advice and decides that small accommodations are an asset in regaining his mobility.

585. Lionni, Leo. *Cornelius: A Fable* (PS–2). Illus. by author. 1983, Pantheon $9.95; LB $9.99. Cornelius is a most unusual crocodile but is not appreciated by his peers.

586. Lionni, Leo. *Fish Is Fish* (K–2). Illus. by author. 1970, Pantheon LB $7.99. A fable about a fish who learns from a frog how to be happy just being himself.

587. Lionni, Leo. *Frederick* (PS–2). Illus. by author. 1967, Pantheon $8.99; paper $2.95. A field mouse appears to be ignoring the coming of winter but actually he is not.

588. Lionni, Leo. *Geraldine, the Music Mouse* (PS–K). Illus. by author. 1979, Pantheon $6.95; LB $6.99. A mouse learns to play lovely music using her tail.

589. Lionni, Leo. *The Greentail Mouse* (PS–3). Illus. by author. 1973, Pantheon LB $8.99. A group of field mice assume new identities when they put on masks.

590. Lionni, Leo. *Inch by Inch* (PS–2). Illus. by author. 1962, Astor-Honor $8.95. When the birds demand that he measure the length of a nightingale's song, this clever, captive inchworm inches his way to freedom.

591. Lionni, Leo. *Let's Make Rabbits: A Fable* (PS–K). Illus. by author. 1982, Pantheon $9.95; LB $9.99. A pencil and a pair of scissors decide to produce two rabbits from wrapping paper.

592. Lionni, Leo. *Swimmy* (PS–1). Illus. by author. 1963, Pantheon LB $6.99; paper $1.95. A remarkable little fish instructs the rest of his school in the art of protection—swim in the formation of a gigantic fish! Beautiful, full-color illustrations.

593. Lloyd, Megan. *Chicken Tricks* (PS–2). Illus. by author. 1983, Harper $8.61; LB $8.89. Chickens try to fool the farmer who demands constant egg production.

594. Lobel, Arnold. *Fables* (2–4). Illus. by author. 1980, Harper $11.49; LB $11.89; paper $4.76. An Americanized Aesop with excellent illustrations. A Caldecott Medal winner.

595. Lobel, Arnold. *Zoo for Mister Muster* (PS–1). Illus. by author. 1962, Harper $9.89. When Mr. Muster can't go to the zoo to visit his animal friends, they all come to visit him in bed at his house. Also use: *Holiday for Mister Muster* (1963, $10.89).

596. Lorenz, Lee. *Hugo and the Spacedog* (PS–1). Illus. 1983, Prentice $10.95. Hugo, a dog, proves to the farm animals that they need a watchdog.

597. Low, Joseph. *Mice Twice* (K–3). Illus. by author. 1980, Atheneum $9.95. Cat invites Mouse to dinner but Mouse brings along Dog.

598. Luttrell, Ida. *Lonesome Lester* (PS–3). Illus. by Megan Lloyd. 1984, Harper $10.53; LB $10.89. Lester, a prairie dog, feels alone and neglected.

599. McLeod, Emilie W. *The Bear's Bicycle* (PS–2). Illus. by David McPhail. 1975, Little $8.95; paper $2.95. A small boy and his teddy bear have an exciting bicycle ride as he gives the bear safety lessons. When the bear, grown to grizzly bear proportions, does not follow the safety rules, the bear suffers the consequences.

600. McNulty, Faith. *The Elephant Who Couldn't Forget* (1–3). Illus. by Marc Simont. 1980, Harper $6.41; LB $8.89. A moral lesson about an elephant who was unable to forgive and forget.

601. McPhail, David. *The Bear's Toothache* (PS–K). Illus. by author. 1972, Little $9.95; Penguin paper $3.95. A very funny story of a little boy's attempt to help extract a bear's tooth and rid him of his toothache.

602. McPhail, David. *Captain Toad and the Motorbike* (1–3). Illus. by author. 1978, Atheneum $9.95. A retired Navy officer wins a motorcycle race.

603. McPhail, David. *Fix-it* (PS–K). 1984, Dutton $7.72. Emma Bear is distraught when the television set won't work.

604. McPhail, David. *Pig Pig Grows Up* (PS–K). Illus. by author. 1980, Dutton $8.95. Pig Pig refuses to stop being treated as a child. Two sequels are: *Pig Pig Rides* (1982, $8.95); *Pig Pig Goes to Camp* (1983, $9.95).

605. McPhail, David. *Stanley, Henry Bear's Friend* (2–4). Illus. by author. 1979, Little $7.95. After a harrowing time in jail, a young raccoon forms a friendship with Henry Bear. Also use: *Henry Bear's Park* (1976, Little $5.95; Penguin paper $2.50).

606. McPhail, David. *That Grand Master Jumping Teacher, Bernard, Meets Jerome, the Great Jumping Glump* (K–3). Illus. by author. 1982, Warne $9.95. A great jumper named Bernard takes on the training of a sorry student named Jerome.

607. McPhail, David. *Where Can an Elephant Hide?* (PS–K). Illus. by author. 1979, Doubleday LB $7.95. Several creatures suggest ways in which Morris can hide from approaching hunters.

608. Maestro, Betsy. *Harriet Goes to the Circus* (PS–1). Illus. by Giulio Maestro. 1977, Crown $6.95. Harriet, an elephant, is determined to be first in line for the best circus seats. Sequels are: *Harriet at Home; Harriet at Play; Harriet at School; Harriet at Work* (all 1984, Crown $2.95).

609. Manushkin, Fran. *Moon Dragon* (K–2). Illus. by Geoffrey Hayes. 1982, Macmillan $8.95. A clever mouse outwits a dragon.

610. Maris, Ron. *Better Move On, Frog!* (PS–2). Illus. by author. 1982, Watts $8.90. Frog searches for a perfect home.

611. Marshall, James. *George and Martha* (PS–1). Illus. by author. 1972, Houghton $7.95; paper $4.50. The friendship of two hippos leads to some very humorous situations. Also use the sequels:

George and Martha Encore (1973, $10.95; paper $2.95); *George and Martha Rise and Shine* (1976, LB $8.95; paper $3.95); *George and Martha One Fine Day* (1978, $6.95; paper $3.95); *George and Martha Tons of Fun* (1980, $8.95); *George and Martha Back in Town* (1984, $9.70).

612. Marshall, James. *The Guest* (K–3). Illus. by author. 1975, Houghton LB $5.95; paper $3.45. Mona Moose develops a friendship with Maurice, a snail.

613. Marshall, James. *What's the Matter with Carruthers? A Bedtime Story* (K–3). Illus. by author. 1972, Houghton $9.95. Carruthers, a very large bear, gets grumpy because it's time for his sleep.

614. Marshall, James. *Willis* (PS–K). Illus. by author. 1974, Houghton LB $6.95. Willis, an alligator, has sensitive eyes and needs sunglasses when he goes sunbathing, but he has no money to buy them. His friends, Bud, Snake, and Lobster, devise very funny ingenious jobs to help him earn the money—19¢ for a pair of glasses!

615. Marshall, James. *Yummers!* (PS–K). Illus. by author. 1973, Houghton $9.95. Emily Pig is worried about her weight, so she goes for a walk for exercise. Unfortunately, the walk is interrupted for several snacks, and the resulting stomachache, Emily Pig suggests, is due to the exercise, not the food!

616. Martin, Bill, Jr. *Brown Bear, Brown Bear, What Do You See?* (PS–1). Illus. by Eric Carle. 1983, Holt $10.45. Many animals see other animals looking at them.

617. Martin, Charles E. *Dunkel Takes a Walk* (PS–1). Illus. by author. 1983, Greenwillow $10.00; LB $9.55. A dachshund has adventures in the forest.

618. Martin, Jacqueline Briggs. *Bizzy Bones and Uncle Ezra* (PS). Illus. by Stella Ormai. 1984, Lothrop $10.50; LB $10.08. A young mouse is afraid that his new house, a shoe, will blow away.

619. Marzollo, Jean. *Uproar on Hollercat Hill* (K–2). Illus. by Steven Kellogg. 1980, Dial $8.95; LB $8.89; paper $3.50. Even in the best of cat families, there are quarrels.

620. Massie, Diane Redfield. *Chameleon Was a Spy* (2–4). Illus. by author. 1979, Harper $9.57; $9.89; Scholastic paper $1.95. Chameleon uses his talents in spy work. Two sequels are: *Chameleon the Spy and the Terrible Toaster Trap* (1982, $9.57; LB $9.89); *Chameleon the Spy and the Case of the Vanishing Jewels* (1984, $9.57; LB $9.89).

621. Mayer, Marianna. *The Unicorn and the Lake* (K–4). Illus. by Michael Hague. 1982, Dial $11.95; LB $11.89. A helpful unicorn purifies a lake so animals may use it.

622. Mayer, Mercer. *Appelard and Liverwurst* (K–2). Illus. by Steven Kellogg. 1978, Scholastic $10.95. Liverwurst, a rhino, helps Appelard plow his fields and raise a bumper crop. A sequel is: *Liverwurst Is Missing* (1981, $10.95).

623. Mayne, William. *The Mouse and the Egg* (PS–2). Illus. by Krystyna Turska. 1981, Greenwillow $12.25; LB $11.76. Grandfather learns he should be thankful for his daily brown egg.

624. Mayne, William, and Bayley, Nicola. *The Patchwork Cat* (K–2). Illus. by Nicola Bayley. 1981, Knopf $9.95; LB $9.99. A cat sets out to find her discarded patchwork quilt.

625. Meddaugh, Susan. *Maude and Claude Go Abroad* (PS–1). Illus. 1980, Houghton LB $7.95. A rhyming story about 2 foxes and an eventful transatlantic crossing.

626. Miles, Miska. *Chicken Forgets* (PS–K). Illus. by Jim Arnosky. 1976, Little $6.95. Chicken is told not to be forgetful this time and to fill his basket with wild blackberries, but he is easily diverted until Robin helps him out by advising what berries are best.

627. Miles, Miska. *Mouse Six and the Happy Birthday* (1–3). Illus. by Leslie Morrill. 1978, Dutton $6.50. When Mouse Six goes out to buy a birthday present for his mother, others think he has run away.

628. Miller, Edna. *Mousekin's Family* (1–3). Illus. by author. 1969, Prentice $9.95; paper $2.50. Complications occur when a little white-footed mouse mistakenly believes she has found a relative. Other titles in the series are: *Mousekin's Golden House* (1964, LB $9.95; paper $3.95); *Mousekin Finds a Friend* (1967, paper $3.95); *Mousekin's Woodland Sleepers* (1970, paper $2.50); *Mousekin's Woodland Birthday* (1974, $9.95); *Mousekin Takes a Trip* (1976, $9.95; paper $3.95); *Mousekin's Close Call* (1980, $9.95; paper $3.95); *Mousekin's Fables* (1982, $9.95); *Mousekin's Mystery* (1983, $10.95).

629. Moeri, Louise. *How the Rabbit Stole the Moon* (K–3). Illus. by Marc Brown. 1977, Houghton LB $7.95. A story about how a rabbit stole a piece of the sun and was responsible for the creation of the moon and stars.

630. Moore, Inga. *The Vegetable Thieves* (K–2). Illus. 1984, Viking $10.95. Two mice discover that robbers are stealing from their vegetable garden.

631. Most, Bernard. *If the Dinosaurs Came Back* (1–3). Illus. by author. 1978, Harcourt $11.95; paper $6.95. All the things that might happen if dinosaurs came back to the world.

632. Murphy, Jill. *Peace at Last* (PS–2). Illus. by author. 1980, Dial $7.95; LB $7.45. Mr. Bear finds many distractions keep him from sleeping. A sequel is: *What Next, Baby Bear?* (1984, Dutton $10.63).

633. Musicant, Elke, and Musicant, Ted. *The Night Vegetable Eater* (1–3). Illus. by Jeni Bassett. 1981, Dodd LB $7.95. Who is eating Rabbit's vegetables at night?

634. Myller, Rolf. *A Very Noisy Day* (PS–1). Illus. by author. 1981, Atheneum LB $9.95. Various word sounds are introduced through the adventures of a dog.

635. Ness, Evaline. *Fierce: The Lion* (PS–2). Illus. by author. 1980, Holiday LB $8.95. Isabel's pet lion wants to give rides to children.

636. Newberry, Clare Turlay. *Marshmallow* (K–3). Illus. by author. 1942, Harper $10.38. Oliver, a bachelor cat, and Marshmallow, a soft white bunny, become playmates. Another cat story written and illustrated by Newberry is: *April's Kittens* (1940, Harper $10.53; LB $10.89).

637. Newsham, Wendy, and Newsham, Ian. *The Monster Hunt* (PS–2). Illus. 1983, David and Charles $9.50. Professor Wrightson finds no monster in Loch Ness but the reader knows better.

638. Nicholson, William. *Clever Bill* (1–3). Illus. by author. 1977, Farrar $5.95. Reprint of a classic first published in England in 1926.

639. Nixon, Joan Lowery. *Magnolia's Mixed-Up Magic* (2–4). Illus. by Linda Bucholtz-Ross. 1983, Putnam $8.95. Magnolia Possum produces some magic spells but can't undo them.

640. Oakley, Graham. *The Church Mouse* (K–2). Illus. by author. 1972, Atheneum $9.95; paper $2.95. The humorous escapades of Arthur, the church mouse, and Samson, the church cat. Sequels are: *The Church Cat Abroad* (1973, $6.95); *The Church Mice and the Moon* (1974, $9.95; paper $2.95); *The Church Mice Adrift* (1977, $7.95; paper $2.95); *The Church Mice at Bay* (1978, $9.95); *The Church Mice in Action* (1983, $11.95).

641. Oakley, Graham. *Hetty and Harriet* (K–3). Illus. by author. 1982, Atheneum LB $12.95. Two chickens, Harriet and her sister, Hetty, leave the barnyard to find a better place to live.

642. Ormondroyd, Edward. *Broderick* (PS–3). Illus. by John Larrecq. 1969, Houghton $6.95; LB $4.77; paper $3.95. Broderick, a mouse, loves to chew books, but one night he stops chewing and reads one. The book is on surfing, and it changes his life!

643. Ormondroyd, Edward. *Theodore* (PS–2). Illus. by John Larrecq. 1966, Parnassus $5.95; paper $3.95. A toy bear accidentally gets washed clean, and his little girl owner does not recognize him until he is properly dirty again. Also use: *Theodore's Rival* (1971, $5.95; LB $4.59).

644. Panek, Dennis. *Catastrophe Cat* (K–2). Illus. by author. 1978, Bradbury $10.95. A mischievous cat has an unexpected adventure.

645. Panek, Dennis. *Detective Whoo* (PS–K). Illus. by author. 1981, Bradbury $10.95. Detective Whoo, a brown owl, sets out to find out who disturbed his sleep.

646. Panek, Dennis. *Matilda Hippo Has a Big Mouth* (K–2). Illus. by author. 1980, Bradbury $10.95. Matilda insults her animal friends but gets her comeuppance.

647. Parker, Nancy W. *Cooper: The McNallys' Big Black Dog* (K–2). Illus. by author. 1981, Dodd LB $7.95. A dog named Cooper is considered a failure until he saves a baby.

648. Parker, Nancy W. *The Ordeal of Byron B. Blackbear* (K–2). Illus. by author. 1979, Dodd $6.95. Byron fools scientists who are out exploring animal hibernation.

649. Patz, Nancy. *Nobody Knows I Have Delicate Toes* (PS–3). Illus. 1980, Watts $12.95. Ben and Elephant in a hilarious adventure.

650. Paul, Jan S. *Hortense* (PS–K). Illus. by Madelaine Gill Linden. 1984, Harper $10.10; LB $10.89. Hortense Hen can't find the eggs entrusted to Robinson Rooster.

651. Pavey, Peter. *I'm Taggarty Toad* (K–2). Illus. by author. 1980, Bradbury $9.95. A boastful toad gets his comeuppance.

652. Payne, Emmy. *Katy No-Pocket* (PS–1). Illus. by H. A. Rey. 1944, Houghton $10.95; paper $4.50. Until Katy finds an apron with pockets, she is very sad, for she has no way in which to carry her baby.

653. Peet, Bill. *Cowardly Clyde* (K–2). Illus. by author. 1979, Houghton $8.95; paper $3.95. A horse named Clyde quivers in fear at the thought of fighting a dragon with his master, Sir Galavant. Other titles by this author and publisher are: *Farewell to Shady Glade* (1966, LB $11.95; paper $3.95); *Ant and the Elephant* (1972, LB $11.95; paper $3.95); *Encore for Eleanor* (1981, $11.95); *The Luckiest One of All* (1982, LB $9.95); *No Such Things* (1983, $10.45); *Pamela Camel* (1984, $11.45).

654. Peet, Bill. *Eli* (1–3). Illus. by author. 1978, Houghton $8.95. An old lion is saved from hunters by playing dead. Others by Bill Peet and published by Houghton are: *Hubert's Hair-Raising Adventure* (1959, LB $11.95; paper $2.50); *Ella* (1964); *Chester the Worldly Pig* (1965); *Burford, the Little Bighorn* (1967); *Kermit the Hermit* (1968); *Cyrus the Unsinkable Sea Serpent* (1975) (all LB $11.95; paper $3.95).

655. Peet, Bill. *Whingdingdilly* (2–4). Illus. by author. 1970, Houghton $11.95. Scamp, tired of leading a dog's life, is transformed by a witch. Some others by this author and publisher are: *Huge Harold* (1961, LB $11.95; paper $3.95); *The Pinkish, Purplish, Bluish Egg* (1963, LB $10.95; paper $3.95); *Randy's Dandy Lions* (1964, LB $11.95; paper $3.95); *Fly, Homer, Fly* (1969, LB $11.95; paper $2.50); *How Droofus the Dragon Lost His Head* (1971, LB $11.95; paper $3.95); *The Spooky Tail of Prewitt Peacock* (1973, LB $11.95; paper $2.50); *Merle the High Flying Squirrel* (1974, LB $11.95; paper $3.95).

656. Peppe, Rodney. *The Mice Who Lived in a Shoe* (PS–K). Illus. 1982, Lothrop $10.75. A family of mice moves into a boot in this variation of the old story.

657. Petersham, Maud, and Petersham, Miska. *The Box with Red Wheels: A Picture Book* (PS–1). Illus. by author. 1949, Macmillan paper $0.95. A sleeping baby is discovered by curious barnyard animals when they investigate a box.

658. Petersham, Maud, and Petersham, Miska. *The Circus Baby* (PS–1). Illus. by author. 1950, Macmillan $10.95. A circus elephant decides that the baby must learn to eat as the clown's family does, with rather disastrous results.

659. Phillips, Louis. *The Brothers Wrong and Wrong Again* (K–3). Illus. by J. Winslow Higginbottom. 1979, McGraw $9.95. A humorous story of 2 brothers who inadvertently tame a dragon who has ravaged the countryside.

660. Piatti, Celestino. *The Happy Owls* (K–3). Trans. from the German. Illus. by author. 1964, Atheneum paper $1.95. Two wise owls try to explain their joy in the changing seasons to the barnyard fowl.

661. Pinkwater, D. Manus. *Bear's Picture* (PS–1). Illus. by author. 1984, Dutton $10.63. A fable about truth and imagination.

662. Pinkwater, D. Manus. *Blue Moose* (1–3). Illus. by author. 1975, Dodd $8.95. A restaurant owner takes in a blue moose as his maitre d' in this comic tale.

663. Pinkwater, D. Manus. *Ducks!* (K–3). Illus. by author. 1984, Little $10.95. A duck who is really an angel grants a boy one wish.

664. Pinkwater, D. Manus. *The Wuggie Norple Story* (1–3). Illus. by Tomie de Paola. 1980, Four Winds $9.95. A nonsense story about the size of animals.

665. Polushkin, Maria. *Morning* (PS–1). Illus. by Bill Morrison. 1983, Four Winds $10.95. A cumulative tale about farm animals awakening.

666. Pomerantz, Charlotte. *The Piggy in the Puddle* (PS–K). Illus. by James Marshall. 1974, Macmillan $8.95. Amusing story of the antics of a pig family enjoying a mud puddle.

667. Potter, Beatrix. *The Complete Adventures of Peter Rabbit* (K–3). Illus. by author. 1982, Warne $9.95. An omnibus of the Peter Rabbit stories.

668. Potter, Beatrix. *The Sly Old Cat* (PS–K). Illus. by author. 1972, Warne $5.95. How Rat outwits Cat, who had planned to eat him for dessert, is described with sly humor.

669. Potter, Beatrix. *The Tale of Peter Rabbit* (K–3). Illus. by author. 1902, Warne $3.95; paper $1.95; Bantam paper $2.25; Scholastic paper $1.95. In spite of his mother's warning, Peter ventures into Mr. McGregor's garden. There are 23 titles in this series.

670. Potter, Beatrix. *The Tale of Peter Rabbit and Other Stories* (K–3). Illus. by Allen Atkinson. 1982, Knopf $16.95. Nine Potter stories newly illustrated.

671. Potter, Beatrix. *The Tale of the Faithful Dove* (K–2). Illus. by Marie Angel. 1970, Warne $4.95. A gentle story of a little pigeon who is chased into a chimney by a hawk. A posthumous manuscript, illustrated and printed in the style and format of the other Potter books.

672. Potter, Beatrix. *Yours Affectionately, Peter Rabbit: Miniature Letters by Beatrix Potter* (PS–2). Illus. by author. 1984, Warne $6.95. Correspondence from some of Potter's favorite characters.

673. Prelutsky, Jack. *The Baby Uggs Are Hatching* (K–4). Illus. by James Stevenson. 1982, Greenwillow $10.25; LB $10.88. A collection of imaginary animals introduced in catchy verse.

674. Prelutsky, Jack. *The Mean Old Mean Hyena* (K–3). Illus. by Arnold Lobel. 1978, Greenwillow $10.95; LB $10.51. The animals who have been victimized by the hyena plan their revenge.

675. Preston, Edna Mitchell. *Where Did My Mother Go?* (K–2). Illus. by Chris Conover. 1978, Four Winds $7.95. Little Cat searches all over town for his mother.

676. Preston, Edna Mitchell, and Cooney, Barbara. *Squawk to the Moon, Little Goose* (K–2). Illus. by Barbara Cooney. 1974, Viking $10.50. A silly but resourceful goose uses her fear of the moon, which she is sure has fallen into the pond, to escape from the clutches of Mr. Fox.

677. Quackenbush, Robert. *Funny Bunnies* (PS–1). Illus. by author. 1984, Ticknor & Fields $12.95. Mama and Papa Bunny have many unexpected guests in their hotel room.

678. Quackenbush, Robert. *Henry's Awful Mistake* (PS–2). Illus. by author. 1981, Dutton $5.50; LB $5.95. Henry, a duck, tries to rid his horse of an ant. A sequel is: *Henry's Important Date* (1982, $5.50; LB $5.95).

679. Quackenbush, Robert. *Moose's Store* (1–3). Illus. by author. 1979, Morrow $9.95; LB $9.55. Beaver decides to modernize Moose's old-fashioned store.

680. Quackenbush, Robert. *Rickshaw to Horror* (1–3). Illus. by author. 1984, Prentice $9.95. Miss Mallard, super sleuth, and an exciting mystery. Others in this series are: *Express Train to Trouble: A Miss Mallard Mystery* (1981, $9.95); *Dig to Disaster* (1982, $9.95); *Gondola to Danger* (1983, $9.95); *Stairway to Doom* (1983, $8.95); *Taxi to Intrigue* (1984, $9.95).

681. Raskin, Ellen. *And It Rained* (K–2). Illus. by author. 1969, Atheneum LB $6.95. Cleverly designed to amuse, the illustrations reveal a comically romantic subplot while some animals try to solve their problems.

682. Raskin, Ellen. *Moose, Goose and Little Nobody* (PS–3). Illus. by author. 1980, Four Winds $8.95. Moose and Goose adopt a homeless waif.

683. Rayner, Mary. *Garth Pig and the Ice Cream Lady* (K–3). Illus. by author. 1977, Atheneum $9.95. A wolf disguised as an ice-cream vendor almost succeeds in making a piglet dinner out of Garth. Other titles in the series are: *Mr. and Mrs. Pig's Evening Out* (1976, $8.95; paper $2.50); *Mrs. Pig's Bulk Buy* (1981, $10.95; paper $3.95).

684. Rey, H. A. *Cecily G and the Nine Monkeys* (K–2). Illus. by author. 1942, Houghton LB $9.95; paper $3.95. A lonely giraffe and 9 homeless monkeys share some uproarious adventures.

685. Rey, H. A. *Curious George* (K–4). Illus. by author. 1941, Houghton LB $9.95; paper $3.95. A small monkey finds himself in difficulties due to his mischievous curiosity. Also use by the same author: *Curious George Takes a Job* (1947); *Curious George Rides a Bike* (1952); *Curious George Gets a Medal* (1957) (all LB $9.95; paper $3.95).

686. Rey, Margaret. *Curious George Flies a Kite* (K–2). Illus. by H. A. Rey. 1958, Houghton LB $9.95; paper $3.95. More predicaments are encountered by this fun-loving monkey. Also use by the same author: *Curious George Goes to the Hospital* (1966, LB $9.95; paper $3.95).

687. Roberts, Bethany. *Waiting-for-Spring Stories* (PS–K). Illus. by William Joyce. 1984, Harper $9.57; LB $9.89. Seven stories that rabbit tells to speed the coming of spring.

688. Robinson, Marileta. *Mr. Goat's Bad Good Idea* (K–2). Illus. by Arthur Getz. 1979, Harper $9.57. Three amusing animal stories that use a Navajo setting.

689. Robinson, Tom. *Buttons* (K–1). Illus. by Peggy Bacon. 1976, Penguin $3.50. An alley cat joins the British upper crust.

690. Roche, P. K. *Good-Bye, Arnold!* (K–2). Illus. by author. 1979, Dial $8.50; LB $8.23. Webster's big brother goes away for a week, and Webster realizes how much he misses him. A sequel is: *Webster and Arnold and the Giant Box* (1980, LB $5.89; paper $2.25).

691. Roche, P. K. *Plaid Bear and the Rude Rabbit Gang* (K–2). Illus. by author. 1982, Dial $9.95; LB $9.89; paper $3.95. Four holiday revelers are harassed by a gang of bullies.

692. Rockwell, Anne. *Henry the Cat and the Big Sneeze* (1–3). Illus. by author. 1980, Greenwillow $8.25; LB $7.92. When Henry the Cat falls into a deep hole, he must use trickery to get out.

693. Ross, Tony. *Towser and Sadie's Birthday* (PS–1). Illus. by author. 1984, Pantheon $4.95; LB $6.99. Towser, a dog, wants to give Sadie, a cat, a present. A sequel is: *Towser and the Terrible Thing* (1984, $4.95; LB $6.99).

694. Sampson, Pamela. *A Mouse Family Album* (PS–2). Illus. by author. 1980, Rand McNally $6.95. A mouse reconstructs his family history from various memorabilia. A sequel is: *The Incredible Invention of Alexander Woodmouse* (1982, $8.95).

695. Saunders, Susan. *Charles Rat's Picnic* (K–3). Illus. by Robert Byrd. 1983, Dutton $8.95. A rat and an armadillo share 4 brief adventures.

696. Schatell, Brian. *Farmer Goff and His Turkey Sam* (PS–2). Illus. by author. 1982, Harper $10.53; LB $10.89. A prize-winning turkey has a passion for pies. A sequel is: *Sam's No Dummy, Farmer Goff* (1984, $9.57; LB $9.89).

697. Schweitzer, Iris. *Hilda's Restful Chair* (PS–K). Illus. by author. 1982, Atheneum LB $9.95. All of Hilda's animal friends come to join her when she rests.

698. Selden, George. *Chester Cricket's Pigeon Ride* (2–4). Illus. by Garth Williams. 1981, Farrar $10.95; Dell paper $1.95. A friendly pigeon gives Chester Cricket a bird's-eye view of Manhattan. A sequel is: *Chester Cricket's New Home* (1983, $10.95).

699. Seuss, Dr. *Horton Hears a Who!* (K–3). Illus. by author. 1954, Random $5.96; LB $6.94. The children's favorite elephant discovers a whole town of creatures so small that they live on a speck of dust. Other titles by Dr. Seuss: *Horton Hatches the Egg* (1940, $6.95; LB $6.99); *If I Ran the Zoo* (1950, $7.95; LB $7.99; paper $2.95); *If I Ran the Circus* (1956, $5.95; LB $6.99; paper $2.95); *Yertle the Turtle and Other Stories* (1958, $7.95; LB $6.99).

700. Seuss, Dr. *Hunches in Bunches* (PS–3). Illus. by author. 1982, Random LB $6.99; paper $5.95. A rhyming story about the problems of making up one's mind. Three other titles by Dr. Seuss are: *Thidwick, the Big-Hearted Moose* (1948, $5.95; LB

$7.99; paper $2.95); *Scrambled Eggs Super!* (1953, LB $7.99; paper $2.95); *I Had Trouble in Getting to Solla Sollew* (1965, $5.95; LB $6.99; paper $2.95).

701. Shannon, George. *Dance Away* (K–1). Illus. by Jose Aruego and Ariane Dewey. 1982, Greenwillow $10.25; LB $10.88. A rabbit's love of dancing helps save some friends from a fox.

702. Sharmat, Marjorie W. *Bartholomew the Bossy* (K–2). Illus. by Normand Chartier. 1984, Macmillan $9.95. Power goes to a young skunk's head when he becomes club president.

703. Sharmat, Marjorie W. *Frizzy the Fearful* (K–2). Illus. by John Wallner. 1983, Holiday $8.95. Through Frizzy's many fears, children can explore their own fears.

704. Sharmat, Marjorie W. *Grumley the Grouch* (PS–3). Illus. by Kay Chorao. 1980, Holiday LB $8.95. Grumley meets Brunhilda, another grouchy badger, and soon they stop complaining.

705. Sharmat, Marjorie W. *I'm Terrific* (PS–1). Illus. by Kay Chorao. 1977, Holiday $8.95; paper $3.95. An amusing story of a bear cub who thinks he is marvelous and insists on telling everyone so.

706. Sharmat, Marjorie W. *Mitchell Is Moving* (1–3). Illus. by Jose Aruego and Ariane Dewey. 1978, Macmillan $9.95. Mitchell, the dinosaur, moves but unexpectedly misses his neighbor Margo.

707. Sharmat, Marjorie W. *Mr. Jameson & Mr. Phillips* (K–3). Illus. by Bruce Degen. 1979, Harper LB $9.89. Two animal friends, leaving the big city, sail away to find a tropical island.

708. Sharmat, Marjorie W. *Sasha the Silly* (K–3). Illus. by Janet Stevens. 1984, Holiday $12.95. A basset hound visits the Classy Canine Salon and is transformed.

709. Sharmat, Marjorie W. *Taking Care of Melvin* (1–3). Illus. by Victoria Chess. 1980, Holiday $8.95. When Melvin gets sick, his friends take care of him, and he learns a lesson.

710. Sharmat, Marjorie W. *The 329th Friend* (K–3). Illus. by Cyndy Szekeres. 1979, Four Winds $8.95. Emery Raccoon invites 328 guests to lunch and ends up making friends with himself.

711. Sharmat, Marjorie W. *Twitchell the Wishful* (1–3). Illus. by Janet Stevens. 1981, Holiday LB $7.95. A mouse must conquer his envy for other people's possessions.

712. Sharmat, Mitchell. *Gregory, the Terrible Eater* (PS–3). Illus. by Jose Aruego and Ariane Dewey. 1980, Four Winds $9.95; Scholastic paper $1.95. Gregory, a young goat, prefers a diet of fruit and vegetables to paper, shoes, and clothing.

713. Sharmat, Mitchell. *The Seven Sloppy Days of Phineas Pig* (K–3). Illus. by Sue Truesdell. 1983, Harcourt $11.95. Phineas is a neat pig and must learn to be sloppy.

714. Silverstein, Shel. *Who Wants a Cheap Rhinoceros?* (K–2). Illus. by author. 1983, Macmillan LB $9.95. All the advantages of owning a rhino.

715. Skurzynski, Gloria. *Honest Andrew* (2–3). Illus. by David Wiesner. 1980, Harcourt $5.95; paper $1.95. Andrew Otter learns that honesty must be tempered with tact.

716. Slate, Joseph. *The Mean, Clean, Giant Canoe Machine* (2–3). Illus. by Lynn Munsinger. 1983, Harper $9.57; LB $9.89. A mean witch steals the piglet's bathtub.

717. Small, David. *Eulalie and the Hopping Head* (PS–2). Illus. by author. 1982, Macmillan $8.95. A mischievous toad inhabits a doll's head as a joke.

718. Smith, Jim. *Alphonse and the Stonehenge Mystery* (1–3). Illus. by author. 1980, Little $8.95. Alphonse le Flic and sidekick Marlo McGrath discover criminals stealing the rocks from Stonehenge.

719. Smith, Jim. *The Frog Band and the Mystery of the Lion Castle* (1–3). Illus. by author. 1979, Little $8.95; paper $3.95. Alphonse the detective solves the mystery of Clarence the Lion's disappearance. Others in the series are: *The Frog Band and the Onion Seller* (1977, $8.95; paper $3.95); *The Frog Band and Durrington Dormouse* (1978, $8.95; paper $3.95); *The Frog Band and the Owlnapper* (1981, $8.95).

720. Smyth, Gwenda. *A Pet for Mrs. Arbuckle* (PS–1). Illus. by Ann James. 1984, Crown $9.95. Mrs. Arbuckle finally chooses the cat from down the street as her pet.

721. Stadler, John. *Animal Cafe* (K–2). Illus. by author. 1980, Bradbury $9.95. Maxwell wonders who is mysteriously buying from his food store.

722. Stadler, John. *Gorman and the Treasure Chest* (K–2). Illus. by author. 1984, Macmillan $12.95. Gorman, the pig-locksmith, is the only one that can open the treasure chest.

723. Stadler, John. *Hooray for Snail!* (K–2). Illus. 1984, Harper $9.57; LB $9.89. Snail has a humorous journey around the bases in a baseball game.

724. Stadler, John. *Rodney and Lucinda's Amazing Race* (K–2). Illus. by Tomi Ungerer. 1981, Bradbury $9.95. Rodney, a car racer, is challenged by Lucinda.

725. Stanley, Diane. *The Conversation Club* (PS–2). Illus. by author. 1983, Macmillan $9.95. Peter Fieldmouse, tired of the Conversation Club, forms a Listening Club.

726. Steig, William. *Amos and Boris* (K–2). Illus. by author. 1971, Farrar $8.95; Penguin paper $2.95.

The friendship between Amos, a seafaring mouse, and Boris, his whale rescuer, whose life, in turn, Amos manages to save.

727. Steig, William. *Doctor De Soto* (K–3). Illus. by author. 1982, Farrar $11.95; Scholastic paper $2.50. A mouse dentist outwits a fox.

728. Steig, William. *Farmer Palmer's Wagon Ride* (K–2). Illus. by author. 1974, Farrar $11.95; Penguin paper $2.95. Farmer Palmer, a pig, and the hired hand, a donkey, have a disastrous ride home from the market in this engaging nonsensical bit of fun.

729. Steig, William. *Gorky Rises* (1–3). Illus. by author. 1980, Farrar $10.95. A frog named Gorky concocts a formula that sends him on a magical journey.

730. Steig, William. *Sylvester and the Magic Pebble* (K–3). Illus. by author. 1969, Windmill paper $4.95. A donkey who collects pebbles finds a red stone that will grant wishes—and off Sylvester goes on a series of adventures. Caldecott Medal, 1969. Also use: *Roland the Minstrel Pig* (1968, Harper $10.89; Windmill paper $2.95).

731. Steig, William. *Tiffky Doofky* (K–2). Illus. by author. 1978, Farrar $7.95. A canine garbage collector awaits a fortune-teller's prophecy to come true.

732. Steiner, Jorg, ed. *The Bear Who Wanted to Be a Bear* (K–3). Illus. by Jorg Muller. 1977, Atheneum $7.95. Amusing colorful pictures enhance this story, first published in Switzerland, of a bear who did not want to be anything other than a bear.

733. Stevens, Carla. *Hooray for Pig!* (K–2). Illus. by R. Bennett. 1974, Houghton $5.95. With the help of Otter, Pig conquers his fear of the water and learns to swim.

734. Stevens, Janet. *Animal Fair* (PS–K). Illus. by author. 1981, Holiday LB $8.95. A panda takes a young boy to an imaginary circus in this adaptation of the popular song.

735. Stevenson, James. *The Bear Who Had No Place to Go* (K–3). Illus. by author. 1972, Harper $10.89. What happens to a bear when he is displaced from the circus by a seal who plays a horn? Finally, Ralph settles down comfortably in a wildlife community where his act is appreciated.

736. Stevenson, James. *Howard* (PS–1). Illus. by author. 1980, Greenwillow LB $10.51. A duck named Howard looses his way and spends the winter in New York City.

737. Stevenson, James. *Monty* (K–2). Illus. by author. 1979, Greenwillow $12.50; LB $12.88; Scholastic paper $1.95. Monty, a crocodile, thinks he is being taken for granted by his friends and goes on a vacation.

738. Stevenson, James. *Wilfred the Rat* (K–2). Illus. by author. 1977, Greenwillow $9.84; Penguin paper $2.95. Wilfred is lonely until he finds 2 friends—Wayne, a squirrel, and Ruppert, a chipmunk—and he forsakes an opportunity to work in the carnival to be with his friends.

739. Stevenson, James. *Winston, Newton, Elton and Ed* (1–3). Illus. by author. 1978, Greenwillow $8.25; LB $7.92. Two stories—one about a squabbling walrus, the other about a marooned penguin.

740. Sutton, Jane. *What Should a Hippo Wear?* (K–2). Illus. by Lynn Munsinger. 1979, Houghton LB $6.95. Bertha has trouble deciding what to wear when invited to a dance by Fred, the giraffe.

741. Tafuri, Nancy. *Have You Seen My Duckling?* (PS–2). Illus. by author. 1984, Greenwillow $10.00; LB $9.55. Mother Duck asks a number of animals if they have seen her missing duckling.

742. Tallon, Robert. *Latouse My Moose* (K–3). Illus. by author. 1983, Knopf $9.95; LB $9.99. A gullible young man buys a rare dog that is really a moose.

743. Taylor, Judy. *Sophie and Jack* (PS–1). Illus. by Susan Gantner. 1983, Putnam $9.95. Two hippo children play hide and seek. Also use: *Sophie and Jack Help Out* (1984, Putnam $8.95).

744. Taylor, Mark. *The Case of the Missing Kittens* (1–3). Illus. by Graham Booth. 1978, Atheneum $8.95. An intrepid dog sets out to find the kittens so cleverly hidden by their mother.

745. Thaler, Mike. *Moonkey* (PS–2). Illus. by Giulio Maestro. 1981, Harper $9.13; LB $10.84. A monkey falls in love with the moon.

746. Thaler, Mike. *Owly* (K–2). Illus. by David Wiesner. 1982, Harper $10.10; LB $9.89. A young owl learns about life in many ways, but learns about love from his mother.

747. Thayer, Jane. *Clever Raccoon* (K–2). Illus. by Holly Keller. 1981, Morrow $10.25; LB $9.84. Mr. and Mrs. Raccoon outwit a farmer and his wife.

748. Thomas, Patricia. *"There Are Rocks in My Socks!" Said the Ox to the Fox* (1–3). Illus. by Mordicai Gerstein. 1979, Lothrop $10.50; LB $10.08. An ox has many problems and so consults his friend, a fox.

749. Titus, Eve. *Anatole and the Cat* (K–2). 1965, McGraw $7.95. One book in the series about an enterprising mouse.

750. Tomlinson, Jill. *Hilda the Hen Who Wouldn't Give Up* (2–4). Illus. by Fernando Krahn. 1980, Harcourt $5.95. Hilda must find a way to a nearby farm to see a new family of chicks.

751. Tompert, Ann. *Little Fox Goes to the End of the World* (K–2). Illus. by John Wallner. 1976, Crown

$8.95. A fox cub pretends that she travels afar and outwits other animals.

752. Tompert, Ann. *Nothing Sticks Like a Shadow* (PS–3). Illus. by Lynn Munsinger. 1984, Houghton $12.95. Rabbit tries to get rid of his shadow.

753. Tresselt, Alvin. *The Frog in the Well* (K–3). Illus. by Roger Duvoisin. 1958, Lothrop $10.80. A foolish but happy frog learns that there is more to the world than just his cool, green, moss-covered home.

754. Turpin, Lorna. *The Sultan's Snakes* (K–2). Illus. by author. 1980, Greenwillow $9.95; LB $9.55. Escaped snakes hide out in the pictures of this humorous book.

755. Udry, Janice May. *Thump and Plunk* (PS–2). Illus. by Ann Schweninger. 1981, Harper $9.57; LB $9.89. Two mouse children quarrel over their dolls.

756. Ungerer, Tomi. *Crictor* (PS–2). Illus. by author. 1958, Harper $10.53; LB $10.89; Scholastic paper $1.95. A boa constrictor becomes the hero of a small French town after he captures a burglar.

757. Ungerer, Tomi. *No Kiss for Mother* (1–3). Illus. by author. 1973, Harper LB $10.89. Piper Paw, an untidy kitten, learns a lesson at the hands of a tough school nurse.

758. Van De Wetering, Janwillem. *Hugh Pine* (2–4). Illus. by Lynn Munsinger. 1980, Houghton $6.95. The story of an inventive and most individualistic porcupine.

759. Van Horn, William. *Harry Hoyle's Giant Jumping Bean* (K–2). Illus. by author. 1978, Atheneum $8.95. Harry the pack rat's enormous collection of oddments is endangered by a giant jumping bean.

760. Van Leeuwen, Jean. *Tales of Oliver Pig* (K–2). Illus. by Arnold Lobel. 1979, Dial $5.89; paper $2.25. Five charming stories about Oliver's adventures. Three sequels are: *More Tales of Oliver Pig* (1981, LB $5.99; paper $2.50); *Amanda Pig and Her Big Brother Oliver* (1982, LB $8.89; paper $3.75); *Tales of Amanda Pig* (1983, $8.89; paper $3.95).

761. Van Woerkom, Dorothy O. *Donkey Ysabel* (1–2). Illus. by Normand Chartier. 1978, Macmillan $6.95. A donkey is afraid that the automobile purchased by her owners will replace her.

762. Varley, Susan. *Badger's Parting Gifts* (1–4). Illus. by author. 1984, Lothrop $10.50; LB $10.08. After initial grief, the animals retain happy memories of their dead friend, Badger.

763. Vincent, Gabrielle. *Ernest and Celestine* (1–3). Illus. by author. 1982, Greenwillow $10.25; LB $10.88. A bear and a mouse child live together in a little home. Other stories with these 2 charming characters are: *Bravo, Ernest and Celestine* (1982, $10.25; LB $10.88); *Ernest and Celestine's Picnic* (1982, $10.88; LB $9.84); *Smile, Ernest and Celestine* (1982, $11.25; LB $11.88).

764. Waber, Bernard. *An Anteater Named Arthur* (PS–2). Illus. by author. 1967, Houghton $4.95; paper $3.95. A mother anteater despairs of her son Arthur, who has problems very much like those of a young boy. Also use: *A Firefly Named Torchy* (1970, Houghton $9.95).

765. Waber, Bernard. *Bernard* (K–3). Illus. by author. 1982, Houghton LB $10.95. When his owners quarrel over his custody, Bernard leaves home.

766. Waber, Bernard. *The House on East 88th Street* (K–2). Illus. by author. 1962, Houghton $11.95; paper $4.95. Adventures of a pet crocodile (Lyle) who lives with a family in a New York City brownstone. Other books about Lyle by the same author and publisher: *Lyle, Lyle, Crocodile* (1965, $8.95; paper $3.95); *Lyle and the Birthday Party* (1966, LB $10.95; paper $2.25); *Lovable Lyle* (1969, LB $10.95; paper $1.95); *Lyle Finds His Mother* (1974, $7.95; paper $2.25).

767. Waber, Bernard. *I Was All Thumbs* (K–2). Illus. by author. 1975, Houghton $10.95. The amusing adventures of Legs, a young octopus, who goes from a laboratory tank to sea, with its attendant dangers.

768. Waber, Bernard. *The Snake: A Very Long Story* (PS). Illus. by author. 1978, Houghton LB $7.95. A long trip brings the snake back home again.

769. Waber, Bernard. *You Look Ridiculous, Said the Rhinoceros to the Hippopotamus* (K–2). Illus. by author. 1966, Houghton $9.95; paper $2.25. The hippopotamus is discontented with her shape and imagines herself with many of the appendages of neighboring animals.

770. Waddell, Martin. *Harriet and the Crocodiles* (3–4). Illus. by Mark Burgess. 1984, Little $10.45. Harriet loses her pet crocodile and sets out to find him.

771. Wagner, Jenny. *The Bunyip of Berkeley's Creek* (PS–2). Illus. by Ron Brooks. 1977, Bradbury $9.95; Penguin paper $2.95. A strange creature called bunyip thinks he is unwanted until he meets his female counterpart.

772. Wagner, Jenny. *John Brown, Rose and the Midnight Cat* (PS–1). Illus. by Ron Brooks. 1978, Bradbury $9.95; Penguin paper $3.25. A widow and her dog accept a cat into their household.

773. Wahl, Jan. *Doctor Rabbit's Lost Scout* (PS–1). Illus. by Cyndy Szekeres. 1979, Random LB $5.99.

A group of animals search for their chipmunk friend who is lost in a forest. Another related story is: *Doctor Rabbit's Foundling* (1977, Pantheon $5.99).

774.   Walsh, Ellen Stoll. *Brunus and the New Bear* (PS–K). 1979, Doubleday $9.95. A favorite stuffed bear becomes jealous when a new arrival tries to take his place.

775.   Watanabe, Shigeo. *I Can Take a Walk!* (PS–K). Illus. by Yasuo Ohtomo. 1984, Putnam $7.95. Little Bear takes his first walk alone. Others in this series are: *I Can Ride It!* (1982, $8.95); *I'm the King of the Castle!* (1982, $7.95; LB $7.99); *Where's My Daddy?* (1982, $8.95; paper $3.95); *I Can Build a House!* (1983, $7.95).

776.   Waterton, Betty. *A Salmon for Simon* (K–3). 1980, Atheneum $8.95. A small Canadian Indian has a great adventure with a live salmon.

777.   Watson, Wendy. *Has Winter Come?* (PS–1). Illus. by author. 1981, Putnam paper $3.95. A family of woodchucks prepares for hibernation.

778.   Watson, Wendy. *Lollipop* (PS). Illus. by author. 1976, Penguin paper $2.95. A rabbit begs for a lollipop, and when his mother says no, he takes one of his pennies and runs off to the store to buy one—but he is so small, no one sees or hears his pleas for a lollipop.

779.   Weinberg, Lawrence. *The Forgetful Bears* (PS–1). Illus. by Paula Winter. 1982, Houghton $8.95; Scholastic paper $1.95. Four bears discover all the things they forgot to bring to a picnic.

780.   Weiss, Leatie. *Funny Feet!* (1–2). Illus. by Ellen Weiss. 1978, Avon paper $1.95. Priscilla, the penguin, tries to cure her awkwardness.

781.   Weiss, Leatie. *My Teacher Sleeps in School* (K–2). Illus. by Ellen Weiss. 1984, Warne $10.95. Because their teacher is always there, 2 elephant children believe their teacher lives in school.

782.   Wells, Rosemary. *Noisy Nora* (PS–1). Illus. by author. 1973, Dial $7.95; Scholastic paper $2.75. Young readers will enjoy the adventures of Nora, who is always loud.

783.   Wells, Rosemary. *Stanley and Rhoda* (PS–K). Illus. by author. 1978, Dial paper $2.95. Stanley copes with the problem of getting along with a difficult younger sister.

784.   Wheeler, Cindy. *Marmalade's Snowy Day* (PS–1). Illus. by author. 1982, Knopf $4.95; LB $8.99. A little cat wants to explore the snow. Sequels are: *Marmalade's Yellow Leaf* (1982); *Marmalade's Nap* (1983); *Marmalade's Picnic* (1983) (all $4.95; LB $8.99).

785.   Wheeler, M. J. *Fox Tales* (1–3). Illus. by Dana Gustafson. 1984, Carolrhoda $7.95. Three very simple stories based on Indian folktales.

786.   Wildsmith, Brian. *Animal Tricks* (PS–1). Illus. by author. 1980, Oxford $7.95. Fanciful antics of animals. Also in this series: *Animal Games; Animal Homes; Animal Shapes* (all 1980, $7.95).

787.   Wildsmith, Brian. *Bear's Adventure* (PS–3). Illus. by author. 1982, Pantheon $9.95; LB $9.99. A bear accidently becomes part of a parade in a big city.

788.   Wildsmith, Brian. *Daisy* (K–2). Illus. by author. 1984, Pantheon $9.95; LB $9.99. The story of how fame in Hollywood changes a simple cow named Daisy.

789.   Wildsmith, Brian. *Hunter and His Dog* (K–2). Illus. by author. 1979, Oxford $9.95. A hunter's dog protects a flock of wild ducks.

790.   Wilson, Bob. *Stanley Bagshaw and the Twenty-Two Ton Whale* (K–3). 1984, Hamish Hamilton $9.95. Stanley and Ted win a fishing contest, thanks to a friendly whale.

791.   Wiseman, Bernard. *Doctor Duck and Nurse Swan* (PS–2). Illus. 1984, Dutton $9.66. Doctor Duck has a zany solution for every animal's ailment.

792.   Wolkstein, Diane. *The Banza: A Haitian Story* (PS–3). Illus. by Marc Brown. 1981, Dial $8.95; LB $8.89; paper $3.95. A tiger and a goat decide to be friends.

793.   Worthington, Phoebe, and Worthington, Selby. *Teddy Bear Baker* (PS). Illus. by author. 1980, Warne $6.95. A day in the life of Teddy Bear Baker. A companion volume is: *Teddy Bear Coalman: A Story for the Very Young* (1980, paper $6.95).

794.   Yeoman, John. *Mouse Trouble* (PS–3). Illus. by Quentin Blake. 1976, Macmillan paper $1.95. A miller brings in a cat to control the mice who have taken over his mill.

795.   Yolen, Jane. *Spider Jane on the Move* (1–3). Illus. by Stefen Bernath. 1980, Putnam $6.99. The adventures of a feisty heroine and her friend Bert Bluebottle.

796.   Zelinsky, Paul O. *The Lion and the Stoat* (1–3). Illus. by author. 1984, Greenwillow $10.00; LB $9.55. A lion and a weasel vie for artistic supremacy.

797.   Zolotow, Charlotte. *Mr. Rabbit and the Lovely Present* (PS–3). Illus. by Maurice Sendak. 1962, Harper $10.89; paper $2.95. A little girl meets Mr. Rabbit, and together they find the perfect birthday gift for her mother.

Fantasies

798.   Ahlberg, Janet, and Ahlberg, Allan. *Each Peach Pear Plum* (PS). Illus. by author. 1979, Viking

$10.95. A pictorial guessing game revealed in pictures and rhymes.

799. Ahlberg, Janet, and Ahlberg, Allan. *Funnybones* (PS–2). Illus. by author. 1981, Greenwillow $11.25; LB $11.88; Scholastic paper $1.95. Three skeletons set out one dark night to frighten somebody in town.

800. Ainsworth, Ruth. *The Mysterious Baba and Her Magic Caravan* (K–5). Illus. by Joan Hickson. 1980, Andre Deutsch $8.95. A fantasy that takes place in the land where unsold toys go.

801. Alexander, Martha. *Marty McGee's Space Lab, No Girls Allowed* (K–2). Illus. by author. 1981, Dial $7.95; LB $7.89; paper $3.25. Rachel and Jenny foil their sexist brother in this fantasy.

802. Anno, Mitsumasa. *Dr. Anno's Magical Midnight Circus* (K–2). Illus. by author. 1972, Weatherhill $6.50. The little people come out at midnight and perform as they would in a real circus.

803. Balian, Lorna. *Leprechauns Never Lie* (K–3). Illus. by author. 1980, Abingdon $7.95. Lazy Ninny Nanny is outwitted by a clever leprechaun.

804. Barrett, Judith. *Cloudy with a Chance of Meatballs* (K–3). Illus. by Ron Barrett. 1978, Atheneum $12.95; paper $2.95. In the land of Chew and Swallow, food falls from the skies.

805. Benjamin, Alan. *A Change of Plans* (PS–K). Illus. by Steven Kellogg. 1982, Four Winds $10.95. The Browns, plus their many, many, animal pets, go for an outing.

806. Bennett, Jill. *Jack and the Robbers* (PS–K). Illus. by Val Biro. 1984, Merrimack $6.95. Jack and his animal friends outwit some robbers.

807. Berson, Harold. *Barrels to the Moon* (K–2). Illus. by author. 1982, Putnam $9.95. The people of Rully, France, decide to unhook the moon and attach it to their church steeple.

808. Bishop, Claire Huchet. *The Man Who Lost His Head* (K–3). Illus. by Robert McCloskey. 1942, Viking $8.95. A man tries several unsatisfactory substitutes for the head he has lost.

809. Bishop, Gavin. *Mrs. McGinty and the Bizarre Plant* (PS–2). Illus. by author. 1983, Merrimack $9.95. Mrs. McGinty becomes famous because of her huge cucumber plant.

810. Blos, Joan W. *Martin's Hats* (K–2). Illus. by Marc Simont. 1984, Morrow $9.00; LB $8.59. Each of Martin's hats brings him a new adventure.

811. Bolliger, Max. *The Most Beautiful Song* (K–2). Illus. by Jindra Capek. 1981, Little $8.95. A king demands that the bird who sang to him in his dream be found.

812. Bowden, Joan Chase. *Why the Tides Ebb and Flow* (1–3). Illus. by Marc Brown. 1979, Houghton LB $12.95. In her search for a hut, Old Woman causes the tides.

813. Brenner, Barbara. *The Prince and the Pink Blanket* (PS–1). Illus. by Nola Langner. 1980, Scholastic $8.95. Prince Hal is deprived of his favorite blanket.

814. Briggs, Raymond. *Jim and the Beanstalk* (4–7). Illus. by author. 1970, Putnam paper $2.95. A humorous, fast-moving sequel to the well-known tale.

815. Bright, Robert. *Georgie and the Robbers* (K–2). Illus. by author. 1963, Doubleday $7.95; paper $2.50. Adventures of Georgie, the friendly little ghost who haunted the Whittaker's attic. Other related titles by the same author and publisher: *Georgie* (1944, $7.95); *Georgie to the Rescue* (1956, $7.95); *Georgie and the Magician* (1966, paper $2.50); *Georgie and the Noisy Ghost* (1971, LB $7.95); *Georgie and the Baby Birds* (1983, $3.95); *Georgie and the Ball of Yarn* (1983, $3.95); *Georgie and the Little Dog* (1983, $3.95); *Georgie and the Runaway Balloon* (1983, $3.95).

816. Bright, Robert. *My Red Umbrella* (PS–1). Illus. by author. 1973, Morrow $8.16. A little girl's umbrella grows so that everyone who wants to can get under it.

817. Brown, Jeff. *Flat Stanley* (1–3). Illus. by Tomi Ungerer. 1964, Harper $10.89. A falling bulletin board flattens Stanley so he is only one-half-inch thick.

818. Brown, Marc. *Witches Four* (PS–1). Illus. by author. 1980, Dutton $5.50; LB $5.95. Four witches lose their magic hats and they are found by 4 homeless cats.

819. Brychta, Alex. *Wishwhat* (K–3). Illus. 1984, Oxford $9.95. Danny finds he has the power to have his wishes granted.

820. Bunting, Eve. *Demetrius and the Golden Goblet* (1–3). Illus. by Michael Hague. 1980, Harcourt $8.95; paper $3.95. A prince and a sponge diver have different attitudes about the sea.

821. Burningham, John. *Avocado Baby* (PS–K). Illus. 1982, Harper $9.57; LB $9.89. A weak baby thrives on avocados.

822. Burningham, John. *Come Away from the Water, Shirley* (K–2). Illus. by author. 1977, Harper $10.53; LB $10.89; paper $3.80. While her parents nap on the beach, Shirley goes adventuring at sea—in her imagination.

823. Calhoun, Mary. *Big Sixteen* (K–3). Illus. by Trina S. Hyman. 1983, Morrow $8.50; LB $7.63.

The story of the southern black folk hero who wore a size 16 shoe.

824. Calhoun, Mary. *Hungry Leprechaun* (K–3). Illus. by Roger Duvoisin. 1962, Morrow $9.12. A fantasy about how a hungry leprechaun changes rocks into the first potatoes found in Ireland.

825. Calhoun, Mary. *The Witch Who Lost Her Shadow* (K–2). 1979, Harper LB $10.89. A lovable old lady loses her cat.

826. Calhoun, Mary. *Wobble the Witch Cat* (PS–1). Illus. 1958, Morrow $8.16. A cat hides a witch's broomstick because he can't ride it.

827. Carrick, Carol. *Old Mother Witch* (1–3). Illus. by Donald Carrick. 1975, Houghton $11.95. A prank on a supposed witch and its aftermath.

828. Chatalbash, Ron. *A Perfect Day for the Movies* (3–5). Illus. by author. 1983, Godine $11.95. Nancy gets a chance to participate in the Saturday afternoon movie.

829. Chorao, Kay. *Lemon Moon* (PS–K). Illus. by author. 1983, Holiday LB $8.95. A boy and his grandma dance with the animal figures on a quilt.

830. Cole, Babette. *The Trouble with Mom* (K–2). Illus. by author. 1984, Putnam $9.95. In this humorous fantasy, a boy has a witch for a mother.

831. Cole, Joanna. *Golly Gump Swallowed a Fly* (PS–3). Illus. by Bari Weissman. 1982, Parents $5.50. A new version of "The Old Woman Who Swallowed a Fly" story.

832. Coombs, Patricia. *Dorrie and the Birthday Eggs* (K–3). Illus. by author. 1971, Lothrop LB $10.88. Magic spells and the birthday theme combine in an enchanting story of little Dorrie and her adventures. Also use: *Dorrie and the Screebit Ghost* (1979, Lothrop $10.00; LB $10.88); *Dorrie and the Blue Witch* (1980, Dell paper $1.75); *Dorrie and the Goblin* (1983, Dell paper $1.75).

833. Coombs, Patricia. *Lisa and the Grompet* (K–3). Illus. by author. 1970, Lothrop LB $11.88. Lisa runs away from home and befriends a strange cuddly creature.

834. Coombs, Patricia. *The Magician and McTree* (K–3). Illus. 1984, Lothrop $9.50; LB $9.12. By accident, a magician causes his cat to speak.

835. Coontz, Otto. *Hornswoggle Magic* (3–5). 1981, Little $8.95. Cassie and Milton want to help Mr. Wiseman and his newsstand concession.

836. Coville, Bruce, and Coville, Katherine. *The Foolish Giant* (1–3). 1978, Harper $8.89. In spite of not being too bright, a giant named Harry saves a town from a wicked wizard.

837. Crowley, Arthur. *The Wagon Man* (K–2). Illus. by Annie Gusman. 1981, Houghton LB $8.95. The wicked Wagon Man takes children to a land of endless play but is eventually foiled by a young boy.

838. Daly, Niki. *Joseph's Other Red Sock* (PS–1). Illus. by author. 1982, Atheneum LB $10.95. Joseph must free his sock from a wiggly monster.

839. Davis, Douglas F. *The Lion's Tail* (1–3). Illus. by Ronald Himler. 1980, Atheneum $8.95. A pseudo folktale involving the Masai and their cattle vs. the lions.

840. Demi. *Liang and the Magic Paintbrush* (2–4). Illus. by author. 1980, Holt $9.95. A boy in Old China finds everything he dreams comes to life.

841. de Paola, Tomie. *Bill and Pete* (K–2). Illus. by author. 1978, Putnam $8.95; paper $4.95. Pete is a toothbrush (alias a bird) who helps young Bill in a series of world misadventures.

842. de Paola, Tomie. *Sing, Pierrot, Sing: A Picture Book in Mime* (PS–2). Illus. by author. 1983, Harcourt $11.95. A group of children comfort Pierrot at his loss of Columbine.

843. de Paola, Tomie. *Songs of the Fog Maiden* (PS–K). Illus. by author. 1979, Holiday $8.95. Poems about the magic of Fog Maiden.

844. De Regniers, Beatrice S. *Waiting for Mama* (K–2). Illus. by Victoria de Larrea. 1984, Houghton LB $9.95. A young girl is left on a park bench while her mother buys groceries, and the time seems never-ending.

845. D'Ignazio, Fred. *Katie and the Computer* (2–4). Illus. by Stan Gilliam. 1980, Creative Computing LB $8.95. Katie enters the world of computers and learns their language.

846. Dillon, Barbara. *The Good-Guy Cake* (2–4). Illus. by Alan Tiegreen. 1980, Morrow $8.75; LB $8.40. Martin eats too much of the "good guy" magic cake and becomes over helpful.

847. Drescher, Henrik. *Simon's Book* (PS–1). Illus. by author. 1983, Lothrop $11.25; LB $11.88. A frightening monster chases Simon through the pages of his drawing pad.

848. Flora, James. *The Great Green Turkey Creek Monster* (K–4). Illus. by author. 1976, Atheneum paper $1.95. The monster is really a many-headed vine that grows out of control in this tall tale.

849. Flora, James. *My Friend Charlie* (K–3). Illus. by author. 1964, Harcourt paper $1.25. Friend Charlie's fabulous escapades: talking to fish, skating on his head while eating noodles, and finding a submarine caught in a wad of bubble gum.

850. Freedman, Sally. *Monster Birthday Party* (PS–1). Illus. by Diane Dawson. 1983, Whitman $8.75. A Victorian child imagines the kind of birthday party he'd really like.

851. Freeman, Don. *The Paper Party* (K–3). Illus. by author. 1974, Viking LB $9.95; Penguin paper $2.50. A boy is invited to a party in a TV set by his favorite puppets.

852. Freeman, Don. *A Rainbow of My Own* (K–3). Illus. by author. 1966, Viking LB $9.95; Penguin paper $3.95. A boy's search for a rainbow ends in his own home.

853. Freeman, Don. *Tilly Witch* (1–3). Illus. by author. 1969, Viking $9.95; Penguin paper $2.95. Tilly attends Miss Fitch's Finishing School for Witches.

854. Gackenbach, Dick. *Harry and the Terrible Whatzit* (PS–2). Illus. by author. 1978, Houghton $7.95; paper $3.95. Harry follows his mother into the dark cellar to confront the terrible 2-headed Whatzit.

855. Gackenbach, Dick. *King Wacky* (PS–2). Illus. by author. 1984, Crown $8.95. King Wacky of the land of Woosey has his head on backwards.

856. Gackenbach, Dick. *McGoogan Moves the Mighty Rock* (1–3). Illus. by author. 1981, Harper $8.95; LB $9.89. A rock asks McGoogan if he will help him get to the sea.

857. Gackenbach, Dick. *Mr. Wink and His Shadow, Ned* (K–3). Illus. by author. 1983, Harper $9.57; LB $9.89. Mr. Wink quarrels with his shadow who then leaves him.

858. Gage, Wilson. *Mrs. Gaddy and the Ghost* (1–3). Illus. by Marylin Hafner. 1979, Greenwillow $8.75; LB $7.92. Mrs. Gaddy tries to get rid of a ghost but relents when she realizes how gentle it is.

859. Galdone, Paul. *The Magic Porridge Pot* (K–3). Illus. by author. 1976, Houghton $7.95. The familiar tale of the magic pot that produces porridge but runs amuck when the words that stop it are forgotten.

860. Galdone, Paul, retel. *The Monster and the Tailor: A Ghost Story* (K–3). Illus. by retel. 1982, Houghton $11.50. A tailor must stitch a pair of trousers in a graveyard.

861. Garrison, Christian. *Little Pieces of the West Wind* (PS–1). Illus. by Diane Goode. 1975, Bradbury $9.95. In this cumulative tale, various people imprison parts of the West Wind until it becomes only a breeze.

862. Gerstein, Mordicai. *Arnold of the Ducks* (K–3). Illus. by author. 1983, Harper $10.10; LB $10.89. A baby boy is adopted by a family of ducks.

863. Gerstein, Mordicai. *Prince Sparrow* (K–3). Illus. by author. 1984, Scholastic $10.95. A young princess gains the title Queen through love of a sparrow.

864. Ginsburg, Mirra. *Where Does the Sun Go at Night?* (PS–1). Illus. by Jose Aruego and Ariane Dewey. 1980, Greenwillow $10.95; LB $10.51. A question-and-answer format is used in this adaptation of an Armenian song.

865. Goffstein, M. B. *Me and My Captain* (K–2). Illus. by author. 1974, Farrar $6.95. A small wooden doll dreams that the captain of a toy boat on the shelf below her comes to visit and asks to marry her.

866. Gorey, Edward. *The Dwindling Party* (K–3). Illus. 1982, Random paper $8.95. One by one, the MacFizzet family is picked off by monsters until only young Neville is left.

867. Gray, Catherine, and Gray, James. *Tammy and the Gigantic Fish* (PS–2). Illus. by William Joyce. 1983, Harper $8.61; LB $8.89. Tammy goes fishing with her father and grandfather.

868. Greene, Carol. *Hinny Winny Bunco* (1–3). Illus. by Jeanette Winter. 1982, Harper $10.10; LB $9.89. As a result of his fiddle and the music it produces, Hinny Winny's fortunes change.

869. Greenfield, Eloise. *Daydreamers* (1–4). Illus. by Tom Feelings. 1981, Dial $11.95; LB $11.89. A celebration of daydreaming and the pleasures it can bring.

870. Haas, Irene. *The Maggie B* (K–2). Illus. by author. 1975, Atheneum $9.95. Beautiful watercolors enhance this story of a little girl and her adventures on an imaginary ship named for her— *The Maggie B.*

871. Hancock, Sibyl. *Esteban and the Ghost* (1–3). Illus. by Dirk Zimmer. 1983, Dial $10.95; LB $10.89. Esteban sets out to find a ghost and collect a reward.

872. Harlow, Joan Hiatt. *Shadow Bear* (K–2). Illus. by Jim Arnosky. 1981, Doubleday LB $7.95. A polar bear cub and a young Eskimo boy meet.

873. Haseley, Dennis. *The Old Banjo* (1–4). Illus. by Stephen Gammell. 1983, Macmillan $9.95. Old musical instruments once more fill the night with music.

874. Hoban, Russell. *Ace Dragon Ltd.* (PS). Illus. by Quentin Blake. 1981, Jonathan Cape $7.50. John takes a fantastic ride with a dragon.

875. Hoban, Russell. *The Great Gum Drop Robbery* (PS–2). Illus. by Colin McNaughton. 1982, Putnam $6.95; LB $6.99. Three young children embark on a series of imaginative adventures.

876. Hoguet, Susan Ramsay. *I Unpacked My Grandmother's Trunk: A Picture Book Game* (PS–3). Illus. 1983, Dutton $9.66. A cumulative tale based on the word game.

877. Horwitz, Elinor. *When the Sky Is Like Lace* (K–2). Illus. by Barbara Cooney. 1975, Harper $10.55. A dreamlike story involving 3 little girls and magical powers.

878. Ivanov, Anatoly. *Ol' Jake's Lucky Day* (PS–K). Illus. 1984, Lothrop $11.50; LB $11.04. Jake spots a hare and dreams of the wealth this could bring him.

879. Janosch. *Hey Presto! You're a Bear!* (PS–1). Trans. by Klauss Flugge. Illus. by author. 1980, Little $8.95. A little boy turns his father into a bear and together they create mayhem.

880. Jaques, Faith. *Tilly's Rescue* (K–2). Illus. by author. 1981, Atheneum $9.95. Tilly, a wooden doll, sets out on her own.

881. Jennings, Michael. *Robin Goodfellow and the Giant Dwarf* (PS–K). Illus. by Tomie de Paola. 1981, McGraw $9.95. The adventures of Robin Goodfellow, a mischievous trickster.

882. Johnson, Jane. *Sybil and the Blue Rabbit* (PS–3). Illus. by author. 1980, Doubleday LB $8.95. Sybil and her stuffed rabbit embark on a magic trip.

883. Johnston, Tony. *Four Scary Stories* (K–2). Illus. by Tomie de Paola. 1980, Putnam paper $4.95. An imp, a goblin, a scalawag, and a young boy each tell an amusing story.

884. Johnston, Tony. *The Witch's Hat* (PS–1). Illus. by Margot Tomes. 1984, Putnam $9.95. A witch loses her hat in a magic pot and has problems retrieving it.

885. Jonas, Ann. *The Quilt* (PS–1). Illus. by author. 1984, Greenwillow $10.25. A girl has a nightmare involving the designs on a quilt.

886. Kahl, Virginia. *The Duchess Bakes a Cake* (PS–2). Illus. by author. 1955, Scribners LB $7.95; paper $0.79. A cake rises into the sky and carries its creator with it in this rhyming book.

887. Keats, Ezra Jack. *Regards to the Man in the Moon* (PS–1). Illus. by author. 1981, Four Winds $12.95. Lewis and his friend visit outer space via their imaginations.

888. Kellogg, Steven. *Ralph's Secret Weapon* (PS–3). Illus. by author. 1983, Dial $10.63; LB $10.89. Ralph's playing is so bad, his aunt thinks it will charm a sea monster.

889. Kennedy, Richard. *The Leprechaun's Story* (K–3). Illus. by Marcia Sewall. 1979, Dutton $10.00. A wily leprechaun wins his freedom from his captor.

890. Kennedy, Richard. *The Lost Kingdom of Karnica* (1–3). Illus. by Uri Shulevitz. 1979, Scribners $8.95. A king is warned that removal of a precious stone from the earth will destroy his kingdom.

891. Kent, Jack. *Jim Jimmy James* (PS). Illus. 1984, Greenwillow $10.00; LB $9.55. A boy's mirror image comes alive.

892. Kherdian, David. *The Animal* (K–3). Illus. by Nonny Hogrogian. 1984, Knopf $10.95; LB $10.99. A strange animal arrived in the midst of ordinary animals.

893. Kimmel, Margaret Mary. *Magic in the Mist* (1–3). Illus. by Trina S. Hyman. 1975, Atheneum $10.95. A young Welsh boy and his toad Jeremy find a dragon.

894. Klein, Robin. *Thing* (1–3). Illus. by Alison Lester. 1983, Merrimack $7.95. Emily finds a pet rock that hatches into a stegosaurus.

895. Krauss, Ruth. *Carrot Seed* (K–1). Illus. by Crockett Johnson. 1945, Harper $6.68; LB $7.64; paper $3.95. A young boy is convinced that the seeds he plants will grow, in spite of his family's doubts.

896. Krauss, Ruth. *Somebody Else's Nut Tree and Other Tales from Children* (K–3). Illus. by Maurice Sendak. 1983, Magic Circle Pr. $6.50. A collection of Ruth Krauss's stories long out of print.

897. Kroll, Steven. *The Candy Witch* (PS–1). Illus. by Marylin Hafner. 1979, Holiday $10.95. A family of witches performs good works except the youngest, who undoes their work.

898. Kroll, Steven. *The Hand-Me-Down Doll* (K–3). Illus. by Evaline Ness. 1983, Holiday $9.95. The adventures of a doll who finally finds a caring owner.

899. Kroll, Steven. *The Tyrannosaurus Game* (PS–3). Illus. by Tomie de Paola. 1976, Holiday $8.95. A group of first graders plays a game involving an imaginary purple tyrannosaurus.

900. Kuskin, Karla. *Just Like Everyone Else* (K–3). Illus. by author. 1982, Harper paper $1.88. Jonathan was ordinary until he spread his arms and flew to school.

901. Laughlin, Florence. *Little Leftover Witch* (2–4). Illus. 1960, Macmillan $8.95; paper $1.50. Felina is stranded on earth when her broomstick breaks.

902. Lester, Helen. *The Wizard, the Fairy and the Magic Chicken* (K–2). Illus. by Lynn Munsinger. 1983, Houghton $9.70. Three friends are in competition with their magic tricks.

903. Lewis, Marjorie. *The Boy Who Would Be a Hero* (K–3). Illus. by Lydia Dabcovich. 1982, Putnam $9.95. After a narrow escape from a witch, a young man decides not to be a hero.

904. Lobe, Mira. *The Snowman Who Went for a Walk* (PS–1). Illus. by Winifried Opgenoorth. 1984, Morrow $10.00; LB $10.55. A snowman heads north so he won't melt.

905. Lobel, Anita. *The Straw Maid* (1–3). Illus. by author. 1983, Greenwillow $9.00; LB $8.59. A young girl is captured by 3 robbers.

906. Lobel, Anita. *Troll Music* (1–3). Illus. by author. 1966, Harper $10.89. A mischievous troll casts a spell over a group of musicians, who thereafter can only produce animal sounds from their instruments. Also use: *Sven's Bridge* (1965, Harper $10.89).

907. Lobel, Arnold. *Prince Bertram the Bad* (PS–2). Illus. by author. 1963, Harper LB $11.89; Scholastic paper $2.25. Bertram is changed into a dragon by a witch.

908. Low, Alice. *Genie and the Witch's Spells* (3–5). Illus. by Lady McCrady. 1982, Knopf LB $4.99; paper $1.95. Genie thinks that a witch has helped her with her school work.

909. Low, Joseph. *Don't Drag Your Feet* . . . (PS–1). Illus. by author. 1983, Atheneum $9.95. Peggy is impatient with her toys until she learns her lesson in a dream.

910. McMillan, Bruce. *Ghost Doll* (K–1). Illus. 1983, Houghton $8.70. Chrissy changes a ghost doll into the real thing.

911. McPhail, David. *The Train* (3–6). Illus. by author. 1977, Little $6.95; Penguin paper $3.95. This fantasy begins with the breaking of an electric train.

912. Manning-Sanders, Ruth. *A Book of Cats and Creatures* (2–6). Illus. by Robin Jacques. 1981, Dutton $9.25. A collection of 18 stories, chiefly fantasies.

913. Mayer, Mercer. *If I Had* . . . (K–3). Illus. by author. 1968, Dial $6.50; LB $6.29; paper $3.25. A small boy has a menagerie of protectors to ward off the bullies.

914. Mayer, Mercer. *Terrible Troll* (K–3). Illus. by author. 1968, Dial $9.95; LB $9.89; paper $2.75. The fantastic adventures of a small boy told with humorous details.

915. Mayne, William. *The Green Book of Hob Stories* (2–3). Illus. by Patrick Benson. 1984, Putnam $7.95. A series of stories about Hob, who can only be seen by children and budgies. Also use: *The Red Book of Hob Stories* (1984, Putnam $7.95).

916. Meddaugh, Susan. *Beast* (K–2). Illus. by author. 1981, Houghton $8.95. Anna frightens a timid monster.

917. Naylor, Phyllis Reynolds. *The Boy with the Helium Head* (K–3). Illus. by Kay Chorao. 1982, Atheneum $11.95. By mistake, Jonathan receives a helium shot and becomes famous.

918. Nixon, Joan Lowery. *If You Say So, Claude* (1–4). Illus. by Lorinda Bryan Cauley. 1980, Warne $9.95; paper $5.95. In a tall tale from Texas, a couple set out in a covered wagon to find a new home.

919. Noble, Trinka Hakes. *Hansy's Mermaid* (PS–2). Illus. by author. 1983, Dial $10.63; LB $10.89. In Holland of some years ago, children find a mermaid trapped in a pool.

920. Noble, Trinka Hakes. *The King's Tea* (K–2). Illus. by author. 1979, Dial $7.50; LB $7.28; paper $3.25. Each character blames the other when the milk in the king's tea is found to be sour.

921. Obrist, Jurg. *The Miser Who Wanted the Sun* (K–2). Illus. by author. 1984, Atheneum $13.95. A miser commissions a tailor to produce a golden robe so he will be like the sun.

922. Palazzo, Tony. *Magic Crayon* (PS–2). Illus. by author. 1967, Lion $6.87; LB $5.98. Imaginative fun for very young readers.

923. Paterson, Diane. *Soap and Suds* (PS). Illus. by author. 1984, Knopf $10.95; LB $10.99. A washerwoman's clean laundry is dirtied by a variety of animals.

924. Peet, Bill. *Big Bad Bruce* (K–3). Illus. by author. 1977, Houghton LB $11.95; paper $3.95. Bruce encounters a witch and is shrunk to the size of a chipmunk.

925. Pienkowski, Jan. *Haunted House* (K–2). Illus. by Jane Walmsley. 1979, Dutton $10.95. All kinds of ghosts emerge from various places in this unusual house.

926. Pienkowski, Jan. *Robot* (1–3). Illus. 1982, Delacorte $9.95. A pop-up book about a mechanical family.

927. Pinkwater, D. Manus. *Devil in the Drain* (K–2). Illus. by author. 1984, Dutton $9.95. A young boy discovers a little devil living in the drain of the kitchen sink.

928. Pinkwater, D. Manus. *Roger's Umbrella* (K–2). Illus. by James Marshall. 1982, Dutton $8.95. Roger finds his umbrella has a life of its own.

929. Plath, Sylvia. *The Bed Book* (PS–3). Illus. by Emily McCully. 1976, Harper $9.59; LB $10.89. Lyric verses that investigate the characteristics of a variety of beds.

930. Porter, David Lord. *Help! Let Me Out!* (2–5). Illus. by David Macaulay. 1982, Houghton LB $8.95. During a ventriloquist trick, Hugo's voice leaves him for its own adventure.

931. Postma, Lidia. *The Witch's Garden* (K–3). Illus. by author. 1979, McGraw $8.95. Seven children pay a visit to a witch and meet an elf.

932. Quin-Harkin, Janet. *Magic Growing Powder* (K–3). Illus. by Arthur Cumings. 1981, Dutton $5.50; LB $5.95. King Max will try anything to grow taller.

933. Raskin, Ellen. *Franklin Stein* (K–2). Illus. by author. 1972, Atheneum paper $1.50. Franklin makes himself an ingenious contraption, which he calls Fred. Everyone sneers at it until it is judged best in the pet show.

934. Raskin, Ellen. *Ghost in a Four-Room Apartment* (K–2). Illus. by author. 1969, Atheneum LB $8.29; paper $1.95. The story of a poltergeist who haunts a 4-room apartment is told on one page, and the reactions of the haunted family are recounted on the facing page.

935. Rayner, Mary. *The Rain Cloud* (PS–1). Illus. by author. 1980, Atheneum $9.95. A cloud with-holds its rain until it can do the most good.

936. Ross, Tony. *I'm Coming to Get You!* (PS–1). Illus. by author. 1984, Dial $10.95. A big hairy monster from another planet is coming to get Tommy Brown.

937. Ryan, Cheli D. *Hildilid's Night* (K–2). Illus. by Arnold Lobel. 1974, Macmillan paper $0.95. A little old lady who hates the night tries vainly to chase it away in this amusing story.

938. Ryder, Joanne. *The Snail Spell* (K–2). Illus. by Lynne Cherry. 1982, Warne LB $10.95. A little boy knows how a snail feels when he shrinks to that size.

939. Sachs, Marilyn. *Fleet-Footed Florence: A Sequel to Matt's Mitt* (K–3). Illus. by Charles Robinson. 1981, Doubleday $8.95. Matt's daughter proves to be a baseball star.

940. Sandburg, Carl. *The Wedding Procession of the Rag Doll and the Broom Handle and Who Was in It* (1–3). Illus. by Harriet Pincus. 1967, Harcourt $10.95; paper $5.25. Illustrated edition of one of the *Rootabaga Stories*.

941. Sendak, Maurice. *In the Night Kitchen* (K–3). Illus. by author. 1970, Harper $14.38; LB $14.89. Mickey discovers that the "night kitchen" is where the wild snacks are.

942. Sendak, Maurice. *Maurice Sendak's Really Rosie* (1–4). Illus. by author. 1975, Harper paper $5.95. A book based on the TV presentation, including 7 songs used in the program.

943. Sendak, Maurice. *Outside Over There* (PS–3). Illus. by author. 1981, Harper $14.38; LB $14.89. Goblins steal Ira's baby sister and leave another made of ice.

944. Sendak, Maurice. *Where the Wild Things Are* (K–3). Illus. by author. 1963, Harper $10.53; LB $10.89. The few moments' wild reverie of a small unruly boy who has been sent supperless to his room. Caldecott Medal, 1964.

945. Seuss, Dr. *Bartholomew and the Oobleck* (K–2). Illus. 1949, Random $4.95; LB $5.99; paper $2.95. What happens when sticky green stuff begins falling instead of snow? Also use: *McElligot's Pool* (1947, Random $6.95; LB $6.99).

946. Seuss, Dr. *The Butter Battle Book* (K–2). Illus. 1984, Random $6.95; LB $7.99. A warning about the nuclear arms race in words and pictures.

947. Seuss, Dr. *On Beyond Zebra!* (K–2). 1955, Random $6.95; LB $6.99. A nonsense alphabet that begins after Z.

948. Sharmat, Marjorie W. *What Are We Going to Do about Andrew?* (PS–1). Illus. by Ray Cruz. 1980, Macmillan $8.95. Andrew's ability to fly and become a hippopotamus at will causes family and social problems.

949. Shulevitz, Uri. *One Monday Morning* (PS–1). Illus. by author. 1967, Scribners $11.95. Royal visitors right out of a small boy's colorful daydream brighten his drab tenement on a rainy day.

950. Shura, Mary Francis. *Happles and Cinna-munger* (3–5). Illus. by Bertram M. Tormey. 1981, Dodd LB $7.95. The Taggert family has problems finding a new housekeeper.

951. Slobodkin, Louis. *Magic Michael* (K–1). Illus. by author. 1944, Macmillan $8.95; paper $0.95. Michael has a vivid imagination and pretends to be all sorts of different people, but the gift of a bicycle changes everything.

952. Spier, Peter. *Bored—Nothing to Do!* (K–3). Illus. by author. 1978, Doubleday $8.95. Two bored boys put together an airplane and fly it.

953. Steig, William. *Caleb and Kate* (PS–3). Illus. by author. 1977, Farrar $11.95; Scholastic paper $1.95. Because he constantly quarrels with his wife, Caleb is transformed into a dog by a witch.

954. Stern, Simon. *Mrs. Vinegar* (PS–1). Illus. 1979, Prentice $7.95. When the Vinegars lose their home, they set out to find another.

955. Stevenson, James. *The Wish Card Ran Out!* (1–3). Illus. by author. 1981, Greenwillow $10.25; LB $9.84. Charlie's birthday goes badly until he gets his International Wish Card.

956. Stevenson, James. *The Worst Person in the World* (1–3). Illus. by author. 1978, Greenwillow

$10.25; LB $11.88. A visiting monster named Ugly makes a grouch change his ways.

957. Stevenson, James. *Yuck!* (K–3). Illus. by author. 1984, Greenwillow $10.25; LB $9.55. A young witch outsmarts 2 witches who spurn her.

958. Strand, Mark. *The Planet of Lost Things* (2–5). Illus. by William Pene du Bois. 1983, Crown $9.95. A boy dreams of going to a planet where the lost things in life reside.

959. Thayer, Jane. *Gus and the Baby Ghost* (K–2). Illus. by Seymour Fleishman. 1972, Morrow $9.12. Gus, the friendly ghost, adopts a baby ghost that he finds on his doorstep and takes the baby to live with him in the historical museum, much to the delight of the visitors. Also use: *Gus Was a Real Dumb Ghost* (1982, Morrow $10.75; LB $9.84).

960. Thorne, Jenny. *My Uncle* (1–4). Illus. by author. 1982, Atheneum $9.95. Uncle encounters fabulous beasts on treetops and under water.

961. Tobias, Tobi. *Jane, Wishing* (1–3). Illus. by Trina S. Hyman. 1977, Viking $8.95. Black and white represent realities, but Jane's delightful fantasies are in glorious color.

962. Turkle, Brinton. *Do Not Open* (1–3). Illus. by author. 1981, Dutton $12.95. Miss Moody finds a bottle on the shore labeled "Do Not Open."

963. Udry, Janice May. *The Moon Jumpers* (K–2). Illus. by Maurice Sendak. 1959, Harper $11.50. The pleasure and enjoyment of 4 children as they dance in the moonlight.

964. Ungerer, Tomi. *The Hat* (K–2). Illus. by author. 1982, Scholastic $11.95. A magical hat brings riches to a penniless man.

965. Ungerer, Tomi. *Moon Man* (K–3). Illus. by author. 1967, Harper LB $12.89; paper $4.95. The man in the moon visits Earth for a night of fun.

966. Ungerer, Tomi. *The Three Robbers* (PS–1). Illus. by author. 1962, Atheneum paper $1.95. A little orphan captured by robbers is delighted to live with them rather than with her wicked aunt, and she persuades them to spend their loot building a new village for other poor orphans.

967. Ungerer, Tomi. *Zeralda's Ogre* (K–2). Illus. by author. 1967, Harper $12.89. Even a child-eating ogre can be reformed if he meets a cook with Zeralda's skill.

968. Vaes, Alain. *The Porcelain Pepper Pot* (PS–1). Illus. by author. 1982, Little $11.95. A pepper pot falls in love with a salt cellar.

969. Van Allsburg, Chris. *Ben's Dream* (2–4). Illus. by author. 1982, Houghton $10.95. Ben dreams that he is in a flood and passing the great landmarks of the world.

970. Van Allsburg, Chris. *Jumanji* (1–4). Illus. by author. 1981, Houghton $11.95. A board game that 2 children play brings out a jungle world.

971. Waber, Bernard. *You're a Little Kid with a Big Heart* (PS–2). Illus. by author. 1980, Houghton LB $8.95. A little girl is granted her wish—to be an adult.

972. Wahl, Jan. *Peter and the Troll Baby* (PS–K). Illus. by Erik Blegvad. 1984, Western $7.95. The troll steals Peter's sister Susanna.

973. Westcott, Nadine Bernard. *The Giant Vegetable Garden* (PS–K). Illus. by author. 1981, Little $8.95; paper $4.95. A mayor gets his town's residents to grow large vegetables.

974. Whiteside, Karen. *Brother Mouky and the Falling Sun* (2–3). Illus. by author. 1980, Harper $7.95; LB $7.89. Mouky is angry with his brother and does not want to resolve the problem.

975. Wildsmith, Brian. *Professor Noah's Spaceship* (K–3). Illus. by author. 1980, Oxford $9.95. A modern Noah takes off to escape the world's pollution.

976. Willard, Nancy. *The Nightgown of the Sullen Moon* (PS–3). Illus. by David McPhail. 1983, Harcourt $11.95. The story of the moon, her nightgown, and why on some nights she doesn't shine.

977. Williams, Jay. *The City Witch and the Country Witch* (K–3). Illus. by Ed Renfro. 1979, Macmillan $9.95. A city witch trades places with her country counterpart and finds that her powers are inappropriate.

978. Williams, Jay. *One Big Wish* (K–2). Illus. by John O'Brien. 1980, Macmillan $8.95. The idea of having an unlimited number of wishes fails to satisfy Fred Butterspoon.

979. Yolen, Jane. *The Girl Who Loved the Wind* (K–3). Illus. by Ed Young. 1972, Harper $10.53; LB $10.89; paper $4.75. An overly protected child discovers that life is not always happy.

980. Yorinks, Arthur. *It Happened in Pinsk* (1–3). Illus. by Richard Egielski. 1983, Farrar $11.95. A self-satisfied man wakes up one morning to find his head is missing.

981. Yorinks, Arthur. *Louis the Fish* (PS–2). Illus. by Richard Egielski. 1980, Farrar $10.95. The story of an unhappy man who is turned into a fish.

982. Zelinsky, Paul O., adapt. *The Maid and the Mouse and the Odd-Shaped House* (PS–2). Illus. by adapt. 1981, Dodd LB $9.95. A house gradually becomes shaped like a cat in this old story told in rhyme.

983. Zemach, Harve, and Zemach, Kaethe. *The Princess and Froggie* (PS–2). Illus. by Margot Zemach. 1975, Farrar $9.95. These brief tales are charmingly presented by the Zemachs and their teenage daughter.

984. Zemach, Margot. *Jake and Honeybunch Go to Heaven* (1–3). Illus. by author. 1982, Farrar $13.95. A controversial (because of charges of stereotyp-ing) picture book about a black working man and his pet mule.

985. Zimelman, Nathan. *If I Were Strong Enough* (K–2). Illus. by Diane Paterson. 1982, Abingdon $9.95. Ebenezer believes he is strong enough to carry a bag of groceries.

Realistic Stories

Real and Almost Real Animals

986. Alexander, Martha. *No Ducks in Our Bathtub* (PS–1). Illus. by author. 1973, Dial $6.89; paper $2.50. David wanted a pet and finally his mother agreed to let him have some fish eggs to hatch. Much to everyone's surprise, and David's joy, 103 tadpoles inhabit the bathtub!

987. Aliki. *At Mary Bloom's* (K–2). Illus. by author. 1976, Greenwillow $9.95; Penguin paper $2.95. When her pet mouse has babies, a little girl shares the excitement with a neighbor's household.

988. Anderson, Clarence W. *Billy and Blaze* (K–2). Illus. by author. 1969, Macmillan $10.95; paper $3.50. An old favorite about Billy who loved horses and his pony Blaze. Three others in the series are: *Blaze and the Gray Spotted Pony* (1968, $10.95; paper $2.95); *Blaze and the Forest Fire* (1969, $10.00; paper $3.95); *Blaze and the Lost Quarry* (1973, paper $2.95).

989. Asch, Frank. *The Last Puppy* (PS–2). Illus. by author. 1980, Prentice $8.95; paper $3.95. An enchanting story of the puppy born last in a large litter.

990. Bahr, Robert. *Blizzard at the Zoo* (1–3). Illus. by Consuelo Joerns. 1982, Lothrop $11.25; LB $11.88. What happens when a terrible winter storm hits the Buffalo Zoo.

991. Baker, Jeannie. *Home in the Sky* (K–3). Illus. by author. 1984, Greenwillow $11.00. The story of a homing pigeon who gets lost.

992. Bartoli, Jennifer. *In a Meadow, Two Hares Hide* (PS–1). Illus. by Takeo Ishida. 1978, Whitman $8.75. Two rabbits help each other survive from their natural enemies.

993. Baskin, Leonard. *Hosie's Zoo* (2–4). Illus. by author. 1981, Viking $10.95. Animals are introduced in pictures and short verses.

994. Bell, Anthea. *The Great Menagerie* (2–6). 1980, Viking $9.95. A variety of animals come to life in this pop-up book from the nineteenth century.

995. Bourne, Miriam Anne. *Raccoons Are for Loving* (PS–1). Illus. by Marion Morton. 1968, Random LB $5.39. A black child holds a raccoon in her arm as her grandmother did many years before.

996. Brenner, Barbara. *A Dog I Know* (K–3). Illus. by Fred Brenner. 1983, Harper $8.61; LB $8.89. A narrator describes his dog in loving terms.

997. Brown, Marcia. *How Hippo!* (K–1). Illus. by author. 1969, Scribners $6.95; paper $0.95. Mother Hippo saves the day for her venturesome Little Hippo, just learning the proper grunts and roars, when a crocodile threatens. Eye-filling, double-page woodcuts.

998. Brown, Margaret Wise. *The Sleepy Little Lion* (PS–2). Illus. by Ylla. 1947, Harper LB $11.89; paper $1.95. A lion cub gets acquainted with other animals.

999. Brown. Margaret Wise. *When the Wind Blew* (PS–2). Illus. by Geoffrey Hayes. 1977, Harper $6.68; LB $7.89. A reissue with new illustrations of the story about an old woman with 17 cats.

1000. Burningham, John. *Cannonball Simp* (K–2). Illus. by author. 1979, Jonathan Cape $8.95. An abandoned dog and a circus clown team up.

1001. Burningham, John. *Harquin: The Fox Who Went Down to the Valley* (K–2). Illus. by author. 1979, Jonathan Cape $8.95. During a hunt, a fox cub saves his family and acquires the squire's cap.

1002. Campbell, Rod. *Dear Zoo* (PS). Illus. by author. 1983, Scholastic $8.95. A youngster keeps sending back the pets requested from a zoo until a puppy arrives.

1003. Campbell, Rod. *Henry's Busy Day* (PS). Illus. by author. 1984, Viking $6.95. A book for toddlers about a mischievous dog.

1004. Carle, Eric. *The Very Hungry Caterpillar* (PS–2). 1969, Putnam $11.95; Scholastic paper $1.95. A caterpillar eats a great deal and then spins its cocoon.

1005. Carrick, Carol. *Lost in the Storm* (K–3). Illus. by Donald Carrick. 1974, Houghton $7.95. The story of a dog, lost overnight in a storm, who is found in the morning by his owner and safely sheltered under a flight of stairs.

1006. Carrick, Carol. *A Rabbit for Easter* (1–3). Illus. by Donald Carrick. 1979, Greenwillow

$10.50; LB $10.08. During Easter vacation, Paul has adventures with the rabbit from kindergarten.

1007.   Carrick, Carol. *Two Coyotes* (K–3). Illus. by Donald Carrick. 1982, Houghton $11.50. Two coyotes face the bleak chore of finding food during the winter.

1008.   Climo, Lindee. *Chester's Barn* (2–4). Illus. by author. 1982, Tundra $13.95; paper $7.95. The story in words and pictures of life in a Prince Edward Island barn on a winter afternoon.

1009.   Dabcovich, Lydia. *Sleepy Bear* (PS–1). Illus. by author. 1982, Dutton $9.50. A bear's hibernation is illustrated in large pictures and a minimum of text.

1010.   d'Aulaire, Ingri, and d'Aulaire, Edgar. *Don't Count Your Chicks* (PS–1). 1973, Doubleday LB $10.95; paper $2.95. An old woman has fun with various animals during a day in the country.

1011.   de Paola, Tomie. *The Kids' Cat Book* (1–3). Illus. by author. 1979, Holiday $10.95; paper $5.95. Patrick learns about the care, feeding, and history of cats when he decides to adopt one.

1012.   Duncan, Jane. *Janet Reachfar and Chickabird* (K–2). Illus. by Mairi Hedderwick. 1978, Seabury $7.95. Janet, a Scottish farm girl, helps an injured baby chick.

1013.   Dunn, Judy. *The Little Puppy* (PS–K). Illus. by Phoebe Dunn. 1984, Random $4.95; paper $1.95. The story of a little boy who must care for his first puppy.

1014.   Ernst, Kathryn F. *Charlie's Pets* (K–2). Illus. by Arthur Cumings. 1978, Crown LB $4.95. Charlie decides to make pets of some cockroaches.

1015.   Ets, Marie Hall. *Just Me* (PS–K). Illus. by author. 1965, Penguin paper $3.50. A little boy imagines he can match the antics of his animal friends as he spends an afternoon at solitary play.

1016.   Ets, Marie Hall. *Play with Me* (PS–K). Illus. by author. 1953, Viking $12.95; LB $12.95; Penguin paper $3.50. A little girl finds a playmate among the meadow creatures when she finally learns to sit quietly and not frighten them.

1017.   Fatio, Louise. *Hector and Christina* (K–2). Illus. by Roger Duvoisin. 1977, McGraw $8.95; LB $7.95. Two animals are rescued from a zoo and allowed to return to their forest home.

1018.   Fisher, Aileen. *Anybody Home?* (K–3). Illus. by Susan Bonners. 1980, Harper $8.61; LB $8.89. A rhyming book about animals and their homes.

1019.   Fisher, Aileen. *Listen Rabbit* (K–2). Illus. by Symeon Shimin. 1964, Harper $10.89. A delightful picture-poetry book describing a small boy's efforts to make friends with a rabbit.

1020.   Flack, Marjorie. *Angus and the Ducks* (K–2). Illus. by author. 1939, Doubleday $7.95. Angus, the Scotch terrier, and his amusing adventures. Other titles in this series are: *Angus and the Cat* (1931, $7.95) and *Angus Lost* (1941, $7.95).

1021.   Florian, Douglas. *A Bird Can Fly* (PS–2). Illus. by author. 1980, Greenwillow $10.95; LB $10.51. A simple introduction to the capabilities of various animals.

1022.   Freeman, Don. *Fly High, Fly Low* (K–3). Illus. by author. 1957, Viking $8.95. Two pigeons make their home in a San Francisco hotel sign.

1023.   Freschet, Berniece. *Five Fat Raccoons* (2–3). Illus. by Irene Brady. 1980, Scribners $9.95. An introduction to raccoon life using fictional techniques.

1024.   Gackenbach, Dick. *A Bag Full of Pups* (PS–1). Illus. by author. 1981, Houghton $9.95; paper $3.95. A little boy would like one of the pups Mr. Mullen is giving away.

1025.   Gackenbach, Dick. *Do You Love Me?* (K–2). Illus. by author. 1975, Houghton $6.95; Dell paper $1.50. Walter has no one to play with, so he tries to make pets of some insects but realizes that wild things need freedom. At last he gets a puppy that needs his love and attention and that he can fondle and cuddle.

1026.   Gag, Wanda. *Millions of Cats* (PS–1). Illus. by author. 1928, Putnam $7.95; paper $2.95. A wonderful picture book about an old man looking for a cat who suddenly finds himself with millions. Also use: *Snippy and Snappy* (1931, Putnam $5.99).

1027.   Gammell, Stephen. *Once Upon MacDonald's Farm . . .* (K–3). Illus. by author. 1981, Four Winds $8.95. MacDonald tries to populate his farm with circus animals.

1028.   George, Jean Craighead. *The Grizzly Bear with the Golden Ears* (K–4). Illus. by Tom Catania. 1982, Harper $10.10; LB $9.89. A bear searches for her lost cub.

1029.   George, Jean Craighead. *The Wounded Wolf* (1–3). Illus. by John Schoenherr. 1978, Harper $10.89. A simple story that abounds in the author's knowledge of animal lore.

1030.   Ginsburg, Mirra. *Mushroom in the Rain* (K–2). Adapted from the Russian of V. Suteyev. Illus. by Jose Aruego and Ariane Dewey. 1974, Macmillan paper $2.50. An ant, huddling under a mushroom in the rain, makes room for a butterfly, a mouse, a sparrow, and finally a rabbit who is being chased by a fox.

1031.   Goble, Paul. *The Girl Who Loved Wild Horses* (K–2). Illus. by author. 1978, Bradbury $11.95. A mystical story of a girl and her love for a black stallion. Caldecott Medal, 1979.

1032. Graham, John. *I Love You, Mouse* (K–2). Illus. by Tomie de Paola. 1976, Harcourt $9.95; paper $1.75. A tender book about how a young boy would feel if he were several different animals.

1033. Graham, Margaret B. *Benjy's Boat Trip* (PS–3). Illus. by author. 1977, Harper $10.53; LB $10.89. A dachshund refuses to be left behind and sets out to find his family, who left on a summer vacation. Another title is: *Benjy's Dog House* (1973, $10.53; LB $10.89).

1034. Gregor, Arthur. *Animal Babies* (PS–1). Illus. by Ylla. 1976, Harper paper $1.95. Baby animals of all sorts.

1035. Gregor, Arthur. *The Little Elephant* (K–2). Illus. by Ylla. 1976, Harper paper $1.95. Baby elephant leads the king's parade.

1036. Griffith, Helen V. *Mine Will, Said John* (PS–3). Illus. by Muriel Batherman. 1980, Greenwillow LB $9.36. John tries out several pets but stoutly maintains he wants a dog.

1037. Hazen, Barbara S. *Tight Times* (2–3). Illus. by Trina S. Hyman. 1979, Viking $9.95. A child is allowed to keep a stray kitten even though there are hard times in the household.

1038. Hazen, Barbara S. *Where Do Bears Sleep?* (PS–2). Illus. by Ian E. Staunton. 1970, Childrens Pr. $8.95. Questions and answers about where various animals sleep; good for storytelling or beginning readers.

1039. Herriot, James. *Moses the Kitten* (PS–3). Illus. by Peter Barrett. 1984, St. Martins $9.95. The story of a stray black kitten and how it was saved.

1040. Hewett, Joan. *The Mouse and the Elephant* (1–3). Illus. by Richard Hewett. 1977, Little $6.95. Photographs answer the question, What if a mouse lived with an elephant?

1041. Hoban, Tana. *One Little Kitten* (PS–1). Illus. 1979, Greenwillow LB $9.95. The activities of a kitten in text and unusual photographs.

1042. Holl, Adelaide. *The Rain Puddle* (PS–K). Illus. by Roger Duvoisin. 1965, Lothrop $10.80. When the barnyard animals see their reflections in a rain puddle, each believes that one of his own kind has fallen into the water.

1043. Ipcar, Dahlov. *Hard Scrabble Harvest* (K–2). Illus. by author. 1976, Doubleday $8.95. Brisk, colorful illustrations and lilting verses describe the assault made on a farmer's crops by both wild and domesticated animals.

1044. John, Naomi. *Roadrunner* (1–4). Illus. by Peter Parnall and Virginia Parnall. 1980, Dutton $8.95. An introduction to the roadrunner and its desert habitat.

1045. Jonas, Ann. *Two Bear Cubs* (1–3). Illus. by author. 1982, Greenwillow $10.00; LB $10.88. A mother bear shepherds her two cubs through some everyday adventures.

1046. Jones, Rebecca C. *The Biggest, Meanest, Ugliest Dog in the Whole Wide World* (PS–K). Illus. by Wendy Watson. 1982, Macmillan $9.95. Jonathan finds out the neighbor's dog isn't so bad after all.

1047. Kahl, Virginia. *Whose Cat Is That?* (K–2). Illus. by author. 1979, Scribners $8.95. Seven different households adopt the same pretty white cat.

1048. Keats, Ezra Jack. *Hi, Cat!* (K–2). Illus. by author. 1969, Macmillan $9.95; paper $3.95. Archie meets a stray cat on his way to see Peter, and when the cat interferes with their show, Archie acknowledges that it "just kinda liked me!" Also with the same central characters: *Pet Show!* (1972, paper $3.95).

1049. Keats, Ezra Jack. *Kitten for a Day* (PS). Illus. 1982, Scholastic $9.95. A puppy spends a day playing with kittens.

1050. Kellogg, Steven. *Pinkerton, Behave!* (K–3). Illus. by author. 1979, Dial paper $3.95. A mischievous Great Dane puppy foils a burglary attempt. A sequel is: *A Rose for Pinkerton* (1981, $11.95; LB $11.89; paper $3.95).

1051. Knight, Hilary. *Where's Wallace?* (PS–K). Illus. by author. 1964, Harper $11.50; LB $11.89. A little orangutan escapes from the zoo and explores the outside world. Children will find him hidden in the pictures of the various places he explores.

1052. Knotts, Howard. *The Summer Cat* (2–3). Illus. by author. 1981, Harper $8.61; LB $8.89. Ben and Annie's cat visits them only in the evening—where is she during the day?

1053. Lipkind, William, and Mordvinoff, Nicolas. *Finders Keepers* (K–3). Illus. by author. 1951, Harcourt $7.95. Two dogs have a dispute over one bone but unite against a common enemy. Caldecott Medal, 1952.

1054. Lobel, Arnold. *The Rose in My Garden* (PS–3). Illus. by Anita Lobel. 1984, Greenwillow $11.00; LB $10.51. A cumulative tale that starts with a bee sleeping on a rose.

1055. Luton, Mildred. *Little Chicks' Mothers and All the Others* (PS–1). Illus. by Mary Maki Rae. 1983, Viking $11.50. A picture book that shows youngsters that animals have mothers too.

1056. McCloskey, Robert. *Make Way for Ducklings* (PS–3). Illus. by author. 1941, Viking $11.50; Penguin paper $2.95. The Mallard family creates a commotion as they search for and find a permanent home in Boston. Caldecott Medal, 1942.

1057. McMillan, Bruce. *Kitten Can . . .* (PS). Illus. by author. 1984, Lothrop $10.50; LB $10.08. Pictures that show all the things a calico kitten can do.

1058. McNulty, Faith. *Mouse and Tim* (K–2). Illus. by Marc Simont. 1978, Harper $8.61; LB $9.89. Tim adopts an abandoned deer mouse as a pet.

1059. Miles, Miska. *Nobody's Cat* (1–3). Illus. by John Schoenherr. 1969, Little $7.95. Episodes in the life of an independent, dignified cat with a keen knowledge of his rough urban environment and how best to cope with it—superb, dramatic drawings.

1060. Modell, Frank. *Seen Any Cats?* (PS–1). Illus. by author. 1979, Greenwillow $9.95; LB $9.55. Two enterprising boys decide to put on their own circus by training their cats.

1061. Modell, Frank. *Tooley! Tooley!* (K–3). Illus. by author. 1979, Greenwillow $10.50; LB $10.08. Milton and Marvin set out to find Tooley, a lost dog.

1062. Munari, Bruno. *Bruno Munari's Zoo* (PS–K). Illus. by author. 1963, Putnam LB $9.99; paper $4.95. Bold and brilliantly colorful animals.

1063. Newman, Nanette. *That Dog!* (1–3). Illus. by Marylin Hafner. 1983, Harper $8.61; LB $8.89. Ben's dog Barnum is the neighborhood nuisance, but when he dies Ben is inconsolable.

1064. Noble, Trinka Hakes. *The Day Jimmy's Boa Ate the Wash* (PS–2). Illus. by Steven Kellogg. 1980, Dial $8.95; LB $8.89. A hilarious story about a class trip to a farm. A sequel is: *Jimmy's Boa Bounces Back* (1984, $10.63; LB $10.89).

1065. Parker, Nancy W. *Puddums: The Cathcarts' Orange Cat* (2–4). Illus. by author. 1980, Atheneum $8.95. Puddums, the cat, gets mysteriously ill and frightens the Cathcarts.

1066. Pender, Lydia. *The Useless Donkeys* (K–3). Illus. by Judith Cowell. 1980, Warne $9.95. A family and their animals survive a flood.

1067. Politi, Leo. *Song of the Swallows* (K–3). Illus. by author. 1949, Scribners $12.95; paper $2.95. Juan rings the mission's bells to welcome the swallows back to San Juan Capistrano. Caldecott Medal, 1950.

1068. Pomerantz, Charlotte. *Buffy and Albert* (1–3). Illus. by Yossi Abolafia. 1980, Greenwillow $8.50; LB $8.55. Two elderly cats are unwanted by Grandpa.

1069. Pomerantz, Charlotte. *Where's the Bear?* (PS). Illus. by Byron Barton. 1984, Greenwillow $10.00; LB $9.55. A picture book involving the search for a bear; the text uses only 7 words.

1070. Primavera, Elise. *Basil and Maggie* (K–3). Illus. by author. 1983, Harper $9.57; LB $9.89. At first Maggie is disappointed with her new pony.

1071. Provensen, Alice, and Provensen, Martin. *The Year at Maple Hill Farm* (PS–1). Illus. by author. 1978, Atheneum $6.95. Month-by-month activities of the animals on a farm. Two sequels are: *A Horse and a Hound, a Goat and a Gander* (1980, LB $9.95; paper $8.29); *An Owl and Three Pussycats* (1981, $11.95; LB $8.79).

1072. Rey, Margaret. *Pretzel* (K–3). Illus. by H. A. Rey. 1944, Harper LB $12.89; paper $3.95. A dachshund named Pretzel woos the dog across the street.

1073. Rice, Eve. *Sam Who Never Forgets* (PS–1). Illus. by author. 1977, Greenwillow $10.51; Penguin paper $3.95. Sam, the zookeeper, feeds all the animals each day, but one day there appears to be nothing for the elephant.

1074. Rojankovsky, Feodor. *Animals on the Farm* (K–2). Illus. by author. 1967, Knopf $7.99. Nineteen common farm animals are pictured and identified.

1075. Roosevelt, Michele Chopin. *Zoo Animals* (PS). Illus. by author. 1983, Random $3.50. A brief introduction to zoo animals for the very young.

1076. Ross, George M. *When Lucy Went Away* (K–3). Illus. by Ingrid Fetz. 1976, Dutton $7.95. A tender story about the disappearance of a pet cat and the children's adjustment to their loss.

1077. Roy, Ron. *Three Ducks Went Wandering* (PS–1). Illus. by Paul Galdone. 1979, Houghton $8.95; Scholastic paper $1.95. Three ducks are oblivious to the dangers all around them when they take a walk.

1078. Rubel, Nicole. *Me and My Kitty* (PS–1). Illus. by author. 1983, Macmillan $7.95. A youngster and her kitty go through a typical day together.

1079. Schweitzer, Byrd Baylor. *Amigo* (K–3). Illus. by Garth Williams. 1963, Macmillan paper $2.95. Francisco, who longs for a pet, finds a wild prairie dog who wishes to tame a boy.

1080. Sharmat, Marjorie W. *Morris Brookside, a Dog* (K–3). Illus. by Ronald Himler. 1973, Holiday $6.95. An elderly couple adopt a stray dog, Morris, who insists on making friends with another very dirty female stray, and finally the old couple relent and adopt her too.

1081. Shub, Elizabeth. *The White Stallion* (2–4). Illus. by Rachel Isadora. 1982, Greenwillow $8.50;

LB $8.88. In this story of pioneers, Gretchen is saved by a mysterious white stallion.

1082. Simon, Norma. *Where Does My Cat Sleep?* (PS–1). Illus. by Dora Leder. 1982, Whitman $7.50. A picture book that shows the many places where a cat can sleep.

1083. Skorpen, Liesel Moak. *Bird* (K–3). Illus. by Joan Sandin. 1976, Harper $10.84. A small boy finds a baby bird and cares for it through one summer until it is ready to fly.

1084. Skorpen, Liesel Moak. *His Mother's Dog* (1–3). Illus. by M. E. Mullin. 1978, Harper LB $9.89. A little boy is crushed when his new dog prefers his mother.

1085. Thaler, Mike. *My Puppy* (K–2). Illus. by Madeleine Fishman. 1980, Harper $5.95; LB $8.89; Scholastic paper $1.50. A young boy can't afford a dog so he buys a leash instead.

1086. Turner, Dona. *My Cat Pearl* (PS–2). Illus. by author. 1980, Harper $8.61; LB $8.89. A description of the everyday activities of a young girl and her cat.

1087. Uchida, Yoshiko. *The Rooster Who Understood Japanese* (1–3). Illus. by Charles Robinson. 1976, Scribners paper $2.89. Little Miyo spends her after-school hours with Mrs. Kitamura, who speaks Japanese to her many pets.

1088. Wagner, Jenny. *Aranea: A Story about a Spider* (K–3). Illus. by Ron Brooks. 1978, Bradbury $8.95. Tells about the painstaking work of spinning a perfect spider's web.

1089. Wahl, Jan. *Tiger Watch* (K–3). Illus. by Charles Mikolaycak. 1982, Harcourt $12.95. Mustapha the hunter has been asked to kill a preying tiger.

1090. Wildsmith, Brian. *Pelican* (PS–2). Illus. by author. 1983, Pantheon $8.95; LB $10.99. A family copes with a pet pelican.

1091. Willard, Nancy. *Papa's Panda* (K–2). Illus. by Lillian Hoban. 1979, Harcourt $5.95. James realizes that it's better to live with a toy panda than a real one.

1092. Winnick, Karen B. *Sandro's Dolphin* (PS–2). Illus. by author. 1980, Lothrop $9.95; LB $9.55. The story of a young boy's friendship with a dolphin.

1093. Yashima, Mitsu, and Yashima, Taro. *Momo's Kitten* (K–3). Illus. by author. 1961, Penguin paper $3.95. Momo must give away her pet cat's 5 kittens.

1094. Ylla. *Two Little Bears* (PS–1). Illus. by author. 1954, Harper LB $12.89. Photographic story of 2 cubs.

1095. Zimelman, Nathan. *The Lives of My Cat Alfred* (K–3). Illus. by Evaline Ness. 1976, Dutton $6.95. Alfred thinks his cat is so special and wise that he might have participated in any number of important events; engagingly illustrated.

Family Stories

1096. Adoff, Arnold. *Black Is Brown Is Tan* (K–3). Illus. by Emily McCully. 1973, Harper LB $10.89. A story in rhyme, which needs to be read aloud for greater understanding, depicts the warmth and companionship of an interracial family.

1097. Ahlberg, Janet, and Ahlberg, Allan. *The Baby's Catalogue* (PS). Illus. by author. 1983, Little $10.50. A list of some of the interests of babies— like Moms and Dads.

1098. Alda, Arlene. *Sonya's Mommy Works* (PS–2). Illus. by author. 1982, Messner $9.79. The adjustment of a six-year-old whose mother takes a job.

1099. Alexander, Martha. *I'll Be the Horse If You'll Play with Me* (PS–2). Illus. by author. 1975, Dial $8.95; LB $8.89; paper $1.95. Bonnie issues her own declaration of independence in this humorous story.

1100. Alexander, Martha. *Nobody Asked Me If I Wanted a Baby Sister* (PS–1). Illus. by author. 1971, Dial $7.95; LB $7.89; paper $3.25. A young boy discovers that he does love his baby sister in spite of the fact that he thinks there is much too much fuss made over her.

1101. Alexander, Martha. *We Never Get to Do Anything* (K–2). Illus. by author. 1970, Dial $7.95; LB $7.89; paper $1.75. On a hot summer day, Adam's plans to go swimming are foiled, but rainfall helps ease the situation.

1102. Alexander, Martha. *When the New Baby Comes, I'm Moving Out* (PS–K). Illus. by author. 1979, Dial $6.95; LB $6.89; paper $2.25. Oliver has many reasons to resent his place being usurped by a new baby.

1103. Armitage, Ronda. *The Bossing of Josie* (PS–K). Illus. by David Armitage. 1980, Dutton $8.50. Everyone in the family, except the baby, seems to boss Josie.

1104. Aylesworth, Jim. *Siren in the Night* (PS–2). Illus. by Tom Centola. 1983, Whitman $7.75. A family reacts to night sounds, including the approach of a fire engine.

1105. Banish, Roslyn. *I Want to Tell You about My Baby* (PS–2). Illus. 1982, Wingbow Pr. paper $5.95. A preschooler talks about her new baby brother.

1106. Barrett, John M. *Daniel Discovers Daniel* (2–3). Illus. by Joe Servello. 1980, Human Sciences

$10.95. Daniel tries to satisfy his father's need for a sports-minded son.

1107. Bauer, Caroline F. *My Mom Travels a Lot* (K–2). Illus. by Nancy W. Parker. 1981, Warne $8.95. The best thing about Mom taking trips is the homecoming.

1108. Baylor, Byrd. *Guess Who My Favorite Person Is* (1–3). Illus. by Robert Andrew Parker. 1977, Scribners $7.95. A sensitive book that celebrates the joy and happiness in listing favorites.

1109. Behrens, June. *Fiesta!* (1–3). Illus. by Scott Taylor. 1978, Childrens Pr. $9.25. The fun of celebrating a Mexican-American family holiday— . Cinco de Mayo.

1110. Blaine, Marge. *The Terrible Thing That Happened at Our House* (K–2). Illus. by John Wallner. 1975, Parents $8.95. Chaos reigns when Mother decides to go back to work and the children have to learn to "cope."

1111. Blume, Judy. *The Pain and the Great One* (PS–1). Illus. by Irene Trivas. 1984, Bradbury $10.95. A brother and sister each explain why they don't get along.

1112. Borack, Barbara. *Grandpa* (PS–2). Illus. by Ben Schecter. 1967, Harper $10.89. Marilyn enjoys a visit with her grandparents and has an especially good time with her grandfather.

1113. Brandenberg, Franz. *Aunt Nina and Her Nephews and Nieces* (PS–2). Illus. by Aliki. 1983, Greenwillow $10.00; LB $9.55. Aunt Nina's cat has a present for each guest—a kitten. Also use: *Aunt Nina's Visit* (1984, Greenwillow $11.00; LB $10.51).

1114. Brandenberg, Franz. *I Wish I Was Sick, Too!* (K–3). Illus. by Aliki. 1976, Greenwillow LB $11.88. Elizabeth is jealous when her brother's illness gets him all sorts of special attention.

1115. Buckley, Helen E. *Grandmother and I* (PS–1). Illus. by Paul Galdone. 1961, Lothrop $10.80. A small girl explains the reasons why Grandmother's lap is better than anyone else's.

1116. Bunin, Catherine, and Bunin, Sherry. *Is That Your Sister? A True Story of Adoption* (K–3). Illus. by author. 1976, NACAC $5.99. Six-year-old Catherine and her sister Carla, both black, are adopted into a white family with 2 boys.

1117. Byars, Betsy. *Go and Hush the Baby* (PS–1). Illus. by Emily McCully. 1971, Viking $10.50. A clever young boy tries to quiet his baby brother.

1118. Caines, Jeannette. *Abby* (PS–1). Illus. by Steven Kellogg. 1973, Harper $9.57; LB $9.89. Abby, a little black girl, is adopted and enjoys hearing about the day she became part of her warm, loving family.

1119. Carle, Eric. *The Secret Birthday Message* (PS–1). Illus. by author. 1972, Harper $10.53; LB $10.89. In a brightly illustrated picture book with intriguing cutouts, a little boy has to decipher the coded message to find his birthday present.

1120. Clifton, Lucille. *Don't You Remember?* (PS–K). Illus. by Evaline Ness. 1973, Dutton $8.50. Four-year-old Denise remembers everything and is very upset when her parents keep putting off what they had promised her.

1121. Delton, Judy. *My Mom Hates Me in January* (K–2). Illus. by John Faulkner. 1977, Whitman $8.25. Mother really doesn't hate Lee Henry in January. What she hates is the weather in January, a sentiment echoed by many adults.

1122. de Paola, Tomie. *Watch Out for the Feet in Your Chicken Soup* (K–2). Illus. by author. 1974, Prentice $9.95; paper $2.50. Joey is a little embarrassed to take his friend Eugene to his old-fashioned Italian grandmother's for a visit, but in spite of her strange foreign ways, both boys pronounce the visit a great success.

1123. Dickinson, Mary. *Alex's Bed* (PS–2). Illus. by Charlotte Firmin. 1980, Dutton $7.95. Alex and his mother try to solve the problem of his cluttered room. Sequels are: *Alex and Roy* (1981); *Alex and the Baby* (1982); *Alex's Outing* (1983) (all Deutsch $9.95).

1124. Douglass, Barbara. *Good as New* (PS–2). Illus. by Patience Brewster. 1982, Lothrop $11.25; LB $11.88. Grandfather restores Grady's damaged teddy bear.

1125. Dragonwagon, Crescent. *I Hate My Brother Harry* (PS–3). Illus. by Dick Gackenbach. 1983, Harper $9.57; LB $9.89. A young girl maintains she hates her older brother but gradually changes her mind.

1126. Dragonwagon, Crescent. *Jemina Remembers* (1–3). Illus. by Troy Howell. 1980, Macmillan $12.95. Jemina takes one last look at the places she enjoyed most the summer she spent with her aunt.

1127. Edelman, Elaine. *I Love My Baby Sister (Most of the Time)* (PS). Illus. by Wendy Watson. 1984, Lothrop $10.50; LB $10.08. A little girl talks about the likes and dislikes involved in having a baby sister.

1128. Edwards, Dorothy. *My Naughty Little Sister and Bad Harry's Rabbit* (PS–2). Illus. by Shirley Hughes. 1981, Prentice $8.95. A young girl solves a problem with her brother's toy rabbit.

1129. Edwards, Linda Strauss. *The Downtown Day* (K–2). Illus. by author. 1983, Pantheon $9.95; LB $9.99. Linda goes shopping with her two aunts but is unhappy with what they want to buy for her.

1130. Ehrlich, Amy. *Zeek Silver Moon* (PS–3). Illus. by Robert Andrew Parker. 1972, Dial $7.95; LB $7.89; paper $1.75. The happiness encountered in everyday living is revealed in scenes of the first 5 years of Zeek Silver Moon's life.

1131. Everton, Macduff. *Elcirco Magico Modelo: Finding the Magic Circus* (K–4). Illus. by author. 1979, Carolrhoda LB $7.95. Ricky spends a summer in Yucatan with his father, a former circus performer.

1132. Farber, Norma. *How Does It Feel to Be Old?* (1–3). Illus. by Trina S. Hyman. 1979, Dutton $9.95; Creative Arts paper $3.95. Grandmother tries to explain to a young girl what it is like to be old.

1133. Flack, Marjorie. *Wait for William* (1–3). Illus. by R. A. Holberg. 1935, Houghton $6.95. William is left behind by his brother and sister, but all is well when he is allowed to ride in the circus parade.

1134. Fleischman, Paul. *The Animal Hedge* (K–3). Illus. by Lydia Dabcovich. 1983, Dutton $9.66. An old farmer who has lost his farm trims his hedge into all sorts of animals.

1135. Friedman, Ina R. *How My Parents Learned to Eat* (2–4). Illus. by Allen Say. 1984, Houghton $12.45. John, an American, and Aiko, a Japanese girl, learn each other's eating habits.

1136. Galbraith, Kathryn Osebold. *Katie Did!* (PS–2). Illus. by Ted Ramsey. 1982, Atheneum $8.95. Mary Rose seeks the attention now showered on her baby brother.

1137. Goffstein, M. B. *Family Scrapbook* (K–3). Illus. by author. 1978, Farrar $6.95. Vignettes of a Jewish family, told by one of the 2 children.

1138. Goffstein, M. B. *Fish for Supper* (PS). Illus. by author. 1976, Dial $5.89; LB $5.49. Grandmother enjoys fishing more than anything else and spends each day doing just that.

1139. Goffstein, M. B. *My Crazy Sister* (K–3). Illus. by author. 1976, Dial $5.95. Two sisters and a baby live in harmony in spite of the preposterous doings of one of the girls.

1140. Goldman, Susan. *Cousins Are Special* (K–2). Illus. by author. 1978, Whitman $7.75. A warm friendship is depicted between 2 cousins.

1141. Gomi, Taro. *Coco Can't Wait!* (PS–1). Illus. by author. 1984, Morrow $10.00; LB $9.55. Coco sets out to visit her grandmother.

1142. Greenfield, Eloise. *Grandmama's Joy* (2–5). Illus. by Carole Byard. 1980, Putnam $8.95. The story of Rhondy and the grandmother who has raised her.

1143. Greenfield, Eloise. *She Come Bringing Me That Little Baby Girl* (K–2). Illus. by John Steptoe. 1974, Harper $10.95. Kevin resents all the attention the new baby is getting; most of all he resents the fact that she is a girl.

1144. Hall, Donald. *The Man Who Lived Alone* (K–3). Illus. by Mary Azarian. 1984, Godine $11.95. The touching story of a mountain man and his cousin, Nan.

1145. Hamilton, Morse. *Big Sisters Are Bad Witches* (K–2). Illus. by Marylin Hafner. 1981, Greenwillow $11.25; LB $11.88. Kate is hoping for a baby brother but is disappointed.

1146. Hamilton, Morse, and Hamilton, Emily. *My Name Is Emily* (PS–1). Illus. by Jenni Oliver. 1979, Greenwillow LB $8.88. When Emily returns home after running away, her father pretends not to recognize her.

1147. Harranth, Wolf. *My Old Grandad* (K–2). Illus. by Christina Opperman-Dimov. 1984, Oxford $8.95. A young boy's grandfather comes to stay with his family but can't adjust to the change.

1148. Hautzig, Deborah. *The Handsomest Father* (K–2). Illus. by Muriel Batherman. 1979, Greenwillow $8.25; LB $7.92. At school, a young girl has fears that her father won't match up to her friends' parents on visiting day.

1149. Hazen, Barbara S. *Even If I Did Something Awful* (K–2). Illus. by Nancy Kincade. 1981, Atheneum $10.95. Mother still loves you even if you are bad.

1150. Hazen, Barbara S. *If It Weren't for Benjamin I'd Always Get to Lick the Icing* (PS–2). Illus. by Laura Hartman. 1979, Human Sciences $11.95. A younger sibling recounts the reasons for his sense of injustice.

1151. Helmering, Doris Wild. *I Have Two Families* (1–3). Illus. by Heidi Palmer. 1981, Abingdon $8.95. A young child comments on her parents' divorce.

1152. Hest, Amy. *The Crack-of-Dawn Walkers* (PS–2). Illus. by Amy Schwartz. 1984, Macmillan $9.95. Sadie and her grandfather have lovely walks alone every other Sunday.

1153. Hill, Elizabeth Starr. *Evan's Corner* (K–3). Illus. by Nancy Grossman. 1967, Holt $8.90; paper $1.45. Evan longs for a place of his own, until his mother points out that there are 8 corners in their 2-room apartment—one for him and each member of the family.

1154. Hines, Anna Grossnickle. *Taste the Raindrops* (PS–2). Illus. by author. 1983, Greenwillow $8.00; LB $7.63. A boy wants to walk in the rain but mother says no.

1155. Hirsch, Karen. *My Sister* (K–2). Illus. by Nancy Inderieden. 1977, Carolrhoda $5.95. A narrator introduces her sister, a retarded girl, whom she loves and protects.

1156. Hoban, Russell. *The Sorely Trying Day* (K–3). Illus. by Lillian Hoban. 1964, Harper $10.89. After a bad day at the office, father has an equally trying time when he returns home.

1157. Hoopes, Lyn Littlefield. *When I Was Little* (PS–K). Illus. by Marcia Sewall. 1983, Dutton $9.95. During a winter walk, a little girl is told by her mother how much she is loved.

1158. Hughes, Shirley. *Alfie Gets in First* (PS–2). Illus. by author. 1982, Lothrop $10.00; LB $10.88. Alfie locks himself in his house. Two sequels are: *Alfie's Feet* (1983); *Alfie Gives a Hand* (1984) (both $8.00; LB $7.63).

1159. Hurd, Edith Thacher. *I Dance in My Red Pajamas* (PS–1). Illus. by Emily McCully. 1982, Harper $10.53; LB $10.89. A little girl stays overnight at her grandparents' house.

1160. Hutchins, Pat. *Happy Birthday, Sam* (1–3). Illus. by author. 1979, Greenwillow $10.51. Sam is disappointed on his birthday morning to discover that he hasn't grown at all.

1161. Hutchins, Pat. *Titch* (K–3). Illus. by author. 1971, Macmillan $9.95. Titch, the youngest in the family, enjoys a moment of triumph. A sequel is: *You'll Soon Grow into Them, Titch* (1983, Greenwillow $9.00; LB $8.59).

1162. Isadora, Rachel. *Jesse and Abe* (K–3). Illus. by author. 1981, Greenwillow $10.25; LB $9.84. Jesse begins to realize how important his grandfather is.

1163. Jukes, Mavis. *Like Jake and Me* (2–3). Illus. by Lloyd Bloom. 1984, Knopf $11.95. Alex and his stepfather explore the meaning of fear.

1164. Keats, Ezra Jack. *Peter's Chair* (PS–1). Illus. by author. 1967, Harper $10.53; LB $10.89; paper $3.80. Distinctive collage technique and a gentle story show Peter emerging from his jealousy of a recent addition to the family to the acceptance of his new role as big brother.

1165. Keller, Holly. *Too Big* (PS–K). Illus. by author. 1983, Greenwillow $9.00; LB $8.59. Henry tries to participate in the activities of his baby brother.

1166. Kellogg, Steven. *Can I Keep Him?* (K–2). Illus. by author. 1971, Dial $8.95; LB $8.89; paper $3.95. Arnold, an incorrigible animal lover, constantly distresses his mother with a wide assortment of pets—real, imaginary, and human.

1167. Knotts, Howard. *Great-Grandfather, the Baby and Me* (K–2). Illus. by author. 1978, Athe-neum $6.95. Great-grandfather helps a young boy adjust to the arrival of a baby sister in the family.

1168. Knox-Wagner, Elaine. *My Grandpa Retired Today* (1–3). Illus. by Charles Robinson. 1982, Whitman LB $9.75. Margery attends a party for her grandfather, a barber, who is retiring.

1169. Kroll, Steven. *If I Could Be My Grandmother* (PS–K). Illus. by Lady McCrady. 1977, Pantheon LB $5.99. A little girl pretends that she is a grandmother and imitates her real-life counterpart.

1170. Kroll, Steven. *Toot! Toot!* (PS–1). Illus. by Anne Rockwell. 1983, Holiday $12.95. A little boy takes an imaginary trip to visit his grandparents.

1171. Langner, Nola. *Freddy My Grandfather* (2–3). Illus. by author. 1979, Scholastic $7.95. A warm account of a young girl's reflections on her grandfather, who lives in her home.

1172. Lapsley, Susan. *I Am Adopted* (PS–K). Illus. by Michael Charlton. 1975, Merrimack $3.95. "Adoption means belonging" is the theme of this very simple story of 2 children who know they are adopted.

1173. Lasky, Kathryn. *My Island Grandma* (K–2). Illus. by Emily McCully. 1979, Warne LB $7.95. An idyllic summer spent by Abbey with her grandmother.

1174. Lasky, Kathryn, and Knight, Maxwell B. *A Baby for Max* (PS–2). Illus. by Christopher G. Knight. 1984, Scribners $11.95. A book about a new addition to the family; illustrated with photographs.

1175. LeRoy, Gen. *Billy's Shoes* (1–3). Illus. by J. Winslow Higginbottom. 1981, McGraw $9.95. Young Billy is fearful he will lose his ability to run with his new shoes.

1176. LeRoy, Gen. *Lucky Stiff!* (1–2). Illus. by J. Winslow Higginbottom. 1981, McGraw $9.95. Anabel wonders if being a baby and getting a lot of attention is really that pleasant.

1177. Lexau, Joan M. *Benjie* (PS–1). Illus. by Don Bolognese. 1964, Dial LB $6.45. Benjie is painfully shy until he forces himself to go out alone to look for Granny's lost earring. Also use: *Benjie on His Own* (1970, Dial LB $9.89).

1178. Lexau, Joan M. *Emily and the Klunky Baby and the Next-Door Dog* (K–2). Illus. by Martha Alexander. 1972, Dial LB $5.47. A little girl takes her baby brother for a ride on a sled and becomes lost. Since she is not allowed to cross streets, she eventually returns home and is not lost at all.

1179. Lobel, Arnold. *A Treeful of Pigs* (K–2). Illus. by Anita Lobel. 1978, Greenwillow $12.50; LB $12.88. A canny wife cures her husband of laziness.

1180. Long, Earlene. *Gone Fishing* (PS–2). Illus. by Richard Brown. 1984, Houghton $10.95. A loving story of a boy's fishing trip with his father.

1181. McCloskey, Robert. *One Morning in Maine* (1–3). Illus. by author. 1952, Viking $9.95; Penguin paper $3.50. An exciting day, the loss of Sal's first tooth, is realistically recaptured by this fine storyteller and in the large, extraordinary blue pencil drawings of Penobscot Bay. Also use: *Blueberries for Sal* (1948, Viking $5.95; Penguin paper $2.95).

1182. MacLachlan, Patricia. *Mama One, Mama Two* (1–3). Illus. by Ruth Bornstein. 1982, Harper $9.13; LB $9.89. Maudie is told why she has two mothers in this gentle story of a foster home.

1183. MacLachlan, Patricia. *The Sick Day* (K–2). Illus. by William Pene du Bois. 1979, Pantheon $6.99. When Emily is sick, her father takes care of and amuses her.

1184. MacLachlan, Patricia. *Through Grandpa's Eyes* (1–3). Illus. by Deborah Ray. 1980, Harper LB $10.89; paper $4.09. John's blind grandfather shares with him the special way he sees and moves in the world.

1185. McPhail, David. *Sisters* (PS–1). Illus. by author. 1984, Harcourt $10.95. Two loving sisters compare their similarities and differences.

1186. Mantinband, Gerda. *Papa and Mama Biederbeck* (2–4). Illus. by Karen Ann Weinhaus. 1983, Houghton $7.70. Four stories about a husband and wife and their household adventures.

1187. Merriam, Eve. *Mommies at Work* (K–1). Illus. by Beni Montresor. 1973, Scholastic paper $1.95. Why Mommy can be like other people and hold down a job.

1188. Moore, Sheila. *Samson Svenson's Baby* (1–4). Illus. by Karen Ann Weinhaus. 1983, Harper $9.57; LB $9.89. Two outsiders in a village fall in love and marry.

1189. Naylor, Phyllis Reynolds. *How Lazy Can You Get?* (2–4). Illus. by Alan Daniel. 1979, Atheneum $9.95. Three children adjust slowly to their strict professional caretaker, Miss Brasscoat.

1190. Ness, Evaline. *Yeck Eck* (1–3). Illus. by author. 1974, Dutton $6.95. Tana Jones gets her wish to adopt babies in this delightfully daffy tale.

1191. Nolan, Madeena Spray. *My Daddy Don't Go to Work* (1–3). Illus. by Jim LaMarche. 1978, Carolrhoda $5.95. A black girl tells of family problems caused by her father's unemployment.

1192. Ormerod, Jan. *One-Hundred-One Things to Do with a Baby* (PS–K). Illus. 1984, Lothrop $10.00; LB $9.55. The whole family decides to amuse the baby.

1193. Osborn, Lois. *My Dad Is Really Something* (1–3). Illus. by Rodney Pate. 1983, Whitman $8.25. Ron's father seems so much better than Harry George's until the truth comes out.

1194. Oxenbury, Helen. *Beach Day* (PS). Illus. by author. 1982, Dial $3.50. A book describing the activities of a toddler on the beach. Others in this series dealing with everyday activities are: *Monkey See, Monkey Do; Shopping Trip* (both 1982, paper $3.50); *The Car Trip; The Checkup; First Day of School* (all 1982 .78).

1195. Oxenbury, Helen. *The Birthday Party* (PS–K). Illus. by author. 1983, Dial $5.78. A guest is more interested in the presents than in the birthday child. Other everyday situations explored by the author are: *Family* (1981, Simon & Schuster paper $3.50); *The Dancing Class; Eating Out* (both 1983, Dial $5.78).

1196. Oxenbury, Helen. *Grandma and Grandpa* (PS). Illus. by author. 1984, Dial $5.95. A toddler's book on a simple visit of grandparents. Other stories of typical family activities are: *Good Night, Good Morning; Mother's Helper* (both 1982, Dial $3.50).

1197. Paterson, Diane. *Hey, Cowboy!* (PS–1). Illus. by author. 1983, Knopf $9.95; LB $9.99. A boy and his sister argue over who is going to ride on Grandpa.

1198. Pincus, Harriet. *Minna and Pippin* (PS–3). Illus. by author. 1972, Farrar $7.95. The pleasures a young girl named Minna receives from naming Pippin, a new doll.

1199. Politi, Leo. *Three Stalks of Corn* (K–4). Illus. by author. 1976, Scribners $6.95. Chicano culture, including some recipes, is included in this story of a girl and her grandmother.

1200. Pomerantz, Charlotte. *The Half-Birthday Party* (K–3). Illus. by DyAnne DiSalvo-Ryan. 1984, Houghton $10.95. To celebrate his sister's reaching 6 months, Daniel has a half-birthday party.

1201. Power, Barbara. *I Wish Laura's Mommy Was My Mommy* (1–3). Illus. by Marylin Hafner. 1979, Harper $8.89; LB $8.61. When roles are reversed, Jennifer is glad to have her own mommy back.

1202. Radin, Ruth Yaffe. *A Winter Place* (PS–2). Illus. by Mattie Lou O'Kelley. 1982, Little LB $13.95. A family goes ice-skating in this well-illustrated picture book.

1203. Rice, Eve. *Benny Bakes a Cake* (PS–1). Illus. by author. 1981, Greenwillow $11.25; LB $11.88. Benny's dog eats his birthday cake and causes a crisis.

1204. Rice, Eve. *New Blue Shoes* (PS–K). Illus. by author. 1975, Penguin paper $3.50. Rebecca insists on blue as the color for her new shoes, but after she purchases them, doubts assail her.

1205. Rice, Eve. *What Sadie Sang* (PS). Illus. by author. 1983, Greenwillow $9.00; LB $8.59. What Sadie, a very young child, sang was a song according to her mother.

1206. Rockwell, Anne. *Can I Help?* (PS). Illus. by Anne Rockwell and Harlow Rockwell. 1982, Macmillan $8.95. A little girl tries to help with chores around the house.

1207. Rockwell, Anne, and Rockwell, Harlow. *Blackout* (2–3). Illus. by author. 1979, Macmillan $6.95. How a family lives through a long power blackout.

1208. Roth, Susan L., and Phang, Ruth. *Patchwork Tales* (PS–2). Illus. by author. 1984, Atheneum $9.95. At nighttime a grandmother tells the story of each block in a quilt.

1209. Ruffins, Reynold. *My Brother Never Feeds the Cat* (PS–K). Illus. by author. 1979, Scribners $7.95. A young girl complains that her brother doesn't have the chores that she has.

1210. Ryder, Joanne. *Beach Party* (K–3). Illus. by Diane Stanley. 1982, Warne $9.95. Dorothy and family have a birthday party at the beach.

1211. Rylant, Cynthia. *When I Was Young in the Mountains* (K–3). Illus. by Diane Goode. 1982, Dutton $9.95. Two children live with their grandparents in this story of poverty in Appalachia.

1212. Sarnoff, Jane. *That's Not Fair* (PS–2). Illus. by Reynold Ruffins. 1980, Scribners LB $10.95. Becky learns the difference between things that can be changed and those that can't.

1213. Schick, Eleanor. *A Piano for Julie* (PS–3). Illus. by author. 1984, Greenwillow $9.00; LB $8.59. What happens in a household when a piano arrives.

1214. Scott, Ann H. *Sam* (PS–1). Illus. by Symeon Shimin. 1967, McGraw $10.95. Each member of this black family is too preoccupied to give any attention to Sam, until they notice his dejection and provide a satisfying job for him to do.

1215. Segal, Lore. *The Story of Old Mrs. Brubeck and How She Looked for Trouble and Where She Found Him* (1–3). Illus. by Marcia Sewall. 1981, Pantheon $8.95. Mrs. Brubeck is overprotective of her granddaughter, Beatrix.

1216. Segal, Lore. *Tell Me a Mitzi* (K–2). Illus. by Harriet Pincus. 1970, Farrar $12.95; paper $1.95. Three hilarious stories about the antics of a city family: a mad trip to Grandma's house, coming down with a cold, and a meeting with the president.

1217. Segal, Lore. *Tell Me a Trudy* (PS–3). Illus. by Rosemary Wells. 1977, Farrar $8.95. A zany

family experiences ordinary situations that somehow become most unusual.

1218. Shannon, George. *The Piney Woods Peddler* (PS–3). Illus. by Nancy Tafuri. 1981, Greenwillow $11.25; LB $11.85. A peddler is unable to fulfill his promise of a silver dollar for his daughter.

1219. Sharmat, Marjorie W. *Sometimes Mama and Papa Fight* (K–3). Illus. by Kay Chorao. 1980, Harper $8.61; LB $8.89. Two youngsters react to their parents' quarreling.

1220. Shulevitz, Uri. *The Treasure* (K–2). Illus. by author. 1979, Farrar $8.95. A man discovers that the most valuable things in life are usually found at home.

1221. Simon, Norma. *I'm Busy Too* (PS–1). Illus. by Dora Leder. 1980, Whitman $8.25. The work activities of preschool children and parents are compared in this picture book.

1222. Skorpen, Liesel Moak. *Mandy's Grandmother* (K–2). Illus. by Martha Alexander. 1975, Dial $4.95; LB $4.58. Mandy learns to love her grandmother as much as her grandmother loves her.

1223. Stanovich, Betty Jo. *Big Boy, Little Boy* (PS–K). Illus. by Virginia Wright-Freirson. 1984, Lothrop $11.00; LB $10.08. David and Grandma share a tender moment.

1224. Stecher, Miriam B. *Daddy and Ben Together* (PS–1). Illus. 1981, Lothrop $11.25; LB $11.88. While Mommy is away, Daddy and Ben spend an enjoyable time together.

1225. Steptoe, John. *Daddy Is a Monster . . . Sometimes* (K–3). Illus. 1980, Harper $9.57; LB $9.89; paper $4.95. Two boys talk about their fathers and agree that they are not so mean after all.

1226. Steptoe, John. *Stevie* (PS–2). Illus. by author. 1969, Harper $9.95; LB $10.89. A small black boy eloquently expresses his resentment at having to share his possessions and mother with a temporary younger boarder who became "kinda like a little brother"; illustrated in bold line and color.

1227. Stock, Catherine. *Emma's Dragon Hunt* (1–3). Illus. by author. 1984, Lothrop $10.00; LB $9.55. A Chinese grandfather explains that Chinese dragons are good dragons.

1228. Strete, Craig Kee. *When Grandfather Journeys into Winter* (1–3). Illus. by Hal Frenck. 1979, Greenwillow LB $10.88. The touching relationship between an American Indian boy and his grandfather.

1229. Tax, Meredith. *Families* (2–3). Illus. by Marylin Hafner. 1981, Little $7.95. A variety of human and animal living situations are explored.

1230. Thomas, Ianthe. *Walk Home Tired, Billy Jenkins* (K–2). Illus. by Thomas Di Grazia. 1974, Harper $9.89. Poor sister Nina tries everything to coax weary Bill Jenkins to walk home, in this warm, tender story.

1231. Thomas, Ianthe. *Willie Blows a Mean Horn* (K–3). Illus. by Ann Toulmin-Rothe. 1981, Harper $7.95; LB $8.89. A young black boy's enthusiasm for jazz.

1232. Tobias, Tobi. *The Dawdlewalk* (PS–2). Illus. by Jeanette Swofford. 1983, Carolrhoda LB $8.95. A mother and son take a leisurely walk to school.

1233. Tobias, Tobi. *Moving Day* (PS–K). Illus. by William Pene du Bois. 1976, Knopf LB $7.99. A stuffed toy bear helps comfort a little girl through the turmoil and fears of moving day.

1234. Van Leeuwen, Jean. *Too Hot for Ice Cream* (K–2). Illus. by Martha Alexander. 1974, Dial $5.95. Everything goes wrong for Sara on this particular day.

1235. Vigna, Judith. *Daddy's New Baby* (PS–2). Illus. by author. 1982, Whitman $8.25. A little girl adjusts to her divorced and remarried father's new baby.

1236. Vineberg, Ethel. *Grandmother Came from Dworitz: A Jewish Story* (2–4). Illus. by Rita Briansky. 1978, Tundra paper $3.95. A simple retelling of an immigration story from Poland to Canada.

1237. Viorst, Judith. *Alexander and the Terrible, Horrible, No Good, Very Bad Day* (K–3). Illus. by Ray Cruz. 1972, Atheneum $9.95; paper $2.50. Alexander wakes up to a bad day and things get progressively worse as the hours wear on, until he thinks he may escape it all and go to Australia.

1238. Viorst, Judith. *I'll Fix Anthony* (PS–3). Illus. by Arnold Lobel. 1969, Harper $10.53; LB $10.89; paper $2.95. A young boy has a field day planning revenge on an older brother.

1239. Waber, Bernard. *But Names Will Never Hurt Me* (PS–1). Illus. by author. 1976, Houghton $9.95. Alison is teased about her last name, but after her family tells her the story of how she was named, she feels better and can even joke about it.

1240. Walter, Mildred Pitts. *My Mama Needs Me* (PS–1). Illus. by Pat Cummings. 1983, Lothrop $9.00; LB $8.59. Jason, a little black boy, wants to help his mother with his new baby sister.

1241. Watson, Wendy. *Jamie's Story* (PS). Illus. by author. 1981, Putnam $6.95. A day in the life of a very young child.

1242. Weiss, Nicki. *Waiting* (PS–2). Illus. by author. 1981, Greenwillow $11.25; LB $11.88. Analee waits impatiently for her mother's return.

1243. Weiss, Nicki. *Weekend at Muskrat Lake* (K–2). Illus. by author. 1984, Greenwillow $10.51. A family vacation in a rented summer cabin.

1244. Wells, Rosemary. *A Lion for Lewis* (K–1). Illus. by author. 1982, Dial $9.95; LB $9.89; paper $3.95. Young Lewis never gets to play any of the good parts when his brother and sister play-act.

1245. Wells, Rosemary. *Unfortunately Harriet* (PS–3). Illus. by author. 1972, Dial $4.95; LB $4.58. Harriet faces problems when she spills varnish in the middle of the family's new rug.

1246. Williams, Barbara. *Kevin's Grandma* (K–2). Illus. by Kay Chorao. 1975, Dutton $9.95; paper $3.95. Kevin's grandma is an unforgettable personality—a real "swinger" when compared with the traditional grandmother type.

1247. Williams, Vera B. *A Chair for My Mother* (PS–2). Illus. by author. 1982, Greenwillow $11.25; LB $11.88; Scholastic paper $3.95. After fire destroys their home, Rose and her mother and grandmother save to buy a nice new chair. Two sequels are: *Something Special for Me* (1983, $10.00; LB $9.55); *Music, Music for Everyone* (1984, $11.50; LB $10.51).

1248. Williams, Vera B. *The Great Watermelon Birthday* (K–2). Illus. 1980, Greenwillow $10.95; LB $10.51. An elderly couple celebrate the birth of a great-grandchild by giving away watermelon.

1249. Winthrop, Elizabeth. *Are You Sad, Mama?* (K–2). Illus. by Donna Diamond. 1979, Harper $8.61; LB $8.89. A young girl tries to cheer up her mother.

1250. Winthrop, Elizabeth. *I Think He Likes Me* (PS–1). Illus. by Denise Saldutti. 1980, Harper LB $9.89. Eliza adjusts to a new baby.

1251. Winthrop, Elizabeth. *Sloppy Kisses* (K–2). Illus. by Anne Burgess. 1980, Macmillan LB $8.95; paper $3.95. Emmy Lou regrets her decision not to allow any more kisses.

1252. Zola, Meguido. *Only the Best* (K–3). Illus. by Valerie Littlewood. 1982, Watts LB $8.95. A father finds that the best gift he can give his new daughter is love.

1253. Zolotow, Charlotte. *Big Brother* (K–3). Illus. by Mary Chalmers. 1960, Harper LB $9.89; paper $1.88. A story about a young girl and her teasing older brother.

1254. Zolotow, Charlotte. *But Not Billy* (PS–K). Illus. by Kay Chorao. 1983, Harper $9.57; LB $9.89. A baby progresses from crying to his first spoken word.

1255. Zolotow, Charlotte. *Do You Know What I'll Do?* (PS–1). Illus. by Garth Williams. 1958, Harper

$9.51; LB $9.89. A little girl explains all the lovely things she is going to do for her baby brother.

1256. Zolotow, Charlotte. *A Father Like That* (K–2). Illus. by Ben Shecter. 1971, Harper $10.53; LB $10.89. A fatherless boy describes in this tender story the kind of father he would like to have.

1257. Zolotow, Charlotte. *If It Weren't for You* (1–3). Illus. by Ben Shecter. 1966, Harper $10.53; LB $10.89. A young boy lists all of the nice things life would provide if he just didn't have a baby brother.

1258. Zolotow, Charlotte. *If You Listen* (K–2). Illus. by Marc Simont. 1980, Harper $8.95; LB $10.89. A girl wonders if her absent father continues to love her.

1259. Zolotow, Charlotte. *May I Visit?* (K–2). Illus. by Erik Blegvad. 1976, Harper $8.61. A little girl imagines what it would be like to be grown up and asks her mother if she may come back for a visit at that time.

1260. Zolotow, Charlotte. *My Grandson Lew* (K–3). Illus. by William Pene du Bois. 1974, Harper $8.61; LB $9.89. Lew and his mother discuss their memories of grandpa in a gentle, poignant story of a family member who has died.

1261. Zolotow, Charlotte. *The Quarreling Book* (K–2). Illus. by Arnold Lobel. 1963, Harper $7.64; LB $7.89; paper $1.85. Father's failure to kiss mother one morning triggers a series of quarrels, but the pet dog sets things right. Also use: *The Hating Book* (1969, Harper $7.64; LB $8.89).

1262. Zolotow, Charlotte. *Say It!* (K–2). Illus. by James Stevenson. 1980, Greenwillow $10.95; LB $10.57. A mood piece about a mother's love for her daughter.

1263. Zolotow, Charlotte. *William's Doll* (PS–3). Illus. by William Pene du Bois. 1972, Harper $8.61; LB $8.89. William wanted a doll, much to his father's dismay, but when Grandma comes to visit she presents William with a doll, saying that now he will have an opportunity to practice being a good father.

Friendship Stories

1264. Aliki. *We Are Best Friends* (K–3). Illus. by author. 1982, Greenwillow $10.25; LB $10.88. Robert is at a loss when his best friend moves away.

1265. Ardizzone, Edward, and Ardizzone, Aingelda. *The Little Girl and the Tiny Doll* (2–4). 1980, Penguin paper $3.95. A tiny doll, discarded by its owner, is finally found by a girl who loves dolls.

1266. Battles, Edith. *What Does the Rooster Say, Yoshio?* (PS–K). Illus. by Toni Hormann. 1978, Whitman $7.75. A Japanese boy and an American girl have difficulty communicating.

1267. Bottner, Barbara. *Horrible Hannah* (K–2). Illus. by Joan Drescher. 1980, Crown LB $6.95. Children confuse a warning about a dog with an evaluation of their new neighbor.

1268. Brown, Marc. *The True Francine* (1–3). Illus. by author. 1981, Little $8.95. Francine discovers the meaning of friendship when she is accused of cheating.

1269. Bunting, Eve. *Clancy's Coat* (K–3). Illus. by Lorinda Bryan Cauley. 1984, Warne $11.95. Clancy regains a friend over his torn coat.

1270. Bunting, Eve. *The Traveling Men of Ballycoo* (1–3). Illus. by Kaethe Zemach. 1983, Harcourt $12.95. Three traveling musicians must face old age and the necessity of settling down.

1271. Charlip, Remy, and Supree, Burton. *Harlequin and the Gift of Many Colors* (K–3). Illus. by Remy Charlip. 1973, Scholastic $7.95. Harlequin can't go to the carnival because he is too poor to have a costume.

1272. Desbarats, Peter. *Gabrielle and Selena* (K–3). Illus. by Nancy Grossman. 1974, Harcourt paper $0.95. When 8-year-old girls, one black, the other white, show up in each other's homes in an exchange of identity for the evening, to their surprise their parents turn the joke on them.

1273. Erskine, Jim. *Bert and Susie's Messy Tale* (PS–K). Illus. by author. 1979, Crown $5.95. Bert and a friend play in a mud puddle and almost miss the flower show.

1274. Goffstein, M. B. *Neighbors* (1–3). Illus. by author. 1979, Harper $8.61; LB $9.89. After several false starts, two women gradually become friends.

1275. Gordon, Shirley. *Happy Birthday Crystal* (1–3). Illus. by Edward Frascino. 1981, Harper $7.95; LB $9.89. Susan is jealous of Crystal's friend, who lives next door.

1276. Hays, Wilma Pitchford. *Yellow Fur and Little Hawk* (2–4). Illus. by Anthony Rao. 1980, Putnam $6.99. Two friends—one American Indian, one white—and the story of a devastating drought.

1277. Hazen, Barbara S. *Why Couldn't I Be an Only Kid Like You, Wigger* (PS–2). Illus. by Leigh Grant. 1975, Atheneum $7.95; paper $1.95. Two views on the advantages and disadvantages of being an only child are whimsically presented.

1278. Heine, Helme. *Merry-Go-Round* (PS–2). Illus. by author. 1980, Barron's $4.95. Three adults alternate their roles on a vacation so they can play with Katie.

1279. Hickman, Martha Whitmore. *My Friend William Moved Away* (PS–1). Illus. by Bill Myers. 1979, Abingdon $7.95. Jimmy misses his friend William.

1280. Hoffman, Phyllis. *Steffie and Me* (K–3). Illus. by Emily McCully. 1970, Harper $9.89. Two children, one black, the other white, enjoy everyday activities together.

1281. Hurwitz, Johanna. *Busybody Nora* (K–2). Illus. by Susan Jeschke. 1976, Morrow $7.63; Dell paper $1.50. Six-year-old Nora lives in an apartment building in New York City and wants to know all her neighbors. Most of them are friendly except for one woman who calls her a busybody.

1282. Hurwitz, Johanna. *New Neighbors for Nora* (2–3). Illus. by Susan Jeschke. 1979, Morrow $8.25; LB $7.92. Nora, hoping to make a new friend, is not too happy when Eugene Spencer Eastman moves into her building.

1283. Kantrowitz, Mildred. *Maxie* (PS–3). Illus. by Emily McCully. 1970, Four Winds $8.95. Maxie is a little old lady who keeps the entire neighborhood on its toes—everyone sets their clocks by her, until one morning Maxie stays in bed. . . .

1284. Keats, Ezra Jack. *Apt. 3* (PS–3). Illus. by author. 1971, Macmillan $13.95. Two brothers, investigating the various sounds of an apartment building, find a friend in Mr. Muntz, the blind man behind the door of Apt. 3.

1285. Keats, Ezra Jack. *Goggles* (K–3). Illus. by author. 1971, Macmillan paper $3.95. Dachshund Willie outmaneuvers some neighborhood bullies trying to confiscate the motorcycle goggles found by Peter. Bold collage paintings perfectly capture inner-city neighborhood scenes.

1286. Keats, Ezra Jack. *A Letter to Amy* (1–3). Illus. by author. 1968, Harper $10.53; LB $10.89. The dilemma faced by a boy who wants to invite a girl to his all-boy birthday party.

1287. Keats, Ezra Jack. *Whistle for Willie* (PS–1). Illus. by author. 1964, Viking $10.95; Penguin paper $3.50. After many false starts, Peter at last learns to whistle.

1288. Levitin, Sonia. *All the Cats in the World* (2–4). Illus. by Charles Robinson. 1982, Harcourt $14.95. A gruff lighthouse keeper takes over the feeding of the birds when Mikila gets sick.

1289. McKee, David. *I Hate My Teddy Bear* (PS–1). Illus. 1984, Houghton $9.95. Two children vie in praise for their teddy bears.

1290. Politi, Leo. *Moy Moy* (PS–3). Illus. by author. 1960, Scribners $7.95. Appealing picture of Moy Moy's life in a Los Angeles Chinese neighborhood.

1291. Politi, Leo. *Pedro, the Angel of Olivera Street* (1–3). Illus. by author. 1946, Scribners $8.95. Olivera Street in Los Angeles is the setting for this story of a small boy who is chosen to play the part of an angel in the Mexican Christmas celebration.

1292. Robison, Deborah. *Bye-Bye, Old Buddy* (PS–3). Illus. by author. 1983, Houghton $9.95. Jenny decides to send her no-longer-needed baby blanket to a name in the telephone book.

1293. Rylant, Cynthia. *Miss Maggie* (K–3). Illus. by Thomas Di Grazia. 1983, Dutton $9.66. The friendship of a young boy and an elderly recluse.

1294. Schulman, Janet. *The Great Big Dummy* (K–2). Illus. by Lillian Hoban. 1979, Greenwillow $8.88; Dell paper $1.25. Out of old clothes and other objects, a girl creates a playmate.

1295. Sharmat, Marjorie W. *Gladys Told Me to Meet Her Here* (K–2). Illus. by Edward Frascino. 1970, Harper $9.89. Irving is waiting for his friend Gladys, who is 10 minutes late.

1296. Sharmat, Marjorie W. *I'm Not Oscar's Friend Anymore* (K–2). Illus. by Tony DeLuna. 1975, Dutton $9.95. Oscar's best friend tells all the reasons why they aren't friends anymore, but Oscar doesn't even remember they had a fight, and normal relations are happily resumed.

1297. Sherman, Ivan. *I Do Not Like It When My Friend Comes to Visit* (PS–2). Illus. by author. 1973, Harcourt $8.95. A little girl voices her displeasure when her friend comes to visit and gets the lion's share of the toys and attention.

1298. Simon, Norma. *Elly the Elephant* (PS–K). Illus. by Stanley Bleifeld. 1982, Whitman LB $9.25. The story of Wendy and her beloved stuffed toy.

1299. Uchida, Yoshiko. *The Birthday Visitor* (1–3). Illus. by Charles Robinson. 1975, Scribners $5.95. At first, Emi, a Japanese-American girl, resents having a visitor from Japan on her birthday.

1300. Udry, Janice May. *Let's Be Enemies* (PS–2). Illus. by Maurice Sendak. 1961, Harper $8.95; LB $9.89. John is tired of James and his bossiness and decides to tell him so, but things are patched up and they remain friends.

1301. Viorst, Judith. *Rosie and Michael* (1–3). Illus. by Lorna Tomei. 1974, Atheneum $10.95; paper $2.95. In spite of the many tricks they play on one another, Rosie and Michael are still friends.

1302. Walter, Mildred Pitts. *Ty's One-Man Band* (PS–2). Illus. by Margot Tomes. 1980, Four Winds $9.95. Andro produces music from a collection of everyday objects.

1303. Weiss, Nicki. *Maude and Sally* (K–3). Illus. by author. 1983, Greenwillow $8.59. Maude is upset when her friend Sally goes to summer camp.

1304. Winthrop, Elizabeth. *Katharine's Doll* (K–3). Illus. by Marylin Hafner. 1983, Dutton $9.95. Katharine and Molly quarrel when only one receives a new doll.

1305. Winthrop, Elizabeth. *That's Mine!* (PS–K). Illus. by Emily McCully. 1977, Holiday $7.95. Two children who quarrel over a block learn the necessity of sharing.

1306. Wittman, Sally. *A Special Trade* (1–3). Illus. by Karen Gundersheimer. 1978, Harper $9.57; LB $9.89. Nelly, now grown, takes old Bartholomew out for a walk as he once took her.

1307. Zalben, Jane Breskin. *Oh, Simple!* (K–2). Illus. by author. 1981, Farrar $9.95. Winifred derides Beasely's inability to spell.

1308. Zolotow, Charlotte. *I Know a Lady* (PS–2). Illus. by James Stevenson. 1984, Greenwillow $10.00; LB $9.55. Sally loves a kind old lady who lives in the neighborhood.

1309. Zolotow, Charlotte. *Janey* (1–3). Illus. by Ronald Himler. 1973, Harper LB $9.89. A little girl misses her best friend who has moved away and reminisces about the things they used to do together.

1310. Zolotow, Charlotte. *The Unfriendly Book* (K–3). Illus. by William Pene du Bois. 1975, Harper $8.89. Bertha finds fault with many of her friends, but Judy always has a compliment for each.

1311. Zolotow, Charlotte. *The White Marble* (K–2). Illus. by Deborah Kogan. 1982, Harper $10.53; LB $9.89. Two young friends share an evening in the park.

School Stories

1312. Allard, Harry. *Miss Nelson Is Missing!* (K–2). Illus. by James Marshall. 1977, Houghton $10.95; Scholastic paper $1.95. When Miss Nelson's students in Room 207 misbehave, she disappears and is replaced by a martinet. A sequel is: *Miss Nelson Is Back* (1982, LB $8.95).

1313. Boyd, Selma, and Boyd, Pauline. *I Met a Polar Bear* (PS–2). Illus. by Patience Brewster. 1983, Lothrop $10.00; LB $10.88. A young boy explains his lateness at school in far-fetched terms.

1314. Breinburg, Petronella. *Shawn Goes to School* (PS–1). Illus. by Errol Lloyd. 1974, Harper $10.89. Shawn's first day at school is described by his older sister.

1315. Brooks, Ron. *Timothy and Gramps* (1–3). 1979, Bradbury $7.95. Gramps's visit to school changes Timothy's classroom status.

1316. Caudill, Rebecca. *A Pocketful of Cricket* (1–3). Illus. by Evaline Ness. 1964, Holt $7.95; paper $2.95. A small boy delights in the countryside around his home, and one day his pet cricket goes to school in his pocket.

1317. Chapman, Carol. *Herbie's Troubles* (K–2). Illus. by Kelly Oechsli. 1981, Dutton $9.25. Herbie must stand up to the school bully, who is making his life miserable.

1318. Chorao, Kay. *Molly's Lies* (K–2). Illus. by author. 1979, Houghton $7.50. Molly copes with the first day of school by telling fibs.

1319. Cohen, Miriam. *Best Friends* (PS–K). Illus. by Lillian Hoban. 1971, Macmillan $9.95; paper $2.50. Kindergarten is the setting for this story of the friendship and disagreements between two boys. By the same author: *The New Teacher* (1972, Macmillan paper $1.25); *First Grade Takes a Test* (1980, Greenwillow $10.95; LB $10.51; Dell paper $1.95); *See You Tomorrow, Charles* (1983, Greenwillow $10.00; LB $9.55).

1320. Cohen, Miriam. *Will I Have a Friend?* (PS–2). Illus. by Lillian Hoban. 1967, Macmillan $9.95; paper $2.50. Jim, a kindergartner, lives out the actual concern that small children have about finding a friend on the first day of school. By the same author and publisher: *No Good in Art* (1980, $11.25; LB $11.88); *Jim Meets the Thing* (1981, $11.25; LB $11.88); *So What?* (1982, $11.25; LB $11.88); *Jim's Dog Muffins* (1984, $10.50; LB $9.55).

1321. Davis, Gibbs. *The Other Emily* (K–2). Illus. by Linda Shute. 1983, Houghton $10.45. Emily loves her name until she encounters another Emily in her class.

1322. Giff, Patricia Reilly. *Next Year I'll Be Special* (K–2). Illus. by Marylin Hafner. 1980, Dutton $7.95. A young girl daydreams of how life will be better in the second grade.

1323. Hamilton-Merrit, Jane. *My First Days of School* (PS–K). Illus. 1982, Messner LB $8.29. Pictures show Kate during her first two days in kindergarten.

1324. Isadora, Rachel. *Willaby* (K–2). Illus. by author. 1977, Macmillan $9.95. Willaby's desire to express himself in drawing causes school complications.

1325. Rockwell, Anne. *When We Grow Up* (1–2). Illus. 1981, Dutton $10.25. A narrator lists what his classmates will be when they grow up.

1326. Rockwell, Harlow. *My Nursery School* (PS). Illus. by author. 1976, Greenwillow $10.95. Clear, simple pictures show the daily activities of a nursery school.

1327. Schwartz, Amy. *Begin at the Beginning* (1–3). Illus. by author. 1983, Harper $8.61; LB $8.89; paper $2.95. Sara has difficulty with her second-grade art show.

1328. Simon, Norma. *I'm Busy, Too* (PS–1). Illus. by Dora Leder. 1980, Whitman LB $9.25. A day-care center child realizes that every member of the family has an important role to play.

1329. Stanek, Muriel. *Starting School* (K–1). Illus. by Betty Deluna and Tony Deluna. 1981, Whitman LB $8.75. The young boy who tells this story gets ready to start school.

1330. Tester, Sylvia Root. *We Laughed a Lot, My First Day of School* (PS–1). Illus. by Frances Hook. 1979, Childrens Pr. $9.95. A Mexican-American boy has an unexpectedly pleasant first day at school.

1331. Wells, Rosemary. *Timothy Goes to School* (PS–1). Illus. by author. 1981, Dial $7.50; LB $7.28; paper $3.95. Timothy's first day at school is almost ruined by a bully, but a friend helps him.

1332. Whitney, Alma Marshak. *Just Awful* (K–2). Illus. by Lillian Hoban. 1971, Childrens Pr. $7.95. James cuts his finger and goes to the school nurse for the first time, with satisfactory results.

1333. Wittman, Sally. *The Wonderful Mrs. Trumbly* (K–3). Illus. by Margot Apple. 1982, Harper $7.64; LB $8.89. Martin feels a special attachment to his new teacher.

1334. Wolf, Bernard. *Adam Smith Goes to School* (PS–1). Illus. 1978, Harper $10.89. Adam's first day in the first grade.

1335. Yashima, Taro. *Crow Boy* (K–3). Illus. by author. 1955, Viking $13.95; Penguin paper $3.95. Distinguished picture book about a shy little Japanese boy who feels like an outsider at school.

Adventure Stories

1336. Adoff, Arnold. *Where Wild Willie* (K–2). Illus. by Emily McCully. 1978, Harper LB $10.89. Willie stays out late exploring the neighborhood.

1337. Armitage, Ronda. *One Moonlit Night* (PS–1). Illus. by David Armitage. 1984, Deutsch $9.95. Tony and his friend Sam spend the night in Tony's new tent.

1338. Benson, Kathleen. *Joseph on the Subway Trains* (2–3). Illus. by Emily McCully. 1981, Addison LB $7.95. Joseph takes the wrong train and finds he's Manhattan-bound.

1339. Blake, Quentin. *Snuff* (K–2). Illus. by author. 1973, Harper $9.95. Snuff is a page who can't seem to master any of the skills needed to

become a knight, but he uses his brain to foil some robbers and thus demonstrates his ability after all.

1340. Bornstein, Ruth. *Of Course a Goat* (PS–K). Illus. 1980, Harper LB $8.89. A boy imagines a journey to the top of a mountain.

1341. Burningham, John. *Mr. Gumpy's Motor Car* (K–3). Illus. by author. 1976, Harper LB $10.89; Penguin paper $3.50. Mr. Gumpy takes his daughter and an assortment of animals for a ride in the country in his old-fashioned touring car. Companion to: *Mr. Gumpy's Outing* (1971, Holt $10.95; Penguin paper $3.50).

1342. Caines, Jeannette. *Just Us Women* (PS–2). Illus. by Pat Cummings. 1982, Harper $9.51; LB $9.89; paper $3.80. A little black girl is looking forward to a car ride she is going to take with her aunt.

1343. Carrick, Carol. *Sleep Out* (K–2). Illus. by Donald Carrick. 1973, Houghton $7.95; paper $3.45. Christopher has an unsettling experience when he spends his first night outdoors in his sleeping bag. Other titles by the same author and publisher are: *The Washout* (1978, $8.95); *The Climb* (1980, $8.95); *Ben and the Porcupine* (1981, $8.95); *Dark and Full of Secrets* (1984, LB $11.95).

1344. Cleary, Beverly. *The Real Hole* (PS–1). Illus. by Mary Stevens. 1960, Morrow $8.59. Four-year-old Jimmy digs a big hole and puts it to good use.

1345. Cohen, Miriam. *Lost in the Museum* (K–1). Illus. by Lillian Hoban. 1978, Greenwillow $10.75; LB $10.32; Dell paper $1.95. Jim and his friends wander away from the group and get lost in the American Museum of Natural History.

1346. Credle, Ellis. *Down, Down the Mountain* (K–3). Illus. 1934, Lodestar $8.25. Two poor children from the Blue Ridge Mountains sell turnips to get new shoes.

1347. Davidson, Amanda. *Teddy at the Seashore* (PS). Illus. 1984, Holt $7.70. A young boy's adventure on the beach.

1348. Delaney, A. *Monster Tracks?* (PS–1). Illus. by author. 1981, Harper $7.95; LB $8.89. Harry thinks he is being followed by a monster when he ventures into the woods on a winter day.

1349. Delton, Judy. *I'm Telling You Now* (PS–1). Illus. by Lillian Hoban. 1983, Dutton $9.66. Artie gets into mischief that his mother has neglected to prevent.

1350. De Regniers, Beatrice S. *Laura's Story* (K–2). Illus. by Jack Kent. 1979, Atheneum $9.95. A reversal story in which a young girl tells her mother a bedtime story.

1351. Devlin, Wende, and Devlin, Harry. *Hang on Hester!* (K–2). Illus. by author. 1980, Lothrop

$9.95; LB $9.55. A spunky heroine finds adventure in a flood.

1352. Douglass, Barbara. *The Great Town and Country Bicycle Balloon Chase* (K–3). Illus. by Carol Newsom. 1984, Lothrop $10.50; LB $10.08. A young girl and her grandfather enter a bicycle race to follow a balloon.

1353. Dyke, John. *Pigwig and the Pirates* (K–2). 1979, Methuen $7.95. Pigwig sets out to rescue his nephew, who has been kidnapped by pirates.

1354. Emberley, Ed. *Klippity Klop* (PS–1). Illus. by author. 1974, Little $5.95. Prince Krispin and his horse Dumpling go adventuring and discover a fierce dragon, which sends them "klickity klackity" back to the castle and safety.

1355. Florian, Douglas. *Airplane Ride* (PS–1). Illus. 1984, Harper $10.53; LB $10.89. A pilot has an adventurous ride in his little biplane.

1356. Gantos, Jack, and Rubel, Nicole. *Greedy Greeny* (PS–1). Illus. 1979, Doubleday LB $8.95. Greeny Monster eats all the food available in the kitchen, including a watermelon, and then has a nightmare.

1357. Gibbons, Gail. *The Missing Maple Syrup Sap Mystery* (K–1). Illus. 1979, Warne $8.95. Mr. and Mrs. Mapleworth solve the mystery of the missing maple sap in an account that also explains how maple syrup is made.

1358. Haller, Danita Ross. *Not Just Any Ring* (2–4). Illus. by Deborah Kogan Ray. 1982, Knopf $9.95; LB $9.99. Nellie climbs the wall of an arroyo to save her grandfather.

1359. Hoban, Russell. *The Flight of Bembel Rudzuk* (1–3). Illus. by Colin McNaughton. 1982, Putnam $6.95. A gang of three youngsters—the Hungry Three—share humorous adventures.

1360. Hoff, Syd. *Slugger Sal's Slump* (1–3). 1979, Windmill $5.95. Sal's baseball career is saved by a last-minute reversal.

1361. Hutchins, Pat. *One-Eyed Jake* (1–3). Illus. by author. 1979, Greenwillow LB $10.51. A terrifying old buccaneer meets a watery end.

1362. Keats, Ezra Jack. *Maggie and the Pirate* (1–3). Illus. by author. 1979, Four Winds $10.95. Maggie tries to find the kidnapper of her pet cricket.

1363. Kellogg, Steven. *The Mystery of the Magic Green Ball* (1–3). Illus. by author. 1978, Dial $8.95; LB $8.89; paper $2.25. A humorous mystery in which Tommy loses his big green ball. Two other titles in the series are: *The Mystery of the Missing Red Mitten* (1974; $7.95; LB $7.89); *The Mystery of the Stolen Blue Paint* (1982, $7.95; LB $7.89).

1364. Lloyd, Errol. *Nini at Carnival* (1–3). Illus. 1979, Harper LB $8.89. A little Jamaican girl enjoys Carnival in this festive book.

1365. McNaughton, Colin. *Soccer Crazy* (1–4). Illus. 1981, Atheneum $8.95. A new player, Bruno, finally proves his worth.

1366. Miles, Miska. *Swim Little Duck* (PS–K). Illus. by Jim Arnosky. 1976, Little $6.95. A little duck goes out to see the world and is joined by a frog, a pig, and a rabbit.

1367. Myers, Walter Dean. *The Black Pearl and the Ghost: Or, One Mystery after Another* (2–4). Illus. by Robert Quackenbush. 1980, Viking $11.50. Two brief mystery stories involving Dr. Aramy and Mr. Dibble.

1368. Parish, Peggy. *Granny and the Desperadoes* (K–2). Illus. by Steven Kellogg. 1970, Macmillan $6.95. Granny captures two outlaws with a gun that doesn't shoot. A sequel is: *Granny and the Indians* (1972, paper $2.25).

1369. Parkin, Rex. *Red Carpet* (K–2). Illus. by author. 1948, Macmillan $8.95. When the red carpet is unrolled to welcome a visiting duke, it keeps on rolling, bringing excitement wherever it goes.

1370. Peet, Bill. *The Caboose Who Got Loose* (K–3). Illus. by author. 1971, Houghton $9.95; paper $3.95. When Katy Caboose is jarred loose from the rest of the train, she gets her wish to be a "cabin in the trees," free from noise and smoke.

1371. Peet, Bill. *Jennifer and Josephine* (1–3). Illus. by author. 1967, Houghton $11.95; paper $3.45. Jennifer, an old touring car, is driven through several adventures by a reckless driver and is accompanied by a friendly cat named Josephine.

1372. Prelutsky, Jack. *What I Did Last Summer* (1–3). Illus. by Yossi Abolafia. 1984, Greenwillow $8.25; LB $7.29. A hero tells, in poetry, what he did last summer.

1373. Quackenbush, Robert. *Detective Mole and the Tip-Top Mystery* (1–3). Illus. by author. 1978, Lothrop $10.25; LB $9.84. Mole investigates why guests are being disturbed at the Tip-Top Inn.

1374. Schertle, Alice. *Bim Dooley Makes His Move* (K–2). Illus. by Victoria Chess. 1984, Lothrop $9.00; LB $8.59. In silent-film format, a story about how a villainous thief is caught.

1375. Schulman, Janet. *Camp Keewee's Secret Weapon* (1–3). Illus. by Marylin Hafner. 1978, Greenwillow LB $6.67. In spite of herself, Jill enjoys summer camp when she becomes the baseball team's pitcher.

1376. Stevenson, James. *"Could Be Worse!"* (K–2). Illus. by author. 1977, Greenwillow $11.25; LB

$10.80; paper $3.50. Grandpa's response to minor catastrophes is always the same.

1377. Stevenson, James. *The Sea View Hotel* (K–2). Illus. by author. 1978, Greenwillow $10.95; LB $10.51; Penguin paper $3.50. A young child's vacation boredom is relieved by an unexpected airplane ride.

1378. Taylor, Mark. *Henry the Explorer* (K–2). Illus. by Graham Booth. 1966, Atheneum paper $1.95. Henry leaves home on an exploring expedition but finds at nightfall that he is hopelessly lost. Also use: *Henry, the Castaway* (1973, paper $1.95); *Henry Explores the Mountains* (1975, LB $9.95).

1379. Van Allsburg, Chris. *The Garden of Abdul Gasazi* (K–3). Illus. by author. 1979, Houghton $11.95. Young Alan wanders into the garden of a retired magician with unexpected results.

1380. Ward, Lynd. *The Biggest Bear* (K–3). Illus. by author. 1952, Houghton $8.95; paper $2.50. Johnny wanted a bearskin on his barn so he went looking for the biggest bear. A Caldecott Award winner.

1381. Williams, Vera B. *Three Days on a River in a Red Canoe* (K–3). Illus. by author. 1981, Greenwillow $11.25; LB $10.80; paper $3.95. A little girl describes a canoe trip with her cousins and their mother.

Personal Problems

1382. Alexander, Martha. *I'll Protect You from the Jungle Beasts* (PS–K). Illus. 1983, Dial $8.95; LB $8.89; paper $1.95. A small boy and his teddy bear take a walk through the frightening woods.

1383. Alexander, Martha. *Maybe a Monster* (PS–K). Illus. 1983, Dial $7.95; LB $7.89. When a young boy sets a trap, there's no telling what he will catch.

1384. Alexander, Martha. *Move Over, Twerp* (PS–1). Illus. by author. 1981, Dial $7.95; LB $7.89; paper $3.25. Jeffrey has a perfect plan to deal with the big boys on the bus.

1385. Andersen, Karen Born. *What's the Matter, Sylvie, Can't You Ride?* (K–2). Illus. by author. 1981, Dial $9.95; LB $9.89. Sylvie has trouble mastering a two-wheel bicycle.

1386. Arthur, Catherine. *My Sister's Silent World* (1–3). Illus. by Nathan Talbot. 1979, Childrens Pr. $9.25. An older girl tells about her 8-year-old deaf sister, Heather.

1387. Babbitt, Natalie. *The Something* (PS–3). Illus. by author. 1970, Farrar $2.95; Dell paper $1.50. Fear of the dark—common in childhood—underlies this fantasy in which the unusual-looking

hero, Milo, comes face-to-face with the dreaded "something."

1388. Berry, Joy Wilt. *Being Destructive* (K–3). Illus. by John Costanza. 1984, Childrens Pr. $6.95. A book that deals with the behavior of children. Others in this series are: *Being Selfish; Disobeying; Fighting; Throwing Tantrums* (all 1984, $6.95).

1389. Bograd, Larry. *Lost in the Store* (K–3). Illus. by Victoria Chess. 1981, Macmillan $9.95. Bruno at first is frightened when he gets lost in a department store, but a friendly worker shows him some special areas like the pet department.

1390. Brown, Margaret Wise. *The Dead Bird* (PS–3). 1958, Addison LB $8.95; paper $1.75. After finding a dead bird, children give it a solemn burial in this book that introduces the concept of death to young people.

1391. Brown, Tricia. *Someone Special Just Like You* (PS–2). Illus. 1984, Holt $11.45. A book that shows that children are children even if they are handicapped.

1392. Bunting, Eve. *The Big Red Barn* (2–3). Illus. by Howard Knotts. 1979, Harcourt $10.32; paper $1.95. When the barn burns one night, this young boy must adjust to a new aluminum one.

1393. Bunting, Eve. *The Happy Funeral* (K–3). Illus. by Vo-Dinh Mai. 1982, Harper $9.57; LB $8.89. How some Chinese-Americans treat death as revealed in the funeral of a young girl's grandfather.

1394. Carrick, Carol. *The Accident* (K–3). Illus. by Donald Carrick. 1976, Houghton $7.95. A story that deals sympathetically and realistically with a child's reaction to the death of his pet dog.

1395. Carrick, Carol. *The Foundling* (PS–3). Illus. by Donald Carrick. 1977, Houghton $7.95. Young Christopher has difficulty adjusting to his dog's death and getting a replacement.

1396. Carrick, Carol. *Patrick's Dinosaurs* (PS–3). Illus. by Donald Carrick. 1983, Houghton $10.95. Patrick is frightened when his brother tells him about dinosaurs.

1397. Carrick, Carol. *Paul's Christmas Birthday* (K–2). Illus. by Donald Carrick. 1978, Greenwillow LB $9.36. Paul's family helps him adjust to having a birthday just before Christmas.

1398. Cazet, Denys. *You Make the Angels Cry* (PS–K). Illus. by author. 1983, Bradbury $12.95. A boy feels guilty when he breaks a cookie jar.

1399. Chess, Victoria. *Poor Esme* (K–2). Illus. by author. 1982, Holiday LB $12.95. Esme wants someone to play with and gets a baby sister instead.

1400. Chevalier, Christa. *Spence and the Sleeptime Monster* (PS–1). Illus. by author. 1984, Whitman

$9.25. Spence is convinced that a monster visits his bedroom at night.

1401.   Cleary, Beverly. *Lucky Chuck* (PS–3). Illus. by J. Winslow Higginbottom. 1984, Morrow $8.00; LB $7.63. Through bitter experience, Chuck learns the principles of bicycle safety.

1402.   Cooney, Barbara. *Miss Rumphius* (PS–3). Illus. by author. 1982, Viking $12.95. Miss Rumphius wonders how she can make the world more beautiful.

1403.   de Paola, Tomie. *Andy: That's My Name* (PS–K). Illus. by author. 1973, Prentice $9.95; LB $3.95. The big boys borrow Andy's name, affixed to his wagon, and in a play on words, add and subtract letters and make other words out of his name.

1404.   de Paola, Tomie. *Marianna May and Nursey* (PS–2). Illus. by author. 1983, Holiday $12.95. Marianna May always gets her white dresses dirty when she plays.

1405.   de Paola, Tomie. *Nana Upstairs and Nana Downstairs* (PS–K). Illus. by author. 1973, Penguin paper $3.95. The love of a child for his grandmother and Tommy's adjustment to her death are told in tender, comfortable terms.

1406.   de Paola, Tomie. *Now One Foot, Now the Other* (K–3). Illus. by author. 1981, Putnam $8.95; paper $3.95. Bobby helps his grandfather recover from a stroke.

1407.   de Paola, Tomie. *Oliver Button Is a Sissy* (K–3). 1978, Harcourt $7.95; paper $3.95. People think Oliver is a sissy until he shines in a talent show as a fine tap dancer.

1408.   De Regniers, Beatrice S. *A Little House of Your Own* (PS). Illus. by Irene Haas. 1954, Harcourt $6.95. An exploration of the many places in which a child can have a secret house.

1409.   Dragonwagon, Crescent. *Always, Always* (1–3). Illus. by Arieh Zeldich. 1984, Macmillan $10.95. A young girl divides her year between her divorced parents.

1410.   Dragonwagon, Crescent. *Will It Be Okay?* (K–2). Illus. by Ben Shecter. 1977, Harper LB $9.89. Mother comforts her daughter by giving her lots of love and suggestions for overcoming her fears.

1411.   Feder, Jane. *The Night-Light* (PS–1). Illus. by Lady McCrady. 1980, Dial $7.50; LB $7.28. Kate wants some light at night because she is fearful of the dark.

1412.   Fujikawa, Gyo. *That's Not Fair!* (PS–2). Illus. by author. 1983, Grosset paper $3.95. Four friends quarrel and make up.

1413.   Goodsell, Jane. *Katie's Magic Glasses* (K–3). Illus. by Barbara Cooney. 1965, Houghton $5.95; paper $2.25. Katie's sight problems are solved when she gets her first glasses.

1414.   Gordon, Sheila. *A Monster in the Mailbox* (2–4). Illus. by Tony DeLuna. 1978, Dutton $8.25. A young boy sends away for a mail-order monster.

1415.   Greenberg, Barbara. *The Bravest Babysitter* (PS–2). Illus. by Diane Paterson. 1977, Dial $6.95; LB $6.46. A baby-sitter's young charge helps her overcome her fear of thunder and lightning.

1416.   Greenfield, Eloise. *Darlene* (K–2). Illus. by George Ford. 1980, Methuen $8.95. A picture book that shows activities a wheelchair-bound girl can enjoy.

1417.   Greenfield, Eloise. *Me and Nessie* (1–3). Illus. by M. Barnett. 1975, Harper $10.89; paper $3.95. A little girl outgrows her need for an imaginary friend in this story told partly in Black English.

1418.   Haley, Gail E. *The Green Man* (2–4). Illus. by author. 1980, Scribners $11.95. A young man learns about life by living in the woods with the animals.

1419.   Hann, Jacquie. *Up Day, Down Day* (K–3). Illus. by author. 1978, Scholastic $6.95. Good days and bad days are experienced by our hero and his friend.

1420.   Hazen, Barbara S. *Two Homes to Live In: A Child's-Eye View of Divorce* (K–2). Illus. by Peggy Luks. 1978, Human Sciences $11.95; paper $4.95. A reassuring view of divorce because now there are 2 homes where there is love.

1421.   Hazen, Barbara S. *Very Shy* (K–2). Illus. by Bonnie Chan. 1983, Human Sciences $11.95. A problem common to many youngsters is explored.

1422.   Hickman, Martha Whitmore. *When Can Daddy Come Home?* (2–4). Illus. by Francis Livingston. 1983, Abingdon $9.50. Everyone seems to know that Anderson's father is in prison for robbery.

1423.   Hoopes, Lyn Littlefield. *Nana* (K–4). Illus. by Arieh Zeldich. 1981, Harper LB $8.89. A young girl's thoughts after her grandmother's death.

1424.   Horwitz, Elinor. *Sometimes It Happens* (1–4). Illus. by Susan Jeschke. 1981, Harper $7.95; LB $8.89. Victor decides he wants to be a hero when he grows up.

1425.   Hughes, Shirley. *David and Dog* (PS–K). Illus. by author. 1978, Prentice paper $2.95. David loses his favorite toy, a stuffed dog, in this English picture book that won the Greenaway Medal.

1426. Hughes, Shirley. *Moving Molly* (1–3). Illus. by author. 1979, Prentice $7.95; paper $2.95. At first Molly is very lonely when her family moves, but things change when she makes new friends of animals and children.

1427. Hurwitz, Johanna. *Superduper Teddy* (K–3). Illus. by Susan Jeschke. 1980, Morrow $8.75; LB $8.50; Dell paper $1.75. Teddy, though only 5, takes his first steps toward independence.

1428. Isadora, Rachel. *Ben's Trumpet* (K–3). Illus. by author. 1979, Greenwillow $10.50. A young black boy dreams of becoming a trumpet player and eventually is taken to a jazz club by a musician.

1429. Jensen, Virginia Allen. *Sara and the Door* (1–3). Illus. by Ann Strugnell. 1977, Childrens Pr. $5.95. A big problem is solved by a little black girl when her coat gets caught in a door.

1430. Jensen, Virginia Allen, and Haller, Dorcas. *What's That?* (PS–1). Illus. 1979, Putnam $10.95. Embossed shapes tell a story in this picture book intended primarily for blind children. Also use (by Virginia Allen Jensen): *Catching: A Book for Blind and Sighted Children with Pictures to Feel as Well as to See* (1983, Putnam paper $12.95).

1431. Jewell, Nancy. *Bus Ride* (1–3). Illus. by Ronald Himler. 1978, Harper LB $7.95. Janie is fearful of riding the bus alone but soon makes a friend.

1432. Joosse, Barbara M. *Spiders in the Fruit Cellar* (PS–2). Illus. by Kay Chorao. 1983, Knopf $9.95; LB $9.99. Elizabeth is afraid of the spiders in the fruit cellar.

1433. Joslin, Sesyle. *What Do You Say, Dear?* (1–3). Illus. by Maurice Sendak. 1958, Childrens Pr. $7.95. Humorous handbook on manners for young ladies and gentlemen of six to eight. Also use: *What Do You Do, Dear?* (1961, Childrens Pr. $7.95).

1434. Keats, Ezra Jack. *Louie* (PS–K). Illus. by author. 1983, Greenwillow $10.50; Scholastic paper $2.25. Louie, a silent child, makes his first friend, a puppet, and is allowed to keep it for his very own.

1435. Keller, Holly. *Cromwell's Glasses* (PS–2). Illus. by author. 1982, Greenwillow $10.00; LB $10.88. Friends make fun of Cromwell's "goggles."

1436. Kellogg, Steven. *Much Bigger Than Martin* (K–2). Illus. by author. 1976, Dial $7.95; LB $7.45; paper $1.95. Henry is upset because his older brother is so much bigger than he is, and Henry tries many ways to overcome this.

1437. Kellogg, Steven. *Won't Somebody Play with Me?* (K–3). Illus. by author. 1972, Dial $9.95; LB $9.89; paper $3.95. It's Kim's birthday, but no one is home to play with her.

1438. Kesselman, Wendy. *Emma* (PS–1). Illus. by Barbara Cooney. 1980, Doubleday $8.95. A 72-year-old lady becomes a famous painter.

1439. Kherdian, David. *Right Now* (1–4). Illus. by Nonny Hogrogian. 1983, Knopf $10.95; LB $10.99. Everyday incidents and problems in the lives of children are pictured.

1440. Klein, Norma. *Girls Can Be Anything* (1–3). Illus. by Roy Doty. 1973, Dutton $8.95; paper $3.95. Marina convinces Sean that one day she could be a doctor, pilot, or president.

1441. Klein, Norma. *Visiting Pamela* (PS–1). Illus. by Kay Chorao. 1979, Dial LB $6.46. Because of her mother's ultimatum, Carrie emerges from her shell and visits a friend.

1442. Krasilovsky, Phyllis. *The Very Little Girl* (K–3). 1953, Houghton LB $7.95; paper $1.49. A very little girl grows until she can become a sister to a baby brother. A companion volume is: *The Shy Little Girl* (1970, LB $6.95; paper $2.95).

1443. Krauss, Ruth. *A Very Special House* (PS–K). Illus. by Maurice Sendak. 1953, Harper LB $10.89. A little boy tells what it would be like in his very special house—no one would ever say "Stop, Stop."

1444. Kroll, Steven. *Friday the 13th* (K–3). Illus. by Dick Gackenbach. 1981, Holiday LB $10.95. Every day seems to be a hard-luck day for Harold.

1445. Larsen, Hanne. *Don't Forget Tom* (1–3). Illus. 1978, Harper $9.89. A 6-year-old mentally retarded child copes with his handicap.

1446. Lasker, Joe. *The Do-Something Day* (PS–2). Illus. by author. 1982, Viking $12.95; Scholastic paper $1.95. When no one pays attention to him, Bernie runs away from home.

1447. Lasker, Joe. *Nick Joins In* (K–3). Illus. by author. 1980, Whitman LB $8.25. Wheelchair-bound Nicky wonders what will happen to him when he goes to a regular school.

1448. Lindgren, Barbro. *Sam's Ball* (PS). Illus. by Eva Eriksson. 1983, Morrow $5.00. A book in which a toddler shares his toy with a kitty. Five others in this series are: *Sam's Car* (1982); *Sam's Cookie* (1982); *Sam's Teddy Bear* (1982); *Sam's Bath* (1983); *Sam's Lamp* (1983) (all Morrow $5.50).

1449. Litchfield, Ada B. *Captain Hook, That's Me* (2–4). Illus. by Sonia O. Lisker. 1982, Walker $8.95; LB $9.85. Judy, who wears a hook, must go to a new school.

1450. Litchfield, Ada B. *Making Room for Uncle Joe* (2–4). Illus. by Gail Owens. 1984, Whitman $9.25. Three children must adjust when a mentally retarded relative comes to stay with them.

1451. Litchfield, Ada B. *Words in Our Hands* (2–4). Illus. by Helen Cogancherry. 1980, Whitman $8.75. Michael describes his life with his deaf parents.

1452. Little, Lessie Jones, and Greenfield, Eloise. *I Can Do It by Myself* (K–2). Illus. by Carole Byard. 1978, Harper $9.57; LB $9.89. A young boy is successful in his first bid for independence.

1453. McDonnell, Christine. *Don't Be Mad, Ivy* (2–3). Illus. by Diane de Groat. 1981, Dial $8.95; LB $8.89; Bantam paper $1.95. Six episodes that recount the misadventures of 7-year-old Ivy Adams.

1454. Marino, Barbara Pavis. *Eric Needs Stitches* (PS–3). Illus. 1979, Childrens Pr. $8.95. A boy must conquer his fears when the doctor says he must have stitches on his knee.

1455. Mayer, Mercer. *You're the Scaredy-Cat* (K–2). Illus. by author. 1974, Four Winds $7.95. Two young boys decide to spend the night camping out in the backyard.

1456. Meddaugh, Susan. *Too Short Fred* (1–3). Illus. by author. 1978, Houghton $5.95. Fred masters situations despite his small stature.

1457. Ness, Evaline. *Sam, Bangs & Moonshine* (K–2). Illus. by author. 1966, Holt $9.70; paper $3.50. A little girl learns to distinguish truth from "moonshine" only after her cat and playmate nearly meet tragedy. Caldecott Medal, 1967.

1458. Peavy, Linda. *Allison's Grandfather* (2–4). Illus. by Ronald Himler. 1981, Scribners $9.95. Erica knows that Allison's beloved grandfather is dying.

1459. Peterson, Jeanne Whitehouse. *I Have a Sister, My Sister Is Deaf* (1–3). Illus. by Deborah Ray. 1978, Harper $10.89; paper $3.80. About a young girl's adjustment to deafness.

1460. Rabe, Berniece. *The Balancing Girl* (PS–3). Illus. by Lillian Hoban. 1981, Dutton $10.25. A paraplegic girl named Margaret delights in balancing things.

1461. Raskin, Ellen. *Spectacles* (K–3). Illus. by author. 1968, Atheneum $10.95; paper $1.95. A spectacle not to be missed is Iris Fogel's misinterpretation of everything she sees . . . until her myopia is corrected. Cleverly illustrated. Meet Iris's friend Chester in: *Nothing Ever Happens on My Block* (1966, Atheneum $7.95; paper $1.95; Scholastic paper $1.50).

1462. Robinet, Harriette Gillem. *Ride the Red Cycle* (3–5). Illus. by David Brown. 1980, Houghton $6.95. Brain-damaged Jerome wants to ride his new red tricycle.

1463. Rockwell, Anne, and Rockwell, Harlow. *Nice and Clean* (PS). Illus. by author. 1984, Macmil-

lan $12.95. A picture book that explores the topic of cleaning the house. Others in the series are: *Out to Sea* (1980, LB $6.95); *My Barber* (1981, $7.95); *Sick in Bed* (1982, $8.95); *The Night We Slept Outside* (1983, $8.95).

1464. Roy, Ron. *Breakfast with My Father* (K–2). Illus. by Troy Howell. 1980, Houghton $7.95. David's parents separate and his father visits him only on Saturdays.

1465. Sendak, Maurice. *Pierre* (K–3). Illus. by author. 1962, Harper LB $9.89. The story about a young boy whose motto is "I don't care."

1466. Seuling, Barbara. *The Triplets* (K–3). Illus. by author. 1980, Houghton $7.95. Triplets try to establish their own identities.

1467. Sharmat, Marjorie W. *A Big Fat Enormous Lie* (PS–1). Illus. by David McPhail. 1978, Dutton $10.25. A small lie becomes a monster that haunts a youngster until he tells the truth.

1468. Sharmat, Mitchell. *Come Home Wilma* (PS–1). Illus. by Rosekrans Hoffman. 1980, Whitman $8.75. A young girl, confined to her room as punishment, imagines her revenge.

1469. Shyer, Marlene Fanta. *Stepdog* (1–3). Illus. by Judith Schermer. 1983, Scribners $10.95. Papa's new wife brings with her a dog that just doesn't fit.

1470. Simon, Norma. *I Was So Mad!* (K–3). Illus. by Dora Leder. 1974, Whitman $8.25. Children catalog the things that make them mad and learn that adults get angry too.

1471. Simon, Norma. *I Wish I Had My Father* (2–4). Illus. by Arieh Zeldich. 1983, Whitman $8.25. A young boy wishes his divorced father was back with him.

1472. Snyder, Zilpha Keatley. *Come on Patsy* (PS–2). Illus. by Margot Zemach. 1982, Atheneum LB $9.95. Patsy is taken advantage of by a friend.

1473. Stanek, Muriel. *Don't Hurt Me, Mama* (1–3). Illus. by Helen Cogancherry. 1983, Whitman $8.25. A simple story of child abuse as seen through the eyes of a child.

1474. Stein, Sara Bonnett. *About Dying* (1–3). Illus. 1974, Walker $8.95; paper $4.95. Sensitive portrayal of the death of a bird and of a grandfather. Also use: *About Handicaps* (1974); *Making Babies* (1974); *About Phobias* (1979); *The Adopted One* (1979); *On Divorce* (1979) (all Walker $8.95; paper $4.95).

1475. Stevens, Carla. *Sara and the Pinch* (1–3). Illus. by John Wallner. 1980, Houghton $6.95. A kindly school custodian helps Sara the trouble-maker.

1476. Tester, Sylvia Root. *Sometimes I'm Afraid* (PS–1). Illus. by Frances Hook. 1979, Childrens Pr. $6.95. An understanding treatment of the fears of a young child.

1477. Townsend, Maryann, and Stern, Ronnie. *Pop's Secret* (1–3). Illus. 1980, Addison LB $7.95. A young boy fondly remembers his dead grandfather.

1478. Vigna, Judith. *Grandma without Me* (PS–2). Illus. by author. 1984, Whitman $9.75. Because of divorce, a young boy will not be spending Thanksgiving with one of his grandmothers.

1479. Viorst, Judith. *The Tenth Good Thing about Barney* (K–2). Illus. by Erik Blegvad. 1971, Atheneum $10.95; paper $2.95. At a backyard funeral, a little boy tries to think of 10 good things to say about his cat, Barney—but can come up with only 9.

1480. Waber, Bernard. *Ira Sleeps Over* (PS–2). Illus. by author. 1972, Houghton $10.95; paper $3.95; Scholastic paper $1.95. When Ira is invited to sleep overnight at Reggie's house, he wants to go, but should he or shouldn't he take along his teddy bear?

1481. Wallace, Ian. *Chin Chiang and the Dragon's Dance* (K–4). Illus. by author. 1984, Atheneum $9.95. Chin Chiang is afraid to dance in the New Year's dragon dance.

1482. Warren, Cathy. *Fred's First Day* (PS–K). Illus. by Pat Cummings. 1984, Lothrop $10.50; LB $10.08. Fred is anxious about his first day at nursery school.

1483. Watanabe, Shigeo. *How Do I Put It On?* (PS). Illus. by Yasuo Ohtomo. 1980, Putnam $8.95; paper $3.95. How to dress oneself; told in simple, noncondescending terms.

1484. Weiss, Nicki. *Chuckie* (PS–K). Illus. by author. 1982, Greenwillow $8.00; LB $7.63. A child's adjustment to a new family member.

1485. Wells, Rosemary. *Peabody* (PS–K). Illus. 1983, Dial $9.95; LB $9.89. Annie loves Peabody, her teddy bear, until she receives Rita, a big doll.

1486. White, Paul. *Janet at School* (2–4). Illus. by Jeremy Finlay. 1978, Harper $10.89. Janet, a victim of spina bifida, is shown, through photographs and text, engaging in various activities.

1487. Williams, Barbara. *Whatever Happened to Beverly Bigler's Birthday?* (2–3). Illus. by Emily McCully. 1979, Harcourt $6.95. Beverly decides to run away when she thinks everyone has forgotten her birthday.

1488. Wolf, Bernard. *Michael and the Dentist* (K–3). Illus. 1980, Scholastic $8.95. Michael's first visit to the dentist isn't as expected.

Other Times, Other Places

1489. Bemelmans, Ludwig. *Madeline's Rescue* (K–3). Illus. by author. 1953, Viking $10.95; Penguin paper $3.95. This Paris adventure of the inimitable Madeline won the 1954 Caldecott Medal. Also use: *Madeline* (1939, Viking $11.95; Penguin paper $3.95); *Madeline and the Bad Hat* (1957, Viking $9.95; Penguin paper $3.95); *Madeline and the Gypsies* (1959, Viking $9.95; Penguin paper $3.95); *Madeline in London* (1961, Viking $13.95; Penguin paper $3.95).

1490. Beskow, Elsa. *Pelle's New Suit* (PS–3). Illus. by author. 1929, Harper $12.89. A Swedish story of the steps in getting a new suit for a small boy, from shearing the lamb to tailoring.

1491. Borchers, Elisabeth. *Dear Sarah* (K–3). Illus. by Wilhelm Schlote. 1981, Greenwillow $12.50; LB $12.88. Sarah's father writes her many letters from various cities in Europe.

1492. Bradley, Helen. *The Queen Who Came to Tea* (1–3). Illus. by author. 1979, Merrimack $11.95. A fond recollection of the great stir when Queen Victoria visited Manchester in 1901.

1493. Bunting, Eve. *Monkey in the Middle* (PS–2). Illus. by Lynn Munsinger. 1984, Harcourt $10.95. A monkey helps patch up a quarrel between two Malaysian coconut pickers.

1494. Carrick, Donald. *Harald and the Giant Knight* (2–4). Illus. by author. 1982, Houghton $10.95. Harald decides to get even with some callous knights who have destroyed his family's farm.

1495. Clymer, Eleanor. *A Search for Two Bad Mice* (2–4). Illus. by Margery Gill. 1980, Atheneum $9.95. An American family visits Hill Top, the home of Beatrix Potter.

1496. Cole, Brock. *The King at the Door* (K–2). Illus. by author. 1979, Doubleday $7.95. Kindness and helpfulness are rewarded in this folklike tale.

1497. Delton, Julie. *My Uncle Nikos* (2–4). Illus. by Marc Simont. 1983, Harper $10.53; LB $10.89. The story of a girl of Athens and her visit to an uncle in a small Greek village.

1498. de Paola, Tomie. *Giorgio's Village* (K–3). Illus. by author. 1982, Putnam $11.95. Six village scenes in Italy are depicted in this pop-up book.

1499. de Paola, Tomie. *The Lady of Guadalupe* (K–3). Illus. by author. 1980, Holiday $12.95; paper $4.95. The legend of the patron saint of Mexico is retold in this excellent picture book.

1500. Dodge, Mary Mapes. *Mary Ann* (PS–2). Illus. by June Amos Grammer. 1983, Lothrop $9.50. A Victorian period piece on the world of dolls.

1501. Domanska, Janina. *What Happens Next?* (K–3). Illus. by author. 1983, Greenwillow $11.25; LB $11.88. A peasant wins his freedom by telling a tall tale.

1502. Ernst, Lisa Campbell. *Sam Johnson and the Blue Ribbon Quilt* (K–3). Illus. by author. 1983, Lothrop $11.25; LB $11.88. The men and the women vie for honors in the quilting contest.

1503. Ets, Marie Hall. *Gilberto and the Wind* (PS–1). Illus. by author. 1963, Viking $9.95; Penguin paper $3.50. A small Mexican boy learns to play with and understand the moods of the wind.

1504. Feeney, Stephanie. *A Is for Aloha* (PS–K). Illus. by Hella Hammid. 1980, Univ. Pr. of Hawaii $7.95. A simple introduction to Hawaii and its many cultures.

1505. Flack, Marjorie. *The Story about Ping* (PS–3). Illus. by Kurt Wiese. 1933, Viking $9.95; Penguin paper $3.50. A little Peking duck spends a harrowing night on the Yangtze River after he is accidently separated from his family.

1506. Francoise. *Minou* (PS–2). Illus. by author. 1962, Scribners $5.95. A little girl journeys through Paris in search of her pet cat.

1507. Gerrard, Jean. *Matilda Jane* (K–3). Illus. by Roy Gerrard. 1983, Farrar $10.95. A little Victorian girl spends a week at the seashore.

1508. Gerrard, Roy. *Sir Cedric* (1–4). 1984, Farrar $11.95. A spoof on knights and the age of chivalry.

1509. Goffstein, M. B. *My Noah's Ark* (K–2). Illus. by author. 1978, Harper $8.61; LB $9.89. An old woman reminisces about an ark and animals that her grandfather had carved.

1510. Green, Norma B. *The Hole in the Dike* (K–2). Illus. by Eric Carle. 1975, Harper $10.53; LB $10.89; Scholastic paper $1.95. Brilliant illustrations accompany this simple retelling of the Mary Mapes Dodge story of the boy who put his finger in the dike and saved his Dutch town.

1511. Hall, Donald. *Ox-Cart Man* (K–3). Illus. by Barbara Cooney. 1979, Viking $12.95; Penguin paper $3.95. The cycle of production and sale of goods in nineteenth-century New England is pictured in human terms. Caldecott Medal, 1980.

1512. Handforth, Thomas. *Mei Li* (1–3). Illus. by author. 1938, Doubleday $8.95. Adventures of a little Chinese girl who decided to go to the New Year's fair in the city. Caldecott Medal, 1939.

1513. Heller, Linda. *The Castle on Hester Street* (PS–2). Illus. by author. 1982, Jewish Publication Society $8.95. Grandparents share with their granddaughter memories of coming to America.

1514. Hertz, Ole. *Tobias Catches Trout* (K–2). Illus. 1984, Carolrhoda $7.95. A picture book set in rural Greenland. Three others in this series are: *Tobias Goes Ice Fishing; Tobias Goes Seal Hunting; Tobias Has a Birthday* (all 1984, $7.95).

1515. Hirsh, Marilyn. *Hannibal and His 37 Elephants* (1–3). Illus. by author. 1977, Holiday $5.95. Hannibal crosses the Alps with earmuffed elephants in this humorous view of history.

1516. Isadora, Rachel. *No, Agatha!* (K–2). Illus. 1980, Greenwillow $10.95; LB $10.51. Agatha finds her ocean trip very restrictive.

1517. Kesselman, Wendy. *There's a Train Going By My Window* (PS–1). Illus. by Tony Chen. 1982, Doubleday $9.95. A train stops at various places around the world.

1518. Krasilovsky, Phyllis. *The Cow Who Fell in the Canal* (PS–1). Illus. by Peter Spier. 1957, Doubleday $7.95; paper $1.95. Detailed watercolor scenes illustrate this amusing tale of Hendrika, a not-so-contented Dutch cow who floated on a raft to the city.

1519. Krasilovsky, Phyllis. *The First Tulips in Holland* (K–3). Illus. by S. D. Schindler. 1982, Doubleday $12.95. A story of how tulips might have been introduced in Holland many years ago.

1520. Lamorisse, Albert. *The Red Balloon* (1–3). Illus. by author. 1956, Doubleday $10.95; paper $2.95. Pascal possesses a magic balloon that leads him on a tour of Paris, and he must defend the balloon from a gang of boys bent on bursting it.

1521. Lasker, David. *The Boy Who Loved Music* (1–3). Illus. by Joe Lasker. 1979, Viking LB $9.95. Karl, a young horn player for Prince Esterhazy, meets Joseph Haydn.

1522. Leech, Jay, and Spencer, Zane. *Bright Fawn and Me* (K–2). Illus. by Glo Coalson. 1979, Harper $10.95. A Cheyenne girl takes care of her little sister at a tribal fair set in the nineteenth century.

1523. Lewin, Hugh. *Jafta* (K–3). Illus. by Lisa Kopper. 1983, Carolrhoda LB $7.95. There are 6 volumes in this set that are about a black South African child and his father. Others are: *Jafta and the Wedding* (1983); *Jafta's Father* (1983); *Jafta's Mother* (1983); *Jafta: The Journey* (1984); *Jafta: The Town* (1984) (all LB $7.95).

1524. Lindgren, Astrid. *The Tomten* (PS–2). Illus. by Harald Wiberg. 1961, Putnam $8.95; LB $5.99; paper $4.95. The friendly troll speaks in Tomten language only animals and children understand. By the same author, illustrator, and publisher: *The Tomten and the Fox* (1965, LB $6.99; paper $4.95).

1525. Lorenz, Lee, retel. *Scornful Simkin* (K–4). Illus. by retel. 1980, Prentice $8.95; paper $3.95. A retelling of the Chaucer tale, "The Reeve's Tale."

1526. Luenn, Nancy. *The Dragon Kite* (1–4). Illus. by Michael Hague. 1982, Harcourt $12.95. Ishikawa is an unusual thief who steals to buy rice for hungry Japanese villagers.

1527. McClenathan, Louise. *My Mother Sends Her Wisdom* (K–3). Illus. by Rosekrans Hoffman. 1979, Morrow $9.75; LB $9.36. A folklike story about a clever peasant woman, set in old Russia.

1528. Mitchell, Barbara. *Tomahawks and Trombones* (1–3). Illus. by George Overlie. 1982, Carolrhoda LB $7.95. A story based on fact about the Moravians in Bethlehem, Pennsylvania.

1529. Nikly, Michelle. *The Emperor's Plum Tree* (K–3). Illus. 1982, Greenwillow $11.25; LB $11.88. Young Musuko loses a friend when a tree is uprooted in their yard for the emperor.

1530. Patterson, Geoffrey. *Chestnut Farm 1860* (K–4). Illus. by author. 1980, Deutsch $8.95. A fiction account of life on an 1860 English farm.

1531. Politi, Leo. *Little Leo* (K–2). Illus. by author. 1951, Scribners $6.95. Little Leo, decked out in a brand-new Indian chief suit, leaves San Francisco to live in Italy and creates great excitement among the children in the town with his tales of the West.

1532. Quin-Harkin, Janet. *Peter Penny's Dance* (K–2). Illus. by Anita Lobel. 1976, Dial $7.95; LB $7.45. Based on an old English ballad, this is the rollicking tale of how Peter Penny danced the hornpipe around the world in 5 years.

1533. Reiser, Joanne. *Hannah's Alaska* (1–3). Illus. by Julie Downing. 1983, Raintree $10.99. Hannah has new neighbors in her Alaskan wilderness home.

1534. Rettich, Margret. *The Voyage of the Jolly Boat* (1–3). Trans. from German by Joy Backhouse. Illus. by author. 1981, Methuen $9.95. The story of three children who survive a storm at sea in Holland in 1686.

1535. Saunders, Susan. *Fish Fry* (K–3). Illus. by S. D. Schindler. 1982, Viking $12.95. East Texas in 1912 and its fish-fry day.

1536. Say, Allen. *The Bicycle Man* (K–3). Illus. by author. 1982, Houghton $11.95; LB $12.45. Two American soldiers in Japan put on a show for a school.

1537. Scott, Ann H. *On Mother's Lap* (PS–K). Illus. by Glo Coalson. 1972, McGraw LB $10.95. A warm, tender story of an Eskimo family and of a young boy's realization that there is enough room on mother's lap for both him and his sister.

1538. Ward, Leila. *I Am Eyes Ni Macho* (PS–1). Illus. by Nonny Hogrogian. 1978, Greenwillow $11.95. A new day and all of nature's wonders are greeted by a Kenyan child.

1539. Waterton, Betty. *Pettranella* (K–3). Illus. by Ann Blades. 1981, Vanguard $8.95. An immigrant girl grows flowers from seeds she brought from Europe.

1540. Weil, Lisl. *To Sail a Ship of Treasures* (K–2). Illus. by author. 1984, Atheneum $10.95. The story of the author-artist's childhood in Vienna.

1541. Yarbrough, Camille. *Cornrows* (1–3). Illus. by Carole Byard. 1979, Putnam $7.95; paper $3.95. Past and present mingle in this discussion of an unusual hairstyle.

1542. Yashima, Taro. *The Village Tree* (PS–K). Illus. by author. 1953, Penguin paper $3.95. A picture of the author's childhood in Japan and the fun he and his friends had by the river where the great tree stood.

1543. Yolen, Jane. *The Seeing Stick* (K–3). Illus. by Remy Charlip and Demetra Maraslis. 1977, Harper $10.53; LB $10.89. By carving pictures on a stick, an old man helps a blind girl to "see" in this tale set in ancient Peking.

Humorous Stories

1544. Aitken, Amy. *Ruby!* (K–2). Illus. by author. 1979, Bradbury $9.95. Ruby daydreams of becoming a rock star, movie queen, and even president.

1545. Alexander, Sue. *Marc the Magnificent* (1–3). Illus. by Tomie de Paola. 1978, Pantheon $4.95; LB $5.99. Marc dreams of being a great magician, but he can't master the first trick.

1546. Alexander, Sue. *Seymour the Prince* (1–2). Illus. by Lillian Hoban. 1979, Pantheon $4.95; LB $5.99. A young boy chosen to be the prince in a production of *Sleeping Beauty* balks at kissing the princess.

1547. Allard, Harry, and Marshall, James. *The Stupids Have a Ball* (K–3). Illus. by James Marshall. 1978, Houghton $8.95; paper $3.95. The whole Stupid family decides to celebrate when the children bring home terrible report cards from school. Two others in the series: *The Stupids Step Out* (1974, $10.95; paper $2.95); *The Stupids Die* (1981, $9.95).

1548. Armitage, Ronda, and Armitage, David. *"Don't Forget, Matilda!"* (PS–K). Illus. by author. 1979, Deutsch $8.95. An unusual day in the Bear family when everyone forgets things.

1549. Artis, Vicki Kimmel. *Pajama Walking* (1–3). Illus. by Emily McCully. 1981, Houghton $6.95. Four humorous tales about two girls spending the night together.

1550. Barrett, Judith. *Animals Should Definitely Not Wear Clothes* (PS–1). Illus. by Ron Barrett.

1970, Atheneum $9.95; paper $2.95. Humorous idea expressed in brief text and comic drawings. A sequel is: *Animals Should Definitely Not Act Like People* (1980, $9.95).

1551. Barrett, Judith. *Benjamin's 365 Birthdays* (K–2). Illus. by Ron Barrett. 1974, Atheneum $7.95; paper $1.95. Benjamin, the bear, is so delighted with his birthday presents that he decides to rewrap them so that he can enjoy one each day throughout the ensuing months.

1552. Barrett, Judith. *Old MacDonald Had an Apartment House* (K–3). Illus. by Ron Barrett. n.d., Atheneum paper $2.95. How an apartment super achieves an apartment farm.

1553. Bishop, Claire Huchet. *Five Chinese Brothers* (1–3). Illus. by Kurt Wiese. 1938, Putnam $7.95. Physically identical in every way, each of the 5 Chinese brothers has one distinguishing trait that saves the lives of all of them.

1554. Blake, Quentin. *Mister Magnolia* (PS). Illus. 1980, Merrimack $8.95. A silly rhyming tale about a bumpkin and his adventures.

1555. Breitner, Sue. *The Bookseller's Advice* (K–3). Illus. by Jane Chambless-Rigie. 1981, Viking $8.95. An aged advice-giver gives strange advice because his hearing is failing.

1556. Buchanan, Joan. *It's a Good Thing* (PS–3). Illus. by Barbara DiLella. 1984, Annick Pr. $10.95; paper $4.95. Two sisters go out for an eventful walk.

1557. Bulla, Clyde Robert. *The Stubborn Old Woman* (2–3). Illus. by Anne Rockwell. 1980, Harper $8.61; LB $8.89. Only by trickery is an old woman convinced that she must leave her crumbling home.

1558. Burningham, John. *Time to Get Out of the Bath, Shirley* (K–2). Illus. by author. 1978, Harper $7.57; LB $9.89. While taking a bath, Shirley daydreams of knights and castles.

1559. Cate, Rikki. *A Cat's Tale* (1–4). Illus. by Shirley Hughes. 1982, Harcourt $9.95. Through a misunderstanding, a recluse receives a number of cats as presents.

1560. Chapman, Carol. *The Tale of Meshka the Kvetch* (PS–2). Illus. by Arnold Lobel. 1980, Dutton $8.95. The complaints of a kvetch come true.

1561. Chevalier, Christa. *Spence Makes Circles* (PS–2). Illus. by author. 1982, Whitman $7.50. Spence wants to draw circles but gets involved with the glue.

1562. Chorao, Kay. *Molly's Moe* (PS–K). Illus. by author. 1976, Houghton $7.50. Molly is continually losing things and when she loses her stuffed

animal Moe, a stegosaurus, she is disconsolate, until she finds him in a bag of potatoes!

1563. Christian, Mary Blount. *The Devil Take You, Barnabas Beane* (1–3). Illus. by Anne Burgess. 1980, Harper $8.61; LB $8.89. Mean old Barnabas Beane thinks he has been placed under a curse.

1564. Crowe, Robert L. *Clyde Monster* (PS–2). Illus. by Kay Chorao. 1976, Dutton $10.75. A humorous, reassuring story about an engaging monster named Clyde, who is afraid of the dark.

1565. de Paola, Tomie. *Helga's Dowry: A Troll Love Story* (K–2). Illus. by author. 1977, Harcourt $8.95; paper $2.95. Helga cannot marry Lars because she has no dowry, but this humorous account tells how she acquires one.

1566. de Paola, Tomie, illus. *Pancakes for Breakfast* (PS–2). 1978, Harcourt $9.95; paper $4.95. The trials and travails of a country woman who decides to make some pancakes.

1567. De Regniers, Beatrice S. *May I Bring a Friend?* (PS–2). Illus. by Beni Montresor. 1964, Atheneum $9.95; paper $2.95. The king and queen invite a small boy to tea, and each time he goes, he takes a friend—a seal, a hippopotamus, and several lions. Caldecott Medal, 1965.

1568. Freeman, Don. *Mop Top* (K–2). Illus. by author. 1955, Viking $10.95; Penguin paper $3.95. Moppy changes his mind about a haircut after being mistaken for a floor mop by a nearsighted shopper.

1569. Gammell, Stephen. *Git Along, Old Scudder* (PS–2). Illus. by author. 1983, Lothrop $10.50; LB $10.08. A backwoodsman uses a homemade map on a trip.

1570. Gerstein, Mordicai. *The Room* (K–3). Illus. by author. 1984, Harper $9.57; LB $9.95. All the different people who rent a specific apartment are pictured.

1571. Gray, Nigel. *It'll Come Out in the Wash* (PS–1). 1979, Harper $9.57; LB $9.89. No matter how large the stains and spills created by the young heroine, Dad has a pat answer.

1572. Haywood, Carolyn. *The King's Monster* (2–3). Illus. by Victor G. Ambrus. 1980, Morrow $9.75; LB $9.36. A young knight discovers that the dreaded monster in the dungeon is only a mouse.

1573. Hazen, Barbara S. *The Gorilla Did It* (PS–1). Illus. by Ray Cruz. 1974, Atheneum $9.95; paper $2.95. A child keeps blaming an imaginary animal—a gorilla—for all the messes in his room.

1574. Hedderwick, Mairi. *Katie Morag Delivers the Mail* (PS–1). Illus. by author. 1984, Bodley Head $9.95. Katie helps her parents deliver the mail on a Scottish island—with disastrous results.

1575. Heide, Florence Parry. *The Problem with Pulcifer* (2–4). Illus. by Judy Glasser. 1982, Harper $9.13; LB $8.89. Pulcifer's problem is that he prefers reading to watching television.

1576. Hickman, Martha Whitmore. *Eeps, Creeps, It's My Room* (2–4). Illus. by Mary Alice Baer. 1984, Abingdon $9.95. Jeffrey finally gets around to cleaning his room.

1577. Hoban, Russell. *How Tom Beat Captain Najork and His Hired Sportsmen* (1–3). Illus. by Quentin Blake. 1974, Atheneum $7.95; paper $1.95. Impish fun in both text and illustrations in this story of Tom, who triumphs over those intent on punishing him. A sequel is: *A Near Thing for Captain Najork* (1976, $7.95).

1578. Hormann, Toni. *Onions, Onions* (2–4). Illus. by Diane Stanley. 1981, Harper $7.95; LB $8.89. A wife insists that onions will keep away evil spirits.

1579. Hughes, Shirley. *George the Babysitter* (1–3). Illus. by author. 1977, Prentice $9.95; paper $3.95. Life becomes an adventure when the new baby-sitter arrives.

1580. Hutchins, Pat. *Clocks and More Clocks* (1–3). Illus. by author. 1970, Macmillan $9.95. An old gentleman has difficulty acquiring a clock that tells the correct time.

1581. Hutchins, Pat. *Don't Forget the Bacon* (K–2). Illus. by author. 1976, Greenwillow $10.80; Penguin paper $2.95. An absentminded child has trouble remembering the shopping list.

1582. Hutchins, Pat. *King Henry's Palace* (K–3). Illus. 1983, Greenwillow $10.00; LB $9.55. Three humorous stories about good King Henry.

1583. Isadora, Rachel. *Max* (K–2). Illus. by author. 1976, Macmillan $9.95; paper $3.95. Max, an avid baseball player, finds that joining his sister's dancing class makes an excellent warm-up for the game.

1584. Jonas, Ann. *Round Trip* (PS–4). Illus. by author. 1983, Greenwillow $8.50; LB $7.63; Scholastic paper $2.50. A book to read forward, backward, and then upside down.

1585. Keats, Ezra Jack. *Jenny's Hat* (K–2). Illus. by author. 1966, Harper $10.53; LB $10.89. Jenny's drab new hat is decorated by her bird friends, who become its trimming.

1586. Kent, Jack. *There's No Such Thing As a Dragon* (K–2). Illus. by author. 1975, Western paper $1.25. In spite of Mother's insistence that there is no such thing as a dragon, this dragon poses many problems for Mother in a highly amusing story.

1587. Kline, Suzy. *Shhhh!* (2–4). Illus. by Dora Leder. 1984, Whitman $9.25. A little girl is told "shhh" by everyone she wants to talk to.

1588. Krasilovsky, Phyllis. *The Man Who Didn't Wash His Dishes* (K–2). Illus. by Barbara Cooney. 1950, Doubleday $7.95. A man learns his lesson when his home becomes so full of dirty dishes that there is no place to sit down.

1589. Krasilovsky, Phyllis. *The Man Who Tried to Save Time* (K–2). Illus. by Marcia Sewall. 1979, Doubleday $6.95. All of a man's strategems for time saving—like eating breakfast the night before—backfire.

1590. Kroll, Steven. *Bathrooms* (1–3). Illus. by Maxie Chambliss. 1982, Avon paper $1.95. Lionel searches for the perfect bathroom.

1591. Kuskin, Karla. *A Boy Had a Mother Who Bought Him a Hat* (K–3). Illus. by author. 1976, Houghton $8.95. A humorous cumulative poem about a boy receiving an amazing array of new possessions.

1592. Levitin, Sonia. *A Single Speckled Egg* (K–3). Illus. by John Larrecq. 1976, Parnassus $6.95. Three foolish farmers are outwitted by their wives in this ridiculous tale told in the folk tradition.

1593. Levitin, Sonia. *Who Owns the Moon?* (K–2). Illus. by John Larrecq. 1973, Parnassus $6.95. Each of three noodle-headed farmers claims to own the moon and is dismayed when it moves—someone has stolen a piece of it! How the sage of the village resolves their quarrel makes a very humorous story.

1594. Lloyd, David. *Bread and Cheese* (K–1). Illus. by Deborah Ward. 1984, Random $1.95. A humorous repetitive story. Others by this author and publisher: *Duck; Hat; Jack and Nelly* (all 1984, $1.95).

1595. Lobel, Arnold. *Ming Lo Moves the Mountain* (PS–3). Illus. by author. 1982, Greenwillow $11.25; LB $11.88; Scholastic paper $1.95. A humorous tale about a man's attempt to move a mountain away from his house.

1596. Lorenz, Lee. *Big Gus and Little Gus* (PS–K). Illus. 1982, Prentice $10.95; paper $5.95. Two tramps in a story of buffoonery; based on folklore.

1597. Lorenz, Lee. *Pinchpenny John* (2–4). Illus. by author. 1981, Prentice $9.95; paper $4.95. A witty story filled with bright cartoon illustrations.

1598. Lorimer, Janet. *The Biggest Bubble in the World* (1–3). Illus. by Diane Paterson. 1982, Watts $3.95; LB $8.60. Harvey and Jeremy chew 400 pieces of gum to create a giant bubble.

1599. McCloskey, Robert. *Burt Dow, Deep-Water Man* (K–3). Illus. by author. 1963, Viking $10.95.

The humorous tale of an old Maine fisherman who caught a whale by the tail and then used a multicolored Band-Aid to cover the hole.

1600. McCloskey, Robert. *Lentil* (K–3). Illus. by author. 1940, Viking $9.95; paper $2.95. Tale of a boy who can't carry a tune, yet learns to play the harmonica.

1601. McGovern, Ann. *Mr. Skinner's Skinny House* (1–3). Illus. by Mort Gerberg. 1980, Four Winds $8.95. A skinny man finds a perfect mate in Ms. Thinner.

1602. McGovern, Ann. *Nicholas Bentley Stoningpot III* (1–3). Illus. by Tomie de Paola. 1982, Holiday LB $11.95. Nicky doesn't want to be rescued when he is marooned on a desert island.

1603. McPhail, David. *Andrew's Bath* (PS–K). Illus. 1984, Little $12.95. Andrew is finally old enough to take his own bath.

1604. Mahy, Margaret. *The Boy Who Was Followed Home* (K–2). Illus. by Steven Kellogg. 1983, Dial paper $3.95. Robert likes hippopotamuses and is delighted when one follows him home.

1605. Manes, Esther, and Manes, Stephen. *The Bananas Move to the Ceiling* (1–3). Illus. by Barbara Samuels. 1983, Watts $3.95; LB $8.50. Through the use of nails and suction cups, the Banana family moves to the ceiling.

1606. Marshall, James. *The Cut-Ups* (K–3). Illus. by author. 1984, Viking $10.95. A pair of young boys gets into all sorts of trouble.

1607. Mayer, Mercer. *What Do You Do with a Kangaroo?* (K–3). Illus. by author. 1974, Four Winds $7.95. A little girl has all kinds of animal problems.

1608. Murphy, Shirley Rousseau. *Tattie's River Journey* (1–3). Illus. by Tomie de Paola. 1983, Dial $11.95; LB $11.89. Tattie is caught in a flood and rescues many animals.

1609. Newell, Hope. *The Little Old Woman Who Used Her Head* (1–3). Illus. by Margaret Ruse. 1973, Lodestar $6.95. Ten amusing but taxing problems are solved through thought by a little old woman.

1610. Oppenheim, Joanne. *Mrs. Peloki's Snake* (1–2). Illus. by Joyce Audy dos Santos. 1980, Dodd LB $9.95. The discovery of a snake in the boys' room causes problems in Mrs. Peloki's classroom. A sequel is: *Mrs. Peloki's Class Play* (1984, $10.95).

1611. Oxenbury, Helen. *The Queen and Rosie Randall* (K–3). Illus. by author. 1979, Morrow $9.75; LB $9.36. A young girl helps her queen entertain the king of Wottermazzy.

1612. Park, Ruth. *When the Wind Changed* (PS–3). Illus. by Deborah Niland. 1981, Putnam $8.95; paper $4.95. Josh makes terrible faces until his father tells him his face will stay that way when the wind changes.

1613. Parker, Nancy W. *Love from Uncle Clyde* (PS). Illus. by author. 1977, Dodd $5.95. Uncle Clyde's birthday gift to Charlie is Elfreda, a purple hippopotamus. A sequel is: *Love from Aunt Betty* (1983, $10.95).

1614. Parker, Nancy W. *Poofy Loves Company* (4–6). Illus. by author. 1980, Dodd LB $7.95. On a visit to a neighbor's house, Sally runs afoul of a large shaggy dog named Poofy.

1615. Pinkwater, D. Manus. *The Big Orange Splot* (K–2). Illus. by author. 1977, Hastings $7.95. A cumulative story about the effects of dropping a can of orange paint on the roof of Mr. Plumbean's house.

1616. Pinkwater, D. Manus. *I Was a Second Grade Werewolf* (K–3). Illus. by author. 1983, Dutton $9.66. No one except Laurence himself believes he has become a werewolf.

1617. Raskin, Ellen. *Who, Said Sue, Said Whoo?* (PS–2). Illus. by author. 1973, Atheneum $8.95; paper $1.95. A little girl, while driving through a jungle, encounters an ever-increasing menagerie of animals.

1618. Rose, Anne. *As Right As Right Can Be* (K–3). Illus. by Arnold Lobel. 1976, Dial paper $1.95. Acquiring new shoelaces leads to buying a new house and furnishings to match, in this nonsense story.

1619. Rosenbloom, Joseph. *Ridiculous Nicholas Riddle Book* (1–3). Illus. by Joyce Behr. 1981, Sterling $7.95; LB $9.99. A day full of riddles for Nicholas. A sequel is: *Ridiculous Nicholas Pet Riddle Book* (1982, $7.95; LB $9.99).

1620. Ross, Dave. *A Book of Hugs* (1–3). Illus. by author. 1980, Harper $5.95. The author describes a variety of hugs, such as people hugs and blanket hugs. A sequel is: *More Hugs!* (1984, $6.95).

1621. Roy, Ron. *The Great Frog Swap* (1–3). Illus. by Victoria Chess. 1981, Random $7.95; LB $7.99. Wally and Marvin hatch an intricate frog-swapping plot that backfires.

1622. Russo, Susan. *Joe's Junk* (1–3). Illus. by author. 1982, Holt $10.25. Joe cleans up his room and has a garage sale.

1623. Sadler, Marilyn. *Alistair's Elephant* (PS–2). Illus. by Roger Bollen. 1983, Prentice $10.95. Alistair is followed home from the zoo by an elephant.

1624. Scheer, Julian, and Bileck, Marvin. *Rain Makes Applesauce* (K–2). Illus. by author. 1964, Holiday $11.95. A series of silly statements nonsensically presented and accompanied by humorous detailed pictures.

1625. Schwartz, Amy. *Bea and Mr. Jones* (K–3). Illus. by author. 1982, Bradbury $9.95; Penguin paper $3.50. Bea is tired of kindergarten and Mr. Jones of his desk job, so they change places.

1626. Schwartz, Amy. *Her Majesty, Aunt Essie* (1–3). Illus. by author. 1984, Bradbury $12.95. Ruthie boasts to her friend Maisie that her aunt is a queen.

1627. Segal, Lore. *All the Way Home* (K–3). Illus. by James Marshall. 1973, Farrar $6.95. Juliet's wailing attracts the attention of some animal friends in this amusing story of a day in the park.

1628. Sendak, Maurice. *Chicken Soup with Rice: A Book of Months* (K–3). Illus. by author. 1962, Harper LB $9.89. A rhyming story that takes one through each of the months with the always suitable chicken soup with rice.

1629. Shannon, George. *Bean Boy* (PS–3). Illus. 1984, Greenwillow $9.00; LB $8.59. A cumulative story about a boy who starts out in life with only a bean.

1630. Sharmat, Marjorie W. *Gila Monsters Meet You at the Airport* (PS–2). Illus. by Byron Barton. 1980, Macmillan $9.95; Penguin paper $3.50. A young boy imagines all sorts of horrible things about his move from New York City.

1631. Shire, Ellen. *The Bungling Ballerinas* (2–4). Illus. by author. 1982, Little $11.95; paper $5.95. In this spoof, a wardrobe mistress conspires to get a leading role in the ballet.

1632. Skorpen, Liesel Moak. *Outside My Window* (PS–2). Illus. by Mercer Mayer. 1968, Harper $8.89. Words and pictures capture the amusingly desperate attempts of a boy to disguise the unacceptable pet—a small bear cub—that he invited in one night.

1633. Slobodkina, Esphyr. *Caps for Sale* (K–3). Illus. by author. 1947, A. & W. LB $7.64; Scholastic paper $2.50. When some monkeys engage in a bit of monkey business, the cap peddler must use his imagination to retrieve his wares.

1634. Smith, Peter. *Jenny's Baby Brother* (PS–2). Illus. by Bob Graham. 1984, Viking $5.95. Jenny doesn't like her baby brother very much.

1635. Spier, Peter. *Oh, Were They Ever Happy!* (1–3). Illus. by author. 1978, Doubleday $9.95. Three children go on a painting spree.

1636. Steig, William. *The Amazing Bone* (K–2). Illus. by author. 1976, Farrar $7.95; Penguin paper $3.50. A bone that talks saves a piglet from being eaten by a fox in this nonsensical and witty story.

1637. Stevens, Kathleen. *Molly, McCullough, and Tom the Rogue* (2–4). Illus. by Margot Zemach. 1983, Harper $10.53; LB $10.89. Tom has been making a living swindling rich farmers until he meets Molly.

1638. Tapic, Pat Decker. *The Lady Who Saw the Good Side of Everything* (K–2). Illus. by Paul Galdone. 1975, Houghton $6.95. An amusing story of a little old lady who was always cheerful in spite of difficulties.

1639. Testa, Fulvio. *If You Seek Adventure* (K–2). Illus. by author. 1984, Dial $10.95. Twelve amusing ways to cure boredom.

1640. Testa, Fulvio. *Never Satisfied* (K–3). Illus. by author. 1982, Faber $10.95. Two boys believe life is boring when all around them is adventure.

1641. Thaler, Mike. *Madge's Magic Show* (1–2). Illus. by Carol Nicklaus. 1978, Avon paper $1.25. Madge has difficulty pulling a rabbit from her hat, particularly when Jimmy heckles her.

1642. Tierney, Hanne. *Where's Your Baby Brother, Becky Bunting?* (5–8). Illus. by Paula Winter. 1979, Doubleday $7.95. A comic view of sibling rivalry brilliantly illustrated.

1643. Tworkov, Jack. *The Camel Who Took a Walk* (K–3). Illus. by Roger Duvoisin. 1951, Dutton $10.95. A beautiful young camel decides to take a walk one morning, unaware that a terrible tiger has plans to pounce on her.

1644. Ungerer, Tomi. *Beast of Monsieur Racine* (K–3). Illus. by author. 1971, Farrar $9.95. Monsieur Racine catches the strange creature that was stealing the fruit from his prize pear tree; when the creature reveals his true identity, a surprise is in store.

1645. Viorst, Judith. *My Mama Says There Aren't Any Zombies, Ghosts, Vampires, Creatures, Demons, Monsters, Fiends, Goblins, or Things* (PS–1). Illus. by Kay Chorao. 1973, Atheneum $10.95; paper $2.95. A humorous story concerned with a child's vivid description of imaginary monsters and his mother's reassurance that they don't exist.

1646. Waber, Bernard. *Nobody Is Perfick* (K–3). Illus. by author. 1971, Houghton $8.95. A nonsense book that explains 8 topics true to childhood, such as a secret diary and a fantastic dream.

1647. Watson, Nancy. *The Birthday Goat* (K–2). Illus. by Wendy Watson. 1974, Harper LB $9.89. A goat family enjoy their day at the carnival until Baby Souci, the youngest goat, is kidnapped.

1648. Watson, Pauline. *The Walking Coat* (PS–3). Illus. by Tomie de Paola. 1980, Walker LB $7.85; paper $3.95. On the first cold day, Scott dons a huge coat that is much too big for him.

1649. Wells, Rosemary. *Abdul* (K–2). Illus. by author. 1975, Dial $7.95. Feisal is very fond of his camel, Gilda, but when she gives birth to Abdul, an animal strangely resembling a horse, he feels disaster has struck.

1650. Willard, Nancy, and de Paola, Tomie. *Simple Pictures Are Best* (PS–3). Illus. by Tomie de Paola. 1977, Harcourt $7.95; paper $2.95. Over a weary photographer's warnings, a couple insist on cluttering their anniversary portrait with all their worldly goods.

1651. Williams, Barbara. *Albert's Toothache* (K–2). Illus. by Kay Chorao. 1974, Dutton $7.95; paper $3.95. Albert, a turtle, claims he has a toothache, but not until Grandma asks him where his tooth aches does Albert realize he is toothless.

1652. Williams, Barbara. *Jeremy Isn't Hungry* (PS–1). Illus. by Martha Alexander. 1978, Dutton $6.95. Davy tries unsuccessfully to pacify his younger brother.

1653. Williams, Jay. *Everyone Knows What a Dragon Looks Like* (K–3). Illus. by Mercer Mayer. 1976, Four Winds $9.95; Scholastic paper $5.95. In this humorous tale told in the folk tradition, the leaders argue about what a dragon looks like, but the people know—"a small, fat, bald old man."

1654. Wood, Audrey. *The Napping House* (PS–2). Illus. by Don Wood. 1984, Harcourt $11.95. A cumulative story about all the members of a household taking a nap except for a flea.

1655. Yaffe, Alan. *The Magic Meatballs* (K–2). Illus. 1979, Dial $6.95; LB $6.46. Marvin tries to change his family's habits through using some magic meat a stranger gives him.

1656. Yeoman, John. *The Wild Washerwomen: A New Folk Tale* (K–3). Illus. by Quentin Blake. 1979, Greenwillow $11.95; LB $11.47. Seven washerwomen are dissatisfied with their jobs and become the terrors of the neighborhood.

1657. Yolen, Jane. *No Bath Tonight* (PS–1). Illus. by Alice Provensen and Martin Provensen. 1978, Viking $7.64; LB $7.89. Grandmother manages to foil Jeremy's decision not to take a bath.

1658. Zalben, Jane Breskin. *A Perfect Nose for Ralph* (PS–1). Illus. by John Wallner. 1980, Putnam $6.95; LB $6.99. A stuffed panda loses his nose and his owner searches for a new one.

1659. Zemach, Harve. *The Judge: An Untrue Tale* (1–3). Illus. by Margot Zemach. 1969, Farrar $11.95. A foolish judge, who would not believe the frantic reports of an unusual, threatening monster in the vicinity, gets his comeuppance in this rhyming tale with catchy refrain.

1660. Zemach, Harve. *A Penny a Look: An Old Story Retold* (K–3). Illus. by Margot Zemach. 1971,

Farrar $11.95. A rascal tries to exploit his brother in a wild money-making scheme.

1661. Zimelman, Nathan. *Positively No Pets Allowed* (K–3). Illus. by Pamela Johnson. 1980, Dutton $7.95. Strange things happen when a city boy receives a gorilla for a pet.

1662. Zion, Gene. *Dear Garbage Man* (K–2). Illus. by Margaret B. Graham. 1957, Harper $10.89. Stan, the new garbage man, finds it impossible to throw away what he has collected.

1663. Zion, Gene. *The Plant Sitter* (PS–2). Illus. by Margaret B. Graham. 1959, Harper paper $1.95; Scholastic paper $2.25. Tommy learns a lot about plants when he volunteers to take care of the neighbor's plants when they go on vacation.

1664. Zion, Gene. *The Summer Snowman* (1–3). Illus. by Margaret B. Graham. 1955, Harper LB $10.89. Henry keeps a snowman in the freezer and brings him out on the Fourth of July. Also use: *Really Spring* (1956, Harper LB $12.89).

Community and Everyday Life

1665. Alexander, Martha. *How My Library Grew by Dinah* (PS–K). Illus. by author. 1983, Wilson $12.00. Dinah and her teddy watch a library being built across the street.

1666. Barton, Byron. *Building a House* (PS–2). Illus. by author. 1981, Greenwillow $10.25; LB $9.84. The stages of building a house are simply presented.

1667. Baylor, Byrd. *The Best Town in the World* (2–4). Illus. by author. 1983, Scribners $11.95. A description of life in a small Texas town back when Father was a child.

1668. Beekman, Dan. *Forest, Village, Town, City* (2–4). Illus. by Bernice Loewenstein. 1982, Harper $10.10; LB $8.89. The development of America from wilderness to metropolis.

1669. Bester, Roger. *Fireman Jim* (K–3). Illus. 1981, Crown $9.95. A photographic introduction to a real-life fireman and his activities.

1670. Bozzo, Maxine Zohn. *Toby in the Country, Toby in the City* (PS–5). Illus. by Frank Modell. 1982, Greenwillow $11.25; LB $11.88. Two youngsters describe the joys of city and country life.

1671. Brodsky, Beverly. *Secret Places* (1–3). Illus. by author. 1979, Harper LB $9.89. A recollection in text and pictures of a city childhood.

1672. Brown, Marc, and Krensky, Stephen. *Dinosaurs, Beware! A Safety Guide* (PS–2). Illus. by author. 1982, Little $12.45; paper $5.70. Sixty safety tips are illustrated with drawings of dinosaurs.

1673. Burton, Virginia L. *The Little House* (1–3). Illus. by author. 1942, Houghton $10.50; paper $2.95. Story of a little house in the country that over the years witnesses change and progress. Caldecott Medal, 1943.

1674. Chlad, Dorothy. *Bicycles Are Fun to Ride* (PS–3). Illus. by Lydia Halverson. 1984, Childrens Pr. $6.95. A story about bicycle riding that stresses safety.

1675. Chwast, Seymour. *Tall City, Wide Country: A Book to Read Forward and Backward* (PS). Illus. by author. 1983, Viking $7.65. Two books in one that treat city and country life.

1676. Corey, Dorothy. *Tomorrow You Can* (PS–K). Illus. by Lois Areman. 1977, Whitman $7.75. A picture book reassuring youngsters that, although today they might not be able to accomplish a great deal, tomorrow they can.

1677. Crews, Donald. *Carousel* (PS–2). Illus. by author. 1982, Greenwillow $11.25; LB $11.88. A ride on a carousel is described in pictures and text.

1678. Crews, Donald. *Parade* (PS–2). Illus. by author. 1983, Greenwillow $9.00; LB $8.59. A picture book celebration of a parade—fire engine and all.

1679. Fair, Sylvia. *The Bedspread* (K–2). Illus. by author. 1982, Morrow $12.25. Two old ladies decide to embroider their bedspreads.

1680. Fisher, Aileen. *Going Barefoot* (K–2). Illus. by Adrienne Adams. 1960, Harper $8.79. A description of the joys of going barefoot and of a child's envy of the many animals and birds that do not have to wear shoes.

1681. Florian, Douglas. *People Working* (K–2). Illus. by author. 1983, Harper $9.57; LB $9.89. A variety of workers are introduced.

1682. Getz, Arthur. *Tar Beach* (K–3). Illus. 1979, Dial $7.95; LB $7.45. Summer in the city including open hydrants and rooftop sunbathing.

1683. Gibbons, Gail. *Department Store* (K–3). Illus. by author. 1984, Harper $9.57; LB $9.89. A day in the life of a department store.

1684. Gibbons, Gail. *Fire! Fire!* (PS–2). Illus. by author. 1984, Harper $9.57; LB $9.89. The various ways a fire is fought.

1685. Gibbons, Gail. *Paper, Paper Everywhere* (PS–2). Illus. by author. 1983, Harcourt $10.95. A picture book that shows how useful and ever-present is paper.

1686. Goffstein, M. B. *A Writer* (PS–3). Illus. 1984, Harper $11.49; LB $11.89. How a writer writes is explained in this picture book.

1687. Henkes, Kevin. *Clean Enough* (PS–2). Illus. by author. 1982, Greenwillow $10.00; LB $10.85. A young boy takes a bath.

1688. Hines, Anna Grossnickle. *Maybe a Band-Aid Will Help* (PS–1). Illus. 1984, Dutton $8.95. Sarah tries to repair her broken doll.

1689. Jordan, June. *Kimako's Story* (K–3). Illus. by Kay Burford. 1981, Houghton LB $6.95. Seven-year-old Kimako explores her neighborhood.

1690. Keats, Ezra Jack. *Dreams* (PS–2). Illus. by author. 1974, Macmillan $9.95. Roberto has difficulty going to sleep on a hot summer night in the city.

1691. Kessler, Ethel, and Kessler, Leonard. *Night Story* (PS–2). Illus. by author. 1981, Macmillan LB $7.95. A truck driver describes night sounds in the city and country.

1692. Knab, Linda Z. *The Day Is Waiting* (PS–K). Illus. by Don Freeman. 1980, Viking $11.50. A celebration of life in rhyme and paintings.

1693. Kuskin, Karla. *The Philharmonic Gets Dressed* (1–4). Illus. by Marc Simont. 1982, Harper $10.10; LB $10.89. One-hundred-five musicians are across town getting ready for a big concert.

1694. Leiner, Katherine. *Ask Me What My Mother Does* (K–2). Illus. 1978, Watts $5.90. A wide variety of occupations are pictured and discussed.

1695. Lenski, Lois. *The Little Farm* (PS–3). Illus. by author. 1942, McKay $5.25. One in the series of Mr. Small and his family stories enjoyed by young children.

1696. Lenski, Lois. *Lois Lenski's Big Book of Mr. Small* (PS). Illus. by author. 1979, McKay $9.95. Three books are included: *Cowboy Small; The Little Farm; Policeman Small.*

1697. Lenski, Lois. *More Mr. Small* (PS). Illus. by author. 1979, McKay $9.95. The three books included are: *The Little Airplane; The Little Auto; The Little Sailboat.*

1698. Maestro, Betsy, and Maestro, Giulio. *On the Town: A Book of Clothing Words* (PS–1). Illus. by author. 1983, Crown LB $8.95. All kinds of clothing are introduced by a dapper man and an elephant.

1699. Martin, Charles E. *Island Winter* (K–3). Illus. by author. 1984, Greenwillow $10.00; LB $9.55. Heather spends an eventful winter even when the summer people leave her island home. A sequel is: *Summer Business* (1984, $10.00; LB $9.55).

1700. Mitchell, Joyce Slayton. *My Mommy Makes Money* (PS–2). Illus. by True Kelley. 1984, Little $9.45. A story about several mothers who have various occupations.

1701. Papajani, Janet. *Museums* (1–4). Illus. 1983, Childrens Pr. $6.95. An introduction to various kinds of museums and what they contain.

1702. Robbins, Ken. *Tools* (PS–K). Illus. by author. 1983, Four Winds $12.95. An introduction in pictures to such tools as the chisel, wrench, and screwdriver.

1703. Rockwell, Anne. *I Like the Library* (PS–3). Illus. by author. 1977, Dutton $9.95. A small boy describes the joys he experiences during his weekly visit to the public library.

1704. Rockwell, Anne. *Our Garage Sale* (PS–K). Illus. by Harlow Rockwell. 1984, Greenwillow $10.00; LB $9.55. The planning and execution of an American tradition, the garage sale, seen through the experiences of two children.

1705. Rockwell, Anne, and Rockwell, Harlow. *Happy Birthday to Me* (PS). Illus. by author. 1981, Macmillan $6.95. A little boy explains what happens on his birthday, including a party.

1706. Rockwell, Anne, and Rockwell, Harlow. *I Play in My Room* (PS). Illus. by author. 1981, Macmillan $6.95. A preschooler shows what is in her room and how she plays there. Other titles in this series are: *I Love My Pets* (1982); *My Back Yard* (1984); *When I Go Visiting* (1984) (all $8.95).

1707. Rockwell, Anne, and Rockwell, Harlow. *The Supermarket* (PS–K). Illus. by author. 1979, Macmillan $8.95. Familiar objects and situations are explored in a trip to a supermarket.

1708. Rockwell, Harlow. *My Kitchen* (PS). Illus. by author. 1980, Greenwillow $11.25; LB $11.88. A simple presentation of the contents of a kitchen and their uses.

1709. Schaaf, Peter. *An Apartment House Close Up* (PS–1). Illus. 1980, Scholastic $7.95. All of the elements of an apartment building from boilers to elevators are explored.

1710. Schertle, Alice. *In My Treehouse* (K–3). Illus. by Meredith Dunham. 1983, Lothrop $10.00; LB $10.88. The story of a boy and his life in a treehouse.

1711. Schick, Eleanor. *City in the Summer* (1–3). Illus. by author. 1969, Macmillan paper $0.95. City summer activities grouped around an old man's trip to the beach with a young boy. Also use: *City in the Winter* (1970, Macmillan paper $0.95).

1712. Spier, Peter. *The Firehouse* (PS). Illus. by author. 1981, Doubleday $3.95. A board book shaped like a firehouse.

1713. Spier, Peter. *People* (2–4). Illus. by author. 1980, Doubleday $10.95. A view of people's varying life-styles and ways of life.

1714. Stecher, Miriam B., and Kandell, Alice S. *Max, the Music-Maker* (PS–1). Illus. 1980, Lothrop $9.95; LB $9.55. In his everyday activities, Max produces a kind of music.

1715. Thomas, Ianthe. *My Street's a Morning Cool Street* (K–2). Illus. by Emily McCully. 1976, Harper $8.61; LB $8.89. A young boy describes in black English what he sees on his way to school.

1716. Yashima, Taro. *Umbrella* (PS–1). Illus. by author. 1958, Viking $10.95; Penguin paper $3.75. A 3-year-old Japanese-American girl, born in New York, longs for a rainy day so she can use her new blue umbrella and red rubber boots.

Transportation and Machines

1717. Barton, Byron. *Airport* (PS–1). Illus. by author. 1982, Harper $10.53; LB $10.89. Common sights at an airport reproduced in drawings and text.

1718. Burton, Virginia L. *Mike Mulligan and His Steam Shovel* (1–3). Illus. by author. 1939, Houghton $9.95; paper $3.95. Thrilling race against time as Mike Mulligan and his steam shovel dig a cellar in one day. Also use: *Katy and the Big Snow* (1943, Houghton $9.95; paper 2.50).

1719. Crews, Donald. *Harbor* (K–2). Illus. by author. 1982, Greenwillow $11.25; LB $11.88. The activities and objects associated with harbors and harbor activities are illustrated.

1720. Crews, Donald. *School Bus* (PS–1). Illus. by author. 1984, Greenwillow $10.00; LB $9.55. Many kinds of school buses pick up children for school.

1721. Ehrlich, Amy. *The Everyday Train* (PS–K). Illus. by Martha Alexander. 1977, Dial $6.95; LB $6.46. Jane runs across the field every day to watch the train go by and wave to the engineer.

1722. Gibbons, Gail. *Boat Book* (PS–1). Illus. by author. 1983, Holiday $11.95. An illustration of all sorts of boats in simple drawings.

1723. Gibbons, Gail. *New Road!* (K–2). Illus. by author. 1983, Harper $9.57; LB $9.89. The process of road construction from start to finish.

1724. Gibbons, Gail. *Trucks* (PS–2). Illus. by author. 1981, Harper $10.53; LB $10.89. A very simple introduction to trucks and what they do.

1725. Gramatky, Hardie. *Hercules: The Story of an Old-Fashioned Fire Engine* (K–3). 1940, Putnam

$5.99. A horse-drawn fire engine becomes a hero when it saves City Hall.

1726. Gramatky, Hardie. *Little Toot* (K–3). Illus. by author. 1939, Putnam $8.95; LB $8.99; paper $4.95. Little Toot, son of the mightiest tug in the harbor, had no ambition until he became a hero during a raging storm. Also use: *Little Toot on the Thames* (1964, Putnam, LB $5.99).

1727. Haddad, Helen R. *Truck and Loader* (PS–3). Illus. by Donald Carrick. 1982, Greenwillow $8.50; LB $8.88. An easily read account of the uses of a front-end loader and dump truck.

1728. Lasky, Kathryn. *Tugboats Never Sleep* (1–3). Illus. by author. 1977, Little $7.95. A young boy visits a tugboat and learns rope talk.

1729. Lenski, Lois. *Little Auto* (K–3). Illus. by author. 1934, Walck $5.25. Adventures of popular Mr. Small.

1730. Maestro, Betsy, and DelVecchio, Ellen. *Big City Port* (PS–2). Illus. by Giulio Maestro. 1983, Four Winds $10.95; Scholastic paper $2.50. A picture book that shows activities in a big city port.

1731. Petty, Kate. *On a Plane* (K–3). Illus. by Aline Riquier. 1984, Watts $8.60. A description of what happens when you go on a passenger airplane.

1732. Piper, Watty. *The Little Engine That Could* (K–2). Illus. by George Hauman and Doris Hauman. 1954, Platt and Munk $4.95; Scholastic paper $2.25. Little Engine saves the day.

1733. Rockwell, Anne. *Boats* (PS–K). Illus. by author. 1982, Dutton $8.95. For a very young audience, an introduction to boats of all sorts. Two others in this series are: *Trucks* (1983, $9.66); *Cars* (1984, $8.69).

1734. Ross, Pat, and Ross, Joel. *Your First Airplane Trip* (K–2). Illus. by Lynn Wheeling. 1981, Lothrop $10.25; LB $9.84. An explanation of what an airplane trip involves from checking in to disembarking.

1735. Scarry, Huck. *On Wheels* (K–2). Illus. 1980, Putnam $7.95; LB $7.99. A picture book on the uses of wheels through the ages.

1736. Seiden, Art. *Trucks* (PS). Illus. by author. 1983, Platt and Munk $3.50. A board book in which several kinds of trucks are identified.

1737. Siebert, Diane. *Truck Song* (PS–1). Illus. by Byron Barton. 1984, Harper $10.53; LB $10.89. Simple rhymes tell of trucks traveling cross-country.

1738. Steptoe, John. *Train Ride* (K–3). Illus. by author. 1971, Harper $10.89; LB $9.89. The adventures of a group of boys traveling from Brooklyn to Times Square on the subway.

1739. Swift, Hildegarde. *Little Red Lighthouse and the Great Gray Bridge* (1–3). Illus. by Lynd Ward. 1942, Harcourt $10.95; paper $4.95. The beacon of the little red lighthouse at the base of the George Washington Bridge in New York City is still needed even after the bridge is built.

Nature and Science

1740. Adoff, Arnold. *Birds: Poems* (K–3). Illus. by Troy Howell. 1982, Harper $10.10; LB $9.89. A book of simple poems about birds.

1741. Bailey, Jill. *Eyes* (PS). Illus. 1984, Putnam $3.95. A small board book shows the eyes of several animals. Other titles in this series are: *Feet; Mouths; Noses* (all 1984, $3.95).

1742. Barklem, Jill. *Autumn Story* (PS–3). Illus. by author. 1980, Putnam $6.95; LB $6.99. The mice of Brambly Hedge celebrate the seasons. Others in this series are: *Spring Story; Summer Story; Winter Story* (all 1980, $6.95; LB $6.99).

1743. Barrett, Judith. *A Snake Is Totally Tail* (PS–3). Illus. by L. S. Johnson. 1983, Atheneum $9.95. Various characteristics of animals are introduced.

1744. Baskin, Leonard. *Leonard Baskin's Miniature Natural History* (1–4). Illus. 1983, Pantheon 4 vols. $9.95 ea. A collection of watercolors on a variety of animals.

1745. Baylor, Byrd. *If You Are a Hunter of Fossils* (PS–1). Illus. by Peter Parnall. 1980, Scribners $9.95; paper $3.95. A story that introduces a sense of long ago.

1746. Baylor, Byrd. *We Walk in Sandy Places* (K–2). Illus. by Marilyn Schweitzer. 1976, Scribners $6.95. The closeness that desert dwellers feel for their environment and its creatures is beautifully described in this photographic prose poem.

1747. Baylor, Byrd. *Your Own Best Secret Place* (2–4). Illus. by Peter Parnall. 1979, Scribners $9.95. A girl shows her secret hiding place, a hollow tree, to other children.

1748. Bess, Clayton. *The Truth about the Moon* (K–3). Illus. by Rosekrans Hoffman. 1983, Houghton $8.70. A young African boy hears both realistic and fanciful explanations for the moon.

1749. Bodecker, N. M. *The Mushroom Center Disaster* (K–2). Illus. by Erik Blegvad. 1974, Atheneum paper $1.95. Beetle comes to Mushroom Center to find a haven, and when disaster strikes, he devises ways of restoring the ecology of the community.

1750. Brown, Marc. *Your First Garden Book* (2–4). Illus. by author. 1981, Little $9.95; paper $4.95. Human and animal gardeners show how to grow simple plants.

1751. Brown, Margaret Wise. *The Country Noisy Book* (PS). Illus. by Leonard Weisgard. 1940, Harper $10.89; paper $1.95. The sounds made by country animals, many of which are left for the child to supply. Also use: *The Indoor Noisy Book* (1942, Harper $10.89; paper $1.95); *The Winter Noisy Book* (1976, Harper paper $1.95).

1752. Brown, Margaret Wise. *Wait Till the Moon Is Full* (PS–1). Illus. by Garth Williams. 1948, Harper $9.57. The fears of night are dispelled in this tender story about raccoons.

1753. Chen, Tony. *Wild Animals* (PS). Illus. 1981, Random $2.95. An attractive board book introducing a few wild animals.

1754. Clifton, Lucille. *The Boy Who Didn't Believe in Spring* (K–2). Illus. by Brinton Turkle. 1978, Dutton $8.25; paper $1.95. An account of a black child's determination to "get me some of this spring."

1755. Cobb, Vicki. *Fuzz Does It!* (1–3). Illus. by Brian Schatell. 1982, Harper $11.06; LB $10.89; paper $4.75. Fibers and their uses are described and a few projects are introduced.

1756. de Paola, Tomie. *Charlie Needs a Cloak* (PS–1). Illus. by author. 1974, Prentice paper $3.95; Scholastic paper $1.95. The facts about cloth making are humorously presented in this story of Charlie, a shepherd.

1757. de Paola, Tomie. *The Cloud Book* (K–3). Illus. by author. 1975, Holiday LB $10.95; paper $5.95. The 10 most common clouds, along with related myths and sayings.

1758. de Paola, Tomie. *The Quicksand Book* (1–3). Illus. by author. 1977, Holiday $10.95; paper $5.95. Science is both informative and entertaining in this story of Jungle Girl, who falls into a patch of quicksand.

1759. Di Fiori, Lawrence. *Baby Animals* (PS). Illus. by author. 1983, Macmillan $2.95. A board book for toddlers. Others in this series are: *The Farm; My First Book; My Toys* (all 1983, $2.95).

1760. Domanska, Janina. *Spring Is* (K–3). Illus. by author. 1976, Greenwillow $11.25; LB $10.80. A book about the seasons as seen by a dachshund.

1761. dos Santos, Joyce Audy. *Sand Dollar, Sand Dollar* (1–3). Illus. by author. 1980, Harper $7.95; LB $7.89. Peter makes a wish on a sand dollar he finds at the beach.

1762. Dragonwagon, Crescent. *Katie in the Morning* (PS–3). Illus. by Betsy Day. 1983, Harper $10.53; LB $10.89. A reflective story of a girl's solitary walk to get a newspaper.

1763. Dunn, Judy. *The Animals of Buttercup Farm* (PS–K). Illus. 1981, Random $5.95. Large photographs of common farm animals.

1764. Dunn, Judy. *The Little Rabbit* (K–2). Illus. 1980, Random paper $3.99. A real rabbit family is introduced in photographs.

1765. Dunn, Phoebe. *Farm Animals* (PS). Illus. 1984, Random $2.95. An introduction to more than 15 farm animals.

1766. Dunrea, Olivier. *Eddy B., Pigboy* (PS–2). Illus. by author. 1983, Atheneum $8.95. A description of Eddy's chores around the farm.

1767. Elliott, Alan C. *On Sunday the Wind Came* (K–2). Illus. by Susan Bonners. 1980, Morrow $9.36. A week of different kinds of winter weather is described.

1768. Fisher, Aileen. *I Stood upon a Mountain* (1–3). Illus. by Blair Lent. 1979, Harper $10.53; LB $11.89. A little girl questions the origins of the earth and receives many different answers.

1769. Fisher, Leonard Everett. *Storm at the Jetty* (K–3). Illus. by author. 1981, Viking $9.95. A description of the coming of a storm and the eventual return to calm.

1770. Freschet, Berniece. *Raccoon Baby* (1–3). Illus. by Jim Arnosky. 1948, Putnam $6.99. The story of raccoon life as seen through the activities of a mother raccoon.

1771. Gibbons, Gail. *The Seasons of Arnold's Apple Tree* (PS–1). Illus. 1984, Harcourt $13.95. Arnold's apple tree is useful in all seasons.

1772. Givens, Janet Eaton. *Just Two Wings* (K–2). Illus. by Susan Elayne Dodge. 1984, Atheneum $8.95. A picture book about bird migration.

1773. Goffstein, M. B. *Natural History* (1–3). Illus. by author. 1979, Farrar $7.95. A gentle look at the earth, its inhabitants, and its problems.

1774. Goudey, Alice E. *The Day We Saw the Sun Come Up* (PS–1). Illus. by Adrienne Adams. 1961, Scribners $8.95. This lovely picture book captures the wonder of sunrise.

1775. Gundersheimer, Karen. *Happy Winter* (PS–2). Illus. by author. 1982, Harper $9.57; LB $9.89. Two little girls enjoy all the delights of playing on a winter day.

1776. Hader, Berta, and Hader, Elmer. *The Big Snow* (PS–3). Illus. by author. 1948, Macmillan paper $3.95. How all the little animals of a country hillside survive a heavy winter storm. Caldecott Medal, 1949.

1777. Heller, Ruth. *Chickens Aren't the Only Ones* (K–2). Illus. 1981, Grosset $5.95. All kinds of animals that lay eggs.

1778. Himler, Ronald. *Wake Up, Jeremiah* (PS–1). Illus. by author. 1979, Harper LB $10.89. A young boy greets a new day.

1779. Hines, Anna Grossnickle. *Come to the Meadow* (PS–3). Illus. 1984, Houghton $9.95. Granny and grandchild enjoy a picnic in the meadow.

1780. Hutchins, Pat. *The Wind Blew* (PS–K). Illus. by author. 1974, Macmillan $10.95. A cumulative story in rhyme describes the havoc wrought by a stiff wind and all the objects it carries away.

1781. Isenbart, Hans-Heinrich. *Baby Animals on the Farm* (PS). Illus. 1984, Putnam $9.95. The young of many farm animals are shown in color photographs.

1782. Kalan, Robert. *Rain* (PS–1). Illus. by Donald Crews. 1978, Greenwillow LB $10.51. A rainstorm described in pictures and brief text.

1783. Keats, Ezra Jack. *The Snowy Day* (PS–1). Illus. by author. 1962, Viking $10.95; Penguin paper $3.50. A young black boy's delight during his first snowfall. Caldecott Medal winner.

1784. Komori, Atsushi. *Animal Mothers* (PS–K). Illus. by author. 1983, Putnam $8.95. How various animals take care of their young.

1785. Krauss, Ruth. *The Growing Story* (PS–2). Illus. by Phyllis Rowand. 1947, Harper $10.53. A little boy watches things grow but doesn't realize until fall that he, too, has grown.

1786. Kuskin, Karla. *A Space Story* (K–2). Illus. by Marc Simont. 1978, Harper LB $9.89. A simple but accurate presentation of material about the solar system.

1787. Lambert, David. *The Seasons* (1–3). Illus. 1983, Watts $8.90. A simple introduction to the "whys" and characteristics of the seasons.

1788. Lapp, Eleanor J. *In the Morning Mist* (K–3). Illus. by David Cunningham. 1978, Whitman $7.75. A pensive account of a boy and his grandfather on an early-morning fishing trip.

1789. Le Tord, Bijou. *Rabbit Seeds* (PS–2). Illus. by author. 1984, Scholastic $9.95. A rabbit farmer shows children the annual growing cycle on a farm.

1790. Levitin, Sonia. *The Fisherman and the Bird* (K–2). Illus. by Francis Livingston. 1982, Houghton LB $10.95. Rico, a fisherman, must stay ashore while a bird's eggs on his mast hatch.

1791. Lilly, Kenneth. *Animal Builders* (PS). Illus. by author. 1984, Random $2.95. An introduction to animals and their ways of building homes of various kinds. Others in this series are: *Animal*

Climbers; Animal Jumpers; Animal Runners; Animal Swimmers (all 1984, $2.95).

1792. Locker, Thomas. *Where the River Begins* (PS–3). Illus. 1984, Dial $15.00. Two boys hike with their grandfather to the source of a river.

1793. McCloskey, Robert. *Time of Wonder* (1–4). Illus. by author. 1957, Viking $13.95. Full-color watercolors illustrate this poetic text describing a summer on the Maine coast and the hurricane that hits it. Caldecott Medal, 1958.

1794. Mack, Gail. *Yesterday's Snowman* (K–2). Illus. by Erik Blegvad. 1979, Pantheon $6.95; LB $6.99. A beautiful snowman is made by a family, but because of rain, the next day it is gone.

1795. McLaughlin, Lissa. *Why Won't Winter Go?* (K–2). Illus. by author. 1983, Lothrop $10.88; LB $10.89. A simple story of the seasons and the final coming of spring.

1796. McNaughton, Colin. *Autumn* (PS). Illus. by author. 1984, Dial $4.81. A simple board book that shows the characteristics of this season. Others in this series are: *Spring; Summer; Winter* (all 1984, $4.81).

1797. Mangin, Marie-France. *Suzette and Nicholas and the Seasons Clock* (PS–K). Illus. by Satomi Ichikawa. 1982, Putnam $8.95. Suzette and brother Nicholas celebrate each of the seasons.

1798. Newton, James R. *A Forest Is Reborn* (2–4). Illus. by Susan Bonners. 1982, Harper $9.57; LB $9.89. How forestland destroyed by fire can be rejuvenated.

1799. Noguere, Suzanne. *Little Raccoon* (2–3). Illus. by Tony Chen. 1981, Holt $12.95. A fictionalized view of a little raccoon's life.

1800. Peet, Bill. *The Wump World* (1–3). Illus. by author. 1970, Houghton $10.95; paper $3.95. An animal parable in which pollution and the waste of natural resources are the main themes.

1801. Peters, Sharon. *Animals at Night* (PS–1). Illus. by Paul Harvey. 1983, Troll $8.89. A book about some animals that remain awake at night.

1802. Prelutsky, Jack. *It's Snowing! It's Snowing!* (1–4). Illus. by Jeanne Titherington. 1984, Greenwillow $10.00; LB $9.55. A few story poems on the experiences and joys of winter.

1803. Rand, Ann, and Rand, Paul. *I Know a Lot of Things* (PS–1). Illus. by author. 1956, Harcourt paper $1.35. A book to help children develop greater awareness and appreciation of their environment.

1804. Ray, Deborah Kogan. *The Cloud* (1–3). Illus. by author. 1984, Harper $12.50. A young girl walks with her mother to the top of a mountain.

1805. Ray, Deborah Kogan. *Fog Drift Morning* (K–4). Illus. by author. 1983, Harper $10.53; LB $10.89. A young girl and her mother share a morning at the seashore.

1806. Rockwell, Anne, and Rockwell, Harlow. *How My Garden Grew* (PS–1). Illus. by author. 1982, Macmillan $7.95. A young child explains how a garden grows.

1807. Roffey, Maureen. *Home Sweet Home* (PS). Illus. by author. 1983, Putnam $7.95. A peek-a-boo book about where animals live.

1808. Ryder, Joanne. *Fog in the Meadow* (K–3). Illus. by Gail Owens. 1979, Harper $9.57; LB $9.89. Small animals find ways to react to the coming of fog.

1809. Rylant, Cynthia. *This Year's Garden* (PS–K). Illus. by Mary Szilagyi. 1984, Macmillan $12.95. A year in the garden in drawings and gentle text.

1810. Santrey, Louis. *Autumn* (PS–2). Illus. 1983, Troll $8.79; paper $2.50. An introduction to what is happening during autumn. Other titles in this series are: *Spring; Summer; Winter* (all 1983, $8.79; paper $2.50).

1811. Schweninger, Ann. *On My Way to Grandpa's* (PS–1). Illus. by author. 1981, Dial LB $7.28. A young girl travels through a storm to visit Grandpa.

1812. Selberg, Ingrid. *Our Changing World: A Revolving Picture Book* (PS–K). Illus. by Andrew Miller. 1982, Putnam $10.95. Various scenes are used to show such phenomena as seasons and night and day.

1813. Selsam, Millicent E. *Night Animals* (K–3). Illus. 1980, Four Winds $8.95. A simple introduction to such nocturnal creatures as the owl.

1814. Seuss, Dr. *The Lorax* (K–3). Illus. by author. 1971, Random $5.95; LB $5.99. The Lorax, a little brown creature, has tried in vain to ward off pollution and ecological blight, but Onceler, who wanted the trees for his business, would not heed the warning.

1815. Shulevitz, Uri. *Dawn* (PS–2). Illus. by author. 1974, Farrar $10.95. A rare, beautiful book describing in simple poetic terms the coming of dawn.

1816. Shulevitz, Uri. *Rain, Rain, Rivers* (PS–2). Illus. by author. 1969, Farrar $8.95. A little girl sits in her attic bedroom while the rain falls, and her imagination takes her to the places touched by the rain—the city, streams, and the sea.

1817. Simon, Seymour. *Animals in Your Neighborhood* (2–3). Illus. 1976, Walker $5.39. The world of nature in city neighborhoods is explored.

1818. Skofield, James. *All Wet! All Wet!* (K–3). Illus. by Diane Stanley. 1984, Harper $10.53; LB $10.89. A small boy takes a walk in the woods on a rainy day.

1819. Todd, Kathleen. *Snow* (PS–1). Illus. by author. 1982, Addison $7.95. Father, son, and dog enjoy a day in the snow.

1820. Tresselt, Alvin. *Hide and Seek Fog* (K–2). Illus. by Roger Duvoisin. 1965, Lothrop LB $9.84. Pastel watercolors quietly reflect obscure seashore scenes as the mysterious, deepening fog rolls in from the sea.

1821. Tresselt, Alvin. *Rain Drop Splash* (K–3). Illus. by Leonard Weisgard. 1946, Lothrop LB $11.04. How the raindrops form a puddle that grows from pond to river and finally joins the sea.

1822. Tresselt, Alvin. *What Did You Leave Behind?* (K–3). Illus. by Roger Duvoisin. 1978, Lothrop $10.95; LB $10.51. Nature's beauties are explored in poetic text and brilliant pictures.

1823. Udry, Janice May. *A Tree Is Nice* (PS). Illus. by Marc Simont. 1956, Harper $9.57; LB $10.89. The many delights to be had in, with, or under a tree: picking apples, raking leaves, swinging, or just sitting in the shade. Caldecott Medal, 1957.

1824. Wegen, Ron. *Sky Dragon* (K–2). Illus. 1982, Greenwillow $11.25; LB $11.85. A cloud that looks like a dragon brings snow.

1825. Wildsmith, Brian. *Seasons* (PS–3). Illus. by author. 1980, Oxford $9.95. A sense of the marvels of the seasons is conveyed in this picture book.

1826. Wolff, Ashley. *A Year of Birds* (PS–K). Illus. 1984, Dodd $10.45. The story of the various birds that visit Ellie's house.

1827. Yektai, Niki. *Sun, Rain* (PS). Illus. by Patience Brewster. 1984, Four Winds $11.95. Using only a few words, this picture book explains what happens when it rains.

1828. Zolotow, Charlotte. *One Step, Two . . .* (PS–K). Illus. by Cindy Wheeler. 1981, Lothrop $10.25; LB $9.85. A quiet story in which a young girl enjoys the sights and sounds of spring.

1829. Zolotow, Charlotte. *The Song* (PS–2). Illus. by Nancy Tafuri. 1982, Greenwillow $11.25; LB $11.88. Susan has a song inside her that changes with the seasons.

1830. Zolotow, Charlotte. *Summer Is . . .* (PS–2). Illus. by Ruth Bornstein. 1983, Harper $9.57; LB $9.89. A poetic tribute to the seasons.

Books for Beginning Readers

1831. Alexander, Sue. *More Witch, Goblin and Ghost Stories* (1–3). Illus. by Jeanette Winter. 1978, Pantheon $7.99. Three friends involved in six entertaining stories. Three other titles in the series are: *Witch, Goblin and Sometimes Ghost: Six Read-Aloud Stories* (1976, $5.99); *Witch, Goblin, and Ghost in the Haunted Woods* (1981, $6.95; LB $7.99); *Witch, Goblin, and Ghost's Book of Things to Do* (1982, $6.95; LB $7.99).

1832. Allen, Marjorie N. *One, Two, Three—Ah—Choo!* (1–3). Illus. by Dick Gackenbach. 1980, Putnam LB $6.99. Wally's allergies forbid a furry pet, so he tries alternatives.

1833. Arnold, Caroline. *The Biggest Living Thing* (1–3). Illus. by author. 1983, Carolrhoda $6.95. An introduction to California's sequoia tree.

1834. Arnold, Caroline. *My Friend from Outer Space* (1–4). Illus. by Carol Nicklaus. 1981, Watts $7.90. Sherry claims she is from outer space and takes her friend on a rocket ship ride.

1835. Averill, Esther. *Captains of the City Streets: A Story of the Cat Club* (1–3). Illus. by author. 1972, Harper $8.89. Two young tramp cats, in spite of their avowed independence, are gradually drawn into the Cat Club. Three other titles by the same author and publisher are: *Jenny's Birthday Book* (1954, $10.89); *The Fire Cat* (1960, $8.89; paper $2.84); *The Hotel Cat* (n.d., paper $2.95).

1836. Ayer, Jacqueline. *Nu Dang and His Kite* (1–4). 1975, Harcourt paper $1.25. A small Thai boy searches for his kite.

1837. Baker, Betty. *Partners* (1–2). Illus. by Emily McCully. 1978, Greenwillow $8.25; LB $7.92. Three Southwest Indian stories about Coyote and Badger are included in this entertaining beginner's book.

1838. Baker, Betty. *Rat Is Dead and Ant Is Sad: Based on a Pueblo Indian Tale* (K–2). Illus. by Mamoru Funai. 1981, Harper $7.64; LB $8.89. An ant believes that her friend Rat is dead in this Pueblo Indian tale.

1839. Baker, Betty. *The Turkey Girl* (2–4). Illus. by Harold Berson. 1983, Macmillan $8.95. Tally's turkeys fashion a gown for her so she can attend a ball.

1840. Baker, Betty. *Worthington Botts and the Steam Machine* (K–3). Illus. by Sal Murdocca. 1981, Macmillan LB $7.95. Worthington Botts wants a machine to do all his chores so he can read.

1841. Bang, Molly, adapt. *Tye May and the Magic Brush* (1–4). Illus. by adapt. 1981, Greenwillow $8.25; LB $7.92. A poor orphan does battle with an evil emperor.

1842. Benchley, Nathaniel. *Feldman Fieldmouse: A Fable* (2–4). Illus. by Hilary Knight. 1970, Harper $10.89; paper $2.95. Beginning readers will enjoy this tale of an orphaned mouse who is rescued by a boy who understands mice.

1843. Benchley, Nathaniel. *A Ghost Named Fred* (1–3). Illus. by Ben Shecter. 1968, Harper LB $8.89; paper $2.95. To get out of the rain, George enters an empty house and meets Fred, an absent-minded ghost.

1844. Benchley, Nathaniel. *Oscar Otter* (K–2). Illus. by Arnold Lobel. 1966, Harper $8.89; paper $2.95. Hilarious words and pictures describe Oscar's fun on the long and perilous slide he builds to get to his pool.

1845. Benchley, Nathaniel. *Red Fox and His Canoe* (1–2). Illus. by Arnold Lobel. 1964, Harper $8.89. Red Fox gets himself a large canoe and picks up so many unusual passengers that it capsizes. Also from the same author and publisher: *The Strange Disappearance of Arthur Cluck* (1967, LB $8.89; paper $2.95).

1846. Benchley, Nathaniel. *The Several Tricks of Edgar Dolphin* (1–2). Illus. by Mamoru Funai. 1970, Harper LB $8.89. When Edgar is captured, he entertains humans with his tricks.

1847. Berenstain, Stanley, and Berenstain, Janice. *Bears in the Night* (1–2). Illus. by author. 1971, Random $4.95; LB $5.99. Bear cubs go on a rampage after being put to bed. The lively cartoon style and simple phrases make this a good book for beginning readers. Also from the same authors and publisher: *Bears on Wheels* (1969, LB $5.99); *The Bear's Almanac* (1973, LB $6.99).

1848. Boegehold, Betty. *Pippa Pops Out: Four Read-Aloud/Read Alone Stories* (K–2). Illus. by Cyndy Szekeres. 1979, Knopf $4.95; LB $5.99. A group of stories about an adventurous mouse. Two other titles in the series are: *Pippa Mouse* (1973, LB $5.99; Dell paper $1.95); *Hurray for Pippa* (1980, LB $5.99).

1849. Boegehold, Betty. *Three to Get Ready* (1–2). Illus. by Mary Chalmers. 1965, Harper LB $8.89. Four humorous stories about 3 mischievous kittens and their mother.

1850. Bonsall, Crosby. *And I Mean It, Stanley* (1–2). Illus. by author. 1974, Harper $7.64; LB $8.89. A small girl playing alone with a pile of junk keeps up a monologue with Stanley, who is behind the fence, telling him of the great "thing" she is making.

1851. Bonsall, Crosby. *The Case of the Scaredy Cats* (1–2). Illus. by author. 1971, Harper $7.64; LB $8.89. What do you do when you find a bevy of girls in your secret clubhouse? Four other mysteries by the same author and publisher are: *The Case of the Hungry Stranger* (1963, LB $8.89); *The Case of the Cat's Meow* (1965, LB $8.89; paper $2.84); *The Case of the Dumb Bells* (1966, LB $8.89; paper $2.84); *The Case of the Double Cross* (1980, $8.61; LB $8.89; paper $2.84).

1852. Bonsall, Crosby. *The Day I Had to Play with My Sister* (K–2). Illus. by author. 1972, Harper $6.76; LB $8.89. An older brother impatiently tries to teach his little sister how to play hide-and-seek, but she can't seem to get the idea of the game.

1853. Bonsall, Crosby. *Mine's the Best* (1–2). Illus. by author. 1973, Harper LB $8.89. Two small boys discover they have identical balloons, and then begins the argument—whose is the best?

1854. Bonsall, Crosby. *Piggle* (1–2). Illus. by author. 1973, Harper $7.64; LB $8.89. Homer goes in search of someone to play games with and finds Bear, who enjoys "Piggle" with him. This rhyming spree of nonsense words will please beginning readers.

1855. Bonsall, Crosby. *Tell Me Some More* (1–3). Illus. by Fritz Siebel. 1961, Harper $8.89. Andrew introduces his friend to the magic of the library.

1856. Bonsall, Crosby. *What Spot?* (1–2). Illus. by author. 1963, Harper LB $8.89; paper $2.95. Puffin says there is nothing in the snow, but walrus thinks otherwise.

1857. Bonsall, Crosby. *Who's a Pest?* (1–3). Illus. by author. 1962, Harper $8.89. Even though his 4 sisters, a lizard, a rabbit, and a chipmunk insist that he's a pest, Homer refuses to believe it.

1858. Boyd, Selma, and Boyd, Pauline. *Footprints in the Refrigerator* (K–2). Illus. by Carol Nicklaus. 1982, Watts $3.95; LB $8.60. Whose footprints appear mysteriously in the refrigerator?

1859. Bram, Elizabeth. *Woodruff and the Clocks* (K–2). Illus. 1980, Dial $5.89; paper $1.95. The story of a boy who enjoys inventing adventures.

1860. Brandenberg, Franz. *Everyone Ready?* (2–3). Illus. by Aliki. 1979, Greenwillow $5.95; LB $5.71. The Fieldmouse children are on a train without their parents. Four related works by the author are: *What Can You Make of It?* (1977); *A Picnic, Hurrah!* (1978); *Six New Students* (1978); *It's Not My Fault* (1980) (all Greenwillow $8.25; LB $7.92).

1861. Brandenberg, Franz. *Leo and Emily* (K–2). Illus. by Aliki. 1981, Greenwillow $8.25; LB $7.92. The friendship between two neighboring children, Leo and Emily. Sequels are: *Leo and Emily's Big Ideas* (1982, $8.50; LB $8.88); *Leo and Emily and the Dragon* (1984, $8.25; LB $7.92).

1862. Brenner, Barbara. *Wagon Wheels* (1–3). Illus. by Don Bolognese. 1978, Harper $8.61; LB $8.99; paper $2.95. The adventures of a black family in Kansas in the 1870s.

1863. Bulla, Clyde Robert. *Daniel's Duck* (1–3). Illus. by Joan Sandin. 1979, Harper $7.64; LB $8.89. In this story for beginning readers, a young boy is hurt when people make fun of his wood carving of a duck.

1864. Bulla, Clyde Robert. *Poor Boy, Rich Boy* (1–3). Illus. by Marcia Sewall. 1982, Harper $8.64; LB $8.89. An orphan boy is found by a rich uncle.

1865. Bunting, Eve. *The Robot Birthday* (2–4). Illus. by Marie DeJohn. 1980, Dutton $7.95. A robot helps ease the problems of twins Pam and Kerry.

1866. Carrick, Carol. *The Empty Squirrel* (1–3). Illus. by Donald Carrick. 1981, Greenwillow $8.25; LB $7.95. A series of simple stories about a boy and his various pets.

1867. Carrick, Carol. *The Longest Float in the Parade* (1–3). Illus. by Donald Carrick. 1982, Greenwillow $8.50; LB $8.98. Floats are being prepared at camp Hi-Ya-Watha for the big parade.

1868. Carrick, Malcolm. *Mr. Tod's Trap* (1–3). Illus. by author. 1980, Harper LB $8.89. A male chauvinist fox trades places with his wife.

1869. Cauley, Lorinda Bryan. *The New House* (2–5). Illus. by author. 1981, Harcourt paper $3.50. A woodchuck family proposes to move to a new house.

1870. Chapman, Carol. *Ig Lives in a Cave* (1–2). Illus. by Bruce Degen. 1979, Dutton $7.95. A young boy growing up in prehistoric times has problems not too different from those of today's children.

1871. Child Study Association, comp. *Read to Me Storybook* (K–2). Illus. by Lois Lenski. 1947, Harper $9.57. A delightful assortment of easy-to-read stories and poems. Also found in: *Read to Me Again* (PS–3), illus. by Garry Mackenzie (1961, $9.57).

1872. Christian, Mary Blount. *April Fool* (1–3). Illus. by Diane Dawson. 1982, Macmillan $8.95. The inhabitants of a medieval town fear the visit of a king.

1873. Christian, Mary Blount. *The Lucky Man* (1–3). Illus. by Glen Rounds. 1979, Macmillan $7.95. A hard-luck hillbilly finally gets the law on his side.

1874. Christian, Mary Blount. *Two-Ton Secret* (2–4). Illus. by Don Madden. 1981, Whitman LB $7.75. Bulldozers are disappearing mysteriously in this easily read book.

1875. Coerr, Eleanor. *The Bell Ringer and the Pirates* (1–3). Illus. by Joan Sandin. 1983, Harper $7.65; LB $8.89. Pio helps save a California mission from pirates and is rewarded by becoming a bell ringer.

1876. Coerr, Eleanor. *The Big Balloon Race* (1–3). Illus. by Carolyn Croll. 1981, Harper $7.64; LB $8.89; paper $2.84. Arill and her mother fly their balloon in a suspenseful race.

1877. Cohen, Miriam. *When Will I Read?* (1–2). Illus. by Lillian Hoban. 1977, Greenwillow $11.25. Jim, a first grader, experiences the joys of learning to read.

1878. Collins, David. *The One Bad Thing about Birthdays* (PS–3). Illus. by David Wiesner. 1981, Harcourt $6.95; paper $2.95. A problem is what to wish for when blowing out the candles on the birthday cake.

1879. Croll, Carolyn. *Too Many Babas* (1–3). Illus. 1979, Harper LB $8.89. Too many cooks spoil the meal in this simple narrative.

1880. Dauer, Rosamond. *Bullfrog Grows Up* (1–4). Illus. by Byron Barton. 1976, Greenwillow $7.92. An easily read story about a frog that 2 mice bring home from a pond.

1881. Degen, Bruce. *The Little Witch and the Riddle* (1–3). Illus. 1980, Harper LB $8.89. Little Lily attempts to solve a riddle to open her grandmother's book of spells.

1882. Delton, Judy. *Brimhall Turns Detective* (1–3). Illus. by Cherie R. Wyman. 1983, Carolrhoda $6.95. Brimhall investigates giant footsteps in the snow.

1883. Delton, Judy. *The Goose Who Wrote a Book* (1–3). Illus. by Catherine Cleary. 1982, Carolrhoda LB $7.95. A goose tries her hand at becoming an author.

1884. Dorros, Arthur. *Pretzels* (1–3). Illus. by author. 1981, Greenwillow $8.50; LB $8.88. Three humorous stories about crew members of the sailing ship, *Bungle*.

1885. Eastman, Patricia. *Sometimes Things Change* (K–1). Illus. by Seymour Fleishman. 1983, Childrens Pr. $6.50. A story on how things in nature change.

1886. Ehrlich, Amy. *Leo, Zack, and Emmie* (1–3). Illus. by Steven Kellogg. 1981, Dial LB $8.89; paper $2.95. An easily read story of the friendship shared by three people.

1887. Farley, Walter. *Little Black, a Pony* (1–3). Illus. by James Schucker. 1961, Random LB $5.99. The story of a boy and a pony who wishes it were big.

1888. Feder, Paula Kurzband. *Where Does the Teacher Live?* (1–2). Illus. by Lillian Hoban. 1979, Dutton $7.95. Three young people try to find out where their teacher lives.

1889. Finsand, Mary Jane. *The Town That Moved* (1–3). Illus. by Reg Sandland. 1983, Carolrhoda $6.95. The true story of a Minnesota town that moved so that mining in the area could continue.

1890. Firmin, Peter. *Basil Brush Goes Flying* (1–3). Illus. by author. 1977, Prentice paper $3.95. An intrepid fox tries several methods in his unsuccessful attempt at flying. Two sequels are: *Basil Brush and the Windmills*; *Basil Brush on the Trail* (both 1980, $7.95).

1891. Freedman, Russell. *When Winter Comes* (K–3). Illus. by Pamela Johnson. 1981, Dutton $8.25. An easily read book that describes the dangers winter brings.

1892. Freschet, Berniece. *Moose Baby* (1–2). Illus. by Jim Arnosky. 1979, Putnam $6.99. Simple text and appropriate pictures enhance 4 short stories about the first experiences of a moose child.

1893. Freschet, Berniece. *Wood Duck Baby* (1–3). Illus. by Jim Arnosky. 1983, Putnam $6.99. A young wood duck is separated from his family for a day.

1894. Gackenbach, Dick. *Hattie Be Quiet, Hattie Be Good* (1–3). Illus. 1977, Harper $7.64; LB $8.89. In the first of the stories, Hattie Rabbit valiantly tries to be quiet for an hour; in the second, she visits a sick friend.

1895. Gackenbach, Dick. *More from Hound and Bear* (1–3). Illus. by author. 1979, Houghton $7.95. Three humorous stories that continue the adventures begun in *Hound and Bear* (1976, $7.95).

1896. Gage, Wilson. *The Crow and Mrs. Gaddy* (1–3). Illus. by Marylin Hafner. 1984, Greenwillow $8.25; LB $7.92. A farmer named Mrs. Gaddy and a crow try to outdo one another with their dirty tricks.

1897. Gage, Wilson. *Squash Pie* (1–3). Illus. by Glen Rounds. 1976, Greenwillow LB $7.92. A mystery: Who is stealing the squash crop? The solution: Who hates squash pie?

1898. Giff, Patricia Reilly. *The Beast in Ms. Rooney's Room* (2–4). 1984, Dell paper $2.25. A volume in the Kids of the Polk Street School series. Another title is: *Fish Face* (1984, paper $2.25).

1899. Gilchrist, Theo E. *Halfway Up the Mountain* (1–3). Illus. by Glen Rounds. 1978, Harper $8.89. An old man and a half-blind woman drive off a bandit.

1900. Greene, Carol. *Hi, Clouds* (K–2). Illus. by Gene Sharp. 1983, Childrens Pr. $6.50. Two children see many objects in clouds in this easy-to-read book. Two others in this series are: *Ice Is . . . Whee!; Shine, Sun!* (both 1983, $6.50). Also use: *Wait, Skates!* by Mildred D. Johnson, illus. by Tom Dunnington (1983, Childrens Pr. $6.50).

1901. Griffith, Helen V. *Alex and the Cat* (K–3). Illus. by Joseph Low. 1982, Greenwillow $8.50; LB $8.88. Alex, a dog, tries to be many other things before he settles for being himself. A sequel is: *More Alex and the Cat* (1983, $9.00; LB $8.59).

1902. Guilfoile, Elizabeth. *Nobody Listens to Andrew* (1–3). Illus. by Mary Stevens. 1957, Scholastic paper $1.50. The reaction of Andrew's elders when he tells them there is a bear in his bed.

1903. Hancock, Sibyl. *Old Blue* (1–3). Illus. by Erick Ingraham. 1980, Putnam LB $6.99. An easily read story about a boy's first trail drive and the lead steer, Old Blue.

1904. Harper, Anita. *How We Work* (1–3). Illus. by Christine Roche. 1977, Harper LB $8.89. Comic-strip type illustrations portray various ways and conditions of human work.

1905. Heilbroner, Joan. *This Is the House Where Jack Lives* (1–2). Illus. by Aliki. 1962, Harper $8.89. The house is involved in a chain of amusing events. Also use: *The Happy Birthday Present* (1961, Harper $8.89).

1906. Heilbroner, Joan. *Tom the TV Cat* (1–2). Illus. by Sal Murdocca. 1984, Random $5.99; paper $2.95. Tom wants to do all the things he sees on TV.

1907. Hill, Eric. *Spot Goes to School* (PS). 1984, Putnam $9.95. A book that tells the story of a young dog. Two others in this series are: *Spot's Birthday Party; Spot's First Walk* (both 1982, $9.95).

1908. Hoban, Lillian. *Arthur's Honey Bear* (1–3). Illus. by author. 1974, Harper $7.64; LB $8.89; paper $2.84. Arthur, a chimp, decides to sell all his old toys except his bear, but his sisters bribe him into parting with Honey Bear. Two others in the series are: *Arthur's Pen Pal* (1976); *Arthur's Prize Reader* (1978) (both $8.61; LB $8.89; paper $2.84).

1909. Hoban, Lillian. *Mr. Pig and Sonny Too* (1–3). Illus. by author. 1977, Harper $7.64; LB $8.89. A dutiful son helps his father in this slapstick delight. Also use: *Mr. Pig and Family* (1980, $7.64; LB $8.89).

1910. Hoban, Lillian. *Ready, Set, Robot!* (2–3). Illus. by author. 1982, Harper $8.61; LB $8.89. A robot, Sol-1, competes in a space race. A sequel is: *The Laziest Robot in Zone One* (1983, $7.64; LB $8.89).

1911. Hoban, Lillian. *Stick-in-the-Mud Turtle* (2–4). Illus. by author. 1977, Greenwillow $8.25. Fred's family wants to keep up with the Joneses when a new turtle family moves next door and fixes up their mudhole.

1912. Hoban, Russell. *Arthur's New Power* (2–3). Illus. by Byron Barton. 1978, Harper $10.53; LB $10.89; Dell paper $1.50. The lovable chimp faces a situation when father states there is to be no more electricity in the house. A sequel is: *Arthur's Funny Money* by Lillian Hoban (1981, Harper $8.61; LB $8.89; paper $2.84).

1913. Hoban, Russell. *Bedtime for Frances* (1–2). Illus. by Garth Williams. 1960, Harper $9.57; LB $9.89; paper $2.95. Frances, a badger, tries every familiar trick to tease her way past bedtime. Others in the series: *Bread and Jam for Frances* (1964, $9.57; LB $9.89); *Bargain for Frances* (1970, $8.67; LB $8.89; paper $2.95).

1914. Hoban, Russell. *Best Friends for Frances* (1–2). Illus. by Lillian Hoban. 1969, Harper $9.57; LB $9.89; paper $2.95. When friend Albert decides that he must exclude girls from his "wondering day" and baseball game, Frances chooses younger sister Gloria as a companion. Also use: *A Baby Sister for Frances* (1964, Harper $9.57; LB $9.89; paper $2.95).

1915. Hoban, Russell. *Tom and the Two Handles* (K–3). Illus. by author. 1965, Harper LB $8.89; paper $2.40. Tom gets some helpful advice when he loses 4 fistfights in a row.

1916. Hoff, Syd. *Albert the Albatross* (1–2). Illus. by author. 1961, Harper LB $8.89. A seabird's unsuccessful search for the ocean is rewarded by accompanying a lady who is going on an ocean trip.

1917. Hoff, Syd. *Barkley* (1–3). Illus. by author. 1975, Harper LB $8.89. An easily read story about a forcibly retired, aging circus dog.

1918. Hoff, Syd. *Danny and the Dinosaur* (K–2). Illus. by author. 1958, Harper $7.64; LB $8.89; paper $2.95. Danny wanted to play and so did the dinosaur. What could have been more natural than for them to leave the museum together? Also from the same author and publisher: *Sammy the Seal* (1959, LB $8.89); *Oliver* (1960, $8.89).

1919. Hoff, Syd. *Grizzwold* (1–2). Illus. by author. 1963, Harper $8.89; paper $2.95. After foresters have destroyed his home, a bear sets out to find a new one.

1920. Hoff, Syd. *Happy Birthday, Henrietta!* (1–3). Illus. 1983, Garrard $6.69. Henrietta is delighted by her surprise birthday party.

1921. Hoff, Syd. *The Man Who Loved Animals* (1–4). Illus. by author. 1982, Putnam $6.99. The story of the man who founded the ASPCA, Henry Bergh.

1922. Hoff, Syd. *Soft Skull Sam* (1–3). Illus. by author. 1981, Harcourt paper $2.95. A boy loves to play soccer but is afraid of a head shot.

1923. Hoff, Syd. *Stanley* (1–3). Illus. by author. 1962, Harper $8.89; paper $2.95. A caveman finds a new home in this inventive tale.

1924. Holland, Marion. *A Big Ball of String* (1–3). Illus. by author. 1958, Beginner Books $5.99. A child dreams of what he would do with a ball of string and then receives one.

1925. Hurd, Edith Thacher. *Come and Have Fun* (1–2). Illus. by Clement Hurd. 1962, Harper $8.89. A mouse refuses the cat's invitation to join him in a series of activities.

1926. Hurd, Edith Thacher. *Johnny Lion's Rubber Boots* (1–2). Illus. by Clement Hurd. 1972, Harper $8.89. A lion cub tries to amuse himself indoors on a rainy day. Others in the series: *Johnny Lion's Book* (1965); *Johnny Lion's Bad Day* (1970) (both $8.89).

1927. Hurd, Edith Thacher. *Last One Home Is a Green Pig* (PS–2). Illus. by Clement Hurd. 1959, Harper $8.89. A lively race between a duck and a monkey. Also use: *Stop, Stop* (1961, Harper $7.64).

1928. Hutchins, Pat. *The Best Train Set Ever* (K–2). Illus. by author. 1978, Greenwillow $8.25; LB $7.92. Three stories that deal with various crises surrounding celebrations.

1929. Hutchins, Pat. *The Tale of Thomas Mead* (1–3). Illus. by author. 1980, Greenwillow $8.25; LB $7.92. Thomas learns to read and suddenly becomes a bookworm.

1930. Jacobs, Francine. *Supersaurus* (1–3). Illus. by D. D. Tyler. 1982, Putnam LB $6.99. The true story of the discovery of bones from a giant dinosaur.

1931. Johnson, Crockett. *Harold and the Purple Crayon* (K–2). Illus. by author. 1955, Harper $8.61; LB $8.89; paper $2.95. A little boy draws all of the things necessary for him to go for a walk. Three sequels are: *Harold's Circus* (n.d.); *Harold's Trip to the Sky* (1957); *A Picture for Harold's Room* (1960) (all LB $9.89; paper $1.95).

1932. Johnston, Tony. *Odd Jobs and Friends* (1–3). Illus. by Tomie de Paola. 1982, Putnam $6.99. Three stories about a boy named Odd Jobs and the tasks he performs.

1933. Keller, Beverly. *When Mother Got the Flu* (1–3). Illus. by Maxie Chambliss. 1984, Putnam $6.99. A young boy tries to play quietly so he won't disturb his mother.

1934. Kennedy, Richard. *The Mouse God* (2–4). Illus. by Stephen Harvard. 1979, Little $6.95. Mice build a church out of a crate at the advice of their mouse god, the cat in disguise.

1935. Kent, Jack. *The Biggest Shadow in the Zoo* (PS–2). Illus. by author. 1981, Parents $5.50; LB $5.95. Goober the elephant loses his shadow.

1936. Kent, Jack. *Hoddy Doddy* (2–3). Illus. by author. 1979, Greenwillow $8.25; LB $7.92. Three cheerful Danish tales about hoddy doddies, or very foolish people.

1937. Kessler, Ethel, and Kessler, Leonard. *Pig's New Hat* (K–2). Illus. by Pat Paris. 1981, Garrard LB $7.47. Pig's desire to decorate her new hat with flowers gets her into trouble. Also use: *Pig's Orange House* (1981, LB $7.47).

1938. Kessler, Leonard. *Here Comes the Strike-Out* (1–2). Illus. by author. 1965, Harper $8.61; LB $8.89; paper $2.95. Bobby always strikes out at bat until his friend Willie helps him to improve his game. Two other sports stories by the same author and publisher are: *Kick, Pass and Run* (1966, $8.61; LB $8.89; paper $2.45); *Last One in Is a Rotten Egg* (1969, LB $8.89).

1939. Kessler, Leonard. *Hey Diddle Diddle* (1–3). Illus. by author. 1980, Garrard LB $7.12. A dozen takeoffs on the old nursery rhyme.

1940. Kessler, Leonard. *Old Turtle's Baseball Stories* (1–3). Illus. by author. 1982, Greenwillow $8.50; LB $8.88. Imaginative stories about some animal greats in baseball. Two other titles by the same author and publisher are: *Super Bowl* (1980, $8.50; LB $8.88); *Old Turtle's Winter Games* (1983, $7.00; LB $6.67).

1941. Klein, Monica. *Backyard Basketball Superstar* (1–3). Illus. by Nola Langner. 1981, Pantheon $6.95; LB $7.99. Jeremy is upset when his sister tries out for his basketball team.

1942. Krasilovsky, Phyllis. *The Man Who Entered a Contest* (1–3). Illus. by Yuri Salzman. 1980, Doubleday LB $6.95. A man enters a baking contest to win a new oven.

1943. Kwitz, Mary DeBall. *Little Chick's Big Day* (K–2). Illus. by Bruce Degen. 1981, Harper $7.64; LB $8.89. Little Chick runs away because she thinks she is too big to take a nap.

1944. Landshoff, Ursula. *Okay, Good Dog* (1–3). Illus. by author. 1978, Harper $7.64; LB $8.89. An introduction to the principles of successful dog training, simply told. A companion volume is: *Cats Are Good Company* (1983, $7.64; LB $8.89).

1945. Lapp, Eleanor J. *The Mice Came In Early This Year* (1–2). Illus. by David Cunningham. 1976, Whitman $7.75. When mice come in early, it means winter is near.

1946. Lawrence, James. *Binky Brothers, Detectives* (1–2). Illus. by Leonard Kessler. 1968, Harper $8.89; paper $2.95. Dinky is younger brother to Pinky with the status of "helper" in their Binky Brothers Detective Agency, until he solves the case of the missing catcher's mitt and becomes a full partner. Also use: *Binky Brothers and the Fearless Four* (1970, Harper LB $8.89).

1947. Le Sieg, Theo. *Ten Apples Up on Top* (K–2). Illus. 1961, Random $4.95; LB $5.99. Three bears try to pile apples on their heads in this nonsense story. Also from the same author and publisher: *I Wish That I Had Duck Feet* (1965); *Eye Book* (1968) (both $4.95; LB $5.99).

1948. Lewis, Thomas P. *Call for Mr. Sniff* (1–3). Illus. by Beth Weiner Woldin. 1981, Harper $7.64; LB $8.89. A hound becomes a super sleuth. A sequel is: *Mr. Sniff and the Motel Mystery* (1984, $8.61; LB $8.89).

1949. Lexau, Joan M. *Come! Sit! Stay!* (K–2). Illus. by Marsha Winborn. 1984, Watts $8.90. The training of a big dog by his young master.

1950. Lexau, Joan M. *I Hate Red Rover* (1–3). Illus. by Gail Owens. 1979, Dutton $7.95. Jill hates the ridicule when she fails in the game of red rover.

1951. Lexau, Joan M. *Miss Happ in the Poison Ivy Case* (1–2). Illus. by Marylin Hafner. 1984, Dial $8.89; paper $3.83. How did Tilly get poison ivy if she wasn't outdoors?

1952. Lexau, Joan M. *The Rooftop Mystery* (1–2). Illus. by Syd Hoff. 1968, Harper $8.89. Trying desperately to avoid transporting sister's doll on moving day, Sam and Albert lose it instead, and in the end prove their worth as junior detectives.

1953. Lobel, Arnold. *Frog and Toad Are Friends* (K–2). Illus. by author. 1970, Harper $7.64; LB $8.89; paper $2.95. Two new friends for the independent reader. Three sequels are: *Frog and Toad Together* (1972, $7.64; LB $8.89; paper $2.95); *Frog and Toad All Year* (1976); *Days with Frog and Toad* (1979) (both $7.64; LB $8.89).

1954. Lobel, Arnold. *Grasshopper on the Road* (1–2). Illus. by author. 1978, Harper $7.64; LB $8.89. A series of short stories, each with a vital message.

1955. Lobel, Arnold. *How the Rooster Saved the Day* (K–2). Illus. by Anita Lobel. 1977, Greenwillow $11.25; paper $2.95. A smart rooster outwits a thief with a series of clever ruses.

1956. Lobel, Arnold. *Mouse Soup* (1–2). Illus. by author. 1977, Harper $8.61; LB $8.89; paper $2.84. When mouse is caught by weasel, who plans to use him for soup, he convinces his captor that "mouse soup must be mixed with stones to make it taste really good."

1957. Lobel, Arnold. *Mouse Tales* (1–2). Illus. by author. 1972, Harper $8.61; LB $8.89; paper $2.95. Seven bedtime stories told by papa mouse to his 7 sons. Lively little drawings add to the humor.

1958. Lobel, Arnold. *Owl at Home* (1–2). Illus. by author. 1975, Harper $7.64; LB $8.89; paper $2.84. Five stories dealing with the humorous and bungling attempts of Owl to be helpful.

1959. Lobel, Arnold. *Small Pig* (K–2). Illus. by author. 1969, Harper $8.89. A dirty little pig in a search for mud ends up in cement.

1960. Lobel, Arnold. *Uncle Elephant* (K–3). Illus. by author. 1981, Harper $8.61; LB $8.89. A nephew and uncle elephant form a friendship.

1961. Lopshire, Robert. *Put Me in the Zoo* (1–3). Illus. by author. 1960, Beginner Books $4.95; LB $4.99. An unusual dog thinks he should be in the zoo, but his talents really mean he should be in a circus.

1962. Low, Joseph. *Benny Rabbit and the Owl* (K–2). Illus. by author. 1978, Greenwillow $8.25; LB $7.92. Benny insists there is an owl in his closet.

1963. Luttrell, Ida. *One Day at School* (2–3). Illus. by Jared D. Lee. 1984, Harcourt $9.95; paper $4.95. Arnold becomes the teacher, and all the teachers are his pupils.

1964. McClintock, Mike. *A Fly Went By* (1–3). Illus. by Fritz Siebel. 1958, Random $4.95; LB $5.99. A cumulative tale about a merry chase started by a fly and involving a cat, dog, sheep, and other animals. Also use: *Stop That Ball!* (1958, Random LB $5.99); *What Have I Got?* (1961, Harper $8.89).

1965. McGuire, Leslie. *This Farm Is a Mess* (1–3). Illus. by author. 1981, Parents $5.50; LB $5.95. The animals take over and clean up Farmer Wood's very messy farm.

1966. McPhail, David. *Snow Lion* (PS–2). Illus. 1983, Dutton $5.50; LB $5.95; paper $1.95. A lion finds it's too hot for him to stay in the jungle.

1967. Margolis, Richard J. *Wish Again Big Bear* (1–4). Illus. by Robert Lopshire. 1974, Macmillan paper $0.95. A variation on the three wishes story involves a bear and a fish. A sequel is: *Big Bear, Spare That Tree* (1980, Greenwillow $8.50; LB $8.88).

1968. Marshall, Edward. *Fox and His Friends* (1–3). Illus. by James Marshall. 1982, Dial LB $7.89; paper $3.25. Fox usually has his sister tagging along but finally gets together alone with his friends. Some sequels are: *Fox in Love* (1982, LB $8.89; paper $3.75); *Fox at School* (1983, $8.89; paper 3.95); *Fox on Wheels* (1983, $8.89; paper $3.95); *Fox All Week* (1984, $8.95; LB $8.89).

1969. Marshall, Edward. *Three by the Sea* (1–3). Illus. by James Marshall. 1981, Dial LB $5.99; paper $2.50. Three friends, Lolly, Spider, and Sam, tell stories by the seashore.

1970. Marshall, Edward. *Troll Country* (1–2). Illus. by James Marshall. 1980, Dial LB $6.89; paper $3.95. Elsie Fay wanders into the woods and outsmarts a troll.

1971. Marzollo, Jean. *Amy Goes Fishing* (1–3). Illus. by Ann Schweninger. 1980, Dial LB $5.89; paper $2.25. A young girl and her father set out to catch a wily catfish, Old Chinny Whiskers.

1972. Marzollo, Jean, and Marzollo, Claudio. *Jed's Junior Space Patrol* (K–3). Illus. by David S. Rose. 1982, Dial LB $7.89; paper $3.25. In this easily read science fiction adventure, Jed's new teddy bear computer saves the day.

1973. Marzollo, Jean, and Marzollo, Claudio. *Red Sun Girl* (1–3). Illus. by Susan Meddaugh. 1983, Dial $8.89; paper $3.83. During Blue Sun, Kiri's family turns into animals but she remains human. A sequel is: *Blue Sun Ben* (1984, $8.89; paper $3.83).

1974. Marzollo, Jean, and Marzollo, Claudio. *Robin of Bray* (1–3). Illus. by Diane Stanley. 1982, Dial LB $8.89; paper $3.83. Robin must use his magical powers to save a princess from the evil Troll King.

1975. Matthias, Catherine. *I Love Cats* (K–1). Illus. by Tom Dunnington. 1983, Childrens Pr. $6.50. The narrator likes many things but cats are best.

1976. Michel, Anna. *Little Wild Chimpanzee* (1–3). Illus. by Peter Parnall and Virginia Parnall. 1978, Pantheon $6.95; LB $7.99. A description of a chimp growing up in a tropical forest.

1977. Minarik, Else Holmelund. *Little Bear* (K–2). Illus. by Maurice Sendak. 1957, Harper $8.61; LB $8.89; paper $2.95. Humorous adventure stories of Mother Bear and Little Bear. Others in the series: *Little Bear's Friend* (1960); *Little Bear's*

Visit (1961, paper $2.95); *A Kiss for Little Bear* (1968) (all $8.61; LB $8.89).

1978. Minarik, Else Holmelund. *No Fighting, No Biting!* (PS–3). Illus. by Maurice Sendak. 1958, Harper $8.61; LB $8.89; paper $2.95. Light-foot and Quick-foot, 2 little alligators, teach Rosa and Willy a lesson.

1979. Moore, Lilian. *Little Raccoon and the Thing in the Pool* (1–2). Illus. by Gioia Faimmenghi. 1963, McGraw $7.95. Little Raccoon overcomes his fear of the pool and catches crayfish for dinner.

1980. Mooser, Stephen. *Funnyman's First Case* (2–4). Illus. by Tomie de Paola. 1981, Watts $8.60. A robber and a waiter exchange old jokes. A sequel is: *Funnyman and the Penny Dodo* (1984, $8.60).

1981. Myrick, Mildred. *The Secret Three* (1–2). Illus. by Arnold Lobel. 1963, Harper $8.89; paper $2.84. Two boys on the mainland and one on an island lighthouse exchange messages in a bottle carried by the tide.

1982. Neasi, Barbara J. *Just Like Me* (K–1). Illus. by Lois Axeman. 1984, Childrens Pr. $6.50. Twins explore their similarities and differences.

1983. Nodset, Joan I. *Come Here, Cat* (K–3). Illus. by Steven Kellogg. 1973, Harper $9.89. A young girl chases a cat around her house and onto the roof in this simple but enjoyable story.

1984. Nodset, Joan I. *Who Took the Farmer's Hat?* (1–2). Illus. by Fritz Siebel. 1963, Harper $10.89; Scholastic paper $1.95. When the wind blows away the farmer's hat, all of the animals think they saw it.

1985. Numeroff, Laura Joffe. *Beatrice Doesn't Want To* (K–3). Illus. by author. 1981, Watts LB $8.60. Beatrice has no use for libraries until she attends a story hour.

1986. Parish, Peggy. *Amelia Bedelia* (1–3). Illus. by Fritz Siebel. 1963, Harper $8.61; LB $8.89; paper $2.84. The adventures of a literal minded housemaid. Other series titles are: *Thank You, Amelia Bedelia* (1964, Harper $8.61; LB $8.89; paper $2.84); *Amelia Bedelia and the Surprise Shower* (1966, Harper $8.64; LB $8.89; paper $2.95); *Good Work, Amelia Bedelia* (1976, Greenwillow $8.50; LB $8.88; Avon paper $2.25).

1987. Parish, Peggy. *The Cats' Burglar* (1–2). Illus. by Lynn Sweat. 1983, Greenwillow $7.00; LB $6.67. Aunt Emma's 9 cats foil a burglary attempt.

1988. Parish, Peggy. *Mr. Adams's Mistake* (K–3). Illus. by Gail Owens. 1982, Macmillan $8.95. Mr. Adams, a nearsighted truant officer, brings a chimp to Miss Nelson's classroom.

1989. Parish, Peggy. *No More Monsters for Me!* (K–3). Illus. by Marc Simont. 1981, Harper $8.61;

LB $8.89. A young girl wants to keep a monster for a pet.

1990.   Parish, Peggy. *Play Ball, Amelia Bedelia* (1–3). Illus. by Wallace Tripp. 1972, Harper $8.61; LB $8.89; paper $2.95. Amelia Bedelia has trouble with baseball lingo. Other series titles are: *Come Back, Amelia Bedelia* (1970, Harper $8.61; LB $8.89; paper $2.95); *Teach Us, Amelia Bedelia* (1977, Greenwillow $8.50; LB $8.88); *Amelia Bedelia Helps Out* (1979, Greenwillow $8.50; LB $8.88; Avon paper $2.25); *Amelia Bedelia and the Baby* (1981, Greenwillow $8.50; LB $8.88; Avon paper $2.25).

1991.   Parish, Peggy. *Too Many Rabbits* (1–3). Illus. by Leonard Kessler. 1974, Macmillan $6.95; Scholastic paper $1.50. Shortly after Miss Molly takes in a stray rabbit, her house is overrun with rabbits, and she must find a new home for them.

1992.   Pearson, Susan. *Molly Moves Out* (1–3). Illus. by Steven Kellogg. 1979, Dial $5.89; paper $2.25. Molly, a rabbit, moves to her own home for peace and quiet but soon gets lonely.

1993.   Peterson, Jeanne Whitehouse. *That Is That* (2–4). Illus. by Deborah Ray. 1979, Harper LB $9.89. Only time can heal the hurt when a girl's father leaves home.

1994.   Petrie, Catherine. *Joshua James Likes Trucks* (PS–1). Illus. by Jerry Warshaw. 1982, Childrens Pr. LB $8.65; paper $2.50. A description of all the trucks that Joshua likes.

1995.   Platt, Kin. *Big Max* (1–2). Illus. by Robert Lopshire. 1965, Harper $8.89; paper $2.95. A modest detective unravels the case of the king's missing elephant in this Mystery I Can Read book.

1996.   Porte, Barbara Ann. *Harry's Visit* (1–3). Illus. by Yossi Abolafia. 1983, Greenwillow $7.00; LB $6.67. Harry is not looking forward to a visit with the Silversteins. A sequel is: *Harry's Dog* (1984, $8.25; LB $7.92).

1997.   Prager, Annabelle. *The Four Getsys and What They Forgot* (1–4). Illus. by Whitney Darrow, Jr. 1982, Pantheon $6.95; LB $7.99. A hilarious tale about a very absentminded family.

1998.   Prager, Annabelle. *The Surprise Party* (1–3). Illus. by Tomie de Paola. 1977, Pantheon $6.95; LB $7.99; Dell paper $0.95. Nicky plans his own surprise party but receives a real surprise in this easily read picture book.

1999.   Quackenbush, Robert. *No Mouse for Me* (K–3). Illus. by author. 1981, Watts LB $8.60. A boy returning a mouse he has bought starts a frantic chase scene.

2000.   Quin-Harkin, Janet. *Helpful Hattie* (1–3). Illus. by Susanna Natti. 1983, Harcourt $9.95; paper $4.95. Hattie tries to help but never succeeds in these 3 stories.

2001.   Rabinowitz, Sandy. *How I Trained My Colt* (1–4). Illus. by author. 1981, Doubleday $6.95. A little girl shows how she taught her colt, Sunny, various skills.

2002.   Rice, Eve. *Papa's Lemonade and Other Stories* (1–2). Illus. by author. 1976, Greenwillow LB $7.92. Five humorous stories about papa and mama and their 5 children—puppies who seem to be a cross between dogs and bears.

2003.   Richter, Alice, and Numeroff, Laura Joffe. *You Can't Put Braces on Spaces* (2–4). Illus. 1979, Greenwillow $8.25; LB $7.92. A boy has doubts about his looks when he has to wear braces.

2004.   Rockwell, Anne. *The Bump in the Night* (1–3). Illus. by author. 1979, Greenwillow $8.25; LB $7.92. Toby befriends a ghost and uncovers a hidden treasure. Two related titles are: *Walking Shoes* (1980, Doubleday LB $6.95); *Thump Thump Thump!* (1981, Dutton $8.25).

2005.   Rockwell, Anne. *The Gollywhopper Egg* (2–4). Illus. by author. 1974, Macmillan $8.95; paper $2.50. A gullible farmer tries to hatch a coconut, thinking that it is a gollywhopper's egg. Three other titles by the author are: *The Story Snail* (1974, Macmillan $8.95); *Honk Honk!* (1980, Dutton $7.95); *Big Bad Goat* (1982, Dutton $8.95).

2006.   Ross, Pat. *M and M and the Haunted House Game* (K–3). Illus. by Marylin Hafner. 1980, Pantheon $6.95; Dell paper $1.75. Mimi and Mandy frighten themselves with their haunted house games. Also use: *Meet M and M* (1980); *M and M and the Big Bag* (1981); *M and M and the Bad News Babies* (1983) (all $6.95; LB $7.99).

2007.   Ross, Pat. *Molly and the Slow Teeth* (1–3). Illus. by Jerry Milord. 1980, Lothrop $9.95; LB $9.55. Will Molly ever lose her baby teeth?

2008.   Roy, Ron. *Awful Thursday* (1–2). Illus. by Lillian Hoban. 1979, Pantheon $6.95; LB $7.89. Jack is afraid that he has ruined his teacher's tape recorder.

2009.   Ruthstrom, Dorotha. *The Big Kite Contest* (1–3). Illus. by Lillian Hoban. 1980, Pantheon $6.95; LB $7.99. Stephen's kite crashes and so does his hope of winning the kite contest.

2010.   Sadler, Marilyn. *It's Not Easy Being a Bunny* (PS–2). Illus. by Roger Bollen. 1983, Random $4.95; LB $5.99. A young rabbit tries to live with other animals. A sequel is: *The Very Bad Bunny* (1984, $4.95; LB $5.95).

2011.   Schick, Eleanor. *Home Alone* (2–3). Illus. 1980, Dial LB $8.89; paper $3.95. A boy copes with the time between getting out of school and his mother's return from work.

2012. Schick, Eleanor. *Joey on His Own* (K–2). Illus. by author. 1982, Dial LB $7.89. Joey's first trip to the store is frightening but rewarding.

2013. Schick, Eleanor. *Rainy Sunday* (PS–3). Illus. by author. 1981, Dial $5.99; paper $2.50. In this easy-to-read book, Jill finds that a rainy Sunday can be a wonderful time to spend with one's parents.

2014. Schick, Eleanor. *Summer at the Sea* (1–3). Illus. by author. 1979, Greenwillow $8.50; LB $8.88. A series of gentle, simple experiences of a girl during a seaside summer.

2015. Schulman, Janet. *The Big Hello* (1–2). Illus. by Lillian Hoban. 1976, Greenwillow $8.50; LB $8.88; Dell paper $0.95. A good book for independent readers about a small girl who prattles to her doll, her dog, and her mother.

2016. Schulman, Janet. *Jack the Bum and the Haunted House* (1–3). Illus. by James Stevenson. 1977, Greenwillow $8.50; LB $8.88. A hobo goes to live in a haunted house, discovers a jewel thief hiding there, and is rewarded with a steady job in this amiable picture book.

• **2017.** Schwartz, Alvin. *Busy Buzzing Bumblebees and Other Tongue Twisters* (1–4). Illus. by Kathie Abrams. 1982, Harper $8.61; LB $8.89; paper $2.84. An easily read book of tongue twisters. Three other humorous books by the same author and publisher are: *Ten Copycats in a Boat and Other Riddles* (1980, $7.64; LB $8.89); *There Is a Carrot in My Ear and Other Noodle Tales* (1982, $8.61; LB $8.89); *In a Dark, Dark Room and Other Scary Stories* (1984, $7.64; LB $8.89).

2018. Seuling, Barbara. *Just Me* (PS–2). Illus. by author. 1982, Harcourt $8.95; paper $3.95. A little girl imagines that she is a horse, a dragon, and then a robot.

2019. Seuss, Dr. *The Cat in the Hat* (1–3). Illus. by author. 1957, Random $4.95; LB $5.99. The story of the fabulous cat that came to visit one rainy day when Mother was away. Also from the same author and publisher: *The Cat in the Hat Comes Back!* (1958); *Foot Book* (1968) (both $4.95; LB $5.99).

2020. Seuss, Dr. *Green Eggs and Ham* (K–3). Illus. 1960, Random $4.95; LB $5.99. A charming nonsense book.

2021. Seuss, Dr. *Hop on Pop* (1–2). Illus. by author. 1963, Random $4.95; LB $5.99. One of the many entertaining, controlled vocabulary stories of Dr. Seuss. Also use: *One Fish, Two Fish, Red Fish, Blue Fish* (1960); *Fox in Sox* (1965) (both Random $4.95; LB $5.99).

2022. Seuss, Dr. *I Can Lick Thirty Tigers Today and Other Stories* (K–3). Illus. 1969, Random $5.95; paper $2.95. The Cat in the Hat tells 3 zany stories.

2023. Seuss, Dr. *I Can Read with My Eyes Shut!* (1–2). Illus. by author. 1978, Random $4.95; LB $5.99. The Cat in the Hat tells us of all the joys of reading.

2024. Seuss, Dr. *Oh Say Can You Say?* (1–3). Illus. by author. 1979, Random $4.95; LB $5.99. Tongue-twisting verses presented by a variety of imaginative creatures.

2025. Shannon, George. *The Gang and Mrs. Higgins* (PS–2). Illus. by Andrew Vines. 1981, Greenwillow $8.25; LB $7.92. An elderly settler outwits a Wild West gang of thieves.

2026. Sharmat, Marjorie W. *Griselda's New Year* (1–2). Illus. by Normand Chartier. 1979, Macmillan $6.95. Six charming misadventures of a goose named Griselda.

2027. Sharmat, Marjorie W. *Mooch the Messy* (1–2). Illus. by Ben Shecter. 1976, Harper LB $8.89. Mooch the rat lives in his messy rat hole, much to the disgust of his father, who comes to visit and tries to reform him but is successful only temporarily.

2028. Sharmat, Marjorie W. *Nate the Great* (1–3). Illus. by Marc Simont. 1972, Putnam LB $6.99; Dell paper $1.95. Nate, a boy detective, puts on his Sherlock Holmes outfit and sets out confidently to solve the mystery of the missing painting. Other titles in the series: *Nate the Great Goes Undercover* (1974); *Nate the Great and the Lost List* (1975); *Nate the Great and the Phony Clue* (1977); *Nate the Great and the Sticky Case* (1978); *Nate the Great and the Missing Key* (1981); *Nate the Great and the Snowy Trail* (1982) (all LB $6.99; paper $1.95).

2029. Sharmat, Marjorie W. *Sophie and Gussie* (1–3). Illus. by Lillian Hoban. 1973, Macmillan $6.95; paper $1.95. An easily read book about the adventures of 2 squirrels.

2030. Sharmat, Marjorie W. *The Story of Bentley Beaver* (1–3). Illus. 1984, Harper $7.65; LB $5.89. The life story of a beaver from birth to death.

2031. Sharmat, Marjorie W. *The Trolls of Twelfth Street* (1–3). Illus. by Ben Shecter. 1979, Putnam $6.99. A troll family is let loose in Manhattan with amazing results.

2032. Sharmat, Marjorie W. *Two Ghosts on a Bench* (K–2). Illus. by Nola Langner. 1982, Harper $9.57; LB $9.89. Five gentle stories about 2 ghosts who haunt a park bench.

2033. Sharmat, Marjorie W. *Uncle Boris and Maude* (1–2). Illus. by Sammis McLean. 1979, Doubleday LB $6.95. Maude Mole tries to rescue Uncle Boris from his frequent attacks of boredom.

2034. Shecter, Ben. *Hester the Jester* (1–3). Illus. by author. 1977, Harper $7.64; LB $8.89. In this amusing book, Hester causes an uproar when she declares she wants to be a jester like her father.

2035. Shiefman, Vicky. *M Is for Move: A Book of Consonants* (K–1). Illus. 1981, Dutton $8.25. Consonants are shown in 22 words and photographs.

2036. Shub, Elizabeth. *Seeing Is Believing* (1–3). Illus. by Rachel Isadora. 1979, Greenwillow $8.25; LB $7.92. Two folktales about leprechauns and pixies retold simply.

2037. Singer, Bill. *The Fox with Cold Feet* (K–2). Illus. by Dennis Kendrick. 1980, Dutton $5.50; LB $5.95. A fox sets out to get a pair of boots to help cure his cold feet.

2038. Sleator, William. *Once, Said Darlene* (1–3). Illus. by Steven Kellogg. 1979, Dutton $7.95. Darlene tells too many tall tales, and her friends revolt.

2039. Springstubb, Tricia. *My Minnie Is a Jewel* (1–3). Illus. by Jim LaMarche. 1980, Carolrhoda LB $6.95. Henry and Minnie are so compatible that they don't know when each other makes mistakes.

2040. Stadler, John. *Cat at Bat* (1–2). Illus. by author. 1979, Dutton $7.95. Simple rhyming words (cub, tub, scrub, etc.) are cleverly used for humorous effect.

2041. Stevens, Carla. *Pig and the Blue Flag* (1–3). Illus. by R. Bennett. 1977, Houghton $6.95. Pig hates gym and is always chosen last for teams; nevertheless, he unexpectedly gains status as an athlete.

2042. Stevenson, James. *Clams Can't Sing* (K–3). Illus. by author. 1980, Greenwillow $8.50; LB $8.88. A group of clams hold a concert.

2043. Stevenson, James. *Fast Friends: Two Stories* (1–3). Illus. by author. 1979, Greenwillow $8.25; LB $7.92; Scholastic paper $1.95. Two short stories involving friendless turtles.

2044. Stolz, Mary. *Emmet's Pig* (1–3). Illus. by Garth Williams. 1959, Harper $8.89. Although he lives in a city apartment, Emmet's greatest wish is to own his own pig.

2045. Thaler, Mike. *It's Me Hippo!* (1–3). Illus. by Maxie Chambliss. 1983, Harper $7.64; LB $8.89. Four short stories about a friendly hippo.

2046. Van Woerkom, Dorothy O. *Harry and Shellburt* (1–3). Illus. by Erick Ingraham. 1977, Macmillan $6.95. The hare and the tortoise engage

in a rematch, but in spite of fresh twists, the results are the same.

2047. Viorst, Judith. *Alexander, Who Used to Be Rich Last Sunday* (K–2). Illus. by Ray Cruz. 1978, Atheneum $9.95; paper $2.50. Alexander spends his dollar gift foolishly penny by penny.

2048. Wiseman, Bernard. *Morris and Boris* (PS–1). Illus. by author. 1974, Dodd $9.95. Serious Boris, the bear, becomes impatient when he unsuccessfully tries to teach silly Morris, the moose, how to play games. Four others in the series are: *Morris Goes to School* (1970, Harper LB $8.89; paper $2.95); *Morris Has a Cold* (1978, Dodd $9.95); *Morris Tells Boris Mother Moose Stories and Rhymes* (1979, Dodd $6.95); *Morris Has a Birthday Party!* (1983, Little $9.00).

2049. Wolcott, Patty. *Double-Decker, Double-Decker, Double-Decker Bus* (PS–1). Illus. by Bob Barner. 1980, Addison $5.95. A young girl creates a bus out of furniture and everyday objects.

2050. Wyler, Rose, and Ames, Gerald. *Magic Secrets* (1–3). Illus. by Talivaldis Stubis. 1968, Scholastic paper $1.50. Easy tricks for the beginning magician.

2051. Yolen, Jane. *Commander Toad and the Planet of the Grapes* (K–3). Illus. by Bruce Degen. 1982, Putnam LB $6.99; paper $4.95. Commander Toad and the crew of the Star Warts are swallowed by giant grapes. Two other titles in the series are: *Commander Toad in Space* (1980); *Commander Toad and the Big Black Hole* (1983) (both LB $6.99; paper $4.95).

2052. Yolen, Jane. *The Giant's Farm* (1–4). Illus. by Tomie de Paola. 1977, Houghton $6.95. A simple easy-to-read book of 4 stories, each involving the 5 giants who run Fe-Fi-Fo-Farm.

2053. Yolen, Jane. *Mice on Ice* (1–3). Illus. by Lawrence Di Fiori. 1980, Dutton $7.95. Mice foil a kidnapping by Rat King and his henchmen.

2054. Zion, Gene. *Harry and the Lady Next Door* (PS–3). Illus. by Margaret B. Graham. 1960, Harper $7.64; LB $8.89; paper $2.95. Harry, a dog, tries to stop the lady next door from singing. Other titles in the series are: *Harry the Dirty Dog* (1956, $9.57; LB $10.89; paper $2.95); *No Roses for Harry* (1958, $10.53; LB $10.89; paper $2.95); *Harry by the Sea* (1965, $10.10; LB $10.89; paper $2.95).

Fiction

General

2055. Arbuthnot, May H., comp. *The Arbuthnot Anthology of Children's Literature* (4–8). Illus. 1976, Lothrop $29.95. A useful collection of some of the best in children's literature.

2056. Association for Childhood Education International. *And Everywhere, Children!* (4–6). 1979, Greenwillow $12.50. An anthology of excerpts from books set in different lands.

2057. Commager, Henry Steele, ed. *The St. Nicholas Anthology* (4–10). Illus. 1983, Crown $6.98. A collection from the fine old children's magazine.

2058. Meyers, Ruth S. et al. *Embers: Stories for a Changing World* (4–9). Illus. 1983, Feminist Pr. $18.95; paper $8.95. A collection of stories, poems, and illustrations about people who conquered problems.

2059. Waugh, Charles G., and Greenberg, Martin, eds. *The Newbery Award Reader* (6–10). 1984, Harcourt $14.95. Excerpts from the works of 18 Newbery Award winners.

Animal Stories

2060. Adams, Laurie, and Coudert, Allison. *Alice and the Boa Constrictor* (3–5). Illus. by Emily McCully. 1983, Houghton $8.70. A fourth grader is disappointed in her new pet—a boa constrictor.

2061. Adler, Carole S. *The Cat That Was Left Behind* (4–6). 1981, Houghton $8.95. A foster child finds a cat that, like himself, needs care.

2062. Adler, Carole S. *Shelter on Blue Barns Road* (6–8). 1981, Macmillan LB $8.95; paper $1.75. Betsy tries to retrain a vicious Doberman.

2063. Anderson, Clarence W. *A Pony for Linda* (1–3). 1951, Macmillan $8.95. How 7-year-old Linda cares for a horse named Daisy and enters her in a horse show.

2064. Anderson, LaVere. *Balto, Sled Dog of Alaska* (3–5). Illus. by Herman Vestal. 1976, Garrard LB $6.89. Based on fact, this is the story of a heroic sled dog and a race to bring serum to a town in Alaska.

2065. Angell, Judie. *A Home Is to Share . . . and Share . . . and Share . . .* (4–6). 1984, Bradbury $10.95. The Muchmore children decide to help save the local animal shelter.

2066. Bagnold, Enid. *National Velvet* (6–9). Illus. by Paul Brown. 1949, Morrow $12.50; LB $11.96; Pocket paper $2.50. The famous novel about a girl who raced her beloved horse in the Grand National.

2067. Balch, Glenn. *Buck, Wild* (4–6). Illus. by Ruth Sanderson. 1976, Harper $9.57. The life story of a wild mustang in Idaho that would rather face death than live in captivity.

2068. Baudouy, Michel-Aime. *Old One Toe* (5–7). Trans. by Marie Ponsot. Illus. by Johannes Troyer. 1959, Harcourt $6.50. Piet, a clever, marauding old fox, who learns how to observe animal life in the forest, and Commandant, a skillful hunter, are the main characters in this exciting story.

2069. Baylor, Byrd. *Coyote Cry* (3–5). Illus. by Symeon Shimin. 1972, Lothrop $10.80. A young shepherd witnesses a coyote trying to raise a collie pup.

2070. Baylor, Byrd. *Hawk, I'm Your Brother* (3–5). Illus. by Peter Parnall. 1976, Scribners $7.95; paper $2.95. A desert boy captures a young hawk, hoping it will teach him how to fly.

2071. Beatty, Patricia. *The Staffordshire Terror* (4–7). 1979, Morrow $9.75; LB $9.36. Cissie tries to find her lost dog Spook, a Staffordshire terrier.

2072. Benchley, Nathaniel. *Kilroy and the Gull* (5–7). Illus. by John Schoenherr. 1977, Harper LB $9.57; paper $2.95. Kilroy, a young killer whale, escapes from an aquarium with the help of Morris, a seagull.

2073. Berends, Polly. *The Case of the Elevator Duck* (3–5). Illus. by James K. Washburn. 1973, Random $6.99. In spite of the rule that no pets are allowed in his housing development, little Gilbert decides to keep a duck in an elevator.

2074. Brady, Irene. *Doodlebug* (2–5). Illus. by author. 1977, Houghton $8.95. Jennifer heals an injured pony and shapes it into a beautiful animal that pulls a cart as if it were trained to do so.

2075. Bunting, Eve. *Jane Martin, Dog Detective* (2–3). Illus. by Amy Schwartz. 1984, Harcourt $13.95. For 25¢ a day, Jane Martin will solve your pet problem.

2076. Burnford, Sheila. *The Incredible Journey* (6–9). Illus. by Carl Burger. 1961, Bantam paper $2.25. The adventures of a Labrador retriever, a terrier, and a Siamese cat, who journey 250 miles through the Canadian wilderness to return home.

2077. Butterworth, W. E. *A Member of the Family* (6–9). 1982, Four Winds $9.95. A beautiful sheep dog becomes vicious.

2078. Byars, Betsy. *The Midnight Fox* (4–6). Illus. by Ann Grifalconi. 1968, Viking $8.95. When Tom spends 2 months on a farm with his aunt and uncle, he never expects that a black fox will become the focus of his life.

2079. Callen, Larry. *Pinch* (5–7). Illus. by Marvin Friedman. 1976, Little $8.95. Training hunting pigs in rural Louisiana is the theme of this amusing story of a boy and his pig, Homer.

2080. Campbell, Barbara. *A Girl Called Bob and a Horse Called Yoki* (3–6). 1982, Dial $11.95; LB $11.89. A black child's efforts to save a horse slated for destruction.

2081. Carner, Charles. *Tawny* (5–7). Illus. by Donald Carrick. 1978, Macmillan $10.95. A 12-year-old boy adjusts to the death of his twin brother through the love of a doe.

2082. Carris, Joan. *Pets, Vets, and Marty Howard* (5–7). 1984, Harper $11.06; LB $10.89. A young boy takes a job in a veterinary clinic.

2083. Carroll, Jeffrey. *Climbing to the Sun* (6–8). 1977, Houghton $6.95. After being swept into a valley, 3 mountain goats journey back to their mountain home.

2084. Chambers, John W. *Fritzi's Winter* (4–6). Illus. by Carole Kowalchuk Odell. 1979, Atheneum $9.95. A Siamese cat fends for herself on Fire Island when her owners leave her behind.

2085. Cohen, Peter Z. *Bee* (3–5). Illus. by Richard Cuffari. 1975, Atheneum LB $6.95. A young boy helps to train a horse and catch a gang of cattle rustlers in this story set in Wyoming.

2086. Cohen, Peter Z. *Calm Horse, Wild Night* (6–8). 1982, Atheneum $10.95. Arley sets out to find his horse who has been kidnapped.

2087. Cohen, Peter Z. *Deadly Game at Stony Creek* (5–7). Illus. by Michael Dease. 1978, Dial $6.95. Cliff is forced to join a hunt for wild dogs that terrorize the countryside.

2088. Cone, Molly. *Mishmash* (3–5). Illus. by Leonard Shortall. 1962, Houghton $10.95; Pocket paper $1.75. A dog, Mishmash, moves in, takes over, and then helps his owner to adjust to a new home. Other series titles: *Mishmash and the Substitute Teacher* (1963, $10.95; Pocket paper $1.95); *Mishmash and the Sauerkraut Mystery* (1965, $8.95; paper $0.95; Pocket paper $1.75); *Mishmash and the Venus Flytrap* (1976, $6.95; Pocket paper $1.75); *Mishmash and the Robot* (1981, $7.95; Pocket paper $1.75); *Mishmash and Uncle Looey* (1979, Pocket paper $1.75); *Mishmash and the Big Fat Problem* (1982, $8.95; Pocket paper $1.95).

2089. Corcoran, Barbara. *Me and You and a Dog Named Blue* (6–8). 1979, Atheneum $8.95. An older woman tries to dominate 15-year-old Maggie.

2090. Corcoran, Barbara. *Sasha, My Friend* (5–9). Illus. by Richard L. Shell. 1973, Atheneum paper $0.95. From Los Angeles to a remote Montana tree farm is a difficult adjustment for a young girl.

2091. Davis, Gibbs. *Fishman and Charly* (6–8). 1983, Houghton $8.70. A lonely boy finds an animal friend in a manatee named Pie.

2092. DeJong, Meindert. *The Almost All-White Rabbity Cat* (3–6). Illus. by Herman Vestal. 1972, Macmillan $8.95. A young boy's boredom is lifted when he meets an apartment house cat.

2093. DeJong, Meindert. *Along Came a Dog* (4–7). Illus. by Maurice Sendak. 1958, Harper $10.89; paper $1.95. The friendship of a timid, lonely dog and a toeless little red hen is the basis for a very moving story, full of suspense.

2094. DeJong, Meindert. *Hurry Home, Candy* (4–6). 1953, Harper LB $10.89; paper $2.95. Candy is a little dog who, after many adventures, finds a home.

2095. DeJong, Meindert. *The Singing Hill* (3–5). Illus. by Maurice Sendak. 1962, Harper $10.89. A small boy gains self-confidence through his love for an old horse.

2096. Denzel, Justin F. *Snowfoot: White Reindeer of the Arctic* (3–5). Illus. by Taylor Oughton. 1976, Garrard $6.89. A Lapp boy assumes the responsibility for raising a wounded white fawn.

2097. de Trevino, Elizabeth. *Nacar, the White Deer* (5–7). Illus. by Enrico Arno. 1963, Farrar $3.95. Lalo, a mute herder, nurses a sickly white deer until the inevitable parting causes a crisis.

2098. Dixon, Paige. *Summer of the White Goat* (5–7). Illus. by Grambs Miller. 1977, Atheneum $5.95. Gordon spends a summer in Glacier National Park observing the mountain goats that live on the high slopes.

2099. Dolan, Sheila. *The Wishing Bottle* (4–5). Illus. by Leslie Morrill. 1979, Houghton $7.95. A girl gets part of her wish and has partial ownership of a pony.

2100. Doty, Jean Slaughter. *Dark Horse* (6–8). Illus. by Dorothy Haskell Chhuy. 1983, Morrow LB $9.50. Abby finds the new horse at High Hickory a fine jumper. Other horse stories by Doty: *Summer Pony* (1973, Macmillan paper $1.95); *The Monday Horses* (1978, Pocket paper $1.75); *The Valley of the Ponies* (1982, Macmillan $8.95); *If Wishes Were Horses* (1984, Macmillan $9.95).

2101. Duncan, Lois. *Hotel for Dogs* (4–6). Illus. by Leonard Shortall. 1971, Avon paper $1.95. Bruce and Liz Walker accumulate so many stray dogs that they set up a hotel for them in an abandoned house.

2102. Dunn, Marylois, and Mayhar, Ardath. *The Absolutely Perfect Horse* (6–8). 1983, Harper $9.95. Annie purchases a broken-down Indian pony to save him from destruction.

2103. Eckert, Allan W. *Incident at Hawk's Hill* (6–9). Illus. by John Schoenherr. 1971, Little $8.95. A 6-year-old boy wanders away from home and is nurtured and protected by a badger.

2104. Estes, Eleanor. *Ginger Pye* (4–6). Illus. by author. 1972, Harcourt $10.95; paper $4.95. Ginger is the Pye family's engaging puppy who mysteriously disappears. Newbery Award winner. Also use: *Pinky Pye* (1958, $7.95; paper $1.75).

2105. Farley, Walter. *Black Stallion* (5–8). 1941, Random $8.95; LB $8.99. A wild Arabian stallion and the boy who trained him. Other series titles: *The Black Stallion Returns* (1945, $9.95); *Son of the Black Stallion* (1947, LB $7.99; paper $2.95).

2106. Fenner, Phyllis R., sel. *Midnight Prowlers: Stories of Cats and Their Enslaved Owners* (6–9). Illus. by George Gershinowitz. 1981, Morrow $11.25; LB $10.89. Ten unusual cat stories for better readers.

2107. Flack, Marjorie. *Walter the Lazy Mouse* (2–4). Illus. by Cyndy Szekeres. 1963, Doubleday $6.95; paper $2.50. Walter is so lazy, he never gets anywhere on time.

2108. Fox, Paula. *The King's Falcon* (4–7). Illus. by Eros Keith. 1969, Bradbury $6.95. King Philip, discontent with the condition of his poor, tiny country, forsakes his kingdom to pursue his real joy in life—falconry.

2109. Gates, Doris. *A Morgan for Melinda* (5–7). 1980, Viking $9.95; Penguin paper $3.95. In spite of her misgivings, Melinda accepts the responsibility for taking care of a horse. A sequel is: *A Filly for Melinda* (1984, $10.95).

2110. Gauch, Patricia Lee. *Kate Alone* (4–7). 1980, Putnam $7.95; Pocket paper $1.95. Kate must decide what to do with her vicious dog.

2111. George, Jean Craighead. *The Cry of the Crow* (5–7). 1980, Harper $10.89; paper $2.95. Mandy finds a helpless baby crow in the woods and tames it.

2112. Gipson, Fred. *Old Yeller* (6–9). Illus. by Carl Burger. 1956, Harper LB $11.89. A powerful story set in the Texas hill country about a 14-year-old boy and the ugly stray dog he comes to love. Also use: *Savage Sam* (1962, Harper LB $11.89; paper $2.50).

2113. Girion, Barbara. *Misty and Me* (4–7). 1979, Scribners $10.95; Scholastic paper $1.95. Unknown to her parents, Kim adopts a puppy from the pound.

2114. Graeber, Charlotte Towner. *Mustard* (3–5). Illus. by Donna Diamond. 1982, Macmillan $9.95; Bantam paper $1.95. Eight-year-old Alex can't face the fact that his cat is getting old.

2115. Graham, Ada, and Graham, Frank. *Jacob and Owl: A Story* (4–6). Illus. 1982, Putnam $9.95. Josh feels less lonely when he finds an injured barn owl.

2116. Griffith, Helen V. *Foxy* (4–6). 1984, Greenwillow $9.00. Jeff believes his dog Foxy is dead, but his neighbor, Amber, knows this isn't true.

2117. Griffiths, Helen. *Blackface Stallion* (5–7). Illus. by Victor G. Ambrus. 1980, Holiday $9.95. Set in northern Mexico, this is the story of a wild stallion.

2118. Griffiths, Helen. *Grip: A Dog Story* (6–8). 1978, Holiday $9.95; Pocket paper $1.75. The English moors, a cruel father, and the love of a dog are elements in this story of the 1930s.

2119. Griffiths, Helen. *Just a Dog* (5–7). Illus. by Victor G. Ambrus. 1976, Pocket paper $1.95. A stray dog roams the streets of Madrid seeking a permanent home.

2120. Griffiths, Helen. *Rafa's Dog* (3–6). 1983, Holiday $9.95. In this novel set in Spain, a lonely boy befriends a stray dog.

2121. Griffiths, Helen. *Running Wild* (6–9). Illus. 1977, Holiday $6.95. Pablo, a young Spanish boy, tries to hide his dog's puppies for fear his grandfather will drown them.

2122. Guillot, Rene. *Grishka and the Bear* (5–7). Trans. by Gwen Marsh. Illus. by Joan Kiddell Monroe. 1960, Harper $8.95. The haunting story of a Siberian boy and his bear cub who escape to the forest together when the bear is to be sacrificed as village ritual demands.

2123. Haas, Dorothy. *Poppy and the Outdoors Cat* (3–5). Illus. by Margot Apple. 1981, Whitman $7.95. Mrs. Flower can't allow her daughter to bring her cat indoors. A sequel is: *Tink in a Tangle* (1984, $7.95).

2124. Haas, Jessie. *Keeping Barney* (5–7). 1982, Greenwillow $11.25; Scholastic paper $1.95. Sarah decides to accept the responsibility of boarding a horse.

2125. Hall, Lynn. *Danza!* (5–8). 1981, Scribners $11.95. Paulo's error causes a near fatal accident for his horse, Danza.

2126. Hall, Lynn. *The Horse Trader* (6–9). 1981, Scribners $9.95. Karen trusts her horse-trading friend until she realizes he is a fraud.

2127. Hall, Lynn. *Megan's Mare* (4–8). 1983, Scribners $9.95. Megan feels a close psychic bond to her new horse, Berry.

2128. Hall, Lynn. *The Mystery of Pony Hollow* (3–5). Illus. by Ruth Sanderson. 1978, Garrard LB $7.68. Sarah puts a prize pony's ghost to rest in this adventure story.

2129. Hall, Lynn. *The Mystery of Pony Hollow Panda* (3–5). Illus. by William Hutchinson. 1983, Garrard LB $7.68. An entertaining story that also contains a baffling mystery.

2130. Hall, Lynn. *Tin Can Tucker* (6–9). 1982, Scribners $10.95. Orphan Ann Tucker finds excitement and a new family at a rodeo.

2131. Hanson, June Andrea. *Summer of the Stallion* (6–8). Illus. by Gloria Singer. 1979, Macmillan $9.95. Janey's relationship with her grandfather is highlighted in this fine love story. A sequel is: *Winter of the Owl* (1980, $9.95; Scholastic paper $1.95).

2132. Harris, Mark Jonathan. *The Last Run* (6–8). 1981, Lothrop $11.25; LB $10.80. Lyle and his grandfather set out to capture a renegade stallion.

2133. Henry, Marguerite. *King of the Wind* (5–8). Illus. by Wesley Dennis. 1948, Rand McNally $8.95; paper $2.95. The horse, Godolphin Arabian, ancestor of Man O'War and founder of the thoroughbred strain. Newbery Award winner, 1949. Also use: *Born to Trot* (1950); *Black Gold* (1957) (both Rand McNally $8.95; paper $2.95).

2134. Henry, Marguerite. *Misty of Chincoteague* (4–7). 1947, Rand McNally $8.95; paper $2.95. Two sequels to this horse story are: *Sea Star* (1949); *Stormy, Misty's Foal* (1963) (both $8.95; paper $2.95).

2135. Henry, Marguerite. *Mustang, Wild Spirit of the West* (6–8). Illus. by Robert Lougheed. 1966, Rand McNally $8.95; paper $2.95. An excellent horse story written by a master.

2136. Henry, Marguerite. *San Domingo: The Medicine Hat Stallion* (4–6). Illus. by Robert Lou-

gheed. 1972, Rand McNally $8.95. Set in the West during mid-nineteenth century, this is the story of a young man who rights a wrong inflicted on his father. Also from the same author and publisher: *Brighty of the Grand Canyon* (1953, $8.95; paper $2.95); *Justin Morgan Had a Horse* (1954, $6.95; paper $2.95).

2137. Holland, Isabelle. *Alan and the Animal Kingdom* (5–7). 1977, Harper $11.95; Dell paper $1.95. Twelve-year-old Sean tries to hide the death of his great aunt (with whom he has been living) so that he can keep his pets.

2138. Holland, Isabelle. *A Horse Named Peaceable* (5–7). 1982, Lothrop $11.25. Twelve-year-old Jessamy searches for her lost horse.

2139. Holmes, Efner Tudor. *Amy's Goose* (2–4). Illus. by Tasha Tudor. 1977, Harper $7.64. Amy nurses a wild goose back to health, but in the spring she must let it go.

2140. Hurd, Edith Thacher. *The Black Dog Who Went into the Woods* (3–4). Illus. by Emily McCully. 1980, Harper LB $9.89. A family accepts the death of the beloved pet dog.

2141. James, Will. *Smoky* (6–8). 1926, Scribners $12.95. The classic horse story; Newbery Award winner, 1927.

2142. Jukes, Mavis. *No One Is Going to Nashville* (3–5). Illus. by Lloyd Bloom. 1983, Knopf $8.95; LB $8.99. Despite Sonia's wishes, her father begins looking for a new home for the stray dog Sonia has found.

2143. Kemp, Gene. *Dog Days and Cat Naps* (3–5). Illus. by Carolyn Dinan. 1982, Faber $11.95. Ten stories about dogs and cats.

2144. Kennedy, Richard. *Song of the Horse* (4–5). Illus. by Marcia Sewall. 1981, Dutton $9.50. A prose poem about a girl and her love for her horse.

2145. Kipling, Rudyard. *The Beginning of the Armadilloes* (1–5). Illus. by Charles Keeping. 1983, Bedrick $8.95. One of the Just So Stories. Others in the series: *The Butterfly That Stamped; The Cat That Walked by Himself; The Crab That Played with the Sea* (all 1983, $8.95).

2146. Kipling, Rudyard. *Elephant's Child* (3–5). Illus. by Leonard Weisgard. 1970, Walker $7.95. A young elephant gains a lesson and a trunk from a crocodile. Also use: *The Elephant's Child*, illus. by Lorinda Bryan Cauley (1983, Harcourt $12.95).

2147. Kipling, Rudyard. *How the Rhinoceros Got His Skin* (3–5). Illus. by Leonard Weisgard. 1974, Walker $7.95. Colorful illustrations complement the humor of a favorite Kipling story for children. Also use: *How the Leopard Got Its Spots* (1972, Walker $7.95).

2148. Kipling, Rudyard. *Jungle Book* (4–7). Illus. by Fritz Eichenberg. 1950, Grosset $8.95; LB $5.95; Airmont paper $1.95. One of many recommended editions of this classic.

2149. Kipling, Rudyard. *Just So Stories* (4–6). Illus. by J. M. Gleeson. 1946, Doubleday $14.95. The classic children's story, illustrated effectively by the eminent artist. Also use: *Just So Stories* (n.d., Airmont $0.95).

2150. Kjelgaard, James A. *Big Red* (6–9). Illus. by Bob Kuhn. 1945, Holiday $10.95; Bantam paper $2.50. Adventures of a champion Irish setter and a trapper's son. Also use: *Irish Red: Son of Big Red* (1951); *Outlaw Red* (1953) (both $10.95; Bantam paper $2.50).

2151. Kjelgaard, James A. *Haunt Fox* (4–8). Illus. by Glen Rounds. 1954, Bantam paper $1.95. A fox is pursued by a boy and his dog; interest shifts from hunter to hunted.

2152. Knight, Eric. *Lassie Come Home* (4–7). Illus. by Don Bolognese. 1940, Holt $8.70; Dell paper $1.75. The classic that conveys the beautiful relationship between a boy and his loyal dog, and the lives of the people of Yorkshire as well.

2153. Levy, Elizabeth. *The Case of the Counterfeit Racehorse* (5–8). 1980, Pocket paper $1.95. A mystery involving the switching of two look-alike horses.

2154. Lippincott, Joseph. *Wilderness Champion* (5–8). Illus. by Paul Branson. 1944, Harper $9.95; LB $9.89. A puppy becomes leader of a wolf pack but is finally reunited with his master. Also use: *The Wahoo Bobcat* (1950, Harper $12.45).

2155. Little, Mary E. *Old Cat and the Kitten* (3–5). Illus. by author. 1979, Atheneum $8.95. Joel must decide the fate of his 2 new pet cats.

2156. London, Jack. *Call of the Wild* (6–9). Illus. by Karen Kezer. 1965, Macmillan $10.95. One of the many recommended editions.

2157. London, Jack. *White Fang* (5–9). 1935, Dent $9.00; Airmont paper $1.25. The classic dog story.

2158. McInerney, Judith Whitelock. *Judge Benjamin: Superdog* (4–6). Illus. by Leslie Morrill. 1982, Holiday $9.95; Pocket paper $1.95. A large St. Bernard tells of his humorous adventures. Two sequels are: *Judge Benjamin: The Superdog Secret* (1983); *Judge Benjamin: The Superdog Rescue* (1984) (both $9.95; paper $1.95).

2159. Mayerson, Evelyn Wilde. *Coydog* (5–7). 1981, Scribners $10.95. A wild coyote crossed with a dog is taken care of by a Greek-American boy, Kiko.

2160. Meyer, Carolyn. *The Luck of Texas McCoy* (6–9). 1984, Atheneum $11.95. Texas's grandfather leaves her his horse ranch.

2161. Miles, Miska. *Jenny's Cat* (3–4). Illus. by Wendy Watson. 1979, Dutton $7.50. Rather than give up her pet cat, Jenny decides to run away with it.

2162. Miles, Miska. *Mississippi Possum* (2–4). Illus. by John Schoenherr. 1965, Little $7.95. A black family and a little gray possum share the same tent when the mighty Mississippi overflows.

2163. Miles, Miska. *Otter in the Cove* (3–5). Illus. by John Schoenherr. 1974, Little $5.95. In a story that contains much fascinating otter lore, Maggie tries to save a small herd of otters that swims into her father's cove from extinction.

2164. Miles, Miska. *Wharf Rat* (2–4). Illus. by John Schoenherr. 1972, Little $6.95. The survival story of an animal despised by humans.

2165. Morey, Walt. *Gentle Ben* (5–7). Illus. by John Schoenherr. 1965, Dutton $9.95; Avon paper $1.95. A warm story of the deep trust and friendship between a boy and an Alaskan bear.

2166. Morey, Walt. *The Lemon Meringue Dog* (5–9). 1980, Dutton $10.95. A narcotics squad dog must prove his worth.

2167. Morey, Walt. *Sandy and the Rock Star* (5–8). 1979, Dutton $10.95. A teenage boy and a cougar share adventures in an island wilderness.

2168. Morey, Walt. *Scrub Dog of Alaska* (4–8). 1971, Dutton $10.95. A pup, abandoned because of his small size, turns out to be a winner. Also use: *Kavik, the Wolf Dog* (1968, Dutton $10.95).

2169. Morey, Walt. *Year of the Black Pony* (5–7). 1976, Dutton $12.95; Scholastic paper $1.95. A family story about a boy's love for his pony in rural Oregon at the turn of the century. Also use: *Runaway Stallion* (1973, Dutton $8.95).

2170. Morgenroth, Barbara. *Impossible Charlie* (4–6). Illus. by Velma Ilsley. 1979, Atheneum $8.95. A young girl receives as a gift a seemingly untrainable horse named Charlie.

2171. Morgenroth, Barbara. *Last Junior Year* (6–9). 1978, Atheneum $6.95. Jackie's new horse, Charlie, proves difficult to train.

2172. Morgenroth, Barbara. *Ride a Proud Horse* (6–8). 1978, Atheneum $8.95. When Corey begins riding lessons with her horse, she finds unexpected benefits.

2173. Morpurgo, Michael. *War Horse* (5–7). 1983, Greenwillow $9.00. A narrative by a horse who highlights his part in World War I.

2174. Mowat, Farley. *The Dog Who Wouldn't Be* (4–7). Illus. by Paul Galdone. 1957, Little $8.95. The humorous story of Mutt, a dog of character and personality, and his boy.

2175. Mowat, Farley. *Owls in the Family* (4–6). Illus. by Robert Frankenberg. 1962, Atlantic/Little $9.95; Bantam paper $1.50. The many adventures of a family that adopts 2 owls.

2176. Mukerji, Dhan Gopal. *Gay Neck: The Story of a Pigeon* (4–8). Illus. 1968, Dutton $10.95. The Newbery Award winner, 1928, this is the story of a boy from India and his brave carrier pigeon during World War I.

2177. North, Sterling. *Rascal: A Memoir of a Better Era* (6–8). Illus. by John Schoenherr. 1984, Dutton $10.63; Avon paper $1.95. Autobiographical memoir of the beauties of nature as experienced by an 11-year-old and his pet raccoon.

2178. North, Sterling. *The Wolfling* (4–6). 1980, Scholastic paper $1.95. A 13-year-old boy raises a wolf pup.

2179. O'Hara, Mary. *My Friend Flicka* (6–9). Illus. by Dave Blossom. 1973, Harper $11.41. The wonderful story of a young boy and his horse.

2180. Parsons, Elizabeth. *The Upside-Down Cat* (3–5). Illus. by Ronald Himler. 1981, Atheneum $9.95. A cat becomes separated from her owners before they leave their Maine summer home.

2181. Pearce, Philippa. *The Battle of Bubble and Squeak* (4–6). Illus. by Alan Baker. 1979, Dutton $8.95. A family story centering around Sid's battle to keep 2 pet gerbils.

2182. Peyton, K. M. *The Team* (6–7). Illus. by author. 1976, Harper $10.95. Ruth's position on the pony club's team is uncertain, particularly because of Peter's competition.

2183. Pinkwater, Jill. *Cloud Horse* (6–8). Illus. by Irene Brady. 1983, Lothrop $9.00. The story of two young women—one Viking, the other contemporary—and their love for the same breed of horses.

2184. Rawlings, Marjorie K. *The Yearling* (6–9). Illus. by N. C. Wyeth. 1938, Scribners $20.00; paper $6.95. The contemporary classic of a boy and a fawn growing up together in the backwoods of Florida.

2185. Rawls, Wilson. *Summer of the Monkeys* (4–6). 1977, Doubleday $10.95; Dell paper $2.50. Jay and his dog spend a summer chasing 29 escaped monkeys.

2186. Rawls, Wilson. *Where the Red Fern Grows* (4–7). 1961, Doubleday $11.95; Bantam paper $2.50. A young boy saves money to buy 2 coon dogs and faces heartbreak when they die.

2187. Rivers-Coffey, Rachel. *A Horse Like Mr. Ragman* (5–7). 1977, Scribners $7.25. A fresh treatment of a tired plot concerning a girl's efforts to change her run-down horse into a winner.

2188. Roberts, Willo Davis. *Eddie and the Fairy Godpuppy* (3–5). Illus. by Leslie Morrill. 1984, Atheneum $10.95. A 10-year-old orphan tries to hide a lost puppy.

2189. Robertson, Keith. *In Search of a Sandhill Crane* (5–8). Illus. by Richard Cuffari. 1973, Viking $9.95; Penguin paper $2.95. Fifteen-year old Link spends an unexpectedly gratifying summer visiting an aunt in the north woods in Michigan.

2190. Rounds, Glen. *The Blind Colt* (4–6). Illus. by author. 1960, Holiday $10.95. Born blind, a mustang colt learns to "see" with his ears and nose. Also use: *Stolen Pony* (1969, Holiday $10.95).

2191. Rounds, Glen. *Blind Outlaw* (4–7). Illus. by author. 1980, Holiday $10.95. A mute boy lassoes a blind horse.

2192. Rounds, Glen. *Wild Appaloosa* (3–6). Illus. by author. 1983, Holiday $10.95. The story of a wild filly and a boy who dreams of one day training such a horse.

2193. Salten, Felix. *Bambi: A Life in the Woods* (5–8). 1926, Buccaneer LB $16.95; Pocket paper $2.95. The growing to maturity of an Austrian deer.

2194. Savitt, Sam. *The Dingle Ridge Fox and Other Stories* (5–7). Illus. by author. 1978, Scholastic paper $1.95. General, appealing stories chiefly about dogs and horses.

2195. Sewell, Anna. *Black Beauty* (4–6). Illus. by Fritz Eichenberg. n.d, Putnam LB $9.95; paper $5.95. One of several recommended editions of this classic horse story.

2196. Shura, Mary Francis. *Mister Wolf and Me* (5–7). Illus. by Konrad Hack. 1979, Dodd $7.95; Scholastic paper $1.95. A German shepherd is accused of sheep killing.

2197. Smith, Doris Buchanan. *Moonshadow of Cherry Mountain* (3–6). 1982, Four Winds $8.95. Moonshadow, a Labrador Retriever, must adjust to having some of his turf taken from him.

2198. Stolz, Mary. *Cat Walk* (3–6). Illus. by Erik Blegvad. 1983, Harper $8.61; LB $8.89. A barn kitten runs away to find a suitable home.

2199. Taylor, Theodore. *The Trouble with Tuck* (5–8). 1981, Doubleday $9.95; Avon paper $2.25. The story of a golden Labrador Retriever who becomes blind.

2200. Terhune, Albert Payson. *Lad: A Dog* (6–9). Illus. 1959, Dutton $9.95; NAL paper $2.25. One of the best-loved dog stories of all times.

2201. Thiele, Colin. *Fight against Albatross Two* (6–8). 1976, Harper LB $10.89. The tragedy to wildlife caused by an oil spill in offshore Australia is explored through the eyes of a 14-year-old Link and his younger sister.

2202. Thiele, Colin. *Storm Boy* (4–6). Illus. by John Schoenherr. 1978, Harper LB $10.89. A boy grieves when his pet pelican is shot by a hunter in this story set in rural Australia.

2203. Thomas, Jane Resh. *The Comeback Dog* (3–6). Illus. by Troy Howell. 1981, Houghton $9.25. Daniel, trying to forget the death of his dog, tries to train an English Setter.

2204. Tolan, Stephanie S. *A Time to Fly Free* (5–8). 1983, Scribners $11.95. Josh becomes friendly with Rafferty, who helps injured birds.

2205. Towne, Mary. *Boxed In* (4–7). 1982, Harper $9.57; LB $9.89. Should Kate sell her beloved horse so he can be used for showing?

2206. Walker, Diana. *Mother Wants a Horse* (6–9). 1978, Harper $8.61; LB $8.89. While training a horse, 16-year-old Joanne gains maturity.

2207. Wallace, Bill. *A Dog Called Kitty* (4–7). 1980, Holiday $9.95. A boy tries to overcome his fear of dogs so he can help a stray.

2208. Warburg, Sandol Stoddard. *Growing Time* (3–4). Illus. by Leonard Weisgard. 1969, Houghton $8.95; paper $1.50. Death is sensitively treated as Jamie's shock, grief, and anger begin slowly to abate when he accepts the helpless new pup and, consequently, the loss of his beloved collie.

2209. Whitley, Mary Ann. *A Circle of Light* (5–8). 1983, Walker $11.95. A young man rides his horse in a desperate attempt to aid his embattled tribesmen.

2210. Worth, Valerie. *Curlicues: The Fortunes of Two Pug Dogs* (3–5). Illus. by Natalie Babbitt. 1980, Farrar $7.95. The story of 2 puppies in a Victorian setting.

Family Stories

2211. Adler, Carole S. *Get Lost Little Brother* (5–7). 1983, Houghton $9.95. Todd has problems with his twin brothers, who are 2 years older.

2212. Adler, Carole S. *The Silver Coach* (4–6). 1979, Putnam $8.95. Chris and her sister adjust to their parents' imminent divorce during a summer with their grandmother.

2213. Alcott, Louisa May. *Little Women* (4–7). Illus. by Anna M. Magagna and Louis Jambor. 1947, deluxe ed. $10.95; paper $6.95. One of the many fine editions of this enduring story. Two sequels are: *Little Men* (n.d., deluxe ed. $9.95, paper $5.95); *Jo's Boys* (1949, J. M. Dent $10.95).

2214. Aliki. *The Two of Them* (K–3). Illus. by author. 1979, Greenwillow $10.95; LB $10.51. A moving story of a tender relationship between a child and her grandfather and of the death of the old man.

2215. Alter, Judy. *After Pa Was Shot* (5–7). 1978, Morrow LB $9.36. Ellsberg's new stepfather turns out to be a dud in this story set in turn-of-the-century Texas.

2216. Amoss, Berthe. *Secret Lives* (5–8). 1979, Little $8.95; Dell paper $1.95. Through some sleuthing, Addie uncovers some unusual information about her dead mother.

2217. Anckarsvärd, Karin. *Doctor's Boy* (4–6). Illus. by Booker Fermin. 1965, Harcourt $5.50. To 10-year-old Jon, the most exciting part of life is accompanying his father, a doctor in rural Sweden, on his rounds in the horse and buggy.

2218. Armstrong, William H. *Sounder* (6–9). Illus. by James Barkley. 1969, Harper $8.95; LB $9.89; paper $1.50. Harsh customs and hard circumstances cripple the bodies of both the dog Sounder and his master. Newbery Award winner. A sequel is: *Sour Land* (1971, LB $10.89; paper $1.25).

2219. Babbitt, Natalie. *The Eyes of the Amaryllis* (4–6). 1977, Farrar $7.95; Bantam paper $1.75. In this story set in an Atlantic coastal village during the late nineteenth century, an 11-year-old girl is drawn into her grandmother's obsession.

2220. Bach, Alice. *A Father Every Few Years* (6–8). 1977, Harper $10.95. Love and anger at an absent stepfather are the focus of this story of adolescence.

2221. Bates, Betty. *Bugs in Your Ears* (5–7). 1977, Holiday $9.95. An eighth grader, named Carrie, adjusts to her new stepfather and his 3 sons.

2222. Bates, Betty. *My Mom, the Money Nut* (5–7). 1979, Holiday $9.95; Pocket paper $1.95. Slowly Fritzi understands why her mother stresses economic security as a future goal.

2223. Bates, Betty. *Say Cheese* (3–5). 1984, Holiday $10.95. Christy's problems worsen when she wins $100 in a radio contest.

2224. Bawden, Nina. *The Peppermint Pig* (4–6). 1975, Harper $10.53; Penguin paper $2.95. This turn-of-the-century novel set in England recounts the adventures of 9-year-old Poll and his family after they move from London to Norfolk.

2225. Beatty, Patricia. *By Crumbs, It's Mine!* (6–8). 1976, Morrow $9.95. After 14-year-old Damaris

Boyd and his family are given a run-down hotel in the Arizona Territory of 1882, the fun begins.

2226. Bell, William Bruce. *A Little Dab of Color* (5–7). 1980, Lothrop $10.95; LB $10.51. Ten-year-old Bruce is fearful of the arrival of Grandma Brown in his household.

2227. Blume, Judy. *The One in the Middle Is the Green Kangaroo* (2–4). Illus. by Amy Aitken. 1981, Bradbury $8.95; Dell paper $1.95. Freddy knows being in the school play will give him the glory he deserves.

2228. Branscum, Robbie. *The Adventures of Johnny May* (4–7). Illus. by Deborah Howland. 1984, Harper $11.06; LB $10.89. As poor as any in the Arkansas hills, Johnny May struggles to provide his grandparents with a real Christmas.

2229. Branscum, Robbie. *Toby, Granny and George* (6–8). Illus. by Glen Rounds. 1976, Doubleday $7.50; Avon paper $1.75. A heartwarming story set in rural Arkansas about a young girl's search for identity.

2230. Bridgers, Sue Ellen. *Home before Dark* (6–9). 1977, Knopf $10.95. Fourteen-year-old Stella and her family settle down on a tobacco farm after years as migrant workers.

2231. Brink, Carol. *Caddie Woodlawn* (4–6). Illus. by Trina S. Hyman. 1973, Macmillan $10.95; paper $2.95. The delightful escapades of a red-haired tomboy and her brothers in early Wisconsin. Newbery Award winner, 1936. Also use: *Magical Melons* (1944, Macmillan $9.95; paper $3.95).

2232. Brink, Carol. *Winter Cottage* (4–6). Illus. by Fermin Rocker. 1974, Macmillan paper $0.95. During the Great Depression, 2 girls and their jobless father winterize a small summer cabin.

2233. Bunting, Eve. *Blackbird Singing* (5–7). Illus. by Stephen Gammell. 1980, Macmillan $8.95; paper $1.95. A division between his parents puts poor Marcus in the middle.

2234. Burch, Robert. *Ida Early Comes over the Mountain* (4–7). 1980, Viking $10.95; Avon paper $1.95. Ida Early becomes the housekeeper for 4 motherless children.

2235. Byars, Betsy. *The Glory Girl* (6–8). 1983, Viking $10.55. Anna is the nonsinging member of a family of gospel singers.

2236. Cameron, Ann. *The Stories Julian Tells* (3–5). Illus. by Ann Strugnell. 1981, Pantheon $8.95; LB $8.99. Six short stories chiefly about the home life of Julian and his family.

2237. Canfield, Dorothy. *Understood Betsy* (4–6). Illus. by Martha Alexander. 1946, Buccaneer $17.95. A new edition of the old favorite about

Elizabeth Ann and the fearful new way of life that awaits her when she goes to live in the wilds of Vermont.

2238. Carlson, Natalie Savage. *The Half Sisters* (4–6). Illus. by Thomas Di Grazia. 1970, Harper paper $2.95. Six sisters growing up on a Maryland farm in 1915.

2239. Chaikin, Miriam. *I Should Worry, I Should Care* (3–5). Illus. by Richard Egielski. 1979, Harper LB $9.89; Dell paper $1.75. The story of a Jewish family's move to a new apartment in Brooklyn. Three sequels are: *Finders Weepers* (1980, $9.57; LB $9.89); *Getting Even* (1982, $10.53; LB $10.89); *Lower, Higher, You're a Liar!* (1984, $11.49; LB $11.89).

2240. Cleary, Beverly. *Ramona the Brave* (3–5). Illus. by Alan Tiegreen. 1975, Morrow $9.50; LB $9.12; Scholastic paper $1.95. Our young heroine experiences the glories and difficulties of being in the first grade and of having a room of her own. Four other series titles are: *Ramona and Her Father* (1977, $10.75; LB $10.32; Dell paper $2.50); *Ramona and Her Mother* (1979, $10.95; LB $10.51; Dell paper $2.50); *Ramona Quimby, Age Eight* (1981, $10.25; LB $9.84; Dell paper $2.50); *Ramona Forever* (1984, $9.95; LB $9.36).

2241. Cleary, Beverly. *Ramona the Pest* (3–5). Illus. by Louis Darling. 1968, Morrow $10.75; LB $10.32; Dell paper $2.50. The fine addition to this popular series follows spirited Ramona Quimby, sister to Beezus and neighbor to Henry, through her kindergarten escapades. Also use: *Beezus and Ramona* (1955); *Ribsy* (1964) (both $10.75; LB $10.32; Dell paper $2.50).

2242. Cleary, Beverly. *Sister of the Bride* (6–8). Illus. by Beth Krush and Joe Krush. 1963, Morrow $12.20; Dell paper $2.50. All the excitement and confusion an approaching wedding brings to a household.

2243. Cleary, Beverly. *Socks* (4–6). Illus. by Beatrice Darwin. 1973, Morrow $10.75; LB $10.32; Dell paper $2.50. What happens when the family cat Socks realizes that his position of importance is threatened by the arrival of a baby.

2244. Cleaver, Vera. *Sugar Blue* (5–7). 1984, Lothrop $11.50. The arrival of a 4-year-old niece changes many family relationships and attitudes.

2245. Cleaver, Vera, and Cleaver, Bill. *I Would Rather Be a Turnip* (5–7). 1971, NAL paper $2.25. Annie prepares to welcome a precocious young boy, Calvin, who is her sister's illegitimate son, into her household.

2246. Cleaver, Vera, and Cleaver, Bill. *The Mock Revolt* (6–9). 1971, Harper $10.89; NAL paper $1.95. During the Great Depression, 13-year-old

Ussy tries to avoid becoming part of the Establishment and gains an understanding of his wish to revolt through his friendship with a migrant family.

2247. Cleaver, Vera, and Cleaver, Bill. *Queen of Hearts* (6–9). 1978, Harper $10.95; Bantam paper $1.75. A young girl must take care of her salty old grandmother after she has a stroke.

2248. Cleaver, Vera, and Cleaver, Bill. *Where the Lilies Bloom* (6–9). Illus. by James J. Spanfeller. 1969, Harper $11.49. Gutsy, sharp Mary Call is determined to fulfill her dying sharecropper father's last request to keep the family together. A sequel is: *Trial Valley* (1977, $10.95).

2249. Clements, Bruce. *Anywhere Else but Here* (6–8). 1980, Farrar $9.95; Dell paper $1.95. Molly must straighten out her home situation before setting out on her own.

2250. Clifton, Lucille. *The Lucky Stone* (3–5). Illus. by Dale Payson. 1979, Delacorte $8.95; LB $8.89. Several stories in the life of a girl's great-grandmother linked by the power of a stone.

2251. Clifton, Lucille. *The Times They Used to Be* (5–6). Illus. by Susan Jeschke. 1974, Holt $4.95. In a series of reminiscences, a young black girl learns about her mother's childhood.

2252. Clymer, Eleanor. *The Get-Away Car* (4–6). 1978, Dutton $8.95; Bantam paper $1.75. Grahm and Maggie plan to escape from domineering Aunt Ruby, who has plans for their future they don't like.

2253. Clymer, Eleanor. *My Mother Is the Smartest Woman in the World* (4–6). Illus. by Nancy Kincade. 1982, Atheneum $8.95. Kathleen's mom runs for mayor.

2254. Cohen, Barbara. *Benny* (4–6). 1977, Lothrop LB $9.84. Twelve-year-old Benny must assume added family responsibilities and make sacrifices when his mother has an operation.

2255. Cohen, Barbara. *The Carp in the Bathtub* (3–4). Illus. by Joan Halpern. 1972, Lothrop $10.25. Two Jewish children decide that the carp in the bathtub should be rescued before it becomes Passover gefilte fish.

2256. Cohen, Barbara. *The Innkeeper's Daughter* (6–9). 1979, Lothrop $10.25; LB $9.84. A gently paced novel of a young girl, her family, and the small hotel that her mother manages.

2257. Cone, Molly. *Call Me Moose* (4–6). Illus. by Bernice Lowenstein. 1978, Houghton $6.95. Awkward Martha tries to find a place in her athletic family.

2258. Conford, Ellen. *And This Is Laura* (4–6). 1977, Little $8.95. A very ordinary girl discovers that she possesses psychic powers.

2259. Conford, Ellen. *The Luck of Pokey Bloom* (4–6). Illus. by Bernice Lowenstein. 1975, Little $8.95; Pocket paper $1.95. The warm, sunny family story about a young girl, who has a compulsive interest in contests, and her brother, who is undergoing the pangs of first love.

2260. Coolidge, Olivia. *Come by Here* (5–7). Illus. by Milton Johnson. 1970, Houghton $9.95. In turn-of-the-century Baltimore, 7-year-old, black Minty Lou learns the difference between visiting relatives and living with them.

2261. Crofford, Emily. *A Matter of Pride* (4–6). Illus. by Jim LaMarche. 1981, Carolrhoda LB $7.95. A family lives through the Great Depression on a cotton plantation in Arkansas. A sequel is: *Stories from the Blue Road* (1982, LB $7.95).

2262. Cunningham, Julia. *Tuppeny* (6–8). 1978, Avon paper $1.95. A strange girl affects the lives of 3 couples, each of whom has lost a daughter.

2263. D'Aulaire, Ingri, and D'Aulaire, Edgar. *Children of the Northlights* (3–5). Illus. by author. 1935, Viking $8.95. A charming book about living in Lapland, as revealed by the lives of 2 children.

2264. De Angeli, Marguerite. *Fiddlestrings* (4–6). Illus. 1974, Doubleday LB $4.95. In this turn-of-the-century novel, a young boy spends a summer with his father on the Steel Pier in Atlantic City.

2265. De Angeli, Marguerite. *Thee, Hannah!* (4–6). Illus. by author. 1940, Doubleday $8.95. Hannah, the youngest in a large Quaker family, loves fine things and has difficulty fitting into the conservative pattern her elders embrace.

2266. Delton, Judy. *Back Yard Angel* (3–5). Illus. by Leslie Morrill. 1983, Houghton $8.95. Ten-year-old Angel O'Leary is saddled with taking care of her little brother.

2267. Delton, Judy. *Only Jody* (3–5). Illus. by Pat Porter. 1982, Houghton $7.95; Dell paper $2.25. Jody finds being a boy in an all-female household sometimes is difficult.

2268. Delton, Judy. *A Walk on a Snowy Night* (1–4). Illus. by Ruth Rosner. 1982, Harper $9.13; LB $10.89. A young girl and her father enjoy a walk in the snow.

2269. Dixon, Jeanne. *Lady Cat Lost* (6–8). 1981, Atheneum LB $9.95. After their father leaves them, the Ferguson family moves to Montana.

2270. Duncan, Jane. *Brave Janet Reachfar* (4–6). Illus. by Mairi Hedderwick. 1975, Houghton $7.95. Scottish farm life is depicted through the adventures of young Janet and her relationship with her tyrannical grandmother.

2271. Edmonds, Walter. *Bert Breen's Barn* (7–9). 1975, Little $9.95. Upstate New York at the turn of the century is the setting for this quaint story of a boy determined to raise a barn on his family's land.

2272. Eisenberg, Phyllis Rose. *A Mitzvah Is Something Special* (2–4). Illus. by Susan Jeschke. 1978, Harper $9.89; LB $8.89. Lisa brings her 2 very different grandmothers together.

2273. Enright, Elizabeth. *Thimble Summer* (4–6). 1976, Holt $11.95; Dell paper $2.25. A small girl on a Wisconsin farm finds a magic thimble. Newbery Award winner, 1939.

2274. Estes, Eleanor. *The Moffats* (4–6). Illus. by Louis Slobodkin. 1941, Harcourt $8.95; paper $5.95. Lively adventures of 4 Connecticut children, their family, and friends. Sequels are: *The Middle Moffat* (1942, $12.95; paper $2.95); *Rufus M* (1943, $8.95); *The Moffat Museum* (1983, $10.95).

2275. Fine, Anne. *The Granny Project* (5–8). 1983, Farrar $9.95. Four British children try to keep their grandmother out of a nursing home.

2276. Fisher, Lois I. *Rachel Vellars, How Could You?* (4–6). 1984, Dodd LB $8.95. Sixth-grader Cory must choose between a new group of friends and Rachel Vellars.

2277. Fitzhugh, Louise. *Nobody's Family Is Going to Change* (5–8). 1974, Farrar $10.95; Dell paper $1.50. There is considerable misunderstanding within a middle-class black family but also much humor and warmth.

2278. Gaines, Ernest J. *A Long Day in November* (4–6). Illus. by Don Bolognese. 1971, Dial LB $5.47. The events of a day as seen through the eyes of a child on a southern sugarcane plantation during the 1940s.

2279. Galbraith, Kathryn Osebold. *Come Spring* (4–6). 1979, Atheneum $8.95. A simple story of the effects on a family of their possible relocation.

2280. Gardam, Jane. *The Hollow Land* (6–8). Illus. by Janet Rawlings. 1982, Greenwillow LB $11.25. Through the experiences of 2 families, life in northern England is explored in 8 stories.

2281. Garner, Alan. *The Stone Book* (3–5). Illus. by Michael Foreman. 1978, Putnam $7.95. An English stonemason shows his daughter a record of history revealed in marks on rocks.

2282. Garner, Alan. *Tom Fobble's Day* (3–5). Illus. by Michael Foreman. 1979, Putnam $7.95. William, grandson of the hero of *Granny Deardun,* lives through World War II in England.

2283. Gates, Doris. *Blue Willow* (4–6). Illus. by Paul Lantz. 1940, Viking $9.95; Penguin paper $3.50. Janey, a child of migrant workers in the San Joaquin Valley of California, longs for a lasting home to "stay" in.

2284. Geras, Adele. *The Girls in the Velvet Frame* (5–7). 1979, Atheneum $8.95. A warm family story set in pre–World War I Jerusalem.

2285. Gerson, Corinne. *How I Put My Mother through College* (6–8). 1981, Atheneum LB $10.95. Jessica and younger brother Ben find mother's career in college troublesome.

2286. Gerson, Corinne. *Son for a Day* (4–6). Illus. by Velma Ilsley. 1980, Atheneum $10.95; Scholastic paper $1.95. Eleven-year-old Danny finds he can be easily "adopted" by families when he visits the Bronx Zoo. A sequel is: *Oh Brother!* (1982, LB $11.95).

2287. Gerson, Corinne. *Tread Softly* (4–6). 1979, Dial $7.95; LB $7.45. An orphaned girl's fantasy about a perfect family prevents her from facing reality.

2288. Glaser, Dianne. *Summer Secrets* (5–7). 1977, Holiday $5.95. While spending a summer with a great-aunt, Worthy gradually learns about her family and particularly about her dead mother.

2289. Goffstein, M. B. *Two Piano Tuners* (3–4). Illus. by author. 1970, Farrar $6.95. Debbie wants to become a piano tuner like her grandfather, but grandpa wants her to become a concert pianist.

2290. Gooding, Kathleen. *The Rainbow Trail* (6–8). 1983, Faber $11.95. Pa and his children move to a cottage in the Welsh hills.

2291. Gordon, Shirley. *The Boy Who Wanted a Family* (2–4). Illus. by Charles Robinson. 1980, Harper $9.89; Dell paper $1.50. Michael spends the first year with his adoptive parent, Miss Gilbert, and finally finds a home.

2292. Greene, Constance C. *I and Sproggy* (4–6). Illus. by Emily McCully. 1978, Viking $11.50; Dell paper $2.50. Adam gradually grows to like his English stepsister, Sproggy.

2293. Greenfield, Eloise. *Sister* (5–7). Illus. by M. Barnett. 1974, Harper $9.57. Four years in a black girl's life, as revealed through scattered diary entries, during which she shows maturation, particularly in her attitude toward her sister.

2294. Hamilton, Gail. *Titania's Lodestone* (6–8). 1975, Atheneum LB $7.95. Priscilla is amazed when the residents of a New England town accept her hippie parents.

2295. Hamilton, Virginia. *Justice and Her Brothers* (6–8). 1978, Greenwillow $12.50; LB $12.88. A slow-moving but compelling study of a young girl's relationship with her older twin brothers. Two sequels: *Dustland* (1980, $12.50, LB $12.88); *The Gathering* (1981, $11.25; LB $11.88).

2296. Hamilton, Virginia. *M. C. Higgins the Great* (6–8). 1974, Macmillan $10.95. The Newbery

Award winner about a 13-year-old black boy growing up in Appalachia as part of a loving family whose future is threatened by a possible mountain slide.

2297. Hartling, Peter. *Oma* (4–6). Illus. 1977, Harper LB $8.61. In an episodic narrative, Kalle shares many warm experiences with his 67-year-old grandmother, Oma.

2298. Hautzig, Esther. *A Gift for Mama* (3–5). Illus. by Donna Diamond. 1981, Viking $8.95. Sara works hard to earn enough money to buy Mama a Mother's Day gift.

2299. Herman, Charlotte. *Our Snowman Had Olive Eyes* (5–7). 1977, Dutton $7.95. This effective novel explores the relationship between a girl and her grandmother when the elderly lady comes to live with the family.

2300. Hirsch, Linda. *You're Going Out There a Kid, but You're Coming Back a Star!* (4–6). Illus. by John Wallner. 1982, Hastings $9.95. Fifth-grader Margaret Dapple faces many adolescent problems.

2301. Holl, Kristi D. *Just Like a Real Family* (4–6). 1983, Atheneum $9.95. June Finch, a 12-year-old, gets involved in a class project to adopt grandparents from a retirement home.

2302. Hopkins, Lee Bennett. *Mama* (4–6). 1978, Dell paper $1.50. A young boy realizes that his mother has become a thief to support the family. A sequel is: *Mama and Her Boys* (1981, Harper $9.13; LB $8.89).

2303. Hunt, Irene. *William* (5–7). 1984, Ace paper $2.25. An orphan black boy, his 2 sisters, and an older girl join forces to produce a self-made family.

2304. Hunter, Evan. *Me and Mr. Stenner* (5–8). 1976, Harper $9.57. Abby's attitudes toward her new stepfather gradually change from resentment to love.

2305. Hurmence, Belinda. *Tough Tiffany* (6–8). 1980, Doubleday $7.95. Tiffany Cox, an 11-year-old black girl, sorts out her feelings toward her family.

2306. Hurwitz, Johanna. *The Law of Gravity* (4–6). Illus. by Ingrid Fetz. 1978, Morrow LB $9.36. Margot tries to get her recluse mother to come out of her shell.

2307. Hurwitz, Johanna. *Rip-Roaring Russell* (2–5). Illus. by Lillian Hoban. 1983, Morrow $8.50; LB $7.63. The exploits of a self-willed 4-year-old.

2308. Inkiow, Dimiter. *Me and My Sister Clara* (4–6). Illus. by Walter Reiner. 1979, Pantheon LB $3.99. A translation from the German of stories about a small boy and his sister.

2309. Jackson, Jacqueline. *The Taste of Spruce Gum* (5–7). Illus. by Lilian Obligado. 1966, Little $6.95. After her father's death, Libby and her mother return to rural Vermont and her father's family whom she never really knew.

2310. Kaplan, Bess. *The Empty Chair* (5–7). 1978, Harper LB $10.89. Beth is dismayed when her Jewish relatives help plan her father's remarriage.

2311. Keller, Beverly. *No Beasts! No Children!* (4–6). 1983, Lothrop $8.00. A father and 3 children plus three dogs cope when mother takes off.

2312. Kennemore, Tim. *Wall of Words* (6–8). 1983, Faber $10.95. When Mr. Tate leaves to write a book, the rest of the family—mother and 4 daughters—must go it alone.

2313. Kingman, Lee. *The Year of the Raccoon* (5–8). 1966, Houghton $8.95. The responsibility and discipline of caring for a pet raccoon ease the inferiority complex that 15-year-old Joey has acquired.

2314. Klein, Norma. *Confessions of an Only Child* (4–6). Illus. by Richard Cuffari. 1974, Dell paper $1.95. Antonia—Toe for short—undergoes many emotional problems anticipating a baby in the family. Also use: *What It's All About* (1975, Dial $5.95; Pocket paper $1.95); *Tomboy* (1978, Scholastic $6.95; Pocket paper $1.95).

2315. Klein, Norma. *Mom, the Wolfman and Me* (5–8). 1972, Pantheon LB $5.99; Avon paper $1.95. Brett has a most unusual mother and, therefore, doesn't mind the state of being fatherless, but the Wolfman changes things.

2316. Klein, Norma. *Naomi in the Middle* (2–4). Illus. by Leigh Grant. 1974, Pocket paper $1.75. What will it be like to be the middle child when the new baby arrives, ponders 7-year-old Naomi in this frank discussion of pregnancy.

2317. Konigsburg, E. L. *Journey to an 800 Number* (5–8). 1982, Atheneum LB $9.95. Maximilian visits with his show biz father and his trained camel.

2318. Landis, James David. *The Sisters Impossible* (5–7). 1979, Knopf LB $6.99; Bantam paper $1.95. Despite her initial aversion to ballet, Lily changes when she begins to take lessons with her sister.

2319. Lee, Virginia. *The Magic Moth* (4–6). Illus. by Richard Cuffari. 1972, Houghton $7.95; paper $2.95. A family's adjustment to the death of Maryanne, one of 5 children, as seen principally through the experiences of her 6-year-old brother.

2320. L'Engle, Madeleine. *Meet the Austins* (5–7). 1961, Dell paper $1.95. The story of a country doctor's family, told by the 12-year-old daughter, and their reaction to having Maggie, a spoiled orphan, come to live with them.

2321. LeRoy, Gen. *Emma's Dilemma* (4–6). 1975, Harper $9.89; paper $1.50. Emma's problem is that she loves her dog Pearl, but unfortunately grandma, who comes to stay, is allergic to dogs.

2322. Levoy, Myron. *The Witch of Fourth Street and Other Stories* (4–7). 1972, Harper $5.95; LB $5.79; paper $2.95. Eight stories about growing up poor on the lower East Side of New York City.

2323. Lexau, Joan M. *Striped Ice Cream* (2–5). Illus. by John Wilson. 1968, Scholastic paper $1.75. The conquest of poverty is realistically portrayed in this warmly told story about a fatherless black family as they work together.

2324. Lindquist, Jennie D. *The Golden Name Day* (3–5). Illus. by Garth Williams. 1955, Harper $10.89. Nancy longs to celebrate her own name day when she spends a summer with her Swedish-American grandparents.

2325. Lively, Penelope. *The House in Norham Gardens* (6–9). 1974, Dutton $8.95. Fourteen-year-old Clare enjoys taking care of a huge old house, 2 elderly adults, and some roomers.

2326. Love, Sandra. *But What about Me?* (3–6). Illus. by Joan Sandin. 1976, Harcourt $8.95. A sixth grader must adjust to her mother's return to work and the discomforts this produces.

2327. Lowry, Lois. *Us and Uncle Fraud* (4–6). 1984, Houghton $10.45. Two children become disillusioned with their Uncle Claude.

2328. McHugh, Elisabeth. *Raising a Mother Isn't Easy* (5–7). 1983, Greenwillow $9.00. Karen, an adopted Korean orphan, has a wonderful relationship with her stepmother. Two sequels are: *Karen's Sister* (1983, $10.00); *Karen and Vicki* (1984, $9.00).

2329. MacLachlan, Patricia. *Cassie Binegar* (4–7). 1982, Harper $9.13; LB $8.89. Cassie is not happy with the disorder in her family situation.

2330. MacLachlan, Patricia. *Seven Kisses in a Row* (2–4). Illus. by Maria Pia Marrella. 1983, Harper $8.61; LB $8.89. Seven stories about 2 youngsters who are cared for by an aunt and uncle.

2331. Maguire, Gregory. *The Lightning Time* (5–7). 1978, Farrar $7.95. After the illness of his mother, David moves to his grandmother's home in northern New York State. A sequel is: *Lights on the Lake* (1981, $10.95).

2332. Mathis, Sharon Bell. *The Hundred Penny Box* (3–5). Illus. by Leo Dillon and Diane Dillon. 1975, Viking $10.95. Old and frail Aunt Dew tells Michael about her experiences through a box that contains a penny for each year of her life.

2333. Mearian, Judy Frank. *Someone Slightly Different* (6–8). 1980, Dial $8.95; LB $8.44. Marty Trevor's grandmother comes to take over the household.

2334. Mearian, Judy Frank. *Two Ways about It* (5–7). 1979, Dial $7.95. Eleven-year-old Annie decides that having her older cousin Lou spend summers with her has a lot of hidden rewards.

2335. Miles, Betty. *Just the Beginning* (4–7). 1976, Avon paper $2.25. Being relatively poor in an upper-class neighborhood causes problems for 13-year-old Catherine Myers.

2336. Miles, Miska. *Aaron's Door* (2–5). Illus. by Alan E. Cober. 1977, Little $6.95. Aaron and his sister are adopted, and they react quite differently toward their new parents.

2337. Moskin, Marietta D. *Rosie's Birthday Present* (1–4). Illus. by David S. Rose. 1981, Atheneum LB $10.95. Through a series of trades, Rosie is able to get a birthday present for her mother.

2338. Nesbit, Edith. *The Railway Children* (3–7). 1975, Dent $9.00; Penguin paper $2.25. Bobbie, Peter, and Phyllis try to solve the mystery of their father's disappearance.

2339. Neville, Emily. *It's Like This, Cat* (7–9). Illus. by Emil Weiss. 1963, Harper $10.53; LB $10.89; paper $2.95. Good picture of New York and city living is presented in the story of Dave and his relationships with his friends and family. Newbery Award winner, 1964. Also use: *Berries Goodman* (1965, Harper paper $2.95).

2340. Nixon, Joan Lowery. *The Gift* (4–6). Illus. by Andrew Glass. 1983, Macmillan $8.95. Brian's Irish great-grandfather tells him stories of leprechauns.

2341. Orgel, Doris. *A Certain Magic* (4–6). 1976, Dial $7.95; paper $1.95. Jenny's reading from her aunt's childhood diary leads to her tracking down some of her aunt's lost friends.

2342. Pascal, Francine. *The Hand-Me-Down Kid* (5–7). 1980, Viking $9.95; Dell paper $2.25. Eleven-year-old Ari feels that other people, including her older sister, are taking advantage of her.

2343. Paterson, Katherine. *Jacob Have I Loved* (6–9). 1980, Harper $8.95; LB $9.89; Avon paper $1.95. A story set in the Chesapeake Bay region about the rivalry between 2 sisters. A Newbery Award winner.

2344. Paulsen, Gary. *Popcorn Days and Buttermilk Nights* (6–9). 1983, Dutton $10.63. A troubled young boy is sent to live with poor relatives on a farm in Minnesota.

2345. Pellowski, Anne. *Willow Wind Farm: Betsy's Story* (3–5). Illus. by Wendy Watson. 1981, Putnam

$8.95. Episodes on a small Wisconsin farm involving Betsy and her family. Sequels are: *Stairstep Farm: Anna Rose's Story* (1981); *First Farm in the Valley: Anna's Story* (1982); *Winding Valley Farm: Annie's Story* (1982) (all $9.95); *Betsy's Up-and-Down* (1983, $10.95).

2346. Perl, Lila. *Annabelle Starr, E.S.P.* (5–8). 1983, Houghton $10.95. Does Annabelle really have E.S.P. as she thinks she has?

2347. Perl, Lila. *Tybbee Trimble's Hard Times* (5–7). 1984, Houghton $10.95. Because of financial problems at home, Tybbee can't go to the circus.

2348. Pevsner, Stella. *And You Give Me a Pain, Elaine* (5–7). 1978, Houghton $7.99; Pocket paper $1.95. Andrea tries to get along with her older sister while trying to adjust to her mother's death.

2349. Pfeffer, Susan Beth. *Kid Power* (4–6). Illus. by Leigh Grant. 1977, Watts $8.90; Scholastic paper $1.95. A spunky, young girl organizes an employment agency for herself and friends when her mother loses her job.

2350. Phipson, Joan. *The Family Conspiracy* (5–6). 1965, Harcourt paper $4.95. Some Australian children try to collect enough money for their mother's operation.

2351. Rabin, Gil. *Changes* (6–9). 1973, Harper LB $10.89. Chris finds many things difficult to adjust to, including his mother's move to Brooklyn and placing his grandfather in a nursing home.

2352. Read, Elfrieda. *Brothers by Choice* (6–9). 1974, Farrar $6.95. Brett tries to resolve the difficulties between his pompous and difficult father and his alienated and older adopted brother, Rocky.

2353. Reynolds, Pamela. *Will the Real Monday Please Stand Up* (6–9). 1975, Pocket paper $1.75. Fourteen-year-old Monday Holliday tells of her brother's encounters with drugs and her growing alienation from her family.

2354. Rinaldo, C. L. *Dark Dreams* (6–9). 1974, Harper $8.61. In this novel set during World War II, Carlo adjusts to a new life with his grandmother.

2355. Rodowsky, Colby F. *Evy-Ivy-Over* (5–7). 1978, Watts $8.90. Slug's grandmother has an unusual gift, which causes embarrassment for the young girl.

2356. Rodowsky, Colby F. *H, My Name Is Henley* (6–8). 1982, Farrar $10.95. Henley's mother Patti is forever on the move.

2357. Rogers, Pamela. *The Rare One* (4–6). 1974, Lodestar $6.95. Josh's tragedy and guilt over the death of an old man he has befriended bring him closer to his own family.

2358. Root, Phyllis, and Marron, Carol A. *Gretchen's Grandma* (K–2). Illus. by Deborah Kogan Ray. 1983, Raintree $10.99. Although they don't speak the same language, Gretchen and her grandmother spend a find day together.

2359. Sachs, Marilyn. *Dorrie's Book* (5–6). Illus. by Ann Sachs. 1975, Doubleday $7.95. For a school assignment, Dorrie writes on how her comfortable "only child" status was upset with the arrival of triplets.

2360. St. Peter, Joyce. *Always Abigail* (4–6). Illus. by Elise Primavera. 1981, Harper $9.13; LB $8.89. Eleven-year-old Abigail not only survives but also unexpectedly enjoys a summer with her aunt.

2361. Shotwell, Louisa R. *Magdalena* (5–7). Illus. by Lilian Obligado. 1971, Dell paper $1.50. Generation and cultural conflicts in a Puerto Rican family involving Magdalena, her grandmother, and the girl's desire to have her pigtails cut.

2362. Sidney, Margaret. *Five Little Peppers and How They Grew* (4–6). Illus. by W. Sharp. n.d., Putnam $9.95; paper $5.95. The classic of 5 children growing up several years ago.

2363. Simon, Norma. *How Do I Feel?* (4–6). Illus. by Joe Lasker. 1970, Whitman $8.95. A small boy has tangled, emotional problems with his twin and his older brother.

2364. Skolsky, Mindy Warshaw. *Carnival and Kopeck and More about Hannah* (3–5). Illus. by Karen Ann Weinhaus. 1979, Harper $7.95; LB $9.89. Hannah's relationship with her grandmother is realistically treated in this convincing novel. Two sequels are: *Hannah Is a Palindrome* (1980, $8.95; LB $8.79); *Hannah and the Best Father on Route 9W* (1982, $11.06; LB $11.89).

2365. Smith, Alison. *Reserved for Mark Anthony Crowder* (5–7). 1978, Dutton $9.95. Mark, a misfit sixth grader, is able to prove himself to his father.

2366. Smith, Janice Lee. *The Monster in the Third Dresser Drawer and Other Stories about Adam Joshua* (3–5). Illus. by Dick Gackenbach. 1981, Harper $8.61; LB $8.89. Adam Joshua faces many everyday problems, including a new baby sister, in these 6 stories. A sequel is: *The Kid Next Door and Other Headaches: Stories about Adam Joshua* (1984, $9.95; LB $9.89).

2367. Smith, Robert Kimmel. *The War with Grandpa* (4–6). Illus. by Richard Lauter. 1984, Delacorte $12.95; LB $12.95; Dell paper $2.25. Peter resents giving up his bedroom to his grandfather.

2368. Sorensen, Virginia. *Miracles on Maple Hill* (4–6). Illus. by Beth Krush and Joe Krush. 1956, Harcourt $7.95; paper $4.95. The story of a troubled family drawn together by the experience of a year of country living. Newbery Award winner, 1957.

2369. Spinelli, Jerry. *Who Put That Hair in My Toothbrush?* (6–8). 1984, Little $12.45. In alternating chapters, a brother and sister tell of their problems and triumphs.

2370. Spyri, Johanna H. *Heidi* (4–6). Illus. by Greta Elgaard. 1962, Western $4.50. A Swiss girl must leave her beloved grandfather. One of many recommended editions of this classic.

2371. Stolz, Mary. *Go and Catch a Flying Fish* (6–8). 1979, Harper $10.53; LB $12.45. Three children face a disturbing future when their mother abandons them. A sequel is: *What Time of Night Is It?* (1981, $10.53).

2372. Stolz, Mary. *Lands End* (5–8). Illus. by Dennis Hermanson. 1973, Harper $12.95. Josh finds an intriguing contrast between his family structure and the casual, relaxed life-style of his new neighbors, the Arthurs.

2373. Strang, Celia. *Foster Mary* (6–8). 1979, McGraw $8.95. The story of Aunt Foster Mary, her husband Alonzo, and the 4 unrelated, unwanted children they have taken in.

2374. Stren, Patti. *There's a Rainbow in My Closet* (4–6). 1979, Harper $10.51. During a visit, Emma's grandmother helps the young girl understand why it's good to be different.

2375. Sunderlin, Sylvia. *Antrim's Orange* (2–4). Illus. by Diane de Groat. 1976, Scribners $1.79. During World War II, a young boy receives a precious orange from visiting grandmother.

2376. Sutton, Jane. *Me and the Weirdos* (4–6). 1981, Harcourt LB $6.95; Bantam paper $1.95. Sandy tries to change her eccentric family but without success.

2377. Taylor, Mildred D. *Roll of Thunder, Hear My Cry* (6–8). Illus. by Jerry Pinkney. 1976, Dial $10.95. Set in rural Mississippi during the Depression, this Newbery Award winner continues the story about black Cassie Logan and her family. Begun in: *Song of the Trees* (1975, $7.95; LB $7.89); continued in: *Let the Circle Be Unbroken* (1981, $14.95; Bantam paper $2.95).

2378. Taylor, Sydney. *All-of-a-Kind Family* (3–6). Illus. by Helen John. 1951, Dell paper $2.25. Warm and moving stories of Jewish family life in New York City. Also use: *More All-of-a-Kind Family* (1954, Dell paper $1.25); *All-of-a-Kind Family Uptown* (1968, Dell paper $1.95); *All-of-a-Kind Family Downtown* (1972, Dell paper $1.75); *Ella of All-of-a-Kind Family* (1978, Dutton $9.95; Dell paper $1.50).

2379. Terris, Susan. *Octopus Pie* (4–6). 1983, Farrar $10.95. Kristen and her sister Mari don't get along, particularly when father brings home an octopus.

2380. Thayer, Marjorie. *The Youngest* (4–5). Illus. by Dale Payson. 1982, Dodd LB $7.95. Nine-year-old Margie envies her grown-up sisters.

2381. Thiele, Colin. *February Dragon* (5–7). 1976, Harper LB $10.89. The Pine family face a new life in a rural Australia after their home is destroyed by the February dragon, a brush fire that gets out of control.

2382. Thomas, Jane Resh. *Elizabeth Catches a Fish* (2–4). Illus. by Joseph Duffy. 1977, Houghton $6.95. For her seventh birthday, Elizabeth receives fishing gear and, with her father, goes on a day-long fishing trip.

2383. Thompson, Jean. *Don't Forget Michael* (3–4). Illus. by Margot Apple. 1979, Morrow $8.75; LB $8.40. Four short stories about Michael and his large family.

2384. Thrasher, Crystal. *The Dark Didn't Catch Me* (6–8). 1975, Atheneum paper $1.95. Young Seely is determined to survive and not let the dark catch her. Four sequels are: *Between Dark and Daylight* (1979, $10.95); *Julie's Summer* (1981); *End of a Dark Road* (1982); *A Taste of Daylight* (1984) (all $12.95).

2385. Tobias, Tobi. *How Your Mother and Father Met, and What Happened After* (3–4). Illus. by Diane de Groat. 1978, McGraw $6.95. A story of courtship, marriage, and the arrival of the first child.

2386. Tolan, Stephanie S. *Grandpa and Me* (4–6). 1978, Scribners $9.95. A young girl must face life with a senile grandfather.

2387. Townsend, John R. *Noah's Castle* (6–9). 1976, Harper $9.57. Interpersonal conflicts within a family are realistically portrayed in this novel set in England in the near future.

2388. Uchida, Yoshiko. *A Jar of Dreams* (4–7). 1981, Atheneum $11.95. A Japanese-American family is disillusioned until Aunt Waka arrives. A sequel is: *The Best Bad Thing* (1983, $9.95).

2389. Voigt, Cynthia. *Dicey's Song* (5–8). 1982, Atheneum $10.95. This story of Dicey's life with her "Gram" in Maryland won a Newbery Award. Preceding it was: *Homecoming* (1981, LB $12.95); a sequel is: *A Solitary Blue* (1983, $10.95).

2390. Walker, Diana. *The Hundred Thousand Dollar Farm* (6–8). 1977, Harper $9.95. An abandoned Australian boy seeks shelter with a Prince Edward Island farm family.

2391. Walker, Diana. *The Year of the Horse* (5–7). 1975, Harper $9.95; paper $2.95. Joanna's year on her grandmother's farm in Ontario provides unexpected rewards.

2392. Wells, Rosemary. *Leave Well Enough Alone* (6–8). 1977, Dial $8.95; Pocket paper $1.95. Fourteen-year-old Dorothy takes a summer job with a wealthy family in Pennsylvania, caring for their spoiled children.

2393. Wiegand, Roberta. *The Year of the Comet* (3–5). 1984, Bradbury $9.95. The events of 1910 as experienced by Sarah and family.

2394. Wiggin, Kate Douglas. *Rebecca of Sunnybrook Farm* (4–7). Illus. by Lawrence Beall Smith. n.d, Houghton $6.95. Rebecca is a spunky, curious girl living in a quiet Maine community of the nineteenth century. One of many editions.

2395. Wilder, Laura Ingalls. *Little House in the Big Woods* (4–7). Illus. by Garth Williams. 1932, Harper $12.45; LB $12.89; paper $2.95. Outstanding story of a log-cabin family in Wisconsin in the late 1800s. Also use: *By the Shores of Silver Lake* (1953); *Farmer Boy* (1953); *Little House on the Prairie* (1953); *Little Town on the Prairie* (1953); *Long Winter* (1953); *On the Banks of Plum Creek* (1953); *These Happy Golden Years* (1953); *The First Four Years* (1971) (all Harper $12.45; LB $12.89; paper $2.95).

2396. Wilder, Laura Ingalls. *West from Home: Letters of Laura Ingalls Wilder, San Francisco* (6–9). 1974, Harper $10.53; LB $10.89; paper $2.95. Laura visited her daughter Rose in San Francisco in the year that the city was preparing a world's fair, and she wrote about her experiences to her husband.

2397. Wright, Betty Ren. *Getting Rid of Marjorie* (4–6). 1981, Holiday $8.95; Scholastic paper $1.95. Emily is upset when her grandfather remarries.

2398. Yep, Laurence. *Child of the Owl* (6–9). 1977, Harper LB $10.89; Dell paper $2.25. Because of family problems, Casey is sent to live with her grandmother in San Francisco's Chinatown.

2399. Yolen, Jane. *Uncle Lemon's Spring* (3–6). Illus. by Glen Rounds. 1981, Dutton $9.25. Uncle Lemon and Letty outwit the mean Preacher Morton in this mountain tale.

2400. Zindel, Bonnie, and Zindel, Paul. *A Star for the Latecomer* (6–9). 1980, Harper $10.53; LB $10.89. A girl's relations with her terminally ill mother are explored in this novel with a ballet setting.

Friendship Stories

2401. Adler, Carole S. *The Magic of the Glits* (5–7). Illus. by Ati Forberg. 1979, Macmillan $9.95. Jeremy, age 12, takes care of 7-year-old Lynette for the summer. A sequel is: *Some Other Summer* (1982, $9.95).

2402. Angell, Judie. *The Buffalo Nickel Blues Band* (5–8). 1982, Bradbury $9.95; Dell paper $2.50. Five youngsters join together to form a band.

2403. Angell, Judie. *Ronnie and Rosie* (5–7). 1977, Bradbury $9.95. Ronnie, a girl, and Rosie, a boy, form a close friendship, particularly after the death of Ronnie's father.

2404. Angell, Judie. *Secret Selves* (6–8). 1979, Bradbury $9.95. A prank phone call leads to two youngsters developing a secret friendship.

2405. Angell, Judie. *Tina Gogo* (5–8). 1978, Bradbury $9.95. Sarajane becomes friendly with an outlandish, irresponsible, but basically insecure young girl.

2406. Angell, Judie. *A Word from Our Sponsor or My Friend Alfred* (5–7). 1979, Bradbury $9.95; Dell paper $1.75. A message about consumerism is delivered in this entertaining novel about a group of boys who take on big business.

2407. Asher, Sandy. *Daughters of the Law* (6–8). 1980, Beaufort Books $7.95; Dell paper $1.95. Denise becomes friends with a Jewish girl who is still suffering from her family's experiences in Nazi Germany.

2408. Asher, Sandy. *Just Like Jenny* (5–8). 1982, Delacorte $9.95; Dell paper $2.50. The story of 2 girls, their friendship, and their training in ballet.

2409. Bargar, Gary W. *Life Is Not Fair* (6–9). 1984, Houghton $11.95. Louis decides to become friends with the black kid who has moved next door.

2410. Bates, Betty. *That's What T.J. Says* (4–6). 1982, Holiday $10.95. A young girl grows to independence through a friendship with another loner.

2411. Beckman, Delores. *My Own Private Sky* (6–8). 1980, Dutton $9.95. A young boy helps his 68-year-old friend recover after an automobile accident.

2412. Beim, Lorraine, and Beim, Jerrold. *Two Is a Team* (K–3). Illus. by Ernest Crichlow. 1945, Harcourt $8.95; paper $1.25. Interracial friendship is the theme of this story of 2 boys.

2413. Berger, Terry. *Special Friends* (3–5). Illus. 1979, Messner $7.95. The story of a friendship between a young girl and an elderly woman.

2414. Billington, Elizabeth. *Getting to Know Me* (4–6). 1982, Warne $8.95. Pete and Billy spend a summer in a small town in Massachusetts.

2415. Billington, Elizabeth. *Part-Time Boy* (4–6). 1980, Warne $7.95. Jamie, a quiet boy, gains self-confidence through a friendship with a most unusual young woman.

2416. Bosse, Malcolm J. *The 79 Squares* (6–9). 1979, Houghton $9.57; LB $10.89. An unusual story of a friendship between a young boy and a dying ex-convict.

2417. Brynildsen, Ken. *School's Out!* (5–8). 1982, Putnam $9.95. The story of 4 boys and their summer adventures.

2418. Bulla, Clyde Robert. *The Cardboard Crown* (2–5). Illus. by Michele Chessare. 1984, Harper $10.95; LB $10.89. Adam tries to help the strange girl who is staying with a neighbor.

2419. Bunting, Eve. *The Empty Window* (3–6). Illus. by Judy Clifford. 1980, Warne $7.95. C.G. wants to catch a wild parrot to give to his dying friend.

2420. Bunting, Eve. *One More Flight* (4–8). 1976, Warne $5.95. A runaway boy finds help and direction in his life from meeting Timmie, who nurses injured birds of prey.

2421. Burch, Robert. *Two That Were Tough* (4–6). Illus. by Richard Cuffari. 1976, Viking $9.95. A story set in rural Georgia about an old man's attachment to children who, like himself, crave independence.

2422. Byars, Betsy. *The Animal, the Vegetable and John D. Jones* (5–8). Illus. by Ruth Sanderson. 1982, Delacorte $9.95; LB $9.89; Dell paper $2.25. Clara and Deanie must share their vacation with the brainy John D.

2423. Byars, Betsy. *The Pinballs* (5–7). 1977, Harper $8.57; LB $8.89. Three misfits in a foster home band together to help lessen their problems.

2424. Calhoun, Mary. *Katie John* (4–6). Illus. by Paul Frame. 1960, Harper LB $10.89. In spite of her worst fears, Katie John has a pleasant time and makes new friends during a summer in a small southern town. Three sequels are: *Depend on Katie John* (1961, LB $10.89); *Honestly, Katie John!* (1963, LB $10.89; paper $2.95); *Katie John and Heathcliff* (1980, LB $9.89; paper $2.95).

2425. Callen, Larry. *Sorrow's Song* (5–7). Illus. by Marvin Friedman. 1979, Little $7.95. In a Four Corners story, Pinch and his friend Sorrow try to save a whooping crane. A sequel is: *The Muskrat War* (1980, $8.95).

2426. Carlson, Natalie Savage. *Ann Aurelia and Dorothy* (4–6). Illus. by Dale Payson. 1968, Harper $9.89. Foster child Ann Aurelia must decide between her foster home, with its experiences of sharing in her black friend Dorothy's stable home life, and her mother.

2427. Carlson, Natalie Savage. *Carnival in Paris* (2–4). Illus. by Fermin Rocker. 1962, Harper $12.89. Children of carnival workers spend their Easter vacation at the Gingerbread Fair.

2428. Carlson, Natalie Savage. *Family under the Bridge* (3–5). Illus. by Garth Williams. 1958, Harper $12.89. Old Armand, a Paris hobo, finds 3 children huddled in his hideaway under the bridge and befriends them.

2429. Carrick, Carol. *Some Friend!* (3–5). Illus. by Donald Carrick. 1979, Houghton $8.95. It is difficult for Mike to accept his friend Rob's overbearing behavior.

2430. Child Study Children's Book Committee, ed. *Friends Are Like That! Stories to Read to Yourself* (2–3). Illus. by Leigh Grant. 1979, Harper $10.53; LB $10.89. Nine stories and 2 poems celebrate friendship in its many facets.

2431. Conford, Ellen. *Me and the Terrible Two* (4–6). Illus. by Charles Carroll. 1978, Little $8.95; Pocket paper $1.75. The *Me* of the title, Dorrie, wages an undeclared war on twin boys who move next door, until she becomes ill and they become her only real friends.

2432. Cooper, Susan. *Dawn of Fear* (5–6). Illus. by Margery Gill. 1970, Harcourt $5.95. Reality must be faced by a group of English boys when one of their friends is killed in an air raid during World War II.

2433. Corcoran, Barbara. *The Winds of Time* (5–7). Illus. by Gail Owens. 1974, Atheneum $7.95. When Gail runs away rather than be forced to live with her Uncle Chad, whom she dislikes, she stumbles into a new life and unexpected kindness and understanding.

2434. Cresswell, Helen. *The Bongleweed* (4–6). 1973, Macmillan $8.95. In this English story, Becky and her friend try to save a strange plant they call the "bongleweed."

2435. Cresswell, Helen. *The Night Watchmen* (4–6). Illus. by Gareth Floyd. 1970, Macmillan $8.95. Henry has time on his hands until he meets 2 fascinating tramps, Josh and Caleb.

2436. Delton, Judy. *Kitty in the Middle* (3–4). Illus. by Charles Robinson. 1979, Houghton $6.95; Dell paper $1.50. An episodic account of 3 fourth-grade girls living through the war in 1942. Two sequels are: *Kitty in the Summer* (1980, $8.95; Dell paper $1.95); *Kitty in High School* (1984, $10.45).

2437. Derman, Martha. *The Friendstone* (6–8). 1981, Dial $8.95; LB $8.44. Sally is fearful of making friends with Evie, a Jewish girl.

2438. Donnelly, Elfie. *Offbeat Friends* (4–6). 1982, Crown $8.95. Eleven-year-old Mari becomes friends with an old lady from a mental home.

2439. Eige, Lillian E. *The Kidnapping of Mister Huey* (6–8). 1983, Harper $9.57; LB $9.89. Young Wally and his elderly friend, Mr. Huey, decide to go on a trip together.

2440. Epstein, Anne Merrick. *Good Stones* (5–7). Illus. by Susan Meddaugh. 1977, Houghton $6.95. During the 1930s in New Hampshire, 2 outcasts—a young part-Indian girl and an ex-convict—try to find a better world together.

2441. Farrar, Susan Clement. *Samantha on Stage* (5–6). Illus. by Ruth Sanderson. 1979, Dial $7.95; LB $7.45. Lizinska and Sam study ballet together.

2442. Feil, Heila. *The Ghost Garden* (4–6). Illus. by Thomas Quirk. 1976, Atheneum $7.95. Death separates 2 girls whose friendship had grown one summer on Cape Cod.

2443. Gaeddert, Louann. *Your Former Friend, Matthew* (3–5). Illus. by Mary Beth Schwark. 1984, Dutton $9.66. Gail finds that suddenly Matthew is no longer interested in their friendship.

2444. Giff, Patricia Reilly. *The Girl Who Knew It All* (3–5). Illus. by Leslie Morrill. 1979, Delacorte $6.95; LB $6.89; Dell paper $1.95. Tracy faces up to the fact that she has reading problems.

2445. Greenberg, Jan. *The Iceberg and Its Shadow* (5–7). 1980, Farrar $8.95; Dell paper $1.75. Anabeth's position as class leader is jeopardized by the arrival of arrogant Mindy.

2446. Greene, Bette. *Philip Hall Likes Me, I Reckon Maybe* (4–6). Illus. 1974, Dial $12.95; LB $12.89; Dell paper $1.95. Beth finds that letting Philip Hall get first place in their class turns out not to be the best way to gain his affection. A sequel is: *Get On Out of Here Philip Hall* (1981, $12.89; LB $12.89; Dell paper $2.25).

2447. Greene, Constance C. *Ask Anybody* (5–7). 1983, Viking $10.95; Dell paper $2.50. "Sky" Sweet forms a friendship with a most unusual girl.

2448. Greene, Constance C. *Dotty's Suitcase* (5–7). 1980, Viking $9.95; Dell paper $2.25. Dotty and her friend Jud find a suitcase full of money.

2449. Greene, Constance C. *Getting Nowhere* (6–8). 1977, Viking $11.50. Fourteen-year-old Mark's bottled-up hatred turns to self-loathing in this powerful novel.

2450. Greene, Constance C. *A Girl Called Al* (5–7). Illus. by Byron Barton. 1969, Viking $10.95; Dell paper $2.25. The friendship between 2 seventh graders and their apartment building superintendent is humorously and deftly recounted. Three sequels are: *I Know You, Al* (1975, $9.95; Dell paper $2.25); *Your Old Pal, Al* (1979, $10.95; Dell paper $1.95); *Al(exandra) the Great* (1982, $10.95; Dell paper $2.25).

2451. Greene, Constance C. *The Unmaking of Rabbit* (4–6). 1972, Viking $9.95. The class outsider overcomes many disappointments and slights to gain a measure of acceptance by his peers and a feeling of confidence.

2452. Grohskopf, Bernice. *Children in the Wind* (6–8). 1977, Atheneum $8.95. Lenora makes friends with 2 different but fascinating girls.

2453. Hahn, Mary D. *Daphne's Book* (6–8). 1983, Houghton $10.95. The story of a friendship between two very different girls.

2454. Hahn, Mary D. *The Sara Summer* (4–6). 1979, Houghton $7.95. Two young girls, Sara and Emily, form a friendship one summer.

2455. Hammer, Charles. *Me, the Beef, and the Bum* (6–9). 1984, Farrar $10.95. Rosie, her pet steer, and a vagrant run away together.

2456. Hanlon, Emily. *The Swing* (5–7). 1979, Bradbury $9.95. Two youngsters, one deaf and the other grieving for a dead father, are brought together at the swing.

2457. Hansen, Joyce. *The Gift-Giver* (4–7). 1980, Houghton $7.95. Doris forms a friendship with a quiet boy, Amir.

2458. Hart, Carole. *Delilah* (3–4). Illus. by Edward Frascino. 1973, Harper $9.89; Avon paper $1.95. A friendly, cozy book about the everyday adventures of an unusual heroine.

2459. Hayes, Sheila. *Speaking of Snapdragons* (4–6). 1982, Lodestar $8.95. Heather feels left out and lonely until she meets an old man named Duffy.

2460. Hermes, Patricia. *Friends Are Like That* (5–8). 1984, Harcourt $12.95. Tracy must make a choice between unconventional Kelly and the popular crowd.

2461. Hoban, Lillian. *I Met a Traveller* (5–7). 1977, Harper LB $9.89. Josie and her newly divorced mother have an extended visit to Israel, where Josie conquers her loneliness.

2462. Holmes, Efner Tudor. *Carrie's Gift* (2–4). Illus. by Tasha Tudor. 1978, Putnam $7.95; LB $7.99. The story of the friendship between a young girl and a lonely old man.

2463. Hurwitz, Johanna. *The Hot and Cold Summer* (4–6). Illus. by Gail Owens. 1984, Morrow $9.00. Rory and Derek wonder about their neighbor's niece, who is spending the summer with her aunt.

2464. Jones, Adrienne. *The Hawks of Chelney* (6–9). Illus. by Stephen Gammell. 1978, Harper $10.95; LB $10.89. A strong, introspective story of an outcast from his tribe and his love for a shipwrecked girl.

2465. Jones, Rebecca C. *Angie and Me* (4–6). 1981, Macmillan $8.95. The story of two girls confined in the same hospital room.

2466. Keller, Beverly. *Fiona's Bee* (2–3). Illus. by Diane Paterson. 1975, Putnam LB $6.99. Fiona accidentally makes a number of friends when she saves a bee from drowning. Also use: *The Bee Sneeze* (1982, Putnam $6.99).

2467. Kemp, Gene. *Gowie Corby Plays Chicken* (4–6). 1980, Faber $9.95. Gowie is reformed through his friendship with Rosie.

2468. Kemp, Gene. *Turbulent Term of Tyke Tiller* (4–6). Illus. by Carolyn Dinan. 1980, Faber $10.95. A humorous English story about Tyke's friendship with Danny, a boy with a speech impediment.

2469. Kerr, M. E. *The Son of Someone Famous* (6–9). 1979, Harper $10.89; NAL paper $2.25. Adam Blessing and Brenda Belle Blossom are 2 outsiders whose problems bring them together in a small-town environment.

2470. Klevin, Jill Ross. *The Turtle Street Trading Co.* (4–6). Illus. by Linda Strauss Edwards. 1982, Delacorte $9.95; LB $9.89; Dell paper $2.25. Four youngsters band together to make enough money to go to Disneyland. A sequel is: *Turtles Together Forever!* (1982, $9.95; LB $9.89; Dell paper $2.25).

2471. Konigsburg, E. L. *Jennifer, Hecate, Macbeth, William McKinley, and Me, Elizabeth* (4–6). Illus. by author. 1967, Atheneum $7.95; paper $2.95. Black Jennifer hazes white newcomer Elizabeth, her apprentice witch, and their amusing amateur sorcery leads to the magic of a firm friendship for 2 loners.

2472. Lampman, Evelyn Sibley. *Three Knocks on the Wall* (5–7). 1980, Atheneum $8.95. A young girl discovers a counterpart who has been kept in hiding by a neighbor.

2473. LeGuin, Ursula. *Very Far from Anywhere Else* (6–8). 1976, Atheneum $6.95. A loner, attending a college he dislikes, forms a friendship with an equally independent girl.

2474. Line, David. *Soldier and Me* (6–8). 1965, Harper $10.89. An English schoolboy befriends a Hungarian refugee, and they join forces in an effort to prevent murder.

2475. Lipp, Frederick J. *Some Lose Their Way* (6–9). 1980, Atheneum $8.95. David gets satisfaction teasing timid Victoria in his eighth-grade class.

2476. Lipsyte, Robert. *The Summerboy* (5–7). 1982, Harper $10.10; LB $10.89; Bantam paper $2.25. A humorous story of growing up. Also use: *Summer Rules* (1981, Harper $10.53; LB $10.89).

2477. Little, Jean. *Look through My Window* (4–6). Illus. by Joan Sandin. 1970, Harper $7.89; paper $2.95. Emily's ideas change when Aunt Deborah's 4 children come to live with Emily's family. A sequel is: *Kate* (1971, $10.89; paper $2.95).

2478. Little, Jean. *Stand in the Wind* (4–6). Illus. 1975, Harper $10.89; paper $2.95. Four young girls share a lake cottage during one summer and gradually lose their animosities.

2479. Magorian, Michelle. *Good Night, Mr. Tom* (6–9). 1982, Harper $12.02; LB $11.89. For better readers, the story of a friendship between an old man and a battered child.

2480. Mark, Jan. *Thunder and Lightnings* (6–9). 1979, Harper $8.95; LB $9.89. Two English boys form a fast friendship in this story set in Norfolk, which won the Carnegie Medal, 1976.

2481. Marney, Dean. *Just Good Friends* (5–8). 1982, Addison LB $9.95. Thirteen-year-old Lou finds two men friends who help him through adolescence.

2482. Mazer, Harry. *Snowbound* (5–7). 1973, Dell paper $1.95. In this survival story, Tony and Cindy spend 11 days together snowbound.

2483. Mazer, Norma Fox. *Mrs. Fish, Ape and Me, the Dump Queen* (5–7). 1980, Dutton $8.95; Avon paper $1.95. Three misfits band together in friendship.

2484. Mills, Claudia. *At the Back of the Woods* (4–6). 1982, Scholastic $7.95. Charisse's friend Emily is afraid a curse has been placed on her.

2485. Milton, Joyce. *Save the Loonies* (6–8). 1983, Scholastic $8.95. Twelve-year-old Jenny spends a week with the family of a friend at their camp in New Hampshire.

2486. Myers, Walter Dean. *Fast Sam, Cool Clyde and Stuff* (6–9). 1975, Viking $10.95. Stuff tells the story of the 116th St. Good People, a group of Harlem teenagers who help each other face problems of growing up.

2487. Neville, Emily. *The Seventeenth-Street Gang* (5–7). Illus. by author. 1966, Harper $9.89; paper $2.95. Hollis and her crew find problems accepting Irving, a new boy in their New York City neighborhood.

2488. Newton, Suzanne. *An End to Perfect* (6–8). 1984, Viking $11.50. The friendship of two girls is tested during a series of family problems.

2489. O'Connor, Jane. *Yours Till Niagara Falls* (4–6). Illus. by Margot Apple. 1979, Hastings $9.95; Scholastic paper $1.95. Abby's summer at camp proves to be unexpectedly rewarding.

2490. Paterson, Katherine. *Bridge to Terabithia* (6–8). Illus. by Donna Diamond. 1977, Harper $9.57; Avon paper $2.25. Jess becomes a close friend of Leslie, a new girl in his school, and suffers agony after her accidental death. Newbery Award winner.

2491. Paulsen, Gary. *Dancing Carl* (6–9). 1983, Bradbury $9.95. The story of two boys and their friendship with a man broken by his World War II experiences.

2492. Peck, Robert Newton. *Soup* (5–7). Illus. by Charles C. Gehm. 1974, Knopf $4.95; LB $6.99; Dell paper $2.25. Rural Vermont in the 1920s is recreated in these reminiscences of the author of the times he spent with his friend Soup. Also use: *Soup and Me* (1975, $4.95; LB $5.99; Dell paper $2.25); *Soup for President* (1978, $5.95; LB $5.99); *Soup's Drum* (1980, $6.95; LB $6.99); *Soup on Wheels* (1981, LB $7.99); *Soup in the Saddle* (1983, $9.95); *Soup's Goat* (1984, $9.95; LB $9.99).

2493. Pfeffer, Susan Beth. *Truth or Dare* (5–7). 1984, Four Winds $9.95. A sixth grader explores the nature of friendship when she sets out to make new friends.

2494. Phipson, Joan. *Horse with Eight Hands* (5–7). 1974, Atheneum $7.50. Four children help a German immigrant, Horst, to open an antique shop in this satisfying novel set in Australia.

2495. Robertson, Mary Elsie. *Tarantula and the Red Chigger* (5–7). 1980, Little LB $7.95. Ben's summer turns brighter when he makes a new friend.

2496. Rock, Gail. *Addie and the King of Hearts* (4–6). Illus. by Charles McVicker. 1976, Knopf LB $5.99. Addie Mills, a seventh grader, tries to avoid Billy, who has a crush on her. Also use: *A Dream for Addie* (1975, Bantam paper $1.95).

2497. Roth, David. *The Hermit of Fog Hollow Station* (4–7). 1980, Beaufort $7.95. After rescuing an old man from a stream, Alex becomes friendly with him.

2498. Roy, Ron. *Frankie Is Staying Back* (3–5). Illus. by Walter Kessell. 1981, Houghton $8.95. Two friends are separated when one moves up to the fourth grade.

2499. Sachs, Elizabeth-Ann. *Just Like Always* (4–6). 1981, Atheneum LB $9.95. Two girls in the hospital for operations become friends. A sequel is: *Where Are You, Cow Patty?* (1984, $10.95).

2500. Sachs, Marilyn. *Beach Towels* (6–9). Illus. by Jim Spence. 1982, Dutton $9.95; Avon paper $2.25. A friendship between a boy and girl slowly evolves from encounters at the beach.

2501. Sachs, Marilyn. *Class Pictures* (5–8). 1980, Dutton $9.95. The story of a lasting friendship between 2 school chums.

2502. Sachs, Marilyn. *Hello . . . Wrong Number* (6–9). Illus. by Pamela Johnson. 1981, Dutton $9.75. A friendship begins because of a misdialed phone call.

2503. Sharmat, Marjorie W. *I Saw Him First* (6–9). 1983, Delacorte $12.95; Dell paper $2.25. Dana has a crush on Seymour but finds that friend Andrea is already dating him.

2504. Shura, Mary Francis. *The Barkley Street Six-Pack* (5–7). 1979, Dodd $7.95. Instant friendship with scheming Natalie proves to be ultimately unsatisfactory for Jane.

2505. Simmons, Anthony. *The Optimists of Nine Elms* (5–6). Illus. by Ben Stahl. 1975, Pantheon LB $5.99. A family story set in England in which 2 children form a tender relationship with an old man and his dog.

2506. Singer, Marilyn. *No Applause, Please* (5–7). 1977, Dutton $7.50. Ruthie and Laurie try to remain friends in spite of rivalry about a singing career.

2507. Snyder, Zilpha Keatley. *The Egypt Game* (5–7). Illus. by Alton Raible. 1967, Atheneum $9.95; paper $2.95. Humor and suspense mark an outstanding story of city children whose safety, while playing at an unsupervised re-creation of an Egyptian ritual, is threatened by a violent lunatic.

2508. Snyder, Zilpha Keatley. *The Velvet Room* (5–6). Illus. by Alton Raible. 1965, Atheneum LB $7.95; paper $1.95. Robin's search to escape the realities of life in a sharecropper's family leads her to new friendships and insights.

2509. Stein, R. Conrad. *Me and Dirty Arnie* (4–6). 1982, Harcourt $9.95. Dan, new to Chicago, finds a friend in streetwise Arnie.

2510. Stolz, Mary. *The Bully of Barkham Street* (4–8). Illus. by Leonard Shortall. 1963, Harper LB $10.89. Eleven-year-old Martin goes through a typical phase of growing up—feeling misunderstood. Also use: *A Dog on Barkham Street* (1960, $10.89).

2511. Stolz, Mary. *Cider Days* (4–5). 1978, Harper $10.53; LB $10.89; paper $1.95. A story of how a friendship between 2 very different girls matures. A sequel to: *Ferris Wheel* (1977, LB $10.89; paper $1.95).

2512. Stolz, Mary. *The Noonday Friends* (4–6). Illus. by Louis Glanzman. 1965, Harper $10.89; paper $2.95. Eleven-year-old Franny's unskilled father is out of work, and the demanded family teamwork leaves her free from chores only during lunch periods.

2513. Stolz, Mary. *A Wonderful, Terrible Time* (4–6). 1967, Harper $10.89. Clear characterizations perceptively reveal the different reactions to a summer camp for 2 black girlfriends of lower-income urban families.

2514. Streatfeild, Noel. *Ballet Shoes* (4–6). Illus. by Richard Floethe. 1937, Dell paper $3.25. Three small girls are adopted by an elderly professor and educated for the stage in a London school of dancing.

2515. Tate, Joan. *Wild Boy* (5–7). Illus. by Susan Jeschke. 1973, Harper LB $9.89. The friendship between 2 boys—one quiet and restrained, the other wild and untamed.

2516. Taylor, Theodore. *The Cay* (5–8). 1969, Doubleday $7.95; Avon paper $1.75. Themes of growing up and survival—black versus white, innocence and distrust versus wisdom and respect—are deftly woven into the saga of a young blind American boy and an old West Indian native, both stranded on a Caribbean cay.

2517. Terris, Susan. *Two P's in a Pod* (5–7). 1977, Greenwillow $11.25; LB $10.80. Sixth-grader Pru finds she is being dominated by her look-alike friend, Penny Hoffman.

2518. Thiele, Colin. *The Shadow on the Hills* (5–8). 1978, Harper $10.53. Farm life in rural Australia is highlighted in this story of a young boy and his encounters with a half-crazed hermit.

2519. Wallace, Barbara Brooks. *Hello, Claudia!* (4–6). 1982, Follett $5.97. Claudia Harper finds a new friend in a neighborhood boy, Duffy. A sequel is: *Claudia and Duffy* (1982, $5.97).

2520. Wallace-Brodeur, Ruth. *Callie's Way* (5–7). 1984, Atheneum $10.95. Callie finds herself through a friendship with a stroke victim.

2521. Walsh, Jill Paton. *Babylon* (K–3). Illus. by Jennifer Northway. 1982, Dutton $9.95. Two Jamaican children and a young English girl share adventures in London.

2522. Westall, Robert. *The Machine Gunners* (5–9). 1976, Greenwillow $11.25. Charles and his young friends conceal a machine gun and a German prisoner in this Carnegie Award-winning novel set in a small town during World War II.

2523. Williams, Barbara. *Tell the Truth Marly Lee* (4–6). 1982, Dutton $9.95. Lee wants to get even with Dennis Cunningham.

2524. Winthrop, Elizabeth. *Miranda in the Middle* (5–7). 1980, Holiday $8.95. The story of the trials and tribulations of the friendship between Phoebe and Miranda.

2525. Winthrop, Elizabeth. *Walking Away* (5–7). Illus. by Noelle Massena. 1973, Harper $9.81. Emily's friend Nina doesn't fit in as expected when the 2 girls spend a summer with Emily's grandparents.

2526. York, Carol Beach. *The Look-a-Like Girl* (4–6). 1980, Beaufort $7.95. Gracie bears an uncanny resemblance to Mrs. Mayfield's dead daughter.

School Stories

2527. Adler, Carole S. *The Once in Awhile Hero* (5–7). 1982, Putnam $8.95. A bully accuses a sensitive boy of being a sissy.

2528. Asher, Sandra F. *Summer Begins* (6–8). 1980, Lodestar $8.95. Summer Smith's editorial in the school newspaper causes a furor.

2529. Bottner, Barbara. *The World's Greatest Expert on Absolutely Everything Is Crying* (3–6). 1984, Harper $10.89. The new girl in fifth grade knows absolutely everything, but Jesse and her friends aren't impressed.

2530. Butterworth, W. E. *Moose, the Thing, and Me* (5–7). 1982, Houghton $9.70. Runt Peters, his sheepdog The Thing, friend Moose, and life at a private school.

2531. Byars, Betsy. *The 18th Emergency* (4–6). Illus. by Robert Grossman. 1973, Penguin paper $2.95. A young boy, nicknamed Mousi, incurs the wrath of the school bully and awaits his inevitable punishment with fear.

2532. Carlson, Natalie Savage. *The Empty Schoolhouse* (3–5). Illus. by John Kaufmann. 1965, Harper $10.89. A 10-year-old black girl in a small Louisiana town endures loneliness and abuse as the first to integrate her school.

2533. Carlson, Natalie Savage. *Luvvy and the Girls* (4–6). Illus. by Thomas Di Grazia. 1971, Harper paper $2.95. In this novel, Luvvy Savage adjusts, sometimes with difficulty, to life at Visitation Academy. A sequel to: *The Half Sisters* (1970, paper $2.95).

2534. Carrick, Carol. *What a Wimp!* (4–6). Illus. by Donald Carrick. 1983, Houghton $9.95. Young Barney enters a new school after his parents' divorce and is confronted by a bully.

2535. Caudill, Rebecca. *Did You Carry the Flag Today, Charley?* (2–5). Illus. by Nancy Grossman. 1966, Holt $6.95; paper $2.95. Contemporary Appalachia is the setting for the activities of Charley, an irrepressibly curious kindergartner, who finally achieves the honor of carrying the school flag for his class.

2536. Chaikin, Miriam. *How Yossi Beat the Evil Urge* (3–5). Illus. by Petra Mathers. 1983, Harper $8.61; LB $8.89. A young Jewish boy in Chassidic Yeshiva likes to make mischief.

2537. Chambers, Aidan. *The Present Takers* (5–8). 1984, Harper $10.53; LB $10.89. In this English story, the victims of a bully take their revenge.

2538. Cheatham, K. Follis. *The Best Way Out* (6–8). 1982, Harcourt $9.95. Once a fine student, Haywood has problems in his new junior high school.

2539. Conford, Ellen. *Dear Lovey Hart, I Am Desperate* (6–7). 1975, Little $8.95; Scholastic paper $1.95. Freshman reporter Carrie Wasserman gets into trouble with her advice column in the school newspaper. A sequel is: *We Interrupt This Semester for an Important Announcement* (1979, $8.95; Scholastic paper $1.95).

2540. Conford, Ellen. *The Revenge of the Incredible Dr. Rancid and His Youthful Assistant Jeffrey* (5–7). 1980, Little $6.70. An 11-year-old boy tries to cope with the class bully.

2541. Cross, Gillian. *The Demon Headmaster* (4–6). Illus. by Gary Rees and Mark Thomas. 1983, Merrimack $6.95. The demonic headmaster at an English school is turning his students into automatons.

2542. Cuyler, Margery. *The Trouble with Soap* (5–7). 1982, Dutton $9.95. Two mischievous friends are transferred to Miss Pringle's exclusive girls' school.

2543. Danziger, Paula. *The Cat Ate My Gymsuit* (6–8). 1974, Delacorte $7.95; LB $7.89; Dell paper $2.25. Marcy will go to any lengths to get out of going to gym and to defend an English teacher she feels has been wrongly dismissed. A sequel is: *There's a Bat in Bunk Five* (1980, $9.95; LB $9.89; Dell paper $2.25).

2544. DeClements, Barthe. *Nothing's Fair in Fifth Grade: A Novel* (4–6). 1981, Viking $10.95; Scholastic paper $1.95. Overweight Elsie steals lunch money to feed her habits. A sequel is: *Seventeen and in-Between* (1984, $11.95).

2545. Estes, Eleanor. *The Hundred Dresses* (3–5). Illus. by Louis Slobodkin. 1944, Harcourt $8.95; paper $4.95. A little Polish girl in an American school finally wins acceptance by her classmates.

2546. Fitzhugh, Louise. *Harriet the Spy* (4–6). Illus. by author. 1964, Harper $10.53; LB $10.89; Dell paper $1.75. Precocious, overprivileged Harriet darts around her Manhattan neighborhood ferreting out and writing down the worst and best on her scene, sparing no one. A provocative sequel, primarily about Harriet's friend Beth, is: *The Long Secret* (1965, $12.45; LB $12.89; Dell paper $1.75).

2547. Foley, June. *It's No Crush, I'm in Love!* (6–9). 1982, Delacorte $9.95; Dell paper $2.50. Annie falls in love with her English teacher.

2548. Gaeddert, Louann. *The Kid with the Red Suspenders* (3–5). Illus. by Mary Beth Schwark. 1983, Dutton $9.66. Hamilton Perkins is accused by a classmate of being overprotected and pampered.

2549. Giff, Patricia Reilly. *Fourth-Grade Celebrity* (3–5). Illus. by Leslie Morrill. 1979, Delacorte $8.95; LB $8.89; Dell paper $1.95. Casey decides that she wants to become famous, and she does, in a most surprising way. Two sequels are: *The Girl Who Knew It All* (1979, $6.95; LB $6.89; Dell paper $1.95); *The Winter Worm Business* (1981, $8.95; LB $8.89; Dell paper $1.95).

2550. Giff, Patricia Reilly. *Today Was a Terrible Day* (2–3). Illus. by Susanna Natti. 1980, Viking $9.95. Ronald is having a terrible day until his teacher writes him an understanding note. A sequel is: *The Almost Awful Play* (1984, $9.95).

2551. Gilson, Jamie. *Thirteen Ways to Sink a Sub* (4–7). Illus. by Linda Strauss Edwards. 1982, Lothrop $10.25; Pocket paper $1.95. The girls in Room 4A challenge the boys to see who can first make their substitute teacher cry. A sequel is: *4B Goes Wild* (1983, $9.00).

2552. Girion, Barbara. *Joshua, the Czar and the Chicken Bone Wish* (4–6). Illus. by Richard Cuffari. 1978, Scribners $10.95. Awkward Joshua gets help from Nicholai Romanoff, Czar of Markova.

2553. Greene, Constance C. *Double-Dare O'Toole* (4–6). 1981, Viking $11.50; Dell paper $2.25. Fix O'Toole is game for anything, particularly when double-dared.

2554. Haynes, Betsy. *The Against Taffy Sinclair Club* (4–6). 1981, Bantam paper $2.25. A group of girls victimizes a classmate. A sequel is: *Taffy Sinclair Strikes Again* (1984, paper $2.25).

2555. Haywood, Carolyn. *"B" Is for Betsy* (3–4). Illus. by author. 1939, Harcourt $9.95; paper $2.50. Betsy's adventures in the first grade. Others in the series: *Betsy and Billy* (1941, $9.55; Pocket paper $2.50); *Back to School with Betsy* (1943, $9.95; Pocket paper $3.95); *Betsy and the Boys* (1945, $7.95; Pocket paper $2.95).

2556. Haywood, Carolyn. *Betsy's Play School* (3–5). Illus. by James Griffin. 1977, Morrow $10.80; Pocket paper $1.75. In this Betsy book, the young heroine manages a summer play school for neighborhood children. Also use: *Betsy's Little Star* (1950, LB $10.80; Pocket paper $1.75); *Betsy and the Circus* (1954, LB $10.80; Pocket paper $1.95); *Betsy's Busy Summer* (1956, $11.28; Pocket paper $1.75); *Betsy's Winterhouse* (1958, $10.80); *Snowbound with Betsy* (1962, Pocket paper $1.75).

2557. Haywood, Carolyn. *Here Comes the Bus!* (2–4). Illus. by author. 1963, Morrow LB $10.80. A first-grader's wonderfully funny adventures on the school bus. Also use the Penny stories: *Here's a*

Penny (1944, Harcourt paper $1.75); *Penny and Peter* (1946, Harcourt $7.95).

2558. Herzig, Alison C., and Mali, Jane L. *A Word to the Wise* (4–6). 1978, Little $7.95; Scholastic paper $1.95. Three friends in a slow reading group discover the world of the thesaurus.

2559. Hopper, Nancy J. *Hang On, Harvey!* (5–7). 1983, Dutton $9.66. Harvey Smucker has many problems in the eighth grade, including coping with Miss Hamilton and the school bully.

2560. Hopper, Nancy J. *Lies* (5–8). 1984, Lodestar $10.95. A teenager tells some whoppers to get and keep the attention of a boy she likes.

2561. Hughes, Dean T. *Nutty for President* (4–6). Illus. by Blanche Sims. 1981, Atheneum LB $9.95. A wheeler-dealer named William Bilks takes charge of the fifth-grade election.

2562. Hurwitz, Johanna. *Tough-Luck Karen* (4–6). Illus. by Diane de Groat. 1982, Morrow $9.75; Scholastic paper $1.95. Karen prefers housework to homework.

2563. Kalb, Jonah. *The Kid's Candidate* (5–6). Illus. by Sandy Kossin. 1975, Houghton $5.95. A 13-year-old becomes a candidate for the school board.

2564. Kerr, M. E. *Is That You, Miss Blue?* (6–9). 1975, Harper LB $10.89; Dell paper $1.75. The chronicle of Flanders Brown's first year in a private prep school during which she meets an amazing group of students and teachers, almost gets expelled, and solves some personal problems.

2565. Korman, Gordon. *The War with Mr. Wizzle* (4–6). 1982, Scholastic paper $1.95. Two friends fear that a computer will change their school. Others in the series: *Beware the Fish!*; *Go Jump in the Pool!*; *This Can't Be Happening at MacDonald Hall!* (all 1982, paper $1.95).

2566. Krensky, Stephen. *The Wilder Plot* (5–7). 1982, Atheneum $10.95. Charlie tries desperately to get out of appearing in the class play.

2567. Langton, Jane. *The Boyhood of Grace Jones* (4–6). Illus. by Emily McCully. 1972, Harper paper $2.95. Grace successfully weathers the perils and pitfalls of adolescence while coping with junior high school. A sequel is: *Her Majesty, Grace Jones* (1974, LB $10.89; paper $2.95).

2568. Levitin, Sonia. *The Mark of Conte* (6–9). Illus. by Bill Negron. 1976, Atheneum $8.95. When Conte receives 2 high school program cards because of a complex error, he decides to become 2 students and complete high school in half the time.

2569. Lewis, Marjorie. *Ernie and the Mile-Long Muffler* (2–4). Illus. by Margot Apple. 1982, Putnam $9.95. Ernie gets his first-grade classmate to learn how to knit.

2570. Littke, Lael. *Trish for President* (6–9). 1984, Harcourt $12.95. In a class president's election, Trish decides to run against the boy she likes.

2571. Lovelace, Maud H. *Betsy-Tacy* (3–4). Illus. by Lois Lenski. 1940, Harper $11.89; paper $1.95. Two 5-year-olds are inseparable at school and at play. One of a popular series. Five sequels are: *Betsy-Tacy and Tib* (1941, LB $11.89; paper $1.95); *Betsy and Tacy Go over the Big Hill* (1942, LB $11.89; paper $2.95); *Betsy and Tacy Go Downtown* (1943, LB $11.89; paper $1.95); *Heaven to Betsy* (1945); *Betsy in Spite of Herself* (1946) (both LB $13.50; paper $2.95).

2572. McNeil, Florence. *Miss P. and Me* (5–7). 1984, Harper $10.53; LB $10.89. Janie has her revenge on a teacher by stealing her prize possession.

2573. McNeill, Janet. *Wait for It and Other Stories* (6–9). 1979, Faber paper $2.95. British school life as seen through the eyes of 12 students.

2574. Martin, Ann M. *Stage Fright* (4–6). 1984, Holiday $10.95. Sara is petrified of speaking before a group.

2575. Miles, Betty. *Maudie and Me and the Dirty Book* (5–7). 1980, Knopf LB $7.99; Avon paper $2.25. Kate, a sixth grader, becomes involved in a censorship case involving a first-grade book about birth.

2576. Nordstrom, Ursula. *The Secret Language* (3–5). Illus. by Mary Chalmers. 1960, Harper $10.89; paper $2.95. Boarding school problems begin to look smaller to shy, homesick Vicky when she and her rebelliously outspoken roommate confound the school with their secret language.

2577. Peck, Robert Newton. *Mr. Little* (4–6). Illus. by Ben Stahl. 1979, Doubleday $8.95. A new teacher takes over for beloved Miss Kellogg.

2578. Perl, Lila. *That Crazy April* (5–7). 1974, Houghton $7.95. An identity crisis occurs when Chris is torn between a liberated mother and a traditional male teacher.

2579. Petersen, P. J. *Would You Settle for Improbable?* (5–8). 1981, Delacorte $8.95; LB $8.44; Dell paper $2.25. Three ninth-grade friends try to rehabilitate Arnold Norberry.

2580. Pevsner, Stella. *Cute Is a Four-Letter Word* (6–8). 1980, Houghton $10.50; Pocket paper $1.95. Clara thinks she is in for a great year—but events prove otherwise.

2581. Pevsner, Stella. *A Smart Kid like You* (5–7). 1975, Houghton $8.95; Pocket paper $1.95. Nina's adjustment to a new junior high school becomes more complicated when she discovers that her math teacher is her new stepmother.

2582. Peyton, K. M. *"Who Sir? Me, Sir?"* (6–9). 1983, Oxford $11.95. A humorous English school story in which 2 different sets of youngsters compete in athletics.

2583. Robinson, Nancy K. *Wendy and the Bullies* (3–5). Illus. by Ingrid Fetz. 1980, Hastings $7.95. Wendy is so frightened by the school bullies that she plays hooky to avoid them.

2584. Rosenblatt, Arthur S. *Smarty* (4–7). 1981, Little $8.95. Stanley decides he will become president of his seventh-grade class.

2585. Ruckman, Ivy. *What's an Average Kid Like Me Doing Way Up Here?* (5–8). 1983, Delacorte $11.95; LB $11.89. Norman tries to save his school from destruction.

2586. Sachar, Louis. *Someday Angeline* (3–5). Illus. by Barbara Samuels. 1983, Avon paper $2.25. An 8-year-old with a high IQ has trouble fitting in.

2587. Sachs, Marilyn. *Amy and Laura* (4–6). Illus. by Tracy Sugarman. 1966, Doubleday $6.95; Scholastic paper $1.95. Two sisters face problems at school and at home.

2588. Sachs, Marilyn. *The Bears' House* (4–7). Illus. by Louis Glanzman. 1971, Doubleday $7.95. A poor girl escapes from reality by living in a fantasy in her classroom.

2589. Sachs, Marilyn. *Veronica Ganz* (4–6). Illus. by Louis Glanzman. 1968, Doubleday LB $6.95. Set in pre–World War II Massachusetts, the contemporary issues faced by this 11-year-old anti-heroine girl bully will appeal to younger girls. A sequel is: *Peter and Veronica* (1969, LB $8.95).

2590. Sharmat, Marjorie W. *Getting Something on Maggie Marmelstein* (3–5). Illus. by Ben Shecter. 1971, Harper LB $10.89. When Thad's mortal enemy, Maggie, sees him cooking and begins teasing him, Tad must find some way of blackmailing her into silence. Two sequels are: *Maggie Marmelstein for President* (1975, LB $10.89; paper $1.95); *Mysteriously Yours, Maggie Marmelstein* (1982, $8.61; LB $9.89; paper $3.80).

2591. Shreve, Susan. *The Flunking of Joshua T. Bates* (3–5). Illus. by Diane de Groat. 1984, Knopf $10.95; LB $10.99. Joshua must face the fact that he flunked the third grade.

2592. Simon, Norma. *We Remember Philip* (2–4). Illus. by Ruth Sanderson. 1979, Whitman $8.25. Sam and his classmates sympathize when the son of a favorite teacher is killed.

2593. Stanek, Lou Willett. *Megan's Beat* (6–9). 1983, Dial $10.95. Megan loses her old friends when she starts writing a school gossip column.

2594. Sutton, Jane. *Not Even Mrs. Mazursky* (3–5). Illus. by Joan Drescher. 1984, Dutton $9.66. Stella realizes that even her idealized former teacher has feet of clay.

2595. Twohill, Maggie. *Who Has the Lucky-Duck in Class 4B?* (3–5). 1984, Bradbury $9.95. A lucky charm works its wonders on a number of classmates.

2596. Ure, Jean. *You Two* (5–7). Illus. by Ellen Eagle. 1984, Morrow $8.75. Because of family financial problems, a young English girl must attend a different school.

2597. Williams, Ursula. *No Ponies for Miss Pobjoy* (6–9). 1976, Lodestar $6.50. At Canterdown School for Girls, the new headmistress is uncomfortable with the "horsey" background.

2598. Windsor, Patricia. *Mad Martin* (5–6). 1976, Harper LB $10.89; paper $1.95. Martin, considered mad by his London schoolmates, is actually only lonely and confused.

2599. Wood, Phyllis Anderson. *Pass Me a Pine Cone* (6–8). Illus. 1982, Westminster $11.95. Because he is the new principal's son, Sam expects some problems at school.

Adventure and Mystery

2600. Adkins, Jan. *Luther Tarbox* (5–7). 1977, Scribners $2.49. In this rollicking sea tale, a sailor helps a number of assorted vessels back to port in a fog.

2601. Adler, Carole S. *The Evidence That Wasn't There* (6–9). 1982, Houghton $10.50. Kim feels that her English teacher is being swindled.

2602. Adler, Carole S. *Shadows on Little Reef Bay* (6–9). 1984, Houghton $10.95. A young girl on a Caribbean island with her mother gets involved in a smuggling ring.

2603. Adler, David A. *Cam Jansen and the Mystery of the Stolen Diamonds* (2–4). Illus. by Susanna Natti. 1980, Viking $7.95; Dell paper $1.75. Cam is captured by diamond thieves but still manages to keep in charge. Some sequels are: *Cam Jansen and the Mystery of the U.F.O.* (1980, $8.95; Dell paper $1.75); *Cam Jansen and the Mystery of the Dinosaur Bones* (1981, $8.95; Dell paper $1.75); *Cam Jansen and the Mystery of the Television Dog* (1981, $7.95; Dell paper $1.75); *Cam Jansen and the Mystery of the Babe Ruth Baseball* (1982, $8.95; Dell paper $1.95); *Cam Jansen and the Mystery of the Gold Coins* (1982, $8.95; Dell paper $1.95); *Cam Jansen and the Mystery of the Circus Clown* (1983, $8.50); *Cam Jansen and the Mystery of the Carnival Prize* (1984, $8.95); *Cam Jansen and the Mystery of the Monster Movie* (1984, $8.60).

2604. Adrian, Mary. *The Fireball Mystery* (3–5). Illus. by Reisie Lonette. 1977, Hastings $6.95. Two youngsters uncover a UFO hoax.

2605. Aiken, Joan. *Midnight Is a Place* (6–8). 1974, Viking $9.95. The sweatshops of industrial-age England form the backdrop of a story about a young boy fighting for his rightful inheritance.

2606. Aiken, Joan. *A Whisper in the Night: Tales of Terror and Suspense* (6–9). 1984, Delacorte $14.95. Thirteen short stories of adventure and mystery.

2607. Aiken, Joan. *The Wolves of Willoughby Chase* (4–6). Illus. by Pat Marriott. 1963, Doubleday $8.95; Dell paper $2.50. A Victorian melodrama about two little girls who outwit their wicked governess-guardian. Two sequels are: *Nightbirds on Nantucket* (1981, Dell paper $1.95); *The Stolen Lake* (1981, Delacorte $10.95).

2608. Alcock, Vivien. *The Sylvia Game* (5–8). 1984, Delacorte $14.95. Friends, Emily and Oliver, fear that their fathers are going to market art forgeries.

2609. Allan, Mabel Esther. *The Horns of Danger* (6–9). 1981, Dodd $7.95. Mysterious doings at the Darkling Farm in the English Midlands.

2610. Allen, Linda. *Lionel and the Spy Next Door* (3–5). Illus. by Margot Apple. 1980, Morrow $8.75; LB $8.40. Lionel is convinced that his new neighbor named Mark Shakespeare is really a spy.

2611. Ames, Mildred. *Philo Potts, or the Helping Hand Strikes Again* (4–6). 1982, Scribners $11.95. Philo and his friend Cristabel are on the track of dognappers.

2612. Anckarsvard, Karin. *The Mysterious School-master* (4–6). Illus. by Paul Galdone. 1959, Harcourt paper $2.95. A fast-moving mystery story about spies in a Swedish coastal town. Also use: *The Robber Ghost* (1961, Harcourt paper $3.95); *The Madcap Mystery* (1970, Harcourt paper $2.75).

2613. Anderson, Mary. *R.I.S.K.* (4–7). 1983, Atheneum $3.95. Three children get involved in a jewel thief racket.

2614. Annixter, Jane, and Annixter, Paul. *The Last Monster* (6–8). 1980, Harcourt $6.95. Ron is determined to kill the grizzly that crippled his father.

2615. Arden, William. *Alfred Hitchcock and the Three Investigators in the Secret of Shark Reef* (4–8). 1979, Random LB $5.39; paper $1.95. Offshore oil drilling, sharks, and a hurricane are elements in this exciting story. One of a large series.

2616. Ashley, Bernard. *A Kind of Wild Justice* (6–9). Illus. by Charles Keeping. 1979, Phillips $10.95. An English story about underworld life set in present-day London.

2617. Asimov, Isaac. *The Key Word and Other Mysteries* (4–6). Illus. by Rod Burke. 1979, Avon paper $1.95. Five short stories about young Larry, an ingenious amateur sleuth.

2618. Atkinson, Linda. *Incredible Crimes* (5–8). 1980, Watts LB $8.90. A brief, uncomplicated mystery for reluctant readers.

2619. Avi. *The History of Helpless Harry: To Which Is Added a Variety of Amusing and Entertaining Adventures* (4–6). Illus. by Paul O. Zelinsky. 1980, Pantheon $8.99. Wit and suspense combine in the free-wheeling adventure-mystery.

2620. Avi. *Man from the Sky* (4–6). 1980, Knopf paper $1.95. Eleven-year-old Jamie spots a thief parachuting from an airplane.

2621. Avi. *Who Stole the Wizard of Oz?* (4–6). 1981, Knopf LB $5.99; paper $1.95. Several books disappear from the Chickertown Library book sale.

2622. Babbitt, Natalie. *Goody Hall* (4–6). Illus. by author. 1971, Farrar $8.95. Gothic mystery told with suspense and humor, centering around the magnificent home of the Goody family.

2623. Babbitt, Natalie. *Kneeknock Rise* (4–7). 1970, Farrar $10.95. Young Egan sets out to see the people-eating Megrimum.

2624. Baird, Thomas. *Finding Fever* (6–9). 1982, Harper $11.06; LB $11.89. Fifteen-year-old Benny and a friend investigate a case of dognapping.

2625. Baudouy, Michel-Aime. *More Than Courage* (6–8). 1966, Harcourt paper $1.65. Mick secretly reconditions an old motorcycle for a cross-country race.

2626. Bawden, Nina. *Devil by the Sea* (5–6). 1976, Harper $10.53. No one believes Hilary when she claims to know the identity of a child murderer in this suspenseful English story.

2627. Bawden, Nina. *Kept in the Dark* (5–9). 1982, Lothrop $10.00; LB $10.75; Scholastic paper $1.95. Three children visiting their grandmother encounter a wicked grandson.

2628. Bawden, Nina. *Runaway Summer* (4–6). 1969, Harper $10.57; Penguin paper $1.50. While visiting relatives, Mary helps hide a young boy who has entered England illegally.

2629. Bawden, Nina. *The Witch's Daughter* (4–6). 1966, Harper $10.53. A blind girl, her brother, and an outcast, called the witch's daughter, find jewels hidden by smugglers.

2630. Beatty, Patricia. *I Want My Sunday Stranger!* (6–8). 1977, Morrow $10.95; LB $10.51. Andrew Lancy's quest to retrieve his horse, stolen by a Confederate soldier, ends at the Battle of Gettysburg.

2631. Beatty, Patricia. *Jonathan Down Under* (5–8). 1982, Morrow $9.50. Our hero, Jonathan Cole, is involved in the Australian gold rush of 1851.

2632. Bellairs, John. *The Treasure of Alpheus Winterborn* (5–7). Illus. by Judith Gwyn Brown. 1978, Harcourt $7.95; Bantam paper $1.95. A boy's family problems encourage him to seek a buried treasure.

2633. Benary-Isbert, Margot. *Blue Mystery* (4–6). Illus. by Enrico Arno. 1957, Harcourt paper $3.95. A beautiful new flower is developed by the heroine's father, and when it is stolen, suspicion falls on an apprentice.

2634. Bernheim, Marc, and Bernheim, Evelyne. *The Drums Speak: The Story of Kofi, a Boy of West Africa* (3–6). Illus. 1972, Harcourt $6.50. Kofi conquers his fear of heights and gains a respected place in his tribe.

2635. Blades, Ann. *A Boy of Tache* (3–5). Illus. 1977, Tundra paper $4.95. A novel of life in Tache, an Indian reservation in northwest Canada, which focuses on a young boy and a trapping expedition.

2636. Bond, Ann Sharpless. *Saturdays in the City* (3–5). Illus. by Leonard Shortall. 1979, Houghton $8.95. A pair of enterprising young boys spends adventurous times in the big city.

2637. Bonham, Frank. *Mystery of the Fat Cat* (5–7). Illus. by Alvin Smith. 1971, Dell paper $2.50. Four Oak Street Boys Club members set out to prove foul play in the death of a cat.

2638. Boutis, Victoria. *Katy Did It* (3–5). Illus. by Gail Owens. 1982, Greenwillow $11.25; LB $11.88. Katy goes on a backpacking weekend with her father.

2639. Brandel, Marc. *The Mystery of the Two-Toed Pigeon* (4–7). 1984, Random LB $5.99; paper $1.95. One of the many adventures in the Alfred Hitchcock and the Three Investigators series.

2640. Branscum, Robbie. *The Murder of Hound Dog Bates* (5–7). 1982, Viking $9.95. Sassafras Bates is convinced that one of his 3 maiden aunts has killed his dog.

2641. Branscum, Robbie. *Three Buckets of Daylight* (3–4). 1978, Lothrop $9.36; LB $9.95. When he steals some apples, Jackie is cursed by a witch.

2642. Brenner, Barbara. *Mystery of the Disappearing Dogs* (4–6). Illus. by Blanche Sims. 1982, Knopf LB $4.99; paper $1.95. Twins, Elena and Michael, set out to find their kidnapped dog.

2643. Bromberg, Andrew. *Computer Overbyte: Plus Two More Codebreakers* (3–6). Illus. by Mary Kornblum. 1982, Greenwillow paper $4.45. Three mysteries featuring Amanda Jones and brother Sherlock. Others in the series: *Flute Revenge: Plus Two More Mysteries; The House on Blackthorn Hill: Plus Two More Mysteries; Rubik's Ruse: Plus Two More Codebreakers* (all 1982, paper $4.45).

2644. Brontë, Charlotte. *Jane Eyre* (6–9). 1983, Putnam $9.95. The immortal love story of Jane and Mr. Rochester in a fine edition.

2645. Brontë, Emily. *Wuthering Heights* (6–9). 1956, Houghton paper $5.50. Heathcliff, Kathy, and their tragic love story in one of many available editions.

2646. Brookins, Dana. *Alone in Wolf Hollow* (5–7). 1978, Houghton $7.95. Two orphans move in with an alcoholic uncle and encounter murder.

2647. Brow, Thea. *The Secret Cross of Lorraine* (5–9). Illus. by Allen Say. 1981, Houghton $8.95. The discovery of a medallion leads to the unraveling of a mystery.

2648. Budbill, David. *Snowshoe Trek to Otter River* (5–9). Illus. 1976, Dial LB $5.47; Bantam paper $1.95. Three complete short stories about 2 boys who camp in the wilderness at different times of the year. A sequel is: *Bones on Black Spruce Mountain* (1978, $7.95; LB $7.89).

2649. Bulla, Clyde Robert. *Down the Mississippi* (4–6). Illus. by Peter Burchard. 1954, Harper $10.53; Scholastic paper $1.75. Various exciting escapades of a farm boy on the Mississippi River.

2650. Bulla, Clyde Robert. *Marco Moonlight* (4–6). 1976, Harper $10.53; Dell paper $1.25. Rich, spoiled Marco meets Flint, a youngster from the neighboring village, and wonders if he could be his brother.

2651. Bunting, Eve. *The Ghost of Summer* (6–8). 1977, Warne $7.95. Kevin tries to find the booty of a hanged highwayman.

2652. Bunting, Eve. *The Skate Patrol* (2–5). Illus. by Don Madden. 1980, Whitman $6.95. James and Milton track down the notorious Creep Thief. Two sequels are: *The Skate Patrol and the Mystery Writer* (1982, $6.50); *The Skate Patrol Rides Again* (1982, LB $7.75).

2653. Bunting, Eve. *Someone Is Hiding on Alcatraz Island* (5–9). 1984, Houghton $10.95. A boy and a young woman ranger are trapped by a gang of thugs on Alcatraz.

2654. Burnham, Sophy. *The Dogwalker* (6–9). 1979, Warne $7.95. Two friends must find a dog with a bomb attached to her collar.

2655. Calhoun, Mary, and Morrill, Leslie. *The Night the Monster Came* (2–5). Illus. by Leslie Morrill. 1982, Morrow $8.75; LB $7.92. Andy believes Bigfoot is on the prowl near his house.

2656. Callen, Larry. *If the World Ends* (4–7). 1983, Atheneum $3.95. A young boy must land a private plane in this exciting adventure.

2657. Cameron, Eleanor. *The Terrible Churnadryne* (4–6). Illus. by Beth Krush and Joe Krush. 1959, Little $8.95. Two children think that a shape in the fog is a prehistoric monster.

2658. Campbell, Hope. *Mystery at Fire Island* (4–7). 1978, Scholastic $8.95; paper $1.95. A satisfying mystery that will hold a reader's attention.

2659. Carey, M. V. *Alfred Hitchcock and the Three Investigators in the Mystery of the Singing Serpent* (4–7). 1972, Random LB $5.39. A fast-paced adventure that is part of a large series.

2660. Carey, M. V. *The Mystery of the Missing Mermaid* (5–7). 1983, Random $5.99; paper $1.95. One of the Alfred Hitchcock and the Three Investigators series.

2661. Carlson, Dale. *Call Me Amanda* (4–6). 1981, Dutton $9.50; Scholastic paper $1.95. When there is a series of thefts, Amanda is fearful she will be accused.

2662. Carlson, Natalie Savage. *Surprise in the Mountains* (2–4). Illus. by Elise Primavera. 1983, Harper $9.57; LB $9.89. A pack rat leaves gold nuggets and helps a solitary prospector.

2663. Cavanna, Betty. *Stamp Twice for Murder* (6–9). 1981, Morrow LB $10.80. Jan and brother Tony encounter danger while vacationing with their family in a French village.

2664. Chambers, Aidan. *Seal Secret* (5–7). 1981, Harper $8.95; LB $8.79. On a vacation in Wales, William tries to free a trapped seal pup.

2665. Chambers, John W. *Finder* (5–8). 1981, Atheneum LB $11.95. Jenny's dog, Finder, involves her in a mystery.

2666. Chambers, John W. *Showdown at Apple Hill* (5–7). 1982, Atheneum LB $9.95. Two children encounter an ex-convict. Also use: *Fire Island Forfeit* (1984, Atheneum $11.95).

2667. Christian, Mary Blount. *The Firebug Mystery* (4–6). 1982, Whitman LB $8.95. Two youngsters investigate a series of mysterious fires.

2668. Christian, Mary Blount. *Sebastian (Super Sleuth) and the Bone to Pick Mystery* (3–5). Illus. by Lisa McCue. 1983, Macmillan $7.95. Sebastian, an English sheepdog, and master John Jones at a fossil dig. Also use: *Sebastian (Super Sleuth) and the Hair of the Dog Mystery* (1982, $6.95); *Sebastian (Super Sleuth) and the Crummy Yummies Caper* (1983, $7.95); *Sebastian (Super Sleuth) and the Santa Claus Caper*; *Sebastian (Super Sleuth) and the Secret of the Skewered Skier* (both 1984, $8.95).

2669. Christopher, Matt. *Stranded* (3–5). Illus. by Gail Owens. 1974, Little $8.70. After a shipwreck, Andy and his guide dog Max are stranded on a small island.

2670. Cleaver, Vera, and Cleaver, Bill. *A Little Destiny* (6–9). 1979, Morrow $11.25; LB $10.80. A spunky heroine tries to avenge her father's death.

2671. Clewes, Dorothy. *Missing from Home* (6–9). 1978, Harcourt $6.95. Two English girls hatch a kidnapping plot to bring their parents back together again.

2672. Clifford, Eth. *The Curse of the Moonraker: A Tale of Survival* (5–8). 1977, Houghton $6.95. Cat, a young cabin boy, tells of the shipwreck of the square-rigger *Moonraker*.

2673. Clifford, Eth. *Help! I'm a Prisoner in the Library* (3–5). Illus. by George Hughes. 1979, Houghton $8.95. Two youngsters are locked in a library after it closes. Two sequels are: *The Dastardly Murder of Dirty Pete* (1981, $7.95); *Just Tell Me When We're Dead!* (1983, $8.70).

2674. Clifford, Eth. *The Strange Reincarnation of Hendrik Verloom* (4–6). 1982, Houghton $8.70. Has Anna's grandfather really been reincarnated?

2675. Clifford, Sandy. *The Roquefort Gang* (2–4). Illus. by author. 1981, Houghton $7.95. A mouse nursemaid sets out to find her two charges who have disappeared.

2676. Climo, Shirley. *Gopher, Tanker, and the Admiral* (4–6). Illus. by Eileen McKeating. 1984, Harper $10.53; LB $10.89. Eleven-year-old Gopher doesn't get along too well with his neighbor, the Admiral, until he becomes a hero.

2677. Clymer, Eleanor. *The Horse in the Attic* (4–6). Illus. by Ted Lewin. 1983, Bradbury $9.95. In their new house, Caroline finds a painting of a horse in the attic.

2678. Clyne, Patricia Edwards. *The Curse of Camp Gray Owl* (5–7). 1981, Dodd LB $7.95. Five friends explore a haunted army artillery range.

2679. Coatsworth, Elizabeth. *The Princess and the Lion* (4–6). Illus. by Evaline Ness. 1963, Pantheon LB $5.99. Adventure and suspense in ancient Abyssinia.

2680. Cohen, Daniel. *The Restless Dead: Ghostly Tales from Around the World* (4–8). Illus. 1984, Dodd $8.95. Eleven ghost stories from around the world.

2681. Conn, Martha Orr. *Crazy to Fly* (6–9). Illus. by Richard Cuffari. 1978, Atheneum $8.95.

Tommy's desire to fly conflicts with his farm work in this story of the early days of aircraft.

2682. Cookson, Catherine. *Lanky Jones* (6–9). 1981, Lothrop $10.25; LB $9.84. Daniel uncovers a sheep stealing racket in this English mystery.

2683. Cool, Joyce. *The Kidnapping of Courtney Van Allen and What's-Her-Name* (5–7). 1981, Random $8.95; LB $8.99; Bantam paper $2.25. Wealthy Courtney and middle-class Jan get involved in a kidnapping plot.

2684. Cooney, Caroline B. *The Paper Caper* (4–6). Illus. by Gail Owens. 1981, Putnam $6.95. During a visit to England, twins become involved in a computer mystery.

2685. Coontz, Otto. *Mystery Madness* (5–7). 1982, Houghton $8.95. In this amusing spoof, Murray erroneously believes his sister committed a crime.

2686. Corbett, Scott. *Captain Butcher's Body* (4–6). Illus. by Geff Gerlach. 1976, Little $7.95. Two cousins are brought together by a story they read of piracy, buried treasures, and the ghost of Captain Butcher.

2687. Corbett, Scott. *Grave Doubts* (6–8). 1982, Little $11.45. Les and Wally wonder if Mr. Canby died of natural causes.

2688. Corbett, Scott. *The Great McGoniggle Rides Shotgun* (2–4). Illus. by Bill Ogden. 1977, Little $6.95; Dell paper $1.25. McGoniggle and friend Ken foil a robbery but in turn receive their due. A sequel is: *The Great McGoniggle Switches Pitches* (1980, $6.95).

2689. Corbett, Scott. *The Red Room Riddle* (4–6). Illus. by Geff Gerlach. 1972, Little $6.95. Scary story of 2 boys in a haunted house in the 1920s.

2690. Corcoran, Barbara. *The Clown* (5–8). 1975, Atheneum $8.95. Lisa uses her American uncle's passport and clothes to smuggle a clown from Russia, who is in danger for political reasons. Also use: *Meet Me at Tamerlane's Tomb* (1975, Atheneum LB $6.95).

2691. Corcoran, Barbara. *The Long Journey* (5–7). Illus. by Charles Robinson. 1970, Atheneum paper $1.25. Laurie rides alone across Montana to get help for her grandfather.

2692. Corcoran, Barbara. *The Person in the Potting Shed* (5–8). 1980, Atheneum $9.95. Dorothy and Franklin discover the body of their gardener in the potting shed.

2693. Corcoran, Barbara. *Which Witch Is Which* (4–6). 1983, Atheneum $3.95. In Salem, Massachusetts, Jennifer and Jack are on the trail of a catnapper.

2694. Corcoran, Barbara. *You're Allegro Dead* (6–8). 1981, Atheneum LB $11.95. Two summer campers uncover mystery and danger at Camp Allegro. A sequel is: *A Watery Grave* (1982, $14.95).

2695. Cotich, Felicia. *Valda* (6–8). 1983, Putnam $9.95. A story about Depression days in Australia and a courageous heroine named Valda.

2696. Crayder, Dorothy. *The Riddles of Mermaid House* (4–6). 1977, Atheneum $7.95. A young girl, having recently moved to a New England seacoast town, tries to discover why the community hates an elderly recluse.

2697. Crayder, Dorothy. *She, the Adventuress* (4–6). Illus. by Velma Ilsley. 1979, Atheneum paper $1.95. Maggie finds fun, adventure, and mystery on her sea trip to visit an aunt in Italy.

2698. Cresswell, Helen. *The Beachcombers* (4–6). 1972, Macmillan $8.95. A missing treasure, a boy held by a group of thieves, and a family of beachcombers are elements combined in this suspenseful adventure.

2699. Cross, Gillian. *The Dark behind the Curtain* (6–9). 1984, Oxford $12.95. A mystery centered around a school production of *Sweeney Todd*.

2700. Curry, Jane Louise. *The Bassumtyte Treasure* (5–7). 1978, Atheneum $9.95. The discovery of hidden treasure enables Tommy to continue to stay with his grandmother.

2701. Curry, Jane Louise. *Ghost Lane* (5–7). 1979, Atheneum $9.95. An English story about a young boy's involvement with a series of art thefts.

2702. Curry, Jane Louise. *The Ice Ghosts Mystery* (4–6). 1972, Atheneum paper $1.95. The Bird family members set out to find their lost father.

2703. Dank, Milton, and Dank, Gloria. *The Computer Caper* (6–9). 1983, Delacorte $12.95; Dell paper $2.25. Six kids expose a phony investment racket.

2704. Davies, Andrew. *Conrad's War* (4–6). 1980, Crown $7.95; Dell paper $2.25. An English boy's fascination with war games leads to exciting, often hilarious situations.

2705. Defoe, Daniel. *Robinson Crusoe* (5–9). Illus. by N. C. Wyeth. 1983, Scribners $17.95. A beautifully illustrated edition of this classic shipwreck story.

2706. Degens, T. *The Game on Thatcher Island* (4–6). 1977, Viking $7.95. On a small island, 3 youngsters narrowly escape serious injury at the hands of sadistic boys.

2707. DeJong, Meindert. *A Horse Came Running* (5–7). Illus. by Paul Sagsoorian. 1970, Macmillan

$9.95. A boy tries to cope with a tornado's effects on his parents, neighbors, and animals.

2708. DeRoo, Anne. *Scrub Fire* (5–7). 1980, Atheneum $9.95. Three children must survive in a New Zealand bush region.

2709. Dickinson, Peter. *Annerton Pit* (6–8). 1977, Little $7.95. Blind, 13-year-old Jake helps free his grandfather and brother from revolutionists.

2710. Dickinson, Peter. *The Gift* (6–9). 1974, Little $8.95. Davy's telepathic gift leads him into a murderous plot in which his father is the scapegoat.

2711. Dicks, Terrance. *The Baker Street Irregulars in the Case of the Missing Masterpiece* (5–6). 1979, Lodestar $7.95. A group of youngsters solves a crime, catches the villain, and prevents a murder. Five other mysteries involving the Baker Street Irregulars are: *The Case of the Blackmail Boys* (1981, $7.95); *The Case of the Cinema Swindle* (1981, $9.25); *The Case of the Crooked Kids* (1981, $7.95); *The Case of the Ghost Grabbers* (1981, $9.25); *The Case of the Cop Catchers* (1982, $9.95).

2712. D'Ignazio, Fred. *Chip Mitchell: The Case of the Stolen Computer Brains* (5–7). Illus. by Larry Pearson. 1983, Lodestar $8.69. Ten cases that can be solved with a slight knowledge of computers. A sequel is: *Chip Mitchell: The Case of the Robot Warriors* (1984, $9.66).

2713. Dixon, Paige. *The Search for Charlie* (5–7). 1976, Atheneum $6.95. In the Montana mountains, Jane participates in a search for her missing younger brother.

2714. Dodd, Wayne. *A Time of Hunting* (6–9). 1975, Houghton $6.95. Several events in young Jess's life change his attitude toward hunting from enthusiasm to abhorrence.

2715. Doty, Jean Slaughter. *The Crumb* (5–7). 1976, Greenwillow $9.84. Cindy finds mystery and adventure when she takes a part-time job at the Ashford stables to help with the expenses caused by her pony, Crumb.

2716. Duncan, Lois. *I Know What You Did Last Summer* (6–9). 1973, Little $8.95; Pocket paper $1.95. The mysterious avenger torments 4 teenagers who have tried to hide their involvement in a hit-and-run death.

2717. Duncan, Lois. *The Third Eye* (6–9). 1984, Little $12.45. Karen uses hidden psychic powers to locate lost children.

2718. Ecke, Wolfgang. *The Face at the Window* (5–9). Trans. from German by Stella Humphries and Vernon Humphries. Illus. by Rolf Rettich. 1979, Prentice $7.95; paper $4.95. Various European settings are used in these short, solve-it-your-self mysteries. A sequel is: *The Invisible Witness* (1981, $9.95).

2719. Ellis, Ella Thorp. *Roam the Wild Country* (6–8). Illus. by Bret Schlesinger. 1967, Atheneum paper $0.95. Top-form action and adventure as men, boys, and horses desperately outrace the herd's almost sure death on Argentina's drought-stricken pampas.

2720. Elmore, Patricia. *Susannah and the Blue House Mystery* (5–7). 1980, Dutton $10.25; Pocket paper $1.95. Susannah, Lucy, and the Knievel solve the mystery of a strange house. A sequel is: *Susannah and the Poison Green Halloween* (1982, $9.95).

2721. Enright, Elizabeth. *Gone-Away Lake* (4–6). Illus. by Beth Krush and Joe Krush. 1957, Harcourt paper $4.95. An abandoned summer colony bordering a swamp leads to a vacation of glorious exploration for Julian and Portia. A sequel is: *Return to Gone-Away* (1973, paper $1.15).

2722. Farley, Carol. *Ms. Isabelle Cornell, Herself* (5–7). 1980, Atheneum $7.95. Ibby must go to live with her new stepfather on an army base in Korea.

2723. Fenner, Phyllis R., ed. *The Endless Dark* (5–8). Illus. by Steve Marchesi. 1977, Morrow LB $9.55. A theme of total isolation runs through these stories.

2724. Fife, Dale. *Destination Unknown* (5–8). 1981, Dutton $9.95. During World War II, Jon stows away on a ship that is crossing the Atlantic.

2725. Fife, Dale. *Follow That Ghost!* (2–4). Illus. by Joan Drescher. 1979, Dutton $9.95. Two amateur sleuths discover that a tapping, troublesome ghost is really a woodpecker.

2726. Fife, Dale. *The Sesame Seed Snatchers* (3–5). Illus. by Sandy Kossin. 1983, Houghton $8.70. Mike and Hank are hired to find out who is stealing the sesame seeds.

2727. Fleischman, Paul. *Finzel the Farsighted* (3–5). Illus. by Marcia Sewall. 1983, Dutton $9.95. Finzel, the fortune-teller, is so near blindness that he becomes an easy prey.

2728. Fleischman, Paul. *The Half-a-Moon Inn* (5–7). Illus. by Kathy Jacobi. 1980, Harper $9.89. A young mute boy sets out to find his mother lost in a violent snowstorm.

2729. Fleischman, Sid. *The Bloodhound Gang and the Case of the Cackling Ghost* (4–6). 1981, Random LB $4.99; paper $1.50. A trio of young detectives, the Bloodhound Gang, uses deductive reasoning to solve baffling crimes. Some sequels are: *The Case of Princess Tomorrow; The Case of the Flying Clock; The Case of the Secret Message* (all 1981); *The Case of the 264-Pound Burglar* (1982) (all LB $4.99; paper $1.50).

2730. Flora, James. *Grandpa's Ghost Stories* (2–4). Illus. by author. 1978, Atheneum $9.95; paper $1.95. Three grisly short stories told by an old man to his grandson.

2731. Flory, Jane. *Miss Plunkett to the Rescue* (3–6). Illus. by Blanche Sims. 1983, Houghton $7.70. The retired third-grade teacher on the trail of an enemy agent.

2732. Fox, Paula. *How Many Miles to Babylon?* (4–6). Illus. by Paul Giovanopoulos. 1980, Bradbury $8.95; Scholastic paper $1.95. Tension and suspense when 10-year-old James Douglas is kidnapped by teenage dog thieves and held captive in an abandoned Coney Island fun house.

2733. Garrigue, Sheila. *All the Children Were Sent Away* (3–5). 1976, Bradbury $8.95. A based-on-fact account of an English girl's evacuation from London to Vancouver, Canada, during World War II.

2734. Gathorne-Hardy, Jonathan. *Airship Ladyship Adventure* (5–7). 1977, Harper $10.53. Jane and her housekeeper take off in her father's airship.

2735. Gathorne-Hardy, Jonathan. *Operation Peeg* (4–6). Illus. by Glo Coalson. 1974, Harper $10.53. A high-spirited adventure story about classmates trapped on a remote Scottish island and a madman trying to take over the world.

2736. George, Jean Craighead. *My Side of the Mountain* (5–7). Illus. by author. 1959, Dutton $8.95; paper $4.75. Sam Gribley spends a winter alone in the Catskill Mountains.

2737. George, Jean Craighead. *River Rats, Inc.* (4–7). 1979, Dutton $8.95; Scholastic paper $1.95. A run down the Colorado River turns into a story of survival.

2738. George, Jean Craighead. *The Talking Earth* (6–9). 1983, Harper $9.57; LB $9.89. A young Seminole girl spends 3 months in the Everglades alone.

2739. Giff, Patricia Reilly. *Have You Seen Hyacinth Macaw?* (4–6). 1984, Delacorte $11.95; LB $11.95; Dell paper $1.75. Abby Jones, a would-be detective, misunderstands clues and thinks her brother is a thief. A sequel is: *Loretta P. Sweeney, Where Are You?* (1984, Dell paper $2.25).

2740. Gipson, Fred. *Curly and the Wild Boar* (4–6). Illus. by Ronald Himler. 1979, Harper $7.64; LB $8.89; paper $1.95. Curly's encounter with a wild boar produces a ripsnorting adventure.

2741. Glaser, Dianne. *Case of the Missing Six* (4–6). 1978, Holiday $6.95. The hiding of a St. Bernard puppy produces unexpected results.

2742. Godden, Rumer. *The Rocking-Horse Secret* (4–6). Illus. by Juliet Stanwell Smith. 1978, Viking $11.50. Tibby solves many problems when she finds a will hidden in a rocking horse.

2743. Gray, Nigel. *The Deserter* (4–6). Illus. by Ted Lewin. 1977, Harper $8.61. Four English children care for an army deserter and help him escape the police.

2744. Gray, Patsey. *Barefoot a Thousand Miles* (5–7). 1984, Walker $10.95. A young Apache boy sets out to retrieve his pet dog taken from the reservation.

2745. Griese, Arnold A. *The Way of Our People* (4–6). Illus. by Haru Wells. 1975, Harper LB $10.89. Set in 1838, this story of an adolescent boy's growth to maturity in an accurate picture of life within the Alaska Anvik community.

2746. Hall, Lynn. *The Mystery of the Schoolhouse Dog* (3–5). Illus. by William Hutchinson. 1979, Garrard $6.89. Is the white dog in the abandoned schoolhouse real or a ghost?

2747. Hamilton, Virginia. *The House of Dies Drear* (5–8). Illus. by Eros Keith. 1968, Macmillan $9.95. First-rate suspense as history professor Small and his young son Thomas investigate their rented house, formerly a station on the Underground Railroad, unlocking the secrets and dangers from attitudes dating back to the Civil War.

2748. Hamre, Leif. *Operation Arctic* (6–7). 1973, Atheneum $4.95. Trying to find their father, 3 children are isolated on a remote Arctic island.

2749. Harrison, Ted. *Children of the Yukon* (2–4). Illus. by author. 1977, Tundra $10.95. Life in present-day Yukon with a little historical material.

2750. Hass, E. A. *Incognito Mosquito, Private Insective* (2–5). Illus. 1982, Lothrop $10.00; LB $10.88. A group of 5 nonsense mysteries involving insect/humans.

2751. Hayes, Geoffrey. *The Alligator and His Uncle Tooth: A Novel of the Sea* (3–5). Illus. by author. 1977, Harper $11.49. Corduroy, an alligator, is fascinated by the sea yarns his old Uncle Tooth tells him.

2752. Haynes, Mary. *Wordchanger* (5–7). 1982, Lothrop $9.00. A machine is invented that can change words in documents in this adventure story.

2753. Heck, Bessie Holland. *Cave-In at Mason's Mine* (4–5). Illus. by Charles Robinson. 1980, Scribners $9.95. Joey must help his father who is trapped in a mine.

2754. Heide, Florence Parry, and Heide, Roxanne. *Mystery of the Forgotten Island* (4–7). Illus. by Seymour Fleishman. 1980, Whitman $8.95; Pocket paper $1.95. Three youngsters discover an unmapped island and its elderly owner. Others in the series: *Mystery of the Mummy's Mask* (1979, $8.95; Pocket paper $1.75); *The Body in the Brillstone Garage* (1980, $8.95).

2755. Hicks, Clifford B. *Alvin's Swap Shop* (4–6). Illus. by Bill Sokol. 1976, Holt $9.70. A casual summer activity suddenly becomes the setting of a real detective activity when Alvin, the Magnificent Brain, takes over. Also use: *Alvin Fernald: Mayor for a Day* (1971); *Alvin Fernald: Foreign Trader* (1972); (both Pocket paper $1.50); *Alvin Fernald, TV Anchorman* (1980, Holt $9.70); *The Wacky World of Alvin Fernald* (1981, Pocket paper $1.95).

2756. Hildick, E. W. *The Case of the Condemned Cat* (4–6). Illus. by Lisl Weil. 1975, Pocket paper $1.95. Who killed the white dove? The McGurk Organization solves another crime. Also use: *Deadline for McGurk: A McGurk Mystery* (1975, Pocket paper $1.95); *The Case of the Nervous Newsboy* (1976); *The Case of the Invisible Dog* (1977); *The Case of the Phantom Frog* (1979); *The Case of the Bashful Bank Robber* (1981) (all Macmillan $9.95; Pocket paper $1.95); *The Case of the Four Flying Fingers* (1981, Pocket paper $1.95).

2757. Hildick, E. W. *The Case of the Secret Scribbler* (3–5). Illus. by Lisl Weil. 1978, Macmillan $9.95; Pocket paper $1.75. Jack McGurk, investigator, foils a robbery. Some sequels include: *The Case of the Snowbound Spy* (1980; LB $9.95); *The Case of the Treetop Treasure* (1980, Macmillan LB $9.95; Pocket paper $1.95); *The Case of the Felon's Fiddle* (1982); *McGurk Gets Good and Mad* (1982); *The Case of the Slingshot Sniper* (1983) (all $9.95).

2758. Hildick, E. W. *Manhattan Is Missing* (4–6). Illus. by Jan Palmer. 1969, Avon paper $1.95. Operation Catnet is initiated by Peter Clarke, his brother Benjie, and friend Hugh in an effort to recover Manhattan, the prized Siamese. Two other mysteries are: *Great Rabbit Rip-Off* (1977, Macmillan $9.95; Pocket paper $1.95); *The Top-Flight Fully-Automated Junior High School Girl Detective* (1979, Pocket paper $1.75).

2759. Hitchcock, Alfred, ed. *Alfred Hitchcock's Daring Detectives* (6–8). Illus. by Arthur Shilstone. 1969, Random paper $2.50. Eleven thrillers from popular writers such as Agatha Christie and Ellery Queen. Also use: *Alfred Hitchcock's Supernatural Tales* (1973, $6.95; paper $2.50).

2760. Hoke, Helen, ed. *Creepies, Creepies, Creepies: A Covey of Quiver and Quaver Tales* (6–9). Illus. by Bill Prosser. 1977, Watts $8.90. A spine-tingling collection of short stories and scenes taken chiefly from adult sources. Also use: *Ghostly, Grim and Gruesome* (1977, Lodestar $7.95); *Ghastly, Ghoulish, Gripping Tales* (1983, Watts $9.90).

2761. Holl, Kristi D. *Mystery by Mail* (4–7). 1983, Atheneum $3.95. Kate is determined to find the blackmailer of herself and her friends.

2762. Holland, Barbara. *Prisoners at the Kitchen Table* (4–6). 1979, Houghton $7.95. Two children are held prisoner in an abandoned house by a kidnapper.

2763. Holland, Isabelle. *The Empty House* (6–9). 1983, Harper $10.10; LB $10.89. Betsy Smith and her brother try to clear their father of a tax-fraud charge.

2764. Holman, Felice. *Slake's Limbo* (5–7). 1974, Scribners $8.95; Dell paper $1.75. Thirteen-year-old Aremis Slake finds an ideal hideaway for 4 months in the labyrinth of the New York subway.

2765. Honness, Elizabeth. *Mystery of the Maya Jade* (5–7). Illus. by Paul Frame. 1971, Harper $8.95. Pam becomes involved with thieves who rob archaeological sites in this story set in modern Guatemala.

2766. Hooks, William H. *The Mystery on Bleeker Street* (3–5). Illus. by Susanna Natti. 1980, Knopf LB $4.99; paper $1.95. Chase Bellards and 78-year-old Babette track down counterfeiters in San Francisco. A sequel is: *The Mystery on Liberty Street* (1982, LB $4.99; paper $1.95).

2767. Hopkins, Lee Bennett, comp. *Witching Time* (4–6). 1977, Whitman $8.75. A suitably scary collection with many humorous situations.

2768. Hopper, Nancy J. *Ape Ears and Beaky* (4–7). 1984, Dutton $10.63. Scott and Beaky solve the mystery of the robberies in a condominium.

2769. Household, Geoffrey. *Escape into Daylight* (6–9). Little $8.95. Carrie, daughter of a famous film star, and young Mike are held prisoner by kidnappers in this English suspense story.

2770. Houston, James. *Frozen Fire* (6–8). Illus. by author. 1977, Atheneum $12.95; paper $2.95. Two boys—one white and one Eskimo—set out on a rescue mission in the Far North. A sequel is: *Black Diamonds: A Search for Arctic Treasure* (1982, $9.95).

2771. Houston, James. *Long Claws: An Arctic Adventure* (4–6). Illus. by author. 1981, Atheneum LB $9.95. Two Eskimo children set out to retrieve the carcass of a caribou.

2772. Hunter, Mollie. *The Third Eye* (6–9). 1979, Harper $10.53; LB $10.89. A young Scottish girl becomes involved in the investigation of the death of an old earl.

2773. Hutchins, Pat. *The Curse of the Egyptian Mummy* (5–7). Illus. by Laurence Hutchins. 1983, Greenwillow $9.00; LB $8.59. A group of English Cub Scouts happen upon a frightening mystery.

2774. Hutchins, Pat. *Follow That Bus!* (2–5). Illus. by Laurence Hutchins. 1977, Greenwillow $10.80. A school picnic becomes a cops-and-robbers chase involving 2 holdup men in this fast-moving English story.

2775. Hutchins, Pat. *The Mona Lisa Mystery* (2–5). Illus. by Laurence Hutchins. 1981, Greenwillow $11.25; LB $10.80. A third-grade's trip from London to Paris ends in the theft of the Mona Lisa.

2776. Hyde, Dayton O. *Island of the Loons* (6–9). 1984, Atheneum $10.95. Jimmy is kidnapped by an escaped convict and kept prisoner on a deserted island.

2777. Jeffries, Roderic. *Police Dog* (6–8). 1965, Harper $10.89. Combination dog and detective story written in the police procedural vain, based on the methods used in England for training police dogs.

2778. Jeffries, Roderic. *Trapped* (5–8). 1972, Harper paper $2.95. Two boys are lost on the mud flats of a river in southeast England during a violent storm.

2779. Johnson, Annabel. *The Grizzly* (5–7). 1964, Harper $9.89; Scholastic paper $2.95. A perceptive story of a father-son relationship in which David, on a camping trip, saves his father's life when a grizzly bear attacks.

2780. Johnson, Annabel, and Johnson, Edgar. *Finders, Keepers* (6–9). 1981, Four Winds $8.95. A brother and sister flee after a nuclear power plant blows up.

2781. Kahn, Joan, ed. *Some Things Weird and Wicked: Twelve Stories to Chill Your Bones* (6–9). 1976, Pantheon $5.95. A batch of varied, excellent thrillers, chiefly from well-known writers.

2782. Keele, Lugman, and Pinkwater, D. Manus. *Java Jack* (4–8). 1980, Harper $7.89. A mystical journey in Indonesia by a 14-year-old boy searching for his parents.

2783. Keller, Beverly. *The Sea Watch: A Mystery* (4–6). 1981, Scholastic $7.95. Fortney Potter unravels a mystery during a cruise.

2784. Kelly, Jeffrey. *Tramp Steamer and the Silver Bullet* (4–7). 1984, Houghton $11.95. Silver and Tramp, 2 friends, share a number of adventures.

2785. Kherdian, David. *It Started with Old Man Bean* (6–8). 1980, Greenwillow $10.95. A secret camping trip turns into an ordeal for 2 youngsters. A sequel is: *Beyond Two Rivers* (1981, $11.25).

2786. Kherdian, David. *The Mystery of the Diamond in the Wood* (5–7). Illus. by Paul Geiger. 1983, Knopf $9.95; LB $9.99. Two boys find a diamond ring in the woods and know they are at the start of an adventure.

2787. Kidd, Ronald. *Sizzle and Splat* (6–9). 1983, Lodestar $10.63. A boy and girl investigate the finances of their faltering youth orchestra.

2788. King, Clive. *The Night the Water Came* (5–7). 1982, Harper $9.50; LB $8.89. A boy survives a cyclone that destroys his Asian island home.

2789. Konigsburg, E. L. *Father's Arcane Daughter* (5–9). 1976, Atheneum $7.95; paper $1.95. When Caroline reappears after an absence of 17 years, everyone wonders if she is really an imposter in this complex suspense tale.

2790. Konigsburg, E. L. *From the Mixed-Up Files of Mrs. Basil E. Frankweiler* (5–7). Illus. by author. 1967, Atheneum $8.95; paper $2.95. Adventure, suspense, detection, and humor are involved when 12-year-old Claudia and her younger brother elude the security guards and live for a week in New York's Metropolitan Museum of Art. Newbery Award winner, 1968.

2791. Kotzwinkle, William. *Trouble in Bugland: A Collection of Inspector Mantis Mysteries* (6–9). Illus. by Joe Servello. 1983, Godine $12.95. An all-insect cast in a take-off on Sherlock Holmes mysteries.

2792. Lane, Carolyn. *Echoes in an Empty Room: And Other Tales of the Supernatural* (5–7). 1981, Holt $7.95. Fifteen stories of encounters with ghosts.

2793. Lasker, Joe. *The Strange Voyage of Neptune's Car* (2–4). Illus. by author. 1977, Viking $11.50. A fictional re-creation of a clipper ship race from New York around Cape Horn to San Francisco.

2794. Lasky, Kathryn. *Jem's Island* (4–6). Illus. by Ronald Himler. 1982, Scribners $10.95. Jem and his father set out on a camping trip via kayak.

2795. Law, Carol Russell. *The Case of the Weird Street Firebug* (3–5). 1980, Knopf $4.99; paper $1.95. Steffi, Mutt, and Jeff track down the origin of several mysterious fires.

2796. Lawrence, Mildred. *Touchmark* (6–8). Illus. by Deanne Hollinger. 1975, Harcourt $7.50. A young girl hopes to become a pewterer's apprentice in pre-Revolutionary Boston.

2797. Leigh, Bill. *The Far Side of Fear* (4–6). 1978, Viking $9.95. A survival story of four youngsters trapped in an underground network.

2798. L'Engle, Madeleine. *The Young Unicorns* (6–9). 1968, Farrar $11.95. Suspense builds as the invention of Dr. Austin's microlaser enmeshes his family in a bizarre plot to use it to control human minds. Also use 2 stories about the O'Keefes: *The Arm of the Starfish* (1965, Farrar 11.95); *Dragons in the Water* (1976, Farrar 10.95; Dell paper 2.50).

2799. Levy, Elizabeth. *Frankenstein Moved In on the Fourth Floor* (2–4). 1979, Harper LB $9.89; paper $2.95. Is the strange Mr. Frank really

Frankenstein? A sequel is: *Dracula Is a Pain in the Neck* (1983, $9.57; LB $9.89; paper $2.95).

2800. Levy, Elizabeth. *The Shadow Nose* (3–5). Illus. by Mordicai Gerstein. 1983, Morrow $8.00; LB $7.63. Lamont and Diana investigate mysterious shadow paintings that appear on Greenwich Village sidewalks.

2801. Levy, Elizabeth. *Something Queer at the Library: A Mystery* (2–4). Illus. by Mordicai Gerstein. 1977, Dell paper $2.75. Jill and Gwen try to track down the person who is mutilating books in the library. Sequels are: *Something Queer on Vacation* (1980, Delacorte $10.95; LB $10.89; Dell paper $1.75); *Something Queer at the Haunted School* (1982, Delacorte $8.95; LB $8.89; Dell paper $1.75); *Something Queer at the Lemonade Stand* (1982, $7.95; LB $7.89; Dell paper $1.75); *Something Queer Is Going On* (1982, Dell paper $1.75); *Something Queer at the Ballpark* (1984, Dell paper $1.95).

2802. McElrath, William N. *Indian Treasure on Rockhouse Creek* (5–8). 1984, Broadman paper $5.95. Three boys go treasure hunting.

2803. McGraw, Eloise. *The Money Room* (5–7). 1981, Atheneum LB $11.95. Scott and his sister set out to find great-grandfather's Money Room.

2804. McHargue, Georgess. *The Talking Table Mystery* (4–6). Illus. by Emanuel Schongut. 1977, Dell paper $1.95. Two youngsters find mystery and excitement when they discover some belongings of a medium in an attic. Another mystery is: *The Turquoise Toad Mystery* (1982, Delacorte $9.95; Dell paper $2.25).

2805. Macken, Walter. *The Flight of the Doves* (5–7). 1968, Macmillan paper $1.95. Two children flee a cruel stepfather in England to find their mother's home in Ireland.

2806. McLean, Andrew, and McLean, Janet. *The Steam Train Crew* (K–2). Illus. 1983, Merrimack $9.95. The crew of a steam train decides to run on time so one of them can be at his granddaughter's birthday party.

2807. MacLeod, Charlotte. *We Dare Not Go A-Hunting* (6–8). 1980, Atheneum $8.95. A mystery story involving a kidnapping on Netaquid Island.

2808. MacMillan, Bruce. *Finest Kind O'Day: Lobstering in Maine* (2–4). Illus. 1977, Harper $8.95. Young Brett spends a day as a helper aboard a lobster boat, the *Ruth M.*

2809. McNulty, Faith. *Hurricane* (2–5). Illus. by Gail Owens. 1983, Harper $8.61; LB $8.89. A hurricane strikes the New England town where John lives.

2810. Majors, G. *Who Would Want to Kill Hallie Panky's Cat?* (4–6). 1981, Hastings $8.95. Someone threatens the life of Hallie's cat, and she sets out to find out who it is.

2811. Manley, Seon. *The Ghost in the Far Garden and Other Stories* (6–9). Illus. by Emanuel Schongut. 1977, Lothrop LB $10.80. Eleven original stories, each of which achieves a fairly high spine-tingle quotient.

2812. Markham, Marion M. *The Halloween Candy Mystery* (2–4). Illus. by Emily McCully. 1982, Houghton LB $7.95. The Dixon twins and their brother solve the mystery of a Halloween thief. Another mystery is: *The Christmas Present Mystery* (1984, Houghton $7.70).

2813. Masterman-Smith, Virginia. *The Great Egyptian Heist* (4–6). 1982, Four Winds $8.95. Angel and friend Billy find diamonds in a pharaoh's coffin.

2814. Masterman-Smith, Virginia. *The Treasure Trap* (5–8). Illus. by Roseanne Litzinger. 1979, Four Winds $8.95. An old man's disappearance sets off a mad treasure hunt.

2815. Mayne, William. *Salt River Times* (6–8). 1981, Greenwillow $11.25. Separate seemingly unrelated stories about various people converge in the solution of a mystery.

2816. Mazer, Harry. *Snow Bound* (6–8). 1973, Dell paper $1.95. Two teenagers are caught in a blizzard in an isolated area.

2817. Mazer, Norma Fox, and Mazer, Harry. *The Solid Gold Kid* (5–9). 1977, Dell paper $1.95. Five adolescents are kidnapped, and each reacts differently to their harrowing situation.

2818. Melwood, Mary. *Nettlewood* (6–8). 1975, Houghton $8.95. In this English novel, the young heroine Lacie explores Nettlewood, a run-down manor house, and uncovers some interesting secrets.

2819. Miles, Miska. *Hoagie's Rifle Gun* (2–4). Illus. by John Schoenherr. 1970, Little $6.95. Hoagie, a boy in Appalachia, and his little brother go hunting for food.

2820. Miller, Ruth. *The City Rose* (4–7). 1977, McGraw $9.95. Mystery and danger are combined in this story of an orphaned black girl's stay with a hostile uncle in a southern rural area.

2821. Milton, Hilary. *Mayday! Mayday!* (5–8). 1979, Watts $8.90. Two boys make their way to safety after a plane wreck.

2822. Milton, Hilary. *Tornado!* (5–9). 1983, Watts $9.90. A mother and two youngsters are caught in the path of a tornado.

2823. Moeri, Louise. *Downwind* (5–7). 1984, Dutton $10.95. A dramatic novel of a near disaster at a nuclear power plant.

2824. Moore, Emily. *Just My Luck* (4–6). 1983, Dutton $10.63. Olivia and Jeffery, two black children, set out to find Mrs. Dingle's lost dog.

2825. Morey, Walt. *Canyon Winter* (5–7). 1972, Dutton $10.95. A hermit helps a young survivor of a plane crash.

2826. Myers, Walter Dean. *Tales of a Dead King* (5–8). 1983, Morrow $8.00. John and Karen investigate the disappearance of an archaeologist in Egypt.

2827. Newman, Robert. *The Case of the Baker Street Irregulars: A Sherlock Holmes Story* (4–6). 1978, Atheneum $8.95; paper $3.95. Young Andrew unexpectedly finds himself teamed up with Sherlock Holmes. Others in this series are: *The Case of the Vanishing Corpse* (1980, $10.95); *The Case of the Somerville Secret* (1981, $12.95); *The Case of the Threatened King* (1982, $10.95); *The Case of the Etruscan Treasure* (1983, $10.95); *The Case of the Frightened Friend* (1984, $10.95).

2828. Newman, Robert. *Night Spell* (5–7). Illus. by Peter Buchard. 1977, Atheneum $8.95. After the death of his parents, Tad moves to a New England coastal town for a summer and encounters an unsolved mystery.

2829. O'Dell, Scott. *Alexandra* (6–9). 1984, Houghton $12.45. Alexandra becomes a sponge diver in Florida to help her family's failing business.

2830. O'Dell, Scott. *The Black Pearl* (6–9). Illus. by Milton Johnson. 1967, Houghton $9.95. A haunting story of Mexican pearl divers and of Manta Diablo, the monster of the sea and owner of the magnificent black pearl.

2831. O'Dell, Scott. *Island of the Blue Dolphins* (5–8). 1960, Houghton $9.95. An Indian girl spends 18 years alone on an island off the coast of California in the 1800s. Newbery Award winner, 1961. A sequel is: *Zia* (1976, $11.95).

2832. O'Dell, Scott. *The 290* (6–8). 1976, Houghton $7.95; Dell paper $1.50. Kim, an American working in a British shipyard during the American Civil War, is approached by his Yankee brother to gather information about *The 290*, a ship destined for the Confederacy.

2833. Okimoto, Jean Davies. *Who Did It, Jenny Lake?* (6–9). 1983, Putnam $10.95. A friend of Jenny's aunt is found dead in a hotel room in Kauai. Is it murder?

2834. Oleksy, Walter. *Quacky and the Haunted Amusement Park* (4–7). 1982, McGraw $8.95. Quacky's dog Puddles disappears, and this begins a dognapping adventure.

2835. Oliver, Stephen Ryan. *The Gitter, the Googer and the Ghost* (3–5). Illus. by Cherie R. Wyman.

1983, Carolrhoda $7.95. Two boys investigate a ghost story in an old house in Maine.

2836. Otis, James. *Toby Tyler: Or Ten Weeks with a Circus* (4–6). 1923, Buccaneer $16.95. A perennial favorite about a subject popular with most children.

2837. Packard, Edward. *ESP McGee* (5–7). Illus. by Larry Ross. 1983, Avon paper $2.25. Introducing a new mystery solver and his sidekick, Matt Terrell. Others in this series: *ESP McGee and the Haunted Mansion* by Jim Lawrence (1983); *ESP McGee and the Mysterious Magician* by Kathryn F. Ernst (1983); *ESP McGee and the Dolphin's Message* by Jesse Rodgers (1984); *ESP McGee and the Ghost Ship* by Ian McMahan (1984); *ESP McGee to the Rescue* by George Shea (1984) (all Avon paper $2.25).

2838. Parish, Peggy. *Pirate Island Adventure* (2–4). 1975, Dell paper $1.50. Three children search for a long-lost family treasure.

2839. Pearce, Philippa. *The Way to Sattin Shore* (5–9). Illus. by Charlotte Voake. 1984, Greenwillow $10.00. Kate learns that the man buried in the family plot is not her father as she has always believed.

2840. Peck, Richard. *Through a Brief Darkness* (6–9). 1973, Viking $9.95; Dell paper $2.25. A suspenseful adventure story in which a young girl is held prisoner by her father's enemies.

2841. Peck, Robert Newton. *Banjo* (4–6). Illus. by Andrew Glass. 1982, Knopf $8.95; LB $8.99. Alvin and friend Banjo are trapped in a mine shaft.

2842. Peyton, K. M. *Going Home* (4–6). Illus. by Huck Scarry. 1982, Putnam $9.95. Milly and Mickey decide to return on their own from France to England.

2843. Phipson, Joan. *Fly into Danger* (6–8). 1977, Atheneum $6.95. A spunky 13-year-old girl tries to foil a scheme to illegally export exotic birds from Australia.

2844. Phipson, Joan. *When the City Stopped* (5–8). 1978, Atheneum $8.95. A group of children copes with a general strike in an Australian city.

2845. Pickering, Mary Tyson. *The Mystery of the Greek Icon* (6–9). 1984, Dodd $10.95. The search for her missing father takes Marty and her boyfriend to Greece.

2846. Place, Marian T. *The Boy Who Saw Bigfoot* (3–5). 1979, Dodd $6.95. When a young fourth grader sights Bigfoot, his adventures begin.

2847. Platt, Kin. *Dracula, Go Home!* (6–9). 1979, Watts $8.90; Dell paper $1.50. A hi-lo book that tells an exciting tale with tongue in cheek.

2848. Platt, Kin. *Frank and Stein and Me* (5–8). 1982, Watts LB $8.90; Scholastic paper $1.95. In this easily read adventure, Jack encounters a smuggling ring on a free trip to Paris.

2849. Platt, Kin. *The Ghost of Hellsfire Street* (5–8). 1980, Delacorte $10.95. Steve and his bulldog Sinbad solve a mystery involving a local election.

2850. Pomerantz, Charlotte. *Detective Poufy's First Case: Or the Missing Battery Operated Pepper Grinder* (3–5). 1976, Bantam paper $1.95. Detective Poufy, alias Rosie Maloon, finds out who broke into her family's house.

2851. Poole, Josephine. *The Visitor* (6–9). 1972, Harper $10.89. Harry is suspicious of his mysterious new tutor, a gaunt, strange man who seems to possess powers over the nearby village.

2852. Prince, Alison. *The Sinister Airfield* (5–7). Illus. by Ellen Thompson. 1983, Morrow $8.00. Three youngsters find a body in the woods in this English thriller. A sequel is: *Night Landings* (1984, $10.00).

2853. Pullman, Philip. *Count Karlstein* (5–7). 1983, Merrimack $10.95. A serving girl tries to save two nieces of the wicked Count Karlstein.

2854. Quackenbush, Robert. *Piet Potter's First Case* (K–3). Illus. by author. 1980, McGraw $7.95. Piet helps his neighbors receive their million dollar inheritance in this easy-to-read mystery. Two sequels are: *Piet Potter Returns* (1980, $7.95); *Piet Potter's Hot Clue* (1982, $9.95).

2855. Ransome, Arthur. *Swallows and Amazons* (4–7). Illus. by author. 1980, Merrimack $12.95. These adventures of the 4 Walker children have been read for many years. Others in the series: *Missee Lee; Peter Duck; Pigeon Post; Secret Water; Swallowdale* (all 1980, $9.95).

2856. Ransome, Arthur. *Winter Holiday* (4–7). Illus. by author. 1980, Merrimack $12.95. Further adventures of the Swallows and Amazons. Some sequels are: *The Big Six; Coot Club; Great Northern; The Picts and the Martyrs* (all 1980, $9.95).

2857. Rardin, Susan Lowry. *Captives in a Foreign Land* (5–9). 1984, Houghton $12.45. Two young Americans are kidnapped by terrorists.

2858. Raskin, Ellen. *The Westing Game* (5–8). 1978, Dutton $11.00; Avon paper $2.25. A convoluted mystery that involves deciphering a will. Newbery Award winner.

2859. Razzi, Jim, and Razzi, Mary. *The Sherluck Bones Mystery-Detective Book #6* (2–4). 1984, Bantam paper $1.95. This is number 6 in a series of books, each containing 6 mysteries with solutions in the back.

2860. Renner, Beverly Hollett. *The Hideaway Summer* (5–7). 1978, Harper $10.89. A survival story of 2 youngsters who spend a summer in the woods.

2861. Rettich, Margret. *The Tightwad's Curse and Other Pleasantly Chilling Stories* (4–6). Trans. by Elizabeth D. Crawford. Illus. by Rolf Rettich. 1979, Morrow $8.75; LB $8.40. A collection of innocent mystery stories translated from the German.

2862. Rice, Eve. *The Remarkable Return of Winston Potter Crisply* (5–7). 1978, Greenwillow $10.95; LB $10.51. Becky and Max trail their brother who, although supposedly at Harvard, is mysteriously on the streets of New York City.

2863. Roach, Marilynne K. *Encounters with the Invisible World* (5–7). Illus. by author. 1977, Harper $9.57. For this reworking of traditional stories, the subtitle is *Being Ten Tales of Ghosts, Witches and the Devil Himself in New England*.

2864. Roberts, Willo Davis. *The Minden Curse* (5–7). Illus. by Sherry Streeter. 1978, Atheneum $8.95. Two youngsters solve a case of petnapping. A sequel is: *More Minden Curses* (1980, $9.95).

2865. Roberts, Willo Davis. *No Monsters in the Closet* (4–7). 1983, Atheneum $3.95. Steve and his puppy Sandy find mystery in an old house.

2866. Roberts, Willo Davis. *The Pet-Sitting Peril* (4–6). 1983, Atheneum $10.95. Nick and friend Stan happen upon a gang of arsonists.

2867. Roberts, Willo Davis. *The View from the Cherry Tree* (5–9). 1975, Atheneum $11.95; paper $1.95. An exciting story of a boy who witnesses a murder but can't find anyone who will believe him.

2868. Rosenbloom, Joseph. *Maximilian, You're the Greatest* (4–6). Illus. 1979, Lodestar $8.95. In each chapter, Maximilian Augustus Adams cracks a new case. A sequel is: *Maximilian Does It Again* (1983, $9.95).

2869. Roth, Arthur. *The Iceberg Hermit* (6–8). 1974, Scholastic paper $2.25. Around 1850, a 17-year-old Scottish lad endures incredible hardships in his struggle for survival when his whaling ship sinks.

2870. Roy, Ron. *Avalanche!* (4–6). Illus. by Robert MacLean. 1981, Dutton $8.25. Two brothers are trapped in an avalanche in Aspen, Colorado. Three other adventure stories are: *Nightmare Island* (1981, $9.25); *I Am a Thief* (1982, $8.95); *Million Dollar Jeans* (1983, $9.47) (all Dutton).

2871. Ruckman, Ivy. *Night of the Twisters* (4–6). 1984, Harper $11.06; LB $10.89. An 11-year-old boy witnesses a series of tornadoes that destroy his Nebraska town.

2872. St. John, Wylly Folk. *Mystery of the Ginger-bread House* (5–7). Illus. by Frank Aloise. 1969, Avon paper $1.95. Two boys solve a mystery involving an abandoned body and missing jewels in modern Atlanta.

2873. Salassi, Otto R. *And Nobody Knew They Were There* (5–8). 1984, Greenwillow $9.00. Two boys try to track down some missing marines.

2874. Scott, Jane. *To Keep an Island* (5–7). Illus. 1983, Atheneum $10.95. Tina, Josh, and Harry spend a night on a deserted island.

2875. Sefton, Catherine. *In a Blue Velvet Dress* (4–7). 1973, Harper LB $9.89; paper $1.25. Jane Reed finds adventure during a holiday with her aunt and uncle.

2876. Sharmat, Marjorie W. *51 Sycamore Lane* (4–6). 1971, Macmillan $9.95. Paul and his friends believe their new neighbor is a spy.

2877. Shearer, John. *Bill Jo Jive and the Walkie-Talkie Caper* (3–4). Illus. by Ted Shearer. 1981, Dell paper $1.75. Billy Jo Jive and his sidekick, Susie Sunset, solve a mystery. One of a lengthy series.

2878. Showell, Ellen Harvey. *The Ghost of Tillie Jean Cassaway* (4–6). Illus. by Stephen Gammell. 1978, Scholastic $8.95. What appear to be ghostly happenings have a logical explanation in this adventure story set in present-day Appalachia.

2879. Shura, Mary Francis. *The Gray Ghosts of Taylor Ridge* (5–7). Illus. by Michael Hampshire. 1978, Dodd $7.95. A boy and his sister find a lost treasure.

2880. Simon, Seymour. *Chip Rogers, Computer Whiz* (4–7). 1984, Morrow $9.00. Chip and Katie solve a mystery using the computer.

2881. Simon, Seymour. *Einstein Anderson: Science Sleuth* (3–6). Illus. by Fred Winkowski. 1980, Viking $9.95; paper $2.50. A series of mysteries solved by a 12-year-old sleuth. Some sequels are: *Einstein Anderson Makes Up for Lost Time* (1981, $8.95); *Einstein Anderson Tells a Comet's Tale* (1981, $9.95); *Einstein Anderson Goes to Bat; Einstein Anderson Lights Up the Sky* (both 1982, $9.95); *Einstein Anderson Sees Through the Invisible Man* (1983, $9.60).

2882. Singer, Marilyn. *The Case of the Sabotaged School Play* (3–5). Illus. by Judy Glasser. 1984, Harper $7.64; LB $7.89. The Bean brothers solve the mystery of who is trying to sabotage the school play.

2883. Sivers, Brenda. *The Snailman* (4–6). Illus. by Shirley Hughes. 1978, Little $6.95. Bullies terrorize a young English boy and his friend, who raises snails.

2884. Skurzynski, Gloria. *Lost in the Devil's Desert* (4–7). Illus. by Joseph M. Scrofani. 1982, Lothrop

$10.00. Kevin is lost in the Utah desert for 3 days. Two other adventure stories by this author are: *Caught in the Moving Mountain; Trapped in the Slickrock Canyon* (both 1984, Lothrop $10.00).

2885. Smith, Carole. *The Hit-and-Run Connection* (3–6). Illus. by Marie DeJohn. 1982, Whitman LB $8.95. Two boys set out to investigate a hit-and-run accident involving a friend.

2886. Sneve, Virginia. *High Elk's Treasure* (4–7). Illus. by Oren Lyons. 1972, Holiday $8.95. Joe discovers a cave and a treasure left there by his great-grandfather, the Sioux warrior High Elk. Also use: *When Thunder Spoke* (1974, Holiday $4.95).

2887. Snyder, Zilpha Keatley. *The Changeling* (5–7). Illus. by Alton Raible. 1970, Atheneum LB $7.95; paper $0.95. A dramatic novel of a talented girl wrongly accused of vandalism and her strange belief that she was a changeling.

2888. Snyder, Zilpha Keatley. *The Headless Cupid* (4–7). 1971, Atheneum $12.95; paper $3.95. Amanda, a student of the occult, upsets her new family. Two sequels are: *The Famous Stanley Kidnapping Case* (1979, $10.95; paper $2.95); *Blair's Nightmare* (1984, $11.95).

2889. Snyder, Zilpha Keatley. *The Truth about Stone Hollow* (5–7). Illus. by Alton Raible. 1974, Atheneum $8.95; paper $1.95. Although the ravine's past remains shrouded in mystery, Amy's and Jason's trips to the haunted hollow make a compelling excursion into the semisupernatural.

2890. Sobol, Donald J. *Angie's First Case* (4–7). Illus. by author. 1981, Four Winds $8.95; Scholastic paper $1.95. Angie and friend Jess are kidnapped while on the track of some house thieves.

2891. Sobol, Donald J. *Encyclopedia Brown, Boy Detective* (3–5). Illus. 1963, Lodestar $9.95; Bantam paper $1.75. Ten-year-old Leroy Brown opens his own detective agency and solves 10 crimes. Some sequels are: *Encyclopedia Brown and the Case of the Secret Pitch* (1965); *Encyclopedia Brown Finds the Clues* (1966) (both Lodestar $8.95; Bantam paper $1.95); *Encyclopedia Brown Gets His Man* (1967, Lodestar $9.95; Bantam paper $1.95); *Encyclopedia Brown Keeps the Peace* (1973, Lodestar $8.95; Bantam paper $1.95); *Encyclopedia Brown and the Case of the Dead Eagles* (1975, Lodestar $9.95; Scholastic paper $1.95); *Encyclopedia Brown Sets the Pace* (1982, Scholastic $7.95; paper $1.95).

2892. Sobol, Donald J. *Encyclopedia Brown Saves the Day* (3–5). Illus. by Leonard Shortall. 1970, Lodestar $8.95; Bantam paper $1.95. This title, as well as other titles in this popular series, consists of a number of short stories told with wit and suspense. Some sequels are: *Encyclopedia Brown Takes the Case* (1971); *Encyclopedia Brown Tracks*

Them Down (1971); *Encyclopedia Brown Shows the Way* (1971) (all Lodestar $8.95; Bantam paper $1.95); *Encyclopedia Brown and the Case of the Midnight Visitor* (1977, Lodestar $9.95; Bantam paper $1.95); *Encyclopedia Brown Carries On* (1980, Four Winds $7.95; Scholastic paper $1.75).

2893. Sorensen, Virginia. *Friends of the Road* (4–6). 1978, Atheneum $6.95. Two daughters of diplomats help make life in Morocco an exciting adventure.

2894. Southall, Ivan. *Ash Road* (5–7). 1978, Greenwillow $10.95; LB $10.51. A group of children are alone and in the path of a devastating fire.

2895. Southall, Ivan. *King of the Sticks* (6–8). 1979, Greenwillow $9.95; LB $9.55. A young boy named Custard is kidnapped because he supposedly has psychic powers. A sequel is: *The Golden Goose* (1981, $12.50).

2896. Speare, Elizabeth. *The Bronze Bow* (6–9). 1961, Houghton $10.95; paper $7.95. A Jewish boy seeks revenge against the Romans who killed his parents, but he finally loses his hatred after he hears the messages and teachings of Jesus. Newbery Award winner.

2897. Sperry, Armstrong. *All Sail Set: A Romance of the Flying Cloud* (5–7). Illus. by author. 1982, Godine paper $8.95. A reissue of the story of a clipper ship race around the Horn.

2898. Sperry, Armstrong. *Call It Courage* (5–8). Illus. by author. 1940, Macmillan $10.95; paper $2.95. The "Crusoe" theme is interwoven with this story of a Polynesian boy's courage in facing the sea he feared. Newbery Award winner, 1941.

2899. Spier, Peter. *Tin Lizzie* (4–6). Illus. by author. 1975, Doubleday $8.95; paper $2.50. The life and adventures of a single Model-T Ford made in 1909 and now a showpiece of an antique car collector.

2900. Stegeman, Janet Allais. *Last Seen on Hopper's Lane* (6–9). 1982, Dial $11.95. Kerry is kidnapped by 2 drug dealers.

2901. Stevenson, Robert Louis. *Treasure Island* (6–9). Illus. by N. C. Wyeth. 1981, Scribners LB $17.95. The classic famous pirate story.

2902. Storr, Catherine. *Kate and the Island* (4–5). Illus. by Gareth Floyd. 1978, Faber $8.95. This recounts the adventures of a young English girl and her attempt at amateur archaeology on a Greek island.

2903. Swindells, Robert E. *The Moonpath and Other Tales of the Bizarre* (4–8). Illus. by Reg Sandland. 1983, Carolrhoda $7.95. Five stories of the occult and mysterious.

2904. Taylor, Theodore. *The Odyssey of Ben O'Neal* (6–8). Illus. by Richard Cuffari. 1977, Avon paper $1.50. Action and humor are skillfully combined in this story of a trip by Ben and his friend Tee to England at the turn of the century. Two others in the series: *Teetoncey* (1974, Doubleday LB $7.95; Avon paper $1.95); *Teetoncey and Ben O'Neal* (1975, Doubleday LB $7.95; Avon paper $1.25).

2905. Taylor, Theodore. *Sweet Friday Island* (6–9). 1984, Scholastic paper $2.25. A young girl and her father are hunted by a madman on a remote island.

2906. Thiele, Colin. *Blue Fin* (6–9). Illus. by Roger Haldane. 1974, Harper $10.89. A 14-year-old's courage and love are put to the test when his father's tuna ship founders off the coast of Australia.

2907. Thiele, Colin. *Fire in the Stone* (6–9). 1974, Harper LB $9.89. Ernie and his aboriginal friend track down an opal thief in this exciting adventure set in Australia.

2908. Thiele, Colin. *The Hammerhead Light* (5–7). 1977, Harper $10.53. A young girl Tess and a 70-year-old man operate an abandoned lighthouse and help save Tess's father from drowning in this exciting Australian novel.

2909. Thomas, Jane Resh. *Courage at Indian Deep* (5–7). 1984, Houghton $9.95. A young boy must help save a ship caught in a sudden storm.

2910. Townsend, John R. *Top of the World* (5–8). Illus. by John Wallner. 1977, Harper $8.95. Two young apartment dwellers court disaster when, unsupervised, they begin walking catwalks in the penthouse garden.

2911. Ullman, James. *Banner in the Sky* (6–9). 1954, Harper $8.89. Rudi wants more than anything else to follow in his father's footsteps as an alpine guide and conquer the unclimbed Citadel Mountain.

2912. Van Iterson, Siny Rose. *The Spirits of Chocamata* (6–8). 1977, Morrow $8.95; LB $8.59. In this suspenseful novel, 2 boys help capture an escaped prisoner on the island of Curacao.

2913. Verne, Jules. *Twenty Thousand Leagues Under the Sea* (6–9). Illus. by W. J. Aylward. 1976, J. M. Dent $9.00. The fantastic adventures of Captain Nemo with a submarine in the 1860s. Also use: *Around the World in Eighty Days* (1956, Dodd $8.95).

2914. Viereck, Philip. *The Summer I Was Lost* (5–7). 1965, Scholastic paper $1.95. A boy survives a harrowing ordeal when he is lost on a mountain.

2915. Voigt, Cynthia. *The Callender Papers* (6–9). 1983, Atheneum $11.95. Jean takes a summer job in the Berkshire hills of Massachusetts and finds adventure and mystery.

2916. Wallace, Barbara Brooks. *Peppermints in the Parlor* (4–6). 1980, Atheneum $10.95. Emily encounters mystery and terror when she goes to her aunt's home in San Francisco.

2917. Wallace, Bill. *Trapped in Death Cave* (5–8). 1984, Holiday $10.95. Gary is convinced his grandpa was murdered to secure a map indicating where some gold is buried.

2918. Wallin, Luke. *Blue Wings* (5–8). 1982, Bradbury $9.95. Fourteen-year-old Mandy helps capture some parrot smugglers.

2919. Warren, William E. *The Graveyard and Other Not-So-Scary Stories* (4–6). Illus. by Edward Frascino. 1984, Prentice $10.95. Four stories that involve reader participation.

2920. Welch, Patricia. *The Day of the Muskie* (2–4). 1984, Faber $11.95. Norm wants desperately to catch a large muskie and win a fishing boat.

2921. Wells, Rosemary. *The Man in the Woods* (6–9). 1984, Dutton $11.60. Helen is involved in a mystery involving drug smuggling.

2922. White, Robb. *Fire Storm* (6–8). 1979, Doubleday LB $6.95. A forest ranger and a 14-year-old boy are trapped by a forest fire.

2923. Whitney, Phyllis A. *Secret of the Stone Face* (5–7). 1977, Westminster $8.95; NAL paper $1.75. While trying to discredit the reputation of her mother's fiance, Jo encounters a mystery. Also use: *Secret of the Spotted Shell* (1967, Westminster $6.95).

2924. Wibberley, Leonard. *Perilous Gold* (6–9). 1978, Farrar $7.95. An action story involving the exploration of a sunken ship in a 2-person submarine.

2925. Willard, Barbara. *The Gardener's Grandchildren* (6–9). Illus. by Gordon King. 1979, McGraw $7.95. Two youngsters find a boy hiding in a cave on a Scottish island.

2926. Wright, Betty Ren. *The Dollhouse Murders* (4–7). 1983, Holiday $10.95. Dolls in a dollhouse come to life in this mystery about long-ago murders.

2927. Wyss, Johann D. *Swiss Family Robinson* (5–8). Illus. by Lynd Ward and Lee Gregori. n.d, Putnam paper $5.96; deluxe ed. $9.95. A family is shipwrecked in this classic story.

2928. Yolen, Jane. *The Boy Who Spoke Chimp* (3–6). Illus. by David Wiesner. 1981, Knopf paper $4.99. Kriss must survive the wilderness after a terrible earthquake.

2929. Yolen, Jane. *Shirlick Holmes and the Case of the Wandering Wardrobe* (3–6). 1981, Putnam $8.95.

Shirli and her 3 friends solve the mystery of the stolen antiques.

2930. York, Carol Beach. *Nothing Ever Happens Here* (6–9). 1980, NAL paper $1.50. Elizabeth's quiet, monotonous life is shattered when new tenants move into the apartment upstairs.

2931. York, Carol Beach. *Remember Me When I Am Dead* (5–7). 1980, Nelson $8.95. Jenny's mother died a year ago, but it appears she is still alive.

2932. York, Carol Beach. *Takers and Returners: A Novel of Suspense* (6–8). 1982, Ace paper $1.95. A group of bored youngsters, led by 15-year-old Julian, tries to enliven their summer by stealing and then returning items.

Sports Stories

2933. Adler, David A. *Jeffrey's Ghost and the Leftover Baseball Team* (3–5). Illus. by Jean Jenkins. 1984, Holt $8.95. A gang of misfit ball players is helped by a ghost.

2934. Altman, Millys N. *Racing in Her Blood* (6–8). 1980, Harper $8.61; LB $8.89. Jane Barton attempts to break into the male-dominated world of auto racing.

2935. Avi. *S.O.R. Losers* (5–7). 1984, Macmillan $9.95. The most inept soccer team in the history of the South Orange River Middle School is formed.

2936. Bonham, Frank. *The Rascals from Haskell's Gym* (5–7). 1977, Dutton $9.95. Sissy's gymnastic team is challenged by a rival group that doesn't play fair.

2937. Cebulash, Mel. *Ruth Marini, Dodger Ace* (6–9). 1983, Lerner $8.95. A novel of the first woman in the Major Leagues. A sequel is: *Ruth Marini of the Dodgers* (1983, $8.95).

2938. Christopher, Matt. *Dirt Bike Racer* (3–5). Illus. by Barry Bomzer. 1979, Little $10.45. Ron finds a bike at the bottom of a lake and begins dirt bike racing. Another sports story is: *Dirt Bike Runaway* (1983, Little $10.45).

2939. Christopher, Matt. *The Dog That Called the Signals* (2–3). Illus. by Bill Ogden. 1982, Little LB $8.95. Because Mike and his dog can read each other's minds, a crucial football game is won. Also from the same author and publisher: *Touchdown for Tommy* (1959, $8.95; paper $3.95); *Catch That Pass!* (1969, $8.95); *The Dog That Stole Football Plays* (1980, $7.95); *The Great Quarterback Switch* (1984, $10.45).

2940. Christopher, Matt. *Shortstop from Tokyo* (3–5). Illus. by Harvey Kidder. 1970, Little $7.95. Stogie feels resentment when a Japanese boy takes his place on the baseball team. Also from the same author and publisher: *The Year Mom Won the Pennant* (1968, $6.95); *The Kid Who Only Hit Homers* (1972, $10.45); *Jinx Glove* (1974, $7.95); *No Arm in Left Field* (1974, $8.95); *The Fox Steals Home* (1978, $8.95); *Wild Pitch* (1980, $7.95).

2941. Christopher, Matt. *Soccer Halfback* (4–6). 1978, Little $8.95; paper $3.95. Everyone wants Jabber to play football, but his favorite sport is soccer.

2942. Cohen, Barbara. *Thank You, Jackie Robinson* (4–6). Illus. by Richard Cuffari. 1974, Lothrop $9.84. A memoir written by Sam about his friendship with an old man and his devotion as a boy to the Brooklyn Dodgers and Ebbets Field.

2943. Cohen, Peter Z. *The Muskie Hook* (3–7). Illus. by Tom O'Sullivan. 1972, Atheneum paper $0.95. In spite of his feelings to the contrary, one day Aaron becomes a real fisherman.

2944. Corbett, Scott. *The Hockey Girls* (4–6). 1976, Dutton $8.95. Irma reluctantly joins the field hockey team coached by an old English teacher Miss Tingery in this humorous and different sports story.

2945. Dygard, Thomas J. *Quarterback Walk-On* (5–8). 1982, Morrow $9.95; Scholastic paper $1.95. Denny, a fourth-string quarterback, must save the day for his college team.

2946. Dygard, Thomas J. *Soccer Duel* (6–9). 1981, Morrow $10.25; LB $9.84. Terry learns true sportsmanship by playing soccer.

2947. Fenner, Carol. *The Skates of Uncle Richard* (3–4). Illus. by Ati Forberg. 1978, Random LB $5.99. Nine-year-old Marsha tries to ice-skate on hand-me-down skates from Uncle Richard.

2948. Foley, Louise M. *Tackle 22* (3–5). Illus. by John Heily. 1978, Dell paper $1.75. Herbie wins the day as a substitute player on the football team.

2949. Frick, C. H. *The Comeback Guy* (4–7). 1965, Harcourt paper $1.45. The story of a young athlete who must cope with defeat.

2950. Gault, William Campbell. *Showboat in the Backcourt* (5–7). 1976, Dutton $7.95. The careers of 2 basketball players from high school to the big leagues.

2951. Giff, Patricia Reilly. *Left-Handed Shortstop* (4–6). Illus. by Leslie Morrill. 1980, Delacorte $9.95; LB $9.89; Dell paper $1.75. Walter tries everything possible not to play baseball.

2952. Hurwitz, Johanna. *Baseball Fever* (3–6). Illus. by Ray Cruz. 1981, Morrow $10.25; LB $9.84; Dell paper $2.25. Mr. Feldman loaths baseball, but his son Ezra loves it.

2953. Ilowite, Sheldon A. *Centerman from Quebec* (4–6). Illus. by Ned Butterfield. 1972, Hastings $6.95. A move from Quebec to Long Island brings difficulties for Jean Nicol's acceptance onto a new hockey team. Also use: *Penalty Killer* (1973, Hastings $6.95).

2954. Kaatz, Evelyn. *Soccer! How One Player Made the Pros* (4–6). Illus. 1981, Little $7.95. A fictional account of how Rick makes out during his first season in pro soccer.

2955. Kalb, Jonah. *The Goof That Won the Pennant* (3–6). Illus. by Sandy Kossin. 1976, Houghton $5.95. Losers become winners in this humorous baseball story.

2956. Knudson, R. R. *Rinehart Lifts* (4–6). 1980, Farrar $9.95. A failure at all sports, Rinehart finds he can excel in weight lifting.

2957. Levy, Elizabeth. *The Tryouts* (4–6). Illus. by Jacquie Hann. 1979, Four Winds $7.95. The boys' basketball team finds that it must accept 2 girls.

2958. Lewis, Marjorie. *Wrongway Applebaum* (2–5). 1984, Putnam $9.95. A clumsy boy becomes the hero of a baseball team.

2959. Park, Barbara. *Skinnybones* (4–6). 1982, Knopf $8.95; LB $8.99; Avon paper $2.25. The story of a little league misfit.

2960. Robison, Nancy. *On the Balance Beam* (4–6). Illus. by Rondi Anderson. 1978, Whitman $6.50. Andrea's dream of becoming a gymnast comes true.

2961. Schulman, Janet. *Jenny and the Tennis Nut* (2–4). Illus. by Marylin Hafner. 1978, Greenwillow $8.25; LB $7.92; Dell paper $1.25. Jenny really wants to be a gymnast in spite of her father's love for tennis.

2962. Slote, Alfred. *The Hotshot* (4–6). Photos by William LaCrosse. 1977, Watts $8.90. A fast-moving, easy-to-read book about a hockey player who slowly learns how to play as part of a team.

2963. Slote, Alfred. *Jake* (5–6). 1971, Harper paper $2.50. Jake claims he is interested only in baseball.

2964. Slote, Alfred. *Matt Gargan's Boy* (4–6). 1975, Harper $10.89; Avon paper $1.95. A baseball story with substance involving Danny, the team's excellent pitcher, his divorced parents, and a young girl who wants to make the team.

2965. Slote, Alfred. *Rabbit Ears* (4–6). 1982, Harper $2.84. Fourteen-year-old Tip is losing his confidence as a baseball player.

2966. Slote, Alfred. *Tony and Me* (4–6). 1974, Harper $9.57; Avon paper $1.75. Bill's new friend Tony is a whiz at baseball, but unfortunately he is also a thief, and this knowledge forces Bill to make a difficult moral decision.

2967. Tolle, Jean Bahor. *The Great Pete Penney* (4–6). 1979, Atheneum $8.95. A leprechaun helps a girl move into major league baseball.

2968. Wallace, Barbara Brooks. *Hawkins and the Soccer Solution* (4–6). Illus. by Gloria Kamen. 1981, Abingdon $7.95. A "gentleman's gentleman" helps coach a soccer team. Others in this series: *Hawkins* (1977, $6.95); *The Contest Kid Strikes Back* (1980, $7.95).

Humorous Stories

2969. Ahlberg, Allan, and Ahlberg, Janet. *Burglar Bill* (3–5). Illus. 1977, Penguin paper $2.95. The arrival of a baby reforms the rambunctious Burglar Bill.

2970. Aiken, Joan. *Arabel and Mortimer* (3–6). Illus. by Quentin Blake. 1981, Doubleday $9.95; Dell paper $2.25. Mortimer, the irrepressible raven, continually causes problems for his 6-year-old mistress. A sequel is: *Mortimer's Cross* (1984, Harper $10.89).

2971. Angell, Judie. *First the Good News* (6–8). 1982, Bradbury $9.95. Five girls decide to interview a TV personality.

2972. Angell, Judie. *In Summertime It's Tuffy* (5–7). 1977, Bradbury $9.95; Dell paper $2.25. The girls in Bunk 10 want to get even with the head counselor.

2973. Angell, Judie. *Suds* (6–9). 1983, Bradbury $9.95. A takeoff on soap operas with a junior high school girl as heroine.

2974. Atwater, Richard, and Atwater, Florence. *Mr. Popper's Penguins* (4–6). Illus. by Robert Lawson. 1938, Little $9.95; Dell paper $2.25. Mr. Popper has to get a penguin from the zoo to keep his homesick penguin company; soon there are 12.

2975. Baron, Nancy. *Tuesday's Child* (4–6). 1984, Atheneum $9.95. Grace wants to play baseball, but her mother wants her to follow a ballet career.

2976. Beatty, Patricia. *That's One Ornery Orphan* (6–8). 1980, Morrow $9.75; LB $9.36. An unconventional orphan is adopted 3 times in this story set in nineteenth-century Texas.

2977. Beckman, Delores. *My Own Private Sky* (4–6). 1980, Dutton $9.95. Arthur Elliot has a real with-it 60-year-old grandmother, who helps him conquer his fear of swimming.

2978. Blume, Judy. *Freckle Juice* (2–5). Illus. by Sonia O. Lisker. 1971, Four Winds $8.95. A gullible second grader pays 50¢ for a recipe to grow freckles.

2979. Blume, Judy. *Starring Sally J. Freedman As Herself* (4–7). 1977, Bradbury $10.95; Dell paper $2.50. A story of a fifth-grader's adventures in New Jersey and Florida in the late 1940s.

2980. Bond, Michael. *A Bear Called Paddington* (3–6). Illus. by Peggy Fortnum. 1960, Houghton $9.95; Dell paper $2.25. An endearing bear with a talent for getting into trouble. Some sequels (published by Houghton and Dell) are: *Paddington Helps Out* (1961, $7.95; paper $1.75); *More about Paddington* (1962, $9.95; paper $1.75); *Paddington at Work* (1967, $8.95; paper $1.50); *Paddington Goes to Town* (1968, $7.95; paper $1.25); *Paddington Abroad* (1972, $9.95; paper $1.25); *Paddington Takes to TV* (1974, $6.95; paper $1.25); *Paddington on Top* (1975, $5.95; paper $1.25).

2981. Bond, Michael. *Paddington on Screen* (3–5). Illus. by Barry Macey. 1982, Houghton $8.95. Further adventures of Paddington, everyone's favorite bear. Four other Paddington stories: *Paddington at Large* (1963, $9.95; Dell paper $1.75); *Paddington Marches On* (1965, $8.95; Dell paper $1.50); *Paddington Takes to the Air* (1971, $7.95); *Paddington Takes the Test* (1980, $8.95; Dell paper $1.95).

2982. Bond, Michael. *Paddington's Storybook* (3–5). Illus. by Peggy Fortnum. 1984, Houghton $12.95. A selection of some of the very best stories published over the past 25 years.

2983. Bond, Michael. *The Tales of Olga de Polga* (4–5). Illus. by Hans Helweg. 1973, Dell paper $2.25; Penguin paper $2.50. Olga, another superb creation by the author of Paddington, is a witty imaginative guinea pig who holds other animals spellbound by her stories. Also use: *Olga Meets Her Match* (1975, Dell paper $2.25; Penguin paper $2.95); *Olga Carries On* (1977, Dell paper $2.25); *The Complete Adventures of Olga de Polga* (1983, Delacorte $16.95).

2984. Bontemps, Arna, and Conroy, Jack. *The Fast Sooner Hound* (2–4). Illus. by Virginia L. Burton. 1942, Houghton $10.95. A long-legged, lop-eared hound dog outruns the Cannon Ball Express.

2985. Brooks, Walter R. *Freddy, the Detective* (3–5). Illus. by Kurt Wiese. 1932, Knopf $6.39; Dell paper $1.75. Freddy, the pig, turns into a supersleuth after reading Sherlock Holmes. One of a long and popular series.

2986. Bunting, Eve. *The Big Cheese* (2–5). Illus. by Sal Murdocca. 1977, Macmillan $8.95. Two sisters acquire a huge cheese and must devise methods of protecting it in this amusing story.

2987. Bunting, Eve. *Karen Kepplewhite Is the World's Best Kisser* (5–7). 1983, Houghton $9.95. Karen decides she must learn to kiss for an upcoming birthday party.

2988. Butterworth, Oliver. *The Enormous Egg* (3–6). Illus. by Louis Darling. 1956, Little $8.95; Dell paper $2.25. The story of a boy whose hen lays a large egg, which hatches a triceratops! A sequel is: *The Narrow Passage* (1973, $7.95).

2989. Butterworth, Oliver. *The Trouble with Jenny's Ear* (4–6). 1960, Little $9.95. A humorous story about 2 ingenious boys who capitalize on their sister's sensitive ear—one that can hear thoughts—to earn money.

2990. Byars, Betsy. *The Cybil War* (4–6). Illus. by Gail Owens. 1981, Viking $9.95; Scholastic paper $1.95. A humorous story about the relationship between two boys and a girl, Cybil.

2991. Callen, Larry. *The Deadly Mandrake* (5–7). Illus. by Larry Johnson. 1978, Little $7.95. This second Four Corner story humorously explores superstition and folksiness in backwoods America.

2992. Carris, Joan. *When the Boys Ran the House* (4–6). Illus. by Carol Newsom. 1982, Harper $9.57; LB $9.89. Four boys take care of the house when both parents are away.

2993. Chew, Ruth. *Wednesday Witch* (3–5). 1972, Holiday $8.95. A witch who travels by vacuum cleaner is featured in this humorous tale. Also use: *The Witch's Gardens* (1979, Hastings $7.95).

2994. Cleary, Beverly. *Ellen Tebbits* (3–5). Illus. by Louis Darling. 1951, Morrow $10.75; LB $10.32; Dell paper $2.50. Eight-year-old Ellen has braces on her teeth, takes ballet lessons, and, worst of all, wears long woolen underwear.

2995. Cleary, Beverly. *Emily's Runaway Imagination* (3–6). Illus. by Beth Krush and Joe Krush. 1961, Morrow $11.95; LB $11.47; Dell paper $2.50. Emily's imagination helps get a library for Pitchfork, Oregon, in the 1920s.

2996. Cleary, Beverly. *Henry Huggins* (3–5). Illus. by Louis Darling. 1950, Morrow $10.32; Dell paper $2.50. Henry is a small boy with a knack for creating hilarious situations. Others in the series: *Henry and Beezus* (1952); *Henry and Ribsy* (1954); *Henry and the Paper Route* (1957) (all Morrow $11.25; LB $10.80; Dell paper $2.50); *Henry and the Clubhouse* (1962, Morrow $10.75; LB $10.32; Dell paper $2.50).

2997. Cleary, Beverly. *Otis Spofford* (3–6). Illus. by Louis Darling. 1953, Morrow $10.75; LB $10.32; Dell paper $2.50. This story of Otis stirring up a little excitement at school is full of humor.

2998. Cleary, Beverly. *Runaway Ralph* (3–5). Illus. by Louis Darling. 1970, Morrow $10.95; LB $10.51; Dell paper $2.50. A motorcyclist mouse finds family life too stifling so he takes to his wheels, only to find that freedom is an evasive thing. Two others in the series: *The Mouse and the Motorcycle* (1965, $10.75; LB $10.32; paper $2.50); *Ralph S. Mouse* (1982, $9.75; LB $8.88; paper $2.50).

2999. Clements, Bruce. *I Tell a Lie Every So Often* (5–8). 1984, Farrar $9.95. The adventures of the 14-year-old narrator, an imaginative bender of the truth, and his older brother on a trip up the Missouri River in 1848.

3000. Clifford, Eth. *Harvey's Horrible Snake Disaster* (3–5). 1984, Houghton $10.45. Harvey tries to disguise the fact that he is petrified of snakes.

3001. Conford, Ellen. *Felicia the Critic* (5–7). Illus. by Arvis Stewart. 1973, Little $7.95; Pocket paper $1.95. Felicia's habit of being bluntly honest gets her into trouble.

3002. Conford, Ellen. *Lenny Kandell, Smart Aleck* (5–8). Illus. by Walter Gaffney-Kessell. 1983, Little $9.50. Lenny longs to be a stand-up comic, but his mouth usually just gets him into trouble.

3003. Conford, Ellen. *The Revenge of the Incredible Dr. Rancid and His Youthful Assistant, Jeffrey* (5–7). 1980, Little $6.70. Jeffrey must confront his fear and challenge a bully.

3004. Conford, Ellen. *Seven Days to a Brand-New Me* (6–9). 1981, Little $8.25; Scholastic paper $1.95. Maddy Kemper tries to change her dull disposition.

3005. Conford, Ellen. *You Never Can Tell* (6–9). 1984, Little $11.45. Katie's crush on a soap opera star turns into reality.

3006. Corbett, Scott. *The Baseball Trick* (3–5). Illus. by Paul Galdone. 1965, Little $7.95. Kirby and his wonderful chemistry set help Fenton hit a home run. Others in the series are: *The Lemonade Trick* (1960, $8.95); *The Mailbox Trick* (1961, $7.95); *The Hairy Horror Trick* (1967, $8.95); *The Case of the Fugitive Firebug* (1969, $6.95); *The Case of the Ticklish Tooth* (1969, $5.95); *The Black Mask Trick* (1976, $6.95); *The Hangman's Ghost Trick* (1977, $7.95; Scholastic paper $1.95).

3007. Coren, Alan. *Arthur the Kid* (4–6). Illus. by John Astrop. 1978, Little $7.95; Bantam paper $2.25. A wild spoof of a shoot-em-up Western adventure. Several sequels are: *Buffalo Arthur* (1978); *Railroad Arthur* (1978); *Arthur's Last Stand* (1979); *Klondike Arthur* (1979); *Arthur and the Great Detective* (1980) (all Little $7.95); *Arthur and the Purple Panic* (1984, Parkwest $6.50).

3008. Corrin, Sara, comp. *A Time to Laugh: Thirty Stories for Young Children* (3–5). Illus. by Gerald Rose. 1980, Faber $6.95. An international collection of humorous stories.

3009. Cresswell, Helen. *Ordinary Jack: Being the First Part of the Bagthorpe Saga* (5–7). 1977, Macmillan $9.95; Avon paper $1.50. Everyone in the English Bagthorpe's family is precociously accomplished—except Jack. Some sequels are: *Absolute Zero* (1979, Avon paper $1.75); *Bagthorpes vs. the World* (1979, $9.95; Avon paper $1.95); *Bagthorpes Unlimited* (1980, Avon paper $1.75); *Bagthorpes Abroad* (1984, $10.95).

3010. Cresswell, Helen. *The Winter of the Birds* (6–9). 1976, Macmillan $10.95. A novel, told from 3 different points of view, about the effects on the residents of an English town when unconventional, delightful Patrick Finn comes to visit.

3011. Dahl, Roald. *Danny: The Champion of the World* (3–5). Illus. by Jill Bennett. 1975, Knopf LB $8.99; Bantam paper $2.50. Nine-year-old Danny helps his father on a poaching expedition to wealthy Mr. Hazell's woods.

3012. De Angeli, Marguerite. *Yonie Wondernose* (2–4). 1944, Doubleday $7.95. A Pennsylvania Amish boy earns his funny name from insatiable curiosity.

3013. Delaney, M. C. *The Marigold Monster* (PS–3). Illus. by Ned Delaney. 1983, Dutton $9.66. Audrey decides to sell her marigold seeds to the local monster.

3014. DeWeese, Gene. *Major Colby and the Unidentified Flapping Object* (5–7). 1979, Doubleday $7.95. When 14-year-old Russ agrees to help a UFO, a whole town gets involved.

3015. Domke, Todd. *Grounded* (4–7). 1982, Knopf $9.95; LB $9.99. Parker's determination to build a glider leads to hilarious results.

3016. du Bois, William Pene. *The Alligator Case* (3–6). Illus. by author. 1965, Harper $12.89. A young boy assumes many identities as he tracks down the villains who disguise themselves as alligators.

3017. du Bois, William Pene. *Lazy Tommy Pumpkinhead* (2–4). Illus. by author. 1966, Harper $12.89. The eccentric performance of gadgets in an all-electric house provides high-voltage hilarity.

3018. du Bois, William Pene. *The 3 Policemen: Or, Young Bottsford of Farbe Island* (3–5). 1960, Viking $8.95. A humorous and intriguing detective story of 3 policemen and young Bottsford, who solve the mystery of the stolen fishing nets on Farbe Island.

3019. du Bois, William Pene. *Twenty-One Balloons* (4–6). Illus. by author. 1947, Viking $9.95; Dell paper $2.25. Truth and fiction are combined in the adventures of a professor who sails around the world in a balloon. Newbery Award winner, 1948.

3020. Durrell, Ann, ed. *Just for Fun* (4–6). 1977, Dutton $8.50. Seven humorous stories by such

popular writers as Lloyd Alexander, Scott Corbett, and Marilyn Sachs.

3021. Farley, Carol. *Loosen Your Ears* (4–6). Illus. by Mila Lazarevich. 1977, Atheneum $7.95. Narrator Josh Hemmer tells humorous anecdotes about his comical farm family. Another Hemmer book is: *Settle Your Fidgets* (1977, $6.95).

3022. Fitzgerald, John D. *The Great Brain* (4–7). Illus. by Mercer Mayer. 1967, Dial $9.95; LB $9.89; Dell paper $2.50. A witty and tender novel in which narrator John recalls the escapades of older brother Tom whose perceptive and crafty schemes set him apart. Some sequels are: *More Adventures of the Great Brain* (1969); *Me and My Little Brain* (1971); *The Great Brain at the Academy* (1972); *The Great Brain Reforms* (1973); *The Return of the Great Brain* (1974); *The Great Brain Does It Again* (1975) (all $9.95; LB $9.89; Dell paper $2.50).

3023. Fitzhugh, Louise. *Sport* (4–6). 1979, Delacourt $8.95; Dell paper $1.75. When an 11-year-old boy is left a sizable fortune, his mother tries to regain his custody.

3024. Fleischman, Sid. *By the Great Horn Spoon* (4–6). Illus. by Eric Von Schmidt. 1963, Little $8.95. Accompanied by Praiseworthy, the butler, an orphan boy named Jack Fogg runs away and becomes involved in the California gold rush of 1849 in this hilarious adventure story.

3025. Fleischman, Sid. *Chancy and the Grand Rascal* (5–7). Illus. by Eric Von Schmidt. 1966, Little $7.95. The boy and his uncle, the grand rascal, combine hard work and quick wits to outsmart a scoundrel, hoodwink a miser, and capture a band of outlaws.

3026. Fleischman, Sid. *The Ghost in the Noonday Sun* (5–7). Illus. by Warren Chappell. 1965, Little $7.95. Pirate story with all the standard ingredients of shanghaied boy, villainous captain, and buried treasure.

3027. Fleischman, Sid. *The Ghost on Saturday Night* (3–5). Illus. by Eric Von Schmidt. 1974, Little $7.95. Ten-year-old Opie's efforts to raise money for a saddle involve him in a ghost-raising session and the recovery of money stolen from a bank.

3028. Fleischman, Sid. *The Hey Hey Man* (4–6). Illus. by Nadine Westcott. 1979, Little $7.95. A tree sprite bests an ornery gold thief.

3029. Fleischman, Sid. *Humbug Mountain* (4–6). Illus. by Eric Von Schmidt. 1978, Little $8.95; Scholastic paper $1.75. A madcap tall tale adventure in the wild West.

3030. Fleischman, Sid. *Jingo Django* (4–6). Illus. by Eric Von Schmidt. 1971, Little $9.95. A humorous adventure story about a young boy who lives in an orphanage in Boston and, after many escapades, finds his real father.

3031. Fleischman, Sid. *McBroom and the Beanstalk* (3–5). Illus. by Walter Lorraine. 1978, Little $7.95. A tall tale in which McBroom enters the World Champion Liar's Competition. Others in the series: *McBroom Tells a Lie* (1976); *McBroom and the Great Race* (1980) (both $7.95); *McBroom Tells the Truth* (1981); *McBroom's Ghost* (1981) (both $7.95; paper $3.95); *McBroom and the Big Wind* (1982); *McBroom the Rainmaker* (1982); *McBroom's Ear* (1982); *McBroom's Zoo* (1982) (all $8.95; paper $3.95); *McBroom's Almanac* (1984, $12.45).

3032. Fleischman, Sid. *Me and the Man on the Moon-Eyed Horse* (3–6). Illus. by Eric Von Schmidt. 1977, Little $7.95. A tall tale about a young boy's humorous involvement with the capture of train wreckers in the frontier days of the West.

3033. Fleischman, Sid. *Mr. Mysterious & Company* (3–5). Illus. by Eric Von Schmidt. 1962, Little $8.95. A traveling magic show during the 1880s makes for an entertaining family story that is also an excellent historical novel.

3034. Gannett, Ruth. *My Father's Dragon* (4–6). Illus. by author. 1948, Random $8.99; Dell paper $1.25. Hilarious adventures of Elmer Elevator. Also use: *The Dragons of Blueland* (n.d., Dell paper $1.25); *Elmer and the Dragon* (1980, Dell paper $1.25).

3035. Gilson, Jamie. *Dial Leroi Rupert* (5–7). Illus. by John Wallner. 1979, Lothrop $9.95; LB $9.55. Mitch's imitation of a local disc jockey gets him into trouble. A sequel is: *Can't Catch Me, I'm the Gingerbread Man* (1981, $11.25; LB $10.80; Pocket paper $1.95).

3036. Gilson, Jamie. *Harvey, the Beer Can King* (4–7). Illus. by John Wallner. 1978, Lothrop $8.00; LB $9.55. Harvey is certain that his collection of beer cans will ensure his victory in the Superkid Contest.

3037. Greene, Constance C. *Isabelle the Itch* (4–6). Illus. by Emily McCully. 1973, Viking $9.95; Dell paper $2.25. Isabelle is a hyperactive fifth grader who expends her energies in many directions, not getting much of anywhere. A sequel is: *Isabelle Shows Her Stuff* (1984, $11.50).

3038. Greenwald, Sheila. *Give Us a Great Big Smile, Rosy Cole* (3–5). Illus. by author. 1981, Little $9.70; Dell paper $1.95. Ten-year-old Rosy discovers she is to be the subject of Uncle Ralph's new book. A sequel is: *Valentine Rosy* (1984, $10.95).

3039. Greenwald, Sheila. *It All Began with Jane Eyre: Or the Secret Life of Franny Dilman* (6–9). 1980, Little $8.95; Dell paper $1.75. A spoof on current

adolescent novels about a girl who really enjoys the classics.

3040. Greenwald, Sheila. *The Mariah Delany Lending Library Disaster* (4–6). 1977, Houghton $8.95. To make extra money, Mariah converts her parents' collection of books into a lending library, but her patrons neglect to return them.

3041. Hale, Lucretia P. *The Peterkin Papers* (5–7). 1960, Sharon paper $3.95. A series of amusing anecdotes about the Peterkin family, including 4 new stories out of print since 1886.

3042. Harris, Robbie H. *Rosie's Razzle Dazzle Deal* (4–6). 1982, Knopf LB $4.99; paper $1.95. Rosie is so lovable that blame for her pranks usually is placed on her brother.

3043. Haywood, Carolyn. *Eddie's Menagerie* (3–5). Illus. by Ingrid Fetz. 1978, Morrow $11.95; LB $11.47; Pocket paper $1.95. Eddie Wilson becomes a volunteer detective for a pet store. Others in the series: *Little Eddie* (1947); *Eddie and the Fire Engine* (1949) (both $10.80); *Eddie's Valuable Property* (1975, $11.25; LB $10.80); *Eddie the Dog Holder* (1980, Pocket paper $1.75); *Eddie's Happenings* (1981, Pocket paper $1.95).

3044. Heide, Florence Parry. *Banana Twist* (4–6). 1978, Holiday $9.95. Jonah tries a flimflam job to get into a prep school and succeeds in spite of his friend Goober. A sequel is: *Banana Blitz* (1983, $9.95).

3045. Heide, Florence Parry. *The Shrinking of Treehorn* (1–3). Illus. by Edward Gorey. 1971, Holiday $8.95. Treehorn has a special talent—he can become smaller by the moment—but nobody notices. Some sequels are: *Treehorn's Treasure* (1981, LB $8.95); *The Adventures of Treehorn* (1983, Dell paper $2.25); *Treehorn's Wish* (1984, $8.95).

3046. Heide, Florence Parry. *Time's Up!* (4–6). Illus. by Marylin Hafner. 1982, Holiday $9.95; Pocket paper $1.95. Noah is unhappy in his new neighborhood until he makes 3 new friends and has some madcap adventures. A sequel is: *Time Flies!* (1984, $10.95).

3047. Hicks, Clifford B. *Pop and Peter Potts* (4–6). 1984, Holt $9.70. A tall tale about a boy and his amazing grandfather.

3048. Hoban, Russell. *The Twenty-Elephant Restaurant* (2–4). Illus. by Emily McCully. 1978, Atheneum $9.95. The buying of a table ends in opening a restaurant.

3049. Hopper, Nancy J. *The Seven and One-Half Sins of Stacey Kendall* (5–7). 1982, Dutton $9.95; paper $2.25. Stacey decides to make some money piercing ears.

3050. Howe, Deborah, and Howe, James. *Bunnicula: A Rabbit-Tale of Mystery* (4–6). Illus. by Alan Daniel. 1979, Atheneum $9.95; Avon paper $2.25. A dog named Harold tells the story of a rabbit many believe to be a vampire. Two sequels by James Howe are: *Howliday Inn* (1982, LB $10.95; Avon paper $2.25); *The Celery Stalks at Midnight* (1983, $10.95; Avon paper $2.50).

3051. Hughes, Dean. *Honestly, Myron* (4–6). Illus. by Martha Weston. 1982, Atheneum LB $9.95. Myron decides only to tell the truth with unforeseen results.

3052. Hunter, Norman. *The Incredible Adventures of Professor Branestawm* (5–8). Illus. by W. Heath Robinson. 1979, Merrimack $9.95. Fourteen absurd stories about a madcap inventor and his loony inventions.

3053. Hurwitz, Johanna. *Aldo Applesauce* (3–4). Illus. by John Wallner. 1979, Morrow $10.50; LB $10.08; Scholastic paper $1.95. Aldo moves to New York City, acquires a new nickname, and a strange friend. Two others in the series are: *Much Ado about Aldo* (1978, $10.95; LB $10.51); *Aldo Ice Cream* (1981, $9.25; LB $8.88).

3054. Hutchins, Pat. *The House That Sailed Away* (3–5). Illus. by Laurence Hutchins. 1975, Greenwillow $10.80. A nonsense novel about an English family's adventures at sea in their uprooted house.

3055. Kennedy, Stephanie. *Hey, Didi Darling* (5–9). 1983, Houghton $9.70. Tammy's all-girl rock band pretends to be boys to get engagements.

3056. Kerr, M. E. *Dinky Hocker Shoots Smack!* (6–9). 1972, Harper LB $10.89; Dell paper $1.95. Dinky, a compulsive eater, tries many ways to gain her parents' attention.

3057. King, Clive. *Me and My Million* (4–6). 1979, Harper LB $9.89. Ringo, a London street urchin, has some amazing and amusing adventures resulting from a learning disability.

3058. Klein, Norma. *A Honey of a Chimp* (4–6). 1980, Pantheon LB $6.99; Pocket paper $1.95. Life in a New York apartment with a chimp isn't easy.

3059. Konigsburg. E. L. *About the B'nai Bagels* (3–6). Illus. by author. 1969, Atheneum LB $10.95; paper $3.50. Poor Mark—his mother is the manager of the Little League Baseball team on which he plays, and his older brother is the coach.

3060. Krantz, Hazel. *100 Pounds of Popcorn* (5–7). Illus. by Charles Geer. 1961, Vanguard $6.95. Andy and his friends go into business when they receive 100 pounds of popcorn and learn about business techniques.

3061. Lawson, Robert. *Ben and Me* (5–8). Illus. by author. 1939, Little $9.95; Dell paper $2.25. The events of Benjamin Franklin's life, as told by his good mouse Amos, who lived in his old fur cap.

3062. Lawson, Robert. *Captain Kidd's Cat* (3–5). Illus. by author. 1984, Little paper $3.95. A narrative recount by McDermot, faithful cat of Captain William Kidd.

3063. Lawson, Robert. *Mr. Revere and I* (5–8). Illus. by author. 1953, Little $9.95; Dell paper $1.25. A delightful account of certain episodes in Revere's life, as revealed by his horse Scheherazade.

3064. Levine, Betty K. *The Great Burgerland Disaster* (6–9). 1981, Atheneum LB $9.95. Myron takes a job at Burgerland to buy a new bicycle.

3065. Lindgren, Astrid. *Pippi Longstocking* (4–6). Illus. by Louis Glanzman. 1950, Viking LB $9.95; Penguin paper $3.50. A little Swedish tomboy who has a monkey and a horse for companions. Also use: *Pippi Goes on Board* (1957); *Pippi in the South Seas* (1959) (both LB $9.95; paper $3.50).

3066. Loeper, John J. *Galloping Gertrude: By Motorcar in 1908* (4–6). Illus. 1980, Atheneum $6.95. An eventful 30-mile trip in the early days of automobiles.

3067. Lowry, Lois. *Anastasia Krupnik* (4–6). 1979, Houghton $9.95; Bantam paper $2.25. A lively romp with an intelligent and articulate 10-year-old girl leading the way. Three sequels are: *Anastasia Again!* (1981, $9.95; Dell paper $2.50); *Anastasia at Your Service* (1982, $9.95; Dell paper $2.25); *Anastasia, Ask Your Analyst* (1984, $9.95).

3068. Lowry, Lois. *The One Hundredth Thing about Caroline* (5–7). 1983, Houghton $8.70. Caroline tries everything and anything to break up her mother's new romance.

3069. Lowry, Lois. *Taking Care of Terrific* (6–9). 1983, Houghton $8.95; Dell paper $1.95. Enid concocts adventures for herself and the young boy with whom she babysits.

3070. McCloskey, Robert. *Homer Price* (3–6). Illus. by author. 1943, Viking $10.95; Penguin paper $2.95. Popular and preposterous adventures of a midwestern boy. Continued in: *Centerburg Tales* (1977, $8.85, Penguin paper $2.95).

3071. McDonnell, Christine. *Toad Food and Measle Soup* (3–5). Illus. by Diane de Groat. 1982, Dial $9.95; LB $9.89; Puffin paper $3.50. Five humorous stories about an engaging family. A sequel is: *Lucky Charms and Birthday Wishes* (1984, Viking $10.95).

3072. MacLachlan, Patricia. *Arthur, for the Very First Time* (4–6). Illus. by Lloyd Bloom. 1980, Harper $9.57; LB $9.89. Arthur spends a summer on the farm of his aunt and uncle.

3073. Manes, Stephen. *Be a Perfect Person in Just Three Days!* (4–6). Illus. by Tom Huffman. 1982, Houghton $8.95; Bantam paper $1.95. Milo Crinkley decides to change his ways via a book he has found in the library.

3074. Marshall, James. *Taking Care of Carruthers* (3–5). Illus. by author. 1981, Houghton $9.95. Three friends try to distract Carruthers from his woes.

3075. Merrill, Jean. *The Pushcart War* (5–7). Illus. by Bonni Solbert. 1964, Childrens Pr. LB $9.95. Mack, driving a Mighty Mammoth, runs down a pushcart belonging to Morris the Florist, and a most unusual war is on!

3076. Merrill, Jean. *The Toothpaste Millionaire* (4–6). Illus. 1974, Houghton LB $9.95. Kate tells the delightful story of a black boy, Rufus, who challenges the entire business community by marketing a product called simply "toothpaste."

3077. Morton, Jane. *I Am Rubber, You Are Glue* (3–6). 1981, Beaufort Books $7.95. Bart tries to help his father who is running for mayor.

3078. Myers, Walter Dean. *Mojo and the Russians* (6–8). 1977, Viking $10.95. A group of friends tries to save one of them from a voodoo spell.

3079. Nostlinger, Christine. *Marrying Off Mother* (5–7). 1982, Harcourt $8.95. Sue tries to find a new father by marrying mother off.

3080. Okimoto, Jean Davies. *Norman Schnurman, Average Person* (5–8). 1982, Putnam $9.95; Dell paper $2.25. Norman's father, a football nut, is less than happy with his son's gridiron performances.

3081. Park, Barbara. *Beanpole* (6–8). 1983, Knopf $9.95; LB $9.99. A seventh grader is teased because she is so tall and thin.

3082. Park, Barbara. *Operation: Dump the Chump* (3–6). 1982, Knopf $8.95; LB $8.99; Avon paper $2.25. Oscar Winkle devises a plan to get rid of his young brother.

3083. Peck, Robert Newton. *Hub* (5–7). Illus. by Ted Lewin. 1979, Knopf LB $5.99. Hub and friend Spooner back their teacher Miss Guppy in the Overland Obstacle Bicycle Race.

3084. Peck, Robert Newton. *Trig* (4–6). 1977, Little $8.70; Dell paper $1.95. Elizabeth Trigman, a tomboy, outwits the boys in this humorous novel set in rural Vermont during the Depression. Some sequels are: *Trig See Red* (1978, $6.95; Dell paper $1.25); *Trig Goes Ape* (1980, $7.95); *Trig or Treat* (1982, $9.70; Dell paper $1.95).

3085. Pettersson, Alan R. *Frankenstein's Aunt* (6–9). 1981, Little $7.95; Avon paper $1.95. Frankenstein's aunt tries to restore the family's good name.

3086. Pevsner, Stella. *Call Me Heller, That's My Name* (4–6). Illus. by Richard Cuffari. 1973, Houghton $7.95; Pocket paper $1.95. A young girl tries to handle an aunt who has suddenly become part of her life.

3087. Pinkwater, D. Manus. *Fat Men from Space* (3–6). Illus. by author. 1977, Dodd $7.95; Dell paper $1.95. Among other adventures, William encounters raiders of junk food from outer space in this nutrition-conscious farce.

3088. Pinkwater, D. Manus. *The Hoboken Chicken Emergency* (3–7). 1977, Prentice $8.95; paper $4.95. A young boy buys a 6-foot, 260-pound chicken in this humorous story.

3089. Pinkwater, D. Manus. *The Magic Moscow* (4–6). Illus. by author. 1980, Four Winds $7.95; Scholastic paper $1.95. A humorous story of an Ice Cream parlor in Hoboken, New Jersey. Two sequels are: *Attila the Pun: A Magic Moscow Story* (1981, $7.95); *Slaves of Spiegel: A Magic Moscow Story* (1982, $8.95).

3090. Pinkwater, D. Manus. *Return of the Moose* (4–6). Illus. by author. 1979, Dodd $8.95. Our hero writes a novel based on his exploits and goes to Hollywood to supervise its filming. A sequel to: *Blue Moose* (1975, $8.95).

3091. Pinkwater, D. Manus. *The Snarkout Boys and the Avocado of Death* (5–8). 1982, Lothrop $11.25. In this zany adventure, Walter and Winston search for Rat Face's missing uncle. A sequel is: *The Snarkout Boys and the Baconburg Horror* (1984, $10.50).

3092. Pinkwater, D. Manus. *The Worms of Kukumlima* (4–7). 1981, Dutton $10.25. Ronald Donald and his grandfather set out to find some intelligent earthworms.

3093. Pinkwater, D. Manus. *Yobgorgle: Mystery Monster of Lake Ontario* (5–7). 1979, Houghton $8.95. A nonsense novel that provides a clear twist to the Flying Dutchman legend.

3094. Raskin, Ellen. *The Mysterious Disappearance of Leon (I Mean Noel)* (4–6). Illus. by author. 1980, Dutton paper $1.95. Humorous saga of Mrs. Carillon's search for her husband Leon (or Noel), who is the joint heir to a soup fortune.

3095. Raskin, Ellen. *The Tattooed Potato and Other Clues* (5–7). 1975, Dutton $9.95; Avon paper $2.25. This zany spoof on detective stories introduces the reader to part-time mystery solver Garson and his assistant, Dickdry Dock.

3096. Ritchie, Barbara. *Ramon Makes a Trade* (3–5). 1959, Parnassus $7.95. Ramon turns out to be a most ingenious trader, as explained in English and Spanish.

3097. Robertson, Keith. *Henry Reed, Inc.* (5–7). Illus. by Robert McCloskey. 1958, Viking $10.95; Dell paper $1.75. Told deadpan in diary form, this story of Henry's enterprising summer in New Jersey present one of the most amusing boys since Tom and Huck. Others in the series: *Henry Reed's Journey* (1963, $11.50; Dell paper $1.75); *Henry Reed's Baby-Sitting Service* (1966, LB $11.50; Dell paper $1.75); *Henry Reed's Big Show* (1970, LB $11.50).

3098. Rockwell, Thomas. *How to Eat Fried Worms* (4–6). Illus. by Emily McCully. 1973, Watts $8.90; Dell paper $2.25. In this very humorous story, Billy takes on a bet—he will eat 15 worms a day. His family and friends help devise ways to cook them.

3099. Rodgers, Mary. *Freaky Friday* (4–7). 1972, Harper $9.57; LB $9.89; paper $1.95. Thirteen-year-old Annabel learns some valuable lessons during the day she becomes her mother. Two sequels are: *A Billion for Boris* (1974, paper $2.95); *Summer Switch* (1982, $9.13; LB $9.89; paper $3.80).

3100. Roos, Stephen. *My Horrible Secret* (4–6). Illus. by Carol Newsom. 1983, Delacorte $10.95; Dell paper $2.25. Warren's big problem is he can't play baseball. Two sequels are: *The Terrible Truth* (1983, $12.95); *My Secret Admirer* (1984, $14.95; LB $14.95).

3101. Rounds, Glen. *The Day the Circus Came to Lone Tree* (3–6). Illus. by author. 1973, Holiday $8.95. The circus's first and last visit to Lone Tree is a disaster when all the animals break loose.

3102. Rounds, Glen. *Mr. Yowder and the Steamboat* (3–6). Illus. by author. 1980, Dell paper $1.25. A tall tale that involves the winning of an ocean liner at cards and the subsequent adventures trying to dock it. Also use: *Mr. Yowder and the Giant Bull Snake* (1978, Holiday $8.95); *Mr. Yowder and the Lion Roar Capsules* (1980, Dell paper $1.25); *Mr. Yowder, the Peripatetic Sign Painter* (1980, Holiday $7.95); *Mr. Yowder and the Train Robbers* (1981, Holiday LB $8.95); *Mr. Yowder and the Windwagon* (1983, Holiday $8.95).

3103. St. John, Glory. *What I Did Last Summer* (4–6). Illus. by Emily McCully. 1978, Atheneum $9.95. Three boys and their family decide to rough it in the backyard.

3104. Salassi, Otto R. *On the Ropes* (6–9). 1981, Greenwillow $11.25. Squint Gains and his sister set out to save their Texas farm.

3105. Schellie, Don. *Kidnapping Mr. Tubbs* (6–9). 1978, Scholastic paper $1.95. Two teenagers abduct an old cowboy, with humorous results.

3106. Sharmat, Marjorie W. *Chasing after Annie* (4–6). Illus. by Marc Simont. 1981, Harper $7.95; LB $8.89. Told through journal and diary entries, this is the story of Richie's efforts to impress Annie.

3107. Sharmat, Marjorie W. *Rich Mitch* (3–6). Illus. by Loretta Lustig. 1983, Morrow $9.00. Mitch finds he has new problems when he wins a $250,000 contest.

3108. Shura, Mary Francis. *Chester* (4–6). 1980, Dodd $7.95. A group of likable kids are outshone by a newcomer named Chester. Two sequels are: *Eleanor* (1983, $8.95); *Jefferson* (1984, $9.45).

3109. Singer, Marilyn. *The Fido Frameup* (4–6). Illus. by Andrew Glass. 1983, Warne $9.95. A spoof on tough detective fiction with a dog for a narrator.

3110. Singer, Marilyn. *Tarantulas on the Brain* (4–6). Illus. by Leigh Grant. 1982, Harper $9.13; LB $9.89; Scholastic paper $1.95. Lizzie believes that a tarantula would make a fine pet.

3111. Smith, Alison. *Help! There's a Cat Washing in Here!* (4–7). Illus. by Amy Rowen. 1981, Dutton $10.25. Young Henry offers to take care of the house while his mother looks for a job.

3112. Spykman, E. C. *Terrible, Horrible Edie* (4–6). 1960, Harcourt paper $2.95. The humorous adventures of a difficult child. A sequel: *Edie on the Warpath* (1966, paper $2.50).

3113. Stevenson, James. *Here Comes Herb's Hurricane!* (3–5). Illus. 1973, Harper LB $8.89. Under Herb's leadership, an animal community prepares for a hurricane in this amusing story.

3114. Supraner, Robyn. *Think about It, You Might Learn Something* (3–7). Illus. by Sandy Kossin. 1973, Houghton $9.95. A fourth grader writes down some of his experiences in this hilarious series of vignettes.

3115. Sutton, Jane. *Confessions of an Orange Octopus* (4–6). Illus. by Jim Spence. 1983, Dutton $9.66. In spite of parental displeasure, Clarence, alias Chooch, pursues his hobby of juggling.

3116. Swinnerton, A. R. *Rocky the Cat* (4–6). Illus. by Jim Arnosky. 1981, Addison LB $7.95. The story of a mild-mannered boy, his tough cat, and their adventures.

3117. Tolan, Stephanie S. *The Great Skinner Strike* (6–8). 1983, Macmillan $8.95. Mother Skinner, a housewife, goes on strike for unfair labor practices.

3118. Tolles, Martha. *Who's Reading Darci's Diary?* (4–6). 1984, Dutton $10.63. Darci has several problems, including a missing diary.

3119. Travers, P. L. *Mary Poppins* (4–7). Illus. by Mary Shepard. 1934, Harcourt $12.95; paper $3.95. Delightful and humorous things happen when Mary Poppins blows in with the east wind to be nurse for the Banks children. Other series titles: *Mary Poppins Opens the Door* (1943, $11.95; paper $4.95); *Mary Poppins in the Park* (1952, $11.95); *Mary Poppins Comes Back* (1955, $11.95; paper $4.95); *Mary Poppins in Cherry Tree Lane* (1982, $9.95; paper $1.95).

3120.   Twain, Mark. *Adventures of Huckleberry Finn* (6–8). Illus. by Donald McKay and Jo Pelseno. n.d, Putnam $8.95; paper $5.95. One of many editions.

3121.   Twain, Mark. *Adventures of Tom Sawyer* (5–8). Illus. by C. Walter Hodges. 1977, Grosset $9.95. One of many fine editions of this American classic.

3122.   Wallace, Barbara Brooks. *The Contest Kid Strikes Again* (4–6). Illus. by Gloria Kamen. 1980, Abingdon LB $7.95. A story involving villainous P. M. Heister and his plot against hero Harvey Small.

3123.   Weber, Judith Eichler. *Lights, Camera, Cats!* (4–6). Illus. by Pat Grant Porter. 1978, Lothrop $10.00; LB $10.88; Pocket paper $1.95. Twelve-year-old Elizabeth auditions her cats for a commercial.

3124.   Willard, Nancy. *The Highest Hit* (3–5). Illus. by Emily McCully. 1978, Harcourt $6.95; Scholastic paper $1.95. A young girl tries to make the *Guinness Book of World Records*.

3125.   Winn, Chris, and Beadle, Jeremy. *Rodney Rootle's Grown-Up Grappler and Other Treasures from the Museum of Outlawed Inventions* (5–9). Illus. 1983, Little $9.95. All kinds of wacky inventions like an automatic clothes-scattering machine.

3126.   Wolkoff, Judie. *Wally* (4–6). 1977, Bradbury $8.95; Scholastic paper $1.95. Michael and Roger promise to keep Wally the lizard in their home without telling their parents.

3127.   Zimelman, Nathan. *Mean Chickens and Wild Cucumbers* (K–3). Illus. by David Small. 1983, Macmillan $9.95. Two quarreling neighbors each decide to build the biggest fence between them.

Fantasy

3128.   Adams, Richard. *The Tyger Voyage* (3–5). Illus. by Nicola Bayley. 1976, Knopf $7.95. Two tigers leave their home for adventures on land and at sea.

3129.   Adler, Carole S. *Footsteps on the Stairs* (5–7). 1982, Delacorte $9.95; Dell paper $2.25. Dodie and Anne pursue 2 ghosts that are haunting their summer home.

3130.   Aiken, Joan. *The Shadow Guests* (5–8). 1980, Delacorte $7.95. Ghosts appear to Cosmo Autry to seek his help in breaking the power of a curse.

3131.   Alcock, Vivien. *The Haunting of Cassie Palmer* (5–8). 1982, Delacorte $9.95. Cassie finds she is blessed with second sight.

3132.   Alcock, Vivien. *The Stonewalkers* (5–8). 1983, Delacorte $12.95. Statues come to life and begin stalking 2 girls.

3133.   Alexander, Lloyd. *The Book of Three* (5–8). 1964, Holt LB $9.70; Dell paper $2.75. Welsh legend and universal mythology are blended in the tale of an assistant pig keeper who becomes a hero. Newbery award winner 1969. Others in the Prydain cycle: *The Black Cauldron* (1965, LB $10.95; paper $2.95); *The Castle of Llyr* (1966, LB $9.95; paper $2.99); *Taran Wanderer* (1967, LB $9.95; paper $3.25); *The High King* (1968, LB $10.99; paper $3.25).

3134.   Alexander, Lloyd. *The Cat Who Wished to Be a Man* (5–6). 1973, Dutton $8.95. A cat named Lionel, turned into a man by a magician, begins combating the corrupt mayor of the town.

3135.   Alexander, Lloyd. *The First Two Lives of Lukas-Kasha* (5–7). 1978, Dutton $11.95; Dell paper $2.25. Lukas awakens to find himself in a strange land.

3136.   Alexander, Lloyd. *The Marvelous Misadventures of Sebastian* (4–7). 1970, Dutton $14.95. Fourth fiddler Sebastian meets many trials while crossing a Graustarkian kingdom to reach the arms of his princess.

3137.   Alexander, Lloyd. *Time Cat: The Remarkable Journeys of Jason and Gareth* (4–6). 1963, Dutton $9.95; Dell paper $1.50. Jason's cat takes him to various times and places.

3138.   Alexander, Lloyd. *Westmark* (5–7). 1981, Dutton $11.95; Dell paper $2.50. Theo flees his city when his master is killed by the king's chief minister. Two sequels are: *The Kestrel* (1983, Dell paper $2.75); *The Beggar Queen* (1984, Dutton $11.95).

3139.   Alexander, Lloyd. *The Wizard in the Tree* (4–6). Illus. by Laszlo Kubinyi. 1975, Dutton $9.95; Dell paper $1.75. A delightful fantasy of a good versus evil struggle involving an orphan, Mallory, his wizard, and their battle against Mrs. Parsel and Squire Scrupnor.

3140.   Allan, Mabel Esther. *Romansgrove* (6–8). Illus. by Gail Owens. 1975, Atheneum $6.95. Two modern-day children find a magic pendant that transports them through time back to 1902.

3141.   Allan, Ted. *Willie the Squowse* (3–5). Illus. by Quentin Blake. 1978, Hastings $6.95. Willie, part mouse, part squirrel, lives in walls between the houses of 2 very different families.

3142.   Ames, Mildred. *Is There Life on a Plastic Planet?* (5–6). 1975, Dutton $9.95. Hollis is intrigued when Mrs. Eudora, owner of a doll shop, makes a lifelike doll substitute of Hollis, but soon her replacement begins taking over her life. Also use: *Without Hats, Who Can Tell the Good Guys?* (1976, Dutton $8.50).

3143. Amoss, Berthe. *The Chalk Cross* (5–7). 1976, Houghton $6.95. A story involving voodoo in New Orleans.

3144. Anastasio, Dina. *A Question of Time* (4–6). Illus. by Dale Payson. 1978, Dutton $8.50; Scholastic paper $1.95. In this fantasy, a young girl finds a connection between a doll collection, a town tragedy, and her own family.

3145. Arkin, Alan. *The Lemming Condition* (4–7). Illus. by Joan Sandin. 1976, Harper $9.57; LB $9.89. Bubber opposes the mass suicide of his companions in this interesting fable.

3146. Arthur, Ruth. *A Candle in Her Room* (5–7). Illus. by Margery Gill. 1972, Atheneum paper $1.95. An evil wooden doll influences 3 generations of a Welsh family until one girl courageously destroys it.

3147. Asch, Frank. *Pearl's Promise* (3–6). Illus. by author. 1984, Delacorte $12.95; LB $12.95. A mouse named Pearl sets out to save her brother from a pet-store python.

3148. Babbitt, Natalie. *The Devil's Storybook* (4–6). Illus. by author. 1974, Farrar $9.95; paper $3.45. Ten stories about outwitting the devil, in this case personified as a middle-aged, vain, but crafty adversary.

3149. Babbitt, Natalie. *The Search for Delicious* (4–7). Illus. by author. 1969, Farrar $9.95. The innocent task of polling the kingdom's subjects for personal food preferences provokes civil war in a zestful spoof of taste and society.

3150. Babbitt, Natalie. *Tuck Everlasting* (4–6). 1975, Farrar $10.95; Bantam paper $2.25. Violence erupts when the Tuck family members discover that their secret about a spring that brings immortality has been discovered.

3151. Bacon, Martha. *Moth Manor: A Gothic Tale* (4–6). Illus. by Gail Burroughs. 1978, Little $6.95. The story of a dollhouse and 3 generations of its owners.

3152. Bailey, Carolyn Sherwin. *Miss Hickory* (4–6). Illus. by Ruth Gannett. 1946, Viking $9.95; Penguin paper $2.95. The adventures of a doll made from an apple branch with a hickory nut head. Newbery Award winner, 1947.

3153. Baker, Betty. *Seven Spells to Farewell* (5–8). 1982, Macmillan $8.95. A young girl, talented at making spells, joins a medicine show.

3154. Ballard, Mignon Franklin. *Aunt Matilda's Ghost* (5–7). 1978, Aurora paper $3.95. A ghost tries to clear the name of a man wrongfully accused of embezzlement.

3155. Banks, Lynne Reid. *The Indian in the Cupboard* (3–5). 1981, Doubleday $9.95; paper $2.25. A magical cupboard turns toys into living things.

3156. Barber, Antonia. *The Ghosts* (4–6). 1969, Pocket paper $2.25. Two youngsters meet ghosts from another country in their garden.

3157. Barrie, J. M. *Peter Pan* (3–6). Illus. by Trina Schart Hyman. 1980, Scribners $14.95. The Darling family, Tinker Bell, and the whole beloved cast of characters in a recommended edition. Also use: *Peter Pan,* illus. by Diane Goode (1983, Random $6.95; LB $7.99).

3158. Baum, L. Frank. *The Wizard of Oz* (3–5). Illus. by Michael Hague. 1982, Holt $18.95. A new edition of this favorite. One of a large series.

3159. Beachcroft, Nina. *The Wishing People* (4–6). 1982, Dutton $10.50. Two wooden figures come to life and grant wishes to Martha and Jonathan.

3160. Beckman, Thea. *Crusade in Jeans* (4–6). 1975, Scribners paper $1.79. By time machine, a boy is transported back to the days of the Children's Crusade.

3161. Bellairs, John. *The Curse of the Blue Figurine* (5–8). 1983, Dial $11.95; LB $11.89; Bantam paper $2.50. A boy steals an ancient book from a church and evil spells begin working. Two sequels are: *The Mummy, the Will, and the Crypt* (1983, $11.95; LB $11.89); *The Spell of the Sorcerer's Skull* (1984, $11.95).

3162. Bellairs, John. *The Dark Secret of Weatherend* (5–8). 1984, Dutton $11.95; LB $11.89. Anthony and his librarian friend, Miss Eells, uncover a secret in a dead man's diary.

3163. Bellairs, John. *The Figure in the Shadows* (5–7). Illus. by Mercer Mayer. 1975, Dial LB $9.89; Dell paper $2.50. Excitement, magic, and suspense are combined in this story of a boy whose new-found ancient coin is actually an evil talisman. Two others in the series: *The House with a Clock in Its Walls* (1973, $10.95; LB $10.89); *The Letter, the Witch and the Ring* (1976, $12.95; paper $2.50).

3164. Benchley, Nathaniel. *Demo and the Dolphin* (4–7). Illus. by Stephen Gammell. 1981, Harper LB $8.89. A young boy and his dolphin visit the site of ancient Greece.

3165. Bennett, Anna Elizabeth. *Little Witch* (3–5). Illus. by Helen Stone. 1953, Harper $10.89; paper $2.95. Minx, the little witch, does not like being a witch's child and wants most of all to go to school.

3166. Bethancourt, T. Ernesto. *The Dog Days of Arthur Cane* (6–9). 1976, Holiday $9.95. Arthur, a schoolboy from Long Island, New York, discovers that he has been turned into a dog.

3167. Bodecker, N. M. *Carrot Holes and Frisbee Trees* (4–6). Illus. by Nina Winters. 1983, Atheneum $12.95. The Plumtree's carrots are so large that they can use them for post-hole diggers.

3168. Bodecker, N. M. *Quimble Wood* (3–5). Illus. by Branka Starr. 1981, Atheneum $9.95. Four Quimbles, or small people, set up a new forest home.

3169. Bond, Nancy. *A String in the Harp* (6–9). 1976, Atheneum $10.95. A young boy discovers a key that allows him to look into the past, in this fantasy about an American family spending a year in Wales.

3170. Bond, Nancy. *The Voyage Begun* (6–9). 1981, Atheneum LB $12.95. A novel set in the near future when America is starving for energy.

3171. Bonham, Frank. *The Friends of the Loony Lake Monster* (4–6). 1972, Dutton $8.95. Gussie protects her pet dinosaur in this fanciful story that combines a resourceful heroine and a lesson about conservation.

3172. Boston, L. M. *The Children of Green Knowe* (4–7). Illus. by Peter Boston. 1955, Harcourt paper $2.95. A small, lonely boy comes to live in an old English country house where the children who played there generations ago sometimes reappear. Sequels are: *The Treasure of Green Knowe* (1958, $8.95; paper $1.95); *A Stranger at Green Knowe* (1961, $9.95; paper $4.95); *An Enemy at Green Knowe* (1979, paper $3.95); *The Stones of Green Knowe* (1976, Atheneum $7.95).

3173. Boston, L. M. *The Guardians of the House* (3–7). Illus. by Peter Boston. 1975, Atheneum $5.95. A Green Knowe story in which a young boy, newly moved from Wales, has adventures in the ancient house.

3174. Boston, L. M. *The Sea Egg* (3–5). Illus. by Peter Boston. 1967, Harcourt $8.95. A brief episode of magic perfectly captured in this seaside adventure of 2 brothers whose egg-shaped rock hatches into a baby merman.

3175. Briggs, Katharine. *Hobberdy Dick* (5–7). 1977, Greenwillow $11.25; LB $11.30. Set in midseventeenth-century England, this is a fantasy about a hobgoblin who guards a country house.

3176. Brittain, Bill. *All the Money in the World* (4–6). 1979, Harper $10.53; LB $10.89; paper $2.84. A leprechaun grants Quentin Stowe his wish for all the money in the world.

3177. Brittain, Bill. *Devil's Donkey* (3–6). Illus. by Andrew Glass. 1981, Harper $10.53; LB $10.89; paper $2.84. Dan'l defies the witches and is turned into a donkey. A sequel is: *The Wish Giver: Three Tales of Coven Tree* (1983, $9.57; LB $9.89).

3178. Brown, Jeff. *A Lamp for the Lambchops* (2–6). Illus. by Lynn Wheeling. 1983, Harper $9.89. A genie-in-training provides madcap adventures for the Lambchops.

3179. Brown, Margaret Wise. *Sneakers: Seven Stories about a Cat* (2–4). Illus. by Jean Charlot. 1979, Addison $6.95. Sneakers, a cat, has several adventures in this old favorite.

3180. Brown, Palmer. *Hickory* (2–4). Illus. by author. 1978, Harper $8.61; LB $8.89. Hickory, a field mouse, is lonely on his own until he makes friends with a grasshopper.

3181. Buchwald, Emilie. *Floramel and Esteban* (3–5). Illus. by Charles Robinson. 1982, Harcourt $9.95. The story of friendship between an egret and a cow.

3182. Bunting, Eve. *The Man Who Could Call Down Owls* (K–3). Illus. by Charles Mikolaycak. 1984, Macmillan $9.95. A fantasy about a man who could communicate with owls.

3183. Burnett, Frances Hodgson. *A Little Princess* (4–6). Illus. by Tasha Tudor. 1962, Harper $12.45; LB $12.89; Dell paper $2.50. Sad story of the penniless orphan whose fortune is finally restored.

3184. Burnett, Frances Hodgson. *The Secret Garden* (4–6). Illus. by Tasha Tudor. 1962, Harper $12.45; Dell paper $2.95. Three children find a secret garden and make it bloom again; the garden, in turn, changes the children.

3185. Butler, Beverly. *Ghost Cat* (6–9). 1984, Dodd $10.95. The ghost of a dead relative haunts Annabel.

3186. Byars, Betsy. *The Winged Colt of Casa Mia* (4–6). Illus. by Richard Cuffari. 1973, Viking $9.95; Avon paper $1.95. In this fantasy, a young boy visits the Texas ranch of his uncle, an ex-stuntman, and encounters a colt with supernatural powers.

3187. Cameron, Eleanor. *The Court of the Stone Children* (5–7). 1973, Dutton $11.50. Nina's move with her family to San Francisco is a disaster until she encounters a young ghost in a small museum.

3188. Campbell, Hope. *Peter's Angel* (3–5). Illus. by Ralph Pinto. 1976, Scholastic $7.95. Monsters drawn on wall posters frighten Peter until 2 mice intervene.

3189. Carew, Jan. *Children of the Sun* (3–5). Illus. by Leo Dillon and Diane Dillon. 1980, Little $9.95. The fate of the 2 children born of the Sun and the Earth Mother is told in this mythlike epic.

3190. Carroll, Lewis. *Alice's Adventures in Wonderland and Through the Looking Glass* (4–7). Illus. by

John Tenniel. 1963, Grosset $9.95. One of many recommended editions.

3191. Cassedy, Sylvia. *Behind the Attic Wall* (6–8). 1983, Harper $11.49; LB $11.89. Maggie Turner, a difficult girl, is contacted by ghosts in the large house where 2 great-aunts live.

3192. Catling, Patrick Skene. *The Chocolate Touch* (3–5). Illus. by Margot Apple. 1979, Morrow LB $9.12. A Midas-story variation in which a boy turns his mother into chocolate.

3193. Chew, Ruth. *Mostly Magic* (3–5). Illus. by author. 1982, Holiday $8.95; Scholastic paper $1.95. Two children find a magic ladder to take them to adventure.

3194. Chew, Ruth. *The Wishing Tree* (3–5). Illus. by author. 1980, Hastings $8.95. Peggy and Brian enter a magical world with a talking cat.

3195. Chew, Ruth. *Witch's Buttons* (2–4). Illus. by author. 1974, Hastings $6.95. The strange button that Sandy and her friend find actually belongs to a witch.

3196. Chew, Ruth. *The Would-Be Witch* (3–5). Illus. by author. 1977, Hastings $6.95. Robin and Andy take midnight rides on a flying dustpan. Also use: *Witch's Broom* (1977, Dodd $6.95; Scholastic paper $1.50).

3197. Clapp, Patricia. *Jane Emily* (5–7). 1969, Lothrop $11.88; Dell paper $1.95. After seeing the image of a dead girl in a crystal ball, Jane becomes possessed by the ghost.

3198. Coatsworth, Elizabeth. *Marra's World* (4–6). Illus. by Krystyna Turska. 1975, Greenwillow $10.25; LB $9.84. A Scottish tale transferred to the Maine coast about a waif cared for by a harsh grandmother.

3199. Coatsworth, Elizabeth. *Pure Magic* (4–6). Illus. by Ingrid Fetz. 1973, Macmillan $8.95; paper $1.25. A fantasy about a friendship between Johnny and Giles, a "werefox."

3200. Coblentz, Catherine C. *The Blue Cat of Castle Town* (3–5). Illus. by Janice Holland. 1983, Countryman paper $5.95. A fantasy, set in Vermont in the 1800s, that tells of a little cat's wanderings and how he changed the course of the town's early history.

3201. Coombs, Patricia. *Dorrie and the Dreamyard Monsters* (2–4). Illus. 1977, Lothrop $10.25; LB $9.84; Dell paper $1.75. Dorrie helps convert fierce monsters into lovable friends in this adventure story for Dorrie fans. Others in the series: *Dorrie and the Haunted House* (1970, LB $11.88; paper $1.50); *Dorrie and the Amazing Magic Elixir* (1974, LB $10.88; paper 1.75); *Dorrie and the Witch's Imp* (1975, $10.88; paper $1.25); *Dorrie and the Witchville Fair* (1980); *Dorrie and the Witches' Camp* (1983) (both $10.00; LB $10.88).

3202. Coontz, Otto. *Isle of the Shape-Shifters* (5–8). Illus. 1983, Houghton $6.70. Theo becomes involved in ancient Indian rites on the island of Nantucket.

3203. Cooper, Susan. *Jethro and the Jumbie* (3–4). Illus. by Ashley Bryan. 1979, Atheneum $7.95. On a Caribbean island, a young boy has a humorous encounter with a jumbie, the ghost of a dead person.

3204. Cooper, Susan. *Seaward* (5–8). 1983, Atheneum $10.95. West follows his mother's dying words and heads seaward to his father.

3205. Cooper, Susan. *Silver on the Tree* (5–7). 1977, Atheneum $11.95; paper $2.95. The fifth and last volume of the series that tells of the final struggle waged by Will Stanton and his friends against the Dark, the powers of evil. The first 4 volumes are: *Over Sea, Under Stone* (1966, Harcourt $10.95; paper $4.95); *The Dark Is Rising* (1973, Atheneum $11.95; paper $2.95); *Greenwitch* (1974, Atheneum $13.95; paper $2.95); *The Grey King* (1975, Atheneum $10.95; paper $3.50).

3206. Corbett, Scott. *The Discontented Ghost* (6–8). 1978, Dutton $10.95. Corbett retells Oscar Wilde's *The Canterville Ghost* in an amusing way.

3207. Corbett, Scott. *The Mysterious Zetabet* (2–4). Illus. by Jon McIntosh. 1979, Little $7.95. In a dream, Zachary Zwicker enters a land with a topsy-turvy alphabet.

3208. Corbett, W. J. *The Song of Pentecost* (5–8). Illus. by Martin Ursell. 1983, Dutton $10.63. A group of animals, lead by Snake, journeys to a new home.

3209. Counsel, June. *A Dragon in Class Four* (3–5). Illus. by Jill Bennett. 1984, Faber $11.95. A fantasy about a group of British children and a dragon.

3210. Coville, Bruce. *The Monster's Ring* (4–6). Illus. by Katherine Coville. 1982, Pantheon $8.95; LB $8.99. A boy finds a ring that turns him into a monster.

3211. Cox, Palmer. *The Brownies: Their Book* (3–5). Illus. by author. 1964, Dover paper $3.95. The classic fantasy reissued.

3212. Crayder, Dorothy. *Joker and the Swan* (3–5). Illus. by Elise Primavera. 1981, Harper $9.50; LB $8.89. A talking dog, Pavlova, and a ballet slipper play important roles in this fantasy.

3213. Cresswell, Helen. *A Game of Catch* (3–5). Illus. by Ati Forberg. 1977, Macmillan $8.95. A time-warp fantasy in which 2 eighteenth-century children play with their contemporary counterparts.

3214. Cresswell, Helen. *The Secret World of Polly Flint* (5–7). Illus. by Shirley Felts. 1984, Macmillan $10.95. In this English fantasy, a young girl meets some inhabitants of a village that disappeared centuries ago.

3215. Cresswell, Helen. *Up the Pier* (5–6). Illus. by Gareth Floyd. 1972, Macmillan $8.95. Carrie meets a boy at a Welsh seaside resort who is trapped in a time warp and wants to leave the present and return to 1921.

3216. Cunningham, Julia. *Macaroon* (4–6). Illus. by Evaline Ness. 1962, Pantheon $6.99; Dell paper $1.50. Fantasy of a raccoon who deliberately sets out to adopt an "impossible" child.

3217. Cunningham, Julia. *Maybe, a Mole* (3–5). Illus. by Cyndy Szekeres. 1974, Pantheon $6.99; Dell paper $0.95. Five stories of survival involving a mole who is ostracized by his own kind because he is able to see.

3218. Cunningham, Julia. *Wolf Roland* (6–8). 1983, Pantheon $9.95. A medieval peddler seeks revenge on a wolf who has destroyed his donkey.

3219. Curry, Jane Louise. *Mindy's Mysterious Miniature* (4–6). Illus. by Charles Robinson. 1970, Harcourt $5.95. Mindy is kidnapped by a strange man who controls the power of miniaturizing people and things. A sequel is: *The Lost Farm* (1974, Atheneum $5.95).

3220. Curry, Jane Louise. *Poor Tom's Ghost* (5–7). 1977, Atheneum $8.95. An actor and his 2 children buy an old country home haunted by the ghost of another Shakespearean actor.

3221. Dahl, Roald. *The BFG* (3–6). Illus. by Quentin Blake. 1982, Farrar $10.95. Sophie is saved by the BFG (Big Friendly Giant) and finds herself in a strange environment.

3222. Dahl, Roald. *Charlie and the Chocolate Factory* (4–6). Illus. by Joseph Schindelman. 1964, Knopf $8.95; LB $8.99; Bantam paper $2.50. A rather morbid tale of Charlie and 4 of his nasty friends who tour Willy Wonka's extraordinary chocolate factory. They all meet disaster except for Charlie, for he has obeyed orders. A sequel is: *Charlie and the Great Glass Elevator* (1972, $8.95; LB $8.99; Bantam paper $2.25).

3223. Dahl, Roald. *Fantastic Mr. Fox* (4–6). Illus. by Donald Chaffin. 1970, Knopf LB $7.99; paper $2.25. Mr. Fox outwits 3 rich mean farmers.

3224. Dahl, Roald. *George's Marvelous Medicine* (4–6). Illus. by Quentin Blake. 1982, Knopf $7.95; LB $7.99; Bantam paper $2.25. George concocts medicine that shrinks his mean grandmother.

3225. Dahl, Roald. *James and the Giant Peach* (4–6). Illus. by Nancy E. Burkert. 1961, Knopf $11.95; LB $11.99; Bantam paper $2.75. James is unhappy living with his mean aunts until a magic potion produces an enormous peach, which becomes a home for him.

3226. Dahl, Roald. *Magic Finger* (3–5). Illus. by William Pene du Bois. 1966, Harper LB $8.61; paper $3.80. An 8-year-old girl mysteriously has the power to punish people for wrongdoing by pointing her finger at them.

3227. Dahl, Roald. *The Witches* (3–6). Illus. by Quentin Blake. 1983, Farrar $10.95. A boy and his grandmamma save English children from being turned into mice by witches.

3228. Dahl, Roald. *The Wonderful Story of Henry Sugar and Six More* (4–6). 1977, Knopf $5.95; LB $6.99; Bantam paper $2.50. Seven tales of fantasy and fun.

3229. Dana, Barbara. *Zucchini* (3–5). Illus. by Eileen Christelow. 1982, Harper $10.10; LB $10.89. The story of a ferret and his escape from the Bronx Zoo.

3230. Davies, Andrew. *Marmalade and Rufus* (3–5). 1983, Crown $8.95. An impulsive girl and ornery donkey team up and create havoc.

3231. Davis, Maggie S. *Grandma's Secret Letter* (4–6). Illus. by John Wallner. 1982, Holiday LB $12.95. A fantasy in which a girl has many adventures on her way to her grandmother's home.

3232. Delaney, M. C. *Henry's Special Delivery* (3–6). Illus. by Lisa McCue. 1984, Dutton $9.66. Henry receives a talking panda in the mail.

3233. Dickinson, Peter. *Giant Cold* (3–5). Illus. by Alan E. Cober. 1983, Dutton $10.95. The reader experiences the fantastic adventures on the trail of Giant Cold.

3234. Dickinson, Peter. *The Iron Lion* (2–4). Illus. by Pauline Baynes. 1984, Harper $10.95. After many trials, a poor boy wins a prize.

3235. Dillon, Barbara. *The Teddy Bear Tree* (PS–K). Illus. by David S. Rose. 1982, Morrow $9.75; LB $8.88. Bertine finds she has a crop of teddy bears to dispose of.

3236. Donovan, John. *Family* (6–9). 1976, Harper LB $10.89. An unusual novel about the flight of 3 apes from the laboratory where they are being held for experiments.

3237. dos Santos, Joyce Audy. *Henri and the Loup-Garou* (K–3). Illus. by author. 1982, Pantheon $8.95; LB $8.99. A forest dweller encounters a monster on his way home.

3238. Doty, Jean Slaughter. *Can I Get There by Candlelight?* (5–7). Illus. by Ted Lewin. 1980,

Macmillan $9.95. A time-lapse story about a girl who magically enters the world of the nineteenth century.

3239. Drury, Roger. *The Champion of Merrimack County* (4–7). Illus. by Fritz Wegner. 1976, Little $9.95. The Buryfield's house is invaded by mice, including a daredevil bicycle rider who uses the bathtub as a track.

3240. Duane, Diane. *So You Want to Be a Wizard* (5–8). 1983, Delacorte $14.95. Nita and friends embark on a journey to retrieve the *Book of Night with Moon.*

3241. Duncan, Jane. *Janet Reachfar and the Kelpie* (4–5). Illus. by Mairi Hedderwick. 1976, Houghton $7.50. A story about young Janet living on a Scottish farm and her belief that a kelpie lives in her well.

3242. Dunlop, Eileen. *The Maze Stone* (6–9). 1983, Putnam $10.95. Sixteen-year-old Hester and her sister fall under the spell of a drama teacher.

3243. Durrell, Gerald. *The Talking Parcel* (4–7). Illus. by Pamela Johnson. 1975, Harper $10.95. Three children journey to Mythologia to recover stolen books of magic.

3244. Eager, Edward. *Knight's Castle* (4–6). Illus. by N. M. Bodecker. 1956, Harcourt paper $2.95. Several children are introduced by an old lead soldier into the fantastic world peopled by characters in Scott's *Ivanhoe.*

3245. Eager, Edward. *Seven-Day Magic* (5–6). Illus. by N. M. Bodecker. 1962, Harcourt $10.95. Magic enters the lives of 5 children through a magic wishing book from the library. Also use: *Half Magic* (1954, Harcourt $8.95; paper $4.95); *Magic or Not?* (1984, Peter Smith $12.75; Harcourt paper $3.95).

3246. Edmondson, Madeleine. *Anna Witch* (3–5). Illus. by William Pene du Bois. 1982, Doubleday $8.95; LB $8.95. Anna, a junior witch, is unable to learn her mother's spells.

3247. Edmondson, Madeleine. *The Witch's Egg* (4–6). Illus. by Kay Chorao. 1974, Houghton $5.95; Dell paper $0.95. A creature who hatches from the witch's egg acts like a human but is really different.

3248. Edwards, Dorothy. *The Witches and the Grinnygog* (3–5). 1983, Faber $9.95. Three witches come to live in Church Alley and seek to be reunited with their unifying totem.

3249. Estes, Eleanor. *The Witch Family* (3–6). Illus. by Edward Ardizzone. 1960, Harcourt $11.95; paper $2.95. Amusing tale of 2 little girls, some fanciful witches, and a bumblebee.

3250. Eustis, Helen. *Mr. Death and the Redheaded Woman* (3–6). Illus. by Reinhard Michl. 1983, Green Tiger paper $6.95. Maude Applegate wants Mr. Death to bring Billy back to life.

3251. Farmer, Penelope. *William and Mary: A Story* (4–6). 1974, Atheneum $5.95. Two youngsters are transported through time to other places.

3252. Field, Rachel. *Hitty: Her First Hundred Years* (4–6). Illus. by Dorothy P. Lathrop. 1937, Macmillan $11.95. America 100 years ago seen through the adventures of a wooden doll. Newbery Award winner, 1930.

3253. Fisher, Paul R. *The Hawks of Fellheath* (6–9). 1980, Atheneum $9.95. Orne and an orphan family set out on a search through a dangerous land ruled by a sorcerer.

3254. Fisher, Paul R. *Mont Cant Gold* (6–9). 1981, Atheneum LB $10.95. A challenging fantasy about Rhian Mont Cant and his desire to unite his land into a single kingdom.

3255. Fleischman, Paul. *The Birthday Tree* (3–4). Illus. by Marcia Sewall. 1979, Harper $9.57. An apple tree mirrors the experiences of a couple's absent son.

3256. Fleming, Ian. *Chitty Chitty Bang Bang* (4–6). Illus. by John Burningham. 1964, Amereon LB $10.85. Chitty Chitty Bang Bang, a magical racing car, flies, floats, and has a real talent for getting the Pott family in and out of trouble.

3257. Flora, James. *Wanda and the Bumbly Wizard* (2–4). Illus. by author. 1980, Atheneum $9.95. Wanda joins forces with an inept wizard to outwit a wicked giant.

3258. Foote, Timothy. *The Great Ringtail Garbage Caper* (4–6). Illus. by Normand Chartier. 1980, Houghton $5.95; Scholastic paper $1.95. The raccoons revolt when garbage collection at a summer resort becomes too efficient.

3259. Gage, Wilson. *Down in the Boondocks* (2–4). Illus. by Glen Rounds. 1977, Greenwillow $7.95; Dell paper $0.95. An easy-to-read rhyming text conveys the story of a near-deaf farmer who is impervious to noise and a robot who isn't.

3260. Gage, Wilson. *The Ghost of Five Owl Farm* (4–6). Illus. by Paul Galdone. 1966, Pocket paper $1.75. Ted finds his vacation on an old farm ruined by his younger twin cousins, and so he creates a ghost to keep them busy—then a REAL ghost furnishes suspense.

3261. Gage, Wilson. *Miss Osborne the Mop* (4–6). Illus. by Paul Galdone. 1963, Pocket paper $1.75. The fun and adventures that result from a girl's finding she has the power to change people and objects into something else and back again.

3262. Garden, Nancy. *Four Crossing* (5–8). 1981, Farrar $9.95; Scholastic paper $1.95. Melissa and new friend Jed think that their town and its inhabitants are under a spell. A sequel is: *Watersmeet* (1983, $10.95).

3263. Gardner, John. *Dragon, Dragon and Other Timeless Tales* (4–6). Illus. by Charles Shields. 1975, Knopf LB $5.99. Four tales that show many folklore derivations as well as the author's originality and inventiveness.

3264. Garner, Alan. *The Owl Service* (5–9). 1981, Ballantine paper $1.95. An unusual pattern in a dinner service unleashes an evil spell in this fantasy set in Wales. Also use: *Elidor* (1981, Ballantine paper $1.95).

3265. Garner, Alan. *The Stone Book* (4–Up). Illus. by Michael Foreman. 1978, Putnam $7.95. A fantasy written by a contemporary master.

3266. Gilman, Dorothy. *The Maze in the Heart of the Castle* (6–9). 1983, Doubleday $11.95. In this allegory for better readers, Colin enters a castle maze to find peace and fulfillment.

3267. Goble, Paul, and Goble, Dorothy. *The Friendly Wolf* (3–5). Illus. 1975, Bradbury $9.95. A fantasy in which 2 lost Plains Indian children are helped back home by a wolf.

3268. Godden, Rumer. *The Dragon of Og* (3–6). Illus. by Pauline Baynes. 1981, Viking $9.95. Ordinarily peaceful, the Dragon of Og is aroused by the new lord of the castle.

3269. Godden, Rumer. *Four Dolls* (3–6). Illus. by Pauline Baynes. 1984, Greenwillow $11.00. Four stories that had previously been published in the 1950s about dolls.

3270. Godden, Rumer. *The Mousewife* (3–5). rev. ed. Illus. by Heidi Holder. 1982, Viking $9.95. The story of a devoted mousewife.

3271. Gordon, John. *The Edge of the World* (5–9). 1983, Atheneum $10.95. Tekken and friend Kit travel to another world peopled by ghosts.

3272. Gormley, Beatrice. *Best Friend Insurance* (5–7). Illus. by Emily McCully. 1983, Dutton $10.95. Maureen finds that her mother has been transformed into a new friend named Kitty.

3273. Gormley, Beatrice. *Fifth Grade Magic* (4–6). Illus. by Emily McCully. 1982, Dutton $9.95; Avon paper $2.25. Gretchen uses the help of an inept fairy godmother to get the lead in the school play.

3274. Gormley, Beatrice. *Mail-Order Wings* (3–5). Illus. by Emily McCully. 1981, Dutton $10.95; Avon paper $2.25. Andrea finds her Wonda-Wings are gradually transforming her into a bird.

3275. Gorog, Judith. *A Taste for Quiet and Other Disquieting Tales* (6–9). 1983, Putnam $9.95. A group of eerie stories for better, more mature readers.

3276. Grahame, Kenneth. *The Wind in the Willows* (All Ages). Illus. by Ernest H. Shepard. 1983, Scribners $17.95. The classic that introduced Mole, Ratty, and Mr. Toad. Three other recommended editions are: Illus. by Michael Hague (1980, Holt $17.95); illus. by John Burningham (1983, Viking $15.75); illus. by Babette Cole (1983, Holt $11.95).

3277. Greaves, Margaret. *Cat's Magic* (5–9). 1981, Harper $9.57; LB $9.89. A cat goddess grants Louise the power to travel through time.

3278. Greaves, Margaret. *A Net to Catch the Wind* (2–4). Illus. by Stephen Gammell. 1979, Harper $9.57; LB $10.89. A king uses his daughter to trap a unicorn.

3279. Green, Phyllis. *Eating Ice Cream with a Werewolf* (4–6). Illus. by Patti Stren. 1983, Harper $9.57; LB $9.89. The babysitter of 12-year-old Brad and his young sister is into witchcraft.

3280. Greene, Jacqueline Dembar. *The Leveller* (5–8). Illus. 1984, Walker $12.95. The story of a Robin Hood-like character, Tom Cook, in eighteenth-century New England.

3281. Greer, Gery, and Ruddick, Bob. *Max and Me and the Time Machine* (5–8). 1983, Harcourt $11.95. Steve and Max travel back in time to England during the Middle Ages.

3282. Haas, Dorothy. *The Bears Upstairs* (4–6). Illus. 1978, Greenwillow $11.25; LB $11.88; Dell paper $1.75. A young girl hides 2 bears who are awaiting relocation to another planet.

3283. Hahn, Mary D. *The Time of the Witch* (5–6). 1982, Houghton $10.50. Laura uses a witch's spell to prevent her parents' divorce.

3284. Haley, Gail E. *Birdsong* (PS–2). Illus. by author. 1984, Crown $10.95. A young girl learns the language of the birds.

3285. Hall, Lynn. *The Mystery of the Caramel Cat* (3–4). Illus. by Ruth Sanderson. 1981, Garrard LB $7.68. While exploring an abandoned mansion, Willie is visited by the ghost of a cat.

3286. Hamilton, Virginia. *The Magical Adventures of Pretty Pearl* (6–10). 1983, Harper $11.06; LB $11.89. A fantasy about a god/child and her experiences in America.

3287. Haynes, Betsy. *The Ghost of Gravestone Hearth* (4–6). 1977, Lodestar $6.95. A 16-year-old ghost comes back to life to recover a buried treasure.

3288. Hearne, Betsy Gould. *South Star* (3–7). Illus. by Trina S. Hyman. 1977, Atheneum $7.95. An odyssey in which a young girl and a resourceful boy accomplish an arduous quest. A sequel is: *Home* (1979, $8.95).

3289. Hildick, E. W. *The Ghost Squad Breaks Through* (5–7). 1984, Dutton $9.66. Ghosts and the ghost squad work together to prevent a crime.

3290. Hill, Donna. *Eerie Animals: Seven Stories* (5–7). Illus. by author. 1983, Atheneum $10.95. Stories about such strange animals as a phantom cat.

3291. Hoban, Russell. *The Mouse and His Child* (2–5). Illus. by Lillian Hoban. 1967, Harper LB $11.89; paper $2.25. A tin toy mouse and his tin son set out to find their friends in this fantasy reminiscent of Tolkien.

3292. Hooks, William H. *Mean Jake and the Devils* (3–5). Illus. by Dirk Zimmer. 1981, Dial $9.95; LB $9.89. Jake is so mean he can outwit the devil in these 3 tales.

3293. Hopkins, Lee Bennett, comp. *Monsters, Ghoulies and Creepy Creatures* (4–6). Illus. by Vera Rosenberry. 1977, Whitman $8.75. Traditional and modern writers and tales are represented in this appealing collection.

3294. Horowitz, Anthony. *The Devil's Door-bell* (6–8). 1984, Holt $11.45. Orphaned Martin discovers he has supernatural powers in this English novel that mixes fact and fancy.

3295. Houghton, Eric. *Steps Out of Time* (5–7). 1980, Lothrop $9.95; LB $9.55. Jonathan is propelled in time where he meets two new friends.

3296. Howe, James. *Morgan's Zoo* (4–6). Illus. by Leslie Morrill. 1984, Atheneum $11.95. Morgan, a set of twins, and a number of animals band together to save a zoo.

3297. Hoyland, John. *The Ivy Garland* (4–6). Illus. by Richard Vicary. 1983, Schocken $9.95. In this English story, an age-old curse threatens the life of a young girl.

3298. Hughes, Richard. *The Wonder-Dog* (4–6). Illus. by Antony Maitland. 1977, Greenwillow $12.25; LB $11.76. A collection of short stories first published from 1932 to 1966.

3299. Hunter, Mollie. *A Furl of Fairy Wind* (3–6). Illus. by Stephen Gammell. 1977, Harper $9.57. Four new stories that rely heavily on the creatures and situations associated with traditional Scottish folklore.

3300. Hunter, Mollie. *The Haunted Mountain* (5–7). Illus. by Laszlo Kubinyi. 1972, Harper $10.89; paper $2.95. MacAllister, with the help of a courageous son and an old dog, overcomes the supernatural forces that control a mountain.

3301. Hunter, Mollie. *The Kelpie's Pearls* (4–6). Illus. by Stephen Gammell. 1976, Harper $9.59. A

spellbinding fantasy, set in the Scottish Highlands, concerning a water sprite.

3302. Hunter, Mollie. *The Knight of the Golden Plain* (4–6). Illus. by Marc Simont. 1983, Harper $10.53; LB $10.89. A boy daydreams that he is a knight out to save a maiden in distress.

3303. Hunter, Mollie. *A Stranger Came Ashore* (6–8). 1975, Harper $10.89; paper $2.95. A fantasy in which the great Selkie, a bull seal of the Shetland islands, takes human form and lures a young girl to his underwater palace.

3304. Hunter, Mollie. *The Wicked One* (5–7). 1977, Harper $10.89; paper $2.95. A fantasy set in the Scottish Highlands in which a forester invokes the ire of a supernatural power.

3305. Hurmence, Belinda. *A Girl Called Boy* (5–8). 1982, Houghton $9.95. A contemporary black girl travels back to the time of slavery.

3306. Irving, Washington. *Rip Van Winkle and the Legend of Sleepy Hollow* (5–7). Illus. by George H. Boughton. 1980, Smith $6.95. A handsome edition of these 2 classics.

3307. Irwin, Hadley. *I Be Somebody* (4–7). 1984, Atheneum $11.95. During the early 1900s, a black family relocates to northern Canada.

3308. Irwin, Hadley. *Moon and Me* (6–8). 1981, Atheneum $9.95. E.J. is not happy staying with her grandparents on their Iowa farm or with a persistent friend named Moon.

3309. Jarrell, Randall. *The Animal Family* (5–7). Illus. by Maurice Sendak. 1965, Pantheon $8.95. Tale of a lonely hunter and how he acquires a family consisting of a mermaid, a bear, a lynx, and, finally, a boy. Also use: *Fly by Night* (1976, Farrar $7.95).

3310. Jarrell, Randall. *The Bat-Poet* (2–4). Illus. by Maurice Sendak. 1964, Macmillan $9.95; paper $2.95. A little-known bat makes up poems during the day to recite to his fellows.

3311. Joerns, Consuelo. *The Midnight Castle* (K–3). Illus. by author. 1983, Lothrop $10.00; LB $9.12. A mouse family explores a toy castle.

3312. Jones, Diana Wynne. *Archer's Goon* (6–10). 1984, Greenwillow $9.00. The Sykes family is threatened by a powerful local family.

3313. Jones, Diana Wynne. *Charmed Life* (4–6). 1978, Greenwillow $6.95. Gwendole tries to obtain supernatural powers from her mysterious guardian. Two sequels are: *The Magicians of Caprona* (1980, $10.95; LB $10.51); *Witch Week* (1982, LB $10.25).

3314. Jones, Diana Wynne. *Power of Three* (5–7). 1977, Greenwillow $11.25; LB $11.88. The story of 3 children and their special gifts.

3315. Jones, Terry. *The Saga of Erik the Viking* (4–6). Illus. by Michael Foreman. 1983, Schocken $15.95. Erik and comrades set sail to find the land where the sun goes at night.

3316. Juster, Norton. *Phantom Tollbooth* (4–6). Illus. by Jules Feiffer. 1961, Random $9.95; paper $2.95. When Milo receives a tollbooth as a gift, he finds that it admits him to a land where many adventures take place. A favorite fantasy.

3317. Karl, Jean. *Beloved Benjamin Is Waiting* (4–6). 1978, Dutton $10.75. Lucinda finds comfort from her loneliness in conversations with the spirit of a long-dead young boy.

3318. Kastner, Erich. *The Little Man* (4–6). Trans. by James Kirkup. Illus. by Rick Schreiter. 1966, Avon paper $1.95. A 2-inch-high orphan with the help of his guardian, a circus magician, eventually becomes the greatest *artiste* in the world. A sequel is: *Little Man and the Big Thief* (1981, paper $1.95).

3319. Katz, Welwyn Wilton. *Witchery Hill* (6–9). 1984, Atheneum $12.95. A novel about witchcraft on the island of Guernsey that involves 2 young people.

3320. Kaufman, Charles. *The Frog and the Beanpole* (5–6). Illus. by Troy Howell. 1980, Lothrop $10.95; LB $10.51. An intelligent frog and a wayward orphan run away together.

3321. Kay, Mary. *A House Full of Echoes* (6–8). 1981, Crown $8.95. A boarding school is the scene of strange supernatural events.

3322. Keller, Beverly. *A Small, Elderly Dragon* (4–6). Illus. by Nola Langner Malone. 1984, Lothrop $10.50. A now-harmless dragon becomes the center of a village's plea for protection in this engaging romp.

3323. Kendall, Carol. *The Gammage Cup* (4–7). Illus. by Erik Blegvad. 1959, Harcourt paper $4.95. Fantasy of the Minnipins, a small people of the "land between the mountains."

3324. Keneally, Thomas. *Ned Kelly and the City of the Bees* (5–7). Illus. by Stephen Ryan. 1981, Godine $11.95; Avon paper $2.25. Ned is made small enough to spend the summer in a beehive.

3325. Kennedy, Richard. *The Blue Stone* (3–5). Illus. by Ronald Himler. 1976, Holiday $8.95. Set in the Middle Ages, this fantasy tells what happens to 2 youngsters after one discovers a stone with magical powers.

3326. Kennedy, Richard. *Crazy in Love* (4–6). Illus. by Marcia Sewall. 1980, Dutton $7.95. An old woman grants Diana her wish of a husband.

3327. Kennedy, Richard. *Inside My Feet: The Story of a Giant* (4–6). Illus. by Ronald Himler. 1979, Harper LB $9.89. Two enormous boots carry off a boy's parents in this thriller.

3328. King-Smith, Dick. *Magnus Powermouse* (4–6). Illus. by Mary Rayner. 1984, Harper $10.53; LB $10.89. Madeleine and Marcus Aurelius, 2 mice, have a huge pushy mouse as a son.

3329. King-Smith, Dick. *The Mouse Butcher* (4–6). Illus. by Margot Apple. 1982, Viking $10.95. Cats take over human roles on a deserted island.

3330. King-Smith, Dick. *Pigs Might Fly* (3–5). Illus. by Mary Rayner. 1982, Viking $10.95; Scholastic paper $1.95. A pig named Daggie Dogfoot saves the day because he can swim.

3331. Klaveness, Jan O'Donnell. *The Griffin Legacy* (6–8). 1983, Macmillan $9.95. Amy encounters 2 ghosts in her grandmother's house.

3332. Kooiker, Leonie. *The Magic Stone* (3–7). Trans. from the Dutch by Richard Winsto and Clara Winsto. Illus. by Carl Hollander. 1978, Morrow $9.75; LB $9.36. A young boy finds a powerful magic stone owned by a group of witches. A sequel is: *Legacy of Magic* (1981, $11.25; LB $10.80).

3333. Kortum, Jeanie. *Ghost Vision* (5–8). Illus. by Dugald Stermer. 1983, Pantheon $10.95; LB $10.99. A Greenland Eskimo realizes that his son has special mystical powers.

3334. Krensky, Stephen. *The Dragon Circle* (4–6). Illus. by A. Delaney. 1977, Atheneum $6.95. The Wynd children are kidnapped by a circle of 5 ancient dragons. A sequel is: *The Witching Hour* (1981, LB $9.95).

3335. Krensky, Stephen. *A Ghostly Business* (4–6). 1984, Atheneum $10.95. Five children visit a house in Boston that is haunted.

3336. Kushner, Donn. *The Violin-Maker's Gift* (5–7). Illus. by Doug Panton. 1982, Farrar $8.95. Gaspard, a violin maker, rescues a magical bird.

3337. Langton, Jane. *The Astonishing Stereoscope* (6–8). Illus. by Erik Blegvad. 1971, Harper $10.89; paper $3.15. A terrible accident reveals to a young boy and girl some of the secrets of life. An earlier book: *The Diamond in the Window* (1962, LB $10.89; paper $2.95).

3338. Langton, Jane. *The Fledging* (5–7). 1980, Harper LB $9.89; paper $2.95. A young girl learns to fly with her Goose Prince. A sequel is: *The Fragile Flag* (1984, $11.49; LB $11.89).

3339. Laurin, Anne. *Perfect Crane* (2–4). Illus. by Charles Mikolaycak. 1982, Harper $8.95; LB $8.79. A magician is dismayed when the crane he has created leaves for fall migration.

3340. Lawson, Robert. *The Fabulous Flight* (4–6). Illus. by author. 1984, Little paper $3.95. Peter becomes so small he can take a trip via a pet seagull.

3341. Lawson, Robert. *Rabbit Hill* (4–7). Illus. by author. 1944, Viking $9.95; Penguin paper $2.95. The small creatures of a Connecticut countryside—each with a distinct personality—create a warm and humorous story. Newbery Award winner, 1945. A sequel: *The Tough Winter* (1954, $8.95; Penguin paper $2.95).

3342. Leach, Maria. *The Thing at the Foot of the Bed and Other Scary Tales* (4–6). Illus. by Kurt Werth. 1959, Dell paper $2.95. Spine-chilling stories about ghosts.

3343. Leeson, Robert. *Genie on the Loose* (5–7). 1984, Hamish Hamilton $11.95. Alec acquires a beer can in which a genie lives.

3344. Levin, Betty. *A Binding Spell* (6–8). 1984, Dutton $10.63. A ghost horse can be seen only by Wren and the recluse Axel.

3345. Levin, Betty. *The Keeping Room* (6–9). 1981, Greenwillow $11.25. A story that intertwines events of the past and present.

3346. Levitin, Sonia. *Beyond Another Door* (5–8). 1977, Atheneum $8.95. A girl encounters an apparition of her dead grandmother in this novel that explores a mother-daughter relationship.

3347. Levy, Elizabeth. *Running Out of Magic with Houdini* (3–5). Illus. by Blanche Sims and Jenny Rutherford. 1981, Knopf LB $4.99; paper $1.95. Through a time lapse, 3 youngsters travel through time to the days of Houdini. Also use: *Running Out of Time* (1980, Knopf LB $4.99; paper $1.95).

3348. Lewis, Clive S. *The Lion, the Witch and the Wardrobe: A Story for Children* (4–7). Illus. by Pauline Baynes. 1950, Macmillan $10.95; paper $2.50. A beautifully written modern tale of the adventures of 4 children who go into the magical land of Narnia. A special edition with illustrations by Michael Hague is: (1983, Macmillan $19.95). Some sequels are: *The Silver Chair* (1967); *The Horse and His Boy* (1969); *The Last Battle* (1969); *Prince Caspian* (1969); *The Voyage of the "Dawn Treader"* (1969); *The Magician's Nephew* (1970) (all $10.95; paper $2.95).

3349. Lewis, Naomi, comp. *The Silent Playmate: A Collection of Doll Stories* (4–6). Illus. by Harold Jones. 1981, Macmillan $9.95. An anthology of excerpts and stories about all sorts of dolls.

3350. Lifton, Betty Jean. *Jaguar, My Twin* (4–6). Illus. by Ann Leggett. 1976, Atheneum $6.50. Legend and reality are mixed in this story of a Mexican Indian boy and his twin animal spirit, the jaguar.

3351. Lindbergh, Anne. *Bailey's Window* (3–6). Illus. by Kinuko Craft. 1984, Harcourt $12.95. A young boy paints a scene into which he enters.

3352. Lindbergh, Anne. *The People in Pineapple Place* (4–6). 1982, Harcourt $10.95. August Brown is still adjusting to his parents' divorce when he meets some people only he can see.

3353. Lindgren, Astrid. *The Brothers Lionheart* (4–6). Illus. by J. K. Lambert. 1975, Viking $9.95. Two brothers are reunited after death in the magical land of Nangiyala.

3354. Lindgren, Astrid. *Ronia, the Robber's Daughter* (4–7). 1983, Viking $12.05. Ronia becomes friendly with the son of her father's rival in this fantasy.

3355. Lisle, Janet Taylor. *The Dancing Cats of Applesap* (4–6). Illus. by Joelle Shefts. 1984, Bradbury $11.95. Melba discovers that the cats at Jigg's Drugstore have a special talent.

3356. Lively, Penelope. *The Ghost of Thomas Kempe* (4–6). Illus. by Antony Maitland. 1973, Dutton $8.95. When his family moves into an old house in an English village, James is blamed when the resident ghost begins to act up.

3357. Lively, Penelope. *The Revenge of Samuel Stokes* (5–7). 1981, Dutton $10.25. A bad-mannered ghost causes problems in this fantasy.

3358. Lively, Penelope. *The Voyage of QV 66* (4–6). Illus. by Howard Jones. 1979, Dutton $7.95. After a flood has destroyed human life on earth, Stanley, a monkey, leads a group of animals on a march to the London Zoo to free the animals.

3359. Locke, Angela. *Mr. Mullett Owns a Cloud* (3–6). Illus. by Ian Newsham. 1983, Merrimack $10.95. The gift of a cloud from Mr. Zeus complicates Mr. Mullett's life.

3360. Lovejoy, Jack. *The Rebel Witch* (4–6). Illus. by Judith Gwyn Brown. 1978, Lothrop $11.95; LB $11.47. Suzie, with a magic wand, tries to foil evil Professor Sinistrari.

3361. Lunn, Janet. *The Root Cellar* (5–8). 1983, Scribners $12.95. An unhappy girl is transported to Canada of 1860.

3362. MacDonald, Betty. *Hello, Mrs. Piggle-Wiggle* (3–5). Illus. by Hilary Knight. 1950, Harper $9.57; paper $2.50. Introducing the lady who loves all children, good or bad. Further adventures are: *Mrs. Piggle-Wiggle's Farm* (1954); *Mrs. Piggle-Wiggle* (1957); *Mrs. Piggle-Wiggle's Magic* (1957) (all $9.57; paper $2.50).

3363. MacDonald, Reby Edmond. *The Ghosts of Austwick Manor* (5–7). 1982, Atheneum $13.95. Two sisters travel back in time and save their brother from an ancient curse.

3364. McGinnis, Lila Sprague. *The Ghost Upstairs* (3–6). Illus. by Amy Rowen. 1982, Hastings LB $9.95. Albert Shook finds a new friend in a ghost named Otis.

3365. McGraw, Eloise. *Joel and the Great Merlini* (3–5). Illus. by Jim Arnosky. 1979, Pantheon LB $5.99. Joel gains new magical powers from a magician named Merlini.

3366. McGraw, Eloise. *A Really Weird Summer* (5–7). Illus. 1977, Atheneum $9.95. While visiting a great-aunt and great-uncle, Nels befriends a strange boy, Alan, who lived in another time.

3367. MacKellar, William. *Kenny and the Highland Ghost* (5–7). Illus. by W. T. Mars. 1980, Dodd $7.95. A young boy tries to remove a curse from a friendly Scottish ghost.

3368. McKillip, Patricia A. *The House on Parchment Street* (5–7). Illus. by Charles Robinson. 1973, Atheneum paper $1.95. Two teenagers—one English, one American—unite to discover the secret behind the basement ghosts.

3369. McKillip, Patricia A. *The Riddle-Master of Hed* (5–8). 1976, Atheneum $8.99. A somewhat complex fantasy of a questing lad who sets out to answer the riddle of the 3 stars on his forehead. A sequel: *Heir of the Sea and Fire* (1977, $9.95).

3370. McKinley, Robin. *Beauty: A Retelling of the Story of Beauty and the Beast* (6–9). 1978, Harper $10.89; LB $9.89. A beautiful retelling of the familiar story.

3371. McKinley, Robin. *The Hero and the Crown* (6–9). 1984, Greenwillow $11.00. A Newbery Award-winning novel set in the mythical kingdom of Damon. Also use: *The Blue Sword* (1982, Greenwillow LB $12.50).

3372. MacLachlan, Patricia. *Tomorrow's Wizard* (3–5). Illus. by Kathy Jacobi. 1982, Harper $9.57; LB $9.89. Six short stories about a wizard, an apprentice, and their horse.

3373. Maguire, Gregory. *The Lightning Time* (6–8). 1978, Farrar $7.95. Through the help of a ghostly spirit, David saves a mountain from developers.

3374. Mahy, Margaret. *The Haunting* (5–7). 1982, Atheneum $10.95; Scholastic paper $1.95. Eight-year-old Barry begins receiving mental messages from an uncle thought dead.

3375. Major, Beverly. *Porcupine Stew* (2–5). Illus. by Erick Ingraham. 1982, Morrow $9.50. A fantasy about a boy traveling to a kingdom of porcupines.

3376. Martin, Graham Dunstan. *Giftwish* (6–8). 1981, Houghton $8.95. Ewan, with the help of a wizard and an enchantress, triumphs over evil.

3377. Masefield, John. *The Box of Delights, or, When the Wolves Were Running* (5–7). 1984, Macmillan $14.95. An abridgment of the novel about a boy pitted against the forces of evil.

3378. Mazer, Norma Fox. *Saturday, the Twelfth of October* (6–8). 1975, Dell paper $1.75. In a time shift, the heroine leaves behind her contemporary problems involving adolescence and lives with a group of prehistoric cave dwellers.

3379. Menuhin, Yehudi, and Hope, Christopher. *The King, the Cat, and the Fiddle* (2–5). Illus. by Angela Barrett. 1983, Holt $10.95. When a king dismisses his fiddlers, gloom settles over the kingdom.

3380. Milne, A. A. *Winnie-the-Pooh* (K–5). Colored by Hilda Scott. Illus. by Ernest H. Shepard. 1974, Dutton $7.95; Dell paper $1.95. The world-famous book that has become a classic. Also use: *The House at Pooh Corner* (1961, Dutton $7.95; Dell paper $1.50); *The Christopher Robin Story Book* (1966, Dutton $7.95).

3381. Moskin, Marietta D. *Dream Lake* (6–8). 1981, Atheneum LB $8.95. A young girl finds herself in the body of an eighteenth-century indentured servant.

3382. Murdocca, Sal. *Sir Hamm and the Golden Sundial* (2–5). Illus. by author. 1982, Delacorte $8.95; LB $8.89. A spoof on the Middle Ages with Sir Hamm, the pig hero.

3383. Murphy, Jill. *The Worst Witch* (4–6). 1980, Schocken $7.95; Avon paper $2.50. Mildred's first year at Miss Cackle's Academy for Witches is a disaster. A sequel is: *The Worst Witch Strikes Again* (1980, $7.95; paper $2.50).

3384. Murray, Marguerite. *The Sea Bears* (4–6). 1984, Atheneum $10.95. Jeanine and her family encounter adventure in a coastal Nova Scotia village.

3385. Myers, Walter Dean. *The Golden Serpent* (3–5). Illus. by Alice Provensen and Martin Provensen. 1980, Viking $9.95. A king is unable to understand the problems in his kingdom.

3386. Naylor, Phyllis Reynolds. *All Because I'm Older* (3–4). Illus. by Leslie Morrill. 1981, Atheneum LB $9.95. An 8-year-old gets blamed for his sibling's mistakes.

3387. Naylor, Phyllis Reynolds. *Shadows on the Wall* (6–9). 1980, Atheneum $8.95. Book One of the York trilogy set in rural Pennsylvania. The other 2 are: *Faces in the Water* (1981); *Footprints at the Window* (1981) (both $9.95).

3388. Naylor, Phyllis Reynolds. *Witch's Sister* (4–6). Illus. by Gail Owens. 1975, Atheneum $8.95. Lynn is convinced that her sister Judith is becoming a witch. Two sequels are: *Witch Water* (1977); *The Witch Herself* (1978) (both $9.95).

3389. Nesbit, Edith. *Five Children and It* (4–6). Illus. by H. R. Miller. 1959, Buccaneer LB $10.95; Penguin paper $2.95. An enchanting story about a group of children who discover a Psammead, a sand fairy, who both enlivens and confuses their lives. Two more stories about the children: *The Phoenix and the Carpet; The Story of the Amulet* (both 1959, Penguin paper $2.95).

3390. Newman, Robert. *The Shattered Stone* (4–7). Illus. by John Gretzer. 1975, Atheneum $6.95. Two youngsters attempt to bring peace to 2 warring kingdoms.

3391. Nichols, Ruth. *A Walk Out of the World* (4–6). Illus. by Trina S. Hyman. 1969, Harcourt $6.95. Judith and Tobit enter a world of 500 years ago after a strange walk in the woods.

3392. Norton, Andre. *Lavender-Green Magic* (4–7). Illus. by Judith Gwyn Brown. 1974, Harper $12.95. A family of black children living north of Boston is drawn into the mysterious colonial past.

3393. Norton, Andre. *Red Hart Magic* (4–7). Illus. by Donna Diamond. 1976, Harper $12.95. Two misfits see their counterparts at 3 periods in English history in this time-warp fantasy.

3394. Norton, Andre, and Miller, Phyllis. *House of Shadows* (5–7). 1984, Atheneum $11.95. While staying with a great-aunt, 3 children learn about the family curse.

3395. Norton, Andre, and Miller, Phyllis. *Seven Spells to Sunday* (4–6). 1979, Atheneum $9.95; Pocket paper $1.95. Two youngsters find a magic mailbox in a junkyard.

3396. Norton, Mary. *Are All the Giants Dead?* (4–6). 1975, Harcourt $6.50; paper $2.50. James journeys to the fairy-tale world of princes, giants, and witches.

3397. Norton, Mary. *Bed-Knob and Broom-Stick* (4–6). Illus. by Erik Blegvad. 1957, Harcourt $10.95; paper $3.95. Charles, Carey, and Paul meet a woman who is studying to become a witch, and she takes them on many exciting but gruesome adventures.

3398. Norton, Mary. *The Borrowers* (4–6). Illus. by Beth Krush and Joe Krush. 1953, Harcourt $7.95; paper $3.95. Little people, no taller than a pencil, live in old houses and borrow what they need from humans. Some sequels are: *The Borrowers Afield* (1955, $7.95; paper $3.95); *The Borrowers Afloat* (1959, $9.95; paper $3.95); *The Borrowers Aloft* (1961, $9.95; paper $4.95); *The Borrowers Avenged* (1982, $12.95; paper $5.95).

3399. Nostlinger, Christine. *Konrad* (4–6). Trans. by Anthea Bell. Illus. by Carol Nicklaus. 1977, Avon paper $1.95. A daffy fantasy about a woman adopting a boy who has been made perfectly in a factory.

3400. O'Brien, Robert C. *Mrs. Frisby and the Rats of NIMH* (5–7). Illus. by Zena Bernstein. 1971, Atheneum $9.95. Saga of a group of rats made literate and given human intelligence by a series of experiments, who escape from their laboratory to found their own community. Newbery Award winner.

3401. O'Connell, Jean S. *The Dollhouse Caper* (3–5). Illus. by Erik Blegvad. 1976, Harper $8.95. A convincing adventure-fantasy about a family of dolls that comes to life when no human is about.

3402. Olson, Helen Kronberg. *The Strange Thing That Happened to Oliver Wendell Iscovitch* (1–4). Illus. by Betsy Lewin. 1983, Dodd $9.95. Oliver Wendell discovers if he holds his breath he can float.

3403. Ormondroyd, Edward. *Castaways on Long Ago* (4–6). Illus. by Ruth Robbins. 1973, Bantam paper $1.95. Three youngsters have an unexpectedly exciting time visiting a farm when they encounter a strange boy from Long Ago Island.

3404. Ormondroyd, Edward. *Time at the Top* (5–7). Illus. by Peggie Bach. 1963, Houghton $8.95. Susan rides an apartment elevator to a floor that is not there and finds herself in the year 1881. A sequel is: *All in Good Time* (1975, $7.95).

3405. Otto, Svend. *The Giant Fish and Other Stories* (3–5). Illus. by author. 1982, Larousse $10.95. Greenland, Ireland, and the Shetland Islands are the locales of these stories.

3406. Parish, Peggy. *Haunted House* (4–6). 1971, Macmillan $9.95; Dell paper $1.95. The Roberts family believes a ghost is loose and nearby.

3407. Park, Ruth. *Playing Beatie Bow* (6–9). 1982, Atheneum LB $12.95; paper $3.50. Abigail Kirk is transported in time to Australia of Victorian times.

3408. Parker, Nancy W. *The Spotted Dog: The Strange Tale of a Witch's Revenge* (2–5). Illus. by author. 1980, Dodd LB $6.95. Some dogs, a mean witch, and a proud family are the ingredients in this English fantasy.

3409. Pascal, Francine. *Hangin' Out with Cici* (6–8). 1977, Viking $9.95; Pocket paper $2.25. Victoria realizes that the girl she meets in Penn Station is really herself as she was in 1944.

3410. Patten, Brian. *Mr. Moon's Last Case* (4–6). Illus. by Mary Moore. 1976, Scribners $1.19. An ex-police officer and a young boy track down Nameon, one of the few dwarfs ever to visit the world of humans.

3411. Pearce, Philippa. *The Shadow Cage, and Other Tales of the Supernatural* (6–8). Illus. by Ted

Lewin. 1977, Harper $9.57. Ten original tales, each set in Britain, that involve various mysterious and exciting elements of the supernatural.

3412.   Pearce, Philippa. *Tom's Midnight Garden* (4–7). Illus. by Susan Einzig. 1984, Harper $11.89. When the clock strikes 13, Tom visits his garden and meets Hatty, a strange mid-Victorian girl.

3413.   Peck, Richard. *The Ghost Belonged to Me* (6–8). 1975, Viking $10.95; Dell paper $2.25. Richard unwillingly receives the aid of his nemesis, Blossom Culp, in trying to solve the mystery behind the ghost of a young girl. Two sequels are: *Ghosts I Have Been* (1977, Viking $11.50; Dell paper $2.50); *The Dreadful Future of Blossom Culp* (1983, Delacorte $12.95).

3414.   Petroski, Catherine. *Beautiful My Mane in the Wind* (3–4). Illus. by Robert Andrew Parker. 1983, Houghton $9.95. A girl who sometimes would like to be a horse shares her daydreams.

3415.   Peyton, K. M. *A Pattern of Roses* (6–9). Illus. by author. 1973, Harper $10.32. In a fantasy set in contemporary England, Tom gains independence from his father while exploring his strange affinity with 2 children from Victorian times.

3416.   Phipson, Joan. *The Watcher in the Garden* (5–8). 1982, Atheneum $10.95. Kitty and a blind recluse find they have unusual ˌpowers of communication.

3417.   Pinkwater, D. Manus. *Alan Mendelsohn, the Boy from Mars* (5–7). 1979, Dutton $9.95; Bantam paper $1.95. Thought control and time warps are humorous elements in this story of misfits at the Bat Masterson Junior High.

3418.   Pomerantz, Charlotte. *The Downtown Fairy Godmother* (3–5). Illus. by Susanna Natti. 1978, Bantam paper $1.75. Olivia discovers that her fairy godmother is a rank amateur at her trade.

3419.   Poole, Josephine. *Moon Eyes* (5–7). 1967, Little $8.95. A battle against the witchcraft of evil Aunt Rhoda.

3420.   Porte, Barbara Ann. *Jesse's Ghost and Other Stories* (4–6). 1983, Greenwillow $9.00. Several stories set in a variety of times and places.

3421.   Postma, Lidia. *The Stolen Mirror* (3–4). Illus. 1976, McGraw $6.95; LB $8.95. A delicate fantasy in which a boy helps a group of people regain their identity.

3422.   Proysen, Alf. *Little Old Mrs. Pepperpot and Other Stories* (3–5). 1960, Astor-Honor $7.95. The story of a woman who can shrink to the size of a pepper pot.

3423.   Raskin, Ellen. *Figgs and Phantoms* (4–6). Illus. 1974, Dutton $10.95; paper $1.95. The family of Figg-Newton has always dreamed of

going to Capri, and in this fantasy, heroine Mona Lisa fulfills the wish.

3424.   Roberts, Willo Davis. *The Girl with the Silver Eyes* (5–7). 1980, Atheneum $10.95; Scholastic paper $1.95. Ten-year-old Katie can move objects by telekinesis.

3425.   Robertson, Mary Elsie. *Jemimallee* (3–5). Illus. by Judith Gwyn Brown. 1977, McGraw $6.95; LB $7.95. A cat-poet tries to keep a giant rat out of the house.

3426.   Rodowsky, Colby F. *The Gathering Room* (5–8). 1981, Farrar $9.95. Mudge is befriended by spirits that live in the cemetery where her parents are caretakers.

3427.   Rodowsky, Colby F. *Keeping Time* (6–9). 1983, Farrar $10.95. A troubled boy finds he is transported in time to sixteenth-century England.

3428.   Rubin, Amy Kateman. *Children of the Seventh Prophecy* (5–7). 1981, Warne $8.95. Alice and Bernard help a troll prince whose father is ailing.

3429.   Rush, Alison. *The Last of Danu's Children* (6–9). 1982, Houghton LB $9.95. Three teenagers are confronted with the forces of evil and a wicked wizard.

3430.   Ruskin, John. *King of the Golden River* (5–8). Illus. by Richard Doyle. 1974, Dover paper $1.95. Two mean brothers incur the wrath of the South-West Wind, Esquire.

3431.   Saint-Exupery, Antoine de. *The Little Prince* (4–7). Trans. by Katherine Woods. Illus. by author. 1967, Harcourt paper $1.95. An original fantasy of a little prince who leaves his planet to discover great wisdom.

3432.   St. John, Wylly Folk. *The Ghost Next Door* (4–7). Illus. by Trina S. Hyman. 1971, Pocket paper $1.95. A family accepts the reality of a beloved member's death in this unusual story.

3433.   Sargent, Sarah. *Weird Henry Berg* (4–6). 1980, Crown $8.95; Dell paper $1.75. Henry, his pet lizard Vincent, friend Millie, and a dragon named Aelf are the main characters in this fantasy.

3434.   Sefton, Catherine. *Emma's Dilemma* (3–5). Illus. by Jill Bennett. 1983, Faber $8.95. A fantasy involving a girl and her transparent twin.

3435.   Selden, George. *The Cricket in Times Square* (3–6). Illus. by Garth Williams. 1960, Farrar $10.95; Dell paper $2.25. A Connecticut cricket is transported in a picnic basket to New York's Time Square. Two sequels are: *Tucker's Countryside* (1969, $9.95; paper $2.25); *Harry Cat's Pet Puppy* (1974, $10.95; paper $2.75).

3436.   Selden, George. *The Genie of Sutton Place* (5–6). 1973, Farrar $10.95; paper $3.45. The summer Tim lives with his Aunt Lucy in Sutton Place, New York City, he evokes his own magical genie who works not only miracles but mishaps.

3437. Selden, George. *Irma and Jerry* (4–6). Illus. by Leslie Morrill. 1982, Avon paper $2.50. A conservative dog and a street-smart cat become friends.

3438. Sendak, Maurice. *Higglety, Pigglety Pop! or There Must Be More to Life* (2–4). Illus. by author. 1967, Harper $10.53; LB $10.89. Jennie, a Sealyham terrier who has everything but wants more, leaves home in search of experience.

3439. Serraillier, Ian. *Suppose You Met a Witch* (2–4). 1973, Little $6.95. Two children are kidnapped by a witch.

3440. Sharp, Margery. *The Rescuers* (3–6). Illus. by Garth Williams. 1959, Little $9.70; Dell paper $1.75. A beguiling fantasy depicting the adventures of 3 courageous, resourceful mice. Also use: *Miss Bianca* (1974, paper $1.25); *The Turret* (1974, Dell paper $1.50); *Bernard the Brave* (1977, Little $9.95; Dell paper $1.95); *Miss Bianca in the Orient* (1978, Dell paper $2.25); *Bernard into Battle: A Miss Bianca Story* (1983, Dell paper $1.75).

3441. Showell, Ellen Harvey. *Cecelia and the Blue Mountain Boy* (4–6). Illus. by Margot Tomes. 1983, Lothrop $9.00; LB $9.50. Cecelia, a musical child, meets a strange boy who plays beautiful fiddle music.

3442. Singer, Isaac Bashevis. *Alone in the Wild Forest* (4–6). Illus. by Margot Zemach. 1971, Farrar $8.95. A magical tale about Joseph, who, with the help of an angel's amulet, wins the hand of a princess.

3443. Singer, Isaac Bashevis. *The Fearsome Inn* (4–7). Illus. by Nonny Hogrogian. 1967, Scribners paper $4.95. Evil is overcome by magic and common sense in a story written in an Eastern European folk manner and superbly illustrated in full color.

3444. Slater, Jim. *Grasshopper and the Unwise Owl* (3–5). Illus. by Babette Cole. 1980, Holt $7.95. A grasshopper saves his mother's home with the help of an owl.

3445. Sleator, William. *Among the Dolls* (3–5). Illus. by Trina S. Hyman. 1975, Dutton $8.95. Vicky is shrunken to doll size and forced to live in her dollhouse with the malicious dolls whose personalities she has created.

3446. Sleator, William. *Blackbriar* (5–8). Illus. by Blair Lent. 1972, Scholastic paper $1.95. Danny and his stepmother move to a mysterious house by the sea in England and encounter many unanswered questions about the place.

3447. Sleator, William. *The Green Futures of Tycho* (5–7). 1981, Dutton $10.25. Tycho finds a device that will allow him to travel back and forth in time.

3448. Sleator, William. *Into the Dream* (5–7). Illus. by Ruth Sanderson. 1979, Dutton $10.95; Scholastic paper $1.95. Two young children discover that they can read each other's minds.

3449. Smith, Dodie. *The Hundred and One Dalmatians* (3–5). 1976, Avon paper $1.95. Pongo and Missis must save the Dalmation puppies captured by Cruella de Vil.

3450. Snyder, Zilpha Keatley. *And All Between* (5–7). Illus. by Alton Raible. 1976, Atheneum $8.95. In this fantasy, a young girl leaves her underground civilization and mingles with the people of the planet Green Sky.

3451. Snyder, Zilpha Keatley. *Black and Blue Magic* (5–7). Illus. by Gene Holtan. 1966, Atheneum $5.95; paper $0.95. A mysterious old man grants a pair of wings to an awkward teenage boy, who embarks on a hilarious series of flights over San Francisco.

3452. Snyder, Zilpha Keatley. *Season of Ponies* (4–7). 1964, Atheneum $3.07; paper $0.95. A magic amulet brings a gypsy boy and magical ponies into Pamela's life.

3453. Sommer-Bodenburg, Angela. *My Friend the Vampire* (3–6). Illus. by Amelie Glienke. 1984, Dial $9.65; LB $9.89. Tony finds he has problems when he befriends a vampire. A sequel is: *The Vampire Moves In* (1984, $9.95; LB $9.89).

3454. Stearns, Pamela. *The Fool and the Dancing Bear* (5–7). Illus. by Ann Strugnell. 1979, Little $8.95. A fool, a bear, and a king embark on a mission to save a kingdom.

3455. Steele, Mary Q. *Journey Outside* (5–8). Illus. by Rocco Negri. 1969, Penguin paper $2.95. Young Dilar, believing that his Raft People in seeking a "Better Place" have been circling endlessly, sets out to discover the origin and fate of his kind.

3456. Steele, Mary Q. *The True Men* (5–8). 1976, Greenwillow LB $10.80. An allegory in which a boy is banished from his tribe when they discover he glows in the dark.

3457. Steele, Mary Q. *Wish, Come True* (4–6). Illus. by Muriel Batherman. 1979, Greenwillow $10.95; LB $10.51; Scholastic paper $1.95. A magic ring allows a brother and sister, Joe and Meg, to have unexpected adventures.

3458. Steig, William. *Abel's Island* (4–6). Illus. 1976, Farrar $7.95; Bantam paper $2.25. A tale of a pampered mouse who must fend for himself after being marooned on an isolated island.

3459. Steig, William. *Dominic* (4–6). Illus. by author. 1972, Farrar $8.95; paper $3.45. A resourceful and engaging hound dog helps a group of animals overcome the wicked Doomsday Gang.

3460. Steig, William. *The Real Thief* (4–5). Illus. by author. 1973, Farrar $8.95. Gawain, a goose, is disgraced when gold and jewels begin disappearing from the Royal Treasury where he is the guard.

3461. Stephens, Mary Jo. *Witch of the Cumberlands* (4–7). Illus. by Arvis Stewart. 1974, Houghton $8.95. Mountain folklore, seances, and charms are interwoven in this story of 3 children who come to live in a rural mining area of Kentucky.

3462. Stolz, Mary. *Cat in the Mirror* (5–8). 1975, Harper LB $11.89; Dell paper $1.95. A time-warp story in which a young girl leaves the New York of today, but faces similar problems in a wealthy household in ancient Egypt.

3463. Sudbery, Rodie. *The Silk and the Skin* (5–8). 1982, Elsevier $8.95. A slightly retarded youngster becomes master of a magical bat that contains a powerful force.

3464. Swift, Jonathan. *Gulliver's Travels* (5–8). Illus. by Willy Pogany. 1983, Morrow $10.50. The many adventures of the fearless Gulliver.

3465. Syfret, Anne, and Syfret, Edward. *Bella* (4–7). 1978, Farrar $9.95. Two girls fall under the spell of a devil doll.

3466. Tannen, Mary. *Huntley Nutley and the Missing Link* (4–6). Illus. by Rob Sauber. 1983, Knopf $9.95; LB $9.99. Huntley discovers a living creature, the ape-human missing link, and brings him into the household.

3467. Tannen, Mary. *The Wizard Children of Finn* (4–6). Illus. by John Burgoyne. 1981, Avon paper $1.95. Fiono and Bran are transported in time to the Ireland of the Celts and Finn McCool. A sequel is: *The Lost Legend of Finn* (1982, Knopf $9.95; LB $9.99; Avon paper $2.25).

3468. Tapp, Kathy Kennedy. *Moth-Kin Magic* (4–6). Illus. by Michele Chessare. 1983, Atheneum $10.95. A fantasy about little people who become part of a science experiment.

3469. Terlouw, Jan. *How to Become King* (6–8). 1977, Hastings $7.95. A 17-year-old undergoes several tests to become king in this satirical fantasy.

3470. Titus, Eve. *Basil of Baker Street* (4–6). 1958, McGraw LB $8.95; Pocket paper $1.75. A clever mystery about a mouse who moves to 221 Baker Street out of admiration of Mr. Holmes. Others in the series: *Basil and the Pigmy Cats* (1973, Pocket paper $1.95); *Basil in Mexico* (1976, McGraw $7.95; Pocket paper $1.75); *Basil and the Lost Colony* (1978, Pocket paper $1.50); *Basil in the Wild West* (1981, McGraw $9.95).

3471. Tolkien, John R. *The Hobbit* (5–7). Illus. by author. 1938, Houghton $6.95; Ballantine paper $1.95. A saga of dwarfs and elves, goblins and trolls in a far-off, long ago land. There is a special edition illustrated by Michael Hague (1984, Houghton $19.45).

3472. Tomalin, Ruth. *Gone Away* (5–6). 1979, Faber $11.95. In this English fantasy, a young girl befriends a ghost living in her boarding house.

3473. Turnbull, Ann. *The Frightened Forest* (4–6). Illus. by Gillian Gaze. 1975, Houghton $7.95. Three children discover the horrible truth behind a freak summer snowstorm.

3474. Van Allsburg, Chris. *The Wreck of the Zephyr* (2–5). Illus. by author. 1983, Houghton $14.95. The story behind the wreck of a sailboat.

3475. Van Leeuwen, Jean. *The Great Rescue Operation* (3–5). Illus. by Margot Apple. 1982, Dial $9.95; LB $9.89. Two mice try to locate their friend who has disappeared in Macy's department store.

3476. Voigt, Cynthia. *Building Blocks* (5–8). 1984, Atheneum $10.95. Inside a fortress his father built him, Braunn meets Kevin, his father as a child.

3477. Wallace, Barbara Brooks. *Miss Switch to the Rescue* (3–6). Illus. by Kathleen Garry McCord. 1981, Abingdon $9.95; Archway paper $1.95. A witch, who is also popular as a fifth-grade substitute teacher, fights her enemy Saturna.

3478. Walsh, Jill Paton. *A Chance Child* (6–8). 1978, Avon paper $1.95. A time-shift story that reveals the horror of child labor practices after the Industrial Revolution.

3479. Wangerin, Walter, Jr. *The Book of the Dun Cow* (6–9). 1978, Harper $8.61. A mature fable of duty, love, and death.

3480. Wangerin, Walter, Jr. *Thistle* (2–4). Illus. by Marcia Sewall. 1983, Harper $8.61; LB $8.89. A potato farmer and his family are menaced by Pudge, a giant potato.

3481. Webster, Joanne. *The Love Genie* (6–8). 1980, Archway paper $1.95. With a genie to help her, Jennie's life becomes even more complex.

3482. Weldrick, Valerie. *Time Sweep* (5–7). Illus. by Ron Brooks. 1978, Lothrop $10.95; LB $10.51. A young Australian boy travels to London in 1862.

3483. Westall, Robert. *The Devil on the Road* (6–9). 1979, Greenwillow $10.95; LB $10.51. An English novel in which a motorcycle vacation becomes a journey back to the seventeenth century.

3484. Westall, Robert. *The Wind Eye* (5–8). 1977, Greenwillow LB $9.55. In a time-warp story, 3 children travel to the Middle Ages in this exciting fantasy that also explores complex family relationships.

3485. Wetterer, Margaret K. *The Giant's Apprentice* (2–4). Illus. by Elise Primavera. 1982, Atheneum LB $9.95. Young Liam is stolen by a giant to work at his blacksmith's forge.

3486. White, E. B. *Charlotte's Web* (PS–3). Illus. by Garth Williams. 1952, Harper $8.61; LB $8.89; paper $2.50. Classic, whimsical barnyard fable about a spider who saves the life of Wilbur the pig. Read about the ever-engaging mouse in: *Stuart Little* (1945, Harper $8.61; LB $8.89; paper $2.50).

3487. White, E. B. *The Trumpet of the Swan* (3–6). Illus. by Edward Frascino. 1970, Harper $9.57; LB $9.89; paper $2.50. Louis, a voiceless trumpeter swan, is befriended by Sam, learns to play a trumpet, and finds fame, fortune, and fatherhood.

3488. Wibberley, Leonard. *The Crime of Martin Coverly* (6–9). 1980, Farrar $9.95. Nicholas Ormsby is visited one evening by a pirate from the past, and suddenly he is transported to the early 1700s.

3489. Willard, Nancy. *The Island of the Grass King: The Further Adventures of Anatole* (4–6). Illus. by David McPhail. 1979, Harcourt $7.95. Anatole goes to the island of the Grass King to find a cure for grandmother's asthma.

3490. Willard, Nancy. *The Marzipan Moon* (4–5). Illus. by Marcia Sewall. 1981, Harcourt $9.95; paper $4.95. A cracked pot given to a parish priest has miraculous powers.

3491. Willard, Nancy. *Uncle Terrible: More Adventures of Anatole* (4–6). Illus. by David McPhail. 1982, Harcourt $9.95. A boy's visit to Uncle Terrible, so named because he is so terribly nice.

3492. Williams, Margery. *The Velveteen Rabbit: Or How Toys Become Real* (2–4). Illus. by Michael Hague. 1983, Holt $11.00; Avon paper $2.50. Love brings a toy rabbit to life. One of many fine editions.

3493. Wiseman, David. *Adam's Common* (6–8). 1984, Houghton $11.45. In doing research to save the Commons in her English town, Peggy is visited by ghosts from the past.

3494. Wiseman, David. *Blodwen and the Guardians* (4–6). 1983, Houghton $6.70. The confrontation between a group of little people and humans in contemporary Britain.

3495. Wiseman, David. *Jeremy Visick* (5–8). 1981, Houghton $8.95. Matthew helps the ghost of young Jeremy find rest.

3496. Wiseman, David. *Thimbles* (5–8). 1982, Houghton $7.95. Two magic thimbles enable Cathy to be transported back to 1819.

3497. Wright, Betty Ren. *Ghosts beneath Our Feet* (4–6). Illus. 1984, Holiday $10.95. Katie's visit to a sick uncle in Michigan involves her in visitations from a ghost.

3498. Wright, Betty Ren. *The Secret Window* (5–7). 1982, Holiday $10.95; Scholastic paper $1.95. Meg discovers that she has psychic powers.

3499. Wrightson, Patricia. *Journey behind the Wind* (6–9). 1981, Atheneum $8.95. Part of an Australian myth/fantasy for better readers. Also use: *The Dark Bright Water* (1979, Atheneum $7.95).

3500. Wrightson, Patricia. *A Little Fear* (6–9). 1983, Atheneum $9.95. A forest gnome, Njimbin, tries to prevent Mrs. Tucker from taking over a rural cottage.

3501. Yep, Laurence. *Dragon of the Lost Sea* (5–8). 1982, Harper $10.53; LB $10.89. Shimmer, a dragon, in the company of a boy, Thorn, sets out to destroy the villain Civet.

3502. Yolen, Jane. *The Acorn Quest* (1–5). Illus. by Susanna Natti. 1981, Harper $10.53; LB $10.89. A humorous spoof on the Arthurian legend of the knights' quest for the Golden Acorn.

3503. Zaring, Jane. *The Return of the Dragon* (3–6). Illus. by Polly Broman. 1981, Houghton $7.95. A dragon must perform 12 good deeds before Twelfth Night.

3504. Zhitkov, Boris. *How I Hunted the Little Fellows* (2–4). Illus. by Paul O. Zelinsky. 1979, Dodd $7.95. Boris believes that little people are living on a miniature steamship.

Science Fiction

3505. Ames, Mildred. *Anna to the Infinite Power* (6–8). 1981, Scribners $11.95; Scholastic paper $1.95. Anna is the product of a cloning experiment in 1990 California.

3506. Anderson, Margaret J. *The Brain on Quartz Mountain* (3–5). Illus. by Charles Robinson. 1982, Knopf LB $4.99; paper $1.95. A young boy realizes that the brain growing in a scientist's lab is trying to take over his body.

3507. Asimov, Isaac. *Mutants* (5–Up). Illus. by William Ersland. 1982, Raintree $8.96. A small collection of science fiction stories. Some others in the series: *Earth Invaded; Mad Scientists; Tomorrow's TV* (all 1982, $8.96).

3508. Asimov, Isaac; Greenberg, Martin; and Waugh, Charles, eds. *Young Mutants* (6–9). 1984, Harper $10.89; paper $7.95. Twelve stories about children and strange mutations. A sequel is: *Young Extra-Terrestrials* (1984, $10.89).

3509. Asimov, Janet, and Asimov, Isaac. *Norby: The Mixed-up Robot* (4–6). 1984, Walker $9.95; LB

$10.85. Jeff, his brother Fargo, and a robot named Norby combat Ing the Ingrate. A sequel is: *Norby's Other Secret* (1984, $9.95).

3510. Beatty, Jerome, Jr. *Maria Looney and the Remarkable Robot* (4–6). Illus. 1978, Avon paper $1.95. Maria goes to summer camp on the moon. Another in this series is: *Maria Looney and the Cosmic Circus* (1978, paper $1.95).

3511. Beatty, Jerome, Jr. *Matthew Looney and the Space Pirates* (3–7). Illus. by Gahan Wilson. 1972, Addison $8.95; Avon paper $1.75. Matthew, a member of the Moon Space Navy, heads an expedition to found a moon colony. Also use: *Matthew Looney's Invasion of the Earth* (1965, LB $8.95; paper $1.95); *Matthew Looney's Voyage to the Earth* (1974, Avon paper $1.95).

3512. Bethancourt, T. Ernesto. *The Mortal Instruments* (6–9). 1977, Holiday $6.95. An adolescent with supernatural powers assumes several guises when he becomes the tool of a sadistic computer installation.

3513. Byars, Betsy. *The Computer Nut* (4–6). 1984, Viking $11.50. Through her computer, Kate encounters an extraterrestrial being.

3514. Cameron, Eleanor. *The Wonderful Flight to the Mushroom Planet* (4–6). Illus. by Robert Henneberger. 1954, Little $9.95. Science fiction combined with magic in the story of 2 boys who take off on a spaceship with a magical man named Tyco Bass. A sequel: *Time and Mr. Bass* (1967, $9.95).

3515. Christopher, John. *Beyond the Burning Lands* (6–9). 1971, Macmillan $9.95; paper $2.75. In this adventure, Luke fulfills a prophecy and becomes prince in an English city-state that has reverted to a feudal organization. The series began with: *The Prince Is Waiting* (1970, paper $2.75); ended with: *The Sword of the Spirits* (1972, $7.95; paper $2.75).

3516. Christopher, John. *Empty World* (6–8). 1978, Dutton $10.95. A boy struggles for survival in a world depopulated by a plague.

3517. Christopher, John. *The White Mountains* (6–9). 1967, Macmillan $9.95; paper $3.95. The first volume of a trilogy in which a young boy escapes from a futuristically mechanized tyranny. The other volumes are: *City of Gold and Lead* (1967, paper $2.75); *Pool of Fire* (1968, $10.95; paper $2.95).

3518. Christopher, John. *Wild Jack* (6–9). 1974, Macmillan $9.50. Clive, a fugitive from his society, is befriended by a latter-day Robin Hood, Wild Jack.

3519. Clark, Margaret Goff. *Barney and the UFO* (5–7). Illus. by Ted Lewin. 1979, Dodd $7.95. An orphan meets a lonely space boy from a UFO. Two sequels are: *Barney in Space* (1981, LB $7.95); *Barney on Mars* (1983, $8.95).

3520. Clarke, Arthur C. *Dolphin Island: A Story of the People of the Sea* (6–9). 1963, Holt $5.95. Johnny Clinton, in the twenty-first century, is shipwrecked and rescued by dolphins.

3521. Collier, James Lincoln. *Planet Out of the Past* (5–8). 1983, Macmillan $10.95. Professor Joher and 3 teenagers explore a planet where life is like our prehistoric times.

3522. Coontz, Otto. *The Night Walkers* (6–9). 1982, Houghton $9.95; Archway paper $2.25. A strange fungus turns Martin and Tony into zombies.

3523. Cooper, Margaret C. *Code Name: Clone* (6–8). 1982, Walker $8.95; LB $9.85. Two clone brothers search for their real father.

3524. Cooper, Margaret C. *Solution: Escape* (6–8). Illus. by Rod Burke. 1980, Walker $8.85; LB $8.85. Steven and Evoon discover they are clones produced by Dr. Zorak.

3525. Corbett, Scott. *The Deadly Hoax* (6–9). 1981, Dutton $9.25. Two high school boys encounter beings from space.

3526. Corbett, Scott. *The Donkey Planet* (4–6). Illus. by Troy Howell. 1979, Dutton $7.95. Two young scientists must bring back samples of a metal from another planet.

3527. Curtis, Philip. *Invasion of the Brain Sharpeners* (4–6). Illus. by Tony Ross. 1981, Random $4.95; paper $1.95. A group of extraterrestrials kidnaps Mr. Browser's dull fifth-grade class.

3528. Curtis, Philip. *Invasion of the Comet People* (4–7). Illus. by Tony Ross. 1983, Knopf $4.99; paper $1.95. Jason Taylor and his family are trying to hide the fact they are from a distant planet.

3529. Dank, Milton, and Dank, Gloria. *The 3-D Traitor* (5–7). 1984, Delacorte $10.95. Science fiction with youthful heroes. Others in the series: *The Computer Caper* (1983, Dell paper $2.25); *A UFO Has Landed* (1983, $12.95; Dell paper $2.25).

3530. de Camp, Catherine Crook. *Creatures of the Cosmos* (4–6). Illus. by Joe Krush. 1977, Westminster $7.95. A collection of 8 stories, each about a strange unearthly animal.

3531. Engdahl, Sylvia Louise. *Enchantress from the Stars* (6–9). Illus. by Rodney Shackell. 1970, Atheneum paper $0.95. A novel that explores 3 worlds at different stages of development.

3532. Engdahl, Sylvia Louise. *This Star Shall Abide* (6–9). Illus. by Richard Cuffari. 1972, Atheneum paper $2.50. A young boy learns the innermost secrets of his planetary civilization in this novel that takes place in the future.

3533. Fenner, Phyllis R., sel. *Wide-Angle Lens: Stories of Time and Space* (6–9). Illus. by Erick Ingraham. 1980, Morrow $9.36; LB $9.75. Ten science fiction stories by such masters as Asimov and Nourse.

3534. Fisher, Leonard Everett. *Noonan: A Novel about Baseball, ESP and Time Warps* (6–9). 1978, Avon paper $1.95. A baseball fantasy in which a pitcher is transported in time from 1896 to 1996.

3535. Fisk, Nicholas. *Escape from Splattersbang* (4–6). 1979, Macmillan $9.95; paper $2.50. Myki and his talking computer are left behind on a hostile planet.

3536. Fisk, Nicholas. *A Rag, a Bone and a Hank of Hair* (6–8). 1982, Crown $8.95. In the twenty-first century, the world must be populated by "reborns" from past centuries.

3537. Harrison, Harry. *The Men from P.I.G. and R.O.B.O.T.* (4–6). 1978, Atheneum $7.95. Two sci-fi stories about galactic use of computers and specially trained pigs.

3538. Hoover, H. M. *The Bell Tree* (6–9). 1982, Viking $11.95. Jenny and her father realize evil forces are at work on the planet Tarin.

3539. Hoover, H. M. *The Delikon* (6–8). 1977, Viking $9.95; Avon paper $1.50. Varina, her faithful guard, and 2 children become involved in a revolution to rid the earth of its rulers, the Delikon.

3540. Hoover, H. M. *The Lost Star* (6–9). 1979, Viking $11.50; Avon paper $1.75. A young astrophysicist visits the planet Balthor.

3541. Hoover, H. M. *The Rains of Eridan* (6–8). 1977, Viking $9.95; Avon paper $1.50. In this novel, Theo tries to solve the mystery of a strange fear that grips people on an Earth-type planet.

3542. Hoover, H. M. *The Shepherd Moon: A Novel of the Future* (6–9). 1984, Viking $11.50. For better readers, a novel that takes place in the forty-eighth century.

3543. Hughes, Monica. *The Guardian of Isis* (6–9). 1982, Atheneum LB $11.95. For mature readers, a science fiction thriller set on the planet Isis. A sequel to: *The Keeper of the Isis Light* (1981, $8.95).

3544. Karl, Jean. *But We Are Not of Earth* (6–9). 1981, Dutton $10.95. Four people are sent to a place like Earth on a mysterious mission.

3545. Karl, Jean. *The Turning Place: Stories of a Future Past* (6–9). 1976, Dutton $9.95. Nine stories that deal with the results of an invasion from a planet called Ciord.

3546. Kesteven, G. R. *The Awakening Water* (6–9). 1979, Hastings $7.95. After humans have destroyed their civilization, the survivors are tranquil-ized into submission, but some known as the Lost Ones try to assert themselves.

3547. Key, Alexander. *The Case of the Vanishing Boy* (5–7). 1979, Pocket paper $1.75. Two children with unusual powers are the subject of a ruthless manhunt.

3548. Key, Alexander. *Escape to Witch Mountain* (5–7). Illus. by Leon B. Wisdom. 1968, Westminster $8.95; Pocket paper $1.95. Tony and Tina flee to the Smokies searching for their true home. A sequel is: *Return from Witch Mountain* (1981, $9.95; paper $1.75).

3549. Key, Alexander. *The Forgotten Door* (5–7). 1965, Westminster $9.95; Scholastic paper $1.95. When little Jon falls to earth from another planet, he encounters suspicion and hostility as well as sympathy.

3550. Kroll, Steven. *Space Cats* (2–4). Illus. by Frisco Henstra. 1979, Holiday LB $5.95; Avon paper $1.95. Alexander is no ordinary cat—he is King on a faraway planet.

3551. Landsman, Sandy. *The Gadget Factor* (5–9). 1984, Atheneum $11.95. Michael and friend Worm devise the ultimate computer game.

3552. Lawrence, Louise. *Calling B for Butterfly* (5–9). 1982, Harper $11.06; LB $11.89. Four teenagers and 2 children are the only survivors of a starliner smashed by an asteroid.

3553. Lawrence, Louise. *Star Lord* (6–9). 1978, Harper $8.95; LB $10.89. A fantasy set in Wales in which a boy hides a stranger from a distant star.

3554. Lee, Robert C. *Timequake* (5–8). 1982, Westminster $9.95. Randy and his cousin travel to the world of 2027.

3555. LeGuin, Ursula. *The Farthest Shore* (6–9). Illus. by Gail Garraty. 1972, Atheneum $9.95. Arren travels with Ged to find and vanquish the power of an evil spirit in this final part of the triology. The first 2 are: *The Wizard of Earth-Sea* (1968, Parnassus $10.95); *The Tombs of Atuan* (1971, Atheneum $10.95).

3556. L'Engle, Madeleine. *A Wrinkle in Time* (6–9). 1962, Farrar $9.95; Dell paper $1.95. A provocative fantasy-science fiction tale of a brother and sister in search of their father, who is lost in the fifth dimension. Newbery Award winner, 1963. Also use: *Wind in the Door* (1974, Farrar $9.95; Dell paper $1.95); *A Swiftly Tilting Planet* (1978); *A Ring of Endless Light* (1980) (both Farrar $9.95).

3557. McCaffrey, Anne. *Dragonsong* (6–9). 1976, Atheneum $10.95. Fifteen-year-old Menolly acquires a band of fire lizards and uses them to achieve her career goal. Two sequels are: *Dragonsinger* (1977, $10.95); *Dragondrums* (1979, $8.95).

3558. MacGregor, Ellen. *Miss Pickerell Goes to Mars* (4–6). Illus. by Paul Galdone. 1951, McGraw $5.72; Pocket paper $1.75. A sprightly old lady and her fantastic escapades. Also use: *Miss Pickerell and the Geiger Counter* (1953); *Miss Pickerell Goes Undersea* (1953); *Miss Pickerell Goes to the Arctic* (1954) (all Pocket paper $1.75).

3559. MacGregor, Ellen, and Pantell, Dora. *Miss Pickerell to the Earthquake Rescue* (3–5). Illus. by Charles Geer. 1977, McGraw $9.95; Pocket paper $1.75. The trusty adventurer sets out to solve the mystery behind a rash of unexplained earthquakes. Also use: *Miss Pickerell Harvests the Sea* (1969); *Miss Pickerell and the Weather Satellite* (1971) (both Pocket paper $1.95); *Miss Pickerell Meets Mr. H.U.M.* (1974, LB $10.95); *Miss Pickerell and the Supertanker* (1978, $9.95; Pocket paper $1.95); *Miss Pickerell Goes on a Dig* (1980, Pocket paper $1.75); *Miss Pickerell on the Moon* (1980, Pocket paper $1.95); *Miss Pickerell Tackles the Energy Crisis* (1980, $9.95; Pocket paper $1.95); *Miss Pickerell Takes the Bull by the Horns* (1980, Pocket paper $1.75); *Miss Pickerell on the Trail* (1982, $8.95); *Miss Pickerell and the Blue Whale* (1983, $9.95).

3560. Manes, Stephen. *That Game from Outer Space: The First Strange Thing That Happened to Oscar Noodleman* (3–6). Illus. by Tony Auth. 1983, Dutton $8.69. Oscar repairs a rocket ship from outer space. A sequel is: *The Oscar J. Noodleman Television Network: The Second Strange Thing That Happened to Oscar Noodleman* (1983, $8.69).

3561. Mason, Anne. *The Dancing Meteorite* (6–9). 1984, Harper $11.89. Sixteen-year-old Kira lives on a space station and befriends some aliens.

3562. Morressy, John. *The Drought on Ziax II* (2–4). Illus. by Stanley Skardinski. 1978, Walker $5.95; LB $5.85. The water supply of the planet Ziax is endangered.

3563. Nastick, Sharon. *Mr. Radagast Makes an Unexpected Journey* (4–7). Illus. by Judy Glasser. 1981, Harper $8.95; LB $8.79; Dell paper $1.75. A seventh-grade class performs an experiment and their teacher disappears.

3564. Ray, N. L. *There Was This Man Running* (6–8). 1981, Macmillan LB $9.95. An alien loses his power source and will kill to retrieve it.

3565. Slobodkin, Louis. *Space Ship under the Apple Tree* (3–5). 1952, Macmillan paper $2.95. Eddie discovers small men in his grandmother's apple tree. Also use: *The Space Ship Returns to the Apple Tree; The Three-Seated Space Ship* (both 1981, paper $2.95).

3566. Slote, Alfred. *Clone Catcher* (6–8). Illus. by Elizabeth Slote. 1982, Harper $10.10; LB $10.89. In 2019, a young man is hired to recapture escaped clones.

3567. Slote, Alfred. *My Robot Buddy* (4–6). 1975, Harper $10.95; Avon paper $2.25. For his tenth birthday, Jack's parents get him his very own Robot Buddy. Sequels are: *My Trip to Alpha I* (1978, $9.57; Avon paper $1.95); *C.O.L.A.R.: A Tale of Outer Space* (1981, $9.57; LB $9.89; Avon paper $2.25); *Omega Station* (1983, $9.57; LB $9.89).

3568. Snyder, Zilpha Keatley. *Below the Root* (5–7). Illus. by Alton Raible. 1975, Atheneum LB $8.95. In a society that has survived the almost total destruction encompassing the world, 13-year-old Raamo sets out to explore a civilization that reportedly lives underground.

3569. Stone, Josephine Rector. *Those Who Fall from the Sun* (6–8). Illus. by Mal Luber. 1978, Atheneum $6.95. Alanna and her family are deported to another planet for their crime of independent thinking.

3570. Sullivan, Mary W. *Earthquake 2099* (5–8). 1982, Dutton $9.95. A story of survival in the year 2099.

3571. Walsh, Jill Paton. *The Green Book* (4–7). Illus. by Lloyd Bloom. 1982, Farrar $8.95. The exodus of a group of Britons from dying earth to another planet.

3572. Walters, Hugh. *The Blue Aura* (6–9). 1979, Faber $13.50. A group of angels from a friendly civilization visits Earth.

3573. Watson, Jane Werner. *The Case of the Vanishing Spaceship* (4–6). 1982, Putnam $9.95. Rick and his father attempt to trace a downed UFO in the Arctic.

3574. Watson, Simon. *No Man's Land* (6–9). 1976, Greenwillow $9.95. A boy tries to rebel against the overly mechanized and regulated existence in the next century.

3575. Wilkes, Marilyn Z. *C.L.U.T.Z.* (4–6). Illus. by Larry Ross. 1982, Dial $9.95; LB $9.89; Bantam paper $1.95. The Pentax family get a new robot that is a clutz.

3576. Willett, John. *The Singer in the Stone* (6–8). 1981, Houghton $6.95. Two young people try to return a sense of questioning to the Plain People of Earth.

3577. Williams, Jay, and Abrashkin, Raymond. *Danny Dunn, Invisible Boy* (4–6). Illus. by Paul Sagsoorian. 1975, Pocket paper $1.95. One of a popular series about an engaging boy and his science fiction adventures. Others in the series are: *Danny Dunn and the Weather Machine* (1959, McGraw $9.95; Pocket paper $1.95); *Danny Dunn and the Smallifying Machine* (1971, Pocket paper $1.95); *Danny Dunn and the Anti-Gravity Paint; Danny Dunn and the Fossil Cave; Danny Dunn and the*

Heat Ray; Danny Dunn and the Homework Machine; Danny Dunn and the Swamp Monster (all 1977, Pocket paper $1.95); *Danny Dunn and the Universal Glue* (1977, McGraw $9.95; Pocket paper $1.95); *Danny Dunn on a Desert Island; Danny Dunn on the Ocean Floor; Danny Dunn, Scientific Detective; Danny Dunn, Time Traveler* (all 1977, Pocket paper $1.95); *Danny Dunn and the Voice from Space* (1979, Pocket paper $2.25).

3578. Williams, Jay. *The Magic Grandfather* (4–6). Illus. by Gail Owens. 1979, Four Winds $8.95; Scholastic paper $1.95. When his grandfather's sorcery misfires, young Sam must undo the damage.

3579. Wismer, Donald. *Starluck* (6–8). 1982, Doubleday LB $9.95. Paul becomes a threat to the Emperor of the Three Hundred Suns.

3580. Yep, Laurence. *Sweetwater* (6–8). Illus. by Julia Noonan. 1973, Harper $10.89; paper $3.13. A novel in which the narrator and his friends are threatened by a group that wants to modernize and change their planet, Harmony.

3581. Yolen, Jane. *The Robot and Rebecca and the Missing Owser* (3–5). Illus. by Lady McCrady. 1981, Knopf LB $4.99; paper $1.95. Rebecca and robot Watson II wonder what happened to their three-legged pet, an owser.

Ethnic Groups

3582. Beatty, Patricia. *Lupita Manana* (6–8). 1981, Morrow $9.95; LB $9.55. Two young Mexicans must travel to the United States to find work.

3583. Bernstein, Joanne E. *Dmitry: A Young Soviet Immigrant* (6–8). Illus. 1981, Houghton $10.95. A Russian-Jewish family leaves the Soviet Union for a life in the United States.

3584. Bethancourt, T. Ernesto. *Where the Deer and the Cantaloupe Play* (6–9). 1981, Oak Tree $7.95. A young New York Latin tries to find himself a place in the Wild West.

3585. Blume, Judy. *Iggie's House* (4–7). 1970, Bradbury $9.95; Dell paper $2.50. A black family moves into Iggie's old house.

3586. Borland, Hal. *When the Legends Die* (6–8). 1963, Harper $9.95; Bantam paper $2.75. A Ute Indian boy faces many problems growing up in Colorado.

3587. Brodie, Deborah, ed. *Stories My Grandfather Should Have Told Me* (3–6). Illus. by Carmela Tal-Baron. 1977, Hebrew $6.95. Twelve stories from a variety of authors that explore many aspects of twentieth-century Jewish life.

3588. Bulla, Clyde Robert. *Indian Hill* (3–4). Illus. by James J. Spanfeller. 1963, Harper $9.95. A young Navajo and his family must adjust to new ways when they move from the reservation to the city.

3589. Chadwick, Roxanne. *Don't Shoot* (5–8). Illus. by Edwin H. Ryan. 1978, Lerner LB $5.95. A young Inuit (Eskimo) boy must decide between saving a polar bear or a cruel hunter.

3590. Coates, Belle. *Mak* (5–8). 1981, Houghton $8.95. Mak is torn between the Indian and white cultures.

3591. Cohen, Barbara. *Bitter Herbs and Honey* (6–9). 1976, Lothrop $9.84. Difficulties and differences are explored in this story of an orthodox Jewish girl growing up in a New Jersey gentile community in 1916.

3592. Cohen, Barbara. *King of the Seventh Grade* (5–7). 1982, Lothrop $11.00. Vic Abrams's secure world becomes unstuck when his mother reveals she is not Jewish, therefore, there will be no Bar Mitzvah.

3593. Cone, Molly. *Number Four* (6–9). 1972, Houghton $6.95. After his brother's death, Benjamin begins to establish his native American identity, as his brother did. Tragedy results in this sensitive and convincing novel.

3594. Dyer, T. A. *The Whipman Is Watching* (5–8). 1979, Houghton $7.95. Children living on an American Indian reservation try to retain their identity in an all-white school.

3595. Forman, James D. *People of the Dream* (6–8). 1972, Farrar $8.95. A novel concerning the flight of Chief Joseph and his Nez Percé people and the gross injustice inflicted on them.

3596. Gardiner, John Reynolds. *Stone Fox* (3–6). Illus. by Marcia Sewall. 1980, Harper $10.53; LB $10.89; paper $2.84. Little Willy competes against the Indian Stone Face in the National Dogsled Races.

3597. Graham, Lorenz. *Return to South Town* (6–9). 1976, Harper $11.49. In this fourth volume of a celebrated series, David Williams, now a doctor, returns to the southern town from which his black family fled years ago.

3598. Haseley, Dennis. *The Scared One* (4–6). Illus. by Deborah Howland. 1983, Warne $10.95. The story of an Indian boy who is living in fear.

3599. Holman, Felice. *The Murderer* (5–7). 1978, Scribners paper $1.95. A young Jewish boy growing up in the days of the Great Depression is bullied by local boys and accused of murdering Christ.

3600. Hooks, William H. *Circle of Fire* (5–8). 1982, Atheneum $12.95. Three friends—a white and 2 black boys—try to thwart an attack on some Irish gypsies by the Klan.

3601. Hunter, Kristin. *The Soul Brothers and Sister Lou* (6–9). 1968, Scribners $12.95; Avon paper $2.25. Louretta Hawkens, a 14-year-old girl, and her friends grow up in an urban ghetto and, in spite of frustration, succeed in creating soul music. Also use: *Guests in the Promised Land* (1973, Scribners $5.95).

3602. Jones, Toeckey. *Go Well, Stay Well* (5–7). 1980, Harper LB $8.89. A white girl in South Africa meets a black girl her own age, and a friendship begins in spite of social pressures.

3603. Karp, Naomi J. *The Turning Point* (5–8). 1976, Harcourt $6.95. Hannah and brother Zach encounter anti-Semitism when their Bronx family moves to the suburbs.

3604. Klein, Norma. *Bizou* (6–8). 1983, Viking $11.10. Bizou, a French child with a black American mother, learns about her family roots.

3605. Lester, Julius. *Long Journey Home* (6–8). 1972, Dial $7.95. Six (based-on-fact) stories concerning slaves, and ex-slaves, and their lives in a hostile America.

3606. Lord, Bette Bao. *In the Year of the Boar and Jackie Robinson* (4–6). Illus. by Marc Simont. 1984, Harper $9.57; LB $9.89. The story of a Chinese girl who leaves China to join her father in New York in 1947.

3607. Madison, Winifred. *Maria Luisa* (4–6). 1971, Harper $8.79. Maria Luisa encounters prejudice against Chicanos when she and her younger brother move to San Francisco to live with an aunt.

3608. Martel, Cruz. *Yagua Days* (K–2). Illus. by Jerry Pinkney. 1976, Dial $8.95. Adam Bure visits for the first time his parents' homeland, Puerto Rico.

3609. Miles, Betty. *All It Takes Is Practice* (4–6). 1976, Knopf $6.95; Dell paper $1.25. The arrival of an interracial family in town upsets the quiet lives of Stuart and his fellow fifth graders.

3610. Mohr, Nicholasa. *Felita* (6–8). Illus. by Ray Cruz. 1979, Dial LB $6.46; Dell paper $1.50. A Puerto Rican family moves from a friendly neighborhood to one where Spanish is not spoken.

3611. Myers, Walter Dean. *It Ain't All for Nothin'* (6–8). 1979, Avon paper $1.75. A 12-year-old boy is cast adrift in Harlem.

3612. Myers, Walter Dean. *The Young Landlords* (6–9). 1979, Viking $11.50. The gang plus the narrator Paul acquire a slum building. Another "gang" book: *Mojo and the Russians* (1977, $10.95).

3613. Place, Marian T., and Preston, Charles G. *Juan's Eighteen-Wheeler Summer* (5–7). 1982, Dodd LB $8.95. A Mexican-American boy spends a summer working with a truck driver to buy a bicycle.

3614. Rogers, Jean. *Goodbye, My Island* (4–6). Illus. by Rie Munoz. 1983, Greenwillow $10.00; LB $10.88. An Eskimo girl describes her doomed community on King Island in Alaska.

3615. Uchida, Yoshiko. *Journey Home* (4–6). Illus. by Charles Robinson. 1978, Atheneum $8.95; paper $2.95. Life of a Japanese-American family after their release from a World War II internment camp.

3616. Waldron, Ann. *The Integration of Mary-Larkin Thornhill* (5–8). 1975, Dutton $8.95. Because her parents insist, a white northern girl must attend a black junior high school.

3617. Wilkinson, Brenda. *Ludell* (5–7). 1975, Harper $12.89. A tender story of a girl's years in the fifth grade in a southern segregated school during the mid-1950s. Two sequels are: *Ludell and Willie* (1977, LB $10.89; Bantam paper $1.75); *Ludell's New York Time* (1980, $8.95; LB $9.89).

3618. Yep, Laurence. *Sea Glass* (6–8). 1979, Harper $10.53; LB $10.89. An awkward Chinese-American boy moves to a new junior high school and has trouble adjusting.

Growing into Maturity

Family Problems

3619. Abercrombie, Barbara. *Cat-Man's Daughter* (5–8). 1983, Harper $10.53; LB $11.06; Scholastic paper $1.95. Kate shuttles between her TV star father in Los Angeles and her mother in New York.

3620. Adler, Carole S. *Fly Free* (6–9). 1984, Putnam $10.95. A young girl learns from her vindictive mother that the man she thought was her father isn't.

3621. Adler, Carole S. *In Our House Scott Is My Brother* (5–8). 1980, Macmillan $9.95; Bantam paper $1.95. The effects of an unsuccessful divorce are explored in this story from the viewpoint of a 13-year-old boy.

3622. Alexander, Anne. *To Live a Lie* (4–6). Illus. by Velma Ilsley. 1975, Atheneum $8.95. Allan and Sam run away from a father they fear, but the consequences are tragic.

3623. Alexander, Sue. *Nadia the Willful* (2–4). Illus. by Lloyd Bloom. 1983, Pantheon $10.95; LB

$10.99. Nadia, a Bedouin child, grieves over her brother's death.

3624. Ames, Mildred. *What Are Friends For?* (5–7). 1978, Scribners $8.95. Amy and Michele share a common bond—they are children of divorce.

3625. Angell, Judie. *What's Best for You: A Novel* (6–9). 1981, Dutton $9.95; Dell paper $2.25. A novel about how each member of a family deals with divorce.

3626. Ashley, Bernard. *A Break in the Sun: A Novel* (6–8). Illus. by Charles Keeping. 1980, Phillips $10.95. Patsy Bligh runs away, and her stepfather begins a search for her.

3627. Avi. *A Place Called Ugly* (6–9). 1981, Pantheon $8.95; LB $8.99; Scholastic paper $1.95. Owen tries to prevent the destruction of his family's summer place.

3628. Bates, Betty. *It Must've Been the Fish Sticks* (5–8). 1982, Holiday $8.95. Brian finds out that his mother is really only his stepmother.

3629. Bauer, Marion Dane. *Foster Child* (5–7). 1977, Houghton $7.95. Rennie is unable to adjust to a foster home and runs away in this touching story.

3630. Bawden, Nina. *The Robbers* (4–6). 1979, Lothrop $10.25; LB $9.84. Nine-year-old Philip joins his divorced father in London and faces identity problems.

3631. Bawden, Nina. *Squib* (4–6). Illus. by Hank Blaustein. 1982, Lothrop $11.25. An English story about an abused child.

3632. Benjamin, Carol Lea. *Nobody's Baby Now* (6–9). 1984, Macmillan $9.95. Olivia must take care of her withdrawn grandmother in this novel for mature readers.

3633. Billington, Elizabeth. *The Move* (5–8). 1984, Warne $9.95. The Black family moves from New York City to the suburbs.

3634. Blue, Rose. *Grandma Didn't Wave Back* (3–5). Illus. by Ted Lewin. 1972, Watts $8.90. Debbie witnesses the degeneration into senility of her beloved grandma and finally accepts the idea of a nursing home.

3635. Blume, Judy. *It's Not the End of the World* (4–7). 1972, Bradbury $9.95; Bantam paper $1.95. Twelve-year-old Karen's world seems to end when her parents are divorced and her older brother runs away.

3636. Bond, Nancy. *Country of Broken Stone* (6–9). 1980, Atheneum $12.95. Penelope, her brother, and her father accompany her new stepmother on an archaeological dig in the north of England.

3637. Brancato, Robin F. *Sweet Bells Jangled Out of Tune* (6–9). 1982, Scholastic paper $1.95. Ellen's grandmother becomes a "bag" lady.

3638. Buchan, Stuart. *When We Lived with Pete* (6–8). 1978, Scribners $2.98. A young boy is responsible for bringing his mother and her former boyfriend together.

3639. Burch, Robert. *Skinny* (4–7). Illus. by Don Sibley. 1970, Dell paper $0.75. The story of a young orphan who works in a hotel run by Miss Bessie.

3640. Byars, Betsy. *The Two-Thousand-Pound Goldfish* (4–6). 1982, Harper $10.10; LB $9.89; Scholastic paper $1.95. Warren can't accept the fact that his mother has rejected him.

3641. Calvert, Patricia. *The Money-Creek Mare* (6–9). 1981, Scribners $9.95. Ella Rae takes charge of her family when her mother leaves.

3642. Carrick, Malcolm. *I'll Get You!* (5–7). 1979, Harper LB $8.89. An English story of a boy who tries to transcend his snobbish parents.

3643. Carris, Joan. *The Revolt of Ten X* (5–7). 1980, Harcourt $7.95. A girl retreats to her computer after her father's death.

3644. Cleaver, Vera, and Cleaver, Bill. *The Kissimmee Kid* (6–8). 1981, Lothrop $9.95; LB $9.55. Evelyn and brother Buell discover that their older brother-in-law is involved in cattle rustling.

3645. Clifford, Eth. *The Killer Swan* (6–9). 1980, Houghton $6.95. Lex is still brooding over his father's suicide and, therefore, can't accept his new stepfather.

3646. Clifford, Mary Louise. *Salah of Sierra Leone* (6–8). Illus. by Elzia Moon. 1975, Harper $9.57. Tribal loyalties conflict with today's culture in this story of a boy in Sierra Leone.

3647. Colman, Hila. *What's the Matter with the Dobsons?* (6–8). 1980, Crown $7.95; Pocket paper $1.95. There is such strife inside the Dobson family that divorce seems imminent.

3648. Cone, Molly. *The Amazing Memory of Harvey Bean* (3–6). Illus. by Robert MacLean. 1980, Houghton $8.95. Harvey's parents are separating, but the blow is softened by a friendship with Mr. and Mrs. Katz.

3649. Culin, Charlotte. *Cages of Glass, Flowers of Time* (6–8). 1979, Bradbury $10.95; Dell paper $2.75. Two friends help Clara adjust to her parents' abuse and alcoholism.

3650. Danziger, Paula. *Can You Sue Your Parents for Malpractice?* (6–9). 1979, Delacorte $8.95; Dell paper $1.95. Quarreling parents and a strong-willed father are only 2 of 14-year-old Lauren's problems.

3651. Danziger, Paula. *The Divorce Express* (6–8). 1982, Delacorte $10.95; Dell paper $2.25. Phoebe commutes between divorced parents.

3652. Danziger, Paula. *The Pistachio Prescription* (6–9). 1978, Delacorte $8.95. A thirteen-year-old talks about her school problem and possible divorce in the family.

3653. Davis, Gibbs. *Maud Flies Solo* (4–6). 1981, Bradbury $8.95. Maud can't understand why her older sister is no longer as close.

3654. Derman, Martha. *And Philippa Makes Four* (5–8). 1983, Scholastic $8.95. Philippa at first rejects her new stepmother.

3655. Dixon, Paige. *Walk My Way* (6–9). 1980, Atheneum $7.95. Kilty, a 14-year-old, flees from an alcoholic father.

3656. Dubelaar, Thea. *Maria* (3–5). Illus. by Mance Post. 1982, Morrow $9.25. Maria faces many family problems including a retarded brother and an emotionally disturbed mother.

3657. Duncan, Lois. *A Gift of Magic* (5–8). Illus. by Arvis Stewart. 1971, Little $8.95; Pocket paper $2.25. A young girl, gifted with extrasensory perception, adjusts to her parents' divorce.

3658. Dunne, Mary Collins. *Hoby and Stub* (5–8). 1981, Atheneum LB $9.95. Hoby runs away from home with a bull terrier puppy.

3659. First, Julia. *I, Rebekah, Take You, the Lawrences* (5–8). 1981, Watts LB $8.90. Rebekah has many problems when she is adopted by the Lawrences.

3660. Fox, Paula. *One-eyed Cat* (6–9). 1984, Macmillan $11.95. A story about a boy growing up in upstate New York and a gift of an air rifle.

3661. Gaeddert, Louann. *Just Like Sisters* (4–7). Illus. by Gail Owens. 1981, Dutton $10.25. When Carrie's cousin comes to stay with her, the friendship doesn't work out.

3662. Gibbons, Faye. *Some Glad Morning* (5–7). 1982, Morrow $10.75. Maude's family tries to get along after they leave their alcoholic father.

3663. Giff, Patricia Reilly. *Rat Teeth* (4–6). Illus. by Leslie Morrill. 1984, Delacorte $12.95; LB $12.95. Radcliffe can't adjust to both his parents' divorce and a new school.

3664. Girion, Barbara. *Like Everybody Else* (6–8). 1980, Scribners $9.95; Dell paper $1.95. Eileen discovers that her mother's new novel contains torrid sex.

3665. Gordon, Shirley. *The Boy Who Wanted a Family* (2–4). Illus. by Charles Robinson. 1980, Harper LB $9.89; paper $1.50. A 7-year-old awaits adoption and endures the terrible anxiety that this involves.

3666. Greenberg, Jan. *A Season In-Between* (6–8). 1979, Farrar $9.95. Carrie's life changes dramatically when it is discovered that her father has cancer.

3667. Greenwald, Sheila. *All the Way to Wit's End* (5–7). 1979, Little $8.95. An old-fashioned family moves to a modern housing development, and 11-year-old Drucilla must readjust.

3668. Gregory, Diana. *The Fog Burns Off by Eleven O'Clock* (6–8). 1981, Addison LB $7.95. During Dedi's summer with her father in southern California, she learns a lot about him and herself.

3669. Harris, Mark Jonathan. *With a Wave of the Wand* (5–7). 1980, Lothrop $11.25; LB $11.89; Scholastic paper $1.95. Magic and reality are intertwined in this novel of a girl's adjustment to her parents' divorce.

3670. Hayes, Sheila. *The Carousel Horse* (5–7). 1978, Lodestar $7.95. A young girl feels the difference in class when her mother becomes the cook for a wealthy family.

3671. Henkes, Kevin. *Margaret and Taylor* (2–4). Illus. by author. 1983, Greenwillow $10.00; LB $10.88. Margaret thrives on being mean to her young brother.

3672. Hermes, Patricia. *You Shouldn't Have to Say Good-bye* (5–8). 1982, Houghton $10.95; Scholastic paper $1.95. Sarah's mother is dying of cancer.

3673. Holland, Isabelle. *Now Is Not Too Late* (5–7). 1980, Lothrop $9.75; LB $10.05. Cathy discovers the identity of her real mother during a summer at her grandmother's.

3674. Hughes, Dean. *Switching Tracks* (6–8). 1982, Atheneum $14.95. Mark believes he was responsible for his father's suicide.

3675. Hurwitz, Johanna. *Dede Takes Charge!* (5–7). Illus. by Diane de Groat. 1984, Morrow $9.00. Dede's life is not the same A.D. (after divorce).

3676. Irwin, Hadley. *Bring to a Boil and Separate* (5–8). 1980, Atheneum $8.95. Katie's traumatic thirteenth summer involves her parents' divorce and an uneasy friendship.

3677. Ish-Kishor, Sulamith. *Our Eddie* (6–9). 1969, Random $4.95; LB $5.99. A powerful story dealing with the effect of an egotistical, fanatical Jewish father on his family and particularly his son, Eddie.

3678. Jacobs, Anita. *Where Has Deedie Wooster Been All These Years?* (6–8). 1981, Delacorte $9.95;

Dell paper $2.25. Deedie finds it is difficult to adjust to her brother's death.

3679. Jones, Penelope. *Holding Together* (4–6). 1981, Bradbury $9.95. Vickie's family unites to fill the gap when their mother dies.

3680. Kenny, Kevin, and Krull, Helen. *Sometimes My Mom Drinks Too Much* (2–4). Illus. by Helen Cogancherry. 1980, Raintree LB $14.25. Young Maureen must face her mother's alcoholism.

3681. Kingman, Lee. *The Refiner's Fire* (6–8). 1981, Houghton $8.95. Sara is forced to live with her artist father and his girl friend Kyra.

3682. Klass, Sheila Solomon. *Nobody Knows Me in Miami* (5–7). 1981, Scribners $9.95. Miriam's aunt and uncle in Miami want to adopt her.

3683. Klass, Sheila Solomon. *To See My Mother Dance* (6–9). 1981, Scribners $10.95. Jessica dreams of meeting her mother who abandoned her.

3684. Klein, Norma. *Robbie and the Leap Year Blues* (4–6). 1981, Dial $9.95; LB $9.89. Robbie alternates weeks with his divorced parents.

3685. Klein, Norma. *Taking Sides* (5–7). 1974, Pantheon $6.95. Nur and her young brother adjust to their parents' divorce; then their father's heart attack further upsets their lives.

3686. Kropp, Paul. *Wilted: A Novel* (6–8). 1980, Dell paper $1.75. Danny's life is a series of ups and downs after his parents separate.

3687. Lindbergh, Anne. *Nobody's Orphan* (4–6). 1983, Harcourt $12.95. Martha believes that she is adopted, though she has no proof.

3688. Little, Jean. *Home from Far* (4–6). Illus. by Jerry Lazare. 1965, Little $7.95. After Jenny's twin brother was killed in an auto accident, her mother brought 2 foster children into their home, one a boy just her age.

3689. Love, Sandra. *Crossing Over* (6–8). 1981, Lothrop $11.25; LB $11.88. Megan learns to communicate with her often gruff father.

3690. Lowry, Lois. *Find a Stranger, Say Goodbye* (6–9). 1978, Houghton $8.95; Pocket paper $1.95. An adopted girl sets out to find her real mother.

3691. McCaffrey, Mary. *My Brother Ange* (3–6). Illus. by Denise Saldutti. 1982, Harper $9.57; LB $9.89. Mick's anger at his younger brother causes an accident.

3692. McLean, Susan. *Pennies for the Piper* (5–7). 1981, Farrar $9.95. A moving story of a young girl alone facing the death of her mother.

3693. Mann, Peggy. *My Dad Lives in a Downtown Hotel* (4–6). Illus. by Richard Cuffari. 1973,

Doubleday $7.95; Avon paper $1.75. Joey tells the story of his adjustment to his parents' separation and their impending divorce.

3694. Masters, Mildred. *The House on the Hill* (3–5). 1982, Greenwillow $10.25. Jenny is faced with a lonely summer when her best friend moves away.

3695. Mathis, Sharon Bell. *Teacup Full of Roses* (6–9). 1972, Viking $10.95. The devastating effect of drugs on a black inner-city family and how addiction causes the death of the youngest son.

3696. Mazer, Norma Fox. *Taking Terri Mueller* (6–9). 1981, Morrow $19.50; Avon paper $2.50. Terri learns that she has been kidnapped by her father.

3697. Moore, Emily. *Something to Count On* (4–5). 1980, Dutton $9.95. Lorraine finds it difficult at school after her parents' divorce.

3698. Morris, Judy K. *The Crazies and Sam* (4–8). 1983, Viking $11.10. Sam is growing up with his father in Washington and is befriended by Ellen, one of the crazies who hangs around the city's parks.

3699. Naylor, Phyllis Reynolds. *The Solomon System* (5–8). 1983, Atheneum $10.95. Ted must face the facts that his older brother has less time for him and his parents are heading for a divorce.

3700. Newfield, Marcia. *A Book for Jodan* (3–4). Illus. by Diane de Groat. 1975, Atheneum $8.95. Nine-year-old Jodan must adjust to the gradual breakup of her parents' marriage and their eventual divorce.

3701. Okimoto, Jean Davies. *It's Just Too Much* (5–8). 1980, Putnam $9.95. Sixth grader Cynthia faces personal problems of growing up plus the remarriage of her mother.

3702. Okimoto, Jean Davies. *My Mother Is Not Married to My Father* (5–7). 1979, Pocket paper $1.75. A story of divorce as seen through the eyes of a sixth-grade girl.

3703. Oppenheimer, Joan L. *Gardine vs. Hanover* (6–9). 1982, Harper $9.13; LB $9.89. Step families are brought together and conflicts begin.

3704. Paige, Harry W. *Johnny Stands* (5–8). 1982, Warne $8.95. Johnny and his Indian grandfather run away to avoid separation.

3705. Park, Barbara. *Don't Make Me Smile* (4–6). 1981, Random LB $8.95; Avon paper $1.95. Charles refuses to face the fact of his parents' divorce.

3706. Perl, Lila. *Dumb Like Me, Olivia Potts* (4–6). 1976, Houghton $10.95; Dell paper $1.50. Olivia, following in the wake of her superbright brother and sister, doubts her own intelligence.

3707. Perl, Lila. *The Telltale Summer of Tina C.* (4–6). 1975, Scholastic paper $1.95. Tina gains self-confidence and tolerance during her visit to her mother and new stepfather.

3708. Pfeffer, Susan Beth. *Starting with Melodie* (5–8). 1982, Scholastic $9.95. The parents of Elaine's best friend are getting a divorce.

3709. Platt, Kin. *Chloris and the Creeps* (6–8). 1973, Dell paper $1.75. Eleven-year-old Chloris gradually adjusts to the "creep" that has married her mother in this story told by her younger sister Jenny. Two sequels are: *Chloris and the Freaks* (1975, Bradbury $9.95; Bantam paper $1.95); *Chloris and the Weirdos* (1978, Bradbury $9.95).

3710. Provost, Gary. *The Pork Chop War* (6–8). 1982, Bradbury $9.95. Brian's hope that his mother will marry Currie is doomed.

3711. Radley, Gail. *Nothing Stays the Same Forever* (5–7). 1981, Crown $8.95. Carrie cannot accept the woman her widowed father wants to marry.

3712. Sachs, Marilyn. *Call Me Ruth* (5–7). 1982, Doubleday $11.95. Ruth, a young immigrant, is in conflict with her mother who wants to keep her Russian-Jewish ways.

3713. Sachs, Marilyn. *A Secret Friend* (4–6). 1978, Doubleday LB $8.95. A broken friendship and overdependence on a parent are two themes explored in this novel.

3714. Sargent, Sarah. *Secret Lies* (5–7). 1981, Crown $8.95; Dell paper $1.95. Elveria is sent to Virginia to live with a large family of cousins.

3715. Seabrooke, Brenda. *Home Is Where They Take You In* (5–7). 1980, Morrow $9.75; LB $9.36. A young girl named Benicia is abandoned by her alcoholic mother.

3716. Sebestyen, Ouida. *IOU's* (6–9). 1982, Little $12.45. Stowe Garrett is summoned to visit a grandfather he doesn't know.

3717. Sloan, Carolyn. *Skewer's Garden* (4–8). 1983, Merrimack $10.95. A gypsy boy decides he must run away from home.

3718. Smith, Doris Buchanan. *Kick a Stone Home* (6–9). 1974, Harper $10.53. Fifteen-year-old Sara already has problems adjusting to her parents' divorce when troubles with dating and boys also begin to plague her.

3719. Snyder, Anne. *First Step* (5–8). 1975, NAL paper $1.75. Being saddled with a divorced, alcoholic mother is almost too much for Cindy until she discovers Alateen.

3720. Snyder, Carol. *The Great Condominium Rebellion* (4–7). Illus. by Anthony Kramer. 1981, Dell paper $2.25. Young visitors to a condo in Florida find the rules oppressive.

3721. Sobol, Harriet Langsam. *My Other-Mother, My Other-Father* (2–4). Illus. 1979, Macmillan $8.95. Children struggle through the problems of their parents' divorces and remarriages.

3722. Springstubb, Tricia. *Which Way to the Nearest Wilderness?* (5–7). 1984, Little $12.45. Eunice prepares to leave home to escape conflicts with her parents.

3723. Stern, Cecily. *A Different Kind of Gold* (6–8). Illus. by Ruth Sanderson. 1981, Harper $11.06; LB $10.89; paper $1.95. Story of a girl growing up in Alaska.

3724. Stolz, Mary. *The Edge of Next Year* (5–8). 1974, Harper LB $11.89; Dell paper $1.50. The painful adjustment by the Woodwards—father and 2 sons—to the tragic death of the mother.

3725. Stolz, Mary. *Leap before You Look* (6–9). 1972, Harper $12.89. Jimmie, the 14-year-old heroine of this perceptive novel, reviews the problems of living through the first year of her parents' divorce.

3726. Sykes, Pamela. *Phoebe's Family* (3–5). 1974, Lodestar $7.95. Phoebe tolerates her family's idiosyncrasies while undergoing a traumatic crush on an older man.

3727. Tate, Eleanora E. *Just an Overnight Guest* (4–6). 1980, Dial $8.95; LB $8.44. Margie's mother takes in a neglected half-white 4-year-old and the trouble begins.

3728. Teibl, Margaret. *Davey Come Home* (3–5). Illus. by Jacqueline Bardner Smith. 1979, Harper LB $8.89. A young boy adjusts to life with his divorced father and a new housekeeper.

3729. Terris, Susan. *No Scarlet Ribbons* (5–8). 1981, Farrar $9.95. Rachel is determined to ruin her mother's new marriage when she feels rejected.

3730. Williams, Barbara. *Mitzi and the Terrible Tyrannosaurus Rex* (2–4). Illus. by Emily McCully. 1982, Dutton $8.95; Dell paper $2.25. Mitzi is apprehensive about her mother's remarriage. Two sequels are: *Mitzi's Honeymoon with Nana Potts* (1983); *Mitzi and Frederick the Great* (1984) (both $9.66).

3731. Wolitzer, Hilma. *Wish You Were Here* (6–8). 1984, Farrar $10.95. Bernie does not want to live with his stepfather and decides to move to Florida with his grandfather.

3732. Wolkoff, Judie. *Happily Ever After . . . Almost* (5–8). 1982, Bradbury $10.95; Dell paper $2.50. Kitty describes her life with her new stepfather and his family.

3733. Wolkoff, Judie. *Where the Elf King Sings* (6–9). 1980, Bradbury $8.95. Marcie's major problem is an alcoholic father.

Personal Problems

3734. Amdur, Nikki. *One of Us* (4–6). Illus. by Ruth Sanderson. 1981, Dial $8.95; LB $8.89. Gradually, Neva adjusts to moving to a new town.

3735. Anderson, Mary. *Step on a Crack* (6–9). 1978, Atheneum $10.95. Family secrets produce childhood trauma and subsequent maturity in young Sarah.

3736. Angell, Judie. *Dear Lola or How to Build Your Own Family* (4–6). 1980, Bradbury $10.95; Dell paper $1.95. Six children run away from their orphanage and form their own family.

3737. Arthur, Ruth. *Miss Ghost* (4–6). 1979, Atheneum $7.95. Elphie, after suffering a number of rejections, finds solace in talking to Miss Ghost.

3738. Ashley, Bernard. *All My Men* (6–8). 1978, Phillips $10.95. Gradually, Paul adjusts to life in a small town far from his native London.

3739. Baker, Betty. *The Spirit Is Willing* (4–7). 1974, Macmillan $12.95. Carrie, a young precursor of the women's rights movement, performs audacious acts in an Arizona town at the end of the eighteenth century.

3740. Bargar, Gary W. *What Happened to Mr. Forster?* (5–8). 1981, Houghton $8.95. Louis's beloved sixth-grade teacher is fired because he is a homosexual.

3741. Bates, Betty. *Picking Up the Pieces* (6–9). 1981, Holiday $8.95; Pocket paper $1.95. Nell loses her beloved Dexter to Lacey.

3742. Bauer, Marion Dane. *Rain of Fire* (5–8). 1983, Houghton $10.95. Steve makes up stories about his brother's World War II exploits.

3743. Bauer, Marion Dane. *Shelter from the Wind* (5–9). 1976, Houghton $7.95. Twelve-year-old Stacy runs away from home and is taken in by gruff old Ella who teaches her about life.

3744. Beatty, Patricia. *Melinda Takes a Hand* (5–7). 1983, Morrow $9.00. Two sisters find themselves stranded in Guldendale, Colorado.

3745. Benjamin, Carol Lea. *The Wicked Stepdog* (4–7). Illus. 1982, Harper $10.53; LB $10.89. Louise is in the midst of puberty problems and her father's remarriage.

3746. Berger, Fredericka. *Nuisance* (5–7). 1983, Morrow $9.50. When her mother remarries, Julie feels like an unwanted nuisance.

3747. Blades, Ann. *Mary of Mile 18* (2–4). Illus. by author. 1978, Tundra $9.95. Mile 18 is in reality a Mennonite community in Canada, and Mary was a student in the school where the author taught.

3748. Blume, Judy. *Are You There God? It's Me, Margaret* (4–6). 1970, Bradbury $9.95. Eleven-year-old Margaret is the daughter of a Jewish father and a Catholic mother.

3749. Blume, Judy. *Otherwise Known as Sheila the Great* (4–6). 1972, Dutton $9.95; Dell paper $2.50. During a summer in New York, Sheila learns a great deal about herself and how to overcome her feelings of inferiority.

3750. Blume, Judy. *Tales of a Fourth Grade Nothing* (3–4). Illus. by Roy Doty. 1972, Dutton $9.25; Dell paper $2.75. Peter Hatcher's trials and tribulations, most of which are caused by his 2-year-old pesky brother, Fudge. A sequel is: *Superfudge* (1980, $9.95; paper $2.25).

3751. Blume, Judy. *Then Again, Maybe I Won't* (5–7). 1971, Bradbury $9.95; Dell paper $2.50. Thirteen-year-old Tony adjusts with difficulty to his family's move to a home in the affluent suburbs of Long Island, New York.

3752. Blume, Judy. *Tiger Eyes: A Novel* (6–9). 1981, Bradbury $10.95; Dell paper $2.50. Davey must deal with reactions to her father's murder.

3753. Bond, Nancy. *The Best of Enemies* (5–7). 1978, Atheneum $9.95. In Concord, Massachusetts, a lonely girl becomes involved in the Patriot's Day pageant. A sequel is: *A Place to Come Back To* (1984, $12.95).

3754. Bonham, Frank. *Durango Street* (6–9). 1965, Dutton $8.95. A novel of gang warfare in the "jungle" of a big city.

3755. Bonsall, Crosby. *The Goodbye Summer* (4–6). 1978, Greenwillow LB $8.88; Pocket paper $1.95. An exciting summer of making and losing friends is experienced by Allie, the lively spirited heroine of this humorous story.

3756. Branscum, Robbie. *Cheater and Flitter Dick* (5–7). 1983, Viking $10.95. Victims of a tornado move in with Cheater and her adopted sharecropper father.

3757. Branscum, Robbie. *The Saving of P.S.* (5–6). Illus. by Glen Rounds. 1977, Dell paper $1.25. The narrator, Priscilla Sue, is a preacher's daughter who must adjust to her father's courting of a pretty widow.

3758. Branscum, Robbie. *Spud Tackett and the Angel of Doom* (5–7). 1983, Viking $11.50. A young mountain boy is convinced by a preacher that the world is coming to an end.

3759. Brenner, Barbara. *A Year in the Life of Rosie Bernard* (4–6). Illus. by Joan Sandin. 1971, Harper $10.89; Avon paper $1.50. Set in Brooklyn during the Great Depression, this is the story of Rosie's adjustment to living with her dead mother's family, attending a new school, and accepting her father's girlfriend.

3760. Brink, Carol. *Bad Times of Irma Baumlein* (4–6). 1972, Macmillan $11.95; paper $3.95. In order to become popular, Irma resorts to lying and stealing.

3761. Buck, Pearl. *The Big Wave* (4–8). 1973, Scholastic paper $1.95. The loss of family and home in a tidal wave reveals the courage of a little Japanese boy.

3762. Bulla, Clyde Robert. *Almost a Hero* (5–8). Illus. by Ben Stahl. 1981, Dutton $9.75. A homeless boy in a boarding school faces his problems.

3763. Bulla, Clyde Robert. *Shoeshine Girl* (3–5). Illus. by Leigh Grant. 1975, Harper $9.57. A somewhat indolent 10-year-old girl matures during a summer working for Al at his shoeshine stand.

3764. Burch, Robert. *D. J.'s Worst Enemy* (4–6). Illus. by Emil Weiss. 1965, Viking $8.95. D.J., growing up in the Depression-poor rural South, discovers by his thoughtless actions that he is his own worst enemy.

3765. Burch, Robert. *Queenie Peavy* (4–7). Illus. by Jerry Lazare. 1966, Viking $9.95. A defiant 13-year-old rescues her future from reform school in a Georgia town of the 1930s.

3766. Byars, Betsy. *After the Goat Man* (5–7). Illus. by Ronald Himler. 1974, Viking $10.95; Penguin paper $2.95. The effects on a number of people of an old man's vehement refusal to sell his home for the building of a superhighway are explored in this convincing novel.

3767. Byars, Betsy. *The Cartoonist* (4–6). Illus. by Richard Cuffari. 1978, Viking $9.95; Dell paper $2.25. Alfie's refuge in his attic room with his cartoons is disrupted by his brother's return.

3768. Byars, Betsy. *Goodbye, Chicken Little* (4–6). 1979, Harper $10.53; LB $10.89; Scholastic paper $1.95. Jennie learns to accept the senseless death of a beloved uncle.

3769. Byars, Betsy. *The House of Wings* (4–6). Illus. by Daniel Schwartz. 1972, Viking $10.95; Penguin paper $2.95. Sammy is distraught when he is left alone with his grandfather, but things get better when a wounded crane is found and must be taken care of.

3770. Byars, Betsy. *The Night Swimmers* (5–6). Illus. by Troy Howell. 1980, Delacorte $9.95; LB $9.89; Dell paper $2.25. An enterprising girl tries to be a housekeeper and to take care of her 2 brothers.

3771. Calhoun, Mary. *The Horse Comes First* (4–6). Illus. by John Gretzer. 1974, Atheneum $6.95. City-raised Randa has trouble adjusting to a summer on her grandfather's Iowa farm.

3772. Calvert, Patricia. *The Stone Pony* (5–8). 1982, Scribners $10.95. Jo Beth seems unable to cope with the death of her older sister.

3773. Cameron, Eleanor. *Julia and the Hand of God* (4–6). Illus. by Gail Owens. 1977, Dutton $9.95. Eleven-year-old Julia, a fledgling writer, is growing up in grandma's crowded apartment in the Berkeley of 1923. Others in the series: *A Room Made of Windows* (1971); *That Julia Redfern* (1982); *Julia's Magic* (1984) (all $10.95).

3774. Cameron, Eleanor. *To the Green Mountains* (5–8). 1975, Dutton $9.95. Thirteen-year-old Kath views a number of adult problems with amazing understanding as she grows up in a small midwestern town where her mother runs a hotel.

3775. Carlson, Dale. *Charlie the Hero* (4–6). 1983, Dutton $8.95. Will 11-year-old Charlie Collins become the hero he desires to be?

3776. Cavanna, Betty. *Going on Sixteen* (6–9). 1946, Westminster $8.95. The problems of a motherless girl's adolescence.

3777. Chambers, John W. *Footlight Summer* (6–9). 1983, Atheneum $10.95. Chris and Sherry join a summer theater as apprentices.

3778. Child Study Association, comp. *Courage to Adventure: Stories of Boys and Girls Growing Up in America* (4–6). Illus. by Reisie Lonette. 1976, Harper $10.53. This anthology, culled chiefly from full-length novels, covers growing up in America from the Revolution to the present.

3779. Childress, Alice. *A Hero Ain't Nothin' But a Sandwich* (6–9). 1973, Putnam $8.95; Avon paper $2.25. Told by various narratives, this is the story of a young Harlem boy, Benjie, and his encounter with drugs. For mature readers.

3780. Clark, Ann Nolan. *To Stand against the Wind* (5–7). 1978, Viking $11.50. A young Vietnamese boy changes his outlook when he leaves his war-torn country for the United States.

3781. Clarke, Joan. *Early Rising* (5–8). 1976, Harper $9.95. Adoring Erica discovers the imperfections in her older half-sister, in this novel set in an English vicarage of the 1880s.

3782. Cleary, Beverly. *Dear Mr. Henshaw* (4–7). Illus. by Paul O. Zelinsky. 1983, Morrow $8.00; LB $7.63; Dell paper $2.50. A Newbery Award winner about a boy who pours out his problems in letters to a writer he greatly admires.

3783. Cleaver, Vera, and Cleaver, Bill. *Dust of the Earth* (6–9). 1975, Harper $10.95. A first-person novel about a 14-year-old growing up in a large, poor family eking out a living as sheep ranchers in the Badlands of South Dakota.

3784. Cleaver, Vera, and Cleaver, Bill. *Ellen Grae* (6–8). Illus. by Ellen Raskin. 1967, NAL paper $1.95. Eleven-year-old Ellen, locally noted for her very amusing tall tales, tries one dramatically painful venture into straight reporting and learns that the truth can be rejected when it is something that adults don't want to believe.

3785. Cleaver, Vera, and Cleaver, Bill. *Grover* (4–7). Illus. by Frederic Marvin. 1970, NAL paper $1.75. After his mother's suicide and his father's resultant breakdown, 10-year-old Grover must face the hard reality of death and trouble.

3786. Cleaver, Vera, and Cleaver, Bill. *Hazel Rye* (6–8). 1983, Harper $11.06; LB $11.89. A young loner meets a couple who changes her life.

3787. Clifford, Eth. *The Rocking Chair Rebellion* (5–7). 1978, Houghton $8.95. Opie, age fourteen, helps some oldsters in an old people's home.

3788. Cohen, Barbara. *Queen for a Day* (5–7). 1981, Lothrop $11.25; LB $11.89. A new boarder helps Gertie lose some of her loneliness.

3789. Cohen, Miriam. *Born to Dance Samba* (4–6). Illus. by Gioia Fiammenghi. 1984, Harper $10.53; LB $10.89. Mario Antonia, who loves to samba, prepares for the annual carnival in Rio.

3790. Colman, Hila. *Confession of a Storyteller* (6–8). 1981, Crown $8.95; Pocket paper $1.95. Annie's crush on her music teacher almost leads to the teacher's destruction.

3791. Colman, Hila. *Diary of a Frantic Kid Sister* (4–6). 1973, Pocket paper $1.95. Sarah has trouble communicating with her family, so she pours out her soul to her diary.

3792. Cone, Molly. *Dance around the Fire* (4–6). Illus. by Marvin Friedman. 1974, Houghton $5.95. Joanne faces problems concerning her commitment to her Jewish religion. Also use: *A Promise Is a Promise* (1964, Houghton $8.95).

3793. Conford, Ellen. *Anything for a Friend* (5–7). 1979, Little $7.95; Pocket paper $1.95. A young girl tries various schemes to make new friends.

3794. Conford, Ellen. *Dreams of Victory* (4–6). Illus. by Gail Rockwell. 1973, Little $8.95; Scholastic paper $1.95. Although Vicky is a shy social misfit, in her fantasies she conquers all.

3795. Conford, Ellen. *Hail, Hail Camp Timberwood* (5–7). Illus. by Gail Owens. 1978, Little $8.95; Pocket paper $1.95. Thirteen-year-old Melanie's first summer at camp.

3796. Conford, Ellen. *If This Is Love, I'll Take Spaghetti* (6–9). 1983, Four Winds $8.95; Scholastic paper $2.25. Nine stories about girls and love problems.

3797. Coolidge, Susan. *What Katy Did* (4–6). 1983, Penguin paper $2.25. Tomboy Katy Carr overcomes a tragic accident in this classic story.

3798. Corcoran, Barbara. *Cabin in the Sky* (6–9). 1976, Atheneum $7.95. New York show biz of the 1950s is the background for this story of a young man from Maine who comes to the big city for a life in the theater.

3799. Corcoran, Barbara. *Make No Sound* (5–7). 1977, Atheneum $6.95. Melody must overcome guilt when, after wishing her older brother harm, he has a serious accident.

3800. Cresswell, Helen. *Dear Shrink* (5–8). 1982, Macmillan $9.95. Three English youngsters are left alone when their parents go on a scientific expedition.

3801. Cunningham, Julia. *Come to the Edge* (5–7). 1977, Avon paper $1.95. An unwanted and cruelly treated young boy eventually finds a home with a kindly sign painter.

3802. Cunningham, Julia. *Dorp Dead* (6–8). Illus. by James J. Spanfeller. 1965, Pantheon LB $6.99; Avon paper $2.25. An orphan is sent away to live with a fanatically meticulous and psychotic carpenter.

3803. Cunningham, Julia. *Flight of the Sparrow* (5–7). 1980, Pantheon $6.95; LB $6.99; Avon paper $1.95. A street waif in Paris steals a picture to save her friend.

3804. Dalgliesh, Alice. *The Bears on Hemlock Mountain* (1–4). Illus. by Helen Sewell. 1952, Scribners paper $2.95. Jonathan ventured over the mountain by himself after dark and discovered the reality of bear existence!

3805. DeClements, Barthe. *How Do You Lose Those Ninth Grade Blues?* (6–9). 1983, Viking $10.55. Elsie thinks she is unloved and unlovable.

3806. Donnelly, Elfie. *So Long, Grandpa* (4–6). Trans. from German by Anthea Bell. 1981, Crown $8.95. Michael must face the fact that his beloved grandfather is dying.

3807. Donovan, John. *Wild in the World* (6–9). 1971, Harper $11.89. After the death of the rest of his family, John Gridley befriends a wolf-dog who remains faithful even after John's death.

3808. Edwards, Page. *Scarface Joe* (6–8). 1984, Scholastic $9.95. While spending a summer in Colorado, a young boy has his first deep feelings for a girl.

3809. Everden, Margery. *The Kite Song* (6–7). 1984, Lothrop $10.00. Jamie is helped by a cousin and a friendly teacher to gain some confidence.

3810. Fairless, Caroline. *Hambone* (3–6). Illus. by Wendy Edelson. 1980, Tundra $8.95. When Jeremy's pig Hambone is slaughtered, he plans a suitable memorial.

3811. Farmer, Penelope. *August the Fourth* (3–6). Illus. by Jael Jordan. 1976, Houghton $5.95; LB $4.77. The effects of World War I on a teenage English girl are described well.

3812. Fisher, Lois I. *Wretched Robert* (3–6). 1982, Dodd LB $7.95. Robert, living with a newly divorced mother, is not as happy as he appears.

3813. Fox, Paula. *Blowfish Live in the Sea* (6–9). 1970, Bradbury $8.95; Scholastic paper $1.95. A touching novel about a boy's reconciliation with his father.

3814. Fox, Paula. *Portrait of Ivan* (5–7). Illus. by Saul Lambert. 1969, Bradbury $8.95. Ivan's world, heretofore austere and numbed, expands while his portrait is painted, to one with the promise of wholeness and hope; a compelling story.

3815. Gauch, Patricia Lee. *Night Talks* (6–9). 1983, Putnam $10.95. Three friends find they are bunkmates at summer camp with a difficult girl.

3816. George, Jean Craighead. *Julie of the Wolves* (5–8). Illus. by John Schoenherr. 1972, Harper $9.59; LB $10.89; paper $1.95. Julie (Eskimo name, Miyax) begins a trek across frozen Alaska and is saved only by the friendship of a pack of wolves. Newbery Award winner.

3817. George, Jean Craighead. *The Summer of the Falcon* (5–8). 1962, Harper paper $2.95. June learns to take responsibility and discipline when she trains her own falcons.

3818. Giff, Patricia Reilly. *The Gift of the Pirate Queen* (4–6). Illus. by Jenny Rutherford. 1982, Delacorte $9.95; LB $9.89; Dell paper $2.25. Grace is looking forward to the arrival of Fiona from Ireland to take care of her family.

3819. Gilson, Jamie. *Do Bananas Chew Gum?* (4–6). 1980, Lothrop $10.00; LB $10.88; Pocket paper $1.95. Sam still can't read, and he is in the sixth grade.

3820. Gipson, Fred. *Little Arliss* (4–5). Illus. by Ronald Himler. 1978, Harper LB $9.89; paper $1.95. Arliss proves his worth even though he is small.

3821. Glaser, Dianne. *The Diary of Trilby Frost* (6–8). 1976, Holiday $9.95. Two turbulent and frequently tragic years in the life of a teenager growing up in turn-of-the-century rural America.

3822. Greene, Bette. *Summer of My German Soldier* (6–9). 1973, Dial $9.95. In a small southern town during World War II, Patty's life gains meaning when she harbors an escaped German soldier. The sequel: *Morning Is a Long Time Coming* (1978, $10.95; Pocket paper $1.95).

3823. Greene, Constance C. *Beat the Turtle Drum* (4–6). Illus. by Donna Diamond. 1976, Viking $11.50; Dell paper $1.75. A young girl must adjust to the accidental death of her beloved younger sister.

3824. Greenwald, Sheila. *The Secret in Miranda's Closet* (3–5). Illus. by author. 1977, Houghton $6.95. Young Miranda hides the fact from her divorced mother, a feminist, that her favorite toy is a doll.

3825. Greenwald, Sheila. *Will the Real Gertrude Hollings Please Stand Up?* (4–6). 1983, Little $10.95. Gertrude has a learning disability, and her aunt, with whom she is living, doesn't understand.

3826. Hall, Lynn. *Flowers of Anger* (5–7). Illus. by Joseph Cellini. 1976, Avon paper $1.95. In spite of protests, Ann plans an act of revenge after a neighbor shoots her horse for trespassing on his land.

3827. Hamilton, Virginia. *Arilla Sun Down* (5–7). 1976, Greenwillow $12.25; LB $11.76. A girl with a dual inheritance—part Black, part American Indian—faces problems in maturing.

3828. Hamilton, Virginia. *Zeely* (4–6). Illus. by Symeon Shimin. 1967, Macmillan $9.95. An 11-year-old black city girl is lightly guided from her daydreams to reality by Zeely, who is as kind as she is tall and beautiful.

3829. Hassler, Jon. *Four Miles to Pinecone* (6–9). 1977, Warne $6.95. Tom faces the dilemma of reporting to the police 2 people—one a good friend—who are guilty of theft.

3830. Haugen, Tormod. *The Night Birds* (2–5). 1982, Delacorte $9.95; LB $9.89. Seven-year-old Jake learns to conquer some of his fears.

3831. Henkes, Kevin. *Return to Sender* (3–5). Illus. by author. 1984, Greenwillow $9.00; LB $8.59. Whitaker writes to his hero Frogman, but it is answered by a mail carrier.

3832. Hentoff, Nat. *Jazz Country* (6–9). 1965, Harper $10.89; paper $2.25. A portrayal of the black jazz world, as seen through the eyes of a teenage white boy whose deepest desire is to be a great trumpet player.

3833. Hermes, Patricia. *Nobody's Fault?* (4–7). 1981, Harcourt $8.95; Dell paper $1.75. Mouse dies and younger sister Emily must adjust.

3834. Hickman, Janet. *The Stones* (5–6). Illus. by Richard Cuffari. 1976, Macmillan $8.95. In a small midwestern town during World War II, a group of boys unjustly persecutes an old German-American man. A sequel is: *The Thunder-Pup* (1981, $8.95).

3835. Hinton, Nigel. *Collision Course* (6–9). 1977, Lodestar $7.95. Ray's joyride on a stolen motorcycle ends in the death of an old woman.

3836. Holl, Kristi D. *Footprints up My Back* (5–7). 1984, Atheneum $10.95. Jean feels that her good nature is being taken advantage of.

3837. Holland, Isabelle. *Abbie's God Book* (4–6). Illus. by James McLaughlin. 1982, Westminster $7.95. The thoughts of a 12-year-old girl and her ideas about God.

3838. Holland, Isabelle. *God, Mrs. Muskrat and Aunt Dot* (3–6). Illus. by Beth Krush and Joe Krush. 1983, Westminster $10.00. Orphaned Rebecca Jones has many problems to overcome.

3839. Holland, Isabelle. *The Man without a Face* (6–9). 1972, Harper $11.96; Dell paper $1.75. Charles seeks Justin McLeod to be his tutor and becomes involved in a close and disturbing relationship.

3840. Howe, James. *A Night without Stars* (5–7). 1983, Atheneum $10.95. A novel about a young girl's hospitalization and serious operation.

3841. Hughes, Dean. *Millie Willenheimer and the Chestnut Corporation* (5–7). 1983, Atheneum $9.95. Millie forms her own business to make some money.

3842. Hughes, Monica. *Hunter in the Dark* (6–9). 1983, Atheneum $9.95. Sixteen-year-old Mick's long hunt for a whitetail buck and his growing-up process.

3843. Hunt, Irene. *Lottery Rose* (6–8). 1976, Scribners $11.95; Ace paper $1.95. Georgie is beaten and cruelly treated by his mother until finally the police rescue him.

3844. Hunt, Irene. *No Promises in the Wind* (5–8). 1981, Ace paper $2.25. During the Great Depression, Josh Grondowski is forced to make his own way in life.

3845. Hunt, Irene. *Up a Road Slowly* (6–9). 1966, Modern Curriculum $4.95; LB $4.98; Ace paper $2.25. Julie goes to live with Aunt Cordelia after her mother's death and finds the adjustment very difficult. Newbery Award winner.

3846. Hurwitz, Johanna. *Once I Was a Plum Tree* (4–5). Illus. by Ingrid Fetz. 1980, Morrow $9.25; LB $8.88. In spite of her parents' indifference, Geraldine becomes aware of her Jewish inheritance.

3847. Irwin, Hadley. *The Lilith Summer* (6–8). 1979, Feminist Pr. $8.95. Twelve-year-old Ellen learns about old age when she "lady sits" with 77-year-old Lilith Adams.

3848. Johnson, Emily R. *Spring and the Shadow Man* (4–6). Illus. by Paul Geiger. 1984, Dodd $9.95. Spring Weldon tries to change her ways when she moves to a new town.

3849. Jones, Penelope. *The Stealing Thing* (4–6). 1983, Bradbury $10.95. Hope's loneliness causes her to steal.

3850. Kidd, Ronald. *Who Is Felix the Great?* (6–9). 1983, Lodestar $10.63. Tim looks up a retired baseball great and encounters disillusionment.

3851. Kingman, Lee. *Break a Leg, Betsy Maybe!* (6–9). 1979, Dell $1.75. Betsy's seventeenth year, in which she falls in love, becomes an actress, and adjusts to a new home.

3852. Kirk, Barbara. *Grandpa, Me and Our House in the Tree* (3–5). Illus. 1978, Macmillan $9.95. The friendship of a boy and his grandfather during the old man's last illness.

3853. Knowles, Anne. *The Halcyon Island* (5–7). 1981, Harper $9.57. Ken tries to conquer his fear of water and other personal problems.

3854. Koff, Richard M. *Christopher* (4–8). Illus. by Barbara Reinertson. 1981, Celestrial Arts $8.95; paper $2.25. A man named Headmaster helps a young boy mature.

3855. Konigsburg, E. L. *Altogether, One at a Time* (4–6). Illus. by Gail E. Haley. 1971, Atheneum LB $7.95; paper $1.25. Four short stories by the Newbery Award-winning writer, each of which explores the theme that compromise is often necessary to appreciate life fully.

3856. Konigsburg, E. L. *Throwing Shadows* (6–9). 1979, Atheneum $9.95; paper $2.95. Five stories that explore the inner character of some interesting young people.

3857. Krumgold, Joseph. *Onion John* (5–8). Illus. by Symeon Shimin. 1959, Harper $12.45; paper $3.80. A Newbery Award winner about a boy's friendship with an old man. Also use the Newbery Award winner: *And Now Miguel* (1953, Harper $12.45; paper $3.80).

3858. Kullman, Harry. *The Battle Horse* (6–8). Trans. from Swedish by George Blecher and Lone Thygesen-Bleeher. 1981, Bradbury $9.95. A symbolic novel about a game where rich kids use their poor counterparts as horses.

3859. Lee, Mildred. *The Rock and the Willow* (6–9). 1963, Lothrop $10.75. A realistic portrayal of a teenager growing up in rural Alabama in 1930, the oldest of a large family, who dreams of becoming a teacher and writer.

3860. Lee, Mildred. *Sycamore Year* (6–8). 1974, Lothrop $11.25; LB $9.55. Fourteen-year-old Wren must make many adjustments during her first year in Sycamore, including coping with her sister's pregnancy.

3861. Levoy, Myron. *Alan and Naomi* (6–9). 1977, Harper $9.57; LB $10.89. A young boy in New York City helps a girl traumatized by Nazi brutality.

3862. Levy, Elizabeth. *Come Out Smiling* (6–8). 1981, Delacorte $8.95. Jenny finds that her favorite counselor at summer camp is gay.

3863. Levy, Elizabeth. *The Computer That Said Steal Me* (5–7). 1983, Scholastic $8.95. Adam steals a computer to keep up with his wealthy friends.

3864. Levy, Elizabeth. *Lizzie Lies a Lot* (4–6). Illus. by John Wallner. 1976, Delacorte $6.95; LB $6.46; Dell paper $2.50. Nine-year-old Lizzie is helped to stop lying by her friend Sara.

3865. Lifton, Betty Jean. *I'm Still Me* (6–8). 1981, Knopf $9.95; LB $9.99. A project in genealogy brings a feeling of self-knowledge to a girl.

3866. Lindgren, Astrid. *Lotta on Troublemaker Street* (3–5). Illus. by Julie Brinckloe. 1984, Macmillan $9.95. Lotta runs away to a neighbor's house but in time returns home.

3867. Lorentzen, Karin. *Lanky Longlegs* (3–6). Illus. by Jan Ormerod. 1983, Atheneum $9.95. Di must reconcile herself to the illness and death of her brother.

3868. Lowry, Lois. *A Summer to Die* (6–8). Illus. by Jenni Oliver. 1977, Houghton $10.95; Bantam paper $2.25. Meg's hostility toward her sister Molly turns to guilt and bewilderment when she learns Molly has a fatal disease.

3869. McCord, Jean. *Turkeylegs Thompson* (6–8). 1979, Atheneum $8.95. A young girl begins life again after a tragic summer.

3870. McGraw, Eloise. *Hideaway* (6–8). 1983, Atheneum $10.95. Disillusioned with his divorced parents, Jerry sets out on his own.

3871. MacLachlan, Patricia. *Unclaimed Treasures* (5–8). 1984, Harper $10.53; LB $10.89. A romantic story of a young girl finding herself.

3872. McLendon, Gloria H. *My Brother Joey Died* (4–6). Illus. 1982, Messner LB $9.29. A photo-essay in fictional form about a death in a family as seen through a girl's eyes.

3873. Major, Kevin. *Hold Fast* (6–8). 1980, Delacorte $9.95; Dell paper $1.75. An orphaned 14-year-old boy in Newfoundland flees from an overbearing uncle.

3874. Manes, Stephen. *Slim Down Camp* (5–7). 1981, Houghton $8.95. Hostile Sam Zimmer goes to a weight-loss camp.

3875. Mann, Peggy. *There Are Two Kinds of Terrible* (5–7). 1979, Avon paper $1.50. Bob lives through his mother's illness and the anguish of her death from cancer.

3876. Mark, Jan. *Nothing to Be Afraid Of* (6–9). 1982, Harper LB $9.89. Seven short stories involving young people and their problems.

3877. Martin, Ann M. *Bummer Summer* (5–7). 1983, Holiday $10.95. Kammey spends an unusual summer at Camp Arrowhead.

3878. Martin, Guenn. *Remember the Eagle Day* (6–8). 1984, Herald Pr. paper $4.95. In this novel set in Alaska, Melanie must adjust to the death of a family friend, Long Jake.

3879. Mauser, Pat Rhoads. *A Bundle of Sticks* (5–7). Illus. by Gail Owens. 1982, Atheneum LB $10.95. Timid Ben must eventually take on a bully.

3880. Mauser, Pat Rhoads. *How I Found Myself at the Fair* (3–5). Illus. by Emily McCully. 1980, Atheneum $8.95. Laura gets lost at a fair and tries various ways to find her friends.

3881. Mazer, Norma Fox. *A Figure of Speech* (6–9). 1973, Dell paper $1.75. The rejection and death of a beloved grandfather are seen through the sensitive eyes of Jenny.

3882. Miles, Betty. *All It Takes Is Practice* (4–6). 1976, Knopf LB $6.99; Dell paper $1.25. Fifth-grader Stuart and his family are upset when an interracial family comes to town.

3883. Miles, Betty. *Looking On* (6–8). 1978, Knopf $6.95; LB $6.99; Avon paper $1.95. A lonely young girl is befriended by a young couple who move into a nearby trailer.

3884. Miles, Betty. *The Real Me* (4–6). 1974, Knopf $6.99; Avon paper $2.25. Barbara decides to fight injustice when a company refuses to let her take over her brother's newspaper delivery route.

3885. Miles, Betty. *The Trouble with Thirteen.* 1979, Knopf LB $6.99; Avon paper $2.25. Annie's life is disrupted by many changes, including a move to New York City.

3886. Miles, Miska. *Annie and the Old One* (2–5). Illus. by Peter Parnall. 1971, Little $9.95. Annie, a young Navajo girl, realizes her wonderful grandmother is dying and tries to put off the inevitable.

3887. Mills, Claudia. *All the Living* (5–8). 1983, Macmillan $9.95. Karla becomes obsessed with death.

3888. Mills, Claudia. *The Secret Carousel* (5–8). 1983, Scholastic $8.95. Lindy wonders if she should follow her sister to New York City or remain in Three Churches, Iowa.

3889. Montgomery, L. M. *Anne of Green Gables* (5–8). Illus. by Jody Lee. 1983, Grosset $9.95; Bantam paper $2.95. The old-fashioned story of an orphan girl and her adventures. Others in this series are available in paperback from Bantam.

3890. Morgan, Alison. *All Kinds of Prickles* (6–8). 1979, Nelson $7.95. Davy's pet goat is killed by his guardians, and this complicates an adjustment to life without his beloved grandfather. A sequel is: *Paul's Kite* (1982, Atheneum $8.95).

3891. Morgan, Alison. *A Boy Called Fish* (6–9). 1973, Harper paper $1.25. A lonely boy takes in a stray dog in this story set in Wales.

3892. Myers, Walter Dean. *Won't Know Till I Get There* (6–9). 1982, Viking $10.95. For better readers, the story of a 14-year-old boy, a new arrival in his home, and his summer working in an old-folks home.

3893. Naylor, Phyllis Reynolds. *Eddie, Incorporated* (4–6). Illus. by Blanche Sims. 1980, Atheneum $9.95. After many tries, a sixth grader finally finds a way to make money.

3894. Naylor, Phyllis Reynolds. *Night Cry* (5–8). 1984, Atheneum $10.95. A 13-year-old Mississippi girl lives alone in the backwoods.

3895. Naylor, Phyllis Reynolds. *A String of Chances* (6–9). 1982, Atheneum $11.95. Evie's sixteenth birthday is one of tragedy and personal growth.

3896. Newton, Suzanne. *M. V. Sexton Speaking: A Novel* (6–9). 1981, Viking $9.95; Fawcett paper $2.25. Orphan Martha Venable takes a job with a local baker.

3897. Oldham, Mary. *The White Pony* (5–7). 1981, Hastings $8.95. Overweight Barbara has a friend in a colt, named Bianco.

3898. Oneal, Zibby. *The Language of Goldfish* (6–8). 1980, Viking $11.50. A novel for better readers of the approaching adolescence of the 13-year-old girl.

3899. Orgel, Doris. *The Mulberry Music* (4–6). Illus. by Dale Payson. 1971, Harper paper $1.95. A moving story of a young girl's difficult adjustment to the death of her beloved grandma.

3900. Osborne, Mary Pope. *Run, Run, As Fast As You Can* (5–7). 1982, Dial $12.95; LB $12.89; Scholastic paper $1.95. Haillie must adjust to a painful rebuff from classmates and the imminent death of her brother.

3901. Pascal, Francine. *My First Love and Other Disasters* (6–8). 1979, Viking $8.95; Dell paper $1.75. First love is encountered in Victoria's summer at the beach.

3902. Paterson, Katherine. *The Great Gilly Hopkins* (4–6). 1978, Harper $9.57; LB $9.89; Avon paper $2.25. Precocious Gilly bounces from one foster home to another.

3903. Paulsen, Gary. *Tracker* (6–9). 1984, Macmillan $9.95. John goes hunting for deer alone because his grandfather, who usually accompanies him, is dying.

3904. Perl, Lila. *Don't Ask Miranda* (5–7). 1979, Houghton $7.95; Dell paper $1.50. Miranda faces many adjustment problems when she moves to a new neighborhood.

3905. Rabe, Berniece. *The Girl Who Had No Name* (6–8). 1977, Dutton $9.95. Girlie is shunted from one home to another because of her father's guilt, in this touching novel set in Depression-time Missouri.

3906. Roberts, Willo Davis. *Don't Hurt Laurie!* (4–6). Illus. by Ruth Sanderson. 1977, Atheneum $9.95; paper $2.95. Seen from the viewpoint of 11-year-old Laurie, this is a harrowing story of child abuse.

3907. Sachs, Marilyn. *A December Tale* (5–7). 1976, Doubleday $7.95. Myra decides to save herself and her younger brother from the constant abuse they receive in their foster home.

3908. Sachs, Marilyn. *A Summer's Lease* (6–9). 1979, Dutton $9.25; Dell paper $1.75. A strong-willed egocentric girl learns to pity and love during a summer when she works at the home of her English teacher.

3909. Shecter, Ben. *Someplace Else* (4–6). 1971, Harper $8.89. Eleven-year-old Arnie has to cope with such problems of growing up as preparing for a bar mitzvah, the loss of a pet, and unwanted attentions from a female admirer.

3910. Shyer, Marlene Fanta. *My Brother, the Thief* (5–7). 1980, Scribners $10.95. A young girl is caught up in her brother's habit of stealing.

3911. Simon, Marcia L. *A Special Gift* (5–7). 1978, Harcourt $6.95. Peter keeps his ballet classes a secret.

3912. Smith, Doris Buchanan. *A Taste of Blackberries* (4–6). Illus. by Charles Robinson. 1973, Harper LB $10.89; Scholastic paper $1.95. Young Jamie dies unexpectedly of a bee sting, and his friends adjust to this loss.

3913. Sorensen, Virginia. *Plain Girl* (4–6). Illus. by Charles Geer. 1955, Harcourt paper $2.95. An Amish girl finds it difficult to accept both her cultural heritage and the world around her.

3914. Stewart, A. C. *Dark Dove* (6–9). 1974, Phillips $10.95. Roddy's constant quarreling with his father leads to his leaving his Scottish home to become a sailor.

3915. Stewart, A. C. *Ossian House* (6–8). 1976, Phillips $10.95. Eleven-year-old John Murray inherits the ancestral home in Scotland and must live there 8 weeks of each year.

3916. Stolz, Mary. *By the Highway Home* (6–9). 1971, Harper $12.95; LB $12.89. Cathy's family moves to Vermont, and there she finds a new life and is able to adjust to her brother's death in Vietnam.

3917. Stolz, Mary. *Ferris Wheel* (4–7). 1977, Harper LB $10.89; paper $1.95. Polly suffers the pangs of preadolescent worries and concerns in this realistic novel set in a small Vermont town.

3918. Valencak, Hannelore. *A Tangled Web* (5–7). Trans. from the German by Patricia Crampton. 1978, Morrow $9.75; LB $9.36. Annie's lies get her into trouble, particularly with an overbearing schoolmate.

3919. Wagner, Jane. *J.T.* (4–6). Photos by Gordon Parks. 1969, Dell paper $2.25. J. T. Gamble lives in Harlem, and his most prized possessions are a tiny portable radio and a stray cat, for whom he has made a home.

3920. Wojciechowska, Maia. *Shadow of a Bull* (5–7). Illus. by Alvin Smith. 1964, Atheneum $10.95. Manolo, surviving son of a great bullfighter, has his own "moment of truth" when he faces his first bull. Newbery Award winner, 1965.

3921. Wolitzer, Hilma. *Toby Lived Here* (5–7). 1978, Farrar $8.95. Two sisters adjust in different ways to a foster home.

3922. Young, Miriam. *Truth and Consequences* (4–6). Illus. by Diane de Groat. 1975, Scholastic paper $1.50. Kim Jones faces unexpected consequences when she makes a vow always to tell the truth.

3923. Zolotow, Charlotte, comp. *An Overpraised Season: 10 Stories of Youth* (6–9). 1973, Harper LB $9.89. Problems of adolescents, particularly relating to adults, are explored in 10 short stories by such authors as Updike, Vonnegut, and Lessing.

Physical and Emotional Problems

3924. Adler, Carole S. *The Shell Lady's Daughter* (6–9). 1983, Putnam $10.95. Kelly's mother has a nervous breakdown and attempts suicide.

3925. Albert, Louise. *But I'm Ready to Go* (6–9). 1976, Bradbury $9.95. In spite of a learning disability, Judy gallantly strikes out on her own to find fame in New York City.

3926. Baldwin, Anne Norris. *A Little Time* (4–6). 1978, Viking $8.95. Ten-year-old Sarah tells about her 4-year-old brother who has Down's syndrome.

3927. Blue, Rose. *Me and Einstein: Breaking through the Reading Barrier* (4–6). Illus. by Peggy Luks. 1979, Human Sciences $10.95; paper $5.95. Bobby, a dyslexic youngster, tries to hide the fact that he can't read.

3928. Blume, Judy. *Blubber* (4–6). 1974, Bradbury $9.95. Jill finds out what it's like to be an outsider when she defends Linda, a classmate who is teased because of her obesity.

3929. Blume, Judy. *Deenie* (5–7). 1974, Bradbury $9.95; Dell paper $2.25. Instead of becoming a model, as her mother wishes, Deenie must cope with sclerosis and wearing a spinal brace.

3930. Bottner, Barbara. *Dumb Old Casey Is a Fat Tree* (2–4). Illus. by author. 1979, Harper LB $9.89. In spite of her weight, Casey still hopes to be a ballet dancer.

3931. Branscum, Robbie. *For Love of Jody* (6–8). Illus. by Allen Davis. 1979, Lothrop $10.95; LB $10.08. Francie, growing up in a poor family, finds it difficult to accept her mentally retarded sister.

3932. Bridgers, Sue Ellen. *All Together Now* (5–7). 1979, Knopf LB $7.99. Twelve-year-old Casey forms a strong friendship with a 30-year-old retarded man.

3933. Byars, Betsy. *The Summer of the Swans* (5–7). Illus. by Ted Coconis. 1970, Viking $10.95; Penguin paper $3.95. The story of a 14-year-old named Sara—moody, unpredictable, and on the brink of womanhood—and how her life changes when her younger, mentally retarded brother disappears. Newbery Award winner, 1971.

3934. Byars, Betsy. *The TV Kid* (3–4). Illus. by Richard Cuffari. 1976, Viking $9.95. In his loneliness, a young boy escapes into the world of television watching and soon has difficulty distinguishing fact from fancy.

3935. Cleaver, Vera, and Cleaver, Bill. *Me Too* (5–7). 1973, Harper $10.95; NAL paper $2.50. Lydia secretly decides to help her twin sister Lorna, who is retarded.

3936. Clifton, Lucille. *My Friend Jacob* (K–3). Illus. by Thomas Di Grazia. 1980, Dutton $9.95. A story of the friendship between 8-year-old Sam and a gentle mentally retarded teenager.

3937. Cohen, Barbara. *My Name Is Rosie* (4–6). 1978, Lothrop $10.95; LB $10.51. Rosie Gold escapes her unhappy life through fantasy.

3938. Cookson, Catherine. *Go Tell It to Mrs. Golightly* (4–6). 1980, Lothrop $10.95; LB $10.50. Nine-year-old Bella, blind and orphaned, comes to her grandfather's home.

3939. Corcoran, Barbara. *Child of the Morning* (6–9). 1982, Atheneum LB $11.95. Susan, who is working with a theatre company, finds she has epilepsy.

3940. Corcoran, Barbara. *A Dance to Still Music* (6–9). Illus. by Charles Robinson. 1974, Atheneum $9.95; paper $1.95. Threatened by her mother with attending a special school for the deaf, Margaret runs away and finds unexpected help.

3941. Coutant, Helen. *The Gift* (2–5). Illus. by Vo-Dinh Mai. 1983, Knopf $9.95; LB $9.99. Marie's dear friend, an old lady, returns from the hospital blind.

3942. Cowley, Joy. *The Silent One* (5–8). Illus. by Hermann Greissle. 1981, Knopf LB $8.99. A deaf mute South Sea Islander tames an albino sea turtle.

3943. Cunningham, Julia. *Burnish Me Bright* (4–6). 1980, Dell paper $1.25. An imaginative mute boy named Auguste is scorned by the inhabitants of the French village where he lives. Also use: *The Silent Voice* (1981, Dutton $11.95; Dell paper $2.50).

3944. Dacquino, Vincent T. *Kiss the Candy Days Good-Bye* (6–8). 1982, Delacorte $9.95; Dell paper $2.25. Jimmy finds that he has diabetes.

3945. Eyerly, Jeannette. *The Seeing Summer* (4–6). Illus. by Emily A. McCauley. 1981, Harper $10.10; LB $9.89. Carey's new neighbor turns out to be blind.

3946. Fassler, Joan. *Howie Helps Himself* (2–4). Illus. by Joe Lasker. 1975, Whitman $8.75. Howie adjusts to cerebral palsy and the use of his wheelchair.

3947. Fox, Paula. *The Stone-Faced Boy* (4–7). Illus. by Donald MacKay. 1968, Bradbury $8.85. Gus, a sensitive and timid middle child in a family of 5, learns to mask his feelings and present a "stone face" to the world.

3948. Froehlich, Margaret Walden. *Hide Crawford Quick* (5–8). 1983, Houghton $9.95. The new baby in the Prayther family is deformed.

3949. Garrigue, Sheila. *Between Friends* (5–7). 1978, Bradbury $9.95. Through her friendship with Dedi, Jill learns about retardation and the value of friendship.

3950. Gillham, Bill. *My Brother Barry* (4–5). Illus. by Laszlo Acs. 1982, Andre Deutsch $9.95. Barry is mentally handicapped in this story set in a small British rural community.

3951. Girion, Barbara. *A Handful of Stars* (6–9). 1981, Scribners $11.95; Dell paper $2.25. Julie discovers she has epilepsy.

3952. Gould, Marilyn. *Golden Daffodils* (5–7). 1982, Addison $10.95. James adjusts to her handicapp resulting from cerebral palsy.

3953. Greene, Constance C. *The Ears of Louis* (3–5). Illus. by Nola Langner. 1974, Viking $9.95. Louis at last finds a solution to the social problems caused by having such large ears that people call his "Sugar Bowl."

3954. Hamilton, Virginia. *The Planet of Junior Brown* (6–9). 1971, Macmillan $8.95. Buddy helps his fellow eighth-grade dropout Junior Brown by taking him to his hangout (his planet) and trying to retain Junior's tentative grip on reality.

3955. Harlan, Elizabeth. *Footfalls* (6–9). 1982, Atheneum $11.95. A young girl interested in track is diminished by her father's serious illness.

3956. Heide, Florence Parry. *Growing Anyway Up* (5–7). 1976, Harper $10.53. A seriously disturbed girl is alienated from her mother and finds difficulty adjusting to her new private school.

3957. Heide, Florence Parry. *Secret Dreamer, Secret Dreams* (6–8). 1978, Harper $10.53. A mentally handicapped girl tells her own secret story.

3958. Hermes, Patricia. *What if They Knew?* (4–6). 1980, Harcourt $10.95; Dell paper $2.25. Jeremy has epilepsy and must adjust to living with her grandparents.

3959. Hermes, Patricia. *Who Will Take Care of Me?* (4–6). 1983, Harcourt $10.95. Mark runs away with his mentally handicapped brother.

3960. Herzig, Alison C., and Mali, Jane L. *A Season of Secrets* (5–8). 1982, Little $9.95. Benji's illness is misunderstood until it is correctly diagnosed as epilepsy.

3961. Holland, Isabelle. *Dinah and the Green Fat Kingdom* (5–7). 1978, Harper $11.95; Dell paper $1.95. Twelve-year-old Dinah agonizes over her weight problem.

3962. Howard, Ellen. *Circle of Giving* (5–7). 1984, Atheneum $9.95. In the Los Angeles of the late 1920s, Jeannie and sister Marguerite meet Francie, a girl with cerebral palsy.

3963. Jones, Rebecca C. *Madeline and the Great (Old) Escape Artist* (4–6). 1983, Dutton $9.66. Madeline discovers she has epilepsy and tries to run away to hide her condition.

3964. Kelley, Sally. *Trouble with Explosives* (5–7). 1976, Bradbury $8.95. With the help of many people, Polly overcomes her stuttering.

3965. Kent, Deborah. *Belonging* (6–8). Illus. by Gary Watson. 1978, Dial $7.95; Ace paper $1.95. A blind teenager finds that being different has its compensations.

3966. Knowles, Anne. *Under the Shadow* (5–8). 1983, Harper $9.57; LB $9.89. Cathy becomes friendly with a boy who has muscular dystrophy.

3967. Konigsburg, E. L. *[George]* (6–9). Illus. by author. 1970, Atheneum $8.95; paper $1.25. George lives inside Ben and in times of mental stress emerges as the dark side of Ben's personality.

3968. Lasker, Joe. *He's My Brother* (2–4). Illus. by author. 1974, Whitman $8.75. Family attitudes and their wonderful treatment of their retarded family member, Jamie, is told by his older brother.

3969. Levine, Edna S. *Lisa and Her Soundless World* (3–5). Illus. by Gloria Kamen. 1984, Human Sciences paper $4.95. The plight of a deaf girl is explored in this gripping, realistic story of Lisa and her problems.

3970. Litchfield, Ada B. *A Cane in Her Hand* (2–4). Ed. by Caroline Rubin. Illus. by Eleanor Mill. 1977, Whitman LB $9.75. A partially sighted girl must adjust to using a cane.

3971. Little, Jean. *From Anna* (4–6). Illus. by Joan Sandin. 1972, Harper $10.89; paper $2.95. Anna's family immigrates to Canada to escape Nazi persecution, and this opens up a new world and a wonderful change for the partially sighted girl.

3972. Little, Jean. *Mine for Keeps* (4–6). Illus. by Lewis Parker. 1962, Little $11.45. The exceptionally well-handled story of Sal, a cerebral palsy victim, who must adjust to her family after being in a special school. The sequel, with Sal's younger sister Meg as the heroine, is: *Spring Begins in March* (1966, $7.95).

3973. Little, Jean. *Take Wing* (5–7). Illus. 1968, Little $8.95. Laurel loves her brother James, who is mentally retarded, but it is not until after her mother's absence that his retardation comes to light and his situation is acknowledged by the family.

3974. Martin, Ann M. *Inside Out* (4–6). 1984, Holiday $10.95. Jonno's little brother James is autistic.

3975. Nixon, Joan Lowery. *Casey and the Great Idea* (5–7). Illus. by Amy Rowen. 1980, Scholastic paper $1.95. Casey, fighter for women's rights, tries to get a 65-year-old flight attendant reinstated.

3976. Parker, Richard. *He Is Your Brother* (5–6). 1976, Scholastic paper $1.75. Eleven-year-old Mike gradually learns to accept and help his autistic brother, Orry.

3977. Payne, Sherry Neuwirth. *A Contest* (3–4). Illus. by Jeff Kyle. 1982, Carolrhoda LB $5.95. Mike, wheelchairbound, goes to a regular school.

3978. Perl, Lila. *Me and Fat Glenda* (6–8). 1972, Houghton $10.50; Pocket paper $1.95. The May-berry family faces middle-class snobs when they move to Havenhurst. A sequel is: *Hey, Remember Fat Glenda?* (1981, $10.50; Pocket paper $2.25).

3979. Petroski, Catherine. *The Summer That Lasted Forever* (6–8). 1984, Houghton $11.45. In times of crises, Molly always retreats into thoughts of her dead mother.

3980. Pevsner, Stella. *Keep Stompin Till the Music Stops* (5–7). 1977, Houghton $10.95. Richard, a dyslexic, must also cope with a bossy aunt who wants to send Grandfather to Florida.

3981. Pfeffer, Susan Beth. *Courage Dana* (4–6). Illus. by Jenny Rutherford. 1983, Delacorte $10.95; Dell paper $2.25. After she courageously saves a boy from an accident, Dana wonders if she really is brave.

3982. Pfeffer, Susan Beth. *Just between Us* (4–7). 1980, Delacorte $9.89; Dell paper $1.95. When and when not to keep a secret is a problem Cass faces.

3983. Pfeffer, Susan Beth. *What Do You Do When Your Mouth Won't Open?* (5–7). Illus. by Lorna Tomei. 1981, Delacorte $8.95; LB $8.44; Dell paper $2.25. Reesa is scared stiff of speaking in public.

3984. Phelan, Terry. *The S. S. Valentine* (4–6). 1979, Scholastic $6.95. Though in a wheelchair, Connie is a success in the class play.

3985. Phipson, Joan. *A Tide Flowing* (5–9). 1981, Atheneum $8.95. A motherless lonely boy becomes friends with a quadriplegic girl.

3986. Piowaty, Kim Kennelly. *Don't Look in Her Eyes* (6–8). 1983, Atheneum $10.95. Jason and his young brother Chad are deserted by their mentally ill mother.

3987. Pollock, Penny. *Keeping It Secret* (4–6). Illus. by Donna Diamond. 1982, Putnam $8.95. Mary Lou, nicknamed Wisconsin, feels embarrassment over wearing a hearing aid.

3988. Potter, Marian. *The Shared Room* (4–5). 1976, Morrow $8.95; LB $8.40. Ali copes with the fact that her mother is in a hospital suffering from mental illness.

3989. Provost, Gary, and Levine-Freidus, Gail. *Good If It Goes* (6–8). 1984, Bradbury $10.95. Through a boy's preparation for his Bar Mitzvah, the reader learns a great deal about this occasion.

3990. Radley, Gail. *CF in His Corner* (6–8). 1984, Scholastic $9.95. Jeff's young brother has cystic fibrosis.

3991. Riley, Jocelyn. *Only My Mouth Is Smiling* (6–9). 1982, Morrow $10.75. Merle and her brother watch the painful descent of their mother into insanity. A sequel is: *Crazy Quilt* (1984, $11.50).

3992. Riskind, Mary. *Apple Is My Sign* (5–6). 1981, Houghton $8.95. A deaf and mute boy is sent to a special school in the early 1900s.

3993. Robinson, Nancy K. *Veronica the Show-Off* (3–4). 1983, Scholastic $7.95; paper $1.95. Veronica goes too far in her efforts to make new friends. Also use: *Just Plain Cat* (1983, Scholastic $7.95).

3994. Robinson, Veronica. *David in Silence* (5–7). Illus. by Victor G. Ambrus. 1965, Harper $8.95. A deaf boy encounters varying reactions when he first shares the usual activities of children who can hear in this realistic, revealing story about this disability.

3995. Robison, Nancy. *Ballet Magic* (4–6). Illus. by Karen Loccisano. 1982, Whitman LB $7.50. Stacey is the tallest girl in her class but is still able to excel in ballet.

3996. Roe, Kathy Gibson. *Goodbye, Secret Place* (6–8). 1982, Houghton $7.95. After an absence of one year, a young girl moves back to her old neighborhood.

3997. Roth, David. *River Runaways* (6–9). 1981, Houghton $7.95. Ted and Michael run away from home, but Michael drowns when their canoe capsizes.

3998. Roy, Ron. *Where's Buddy?* (3–5). Illus. by Troy Howell. 1982, Houghton $8.95. Mike must take care of his diabetic brother.

3999. Rubinstein, Robert E. *When Sirens Scream* (6–9). 1981, Dodd LB $7.95. Ned's pro-nuclear energy ideas change after an incident in the plant.

4000. Russ, Lavinia. *Over the Hills and Far Away* (6–9). 1968, Harcourt $5.50. In the Midwest of 1917, Peakie Maston, a spirited, independent-minded adolescent, finds the process of growing up painful. A sequel is: *The April Age* (1975, Atheneum $5.25).

4001. Sachs, Marilyn. *Fourteen* (5–8). 1983, Dutton $9.66. Fourteen-year-old Rebecca faces the problems of adolescence.

4002. Sallis, Susan. *An Open Mind* (6–9). 1978, Harper $8.95; LB $10.53. David learns to get along with a variety of people, including youngsters in a school for special children.

4003. Schwartz, Joel L. *Upchuck Summer* (4–7). Illus. by Bruce Degen. 1982, Delacorte $9.95; LB $9.89; Dell paper $2.25. Richie changes as a result of a summer at camp.

4004. Shreve, Susan. *Family Secrets: Five Very Important Stories* (3–4). Illus. by Richard Cuffari. 1979, Knopf LB $6.99; Dell paper $1.75. Five essaylike ruminations on serious subjects by a young boy named Sammy. A sequel is: *The Bad Dreams of a Good Girl* (1982, $8.95; LB $8.99; Avon paper $2.25).

4005. Shyer, Marlene Fanta. *Adorable Sunday* (5–8). 1983, Scribners $11.95. Thirteen-year-old Sunday becomes a model, and her troubles begin.

4006. Shyer, Marlene Fanta. *Welcome Home, Jellybean* (5–7). 1978, Scribners $9.95. Twelve-year-old Neil encounters a near-tragic situation when his older retarded sister comes home to stay.

4007. Singer, Marilyn. *It Can't Hurt Forever* (5–7). Illus. by Leigh Grant. 1978, Harper LB $10.89; paper $2.95. Ellie survives a harrowing experience as a heart patient in a hospital.

4008. Skorpen, Liesel Moak. *Grace* (5–7). 1984, Harper $11.06; LB $10.89. A young girl reluctantly befriends an old lady who is her neighbor.

4009. Slepian, Jan. *The Alfred Summer* (6–9). 1980, Macmillan $8.95; Scholastic paper $1.95. Four youngsters with various problems construct a boat to use at Coney Island. A sequel is: *Lester's Turn* (1981, LB $8.95).

4010. Slepian, Jan. *The Night of the Bozos* (6–9). 1983, Dutton $10.63. Thirteen-year-old George, older Uncle Hibbie, and Lolly are introduced to the circus world.

4011. Slote, Alfred. *Hang Tough, Paul Mather* (4–7). 1973, Harper $10.95; Avon paper $1.75. Paul recollects from his hospital bed the details of his struggle with leukemia. Told candidly and without sentimentality.

4012. Smith, Anne Warren. *Blue Denim Blues* (6–8). 1982, Atheneum $9.95. Shy Janet Donovan gets a job as a nursery school assistant for the summer.

4013. Smith, Doris Buchanan. *Kelly's Creek* (4–6). Illus. by Alan Tiegreen. 1975, Harper $12.45. Through the help of an older boy, Kelly gains confidence and partially overcomes the effects of the physical handicap that has produced his lack of coordination.

4014. Smith, Doris Buchanan. *Last Was Lloyd* (3–6). 1981, Viking $9.95; Dell paper $1.75. Overprotected Lloyd must learn to be on his own at school. A sequel is: *The First Hard Times* (1983, $9.95).

4015. Smith, Doris Buchanan. *Laura Upside-Down* (6–8). 1984, Viking $11.50. A fine portrait of a young girl facing some problems in growing up.

4016. Smith, Nancy Covert. *The Falling-Apart Winter* (5–7). 1982, Walker $9.95; LB $10.85. A boy must cope with his mother's mental breakdown.

4017. Smith, Robert Kimmel. *Jelly Belly* (4–6). Illus. by Bob Jones. 1982, Dell paper $2.25. A boy is sent to a weight-loss camp by his parents.

4018. Snyder, Carol. *Memo: To Myself When I Have a Teenage Kid* (6–8). 1983, Putnam $10.95. Fourteen-year-old Karen is growing up ungracefully.

4019. Snyder, Zilpha Keatley. *The Witches of Worm* (5–8). Illus. by Alton Raible. 1972, Atheneum paper $2.95. A deeply disturbed girl believes that her selfish and destructive acts are caused by bewitchment.

4020. Sobol, Harriet Langsam. *My Brother Steven Is Retarded* (2–4). Photos by Patricia Agre. 1977, Macmillan $8.95. Eleven-year-old Beth describes candidly and unflinchingly her conflicting emotions about her retarded older brother.

4021. Spence, Eleanor. *The Nothing Place* (5–7). Illus. by Geraldine Spence. 1973, Harper $10.89. Glen, a deaf boy, is insulted when his friends collect money to buy him a hearing aid in this Australian novel.

4022. Spencer, Zane, and Leech, Jay. *Cry of the Wolf* (5–8). 1977, Westminster $7.95. Jim slips into self-pity after an accident that kills his father and leaves him unable to walk.

4023. Spinelli, Jerry. *Space Station Seventh Grade* (5–8). 1982, Little $11.95; Dell paper $2.50. For mature readers, the story of a boy's bout with puberty.

4024. Steele, Mary Q. *The Life (and Death) of Sara Elizabeth Harwood* (5–8). 1980, Greenwillow $10.00; LB $10.88. Sara becomes so disgusted with herself she thinks of suicide.

4025. Sullivan, Mary Ann. *Child of War* (6–8). 1984, Holiday $10.95. The story of a young girl whose life disintegrates in the war in northern Ireland.

4026. Tate, Joan. *Luke's Garden and Gramp: Two Short Novels* (6–8). 1981, Harper LB $8.89. Two short novels—the first tragic, the second hopeful.

4027. Thomas, William E. *The New Boy Is Blind* (3–5). Illus. 1980, Messner LB $7.79. Ricky, a blind and overprotected boy, must make his own way at school.

4028. Tolan, Stephanie S. *The Liberation of Tansy Warner* (6–9). 1980, Scribners $9.95; Dell paper $1.95. When mother deserts the family, Tansy must adjust and find her own identity.

4029. Ure, Jean. *Supermouse* (5–7). Illus. by Ellen Eagle. 1984, Morrow $8.00. An English novel about two sisters, a have and a have-not.

4030. Van Leeuwen, Jean. *Benjy and the Power of Zingies* (3–5). Illus. by Margot Apple. 1982, Dial $9.95; LB $9.89. Benjy is tired of being pushed around by the class bully. A sequel is: *Benjy in Business* (1983, $10.63; LB $10.89).

4031. Vogel, Ilse-Margaret. *Farewell, Aunt Isabelle* (5–7). Illus. by author. 1979, Harper LB $8.89. The twins, Erika and Inge, form a friendship with their mentally ill Aunt Isabelle.

4032. Vogel, Ilse-Margaret. *My Twin Sister Erika* (5–7). Illus. by author. 1976, Harper $8.89. Inge's relations with her identical twin reach a tragic conclusion when Erika dies. A sequel is: *Tikhon* (1984, $10.53; LB $10.89).

4033. Waldorf, Mary. *Jake McGee and His Feet* (3–5). Illus. by Leonard Shortall. 1980, Houghton $5.95. A believable story about a boy who has trouble reading and whose feet always get him into trouble.

4034. Wallace-Brodeur, Ruth. *The Kenton Year* (4–6). 1980, Atheneum $9.95. Mandy grows to accept her father's death after a move to Vermont.

4035. Wallace-Brodeur, Ruth. *One April Vacation* (4–6). 1981, Atheneum $9.95. A girl contemplates the possibility of her own death.

4036. Weik, Mary Hays. *The Jazz Man* (4–6). Illus. by Ann Grifalconi. 1966, Atheneum paper $1.95. The heartrending story of crippled Zeke, who never leaves his Harlem apartment and whose only delight is in watching the jazz man play his piano in a nearby apartment.

4037. Weiman, Eiveen. *It Takes Brains* (5–7). 1982, Atheneum LB $10.95. A bright girl does not succeed in school until she is properly challenged.

4038. Weiman, Eiveen. *Which Way Courage* (5–7). 1981, Atheneum LB $8.95. Courage Kuntzler questions her Amish faith.

4039. Weltner, Linda R. *Beginning to Feel the Magic* (5–7). 1981, Little $8.95. A sixth-grader's concerns about popularity, family problems, and boys are well presented.

4040. Young, Helen. *What Difference Does It Make, Danny?* (4–6). Illus. by Quentin Blake. 1980, Dutton $7.95. The story of a 9-year-old boy who suffers from epilepsy.

Historical Fiction

Africa

4041. Bess, Clayton. *Story for a Black Night* (5–8). 1982, Parnassus $7.95. Smallpox comes to a Liberian village.

4042. Christopher, John. *Dom and Va* (6–8). 1973, Macmillan $7.95. A power struggle between fierce hunters and peaceful farmers, set in the Africa of 5,000 years ago.

4043. Emecheta, Buchi. *The Moonlight Bride* (6–8). 1983, Braziller $7.95; paper $4.95. Two young African girls encounter a python in the forest.

4044. Myers, Walter Dean. *The Legend of Tarik* (6–8). 1981, Viking $9.95; Scholastic paper $1.95. An epic novel for better readers set in medieval North Africa.

4045. Ray, Mary. *The Windows of Elissa* (6–8). 1982, Faber $11.95. A novel that takes place in the beseiged city of Carthage during the third century B.C.

4046. Schlein, Miriam. *I, Tut: The Boy Who Became Pharaoh* (3–5). Illus. by Erik Hilgerdt. 1978, Four Winds $8.95. The story of the young Pharaoh first told by himself and continued after his death by a friend.

Asia

4047. Anderson, Margaret J. *Light in the Mountain* (6–9). 1982, Knopf LB $9.95. A novel about a primitive tribe's conquest of a new land.

4048. Bunting, Eve. *Magic and the Night River* (2–4). Illus. by Allen Say. 1978, Harper $9.57. A boy and his grandfather fish with cormorants on the coast of Japan.

4049. Chrisman, Arthur B. *Shen of the Sea* (4–6). Illus. by Else Hasselriis. 1926, Dutton $13.95. These engaging short stories of Chinese life received the Newbery Award, 1926.

4050. Huynh, Quang Nhuong. *The Land I Lost: Adventures of a Boy in Vietnam* (5–8). Illus. by Vo-Dinh Mai. 1982, Harper $10.10; LB $9.89. The story of a boy's growing up in rural Vietnam before the war.

4051. Lattimore, Eleanor F. *Little Pear* (K–3). Illus. by author. 1968, Harcourt paper $2.95. A young boy growing up in China during the 1920s.

4052. Lewis, Elizabeth Forman. *Young Fu of the Upper Yangtze* (5–8). Illus. by Ed Young. 1973, Holt $9.75. Young Fu must pay back a debt of $5 or face public shame. Newbery Award winner.

4053. Namioka, Lensey. *Valley of the Broken Cherry Trees* (4–6). 1980, Delacorte $8.95. Two sixteenth-century samurai get involved in plots and intrigue.

4054. Paterson, Katherine. *The Master Puppeteer* (6–9). Illus. by Haru Wells. 1976, Harper $10.51; Avon paper $1.95. Feudal Japan is the setting for this story about a young apprentice puppeteer and his search for a mysterious bandit.

4055. Paterson, Katherine. *Of Nightingales That Weep* (6–9). Illus. by Haru Wells. 1974, Harper $10.51; Avon paper $1.95. A story set in feudal Japan tells of Takiko, a samurai's daughter, who is sent to the royal court when her mother remarries.

4056. Paterson, Katherine. *The Sign of the Chrysanthemum* (5–7). Illus. by Peter Landa. 1973, Harper $10.51; Avon paper $1.75. At the death of his mother, a young boy sets out to find his samurai father in twelfth-century Japan.

4057. Say, Allen. *The Ink-Keeper's Apprentice* (6–8). 1979, Harper $7.95; LB $10.89. A post–World War II glimpse of Tokyo by a boy set to immigrate to the United States.

4058. Wartski, Maureen Crane. *A Boat to Nowhere* (4–5). 1980, Westminster $9.95. An adventure story about the Vietnamese "boat people."

4059. Yolen, Jane. *Children of the Wolf* (6–9). 1984, Viking $11.50. The story of a Christian missionary and his experiences with two feral children in India during the 1920s.

Europe

4060. Almedingen, E. M. *The Crimson Oak* (5–7). 1983, Putnam $9.95. The story of a boy growing up in Czarist Russia.

4061. Baer, Edith. *A Frost in the Night* (6–9). 1980, Pantheon LB $8.99. Reminiscences of Jewish life in prewar Germany.

4062. Behn, Harry. *The Faraway Lurs* (6–9). 1981, G. K. Hall $9.95; Putnam paper $4.95. A tragic love story set in prehistoric days.

4063. Benchley, Nathaniel. *Beyond the Mists* (6–9). 1975, Harper LB $10.95. The story of an eleventh-century Norseman, Gunnar Egilsen, and his involvement with the explorations of Leif Ericson.

4064. Bloch, Marie. *Aunt America* (4–7). Illus. by Joan Berg. 1972, Atheneum paper $0.95. Lenya, growing up in a Ukrainian town, is visited by her aunt from America.

4065. Burstein, Chaya M. *Joseph and Anna's Time Capsule: A Legacy from Old Jewish Prague* (3–6). Illus. by Nancy Edwards Calder. 1984, Summit $8.70. Through the story of two children, Jewish history and artifacts of nineteenth-century Prague are introduced.

4066. Carlson, Natalie Savage. *The Happy Orpheline* (3–5). Illus. by Garth Williams. 1957, Harper LB $12.89. Brigitte, happy in a French orphanage, tries to avoid being adopted. Two sequels are: *The Orphelines in the Enchanted Castle* (1964, $12.89); *A Grandmother for the Orphelines* (1980, $10.53; LB $10.89).

4067. Clark, Margery. *Poppy Seed Cakes* (2–4). Illus. by Maud Petersham and Miska Petersham. 1924, Doubleday $9.95. A great favorite with young children, this is the story of small Andrewshek and his Auntie Natushka, who journey to America and find themselves neighbors in New York.

4068. Degens, T. *The Visit* (6–9). 1982, Viking $10.95. A novel set in Germany that contrasts events in the Nazi era with contemporary issues.

4069. DeJong, Meindert. *Journey from Peppermint Street* (3–5). Illus. by Emily McCully. 1968, Harper paper $3.95. A small boy's first journey away from his Dutch village by the sea is recounted with warmth and understanding.

4070. DeJong, Meindert. *Shadrach* (2–4). Illus. by Maurice Sendak. 1953, Harper $10.89; paper $1.95. Based on the author's own childhood in the Netherlands, this tells of Davie's great joy when his grandfather promises him a real rabbit for his very own pet and the anxious days until it finally arrives.

4071. DeJong, Meindert. *Wheel on the School* (4–7). Illus. by Maurice Sendak. 1954, Harper $13.41; LB $13.89; paper $2.95. The storks are brought back to their island by the schoolchildren in a Dutch village.

4072. de Trevino, Elizabeth. *I, Juan de Pareja* (6–9). 1965, Farrar $9.95. Through the eyes of his devoted black slave, Juan de Pareja, the character of the artist Velasquez is revealed. Newbery Award winner.

4073. Dickinson, Peter. *The Dancing Bear* (6–9). Illus. by David Smee. 1973, Little $6.95. The slave Silvester and his trained bear survive the sacking of Byzantium by the Huns in A.D. 558.

4074. Dodge, Mary Mapes. *Hans Brinker: Or the Silver Skates* (5–8). Illus. by G. W. Edwards. 1915, Putnam $9.95. Hans hopes to enter the racing contest and win the silver skates; one of several fine editions of this story set in the Netherlands.

4075. Fenton, Edward. *The Refugee Summer* (6–9). 1982, Delacorte $10.95. The Greco-Turkish War touches the life of young Nikolas in this novel set in Athens in 1922.

4076. Garcia, Ann O'Neal. *Spirit on the Wall* (5–8). 1982, Holiday $9.95. A novel dealing with the cavemen of prehistoric times.

4077. Graham, Harriet. *The Ring of Zoraya* (5–7). 1982, Atheneum LB $9.95. An adventure-mystery set in nineteenth-century Russia.

4078. Gray, Elizabeth Janet. *Adam of the Road* (6–9). Illus. by Robert Lawson. 1942, Viking $12.95. Adventure of a thirteenth-century minstrel boy. Newbery Award winner, 1943.

4079. Griffiths, Helen. *The Last Summer: Spain 1936* (5–7). Illus. by Victor G. Ambrus. 1979, Holiday $7.95. A boy and his horse are swept into the Spanish Civil War. A sequel is: *Dancing Horses* (1982, $9.95).

4080. Griffiths, Helen. *The Mysterious Appearance of Agnes* (6–8). Illus. by Victor G. Ambrus. 1975, Holiday $9.95. A young girl is accused of witchcraft in this powerful novel set in sixteenth-century Germany.

4081. Hamori, Laszlo. *Dangerous Journey* (6–9). Illus. by W. T. Mars. 1966, Harcourt paper $1.75. A dramatic escape story of 2 Hungarian boys who jump the iron curtain to Austria.

4082. Harris, Rosemary. *Janni's Stork* (3–5). Illus. by Juan Wijngaard. 1984, Bedrick $10.95. In seventeenth-century Holland, Janni hopes for luck by getting a stork for his roof.

4083. Haugaard, Erik C. *Chase Me, Catch Nobody* (5–9). 1980, Houghton $8.95. A young Danish boy takes an adventure-filled trip into Nazi Germany in 1937.

4084. Haugaard, Erik C. *Hakon of Rogen's Saga* (6–8). Illus. by Leo Dillon and Diane Dillon. 1963, Houghton paper $0.95. Through his uncle's treachery, orphaned Hakon is temporarily deprived of his birthright to Rogen Island in Norway during the time of the Vikings.

4085. Holman, Felice. *The Wild Children* (6–9). 1983, Scribners $11.95. Set in revolutionary Russia, this is the story of a gang of street kids in Moscow.

4086. Ish-Kishor, Sulamith. *A Boy of Old Prague* (5–8). Illus. by Ben Shahn. 1980, Scholastic paper $1.75. First-person story of a peasant boy born in 1540 and how he is affected by life in the ghetto of Prague.

4087. Kelly, Eric P. *The Trumpeter of Krakow* (5–8). Illus. by Janina Domanska. 1928, Macmillan $11.95; paper $4.00. Mystery surrounds a precious jewel and the youthful patriot who stands watch over it in a church tower in this novel of fifteenth-century Poland. Newbery Award winner, 1929.

4088. Konigsburg, E. L. *A Proud Taste for Scarlet and Miniver* (6–9). Illus. by author. 1973, Atheneum $9.95; paper $1.95. The life of Eleanor of Aquitaine as told by different members of her entourage; written with wit and style.

4089. Konigsburg, E. L. *The Second Mrs. Giaconda* (6–9). 1975, Atheneum $9.95; paper $1.95. A fictional series of episodes involving Leonardo da Vinci, his enterprising apprentice, and the story behind the Mona Lisa.

4090. Lasky, Kathryn. *The Night Journey* (4–7). Illus. by Trina S. Hyman. 1981, Warne $8.95.

Nana tells her great-granddaughter about her escape from Czarist Russia.

4091. Mark, Michael. *Toba* (5–7). Illus. by Neil Waldman. 1984, Bradbury $10.95. Life in a Polish village in 1910 as seen through the experiences of a young Jewish girl.

4092. Millstead, Thomas. *Cave of the Moving Shadows* (6–8). 1979, Dial $7.95. A boy grows to maturity in prehistoric times.

4093. Monjo, F. N. *The House on Stink Alley* (3–5). Illus. by Robert Quackenbush. 1977, Dell paper $1.25. Mr. Brewster plans to move his family to America on the *Mayflower*.

4094. Ofek, Uriel. *Smoke over Golan* (6–8). Illus. by Lloyd Bloom. 1979, Harper LB $9.89. The battle on Golan Heights as seen through the eyes of a young Israeli.

4095. Pyle, Howard. *Otto of the Silver Hand* (6–9). Illus. by author. 1916, Dover paper $3.50. Life in feudal Germany, the turbulence and cruelty of robber barons, and the peaceful scholarly pursuits of the monks are presented in the story of the kidnapped son of a robber baron.

4096. Robbins, Ruth. *The Emperor and the Drummer Boy* (3–6). Illus. by Nicholas Sidjakov. 1962, Parnassus $4.95; LB $5.38. A young drummer boy waits at Napoleon's side for the safe return of his friend, who floats ashore clinging to his drum.

4097. Seredy, Kate. *The Good Master* (4–6). Illus. by author. 1935, Viking $11.50. Warm and humorous story of a city girl on her uncle's farm in prewar Hungary.

4098. Skurzynski, Gloria. *Manwolf* (6–8). 1981, Houghton $9.95. For mature readers, a story set in medieval Poland about a boy's disfigurement.

4099. Skurzynski, Gloria. *What Happened in Hamelin* (5–7). 1979, Scholastic $9.95. A retelling of the Pied Piper story as narrated by one of the survivors.

4100. Steele, William O. *The Magic Amulet* (4–6). 1979, Harcourt $6.95. A story, set in prehistoric times, features a resourceful hero and such animals as saber-toothed tigers and mammoths.

4101. Tene, Benjamin. *In the Shade of the Chestnut Tree* (6–9). Illus. by Richard Sigberman. 1981, Jewish Publication Society $8.95. Jewish children growing up in Warsaw between the wars.

4102. Winterfeld, Henry. *Detectives in Togas* (5–7). Illus. by Charlotte Kleinert. 1956, Harcourt paper $2.25. A jolly mystery story set in ancient Rome, involving a group of schoolboys unjustly accused of defacing a temple. A sequel is: *Mystery of the Roman Ransom* (1971, paper $1.75).

4103. Yarbro, Chelsea Quinn. *Locadio's Apprentice* (6–9). 1984, Harper $12.02; LB $11.89. An historical novel that ends with the eruption of Vesuvius and the destruction of Pompeii.

Great Britain and Ireland

4104. Allan, Mabel Esther. *The Mills Down Below* (6–8). 1981, Dodd $7.95. A novel set in Victorian England about industrialism and the beginnings of feminism.

4105. Anderson, Margaret J. *Journey of the Shadow Bairns* (5–8). 1980, Scholastic paper $1.95. Two youngsters embark on a lonely journey to Canada in this novel set in 1903.

4106. Avery, Gillian. *Ellen and the Queen* (3–5). Illus. by Krystyna Turska. 1975, Lodestar $5.95. A slight but amusing story of wish fulfillment in which a young girl is able to see Queen Victoria.

4107. Bibby, Violet. *Many Waters Cannot Quench Love* (6–8). 1975, Morrow $8.59. In this story set in seventeenth-century England, a girl loves someone other than her betrothed.

4108. Briggs, Katharine. *Kate Crackernuts* (6–8). 1980, Greenwillow $13.75. Two Kates—one wild, one mild—are involved in witchcraft and intrigue in seventeenth-century Scotland.

4109. Bulla, Clyde Robert. *The Beast of Lor* (4–6). Illus. by Ruth Sanderson. 1977, Harper $9.57. The story of the friendship between a boy and an elephant brought to England during the Roman conquest.

4110. Bulla, Clyde Robert. *The Sword in the Tree* (2–5). Illus. by Paul Galdone. 1956, Harper $10.53. A simply written account of knighthood at the time of King Arthur.

4111. Bunting, Eve. *The Haunting of Kildoran Abbey* (6–8). 1978, Warne $7.95. Twins join a gang of waifs to survive in famine-stricken Ireland of 1847.

4112. Clarke, Pauline. *Torolv the Fatherless* (6–9). Illus. by Cecil Leslie. 1978, Faber $6.95. An English historical novel set during the reign of Ethelred the Unready.

4113. Clements, Bruce. *Prison Window, Jerusalem Blue* (6–8). 1977, Farrar $7.95. In the year 1031, a brother and sister from the south shore of England become slaves of the Vikings.

4114. De Angeli, Marguerite. *The Door in the Wall* (5–7). Illus. by author. 1949, Doubleday $10.95. Crippled Robin proves his courage in plague-ridden nineteenth-century London. Newbery Award winner, 1950.

4115. Garfield, Leon. *Footsteps* (5–8). 1980, Delacorte $8.95. A mystery set in the back alleys of Victorian London.

4116. Garfield, Leon. *The Night of the Comet: A Courtship Featuring Bostock and Harris* (6–8). 1979, Delacorte $8.95; LB $8.44. Three unusual love stories culminate on the night a comet is due.

4117. Geras, Adele. *Apricots at Midnight and Other Stories from a Patchwork Quilt* (4–6). Illus. by Doreen Caldwell. 1982, Atheneum $10.95. Every patch in the quilt reminds Aunt Penny of another story.

4118. Graves, Robert. *An Ancient Castle* (4–6). Illus. by Elizabeth Graves. 1982, Michael Kesend $10.95. A novel of heroes, villains, and buried treasures set in pre-World War I Britain.

4119. Haugaard, Erik C. *A Boy's Will* (4–6). Illus. by Troy Howell. 1983, Houghton $8.95. A novel set on a coastal Irish island during the American Revolution.

4120. Haugaard, Erik C. *Cromwell's Boy* (6–8). 1978, Houghton $7.95. Thirteen-year-old Oliver fights with Cromwell against King Charles. A sequel to: *A Messenger for Parliament* (1976, $6.95).

4121. Hunter, Mollie. *The Stronghold* (6–9). 1974, Harper $10.53; LB $10.89. In this historical novel set in northern Scotland, a young crippled boy discovers a way to withstand the devastating raids by the Romans.

4122. Hunter, Mollie. *You Never Knew Her As I Did!* (6–9). 1981, Harper $11.49; LB $10.89. An historical novel for better readers dealing with the life of Mary, Queen of Scots.

4123. King, Clive. *Ninny's Boat* (5–8). Illus. by Ian Newsham. 1981, Macmillan $9.95. A young boy sets out to discover his true identity in fifth-century Britain.

4124. Kusan, Ivan. *The Mystery of Green Hill* (4–6). Illus. by Kermit Adler. 1966, Harcourt paper $3.95. Five boys set out to catch the thieves who are plundering their village after World War II.

4125. Langford, Sondra Gordon. *Red Bird of Ireland* (6–8). 1983, Atheneum $10.95. In Ireland in 1846, a young girl must adjust to several crises in her family and the potato famine.

4126. Lively, Penelope. *Fanny's Sister* (3–5). Illus. by Anita Lobel. 1980, Dutton $7.95. Fanny wishes her nearest sibling would disappear in this gentle tale set in Victorian days.

4127. MacDonald, George. *Sir Gibbie* (4–6). 1979, Schocken $9.95; paper $4.95. The story of a Scottish waif and the triumph of love over hardship.

4128. McGraw, Eloise. *Master Cornhill* (6–9). Illus. 1973, Atheneum $6.25. A young boy is left without family or funds when the plague hits, in this historical novel set in London.

4129. Minard, Rosemary. *Long Meg* (3–6). Illus. by Philip Smith. 1982, Pantheon $8.95. Meg, in disguise as a man, joins Henry VIII's army fighting in France.

4130. Moskin, Marietta D. *A Royal Gift* (3–4). Illus. by Catherine Stock. 1982, Putnam LB $6.99. A story based on a tale surrounding the marriage of the Duke of York in England in 1923.

4131. Pierce, Tamora. *Alanna: The First Adventure* (5–8). 1983, Atheneum $13.95. During the Middle Ages, a young girl changes places with her brother so she can become a knight. A sequel is: *In the Hand of the Goddess* (1984, $12.95).

4132. Pyle, Howard. *Men of Iron* (5–8). 1930, Airmont paper $1.95. Brave deeds and knightly adventure in England—an old favorite.

4133. Schlee, Ann. *Ask Me No Questions* (6–9). 1982, Holt $14.50. In Victorian England, young Laura tries to help those youngsters kept in an asylum.

4134. Schlee, Ann. *The Consul's Daughter* (5–8). 1972, Atheneum $4.50. A 14-year-old girl becomes involved with the British fleet's bombardment in Algiers in 1816.

4135. Strauss, Victoria. *The Lady of Rhuddesmere* (6–9). 1982, Warne LB $8.95. A lengthy historical novel set in medieval Britain.

4136. Sutcliff, Rosemary. *Blood Feud* (6–8). 1977, Dutton $7.50. Two young men, Jestyn and Thormod, set out to avenge the murder of Thormod's father in tenth-century Europe.

4137. Sutcliff, Rosemary. *Frontier Wolf* (6–8). 1981, Dutton $11.50. Alexius Flavius is sent to lead a fierce band of warriors in Roman Britain.

4138. Sutcliff, Rosemary. *Song for a Dark Queen* (6–9). 1979, Harper $10.95. A novel for mature readers about Queen Boadicea and her revolt against the Roman conquerors.

4139. Sutcliff, Rosemary. *Sun Horse, Moon Horse* (6–8). Illus. by Shirley Felts. 1978, Dutton $9.95. A boy sacrifices himself for his people in pre-Roman Britain.

4140. Townsend, John R. *Dan Alone* (6–8). 1983, Harper $9.57; LB $9.89. The story of an 11-year-old boy alone in a British city between the wars.

4141. Turner, Ann. *The Way Home* (6–9). 1982, Crown $8.95. Anne flees to a marsh during the Black Plague in England in the fourteenth century.

Latin America

4142. Baker, Betty. *Walk the World's Rim* (6–8). 1965, Harper $10.89; paper $2.95. Colonial Mexico and the Indian life are the background for this engrossing story of Cabeza de Vaca and his black slave's trek from eastern Texas to Mexico.

4143. Bulla, Clyde Robert. *The Poppy Seeds* (2–4). Illus. by Jean Charlot. 1955, Harper $10.53. A young Indian boy in Mexico plants poppy seeds throughout the village.

4144. Clark, Ann Nolan. *Secret of the Andes* (4–8). Illus. by Jean Charlot. 1952, Viking $10.50; Penguin paper $2.95. Cusi, a young Inca boy, tends a precious llama herd high in the Peruvian mountains and ponders his future. Newbery Award winner, 1953.

4145. Mangurian, David. *Children of the Incas* (3–6). Illus. 1979, Four Winds $9.95. The story of a poor boy growing up in a little town in Peru.

4146. O'Dell, Scott. *The King's Fifth* (6–9). Illus. by Samuel Bryant. 1966, Houghton $10.95. A powerful story of the young mapmaker, Esteban, whose search for knowledge was clouded by his lust for gold.

4147. O'Dell, Scott. *The Treasure of Topo-el-Bampo* (K–4). Illus. by Lynd Ward. 1972, Houghton $4.95. Two donkeys make a very poor Mexican village rich.

United States

Indians of North America

4148. Armer, Laura A. *Waterless Mountain* (5–7). Illus. by author. 1931, McKay $10.95. Story of a young Navaho boy who feels keenly the beauty and power of his heritage, although he lives on the fringe of white civilization. Newbery Award winner, 1932.

4149. Baker, Betty. *Shaman's Last Raid* (6–9). 1973, Harper $10.89. Two modern Apache children try to ignore the old Indian ways.

4150. Bulla, Clyde Robert, and Syson, Michael. *Conquista!* (3–5). Illus. by Ronald Himler. 1978, Harper $9.57; LB $9.89. A young Indian boy encounters his first horse, a refugee from the Coronado expedition.

4151. Carlson, Natalie Savage. *Alphonse, That Bearded One* (3–5). Illus. by Nicolas Mordvinoff. 1954, Harcourt $7.95. A bear makes peace with the Iroquois.

4152. Crompton, Anne Eliot. *The Ice Trail* (4–7). 1980, Methuen $9.50. Two outcasts from an Indian tribe survive a hard winter.

4153. Griese, Arnold A. *At the Mouth of the Luckiest River* (4–6). Illus. by Glo Coalson. 1973, Harper LB $9.89. A young Indian boy, growing up around Lake Athalasea in the late 1800s, makes enemies with the tribe's powerful medicine man.

4154. Lampman, Evelyn Sibley. *White Captives* (5–6). 1975, Atheneum $6.95. The fictional story of Olive Oatman's 5 years as a captive, first of the Apaches and later the Mohaves.

4155. Osborne, Chester G. *The Memory String* (5–8). 1984, Atheneum $11.95. A novel of how the Indians might have moved from Siberia to Alaska 30,000 years ago.

4156. Richter, Conrad. *Light in the Forest* (6–8). Illus. by Warren Chappell. 1966, Knopf $11.95; Bantam paper $1.95. A young white boy is captured by Indians and, after becoming a true tribe member, is suddenly returned to his parents. A companion volume is: *Country of Strangers* (1966, $9.95).

4157. Rockwood, Joyce. *Groundhog's Horse* (4–6). Illus. by Victor Kalin. 1978, Holt $9.70. An eleven-year-old Cherokee decides to rescue his horse when it is stolen by the Crees.

4158. Sneve, Virginia. *Jimmy Yellow Hawk* (3–5). Illus. by Oren Lyons. 1972, Holiday $8.95. A good picture of contemporary Indian life and of Little Jim's success in trapping a mink and earning his father's approval.

4159. Steele, William O. *The War Party* (4–6). Illus. by Lorinda Bryan. 1978, Harcourt $4.95. A young Indian brave understands the cruelty of war when he is wounded during his first war party.

4160. Thompson, Jean. *Brother of the Wolves* (6–8). Illus. by Steve Marchesi. 1978, Morrow $9.75; LB $9.36. A young Indian boy raised by wolves returns to his tribe.

Colonial Period

4161. Avi. *Encounter at Easton* (5–7). 1980, Pantheon LB $6.99. The story about the fate of 2 runaway indentured servants in eighteenth-century America. A sequel to: *Night Journeys* (1979, $6.95).

4162. Bulla, Clyde Robert. *Charlie's House* (3–5). Illus. by Arthur Dorros. 1983, Harper $10.10; LB $10.89. Charlie Brig is shipped as an indentured servant from England to Colonial America.

4163. Bulla, Clyde Robert. *John Billington, Friend of Squanto* (2–4). Illus. by Peter Burchard. 1956, Harper $10.53. The story of the early days of the Plymouth colony. John is captured but released when Squanto intercedes.

4164. Bulla, Clyde Robert. *A Lion to Guard Us* (3–6). 1981, Harper $11.49; LB $11.89; paper

$1.95. Three motherless children sail for America to be united with their father in the Jamestown, Virginia, colony.

4165. Clapp, Patricia. *Constance: A Story of Early Plymouth* (6–9). 1968, Lothrop $10.32. Historical novel based on a journal that records a girl's journey from London at the age of 15 and the hardships and stern pleasures of colonial life in Massachusetts.

4166. Clapp, Patricia. *Witches' Children: A Story of Salem* (6–9). 1982, Lothrop $11.25. In July 1692, Mary Warren and 9 other girls are "possessed" in Salem.

4167. Dalgliesh, Alice. *Courage of Sarah Noble* (3–5). Illus. by Leonard Weisgard. 1954, Scribners LB $6.95; paper $5.95. The true story of a brave little girl who in 1707 went with her father into the wilds of Connecticut.

4168. Edmonds, Walter. *The Matchlock Gun* (5–7). Illus. by Paul Lantz. 1941, Dodd $11.95. Exciting, true story of a courageous boy who protected his mother and sister from the Indians of the Hudson Valley. Newbery Award winner, 1942.

4169. Petry, Ann. *Tituba of Salem Village* (6–9). 1964, Harper $14.38. The story of the slave Tituba and her husband, John Indian, from the day they were sold in the Barbados until the tragic Salem witchcraft trials.

4170. Speare, Elizabeth. *The Sign of the Beaver* (6–9). 1983, Houghton $8.95; Dell paper $2.50. In Maine in 1768, Matt, though only 12, must protect his family.

4171. Speare, Elizabeth. *The Witch of Blackbird Pond* (6–9). 1958, Houghton $10.95. Historical romance set in Puritan Connecticut with the theme of witchcraft. Newbery Award winner. Also use: *Calico Captive* (1957, Houghton $9.95).

4172. Starkey, Marion L. *The Visionary Girls: Witchcraft in Salem Village* (6–9). 1973, Little $7.95. A fictionalized account of the Salem witch trials.

The Revolution

4173. Collier, James Lincoln, and Collier, Christopher. *The Bloody Country* (6–9). 1976, Four Winds $8.95. Ben Buck narrates this story of the hardships endured by his Connecticut family after their resettlement in Pennsylvania at the time of the Revolution.

4174. Collier, James Lincoln, and Collier, Christopher. *Jump Ship to Freedom* (6–9). 1981, Delacorte $10.95. A young slave tries to buy his freedom. Two sequels are: *War Comes to Willy Freeman* (1983, $10.95); *Who Is Carrie?* (1984, $14.95).

4175. Collier, James Lincoln, and Collier, Christopher. *My Brother Sam Is Dead* (6–9). 1974, Four Winds $9.95; paper $2.25. The story, based partially on fact, of a Connecticut family divided in loyalties during the Revolutionary War.

4176. Collier, James Lincoln, and Collier, Christopher. *The Winter Hero* (6–9). 1978, Four Winds $8.95. A fictionized account of Shays's Rebellion set in the Massachusetts of 1787.

4177. Finlayson, Ann. *Rebecca's War* (5–8). Illus. by Sherry Streeter. 1972, Warne $5.95. Philadelphia during the Revolutionary War, where 14-year-old Rebecca tries to hide military secrets from British soldiers billeted in her home.

4178. Forbes, Esther. *Johnny Tremain: A Novel for Old and Young* (6–9). Illus. by Lynd Ward. 1943, Houghton $8.95; Dell paper $2.95. Story of a young silversmith's apprentice, who plays an important part in the American Revolution. Newbery Award winner, 1944.

4179. Fritz, Jean. *The Cabin Faced West* (3–6). Illus. by Feodor Rojankovsky. 1958, Putnam $8.95. The western Pennsylvania territory of 1784 is a very lonely place for Ann until General Washington comes to visit.

4180. Fritz, Jean. *Early Thunder* (6–9). Illus. by Lynd Ward. 1967, Putnam $9.95. In 1775, the early thunder of the Revolution was heard in Massachusetts, and the town of Salem was divided into contradictory factions.

4181. Fritz, Jean. *George Washington's Breakfast* (3–5). Illus. by Paul Galdone. 1969, Putnam LB $5.99; paper $4.95. George W. Allen knows all there is to know about our first president—except what he had for breakfast.

4182. Gauch, Patricia Lee. *This Time, Tempe Wick?* (2–5). 1974, Putnam $6.95. Tempe (Temperance) Wick helped the Revolutionary soldiers who camped on her farm in New Jersey in 1780, until they tried to steal her horse, and then she got mad.

4183. O'Dell, Scott. *Sarah Bishop* (5–8). 1980, Houghton $10.95; Scholastic paper $1.95. A first-person narrative of a girl who lived through the American Revolution and its toll of suffering and misery.

4184. Steele, William O. *The Man with the Silver Eyes* (5–7). 1976, Harcourt $5.95. A young American Indian boy gradually develops a respect for a peace-loving white man in this story set in Tennessee during the Revolutionary War.

4185. Wibberley, Leonard. *John Treegate's Musket* (6–9). 1959, Farrar $6.95. Story of a young boy apprenticed to a maker of barrel staves in Boston in 1769 and his adventures in the Revolutionary War.

The Young Nation, 1789–1861

4186. Avi. *Emily Upham's Revenge* (4–6). Illus. by Paul O. Zelinsky. 1978, Pantheon LB $6.99. Subtitle: *How Deadwood Dick Saved the Banker's Niece: A Massachusetts Adventure.*

4187.   Blos, Joan W. *A Gathering of Days: A New England Girl's Journal, 1830–32* (6–9). 1979, Scribners $10.95; paper $2.95. A fictional diary kept by 13-year-old Catherine Cabot who is growing up in the town of Meredith, New Hampshire. Newbery Award winner, 1979.

4188.   Bourne, Miriam Anne. *Uncle George Washington and Harriot's Guitar* (3–5). Illus. by Elise Primavera. 1983, Putnam $8.95. Fourteen-year-old Harriot Washington asks her famous uncle for a guitar.

4189.   Brady, Esther W. *The Toad on Capital Hill* (4–6). 1978, Crown $6.95. A young boy and his stepbrother are in the line of advancing British troops in 1814.

4190.   Fleischman, Paul. *Path of the Pale Horse* (6–9). 1983, Harper $9.95. In disease-ridden Philadelphia in 1793, 14-year-old Lep has a series of adventures.

4191.   Fox, Paula. *The Slave Dancer* (6–9). Illus. by Eros Keith. 1973, Bradbury $10.95. Fourteen-year-old Jessie is kidnapped and press-ganged aboard an American slave ship bound for Africa. Newbery Award winner.

4192.   Fritz, Jean. *Brady* (4–7). Illus. by Lynd Ward. 1960, Putnam $7.95. When Brady discovers his father is an Underground Railroad agent, he learns to control his tongue and form his own opinion about slavery.

4193.   Loeper, John J. *The Golden Dragon* (5–6). 1978, Atheneum $6.95. A fictional account of a clipper ship's voyage from New York to San Francisco in the midnineteenth century.

4194.   Lord, Athena V. *A Spirit to Ride the Whirlwind* (6–9). 1981, Macmillan $10.95. Twelve-year-old Bennie becomes a mill worker in Lowell, Massachusetts, in 1836.

4195.   Monjo, F. N. *The Drinking Gourd* (2–4). Illus. by Fred Brenner. 1970, Harper LB $8.89; paper $2.95. A New England white boy helps a black family escape on the Underground Railroad.

4196.   Smucker, Barbara. *Runaway to Freedom* (3–5). Illus. by Charles Lilly. 1978, Harper paper $1.95. Two slave girls try to reach Canada and freedom.

4197.   Steele, William O. *The Lone Hunt* (5–7). Illus. by Paul Galdone. 1976, Harcourt paper $1.75. Story of early Tennessee and an 11-year-old boy's hunt for the last buffalo in the Cumberland Mountains. Another pioneer story by the author and publisher: *The Buffalo Knife* (1968, paper $2.95).

4198.   Turkle, Brinton. *Rachel and Obadiah* (3–4). Illus. by author. 1978, Dutton $8.95. Obadiah and his sister, Rachel, vie to be first with the news of a ship's arrival in port. Also use: *Thy Friend, Obadiah* (1969, Viking $10.95; Penguin paper $3.95).

4199.   Yep, Laurence. *The Mark Twain Murders* (5–8). 1982, Four Winds $8.95. A youthful Mark Twain and a sea urchin solve a mystery in the San Francisco of Lincoln's day. A sequel is: *The Tom Sawyer Fires* (1984, Morrow $10.00).

Westward Expansion and Pioneer Life

4200.   Beatty, Patricia. *The Bad Bell of San Salvador* (5–8). 1973, Morrow LB $10.80. Early California is re-created in this story of Jacinto, who wants to recover his true Comanche birthright.

4201.   Beatty, Patricia. *Eight Mules from Monterey* (6–8). 1982, Morrow $10.75. Mrs. Ashmore, a new librarian, delivers a book collection to Big Tree Junction via mule.

4202.   Beatty, Patricia. *Hail Columbia* (5–8). Illus. by Liz Dauber. 1970, Morrow $10.08. The Oregon of the 1890s is the unlikely setting for a visit from Aunt Columbia, a spirited, liberated suffragist, but nieces Louisa and Rowena are delighted.

4203.   Beatty, Patricia. *Wait for Me, Watch for Me, Eula Bee* (6–8). 1978, Morrow $10.75; LB $10.32. Two children are taken captive by Comanche Indians in Texas in 1861.

4204.   Brenner, Barbara. *On the Frontier with Mr. Audubon* (5–8). Illus. 1977, Putnam $8.95. A thoroughly researched account of a frontier journey, described by a 13-year-old apprentice to Audubon, the great nature artist.

4205.   Byars, Betsy. *Trouble River* (3–6). Illus. by Rocco Negri. 1969, Viking $10.95; Scholastic paper $1.95. Dewey uses his canoe to escape Indians.

4206.   Calvert, Patricia. *The Snowbird* (5–8). 1980, Scribners $9.95. Orphaned Willana and her brother travel to the Dakota Territory to join their uncle and his wife.

4207.   Flory, Jane. *The Great Bamboozlement* (4–6). Illus. by author. 1982, Houghton $7.95. Serena's Ma and Pa disagree on whether farming or storekeeping should be their life's work.

4208.   Holling, Holling C. *Tree in the Trail* (4–7). Illus. by author. 1942, Houghton LB $15.95. The history of the Santa Fe Trail, described through the life of a cottonwood tree, a 200-year-old landmark to travelers and a symbol of peace to the Indians.

4209.   Keith, Harold. *The Obstinate Land* (6–8). 1977, Harper $9.95. A realistic portrait of the

Romberg family's struggle to gain a livelihood from the hostile land of the Cherokee Strip.

4210. Kirby, Susan E. *Ike and Porker* (4–6). 1983, Houghton $8.70. Ike is determined that he will accompany his father on a hog drive.

4211. Lasky, Kathryn. *Beyond the Divide* (6–10). 1983, Macmillan $11.95. Merebah, an Amish girl, and her father travel west on a wagon train.

4212. Levitin, Sonia. *The No-Return Trail* (5–7). 1978, Harcourt $6.95. Seventeen-year-old Nancy Kelsey, a wife and mother, accompanies a wagon train to California in 1841.

4213. Meadowcroft, Enid. *By Wagon and Flatboat* (5–7). Illus. by Minon MacKnight. 1938, Harper $10.95. The Burd family travels from Pennsylvania to Ohio by flatboat.

4214. Moeri, Louise. *Save Queen of Sheba* (5–7). 1981, Dutton $9.95. Young David survives a wagon train massacre and must take care of his young sister.

4215. Monjo, F. N. *Indian Summer* (1–2). Illus. by Anita Lobel. 1968, Harper $8.89. Matt and Toby, in charge of protecting the family while pa is away fighting the British, suspect their cabin will soon be a target for Kentucky's Indians.

4216. Moore, Ruth Nulton. *Wilderness Journey* (4–6). Illus. by Allan Eitzen. 1979, Herald Pr. paper $4.50. Two Irish boys travel over a mountainous wilderness from Philadelphia to Pittsburgh to join their mother.

4217. Mooser, Stephen. *Orphan Jeb at the Massacree* (3–5). Illus. by Joyce Audy dos Santos. 1984, Knopf $9.95; LB $9.99. In a novel set in the American west in the mid-1850s, Jeb sets out to find his missing father.

4218. O'Dell, Scott. *Carlota* (6–9). 1977, Houghton $10.95; Dell paper $1.50. After the Mexican-American War, a brave California group, including the enterprising heroine Carlota, who wishes independence, does battle with the U.S. Army.

4219. Paige, Harry W. *Shadow on the Sun* (5–8). 1984, Warne $9.95. Should the son of Billy the Kid avenge his father's death?

4220. Potter, Marian. *Blatherskite* (5–7). 1980, Morrow $8.75; LB $8.40. A talkative young girl in Depression Missouri proves her worth.

4221. St. George, Judith. *The Halo Wind* (5–7). 1978, Putnam $8.95. Hardship on a wagon train to Oregon, as experienced by Ella Jane, a 13-year-old pioneer.

4222. Stevens, Carla. *Trouble for Lucy* (4–6). Illus. by Ronald Himler. 1979, Houghton $8.95. Lucy's pup Finn causes trouble during a wagon trip to the Oregon territory.

4223. Stone, Nancy. *Dune Shadow* (5–7). 1980, Houghton $7.95. Serena, her grandmother, and a neighborhood girl are alone as winter approaches their Lake Michigan home in the 1850s.

4224. Wallin, Luke. *In the Shadow of the Wind* (6–10). 1984, Bradbury $11.95. The conflicts between the white settlers and the Cree Indians in Alabama in 1835.

4225. Wisler, G. Clifton. *Winter of the Wolf* (6–10). 1981, Nelson $8.95. A novel of friendship between a white boy and a young Comanche in rural Texas in 1864.

Civil War

4226. Beatty, Patricia. *Turn Homeward Hannalee* (6–8). 1984, Morrow $10.00. The story of a group of mill workers who become displaced persons during the Civil War.

4227. Cummings, Betty Sue. *Hew against the Grain* (6–9). 1977, Atheneum $6.95. The story of the ravages of the Civil War on a divided Virginia family, as expressed by the youngest daughter.

4228. Hickman, Janet. *Zoar Blue* (6–9). 1978, Macmillan $8.95. A pacifist community and the effects of the Civil War on it as experienced by a young girl.

4229. Hunt, Irene. *Across Five Aprils* (6–8). 1964, Ace paper $2.25. A young boy's experiences during the Civil War in the backwoods of southern Illinois. One brother joins the Union forces, the other the Confederacy, and the family is divided.

4230. Keith, Harold. *Rifles for Watie* (6–9). 1957, Harper $12.95. Life of a Union soldier and spy fighting the Civil War in the West. Newbery Award winner, 1958.

4231. O'Dell, Scott. *Sing Down the Moon* (5–8). 1970, Houghton $9.95. The tragic forced march of the Indians to Fort Sumner in 1864, told by a young Navajo girl.

4232. Sneve, Virginia. *Betrayed* (5–7). 1974, Holiday $5.95. This bitter, graphic account of Indian-white conflicts during the Civil War is based on fact.

4233. Steele, William O. *The Perilous Road* (5–7). Illus. by Paul Galdone. 1954, Harcourt paper $3.95. Chris, a Yankee-hating Tennessee mountain boy, learns by experience the futility of war, in this fast-paced Civil War story.

4234. Wisler, G. Clifton. *Thunder on the Tennessee* (6–9). 1983, Dutton $10.53. A young boy witnesses the horror of war after he joins the Confederate Army. A sequel is: *Buffalo Moon* (1984, $10.63).

Reconstruction to World War II: 1865–1941

4235. Avi. *Shadrach's Crossing* (5–8). 1983, Pantheon $10.95; LB $10.99. An adventure story of smuggling during Prohibition days.

4236. Babbitt, Natalie. *Phoebe's Revolt* (K–2). Illus. by author. 1968, Farrar $7.95; paper $3.45. The story of a stubborn little girl set in the gaslight era.

4237. Baker, Betty. *The Night Spider Case* (4–6). 1984, Macmillan $9.95. A rousing adventure story set in turn-of-the-century New York City.

4238. Beatty, Patricia. *Lacy Makes a Match* (5–7). 1979, Morrow $11.50. California in 1893 is the setting of this story of a girl trying to marry off her older brothers.

4239. Bolton, Carole. *Never Jam Today* (6–9). 1971, Atheneum paper $0.95. Young Maddy works for the suffragettes in this novel set in America during 1917.

4240. Branscum, Robbie. *The Ugliest Boy* (5–7). Illus. by Mike Eagle. 1978, Lothrop $10.75; LB $10.32. Reb struggles through growing-up pangs during the Great Depression in rural Arkansas.

4241. Brown, Irene Bennett. *Before the Lark* (5–7). 1982, Atheneum $10.95. Jocey and her grandmother begin farming in Kansas during the 1880s.

4242. Burch, Robert. *Wilkin's Ghost* (5–7). Illus. by Lloyd Bloom. 1978, Viking $9.95. Wilkin befriends an older boy who was once accused of theft, in a story set in Georgia during 1935.

4243. Burchard, Peter. *Digger: A Novel* (6–9). 1980, Putnam $8.95. An adventure-filled novel about a newsboy in the New York City of 1871.

4244. Callaway, Kathy. *The Bloodroot Flower* (6–8). 1982, Knopf $9.95; LB $9.99. A turn-of-the-century story about a courageous heroine and her family tragedies.

4245. Cohen, Barbara. *Gooseberries to Oranges* (2–4). Illus. by Beverly Brodsky. 1982, Lothrop $11.88; LB $10.80. A little Jewish girl leaves Russia to join her father in this country.

4246. Constant, A. Wilson. *Does Anybody Care about Lou Emma Miller?* (5–7). 1979, Harper $10.53; LB $10.89. A family novel set in Kansas prior to World War I that also highlights a girl's growing pains.

4247. Cross, Helen Reeder. *Isabella Mine* (5–7). Illus. by Catherine Stock. 1982, Lothrop $11.25. A family and their life in a Tennessee mining town in 1930.

4248. Cummings, Betty Sue. *Now, Ameriky* (5–8). 1979, Atheneum $9.95. Brigid Ni Cleary comes to America from Ireland to raise passage money for the rest of the family.

4249. De Angeli, Marguerite. *Copper-Toed Boots* (3–6). Illus. by author. 1938, Doubleday $5.95. American family life in the early twentieth century.

4250. De Angeli, Marguerite. *Henner's Lydia* (3–5). Illus. by author. 1963, Doubleday $9.95. A little Amish girl and her family on a farm in Pennsylvania.

4251. Ellison, Lucile Watkins. *Butter on Both Sides* (4–6). Illus. by Judith Gwyn Brown. 1979, Scribners $7.95. A family story set in rural Alabama during the early 1900s. Two sequels are: *The Tie That Binds* (1981); *A Window to Look Through* (1982) (both $9.95).

4252. Gessner, Lynne. *Navajo Slave* (5–7). 1976, Harvey House LB $7.49. The story of a Navajo boy after the Civil War and his escape from slavery in New Mexico.

4253. Goldsmith, Ruth M. *Phoebe Takes Charge* (6–9). 1983, Atheneum $11.95. Eighteen-year-old Phoebe takes charge of the household in New England of 1926.

4254. Haynes, Mary. *Pot Belly Tales* (3–6). Illus. by Michael J. Deraney. 1982, Lothrop $11.25; LB $11.88. Ten stories that take place at various times in our history.

4255. Huntington, Lee Pennock. *Maybe a Miracle* (4–6). Illus. by Neil Waldman. 1984, Putnam $9.95. Eleven-year-old Dorcus tries to help a childless couple during the Depression years.

4256. Hurwitz, Johanna. *The Rabbi's Girls* (4–7). Illus. by Pamela Johnson. 1982, Morrow $9.75. The 5 Jewish Levin sisters are growing up in 1924 Ohio.

4257. Kelly, Rosalie. *Addie's Year* (4–6). 1981, Beaufort $9.95. A period piece set in a small U.S. town in the 1920s.

4258. Lenski, Lois. *Strawberry Girl* (4–6). Illus. by author. 1945, Harper $11.49; Dell paper $2.75. Lively adventures of a little girl, full of the flavor of the Florida lake country. Other regional stories in this series: *Judy's Journey* (1947); *Prairie School* (1951) (both $11.89).

4259. Mays, Lucinda. *The Other Shore* (6–9). 1979, Atheneum $8.95. An immigrant Italian girl arrives in the United States with her family in 1911.

4260. Miles, Betty. *I Would if I Could* (3–6). 1982, Knopf LB $8.99; paper $2.25. During 1930, a 10-year-old girl spends a summer visiting grandmother in rural Ohio.

4261. Moskin, Marietta D. *Day of the Blizzard* (3–4). Illus. by Stephen Gammell. 1978, Putnam $7.95. A 12-year-old girl's experiences in New York City during the blizzard of 1888.

4262. Naylor, Phyllis Reynolds. *Walking through the Dark* (6–9). 1976, Atheneum $6.95. The effects of poverty caused by the Great Depression, as seen through the eyes of an adolescent girl.

4263. Olsen, Violet. *The Growing Season* (5–7). 1982, Atheneum $10.95. Marie finds it hard growing up on an Iowa farm during the Depression.

4264. Peck, Robert Newton. *The Day No Pigs Would Die* (6–9). 1972, Knopf $11.95; Dell paper $2.25. A gentle story about a 12-year-old Vermont farm boy.

4265. Potter, Marian. *A Chance Wild Apple* (5–7). 1982, Morrow $10.75. A Depression story of Missouri farm life as seen from the viewpoint of a young girl.

4266. Sawyer, Ruth. *Roller Skates* (4–6). Illus. by Valenti Angelo. 1936, Dell paper $2.25. A little girl explores New York City on roller skates in the 1890s. Newbery Award winner, 1937.

4267. Sebestyen, Ouida. *Words by Heart* (5–7). 1979, Little $8.95; Bantam paper $1.95. Race relations are explored when a black family moves to an all-white community during the Reconstruction Era.

4268. Snyder, Carol. *Ike and Mama and the Once-in-a-Lifetime Movie* (4–6). Illus. by Charles Robinson. 1981, Putnam $7.95. Growing up in New York in the early 1900s. Two others in the series: *Ike and Mama and the Block Wedding* (1979, $7.95); *Ike and Mama and Trouble at School* (1983, $9.95).

4269. Stevens, Carla. *Anna, Grandpa, and the Big Storm* (2–4). Illus. by Margot Tomes. 1982, Houghton $7.95. A family story that takes place during the famous blizzard of 1888 in New York City.

4270. Talbot, Charlene Joy. *An Orphan for Nebraska* (4–6). 1979, Atheneum $10.95. An orphaned Irish immigrant boy is sent west in the 1870s.

4271. Weik, Mary Hays. *A House on Liberty Street* (5–8). Illus. by Ann Grifalconi. 1973, Atheneum $4.50. An inspiring story based on fact about an immigrant's contributions to America.

4272. Wiegand, Roberta. *The Year of the Comet* (5–6). 1984, Bradbury $9.95. The story of a young girl growing up in rural Nebraska in the early 1900s.

4273. Yep, Laurence. *Dragonwings* (5–9). 1977, Harper LB $10.89; paper $2.95. A young Chinese

boy adjusts to life in San Francisco during the time of the earthquake.

World War II

4274. Allan, Mabel Esther. *A Dream of Hunger Moss* (7–9). 1983, Dodd $10.95. At the time of the outbreak of World War II, 2 Liverpool children spend time in the countryside.

4275. Anderson, Margaret J. *Searching for Shona* (4–6). 1978, Knopf LB $6.99. In England during World War II, two girls exchange places; one goes to Scotland, the other to Canada.

4276. Bawden, Nina. *Carrie's War* (4–6). 1973, Harper $10.89; Penguin paper $1.95. Twelve-year-old Carrie and her younger brother are evacuated from London to a small Welsh town.

4277. Bishop, Claire Huchet. *Twenty and Ten* (4–6). Illus. by William Pene du Bois. 1984, Peter Smith $12.50; Penguin paper $2.95. A nun and 20 French children hide 10 young refugees from the Nazis.

4278. Bloch, Marie. *Displaced Person* (6–9). Illus. by Allen Davis. 1978, Morrow $11.95; LB $10.32. A Ukrainian boy flees a German refugee camp in the final days of World War II.

4279. Degens, T. *Transport 7-41-R* (6–9). 1974, Viking $11.50; Dell paper $1.50. A nightmarish trip through Post–World War II Germany by a young refugee girl.

4280. DeJong, Meindert. *The House of Sixty Fathers* (6–9). Illus. by Maurice Sendak. 1956, Harper LB $10.89. Tien Pao and his pig, Glory-of-the-Republic, journey to find his parents in Japanese-occupied China.

4281. Donaldson, Margaret. *Journey into War* (4–6). 1980, Andre Deutsch $7.95. A young girl tries to find her father in World War II Europe.

4282. Fife, Dale. *North of Danger* (5–7). Illus. by Haakon Saether. 1978, Dutton $8.95; Scholastic paper $1.50. A boy's adventures in Norway during World War II.

4283. Frascino, Edward. *Eddie Spaghetti* (3–5). 1978, Harper $9.57. Growing up in Yonkers, New York, during the 1940s. A sequel is: *Eddie Spaghetti on the Homefront* (1983, $9.57; LB $9.89).

4284. Gillham, Bill. *Home before Long* (4–6). Illus. by Francis Mosley. 1984, Andre Deutsch $10.95. Two British children leave London and Dorset during the air raids of World War II.

4285. Griese, Arnold A. *The Wind Is Not a River* (4–6). Illus. by Glo Coalson. 1978, Harper LB $10.89. A World War II story about 2 children who help a wounded Japanese soldier in the Aleutian Islands.

4286. Holm, Anne. *North to Freedom* (6–8). 1984, Peter Smith $13.25; Harcourt paper $4.95. A boy who has never known anything except life in a concentration camp makes his way across Europe alone and escapes to freedom.

4287. Kerr, Judith. *When Hitler Stole Pink Rabbit* (4–7). Illus. by author. 1972, Putnam $8.95. Based on incidents in the author's life, this is an exciting story of a German-Jewish family and their escape from Nazi Germany. A sequel is: *The Other Way Round* (1975, $8.95).

4288. Levitin, Sonia. *Journey to America* (5–8). Illus. by Charles Robinson. 1970, Atheneum paper $0.95. A Jewish mother and her 3 daughters flee Nazi Germany in 1938 for a long and difficult journey to join their father in America.

4289. Lowry, Lois. *Autumn Street* (6–9). 1980, Houghton $8.95. Six-year-old Elizabeth, her sister, and mother go to live with grandmother in Pennsylvania during World War II.

4290. McSwigan, Marie. *Snow Treasure* (4–7). Illus. by Mary Reardon. 1942, Dutton $9.95; Scholastic paper $1.95. Children smuggle gold out of occupied Norway on their sleds.

4291. Orgel, Doris. *The Devil in Vienna* (6–8). 1978, Dial $7.95. A novel based on fact that centers around the Nazi occupation of Austria.

4292. Orlev, Uri. *The Island on Bird Street* (5–7). 1984, Houghton $10.95. A young Jewish boy inside a Warsaw ghetto during World War II.

4293. Oz, Amos. *Soumchi* (5–8). Trans. by author and Penelope Farmer. Illus. by William Papas. 1981, Harper LB $8.79. In Jerusalem just after World War II, an 11-year-old boy tells his story.

4294. Pelgrom, Els. *The Winter When Time Was Frozen* (5–7). Trans. from Dutch by Maryka Rudnik and Raphael Rudnik. 1980, Morrow $11.95;

LB $11.47. A Dutch girl and her father during the Allied invasion of Europe during World War II.

4295. Reiss, Johanna. *The Upstairs Room* (5–8). 1972, Harper $10.95. Two young Jewish girls are hidden for over 2 years in the home of a simple Dutch peasant during the German occupation. A sequel is: *The Journey Back* (1976, $10.95).

4296. Sachs, Marilyn. *A Pocket Full of Seeds* (5–7). Illus. by Ben Stahl. 1973, Doubleday $6.95. A family of French Jews suffer the heartache of persecution during World War II.

4297. Schellie, Don. *Shadow and the Gunner* (4–6). 1982, Scholastic $9.95. A remembrance of World War II—of friendship, parting, and death.

4298. Serraillier, Ian. *The Silver Sword* (6–8). Illus. by C. Walter Hodges. 1959, Phillips $10.95. A World War II story of Polish children who are separated from their parents and finally reunited.

4299. Smith, Doris Buchanan. *Salted Lemons* (4–6). 1980, Four Winds $9.95. Darby is a new girl in town but soon makes friends in this novel set during World War II.

4300. Streatfeild, Noel. *When the Sirens Wailed* (4–6). Illus. by Judith Gwyn Brown. 1976, Random LB $6.99. The story of a cockney family separated during the London blitz.

4301. Terlouw, Jan. *Winter in Wartime* (6–9). 1976, McGraw $7.95. Young Michiel takes care of a wounded British airman in the Netherlands during World War II.

4302. Todd, Leonard. *The Best Kept Secret of the War* (5–7). 1984, Knopf $9.95; LB $9.99. A young boy growing up in North Carolina during World War II.

4303. Walsh, Jill Paton. *Fireweed* (6–9). 1969, Avon paper $1.75. A story of 2 young people in London during the World War II blitz, who fall in love but must part since Bill will not be accepted by Julie's wealthy family.

Mysteries, Monsters, and Curiosities

4304. Ardley, Neil. *Fact or Fantasy?* (4–6). Illus. 1982, Watts $8.90. Life in the coming century is explored through such topics as clones and UFOs.

4305. Arnold, Oren. *What's in a Name: Famous Brand Names* (5–8). 1979, Messner $7.79. Stories behind such names as Coca Cola and Ivory Soap.

4306. Aylesworth, Thomas G. *Science Looks at Mysterious Monsters* (5–8). Illus. 1982, Messner LB $9.79. A discussion of what we know about such monsters as Bigfoot and the Abominable Snowman. Also use: *Bigfoot: America's Number One Monster* by Daniel Cohen (1982, Pocket paper $1.75).

4307. Aylward, Jim. *You're Dumber in the Summer* (2–5). Illus. by Jane Chambless-Rigie. 1980, Avon paper $2.25. A collection of most unusual facts. A sequel is: *Your Burro Is No Jackass!* (1981, paper $2.25).

4308. Baldwin, Margaret. *Fortune Telling* (2–5). 1984, Messner $9.29. A great variety of fortune-telling techniques are explored.

4309. Bendick, Jeanne. *Scare a Ghost, Tame a Monster* (4–6). Illus. by author. 1983, Westminster $11.95. Beliefs and superstitions about ghosts, monsters, and supernatural beings.

4310. Berger, Melvin. *The Supernatural: From ESP to UFO's* (6–9). Illus. 1977, Harper $9.57. Basic material on an intriguing subject is well presented.

4311. Blumberg, Rhoda. *Witches* (5–8). Illus. 1979, Watts $8.90. A history of witchcraft and the horrendous witch-hunts in Europe and America. Also use: *Devils and Demons* (1982, Watts LB $8.90).

4312. Branley, Franklyn M. *Age of Aquarius: You and Astrology* (4–6). Illus. by Leonard Kessler. 1979, Harper $10.53; LB $10.89. An explanation of the 12 zodiac signs and a world history of astrology are included in this account.

4313. Branley, Franklyn M. *A Book of Flying Saucers for You* (3–4). Illus. by Leonard Kessler. 1973, Harper $9.89. A report on the phenomena considered flying saucers and details on probable explanations.

4314. Calhoun, Mary. *Medicine Show: Conning People and Making Them Like It* (6–9). Illus. 1976, Harper LB $9.89. An entertaining survey of the confidence games practiced in medicine shows from the mid-nineteenth century to the 1940s.

4315. Campbell, Hannah. *Why Did They Name It?* (3–6). Illus. 1964, Fleet $8.95. The stories behind such brand names as Sanka and Kodak.

4316. Christensen, Nancy. *Monsters: Creatures of Mystery* (2–4). Illus. by Pamela Baldwin Ford. 1980, Platt $5.95; LB $11.85. A brief introduction to various monsters.

4317. Cohen, Daniel. *America's Very Own Monsters* (2–4). Illus. by Tom Huffman. 1982, Dodd $7.95. Ten monsters introduced simply for young readers. Also use: *Science Fiction's Greatest Monsters* (1980, Dodd $8.95).

4318. Cohen, Daniel. *The Body Snatchers* (6–8). Illus. 1975, Harper $10.10; paper $2.95. The spine-tingling, fascinating subject of the history of grave robbing, handled with taste. Also use: *The Tomb Robbers* (1980, McGraw $10.95).

4319. Cohen, Daniel. *Creatures from UFO's* (6–8). Illus. 1978, Dodd $9.57. A collection of stories of encounters with aliens, often in the words of the original observers.

4320. Cohen, Daniel. *Curses, Hexes and Spells* (5–7). Illus. 1974, Harper $8.89. A lively discussion of all sorts of creepy phenomena and evil magic. Also use: *Famous Curses* (1979, Dodd $8.95; Pocket paper $1.95); *Masters of Horror* (1984, Houghton $11.95).

4321. Cohen, Daniel. *Frauds, Hoaxes and Swindles* (4–7). Illus. 1979, Dell paper $1.50. A book that tells about the people behind some great hoaxes.

4322. Cohen, Daniel. *The World's Most Famous Ghosts* (6–9). 1978, Dodd $8.95; Pocket paper $2.25. A report in 10 short chapters of better-known incidents accredited to ghosts. Also use: *Real Ghosts* (1977, Dodd $8.95; Pocket paper $1.95); *Young Ghosts* (1978, Dutton $7.95); *Ghostly Terrors* (1981, Dodd LB $8.95; Pocket paper $1.95).

4323. Cornell, James C. *Nature at Its Strangest* (5–9). Illus. 1974, Sterling $7.95; LB $9.99. A wonderful browsing book on strange, short-lived natural phenomena, such as stones suddenly pushing out of the ground in an Oklahoma pasture.

4324. Dolan, Edward F., Jr. *Great Mysteries of the Air* (4–7). Illus. 1983, Dodd $8.95. Unsolved mysteries dealing with aviation, such as the disappearance of Amelia Earhart. Also use: *Great Mysteries of the Sea* (1984, Dodd $8.95).

4325. Edelson, Edward. *Great Animals of the Movies* (5–8). Illus. 1980, Doubleday LB $8.95. A history and profile of the most important animals—real and imaginary—that have appeared in movies.

4326. Feinman, Jeffrey. *Freebies for Kids* (4–9). 1983, Simon & Schuster paper $4.95. All kinds of free materials are listed here under such subject headings as careers, pets, and health.

4327. Fisher, Leonard Everett. *Star Signs* (3–6). Illus. by author. 1983, Holiday LB $13.95. An introduction to astrology.

4328. Giblin, James, and Ferguson, Dale. *The Scarecrow Book* (2–5). Illus. 1980, Crown $8.95. The history and present status of various crow-scaring devices.

4329. Haislip, Barbara. *Stars, Spells, Secrets and Sorcery: A Do-It-Yourself Book of the Occult* (6–7). Illus. 1976, Little $10.95. Many types of Asian occult phenomena, including I Ching and Tarot cards, are explored.

4330. Hayman, LeRoy. *Thirteen Who Vanished* (4–6). 1979, Messner $8.29. True stories about famous people such as Amelia Earhart and Judge Crater, who disappeared mysteriously.

4331. Hazen, Barbara S. *Last, First, Middle and Nick: All about Names* (3–6). Illus. by Sam Weissman. 1979, Prentice $7.95. A book about how names originated, their meanings, trends in naming, and how names can be changed.

4332. Kettelkamp, Larry. *Haunted Houses* (4–6). Illus. by author. 1969, Morrow $8.95; LB $8.59. The author documents 10 case histories where ghosts or poltergeists have made their presence known, and speculates on the reasons for these supernatural occurrences. Also use: *Mischievous Ghosts: The Poltergeist and PK* (1980, Morrow $8.75; LB $8.50).

4333. Kettelkamp, Larry. *Investigating Psychics: Five Life Histories* (5–9). Illus. 1977, Morrow $8.59. Parapsychology is examined through the lives of several psychics who have worked with scientists to explain this phenomenon. Also use: *Sixth Sense* (1970, Morrow $8.59).

4334. Knight, David C. *Those Mysterious UFO's* (4–6). Illus. 1975, Parents LB $9.95. A history of mysterious objects that people have seen in the sky.

4335. Lauber, Patricia. *Mystery Monsters of Loch Ness* (3–5). Illus. 1978, Garrard $7.22. A report by an author who obviously believes that such a creature exists.

4336. Lopshire, Robert. *The Biggest, Smallest, Fastest, Tallest Things You've Ever Heard Of* (1–3). 1980, Harper $8.95; LB $8.89. A junior version of Guinness in question-and-answer format.

4337. McGowen, Tom. *Encyclopedia of Legendary Creatures* (4–6). Illus. by Victor G. Ambrus. 1982, Rand McNally $8.95. More than 100 supernatural beings like leprechauns and zombies are described.

4338. McHargue, Georgess. *Meet the Werewolf* (2–5). Illus. by Stephen Gammell. 1976, Harper $10.53; Dell paper $2.95. Stories, legends, and other materials are entertainingly presented. Also use: *Meet the Vampire* (1979, Harper $10.89; Dell paper $1.95); *Meet the Witches* (1984, Harper $10.53; LB $10.89).

4339. McLoone, Margo, and Siegel, Alice. *The Kids' Book of Lists* (4–7). 1980, Holt $9.95. A trivia book that deals with accomplishments of children.

4340. McWhirter, Norris, ed. *Guinness Book of Amazing Animals* (4–6). Illus. by Bill Hinds. 1982, Sterling $6.95; LB $8.99. Ninety-two record-holding animals are introduced.

4341. McWhirter, Norris, ed. *Guinness Book of World Records* (4–9). 1984, Bantam paper $3.95. The one and only Guinness.

4342. Maynard, Christopher. *All about Ghosts* (4–7). Illus. 1978, EMC $7.95. An introduction to this fascinating subject; great for browsing.

4343. Meltzer, Milton. *A Book about Names* (5–8). 1984, Harper $11.06; LB $10.89. Subtitle: "In which customs, traditions, law, myth, history, folklore, foolery, legend, fashion, nonsense, symbol, taboo help explain how we got our names and what they mean."

4344. Mooser, Stephen. *Into the Unknown: Nine Astounding Stories* (3–6). Illus. 1980, Harper LB $9.89. Nine accounts, somewhat fictionalized, of unexplained occurrences involving ESP, reincarnation, and so forth.

4345. Murphy, Jim. *Weird and Wacky Inventions* (4–6). Illus. 1978, Crown $9.95. Unusual and bizarre gizmos from the Patent Office are described.

4346. Nevins, Ann. *Super Stitches: A Book of Superstitions* (4–6). Illus. 1983, Holiday $8.95. An explanation of common superstitions arranged by categories such as "good luck" and "bad luck."

4347. O'Neill, Catherine. *Amazing Mysteries of the World* (3–8). Illus. 1983, National Geographic

Society $6.95; LB $8.50. Stonehenge, Easter Island, and Bigfoot are three of the many mysteries explored.

4348. Phillips, Louis. *The World by Sevens: A Kid's Book of Lists* (5–7). Illus. 1981, Watts LB $8.90. A book of curiosities arranged in lists of 7 facts each.

4349. Place, Marian T. *Bigfoot All Over the Country* (5–9). 1978, Dodd $7.95. A detailed, often fascinating account of the search for Sasquatch. Also use: *On the Track of Bigfoot* (1974, Dodd $10.95).

4350. Pringle, Laurence. *"The Earth Is Flat"—and Other Great Mistakes* (5–8). Illus. by Steve Miller. 1983, Morrow $8.00; LB $7.63. The story of some of the greatest mistakes for which mankind has been responsible.

4351. Quinn, John R. *Nature's World Records* (3–6). Illus. by author. 1977, Walker $5.95; LB $5.85. Nature's slowest, fastest, and so forth, are listed in this chronicle of the unusual.

4352. Rabinowich, Ellen. *The Loch Ness Monster* (3–5). Illus. by Sally Law. 1979, Watts $8.60. Fact and theory are divided equally in this well-illustrated account.

4353. Rudley, Stephen. *The Abominable Snowcreature* (6–9). Illus. 1978, Watts $8.90. An account of the sightings and existing evidence involving the mysterious creature of the Himalayas.

4354. Sarnoff, Jane. *If You Were Really Superstitious* (3–6). Illus. by Reynold Ruffins. 1980, Scribners $7.95. Superstitions are arranged by subjects and given a clever, humorous treatment.

4355. Schwartz, Alvin. *Cross Your Fingers, Spit in Your Hat: Superstitions and Other Beliefs* (4–6). Illus. by Glen Rounds. 1974, Harper $10.10; paper $2.95. An amazing collection of information on a variety of superstitions.

4356. Seuling, Barbara. *You Can't Eat Peanuts in Church and Other Little-Known Laws* (4–7). Illus. by author. 1975, Doubleday $6.95; paper $2.50. A collection of unusual laws gathered from all parts of the United States.

4357. Simon, Seymour. *Creatures from Lost Worlds* (6–9). Illus. 1979, Harper $9.57; LB $9.89. Surveys worlds created in movies, books, and television and tells about the strange beings found there.

4358. Simon, Seymour. *Mad Scientists, Weird Doctors, and Time Travelers in Movies, TV, and Books* (4–8). Illus. 1981, Harper $7.95. An introduction to monsters in the mass media.

4359. Simon, Seymour. *Strange Mysteries from around the World* (3–5). Illus. 1980, Four Winds $8.95. Ten strange phenomena are described, with possible explanations.

4360. Sobol, Donald J. *Disaster* (5–8). 1979, Pocket paper $1.95. Events from the Black Death to a 1970 cyclone in East Pakistan are chronicled.

4361. Sobol, Donald J. *Encyclopedia Brown's Book of Wacky Spies* (5–8). Illus. by Ted Enik. 1984, Morrow $9.50; Bantam paper $1.95. Unusual and curious stories about spies. Also use: *Encyclopedia Brown's Book of Wacky Crimes* (1982, Lodestar $8.95; Bantam paper $1.95).

4362. Sobol, Donald J. *Encyclopedia Brown's Record Book of Weird and Wonderful Facts* (5–8). 1979, Delacorte LB $9.89; Dell paper $2.50. A delightful collection of astonishing information. Also use: *Encyclopedia Brown's Second Record Book of Weird and Wonderful Facts* (1981, Delacorte LB $8.89; Dell paper $1.95).

4363. Taves, Isabella. *True Ghost Stories* (5–7). Illus. by Michael Deas. 1978, Watts $6.90. Six supposedly true supernatural tales.

4364. Wilding-White, Ted. *All about UFO's* (4–7). Illus. 1978, EMC $7.95. An entertaining account of UFOs—probable cause and how to make one.

4365. Wise, William. *Monsters from Outer Space* (3–4). Illus. by Richard Cuffari. 1979, Putnam $6.89. UFOs and other phenomena are discussed objectively and with candor.

Mythology

General and Miscellaneous

4366. Bernstein, Margery, and Kobrin, Janet. *The First Morning: An African Myth Retold* (2–3). Illus. by Enid Warner Romanek. 1976, Scribners paper $3.19. Stark, dramatic illustrations accompany this simple retelling of an African myth that recounts how light came to the world.

4367. Bernstein, Margery, and Kobrin, Janet. *The Summer Maker: An Ojibway Indian Myth* (2–3). Illus. by Anne Burgess. 1977, Scribners paper $1.19. Ojug, the fisher, sets out with several friends in search of summer.

4368. Gifford, Douglas. *Warriors, Gods and Spirits from Central and South American Mythology* (5–8). Illus. by John Sibbick. 1983, Schocken $15.45. Starting with the Incas and Aztecs, this is a collection of South and Central American folklore.

4369. Hamilton, Edith. *Mythology* (6–9). Illus. by Steele Savage. 1942, Little $12.95; NAL paper $2.95. A book of Greek, Roman, and Norse myths, modern in language, sound in scholarship.

4370. Harris, Geraldine. *Gods and Pharaohs from Egyptian Mythology* (5–8). Illus. by David O'Connor and John Sibbick. 1983, Schocken $15.45. A collection of myths and legends from ancient Egypt.

4371. McDermott, Beverly Brodsky. *Sedna: An Eskimo Myth* (K–3). Illus. by author. 1975, Viking $11.50. Food is denied starving Eskimos until they pay proper homage to the sea spirit, Sedna.

4372. McDermott, Gerald. *Arrow to the Sun: A Pueblo Indian Tale* (K–3). Illus. by author. 1974, Viking $10.95; Penguin paper $3.95. Brilliant colors effectively highlight this adaptation of a Pueblo myth—the search by a young Indian boy for his father, the Sun. Caldecott medal winner.

4373. Marriott, Alice Lee, and Rachlin, Carol K. *American Indian Mythology* (5–7). 1968, NAL paper $2.95. Folktales and myths representing seven tribes are presented in an easily read anthology.

4374. Rose, Anne. *Spider in the Sky* (1–3). Illus. by Gail Owens. 1978, Harper LB $8.89. An American Indian myth on how Grandmother Spider brought fire and light to the animals.

Classical

4375. Barth, Edna. *Cupid and Psyche: A Love Story* (4–6). Illus. by Ati Forberg. 1976, Houghton $10.95. The Greek myth adroitly retold and highlighted with tasteful wash drawings.

4376. Benson, Sally. *Stories of the Gods and Heroes* (4–6). Illus. by Steele Savage. 1940, Dial $9.95; Dell paper $1.75. A selection of tales of the Trojan War based on *The Age of Fable* by Bulfinch.

4377. Billout, Guy. *Thunderbolt and Rainbow: A Look at Greek Mythology* (4–7). Illus. 1981, Prentice $9.95. Retelling with modern trappings of several Greek myths.

4378. Colum, Padraic. *The Golden Fleece and the Heroes Who Lived Before Achilles* (5–7). Illus. by Willy Pogany. 1983, Macmillan paper $5.95. Jason's search for the Golden Fleece incorporates some of the best-known myths and legends of ancient Greece.

4379. Coolidge, Olivia. *Greek Myths* (4–7). Illus. by Eduard Sandoz. 1949, Houghton $10.95. Twenty-seven well-known myths dramatically retold with accompanying illustrations.

4380. D'Aulaire, Ingri, and D'Aulaire, Edgar. *D'Aulaires' Book of Greek Myths* (3–6). Illus. by author. 1962, Doubleday $14.95; paper $6.95. Full-color pictures highlight these brief stories, which are excellent for first readers in mythology.

4381. Evslin, Bernard. *Hercules* (5–8). Illus. by Jos. A. Smith. 1984, Morrow $10.00. An exciting account of many of Hercules' adventures.

4382. Fisher, Leonard Everett. *The Olympians: Great Gods and Goddesses of Ancient Greece* (3–5). Illus. 1984, Holiday $14.95. The stories behind 12 of the gods and goddesses of ancient Greece.

4383. Gates, Doris. *A Fair Wind for Troy* (5–8). 1976, Viking $9.95; Penguin paper $2.95. A retelling of legends connected with the Trojan War.

4384. Gates, Doris. *Lord of the Sky: Zeus* (3–6). Illus. by Robert Handville. 1972, Viking $9.95; Penguin paper $2.95. In the first of a series, the author has retold simply and directly myths in which Zeus plays a central part. Also use: *The*

Golden God: Apollo (1973, Viking $9.95; Penguin paper $2.95).

4385. Gates, Doris. *Mightiest of Mortals: Heracles* (4–6). Illus. by Richard Cuffari. 1975, Viking $9.95; Penguin paper $2.95. All of the tales of Heracles are presented in logical order in a breezy, informal style.

4386. Gates, Doris. *The Warrior Goddess Athena* (4–6). Illus. by Don Bolognese. 1972, Viking $9.95; Penguin paper $2.95. A spirited retelling of the myths associated with Athena. Also use: *Two Queens of Heaven: Aphrodite and Demeter* (1974, Viking $9.95; Penguin paper $2.95).

4387. Green, Roger L. *Tales of Greek Heroes* (4–6). 1974, Penguin paper $2.95. Stories in this volume include those about Prometheus, Dionysus, Perseus, and Heracles. Also use: *The Tale of Troy* (1974, Penguin paper $2.95); *The Tale of Thebes* (1977, Cambridge paper $6.50).

4388. Hawthorne, Nathaniel. *Wonderbook and Tanglewood Tales* (5–7). 1853; 1972, Houghton $9.95. This is a highly original retelling of the Greek myths.

4389. Hodges, Margaret. *Persephone and the Springtime: Myths of the World* (K–3). Illus. by Arvis Stewart. 1973, Little $5.95. A gentle retelling of the origins of springtime that occurred when Persephone was released from Hades.

4390. Kingsley, Charles. *The Heroes: Or Greek Fairy Tales for My Children* (5–7). Illus. by H. M. Brock. 1980, Mayflower $8.95. A classic retelling of three Greek myths—those about Perseus, Jason, and Theseus.

4391. Land, Andrew. *Tales of Troy and Greece* (5–8). Illus. by Edward Bawden. 1978, Faber paper $2.95. Tales from the Iliad retold for young people.

4392. Lurie, Alison, retel. *The Heavenly Zoo: Legends and Tales of the Stars* (4–6). Illus. by Monika Beisner. 1980, Farrar $9.95. A retelling of 16 legends involved with star groupings.

4393. McDermott, Gerald, retel. *Daughter of Earth: A Roman Myth* (1–4). Illus. by retel. 1984, Delacorte $15.00. A retelling of the myth of Ceres, the earth mother, and her daughter Proserpina.

4394. McDermott, Gerald. *Sun Flight* (3–6). Illus. by author. 1980, Four Winds $10.95. A retelling of the myth of Daedalus and Icarus.

4395. McLean, Mollie, and Wiseman, Anne. *Adventures of Greek Heroes* (4–6). Illus. by W. T. Mars. 1961, Houghton paper $4.50. Easily read version of myths involving such heroes as Jason, Hercules, and Theseus.

4396. Naden, C. J. *Jason and the Golden Fleece* (2–4). Illus. by Robert Baxter. 1980, Troll LB $8.79; paper $2.50. One of a series of retold myths. Others by the same author and publisher are: *Pegasus, the Winged Horse; Perseus and Medusa; Theseus and the Minotaur* (all 1980, LB $8.79; paper $2.50).

4397. Proddow, Penelope. *Art Tells a Story: Greek and Roman Myths* (4–9). Illus. 1979, Doubleday LB $7.95. Works of various artists are used to illustrate classic myths.

4398. Richardson, I. M. *The Adventures of Eros and Psyche* (3–6). Illus. by Robert Baxter. 1983, Troll $8.79; paper $2.50. How Psyche is able to prove her love for Eros in this retelling of the Greek myth. Others by this author and publisher are: *The Adventures of Hercules* (1983); *Demeter and Persephone: The Season of Time* (1983); *Prometheus and the Story of Fire* (1983) (all LB $8.79; paper $2.50).

4399. Usher, Kerry. *Heroes, Gods and Emperors from Roman Mythology* (5–8). Illus. by John Sibbick. 1984, Schocken $15.45. The story of the *Aeneid* plus those of the Tarquino and Romulus and Remus are 3 of the legends retold here.

4400. Vautier, Ghislaine. *The Shining Stars: Greek Legends of the Zodiac* (4–6). Illus. by Jacqueline Bezencon. 1981, Cambridge $10.95. The Greek legends in the origin of each sign of the zodiac are retold.

Scandinavian

4401. Colum, Padraic. *Children of Odin* (4–6). 1930; 1962, Macmillan $10.95; paper $5.95. Collection of Norse sagas.

4402. Coolidge, Olivia. *Legends of the North* (5–7). Illus. by Eduard Sandoz. 1951, Houghton $13.95. This is a fine collection of Norse myths that includes those about Thor.

4403. D'Aulaire, Ingri, and D'Aulaire, Edgar. *Norse Gods and Giants* (4–6). Illus. by author. 1967, Doubleday $12.95. A vigorous retelling of many of the Norse myths, illustrated with bold, colorful lithographs.

4404. Green, Roger L. *The Myths of the Norsemen* (4–6). Illus. by Brian Wildsmith. 1970, Penguin paper $2.95. The great Norse myths woven into a continuous narrative.

4405. Synge, Ursula. *Land of Heroes: A Retelling of the Kalevala* (6–9). 1978, Atheneum $6.95. A spellbinding but complex retelling of the Finnish national epic.

Religion

General and Miscellaneous

4406. Asimov, Isaac. *Animals of the Bible* (3–7). Illus. 1978, Doubleday $9.95. The kinds and uses of animals mentioned in the Bible.

4407. Bahree, Patricia. *The Hindu World* (5–7). Illus. 1984, Silver Burdett $9.75. An introduction to various aspects of this faith and its place in the world today.

4408. Berger, Gilda. *Religion* (4–8). Illus. by Annee Canevari Green. 1983, Watts LB $8.90. An alphabetically arranged book from Abraham to Zoroastrianism.

4409. Charing, Douglas. *The Jewish World* (5–7). Illus. 1984, Silver Burdett $9.75. An explanation of the religious, social, and historical aspects of this faith.

4410. Daves, Michael. *Young Reader's Book of Christian Symbolism* (5–8). Illus. by Gordon Laite. 1967, Abingdon $10.95. The "history and description of symbolism in the Protestant church."

4411. Edmonds, I. G. *Buddhism* (5–8). Illus. 1978, Watts $8.90. As well as background information, this simple survey discusses the role of Buddhism in the world today.

4412. Edmonds, I. G. *Hinduism* (3–6). Illus. 1979, Watts $8.90. A basic introduction to the world's third largest religion.

4413. Faber, Doris. *The Perfect Life: The Shakers in America* (6–9). Illus. 1974, Farrar $6.95. The author astutely appraises this communal movement that anticipated the concerns of modern back-to-nature advocates.

4414. Fellows, Lawrence. *A Gentle War: The Story of the Salvation Army* (5–8). Illus. 1979, Macmillan $9.95. A narrative that traces the history and present status of the Salvation Army.

4415. Haskins, James. *Religions* (6–9). 1973, Harper $10.53. The history, founders, and practices of 5 religions—Buddhism, Christianity, Hinduism, Islam, and Judaism—are described in this introductory survey.

4416. Moskin, Marietta D. *In Search of God: The Story of Religion* (6–9). Illus. 1979, Atheneum $10.95. An account that explores the many ways men and women have searched for a meaning to life.

4417. Rice, Edward. *American Saints and Seers: American-Born Religions and the Genius behind Them* (6–9). 1982, Four Winds $11.95. A look at such native religions as Mormonism and Christian Science.

4418. Rice, Edward. *Ten Religions of the East* (6–9). Illus. 1978, Four Winds $9.95. The history and principal teachers of 10 Eastern faiths, including some, such as Cao Dai and Bon, rarely written about.

4419. Seeger, Elizabeth. *Eastern Religions* (6–8). Illus. 1973, Harper $12.50. The lives and teachings of Buddha, Confucius, and Lao-tse are highlighted in this well-organized, valuable account.

4420. Serage, Nancy. *The Prince Who Gave Up a Throne* (4–6). Illus. by Kazue Mizumura. 1966, Harper $11.49. The life of Buddha and the meaning of his teachings.

4421. Synge, Ursula. *The Giant at the Ford and Other Legends of the Saints* (6–8). Illus. by Shirley Felts. 1980, Atheneum $9.95. A retelling of several legends associated with the lives of the saints.

4422. Tames, Richard. *The Muslim World* (5–7). Illus. 1984, Silver Burdett $9.75. An introduction to this faith and its influence in the world today.

4423. Terrien, Samuel. *The Golden Bible Atlas* (4–7). Illus. 1957, Western $8.95. Colorful maps of the Holy Land, faithfully reproduced.

4424. Yolen, Jane. *Simple Gifts: The Story of the Shakers* (5–7). Illus. by Betty Fraser. 1976, Viking $9.95. A brief account of the Shaker way of life.

Bible Stories

4425. Asch, Sholem. *In the Beginning: Stories from the Bible* (4–6). Illus. by Eleanor Klemm. 1979, Schocken paper $3.95. A retelling of Old Testament stories such as those of Adam and Eve, Noah, and the Tower of Babel.

4426. Bull, Norman J. *One-Hundred Bible Stories* (5–8). Illus. by Val Biro. 1983, Abingdon $7.95. A clear and direct retelling of well-known and less well-known Bible stories.

4427. Bull, Norman J. *The Story of Jesus* (3–5). Illus. by Mike Codd. 1982, Abingdon $13.95. The life of Jesus plus a section on life in the first century.

4428. Chaikin, Miriam. *Joshua in the Promised Land* (4–8). Illus. by David Frampton. 1982, Houghton $11.50. The story of Moses' success and the Israelites journey to the Holy Land.

4429. Christie-Murray, David. *The Illustrated Children's Bible* (3–6). Illus. by Ken Petts and Norma Burgin. 1983, Putnam $12.95. The retelling of famous Bible stories is interspersed with historical asides. historical asides.

4430. Cohen, Barbara. *The Binding of Isaac* (2–4). Illus. by Charles Mikolaycak. 1978, Lothrop $10.95; LB $10.51. Isaac, as an old man, tells the story of himself and Abraham.

4431. Cohen, Barbara. *I Am Joseph* (3–4). Illus. by Charles Mikolaycak. 1980, Lothrop $12.88; LB $12.39. The story of the biblical Joseph in simple, dignified text and color pencil drawings.

4432. de Paola, Tomie. *Noah and the Ark* (PS–2). Illus. by author. 1983, Winston $12.95; paper $5.95. A straightforward retelling.

4433. Efron, Olsen. *Bible Stories You Can't Forget: No Matter How Hard You Try* (5–Up). 1979, Dell paper $1.25. Eight Bible stories retold with humor and wit.

4434. Farber, Norma. *Where's Gomer?* (K–3). Illus. by William Pene du Bois. 1974, Dutton $9.95. Gomer, son of Japheth, son of Noah, is missing when it is time to board the ark.

4435. Fisher, Leonard Everett, adapt. *The Seven Days of Creation* (PS–3). Illus. by adapt. 1981, Holiday LB $12.95. The story of creation told with striking illustrations.

4436. Garfield, Leon. *King Nimrod's Tower* (3–4). Illus. by Michael Bragg. 1982, Lothrop $11.25. A very loose retelling of the Tower of Babel story.

4437. Haubensak-Tellenbach, Margrit. *The Story of Noah's Ark* (K–3). Illus. by Erna Emhardt. 1983, Crown $9.95. A humanized retelling of the Flood story.

4438. Hewitt, Kathryn. *Two by Two: The Untold Story* (4–6). Illus. 1984, Harcourt $12.95. A hilarious retelling of the Ark story.

4439. Hirsh, Marilyn. *The Tower of Babel* (PS–2). Illus. by author. 1981, Holiday LB $6.95. The Genesis story explained and illustrated.

4440. Hutton, Warwick. *Jonah and the Great Fish* (PS–4). Illus. by author. 1984, Atheneum $12.95. A fine retelling of the biblical story with equally good pictures.

4441. Hutton, Warwick. *Noah and the Great Flood* (1–3). Illus. by author. 1977, Atheneum $12.95. The version of the Flood from the King James Bible is excellently illustrated by a master artist.

4442. Lenski, Lois. *Mr. and Mrs. Noah* (PS–1). Illus. by author. 1948, Harper $8.61; LB $8.89. A charming retelling of the Flood story.

4443. Proddow, Penelope. *Art Tells a Story: The Bible* (4–9). Illus. 1979, Doubleday $7.95. Bible stories are represented through the work of famous artists.

4444. Reed, Gwendolyn E. *Adam and Eve* (1–3). Illus. by Helen Siegl. 1968, Lothrop $10.51. The creation story and life in the Garden of Eden are re-created with dignity.

4445. Singer, Isaac Bashevis. *The Wicked City* (4–8). Illus. by Leonard Everett Fisher. 1972, Farrar $6.95. An unusual retelling of the story of Lot in Sodom from the book of Genesis.

4446. Spier, Peter, illus. *Noah's Ark* (PS–K). 1977, Doubleday $7.90; paper $3.95. Vital, humorous, detailed pictures present a panorama of the animals and their voyage in the Ark. Caldecott Medal, 1977.

4447. Stoddard, Sandol. *The Doubleday Illustrated Children's Bible* (4–6). Illus. by Tony Chen. 1983, Doubleday $14.95. A retelling of 108 episodes in a single narrative.

4448. Tudor, Tasha, illus. *The Lord Is My Shepherd* (All Ages). 1980, Putnam $6.95. An illustrated edition of the Twenty-third Psalm.

4449. Wangerin, Walter. *The Bible: Its Story for Children* (5–7). Illus. 1981, Rand McNally $12.95; LB $12.97. A collection of stories from both the Old and New Testaments.

4450. Webber, Andrew Lloyd, and Rice, Tim. *Joseph and the Amazing Technicolor Dreamcoat* (5–9). Illus. by Quentin Blake. 1982, Holt $11.50. The text of the musical based on the Old Testament story.

4451. Weil, Lisl. *Esther* (K–2). Illus. by author. 1980, Atheneum $9.95. The story of how Esther saved the Hebrews.

4452. Weil, Lisl. *The Very First Story Ever Told* (PS–2). Illus. by author. 1976, Atheneum $7.95. The Genesis account of creation retold in simple text and pictures.

Nativity

4453. Baker, Laura N. *Friendly Beasts* (PS–2). Illus. by Nicholas Sidjakov. 1957, Houghton $4.95. The story of the animals that waited in wonder in the Bethlehem stable for the Christ Child's birth.

4454. Bierhorst, John, trans. *Spirit Child: A Story of the Nativity* (PS–2). Illus. by Barbara Cooney. 1984, Morrow $11.60; LB $11.04. An Aztec account of the Nativity.

4455. Brown, Margaret Wise. *Christmas in the Barn* (PS–1). Illus. by Barbara Cooney. 1952, Harper $8.95. A beautiful retelling of the Nativity story with effective illustrations.

4456. de Paola, Tomie. *The First Christmas* (PS–3). Illus. by author. 1984, Putnam $12.95. Six vignettes illustrated with pop-up pictures depict the Nativity story.

4457. de Paola, Tomie. *The Story of the Three Wise Kings* (PS–2). Illus. by author. 1983, Putnam $10.95; paper $4.59. The timeless tale of the Magi and their journey.

4458. Kurelek, William. *A Northern Nativity: Christmas Dreams of a Prairie Boy* (1–3). Illus. 1976, Tundra $14.95; paper $7.95. Twenty paintings of the Holy Family transferred to various locales, accompanied by a lyrical text.

4459. Petersham, Maud, and Petersham, Miska. *The Christ Child: As Told by Matthew and Luke* (K–3). Illus. 1931, Doubleday $10.95; paper $4.95. With outstanding illustrations, this story uses direct quotations from the Bible.

4460. Pienkowski, Jan, illus. *Christmas* (1–6). 1984, Knopf $17.95. The story of Christmas as told in various books of the King James Bible.

4461. Trimby, Elisa, illus. *The Christmas Story* (PS–3). 1984, Lothrop $10.00. The story of the Nativity using the King James Bible version.

4462. Weil, Lisl, retel. *The Story of the Wise Men and the Child* (2–4). Illus. by retel. 1981, Atheneum $9.95. The part of the Nativity story as retold from the Gospel of Matthew.

4463. Winthrop, Elizabeth, adapt. *A Child Is Born: The Christmas Story* (All Ages). Illus. by Charles Mikolaycak. 1983, Holiday $14.95. The story of Christmas adapted from the King James version of the Bible, beautifully illustrated.

Prayers

4464. Field, Rachel. *Prayer for a Child* (1–3). Illus. by Elizabeth Orton Jones. 1944, Macmillan $7.95; paper $3.95. A prayer bespeaking the faith, hope, and love of little children. Caldecott Medal, 1945.

4465. Haywood, Carolyn. *Make a Joyful Noise!* (2–6). Illus. by Lane Yerkes. 1984, Westminster $11.95. A collection of Bible verses for children.

4466. Larrick, Nancy, sel. *Tambourines! Tambourines to Glory! Prayers and Poems* (PS–6). Illus. by Geri Greinke. 1982, Westminster $8.95. A collection of 76 religious poems.

4467. Magagna, Anna M., illus. *First Prayers* (PS–3). 1983, Macmillan $7.95. About 35 prayers for young children on a variety of subjects.

4468. Tudor, Tasha. *First Prayers* (K–3). Illus. by author. 1952, McKay $3.50. A small-sized, simple book with prayers for different times of the day. Also use: *First Graces* (1955, McKay $3.50).

4469. Wilkin, Eloise, illus. *Prayers for a Small Child* (K–1). 1984, Random $3.95; LB $4.99. A collection of nondenominational prayers for the young.

Holidays and Holy Days

General and Miscellaneous

4470. Alexander, Sue. *Small Plays for Special Days* (2–4). Illus. by Tom Huffman. 1977, Houghton $8.95. Short 2-character plays for many holidays.

4471. Anderson, Norman D., and Brown, Walter R. *Fireworks! Pyrotechnics on Display* (3–6). Illus. 1983, Dodd $9.95. A history of fireworks and their association with Fourth of July festivities.

4472. Barth, Edna. *Shamrocks, Harps and Shillelaghs: The Story of St. Patrick's Day Symbols* (3–5). Illus. by Ursula Arndt. 1977, Houghton $9.95. Customs and symbols associated with St. Patrick's Day, with the origin of each explained.

4473. Behrens, June. *Gung Hay Fat Choy: Happy New Year* (2–4). Illus. 1982, Childrens Pr. $10.35. A description of the Chinese New Year and how it is celebrated.

4474. Bradley, Virginia. *Holidays on Stage: A Festival of Special-Occasion Plays* (5–7). 1981, Dodd LB $10.95. Ten plays, each on a different holiday.

4475. Brenner, Martha. *Fireworks Tonight!* (5–9). Illus. 1984, Hastings $10.95. A comprehensive history of fireworks, including information about the industry and the care that must be taken when using fireworks.

4476. Brown, Marc. *Arthur's April Fool* (PS–2). Illus. by author. 1983, Little $13.45. Arthur is afraid he will forget his magic tricks prepared for the April Fools' Day show.

4477. Bulla, Clyde Robert. *Washington's Birthday* (1–4). Illus. by Don Bolognese. 1967, Harper $9.89. A brief biography of Washington plus a description of the many ways his birthday is celebrated.

4478. Bunting, Eve. *St. Patrick's Day in the Morning* (PS–2). Illus. by Jan Brett. 1980, Houghton $10.95; paper $3.95. A story about how a young boy celebrates St. Patrick's Day.

4479. Burnett, Bernice. *Holidays* (4–7). 1983, Watts $8.90. Brief background on many holidays, foreign and domestic.

4480. Cantwell, Mary. *St. Patrick's Day* (1–3). Illus. by Ursula Arndt. 1967, Harper $9.89. The life of St. Patrick and how his day is celebrated around the world.

4481. Cheng, Hou-Tien. *The Chinese New Year* (K–3). 1976, Holt $7.95. Various facets and meanings of the cycle of animal signs and the festivities surrounding the celebration of the Chinese New Year.

4482. Cole, Ann, et al. *A Pumpkin in a Pear Tree: Creative Ideas for Twelve Months of Holiday Fun* (4–7). Illus. by Debby Young. 1976, Little $10.95; paper $6.95. Games and other activities for various holidays.

4483. Dobler, Lavinia. *Customs and Holidays around the World* (5–8). Illus. by Josephine Little. 1962, Fleet $9.50. Survey of holidays arranged by season, with a detailed index for specific holidays.

4484. Epstein, Sam, and Epstein, Beryl. *Spring Holidays* (4–6). Illus. by Ted Schroeder. 1964, Garrard $6.56. A simple description of various spring holidays, such as April Fools' Day and Groundhog Day.

4485. Gaer, Joseph. *Holidays around the World* (6–9). Illus. by Anne Marie Jauss. 1953, Little $7.95. An account of the origin and observance of holidays in the Buddhist, Jewish, Hindu, Christian, and Muslim religions. The last chapter concerns United Nations Day.

4486. Giblin, James. *Fireworks, Picnics, and Flags* (3–6). Illus. by Ursula Arndt. 1983, Houghton $10.95; paper $3.95. A history of the Fourth of July holiday and how it was and is celebrated.

4487. Glovach, Linda. *The Little Witch's Birthday Book* (3–5). Illus. 1981, Prentice $7.95; paper $4.95. A handbook for birthday-party givers with many activities suitable for any time.

4488. Glovach, Linda. *The Little Witch's Spring Holiday Book* (3–5). Illus. 1983, Prentice $8.95. Spring holidays, including Easter and Passover, are introduced, and many simple craft projects are included.

4489. Graves, Charles P. *Fourth of July* (2–5). Illus. by Ken Wagner. 1963, Garrard $7.56. Interesting descriptions of the many patriotic symbols associated with this day.

4490. Greene, Carol. *Holidays around the World* (1–4). Illus. 1982, Childrens Pr. $6.95. A simple introduction to some of the world's most important holidays; many illustrations and large type.

4491. Groh, Lynn. *New Year's Day* (1–3). Illus. by Leonard Shortall. 1964, Garrard $7.56. How and why New Year's Day is celebrated all over the world.

4492. Hautzig, Esther. *Holiday Treats* (5–8). Illus. by Yaroslava. 1983, Macmillan $9.95. Forty recipes for 16 different holidays.

4493. Haywood, Carolyn. *Happy Birthday from Carolyn Haywood* (2–4). Illus. by Wendy Watson. 1984, Morrow $9.50. Mini-stories dealing with birthdays.

4494. Janice. *Little Bear's New Year's Party* (PS–K). Illus. by Mariana. 1973, Lothrop LB $11.88. Little Bear and his friends have never been invited to a New Year's party and decide to have one of their own.

4495. Kelley, Emily. *April Fools' Day* (2–4). Illus. by C. A. Nobens. 1983, Carolrhoda $6.95. A history of April Fools' Day and how it is celebrated in various countries.

4496. Kelley, Emily. *Happy New Year* (2–4). Illus. by Priscilla Kiedrowski. 1984, Carolrhoda $7.95. A description of 6 different New Year's celebrations throughout the world.

4497. Kessel, Joyce K. *St. Patrick's Day* (1–4). Illus. by Cathy Gilchrist. 1983, Carolrhoda LB $7.95. The story of St. Patrick and details on how his day is celebrated.

4498. Larrick, Nancy. *Poetry for Holidays* (4–6). Illus. by Kelly Oechsli. 1966, Garrard $6.69. A variety of poems describing 10 well-known holidays, including a birthday.

4499. Livingston, Myra Cohn, ed. *Callooh! Callay! Holiday Poems for Young Readers* (4–6). Illus. by Janet Stevens. 1978, Atheneum $7.95. A lovely collection of poems about holidays and anniversaries.

4500. Livingston, Myra Cohn, ed. *O Frabjous Day! Poetry for Holidays and Special Occasions* (5–8). 1977, Atheneum $9.95. A splendid anthology arranged by headings "To Honor," "To Celebrate," and "To Remember," rather than the conventional chronological approach.

4501. Manning-Sanders, Ruth, ed. *Festivals* (3–6). Illus. by Raymond Briggs. 1973, Dutton $8.95. An anthology of prose and poetry arranged chronologically by monthly holidays. A month-by-month account of the world's most famous holidays as seen through the eyes of famous writers.

4502. Modell, Frank. *Goodbye Old Year, Hello New Year* (PS–2). Illus. by author. 1984, Greenwillow $10.00; LB $9.55. Marvin and Milton are a little late in celebrating New Year's.

4503. Perl, Lila. *Candles, Cakes and Donkey Tales: Birthday Symbols and Celebrations* (4–8). Illus. by Victoria de Larrea. 1984, Houghton $11.95; paper $4.95. The traditions behind birthday celebrations, plus ways to enjoy birthdays.

4504. Perl, Lila. *Pinatas and Paper Flowers: Holidays of the Americas in English and Spanish* (4–8). Illus. by Victoria de Larrea. 1983, Houghton $11.50; paper $4.50. Eight Hispanic holidays are highlighted in this bilingual volume.

4505. Phelan, Mary Kay. *The Fourth of July* (1–3). Illus. by Symeon Shimin. 1966, Harper $9.89. The origins of the Declaration of Independence and information on its signers.

4506. Phelan, Mary Kay. *Mother's Day* (1–3). Illus. by Aliki. 1965, Harper $9.89. A brief history of this holiday from its origins to its spread around the world.

4507. Quackenbush, Robert, ed. *The Holiday Song Book* (3–7). Illus. by ed. 1977, Lothrop $12.95; LB $12.39. Over 100 songs arranged under various holidays.

4508. Rabe, Olive. *United Nations Day* (1–3). Illus. by Aliki. 1965, Harper $7.21. The significance of this day is explained through a description of the United Nations and its work.

4509. Scott, Geoffrey. *Labor Day* (1–4). Illus. by Cherie R. Wyman. 1982, Carolrhoda LB $7.95. A simple book about the first Labor Day.

4510. Scott, Geoffrey. *Memorial Day* (1–4). Illus. by Peter E. Hanson. 1983, Carolrhoda $6.95. The origins of Memorial Day and the Civil War are discussed.

4511. Showers, Paul. *Columbus Day* (1–3). 1965, Harper $10.84. The beginnings of this national holiday and how it is celebrated today.

4512. Tudor, Tasha. *Tasha Tudor's Sampler: A Tale for Easter/Pumpkin Moonshine/The Dolls' Christmas* (PS–3). 1977, McKay $9.95. Three holiday stories originally published separately in 1938, 1941, and 1950.

4513. Tudor, Tasha. *A Time to Keep* (PS–3). Illus. by author. 1977, Rand McNally $7.95. Subtitled "The Tasha Tudor Book of Holidays": the author reminisces about her family's New England festivities.

Christmas

4514. Barth, Edna. *Holly, Reindeer and Colored Lights: The Story of the Christmas Symbols* (3–6). Illus.

by Ursula Arndt. 1971, Houghton $8.95; paper $3.95. Christmas and its symbols from around the world.

4515. Cooney, Barbara. *Christmas* (2–4). Illus. by author. 1967, Harper LB $10.89. A serene and joyful book about Christmas, its background and significance.

4516. Cuyler, Margery. *The All-Around Christmas Book* (3–6). Illus. by Corbett Jones. 1982, Holt $11.95; paper $4.95. Christmas customs are explained and information is given on holiday cooking and crafts.

4517. de Paola, Tomie. *The Family Christmas Tree Book* (PS–3). Illus. by author. 1980, Holiday LB $10.95; paper $5.95. The story of Christmas tree traditions, including a history of ornaments.

4518. Gibbons, Gail. *Christmas Time* (PS). Illus. 1982, Holiday $11.95. A simple explanation of the origins and traditions associated with Christmas.

4519. Hawkins, Robert. *The Christmas Tree Farm* (3–6). Illus. 1981, Messner LB $9.29. The history of Christmas trees and a discussion of how they are grown on farms.

4520. Herda, D. J. *Christmas* (4–7). Illus. 1983, Watts $8.90. The basic story of Christmas and ways it is celebrated.

4521. Patterson, Lillie. *Christmas Feasts and Festivals* (3–4). Illus. by Cliff Schule. 1968, Garrard $7.56. A simple account of many ways in which Christmas is celebrated and how these customs originated.

4522. Sawyer, Ruth. *Joy to the World: Christmas Legends* (3–6). Illus. by Trina S. Hyman. 1966, Little $7.95. Legends from Arabia, Serbia, Ireland, and Spain, accompanied by a Christmas carol for each of the 6 stories.

4523. Spier, Peter. *Peter Spier's Christmas!* (PS–K). Illus. by author. 1983, Doubleday $9.95. The spirit of Christmas is captured in these illustrations without words.

4524. Stevens, Patricia Bunning. *Merry Christmas! A History of the Holiday* (6–9). Illus. 1979, Macmillan $10.95. An examination of both historical and contemporary customs associated with this holiday in various countries.

4525. Tudor, Tasha, ed. *Take Joy: The Tasha Tudor Christmas Book* (1–6). Illus. by ed. 1966, Collins $10.95; LB $10.99. An anthology of Christmas stories, poems, carols, lore, and legend carefully selected and lovingly illustrated.

4526. Willson, Robina Beckles. *Merry Christmas: Children at Christmastime around the World* (PS–5). Illus. by Satomi Ichikawa. 1983, Putnam $12.95.

The Nativity story is presented plus traditions and customs from around the world.

Fiction

4527. Adams, Adrienne. *The Christmas Party* (1–3). Illus. by author. 1978, Scribners $10.95; paper $2.95. An Easter bunny helps prepare for a Christmas party.

4528. Agee, Jon. *If Snow Falls: A Story for December* (PS). Illus. by author. 1982, Pantheon $5.95; LB $6.99. A young boy dreams of a Santa Claus–like man in his workshop.

4529. Andersen, Hans Christian. *The Fir Tree* (2–4). Illus. by Nancy E. Burkert. 1970, Harper $9.57; LB $10.89. Exquisitely detailed color pictures add distinction to this favorite Christmas story.

4530. Asbjornsen, Peter C. *Cat on the Dovrefell: A Christmas Tale* (1–3). Illus. by Tomie de Paola. 1979, Putnam $8.95; paper $3.95. A Finmark man and his bear frighten off the trolls who have spoiled many Christmases for the Halvor family.

4531. Baker, Betty. *Santa Rat* (2–4). Illus. by Tom Huffman. 1980, Greenwillow $11.25; LB $11.88. Several animals prepare to celebrate Christmas for the first time.

4532. Bonsall, Crosby. *Twelve Bells for Santa* (1–3). Illus. 1977, Harper $7.64; LB $8.89. When Santa disappears, 3 children start out for the North Pole to find him, in this easily read book.

4533. Briggs, Raymond. *Father Christmas* (K–3). Illus. by author. 1973, Putnam $9.95; Penguin paper $3.95. Christmas Eve, as Santa sees it, is pictured by the author-artist (winner of the Kate Greenaway Medal) in full-color, comic-strip style. Also use: *Father Christmas Goes on a Holiday* (1975, Penguin paper $3.95).

4534. Bright, Robert. *Georgie's Christmas Carol* (K–2). 1975, Doubleday $7.95. Georgie, the friendly ghost, organizes an unusual Christmas surprise for 2 children and their uncle, gloomy Mr. Glooms, who has never celebrated Christmas before.

4535. Brown, Marc. *Arthur's Christmas* (K–2). Illus. by author. 1984, Little $12.95. Arthur, an anteater, has a series of Christmas adventures.

4536. Burch, Robert. *Christmas with Ida Early* (5–7). 1983, Viking $10.95. A preacher involves Ida in a Christmas pageant in this amusing story.

4537. Caudill, Rebecca. *A Certain Small Shepherd* (3–6). Illus. by William Pene du Bois. 1965, Holt $8.95; paper $3.95. A mute boy gets an opportunity to play one of the shepherds in a Christmas pageant. Also use: *A Pocketful of Cricket* (1964, Holt $7.95; paper $2.95).

4538.   Cazet, Denys. *Christmas Moon* (PS–2). Illus. by author. 1984, Bradbury $12.95. A Christmas moon helps a rabbit forget his sadness at the death of his grandfather.

4539.   Chalmers, Mary. *Merry Christmas, Harry* (PS–2). Illus. by author. 1977, Harper paper $1.44. Harry, a small cat, asks Santa for a kitten.

4540.   Chapman, Jean. *The Sugar-Plum Christmas Book: A Book for Christmas and All the Days of the Year* (3–5). Illus. by Deborah Niland. 1982, Childrens Pr. $12.95. Poems and fiction plus lore and activities related to Christmas.

4541.   Climo, Shirley. *The Cobweb Christmas* (K–3). Illus. by Joe Lasker. 1982, Harper $10.58; LB $10.89. Spiders turn Tante's Christmas tree into a glistening thing of beauty.

4542.   Cooney, Barbara, adapt. *The Little Juggler* (1–4). Illus. by adapt. 1982, Hastings $9.95. The French folktale of the juggler who wants to do something special for Christ at Christmas.

4543.   Corrin, Sara, and Corrin, Stephen, eds. *The Faber Book of Christmas Stories* (6–9). Illus. by Jill Bennett. 1984, Faber $9.95. Fourteen stories are here, including an abridgment of Dickens's *Christmas Carol.*

4544.   Corrin, Sara, and Corrin, Stephen, eds. *Round the Christmas Tree* (K–4). Illus. by Jill Bennett. 1983, Faber $8.95. Sixteen stories, many of them fairy tales, about Christmas.

4545.   Dalgliesh, Alice. *Christmas: A Book of Stories Old and New* (4–7). Illus. by Hildegard Woodward. 1962, Scribners $9.95. A standard collection of stories and poems that have delighted children for years.

4546.   Davidson, Amanda. *Teddy's First Christmas* (PS). Illus. by author. 1982, Holt $7.95. Teddy crawls out of his box under the Christmas tree to explore.

4547.   Davies, Valentine. *Miracle on 34th Street* (3–6). Illus. by Tomie de Paola. 1984, Harcourt $16.95. An old man named Kris Kringle is hired as the Macy Santa Claus.

4548.   De Angeli, Marguerite. *The Lion in the Box* (4–6). Illus. by author. 1975, Doubleday $6.95. The 5 children in the poor, fatherless Scher family prepare for Christmas in a novel set in turn-of-the-century New York.

4549.   de Paola, Tomie, ed. *The Clown of God* (K–3). Illus. by author. 1978, Harcourt $10.95; paper $6.95. On Christmas Eve, a juggler gives to a statue of Christ his only possession, the gift of his art.

4550.   de Paola, Tomie, retel. *The Legend of Old Befana* (PS–3). Illus. by retel. 1980, Harcourt paper $3.95. The legend of the old lady who is still searching for the Christ child.

4551.   Dickens, Charles. *A Christmas Carol* (6–9). Illus. by Trina S. Hyman. 1983, Holiday $14.95. A handsome edition of this classic. Two other recommended editions are: Illus. by Greg Hildebrandt (1983, Simon & Schuster $11.50; Messner LB $11.97); illus. by Michael Foreman (1983, Dutton $12.58).

4552.   Duvoisin, Roger. *Petunia's Christmas* (K–3). Illus. by author. 1952, Knopf $7.99. Petunia, the beloved goose, decides to rescue Charles, a gander, destined for a Christmas dinner table.

4553.   Erickson, Russell E. *Warton's Christmas Eve Adventure* (2–4). Illus. by Lawrence Di Fiori. 1977, Lothrop LB $9.84; Dell paper $1.50. Warton's attempts to fill the hours until he can open his Christmas presents lead to some exciting adventures.

4554.   Estes, Eleanor. *The Coat-Hanger Christmas Tree* (4–6). Illus. by author. 1973, Atheneum paper $1.95. Marianna and her brother decide on a substitute when their mother forbids them to have a Christmas tree.

4555.   Ets, Marie Hall, and Labastida, Aurora. *Nine Days to Christmas* (K–2). Illus. 1959, Viking $11.95. Kindergartner Ceci is old enough to have her first posada—one of the 9 special parties held in Mexico, one a day preceding the day of Christmas. Caldecott Medal.

4556.   Farber, Norma. *How the Hibernators Came to Bethlehem* (K–3). Illus. by Barbara Cooney. 1980, Walker LB $7.85. Animals are summoned to Bethlehem on the first Christmas Eve.

4557.   Gackenbach, Dick. *Claude the Dog: A Christmas Story* (K–3). Illus. by author. 1982, Houghton $7.95; paper $3.60; Scholastic paper $1.50. Claude gives away all his presents but gets an even better one from his master.

4558.   Gammell, Stephen. *Wake Up, Bear . . . It's Christmas!* (PS–1). Illus. by author. 1981, Lothrop $11.25; LB $11.88. A bear is afraid he will sleep through Christmas.

4559.   Gantos, Jack. *Rotten Ralph's Rotten Christmas* (K–2). Illus. by Nicole Rubel. 1984, Houghton $12.95. This miserable cat is determined that Sarah's Christmas will also be miserable.

4560.   Garfield, Leon. *Fair's Fair* (1–4). Illus. by S. D. Schindler. 1983, Doubleday $10.95; LB $10.95. A Christmas story about 2 children who are brought by a dog to a mysterious house in London.

4561.   Gartschev, Ivan. *The Christmas Train* (1–3). Illus. by author. 1984, Little $12.45. A young girl sacrifices her Christmas tree to prevent a train wreck.

4562. Goodall, John S., illus. *An Edwardian Christmas* (K–3). 1978, Atheneum $8.95. A wordless book about celebrating Christmas during Edwardian times.

4563. Grahame, Kenneth. *Mole's Christmas: Or Home Sweet Home* (3–6). Illus. by Beverley Gooding. 1983, Prentice $10.95. A picture book rendition of the fifth chapter of *Wind in the Willows*.

4564. Hays, Wilma Pitchford. *Christmas on the Mayflower* (3–5). Illus. by Roger Duvoisin. 1956, Putnam $5.99. Giles, a young boy on the *Mayflower*, is about to go ashore and gather presents for Christmas.

4565. Hoban, Lillian. *Arthur's Christmas Cookies* (1–2). Illus. by author. 1972, Harper $8.61; LB $8.89; paper $2.95. What can Arthur give his parents for Christmas? Christmas cookies such as he learned to bake in Cub Scouts are the answer, but a hilarious mix-up occurs when salt is used instead of sugar.

4566. Hoban, Lillian. *It's Really Christmas* (K–2). Illus. by author. 1982, Greenwillow $11.25; LB $11.88. A mouse family celebrates Christmas in July to help cheer an ailing member.

4567. Hoban, Russell. *Emmet Otter's Jug-Band Christmas* (K–3). Illus. by Lillian Hoban. 1971, Parents $4.95. Emmet Otter and his Ma just manage to scrape along—by taking in laundry and doing odd jobs—but still manage to have the "best Christmas ever."

4568. Hoban, Russell. *The Mole Family's Christmas* (K–3). Illus. by Lillian Hoban. 1969, Four Winds $8.95. A mole family receives a telescope for Christmas with amazing and amusing results.

4569. Hoff, Syd. *Santa's Moose* (K–3). Illus. by author. 1979, Harper $7.64; LB $8.89. Milton, a big clumsy moose, helps Santa one Christmas.

4570. Janice. *Little Bear's Christmas* (PS–K). Illus. by Mariana. 1964, Lothrop $9.84. Little Bear's Christmas Eve trip with Santa and the surprise party that awaits his homecoming.

4571. Johnston, Tony. *Little Mouse Nibbling* (PS–K). Illus. by Diane Stanley. 1979, Putnam $8.95. A shy mouse, a cricket, and 3 carolers share a Christmas together.

4572. Joslin, Sesyle, and Weisgard, Leonard. *Baby Elephant and the Secret Wishes* (3–6). Illus. by Leonard Weisgard. 1962, Harcourt $6.50. Baby Elephant makes Christmas presents that family members really want.

4573. King, B. A. *The Very Best Christmas Tree* (4–6). Illus. by Michael McCurly. 1984, Godine

$8.95. A family gets together to choose the tree that is just right.

4574. Kroeber, Theodora. *A Green Christmas* (K–3). Illus. by John Larrecq. 1967, Parnassus $6.95. Children new to California discover that Santa Claus will visit places without snow.

4575. Kroll, Steven. *Santa's Crash-Bang Christmas* (K–3). Illus. by Tomie de Paola. 1977, Holiday $10.95. Santa's blunderings are graciously repaired by his faithful elf Gerald.

4576. Kunnas, Mauri, and Kunnas, Tarja. *Santa Claus and His Elves* (1–3). Illus. 1982, Harmony $7.95. A description of how Santa and his helpers spend the year getting ready for Christmas.

4577. Lindgren, Astrid. *Christmas in Noisy Village* (K–2). 1981, Penguin paper $3.95. Children of 3 neighboring farms share the joys of Christmas in a Swedish setting.

4578. Lindgren, Astrid. *Christmas in the Stable* (PS–2). Illus. by Harald Wiberg. 1962, Putnam LB $6.99. A mother tells her child the story of the birth of Jesus, and the child projects the tale into her own present-day farm-life setting.

4579. Low, Joseph. *The Christmas Grump* (PS–3). Illus. by author. 1977, Atheneum $7.95. A Scroogelike mouse is transformed by the kindness of Santa Claus.

4580. McGinley, Phyllis. *The Year without a Santa Claus* (K–3). Illus. by Kurt Werth. 1957, Harper $11.49; LB $11.89. An old favorite now reissued.

4581. MacKellar, William. *The Silent Bells* (4–6). Illus. by Ted Lewin. 1978, Dodd $6.95. A charming Christmas story set in Switzerland.

4582. Manushkin, Fran. *The Perfect Christmas Picture* (PS–3). Illus. by Karen Ann Weinhaus. 1980, Harper $7.64; LB $8.89. An easily read story of Mr. Green, who wants to photograph his family for a Christmas picture.

4583. Miller, Edna. *Mousekin's Christmas Eve* (K–3). Illus. by author. 1965, Prentice $9.95; paper $2.50. Mousekin finds a new home and visits a stable where a baby sleeps in a manger.

4584. Moeri, Louise. *Star Mother's Youngest Child* (PS–2). Illus. by Trina S. Hyman. 1975, Houghton $6.95; paper $2.50. An old woman and a star child celebrate Christmas.

4585. Naylor, Phyllis Reynolds. *Old Sadie and the Christmas Bear* (K–3). Illus. by Patricia Montgomery Newton. 1984, Atheneum $11.95. Amos, a hibernating bear, wakens to share a Christmas with Old Sadie.

4586. Nixon, Joan Lowery. *The Christmas Eve Mystery* (2–3). Illus. by Jim Cummins. 1981, Whitman LB $7.75. A mystery that begins in a barn on Christmas Eve.

4587. Noble, Trinka Hakes. *Apple Tree Christmas* (K–3). Illus. by author. 1984, Dial $10.63; LB $10.89. A nineteenth-century Christmas made special by the gift of an apple tree.

4588. O. Henry. *The Gift of the Magi* (6–8). Illus. by Rita Marshall. 1983, Childrens Book Co. $8.95. The familiar story of marital sacrifice with unusual illustrations.

4589. Oakley, Graham. *The Church Mice at Christmas* (K–3). Illus. 1980, Atheneum $10.95. The church mice are unable to raise the necessary money for a Christmas party.

4590. Olson, Arielle North. *Hurry Home Grandma!* (K–2). Illus. by Lydia Dabcovich. 1984, Dutton $9.66. An explorer-grandmother returns in time for Christmas.

4591. Parker, Nancy W. *The Christmas Camel* (PS–2). Illus. by author. 1983, Dodd $10.95. Uncle Clyde sends a gift of Fafa, a camel, from the Holy Land.

4592. Paterson, Katherine. *Angels and Other Strangers: Family Christmas Stories* (5–8). 1979, Harper $11.06; Avon paper $1.95. Nine stories that explore various meanings of Christmas and what it should represent to people.

4593. Pearson, Susan. *Karin's Christmas Walk* (K–3). Illus. by Trinka Hakes Noble. 1980, Dial $9.95; LB $9.89; paper $3.95. Karin looks forward to the Christmas Eve visit from her favorite uncle.

4594. Plume, Ilse. *The Story of Befana: An Italian Christmas Tale* (K–3). Illus. by author. 1981, Godine $11.95. The Italian legend about the witch who delivers presents to children at Christmas.

4595. Politi, Leo. *Pedro, the Angel of Olivera Street* (PS–2). Illus. by author. 1946, Scribners $8.95. A touching story of a young boy's part in a Christmas pageant in the Mexican-American section of Los Angeles.

4596. Prelutsky, Jack. *It's Christmas* (2–4). Illus. by Marylin Hafner. 1981, Greenwillow $8.50; LB $8.88. A group of simple original poems that celebrate the joys of Christmas.

4597. Raskin, Ellen. *Twenty-Two, Twenty-Three* (K–3). Illus. by author. 1976, Atheneum $7.95. The author concocts the holiday message "Merry Christmas," with nonsensically dressed animals.

4598. Robinson, Barbara. *The Best Christmas Pageant Ever* (4–6). Illus. by Judith Gwyn Brown. 1972, Avon $8.61; LB $8.89; paper $2.25. When a family of unrestrained children take over the church Christmas pageant, the results are hilarious.

4599. Rock, Gail. *The House without a Christmas Tree* (4–6). Illus. by Charles C. Gehm. 1974, Knopf $6.99. A conflict between a father and daughter about having a Christmas tree.

4600. Rydberg, Viktor. *The Christmas Tomten* (K–3). Illus. by Harald Wiberg. 1981, Putnam $9.95. A Christmas story about the old Swedish elf, the Tomten.

4601. Scarry, Richard. *Best Christmas Book Ever!* (K–3). Illus. by author. 1981, Random $4.95. Stories, songs, and various activities are featured in usual Scarry fashion.

4602. Schweninger, Ann. *Christmas Secrets* (PS–K). Illus. by author. 1984, Viking $9.95. A family of bunnies enjoys Christmas and the winter in these three short stories.

4603. Seuss, Dr. *How the Grinch Stole Christmas* (K–3). Illus. by author. 1957, Random $5.95; LB $6.99. A rhyming book about a queer creature, the Grinch, who plans to do away with Christmas.

4604. Slate, Joseph. *How Little Porcupine Played Christmas* (PS–K). Illus. by Felicia Bond. 1982, Harper $8.61; LB $8.89. Little Porcupine saves the day at the Christmas play.

4605. Stevenson, James. *The Night after Christmas* (K–3). Illus. 1981, Greenwillow $11.25; LB $11.88. Old toys, discarded after Christmas, find a new home.

4606. Stone, Bernard. *A Day to Remember* (K–3). Illus. by Anton Pieck. 1981, Four Winds $10.95. Sights seen on a nineteenth-century visit to a Dutch town before the feast of St. Nicholas.

4607. Thayer, Jane. *The Puppy Who Wanted a Boy* (K–3). Illus. by Seymour Fleishman. 1958, Morrow $9.12. A lonely puppy wanted a boy for Christmas more than anything else in the world and got 50 boys when he reached the orphan home.

4608. Theroux, Paul. *A Christmas Card* (5–8). Illus. by John Lawrence. 1978, Houghton $5.95. A magical Christmas card adds charm to this story of a family lost in a snowstorm.

4609. Tudor, Tasha. *The Doll's Christmas* (1–4). Illus. by author. 1950, McKay $6.95; LB $4.50. Two dolls celebrate Christmas together.

4610. Uttley, Alison. *Stories for Christmas* (4–6). Illus. by Gavin Rowe. 1977, Penguin paper $2.95. A selection of 12 stories about old-fashioned Christmas celebrations, culled from the anthologies of this prolific English author.

4611. Van Leeuwen, Jean. *The Great Christmas Kidnapping Caper* (3–5). Illus. by Steven Kellogg. 1975, Dial $10.95; LB $10.89; Dell paper $1.50. A group of mice who live in a dollhouse at Macy's solve the mystery of the disappearance of Santa Claus.

4612. Vincent, Gabrielle. *Merry Christmas, Ernest and Celestine* (K–2). Illus. by author. 1984, Greenwillow $11.50; LB $11.04. The beloved bear and mouse want to have a Christmas party but have no money.

4613. Watson, Clyde. *How Brown Mouse Kept Christmas* (PS–3). Illus. by Wendy Watson. 1980, Farrar $7.95. When the people go to bed, mice come out to celebrate Christmas.

4614. Watson, Wendy. *The Bunnies' Christmas Eve: A Peek-Through Pop-Up Book* (PS–2). Illus. 1983, Putnam $11.95. A pop-up book about a rabbit family at Christmas.

4615. Wells, Rosemary. *Morris's Disappearing Bag: A Christmas Story* (PS–K). Illus. 1975, Dial $9.95; LB $9.89; paper $2.50. Morris, a rabbit, finds one more present under the Christmas tree—a bag that makes him invisible, and then he becomes the envy of his brothers and sisters.

4616. Wenning, Elizabeth. *The Christmas Mouse* (PS–3). Illus. by Barbara Remington. 1959, Holt $9.95. Kaspar, the church mouse, plays a part in the first singing of "Silent Night" in a little Austrian village.

4617. Wiggin, Kate Douglas. *The Birds' Christmas Carol* (3–5). Illus. by Jessie Gillespie. 1941, Houghton $8.95; memorial ed. $9.95. A beautiful edition of a story first published in 1888.

4618. Wiseman, Bernard. *Christmas with Morris and Boris* (1–3). Illus. by author. 1983, Little $10.45. Boris the Bear and Morris the Moose share a Christmas.

4619. Zalben, Jane Breskin. *Porcupine's Christmas Blues* (K–2). Illus. by author. 1982, Putnam $9.95. Porcupine discovers how good friends add to Christmas.

4620. Zolotow, Charlotte. *The Beautiful Christmas Tree* (K–3). Illus. by Ruth Robbins. 1983, Houghton LB $6.95; paper $3.95. With loving care, an old man nurtures a pine tree and brings to life the real spirit of Christmas.

Crafts

4621. Corwin, Judith Hoffman. *Christmas Fun* (3–6). Illus. by author. 1982, Messner LB $9.29; paper $5.95. A collection of simple projects that are useful for this holiday, including designs for gifts and decorations.

4622. Coskey, Evelyn. *Christmas Crafts for Everyone* (6–9). Illus. by Roy Wallace. 1976, Abingdon $8.95. The projects, complete with explicit, step-by-step directions, are based on Christmas customs from various parts of the world.

4623. Fowler, Virginie. *Christmas Crafts and Customs around the World* (5–9). Illus. by author. 1984, Prentice $10.95. A book of interesting craft projects that also introduce holiday customs.

4624. Glovach, Linda. *The Little Witch's Christmas Book* (3–5). Illus. 1974, Prentice paper $4.95. A pleasant, breezy presentation of simple projects, games, and recipes for the holiday season.

4625. Krahn, Fernando. *The Biggest Christmas Tree on Earth* (1–3). Illus. by author. 1978, Little $5.95. A wordless picture book about decorating a Christmas tree.

4626. Meyer, Carolyn. *Christmas Crafts: Things to Make the 24 Days Before Christmas* (5–8). Illus. by Anita Lobel. 1974, Harper $10.53. Beginning with December 1, this attractive "how to" book gives instructions for each day, until the making of a chocolate Yule log on Christmas Eve.

4627. Parish, Peggy. *December Decorations* (1–4). Illus. by Barbara Wolff. 1975, Macmillan $9.95. Projects for several winter holidays are included in this easy-to-use manual.

4628. Pettit, Florence H. *Christmas All around the House: Traditional Decorations You Can Make* (6–9). Illus. by Wendy Watson. 1976, Harper $14.38. Detailed instructions help demonstrate these interesting, simple projects from around the world.

4629. Purdy, Susan. *Christmas Gifts Good Enough to Eat!* (4–Up). Illus. by author. 1981, Watts LB $9.40. Easy instructions plus packaging hints. Also use: *Christmas Cooking around the World* (1983, Watts $9.90).

4630. Purdy, Susan. *Christmas Gifts You Can Make* (4–7). Illus. 1976, Harper $10.89; paper $4.95. Instructions are simple, materials readily available, and finished products look appropriately festive.

4631. Supraner, Robyn. *Merry Christmas! Things to Make and Do* (1–3). Illus. by Renzo Barto. 1981, Troll LB $8.11; paper $1.95. Many festive activities and crafts for the holiday are outlined.

4632. Tichenor, Tom. *Christmas Tree Crafts* (6–7). Illus. 1975, Harper $9.57. Easy-to-make ornaments that can be produced from readily available materials.

4633. Weiss, Ellen. *Things to Make and Do for Christmas* (3–5). 1980, Watts $8.90; paper $3.95. A book of activities that range from making cards to growing a mini-tree.

Music

4634. Cusack, Margaret, illus. *The Christmas Carol Sampler* (3–8). 1983, Harcourt $10.95. Words and music to 13 Christmas carols, illustrated with appropriate scenes.

4635.   de Paola, Tomie, illus. *The Friendly Beasts: An Old English Christmas Carol* (K–3). 1981, Putnam $10.95; paper $4.95. A charmingly illustrated version of this carol.

4636.   Domanska, Janina. *Din Dan Don, It's Christmas* (PS–3). Illus. by author. 1975, Greenwillow $9.95. The story of the first Christmas as told in this traditional Polish carol, stunningly illustrated with paintings that resemble a medieval illuminated manuscript.

4637.   Jeffers, Susan, illus. *Silent Night* (2–5). 1984, Dutton $12.95. A lush setting of the Christmas carol.

4638.   Keats, Ezra Jack, illus. *The Little Drummer Boy* (2–4). 1972, Macmillan paper $3.95. The lyrics of this popular Christmas song are well illustrated.

4639.   Knight, Hilary. *The Twelve Days of Christmas* (K–3). Illus. by author. 1981, Macmillan $9.95. The traditional folk song with animals as participants.

4640.   Langstaff, John, comp. *The Season for Singing: American Christmas Songs and Carols* (All Ages). Musical settings by Seymour Barak. 1974, Doubleday $8.95. Piano and guitar arrangements accompany this collection of American Christmas carols.

4641.   Lobel, Adrianne. *A Small Sheep in a Pear Tree* (K–3). Illus. by author. 1977, Harper $7.64; LB $8.89. When the word *sheep* is substituted for the names of each of the gifts in "The Twelve Days of Christmas," an amusing new twist results.

4642.   Pearson, Tracey Campbell, illus. *We Wish You a Merry Christmas: A Traditional Christmas Carol* (K–3). 1983, Dial $8.69; LB $8.89. A humorous rendition of this popular carol.

4643.   Schneider, Erika, illus. *The Twelve Days of Christmas* (1–Up). 1984, Picture Book Studio USA $4.95. A beautifully illustrated edition of this carol.

4644.   Varnum, Brooke Minarik. *Play and Sing . . . It's Christmas!* (1–4). Illus. by Emily Arnold McCully. 1980, Macmillan $10.95; paper $5.95. Subtitle: "A piano book of easy-to-play carols."

4645.   Wildsmith, Brian. *Brian Wildsmith's The Twelve Days of Christmas* (2–5). Illus. by author. 1972, Watts paper $2.95. With his usual dazzling color, Wildsmith pictures all the strange presents "my true love gave to me."

Plays

4646.   Kamerman, Sylvia E., ed. *Christmas Play Favorites for Young People* (1–8). 1982, Plays paper $8.95. Eighteen plays from the pages of *Play* magazine.

4647.   Kamerman, Sylvia E., ed. *On Stage for Christmas* (3–7). 1978, Plays $13.95. Subtitle: *A Collection of Royalty Free One-Act Christmas Plays for Young People.*

Poetry

4648.   Barth, Edna, ed. *A Christmas Feast: An Anthology of Poems, Sayings, Greetings and Wishes* (4–6). Illus. by Ursula Arndt. 1979, Houghton $10.60. A collection of Christmas poetry divided into 20 sections like "Christmas Is Coming" and "The Three Kings."

4649.   Frost, Frances Mary. *Christmas in the Woods* (K–3). Illus. by Aldren A. Watson. 1976, Harper $7.95. Reissue of a lovely poem, beautifully illustrated, about the animals in the woods on Christmas night.

4650.   Harrison, Michael, and Stuart-Clark, Christopher, eds. *The Oxford Book of Christmas Poems* (4–9). Illus. 1984, Merrimack $12.95. A collection of 120 British and American poems about Christmas and how we celebrate it.

4651.   Hopkins, Lee Bennett. *Sing Hey for Christmas Day* (K–3). Illus. by Laura Jean Allen. 1975, Harcourt $7.95. A selection of short poems in celebration of the Christmas season.

4652.   Livingston, Myra Cohn, sel. *Christmas Poems* (PS–3). Illus. by Trina S. Hyman. 1984, Holiday $12.95. A collection of 18 poems, half of which were commissioned for the volume.

4653.   Livingston, Myra Cohn, ed. *Poems of Christmas* (5–9). 1980, Atheneum $10.95. A collection of over 100 poems from varied sources and times.

4654.   McGinley, Phyllis. *A Wreath of Christmas Legends* (5–8). Illus. by Leonard Weisgard. 1967, Macmillan $8.95. Some of the legendary miracles associated with the birth of Christ form the inspiration for excellent poetry.

4655.   Moore, Clement. *The Night Before Christmas* (PS–3). Illus. by Arthur Rackham. 1977, Doubleday $7.95. A lovely edition of this popular and loved Christmas poem. Two newer editions are: Illus. by Tomie de Paola (1980, Holiday $12.95; paper $4.95); illus. by Anita Lobel (1984, Knopf $9.95; LB $10.99).

4656.   Thomas, Dylan. *A Child's Christmas in Wales* (5–9). Illus. by Fritz Eichenberg. 1959, New Directions $10.95. A prose poem about the poet's childhood in a small Welsh village. Another edition is: Illus. by Edward Ardizzone (1980, Godine $10.95).

Easter

4657. Barth, Edna. *Lilies, Rabbits and Painted Eggs: The Story of the Easter Symbols* (3–6). Illus. by Ursula Arndt. 1970, Houghton $8.95; paper $3.95. The pagan and Christian origins of many of the celebrations associated with Easter.

4658. Berger, Gilda. *Easter and Other Spring Holidays* (4–7). Illus. 1983, Watts $8.90. The origins and ways of observing Easter, plus several Jewish holidays, including Passover.

4659. Chapman, Jean. *Pancakes and Painted Eggs: A Book for Easter and All the Days of the Year* (3–5). Illus. by Kilmeny Niland. 1982, Childrens Pr. $12.95. Stories, poems, and activities related to Easter.

4660. Cole, Marion, and Cole, Olivia H. *Things to Make and Do for Easter* (3–4). 1979, Watts $8.99. Stories about and projects for Easter.

4661. Corwin, Judith Hoffman. *Easter Fun* (2–4). Illus. by author. 1984, Messner $9.29; paper $5.95. Foods and crafts associated with this holiday are highlighted.

4662. Coskey, Evelyn. *Easter Eggs for Everyone* (5–8). Illus. 1973, Abingdon $8.95. Directions for making and decorating Easter eggs, plus a description of the customs and games associated with them.

4663. Fisher, Aileen. *Easter* (3–5). Illus. by Ati Forberg. 1968, Harper $9.89. Easter customs in the Christian faith, some secular, some religious.

4664. Milhous, Katherine. *The Egg Tree* (PS–3). Illus. by author. 1950, Scribners $11.95; paper $2.95. This picture book tells how to make a delightful Easter egg tree. Caldecott Medal.

4665. Patterson, Lillie. *Easter* (3–5). Illus. by Kelly Oechsli. 1966, Garrard $7.56. A retelling of the Easter story, plus a description of how Easter is celebrated in various parts of the world.

4666. Sockman, Ralph W. *The Easter Story for Children* (2–4). Illus. by Gordon Laite. 1966, Abingdon $6.95. A simple account of the events described in the Bible that are associated with Easter.

Fiction

4667. Adams, Adrienne. *The Easter Egg Artists* (PS–2). 1976, Scribners $12.95; paper $2.95. A rabbit family paints 100 dozen eggs for Easter, helped greatly by the son's flair for comic design.

4668. Friedrich, Priscilla, and Friedrich, Otto. *The Easter Bunny That Overslept* (PS–1). Illus. by Adrienne Adams. 1983, Lothrop LB $10.88. Santa Claus helps a tardy Easter bunny who has trouble getting up on time.

4669. Gackenbach, Dick. *Hattie, Tom and the Chicken Witch* (1–3). 1980, Harper $7.64; LB $8.89. A book that proves both chickens and rabbits are important to Easter.

4670. Harper, Wilhelmina. *Easter Chimes: Stories for Easter and the Spring Season* (3–5). Illus. by Hoot Von Zitzewitz. 1967, Dutton $8.95. The celebration of Easter in many countries.

4671. Heyward, DuBose. *The Country Bunny and the Little Gold Shoes* (K–3). Illus. by Marjorie Flack. 1939, Houghton $10.95; paper $4.95. Cottontail, the mother of 21 bunnies, finally realizes her great ambition to be an Easter bunny.

4672. Hoban, Lillian. *The Sugar Snow Spring* (PS–3). Illus. by author. 1973, Harper LB $9.89. The Easter Bunny saves a mouse family hard pressed by an ever-watchful barn cat.

4673. Kroll, Steven. *The Big Bunny and the Easter Eggs* (K–3). Illus. by Janet Stevens. 1982, Holiday $12.95. Wilbur, the Easter bunny, gets sick, and who will do his job?

4674. Roser, Wiltrud. *Everything about Easter Rabbits* (K–3). Illus. by author. 1973, Harper LB $9.89; paper $3.25. A nonsense book about all kinds of Easter rabbits, including the "Genuine, Original Easter Rabbit."

4675. Stevenson, James. *The Great Big Especially Beautiful Easter Egg* (K–3). Illus. by author. 1983, Greenwillow $10.00; LB $9.55. Grampa, as a young man, sets out to find an especially large egg.

4676. Zolotow, Charlotte. *The Bunny Who Found Easter* (K–3). Illus. by Betty Peterson. 1959, Houghton $6.95; paper $3.95. A confused little rabbit searches for Easter thinking it is a place, not a time.

Halloween

4677. Barkin, Carol, and James, Elizabeth. *The Scary Halloween Costume Book* (3–6). Illus. by Katherine Coville. 1983, Lothrop $8.00; LB $7.63. A book of easy-to-make Halloween costumes.

4678. Barth, Edna. *Witches, Pumpkins and Grinning Ghosts: The Story of the Halloween Symbols* (3–6). Illus. by Ursula Arndt. 1972, Houghton $8.95; paper $3.95. The origins of Halloween and how it is celebrated in many countries.

4679. Borten, Helen. *Halloween* (1–3). Illus. by author. 1965, Harper $9.89. The origins of the holiday and of various Halloween customs.

4680. Brewton, John E. et al., comps. *In the Witch's Kitchen: Poems for Halloween* (3–6). Illus. by Harriett Barton. 1980, Harper $10.89. A collection of 46 poems from a variety of sources, but all about Halloween.

4681. Corwin, Judith Hoffman. *Halloween Fun* (3–6). Illus. 1983, Messner $9.29; paper $5.95. A wide variety of holiday activities, including party hints and projects.

4682. Dobrin, Arnold. *Make a Witch, Make a Goblin: A Book of Halloween Crafts* (3–5). Illus. 1977, Four Winds $8.95. Costumes, masks, party favors, food, and puppets are only a few of the creative projects for the young hobbiest.

4683. Emberley, Ed. *Ed Emberley's Big Orange Drawing Book* (2–5). 1980, Little $9.95; paper $5.95. Emberley teaches you to draw many orange things, mostly associated with Halloween.

4684. Gibbons, Gail. *Halloween* (PS–1). Illus. 1984, Holiday $12.95. Halloween history and traditions are explained in this simple picture book.

4685. Glovach, Linda. *Little Witch's Halloween Book* (3–5). Illus. 1975, Prentice $7.95; paper $4.95. Simple directions for a variety of Halloween activities, including games, favors, and costumes.

4686. Herda, D. J. *Halloween* (4–7). Illus. 1983, Watts $8.90. The origin of Halloween, some ghost stories, and tips for planning a party.

4687. Hopkins, Lee Bennett, ed. *Hey-How for Halloween* (3–6). Illus. by Janet McCaffery. 1974, Harcourt $4.95. A varied and appealing selection of poems about happenings and creatures associated with Halloween.

4688. Kessel, Joyce K. *Halloween* (2–4). Illus. by Nancy Carlson. 1980, Carolrhoda LB $6.95. A book for beginning readers about the origins of many traditions connected with Halloween.

4689. Marks, Burton, and Marks, Rita. *The Spook Book* (3–5). Illus. by Lisa Campbell Ernst. 1981, Lothrop $11.25; LB $11.88. All sorts of projects for Halloween and ideas for a fine Halloween party.

4690. Patterson, Lillie. *Halloween* (2–5). Illus. 1965, Garrard $7.56. Well-selected facts about the historical background of the holiday.

4691. Prelutsky, Jack. *It's Halloween* (1–3). Illus. by Marylin Hafner. 1977, Greenwillow $8.25; LB $7.92; Scholastic paper $1.95. Thirteen brief and easily read poems explore various aspects of this scary holiday.

4692. Supraner, Robyn. *Happy Halloween! Things to Make and Do* (1–3). Illus. by Renzo Barto. 1981, Troll $8.11; paper $1.95. Games, decorations, disguises, and more.

Fiction

4693. Adams, Adrienne. *A Woggle of Witches* (PS–3). Illus. by author. 1982, Scribners $11.95. The activities of a group of witches on Halloween night as they go about their business of dining on bat stew and riding on a broom.

4694. Anderson, Lonzo. *The Halloween Party* (PS–2). Illus. by Adrienne Adams. 1974, Scribners $8.95; paper $2.95. Faraday Folson almost becomes part of 2 witches' stew in this Halloween story.

4695. Asch, Frank. *Popcorn: A Frank Asch Bear Story* (PS–K). Illus. 1979, Parents $5.50. Sam Bear decides to pop everyone's popcorn at a Halloween party.

4696. Avi. *No More Magic* (4–6). 1975, Pantheon LB $6.99. Chris encounters many mysterious events one Halloween night.

4697. Barton, Byron. *Hester* (PS–1). Illus. by author. 1975, Greenwillow $10.80; Penguin paper $3.50. A crocodile goes out spooking on Halloween.

4698. Bond, Felicia. *The Halloween Performance* (PS–K). Illus. by author. 1983, Harper $4.76; LB $7.89. A small book about Roger, a mouse, and his class Halloween play.

4699. Bradbury, Ray. *The Halloween Tree* (5–7). 1972, Bantam paper $2.25. Boys visit a deserted house and find a pumpkin tree.

4700. Bridwell, Norman. *Clifford's Halloween* (PS–1). Illus. by author. 1970, Scholastic paper $1.25. Halloween adventures of a big red dog.

4701. Bright, Robert. *Georgie's Halloween* (PS–2). Illus. by author. 1958, Doubleday $7.95; paper $2.50. A shy ghost gets a surprise from his friends.

4702. Brown, Marc. *Arthur's Halloween* (PS–2). Illus. by author. 1982, Little LB $12.45; paper $3.70. Arthur must find courage to help his sister on Halloween.

4703. Carlson, Nancy. *Harriet's Halloween Candy* (PS–K). Illus. 1982, Carolrhoda $7.95; Penguin paper $3.95. A childlike dog overeats on Halloween candy.

4704. Carlson, Natalie Savage. *The Night the Scarecrow Walked* (3–4). Illus. by Charles Robinson. 1979, Scribners $7.95. On Halloween night, before the eyes of 2 disbelieving youngsters, a scarecrow moves from its post.

4705.   Carlson, Natalie Savage. *Spooky Night* (PS–3). Illus. by Andrew Glass. 1982, Lothrop $11.25; LB $11.88. On Halloween, a witch comes to reclaim her cat, which has been adopted by the Bascombs.

4706.   Chetwin, Grace. *On All Hallow's Eve* (4–6). 1984, Lothrop $10.00. Two children are transported to a different world on Halloween night.

4707.   Coombs, Patricia. *Dorrie and the Halloween Plot* (2–4). Illus. 1976, Lothrop $9.84; Dell paper $1.75. Dorrie foils a plot to kidnap the Great Sorceress.

4708.   Cuyler, Margery. *Sir William and the Pumpkin Monster* (2–3). Illus. by Marsha Winborn. 1984, Holt $9.95. In this turnabout story, it is the ghost who gets the scare.

4709.   Davis, Maggie S. *Rickety Witch* (PS–1). Illus. by Kay Chorao. 1984, Holiday $9.95. A sweet old witch experiences a special Halloween.

4710.   Dillon, Barbara. *What's Happened to Harry?* (3–5). Illus. by Chris Conover. 1982, Morrow $8.75. Harry is changed into a dog by a hateful witch.

4711.   Embry, Margaret. *The Blue-Nosed Witch* (2–4). 1956, Holiday $6.95; Bantam paper $1.95. A witch meets a group of children out on Halloween night.

4712.   Freeman, Don. *Space Witch* (K–3). Illus. by author. 1979, Viking LB $11.95; paper $3.95. A witch builds a spaceship to frighten creatures on other planets on Halloween.

4713.   Godden, Rumer. *Mr. McFadden's Halloween* (4–6). 1975, Viking $9.95. A young girl befriends a grumpy old man.

4714.   Greene, Carol. *The Thirteen Days of Halloween* (K–5). Illus. by Tom Dunnington. 1983, Childrens Pr. $6.95. A Halloween-oriented spoof on the "Twelve days of Christmas."

4715.   Hamilton, Virginia. *Willie Bea and the Time the Martians Landed* (5–8). 1983, Greenwillow $11.00. A story built around the Halloween night on which Orson Welles made his famous invasion-from-Mars broadcast.

4716.   Hautzig, Deborah. *Little Witch's Big Night* (1–2). Illus. by Marc Brown. 1984, Random $5.99; paper $2.95. Little Witch has a better Halloween than she expected.

4717.   Haywood, Carolyn. *Halloween Treats* (3–4). Illus. by Victoria de Larrea. 1981, Morrow $11.25; LB $10.80. Nine short stories about Halloween adventures.

4718.   Hoban, Lillian. *Arthur's Halloween Costume* (1–3). Illus. by author. 1984, Harper $8.61; LB $8.89. Arthur is annoyed because no one understands his Halloween costume.

4719.   Jasner, W. K. *Which Is the Witch?* (1–3). Illus. by Victoria Chess. 1979, Random $6.95; LB $7.99. Jenny trades places with a real witch on Halloween night in this easily read account.

4720.   Johnston, Tony. *The Vanishing Pumpkin* (PS–2). Illus. by Tomie de Paola. 1983, Putnam LB $9.95; paper $4.59. An old man and an old woman set out on Halloween to find their pumpkin.

4721.   Kahl, Virginia. *Gunhilde and the Halloween Spell* (K–3). Illus. by author. 1975, Scribners $6.95; paper $2.95. Gunhilde's unraveled scarf is used to effect a rescue after she and her sisters have been turned into toads by a wicked witch.

4722.   Keats, Ezra Jack. *The Trip* (1–3). Illus. by author. 1978, Scholastic paper $2.95. Halloween proves to be a time when Louis isn't lonely anymore.

4723.   Kellogg, Steven. *The Mystery of the Flying Orange Pumpkin* (PS–2). Illus. by author. 1980, Dial $6.95; LB $6.89. Neighborhood children play a Halloween prank on mean Mr. King.

4724.   Kessler, Ethel, and Kessler, Leonard. *Grandpa Witch and the Magic Doobelator* (K–3). Illus. by author. 1981, Macmillan $8.95. Grandpa Witch has a machine that doubles everything.

4725.   Kraus, Robert. *How Spider Saved Halloween* (K–3). Illus. by author. 1980, Four Winds $7.95. Spider saves the fun of Halloween by creating an ingenious disguise.

4726.   Kroll, Steven. *The Biggest Pumpkin Ever* (PS–2). Illus. by Jeni Bassett. 1984, Holiday $12.95. Two mice hope to grow the largest pumpkin ever for Halloween.

4727.   Maestro, Giulio. *Halloween Howls: Riddles That Are a Scream* (2–5). 1983, Dutton $8.69. There are almost 60 riddles related to Halloween in this collection.

4728.   Manushkin, Fran. *Hocus and Pocus at the Circus* (1–3). Illus. by Geoffrey Hayes. 1983, Harper $7.64; LB $8.89. Two witches decide to go to the circus on Halloween night in this easy-to-read book.

4729.   Marshall, Edward. *Space Case* (K–2). Illus. by James Marshall. 1980, Dial LB $7.45; paper $3.95. Strange things happen when a space creature visits Earth on Halloween.

4730.   Massey, Jeanne. *The Littlest Witch* (K–2). Illus. by Adrienne Adams. 1959, Knopf $5.99. A small witch's disobedience loses her a chance to fly to the moon.

4731.   Mooser, Stephen. *The Ghost with the Halloween Hiccups* (1–3). Illus. by Tomie de Paola. 1977,

Avon paper $1.95. Penny's hiccups are cured only by being frightened by 2 costumed kids.

4732. Prager, Annabelle. *The Spooky Halloween Party* (1–3). Illus. by Tomie de Paola. 1981, Pantheon $6.95; LB $7.99. On Halloween, Albert finds himself surrounded by frightening creatures he doesn't know.

4733. Prelutsky, Jack. *It's Halloween* (1–3). Illus. by Marylin Hafner. 1977, Greenwillow LB $8.88. An easy-to-read book of 12 illustrated poems about the traditions of Halloween.

4734. Quackenbush, Robert. *Detective Mole and the Halloween Mystery* (K–3). Illus. by author. 1981, Lothrop $10.25; LB $9.84. Detective Mole sets out to solve the mystery of the missing jack-o'-lantern.

4735. Rockwell, Anne. *A Bear, a Bobcat and Three Ghosts* (1–2). Illus. 1977, Macmillan $6.95. Halloween tricks abound in this tale of children frightening those who should frighten them.

4736. Rose, David S. *It Hardly Seems Like Halloween* (K–1). Illus. by author. 1983, Lothrop $9.50; LB $9.12. On Halloween, a boy is unaware of all the monsters gathering around him.

4737. Schertle, Alice. *Hob Goblin and the Skeleton* (K–3). Illus. by Katherine Coville. 1982, Lothrop $10.00; LB $10.88. Hob Goblin needs a new helper, but Halloween night is not the time to find one.

4738. Schulman, Janet. *Jack the Bum and the Halloween Handout* (2–4). Illus. by James Stevenson. 1977, Greenwillow $8.50; LB $8.88; UNICEF paper $2.00. On Halloween night, a hobo learns the meaning of UNICEF.

4739. Schweninger, Ann. *Halloween Surprises* (PS–2). Illus. by author. 1984, Viking $10.95. The Rabbit children plan and make their witch costumes.

4740. Stevenson, James. *That Terrible Halloween Night* (PS–3). Illus. by author. 1980, Greenwillow $10.95; LB $10.51. Grampa tells how he was frightened one Halloween night.

4741. Wiseman, Bernard. *Halloween with Morris and Boris* (PS–K). Illus. by author. 1975, Dodd $6.95; paper $1.95. Two friends enjoy Halloween together in this easily read story.

4742. Zimmer, Dirk. *The Trick-or-Treat Trap* (K–2). Illus. by author. 1982, Harper $9.13; LB $7.89. Three young Halloween revelers find themselves in strange company.

4743. Zolotow, Charlotte. *A Tiger Called Thomas* (1–3). Illus. by Kurt Werth. 1963, Lothrop $10.32. A new boy in the neighborhood ventures out on Halloween in his tiger suit and discovers new friends.

Thanksgiving

4744. Anderson, Joan. *The First Thanksgiving Feast* (2–6). Illus. 1984, Houghton $12.95. A re-creation of life with the Pilgrims from the Mayflower to the first Thanksgiving.

4745. Baldwin, Margaret. *Thanksgiving* (4–7). Illus. 1983, Watts $8.90. The story of the Pilgrims is retold, with ways in which we celebrate this holiday.

4746. Barth, Edna. *Turkeys, Pilgrims and Indian Corn: The Story of the Thanksgiving Symbols* (3–6). 1975, Houghton $9.95; paper $4.95. Historical details about the origin of this festival and how we celebrate it today.

4747. Bartlett, Robert Merrill. *Thanksgiving Day* (1–3). Illus. by W. T. Mars. 1965, Harper $9.89. An introduction to the harvest festival and, in particular, Thanksgiving in America.

4748. Behrens, June. *Feast of Thanksgiving* (1–3). Illus. by Anne Siberell. 1974, Childrens Pr. $9.25. A 2-act play about the first Thanksgiving dinner.

4749. Child, Lydia Maria. *Over the River and Through the Wood* (1–3). Illus. by Brinton Turkle. 1974, Putnam $8.95; Scholastic paper $1.95. A favorite song of a family's Thanksgiving visit to their grandparents' house.

4750. Corwin, Judith Hoffman. *Thanksgiving Fun* (2–4). Illus. 1984, Messner $9.29; paper $5.95. A number of Thanksgiving projects are outlined, including a big dinner.

4751. Gibbons, Gail. *Thanksgiving Day* (PS–2). Illus. by author. 1983, Holiday $11.95. A very simple introduction to Thanksgiving Day.

4752. Glovach, Linda. *Little Witch's Thanksgiving Book* (1–4). Illus. by author. 1976, Prentice LB $7.95; paper $3.95. An informative book that deals with the history, crafts, recipes, and games surrounding the Thanksgiving holiday.

4753. Hopkins, Lee Bennett, ed. *Merrily Comes Our Harvest In: Poems for Thanksgiving* (2–4). Illus. by Ben Shecter. 1978, Harcourt $4.95. A collection of 20 poems dealing with Thanksgiving.

4754. Prelutsky, Jack. *It's Thanksgiving* (PS–4). Illus. by author. 1982, Greenwillow $8.50; LB $8.88. Twelve poems covering various aspects of Thanksgiving.

Fiction

4755. Brown, Marc. *Arthur's Thanksgiving* (K–3). Illus. by author. 1983, Little $10.95. Arthur is made director of his class Thanksgiving play.

4756. Cohen, Barbara. *Molly's Pilgrim* (2–5). Illus. by Michael J. Deraney. 1983, Lothrop $9.00;

LB $8.59. At Thanksgiving time, Molly begins to feel proud of her Jewish heritage.

4757. Dalgliesh, Alice. *The Thanksgiving Story* (PS–4). Illus. by Helen Sewell. 1954, Scribners paper $2.95. The Hopkins family's experiences on the *Mayflower* to the first Thanksgiving.

4758. Janice. *Little Bear's Thanksgiving* (K–2). Illus. by Mariana. 1967, Lothrop $9.84. Little Bear is taught the meaning of Thanksgiving by many of his forest friends.

4759. Kroll, Steven. *One Tough Turkey: A Thanksgiving Story* (PS–3). Illus. by John Wallner. 1982, Holiday $10.95. The turkeys naturally don't feel that the Pilgrims should have had turkey on Thanksgiving.

4760. Quackenbush, Robert. *Sheriff Sally Gopher and the Thanksgiving Caper* (K–4). Illus. by author. 1982, Lothrop $10.00; LB $10.88. Pebble Junction is looking for a symbol for its Thanksgiving corn feast.

4761. Rock, Gail. *The Thanksgiving Treasure* (4–6). Illus. by Charles C. Gehm. 1974, Knopf LB $6.99; Bantam paper $1.75. Addie's desire to rekindle the spirit of friendship at Thanksgiving produces an unexpected reward.

4762. Williams, Barbara. *Chester Chipmunk's Thanksgiving* (4–6). 1978, Dutton $9.95. Chester's invitation to share his Thanksgiving pecan pie is turned down by everyone except Oswald Opossum.

Valentine's Day

4763. Barth, Edna. *Hearts, Cupids and Red Roses: The Story of the Valentine Symbols* (4–6). Illus. by Ursula Arndt. 1982, Houghton paper $3.95. A fascinating compilation of facts and lore about St. Valentine's Day.

4764. Brown, Fern G. *Valentine's Day* (4–7). Illus. 1983, Watts $8.90. A history of this holiday, plus information about the greeting card industry.

4765. Bulla, Clyde Robert. *St. Valentine's Day* (1–3). Illus. by Valenti Angelo. 1965, Harper $9.89. An explanation of the legends and celebrations associated with this holiday.

4766. Corwin, Judith Hoffman. *Valentine Fun* (3–6). Illus. by author. 1982, Messner $9.29; paper $4.95. Recipes and craft projects highlight this book of activities.

4767. de Paola, Tomie. *Things to Make and Do for Valentine's Day* (1–3). Illus. 1976, Watts $8.90. Games, crafts, and recipes dealing with this day are included with easily followed instructions.

4768. Glovach, Linda. *Little Witch's Valentine Book* (2–4). Illus. by author. 1984, Prentice $8.95. A wide variety of craft projects designed to help brighten Valentine's Day.

4769. Guilfoile, Elizabeth. *Valentine's Day* (2–5). 1965, Garrard $7.56. The beginnings of and ways to celebrate Valentine's Day, in an easily read book.

4770. Hopkins, Lee Bennett, ed. *Good Morning to You, Valentine* (2–5). Illus. by Tomie de Paola. 1976, Harcourt $5.95. Poems, jingles, and couplets gaily illustrated on subjects related to this holiday.

4771. Kessel, Joyce K. *Valentine's Day* (2–4). Illus. by Karen Ritz. 1981, Carolrhoda LB $7.95. An easily read account of the origins of this holiday and the traditions surrounding it.

4772. Prelutsky, Jack. *It's Valentine's Day* (1–4). Illus. by Yossi Abolafia. 1983, Greenwillow $7.00; LB $6.67. Bright, humorous poems in celebration of love and Valentine's Day.

4773. Sandak, Cass R. *Valentine's Day* (2–4). Illus. by Michael Deas. 1980, Watts LB $8.90. A simple introduction to this holiday and the customs surrounding it.

4774. Supraner, Robyn. *Valentine's Day: Things to Make and Do* (1–3). Illus. by Renzo Barto. 1981, Troll LB $8.11; paper $1.95. Interesting holiday crafts are outlined.

4775. Yaroslava, ed. *I Like You, and Other Poems for Valentine's Day* (3–5). Illus. by author. 1976, Scribners $6.95. Poems for children and adults on the vagaries of love, handsomely anthologized.

Fiction

4776. Adams, Adrienne. *The Great Valentine's Day Balloon Race* (K–3). Illus. by author. 1980, Scribners $12.95. Two rabbits plus the Abbot family construct a balloon for a Valentine's Day race.

4777. Balian, Lorna. *A Sweetheart for Valentine* (K–3). Illus. by author. 1979, Abingdon $16.95. An original, highly imaginative explanation of the origins of Valentine's Day.

4778. Brown, Marc. *Arthur's Valentine* (K–3). Illus. by author. 1980, Little $9.95; Avon paper $1.95. Who is sending Arthur valentines?

4779. Bunting, Eve. *The Valentine Bears* (K–3). Illus. by Jan Brett. 1983, Houghton $9.95. Mr. and Mrs. Bear decide not to sleep through Valentine's Day this year.

4780. Cohen, Miriam. *Bee My Valentine!* (1–3). Illus. by Lillian Hoban. 1978, Greenwillow $10.95; LB $10.51; Dell paper $1.95. George is dismayed when he doesn't receive as many valentines as his friends.

4781. Modell, Frank. *One Zillion Valentines* (PS–2). Illus. by author. 1981, Greenwillow $11.25; LB $11.88. Milton and Marvin distribute their homemade hearts to the neighborhood.

4782. Murphy, Shirley Rousseau. *Valentine for a Dragon* (K–3). Illus. by Kay Chorao. 1984, Atheneum $11.95. A little demon falls in love with a lady dragon.

4783. Nixon, Joan Lowery. *The Valentine Mystery* (1–3). Illus. by Jim Cummins. 1979, Whitman $6.95. Susan, with the help of her brothers, finds out who has sent her an anonymous valentine.

4784. Sharmat, Marjorie W. *The Best Valentine in the World* (K–3). Illus. by Lilian Obligado. 1982, Holiday $10.95. Ferdinand and Florette Fox celebrate Valentine's Day together.

4785. Williams, Barbara. *A Valentine for Cousin Archie* (K–2). Illus. by Kay Chorao. 1981, Dutton $8.95. A forest creature gets involved in celebrating Valentine's Day.

Jewish Holy Days

4786. Adler, David A. *A Picture Book of Hanukkah* (K–3). Illus. by Linda Heller. 1982, Holiday $9.95. The origins of this Jewish holiday and ways to celebrate it.

4787. Adler, David A. *A Picture Book of Jewish Holidays* (PS). Illus. by Linda Heller. 1981, Holiday LB $9.95. A very simple explanation of the major Jewish holy days.

4788. Adler, David A. *A Picture Book of Passover* (PS–3). Illus. by Linda Heller. 1982, Holiday $9.95. A book that tells the history of Passover and ways in which it is celebrated.

4789. Becker, Joyce. *Hanukkah Crafts* (4–8). Illus. by author. 1978, Hebrew $9.95; paper $6.95. Directions for creating more than 200 different objects.

4790. Becker, Joyce. *Jewish Holiday Crafts* (5–8). Illus. by author. 1977, Hebrew $9.95; paper $6.95. Simple craft projects—mainly, but not always, directly related to Jewish religious holidays—are clearly described in words and pictures.

4791. Burns, Marilyn. *The Hanukkah Book* (4–7). Illus. by Martha Weston. 1981, Four Winds $8.95. Not only the history and traditions of this day but also attitudes Jewish children have about Christmas are discussed. Also use: *Hanukkah: Festivals and Holidays* by June Behrens (1983, Childrens Pr. $6.95).

4792. Burstein, Chaya M. *The Jewish Kids Catalog* (3–7). Illus. 1983, Jewish Publication Society paper $10.95. An introduction to Jewish holidays, traditions, and crafts.

4793. Cedarbaum, Sophia N. *Passover: Festival of Freedom* (2–4). Illus. by Clare Ross and John Ross. 1960, American Hebrew Cong. $3.50. One of a series that includes many Jewish holidays.

4794. Chaikin, Miriam. *Light Another Candle: The Story and Meaning of Hanukkah* (3–6). Illus. by Demi. 1981, Houghton $10.50; paper $3.95. A simple explanation of the holiday and how it is celebrated around the world.

4795. Chaikin, Miriam. *Make Noise, Make Merry: The Story and Meaning of Purim* (3–6). Illus. by Demi. 1983, Houghton $10.95. The origin and ways of celebrating this happy holiday.

4796. Chaikin, Miriam. *The Seventh Day: The Story of the Jewish Sabbath* (4–7). Illus. by David Frampton. 1980, Schocken paper $4.95. This is not only an account of the Jewish Sabbath but also the story of Genesis and Exodus.

4797. Chaikin, Miriam. *Shake a Palm Branch: The Story and Meaning of Sukkot* (3–6). Illus. by Marvin Friedman. 1984, Houghton $12.95. The Jewish fall harvest festival and the customs associated with it are explained.

4798. Cone, Molly. *The Jewish New Year* (1–3). Illus. by Jerome Snyder. 1966, Harper $9.89. An interesting and enlightening account of the meaning and customs associated with this holiday.

4799. Cone, Molly. *Purim* (1–3). Illus. by Helen Borten. 1967, Harper $9.89. A simple retelling of how Queen Esther saved her people and how this event is commemorated.

4800. Cuyler, Margery. *Jewish Holidays* (3–5). Illus. 1978, Holt $6.95. The history and significance of 9 important Jewish holidays.

4801. Drucker, Malka. *Hanukkah: Eight Nights, Eight Lights* (4–8). Illus. by Brom Hoban. 1980, Holiday LB $9.95. A thorough sourcebook on this joyous Jewish holiday.

4802. Drucker, Malka. *Passover: A Season of Freedom* (5–7). Illus. by Brom Hoban. 1981, Holiday LB $9.95. An explanation of the rituals behind this important Jewish holiday.

4803. Drucker, Malka. *Rosh Hashanah and Yom Kippur: Sweet Beginnings* (5–7). Illus. 1981, Holiday LB $8.95. A comprehensive volume that includes background material, activities, and prayers.

4804. Drucker, Malka. *Shabbat: A Peaceful Island* (4–8). Illus. by Brom Hoban. 1983, Holiday $11.95. The story of the Jewish Sabbath.

4805. Drucker, Malka. *Sukkot: A Time to Rejoice* (4–6). Illus. by Brom Hoban. 1982, Holiday LB $10.95. The story of this happy Jewish holiday.

4806. Epstein, Morris. *All about Jewish Holidays and Customs* (4–6). Illus. by Arnold Lobel. 1969, Ktav paper $6.95. A history and presentation of the customs involved with all of the major Jewish holidays.

4807. Greenfeld, Howard. *Bar Mitzvah* (5–9). Illus. by Elaine Grove. 1981, Holt $7.95. The fundamentals of this ceremony and how they differ in various branches of Judaism.

4808. Greenfeld, Howard. *Passover* (4–6). Illus. by Elaine Grove. 1978, Holt $6.95. The history, traditions, and meaning of this important holiday. Also use: *Chanukah* (1976, Holt $6.95).

4809. Greenfeld, Howard. *Purim* (4–6). Illus. by Elaine Grove. 1983, Holt $9.70. The story of the origins of this joyous holiday.

4810. Greenfeld, Howard. *Rosh Hashanah and Yom Kippur* (5–7). Illus. by Elaine Grove. 1979, Holt $6.95. The origin, significance, and means of observing these 2 important Jewish holy days are well presented.

4811. Hirsh, Marilyn. *The Hanukkah Story* (K–2). Illus. by author. 1977, Hebrew $7.95. A simple narrative with full-page illustrations explains the origins of Hanukkah.

4812. Hirsh, Marilyn. *I Love Hanukkah* (PS–3). Illus. by author. 1984, Holiday $11.95. A grandfather tells his grandson about Hanukkah.

4813. Metter, Bert. *Bar Mitzvah, Bat Mitzvah: How Jewish Boys and Girls Come of Age* (5–8). Illus. by Marvin Friedman. 1984, Houghton $10.95; paper $3.95. An explanation of the Jewish coming-of-age ceremonies.

4814. Simon, Norma. *Hanukkah* (1–3). Illus. by Symeon Shimin. 1966, Harper LB $10.89. An informative and dignified account of the story of Hanukkah; the Festival of Lights and the rituals and customs observed on this holy holiday. Also use: *The Complete Book of Hanukkah* by Kinneret Chiel (1959, Ktav $5.95).

4815. Simon, Norma. *Passover* (1–3). Illus. by Symeon Shimin. 1965, Harper LB $10.89. The origin of Passover in Egypt and how it is celebrated by Jews today.

Fiction

4816. Adler, David A. *The House on the Roof: A Sukkoth Story* (K–4). 1976, Hebrew $6.95; Kar-Ben paper $4.95. An old man hauls all sorts of material into his apartment and builds a Sukkah to celebrate the holiday of Sukkoth.

4817. Aleichem, Sholem. *Hanukkah Money* (K–3). Illus. by Uri Shulevitz. 1978, Greenwillow $10.95; LB $10.51. A young boy and his brother participate in the celebration of Hanukkah in this charming story.

4818. Aleichem, Sholem. *Holiday Tales of Sholem Aleichem* (4–6). 1979, Scribners $10.95. Seven diverse tales that deal with Jewish holidays.

4819. Cohen, Barbara. *Here Come the Purim Players!* (2–4). Illus. by Beverly Brodsky. 1984, Lothrop $11.50; LB $11.04. A story of celebrating Purim in medieval Prague.

4820. Cohen, Barbara, retel. *Yussel's Prayer: A Yom Kippur Story* (2–5). Illus. by Michael J. Deraney. 1981, Lothrop $11.25; LB $11.88. An orphan boy wants to participate in Yom Kippur like others in the village.

4821. Goffstein, M. B. *Laughing Latkes* (K–3). Illus. 1980, Farrar $6.95. A charming story about the joy that abounds at Hanukkah.

4822. Hirsh, Marilyn. *Potato Pancakes All Around: A Hanukkah Tale* (1–3). 1978, Hebrew paper $5.50. A humorous story about making pancakes for Hanukkah.

4823. Shulevitz, Uri. *The Magician* (K–2). Adapt. from the Yiddish of I. L. Peretz. Illus. 1973, Macmillan paper $1.95. A Passover story based on a Yiddish folk legend about Elijah disguised as a magician.

4824. Singer, Isaac Bashevis. *The Power of Light* (4–7). Illus. by Irene Lieblich. 1980, Farrar $10.95. A collection of 8 charming, original stories celebrating Hanukkah, the Feast of Lights.

4825. Suhl, Yari. *The Purim Goat* (3–6). Illus. by Kaethe Zemach. 1980, Four Winds $7.95. A young boy teaches his goat a trick so he will not be butchered.

4826. Sussman, Susan. *There's No Such Thing as a Chanukah Bush* (3–5). Illus. by Charles Robinson. 1983, Whitman $6.95. The difference between believing in a holiday and helping others celebrate is brought out in this story.

4827. Taylor, Sydney. *Danny Loves a Holiday* (2–5). Illus. by Gail Owens. 1980, Dutton $8.95. A story for each of 11 different Jewish holidays.

Jokes, Riddles, Puzzles, Word Games

Jokes and Riddles

4828. Adler, David A. *The Carsick Zebra and Other Animal Riddles* (K–3). Illus. by Tomie de Paola. 1983, Holiday $8.95. A wonderful collection of animal riddles, humorously illustrated.

4829. Beisner, Monika. *Book of Riddles* (2–4). Illus. by author. 1983, Farrar $11.95. The answers to these 101 riddles are found in the illustrations.

4830. Berger, Melvin, and Handelsman, J. B. *The Funny Side of Science* (4–7). Illus. 1973, Harper $9.57. Jokes and riddles dealing with science.

4831. Bernstein, Joanne E. *Fiddle with a Riddle* (3–6). Illus. by Giulio Maestro. 1979, Dutton $9.25. A simple guide on how to write your own riddles, with many examples.

4832. Bernstein, Joanne E., and Cohen, Paul. *Un-Frog-Getable Riddles* (4–6). Illus. by Alexandra Wallner. 1981, Whitman LB $7.75. A collection of howlers about frogs.

4833. Bernstein, Joanne E., and Cohen, Paul. *Unidentified Flying Riddles* (2–5). Illus. by Meyer Seltzer. 1983, Whitman $6.95. Outer space is the inspiration for these riddles.

4834. Bishop, Ann. *Hello, Mr. Chips!* (5–8). Illus. by Jerry Warshaw. 1982, Lodestar $8.95; paper $3.95. A collection of jokes, riddles, etc., involving computers.

4835. Brown, Marc. *Spooky Riddles* (1–4). Illus. by author. 1983, Random $4.95; LB $5.99. Simply read riddles involving ghosts, vampires, etc.

4836. Brown, Marc. *What Do You Call a Dumb Bunny? And Other Rabbit Riddles, Games, Jokes and Cartoons* (2–3). Illus. by author. 1983, Little $9.95; paper $3.95. An unusual collection of rabbit humor.

4837. Cerf, Bennett. *Bennett Cerf's Book of Animal Riddles* (K–2). Illus. by Roy McKie. 1964, Random $4.95; LB $5.99. Easily read riddles that are very popular with young children. Also use: *Bennett Cerf's Book of Riddles* (1960, $4.95; LB $5.99).

4838. Charlip, Remy. *Arm in Arm, a Collection of Connections, Endless Tales, Restorations, and Other Echolalia* (All Ages). Illus. 1969, Four Winds $9.95. All sorts of wordplay and nonsense rhymes.

4839. Clark, David Allen. *Jokes, Puns, and Riddles* (3–7). Illus. by Lionel Kalish. 1968, Doubleday $5.95. A collection that will "tickle the funny bones" of young children.

4840. Cole, William. *Give Up? Cartoon Riddle Rhymers* (3–6). Illus. by Mike Thaler. 1978, Avon paper $1.95. A collection of riddles with rhyming answers.

4841. Corbett, Scott. *Jokes to Read in the Dark* (4–6). Illus. by Annie Gusman. 1980, Dutton $10.95. A fine collection of sure-fire jokes.

4842. Corbett, Scott. *Jokes to Tell Your Worst Enemy* (3–6). Illus. by Annie Gusman. 1984, Dutton $9.66. Jokes so terrible they're funny.

4843. Cunningham, Bronnie. *The Best Book of Riddles, Puns and Jokes* (3–7). Illus. by Amy Aitken. 1979, Doubleday LB $7.95. More than 1,000 jokes, etc., are crammed into this collection.

4844. Duncan, Riana. *A Nutcracker in a Tree: A Book of Riddles* (1–6). Illus. by author. 1981, Delacorte $8.95; LB $8.44. A series of riddles, English in tone, asked in rhyme.

4845. Eckstein, Joan, and Gleit, Joyce. *The Best Joke Book for Kids* (7–12). Illus. by Joyce Behr. 1977, Avon paper $2.25. A general joke book.

4846. Emrich, Duncan, comp. *The Hodge-Podge Book* (2–6). Illus. by Ib Ohlsson. 1972, Four Winds $14.95. A bit of everything—games, jokes, tongue twisters, even medical advice—is included in this charming nonsense book.

4847. Emrich, Duncan. *The Whim-Wham Book* (3–5). Illus. by Ib Ohlsson. 1975, Four Winds $9.95. A miscellany of jokes, superstitions, camp songs, riddles, and more.

4848. Gerler, William R. *A Pack of Riddles* (1–3). Illus. by Giulio Maestro. 1975, Dutton $6.95. A refreshingly hilarious collection of riddles about animal life.

4849. Gomez, Victoria. *Scream Cheese and Jelly: Jokes, Riddles and Puns* (2–3). Illus. by Joel Schick. 1979, Lothrop $9.28; LB $8.88. All sorts of puns and jokes about words.

4850. Gounaud, Karen J. *A Very Mice Joke Book* (2–5). Illus. by Lynn Munsinger. 1981, Houghton

$6.95; paper $2.95. A small joke book dealing with mice.

4851. Hall, Katy, and Eisenberg, Lisa. *Fishy Riddles* (1–4). Illus. by Simms Taback. 1983, Dial $8.89; paper $3.83. An easy-to-read book of riddles on ocean life.

4852. Hoff, Syd. *Syd Hoff's Joke Book* (2–4). Illus. by author. 1972, Putnam $5.99. Riddles and other kinds of jokes, many of them old standbys.

4853. Hoke, Helen, ed. *Jokes, Jokes, Jokes* (5–7). Illus. by Richard Erdoes. 1954, Watts $8.40. A collection divided into subjects.

4854. Jensen, Virginia Allen, and Elman, Polly. *Red Thread Riddles* (K–6). Illus. by author. 1980, Putnam $10.95. A spiral-bound book of riddles that can be read by both sighted and blind children.

4855. Keller, Charles. *Ballpoint Bananas and Other Jokes for Children* (3–6). Illus. by David Barrios. 1973, Prentice paper $4.95. Zany American riddles, rhymes, and contemporary jokes. Two sequels are: *More Ballpoint Bananas* (1977, $7.95; paper $3.95); *Still Going Bananas* (1982, paper $3.95).

4856. Keller, Charles, comp. *Grime Doesn't Pay: Law and Order Jokes* (3–5). Illus. by Jack Kent. 1984, Prentice $8.95. A collection of over 100 cops and robbers jokes.

4857. Keller, Charles. *Llama Beans* (2–6). Illus. by Dennis Nolan. 1979, Prentice $7.95. Thirty-one clever riddles about animals.

4858. Keller, Charles, comp. *Norma Lee I Don't Knock on Doors: Knock Knock Jokes* (3–6). Illus. by Paul Galdone. 1983, Prentice $7.95. About 100 knock-knock jokes of various levels of difficulty.

4859. Keller, Charles. *The Nutty Joke Book* (2–6). Illus. by Jean Claude Swares. 1978, Prentice paper $3.95. A collection of jokes about nuts.

4860. Keller, Charles. *Oh, Brother! And Other Family Jokes* (4–6). Illus. by Edward Frascino. 1982, Prentice $7.95. A collection of rib-ticklers about families.

4861. Keller, Charles. *Ohm on the Range: Robot and Computer Jokes* (3–7). Illus. by Arthur Cumings. 1982, Prentice $7.95. Jokes about various forms of automation.

4862. Keller, Charles. *Remember the A La Mode! Riddles and Puns* (3–6). Illus. by Lee Lorenz. 1983, Prentice $8.95. A humorous collection arranged by the type of question asked.

4863. Keller, Charles. *School Daze* (2–6). Illus. by Sam Q. Quissman. 1979, Prentice paper $3.95. Zany jokes and cartoons about school.

4864. Keller, Charles, and Baker, Richard. *The Star-Spangled Banana and Other Revolutionary Riddles* (3–6). Illus. by Tomie de Paola. 1974, Prentice paper $3.95. Outrageous puns and jokes that celebrate the Spirit of '76. Also use: *The Silly Song Book* (1976, Prentice paper $2.95).

4865. Kohl, Marguerite, and Young, Frederica. *Jokes for Children* (4–8). Illus. by Bob Patterson. 1963, Hill & Wang $8.95. Over 650 rhymes, riddles, puns, and jokes.

4866. Leach, Maria. *Riddle Me, Riddle Me, Ree* (3–6). Illus. by William Wiesner. 1970, Viking $5.95. Over 200 riddles originating in folklore with a selection of jokes appended.

4867. Leeming, Joseph. *Riddles, Riddles, Riddles* (4–6). Illus. by S. Lane Miller. 1953, Watts $8.90. Contains enigmas, anagrams, puns, puzzles, quizzes, conundrums.

4868. Leonard, Marcia. *Cricket's Jokes, Riddles and Other Stuff* (2–6). Illus. 1977, Random $3.95; LB $3.99. Lots of knock-knocks, elephant jokes, and tongue twisters in this funny, funny book.

4869. Levine, Caroline Anne. *Knockout Knock Knocks* (2–4). Illus. by Giulio Maestro. 1978, Dutton $6.95; paper $1.95. A very humorous collection of 61 knock-knock jokes.

4870. Levine, Caroline Anne. *The Silly Kid Joke Book* (2–4). Illus. by Giulio Maestro. 1983, Dutton $9.66. A joke book in which the word *silly* is used in each riddle.

4871. Low, Joseph. *Beastly Riddles: Fishy, Flighty and Buggy, Too* (K–2). Illus. by author. 1983, Macmillan $9.95. A collection of simple animal riddles.

4872. Low, Joseph. *Five Men under One Umbrella and Other Ready-to-Read Riddles* (1–3). Illus. by author. 1975, Macmillan $6.95. Lots of fun in this collection of jokes, humorously illustrated.

4873. Low, Joseph. *What If . . . ?* (2–5). Illus. by author. 1976, Atheneum $6.95. An exploration of 14 fanciful encounters, such as how to behave if a shark invites you for a swim.

4874. McMillan, Bruce A., and McMillan, Brett. *Puniddles* (2–4). Illus. 1982, Houghton LB $7.95; paper $2.95. Objects in photographs are used to illustrate word combinations.

4875. Maestro, Giulio. *A Raft of Riddles* (1–5). Illus. by author. 1982, Dutton $8.95. More than 50 riddles presented with cartoonlike drawings.

4876. Maestro, Giulio. *Riddle Romp* (1–4). Illus. by author. 1983, Houghton $10.95; paper $3.95. A fine collection of riddles not found in other collections.

4877. Maestro, Giulio. *What's a Frank Frank? Tasty Homograph Riddles* (2–4). Illus. by author. 1984, Houghton $11.95; paper $3.95. Riddles that rely on wordplay.

4878. Manes, Stephen. *Socko! Every Riddle Your Feet Will Ever Need* (2–4). Illus. by Nurit Karlin. 1982, Putnam $5.95. Thirty pages of jokes involving the feet.

4879. Morrison, Lillian. *Black Within and Red Without* (4–6). Illus. by Jo Spier. 1953, Harper $9.95. Riddles from all over, for all ages.

4880. Phillips, Louis. *How Do You Get a Horse Out of the Bathtub? Profound Answers to Preposterous Questions* (4–8). Illus. by James Stevenson. 1983, Viking $9.60; Penguin paper $3.95. A spoof of the "Dear Abby" column that is bound to please.

4881. Phillips, Louis. *The Upside Down Riddle Book* (K–3). Illus. by Beau Gardner. 1982, Lothrop $10.00; LB $10.88. The reader must turn the book around to find the clever answers.

4882. Rockwell, Thomas. *The Portmanteau Book* (5–7). Illus. by Gail Rockwell. 1974, Little paper $3.95. A charming sampling of puzzles, humorous recipes, and other amusements.

4883. Roop, Peter, and Roop, Connie. *Space Out! Jokes about Outer Space* (K–3). Illus. by Joan Hanson. 1984, Lerner $5.95. A small-format joke book with plenty of laughs. Two other books in this series: *Go Hog Wild! Jokes for Down on the Farm; Out to Lunch! Jokes about Food* (both 1984, $5.95).

4884. Rosenbloom, Joseph. *Biggest Riddle Book in the World* (3–6). Illus. by Joyce Behr. 1976, Sterling $8.95; LB $10.99; paper $3.95. About 2,000 old and new riddles arranged under various subjects and amusingly illustrated.

4885. Rosenbloom, Joseph. *Ridiculous Nicholas Haunted House Riddles* (2–5). Illus. by Joyce Behr. 1984, Sterling $7.95; LB $9.99. Riddles involving a visit to a haunted house.

4886. Rosenbloom, Joseph. *Sports Riddles* (2–5). Illus. by Sam Weissman. 1982, Harcourt $8.95. A collection of riddles divided by various sports.

4887. Rosenbloom, Joseph. *The Zaniest Riddle Book in the World* (3–6). Illus. by Sanford Hoffman. 1984, Sterling $7.95; LB $9.99. A riddle book arranged by topics.

4888. Ross, Dave, and Kinzel, Dottie. *Rat Race and Other Rodent Jokes* (2–4). Illus. 1983, Morrow $8.00; LB $7.63. A collection of jokes about mice and their relatives.

4889. Sarnoff, Jane. *What? A Riddle Book* (2–4). Illus. by Reynold Ruffins. 1974, Scribners $9.95; paper $1.29. A delightful collection of daffy riddles grouped by various subjects.

4890. Sarnoff, Jane, and Ruffins, Reynold. *I Know! A Riddle Book* (1–4). Illus. by Reynold Ruffins. 1976, Scribners $7.95. A joyful collection of old and new riddles arranged by general subjects.

4891. Schwartz, Alvin, comp. *Witcracks: Jokes and Jests from American Folklore* (3–6). Illus. by Glen Rounds. 1973, Harper $9.89. All sorts of humor associated with America's past, from old riddles to knock-knock jokes.

4892. Steig, William. *C D B!* (3–6). Illus. by author. 1968, Simon & Schuster paper $2.95. When each set of letters and/or numbers is repeated aloud and riddle buffs apply a bit of imagination, the amusing caption accompanying each cartoon becomes apparent. Also use: *C D C* (1984, Farrar $6.95).

4893. Sterne, Noelle. *Tyrannosaurus Wrecks: A Book of Dinosaur Riddles* (2–6). Illus. 1979, Harper LB $9.89; paper $2.95. Many short riddles, all dealing amusingly with prehistoric animals.

4894. Thaler, Mike. *The Yellow Brick Toad* (3–5). 1978, Pocket paper $1.50. Subtitle: "Funny Frog Cartoons, Riddles and Silly Stories."

4895. Thorndike, Susan. *The Electric Radish and Other Jokes* (2–3). Illus. by Ray Cruz. 1973, Doubleday $5.95. A wacky collection of jokes accompanied by suitably flamboyant illustrations.

4896. Wallner, Alexandra. *Ghoulish Giggles and Monster Riddles* (2–4). Illus. by author. 1982, Whitman $6.50. A riddle book featuring all sorts of monsters and cartoon drawings.

4897. Watson, Clyde. *Quips and Quirks* (3–6). Illus. by Wendy Watson. 1975, Harper $9.57. A collection of epithets from such standbys as "Smart-alack" to the more esoteric "Grizzleguts."

4898. White, Laurence B., Jr., and Broekel, Ray. *The Surprise Book* (4–6). Illus. by Will Winslow. 1981, Doubleday LB $7.95. A fine selection of jokes and riddles.

4899. Ziegler, Sandra K., comp. *Jokes and More Jokes* (1–5). Illus. by Diana L. Magnuson. 1983, Childrens Pr. $6.95. In addition to many jokes, this gives a history of humor. Another informative book in this series is: *Knock-Knocks, Limericks and Other Silly Sayings* (1983, $6.95).

4900. Zimmerman, Andrea Griffin. *The Riddle Zoo* (2–4). Illus. by Giulio Maestro. 1981, Dutton $9.25. A collection of 50 riddles dealing with animals.

Puzzles

4901. Adler, Irving. *The Adler Book of Puzzles and Riddles* (1–3). Illus. by Peggy Adler. 1962, Day

$10.89. A simple collection of entertaining puzzles for very young readers.

4902. Adler, Peggy. *Geography Puzzles* (4–7). Illus. by author. 1979, Watts $6.90. A fine collection of puzzles, most of which involve geographical concepts.

4903. Brandreth, Gyles. *Brain-Teasers and Mind-Benders* (4–6). Illus. by Ann Axworthy. 1979, Sterling $7.95. All sorts of puzzles with answers.

4904. Brown, Osa. *The Metropolitan Museum of Art Activity Book* (3–6). Illus. 1983, Random $6.95. An activity book of puzzles, games, and activities involving the collection of the Metropolitan Museum of Art.

4905. Burns, Marilyn. *The Book of Think (or How to Solve a Problem Twice Your Size)* (5–7). Illus. by Martha Weston. 1976, Little $8.95; LB $6.78. A stimulating collection of puzzles to make children think; informally and entertainingly presented.

4906. Churchill, E. Richard. *I Bet I Can: I Bet You Can't* (3–6). Illus. by Sanford Hoffman. 1983, Sterling $6.95; LB $7.49. A collection of tricks, stunts, and puzzles.

4907. Demi. *Where Is it?* (2–4). Illus. by author. 1980, Doubleday LB $9.95. A puzzle book using hidden figures in puzzles.

4908. Doty, Roy, and Rether, David. *Fun to Go: A Take Along Activity Book* (4–6). Illus. 1982, Macmillan paper $4.95. A treasury of activities for children on trips.

4909. Fletcher, Helen Jill. *Put on Your Thinking Cap* (4–8). Illus. by Quentin Blake. 1968, Harper LB $10.89. A collection of 108 brainteasers, including mazes, perceptual and verbal problems, scrambled words, and riddles. Also use: *Puzzles and Quizzles* (1971, Harper LB $10.89).

4910. Hass, E. A. *Come Quick, I'm Sick* (4–6). Illus. 1982, Atheneum paper $2.95. An activity book for those confined to bed.

4911. Lamb, Geoffrey. *Pencil and Paper Tricks* (5–7). 1979, Lodestar $9.25. All kinds of ways to amuse oneself or friends with only a pencil and paper.

Word Games

4912. Brandreth, Gyles. *The Biggest Tongue Twister Book in the World* (4–6). Illus. by Alex Chin. 1978, Sterling $6.95; LB $9.99; paper $2.95. Hundreds of twisters (mostly one-liners) plus cartoonlike drawings make this a most enjoyable book.

4913. Schwartz, Alvin, comp. *A Twister of Twists, a Tangler of Tongues* (4–7). Illus. by Glen Rounds. 1972, Harper $10.10; paper $1.95. A browsing book of tongue twisters in different languages. Also use: *Tomfoolery: Trickery and Foolery with Words* (1973, Harper $10.10).

4914. Tremain, Ruthven. *Teapot, Switcheroo, and Other Silly Word Games* (2–4). Illus. 1979, Greenwillow $8.25; LB $7.92. Riddles, knock-knocks, and interesting word origins are included in this enjoyable collection.

Hobbies

General and Miscellaneous

4915. Adkins, Jan. *The Art and Industry of Sandcastles* (4–6). 1982, Walker $7.95; paper $4.95. Subtitle: "Being an illustrated guide to basic constructions along with information devised by one Jan Adkins, a wily fellow."

4916. Albert, Burton. *Clubs for Kids* (3–6). Illus. 1983, Ballantine paper $4.95. Information on 50 clubs, encompassing a variety of hobby interests, that children can join.

4917. Butler, William Vivian. *The Young Detective's Handbook* (5–8). Illus. by Lucinda Landon. 1981, Little $8.95. All kinds of techniques and activities for the amateur detective.

4918. Duda, Margaret B. *Collections for Kids* (5–8). Illus. 1982, Oak Tree $17.95. A guide to collecting everything from stamps to postcards.

4919. Hawkins, Jim W. *Cheerleading Is for Me* (3–5). Illus. 1981, Lerner LB $7.95. A well-illustrated narration. Also use: *Baton Twirling Is for Me* (1982, Lerner LB $7.95).

4920. Hussey, Lois J., and Pessino, Catherine. *Collecting for the City Naturalist* (4–6). Illus. by Barbara Neill. 1975, Harper $9.57. This survey stresses techniques of collecting and preserving a wide variety of nature specimens.

4921. Kettelkamp, Larry. *Song, Speech and Ventriloquism* (5–8). 1967, Morrow LB $8.59. The structure and function of the speech organs and the formation of speech sounds with explicit instructions in ventriloquism.

4922. Kuslan, Richard David, and Kuslan, Louis I. *Ham Radio: An Introduction to the World Beyond* (6–8). Illus. 1981, Prentice $10.95. Through father-son discussions, the world of ham radio operation is revealed.

4923. McLoone, Margo, and Siegel, Alice. *Sports Cards: Collecting, Trading and Playing* (4–6). Illus. 1979, Harper LB $4.95. An introduction to this hobby illustrated with many examples.

4924. Newman, Frederick R. *Zounds! The Kid's Guide to Sound Making* (3–7). Illus. by Elwood H. Smith. 1983, Random paper $4.95. How to imitate birds, animals, musical instruments, and general voices.

4925. Taylor, Paula. *The Kids' Whole Future Catalog* (5–7). Illus. 1982, Random LB $7.99; paper $6.95. Sources of information are given for materials interesting to youngsters, plus projects and puzzles.

4926. Waltner, Willard, and Waltner, Elma. *The New Hobbycraft Book* (4–6). Illus. 1963, Lantern $6.70. A basic introduction to various hobbies and projects involving each.

4927. Zubrowski, Bernie. *A Children's Museum Activity Book: Bubbles* (4–6). Illus. by Joan Drescher. 1979, Little $6.95; paper $4.70. Bubble blowing is used to create many activities.

Cooking

4928. Better Homes and Gardens, eds. *Better Homes and Gardens Step-by-Step Kids' Cook Book* (4–7). Illus. 1984, Meredith $5.95. A well-organized cookbook that gives cooking tips and recipes that move from the simple to the complex.

4929. Bisignano, Alphonse. *Cooking the Italian Way* (5–9). Illus. 1982, Lerner LB $8.95. An introduction to the food and customs of the country, plus several easy recipes. Others in the series: *Cooking the Mexican Way* by Rosa Coronado; *Cooking the English Way* by Barbara W. Hill; *Cooking the Norwegian Way* by Sylvia Munsen; *Cooking the French Way* by Lynn Marie Waldee; *Cooking the Chinese Way* by Ling Yu (all 1982, Lerner LB $8.95); *Cooking the Japanese Way* (1983, Lerner $7.95) by Reiko Weston.

4930. Borghese, Anita. *The Down to Earth Cookbook.* (4–6). 1980, Scribners $9.95. Cooking the natural way with simple, direct instructions.

4931. Cooper, Terry Touff, and Ratner, Marilyn. *Many Hands Cooking: An International Cookbook for Girls and Boys* (4–7). Illus. by Tony Chen. 1974, Harper $6.50. Produced with the cooperation of the U.S. Committee for UNICEF, this is an interesting collection of recipes from all over the world. Also use: *Many Friends Cooking: An International Cookbook for Boys and Girls* (1980, UNICEF paper $6.00).

4932. George, Jean Craighead. *The Wild, Wild Cookbook: A Guide for Young Wild-Food Foragers* (5–9). Illus. by Walter Kessell. 1982, Harper $10.10; LB $10.89; paper $4.76. All sorts of edible wild plants are introduced, plus recipes.

4933. Haines, Gail Kay. *Baking in a Box, Cooking on a Can* (5–7). Illus. by Margot Apple. 1981, Morrow $8.88. A manual on outdoor cooking.

4934. Henry, Edna. *Native American Cookbook* (3–7). Illus. 1983, Messner $8.79. A collection of recipes and lore about North American Indian cooking.

4935. John, Sue. *The Bread Basket Cookbook* (4–7). Illus. 1982, Putnam paper $6.95. Easy-to-follow instructions plus good illustrations are in this beginning cookbook. By the same author: *The Special Days Cookbook* (1982, Putnam $6.95).

4936. Jones, Judith, and Jones, Evan. *Knead It, Punch It, Bake It! Make Your Own Bread* (5–7). Illus. by Lauren Jarrett. 1981, Harper $11.06; LB $10.89. A collection of recipes, fully explained, on how to make a variety of breads.

4937. McCleary, Julia G. *Cooking Metric Is Fun* (5–8). Illus. by Jan Pyk. 1979, Harcourt $8.95. Recipes from breakfast dishes to desserts presented in metric measurements with many cooking hints.

4938. MacGregor, Carol. *The Storybook Cookbook* (3–6). Illus. by Ray Cruz. 1967, Prentice paper $1.95. Twenty-two recipes inspired by literary characters, such as "Captain Hook—poison cake."

4939. Meyer, Carolyn. *The Bread Book: All about Bread and How to Make It* (4–7). Illus. by Trina S. Hyman. 1971, Harcourt paper $1.95. The importance of bread from early times, its place in religious ceremonies, and the many forms in which it has been made.

4940. Moore, Eva. *The Cookie Book* (3–5). Illus. by Talivaldis Stubis. 1973, Houghton $9.95; Scholastic paper $1.95. A simple book giving clear instructions for 12 cookie recipes for special holidays.

4941. Moore, Eva. *The Great Banana Cookbook for Boys and Girls* (3–6). Illus. by Susan Russo. 1983, Houghton $10.95. A cookbook involving recipes with bananas.

4942. Noad, Susan Strand. *Recipes for Science Fun* (4–6). Illus. by Arnold Dobrin. 1979, Watts $7.90. Recipes that are not only representative of sound nutrition, but also demonstrate basic scientific principles.

4943. Ogren, Sylvia. *Shape It and Bake It: Quick and Simple Ideas for Children from Frozen Bread Dough* (5–9). Illus. 1981, Dillon LB $9.95. Directions are given to young bakers for turning dough into delectables.

4944. Paul, Aileen, and Hawkins, Arthur. *Kids Cooking: The Aileen Paul Cooking School Cookbook* (3–6). 1970, Doubleday $7.95. A lively, well-organized introduction to cooking with easily followed recipes and plenty of background information.

4945. Penner, Lucille Recht. *The Colonial Cookbook* (4–7). Illus. 1976, Hastings $8.95. Interspersed with several easily followed recipes is interesting material on how colonists lived and ate. Also use: *Slumps, Grunts and Snickerdoodles: What Colonial America Ate and Why* by Lila Perl (1975, Houghton $8.95).

4946. Perl, Lila. *The Hamburger Book: All about Hamburgers and Hamburger Cookery* (5–9). Illus. by Ragna Tischler Goddard. 1974, Houghton $8.95. Information on national dishes around the world and various schools of cooking is included with many ground-beef recipes.

4947. Perl, Lila. *Hunter's Stew and Hangtown Fry: What Pioneer America Ate and Why* (5–8). Illus. by Richard Cuffari. 1977, Houghton $8.95. Eating habits and preferences, cooking techniques, and 20 recipes are included in this volume.

4948. Pfommer, Marian. *On the Range: Cooking Western Style* (3–6). Illus. by David Marshall. 1981, Atheneum LB $8.95. An imaginative cookbook on how to prepare food outdoors.

4949. Pinkwater, Jill. *The Natural Snack Cookbook: Good Things to Eat* (5–9). Illus. 1975, Four Winds $14.95. Recipes for healthy eating.

4950. Rockwell, Anne. *The Mother Goose Cookie–Candy Book* (1–3). Illus. by author. 1983, Random $5.95; LB $6.99. A basic dessert cookbook to be used with supervision.

4951. Scherie, Strom. *Stuffin' Muffin: Muffin Pan Cooking for Kids* (4–6). Illus. by Dave Ferry. 1982, Young People's Pr. paper $9.95. A variety of foods without sugar or salt that can be made in muffin tins.

4952. Schroeder, Rosella J., and Sanderson, Marie C. *It's Not Really Magic: Microwave Cooking for Young People* (5–8). Illus. 1981, Dillon LB $9.95. A selection of recipes from breakfast to dinner plus snacks, all using the microwave oven.

4953. Schwartz, Paula Dunaway. *You Can Cook: How to Make Good Food for Your Family and Friends* (5–8). Illus. by Byron Barton. 1976, Atheneum $7.95. Basic recipes and complete menus are given simply and logically.

4954. Shapiro, Rebecca. *A Whole World of Cooking* (5–9). Illus. by author. 1972, Little $7.95. One or 2 recipes from each part of the world are included in this geographical cook's tour.

4955. Solomon, Hannah. *Bake Bread!* (5–7). Illus. 1976, Harper $9.57. Procedures used in bread making are clearly explained along with basic recipes.

4956. Steinkoler, Ronnie. *A Jewish Cookbook for Children* (4–7). Illus. by Sonja Glassman. 1980, Messner LB $7.79. Many traditional Jewish dishes arranged by holiday.

4957. Supraner, Robyn. *Quick and Easy Cookbook* (1–3). Illus. by Renzo Barto. 1981, Troll LB $8.11; paper $1.95. A good introductory cookbook with 22 recipes.

4958. Van der Linde, Polly, and Van der Linde, Tasha. *Around the World in Eighty Dishes* (3–7). Illus. by Horst Lemke. 1971, Scroll $9.95. The compilers and testers of these recipes from many continents are 2 little girls, 8 and 10 years old.

4959. Walker, Barbara M. *The Little House Cookbook* (5–7). Illus. by Garth Williams. 1979, Harper $10.00; LB $10.89. Frontier food, such as green pumpkin pie from the Little House books, served up in tasty, easily used recipes.

4960. Warner, Margaret Brink, and Hayword, Ruth Ann. *What's Cooking? Recipes from around the World* (5–8). 1981, Little $10.95. Eighty-nine recipes from teenagers around the world are given in simple terms.

4961. Williams, Barbara, and Williams, Rosemary. *Cookie Craft* (4–7). Illus. 1977, Holt $7.95; paper $3.50. Subtitle: *No-Bake Designs for Edible Party Favors and Decorations.*

4962. Williams, Vera B. *It's a Gingerbread House: Bake It, Build It, Eat It!* (2–4). 1978, Greenwillow $8.25; LB $7.92. How to build a gingerbread house from simple materials.

4963. Wishik, Cindy S. *Kids Dish It Up . . . Sugar-Free: A Versatile Teaching Tool for Beginning Cooks* (3–5). Illus. 1982, Peninsula paper $8.95. From soup to nuts with sugar-free recipes.

4964. Zweifel, Frances. *Pickle in the Middle and Other Easy Snacks* (1–3). Illus. by author. 1979, Harper $7.64; LB $8.89. A simple how-to cookbook on the preparation of easily prepared treats.

Gardening

4965. Jobb, Jamie. *My Garden Companion* (4–7). Illus. by Martha Weston. 1977, Scribners $9.95; paper $4.95. Subtitle: "A Complete Guide for the Beginner with a Special Emphasis on Useful Plants and Instructive Planting in the Wayside, Dooryard, Patio, Rooftop and Vacant Lot."

4966. Johnsen, Jan. *Gardening without Soil* (5–7). Illus. 1979, Harper LB $8.89. An introduction to

hydroponics, including a number of projects that can be carried out at home.

4967. Johnson, Hannah Lyons. *From Seed to Salad* (2–4). Illus. 1978, Lothrop $10.51. A beginning do-it-yourself guide to gardening.

4968. Mandry, Kathy. *How to Grow a Jelly Glass Farm* (K–3). Illus. by Joe Toto. 1974, Pantheon $5.99. Fourteen simple indoor garden projects are described.

4969. Mintz, Lorelie. *Vegetables in Patches and Pots: A Child's Guide to Organic Vegetable Gardening* (4–7). Illus. 1976, Farrar $6.95. A basic introductory guide to gardening, written with wit and enthusiasm.

4970. Murphy, Louise. *My Garden: A Journal for Gardening around the Year* (4–7). Illus. by Lisa Campbell Ernst. 1980, Scribners $8.95. An almanac and anthology about the wonders and delights of gardening.

4971. Paul, Aileen. *Kids Outdoor Gardening* (3–6). Illus. 1978, Doubleday $7.95. The hows and whys of simple outdoor gardening are well covered.

4972. Rockwell, Harlow. *The Compost Heap* (1–3). Illus. by author. 1974, Doubleday LB $4.95. How a leaf pile changes into garden riches is described in text and drawings.

4973. Wickers, David, and Tuey, John. *How to Make Things Grow* (4–7). 1972, Scholastic paper $1.50. After introductory sections on how plants live, there are chapters on planting and cultivating for both indoor and outdoor gardeners.

Magic

4974. Baker, James W. *Illusions Illustrated: A Professional Magic Show for Young Performers* (5–8). Illus. by Jeanette Swofford. 1984, Lerner $10.95. Directions on how to put on a magic show with 10 different tricks.

4975. Broekel, Ray, and White, Laurence B., Jr. *Abra-Ca-Dazzle: Easy Magic Tricks* (3–5). Illus. by Mary Thelen. 1982, Whitman LB $9.25. Twenty-five simple but impressive tricks for the beginner.

4976. Broekel, Ray, and White, Laurence B., Jr. *Hocus Pocus: Magic You Can Do* (4–6). Illus. by Mary Thelen. 1984, Whitman $9.95. Twenty simple tricks for beginners.

4977. Broekel, Ray, and White, Laurence B., Jr. *Now You See It: Easy Magic for Beginners* (3–5). Illus. by Bill Morrison. 1979, Little $6.95. Forty proven magic tricks good for amateur shows.

4978. Brown, Bob. *How to Fool Your Friends* (3–6). Illus. 1978, Western $10.69; paper $1.95. Amateur magicians will delight in the 46 different tricks and puzzles presented in this book.

4979. Cobb, Vicki. *Magic . . . Naturally* (4–6). Illus. by Lance R. Miyamoto. 1976, Harper $10.53; paper $2.95. The scientific explanation behind some tricks and ways to perform them.

4980. Dolan, Edward F., Jr. *Let's Make Magic* (4–6). Illus. 1981, Doubleday $7.95; LB $8.90. More than 40 simple tricks are introduced.

4981. Kettelkamp, Larry. *Magic Made Easy* (4–7). Illus. by Loring Eutemey. 1981, Morrow $9.95; LB $9.55. An introduction to magic including a number of simple tricks.

4982. Kraske, Robert. *Magicians Do Amazing Things* (2–4). Illus. by Richard Bennett. 1979, Random $3.95; LB $4.99. Kraske reveals the secrets behind 6 great tricks, including one of Houdini's most famous.

4983. Kronzek, Allan Z. *The Secrets of Alkazar: A Book of Magic* (5–Up). Illus. by Tom Huffman. 1980, Four Winds $9.95. An introduction to the magician Alkazar, his techniques, and his tricks.

4984. Michalski, Martin. *Magic Made Easy* (6–9). Illus. 1978, Lodestar $8.95. More than 70 different tricks are presented, plus details on how to prepare for a show.

4985. Permin, Ib. *Hokus Pokus: With Wands, Water and Glasses* (5–8). Illus. 1978, Sterling $6.95; LB $6.69. Over 25 tricks for the beginning magician, plus hints for their artful execution.

4986. Reisberg, Ken. *Card Tricks* (2–3). Illus. by Arline Oberman and Marvin Oberman. 1980, Watts LB $8.90. A slim, easily read book of tricks that are easy to master.

4987. Rigney, Francis. *A Beginner's Book of Magic* (4–6). Illus. 1963, Devin $4.95. Subtitle: "The Do-It-Yourself Book of Tricks, Magic and Stunts."

4988. Shalit, Nathan. *Science Magic Tricks* (5–8). Illus. by Helen Cerra Ulan. 1981, Holt $9.95; paper $3.95. Many science tricks are presented with hints on how to combine them into a show.

4989. Sheridan, Jeff. *Nothing's Impossible: Stunts to Entertain and Amaze* (5–8). Illus. 1982, Lothrop $9.00. A number of tricks and feats bound to amaze and amuse.

4990. Stoddard, Edward. *Magic* (5–8). Illus. by Robin King. 1983, Watts $8.90. The best and simplest tricks, each one a real mystery.

4991. Supraner, Robyn. *Magic Tricks You Can Do!* (1–3). Illus. by Renzo Barto. 1981, Troll LB $8.11; paper $1.95. A beginner's book of magic.

4992. White, Laurence B., Jr. *Science Toys and Tricks* (1–3). Illus. by Marc Tolan Brown. 1980, Addison paper $4.95. An easily read collection of over 40 simple tricks.

Model Making

4993. Berliner, Don. *Flying-Model Airplanes* (4–6). Illus. 1982, Lerner $7.95. A description of the many types of model airplanes that are available.

4994. Berliner, Don. *Scale-Model Airplanes* (4–7). Illus. 1982, Lerner LB $7.95. The story of making model airplanes and directions for assembling them.

4995. Berman, Paul. *Make-Believe Empire: A How-to Book* (4–7). Illus. 1982, Atheneum LB $8.95. A book on how to construct a medieval city.

4996. Blocksma, Mary, and Blocksma, Dewey. *Easy-to-Make Spaceships That Really Fly* (2–5). Illus. by Marisabina Russo. 1983, Prentice $9.95. A variety of models of spaceships are described that can be made from such materials as paper plates and straws.

4997. Curry, Barbara A. *Model Aircraft* (4–6). Illus. 1979, Watts $8.90. A variety of simple models are included, including some folded paper planes.

4998. Gilmore, H. H. *Model Planes for Beginners* (6–9). Illus. 1957, Harper LB $8.89. Plans for building simplified model planes.

4999. Gilmore, H. H. *Model Rockets for Beginners* (4–8). 1961, Harper $8.89. History of rockets, with plans for building simplified models of American and Soviet types.

5000. Herda, D. J. *Model Boats and Ships* (5–7). Illus. 1982, Watts LB $8.90. A fine introduction to the construction of several models of boats and ships. Others in this series: *Model Cars and Trucks* and *Model Railroads* (both 1982, Watts LB $8.90) by D. J. Herda; *Model Cars* (1981, Lerner LB $7.95) by Richard L. Knudson; *Model Historical Aircraft* (1982, Watts LB $8.90) by Barbara A. Curry.

5001. Maginley, C. J. *Historic Models of Early America: And How to Make Them* (5–8). Illus. by James MacDonald. 1966, Harcourt paper $0.60. Simple directions for making such objects from the past as articles of furniture, utensils, and several buildings.

5002. Olney, Ross R. *Out to Launch: Modern Rockets* (5–9). Illus. 1979, Lothrop $9.84; LB $6.96. This clear introduction to a growing hobby covers the subject from construction information to recovery problems.

5003. Ross, Dave. *Making Space Puppets* (2–4). Illus. 1980, Watts LB $8.90. Simple craft projects for science fiction fans. Two others are: *Making Robots*; *Making UFO's* (both 1980, $8.90).

5004. Ross, Frank, Jr. *Antique Car Models: Their Stories and How to Make Them* (5–8). Illus. 1978, Lothrop $11.95; LB $11.47. Four antique cars are introduced and plans are supplied to make models of them.

5005. Ross, Frank, Jr. *The Tin Lizzie: A Model-Making Book* (5–8). Illus. 1980, Lothrop $12.50; LB $12.88. A book on how to build 4 replicas of Henry Ford's automobile.

5006. Simon, Seymour. *The Paper Airplane Book* (3–6). Illus. by Byron Barton. 1971, Viking $9.50; Penguin paper $2.95. Using how to make paper airplanes as the take-off point, the author explains why planes fly and how changes in their construction can cause variations in flight.

5007. Weiss, Harvey. *How to Run a Railroad: Everything You Need to Know about Model Trains* (5–9). Illus. 1977, Harper $10.95; paper $4.76. A thorough description of this popular hobby from purchasing or building the components to various aspects of assembling and operating the system.

5008. Weiss, Harvey. *Model Airplanes and How to Build Them* (5–8). 1975, Harper $12.45. A well-organized, easily used presentation.

5009. Weiss, Harvey. *Model Buildings and How to Make Them* (5–8). Illus. by author. 1979, Harper $10.53. Plans and techniques for constructing a variety of buildings.

5010. Weiss, Harvey. *Model Cars and Trucks and How to Build Them* (4–7). Illus. 1974, Harper $12.45. A beginner's book that gives exact and clear directions and advice concerning tools, techniques, and projects to the novice in the model car hobby.

5011. Weiss, Harvey. *Ship Models and How to Build Them* (5–9). Illus. 1973, Harper $8.95. Following background information on tools and materials, projects are introduced with clear, step-by-step directions.

Photography and Filmmaking

5012. Andersen, Yvonne. *Make Your Own Animated Movies* (5–8). Illus. 1970, Little $10.95. A thorough survey of the preparation techniques and the actual filming of animated films.

5013. Czaja, Paul Clement. *Writing with Light: A Simple Workshop in Basic Photography* (6–9). Illus. 1973, Viking $6.95. Along with the basics of photography, this work tells how to make images with light.

5014. Davis, Edward E. *Into the Dark* (6–9). 1979, Atheneum $9.95. Subtitle: "A Beginner's Guide to Developing and Printing Black and White Negatives."

5015. Fischer, Robert. *Trick Photography: Crazy Things You Can Do with Cameras* (6–8). Illus. 1981, Dutton $9.95; paper $5.95. Tricks with lighting, lenses, mirrors, and so on, are explored.

5016. Forbes, Robin. *Click: A First Camera Book* (3–5). Illus. 1979, Macmillan paper $2.95. An interesting guide to would-be shutterbugs.

5017. Freeman, Tony. *Photography* (1–4). Illus. 1983, Childrens Pr. $7.95. An introductory volume that stresses photography as a hobby.

5018. Herda, D. J. *Photography: Take a Look* (4–6). Illus. 1977, Raintree $13.30. The parts of a camera and a simple guide to taking good pictures.

5019. Horvath, Joan. *Filmmaking for Beginners* (6–9). Illus. 1974, Lodestar $9.95. An award-winning filmmaker explains simply and directly the various facets of this subject.

5020. Leen, Nina. *Taking Pictures* (2–5). Illus. 1977, Holt LB $6.95; paper $1.75. An easily understood introduction to photography illustrated with both good and bad examples.

5021. Noren, Catherine. *The Way We Looked: The Meaning and Magic of Family Photographs* (6–9). Illus. 1983, Dutton $10.63. How to study family photos and what they reveal about the subjects.

5022. Owens-Knudsen, Vick. *Photography Basics* (5–9). Illus. 1983, Prentice $8.95. The story of photography and a description of various cameras in use today.

5023. Sandler, Martin W. *The Story of American Photography* (6–9). Illus. 1979, Little $19.95. A fascinating account for the better reader.

Stamp and Coin Collecting

5024. Hobson, Burton. *Coin Collecting as a Hobby* (5–8). Illus. 1982, Sterling $8.95; LB $10.99. A good book for the beginning collector.

5025. Hobson, Burton. *Getting Started in Stamp Collecting* (5–8). Illus. 1982, Sterling $8.95; LB $10.99. An excellent beginner's guide. Also use: *Collecting Stamps* by Paul Villiard (1975, NAL paper $2.95).

5026. Jacobsen, Karen. *Stamps* (1–4). Illus. 1983, Childrens Pr. $7.95. The history and use of stamps in a simple, well-organized account.

5027. Reinfeld, Fred, and Hobson, Burton. *How to Build a Coin Collection* (4–8). Illus. 1977, Sterling $8.95; LB $10.99. A basic, comprehensive guide for the beginner.

5028. Rosenfeld, Sam. *The Story of Coins* (5–8). 1968, Harvey House paper $7.29. The interesting stories behind some of the world's most famous coins.

Crafts

General and Miscellaneous

5029. Arnold, Susan. *Eggshells to Objects: A New Approach to Egg Craft* (5–8). Illus. by author. 1979, Holt $7.95. A craft book that gives about 30 different projects using egg shells.

5030. Arnold, Wesley F., and Cardy, Wayne C. *Fun with Next to Nothing* (4–6). Illus. by author. 1962, Harper $10.89. Subtitle: "Handicraft Projects for Boys and Girls."

5031. Barwell, Eve. *Make Your Pet a Present* (4–7). Illus. by Giulio Maestro. 1977, Lothrop $10.75. How to make gifts for a dog, cat, bird, or other pet.

5032. Beard, D. C. *The American Boys' Handy Book: What to Do and How to Do It* (5–7). 1983, Godine paper $9.95. A facsimile edition of a manual first published in 1882.

5033. Bernstein, Bonnie. *Writing Crafts Workshop* (4–7). Illus. 1982, Pitman paper $5.95. All kinds of crafts related to writing, such as bookbinding and illuminating letters, are outlined.

5034. Caney, Steven. *Kids' America* (4–6). Illus. 1978, Workman paper $7.95. A potpourri of crafts, puzzles, facts, and fun about the United States.

5035. Caney, Steven. *Steven Caney's Play Book* (3–5). Illus. 1975, Workman $9.95; paper $5.95. All sorts of activities involving discarded or inexpensive materials, thoroughly and clearly presented.

5036. Cobb, Vicki. *The Secret Life of School Supplies* (5–8). Illus. by Bill Morrison. 1981, Harper $9.57; LB $8.89. The author shows how common school supplies like paste and paper can be made. Also use: *The Secret Life of Hardware: A Science Experiment Book* (1982, Harper $9.57; LB $9.89).

5037. Cole, Ann, et al. *Children Are Children Are Children* (4–7). Illus. by Lois Axeman. 1978, Little $11.95; paper $7.95. Subtitle: "An Activity Approach to Exploring Brazil, France, Iran, Japan, Nigeria and the U.S.S.R." A book of games, crafts, and projects.

5038. Cooper, Michael. *Things to Make and Do for George Washington's Birthday* (4–8). 1978, Watts $8.90. Facts about Washington, plus a number of appropriate projects.

5039. Crook, Beverly Courtney. *Invite a Bird to Dinner: Simple Feeders You Can Make* (4–6). Illus. 1978, Lothrop $9.95; LB $9.55. A variety of projects are described involving construction of many bird feeders from everyday materials.

5040. D'Amato, Janet. *Who's Horn? What's an Antler? Crafts of Bone and Horn* (5–7). Illus. 1982, Messner LB $9.29. An explanation of what horns and antlers are and how they are used in carving projects.

5041. Eckstein, Joan, and Gleit, Joyce. *Fun with Making Things* (4–6). Illus. 1979, Avon paper $1.50. Fifty projects for young people from finger puppets to hanging plants.

5042. Ellison, Virginia H. *The Pooh Get-Well Book* (2–5). Illus. by Ernest H. Shepard. 1975, Dell paper $1.25. Subtitle: "Recipes and Activities to Help You Recover from Wheezles and Sneezles."

5043. Fiarotta, Phyllis, and Fiarotta, Noel. *Confetti: The Kids' Make-It-Yourself, Do-It-Yourself Party Book* (4–7). Illus. 1978, Workman paper $5.95. Hundreds of ideas for throwing 22 different kinds of parties.

5044. Fowler, Virginie. *Folk Arts around the World and How to Make Them* (6–9). Illus. by author. 1981, Prentice $10.95; paper $5.95. Thirty-five projects using common materials are included.

5045. Gelman, Rita Golden, and Buxbaum, Susan Kovacs. *Boats That Float* (1–4). Illus. by Marilyn MacGregor. 1981, Watts LB $8.90. A number of easy projects are described involving making boats.

5046. Greene, Peggy. *Things to Make* (2–5). Illus. by Bill Duggin. 1981, Random $4.99. All sorts of projects created from common household items.

5047. Haas, Carolyn, et al. *Backyard Vacation: Outdoor Fun in Your Own Neighborhood* (4–6). Illus. by Roland Rodegast. 1980, Little $9.95; paper $5.95. A book of outdoor activities that include projects, games, and crafts.

5048. Haldane, Suzanne. *The See-Through Zoo: How Glass Animals Are Made* (3–6). Illus. 1984, Pantheon $9.95; LB $9.99. A visit to a glass factory and a description of how glass animals are made.

5049. Hautzig, Esther. *Let's Make More Presents: Easy and Inexpensive Gifts for Every Occasion* (4–7). Illus. by Ray Skibinski. 1973, Macmillan $9.95. All sorts of presents from food to home gifts are presented in this fine sequel to *Let's Make Presents* (1962, Harper $11.49).

5050. Hogrogian, Nonny. *Handmade Secret Hiding Places* (3–5). Illus. by author. 1975, Overlook Pr. $6.50. The construction of 6 hiding places from a mud hut to a hideaway made from blankets over chairs is described in words and pictures.

5051. Kerina, Jane. *African Crafts* (5–8). Illus. by Tom Feelings and Marylyn Katzman. 1970, Lion LB $7.95. Many projects arranged geographically by the region in Africa where they originated.

5052. Linsley, Leslie. *Air Crafts: Playthings to Make and Fly* (3–5). Illus. 1982, Lodestar $8.95. Various activities are described including making boomerangs and whirligigs.

5053. Marks, Mickey Klar. *Op-Tricks: Creating Kinetic Art* (5–9). Illus. 1972, Harper $8.89. A group of projects that create fascinating optical effects, most using material found around the house.

5054. Parish, Peggy. *Beginning Mobiles* (2–4). Illus. by Lynn Sweat. 1979, Macmillan $8.95. A simple book of projects involving readily available materials presented in an easy-to-follow format.

5055. Rahn, Joan Elma. *Seven Ways to Collect Plants* (5–7). Illus. 1978, Atheneum $8.95. A fine introduction to this hobby with special hints on collecting, drying, and pressing specimens.

5056. Robinson, Jeri. *Activities for Anyone, Anytime, Anywhere* (1–4). Illus. 1983, Little $13.95; paper $5.95. A book for adults outlining all kinds of activities from clay to shadow puppets.

5057. Rockwell, Harlow. *I Did It* (1–3). Illus. 1973, Macmillan $8.95. Very simple projects for the beginning crafter.

5058. Sattler, Helen R. *Recipes for Art and Craft Materials* (3–Up). Illus. by author. 1973, Lothrop LB $11.88. Formulas for making craft materials like paints and pastes.

5059. Schwartz, Alvin. *The Rainy Day Book* (1–6). 1973, Simon & Schuster paper $2.45. Many games, activities, and craft ideas as well as dramatics, music, and science experiments make up this helpful book for children and harassed parents.

5060. Simons, Robin. *Recyclopedia: Games, Science Equipment and Crafts from Recycled Materials* (5–9). Illus. by author. 1976, Houghton $9.95; paper $5.95. Clear directions complemented by good illustrations characterize this book of interesting projects using waste materials.

5061. Supraner, Robyn. *Fun-to-Make Nature Crafts* (1–3). Illus. by Renzo Barto. 1981, Troll LB $8.11; paper $1.95. Simple, easy-to-make projects from toys to terrariums.

5062. Supraner, Robyn. *Rainy Day Surprises You Can Make* (1–3). Illus. by Renzo Barto. 1981, Troll LB $8.11; paper $1.95. Simple handicrafts made with accessible materials.

5063. Trivett, Daphne, and Trivett, John. *Time for Clocks* (6–8). Illus. 1979, Harper $10.89. Plans are included for several easy-to-make clocks.

5064. Van Ryzin, Lani. *A Patch of Earth* (4–5). Illus. by Caren Caraway. 1981, Messner LB $7.59. Directions on how to construct miniature landscapes using common objects.

5065. Weiss, Harvey. *How to Make Your Own Books* (5–9). Illus. by author. 1974, Harper $10.51. Details on how to make various types and parts of books.

5066. Wiseman, Ann. *Making Things Book 2: Handbook of Creative Discovery* (4–Up). Illus. 1975, Little paper $7.95. Clear directions for making such articles as Tiffany lamp shades and string bikinis from materials found around the house. Also use: *Making Things* (1973, Little $12.95; paper $7.95).

American Historical Crafts

5067. Hoople, Cheryl G. *The Heritage Sampler: A Book of Colonial Arts and Crafts* (5–7). Illus. by Richard Cuffari. 1975, Dial LB $6.46. Each chapter deals with a different colonial craft, followed by simple instructions on projects that can be done today.

5068. Parish, Peggy. *Let's Be Early Settlers with Daniel Boone* (2–4). Illus. by Arnold Lobel. 1976, Harper LB $9.89. Easy-to-follow directions for making many items associated with pioneer days. Also use: *Let's Be Indians* (1962, Harper $9.89).

Clay and Other Modeling Crafts

5069. Gilbreath, Alice. *Slab, Coil and Pinch: A Beginner's Pottery Book* (3–5). Illus. by Barbara Fiore. 1977, Morrow $9.75; LB $8.16. Very simple projects for the beginning potter using self-hardening clay or terra-cotta.

5070. Weiss, Harvey. *Ceramics from Clay to Kiln* (5–7). Illus. 1964, Addison $12.56. An excellent beginning book that stresses creativity.

Costume Making

5071. Barwell, Eve. *Disguises You Can Make* (4–6). Illus. by Richard Rosenblum. 1977, Lothrop $10.80. With simple materials and instructions, youngsters can transform themselves into such creatures as Martians, monsters, or witches.

5072. Bruun-Rasmussen, Ole, and Petersen, Grete. *Make-Up, Costumes and Masks for the Stage* (5–9). Illus. 1976, Sterling $12.95; LB $15.69; paper $7.95. A useful compilation of material on backstage skills for putting on plays.

5073. Chernoff, Goldie Taub. *Easy Costumes You Don't Have to Sew* (3–6). Illus. by Margaret A. Hartelius. 1977, Four Winds $7.95. Paper bags, cartons, and old cloth are 3 of the materials used in making these simple costumes.

5074. Haley, Gail E. *Costumes for Plays and Playing* (4–6). Illus. by author. 1979, Methuen $9.95. Colorful illustrations highlight this introduction to costume making.

5075. Mooser, Stephen. *Monster Fun* (4–6). Illus. by Dana Herkelrath. 1979, Messner $7.29. An activity book that tells youngsters how to become make-believe monsters.

5076. Schnurnberger, Lynn. *Kings, Queens, Knights and Jesters: Making Medieval Costumes* (4–8). Illus. 1978, Harper $12.45; LB $12.89. This book presents an introduction to the clothing of the Middle Ages and directions for making several examples.

Drawing and Painting

5077. Ames, Lee J. *Draw, Draw, Draw* (4–6). 1962, Doubleday $8.95. Easy-to-follow instructions on how to draw common objects.

5078. Ames, Lee J. *Draw Fifty Airplanes, Aircraft and Spacecraft* (3–7). Illus. 1977, Doubleday $8.95. Simple directions for drawing various airborne articles, from the Wright brothers' plane to the Saturn V rocket. Also use: *Draw Fifty Boats, Ships, Trucks and Trains* (1970, $8.95); *Draw Fifty Vehicles* (1978, paper $3.50); *Draw Fifty Buildings and Other Structures* (1980, $8.95).

5079. Ames, Lee J. *Draw Fifty Dogs* (4–6). Illus. by author. 1981, Doubleday $8.95. Six steps are used to draw several species. Also use: *Draw Fifty Animals* (1974); *Draw Fifty Dinosaurs and Other Prehistoric Animals* (1977) (both $8.95); *Draw Fifty Horses* (1984, $9.95).

5080. Ames, Lee J. *Draw Fifty Famous Cartoons* (4–6). 1979, Doubleday $8.95; paper $3.99. How to draw such characters as Dick Tracy and the Flintstones. Also use: *Make Twenty-five Crayon Drawings of the Circus; Make Twenty-five Felt-tip Drawings Out West* (both 1980, $8.95).

5081. Ames, Lee J. *Draw Fifty Monsters, Creeps, Superheroes, Demons, Dragons, Nerds, Dirts, Ghouls, Giants, Vampires, Zombies and Other Curiosa* (4–6). Illus. by author. 1983, Doubleday $8.95. How to draw a variety of curiosities. Also use: *How to Draw Star Wars Heroes, Creatures, Spaceships, and Other Fantastic Things* (1984, Random paper $4.95).

5082. Arnosky, Jim. *Drawing from Nature* (5–9). Illus. by author. 1982, Lothrop $11.75. A book of techniques on how to draw landscapes and animals.

5083. Arnosky, Jim. *Drawing Life in Motion* (3–6). Illus. by author. 1984, Lothrop $10.00. The author explains with many examples how to capture motion when drawing plants and animals.

5084. Benjamin, Carol Lea. *Cartooning for Kids* (3–6). Illus. by author. 1982, Harper LB $9.89; paper $3.80. Instructions are given for easily drawn cartoons using circles, curves, and lines.

5085. Bolognese, Don. *Drawing Dinosaurs and Other Prehistoric Animals* (4–5). Illus. by author. 1982, Watts LB $8.95; paper $4.95. Basic rules for sketching are introduced, then specific examples are given. Two others in this series: *Drawing Horses and Foals* (1977, LB $8.90; paper $4.95); *Drawing Spaceships and Other Spacecraft* (1982, $8.90).

5086. Emberley, Ed. *Ed Emberley's Big Green Drawing Book* (2–4). Illus. by author. 1979, Little $11.45; paper $6.70. A do-it-yourself drawing book using basic shapes, explained by a master. Also use: *Ed Emberley's Big Purple Drawing Book* (1981, $10.45; paper $5.95).

5087. Emberley, Ed. *Ed Emberley's Drawing Book: Make a World* (2–4). Illus. by author. 1972, Little $6.95. Illustrations and examples on how to draw objects from flags to faces. A companion to the author's *Drawing Book of Animals* (1970, $7.95). Also use: *Ed Emberley Little Drawing Book of Birds; Ed Emberley Little Drawing Book of Farms; Ed Emberley Little Drawing Book of Trains* (all 1973, paper $1.00).

5088. Emberley, Ed. *Ed Emberley's Great Thumbprint Drawing Book* (1–4). 1977, Little $9.25. How to make faces and other objects by adding lines to thumbprints. Also use: *Drawing with Numbers and Letters* by Rebecca Emberley (1981, Little $7.95).

5089. Frame, Paul. *Drawing Cats and Kittens* (6–8). Illus. 1979, Watts LB $8.90. A detailed explanation of how to draw cats that emphasizes the need to practice. Also use: *Drawing Dogs and Puppies* (1978); *Drawing the Big Cats* (1981); *Drawing Sharks, Whales, Dolphins and Seals* (1983) (all LB $8.90).

5090. Hawkinson, John. *Collect, Print and Paint from Nature* (2–4). Illus. by author. 1963, Whitman

$8.25. Basic instructions for leaf printing, spatter painting, and elementary brush techniques.

5091. Kilroy, Sally. *Copycat Drawing Book* (1–4). Illus. by author. 1981, Dial LB $7.89; paper $3.95. Drawing of common objects is made simple in this attractive manual.

5092. Rauch, Hans-Georg. *The Lines Are Coming: A Book about Drawing* (2–6). Illus. 1978, Scribners $8.95. A description of various kinds of lines and how each can be used in the art of drawing.

5093. Weiss, Harvey. *Pencil, Pen and Brush: Drawings for Beginners* (5–7). 1974, Scholastic paper $1.95. Basic techniques and step-by-step directions on drawing from photographs.

5094. Zaidenberg, Arthur. *How to Draw People! A Book for Beginners* (7–9). 1952, Vanguard $7.95. Two other books by this master teacher are: *How to Draw Cartoons: A Book for Beginners* (1959, Vanguard $7.95); *How to Draw Heads and Faces* (1966, Harper $10.89).

5095. Zaidenberg, Arthur. *How to Draw with Pen and Brush: A Book for Beginners* (4–7). 1965, Vanguard $7.95. An explanation with examples on various effects that can be created with pens and paintbrushes.

Masks and Mask Making

5096. Hunt, Kari, and Carlson, Bernice W. *Masks and Mask Makers* (5–7). 1961, Abingdon $7.95. Stories behind the masks used in primitive and modern societies, with instructions for making some of them.

5097. Meyer, Carolyn. *Mask Magic* (4–6). Illus. by Melanie G. Arwin. 1978, Harcourt $7.95. A simple guide to mask making and the relation of masks to many of our celebrations.

5098. Price, Christine. *The Mystery of Masks* (6–8). Illus. 1978, Scribners paper $1.98. A description of masks and their relation to the cultures that made and used them.

5099. Supraner, Robyn. *Great Masks to Make* (1–3). Illus. by Renzo Barto. 1981, Troll LB $8.11; paper $1.95. Bright, full-color illustrations highlight this simple craft book.

Paper Crafts

5100. Araki, Chiyo. *Origami in the Classroom* (4–7). Illus. 1965, Tuttle $8.95. In 2 volumes; each deals with paper crafts for 2 of the seasons. Also use: *The ABC's of Origami* by Claude Sarasas (1964, Tuttle $7.75).

5101. Borja, Robert, and Borja, Corinne. *Making Chinese Papercuts* (4–7). Illus. by authors. 1980, Whitman $9.25. A clear explanation of an ancient art with many examples and photographs.

5102. Bottomley, Jim. *Paper Projects for Creative Kids of All Ages* (4–6). 1963, Little $12.45; paper $8.70. An activity book that presents many projects using paper.

5103. Emberley, Ed. *Ed Emberley's Crazy Mixed-Up Face Game* (1–5). Illus. by author. 1981, Little $9.70; paper $4.95. A paper game that results in an assortment of strange faces.

5104. Fowler, Virginie. *Paperworks: Colorful Crafts from Picture Eggs to Fish Kites* (5–7). Illus. by author. 1982, Prentice $8.95. Many interesting projects, including block printing and papier-mache, are described.

5105. Gilbreath, Alice. *Simple Decoupage: Having Fun with Cutouts* (4–6). Illus. 1978, Morrow $8.25; LB $7.92. Thirteen inexpensive projects are described in detail and with simple instructions.

5106. Grummer, Arnold E. *Paper by Kids* (5–7). Illus. 1980, Dillon LB $9.95. A clear, well-organized guide to papermaking.

5107. Judy, Susan, and Judy, Stephen. *Gifts of Writing: Creative Projects with Words and Art* (4–7). Illus. by author. 1980, Scribners $10.95. Craft projects that involve making such materials associated with writing as cards, posters, and stationery.

5108. Linsley, Leslie. *Decoupage for Young Crafters* (3–6). Illus. by Jon Aron. 1977, Dutton $7.95. Nine projects ranging from simple to more difficult are thoroughly presented and well illustrated.

5109. Munthe, Nelly. *Meet Matisse* (4–7). Illus. by Rory Kee. 1983, Little $10.95. This book focuses on a special cutout technique used by Matisse.

5110. Supraner, Robyn. *Fun with Paper* (1–3). Illus. by Renzo Barto. 1981, Troll LB $8.11; paper $1.95. Simple projects with easy directions.

5111. West, Robin. *Paper Circus: How to Create Your Own Circus* (3–5). Illus. by Priscilla Kiedrowski. 1983, Carolrhoda $9.95. All sorts of circus models that can be made with construction paper.

Printmaking

5112. Cross, Jeanne. *Simple Printing Methods* (6–9). Illus. 1972, Phillips $10.95. An introduction to printmaking techniques, mainly using materials found around the house. Well illustrated with many examples in color.

5113. Haddad, Helen R. *Potato Printing* (4–6). Illus. by author. 1981, Harper $9.13; LB $10.89. A clearly presented introduction plus many ideas for advanced work.

5114. MacStravic, Suellen. *Print Making* (3–5). Illus. by George Overlie. 1973, Lerner $3.95. The techniques used in making various kinds of prints and an introduction in clear, simple text with informative illustrations.

5115. Pettit, Florence H. *The Stamp-Pad Printing Book* (4–6). Illus. by author. 1979, Harper $8.61. How to make a variety of objects, for example, posters and bookmarks, from stamps cut from erasers.

Sewing and Needle Crafts

5116. Barkin, Carol, and James, Elizabeth. *Slapdash Alterations: How to Recycle Your Wardrobe* (5–7). Illus. 1977, Lothrop $9.75; LB $9.36. A simple, do-it-yourself guide to remodeling girl's clothes. Also use: *Slapdash Sewing* (1975, $8.88).

5117. Bradley, Duane. *Design It, Sew It, and Wear It* (5–8). Illus. by Judith Hoffman Corwin. 1979, Harper $10.89. Subtitle: *How to Make Yourself a Super Wardrobe without Commercial Patterns.*

5118. Cone, Ferne Geller. *Crazy Crocheting* (4–6). Illus. by Rachael Osterlof. 1981, Atheneum LB $12.95. A simple introduction to crocheting using any available string or yarn.

5119. Corrigan, Barbara. *I Love to Sew* (4–7). Illus. 1974, Doubleday $6.95. Hand and machine sewing and a variety of projects are introduced in this informative book.

5120. Hodgson, Mary Anne, and Paine, Josephine Ruth. *Fast and Easy Needlepoint* (4–7). Illus. 1979, Doubleday $7.95. A basic introduction that includes directions for 10 different stitches.

5121. Katz, Ruth J. *Make It and Wear It* (6–9). Illus. by Sharon Tondreau. 1981, Walker $7.95; LB $8.85. Simple directions and materials for 22 wardrobe accessories.

5122. Kelly, Karin. *Weaving* (4–6). Illus. by George Overlie. 1973, Lerner $3.95. Directions for making a cardboard loom and simple weaving projects using it.

5123. Rubenstone, Jessie. *Knitting for Beginners* (5–8). Illus. 1973, Harper paper $2.95. Beginning with the most simple procedures, the author proceeds to more complicated stitches and projects. Good use of photographs. Also use: *Crochet for Beginners* (1974, Harper $8.61).

5124. Sommer, Elyse, and Sommer, Joellen. *Patchwork, Applique, and Quilting Primer* (4–8). Illus.

by Giulio Maestro. 1975, Lothrop $9.84. These historic crafts are introduced through a series of useful projects.

5125. Von Wartburg, Ursula. *The Workshop Book of Knitting* (4–7). Illus. 1978, Atheneum $9.95; paper $4.95. An easily understood book of patterns that includes toys and animals and articles of clothing that are knitted.

Toys and Dolls

5126. Glubok, Shirley. *Dolls' Houses: Life in Miniature* (6–9). Illus. 1984, Harper $14.90; LB $14.89. An examination of 26 dollhouses and how they reflect the architecture and life-styles of various times.

5127. Horwitz, Joshua. *Doll Hospital* (2–4). Illus. 1983, Pantheon $10.95; LB $10.99. A step-by-step account of how dolls are repaired at a doll hospital.

5128. Huff, Vivian. *Let's Make Paper Dolls* (2–3). Illus. 1978, Harper $7.89. Simple instructions and clear photographs help youngsters make paper dolls of various sizes.

5129. Joseph, Joan. *Folk Toys around the World and How to Make Them* (6–8). Illus. 1972, UNICEF paper $3.50. Detailed plans for making 18 toys from different countries.

5130. Lasky, Kathryn. *Dollmaker: The Eyelight and the Shadow* (6–9). Illus. 1981, Scribners $11.95. An introduction to Carole Bowling and her craft of doll-making.

5131. Morton, Brenda. *Do-It-Yourself Dinosaurs: Imaginative Toy Craft for Beginners* (4–6). Illus. by author. 1973, Taplinger $6.95. This book on stuffed toys describes how to make a dozen dinosaurs and other prehistoric creatures.

5132. Nicklaus, Carol. *Making Dolls* (1–4). Illus. by author. 1981, Watts LB $8.90. Simple instructions introduce several easy doll-making projects.

5133. Roche, P. K. *Dollhouse Magic: How to Make and Find Simple Dollhouse Furniture* (3–5). Illus. by Richard Cuffari. 1977, Dial $9.95; LB $9.89; paper $2.95. Clear instructions and step-by-step sketches introduce this fascinating craft to the novice.

5134. Schnurnberger, Lynn. *A World of Dolls That You Can Make* (4–6). Illus. by Alan Robert Showe. 1982, Harper LB $16.89; paper $9.57. Instructions are given for making a total of 14 dolls.

5135. Waltner, Willard, and Waltner, Elma. *Hobbycraft Toys and Games* (4–6). Illus. n.d., Lantern $6.70. A basic book for the beginner.

Woodworking

5136. Brown, William F. *Wood Works: Experiments with Common Wood and Tools* (5–8). Illus. by M. G. Brown. 1984, Atheneum $11.95. Several projects that introduce woodworking and scientific principles.

5137. Gibbons, Gail. *Tool Book* (K–3). Illus. by author. 1982, Holiday $11.95. An introduction to various simple tools and their uses.

5138. Herda, D. J., and Herda, Judy. *Carpentry for Kids* (4–7). Illus. 1980, Messner LB $7.79. Eight projects are described plus the tools and techniques needed.

5139. Lasson, Robert. *If I Had a Hammer: Woodworking with Seven Basic Tools* (5–8). Illus. by Jeff Murphy. 1974, Dutton $8.95. Basic tools, how to use them, and several simple projects are given in this useful introduction to the craft.

5140. Rockwell, Anne. *The Toolbox* (1–2). Illus. by Harlow Rockwell. 1971, Macmillan $10.95; paper $2.25. A description of each tool in the toolbox and what it does, told in simple language and illustrated with exact pictures.

5141. Torre, Frank D. *Woodworking for Kids* (6–9). Illus. 1978, Doubleday $7.95. Photographs help amplify this introduction to basic tools and a few interesting projects.

5142. Walker, Les. *Carpentry for Children* (6–9). Illus. 1982, Overlook Pr. $15.95. Carpentry basics are explained plus simple projects.

5143. Walker, Les. *Housebuilding for Children* (4–7). Illus. 1977, Overlook Pr. $14.95. The construction of 6 different kinds of houses, including a tree house, is clearly described in text and pictures.

5144. Weiss, Harvey. *Hammer and Saw: An Introduction to Woodworking* (4–8). Illus. by author. 1981, Harper $9.57; LB $9.89. An account that contains not only simple projects but also information on tools and their uses.

5145. Yates, Raymond F. *The Boys' Book of Tools* (4–6). Illus. 1957, Harper $8.89. An explanation of the types and uses of many household tools.

Sports and Games

General and Miscellaneous

5146. Benson, Rolf. *Skydiving* (6–9). Illus. 1979, Lerner $7.95. Free-fall forms, equipment, and jumping techniques. Also use: *Hang Gliding* by Otto Penzler (1976, Troll $8.79; paper $2.50).

5147. Boccaccio, Tony. *Racquetball Basics* (5–8). Illus. 1979, Prentice $8.95. The history of this increasingly popular sport, as well as rules and the types of equipment needed. Also use: *Racquetball* by George S. Fichter (1979, Watts $8.90); *Racquetball Is for Me* by Mark Lerner (1983, Lerner $6.95).

5148. Colby, C. E. *First Rifle* (4–6). Illus. 1954, Putnam $5.99. A heavily illustrated title with a minimum of text.

5149. Coombs, Charles. *Hot-Air Ballooning* (5–9). Illus. 1981, Morrow $10.25; LB $9.84. A description of the history, equipment, and training necessary, as well as techniques connected with this sport. Also use: *Hot Air Ballooning* by Peter B. Mohn (1975, Crestwood House LB $7.95); *Balloon Trip: A Sketchbook* by Huck Scarry (1983, Prentice $10.95).

5150. Emberley, Michael. *The Sports Equipment Book* (3–6). Illus. 1982, Little $9.95. A handbook on the equipment needed in various sports.

5151. Ferretti, Fred. *The Great American Book of Sidewalk, Stoop, Dirt, Curb and Alley Games* (3–6). Illus. 1975, Workman $3.95. Sixty American street games described by a clear text as well as photographs and diagrams.

5152. Fisher, Leonard Everett. *The Sports: Nineteenth Century American Series* (5–8). Illus. by author. 1980, Holiday LB $7.95. A description of nineteenth-century sports in America, beginning with the formal establishment of baseball in 1845.

5153. Fodor, R. V., and Taylor, G. J. *Junior Body Building: Growing Strong*. Illus. 1982, Sterling $8.95; LB $8.29; paper $4.95. Strength building exercises, as well as weight training, are given.

5154. Freeman, Tony. *An Introduction to Radio-Controlled Sailplanes* (3–6). Illus. 1979, Childrens Pr. $10.60. A brief introduction that includes material on equipment and techniques.

5155. Friedberg, Ardy. *My Greatest Day in Sports* (5–9). 1983, Scholastic paper $1.95. Fourteen athletes choose their greatest day.

5156. Gemme, Leila Boyle. *T-Ball Is Our Game* (1–3). Illus. 1978, Childrens Pr. LB $9.95. T-ball introduced in a simple, less-than-100-word text.

5157. Gould, Marilyn. *Playground Sports: A Book of Ball Games* (2–4). Illus. 1978, Lothrop $12.50; LB $12.88. Rules and techniques are given for a variety of games, including tetherball and beanbag games.

5158. Hargrove, Jim, and Johnson, Sylvia A. *Mountain Climbing* (4–7). Illus. 1983, Lerner $7.95. An introduction to mountain climbing, the techniques, equipment, and dangers. Also use: *Rock Climbing Is for Me* by Tom Hyden and Tim Anderson (1984, Lerner $7.95).

5159. Herda, D. J. *Roller Skating* (4–6). Illus. 1979, Watts LB $8.90. An excellent introduction to this sport, stressing safety. Also use: *Roller Skating!* by Ross R. Olney and Chan Bush (1979, Lothrop $11.25; LB $11.88); *Better Roller Skating for Boys and Girls* by George Sullivan (1980, Dodd LB $8.95; paper $2.95).

5160. Keith, Harold. *Sports and Games* (6–8). 1976, Harper $9.95. A basic guide to a variety of recreational activities. Also use: *The Concise Encyclopedia of Sports* by Gerald Newman (1979, Watts $8.95).

5161. Knudson, R. R. *Muscles!* (5–8). Illus. 1983, Avon paper $1.95. An introduction for young people to weight lifting that stresses moderation.

5162. Liss, Howard. *The Giant Book of More Strange but True Sports Stories* (4–6). Illus. by Joe Mathieu. 1983, Random LB $5.99; paper $4.95. There are 150 incredible but true events retold in a dozen different sports.

5163. Lyttle, Richard B. *The Games They Played: Sports in History* (6–9). Illus. by author. 1982, Atheneum $11.95. The beginnings of many of our present sports, such as skiing and archery.

5164. McWhirter, Norris. *Guinness Book of Sports Spectaculars* (3–6). Illus. by Bill Hinds. 1982, Sterling $6.95; LB $8.99. Unusual accomplishments in a variety of sports are chronicled.

5165. Morrison, Susan Dudley. *Balls* (4–7). Illus. 1983, Crestwood House LB $8.95. The story of how the many different balls used in sports are made. Also use: *Shoes for Sport* (1983, Crestwood House LB $8.95).

5166. Olney, Ross R. *Tricky Discs* (4–6). 1979, Lothrop $10.50; LB $10.08. The origin, use, and care of the Frisbee and other flying discs. Also use: *Frisbee Disc Flying Is for Me* by Tom Moran (1982, Lerner LB $7.95).

5167. Preston-Mauks, Susan. *Field Hockey Is for Me* (3–5). Illus. 1983, Lerner LB $7.95. Alison tells of her experiences in field hockey and how the game is played. Also use: *Better Field Hockey for Girls* by George Sullivan (1981, Dodd LB $8.95).

5168. Ravielli, Anthony. *What Is Golf?* (3–6). Illus. by author. 1976, Atheneum $6.95. An interesting introduction to the sport, which includes a history and description of techniques. Also use: *Golf Is for Me* by Mark Lerner (1982, Lerner LB $9.95).

5169. Reynolds, Robert E. *Lacrosse Is for Me* (3–5). Illus. 1984, Lerner $7.95. A young narrator tells about the basics of this sport.

5170. Rockwell, Anne. *Games and How to Play Them* (2–4). Illus. by author. 1973, Harper $9.57; LB $9.89. Forty-three popular children's indoor and outdoor games are described, and clear, simple illustrations given for their execution.

5171. Savitz, Harriet May. *Wheelchair Champions* (5–7). 1978, Harper $11.06. Subtitle: *A History of Wheelchair Sports.*

5172. Siegel, Alice, and McLoone, Margo. *It's a Girl's Game Too* (5–8). Illus. by Lisa Campbell Ernst. 1980, Holt $7.95. A book about women's contribution to sports and explanation of 18 different sports.

5173. Sobol, Donald J. *Encyclopedia Brown's Book of Wacky Sports* (4–7). 1984, Morrow $9.25; Bantam paper $1.95. A collection of strange but true sports stories.

5174. Sullivan, George. *Better Volleyball for Girls* (6–9). Illus. 1979, Dodd $8.95; paper $2.95. Basic volleyball strategies are described in this useful guide. Also use: *Volleyball Is for Me* by Art Thomas (1980, Lerner LB $6.95).

5175. Thomas, Art. *Archery Is for Me* (3–5). Illus. 1981, Lerner LB $7.95. A simple introduction with glossary and illustrations told in a first-person format.

5176. Thomas, Art. *Fencing Is for Me* (3–6). Illus. 1982, Lerner $7.95. An introduction to a sport that is founded in history.

5177. Tinkelman, Murray. *Rodeo: The Great American Sport* (5–7). Illus. 1982, Greenwillow LB $11.88; paper $7.00. A description of many events found at a rodeo, told mainly in photographs. Also

use: *Cowgirl* by Murray Tinkelman (1984, Greenwillow $9.25; LB $8.59); *Rodeos* by James W. Fain (1983, Childrens Pr. LB $10.60).

5178. Wulffson, Don L. *How Sports Came to Be* (3–5). 1980, Lothrop $10.00; LB $10.88. Short accounts that trace the history of such sports as bowling and badminton.

Automobile Racing

5179. Abodaher, David J. *Great Moments in Sports Car Racing* (4–8). Illus. 1981, Messner $8.29. A history of the sport beginning in France in 1894.

5180. Coombs, Charles. *Drag Racing* (6–9). 1970, Morrow $8.59. An excellent introduction that covers such aspects as drag racing history, types of cars, and a sample race. Also use: *Drag Racing: Then and Now* by Edward Radlauer (1983, Childrens Pr. $7.95).

5181. Dolan, Edward F., Jr. *Great Moments in the Indy 500* (4–6). Illus. 1982, Watts LB $8.90. An easily read, well-illustrated account of some exciting moments in this sport's event. Also use: *The Indy 500* by Jim Murphy (1983, Houghton $11.95).

5182. Edmonds, I. G. *Funny Car Racing for Beginners* (5–8). Illus. 1982, Holt $11.50. A lively narrative that describes both the important cars and their drivers.

5183. Knudson, Richard L. *Land Speed Record-Breakers* (3–6). Illus. 1981, Lerner LB $7.95. An account of the history of automobile racing and speed records.

5184. Knudson, Richard L. *Rallying* (3–6). Illus. 1981, Lerner LB $7.95. What is involved in a car rally and different types of rallies are described.

5185. Leder, Jane Mersky. *Champ Cars* (4–7). Illus. 1983, Crestwood $8.95. The story of how expensive racing cars are made.

5186. Lerner, Mark. *Quarter-Midget Racing Is for Me* (3–5). Illus. 1981, Lerner LB $7.95. Quarter-midget racing is explained in a first-person narrative.

5187. McFarland, Kenton, and Sparks, James C., Jr. *Midget Motoring and Karting* (6–9). Illus. by Denys McMains. 1961, Dutton $11.95. An old but still interesting book on this sport. Also use: *Karting: Racing's Fast Little Cars* by Rosemary G. Washington (1980, Lerner $6.95; LB $7.95); *Karts and Karting* by George S. Fichter (1982, Watts LB $8.90).

5188. Olney, Ross R. *Drama on the Speedway* (5–9). Illus. 1978, Lothrop $10.00; LB $10.88. An exciting re-creation of some important automobile races.

5189. Olney, Ross R. *How to Understand Auto Racing* (5–9). Illus. 1979, Lothrop $11.25. This often confusing sport is introduced in a concise manner.

5190. Olney, Ross R. *Illustrated Auto Racing Dictionary for Young People* (4–8). Illus. by Dave Ross. 1981, Prentice paper $2.50. A helpful compendium of auto racing terms.

5191. Olney, Ross R. *Modern Racing Cars* (6–9). Illus. 1978, Dutton $10.95. A variety of racing cars are described in text and in excellent black-and-white photos. Also use: *Racing Cars* by Alice Fields (1981, Watts LB $8.60).

5192. Radlauer, Edward. *Dirt Riders* (3–6). Illus. 1983, Childrens Pr. $7.95. An introduction to this sport in easy text and many photos.

5193. Radlauer, Edward. *Soap Box Racing* (1–4). Illus. 1973, Childrens Pr. $9.25; paper $2.95. Instructions on how to build a racer and enter derbies. Also use: *Soap Box Derby Racing* by Sylvia A. Rosenthal (1980, Lothrop LB $9.55).

5194. Sheffer, H. R. *Race Cars* (4–6). Illus. 1982, Crestwood LB $7.95. Historical coverage on a wide range of racing cars.

5195. Wilkinson, Sylvia. *Can-Am* (4–7). Illus. 1981, Childrens Pr. LB $11.25; paper $3.95. An account of the Canadian-American Challenge Cup. Others in this series: *Stock Cars* (1981, $6.95); *Super Vee* (1981, LB $11.25; paper $3.95); *Champ Cars* (1982, $7.95); *Endurance Racing* (1982, LB $11.25; paper $3.95); *Trans-Am* (1983, $7.95).

Baseball

5196. Aaseng, Nathan. *Baseball: You Are the Manager* (5–8). Illus. 1983, Lerner $8.95; Dell paper $1.95. Based on a real game, the reader must make decisions concerning plays.

5197. Arnow, Jan. *Louisville Slugger: The Making of a Baseball Bat* (4–6). Illus. 1984, Pantheon $11.95; LB $11.95. The story of the baseball bats made by the firm of Hillerich and Bradsby.

5198. Broekel, Ray. *Baseball* (1–4). Illus. 1982, Childrens Pr. $10.60; paper $3.95. A clear, nicely organized introduction to this sport.

5199. Brondfield, Jerry. *Baseball's Hall of Fame* (4–9). Illus. 1983, Scholastic paper $1.95. A history of the Hall of Fame, biographies of some members, and how they are elected.

5200. Campanis, Al. *Play Ball with Roger the Dodger* (3–6). Illus. by Syd Hoff. 1980, Putnam paper $3.95. Roger shows young baseball players how to play ball.

5201. Cebulash, Mel. *Baseball Players Do Amazing Things* (2–4). Illus. 1973, Random $3.95; LB $4.99. A fascinating book of records involving various aspects of the sport.

5202. Coombs, Charles. *Be a Winner in Baseball* (5–7). Illus. 1973, Morrow $10.32. After introductory material on the history and rules of the game, there are separate chapters on such skills as pitching and hitting.

5203. Dickmeyer, Lowell A. *Baseball Is for Me* (2–3). Illus. 1978, Lerner $6.95. A simple introduction to the sport told in the first person.

5204. Dolan, Edward F., Jr. *Great Moments in the World Series* (3–5). Illus. 1982, Watts LB $8.90. Highlights of almost 100 years of this sporting event. Also use: *Greatest World Series Thrillers* by Ray Robinson (1965, Random LB $3.69); *Memorable World Series Moments* by Nathan Aaseng (1982, Lerner $6.95); *World Series Heroes and Goats: The Men Who Made History in America's October Classics* by Joe Gergen (1982, Random paper $1.95).

5205. Dyer, Mike. *Getting into Pro Baseball* (6–9). Illus. 1979, Watts $8.40. A realistic account that stresses the college route.

5206. Epstein, Sam, and Epstein, Beryl. *The Game of Baseball* (3–6). 1965, Garrard $7.12. A basic introduction to the sport, its origin, rules, and history.

5207. Hollander, Zander, ed. *The Baseball Book: A Complete A to Z Encyclopedia of Baseball* (5–9). Illus. 1982, Random LB $8.99; paper $5.95. A compendium of facts and statistics on every aspect of this sport.

5208. Hollander, Zander, ed. *Home Run: Baseball's Greatest Hits and Hitters* (4–9). Illus. 1984, Random paper $2.50. Home run records and profiles of famous home run hitters are given.

5209. Jaspersohn, William. *The Ballpark* (4–7). Illus. 1980, Brown $10.95; paper $4.95. Subtitle: *One Day behind the Scenes at a Major League Game.*

5210. Jobe, Frank W., and Moynes, Diane Radovich. *The Official Little League Fitness Guide* (3–6). Illus. 1984, Simon & Schuster paper $5.95. Jobe, the physician for the Los Angeles Dodgers, has written a book for coaches, parents, and players.

5211. Kalb, Jonah. *The Easy Baseball Book* (1–3). Illus. by Sandy Kossin. 1976, Houghton $6.95. A beginner's guide with easy-to-read directions in short, simple sentences. For older readers use: *How to Play Baseball Better Than You Did Last Season* (1974, Macmillan paper $1.50).

5212. Madison, Arnold. *How to Play Girls' Softball* (5–7). Illus. 1981, Messner LB $9.79. A useful guide that touches on such topics as skills, techniques, and equipment.

5213. Murphy, Jim. *Baseball's All-Time All-Stars* (5–9). Illus. 1984, Houghton $10.95. Two "perfect" teams are chosen—one from the National League and the other from the American League. Also use: *Tom Seaver's All-Time Baseball Greats* by Tom Seaver and Martin Appel (1984, Wanderer $8.95).

5214. Reichler, Joseph L. *Fabulous Baseball Facts, Feats, and Figures* (4–7). Illus. 1981, Macmillan paper $7.95. A history of the sport, plus tables concerning teams and records.

5215. Ritter, Lawrence S. *The Story of Baseball* (5–9). Illus. 1983, Morrow $12.00; paper $8.50. The book explains the fundamentals and introduces the reader to famous past players.

5216. Sullivan, George. *The Art of Base-Stealing* (5–9). Illus. 1982, Dodd LB $10.95. A history of base stealing, plus various techniques and details.

5217. Sullivan, George. *Better Baseball for Boys* (5–9). Illus. 1981, Dodd LB $8.95; paper $2.95. Hitting, running, and position plays are included in this account.

5218. Walker, Henry. *Illustrated Baseball Dictionary for Young People* (4–8). Illus. by Leonard Kessler. 1978, Prentice paper $2.50. Terms clearly defined for fans and young players.

5219. Washington, Rosemary G. *Softball Is for Me* (2–5). Illus. 1982, Lerner LB $7.95. The basic rules and functions of each playing position are discussed.

Basketball

5220. Aaseng, Nathan. *Basketball: You Are the Coach* (4–6). Illus. 1983, Lerner $8.95; Dell paper $1.95. To win the game, crucial decisions must be made by the reader.

5221. Aaseng, Nathan. *College Basketball: You Are the Coach* (5–8). Illus. 1984, Lerner $8.95. The reader must make the choices that will or will not win the game.

5222. Antonacci, Robert J., and Barr, Jene. *Basketball for Young Champions* (4–7). 1979, McGraw $9.95. An excellent overview of the game for boys and girls with a section on wheelchair basketball.

5223. Clark, Steve. *Illustrated Basketball Dictionary for Young People* (4–6). Illus. by Frank Baginski. 1978, Prentice paper $2.50. Engaging, often humorous drawings add a light touch to this introduction to plays and terms essential in basketball.

5224. Dickmeyer, Lowell A. *Basketball Is for Me* (2–4). Illus. 1980, Lerner LB $6.95. The basics of basketball told through the fact that Jenny's school gym class is studying the sport.

5225. Dolan, Edward F., Jr. *Great Moments in the NBA Championships* (5–7). Illus. 1982, Watts LB $8.90. A book that highlights several important games over the past several years.

5226. Morris, Greggory. *Basketball Basics* (4–6). Illus. by Tim Engelland. 1976, Prentice $6.95; paper $2.50. A player and coach explain 4 specific skills to young players.

5227. Rosenthal, Bert. *Basketball* (2–4). Illus. 1983, Childrens Pr. $6.95. For the very young reader, an introduction utilizing many color photographs and a glossary.

5228. Sullivan, George. *Better Basketball for Girls* (5–7). Illus. 1978, Dodd paper $2.95. A clear exposition along with material that will encourage the female athlete. Also use: *Better Basketball for Boys* (1980, Dodd LB $8.95; paper $2.95).

Bicycles

5229. Loeper, John J. *Away We Go! On Bicycles in 1898* (5–8). 1982, Atheneum LB $9.95. A history of bicycles, plus pertinent safety tips.

5230. Monroe, Lynn Lee. *The Old-Time Bicycle Book* (2–4). Illus. by George Overlie. 1979, Carolrhoda $6.95. A beginner's history of the bicycle, carefully and imaginatively illustrated. Also use: *Two Hundred Years of Bicycles* by Jim Murphy (1983, Harper $9.57; LB $9.89).

5231. Olney, Ross R. *Riding High: Bicycling for Young People* (6–9). Illus. 1981, Lothrop $11.25; LB $11.88. A practical guide that covers choosing a bike, maintaining it, and bicycle sports.

5232. Pursell, Thomas F. *Bicycles on Parade: A Brief History* (4–6). Illus. 1980, Lerner LB $7.95. A history of bicycles, plus a glimpse into the future.

5233. Radlauer, Edward. *Some Basics about Bicycles* (4–8). Illus. 1978, Childrens Pr. $9.65. An easily read account with many color photographs.

5234. Sarnoff, Jane, and Ruffins, Reynold. *A Great Bicycle Book* (4–7). Illus. 1976, Scribners $8.95. A lucid introduction to many aspects of the subject with good coverage on maintenance and repair.

5235. Thomas, Art. *Bicycling Is for Me* (3–5). Illus. 1979, Lerner $6.95. A young narrator describes the basics of this sport. Also use: *Better Bicycling for Boys and Girls* by George Sullivan (1974, Dodd $8.95).

5236. Wilhelm, Tim, and Wilhelm, Glenda. *Bicycling Basics* (5–8). Illus. 1982, Prentice $9.95. How to pick a bike and ride it in safety.

Bowling

5237. Lerner, Mark. *Bowling Is for Me* (3–5). Illus. 1981, Lerner LB $7.95. A first-person account of the basic rules and techniques of this sport.

5238. Pezzano, Chuck. *Bowling Basics* (4–7). Illus. 1984, Prentice $9.95. A fine beginner's book, with a history of the sport and tips from the pros.

Camping and Backpacking

5239. Boy Scouts of America. *Boy Scout Fieldbook* (5–9). Illus. 1967, Boy Scouts of America paper $3.95. A practical guide to camping that has become a standard text throughout the years.

5240. McManus, Patrick F. *Kid Camping from Aaaaiii! to Zip* (5–7). Illus. by Roy Doty. 1979, Lothrop $10.00; LB $10.88. A practical camping guide presented in an amusing way.

5241. Neimark, Paul G. *Camping and Ecology* (6–8). Illus. by Tom Dunnington. 1981, Childrens Pr. LB $9.95. Useful information presented with many illustrations. Two others in this series: *Hiking and Exploring; Survival* (both 1981, LB $9.95).

5242. Poynter, Margaret. *Search and Rescue: The Team and the Missions* (6–8). Illus. 1980, Atheneum $8.95. A book about volunteer mountain search and rescue teams. Also use: *Handbook for Emergencies: Coming Out Alive* by Anthony Greenback (1976, Doubleday $8.95).

5243. Randolph, John. *Backpacking Basics* (5–7). Illus. 1982, Prentice $8.95. An introduction that includes sections on equipment, safety, and good areas for the sport.

5244. Thomas, Art. *Backpacking Is for Me* (3–6). 1980, Lerner LB $6.95. Mike goes backpacking with his older brother and learns the fundamentals.

Chess

5245. Carroll, David. *Make Your Own Chess Set* (5–8). Illus. 1975, Prentice paper $2.95. History and description of each chess piece, plus directions for making 30 different chess sets from such materials as screws, papers, and gumdrops.

5246. Langfield, Paul. *A Picture Guide to Chess* (3–7). Illus. 1977, Harper $10.10. Basic principles and strategies are described with the beginner in mind.

5247. Lombardy, William, and Marshall, Bette. *Chess for Children: Step by Step* (5–8). Illus. 1977,

Little $12.95; LB $7.95. A clear introduction that makes the rudiments of this complex game extremely clear.

5248. Pandolfini, Bruce. *Let's Play Chess! A Step-by-Step Guide for Beginners* (6–9). Illus. 1980, Messner LB $7.79; paper $3.95. A U.S. national chess master presents the fundamentals. Also use: *The Royal Game* by Edith L. Weart (1948, Vanguard $6.95).

5249. Sarnoff, Jane, and Ruffins, Reynold. *The Chess Book* (3–5). 1973, Scribners $6.95. The basic elements of chess and vignettes from its history are told in this entertaining account.

Fishing

5250. Arnosky, Jim. *Freshwater Fish and Fishing* (4–8). Illus. by author. 1982, Four Winds $8.95. An outstanding introduction to this sport, with detailed watercolors and lyrical text.

5251. Evanoff, Vlad. *A Complete Guide to Fishing* (6–8). Illus. 1981, Harper $9.95; LB $10.89. A book that shows how to catch both fresh and saltwater fish.

5252. Neimark, Paul G. *Fishing* (6–8). Illus. by Tom Dunnington. 1981, Childrens Pr. LB $9.95. A straightforward, well-illustrated guide to this sport.

5253. Randolph, John. *Fishing Basics* (4–7). Illus. by Art Seiden. 1981, Prentice $9.95. In addition to equipment and fishing techniques, this volume discusses fish and their habitats.

5254. Thomas, Art. *Fishing Is for Me* (3–5). Illus. 1980, Lerner LB $6.95. Two friends, Kevin and Virgil, share with the reader their tips on fishing.

Football

5255. Aaseng, Nathan. *College Football: You Are the Coach* (5–8). Illus. 1984, Lerner $8.95. Actual games are used in this reader participation book.

5256. Aaseng, Nathan. *Football: You Are the Coach* (4–6). Illus. 1983, Lerner $8.95; Dell paper $1.95. Important coaching decisions are left to the reader to make.

5257. Antonacci, Robert J., and Barr, Jene. *Football for Young Champions* (4–7). Illus. by Rus Anderson. 1976, McGraw $10.95. Formations, positions, and basic skills are interestingly presented.

5258. Berger, Melvin. *The Photo Dictionary of Football* (4–7). 1980, Methuen $8.95. Forty-nine entries are explained in text and pictures. Also use: *Illustrated Football Dictionary for Young People* by Joseph Olgin (1975, Prentice paper $2.50).

5259. Broekel, Ray. *Football* (1–4). Illus. 1982, Childrens Pr. LB $10.60; paper $3.95. A colorfully illustrated introduction for primary grades.

5260. Coombs, Charles. *Be a Winner in Football* (5–7). Illus. 1974, Morrow $8.16; paper $2.45. A useful guide to football basics. Also use: *How to Play Better Football* by C. Paul Jackson (1972, Harper $10.89).

5261. Dickmeyer, Lowell A. *Football Is for Me* (3–5). Illus. 1979, Lerner $7.95. A first-person account that enthusiastically introduces the sport.

5262. Dolan, Edward F., Jr. *Great Moments in the Super Bowl* (5–7). Illus. 1982, Watts LB $8.90. Highlights from the Super Bowl games, 1967 through 1981. Also use: *More Strange but True Football Stories* by Zander Hollander (1973, Random $4.39); *Touchdown! Football's Most Dramatic Scoring Feats* by Phyllis Hollander and Zander Hollander (1982, Random paper $1.95).

5263. Fox, Larry. *Football Basics* (4–7). Illus. by Bill Gow. 1982, Prentice $9.95. Equipment, techniques, and safety tips are discussed, and a glossary is appended.

5264. McCallum, John Dennis. *Getting into Pro Football* (6–9). Illus. 1979, Watts $8.40. A complete rundown, including physical preparedness and game strategies.

5265. Sullivan, George. *Better Football for Boys* (6–9). Illus. 1980, Dodd $8.95; paper $2.95. A handbook that concentrates on how to play the various positions.

5266. Sullivan, George. *Quarterback* (5–7). Illus. 1982, Harper $9.57; LB $9.89. Tips and advice for the beginning quarterback.

5267. Ward, Don. *Super Bowl I: Green Bay Packers vs. Kansas City Chiefs, January 15, 1967, Los Angeles Memorial Coliseum* (3–6). Illus. 1983, Childrens Book Co. LB $8.95. A profile of this first Super Bowl game. Also use: Don Ward's *Super Bowl II; Super Bowl XI; Super Bowl XV; Super Bowl XVI; Super Bowl XVII;* Al Rowland's *Super Bowl IV; Super Bowl VI; Super Bowl VIII;* Richard Rambeck's *Super Bowl VII; Super Bowl X; Super Bowl XII; Super Bowl XIII; Super Bowl XIV;* Frank MacDonald's *Super Bowl III;* and Jim Moore's *Super Bowl IX* (all 1983, Childrens Book Co. LB $8.95).

Gymnastics

5268. Guraedy, I. *Illustrated Gymnastics Dictionary for Young People* (4–8). Illus. by Michael Snyder.

n.d., Prentice paper $2.50. A glossary of terms plus illustrations on this fast growing sport.

5269. Krementz, Jill. *A Very Young Gymnast* (4–6). Illus. by author. 1978, Knopf $12.95. Ten-year-old Torrance York tells of her training that led to a place in the Junior Olympics.

5270. Olney, Ross R. *Gymnastics* (4–6). Illus. by Mary Ann Duganne. 1980, Avon paper $1.75. An introduction that includes types of events, equipment, and necessary training.

5271. Sullivan, George. *Better Gymnastics for Girls* (4–9). Illus. 1977, Dodd $8.95. Fundamentals of the sport are well presented through text and many photographs. Also use: *Some Basics about Women's Gymnastics* by Edward Radlauer and Ruth Shaw Radlauer (1980, Childrens Pr. LB $9.25; paper $2.95).

5272. Traetta, John, and Traetta, Mary Jean. *Gymnastics Basics* (4–7). Illus. by Bill Gow. 1979, Prentice $8.95; paper $3.95. Maneuvers and techniques are included in this well-written introduction to the sport.

Horsemanship

5273. Coombs, Charles. *Be a Winner in Horsemanship* (4–6). 1976, Morrow $8.95; LB $8.59. How to choose and take care of a horse.

5274. Haney, Lynn. *Show Rider* (5–7). Illus. 1982, Putnam $11.95; paper $5.95. The story of the young horsewoman, Kerri Cibbarelli.

5275. Krementz, Jill. *A Very Young Rider* (3–6). Illus. by author. 1977, Knopf $12.95. The story of a 10-year-old girl passionately caught up in the world of horses.

5276. O'Connor, Karen. *Try These on for Size Melody!* (3–5). Illus. 1983, Dodd $9.95. In this nonfiction account, Melody, a horse, gets a new set of horseshoes.

5277. Pervier, Evelyn. *Horsemanship: Basics for Beginners* (6–8). Illus. 1984, Messner $9.29. Advice for beginners on riding and horse care. For experienced riders: *Horsemanship: Basics for Intermediate Riders; Horsemanship: Basics for More Advanced Riders* (both 1984, Messner $9.29).

5278. Roth, Harold. *A Day at the Races* (3–6). Illus. 1983, Pantheon $10.95; LB $10.99. A behind-the-scenes look at a racetrack.

5279. Shapiro, Neal, and Lehrman, Steve. *World of Horseback Riding* (6–8). 1976, Atheneum $6.95. A brief introduction for the would-be horse owner. Also use: *Horseback Riding Is for Me* by Art Thomas and Emily Blackburn (1981, Lerner LB $7.95).

5280. Van Steenwyk, Elizabeth. *Illustrated Horseback Riding Dictionary for Young People* (5–9). Illus. by Eric Lurio. 1980, Prentice paper $2.50. A fine guidebook in glossary format.

5281. Winter, Ginny L. *The Riding Book* (K–3). Illus. by author. 1963, Astor-Honor $5.95. An introductory account for the very young rider.

Ice Hockey

5282. Aaseng, Nathan. *Hockey: You Are the Coach* (4–6). Illus. 1983, Lerner $8.95; Dell paper $1.95. The reader must make decisions concerning the right plays.

5283. Coombs, Charles. *Be a Winner in Ice Hockey* (5–8). Illus. 1974, Morrow paper $2.45. A do-it-yourself sports book with many fine tips on how to improve one's game, along with a history of the sport, its rules, and regulations.

5284. Dickmeyer, Lowell A. *Hockey Is for Me* (2–3). Illus. 1978, Lerner $7.95. A young boy, Ryan, introduces the reader to this growing, popular sport.

5285. Gemme, Leila Boyle. *Hockey Is Our Game* (1–3). Illus. 1979, Childrens Pr. $9.25; paper $2.95. A picture-book format is used to introduce this sport in easily read text.

5286. Kalb, Jonah. *The Easy Hockey Book* (3–5). Illus. by Bill Morrison. 1977, Houghton $6.95. A collection of sound advice on various aspects of the game.

5287. MacLean, Norman. *Hockey Basics* (4–8). Illus. by Bill Gow. 1983, Prentice $8.95. Skills, techniques, and equipment are presented in this introduction to hockey basics.

5288. Walker, Henry. *Illustrated Hockey Dictionary for Young People* (5–9). Illus. by Frank Baginski. 1978, Prentice paper $2.50. An introduction to this sport through an explanation of terms.

Ice Skating

5289. Dickmeyer, Lowell A., and Rolens, Lin. *Ice Skating Is for Me* (2–3). Illus. 1980, Lerner $7.95. A first-person narrative about learning the basics of ice skating.

5290. Faulkner, Margaret. *I Skate!* (5–8). Illus. by author. 1979, Little $8.95. Competitive skating as seen through the eyes of an 11-year-old girl and many photographs.

5291. Haney, Lynn. *Skaters: Profile of a Pair* (4–7). Illus. 1983, Putnam $10.95. A nonfiction account of the life of 2 figure skaters.

5292. Krementz, Jill. *A Very Young Skater* (4–7). Illus. by author. 1979, Knopf $10.95. Family support is stressed in this account of 10-year-old Katherine Healy, an amateur figure skater.

5293. Sullivan, George. *Better Ice Skating for Boys and Girls* (5–9). 1976, Dodd $8.95; paper $2.95. Practical pointers are given along with basic information.

5294. Van Steenwyk, Elizabeth. *Illustrated Skating Dictionary for Young People* (4–8). Illus. by Dave Ross. 1980, Harvey House LB $7.29; paper $2.50. Clear definitions plus engaging drawings highlight this book.

5295. Winter, Ginny L. *The Skating Book* (K–3). Illus. by author. 1963, Astor-Honor $5.95. A beginning account for the young skater.

Indoor Games

5296. Belton, John, and Cramblit, Joella. *Solitaire Games* (4–7). Illus. 1975, Raintree LB $13.30. Simple, step-by-step directions for 9 forms of solitaire.

5297. Cole, Ann et al. *Purple Cow to the Rescue* (PS–5). Illus. by True Kelley. 1982, Little $12.95; paper $8.95. A delightful book of ideas for games in a variety of situations.

5298. Grayson, Marion F. *Let's Do Fingerplays* (PS–2). Illus. by Nancy Weyl. 1962, Luce $9.95. Comprehensive collection of finger plays under such headings as "Things That Go," "Animal Antics," and "Holidays." Also use: *Finger Rhymes* by Marc Brown (1980, Dutton $9.95).

5299. Gryski, Camilla. *Cat's Cradle, Owl's Eyes: A Book of String Games* (4–Up). Illus. by Tom Sankey. 1984, Morrow paper $6.95. Explanations of 21 string figures, plus variations.

5300. Jaureguiberry, Martine. *The Wonderful Rainy Week* (K–3). Illus. by Satomi Ichikawa. 1983, Putnam $8.95. Several children have fun on rainy days through simple projects.

5301. Prieto, Mariana B., ed. *Play It in Spanish: Spanish Games and Folk Songs for Children* (1–4). Illus. by Regina Shekerjian. 1973, Day LB $10.89. Songs and games in Spanish and a free English translation.

5302. Reisberg, Ken. *Card Tricks* (1–3). 1980, Watts LB $8.90. The necessary tactics for card tricks. Also use: *Card Games* by John Belton and Joella Cramblit (1976, Raintree LB $13.30).

5303. Stern, Don. *Backgammon* (5–9). 1977, Watts LB $8.90. A fine introduction to this game that involves both skill and chance.

5304. Tashjian, Virginia A. *Juba This and Juba That* (PS–4). Illus. by Victoria de Larrea. 1969, Little $8.95. A package of "story-hour stretchers," delightful group activity entertainment in this silly, superb assemblage of chants, rhymes, poetry, stories, songs, riddles, finger plays, and tongue twisters.

5305. Zaslavsky, Claudia. *Tic Tac Toe and Other Three-in-a-Row Games from Ancient Egypt to the Modern Computer* (4–6). Illus. by Anthony Kramer. 1982, Harper $9.50; LB $9.89. A rundown of 3-in-a-row games and how to play them.

Kite Making and Flying

5306. Marks, Burton, and Marks, Rita. *Kites for Kids* (4–8). Illus. by Lisa Campbell Ernst. 1980, Lothrop $9.95; LB $9.55. A guide to building several different models as well as tips for flying.

5307. Moran, Tom. *Kite Flying Is for Me* (3–5). Illus. 1984, Lerner $6.95. Told in the first person, this is an introduction to the construction and flying of kites.

5308. Thiebault, Andre. *Kites and Other Wind Machines* (6–8). Illus. 1983, Sterling $9.95; LB $9.29. Kites, and how to make them, and other forms of wind machines are discussed.

Motorcycles and Motor Bikes

5309. Alth, Max. *Motorcycles and Motorcycling* (5–6). Illus. 1979, Watts $8.90. The history, uses, and parts of motorcycles are covered, as well as a rundown on the many variations available today.

5310. Baumann, Elwood D. *An Album of Motorcycles and Motorcycle Racing* (6–9). Illus. 1982, Watts $8.90. A history of motorcycles, plus pictures of many models.

5311. Bygrave, Mike, and Dowdall, Mike. *Motorcycle* (5–7). 1978, Watts $7.90. Sparse text and ample photos make this an interesting volume. Also use: *Cycles* by H. R. Sheffer (1983, Crestwood $7.95).

5312. Coombs, Charles. *BMX: A Guide to Bicycle Motocross* (5–8). Illus. 1983, Morrow $9.50. Begun in the late 1960s, bicycle motocross is now an organized sport, and this is a guide to it. Also use: *Better BMX Riding and Racing for Boys and Girls* by George Sullivan (1984, Dodd LB $8.95; paper $2.95); *BMX* by Dave Spurdens (1984, Sterling $7.95; paper $3.95); *The Complete Book of BMX* by Bob Osborn (1984, Harper paper $11.95).

5313. Coombs, Charles. *Mopeding* (6–8). Illus. 1978, Morrow $8.75; LB $8.40. The construction, operation, and maintenance of these little vehicles are described.

5314. Jefferis, David. *Trailbikes* (2–4). Illus. 1984, Watts $8.60. An introduction to motorcycles and the sports connected with them.

5315. Moran, Tom. *Bicycle Motocross Is for Me* (3–6). Illus. 1982, Lerner LB $7.95. Kevin explains the techniques of bicycle motocross.

5316. Puleo, Nicole. *Motorcycle Racing* (6–8). Illus. 1973, Lerner $7.95. The events associated with various types of motorcycle races are fully described.

5317. Rich, Mark. *Custom Cycles* (4–7). Illus. 1981, Childrens Pr. LB $10.60; paper $2.95. An account of the types of construction of special motorcycles.

5318. Yaw, John, and Rae, Rusty. *Grand National Championship Races* (5–9). Illus. 1978, Lerner $7.95. A history of various important motorcycle races.

Olympic Games

5319. Arnold, Caroline. *The Summer Olympics* (4–6). Illus. 1983, Watts LB $8.60. Concise descriptions of all Olympic events. By the same author: *The Winter Olympics* (1983, Watts LB $8.60). Also use: *The Summer Olympics* by Frank Litsky (1979, Watts LB $8.60).

5320. Durant, John. *Highlights of the Olympics from Ancient Times to the Present* (5–9). Illus. 1977, Hastings paper $5.95. A standard work that includes material on the 1976 games at Innesbruck and Montreal.

5321. Fradin, Dennis B. *Olympics* (1–4). Illus. 1983, Childrens Pr. $7.95. The past and present of Olympic games are introduced in this simple account.

5322. Glubok, Shirley, and Tamarin, Alfred. *Olympic Games in Ancient Greece* (5–8). Illus. 1976, Harper $11.89; paper $4.95. Using a fictitious Olympiad set in the fifth century B.C., the author offers a great deal of background information in an imaginative, satisfying way.

Running and Jogging

5323. Asch, Frank, and Asch, Jan. *Running with Rachel* (3–5). Illus. 1979, Dial LB $9.89; paper $3.95. A young girl's introduction to techniques and equipment involved in the sport of running.

5324. Neff, Fred. *Running Is for Me* (2–4). Illus. 1980, Lerner LB $6.95. By Stephanie jogging with her mother, the reader learns about running.

5325. Olney, Ross R. *The Young Runner* (6–9). Illus. 1978, Morrow $9.95; LB $9.55. An effective, sensible introduction to this subject for both boys and girls.

5326. Sullivan, George. *Better Cross-Country Running for Boys and Girls* (5–8). Illus. 1983, Dodd $8.95; paper $2.95. An introduction to cross-country racing, equipment, and techniques.

Sailing and Boating

5327. David, Andrew, and Moran, Tom. *River Thrill Sports* (5–7). Illus. 1983, Lerner $7.95. Sports that involve canoes, rafts, and kayaks are discussed.

5328. Jones, Claire. *Sailboat Racing* (3–6). Illus. 1981, Lerner LB $6.95. Parts of boats, jargon, and types of races are explained, plus an introduction to the sport.

5329. Moran, Tom. *Canoeing Is for Me* (3–5). Illus. 1984, Lerner $6.95. A first-person narrative and many black-and-white photos introduce this sport.

5330. Slocombe, Lorna. *Sailing Basics* (5–8). Illus. 1982, Prentice $8.95. A good introductory volume, which also contains a glossary.

5331. Vandervoort, Thomas J. *Sailing Is for Me* (3–5). Illus. 1981, Lerner LB $7.95. Told by a single narrator, this is a basic guide with suitable illustrations and a glossary.

Self-Defense

5332. Knudson, R. R. *Punch!* (5–8). Illus. 1983, Avon paper $1.95. An introduction to boxing and how to train both at home and in the gym.

5333. Kozuki, Russell. *Junior Karate* (5–7). Illus. 1971, Sterling $8.95; LB $10.99; Pocket paper $1.95. An easily understood beginning book with information on such aspects as stances, blocks, and kicks. Also use: *Karate for Young People* (1974, Sterling $8.95; LB $10.99; paper $4.95).

5334. Neff, Fred. *Karate Is for Me* (2–4). Illus. 1980, Lerner LB $6.95. Through Becky studying karate, the reader learns about the sport.

5335. Ribner, Susan, and Chin, Richard. *The Martial Arts* (5–8). Illus. 1978, Harper $11.89; paper $4.76. The principles and history of such activities as judo and karate.

5336. Sullivan, George. *Better Karate for Boys* (5–8). Illus. 1983, Dodd $8.95; paper $2.95. An introduction with a glossary and many illustrations.

5337. Thomas, Art. *Wrestling Is for Me* (3–5). Illus. 1979, Lerner $6.95. A young enthusiast describes the basics of this sport.

5338. Thomas, Art, and Storms, Laura. *Boxing Is for Me* (4–6). Illus. 1982, Lerner LB $7.95. Through a young narrator, this sport is introduced. Two other introductory books are: *Better Boxing for Boys* by George Sullivan (1966, Dodd $8.95); *How to Box: A Guide for Beginners* by Edward R. Ricciuti (1982, Harper $11.05; LB $10.89).

Skateboarding

5339. Dickmeyer, Lowell A. *Skateboarding Is for Me* (2–3). Illus. 1978, Lerner $7.95. Many fine black-and-white photographs introduce this sport.

5340. Reiser, Howard. *Skateboarding* (5–8). Illus. 1979, Watts $8.90. This relatively new sport is given a good introductory treatment that stresses safety.

Skiing

5341. Chappell, Annette Jo. *Skiing Is for Me* (2–3). Illus. 1978, Lerner LB $7.95. A first-person account that introduces this sport.

5342. Marozzi, Al. *Skiing Basics* (3–5). Illus. 1980, Prentice $8.95; paper $4.95. A useful manual that covers practice, skills, and equipment.

5343. Sullivan, George. *Cross-Country Skiing: A Complete Beginner's Book* (5–8). Illus. 1980, Messner LB $8.49. A thorough guide to this fast-growing sport. Also use: *Cross-Country Skiing Is for Me* by Rosemary G. Washington (1982, Lerner LB $7.95).

5344. Tinker, Gene. *Let's Learn Ski Touring: Your Guide to Cross-Country Fun* (6–8). Illus. 1972, Walker $4.95; LB $4.85. An introduction to all aspects of cross-country skiing.

5345. Walter, Claire. *Illustrated Skiing Dictionary for Young People* (4–8). 1981, Prentice paper $2.50. Simple basic definitions are included with humorous drawings.

Soccer

5346. Coombs, Charles. *Be a Winner in Soccer* (5–8). Illus. 1977, Morrow $8.95; LB $9.84. Soccer basics explained in a simple, relaxed style for boys and girls; illustrated with fine black-and-white photos.

5347. Dickmeyer, Lowell A. *Soccer Is for Me* (2–3). Illus. 1978, Lerner $6.95. Basic rules and techniques simply presented.

5348. Fichler, Stanley I., and Friedman, Richard. *Getting into Pro Soccer* (6–9). Illus. 1979, Watts LB $8.40. Nutritional requirements, safety precautions, and game strategies are only 3 of the many topics covered.

5349. Gardner, James. *Illustrated Soccer Dictionary for Young People* (5–8). Illus. by Dave Ross. 1978, Prentice paper $2.50. Basic, clear, and helpful.

5350. Gemme, Leila Boyle. *Soccer Is Our Game* (1–3). Illus. 1979, Childrens Pr. $9.25; paper $2.95. An easily read introduction with many action photographs.

5351. Jackson, C. Paul. *How to Play Better Soccer* (3–7). Illus. 1978, Harper $9.89. A thorough account that is enlivened by fine illustrations.

5352. Laitin, Ken, and Laitin, Steve. *The World's Number One Best Selling Soccer Book* (4–9). Illus. 1979, Messner LB $9.79; Soccer for Americans paper $5.95. The authors—both teenagers—give enthusiastic advice to the novice.

5353. Sullivan, George. *Better Soccer for Boys and Girls* (4–7). Illus. 1978, Dodd $8.95; paper $2.95. A fine introduction to the sport and basic playing techniques.

5354. Toye, Clive. *Soccer* (4–7). 1969, Watts LB $8.90. A brief but useful introduction to the sport. Also use: *Soccer* by Bert Rosenthal (1983, Childrens Pr. $6.95).

5355. Yannis, Alex. *Soccer Basics* (5–7). Illus. by Bill Gow. 1982, Prentice $9.95. Team positions and rules are outlined in this introduction to soccer.

Surfing and Water Skiing

5356. Coombs, Charles. *Be a Winner in Windsurfing* (6–9). Illus. 1982, Morrow $10.25. An overview of this sailboat/surfboard sport. Also use: *Windsurfing: A Complete Guide* by Ross R. Olney (1982, Walker $9.95; LB $10.85).

5357. Freeman, Tony. *Beginning Surfing* (4–7). Illus. 1980, Childrens Pr. LB $10.00. Beautiful, color action photographs highlight this account. Also use: *Surf-Riding* by H. Arthur Klein (1972, Harper $7.64).

5358. Radlauer, Edward. *Some Basics about Water Skiing* (5–7). Illus. 1980, Childrens Pr. LB $9.25; paper $2.95. Basic equipment, techniques, and safety measures are discussed.

Swimming and Diving

5359. Briggs, Carole S. *Diving Is for Me* (4–6). Illus. 1983, Lerner $7.95. A first-person narrative that gives basics and explains special dives.

5360. Briggs, Carole S. *Skin Diving Is for Me* (3–5). Illus. 1981, Lerner LB $7.95. Told in a first-person account, basic information is given.

5361. Briggs, Carole S. *Sport Diving* (4–7). Illus. 1982, Lerner LB $7.95. A fine introduction to scuba diving.

5362. Chiefari, Janet, and Wightman, Nancy. *Better Synchronized Swimming for Girls* (5–9). Illus. 1981, Dodd LB $8.95. A fine combination introduction and advanced manual to this sport that relies heavily on timing and technique. Also use: *Synchronized Swimming Is for Me* by Susan Preston-Mauks (1983, Lerner LB $7.95).

5363. Dickmeyer, Lowell A. *Swimming Is for Me* (3–6). Illus. 1980, Lerner LB $6.95. Simple clear instructions are given in a large format.

5364. Gleasner, Diana C. *Illustrated Swimming, Diving and Surfing Dictionary for Young People* (3–6). 1980, Prentice LB $7.29; paper $2.50. Humorous drawings enhance the definitions.

5365. Mohn, Peter B. *Scuba Diving and Snorkeling* (5–7). Illus. 1975, Crestwood LB $7.95. Photographs enliven this introduction to 2 underwater sports.

5366. Orr, C. Rob, and Tyler, Jane B. *Swimming Basics* (4–7). Illus. 1980, Prentice $8.95; paper $4.95. Four basic strokes are thoroughly explained in text and pictures.

5367. Robison, Nancy. *Games to Play in the Pool* (4–8). Illus. 1980, Lothrop $11.95; LB $11.47. More than 70 games to play in the swimming pool are described.

5368. Sullivan, George. *Better Swimming for Boys and Girls* (4–8). Illus. 1982, Dodd LB $8.95; paper $2.95. A manual for those who have already mastered the basics.

Tennis

5369. Coombs, Charles. *Be a Winner in Tennis* (4–6). 1975, Morrow paper $2.45. The history, equipment, and techniques associated with the sport are well presented. Also use: *Better Tennis for Boys and Girls* by Harry Hopman (1972, Dodd LB $8.95).

5370. Dickmeyer, Lowell A. *Tennis Is for Me* (2–3). Illus. 1978, Lerner $6.95. Through a first-person narration, introductory material is presented on this sport.

5371. Sweeney, Karen O'Connor. *Illustrated Tennis Dictionary for Young People* (4–8). Illus. by Dave Ross. 1979, Prentice paper $2.50. All important tennis terms are defined with amusing illustrations.

Track and Field

5372. Dickmeyer, Lowell A. *Track Is for Me* (3–5). Illus. 1979, Lerner LB $7.95. A first-person account of a track meet that can serve as a good introduction to this sport.

5373. Emert, Phyllis. *Illustrated Track and Field Dictionary for Young People* (4–Up). 1981, Prentice paper $2.50. A glossary filled with illustrations and good explanations.

5374. Ryan, Frank. *Jumping for Joy* (6–8). Illus. by Elizabeth T. Hall. 1980, Scribners $2.49. A history and description of several track and field sports.

5375. Sullivan, George. *Better Field Events for Girls* (5–9). Illus. 1982, Dodd LB $8.95. Several events are discussed, plus training techniques and safety hints.

5376. Sullivan, George. *Better Track for Girls* (6–9). Illus. 1981, Dodd LB $8.95; paper $2.95. All sorts of topics are covered, including such events as sprinting, hurdles, and long-distance running.

The Arts and Language

Art and Architecture

General and Miscellaneous

5377. Baron, Nancy. *Getting Started in Calligraphy* (4–7). Illus. by author. 1979, Sterling $14.95; LB $17.79. A well-organized text from an experienced teacher of lettering.

5378. Conner, Patrick. *People at Home* (6–9). Illus. 1982, Atheneum $11.95. Paintings are used to show various aspects of human life. Also use: *People at Work* by Patrick Conner; *Faces (Looking at Art)* by Giles Waterford (both 1982, Atheneum $11.95).

5379. Cumming, Robert. *Just Look . . . A Book about Paintings* (5–8). Illus. 1980, Scribners $12.95. Elements of paintings such as color and perspective are shown through an analysis of some great paintings. A companion volume is: *Just Imagine: Ideas in Painting* (1982, Scribners $12.95).

5380. Fine, Joan. *I Carve Stone* (5–9). Illus. 1979, Harper LB $9.89. A 300-pound marble block becomes a work of art in this excellently illustrated account.

5381. Fisher, Leonard Everett. *Alphabet Art: Thirteen ABCs from Around the World* (5–9). Illus. 1978, Four Winds $10.95. Thirteen alphabets—from Arabic to Tibetan—are pictured with their English equivalents.

5382. Glubok, Shirley. *The Art of Photography* (5–8). Illus. 1977, Macmillan $10.95. Primarily an account of great photographers and their work, beginning with Daguerre and ending with many modern masters.

5383. Goffstein, M. B. *An Artist* (2–5). Illus. by author. 1980, Harper $9.57; LB $9.89. The story of how an artist creates.

5384. Grigson, Geoffrey, and Grigson, Jane. *Shapes and Stories: A Book about Pictures* (5–7). Illus. 1965, Vanguard $9.95. The contents of specific pictures are analyzed in this unusual book.

5385. Holme, Bryan. *Creatures of Paradise: Pictures to Grow Up With* (4–9). Illus. 1980, Oxford $14.95. A collection of 117 artworks depicting animals and birds.

5386. Janson, Horst Woldemar, and Janson, Dora Jane. *The Story of Painting from Cave Painting to Modern Times* (6–9). 1977, Abrams, rev. ed. paper $7.95. This basic history has a larger, more attractive format than the 1962 edition and also contains updated material.

5387. Pratson, Frederick J. *The Special World of the Artisan* (6–8). Illus. 1974, Houghton $5.95. Important aspects of the work of 5 craftsmen—potter, woodcarver, glassblower, instrument maker, and weaver.

5388. Williams, Diane. *Demons and Beasts in Art* (4–6). Illus. 1970, Lerner LB $5.95. Fantastic creatures are portrayed as they exist in various art forms. Also use: *Sports and Games in Art* by Barbara Shissler (1966, Lerner LB $5.95).

The Ancient World

5389. Glubok, Shirley. *The Art of Ancient Rome* (4–7). Illus. 1965, Harper $10.89. A variety of forms introduce Roman art, including statues, mosaics, and monuments. Also use: *The Art of the Etruscans* (1967, Harper LB $11.89).

5390. Glubok, Shirley. *The Art of Egypt under the Pharaohs* (4–7). Illus. by Gerard Nook. 1980, Macmillan $10.95. An introduction to the buildings and crafts of the ancient Egyptians.

5391. Macaulay, David. *City: A Story of Roman Planning and Construction* (6–9). Illus. by author. 1974, Houghton $14.95; paper $5.95. The imaginary Roman city of Verbonia is constructed through accurate and finely detailed drawings.

5392. Macaulay, David. *Pyramid* (5–9). Illus. by author. 1975, Houghton $12.95; paper $5.95. The engineering and architectural feats of the Egyptians are explored with detailed drawings.

Middle Ages and Renaissance

5393. Macaulay, David. *Castle* (5–9). Illus. by author. 1977, Houghton $13.95; paper $6.95. Another of the author's brilliant, detailed works, this one on the planning and building of a Welsh castle.

5394. Macaulay, David. *Cathedral: The Story of Its Construction* (6–9). Illus. by author. 1973, Houghton $14.95; paper $5.95. Gothic architecture as seen through a detailed examination of the construction of an imaginary cathedral.

5395. Unstead, R. J., ed. *See Inside a Castle* (5–7). Illus. by Dan Escott, Brian Lewis, and Richard Hook. 1979, Watts $9.40. A profusely illustrated glimpse into the architecture and activities associated with a medieval castle.

5396. Watson, Percy. *Building the Medieval Cathedrals* (6–9). Illus. 1979, Lerner $6.95. The materials and methods of construction are thoroughly presented.

Africa

5397. Price, Christine. *Dancing Masks of Africa* (2–4). Illus. by author. 1975, Scribners paper $1.79. A picture book about the types and functions of masks in African culture.

Indian Arts and Crafts

5398. Baylor, Byrd. *When Clay Sings* (2–5). Illus. by Tom Bahti. 1972, Scribners paper $2.95. An exploration of the designs that originally appeared on the pottery of the Indians of the Southwest.

5399. Bernstein, Bonnie, and Blair, Leigh. *Native American Crafts Workshop* (6–8). Illus. 1982, Pitman Learning paper $5.95. All kinds of crafts are outlined from pottery to cooking.

5400. Blood, Charles L. *American Indian Games and Crafts* (1–4). Illus. by Lisa Campbell Ernst. 1981, Watts LB $8.90. Simple adaptations of projects involving Indian crafts.

5401. Brindze, Ruth. *The Story of the Totem Pole* (5–7). Illus. by Yeffe Kimball. 1951, Vanguard $9.95. History and symbolism of the totem pole are woven into stories.

5402. D'Amato, Janet, and D'Amato, Alex. *Indian Crafts* (1–4). Illus. by author. 1968, Lion $7.95. An excellent introduction to Indian crafts through projects and activities.

5403. Glubok, Shirley. *The Art of the North American Indian* (4–7). Illus. 1964, Harper $9.95. A general survey of the arts and artifacts of the North American Indian, illustrated with striking photographs.

5404. Glubok, Shirley. *The Art of the Southeastern Indians* (4–7). Illus. 1978, Macmillan $10.95. Artifacts and accompanying information are introduced by text and striking black-and-white photographs.

5405. Glubok, Shirley. *The Art of the Woodland Indians* (4–6). Illus. by Alfred Tamarin. 1976, Macmillan $10.95. Part of Glubok's useful, low-keyed series on the arts and crafts of American Indians.

5406. Whiteford, Andrew Hunter. *North American Indian Arts* (5–9). Illus. by Vern Schaffer. 1970, Western paper $2.95. A presentation of the arts and crafts of North American Indians.

United States

5407. Gladstone, M. J. *A Carrot for a Nose: The Form of Folk Sculpture on America's City Streets and Country Roads* (5–8). Illus. 1974, Scribners $1.99. Folk sculpture found out of doors, from weather vanes and snowmen to gravestones and scarecrows, described in text and copious illustrations.

5408. Glubok, Shirley. *The Art of Colonial America* (4–7). Illus. 1970, Macmillan $10.95. A history of fine and decorative arts in the early days of the colonies. Also use: *The Art of the New American Nation* (1972, Macmillan $10.95).

5409. Glubok, Shirley. *The Art of the Comic Strip* (4–7). Illus. 1979, Macmillan $12.95. The history of the newspaper comic strip in America arranged in chronological order.

5410. Glubok, Shirley. *The Art of the Spanish in the United States and Puerto Rico* (4–7). Illus. 1972, Macmillan $10.95. Three centuries of Spanish domination in colonial America as reflected in art objects.

Communication

General and Miscellaneous

5411. Gibbons, Gail. *The Post Office Book: Mail and How It Moves* (K–3). Illus. by author. 1982, Harper $9.13; LB $8.89. A simple description of how the post office works.

5412. Wolverton, Ruth, and Wolverton, Mike. *The News Media* (4–6). Illus. 1981, Watts LB $8.90. An account that explores the role of radio, TV, and print media in news gathering.

Signs and Symbols

5413. Charlip, Remy, and Ancona, Mary Beth. *Handtalk* (3–6). Illus. by George Ancona. 1974, Four Winds $10.95. Subtitle: *An ABC of Finger Spelling and Sign Language.*

5414. Esterer, Arnulf K., and Esterer, Louise A. *Saying It without Words: Signs and Symbols* (4–6). Illus. 1980, Messner LB $7.29. Popular trademarks, acronyms, and signs are identified and explained.

5415. Fronval, George, and Dubois, Daniel. *Indian Signs and Signals* (5–9). Illus. 1979, Sterling $16.95; LB $19.99. An explanation of over 800 signs grouped under subjects.

5416. Hofsinde, Robert. *Indian Picture Writing* (4–7). Illus. by author. 1959, Morrow LB $9.36. A brief history of Indian picture writing, with almost 250 symbols. Also use: *Indian Sign Language* (1956, Morrow $9.36).

5417. Stein, Harry. *How to Interpret Visual Resources* (6–8). Illus. 1983, Watts $9.40. Charts, graphs, and other forms of visual displays are discussed.

Codes and Cyphers

5418. Albert, Burton. *Codes for Kids* (3–5). 1982, Penguin paper $2.95. Codes developed on such bases as maps, letters, and numbers. Followed by: *More Codes for Kids* (1979, Whitman LB $9.25).

5419. Babson, Walt. *All Kinds of Codes* (4–6). Illus. by Constance Ftera. 1976, Four Winds $8.95. A fascinating collection of material on a variety of codes.

5420. Bielewicz, Julian A. *Secret Languages: Communicating in Codes and Ciphers* (6–8). Illus. 1980, Lodestar $7.95. The history and current practices in using and developing codes and cyphers.

5421. Garden, Nancy. *The Kids' Code and Cipher Book* (6–8). Illus. 1981, Holt paper $4.95. A variety of writing systems—old and new—are introduced.

5422. James, Elizabeth, and Barkin, Carol. *How to Keep a Secret: Writing and Talking in Code* (6–8). Illus. 1978, Lothrop $9.55; Dell paper $1.25. Both well-known and obscure codes are described with decoding information given in an appendix.

5423. Laffin, John. *Codes and Ciphers: Secret Writing through the Ages* (6–8). Illus. 1964, Harper $10.53. The fascinating history of the development of codes.

5424. Peterson, John. *How to Write Codes and Send Secret Messages* (2–4). Illus. by Bernice Myers. 1973, Scholastic paper $1.75. An easily read book on coding and decoding secret messages.

5425. Rothman, Joel, and Tremain, Ruthven. *Secrets with Ciphers and Codes* (2–4). Illus. 1972, Macmillan paper $1.25. Many examples are given, as well as the difference between codes and ciphers.

5426. Sarnoff, Jane, and Ruffins, Reynold. *The Code and Cipher Book* (3–6). 1975, Scribners paper $2.95. A lighthearted look at codes and ciphers.

5427. Zim, Herbert S. *Codes and Secret Writing* (5–8). Illus. 1948, Morrow $9.36. Children love this fun book, which shows them how to encode and decode messages, how to write and read secret languages, and how to use invisible writing to send messages.

Flags

5428. Crouthers, David D. *Flags of American History* (3–6). 1973, Hammond $6.95. The story of 89 flags associated with our history.

5429. Parish, Thomas. *The American Flag* (4–6). 1973, Simon & Schuster $7.95. The story of our flag.

5430. Thompson, Brenda, and Giesen, Rosemary. *Flags* (2–3). Illus. by David Brogan and Rosemary Giesen. 1977, Lerner $4.95. A selection of national sports flags and other flags and their meanings.

Language and Languages

5431. Adkins, Jan. *Letterbox: The Art and History of Letters* (5–9). Illus. by author. 1981, Walker $10.95; LB $11.85. The evolution of letters from pictographs to today's letters.

5432. Cooper, Lee, and McIntosh, Clifton. *Fun with French* (4–7). Illus. by Ann Atene. 1963, Little $8.95. French words are introduced by pictures, stories, and songs. Others in the series: *Fun with Spanish* (1960, $9.70); *Fun with German* (1965, $10.45); *More Fun with Spanish* (1967, $9.70).

5433. Frasconi, Antonio. *See and Say: A Picture Book in Four Languages* (1–3). 1972, Harcourt paper $1.35. Colored woodcuts of familiar objects identified in French, Spanish, Italian, and English, with pronunciation guide.

5434. Greene, Carol. *Language* (1–4). Illus. 1983, Childrens Pr. $7.95. How language developed and its uses and variations are described simply.

5435. Hautzig, Esther. *In the Park: An Excursion in Four Languages* (1–4). Illus. by Ezra Jack Keats. 1968, Macmillan $8.95. The fun of a park in New York City, Paris, Moscow, or Madrid is simply expressed in the languages native to each. Also use: *At Home: A Visit in Four Languages* (1968, Macmillan $9.95).

5436. Ogg, Oscar. *The 26 Letters* (4–6). Illus. 1971, Harper $13.41. The story behind our alphabet, fascinatingly told.

5437. Schwartz, Alvin. *The Cat's Elbow and Other Secret Languages* (4–7). Illus. by Margot Zemach. 1982, Farrar $9.95. Several secret languages are explained.

5438. Wolff, Diane. *Chinese Writing: An Introduction* (4–6). Calligraphy by Jeanette Chien. 1975, Holt $7.95; paper $2.75. An explanation of Chinese characters, their formation, and meaning.

Words

5439. Adelson, Leone. *Dandelions Don't Bite: The Story of Words* (3–5). Illus. by Lou Myers. 1972, Pantheon $6.99. In 9 chapters, humorously illustrated, this is an introduction to the origin of words and their meaning.

5440. Asimov, Isaac. *Words from the Myths* (5–9). Illus. by William Barss. 1961, Houghton $9.95; NAL paper $1.95. Excellent essays on modern words derived from classical myths, with emphasis on scientific vocabulary.

5441. Baer, Edith. *Words Are Like Faces* (PS–3). Illus. by Karen Gundersheimer. 1980, Pantheon $4.95. The uses of words are described in verse and pictures.

5442. Barrol, Grady. *The Little Book of Anagrams* (2–5). Illus. 1978, Harvey House $4.29. An explanation of what anagrams are, plus 60 entertaining examples.

5443. Basil, Cynthia. *Breakfast in the Afternoon: Another Beginning Word Book* (K–2). Illus. 1979, Morrow $8.88. An easy-to-read introduction to the origins of several familiar words.

5444. Basil, Cynthia. *How Ships Play Cards: A Beginning Book of Homonyms* (1–3). Illus. by Janet McCaffery. 1980, Morrow $9.75; LB $9.36. The author uses riddles to introduce words that look and sound alike.

5445. Basil, Cynthia. *Nailheads and Potato Eyes: A Beginning Word Book* (3–5). Illus. by Janet McCaffery. 1976, Morrow $9.36. A quiz book that teaches meanings of words while entertaining the reader.

5446. Bossom, Naomi. *A Scale Full of Fish and Other Turnabouts* (PS–2). Illus. by author. 1979, Greenwillow $10.50; LB $10.08. Word play using homonyms done with imaginative text and woodcuts.

5447. Carle, Eric. *My Very First Book of Words* (PS–1). Illus. by author. 1974, Harper $3.95. A nicely illustrated beginning word book.

5448. Cox, James A. *Put Your Foot in Your Mouth and Other Silly Sayings* (3–5). Illus. by Sam Weissman. 1980, Random $7.95; LB $12.95; paper $4.95. The origins of such expressions as "pay through the nose" are described.

5449. Daly, Kathleen N. *The Macmillan Picture Wordbook* (PS–K). Illus. by John Wallner. 1982, Macmillan $7.95. Several common words are introduced under broad headings.

5450. Espy, Willard R. *A Children's Almanac of Words at Play* (4–6). 1982, Crown $15.95; paper $8.95. A compendium of stories, jokes, riddles, and poems about words.

5451. Hanson, Joan. *More Similes: Roar Like a Lion, as Loud as Thunder . . .* (1–2). 1979, Lerner $4.95. A simple introduction to similes.

5452. Hughes, Shirley, comp. *Over the Moon: A Book of Sayings* (3–5). Illus. by comp. 1980, Faber $6.95. Some 50 expressions plus explanations are examined.

5453. Hunt, Bernice K. *Your Ant Is a Which: Fun with Homophones* (4–6). 1976, Harcourt paper $1.65. An amusing language book.

5454. Kohl, Herbert. *A Book of Puzzlements: Play and Invention with Language* (4–8). 1982, Schocken $17.95. A book of word games and rhymes.

5455. Leigh, Tom, illus. *The Sesame Street Word Book* (PS–1). 1983, Western $9.95; LB $11.95. Over 1,000 words are introduced in cartoonlike illustrations.

5456. Morris, Christopher G., ed. *Macmillan Very First Dictionary: A Magic World of Words* (K–3). Illus. 1983, Macmillan $10.95. Over 1,500 words are introduced with 500 illustrations.

5457. Nevins, Ann. *From the Horse's Mouth* (4–6). 1981, Prentice paper $2.50. The origin of about 150 expressions is explained.

5458. Rudin, Ellen, and Salmon, Marilyn, comps. *My Picture Dictionary* (PS–1). Illus. by Elizabeth B. Rodger. 1984, Western $8.95; paper $4.95. A book of words for beginning readers.

5459. Sarnoff, Jane. *Words: A Book about the Origins of Everyday Words and Phrases* (5–8). Illus. by Reynold Ruffins. 1981, Scribners $9.95. A list of word origins arranged by subjects such as sports and names.

5460. Schwartz, Alvin, ed. *Chin Music: Tall Talk and Other Talk Collected from American Folklore* (4–6). Illus. by John O'Brien. 1979, Harper $10.10; LB $9.89; paper $3.95. An alphabetical glossary of our slang and dialect from 1815 to 1950.

5461. Steckler, Arthur. *One-Hundred-One More Words and How They Began* (4–6). Illus. by James Flora. 1981, Doubleday $8.95. A book of interesting word origins.

5462. Terban, Marvin. *Eight Ate: A Feast of Homonym Riddles* (2–3). Illus. by Giulio Maestro. 1982, Houghton $10.95; paper $2.95. A question-and-answer approach to introducing a variety of homonyms.

5463. Terban, Marvin. *I Think I Thought: And Other Tricky Verbs* (2–5). Illus. by Giulio Maestro. 1984, Houghton $10.95; paper $3.95. The past tense of irregular verbs is introduced.

5464. Terban, Marvin. *In a Pickle and Other Funny Idioms* (3–6). Illus. by Giulio Maestro. 1983, Houghton $10.95; paper $3.95. Common idioms are explained, and their origins are given.

5465. Thayer, Jane. *Try Your Hand* (1–3). Illus. by Joel Schick. 1980, Morrow $8.75; LB $8.40. This work uses riddles and phrases to show several meanings for the word *hand.*

5466. Weiss, Ann E. *What's That You Said? How Words Change* (K–3). Illus. by Jim Arnosky. 1980, Harcourt $6.95; paper $2.25. Derivations of simple words in an easy-to-read format.

5467. Wilbur, Richard. *Opposites* (5–7). Illus. by author. 1973, Harcourt paper $1.75. Through verses and cartoonlike illustrations, a series of antonyms are given for words.

Books and Printing

5468. Ahlstrom, Mark E. *Books* (5–7). Illus. 1983, Crestwood $8.95. An account of how books are made.

5469. Behrman, Carol H. *The Remarkable Writing Machine* (3–6). Illus. 1981, Messner LB $8.59. A fascinating history of the typewriter.

5470. Carey, Helen H., and Greenberg, Judith E. *How to Read a Newspaper* (6–8). Illus. 1983, Watts $9.40. Types of newspaper items and how news is gathered and written are explained.

5471. Cosner, Sharon. *"Paper" through the Ages* (2–5). 1984, Carolrhoda LB $7.95. An easy-to-read history of paper.

5472. Greenfeld, Howard. *Books: From Writer to Reader* (5–8). Illus. 1976, Crown paper $4.95. A beautifully illustrated, comprehensive account of how books are made.

5473. Jaspersohn, William. *Magazine: Behind the Scenes at Sports Illustrated* (6–9). Illus. 1983, Little $12.95. How an important magazine is put together.

5474. Kehoe, Michael. *The Puzzle of Books* (3–6). Illus. 1982, Carolrhoda LB $7.95. The story of how a book is made.

5475. Koral, April. *Headlines and Deadlines* (4–8). 1981, Messner $9.29. How a newspaper operates from the viewpoint of the *New York Daily News.*

5476. Simon, Irving B. *The Story of Printing: From Wood Blocks to Electronics* (6–9). Illus. 1965, Harvey House $7.29. A history of printing for the more mature reader. For a younger group use: *Pencil to Press: How This Book Came to Be* by Marjorie Spector (1975, Lothrop $9.84).

Writing and Speaking

5477. Carey, Helen H., and Greenberg, Judith E. *How to Use Primary Sources* (6–8). Illus. 1983, Watts $9.40. The use of documents, photographs, etc., in data collecting is described.

5478. Carey, Helen H., and Hanka, Deborah R. *How to Use Your Community As a Resource* (6–8). Illus. 1983, Watts $9.40. How to use your community as a source of information for reports is discussed.

5479. Cassedy, Sylvia. *In Your Own Words: A Beginner's Guide to Writing* (6–9). 1979, Doubleday LB $8.95. A thorough but basic guide to creative writing.

5480. Cosman, Anna. *How to Read and Write Poetry* (4–7). Illus. 1979, Watts $8.90. A simple introduction to the writing of poetry.

5481. Dubrovin, Vivian. *Write Your Own Story* (5–8). 1984, Watts $8.90. Practical tips are given on how to write fiction.

5482. Greenberg, Judith E., and Carey, Helen H. *How to Participate in a Group* (6–8). Illus. 1983, Watts $9.40. The skills involved in group participation are discussed.

5483. Hardendorff, Jeanne B. *Libraries and How to Use Them* (4–6). Illus. 1979, Watts $8.90. A logically organized guide to such areas as classification systems, the card catalog, and basic reference books.

5484. James, Elizabeth, and Barkin, Carol. *How to Write a Great School Report* (4–6). Illus. 1983, Lothrop $7.63; paper $5.00. A simple, well-organized account that starts with choosing the topic and ends with the final presentation. For an older group use: *How to Write a Report* by Gerald Newman (1980, Watts LB $7.90).

5485. Petersen, David. *Newspapers* (1–4). Illus. 1983, Childrens Pr. $7.95. The parts of the newspaper and its many functions are introduced for very young readers.

5486. Tchudi, Susan, and Tchudi, Stephen. *The Young Writer's Handbook* (6–9). Illus. 1984, Scribners $12.95. Advice and hints on all kinds of writing—from letters, to school reports, to fiction and poetry.

Music

General

5487. Bierhorst, John. *A Cry from the Earth: Music of the North American Indians* (6–8). 1979, Four Winds $12.95. An informative account of the part played by music in the lives of American Indians interspersed with many examples.

5488. Botsford, Ward. *The Pirates of Penzance: The Story of the Gilbert and Sullivan Operetta* (6–9). Illus. by Edward Sorel. 1981, Random $8.95; LB $9.99. A retelling of the operetta plot, plus lyrics.

5489. Chiefari, Janet. *Introducing the Drum and Bugle Corps* (6–8). Illus. 1982, Dodd $10.95. Through the eyes of Kim McCann, the history and activities of a drum and bugle corps are explored.

5490. Fichter, George S. *American Indian Music and Musical Instruments* (4–8). Illus. 1978, McKay $8.95. Includes material not only on music, but even directions on how to make and decorate some musical instruments.

5491. Greene, Carol. *Music* (1–4). Illus. 1983, Childrens Pr. $7.95. A broad subject is introduced for primary grades in text and photos.

5492. Hofmann, Charles. *American Indians Sing* (3–6). Illus. by Nicholas Amrostia. 1967, Harper $14.38. A beautifully illustrated book that explains how and why the American Indian made music.

5493. Prokofiev, Sergei. *Peter and the Wolf* (PS–3). Trans. by Maria Carlson. Illus. by Charles Mikolayeak. 1982, Viking $12.95. The story of the fairy tale that is the basis of Prokofiev's music. Also use: *Peter and the Wolf*, illus. by Erna Voigt (1980, Godine $10.95).

5494. Walther, Tom. *Make Mine Music* (5–9). Illus. by author. 1981, Little $11.45; paper $5.95. This book deals with principles of sound and a history of musical instruments.

Folk Songs and Ballads

5495. Aliki. *Hush Little Baby* (1–3). Illus. by author. 1968, Prentice $8.95; paper $3.95. This old English folk song is reprinted with colorful drawings and the original music. Also use: *Hush Little Baby* by Jeanette Winter (1984, Pantheon $10.95; LB $10.99).

5496. Berger, Melvin. *The Story of Folk Music* (6–9). 1976, Phillips LB $11.95. How and why American folk music evolved, with biographical information on singers from Woody Guthrie to John Denver.

5497. Engvick, William. *Lullabies and Night Songs* (K–3). Illus. by Maurice Sendak. 1965, Harper $22.50; LB $21.89. A collection of the poet's verses and those of others set to music by Alec Wilder.

5498. Glazer, Tom. *Eye Winker, Tom Tinker, Chin Chopper* (1–3). Illus. by Ronald Himler. 1973, Doubleday $10.95; paper $3.95. Fifty wonderful songs complete with finger plays. A sequel is: *Do Your Ears Hang Low? Fifty More Musical Fingerplays* (1980, $11.90).

5499. Glazer, Tom. *On Top of Spaghetti* (K–5). Illus. by Tom Garcia. 1982, Doubleday $9.95. The popular takeoff on *On Top of Old Smokey*.

5500. Graboff, Abner. *Old MacDonald Had a Farm* (K–3). Illus. by author. 1973, Scholastic paper $3.95. The ever-popular cumulative song about farm animals and implements. Another version is: *Old MacDonald Had a Farm* by Tracey Campbell Pearson (1984, Dial $9.66; LB $9.89).

5501. Ipcar, Dahlov. *The Cat Came Back* (K–3). Illus. by author. 1971, Knopf LB $5.99. An amusing story of a cat that is able to overcome all odds.

5502. Langstaff, John. *Frog Went A-Courtin'* (K–3). Illus. by Feodor Rojankovsky. 1955, Harcourt $12.95; paper $5.95. A rollicking folk song with matching illustrations.

5503. Langstaff, John. *Oh, A-Hunting We Will Go* (K–3). Illus. by Nancy W. Parker. 1974, Atheneum $11.95. Old and new verses have been combined to make this the definitive version of the folk song.

5504. Langstaff, John. *Sweetly Sings the Donkey* (K–3). Illus. by Nancy W. Parker. 1976, Atheneum $6.95. Subtitle: *Animal Rounds for Children to Sing or Play on Recorders*.

5505. Quackenbush, Robert. *Skip to My Lou* (1–3). Illus. by author. 1975, Harper $9.95. A disastrous engagement party is portrayed in this classic folk song.

5506. Quackenbush, Robert. *There'll Be a Hot Time in the Old Town Tonight* (K–3). 1974, Harper $9.57. The old standard, complete with bold, colorful illustrations.

5507. Seeger, Ruth C. *American Folk Songs for Children* (2–6). Illus. by Barbara Cooney. 1948, Doubleday $14.95; paper $5.95. All types of songs, including chants and ballads, that will delight and amuse children.

5508. Shoemaker, Kathryn, illus. *Children, Go Where I Send Thee: An American Spiritual* (K–4). 1980, Winston paper $6.95. A spiritual, originally sung by slaves, is reproduced with its lyrics, music, and history.

5509. Spier, Peter. *The Erie Canal* (K–3). Illus. by author. 1970, Doubleday $10.95. A folk song describing life on the Erie Canal in the 1850s.

5510. Spier, Peter. *The Fox Went Out on a Chilly Night* (K–3). Illus. by author. 1961, Doubleday $10.95. The old folk song about a fox's journey to catch the famous plump goose.

5511. Spier, Peter. *London Bridge Is Falling Down* (K–3). Illus. by author. 1967, Doubleday paper $1.95. The Mother Goose rhyme set to music with accompanying historical sketch.

5512. Taylor, Mark. *Jennie Jenkins* (K–3). Illus. by Glen Rounds. 1974, Little $5.95. A humorous old folk tune about Jennie and her antics at the Nettle Bottom Ball.

5513. Westcott, Nadine. *I Know an Old Lady Who Swallowed a Fly* (2–4). Illus. by author. 1980, Little $9.95. A newly illustrated edition of this outrageously funny song.

5514. Zemach, Harve. *Mommy, Buy Me a China Doll* (K–2). Illus. by Margot Zemach. 1975, Farrar $8.95. Little Eliza Lou thinks up all sorts of ways in which she can get a China doll.

Musical Instruments

5515. Anderson, David. *The Piano Makers* (4–7). Illus. 1982, Pantheon $10.95; LB $10.99. A thorough, well-illustrated account of how a piano is made.

5516. Berger, Melvin. *The Trumpet Book* (5–9). Illus. 1978, Lothrop $10.50; LB $10.08. The author discusses such topics as the instrument's history and construction, as well as important music for it.

5517. Dietz, Betty W. *Musical Instruments of Africa* (6–8). Illus. 1965, Harper $15.00. Subtitle: *Their Nature, Use and Place in the Life of a Deeply Musical People.*

5518. English, Betty Lou. *You Can't Be Timid with a Trumpet: Notes from the Orchestra* (4–8). Illus. by Stanley Skardinski. 1980, Lothrop $10.95; LB $10.51. Eighteen musicians talk about playing their instruments.

5519. Greene, Richard C. *The King of Instruments* (3–6). Illus. 1982, Carolrhoda LB $7.95. A description of the pipe organ and how it works.

5520. Kettelkamp, Larry. *Electronic Musical Instruments: What They Do and How They Work* (6–9). Illus. 1984, Morrow $9.00. A rather complex introduction to electronic instruments.

5521. Mandell, Muriel, and Woods, Robert E. *Make Your Own Musical Instruments* (4–6). Illus. 1959, Sterling $8.95; LB $10.99; paper $4.95. Easy-to-follow directions highlight this simple account.

5522. Posell, Elsa Z. *This Is an Orchestra* (4–7). Illus. 1973, Houghton $9.95. In addition to describing and showing the instruments of the orchestra, this book contains important information on choosing and buying an instrument and building a home record collection.

5523. Stevens, Bryna. *Ben Franklin's Glass Armonica* (2–4). Illus. by Priscilla Kiedrowski. 1983, Carolrhoda $6.95. How Benjamin Franklin invented the glass armonica.

5524. Swears, Linda. *Discovering the Guitar: Teach Yourself to Play* (4–6). Illus. 1981, Morrow $9.36; paper $6.95. A history of the guitar, plus simple songs to play.

5525. Wiseman, Ann. *Making Musical Things* (3–6). Illus. 1979, Scribners $8.95. A step-by-step manual in making musical instruments from such objects as milk cartons.

National Anthems and Patriotic Songs

5526. Bangs, Edward. *Yankee Doodle* (1–4). Illus. by Steven Kellogg. 1976, Four Winds $9.95. Music and text of the famous song, with colorful illustrations.

5527. Browne, C. A. *The Story of Our National Ballads* (5–8). 1960, Harper $12.95. The songs, plus biographical and historical information.

5528. Lyons, John Henry. *Stories of Our American Patriotic Songs* (4–7). Illus. by Jacob Landau. n.d., Vanguard $8.95. Material behind 10 of America's favorite songs, plus the words and music.

5529. Spier, Peter. *The Star Spangled Banner* (K–6). Illus. 1973, Doubleday $8.95. Many of the pictures show the battle scenes that inspired Francis Scott Key's immortal verses.

Songs and Singing Games

5530. Bierhorst, John. *Songs of the Chippewa* (4–8). Illus. by Joe Servello. 1974, Farrar $6.95. Seventeen songs of various types, such as lullabys and love songs, are included in this handsomely illustrated book.

5531. Bley, Edgar S. *The Best Singing Games for Children of All Ages* (1–5). Illus. by Patt Willen. 1959, Sterling $10.95; LB $13.29. Presents 50 children's songs that can be acted out as games.

5532. Boy Scouts of America. *Cub Scout Songbook* (4–6). 1969, Boy Scouts of America paper $0.85. Words to 150 songs that are sung to popular tunes.

5533. Bryan, Ashley. *Walk Together Children* (2–5). Illus. by author. 1974, Atheneum $7.95. A collection of 24 black American spirituals with background historical information. A companion volume is: *I'm Going to Sing: Black American Spirituals, Volume Two* (1982, Atheneum $10.95).

5534. Carroll, Lewis. *Songs from Alice: Alice in Wonderland and Through the Looking Glass* (4–6). Music by Don Harper. Illus. by Charles Folkard. 1979, Holiday $8.95. Nineteen newly composed songs for Lewis Carroll's classics.

5535. Conover, Chris. *Six Little Ducks* (1–3). Illus. by author. 1976, Harper $9.57; LB $9.89. A little duck leads his friends to market in this simple song.

5536. Emberley, Barbara. *Drummer Hoff* (K–3). Illus. by Ed Emberley. 1967, Prentice $9.95; paper $4.95. The classic song about the assembling of a cannon. Caldecott Medal.

5537. Fowke, Edith. *Sally Go Round the Sun: Three Hundred Children's Songs, Rhymes and Games* (K–6). Illus. by Carlos Marchiori. 1970, Doubleday $12.95. Many types of simple songs are presented with chords and piano accompaniments.

5538. Garson, Eugenia, ed. *The Laura Ingalls Wilder Songbook* (4–6). Illus. by Garth Williams. 1968, Harper $15.00; LB $14.89. Sixty-two songs from the Little House books.

5539. Girl Scouts of the U.S.A. *Brownies' Own Songbook* (4–6). 1968, Girl Scouts of the U.S.A. paper $2.00. A total of 45 singing games and songs is included.

5540. Hart, Jane, comp. *Singing Bee! A Collection of Favorite Children's Songs* (PS–3). Illus. by Anita Lobel. 1982, Lothrop $16.00. A collection of 125 simple songs with piano and guitar arrangements.

5541. John, Timothy, ed. *The Great Song Book* (1–6). Illus. by Tomi Ungerer. 1978, Doubleday $14.95. A collection of 68 favorite songs in simple arrangements with guitar chords.

5542. Kennedy, Jimmy. *The Teddy Bears' Picnic* (PS–1). Illus. by Alexandra Day. 1983, Green

Tiger $14.95. A record is included of this now classic song.

5543. Miller, Carl. *Sing Children Sing* (2–5). Illus. 1972, UNICEF paper $3.50. Subtitle: *Songs, Dances and Singing Games of Many Lands and Peoples.* Also use: *Rockabye Baby: Lullabies from Many Nations and Peoples* (1975, UNICEF paper $3.50).

5544. Mitchell, Cynthia. *Halloweena Hecatee, and Other Rhymes* (1–3). Illus. by Eileen Browne. 1979, Harper LB $9.89. A book of jump rope rhymes from 10 to 112 jumps in length.

5545. Mossman, Tam, ed. *The Family Car Songbook* (4–9). 1983, Running Pr. LB $12.90; paper $4.95. A book designed for the glove compartment that contains 57 standard songs.

5546. Nelson, Esther L. *The Funny Songbook* (3–7). Illus. by Joyce Behr. 1984, Sterling $11.95; LB $14.97. A collection of 60 humorous songs usually to familiar melodies.

5547. Nelson, Esther L. *Singing and Dancing Games for the Very Young* (K–3). Illus. by Minn Matsuda. 1977, Sterling $10.95; LB $13.29; paper $7.95. Over 40 songs with accompanying activities.

5548. Powell, Harriet. *Game-Songs with Prof. Dogg's Troupe* (PS–3). Illus. by David McKee. 1984, Sterling paper $7.95. A spiral-bound songbook from England.

5549. Stobbs, William. *There's a Hole in My Bucket* (K–2). Illus. 1983, Merrimack $5.95. The visualization of a charming folk song.

5550. Watson, Clyde. *Father Fox's Feast of Songs* (PS–6). Illus. by Wendy Watson. 1983, Putnam $10.95; paper $5.95. Poems from the author's *Catch Me and Kiss Me* and *Father Fox's Pennyrhymes* set to music.

5551. Wessells, Katharine Tyler. *The Golden Song Book* (3–6). Illus. by Gertrude Elliott. 1981, Western $5.95. Words and music for 56 favorite songs for children, with suggestions for singing games.

5552. Winn, Marie. *The Fireside Book of Children's Songs* (K–5). Illus. by John Alcorn. 1966, Simon & Schuster $12.95. More than 100 songs in this collection, including nursery songs and games.

5553. Winn, Marie. *The Fireside Book of Fun and Game Songs* (2–6). Illus. by Whitney Darrow, Jr. 1974, Simon & Schuster $14.95. All sorts of playful songs are included, such as question-and-answer songs and riddles. Also use: *What Shall We Do and Allee Galloo: Playsongs and Singing Games for Young Children* (1971, Harper $12.89).

5554. Zuromskis, Diane S., illus. *The Farmer in the Dell* (PS–1). 1978, Little $6.95. The familiar singing game presented with fresh drawings.

Performing Arts

Circuses, Fairs, and Parades

5555. Anderson, Norman D., and Brown, Walter R. *Ferris Wheels* (5–8). Illus. 1983, Pantheon $10.95; LB $10.99. The history of the original versions of Ferris wheels, from the seventeenth century to the present.

5556. Boring, Mel. *Clowns: The Fun Makers* (6–8). Illus. 1980, Messner LB $8.29. A discussion of the people who have made us laugh through the ages.

5557. Distad, Audree. *Come to the Fair* (5–8). Illus. 1977, Harper LB $9.89. A glimpse of the activities, many utilizing 4-H groups, that involve youngsters and the South Dakota State Fair.

5558. Fenten, Barbara, and Fenten, D. X. *The Team behind the Great Parades* (4–6). Illus. 1981, Westminster $9.95. What goes into making a great parade like the one at Rose Bowl time.

5559. Harmer, Mabel. *The Circus* (2–3). Illus. 1981, Childrens Pr. LB $10.60. A simple account with many color photographs.

5560. Hintz, Martin. *Circus Workin's* (3–5). Illus. 1980, Messner LB $7.79. A book on how the circus works from advance work to packing up after a performance.

5561. Klayer, Connie, and Kuhn, Joanna. *Circus Time! How to Put on Your Own Show* (4–6). Illus. by Carol Nicklaus. 1979, Lothrop $11.25; LB $11.88. A fascinating account that covers all topics from publicity to the opening performance.

5562. Meggendorfer, Lothar. *International Circus* (2–6). 1980, Viking $8.95. A pop-up book first published in Germany in 1887.

5563. Pierce, Jack. *The State Fair Book* (1–4). Illus. 1980, Carolrhoda LB $7.95. A description of the activities and events at the Minnesota State Fair.

5564. Prelutsky, Jack. *Circus* (K–3). Illus. by Arnold Lobel. 1974, Macmillan $8.95; paper $2.50. Vivid illustrations and swinging verses capture the vitality of the circus.

5565. Thomas, Art. *Merry-Go-Rounds* (K–2). Illus. by George Overlie. 1981, Carolrhoda LB $7.95. A nicely illustrated simple history of these entertainment park fixtures.

5566. Van Steenwyk, Elizabeth. *Behind the Scenes at the Amusement Park* (4–6). Illus. 1983, Whitman $9.95. An account of the activities and jobs associated with running an amusement park.

5567. Wildsmith, Brian. *The Circus* (PS–3). Illus. by author. 1970, Oxford $7.95. Bold and brilliant colors create a wonderful world of an imaginary circus.

Dance

5568. Ancona, George. *Dancing Is* (K–3). Illus. 1981, Dutton $10.75. A first glimpse of dancing through many black-and-white photos.

5569. Baylor, Byrd. *Sometimes I Dance Mountains* (K–3). Illus. by Kenneth Longtemps. 1973, Scribners $5.95. Emotions and objects are expressed by a dancer's movements.

5570. Berger, Melvin. *The World of Dance* (6–9). Illus. 1978, Phillips $11.95. An overview of the subject that begins in prehistoric times and ends with today's social dancing and ballet.

5571. Chappell, Warren. *The Nutcracker* (2–5). Illus. 1958, Knopf $7.99. Beautifully designed picture book with the principal musical themes and story.

5572. Cleaver, Elizabeth. *Petrouchka* (4–7). Illus. by author. 1980, Atheneum $12.95. The story of the ballet using puppet figures.

5573. Collard, Alexandra. *Two Young Dancers: Their World of Ballet* (6–9). Illus. 1984, Messner $10.29. Two 15-year-old ballet dancers—Shane and Melissa—tell their stories.

5574. Diamond, Donna. *Swan Lake* (3–6). Illus. by author. 1980, Holiday $9.95. The story of one of the world's most famous ballets.

5575. Goulden, Shirley. *The Royal Book of Ballet* (5–8). Illus. by Maraja. 1964, Modern Curriculum $7.95. The stories of 6 well-known ballets, beautifully illustrated.

5576. Gross, Ruth Belov. *If You Were a Ballet Dancer* (3–5). Illus. 1980, Dial $8.95; LB $8.89.

Basic questions are answered about ballet, with accompanying photographs.

5577. Hammond, Mildred. *Square Dancing Is for Me* (4–6). Illus. 1983, Lerner $6.95. Michelle and her cousin Andrew explain the basic steps and terminology of square dancing.

5578. Haney, Lynn. *I Am a Dancer* (4–7). Illus. 1981, Putnam $8.95; paper $4.95. Three youngsters—a girl and 2 boys—enter the training world of the ballet dancer.

5579. Isadora, Rachel. *My Ballet Class* (1–3). Illus. by author. 1980, Greenwillow $9.95; LB $9.55. The first-person account that traces a young girl's actions during a ballet class.

5580. Isadora, Rachel. *Opening Night* (K–3). Illus. by author. 1984, Greenwillow $10.50; LB $9.55. How a young ballet dancer feels on opening night in text and photographs.

5581. Jessel, Camilla. *Life at the Royal Ballet School* (6–9). Illus. by author. 1979, Methuen $12.95. An account of the trials and tribulations involved in becoming a ballet dancer.

5582. Maiorano, Robert, and Isadora, Rachel. *Backstage* (PS). Illus. 1978, Greenwillow $9.55. A girl goes backstage at a ballet theater.

5583. Price, Christine. *Dance on the Dusty Earth* (4–7). Illus. by author. 1979, Scribners $2.98. The origins and history of primitive dance.

5584. Sorine, Stephanie Riva. *At Every Turn! It's Ballet* (2–5). Illus. 1981, Knopf $8.95; LB $8.99. Photographs show many of the movements associated with ballet.

5585. Sorine, Stephanie Riva. *Imagine That! It's Modern Dance* (2–5). Illus. 1981, Knopf $8.95; LB $8.99. In photographs, 3 young girls show several free-form movements.

5586. Sorine, Stephanie Riva. *Our Ballet Class* (2–4). Illus. 1981, Knopf LB $8.99; paper $4.95. A photo essay about a weekly ballet class.

5587. Streatfeild, Noel. *A Young Person's Guide to the Ballet* (4–7). Illus. by Georgette Bordier. 1975, Warne $11.95. An excellent introduction to this art form, organized around the experiences of a young boy and girl who enter ballet school.

5588. Walker, Katherine Sorley, and Butler, Joan. *Ballet for Boys and Girls* (4–7). Illus. 1980, Prentice $9.95. An entertaining and enlightening introduction to the world of ballet.

5589. Werner, Vivian. *Ballet: How It All Began* (6–8). Illus. 1982, Atheneum $10.95. The history of ballet from its beginnings in France to modern times.

5590. Zeck, Gerry. *I Love to Dance: A True Story about Tony Jones* (3–6). Illus. 1982, Carolrhoda

$8.95. A young boy shows why he loves to dance and tells his plans for the future.

Motion Pictures and Television

5591. Beal, George. *See Inside a Television Studio* (3–5). Illus. 1978, Watts LB $9.40. Topics such as satellite broadcasting and special effects are covered in this simple account.

5592. Cheney, Glenn Alan. *Television in American Society* (6–8). 1983, Watts $8.90. Such topics as who decides on what programs to air and how the industry works are addressed.

5593. Clemens, Virginia Phelps. *Behind the Film-making Scene* (6–9). Illus. 1982, Westminster $12.95. A realistic picture of what goes into making a movie.

5594. Drucker, Malka, and James, Elizabeth. *Series TV: How a Television Show Is Made* (5–9). Illus. 1983, Houghton $11.95. An inside look on how a TV series is conceived and carried out.

5595. Edelson, Edward. *Great Monsters of the Movies* (6–9). Illus. 1973, Pocket paper $1.75. Vampires and zombies share space with Frankenstein and King Kong in this popular work. Also use: *The Funny Men of the Movies* (1976, Doubleday LB $7.95).

5596. Edelson, Edward. *Tough Guys and Gals of the Movies* (6–9). Illus. 1978, Doubleday $6.95. A history that covers the field from von Stroheim to Clint Eastwood and Harlow to Jane Fonda.

5597. Fradin, Dennis B. *Movies* (1–4). Illus. 1983, Childrens Pr. $7.95. A good introduction for young readers of a very broad subject.

5598. Gleasner, Diana C. *The Movies (Inventions That Changed Our Lives)* (4–6). Illus. 1983, Walker $7.95; LB $8.85. A history of moviemaking.

5599. Ireland, Karin. *Hollywood Stunt People* (5–8). Illus. 1980, Messner LB $8.79. The work of 12 people who risk their lives for our entertainment. Also use: *Movie Stunts and the People Who Do Them* by Gloria D. Miklowitz (1980, Harcourt paper $3.95).

5600. Jones, Eurfron Gwynne. *Television Magic* (2–7). Illus. 1978, Viking $11.50. Many illustrations and simple text highlight this account of how various television shows are produced.

5601. LeBaron, John, and Miller, Philip. *Portable Video: A Production Guide for Young People* (6–9). Illus. 1982, Prentice $10.95; paper $5.95. A practical guide to the use of portable video equipment.

5602. Molina, Maria. *Menudo* (5–7). Illus. 1984, Messner $8.79. The phenomenal story of the young 6-member Puerto Rican music group.

5603. Mooser, Stephen. *Lights! Camera! Scream! How to Make Your Own Monster Movies* (6–8). Illus. 1983, Messner $10.29. First, how to make movies, second, how to make a horror film.

5604. O'Connor, Jane, and Hall, Katy. *Magic in the Movies: The Story of Special Effects* (5–9). Illus. 1980, Doubleday $9.95; LB $9.90. The story of how special effects are accomplished in the movies.

5605. Thurman, Judith, and David, Jonathan. *The Magic Lantern: How Movies Got to Move* (4–6). Illus. 1978, Ahteneum $8.95. A history of early moviemaking that begins with the Chinese 1,000 years ago.

Play Production

5606. Fischer, Robert. *Getting Your Act Together* (5–8). Illus. 1982, Messner $8.79. Advice for young would-be actors.

5607. Judy, Susan, and Judy, Stephen. *Putting On a Play: A Guide to Writing and Producing Neighborhood Drama* (4–8). Illus. 1982, Scribners $12.95. A guide to producing all sorts of theatricals, including puppet plays and radio dramas.

5608. Powers, Bill. *Behind the Scenes of a Broadway Musical* (5–8). Illus. 1982, Crown $13.95. The making of the musical *Really Rosie* from Maurice Sendak's work.

Puppets and Marionettes

5609. Ackley, Edith F. *Marionettes: Easy to Make! Fun to Use!* (5–9). Illus. by Marjorie Flack. 1939, Harper $11.89. Guide includes full-size patterns and 5 marionette plays.

5610. Gates, Frieda. *Easy to Make Puppets* (1–3). Illus. 1981, Prentice paper $3.95. A simple guide for beginners.

5611. Holz, Loretta. *The Christmas Spider: A Puppet Play from Poland and Other Traditional Games, Crafts, and Activities* (3–6). Illus. by Charles Mikolaycak. 1980, Putnam $5.95; LB $5.99. A craft book on various Polish holidays; requires adult supervision.

5612. Lynch-Watson, Janet. *The Shadow Puppet Book* (4–7). Illus. 1980, Sterling $10.95; LB $13.29. A thorough and fascinating introduction to the world of shadow puppetry.

5613. Pels, Gertrude. *Easy Puppets: Making and Using Hand Puppets* (3–6). Illus. by Albert Pels. 1951, Harper $9.57. Easy and simple directions.

5614. Politi, Leo. *Mr. Fong's Toy Shop* (1–3). Illus. by author. 1978, Scribners $6.95. In preparing children to celebrate the Moon Festival, Mr. Fong shows them how to make puppets.

5615. Supraner, Robyn, and Supraner, Lauren. *Plenty of Puppets to Make* (1–3). Illus. by Renzo Barto. 1981, Troll LB $8.11; paper $1.95. A book about 11 easy-to-make puppets.

Shakespeare

5616. Brown, John R. *Shakespeare and His Theatre* (6–9). Illus. by David Gentleman. 1982, Lothrop $12.50. A vivid description of the Globe Theatre and of the people involved with it.

5617. Chute, Marchette. *An Introduction to Shakespeare* (6–9). 1957, Dutton $9.95. An exciting and informative presentation of the way in which Shakespeare's plays were written, costumed, and staged.

5618. Chute, Marchette. *Stories from Shakespeare* (6–9). 1971, NAL paper $3.50. An illuminating guide for the young person reading Shakespeare for the first time.

5619. Hodges, C. Walter. *Shakespeare's Theatre* (6–9). Illus. by author. 1980, Putnam paper $5.95. The development of English drama from its origins in medieval religious observance to mystery and morality plays to Shakespeare's Globe Theatre.

5620. Lamb, Charles, and Lamb, Mary. *Tales from Shakespeare* (4–8). Illus. by Elinore Blaisdell. 1982, Biblio Distributors $9.95; paper $2.95. The classic retelling of several of Shakespeare's most popular plays.

5621. Miles, Bernard. *Favorite Tales from Shakespeare* (5–8). Illus. by Victor G. Ambrus. 1977, Rand McNally $11.95. Five popular plays rewritten in prose by an English actor.

Plays

5622. Alexander, Sue. *Small Plays for You and a Friend* (1–3). Illus. by Olivia H. Cole. 1974, Houghton $6.95. Five simple skits, each involving only 2 characters, are presented in easily read language.

5623. Bradley, Alfred, and Bond, Michael. *Paddington on Stage* (3–5). Illus. by Peggy Fortnum. 1977, Houghton $8.95. Seven short plays about the adventures of the bear who always gets in and out of trouble.

5624. Carlson, Bernice W. *Let's Find the Big Idea* (2–5). Illus. by Bettye Beach. 1982, Abingdon $8.95. Playlets and skits that contain important themes.

5625. Childress, Alice. *When the Rattlesnake Sounds* (5–9). Illus. 1975, Putnam $6.95. A one-act play based on Harriet Tubman's experience one summer as a laundress in a New Jersey resort hotel.

5626. Davis, Ossie. *Escape to Freedom: A Play about Young Frederick Douglass* (6–9). 1978, Viking $11.50. A drama with music based on the life of the famous slave and his struggle for freedom.

5627. Hughes, Ted. *The Tiger's Bones and Other Plays for Children* (5–8). Illus. by Alan E. Cober. 1974, Viking LB $9.95. Five plays based chiefly on such traditional stories as "Orpheus" and "Beauty and the Beast."

5628. Jennings, Coleman A., and Harris, Aurand, eds. *Plays Children Love: A Treasury of Contemporary and Classic Plays for Children* (5–8). Illus. by Susan Swan. 1981, Doubleday $16.95. A group of plays requiring royalties based on such stories as *Sleeping Beauty* and *Pinocchio.*

5629. Miller, Helen L. *First Plays for Children* (3–7). 1971, Plays $12.00. A useful collection of nonroyalty plays.

5630. Nolan, Paul T. *Folk Tale Plays Round the World: A Collection of Royalty-Free, One-Act Plays about Lands Far and Near* (4–7). 1982, Plays paper $6.95. Johnny Appleseed and Robin Hood are heroes featured in 2 of the 17 plays in this collection.

5631. Thane, Adele. *Plays from Famous Stories and Fairy Tales* (4–6). 1983, Plays paper $12.95. Twenty-eight, royalty-free, one-act plays adapted from favorite children's stories.

Poetry

General

5632. Abercrombie, Barbara. *The Other Side of a Poem* (3–6). Illus. 1977, Harper LB $10.89. Such headings as "mysteries or puzzles," "ordinary things," and "poems make pictures" are used.

5633. Adoff, Arnold. *All the Colors of the Race* (4–7). Illus. by John Steptoe. 1982, Lothrop $11.25; LB $11.88. Poems that deal with the many races of mankind.

5634. Adoff, Arnold. *Eats* (4–6). Illus. by Susan Russo. 1979, Lothrop $11.25; LB $11.88. A joyous collection that praises such morsels as apple pie and newly baked bread.

5635. Adoff, Arnold. *OUTside INside Poems* (3–6). Illus. by John Steptoe. 1981, Lothrop $11.25; LB $11.88. Poems that deal with the dreams of a young baseball player.

5636. Adoff, Arnold. *Today We Are Brother and Sister* (3–5). Illus. by Glo Coalson. 1981, Lothrop $11.25; LB $11.88. A brother and sister share experiences visiting a Caribbean island in this series of poems.

5637. Adshead, Gladys L., and Duff, Annis, eds. *An Inheritance of Poetry* (5–7). Illus. by Nora S. Unwin. 1948, Houghton $7.95. An excellent anthology on a wide variety of subjects.

5638. Aiken, Joan. *The Skin Spinners: Poems* (5–8). Illus. by Ken Rinciari. 1976, Viking $12.50. A collection of the poet's verse about everyday things and experiences.

5639. Asch, Frank. *City Sandwich* (1–3). Illus. 1978, Greenwillow $9.95; LB $9.55. A book of poems and sketches to inspire and amuse city lovers.

5640. Bennett, Jill, sel. *Days Are Where We Live and Other Poems* (K–3). Illus. by Maureen Roffey. 1982, Lothrop $10.00. A collection of simple poems illustrated in picture book format.

5641. Bennett, Jill, comp. *Roger Was a Razor Fish and Other Poems* (1–4). Illus. by Maureen Roffey. 1981, Lothrop $10.25. Twenty-two selections from a variety of authors on a number of subjects.

5642. Bennett, Jill, sel. *Tiny Tim: Verses for Children* (PS–3). Illus. by Helen Oxenbury. 1982, Delacorte $10.95; LB $10.89. A collection of well-illustrated short verses, many of them humorous.

5643. Bodecker, N. M. *Pigeon Cubes and Other Verse* (4–6). Illus. by author. 1982, Atheneum $10.95. A group of poems about the joys and frustrations of everyday life.

5644. Brewton, Sara, and Brewton, John E., comps. *America Forever New: A Book of Poems* (5–8). 1968, Harper $6.50. Poetry from the days of Emily Dickinson to the present.

5645. Browning, Robert. *The Pied Piper of Hamelin* (4–6). Illus. by C. Walter Hodges. 1971, Warne $10.95. The piper's revenge on the town of Hamelin in text and richly dramatic, full-colored illustrations.

5646. Cole, Joanna, sel. *A New Treasury of Children's Poetry: Old Favorites and New Discoveries* (1–6). Illus. by Judith Gwyn Brown. 1984, Doubleday $12.95. A family collection of 210 poems for preschoolers through the middle grades.

5647. Cooney, Barbara, illus. *Chanticleer and the Fox* (1–4). Illus. 1958, Harper $10.53; LB $11.89; paper $3.80. Chaucer's *Nun's Priest Tale* adapted by the illustrator. Caldecott Medal, 1959.

5648. Corrin, Sara, and Corrin, Stephen, eds. *Once Upon a Rhyme: 101 Poems for Young Children* (2–5). Illus. by Jill Bennett. 1982, Faber $11.95. Poems old and new—mainly narrative or funny—divided by category.

5649. Cummings, E. E. *Hist Whist and Other Poems for Children* (3–6). Illus. by David Calsada. 1983, Liveright $10.95. A collection of 20 imaginative poems for children.

5650. De Angeli, Marguerite. *Friendship and Other Poems* (5–7). 1981, Doubleday $6.95. A collection of short verses on a variety of subjects.

5651. De La Mare, Walter, ed. *Come Hither* (4–8). Illus. by Warren Chappell. 1957, Knopf $25.00. A distinguished collection of over 500 rhymes and poems for the young of all ages.

5652. De La Mare, Walter. *Peacock Pie* (3–6). Illus. by Barbara Cooney. 1980, Faber paper $3.25. Dancing rhymes of fairies, witches, and farmers.

5653. Dickinson, Emily. *Poems for Youth* (5–7). Illus. by George Hauman and Doris Hauman. 1934, Little $7.95. A wonderful introduction to the simpler poems of this master.

5654. Duncan, Lois. *From Spring to Spring* (4–6). Illus. 1982, Westminster $10.95. Forty-one poems with religious themes.

5655. Dunning, Stephen; Lueders, Edward; and Smith, Hugh, eds. *Reflections on a Gift of Watermelon Pickle and Other Modern Verse* (6–9). Illus. 1966, Lothrop $11.25; LB $11.88. An attractive volume of 114 expressive poems by recognized modern poets, illustrated with striking photographs.

5656. Dunning, Stephen; Lueders, Edward; and Smith, Hugh, eds. *Some Haystacks Don't Even Have Any Needle and Other Complete Modern Poems* (6–9). Illus. 1969, Lothrop $12.50. For the "now generation"—an anthology of more than 125 poems by such masters as Roethke, Yevtushenko, Updike, and McKuen.

5657. Ferris, Helen, ed. *Favorite Poems Old and New* (4–6). Illus. by Leonard Weisgard. 1957, Doubleday $14.95. A book brimming with all kinds of poetry—lyrics, rhymes, doggerel, songs.

5658. Field, Eugene. *Wynken, Blynken and Nod* (K–2). Illus. by Barbara Cooney. 1980, Hastings $6.95. The famous poem illustrated in simple white on black. Another recommended edition is: *Wynken, Blynken and Nod*, illus. by Susan Jeffers (1982, Dutton $9.95).

5659. Fisher, Robert, ed. *Ghosts Galore: Haunting Verse* (4–8). Illus. by Rowena Allen. 1983, Faber $8.95. Fifty-six poems are included in this British publication.

5660. Fleming, Alice, ed. *America Is Not All Traffic Lights: Poems of the Midwest* (5–8). Illus. 1976, Little $6.95. Poets from the more rural areas, such as Carl Sandburg and Sherwood Anderson, are represented in this unique collection.

5661. Foster, John, comp. *A First Poetry Book* (3–7). Illus. by Chris Orr et al. 1982, Merrimack $9.95; paper $4.95. A fine collection of poetry with an English emphasis. Followed by: *A Second Poetry Book* (1982); *A Third Poetry Book* (1983); *A Fourth Poetry Book* (1983) (all $9.95; paper $4.95).

5662. Frank, Josette, sel. *Poems to Read to the Very Young* (PS). Illus. by Eloise Wilkin. 1982, Random LB $6.99; paper $6.95. A collection of short simple verses, many of them old favorites.

5663. Frost, Robert. *Stopping by Woods on a Snowy Evening* (K–4). Illus. by Susan Jeffers. 1978, Dutton $10.95. A richly illustrated version of Frost's most famous poem.

5664. Frost, Robert. *A Swinger of Birches: Poems of Robert Frost for Young People* (4–7). Illus. by Peter

Koeppen. 1982, Stemmer $17.95; paper $9.95. A collection of 38 poems suitable for young people.

5665. Frost, Robert. *You Come Too: Favorite Poems for Young Readers* (5–7). Illus. by Thomas W. Nason. 1959, Holt $8.70. A collection of some of the best-loved Frost poems illustrated with wood engravings. Also use: *The Road Not Taken* (1951, Holt $13.00).

5666. Geismer, Barbara, and Suter, Antoinette B. *Very Young Verses* (PS–1). Illus. by Mildred Bronson. 1945, Houghton $7.95. A pleasant collection for the very young, arranged by such subjects as seasons, bugs, weather.

5667. Giovanni, Nikki. *Vacation Time: Poems for Children* (2–4). 1980, Morrow $5.95; paper $4.95. A collection of simple poems about going on vacation.

5668. Greenfield, Eloise. *Honey, I Love, and Other Love Poems* (2–4). Illus. by Diane Dillon and Leo Dillon. 1978, Harper $7.95; LB $8.89. Sixteen poems on family love and friendship as experienced by a black girl.

5669. Hill, Helen, et al., eds. *Straight on Till Morning: Poems of the Imaginary World* (5–7). Illus. by Ted Lewin. 1977, Harper $13.95. Mystery and marvel in selections chiefly from modern writers.

5670. Hoberman, Mary Ann. *Yellow Butter, Purple Jelly, Red Jam, Black Bread: Poems* (PS–2). Illus. by Chaya M. Burstein. 1981, Viking $9.50. Playful poems that celebrate everyday things.

5671. Holman, Felice. *At the Top of My Voice: And Other Poems* (2–4). Illus. by Edward Gorey. 1970, Scribners $5.95. A pleasant collection of short poems entwined by Gorey's elegant illustrations.

5672. Hopkins, Lee Bennett, sel. *By Myself* (3–6). Illus. by Glo Coalson. 1980, Harper $7.95; LB $8.89. A collection of 16 poems about self-fulfillment and independence.

5673. Hopkins, Lee Bennett. *Circus! Circus!* (K–4). Illus. by John O'Brien. 1982, Knopf LB $9.99. Seventeen short poems about the circus.

5674. Hopkins, Lee Bennett, ed. *Go to Bed! A Selection of Bedtime Poems* (K–3). Illus. 1979, Knopf $5.99. A reassuring book of 20 poems to fit all moods at bedtime.

5675. Hopkins, Lee Bennett. *Love and Kisses* (4–8). Illus. by Kris Boyd. 1982, Houghton $8.95; paper $3.95. A collection of 25 love poems.

5676. Hopkins, Lee Bennett, ed. *Me! A Book of Poems* (K–2). Illus. by Talivaldis Stubis. 1970, Houghton $7.95. Simple poems chiefly by contemporaries on subjects familiar to youngsters.

5677. Hopkins, Lee Bennett. *Morning, Noon and Nighttime, Too* (2–5). Illus. by Nancy Hannans.

1980, Harper $7.95; LB $9.89. Poetry that tracks children through a normal school day.

5678. Hopkins, Lee Bennett. *A Song in Stone: City Poems* (2–5). Illus. 1983, Harper $9.95. Twenty short poems and photos on city life.

5679. Hopkins, Lee Bennett. *Surprises* (K–4). Illus. by Megan Lloyd. 1984, Harper $8.61; LB $8.89. A collection of simple poems for beginning readers.

5680. Hughes, Ted. *Moon-Whales and Other Moon Poems* (6–9). Illus. by Leonard Baskin. 1976, Viking $12.95. In an exuberant burst of imagination, the famous British poet invents a series of strange, sometimes grotesque moon creatures.

5681. Janeczko, Paul B, ed. *Postcard Poems: A Collection of Poetry for Sharing* (6–8). 1979, Bradbury $9.95. Very short poems (104) chosen to attract nonpoetry readers.

5682. Kennedy, X. J, and Kennedy, Dorothy M. *Knock at a Star: A Child's Introduction to Poetry* (4–6). Illus. by Karen Ann Weinhaus. 1982, Little LB $12.95. A collection of 150 poems, plus advice on writing one's own.

5683. Kuskin, Karla. *Dogs and Dragons, Trees and Dreams: A Collection of Poems* (3–6). 1980, Harper LB $10.89. A welcome reissue of poems that had appeared previously in the author's works.

5684. Kuskin, Karla. *Near the Window Tree* (3–4). Illus. 1975, Harper $10.89. A small collection of light verse with each poem prefaced by notes on its origin and background. Also use: *Any Me I Want to Be* (1972, Harper $10.89).

5685. Langstaff, John. *The Two Magicians* (K–3). Illus. by Fritz Eichenberg. 1973, Atheneum $4.95. A witch transforms a young magician in this adaptation of an early English ballad.

5686. Larrick, Nancy, ed. *Bring Me All of Your Dreams* (6–9). Illus. 1980, Evans $7.95. A beautiful collection of dream poems from a variety of times and cultures.

5687. Larrick, Nancy, ed. *Crazy to Be Alive in Such a Strange World: Poems about People* (5–9). Illus. 1977, Evans $7.95. The complexity of human beings is explored in this anthology of chiefly contemporary poetry.

5688. Larrick, Nancy, ed. *I Heard a Scream in the Street: Poems by Young People in the City* (5–8). Illus. 1970, Evans $7.95. Almost 80 poems by young people in 23 different cities are presented from a variety of sources. Also use: *On City Streets* (1968, Evans $7.95).

5689. Larrick, Nancy, ed. *Piping Down the Valleys Wild* (1–5). 1982, Dell paper $2.95. Animals,

children, and the seasons are represented in this fine collection culled from a variety of sources.

5690. Lawrence, D. H. *Birds, Beasts and the Third Thing: Poems* (4–6). Illus. by Alice Provensen and Martin Provensen. 1982, Viking $12.95. A selection of 23 of the author's poems, beautifully illustrated.

5691. Lewis, Richard, ed. *Miracles: Poems by Children of the English-Speaking World* (4–9). Illus. 1966, Simon & Schuster $9.95. Poems on a variety of subjects by children from 4 to 13.

5692. Livingston, Myra Cohn. *The Way Things Are and Other Poems* (5–7). Illus. by Jenni Oliver. 1974, Atheneum $4.95. Everyday things in a preadolescent's life are evoked in these simple verses.

5693. Livingston, Myra Cohn. *Why Am I Grown So Cold? Poems of the Unknowable* (5–9). 1982, Atheneum $13.95. An excellent collection of poetry on the fanciful and supernatural.

5694. Longfellow, Henry Wadsworth. *The Children's Own Longfellow* (5–8). Illus. 1920, Houghton $9.95. Eight selections from the best-known and best-loved of Longfellow's poems.

5695. Longfellow, Henry Wadsworth. *Hiawatha* (K–3). Illus. by Susan Jeffers. 1983, Dial $11.60; LB $11.89. A beautifully illustrated version of sections of Longfellow's poem.

5696. McCord, David. *Away and Ago: Rhymes of the Never Was and Always Is* (4–7). Illus. by Leslie Morrill. 1975, Little $6.95. Fifty poems on a variety of subjects important in childhood, from kings to baseball. Others in this series are: *Far and Few: Rhymes of the Never Was and Always Is* (1952, $6.95); *All Day Long: Fifty Rhymes of the Never Was and Always Is* (1966, $6.95); *For Me to Say: Rhymes of the Never Was and Always Is* (1970, $5.95); *Speak Up: More Rhymes of the Never Was and Always Is* (1980, $7.95).

5697. McCord, David. *One at a Time: His Collected Poems for the Young* (3–8). Illus. by Henry B. Kane. 1977, Little $12.95. All 7 of the poet's anthologies in one handsome volume.

5698. McCord, David. *The Star in the Pail* (K–3). Illus. by Marc Simont. 1975, Little $8.95. A beautifully illustrated collection suitable for very young children.

5699. Margolis, Richard J. *Secrets of a Small Brother* (2–5). Illus. by Donald Carrick. 1984, Macmillan $9.95. The joys and sorrows of being a younger brother are portrayed in these poems.

5700. Merriam, Eve. *Rainbow Writing* (4–8). 1976, Atheneum $6.95. A fine collection of poems, many dealing with contemporary concerns.

5701. Merriam, Eve. *A Word or Two with You: New Rhymes for Young Readers* (3–5). Illus. by John Nez.

1981, Atheneum LB $9.95. A collection of light verses about everyday things.

5702. Millay, Edna St. Vincent. *Edna St. Vincent Millay's Poems Selected for Young People* (6–9). Illus. by Ronald Keller. 1979, Harper $9.57. An excellent selection of poems in a beautifully designed book.

5703. Moore, Lilian, comp. *Go with the Poem* (4–8). 1979, McGraw $10.95. A choice collection of poems mostly by modern writers, on such subjects as sports and the seasons.

5704. Moore, Lilian. *I Feel the Same Way* (1–4). Illus. by Robert Quackenbush. 1967, Atheneum paper $1.95. Poems of city and suburb, nature and human nature recapture universal childhood experiences.

5705. Moore, Lilian. *Something New Begins: New and Selected Poems* (4–7). Illus. by Mary Jane Dunton. 1982, Atheneum $10.95. A delightful selection of 85 poems by this author concerning everyday experiences.

5706. Moore, Lilian. *Think of Shadows* (2–6). Illus. by Deborah Robison. 1980, Atheneum $9.95. Seventeen short poems about shadows.

5707. Morrison, Lillian. *Overheard in a Bubble Chamber and Other Science Poems* (6–9). Illus. by Eyre de Lanux. 1981, Lothrop $11.25; LB $11.88. Original poems grouped under 5 subjects.

5708. Morton, Miriam, ed. *The Moon Is Like a Silver Sickle: A Celebration of Poetry by Russian Children* (5–9). Illus. by Eros Keith. 1972, Simon & Schuster $4.95. Ninety-two poems that cover a wide range of moods and emotions.

5709. Noyes, Alfred. *The Highwayman* (5–9). Illus. by Charles Mikolaycak. 1983, Lothrop $10.00; LB $10.88. An exciting narrative poem, nicely illustrated.

5710. O'Neill, Mary. *Hailstones and Halibut Bones* (PS–3). Illus. by Leonard Weisgard. 1961, Doubleday $8.95; paper $3.50. Imaginative poems about color.

5711. Plotz, Helen, ed. *The Gift Outright: America to Her Poets* (6–9). 1977, Greenwillow LB $11.76. An anthology of 88 American writers that supplies an excellent introduction from colonial times to the present.

5712. Plotz, Helen, comp. *Gladly Learn and Gladly Teach: Poems of the School Experience* (6–8). 1981, Greenwillow $11.25. A wide variety of poems about schools and learning.

5713. Plotz, Helen, ed. *Imagination's Other Place: Poems of Science and Mathematics* (6–9). 1955, Harper $14.38. A useful collection on subjects usually not considered poetic fare.

5714. Plotz, Helen, comp. *Life Hungers to Abound: Poems of the Family* (6–9). 1978, Greenwillow $11.95; LB $11.47. A fine, quite mature collection of poems on familial relationships.

5715. Plotz, Helen, sel. *Saturday's Children: Poems of Work* (6–Up). 1982, Greenwillow $11.25. A collection of poetry about all kinds of work.

5716. Plotz, Helen. *This Powerful Rhyme: A Book of Sonnets* (6–9). 1979, Greenwillow $10.95; LB $10.51. About 130 sonnets are presented from a variety of authors ranging from Shakespeare to Edmund Wilson.

5717. Pomerantz, Charlotte. *If I Had a Paka: Poems in Eleven Languages* (PS–3). Illus. by Nancy Tafuri. 1982, Greenwillow $11.25; LB $11.88. Short poems that rely on foreign words for meaning and rhyme.

5718. Pomerantz, Charlotte. *The Tamarindo Puppy, and Other Poems* (K–2). Illus. by Byron Barton. 1980, Greenwillow $11.25; LB $10.88. A bilingual poetry book that intersperses Spanish words with English.

5719. Prelutsky, Jack. *Nightmares: Poems to Trouble Your Sleep* (5–9). Illus. by Arnold Lobel. 1976, Greenwillow $11.25; LB $10.80. Shuddery, macabre poems that will frighten but amuse a young audience. A sequel is: *The Headless Horseman Rides Tonight: More Poems to Trouble Your Sleep* (1980, $10.95; LB $10.51).

5720. Prelutsky, Jack, sel. *The Random House Book of Poetry for Children* (2–6). Illus. by Arnold Lobel. 1983, Random $13.95; LB $13.99. Old standbys and new gems are included in this fine anthology.

5721. Prelutsky, Jack. *The Snopp on the Sidewalk and Other Poems* (3–6). Illus. by Byron Barton. 1977, Greenwillow $9.84. Twelve wildly imaginative poems about strange imaginary beasts that bring to mind the Jabberwocky.

5722. Riley, James Whitcomb. *Little Orphan Annie* (1–3). Illus. by Diane Stanley. 1983, Putnam $8.95. The poem about a servant girl and the scary stories she tells.

5723. Rossetti, Christina. *Sing-Song: A Nursery Rhyme Book* (K–3). Illus. by Arthur Hughes. 1969, Dover paper $3.00. Many of the poems are about small creatures and familiar objects and have a singing quality that young children enjoy.

5724. Russo, Susan, comp. *The Moon's the North Wind's Cooky: Night Poems* (K–3). 1979, Lothrop $10.00; LB $10.88. Fourteen poems about the night and its charm.

5725. Rylant, Cynthia. *Waiting to Waltz: A Childhood* (5–8). Illus. by Stephen Gammell. 1984, Bradbury $10.95. A collection of 30 poems about growing up in a small town in Appalachia.

5726. Sandburg, Carl. *Rainbows Are Made* (5–8). Illus. by Fritz Eichenberg. 1982, Harcourt $12.95; paper $6.95. Seventy poems by one of America's greatest poets.

5727. Sandburg, Carl. *Wind Song* (4–7). Illus. by William A. Smith. 1960, Harcourt $5.95; paper $1.50. Sandburg selects his own poetry for children. Also use: *Early Moon* (1978, Harcourt $9.95; paper $1.95).

5728. Schwartz, Delmore. *"I Am Cherry Alive," the Little Girl Sang* (PS–2). Illus. by Barbara Cooney. 1979, Harper LB $9.89. A poem that celebrates the joys of being alive.

5729. Silverstein, Shel. *Where the Sidewalk Ends* (3–6). Illus. by author. 1974, Harper LB $12.45. The author explores various facets and interests of children, with appropriate cartoonlike drawings. Also use: *A Light in the Attic* (1981, Harper $13.50; LB $13.89).

5730. Starbird, Kaye. *The Covered Bridge House* (4–6). Illus. by Jim Arnosky. 1979, Four Winds $7.95. A lively collection of both lyric and narrative poems.

5731. Stevenson, Robert Louis. *A Child's Garden of Verses* (K–4). Illus. by Gyo Fujikawa. 1957, Putnam $6.95. Verses known and loved by generations of young people, brilliantly illustrated. Other recommended editions are: *A Child's Garden of Verses*, illus. by Erik Blegvad (1978, Random LB $4.99; paper $1.50); *A Child's Garden of Verses*, illus. by Tasha Tudor (1981, Rand McNally $9.95; LB $7.95).

5732. Streich, Corrine, sel. *Grandparents' House* (1–4). 1984, Greenwillow $12.00. A collection of 15 short poems from many cultures about grandparents.

5733. Thurman, Judith. *Flashlight and Other Poems* (1–5). Illus. by Reina Rudel. 1976, Atheneum $6.95. A fine little collection that explores many aspects of growing up in the city.

5734. Townsend, John R., ed. *Modern Poetry* (6–9). Illus. 1974, Harper $12.95. A well-balanced discriminating collection of important poems and poets from the 1940s through the 1960s.

5735. Tudor, Tasha, ed. *Wings from the Wind* (3–6). Illus. by editor. 1964, Harper $7.89. From Mother Goose to Shakespeare in an enchanting collection of 65 poems.

5736. Untermeyer, Louis, ed. *A Galaxy of Verse* (2–6). 1978, Evans $7.95. A varied collection of English and American verse.

5737. Viorst, Judith. *If I Were in Charge of the World and Other Worries: Poems for Children and Their Parents* (5–8). Illus. by Lynne Cherry. 1981, Atheneum LB $12.95; paper $3.95. Situations that vex are explored in these 41 poems.

5738. Wallace, Daisy, ed. *Fairy Poems* (3–5). Illus. by Trina S. Hyman. 1980, Holiday $6.95. A collection that includes poems by such writers as Tolkien, Farjeon, and De La Mare.

5739. Wallace, Daisy, comp. *Ghost Poems* (4–7). Illus. by Tomie de Paola. 1979, Holiday $8.95. New and old poems to delight and frighten young readers.

5740. Wallace, Daisy, ed. *Giant Poems* (K–3). Illus. by Margot Tomes. 1978, Holiday $5.95. A collection of poems about giants and ogres.

5741. Wallace, Daisy, ed. *Witch Poems* (3–6). Illus. by Trina S. Hyman. 1976, Holiday $8.95. Eighteen poems chosen from several different sources on a wide variety of witches.

5742. Whitman, Walt. *Overhead the Sun: Lines from Walt Whitman* (PS–3). Illus. by Antonio Frasconi. 1969, Farrar $6.95. Striking colored woodcuts illustrate brief excerpts from the poet's *Leaves of Grass*.

5743. Willard, Nancy. *A Visit to William Blake's Inn: Poems for Innocent and Experienced Travelers* (2–5). Illus. by Alice Provensen and Martin Provensen. 1981, Harcourt $12.95; paper $5.95. A collection of poems that won the Newbery Award.

5744. Worth, Valerie. *More Small Poems* (4–7). Illus. by Natalie Babbitt. 1976, Farrar $5.95. Simple poems about everyday things that reveal the poet's skill and fertile imagination. Also use: *Still More Small Poems* (1978, Farrar $6.95).

Animals

5745. Adoff, Arnold. *Friend Dog* (2–4). Illus. by Troy Howell. 1980, Harper $8.95; LB $8.79. A subtly illustrated poem about a girl and her pet dog.

5746. Armour, Richard. *Strange Monsters of the Sea* (2–4). Illus. by Paul Galdone. 1979, McGraw $10.95. Lighthearted verses about real and imaginary sea creatures.

5747. Baylor, Byrd. *Desert Voices* (3–6). Illus. by Peter Parnall. 1981, Scribners $11.95. A series of poems written from the viewpoint of various desert creatures.

5748. Blegvad, Lenore, ed. *Mittens for Kittens and Other Rhymes about Cats* (K–3). Illus. by Erik Blegvad. 1974, Atheneum $5.95. Twenty-five charming poems about cats in a nicely illustrated volume.

5749. Brewton, John E., ed. *Under the Tent of the Sky* (4–6). Illus. by Robert Lawson. 1937, Macmillan $9.95. All kinds of animals parade through this anthology.

5750. Cole, William, comp. *An Arkful of Animals: Poems for the Very Young* (3–5). Illus. by Lynn Munsinger. 1978, Houghton $6.95. A fine collection of humorous poems about animals.

5751. Cole, William, ed. *Good Dog Poems* (4–7). Illus. by Ruth Sanderson. 1980, Scribners $9.95. A collection that explores various aspects of dogdom.

5752. De Regniers, Beatrice S. *It Does Not Say Meow: And Other Animal Riddle Rhymes* (PS–K). Illus. by Paul Galdone. 1972, Houghton $10.95; paper $3.95. Simple rhymes give the clue to the familiar animals pictured on the following pages. The game-playing format will please young children.

5753. Farber, Norma. *Never Say Ugh to a Bug* (4–7). Illus. by Jose Aruego. 1979, Greenwillow LB $11.88. Humorous verses about a species that interests young people.

5754. Fisher, Aileen. *Rabbits, Rabbits* (PS–3). Illus. by Gail Niemann. 1983, Harper $9.57; LB $9.89. A rabbit's life is captured in 21 poems.

5755. Gardner, John. *A Child's Bestiary* (1–3). Illus. 1977, Knopf $4.95; LB $5.99. Sixty humorous and sophisticated poems about animals illustrated by the author and several members of his family.

5756. Hopkins, Lee Bennett, sel. *A Dog's Life* (4–6). Illus. by Linda Rochester Richards. 1983, Harcourt $9.95. An anthology of 23 brief poems about dogs and puppies.

5757. Hopkins, Lee Bennett, ed. *My Mane Catches the Wind* (4–6). Illus. by Sam Savitt. 1979, Harcourt $8.95. Twenty-two poems about horses.

5758. Kherdian, David. *Country Cat, City Cat* (K–4). Illus. by Nonny Hogrogian. 1978, Four Winds $5.95. Twenty-one poems about various animals in a variety of settings.

5759. Prelutsky, Jack. *Zoo Doings: Animal Poems* (3–6). Illus. by Paul O. Zelinsky. 1983, Greenwillow $10.00; LB $10.88. A collection of animal verses previously published by this poet.

5760. Steele, Mary Q. *The Fifth Day* (4–7). Illus. by Janina Domanska. 1978, Greenwillow $11.25; LB $11.88. A collection of poems about all the creatures on the earth after the fifth day of creation.

5761. Yolen, Jane. *How Beastly!* (2–4). Illus. by James Marshall. 1980, Putnam $8.95. This book of imaginative poetry introduces a menagerie through clever rhymes.

Black Poetry

5762. Adoff, Arnold. *Big Sister Tells Me That I'm Black* (3–5). Illus. by Lorenzo Lynch. 1976, Holt $5.95. Sister tells her younger brother in poem form that he should feel strength and pride in his blackness.

5763. Adoff, Arnold, ed. *My Black Me: A Beginning Book of Black Poetry* (3–6). 1974, Dutton $8.50. An anthology by black writers, stressing the positive aspects of blackness, pride, and joy. Also use: *I Am the Darker Brother: An Anthology of Modern Poems by Negro Americans* (1968, Macmillan $10.95; paper $4.95).

5764. Brooks, Gwendolyn. *Bronzeville Boys and Girls* (2–5). Illus. by Bonni Solbert. 1956, Harper LB $9.89. Everyday experiences of black children growing up in Chicago are revealed in these simple poems.

5765. Clifton, Lucille. *Everett Anderson's Year* (K–2). Illus. by Ann Grifalconi. 1974, Holt $6.95. Twelve poems describe the events of the seventh year in Everett's life. Also use: *Everett Anderson's 1–2–3* (1977, $6.95); *Everett Anderson's Goodbye* (1983, $9.70).

5766. Fufuka, Karama. *My Daddy Is a Cool Dude* (2–5). Illus. by Mahiri Fufuka. 1975, Dial $6.95; LB $6.89. A collection of 27 poems that explores life in an urban black neighborhood.

5767. Giovanni, Nikki. *Ego-Tripping and Other Poems for Young People* (6–9). Illus. by George Ford. 1974, Lawrence Hill $8.50; paper $5.95. A selection of poems from the author's works, which she thinks are particularly relevant to young people today. Also use: *Spin a Soft Black Song* (1971, Hill & Wang $7.95).

5768. Grimes, Nikki. *Something on My Mind* (3–5). Illus. by Tom Feelings. 1978, Dial $8.99; LB $8.44. A collection of poems about the black experience.

5769. Michels, Barbara, and White, Bettye, eds. *Apples on a Stick: The Folklore of Black Children* (3–6). Illus. by Jerry Pinkney. 1983, Putnam $10.95. Street verses collected from black children in Houston, Texas.

Haiku

5770. Atwood, Ann. *Haiku: The Mood of the Earth* (5–8). Illus. by author. 1971, Scribners $9.95; paper $4.95. Beautiful color photographs give a visual interpretation to each poem.

5771. Atwood, Ann. *Haiku: Vision in Poetry and Photography* (4–7). Illus. by author. 1977, Scribners $7.95. A lyrical book that tries to elicit responses to the beauty and wonder of nature.

5772. Behn, Harry, trans. *Cricket Songs: Japanese Haiku* (4–6). Illus. 1964, Harcourt $6.95. The unrhymed 17-syllable verse, accompanied by many Japanese paintings.

5773. Caudill, Rebecca. *Wind, Sand and Sky* (3–6). Illus. by Donald Carrick. 1976, Dutton $8.95. An enchanting collection of Haiku poetry.

5774. Lewis, Richard, ed. *In a Spring Garden* (K–4). Illus. by Ezra Jack Keats. 1965, Dial $12.95; LB $12.89; paper $3.95. A beautifully illustrated collection of Haiku in which the verses follow a day of spring.

5775. Livingston, Myra Cohn. *O Sliver of Liver: Together with Other Triolets, Cinquains, Haiku, Verses and a Dash of Poems* (4–6). Illus. by Van Bynbach. 1979, Atheneum $9.95. Personal reactions in poetry to everyday events and objects.

5776. Mizumura, Kazue. *Flower Moon Snow: A Book of Haiku* (2–5). Illus. by author. 1977, Harper LB $9.89. Thirty Haiku written by the brilliant Japanese-born American author and artist.

5777. Mizumura, Kazue. *If I Were a Cricket . . .* (K–3). 1973, Harper LB $9.89. A lovely collection of Haiku poetry.

Humorous Poetry

5778. Belloc, Hilaire. *The Bad Child's Book of Beasts* (3–6). Illus. by Wallace Tripp. 1982, Sparhawk paper $4.95. A reissue of an old favorite.

5779. Belloc, Hilaire. *Cautionary Tales* (2–5). Illus. by Lord Basil Blackwood. 1980, Gregg $5.95. A collection of witty stories on good manners told in verse.

5780. Bodecker, N. M. *Hurry, Hurry, Mary Dear! And Other Nonsense Poems* (2–5). Illus. by author. 1976, Atheneum $6.95. The rhythm and humor of the poetry, together with the droll illustrations, make this collection immediately appealing to children.

5781. Bodecker, N. M. *Let's Marry, Said the Cherry and Other Nonsense Poems* (4–6). Illus. by author. 1974, Atheneum paper $1.95. An excellent book for browsing, filled with daffy nonsense verses humorously illustrated with line drawings.

5782. Bodecker, N. M. *A Person from Britain Whose Head Was the Shape of a Mitten and Other Limericks* (3–5). Illus. by author. 1980, Atheneum $7.95. A humorous collection accompanied by equally amusing drawings.

5783. Bodecker, N. M. *Snowman Sniffles and Other Verse* (2–5). Illus. by author. 1983, Atheneum $8.95. A collection of humorous verses by this author.

5784. Brewton, John E., and Blackburn, Lorraine A. *They've Discovered a Head in the Box for the Bread and Other Laughable Limericks* (3–5). Illus. 1978, Harper $10.89. A surefire hit for introducing limericks to children.

5785. Brewton, Sara; Brewton, John E.; and Blackburn, Meredith G., III, eds. *My Tang's Tungled and Other Ridiculous Situations* (4–6). Illus. by Graham Booth. 1973, Harper $11.95. Nonsense verse, tongue twisters, and other humorous poems brought together in an irresistible collection. Also use: *Laughable Limericks* (1965, Harper $11.95).

5786. Brewton, Sara; Brewton, John E.; and Blackburn, Meredith G., III, eds. *Of Quarks, Quasers and Other Quirks: Quizzical Poems for the Supersonic Age* (5–8). Illus. by Quentin Blake. 1977, Harper $11.95. Contemporary poems that poke fun at such modern innovations as transplants and water beds. Also use: *Shrieks at Midnight* (1969, Harper $11.95).

5787. Cameron, Polly. *"I Can't" Said the Ant* (PS–2). Illus. by author. 1961, Putnam LB $7.99. Delightful nonsense poem of an ant's attempts to solve a kitchen crisis.

5788. Carroll, Lewis. *The Hunting of the Snark* (4–6). Illus. by Marvin Peake. 1970, Merrimack $4.95. Carroll's nonsense poem is imaginatively illustrated in this oversize book. Another recommended edition is: *The Hunting of the Snark*, illus. by Henry Holiday (1980, Mayflower $7.95).

5789. Carroll, Lewis. *Jabberwocky* (K–3). Illus. by Jane Breskin. 1977, Warne $9.95. Carroll poems and extracts from the Alice books delicately illustrated.

5790. Ciardi, John. *Fast and Slow: Poems for Advanced Children of Beginning Parents* (1–4). Illus. by Becky Gaver. 1974, Houghton $6.95; paper $1.95. Humorous, often witty poems for children by a master.

5791. Ciardi, John. *I Met a Man* (K–1). Illus. by Robert Osburn. 1961, Houghton LB $8.95. Lighthearted nonsense poems for the beginning reader. Also use: *The Man Who Sang the Sillies* (1961, Harper LB $9.89).

5792. Ciardi, John. *You Read to Me: I'll Read to You* (4–6). Illus. by Edward Gorey. 1961, Harper $9.57; LB $9.89. A collection of original verse for both adults and children.

5793. Cole, William, ed. *Oh, Such Foolishness* (4–6). Illus. by Tomie de Paola. 1978, Harper $9.37. Humorous poems with illustrations to match. Also use: *Oh, That's Ridiculous* (1972, Viking $8.89).

5794. Cole, William, sel. *Poem Stew* (2–6). Illus. by Karen Ann Weinhaus. 1981, Harper $10.89; LB

$9.98; paper $3.95. A collection of 57 witty poems about food.

5795. Kennedy, X. J. *One Winter Night in August and Other Nonsense Jingles* (3–6). Illus. by David McPhail. 1975, Atheneum $5.95. More than 50 charmingly humorous poems written for youngsters.

5796. Kennedy, X. J. *The Phantom Ice Cream Man: More Nonsense Verse* (3–5). Illus. by David McPhail. 1979, Atheneum $7.95. Contemporary nonsense verse on a variety of subjects.

5797. Knight, Hilary. *Hilary Knight's the Owl and the Pussy-Cat* (PS–3). Illus. by author. 1983, Macmillan $12.95. An imaginative retelling of Lear's original poem.

5798. Lear, Edward. *Complete Nonsense Book* (4–6). Illus. by author. 1943, Dodd $8.95. Verse, prose, drawings, alphabets, and other amusing absurdities. Also use: *A Book of Nonsense* (1980, Viking $9.95); *The Nonsense Verse of Edward Lear* (1984, Harmony $8.95).

5799. Lear, Edward. *How Pleasant to Know Mr. Lear! Edward Lear's Selected Works* (5–9). Sel. by Myra Cohn Livingston. Illus. by author. 1982, Holiday $11.95. A selection of the nonsense verse by this master.

5800. Lear, Edward. *The Owl and the Pussycat* (PS–3). Illus. by Barbara Cooney. 1969, Little $6.95. Elegant full-page illustrations enliven this well-loved poem. Another recommended edition is: *The Owl and the Pussycat*, illus. by Janet Stevens (1983, Holiday $12.95).

5801. Lear, Edward. *The Pelican Chorus* (PS–2). Illus. by Leslie Brooke. 1907, Warne $5.95. A picture book version of Lear's rollicking nonsense poem with 4-color drawings of the birds in all their finery along their beloved Nile, complete with a pelican-headed sphinx.

5802. Lear, Edward. *The Scroobious Pip* (2–5). Completed by Ogden Nash. Illus. by Nancy E. Burkert. 1968, Harper $11.49. Animals of the world are attracted to the strange, inscrutable creature in one of Lear's most engaging nonsense poems.

5803. Lee, Dennis. *Garbage Delight* (K–4). Illus. by Frank Newfeld. 1978, Houghton $7.95. Nonsense poems from a fine Canadian writer.

5804. Livingston, Myra Cohn. *A Lollygag of Limericks* (5–7). Illus. by Joseph Low. 1978, Atheneum $9.95. A lively collection humorously illustrated.

5805. Lobel, Arnold. *The Book of Pigericks: Pig Limericks* (1–4). Illus. by author. 1983, Harper $9.57; LB $9.89. Thirty-eight limericks about pigs.

5806. Lyfick, Warren, ed. *The Little Book of Limericks* (3–5). Illus. by Chris Cummings. 1978,

Harvey House $4.29. A happy book that contains over 70 limericks and many cartoonlike drawings.

5807. Merriam, Eve. *The Birthday Cow* (2–3). Illus. by Guy Michel. 1978, Knopf LB $6.99. Fifteen humorous poems that use nonsense situations and sounds.

5808. Milne, A. A. *When We Were Very Young* (PS–3). Illus. by Ernest H. Shepard. 1961, Dutton $7.95; Dell paper $1.95. Whimsical nonsense verses that have enchanted 3 generations. Also use: *Now We Are Six* (1961, Dutton $5.95; Dell paper $1.50).

5809. Morrison, Lillian, ed. *Best Wishes Amen: A New Collection of Autograph Verses* (4–8). Illus. by Loretta Lustig. 1974, Harper $10.95. A beguiling collection of jokes, jibes, and verses. Also use the worthy companion volume: *Yours Till Niagara Falls* (1950, $10.53).

5810. Morrison, Lillian, ed. *A Diller, a Dollar: Rhymes and Sayings for the Ten O'Clock Scholar* (5–8). 1955, Harper $7.95. All kinds of humorous schoolroom rhymes and folk sayings. Also use: *Remember Me When This You See* (1961, Harper 10.95).

5811. Morrison, Lillian. *Who Would Marry a Mineral? Riddles, Runes, and Love Tunes* (4–7). 1978, Lothrop $10.00; LB $10.88. Nonsense verses filled with word play and fun.

5812. Nash, Ogden. *Custard and Company* (4–7). Illus. by Quentin Blake. 1980, Little $9.95. A gathering of 128 pages of child-pleasing poems.

5813. Nash, Ogden. *Parents Keep Out: Elderly Poems for Youngerly Readers* (6–9). Illus. by Barbara Corrigan. 1951, Little $7.95. A lively collection of humorous poetry.

5814. Ness, Evaline, ed. *Amelia Mixed the Mustard, and Other Poems* (3–5). Illus. by author. 1975, Scribners $7.95. Twenty poems about independent and outrageous girls.

5815. Nolan, Dennis. *Wizard McBean and His Flying Machine* (1–3). Illus. by author. 1977, Prentice LB $7.75; paper $3.95. Through nonsense rhymes, this cumulative tale tells how a man rids himself of one pest after another.

5816. Petersham, Maud, and Petersham, Miska, eds. *The Rooster Crows: A Book of American Rhymes and Jingles* (K–2). 1945, Macmillan $11.95. This Caldecott Medal winner is a diverting book for browsing.

5817. Prelutsky, Jack. *The New Kid on the Block: Poems* (3–6). Illus. by James Stevenson. 1984, Greenwillow $9.00; LB $8.59. A collection of over 100 humorous poems by this prolific master.

5818. Prelutsky, Jack. *The Queen of Eene* (K–3). Illus. by Victoria Chess. 1978, Greenwillow LB

$10.51. Humorous imaginative poems cleverly illustrated.

5819. Prelutsky, Jack. *Rolling Harvey Down the Hill* (1–3). Illus. by Victoria Chess. 1980, Greenwillow $10.95; LB $10.31. Humorous verses about everyday mischief, illustrated with black-and-white drawings.

5820. Prelutsky, Jack. *The Sheriff of Rottenshot* (2–4). Illus. by Victoria Chess. 1982, Greenwillow $10.00; LB $10.88. A collection of the author's humorous poetry, with many a well-turned rhyme.

5821. Rosen, Michael. *Quick, Let's Get Out of Here* (3–6). Illus. by Quentin Blake. 1984, Andre Deutsch $10.95. A collection of funny poems dealing with boyish daydreams.

5822. Silvis, Craig. *Rat Stew* (3–6). Illus. by Annie Gusman. 1979, Houghton LB $6.95. Unusual love poems served up in a delicious concoction.

5823. Tripp, Wallace, ed. *A Great Big Ugly Man Came Up and Tied His Horse to Me: A Book of Nonsense Verse* (K–3). Illus. by editor. 1973, Little $7.95; paper $5.95. The hilarious drawings that accompany this selection of nonsense verses make this an especially entertaining book.

5824. Watson, Clyde. *Catch Me and Kiss Me and Say It Again* (K–2). Illus. by Wendy Watson. 1983, Putnam $10.95; paper $5.95. A collection of rhymes to accompany such activities as brushing teeth or clipping fingernails.

5825. Watson, Clyde. *Father Fox's Penny-Rhymes* (PS–2). Illus. by Wendy Watson. 1971, Harper $10.53; LB $10.89; Scholastic paper $2.25. Footstomping, clap-along nonsense rhymes, with witty watercolors and pen-and-ink illustrations that feature snatches of conversation in cartoonlike balloons. Also use: *Tom Fox and the Apple Pie* (1972, Harper $6.68; LB $7.89).

5826. Withers, Carl. *Favorite Rhymes from a Rocket in My Pocket* (2–5). 1970, Scholastic paper $1.50. Some charming poems from a standard work for young readers.

5827. Yolen, Jane. *How Beastly! A Menagerie of Nonsense Poems* (3–6). Illus. by James Marshall. 1980, Collins $8.95. A zooful of humorous verses about animals.

Indians of North America

5828. Bierhorst, John, ed. *In the Trail of the Wind: American Indian Poems and Ritual Orations* (5–9). 1971, Farrar $6.95. From a large number of North and South American Indian tribes comes this collection of chants, songs, and prayers. Also use:

The Sacred Path: Spells, Prayers and Power Songs of the American Indians (1983, Morrow $9.00).

5829. Wood, Nancy, ed. *Many Winters: Prose and Poetry of the Pueblos* (5–9). Illus. by Frank Howell. 1974, Doubleday $10.95. Sayings by the elders of the Taos Indians presented with accompanying realistic portraits.

Nature and the Seasons

5830. Asch, Frank. *Country Pie* (2–4). Illus. by author. 1979, Greenwillow $11.25; LB $11.88. Fourteen poems about nature. A companion volume is: *City Sandwich* (1978, $10.00; LB $10.88).

5831. Baylor, Byrd. *The Way to Start a Day* (3–5). Illus. by Peter Parnall. 1978, Scribners $10.95. A poetic tribute to the many ways people have greeted a new day.

5832. Behn, Harry. *Crickets and Bullfrogs and Whispers of Thunder: Poems* (K–5). Illus. by author. 1984, Harcourt $11.59. Fifty poems about nature, fantasy, and beauty.

5833. Esbensen, Barbara Juster. *Cold Stars and Fireflies: Poems of the Four Seasons* (4–7). Illus. by Susan Bonners. 1984, Harper $10.53; LB $10.89. Forty-three poems arranged by season.

5834. Fisher, Aileen. *Out in the Dark and Daylight* (K–5). Illus. by Gail Owens. 1980, Harper $9.57; LB $9.89. A collection of poems that celebrate commonplace items and situations.

5835. Greenaway, Kate. *Marigold Garden* (PS–K). Illus. by author. 1910, Warne $8.95. Flower verses written in simple rhyme for young children, beautifully illustrated.

5836. Hazeltine, Alice I., and Smith, Elva, eds. *The Year Around: Poems for Children* (4–6). Illus. by Paula Hutchison. 1956, Arno $15.00. A collection of seasonal poems.

5837. Hill, Helen et al., sels. *Dusk to Dawn: Poems of Night* (4–6). Illus. by Anne Burgess. 1981, Harper $9.95; LB $9.89. A collection of 35 poems about the night.

5838. Hopkins, Lee Bennett, sel. *Moments: Poems about the Seasons* (5–8). Illus. by Michael Hague. 1980, Harcourt $8.95. A series of poems from various authors about each of the seasons.

5839. Hopkins, Lee Bennett, sel. *The Sky Is Full of Song* (1–6). Illus. by Dirk Zimmer. 1983, Harper $9.57; LB $9.89. A collection of 38 short poems about the seasons.

5840. Hughes, Ted. *Season Songs* (6–9). Illus. by Leonard Baskin. 1975, Viking $11.95. A collection by a leading British poet, arranged by season and illustrated by simple mood pictures.

5841. Larrick, Nancy, ed. *Room for Me and a Mountain Lion: Poetry of Open Space* (5–8). Illus. 1974, Evans $7.95. A collection of nature poems arranged under such headings as woods and mountains.

5842. Livingston, Myra Cohn. *A Circle of Seasons* (3–5). Illus. by Leonard Everett Fisher. 1982, Holiday LB $12.95. A group of poems that brings the seasons to life.

5843. Livingston, Myra Cohn. *Sky Songs* (3–6). Illus. by Leonard Everett Fisher. 1984, Holiday $14.95. Fourteen poems about the sky and the universe.

5844. Moss, Elaine, ed. *From Morn to Midnight* (PS–3). Illus. by Satomi Ichikawa. 1977, Harper $8.95. Twenty-one brief verses by well-known poets, each dealing with a particular time of day and illustrated with watercolor paintings.

5845. Moss, Howard. *Tigers and Other Lilies* (4–6). Illus. by Frederick Henry Belli. 1977, Atheneum $5.95. Some 25 whimsical poems about plants that have animal names, such as spiderwort and dandelion.

5846. Parker, Elinor, ed. *Echoes of the Sea* (5–7). Illus. by Jean Vallario. 1977, Scribners paper $1.29. A far-ranging, rich collection about the sea.

5847. Russo, Susan, sel. *The Ice Cream Ocean: And Other Delectable Poems of the Sea* (K–4). Illus. by sel. 1984, Lothrop $10.00; LB $9.55. A humorous collection of poems about the sea and sea life.

5848. Updike, John. *A Child's Calendar* (3–6). Illus. by Nancy E. Burkert. 1965, Knopf $4.99. Twelve poems—one for each month—by this noted writer.

Sports

5849. Adoff, Arnold. *I Am the Running Girl* (3–5). Illus. by Ronald Himler. 1979, Harper $8.61; LB $10.89. A series of poems that celebrate the joy and wonder of running.

5850. Fleming, Alice, ed. *Hosannah the Home Run! Poems about Sports* (5–9). Illus. 1972, Little $7.95. About 20 sports are represented in this collection that reveals various attitudes toward the subject: notes on authors included.

5851. Morrison, Lillian, ed. *The Sidewalk Racer and Other Poems of Sports and Motion* (5–9). Illus. 1977, Lothrop $10.25; LB $9.84. Excellent collection of action poems that vary from the standpoint of the participant to that of the audience.

5852. Morrison, Lillian, ed. *Sprints and Distances: Sports in Poetry and the Poetry of Sport* (5–8). Illus. by Clare Ross and John Ross. 1965, Harper $11.49. A very popular anthology including a wide range of moods and sources, with emphasis on sports popular in the United States.

5853. Thayer, Ernest Lawrence. *Casey at the Bat* (4–7). Illus. by Paul Frame. 1964, Prentice paper $2.50. Joyless Mudville re-created in a picture book format. Another recommended edition is illustrated by Wallace Tripp (1978, Putnam $7.95; paper $3.95).

Fairy Tales

5854. Alexander, Lloyd. *The Town Cats and Other Tales* (4–6). Illus. by Laszlo Kubinyi. 1977, Dutton $9.95; Dell paper $1.50. Eight original tales involving very wise cats.

5855. Andersen, Hans Christian. *Eighty Fairy Tales* (4–7). 1982, Pantheon $14.95. An excellent collection of Andersen's best.

5856. Andersen, Hans Christian. *The Emperor's New Clothes* (2–4). Illus. by Virginia Burton. 1962, Houghton $7.95; paper $2.50. Three other recommended editions of *The Emperor's New Clothes* are: Illus. by Jack Delano and Irene Delano (1971, Random $4.95; LB $5.99); illus. by Anne Rockwell (1982, Harper $9.57; LB $9.89); illus. by Nadine Bernard Westcott (1984, Little $13.45; paper $3.70).

5857. Andersen, Hans Christian. *Hans Andersen: His Classic Fairy Tales* (3–6). Trans. by Erik Haugaard. Illus. by Michael Foreman. 1978, Doubleday $14.95. Eighteen tales retold from this new translation. Other editions include: *Hans Andersen's Fairy Tales,* illus. by Sumiko (1980, Schocken $9.95); *Fairytales: Michael Hague's Favorite Hans Christian Andersen Fairy Tales,* illus. by Michael Hague (1981, Holt $16.95).

5858. Andersen, Hans Christian. *Hans Clodhopper* (K–3). Illus. by Leon Shtainmets. 1975, Harper $10.53. The youngest and least likely of 3 sons wins the princess in this classic fairy tale.

5859. Andersen, Hans Christian. *The Little Match Girl* (4–6). Illus. by Blair Lent. 1968, Houghton LB $10.95; paper $1.95. The touching story of the lonely, shivering little match girl who sees visions in the flames of the matches she cannot sell.

5860. Andersen, Hans Christian. *The Little Mermaid* (2–5). Illus. by Chihiro Iwasaki. 1984, Neugebauer $11.95. A fine retelling of this story of pathos.

5861. Andersen, Hans Christian. *The Nightingale* (K–4). Illus. by Nancy E. Burkert. 1965, Harper $12.45; LB $12.89. The mood of the story is supported by 8 magnificent full-page reproductions of paintings. Another recommended edition is: *The Nightingale,* illus. by Lisbeth Zwerger (1984, Neugebauer $11.95; paper $7.50).

5862. Andersen, Hans Christian. *The Princess and the Pea* (K–3). Illus. by Paul Galdone. 1978, Houghton $10.95. A story of the supersensitive princess given a new look. Another edition is: *The Princess and the Pea,* illus. by Janet Stevens (1982, Holiday LB $10.95).

5863. Andersen, Hans Christian. *The Red Shoes* (1–4). Illus. by Chirhiro Iwasaki. 1983, Neugebauer $11.95. A simple retelling of the story of a doomed dancer. Another edition is: *The Red Shoes,* illus. by Katie Thamer (1982, Green Tiger paper $9.95).

5864. Andersen, Hans Christian. *The Snow Queen* (4–6). Adapt. by Naomi Lewis. Illus. by Errol LeCain. 1979, Viking $10.95; Penguin paper $2.95. A new version of this tale, accompanied by enchanting illustrations. Another edition is: *The Snow Queen,* illus. by Susan Jeffers (1982, Dial $12.95; LB $12.89).

5865. Andersen, Hans Christian. *The Steadfast Tin Soldier* (6–8). Illus. by Paul Galdone. 1979, Houghton $8.95. Courage and tragedy are mingled in this classic tale newly illustrated. Three other recommended editions of *The Steadfast Tin Soldier* are: Illus. by Thomas Di Grazia (1982, Prentice $8.95); illus. by George Lemoine (1983, Creative Ed. $9.95); illus. by Alain Vaes (1983, Little $13.45).

5866. Andersen, Hans Christian. *The Swineherd* (1–4). Trans. from Danish by Anthea Bell. Illus. by Lisbeth Zwerger. 1982, Morrow $10.75; LB $9.84. A prince disguises himself as a swineherd to win a princess.

5867. Andersen, Hans Christian. *Thumbelina* (K–2). Retold by Amy Ehrlich. Illus. by Susan Jeffers. 1979, Dial $11.95; LB $11.89. A lavishly illustrated edition of this ever-popular tale. Another edition is: *Thumbelina,* illus. by Lisbeth Zwerger (1980, Morrow $11.95; LB $11.47).

5868. Andersen, Hans Christian. *The Ugly Duckling* (K–3). Trans. by R. P. Keigwin. Illus. by Adrienne Adams. 1965, Scribners $8.95; paper $2.95. A lovely edition of this standard classic.

5869. Andersen, Hans Christian. *The Wild Swans* (K–2). Retold by Amy Ehrlich. Illus. by Susan Jeffers. 1981, Dial $10.95; LB $10.89. The purity of a gentle princess triumphs over evil. Another fine edition is: *The Wild Swans*, illus. by Angela Barrett (1984, Harper $11.59).

5870. Bolliger, Max. *The Lonely Prince* (PS–3). Illus. by Jurg Obrist. 1982, Atheneum LB $12.95. Prince William discovers what he really needs is a friend.

5871. Bomans, Godfried. *The Wily Witch and All the Other Tales and Fables* (4–7). Trans. by Patricia Crampton. Illus. by Wouter Hoogendijk. 1977, Stemmer $9.95. Works of the popular Dutch author, brilliantly translated.

5872. Bulla, Clyde Robert. *My Friend the Monster* (3–5). Illus. by Michele Chessare. 1980, Harper $10.53; LB $10.89. Prince Hal tries to gain access to a mountain where he believes monsters live.

5873. Coatsworth, Elizabeth. *The Cat Who Went to Heaven* (4–6). Illus. by Lynd Ward. 1967, Macmillan $9.95; paper $3.95. A charming legend of a Japanese artist, his cat, and a Buddhist miracle. Newbery Award, 1930.

5874. Collodi, Carlo. *The Adventures of Pinocchio* (3–6). Illus. by Fritz Kredel. 1946, Putnam deluxe ed. $9.95; paper $5.95. One of many recommended editions. Others are: *The Adventures of Pinocchio*, illus. by Frank Baber (1982, Rand McNally $9.95); illus. by Diane Goode (1983, Random $6.95; LB $7.99); *The Adventures of Pinocchio: Tale of a Puppet*, illus. by Troy Howell (1983, Lothrop $17.00).

5875. Coombs, Patricia. *The Magic Pot* (K–3). Illus. by author. 1977, Lothrop LB $11.88. After an old man finds a magic pot by the side of a road, unexpected events occur.

5876. Corrin, Sara, and Corrin, Stephen, eds. *The Faber Book of Modern Fairy Tales* (4–6). Illus. by Ann Strugnell. 1982, Faber $15.50. Fifteen stories by such authors as Joan Aiken and James Thurber.

5877. Dickens, Charles. *The Magic Fishbone* (2–5). Illus. by Louis Slobodkin. 1953, Vanguard $8.95. A young princess is given a magic fishbone by a fairy.

5878. Flory, Jane. *The Lost and Found Princess* (2–4). Illus. by author. 1979, Houghton $5.95. A woman, a dragon, and a cat form a team and set out to find a lost princess.

5879. Fox, Paula. *The Little Swineherd and Other Tales* (4–7). Illus. by Leonard Lubin. 1981, Dell paper $1.75. A collection of 5 original fable fairy tales impressively told.

5880. Garner, Alan. *Alan Garner's Fairytales of Gold* (3–5). Illus. by Michael Foreman. 1980, Putnam $15.95. Four tales, each with a golden item in it.

5881. Grahame, Kenneth. *The Reluctant Dragon* (2–4). Illus. by Ernest H. Shepard. 1953, Holiday $6.95. Tongue-in-cheek story of a boy who makes friends with a peace-loving dragon. Another fine edition is: *The Reluctant Dragon*, illus. by Michael Hague (1983, Holt $11.50).

5882. Gray, Nicholas Stuart. *A Wind from Nowhere* (4–6). 1979, Faber $9.50. A delightful collection of fairy tales from various sources.

5883. Haviland, Virginia, ed. *The Fairy Tale Treasury* (4–6). Illus. by Raymond Briggs. 1980, Putnam $12.95. A handsome collection of 32 mostly familiar stories (many appeared previously in the compiler's well-known "Favorite Fairy Tales" series), illustrated by a distinguished artist.

5884. Jeffers, Susan. *Wild Robin* (2–4). Illus. by author. 1976, Dutton $9.95. A young boy captured by fairies is rescued by his sister.

5885. Kaye, M. M. *The Ordinary Princess* (4–6). Illus. by author. 1984, Doubleday $11.95. A young princess discovers there are many advantages to being ordinary.

5886. Kennedy, Richard. *The Dark Princess* (4–6). Illus. by Donna Diamond. 1978, Holiday $7.95. A fool sacrifices his life to help a blind princess.

5887. Lang, Andrew, comp. *Blue Fairy Book* (4–6). Ed. by Brian Alderson. 1978, Viking $14.95; Dover paper $5.00; Airmont paper $1.25. A new edition of this classic collection. Other "color" Fairy Books are: *Brown Fairy Book* (n.d., Dover paper $5.00); *Crimson Fairy Book* (1966, Dover paper $5.00); *Green Fairy Book* (1978, Viking $14.95; Dover paper $5.00; Airmont paper $0.75); *Grey Fairy Book* (n.d., Dover paper $5.00); *Lilac Fairy Book* (1968, Dover paper $4.50); *Olive Fairy Book* (1968, Peter Smith $13.25; Dover paper $4.50); *Orange Fairy Book* (1968, Dover paper $4.95); *Pink Fairy Book* (1982, Viking $14.95; Dover paper $5.00); *Red Fairy Book* (1960, Random LB $3.99; Viking $14.95; Dover paper $5.00); *Violet Fairy Book* (n.d., Peter Smith $13.50; Dover paper $5.00); *Yellow Fairy Book* (1980, Viking $14.95; Dover paper $5.00).

5888. Lang, Andrew. *The Rainbow Fairy Book: A Selection of Outstanding Fairy Tales from the Color Fairy Books* (4–6). Illus. by Margery Gill. 1977, Schocken paper $3.95. A fine selection from the author's collection first published in the 1880s and 1890s.

5889. Luenn, Nancy. *The Ugly Princess* (4–7). Illus. by David Wiesner. 1981, Little $6.95. A Princess, made ugly by a curse, finds the true nature of beauty.

5890. MacDonald, George. *The Complete Fairy Tales of George MacDonald* (4–7). Illus. by Arthur Hughes. 1979, Schocken LB $10.95; paper $5.50. A classic work reprinted with the original illustrations.

5891. MacDonald, George. *The Princess and the Goblin* (4–6). Illus. by Peter Wane. 1980, Zondervan $6.95; 1984, Cook $12.95; paper $1.95; Penguin paper $2.25. The classic fairy tale about a Princess and a miner's son who outwit a goblin. The sequel is: *The Princess and Curdie* (1980, Zondervan $6.95; Penguin paper $2.95).

5892. McKinley, Robin. *The Door in the Hedge* (6–8). 1981, Greenwillow $11.25. A sensitive retelling of 4 fairy tales.

5893. Moeri, Louise. *The Unicorn and the Plow* (2–4). Illus. by Diane Goode. 1982, Dutton $8.95. A starving farmer fears he will have to kill his oxen for food.

5894. Morel, Eve, ed. *Fairy Tales* (PS–2). Illus. by Gyo Fujikawa. 1980, Grosset $7.65; paper $1.95. A collection of tales including *Cinderella* and *Little Red Riding Hood.*

5895. Nesbit, Edith. *The Last of the Dragons* (4–6). Illus. by Peter Firmin. 1980, McGraw $8.95. Who will slay the last dragon on earth?

5896. Pyle, Howard. *King Stork* (K–3). Illus. by Trina S. Hyman. 1973, Little $8.95. New illustrations highlight this story from *The Wonder Clock.*

5897. Pyle, Howard. *Pepper and Salt* (4–6). Illus. by author. 1941, Harper LB $11.89. Clever and delightful stories based on old tales, a popular favorite.

5898. Pyle, Howard. *The Wonder Clock: Or Four and Twenty Marvelous Tales* (4–6). Illus. by author. 1915, Dover paper $5.95. Tales for each hour in the day, told by figures on a clock.

5899. Rackham, Arthur, ed. *The Arthur Rackham Fairy Book* (2–5). Illus. by editor. 1950, Harper $12.45. Twenty-three favorite fairy and folktales.

5900. Reesink, Marijke. *The Princess Who Always Ran Away* (1–3). Illus. by Francoise Tresy. 1981, McGraw $9.95. A fairy story about a cruel king's daughter and her desire to be free.

5901. Sandburg, Carl. *Rootabaga Stories* (4–6). Illus. by Maud Petersham and Miska Petersham. 1951, Harcourt $14.95; Part I paper $3.95; Part II paper $2.50. A collection of modern tales from Rootabaga country.

5902. Savryn, L, ed. *Once Upon a Cat* (1–4). Illus. by Kathy Mitchell. 1983, Putnam paper $5.95. Four fairy tales about cats, including *Puss in Boots* and *Dick Whittington,* plus one poem, "The Owl and the Pussycat."

5903. Stearns, Pamela. *The Mechanical Doll* (4–6). Illus. by Trina S. Hyman. 1979, Houghton LB $6.95. A modern fairy tale of a young musician's love for a mechanical doll.

5904. Thurber, James. *Many Moons* (4–5). Illus. by Louis Slobodkin. 1944, Harcourt $12.95; paper $3.95. A little princess who wanted the moon and how her wish came true. Also use: *The Great Quillow* (1984, Peter Smith $11.75; Harcourt paper $1.95).

5905. Thurber, James. *The White Deer* (6–7). Illus. by author. 1945, Harcourt paper $3.95. Three princes, a princess, and magic occurrences in this modern fairy tale.

5906. Tregarthen, Enys. *The Doll Who Came Alive* (1–4). Illus. by Nora S. Unwin. 1972, Harper $10.10. A kindly sailor gives an orphan girl a doll that comes alive in this Cornish tale.

5907. Ungerer, Tomi. *Allumette: A Fable, with Due Respect to Hans Christian, the Grimm Brothers, and the Honorable Ambrose Bierce* (K–2). Illus. 1982, Four Winds $11.95. A dying match girl brings some good into the world.

5908. Wilde, Oscar. *The Birthday of the Infanta and Other Tales* (4–6). Illus. by Beni Montresor. 1982, Atheneum $14.95. Five fairy tales, including *The Selfish Giant* and *The Happy Prince.*

5909. Wilde, Oscar. *The Happy Prince* (3–6). Illus. by Jean Claverie. 1981, Oxford $14.95. A statue gives away its finery in this story of sacrifice. Another edition is: *The Happy Prince and Other Stories* (1968, Dent $11.00; Penguin paper $2.25).

5910. Wilde, Oscar. *The Selfish Giant* (4–6). Illus. by Michael Foreman and Friere Wright. 1978, Methuen $8.95. Many full-color illustrations enliven this classic story. One other edition is: *The Selfish Giant,* illus. by Lisbeth Zwerger (1984, Neugebauer $11.95).

5911. Wilde, Oscar. *The Star Child: A Fairy Tale* (2–3). Illus. by Fiona French. 1979, Four Winds $9.95. An abandoned child searches for his mother.

5912. Williams, Jay. *The Water of Life* (PS–3). Illus. by Lucinda McQueen. 1980, Four Winds $8.95. The king asks a generous fisherman to find the water of life.

5913. Yolen, Jane. *The Girl Who Cried Flowers, and Other Tales* (5–6). Illus. by David Palladini. 1974, Harper $10.53; LB $10.89; Schocken paper $5.95. New wine in old bottles describes these 5 original tales that rely on plot elements and situations loved by all. Seven more tales are in: *The Hundredth Dove and Other Tales* (1977, Harper $10.53).

5914. Yolen, Jane. *The Magic Three of Solatia* (5–7). Illus. by Julia Noonan. 1974, Harper $9.13. Wizard's spells, the struggle between good and evil, and the magic of the guest are familiar elements in this 4-part fantasy.

5915. Yolen, Jane. *Sleeping Ugly* (2–4). Illus. by Diane Stanley. 1981, Putnam $6.99; paper $4.95. A clever and entertaining switch on the Sleeping Beauty story.

Folklore

General

5916. Colwell, Eileen, ed. *The Magic Umbrella and Other Stories for Telling* (4–7). Illus. by Shirley Felts. 1977, Merrimack $9.95. This fine collection stretches from Greek and Norse legends to more modern tales. A companion volume is: *Humblepuppy and Other Stories for Telling* (1980, Bodley Head $9.95).

5917. Crouch, Marcus, comp. *The Whole World Storybook* (4–6). Illus. by William Stobbs. 1983, Merrimack $12.95. A collection of 25 folktales from around the world.

5918. Hadley, Eric, and Hadley, Tessa. *Legends of the Sun and Moon* (2–6). Illus. by Jan Nesbitt. 1983, Cambridge Univ. Pr. $9.95. A collection of folktales on the moon and sun from all over the world.

5919. Jagendorf, M. A., ed. *Noodlehead Stories from Around the World* (4–8). Illus. by Shane Miller. 1957, Vanguard $10.95. Sixty-five funny folktales from 36 countries.

5920. Leach, Maria, ed. *The Lion Sneezed: Folktales and Myths of the Cat* (4–6). Illus. by Helen Siegl. 1977, Harper $10.53. Twenty short stories, plus riddles and proverbs, are illustrated with unusual woodcuts in this endearing tribute to the cat.

5921. Leach, Maria, ed. *Noodles, Nitwits and Numskulls* (5–7). Illus. by Kurt Werth. 1979, Dell paper $1.25. A collection of tales and riddles from many countries.

5922. Leach, Maria, ed. *Whistle in the Graveyard: Folktales to Chill Your Bones* (4–6). Illus. by Ken Rinciari. 1982, Penguin paper $3.50. A collection about ghosts that will satisfy young readers intent on getting a good scare from their reading.

5923. Lurie, Alison. *Clever Gretchen, and Other Forgotten Folk Tales* (4–6). Illus. by Margot Tomes. 1980, Harper LB $10.89. Fourteen folktales, each with active forceful heroines.

5924. Manning-Sanders, Ruth. *A Book of Spooks and Spectres* (5–7). Illus. by Robin Jacques. 1980, Dutton $10.95. Twenty-three entertaining ghost stories from around the world.

5925. Mayo, Margaret, ed. *The Book of Magical Horses* (4–6). Illus. by Victor G. Ambrus. 1977, Hastings $6.95. Thirteen tales from various sources, all dealing with enchanted horses.

5926. Minard, Rosemary, ed. *Womenfolk and Fairy Tales* (4–6). Illus. by Suzanna Klein. 1975, Houghton $11.95. In each of these 18 stories, the female characters triumph because of wit, spunk, and courage.

5927. Phelps, Ethel Johnston. *The Maid of the North* (2–6). 1981, Holt paper $6.00. A collection of folktales from around the world.

5928. Phelps, Ethel Johnston. *Tatterhood and Other Tales* (3–6). Illus. by Pamela Baldwin Ford. 1978, Feminist Pr. $11.95; paper $5.95. Tales in which women play a vital and decisive role.

5929. Rockwell, Anne, ed. *The Three Bears and Fifteen Other Stories* (1–4). Illus. by editor. 1975, Harper $12.02; LB $12.89; paper $7.64. Folktales from England and stories from the Grimm collections are the sources of these charmingly illustrated stories.

5930. Rojankovsky, Feodor, ed. *The Tall Book of Nursery Tales* (K–2). Illus. by editor. 1944, Harper $6.68; LB $7.89. Twenty-four traditional tales in an unusual format.

Africa

5931. Aardema, Verna, retel. *Bringing the Rain to Kapiti Plain: A Nandi Tale* (PS–2). Illus. by Beatriz Vidal. 1981, Dial $9.95; LB $9.45; paper $3.95. A rhyming book on how the rain was brought to an African plain.

5932. Aardema, Verna. *Half-a-Ball-of-Kenki: An Ashanti Tale* (K–2). Illus. by Diane S. Zuromskis. 1979, Warne $8.95. How leopards gained their spots and why flies sit on leaves are explained in this Ashanti folktale.

5933. Aardema, Verna. *Oh Kojo! How Could You! An Ashanti Tale* (K–3). Illus. by Marc Brown. 1984, Dial $10.63; LB $10.89. Ananse meets his match in Kojo, a handsome lazy fellow.

5934. Aardema, Verna, retel. *The Vingananee and the Tree Toad: A Liberian Tale* (PS–4). Illus. by Ellen

Weiss. 1983, Warne $12.95. A Liberian folktale about the animal's war against a monster.

5935. Aardema, Verna, retel. *What's So Funny, Ketu?* (K–3). Illus. by Marc Brown. 1982, Dial $9.95; LB $9.89. A secret joke almost leads to disaster in this comic Sudanese folktale.

5936. Aardema, Verna, ed. *Who's in Rabbit's House? A Masai Tale* (K–3). Illus. by Leo Dillon and Diane Dillon. 1977, Dial $11.95; LB $11.89. Rabbit's friends try to evict a mysterious Long One who has moved into her house.

5937. Aardema, Verna, ed. *Why Mosquitoes Buzz in People's Ears: A West African Tale* (K–3). Illus. by Leo Dillon and Diane Dillon. 1975, Dial $11.95; LB $11.89; paper $3.95. Bold, stylized paintings illustrate this tale of a mosquito who tells a whopping lie, thus setting off a chain of events. Caldecott Medal, 1976.

5938. Appiah, Peggy. *Tales of an Ashanti Father* (2–7). Illus. by Mora Dickson. 1981, Andre Deutsch $8.95. Twenty-two stories about trickster Ananse.

5939. Arkhurst, Joyce Cooper. *The Adventures of Spider: West African Folktales* (4–7). Illus. by Jerry Pinkney. 1964, Little $7.95. Six humorous stories featuring the crafty spider.

5940. Berger, Terry. *Black Fairy Tales* (4–6). n.d, Atheneum paper $3.50. A collection of tales from Africa.

5941. Bryan, Ashley. *Beat the Story-Drum, Pum-Pum* (K–4). Illus. by author. 1980, Atheneum $10.95. A retelling of 5 Nigerian folktales.

5942. Bryan, Ashley. *The Ox of the Wonderful Horns and Other African Folktales* (1–5). Illus. by author. 1971, Atheneum $8.95. Four amusing short stories about animals trying to outwit one another.

5943. Carew, Jan. *The Third Gift* (3–5). Illus. by Leo Dillon and Diane Dillon. 1974, Little $8.95. An African folktale about the valuable gifts a tribe receives from the young men who climb to the peak of Nameless Mountain.

5944. Courlander, Harold. *The Crest and the Hide: And Other African Stories of Heroes, Chiefs, Bards, Hunters, Sorcerers and Common People* (5–7). Illus. by Monica Vachula. 1982, Putnam $11.95. A collection of 20 lively African tales.

5945. Courlander, Harold. *The King's Drum and Other African Stories* (4–6). Illus. by Enrico Arno. 1970, Harcourt paper $3.95. Humorous tales of wise and foolish people and animals.

5946. Dayrell, Elphinstone. *Why the Sun and the Moon Live in the Sky* (K–2). Illus. by Blair Lent. 1977, Houghton LB $7.95; paper $1.95. Stylized

illustrations add to the distinction of this simply told adaptation of a Nigerian folktale.

5947. Domanska, Janina. *The Tortoise and the Tree* (PS–2). Illus. by author. 1978, Morrow LB $11.95. A Bantu tale about a tortoise who punishes animals who have abused him.

5948. Gerson, Mary-Joan. *Why the Sky's Far Away: A Folktale from Nigeria* (1–3). Illus. by Hope Meryman. 1974, Harcourt $8.95. When people begin misusing the generosity of the sky, it moves away.

5949. Guirma, Frederic. *Princess of the Full Moon* (4–6). Illus. by author. 1970, Macmillan $9.95. Many of the standard elements of the fairy tale—a beautiful princess, evil prince, and trusting, simple shepherd—are found in this African story.

5950. Hadithi, Mwenye. *Greedy Zebra* (PS). Illus. by Adrienne Kennaway. 1984, Little $10.45. A story from Kenya on how the zebra got its stripes.

5951. Haley, Gail E. *A Story, a Story* (1–4). Illus. by author. 1970, Atheneum LB $12.95; paper $3.50. How African "spider stories" began is traced back to the time when Ananse, the Spider Man, made a bargain with the Sky God. Caldecott Medal, 1971.

5952. McDermott, Gerald. *Anansi, the Spider: A Tale from the Ashanti* (K–3). Illus. by author. 1972, Holt $10.95. Because Anansi and his sons quarrel, the moon remains in the sky.

5953. McDermott, Gerald. *The Magic Tree: A Tale from the Congo* (K–3). Illus. by author. 1977, Penguin paper $3.95. A young boy discovers a magic tree but loses its riches when he tells its secrets; adapted from the author's film.

5954. Manniche, Lise, trans. *The Prince Who Knew His Fate: An Ancient Egyptian Tale* (2–5). Illus. by trans. 1982, Putnam $10.95. An Egyptian folktale completed by the translator.

5955. Pitcher, Diana, retel. *Tokoloshi: African Folk Tales Retold* (4–6). Illus. by Meg Rutherford. 1981, Celestial Arts $9.95. Creation stories and "why" tales from the Bantu culture.

5956. Rose, Anne. *Pot Full of Luck* (K–2). Illus. by Margot Tomes. 1982, Lothrop $11.25; LB $11.88. A wise man puts his common sense in a pot and then finds he is foolish in this Ashanti tale.

5957. Serwadda, W. Moses. *Songs and Stories from Uganda* (3–5). Illus. by Leo Dillon and Diane Dillon. 1974, Harper $10.53; LB $10.89. A mixture of folk materials from Uganda, including songs in the native language (with translations) and a description of accompanying dance steps.

5958. Smith, Bob, ed. *Old African Tales Told Again* (4–5). Illus. by Dorothy Jungels. 1978, Academy

$5.95. A cross section of short tales from many African regions.

Asia

5959. Asian Cultural Centre of Unesco, eds. *Folk Tales from Asia for Children Everywhere: Book Three* (2–5). Illus. 1975, Weatherhill $6.50. Nine tales with a wide range of folk themes.

5960. Otsuka, Yuzo, retel. *Suho and the White Horse: A Legend of Mongolia* (K–4). Illus. by Suekichi Akaba. 1981, Viking $10.95. The story of a young herdsman's love for his white horse in this Mongolian folktale.

5961. Seros, Kathleen, adapt. *Sun and Moon: Fairy Tales from Korea* (2–5). Illus. by Norman Sibley and Robert Krause. 1983, Hollym LB $14.50. A collection of 7 stories from Korea.

5962. Timpanelli, Gioia, retel. *Tales from the Roof of the World: Folktales of Tibet* (3–6). Illus. by Elizabeth Kelly Lockwood. 1984, Viking $11.50. Four Tibetan folktales that tell of a foreign culture and religion.

China

5963. Carpenter, F. R. *Tales of a Chinese Grandmother* (5–7). Illus. by Malthe Hasselrus. 1973, Tuttle paper $6.95. A boy and a girl listen to 30 classic Chinese tales.

5964. Hume, Lotta Carswell. *Favorite Children's Stories from China and Tibet* (3–6). Illus. by Io Koon-Chiu. 1962, Tuttle $13.50. An enjoyable retelling of 19 tales from the East, many with an uncanny resemblance to Western counterparts.

5965. Jagendorf, M. A., and Weng, Virginia. *The Magic Boat and Other Chinese Folk Tales* (4–7). Illus. by Wan-Go Weng. 1980, Vanguard $11.95. A collection of 33 folktales chiefly from the Han-Chinese people.

5966. Kendall, Carol, and Li, Yao-wen. *Sweet and Sour: Tales from China* (5–7). Illus. 1979, Houghton $7.95. A choice collection of some enchanting Chinese folktales.

5967. Lee, Jeanne M., retel. *Legend of the Li River: An Ancient Chinese Tale* (K–3). Illus. by retel. 1983, Holt $11.45. The legend of how rocky hills became the border of the Li River in China.

5968. Lee, Jeanne M., retel. *Legend of the Milky Way* (K–3). Illus. by retel. 1982, Holt $11.50. The Chinese legend of how the stars Vega and Altair were born.

5969. Louie, Ai-Ling, retel. *Yeh-Shen: A Cinderella Story from China* (2–6). Illus. by Ed Young. 1982, Putnam $10.95. A Chinese story about a poor girl living with her cruel stepmother and stepsisters.

5970. Ludwig, Lyndell. *The Shoemaker's Gift: From an Ancient Chinese Folktale* (1–3). Illus. by author. 1983, Creative Arts paper $4.95. A shoemaker makes a wonderful pair of leather boots for his king in this Chinese folktale. Also use: *Ts'ao Chung Weighs an Elephant* (1983, Creative Arts paper $4.95).

5971. Mosel, Arlene. *Tikki Tikki Tembo* (K–2). Illus. by Blair Lent. 1968, Holt $9.70. Explains why the Chinese no longer honor their firstborn with an unusually long name.

5972. Sadler, Catherine Edwards, retel. *Treasure Mountain: Folktales from Southern China* (4–6). Illus. by Cheng Mung Yun. 1982, Atheneum $11.95. A collection of 6 stories from China in which good triumphs over evil.

5973. Wolkstein, Diane. *The Magic Wings: A Tale from China* (K–3). Illus. by Robert Andrew Parker. 1983, Dutton $10.95. A folktale about a group of girls who long to fly in the spring.

5974. Wolkstein, Diane. *White Wave: A Chinese Tale* (3–7). Illus. by Ed Young. 1979, Harper $9.57; LB $9.89. A subdued story of a young boy's encounter with the goddess who promised him supernatural help.

5975. Yolen, Jane. *The Emperor and the Kite* (K–3). Illus. by Ed Young. 1967, Collins $6.99. Unusual, vibrant illustrations using an ancient, intricate Oriental papercut technique enhance this version of the Chinese legend about the unshakable loyalty of the emperor's smallest daughter.

Japan

5976. Bang, Molly. *Dawn* (3–5). 1983, Morrow $9.50. A variation on the Orpheus story via a Japanese tale.

5977. Garrison, Christian. *The Dream Eater* (K–2). Illus. by Diane Goode. 1978, Bradbury $10.95. Yukio meets a creature who eats bad dreams in this Japanese folktale.

5978. Haviland, Virginia, ed. *Favorite Fairy Tales Told in Japan* (3–5). Illus. by George Suyeoka. 1967, Little $7.95. An excellent collection about animals and people, nicely illustrated.

5979. Ike, Jane Hori, and Zimmerman, Baruch. *A Japanese Fairy Tale* (1–4). Illus. by Jane Hori Ike. 1982, Warne $10.95. A Japanese man loses his good looks so that his bride-to-be can be beautiful.

5980. McDermott, Gerald. *The Stone Cutter: A Japanese Folktale* (K–3). Illus. by author. 1975, Viking $12.50; Penguin paper $3.50. The familiar tale of the stone cutter who kept demanding greater power is brilliantly illustrated with colorful, stylized collage paintings.

5981. Mosel, Arlene. *The Funny Little Woman* (PS–4). Illus. by Blair Lent. 1972, Dutton $8.95; paper $3.95. A Japanese folktale about a little woman whose pursuit of a rice dumpling that falls from her table leads to her capture by wicked people.

5982. Newton, Patricia Montgomery. *The Five Sparrows: A Japanese Folktale* (PS–3). Illus. by author. 1982, Atheneum $11.95. An old woman is rewarded for kindness to an injured sparrow.

5983. Stamm, Claus. *Three Strong Women: A Tall Tale from Japan* (3–5). Illus. by Kazue Mizumura. 1962, Penguin paper $2.50. A conceited wrestler meets his match in 3 women.

5984. Uchida, Yoshiko. *Magic Listening Cap: More Folk Tales from Japan* (4–6). Illus. by author. 1983, Harcourt $1.95. Japanese folktales retold with charm and simplicity.

5985. Winthrop, Elizabeth. *Journey to the Bright Kingdom* (3–5). Illus. by Charles Mikolaycak. 1979, Holiday $7.95. A blind woman is granted a look at her daughter in this retelling of a Japanese folktale.

5986. Yagawa, Sumiko, retel. *The Crane Wife* (2–4). Trans. from Japanese by Katherine Paterson. Illus. by Suekichi Akaba. 1981, Morrow $11.25. A farmer marries a beautiful girl who is actually a transformed crane.

5987. Zemach, Kaethe. *The Beautiful Rat* (K–2). Illus. by author. 1979, Four Winds $8.95. A mother rat prods her husband into finding a suitable son-in-law for her daughter.

India

5988. Bang, Betsy. *The Cucumber Stem* (K–2). Illus. by Tony Chen. 1980, Greenwillow $8.50; LB $8.88. A magical boy must marry the rajah's daughter in this Bengali folktale.

5989. Bang, Betsy, tr. and adapt. *The Demons of Rajpur: Five Tales from Bengal* (3–5). Illus. by Molly Bang. 1980, Greenwillow $10.95; LB $10.51. Five stories filled with magic, drama, and adventure.

5990. Bang, Betsy, ed. *The Old Woman and the Rice Thief* (K–3). Illus. by Molly Bang. 1978, Greenwillow $10.95; LB $10.51. An old woman sets out to catch the thief who has stolen her rice in this Bengali tale.

5991. Bang, Betsy. *Tuntuni, the Tailor Bird* (1–3). Illus. by Molly Bang. 1978, Greenwillow $8.50; LB $8.88. Two animal stories based on a Bengali folktale.

5992. Beach, Milo Cleveland. *The Adventures of Rama* (4–6). Illus. 1983, Smithsonian Institution $15.00. Tales from the Hindu epic Ramayana.

5993. Brown, Marcia. *The Blue Jackal* (1–3). Illus. by author. 1977, Scribners paper $2.89. After falling into a vat of indigo dye, a jackal is regarded as king, in this retelling of an East Indian tale.

5994. Brown, Marcia. *Once a Mouse . . . a Fable Cut in Wood* (PS–3). 1961, Scribners $12.95; paper $2.95. A hermit, gifted with magical powers, ponders the idea of big vs. little. Caldecott Medal winner.

5995. Crouch, Marcus. *The Ivory City: And Other Stories from India and Pakistan* (4–6). Illus. by William Stobbs. 1981, Merrimack $11.95. A fine collection of folktales filled with demons, tigers, and lovely princesses.

5996. Duff, Maggie. *Rum Pum Pum: A Folktale from India* (K–2). Illus. by Jose Aruego and Ariane Dewey. 1978, Macmillan $8.95. Blackbird beats his drum and outwits a greedy king.

5997. Galdone, Paul. *The Monkey and the Crocodile: A Jataka Tale from India* (K–3). Illus. by author. 1969, Houghton $7.50. A crocodile decides he will catch a monkey.

5998. Godden, Rumer, retel. *The Valiant Chatti-Maker* (3–5). Illus. by Jeroo Roy. 1983, Viking $9.60. Set in India, this is the story of a potter who becomes an accidental and unwilling hero.

5999. Haviland, Virginia. *Favorite Fairy Tales Told in India* (3–5). Illus. by Blair Lent. 1973, Little $7.95. A fine standard collection of tales from India.

6000. Jacobs, Joseph. *Indian Fairy Tales* (3–6). Illus. by John D. Batten. 1969, Dover paper $4.50. A standard collection by the well-known authority.

6001. Littledale, Freya. *The Magic Plum Tree* (K–3). Illus. by Enrico Arno. 1981, Crown LB $7.95. Three princes who see a plum tree in different seasons disagree about its appearance.

6002. Singh, Jacquelin. *Fat Gopal* (K–3). Illus. by Demi. 1984, Harcourt $12.95. Seemingly impossible tasks are taken on by the court clown, Fat Gopal.

Southeast Asia

6003. Ginsburg, Mirra, ed. *Little Rystu* (4–6). Illus. by Tony Chen. 1978, Greenwillow $11.25;

LB $11.88. A Central Asian tale about an evil Khan who has enslaved some animals.

6004. Vuong, Lynette Dyer. *The Brocaded Slipper and Other Vietnamese Tales* (5–7). Illus. by Vo-Dinh Mai. 1982, Addison LB $9.95. Five Vietnamese fairytales, some of which are similar to our own.

Australia and the Pacific Islands

6005. Aruego, Jose, and Dewey, Ariane. *A Crocodile's Tale: A Philippine Folk Story* (K–2). 1976, Scholastic paper $1.95. A clever humorous story tells how a small boy saves himself from a wily crocodile, whose life he has just saved.

6006. Brown, Marcia. *Backbone of the King: The Story of Paka'a and His Son Ku* (5–7). Illus. by author. 1984, Univ. of Hawaii $12.95. A reissue of the book based on a Hawaiian legend of a boy who wants to help his exiled father.

6007. Galdone, Paul. *The Turtle and the Monkey: A Philippine Tale* (K–2). Illus. by author. 1983, Houghton $11.95. Turtle asks monkey to help him save a banana tree.

6008. Gittins, Anne. *Tales from the South Pacific Islands* (4–6). Illus. by Frank Rocca. 1977, Stemmer $4.95. Twenty-two folktales from such places as Fiji and Samoa in which the sea and its creature play pominent roles.

6009. Williams, Jay. *The Surprising Things Maui Did* (K–3). Illus. by Charles Mikolaycak. 1979, Four Winds $9.95. A retelling of the fantastic exploits of Maui, a god in Hawaiian folklore.

Europe

Great Britain and Ireland

6010. Azarian, Mary, retel. *The Tale of John Barleycorn: Or from Barley to Beer* (3–6). Illus. by retel. 1983, Godine $12.95; paper $6.95. Set in the Middle Ages, this is John Barleycorn's life from barley to beer.

6011. Brooke, L. Leonard. *Golden Goose Book* (1–3). 1977, Warne $7.95. Four favorite folktales are included in this volume, beautifully illustrated.

6012. Brown, Marcia. *Dick Whittington and His Cat* (K–4). Illus. 1950, Scribners $7.95. The familiar story of the boy who went to London to seek his fortune.

6013. Calhoun, Mary. *Jack the Wise and the Cornish Cuckoos* (1–3). 1978, Morrow $9.75; LB $9.36. A series of nonsensical adventures makes Jack the most respected man in town.

6014. Cauley, Lorinda Bryan, retel. *The Cock, the Mouse, and the Little Red Hen* (PS–2). Illus. by retel. 1982, Putnam $9.95; paper $4.95. The Little Red Hen succeeds in spite of her lazy friends.

6015. Cauley, Lorinda Bryan, retel. *Goldilocks and the Three Bears* (PS–2). Illus. by retel. 1981, Putnam $10.95; paper $4.95. A charming retelling of this classic.

6016. Cauley, Lorinda Bryan, retel. *Jack and the Beanstalk* (1–3). Illus. by retel. 1983, Putnam $10.95; paper $4.95. The traditional tale told in a straightforward manner.

6017. Climo, Shirley, retel. *Piskies, Spriggans, and Other Magical Beings: Tales from the Droll-Teller* (2–4). Illus. by Lester Abrams. 1980, Harper $8.95; LB $9.89. A retelling of 9 Cornish folktales.

6018. Colum, Padraic, ed. *A Treasury of Irish Folklore* (6–9). 1969, Crown $14.95. A marvelous collection of traditional Irish tales.

6019. Cooper, Susan, retel. *The Silver Cow: A Welsh Tale* (K–4). Illus. by Warwick Hutton. 1983, Atheneum $11.95. A greedy farmer inherits a silver cow from his son, who received it for his harp playing.

6020. Creswick, Paul. *Robin Hood* (6–8). Illus. by N. C. Wyeth. 1984, Scribners $18.95. A classic edition now reissued.

6021. Crossley-Holland, Kevin, trans. *Beowulf* (6–9). Illus. by Charles Keeping. 1984, Merrimack $11.95. The English epic folktale retold in prose form.

6022. Curley, Daniel. *Billy Beg and the Bull* (4–6). Illus. by Frank Bozzo. 1978, Harper $6.95. Billy Beg performs good works as he wanders the globe in this Irish folktale.

6023. De La Mare, Walter, retel. *Molly Whuppie* (K–3). Illus. by Errol LeCain. 1983, Farrar $10.95. Molly and her 2 sisters are sent into a forest where they encounter a giant.

6024. de Paola, Tomie, retel. *Fin M'Coul: The Giant of Knockmany Hill* (PS–3). Illus. by retel. 1981, Holiday LB $12.95; paper $5.95. Fin's wife saves him from the most feared giant in Ireland.

6025. du Bois, William Pene, retel. *The Three Little Pigs* (PS–1). Illus. by retel. 1962, Viking $7.95; paper $2.50. The old folktale told in verse. Four other recommended editions are: *The Three Little Pigs*, illus. by Paul Galdone (1972, Houghton $9.95); *The Story of the Three Little Pigs*, illus. by Lorinda Bryan Cauley (1980, Putnam $8.95; paper $3.95); *The Three Little Pigs*, illus. by Rodney Peppe (1980, Lothrop $10.95; LB $9.36); *The Three Little*

Pigs, illus. by Erik Blegvad (1980, Atheneum $8.95).

6026. Elkin, Benjamin. *Six Foolish Fishermen* (K–3). Illus. by Bernice Myers. n.d., Scholastic paper $1.50. A folktale about 6 fishermen and their counting dilemma.

6027. Francois, Andre, illus. *Jack and the Beanstalk: English Fairy Tale* (3–6). 1983, Childrens Book Co. $9.95. For an older audience, this is a faithful version of the original. Another recommended edition is: *Jack and the Beanstalk,* illus. by Tony Ross (1981, Delacorte $8.95; LB $8.44).

6028. Gackenbach, Dick, retel. *Arabella and Mr. Crack: An Old English Tale* (K–3). Illus. by retel. 1982, Macmillan $8.95. Arabella must learn Mr. Crack's strange vocabulary.

6029. Galdone, Paul. *The Gingerbread Boy* (PS–1). Illus. by author. 1983, Houghton paper $3.95. Humorous and vigorous illustrations enhance this favorite folktale of the adventures of a runaway gingerbread boy.

6030. Galdone, Paul. *Henny Penny* (K–2). Illus. by author. 1968, Houghton $10.95; paper $4.95. A retelling of the favorite cumulative folktale of the hen who thought the sky was falling.

6031. Galdone, Paul. *King of the Cats: A Ghost Story by Joseph Jacobs* (K–2). Illus. by author. 1980, Houghton $9.95. A grave digger relates a strange story to his wife and pet cat, Tom.

6032. Galdone, Paul. *The Little Red Hen* (K–2). Illus. by author. 1973, Houghton $9.95. A little hen works for her lazy housemates in this reworking of the old tale. Another fine edition is: *The Little Red Hen: An Old Story* by Margot Zemach (1983, Farrar $10.95).

6033. Galdone, Paul. *The Three Bears* (K–2). Illus. by author. 1972, Scholastic paper $1.95. The illustrations for this familiar story are large, colorful, and humorous; excellent to use with a group.

6034. Galdone, Paul. *The Three Sillies* (PS–3). Illus. by author. 1981, Houghton $9.95. A nonsense story that is full of fun.

6035. Galdone, Paul. *What's in Fox's Sack?* (K–2). Illus. by author. 1982, Houghton $9.95. A sly fox gets its comeuppance.

6036. Gammell, Stephen, retel. *The Story of Mr. and Mrs. Vinegar* (PS–2). Illus. by retel. 1982, Lothrop $10.00; LB $10.88. Mr. Vinegar trades a crock of gold for a walking stick.

6037. Green, Roger L. *Adventures of Robin Hood* (4–6). 1956, Penguin paper $2.95. A classic retelling of stories involving Robin and his merry men.

6038. Green, Roger L. *King Arthur and His Knights of the Round Table* (5–7). 1974, Penguin paper $2.95. The famous deeds of this worthy King and his Knights.

6039. Guard, David. *Dierdre: A Celtic Legend* (5–8). Illus. by Gretchen Guard. 1977, Celestial Arts $9.95. A Druid correctly foretold at Dierdre's birth that her beauty would bring only death and destruction.

6040. Harper, Wilhelmina. *The Gunniwolf* (K–2). Illus. by William Wiesner. 1967, Dutton $9.95. A variation on an old folktale of the little girl who wandered into the jungle searching for flowers when suddenly up rose the fierce gunniwolf.

6041. Hastings, Selina. *Sir Gawain and the Green Knight* (3–7). Illus. by Juan Wijngaard. 1981, Lothrop $11.25. A nicely illustrated retelling of the Arthurian legend.

6042. Haviland, Virginia, ed. *Favorite Fairy Tales Told in Scotland* (3–5). Illus. by Adrienne Adams. 1963, Little $6.95. A beautifully illustrated collection of some of the Scottish folk and fairy tales.

6043. Hodges, Margaret. *St. George and the Dragon: A Golden Legend* (2–5). Illus. by Trina S. Hyman. 1984, Little $13.45. A reworking of the English tale as it appeared in Edmund Spensor's *Fairie Queen.* Caldecott Medal winner, 1984.

6044. Jacobs, Joseph. *Celtic Fairy Tales* (3–6). Illus. by John D. Batten. 1968, Dover paper $4.50. A classic collection. Followed by: *More Celtic Fairy Tales* (1969, paper $3.95).

6045. Jacobs, Joseph. *English Fairy Tales* (1–3). Illus. by John D. Batten. 1969, Dover paper $4.50. A standard collection by a master storyteller.

6046. Lobel, Anita. *The Pancake* (2–3). Illus. by author. 1978, Greenwillow $8.25. The familiar tale of how a pancake escapes being eaten.

6047. Mayer, Marianna. *The Black Horse* (2–4). Illus. by Katie Thamer. 1984, Dial $10.63; LB $10.89. A king's son rescues a princess with the help of a magic horse.

6048. Pyle, Howard. *Some Merry Adventures of Robin Hood* (5–8). Illus. by author. 1967, Watts $20.00. Stories about Robin Hood and the inhabitants of Sherwood Forest.

6049. Pyle, Howard, ed. *The Story of King Arthur and His Knights* (6–9). Illus. by ed. 1984, Scribners $14.95. One of the most famous editions of these classic stories. A sequel is: *The Story of the Champions of the Round Table* (1984, $14.95).

6050. Reeves, James. *English Fables and Fairy Stories* (3–6). 1954, Oxford $14.95. Nineteen beautiful retellings of such standard English tales as "Jack and the Beanstalk."

6051. Riordan, James. *Tales of King Arthur* (5–9). Illus. by Victor G. Ambrus. 1982, Rand McNally $11.95. A spirited retelling of the Arthurian legend.

6052. Robbins, Ruth, ed. *Taliesin and King Arthur* (3–6). Illus. 1970, Parnassus $4.75; LB $4.59. How Taliesin, a poet of Welsh legend, delighted King Arthur with his songs and stories.

6053. Seuling, Barbara. *The Teeny Tiny Woman: An Old English Ghost Tale* (K–3). Illus. by author. 1976, Viking LB $11.50; Penguin paper $2.95. A picture book version of the classic story about the little woman and her soup bone. Another edition is: *The Teeny-Tiny Woman* illus. by Paul Galdone (1984, Houghton $11.95).

6054. Steel, Flora Annie. *Tattercoats: An Old English Tale* (K–3). Illus. by Diane Goode. 1976, Bradbury $10.95. An English folktale reminiscent of the Cinderella theme, beautifully illustrated in full-color paintings.

6055. Sutcliff, Rosemary. *The High Deeds of Finn McCool* (1–4). Illus. by Michael Charlton. 1976, Penguin paper $2.95. Fourteen tales featuring the exploits of Finn, the legendary Irish hero.

6056. Sutcliff, Rosemary. *The Light beyond the Forest: The Quest for the Holy Grail* (4–7). 1980, Dutton $10.95. An imaginative retelling of the quest of Sir Galahad and other Knights for the Holy Grail. Two sequels are: *The Sword and the Circle: King Arthur and the Knights of the Round Table* (1981, $12.50); *The Road to Camlann: The Death of King Arthur* (1982, $11.50).

6057. Wahl, Jan. *Needle and Noodle and Other Silly Stories* (PS–1). Illus. by Stan Mack. 1979, Pantheon $6.99. Six nonsense stories based on old English folktales.

6058. Wetterer, Margaret K. *The Mermaid's Cape* (2–4). Illus. by Elise Primavera. 1981, Atheneum $8.95. The Irish folktale of the capture of a mermaid and its consequences.

6059. Wetterer, Margaret K. *Patrick and the Fairy Thief* (1–3). Illus. by Enrico Arno. 1980, Atheneum $7.95. Patrick breaks the spell that has kept his mother a prisoner of the leprechauns.

6060. Wright, Freire, and Foreman, Michael. *Seven in One Blow* (K–2). Illus. by Michael Foreman. 1981, Random LB $4.99; paper $1.25. The humorous account of a little tailor and his encounter with 7 giants.

6061. Zemach, Harve. *Duffy and the Devil: A Cornish Tale Retold* (1–3). Illus. by Margot Zemach. 1973, Farrar $10.95. A variant of "Rumpelstiltskin," this folktale is told with humor and verve and boldly illustrated. Caldecott Medal, 1974.

Spain and Portugal

6062. Davis, Robert. *Padre Porko: The Gentlemanly Pig* (4–6). Illus. by Fritz Eichenberg. 1948, Holiday $6.95. Eleven Spanish stories about a surprisingly wise pig who helps many creatures in trouble.

6063. Duff, Maggie, adapt. *The Princess and the Pumpkin: Adapted from a Majorca Tale* (PS–3). Illus. by Catherine Stock. 1980, Macmillan LB $9.95. Will anyone be able to make the sad Princess laugh again?

France

6064. Berson, Harold, adapt. *Charles and Claudine* (1–4). Illus. by adapt. 1980, Macmillan $9.95. An angry witch turns Claudine into a frog.

6065. Brown, Marcia. *Stone Soup* (1–4). Illus. by author. 1982, Scribners $11.95; paper $3.95. An old French tale about 3 soldiers who make soup from stones.

6066. Carlson, Natalie Savage. *King of the Cats and Other Tales* (2–6). Illus. by David Frampton. 1980, Doubleday LB $7.95. Eight short stories inspired by the folklore of Brittany.

6067. Harris, Rosemary. *Beauty and the Beast* (3–5). Illus. by Errol LeCain. 1980, Doubleday LB $7.95. A concise retelling made memorable by dazzling pictures. Two other versions are: *Beauty and the Beast* by Marianna Mayer, illus. by Mercer Mayer (1978, Four Winds $10.95); *Beauty and the Beast* by Deborah Apy, illus. by Michael Hague (1983, Holt $12.95).

6068. Holman, Felice, and Valen, Nanine. *The Drac: French Tales of Dragons and Demons* (4–6). Illus. by Stephen Walker. 1975, Scribners paper $1.29. Five fearsome, fanciful fables from French folklore.

6069. La Fontaine, Jean de. *The Miller, the Boy, and the Donkey* (K–3). Illus. by Brian Wildsmith. Oxford paper $7.95. This is Brian Wildsmith's version of the fable about a Miller trying to get his donkey to market. Also use: *The Rich Man and the Shoemaker* (1965, Oxford paper $6.95).

6070. Perrault, Charles. *Cinderella* (PS–2). Illus. by Paul Galdone. 1978, McGraw $10.95. An action-filled, lighthearted retelling of this classic. Other recommended editions are: *Cinderella*, illus. by Errol LeCain (1977, Penguin paper $3.95); *Cinderella: Or, the Little Glass Slipper*, illus. by Marcia Brown (1982, Scribners paper $2.95); *Cinderella*, illus. by Roberto Innocenti (1984, Childrens Book Co. $9.95).

6071. Perrault, Charles. *The Glass Slipper: Charles Perrault's Tales of Times Past* (4–7). Illus. by Mitchell

Miller. 1981, Four Winds $14.95. A new translation of tales by Perrault including *Little Red Riding Hood* and *The Sleeping Beauty*.

6072. Perrault, Charles. *Perrault's Complete Fairy Tales* (4–6). Illus. by Heath Robinson. 1982, Dodd paper $5.95. Fourteen tales in an excellent translation from the French.

6073. Perrault, Charles. *Perrault's Fairy Tales* (4–6). Illus. by Gustave Dore. 1969, Dover paper $4.00. A classic edition with illustrations by the French master.

6074. Perrault, Charles. *Puss in Boots* (K–3). Illus. by Marcia Brown. 1952, Scribners $8.95. A favorite French folktale. Another edition is: *Puss in Boots*, illus. by Paul Galdone (1976, Houghton $7.95; paper $3.95).

6075. Perrault, Charles. *Sleeping Beauty and Other Favourite Fairy Tales* (4–6). Illus. by Michael Foreman. 1984, Schocken $12.95. Ten tales that could be used with older children. Another edition is: *The Sleeping Beauty*, illus. by Warren Chappell (1982, Schocken paper $5.95).

6076. Perrault, Charles. *Sleeping Beauty in the Woods* (4–6). Illus. by John Collier. 1984, Childrens Book Co. $9.95. A new edition of this favorite story.

6077. Perrault, Charles. *Tom Thumb: A Tale* (K–3). Retold by Lidia Postma. Illus. by retel. 1983, Schocken $10.95. The French tale of the small boy who saves his brothers.

6078. Plante, Patricia, and Bergman, David. *The Turtle and the Two Ducks: Animal Fables Retold from La Fontaine* (K–3). Illus. by Anne Rockwell. 1981, Harper $9.13; LB $8.89. A retelling of 11 short fables.

6079. Rockwell, Anne. *Poor Goose: A French Folktale* (K–3). Illus. by author. 1976, Harper $10.53; LB $10.89. A cumulative story about a goose's travels in search of peppermint tea to relieve her headache.

6080. Scribner, Charles, Jr. *The Devil's Bridge* (2–4). Illus. by Evaline Ness. 1978, Scribners $7.95. A French folktale about a bridge where one must forfeit one's soul to cross.

6081. Sewall, Marcia. *The Cobbler's Song: A Fable* (2–4). Illus. by author. 1982, Dutton $8.95. A cobbler finds that the gift of wealth makes him unhappy.

Germany

6082. Grimm Brothers. *The Bear and the Kingbird: A Tale from the Brothers Grimm* (K–3). Trans. by Lore Segal. Illus. by Chris Conover. 1979, Farrar $8.95.

Animals of the sky vs. those of the earth and sea, in a battle with amazing consequences.

6083. Grimm Brothers. *The Best of Grimm's Fairy Tales* (K–3). Trans. by Anthea Bell and Anne Rogers. Illus. by Svend Otto S. 1979, Larousse LB $10.95. A collection made noteworthy by its full-color illustrations. Another recommended edition is: *Favorite Tales from Grimm*, illus. by Mercer Mayer (1982, Four Winds $15.95).

6084. Grimm Brothers. *The Brave Little Tailor* (1–3). Adapt. and illus. by Robert San Souci. 1982, Doubleday $10.95. The boastful tailor is reborn.

6085. Grimm Brothers. *The Bremen Town Musicians* (K–4). Trans. by Elizabeth Shub. Illus. by Janina Domanska. 1980, Greenwillow $11.25; LB $11.89. Four animals frighten away robbers. Another version is: *The Bremen Town Musicians*, illus. by Ilse Plume (1980, Doubleday $10.95).

6086. Grimm Brothers. *Cinderella* (1–3). Retold and illus. by Nonny Hogrogian. 1981, Greenwillow $10.25; LB $10.88. Excellent illustrations highlight this edition.

6087. Grimm Brothers. *The Complete Grimm's Fairy Tales* (4–6). Illus. by Josef Scharl. 1974, Pantheon $17.50; paper $6.95. Based on Margaret Hunt's translation, this has become the standard edition of these perennial favorites.

6088. Grimm Brothers. *The Devil with the Three Golden Hairs* (K–5). Illus. by Nonny Hogrogian. 1983, Knopf $10.95; LB $10.99. In order to keep his princess bride, a young man must collect 3 golden hairs from the devil's head.

6089. Grimm Brothers. *The Elves and the Shoemaker* (PS–K). Retold and illus. by Paul Galdone. 1984, Houghton $11.95. A poor shoemaker is visited by elves at night. Another edition is: *The Elves and the Shoemaker*, illus. by Brinton Turkle (1975, Four Winds $5.95; Scholastic paper $2.50).

6090. Grimm Brothers. *The Fisherman and His Wife* (2–3). Trans. by Randall Jarrell. Illus. by Margot Zemach. 1980, Farrar $10.95. This classic story of the effects of greed on 2 people is superbly told.

6091. Grimm Brothers. *The Frog Prince and Other Stories* (4–6). Illus. by Walter Crane. 1981, Smith $10.95. Several famous tales illustrated by a master.

6092. Grimm Brothers. *Hans in Luck* (PS–1). Illus. by Paul Galdone. 1980, Parents $4.95; LB $5.95. A retelling of the well-loved story.

6093. Grimm Brothers. *Hansel and Gretel* (3–5). Trans. by Charles Scribner. Illus. by Adrienne Adams. 1975, Scribners LB $6.95; paper $2.95. Handsomely complemented by atmospheric paintings. Other recommended editions of *Hansel and Gretel* are: Illus. by Lisbeth Zwerger (1980, Morrow LB $10.95; Neugebauer paper $7.50); illus. by Susan Jeffers (1980, Dial $12.95; LB $12.89); illus. by Anthony Browne (1982, Watts LB $8.95); illus. by Paul Galdone (1982, McGraw $11.95); illus. by Monique Felix (1984, Childrens Book Co. $9.95); illus. by Otto S. Svend (1984, Larousse $8.95); illus. by Paul O. Zelinsky (1984, Dodd $12.95).

6094. Grimm Brothers. *Jorinda and Joringel* (2–3). Ed. by Wanda Gag. Illus. by Margot Tomes. 1978, Putnam $6.95. A maid is changed into a nightingale in this classic retelling of the familiar folktale.

6095. Grimm Brothers. *The Juniper Tree and Other Tales from Grimm* (4–8). Sel. and trans. by Lore Segal. Illus. by Maurice Sendak. 1973, Farrar paper $4.95. A 2-volume cornucopia of stories—popular and lesser known—with 4 additional stories translated by Randall Jarrell. Another recommended edition is: *Rare Treasures from Grimm: Fifteen Little-Known Tales*, illus. by Erik Blegvad (1981, Doubleday $12.95; LB $13.90).

6096. Grimm Brothers. *King Grisly-Beard* (K–3). Illus. by Maurice Sendak. 1978, Penguin paper $2.95. Lovely humorous pictures make this a delightful picture book version of the folktale.

6097. Grimm Brothers. *Little Brother and Little Sister* (K–3). Illus. by Barbara Cooney. 1982, Doubleday $10.95. A sister's caring for her child and her brother brings her back the gift of life.

6098. Grimm Brothers. *Little Red Cap* (K–4). Illus. by Lisbeth Zwerger. 1983, Morrow $9.50; LB $9.59. A fine retelling of this classic story.

6099. Grimm Brothers. *Little Red Riding Hood* (K–2). Illus. by Paul Galdone. 1974, McGraw $12.95; LB $10.95. A retelling of the favorite tale about a little girl and her encounter with a wolf. Another fine version is: *Little Red Riding Hood*, retold and illus. by Trina S. Hyman (1983, Holiday $13.95).

6100. Grimm Brothers. *Mrs. Fox's Wedding* (PS–2). Retold by Sara Corrin and Stephen Corrin. Illus. by Errol LeCain. 1980, Penguin paper $2.95. Loosely based on 2 Grimm tales, this is the story of Mrs. Fox's search for a second husband.

6101. Grimm Brothers. *Nibble Nibble Mousekin* (K–3). Illus. by Joan Walsh Anglund. 1977, Harcourt paper $4.95. A version of the *Hansel and Gretel* story.

6102. Grimm Brothers. *Rapunzel* (1–4). Illus. by Trina S. Hyman (1982, Holiday $12.95. The famous tale of the captive princess and her fabulous hair. Another version is: *Rapunzel*, illus. by Michael Hague (1984, Childrens Book Co. $9.95).

6103. Grimm Brothers. *Rumpelstiltskin* (PS–2). Illus. by Donna Diamond. 1983, Holiday $9.95. A fine retelling of this favorite German tale. Another fine version is: *Rumpelstiltskin*, illus. by John Wallner (1984, Prentice $10.95).

6104. Grimm Brothers. *The Seven Ravens* (K–3). Trans. by Elizabeth D. Crawford. Illus. by Lisbeth Zwerger. 1981, Morrow $11.25; LB $10.89; Neugebauer paper $7.95. In this classic, a girl's brothers are turned to ravens when she is born.

6105. Grimm Brothers. *The Shoemaker and the Elves* (K–2). Illus. by Adrienne Adams. 1982, Scribners $11.95; paper $2.95. A favorite German tale illustrated with soft watercolors. One other edition is: *The Shoemaker and the Elves*, illus. by Cynthia Birrer and William Birrer (1983, Lothrop $11.25; LB $11.88).

6106. Grimm Brothers. *The Sleeping Beauty* (K–2). Illus. by Warwick Hutton. 1979, Atheneum $9.95. A handsome understated version of this story. Two other fine editions are: *The Sleeping Beauty*, illus. by Trina S. Hyman (1977, Little $10.95); *The Sleeping Beauty*, retold and illus. by Mercer Mayer (1984, Macmillan $14.95).

6107. Grimm Brothers. *Snow White and Rose Red* (K–3). Illus. by John Wallner. 1984, Prentice $10.95. The story of 2 sisters and a brown bear, who is a prince under a spell. Two other editions of *Snow White and Rose Red* are: Illus. by Adrienne Adams (1964, Scribners $5.95); illus. by Roland Topor (1984, Childrens Book Co. $9.95).

6108. Grimm Brothers. *Snow White and the Seven Dwarfs* (1–4). Trans. and illus. by Wanda Gag. 1938, Putnam LB $6.99. The famous story of caring dwarfs and their lovely charge. Two other versions are: *Snow White and the Seven Dwarfs*, illus. by Nancy Ekholm Burkert (1972, Farrar $8.95); *Snow White and the Seven Dwarfs*, illus. by Susan Jeffers (1981, Four Winds LB $9.95).

6109. Grimm Brothers. *The Sorcerer's Apprentice* (3–5). Ed. by Wanda Gag. Illus. by Margot Tomes. 1979, Putnam $6.95. A newly illustrated version of the classic story from the Grimm Brothers.

6110. Grimm Brothers. *Thorn Rose or the Sleeping Beauty* (K–3). Illus. by Errol LeCain. 1977, Bradbury $8.95. Illustrations that resemble medieval tapestries enhance this classic tale.

6111. Grimm Brothers. *The Three Feathers* (5–8). Illus. by Eleanore Schmid. 1984, Childrens Book Co. $9.95. A version for older readers that is faithful to the original.

6112. Grimm Brothers. *The Twelve Dancing Princesses* (4–6). Illus. by Errol LeCain. 1978, Viking $12.50; Penguin paper $2.95. A handsomely illustrated and richly told version of this classic tale.

Another edition is: *The Twelve Dancing Princesses,* illus. by Adrienne Adams (1980, Holt paper $2.95).

6113. Grimm Brothers. *Wanda Gag's The Six Swans* (2–4). Illus. by Margot Tomes. 1982, Putnam $8.95. A young princess tries to free her brothers, who have been placed under a spell.

6114. Hoffman, E. T. A. *The Nutcracker* (5–6). Adapt. by Alexandre Dumas. Trans. by Douglas Monro. Illus. by Phillida Gili. 1978, Oxford $12.95. The retelling of the Hoffman story. Other versions are: *The Nutcracker,* illus. by Kay Chorao (1979, Dutton $6.95); *The Nutcracker,* illus. by Rachel Isadora (1982, Macmillan $11.95).

6115. Hoffman, E. T. A. *The Nutcracker* (4–6). Illus. by Maurice Sendak. 1984, Crown $19.95. A brilliant, new rendition of this favorite story.

6116. Hoffman, E. T. A. *The Nutcracker and the Mouse King* (3–6). Trans. by Anthea Bell. Illus. by Lisbeth Zwerger. 1983, Neugebauer $12.95. The story on which the famous ballet was based.

6117. Hoffman, E. T. A. *The Strange Child* (3–5). Adapt. by Anthea Bell. Illus. by Lisbeth Zwerger. 1984, Neugebauer $12.95. A reworking of the Hoffman story of 2 children who fall under magic spells.

6118. Hutton, Warwick, adapt. *The Nose Tree* (1–4). Illus. by adapt. 1981, Atheneum $11.95. A princess gets her comeuppance after tricking some soldiers out of their possessions.

6119. Jagendorf, M. A. *Tyll Ulenspiegel's Merry Pranks* (4–6). Illus. by Fritz Eichenberg. 1938, Vanguard $8.95. Thirty-seven stories of the irrepressible hero of German folklore.

6120. Koenig, Alma Johanna. *Gudrun* (6–9). 1979, Lothrop $11.88; LB $10.80. A thirteenth-century German epic of medieval derring-do.

6121. Rockwell, Anne. *The Old Woman and Her Pig and Ten Other Stories* (PS–1). Illus. by author. 1979, Harper $10.95; LB $10.89. A collection of some favorite folktales.

Scandinavia

6122. Asbjornsen, Peter C. *East of the Sun and West of the Moon* (4–6). Retold by Kathleen Hague and Michael Hague. Illus. by Michael Hague. 1980, Harcourt $9.95; paper $4.95. A poor farmer gives his daughter to a strange white bear in this Norwegian folktale. Another recommended edition is: *East of the Sun and West of the Moon,* illus. by Mercer Mayer (1980, Four Winds $12.95).

6123. Asbjornsen, Peter C., and Moe, Jorgen. *Norwegian Folk Tales* (3–6). Illus. by Erik Werenski-old and Theodor Kittelsen. 1978, Vanous $20.00.

This edition retains the original illustrations from the 1845 edition.

6124. Asbjornsen, Peter C., and Moe, Jorgen. *The Squire's Bride* (3–5). Illus. by Marcia Sewall. 1975, Atheneum $6.95. A wily peasant girl outwits a squire intent on marrying her in this retelling of a classic Norwegian folktale.

6125. Asbjornsen, Peter C., and Moe, Jorgen. *The Three Billy Goats Gruff* (PS–1). Illus. by Marcia Brown. 1957, Harcourt $10.95. A troll meets his match. Two other recommended editions of *The Three Billy Goats Gruff* are: Illus. by Paul Galdone (1973, Houghton $8.95; paper $3.45); and illus. by Susan Blair (1970, Scholastic paper $1.50).

6126. Barth, Edna. *Balder and the Mistletoe: A Story for the Winter Holidays* (4–6). Illus. by Richard Cuffari. 1979, Houghton $10.95. A masterful retelling of the Norse legend of the death of Balder by the cunning of Loki.

6127. Crossley-Holland, Kevin, ed. *The Faber Book of Northern Folktales* (5–7). Illus. by Alan Howard. 1981, Faber $11.95; paper $5.95. A collection of 35 tales from 11 Northern European cultures. Also use: *Faber Book of Northern Legends* (1979, Faber, $11.95; paper $5.95).

6128. D'Aulaire, Ingri, and D'Aulaire, Edgar. *D'Aulaires' Trolls* (3–5). Illus. by author. 1972, Doubleday $8.95; paper $2.95. The many types and activities of trolls are described along with several troll stories—served up by 2 master artists.

6129. D'Aulaire, Ingri, and D'Aulaire, Edgar. *The Terrible Troll Bird* (K–3). Illus. by author. 1976, Doubleday $8.95. A new edition of the 1933 picture book.

6130. Gross, Ruth Belov. *The Girl Who Wouldn't Get Married* (K–2). Illus. by Jack Kent. 1983, Four Winds $9.95. A girl who doesn't want to get married sends a horse in her place.

6131. Hague, Kathleen, and Hague, Michael. *The Man Who Kept House* (PS–6). Illus. by author. 1981, Harcourt $12.95; paper $5.95. In this folktale from Norway, a farmer and his wife exchange places.

6132. Lundbergh, Holder, trans. *Great Swedish Fairy Tales* (4–6). Illus. by John Bauer. 1973, Delacorte paper $10.95. A collection of enchanting stories in which various sorts of trolls play important roles.

6133. McGovern, Ann. *Half a Kingdom: An Icelandic Folktale* (K–3). Illus. by Nola Langner. 1977, Scholastic paper $1.75. A poor peasant girl rescues a noble prince in this unusual folktale.

Greece and Italy

6134. Aesop. *Aesop's Fables* (3–Up). Illus. by Heidi Holder. 1981, Viking $13.50. A fine new edition of this classic.

6135. Aesop. *The Caldecott Aesop: Twenty Fables* (6–9). Intro. by Michael Patrick Hearn. Illus. by Randolph Caldecott. 1978, Doubleday $12.95. A classic edition worthy of rescuing through facsimile printing.

6136. Aesop. *The Exploding Frog and Other Fables from Aesop* (4–6). Retold by John McFarland. Illus. by James Marshall. 1981, Little $11.95; paper $6.95. A modern retelling of these fables.

6137. Aesop. *Fables of Aesop* (4–6). Ed. by Joseph Jacobs. Illus. by David Levine. 1966, Macmillan $8.95; Schocken paper $4.95. One of many recommended editions of this classic.

6138. Aesop. *The Hare and the Tortoise* (K–3). Illus. by Paul Galdone. 1962, McGraw LB $12.95. A picture book retelling of one of the classic races of all time—between the hare and the tortoise— with an outcome that surprised even the hare. Also use: *Three Aesop Fox Fables* (1971, Houghton $10.95).

6139. Aesop. *Once in a Wood* (1–3). Illus. by Eve Rice. 1979, Greenwillow $8.50; LB $8.88. Ten tales from Aesop cleverly retold for beginning readers.

6140. Aesop. *The Tortoise and the Hare: An Aesop Fable* (PS–K). Illus. by Janet Stevens. 1984, Holiday $12.95. An updated charming retelling of the classic fable.

6141. Aesop. *The Town Mouse and the Country Mouse* (PS–1). Illus. by Lorinda Bryan Cauley. 1984, Putnam $11.95; paper $4.95. The classic story faithfully and entertainingly retold.

6142. Aliki. *The Twelve Months: A Greek Folktale* (K–3). Illus. 1978, Greenwillow $10.95. Twelve gifts suitably humble a greedy woman.

6143. Basile, Giambattista. *Petrosinella: A Neapolitan-Rapunzel* (2–5). Illus. by Diane Stanley. 1981, Warne $11.95. A Rapunzel-like story that originated in Italy.

6144. Cauley, Lorinda Bryan, retel. *The Goose and the Golden Coins* (K–3). Illus. by retel. 1981, Harcourt paper $5.95. Two maidens befriend a goose who lays gold coins.

6145. de Paola, Tomie. *The Mysterious Giant of Barletta: An Italian Folktale*. Illus. by author. 1984, Harcourt $12.95. A statue of an old lady saves the town from marauders.

6146. de Paola, Tomie. *The Prince of the Dolomites* (5–8). Illus. by author. 1980, Harcourt $8.95; paper $4.50. An Italian folktale about the winning of a moon princess.

6147. Haviland, Virginia, ed. *Favorite Fairy Tales Told in Greece* (3–6). Illus. by Nonny Hogrogian. 1970, Little $6.95. A delightful collection with most unusual characters.

6148. Haviland, Virginia. *Favorite Fairy Tales Told in Italy* (4–6). Illus. by Evaline Ness. 1965, Little $6.95. A varied collection, charmingly illustrated.

6149. Jagendorf, M. A. *The Priceless Cats and Other Italian Folk Stories* (4–6). Illus. by Gioia Fiammenghi. 1956, Vanguard $7.95. Retellings of old Italian lore.

6150. Zemach, Harve. *Awake and Dreaming* (PS–3). Illus. by Margot Zemach. 1970, Farrar $8.95. A Tuscan legend of a man who has nightmares and makes a bargain with the King of the Land of Pleasant Dreams.

Central and Eastern Europe

6151. Bawden, Nina. *William Tell* (2–4). Illus. by Pascale Allamand. 1981, Lothrop $11.25; LB $11.88. A retelling of the Swiss folktale of Tell's defiance of cruel Gessler.

6152. Domanska, Janina. *King Krakus and the Dragon* (K–3). Illus. by author. 1979, Greenwillow $12.50; LB $12.88. A Polish folktale that tells how a young apprentice slays a fierce dragon.

6153. Gag, Wanda. *Gone Is Gone: Or, the Story of a Man Who Wanted to Do Housework* (K–3). Illus. by author. 1935, Putnam $5.95. An old Bohemian tale about the problems that confront a bumbling man when he is overconfident about his abilities as a housekeeper.

6154. Galdone, Joanna. *The Little Girl and the Big Bear* (PS–2). Illus. by Paul Galdone. 1980, Houghton $8.95. A lost girl seeks refuge in a hut where a bear lives.

6155. Galdone, Paul. *The Amazing Pig: An Old Hungarian Tale* (K–3). Illus. by author. 1981, Houghton $8.95. A king promises his daughter to the man who can tell an unbelievable story.

6156. Reid, Barbara, and Reid, Eva. *The Cobbler's Reward* (K–3). Illus. by Charles Mikolaycak. 1978, Macmillan $9.95. Janek, a cobbler, tries to rescue a maiden held prisoner by a witch in this Polish folktale.

6157. Seredy, Kate. *The White Stag* (5–9). Illus. by author. 1937, Viking $10.95; Penguin paper $3.50. A legendary account of the westward migration of the Hungarians to new lands. Newbery medal 1938.

6158. Severo, Emoke de Papp, trans. *The Good-Hearted Youngest Brother: An Hungarian Folktale* (2–5). Illus. by Diane Goode. 1981, Bradbury

$10.95. Through kindness, a young man breaks a wicked enchantment.

6159. Wood, Ruzena. *The Palace of the Moon and Other Tales from Czechoslovakia* (4–6). Illus. by Krystyna Turska. 1981, Andre Deutsch $9.95. A collection of tales, many good for storytelling.

Russia

6160. Afanasyev, Alexander, ed. *Russian Fairy Tales* (4–7). Illus. by Alexander Alexeieff. 1975, Pantheon $14.95; paper $6.95. The definitive collection of folktales reissued in the 1945 edition. Also use by the same compiler: *Russian Folk Tales* (1980, Random $14.95).

6161. Afanasyev, Alexander. *Soldier and Tsar in the Forest: A Russian Tale* (K–3). Trans. by Richard Lourie. Illus. by Uri Shulevitz. 1972, Farrar $8.95. Handsome, brilliant illustrations accompany this story of a soldier who saves the tsar's life and is rewarded by being made a general.

6162. Aiken, Joan. *The Kingdom under the Sea and Other Stories* (5–7). Illus. by Jan Pienkowski. 1979, Merrimack $12.95. A retelling of 11 magical folktales from Eastern Europe.

6163. Bider, Djemma. *The Buried Treasure* (K–3). Illus. by Debby L. Carter. 1982, Dodd $10.95. A father tricks his lazy sons into becoming fine gardeners.

6164. Carey, Bonnie, trans. *Grasshopper to the Rescue: A Georgian Story* (1–3). Illus. by Lady McCrady. 1979, Morrow $9.25; LB $8.88. An ant falls in the water and the grasshopper sets up a rescue operation in this Russian tale.

6165. Cohen, Barbara. *The Demon Who Would Not Die* (3–5). Illus. by Anatoly Ivanov. 1982, Atheneum $11.95. A man loses his girlfriend because a demon wants her for himself.

6166. Cole, Joanna. *Bony-Legs* (1–4). Illus. by Dirk Zimmer. 1983, Four Winds $8.95. A simply read story based on the Russian Baba Yaga.

6167. De Regniers, Beatrice S. *Little Sister and the Month Brothers* (K–3). Illus. by Margot Tomes. 1976, Houghton $8.95. A delightful retelling of an old Slavic tale reminiscent of the Cinderella theme.

6168. Domanska, Janina, retel. *Marek, the Little Fool* (PS–2). Illus. by retel. 1982, Greenwillow $11.25; LB $11.88. Marek is unable to do anything right.

6169. Domanska, Janina. *A Scythe, a Rooster, and a Cat* (1–4). Illus. by author. 1981, Greenwillow $11.25; LB $11.88. A folktale about the 3 sons of a peasant, who each receive part of his worldly goods.

6170. Ginsburg, Mirra, ed. *The Fisherman's Son: Adapted from a Georgian Folktale* (1–3). Illus. by Tony Chen. 1979, Greenwillow $12.25; LB $11.88. A fisherman's son wins the hand of his love by avoiding her magical mirror in this Georgian tale.

6171. Ginsburg, Mirra. *Good Morning, Chick* (PS–K). Illus. by Byron Barton. 1980, Greenwillow $10.95; LB $10.51; Scholastic paper $1.95. A Russian folktale about a chick who must learn his identity.

6172. Ginsburg, Mirra. *The Magic Stove* (K–3). Illus. by Linda Heller. 1983, Putnam $10.95. A king takes a magic pie-making stove from an old man and woman.

6173. Ginsburg, Mirra. *The Night It Rained Pancakes* (K–2). Illus. by Douglas Florian. 1980, Greenwillow $8.25; LB $7.92. Ivan tries to make his brother look like a fool in order to retain a pot of gold.

6174. Ginsburg, Mirra. *The Strongest One of All* (K–3). Illus. by Jose Aruego and Ariane Dewey. 1977, Greenwillow LB $10.80. A little lamb sets out to find "the strongest one of all" in this story based on a Caucasian folktale.

6175. Ginsburg, Mirra. *The Twelve Clever Brothers and Other Fools* (3–5). Illus. by Charles Mikolaycak. 1979, Harper LB $10.89. Russian tales of absurd, nonsensical situations and characters.

6176. Hall, Amanda. *The Gossipy Wife: Adapted from a Russian Folk Tale* (K–2). Illus. 1984, Harper $10.45. Can Ivan prevent his wife from telling the story of their good fortune?

6177. Hogrogian, Nonny. *The Contest* (3–5). Illus. by author. 1976, Greenwillow $11.47. Adaptation of the folktale about 2 robbers who discover that they are engaged to the same girl.

6178. Hogrogian, Nonny. *One Fine Day* (K–3). Illus. by author. 1971, Macmillan $10.95; paper $2.95. Based on an Armenian folktale, this cumulative story is ideal for reading aloud. Caldecott winner.

6179. Isele, Elizabeth. *The Frog Princess* (K–3). Illus. by Michael Hague. 1984, Harper $10.53; LB $10.89. Ivan must marry whomever finds his arrow, and a frog does.

6180. Kemp, Moira. *The Firebird* (K–3). Illus. 1984, Godine $10.95. A retelling with embellishments of this Russian tale.

6181. Maguire, Gregory. *The Dream Stealer* (3–5). 1983, Harper $9.57; LB $9.89. Several Russian folktales are combined in this story about young Pasha and Lisette.

6182. Marshak, Samuel, retel. *The Month-Brothers: A Slavic Tale* (K–4). Illus. by Diane

Stanley. 1983, Morrow $10.45; LB $10.08. A folktale involving such familiar elements as a girl and a mean stepmother.

6183. Mikolaycak, Charles. *Babushka: An Old Russian Folktale* (PS–2). Illus. by author. 1984, Holiday $14.95. Babushka refuses to leave her home to search for the Christ child.

6184. Ransome, Arthur. *The Fool of the World and the Flying Ship* (1–4). Illus. by Uri Shulevitz. 1968, Farrar $10.95. Colorful, panoramic scenes extend this retelling of a popular Russian folktale about a simple peasant boy who acquires a flying ship. Caldecott Medal winner. Also use: *Peter's Russian Tales* (1984, Merrimack $13.95).

6185. Reyher, Becky. *My Mother Is the Most Beautiful Woman in the World* (2–5). Illus. by Ruth Gannett. 1945, Lothrop $10.32. A girl tries to find her mother in this Russian setting.

6186. Riordan, James, ed. *Tales from Central Russia: Russian Tales, Volume One* (5–8). Illus. by Krystyna Turska. 1979, Viking $12.50. A selection from Afanasyev's stories.

6187. Riordan, James. *The Three Magic Gifts* (1–4). Illus. by Errol LeCain. 1980, Oxford $11.95. The revenge of a poor man on his wealthy brother.

6188. Robbins, Ruth. *Baboushka and the Three Kings* (2–Up). Illus. by Nicholas Sidjakov. 1960, Parnassus $5.95; LB $7.95. The Russian legend of the old woman who refused to follow the 3 kings in search of the Holy Child. Caldecott Medal, 1961.

6189. Silverman, Maida. *Anna and the Seven Swans* (K–2). Illus. by David Small. 1984, Morrow $11.00; LB $10.51. Anna saves her brother from the clutches of Baba Yaga.

6190. Small, Ernest. *Baba Yaga* (1–3). Illus. by Blair Lent. 1966, Houghton $9.95. A simplified version of the tale of the evil Russian witch who flies in a mortar and pestle and lives in a hut supported by chicken legs.

6191. Stern, Simon, retel. *Vasily and the Dragon: An Epic Russian Fairy Tale* (3–6). Illus. by retel. 1983, Merrimack $9.95. A miser tries to kill the youngster who will one day inherit his wealth.

6192. Tolstoy, Leo. *The Fool* (5–7). Illus. 1981, Schocken $5.95. A retelling in rhyme of a classic Russian folktale.

6193. Tresselt, Alvin, ed. *The Mitten* (K–2). Illus. by Yaroslava. 1964, Lothrop $10.80. An old Ukrainian folktale about a little boy and his lost mitten.

6194. Winter, Jeanette. *The Girl and the Moon Man: A Siberian Tale* (2–4). Illus. by author. 1984, Pantheon $10.95; LB $10.99. The moon wants to kidnap an Arctic girl to live with him.

6195. Zemach, Harve. *Salt: A Russian Tale* (1–3). Illus. by Margot Zemach. 1977, Farrar $7.95. A picture book version of a Russian folktale that tells how Ivan the Fool introduces salt to the King and wins the hand of the princess.

Jewish Folklore

6196. Aronin, Ben. *The Secret of the Sabbath Fish* (1–3). Illus. by Shay Rieger. 1979, Jewish Publication Society $5.95. The preparation of gefilte fish reminds a Jewish woman about the sorrows of her people in this eastern European tale.

6197. Gershator, Phillis. *Honi and His Magic Circle* (K–3). Illus. by Shay Rieger. 1980, Jewish Publication Society $6.95. A Talmudic story about Honi who sowed seeds throughout Israel.

6198. Hirsh, Marilyn. *Could Anything Be Worse? A Yiddish Tale* (K–3). Illus. by author. 1974, Holiday $8.95. A man dissatisfied with all the noise and confusion in his household asks the rabbi for advice, with humorous results.

6199. Hirsh, Marilyn. *The Rabbi and the Twenty-Nine Witches: A Talmudic Legend* (K–3). Illus. by author. 1981, Holiday $8.95; Scholastic paper $1.50. Through the efforts of a wise rabbi, village people are able to rid themselves of 29 witches.

6200. Kimmel, Eric A. *Hershel of Ostropol* (3–5). Illus. by Arthur Friedman. 1982, Jewish Publication Society $7.95. These tales are derived from Jewish tales about a man who lives by his wits.

6201. McDermott, Beverly Brodsky. *The Golem: A Jewish Legend* (4–6). 1975, Harper $10.53. The Jewish folktale about the strange creature created by a rabbi to combat evil.

6202. Rose, Anne, ed. *The Triumph of Fuzzy Fogtop* (1–3). Illus. by Tomie de Paola. 1979, Dial paper $2.95. Three simple, humorous stories set in eastern Europe derived from Jewish folklore.

6203. Singer, Isaac Bashevis. *Elijah the Slave* (PS–3). Illus. by Antonio Frasconi. 1970, Farrar $7.95; Scholastic paper $1.95. Retelling of a Hebrew legend.

6204. Singer, Isaac Bashevis. *The Fools of Chelm and Their History* (5–6). Illus. by Uri Shulevitz. 1973, Farrar $9.95. Nonsense stories about the village that is the setting of other Singer tales.

6205. Singer, Isaac Bashevis. *Mazel and Shlimazel: Or the Milk of a Lioness* (3–5). Illus. by Margot Zemach. 1967, Farrar $8.95. The fate of a peasant and a princess depends on a battle between good and evil spirits.

6206. Singer, Isaac Bashevis. *Naftali the Storyteller and His Horse, Sus, and Other Stories* (5–8). Illus. by

Margot Zemach. 1976, Farrar $10.95. Singer's favorite town, Chelm, where fools reign supreme, is the setting for many of these stories.

6207. Singer, Isaac Bashevis. *Stories for Children* (4–7). 1984, Farrar $13.95. A collection of stories that draw on Yiddish folklore.

6208. Singer, Isaac Bashevis. *When Shlemiel Went to Warsaw and Other Stories* (4–7). Illus. by Margot Zemach. 1968, Farrar $8.95. Illustrations and the 8 stories retold here delightfully reveal the distinctive people of Chelm and their extraordinary, universally exportable wisdom.

6209. Singer, Isaac Bashevis. *Zlateh the Goat and Other Stories* (4–6). Illus. by Maurice Sendak. 1966, Harper $12.95; LB $12.89. Warm, humorous, and ironical stories based on middle European Jewish folklore and on the author's childhood memories.

6210. Zemach, Margot. *It Could Always Be Worse: A Yiddish Folktale* (K–3). Illus. by author. 1976, Farrar $10.95; Scholastic paper $1.95. A Yiddish version of an old tale with colorful, humorous illustrations.

Middle East

6211. Bell, Anthea, trans. *Stories of the Arabian Nights* (4–6). Illus. by Giannini. 1983, Bedrick $12.95. Six stories are retold including *Aladdin* and *Ali Baba*.

6212. Cohen, Barbara, and Lovejoy, Bahijia. *Seven Daughters and Seven Sons* (6–8). 1982, Atheneum $10.95. An Arabian folktale about an ingenious young girl and how she saved her family.

6213. Green, Roger L. *Tales of Ancient Egypt* (6–9). Illus. by Elaine Raphael. 1968, Penguin paper $2.95. Some of the oldest stories known.

6214. Lang, Andrew, retel. *Aladdin and the Wonderful Lamp* (3–5). Illus. by Errol LeCain. 1981, Viking $12.50; Penguin paper $3.95. An excellently retold and illustrated tale from *The Arabian Nights*. Another recommended edition is: *Aladdin and the Wonderful Lamp*, illus. by Leonard Lubin (1982, Delacorte $10.95; LB $10.89).

6215. Manniche, Lise, trans. *How Djadja-Emankh Saved the Day: A Tale from Ancient Egypt* (4–6). Illus. by trans. 1977, Harper $8.95. An ancient Egyptian fantasy resembling the original in format and paper.

6216. Skurzynski, Gloria. *Two Fools and a Faker: Three Lebanese Folktales* (1–3). Illus. by William Papas. 1977, Lothrop $10.50. Three rollicking stories about buffoonish characters in humorous situations.

6217. Travers, P. L. *Two Pairs of Shoes* (4–6). Illus. by Leo Dillon and Diane Dillon. 1980, Viking $10.95. Two stories from the East about the part shoes play in the lives of 2 men.

Middle America

Mexico and Central America

6218. Aardema, Verna. *The Riddle of the Drum: A Tale from Tizapan, Mexico* (K–3). Illus. by Tony Chen. 1979, Four Winds $8.95. A handsome prince solves a thorny problem to win the hand of a princess.

6219. Baker, Betty. *No Help at All* (1–2). Illus. by Emily McCully. 1978, Greenwillow $8.50; LB $8.88. The West Wind of Maya has trouble finding a suitable helper.

6220. Bierhorst, John, ed. *The Hungry Woman: Myths and Legends of the Aztecs* (6–9). Illus. 1984, Morrow $10.00. A collection of myths that also reveal a great deal of the culture and history of the Aztecs.

6221. Kurtycz, Marcos, and Kobeh, Ana Garcia. *Tigers and Opossums: Animal Legends* (2–4). Illus. 1984, Little $12.45. Six Mexican folktales involving animals and birds.

Puerto Rico and Other Caribbean Islands

6222. Belpre, Pura. *Once in Puerto Rico* (3–6). Illus. by Christine Price. 1973, Warne $7.95. Sixteen short tales gathered by a master storyteller who was educated in Puerto Rico. Also use: *Dance of the Animals* (1972, Warne LB $4.95).

6223. Belpre, Pura. *Perez and Martina* (2–3). Illus. by Carlos Sanchez. 1961, Warne $7.95. A charming Puerto Rican folktale that has been handed down orally.

6224. Belpre, Pura. *The Rainbow-Colored Horse* (4–6). Illus. by Antonia Martorell. 1978, Warne LB $8.95. A favorite story from Puerto Rico about a man who wins a bride with the help of an enchanted horse.

6225. Bryan, Ashley, ed. *The Dancing Granny* (K–3). Illus. by ed. 1977, Atheneum $8.95. Granny Anika, who loves to dance, beats the traditional character, Spider Ananse, pictured in this adaptation as a tall, vigorous man.

6226. Chardiet, Bernice. *Juan Bobo and the Pig: A Puerto Rican Folktale Retold* (1–3). Illus. by Hope

Meryman. 1973, Walker $5.95; LB $5.85. Juan Bobo plays a trick on the family pig.

6227. Sherlock, Philip M. *Anansi, the Spider Man: Jamaican Folktale* (4–6). Illus. by Marcia Brown. 1954, Harper $13.50. Tales of a famous Caribbean folk hero. Also use: *West Indian Folk Tales* (1960, Oxford $14.95).

6228. Wolkstein, Diane, comp. *The Magic Orange Tree and Other Haitian Folktales* (5–8). Illus. by Elsa Hanriquez. 1978, Schocken paper $5.95. A magical collection of outstanding folktales.

South America

6229. Dewey, Ariane. *The Thunder God's Son: A Peruvian Folktale* (PS–3). Illus. by author. 1981, Greenwillow $10.25; LB $9.84. Acuri, son of the Thunder God, visits earth in this Peruvian folktale.

6230. Finger, Charles J. *Tales from Silver Lands* (4–6). Illus. by Paul Honore. 1924, Doubleday $13.95. Folklore from South America. Newbery medal winner, 1925.

6231. Jagendorf, M. A., and Boggs, R. S. *The King of the Mountains* (4–6). Illus. by Carybe. 1960, Vanguard $10.95. Favorite tales of Latin American peoples.

North America

Canada

6232. Carlson, Natalie Savage. *The Talking Cat: And Other Stories of French Canada* (4–6). Illus. by Roger Duvoisin. 1952, Harper LB $10.89. Seven delightful stories from early pioneer life in Quebec.

6233. Coatsworth, Elizabeth. *Pure Magic* (3–6). Illus. by Ingrid Fetz. 1973, Macmillan $8.95. Young Giles has the ability to transform himself into a fox, in this retelling of an old legend now set in French Canada.

Eskimo

6234. Hewitt, Garnet. *Ytek and the Arctic Orchid: An Inuit Legend* (3–5). Illus. by Heather Woodall. 1981, Vanguard $10.95. A shaman's son must prove himself by a series of ordeals.

6235. Houston, James. *Tikta'liktak: An Eskimo Legend* (4–6). Illus. by author. 1965, Harcourt $9.95. Legend of a young Eskimo hunter who is carried out to sea on a drifting ice floe with only his bow and arrows and a harpoon. Also use: *The White Archer: An Eskimo Legend* (1979, Harcourt paper $2.25).

6236. San Souci, Robert. *Song of Sedna* (2–5). Illus. by Daniel San Souci. 1981, Doubleday $9.95. An Eskimo maiden, tricked and betrayed, becomes goddess of the sea.

Indians of North America

6237. Baker, Betty. *And Me, Coyote!* (K–3). Illus. by Maria Horvath. 1982, Macmillan $8.95. Creation myths from California form the basis of this story of World Maker and helper Coyote.

6238. Baker, Olaf. *Where the Buffalos Begin* (4–6). Illus. by Stephen Gammell. 1981, Warne $8.95; paper $5.95. A retelling of the American Indian legend of the boy who led a stampeding buffalo herd away from his people.

6239. Baylor, Byrd. *And It Is Still That Way: Legends Told by Arizona Indian Children* (2–4). 1976, Scribners $7.95. These legends and folktales were told to the compiler.

6240. Baylor, Byrd. *A God on Every Mountain Top: Stories of Southwest Indian Sacred Mountains* (4–5). Illus. by Carol Brown. 1981, Scribners $9.95. Creation myths and other legends from 5 Indian tribes.

6241. Bierhorst, John, ed. *The Whistling Skeleton: American Tales of the Supernatural* (4–6). Collected by George Bird Grinnell. Illus. by Robert Andrew Parker. 1982, Four Winds $12.95. Nine stories from the Plains Indians.

6242. Bierhorst, John, and Schodcraft, Henry, eds. *Ring in the Prairie* (K–3). Illus. by Leo Dillon and Diane Dillon. 1970, Dial $7.95; paper $1.95. A Shawnee legend about a young warrior in love with the daughter of a star.

6243. Bruchac, Joseph. *Stone Giants and Flying Heads: Adventure Stories from the Iroquois* (3–6). Illus. 1979, Crossing Pr. $10.95. Eight selections in prose and free verse.

6244. Crompton, Anne Eliot. *The Winter Wife: An Abenaki Folktale* (2–4). Illus. by Robert Andrew Parker. 1975, Little $8.95. An Indian trapper gains a companion for the winter when a strange, quiet woman appears at his wigwam.

6245. de Paola, Tomie, retel. *The Legend of the Bluebonnet: An Old Tale of Texas* (K–3). Illus. by retel. 1983, Putnam $10.95; paper $4.95. This book retells the Comanche Indian story of the origin of the Texas bluebonnet flower.

6246. DeWit, Dorothy, ed. *The Talking Stone* (6–8). 1979, Greenwillow $11.95; LB $11.45.

Subtitle: *An Anthology of Native American Tales and Legends.*

6247. Erdoes, Richard. *The Sound of the Flutes and Other Indian Legends* (5–7). Illus. by Paul Goble. 1976, Pantheon LB $6.99. A collection of tales, some based on fact, gathered from the Plains Indians.

6248. Fritz, Jean. *The Good Giants and the Bad Pukwudgies* (1–4). Illus. by Tomie de Paola. 1982, Putnam $10.95; paper $5.95. Old legends are used to explain the formation of Cape Cod and nearby islands.

6249. Goble, Paul. *Buffalo Women* (4–6). Illus. by author. 1984, Bradbury $12.95. A legend from the Plains Indians about a buffalo that turns into a beautiful girl.

6250. Goble, Paul. *The Gift of the Sacred Dog* (2–4). Illus. by author. 1980, Bradbury $10.95. A boy brings to his starving people the gift of horses.

6251. Goble, Paul, retel. *Star Boy* (2–4). Illus. by retel. 1983, Bradbury $12.95. An Indian legend on how Star Boy was able to rid himself of a disfiguring scar.

6252. Gustafson, Anita, retel. *Monster Rolling Skull and Other Native American Tales* (3–8). Illus. by John Stadler. 1980, Harper LB $7.89. Coyote is both narrator and character in these 9 American Indian folktales.

6253. Harris, Christie. *Mouse Woman and the Vanished Princesses* (4–6). Illus. by Douglas Tait. 1976, Atheneum $7.95. Six legends from the Indians of the Northwest about the rescue of princesses by a small supernatural creature who often assumes the shape of a mouse. Two sequels are: *Mouse Woman and the Mischief-Makers* (1977); *Mouse Woman and the Muddleheads* (1979) (both $7.95).

6254. Harris, Christie. *Once More upon a Totem* (4–7). Illus. by Douglas Tait. 1973, Atheneum $5.95. West Coast Indian legends retold with excitement and a sense of wonder. Two related titles are: *The Trouble with Adventurers* (1982, Atheneum LB $10.95); *The Trouble with Princesses* (1982, Atheneum $9.95).

6255. Highwater, Jamake. *Anpao: An American Indian Odyssey* (5–8). Illus. by Fritz Scholder. 1977, Harper $12.45; paper $3.95. A young hero encounters great danger on his way to meet his father, the Sun, in this dramatic American Indian folktale.

6256. Hillerman, Tony, ed. *The Boy Who Made Dragonfly: A Zuni Myth* (5–7). Illus. by Laszlo Kubinyi. 1972, Harper LB $9.89. A Zuni boy and his little sister are left behind by their tribe and survive hunger and deprivation through the intervention of the Cornstalk Being.

6257. Hodges, Margaret, ed. *The Fire Bringer: A Paiute Indian Legend* (3–5). Illus. by Peter Parnall. 1972, Little $6.95. The coyote helps a Paiute boy withstand the cold of winter by stealing a brand from the Fire Spirits.

6258. Martin, Frances Gardiner. *Raven-Who-Sets-Things-Right: Indian Tales of the Northwest Coast* (5–7). Illus. by Dorothy McEntee. 1975, Harper LB $9.89. Nine tales retold with handsome illustrations and preparatory material on the origin of each story.

6259. Mobley, Jane. *The Star Husband* (5–7). Illus. by Anna Vojtech. 1979, Doubleday LB $8.95. An Indian legend of a girl who leaves earth to fulfill a desire for a star husband.

6260. Robbins, Ruth, retel. *How the First Rainbow Was Made: An American Indian Tale* (1–3). Illus. by retel. 1980, Houghton $8.95. The Shasta Indians approach a wise coyote to get the rain to stop.

6261. Robinson, Gail, retel. *Raven the Trickster: Legends of the North American Indians* (4–6). Illus. by Joanna Troughton. 1982, Atheneum $8.95. Nine stories featuring Raven, the Northwest Coast Indian trickster.

6262. San Souci, Robert. *The Legend of Scarface: A Blackfeet Indian Tale* (2–4). Illus. by Daniel San Souci. 1978, Doubleday $9.95. A young brave travels to the land of the Sun to seek permission to marry the maiden he loves.

6263. Siberell, Anne. *Whale in the Sky* (PS–2). 1982, Dutton $10.95. Thunderbird removes Whale from the sea to save the salmon for the Indians.

6264. Sleator, William. *The Angry Moon.* K–3. Illus. by Blair Lent. 1981, Little $4.95. Tlingit Indian legend in which a little boy, with the aid of his grandmother's magic, rescues a girl held captive by the angry moon.

6265. Steptoe, John, retel. *The Story of Jumping Mouse: A Native American Legend* (1–4). Illus. by retel. 1984, Lothrop $12.00; LB $11.47. The legend of the mouse who, because of good acts, is transformed into an eagle.

United States

6266. Bang, Molly. *Wiley and the Hairy Man* (2–4). Adapted from an American folktale. Illus. by author. 1976, Macmillan $7.95. In this story from Alabama, Wiley's mother helps him outwit the Hairy Man, a terrible swamp creature.

6267. Barth, Edna. *Jack-O-Lantern* (3–5). Illus. by Paul Galdone. 1974, Houghton $8.95; paper $3.95. A retelling of the old legend about Mean

NORTH AMERICA 281

Jack and what happens when he is refused admittance to both heaven and hell.

6268. Blassingame, Wyatt. *Pecos Bill and the Wonderful Clothesline Snake* (1–3). Illus. by Herman Vestal. 1978, Garrard $6.69. Make-believe snakes are introduced by the legendary cowboy.

6269. Chase, Richard. *Grandfather Tales* (4–6). Illus. by Berkeley Williams. 1948, Houghton $12.95. Folktales gathered from the South. Also use: *The Jack Tales* (1943, Houghton $10.95).

6270. Cohen, Daniel. *Southern Fried Rat and Other Gruesome Tales* (6–9). Illus. by Peggy Brier. 1983, Dutton $9.95. Grisly folktales—some funny, some gruesome.

6271. Crompton, Anne Eliot. *The Lifting Stone* (1–3). 1978, Holiday $7.95. Mandy Jane will marry whomever can lift a massive stone.

6272. Davis, Hubert, ed. *A January Fog Will Freeze a Hog and Other Weather Folklore* (2–4). Illus. by John Wallner. 1977, Crown LB $6.95. Weather sayings that are part of the folklore of the United States, handsomely illustrated with stylized drawings.

6273. Dewey, Ariane. *Febold Feboldson* (1–3). Illus. 1984, Greenwillow $10.00; LB $9.55. A tall tale about the first farmer to settle in Nebraska.

6274. Dewey, Ariane. *Pecos Bill* (2–4). Illus. 1983, Greenwillow $9.00. Tall tales about the deeds of a legendary hero.

6275. Duff, Maggie. *Dancing Turtle* (2–4). Illus. by Maria Horvath. 1981, Macmillan LB $8.95. Turtle is able to outwit the wily Fox who has captured her.

6276. Galdone, Joanna. *The Amber Day: A Very Tall Tale* (K–3). Illus. by Paul Galdone. 1978, McGraw $9.95. A husband and wife are changed into half-human/half-mules because of their quarreling.

6277. Galdone, Joanna. *The Tailypo: A Ghost Story* (1–3). Illus. by Paul Galdone. 1977, Houghton $8.95. In this ghostly story, a mysterious creature returns to retrieve his tail, cut off by an old man.

6278. Galdone, Paul. *The Greedy Old Fat Man: An American Folk Tale* (3–5). Illus. by author. 1983, Houghton $10.45. A fat man consumes everything he sees until he bursts.

6279. Harris, Joel Chandler. *Brer Rabbit* (3–5). Illus. by William Stobb. 1978, Merrimack $8.95. A retelling and simplifying of 23 of Uncle Remus's most famous stories. Another recommended edition is: *The Adventures of Brer Rabbit*, illus. by Frank Baber (1980, Rand McNally $9.95).

6280. Jagendorf, M. A. *Folk Stories of the South* (4–7). Illus. by Michael Parks. 1973, Vanguard $9.95. A satisfying collection of folklore—including tall tales, Indian legends, and old ghost stories—arranged by states. Also use: *New England Bean Pot* (1948, Vanguard $7.95).

6281. Jagendorf, M. A. *The Ghost of Peg-Leg Peter and Other Stories of Old New York* (4–6). Illus. by Lino Lipinsky. 1965, Vanguard $7.95. A wonderful collection of stories, some dating back to the original Dutch settlers.

6282. Jaquith, Priscilla, retel. *Bo Rabbit Smart for True: Folktales from the Gullah* (K–3). Illus. by Ed Young. 1981, Putnam LB $9.99. Four tales from the sea islands of Georgia and South Carolina that date back to the days of slavery.

6283. Keats, Ezra Jack. *John Henry: An American Legend* (1–3). Illus. by author. 1965, Pantheon $9.99. Large, bold figures capture the spirit of the hero who was born with a hammer in his hand.

6284. Kellogg, Steven. *Paul Bunyan: A Tall Tale* (K–4). Illus. by author. 1984, Morrow $12.88. Several stories about Paul and the blue ox Babe, all wittily illustrated.

6285. Leach, Maria. *The Luck Book* (3–6). 1979, Dell paper $1.50. A fascinating collection of folklore connected to luck and its symbols, e.g., the number 13.

6286. Lent, Blair. *John Tabor's Ride* (1–3). Illus. by author. 1966, Little $6.95. A tall tale based on a New England legend in which a shipwrecked old man is given a wild ride home on the back of a whale.

6287. Lester, Julius. *The Knee-High Man and Other Tales* (K–2). Illus. by Ralph Pinto. 1972, Dial $5.95; LB $5.47. Six black American folktales concerned with animals make this an appealing selection for reading aloud or storytelling to younger readers.

6288. McCormick, Dell J. *Paul Bunyan Swings His Axe* (4–6). Illus. by author. 1936, Caxton $6.95; Scholastic paper $1.95. The stories of the giant woodsman and his great blue ox named Babe are favorites among American folktales.

6289. Maitland, Antony. *Idle Jack* (1–3). Illus. by author. 1979, Farrar $8.95. A neer-do-well finds unexpected fame in this old folktale.

6290. Rounds, Glen. *The Morning the Sun Refused to Rise: An Original Paul Bunyan Tale* (2–4). Illus. by author. 1984, Holiday $9.95. Paul Bunyan changes the geography of North America to save the earth from the Great Blizzard.

6291. Rounds, Glen. *Ol' Paul, the Mighty Logger* (3–6). Illus. by author. 1976, Holiday $10.95. Subtitle: *A True Account of the Seemingly Incredible Exploits and Inventions of the Great Paul Bunyan, Properly Illustrated by Drawings Made at the Scene by the Author.*

6292. Sawyer, Ruth. *Journey Cake, Ho!* (K–3). Illus. by Robert McCloskey. 1953, Viking $9.95; Penguin paper $3.95. Retelling of the old folktale of Johnny and his chase after a journey cake that rolls away singing a taunting verse.

6293. Schwartz, Alvin, comp. *Flapdoodle: Pure Nonsense from American Folklore* (5–7). Illus. by John O'Brien. 1980, Harper $9.57; paper $3.95. A collection of nonsense sayings and riddles gathered from American folklore.

6294. Schwartz, Alvin, ed. *Kickle Snifters and Other Fearsome Critters Collected from American Folklore* (3–5). Illus. by Glen Rounds. 1976, Harper $10.10. A dictionary of beasts found chiefly in American tall tales with descriptions and amusing illustrations.

6295. Schwartz, Alvin, sel. *Scary Stories to Tell in the Dark* (3–8). Illus. by Stephen Gammell. 1981, Harper $10.10; LB $9.89; paper $4.95. Ghost stories collected from American folklore. A sequel is: *More Scary Stories to Tell in the Dark* (1984, $10.89).

6296. Schwartz, Alvin, comp. *Unriddling: All Sorts of Riddles to Puzzle Your Guessery, Collected from American Folklore* (4–8). Illus. by Sue Truesdell. 1983, Harper $9.57; LB $9.89. A collection of riddles from our history, plus many background descriptions.

6297. Schwartz, Alvin, ed. *Whoppers: Tall Tales and Other Lies Collected from American Folklore* (3–5). 1975, Harper $8.95. A collection of long and short humorous tales from a number of sources.

6298. Stoutenberg, Adrien. *American Tall Tales* (3–7). 1966, Viking LB $12.95; Penguin paper $3.50. Eight tales about such heroes as Paul Bunyan, Pecos Bill, and Johnny Appleseed.

6299. Taylor, Mark. *Young Melvin and Bulger* (3–7). Illus. by Jan Brett. 1981, Doubleday LB $8.95. A tall tale about Young Melvin and his foxhound Bulger.

History and Geography

General

6300. Arnold, Guy, and Trease, Geoffrey. *Datelines of World History* (5–8). Illus. 1983, Watts $12.90. A useful guide to world history.

6301. Bell, Neill. *The Book of Where, or How to Be Naturally Geographic* (4–7). Illus. by Richard Wilson. 1982, Little $10.95; paper $6.95. A collection of activities that make one aware of the study of geography.

6302. Foster, Genevieve. *Birthdays of Freedom: From Early Egypt to July 4, 1776* (6–9). Illus. by author. 1974, Scribners $6.95. Great historical events from prehistoric times to July 4, 1776.

6303. Hauptly, Denis J. *The Journey from the Past: A History of the Western World* (6–9). 1983, Atheneum $12.95. A period of 400 million years is covered with particular emphasis on Western civilization.

6304. Hogan, Paula Z. *The Compass* (4–7). Illus. by David Wood. 1982, Walker $7.95; LB $8.85. The story of an invention that changed history.

6305. Lyttle, Richard B. *The Golden Path: The Lure of Gold through History* (6–9). Illus. by author. 1983, Atheneum $11.95. How the lure of gold has changed world history.

6306. Marrin, Albert. *The Sea Rovers: Pirates, Privateers, and Buccaneers* (6–9). 1984, Atheneum $13.95. Three hundred years of skulduggery on the high seas.

6307. Sandak, Cass R. *Museums: What They Are and How They Work* (4–7). Illus. 1981, Watts $8.90. A description of museums, their types and functions.

6308. Sterling Publishers. *Lebanon in Pictures* (4–7). Illus. 1978, Sterling paper $2.95. Part of the Sterling Visual Geographies series, which has volumes on approximately 40 countries of the world. Each book is 64 pages long and contains about 100 photos.

6309. Van Loon, Hendrik W. *The Story of Mankind* (6–9). 1972, Liveright $16.95. This famous history of the development of civilization won the first Newbery Medal in 1922.

6310. Weitzman, David. *My Backyard History Book* (4–7). 1975, Little $9.95; paper $5.95. A guide to re-creating history that occurred close to home by interviewing, for example, family and friends.

Maps and Mapmaking

6311. Broekel, Ray. *Maps and Globes* (1–4). Illus. 1983, Childrens Pr. $7.95. A well-illustrated introduction to maps and how to read them.

6312. Brown, Lloyd. *Map Making: The Art That Became a Science* (5–7). Illus. 1960, Little $10.95. The history of mapmaking from early times to the present, including an explanation of the methods and instruments used by the cartographer.

6313. Carey, Helen H. *How to Use Maps and Globes* (6–8). Illus. 1983, Watts $9.40. A discussion of the types of maps and the material they include.

6314. Cartwright, Sally. *What's in a Map?* (K–2). Illus. by Dick Gackenbach. 1976, Putnam $6.99. An excellent book for beginning map work with young children, written by a science teacher.

6315. Dicks, Brian, ed. *The Children's World Atlas* (4–7). Illus. 1981, Celestial Arts $9.95. Because of the amount of text included, this is almost a geography book.

6316. Madden, James F. *The Wonderful World of Maps* (3–5). Illus. 1977, Hammond $6.95. An atlas plus an introductory section on how to read maps.

6317. Oglivie, Bruce, and Waitley, Douglas. *Rand McNally Picture Atlas of the World* (3–5). 1979, Rand McNally $9.95. A useful atlas that contains comprehensive textual material as well as excellent maps.

6318. Tivers, Jacqueline, and Day, Michael. *The Viking Children's World Atlas* (3–4). Illus. 1983, Viking $6.95. A clearly presented atlas with maps of products and topography as well as political divisions.

6319. Townson, W. D. *Illustrated Atlas of the World in the Age of Discovery 1453–1763* (4–6). Illus. 1981, Watts $12.90. An extensive text accompanies the maps and many graphics.

Paleontology

6320. Aliki. *Digging Up Dinosaurs* (2–4). Illus. by author. 1981, Harper $10.53; LB $10.89. This book answers the question "How do dinosaurs get into museums?"

6321. Aliki. *Fossils Tell of Long Ago* (2–3). Illus. by author. 1972, Harper $10.89; paper $3.80. A good introduction to fossils, how they are formed, what they can reveal about the past, and where they might be found, written simply enough for the beginning reader.

6322. Aliki. *My Visit to the Dinosaurs* (2–3). Illus. by author. 1969, Harper LB $10.89; paper $2.95. A beginning science book that serves as an introduction to the subject. Also use: *The Dinosaur Story* by Joanna Cole (1974, Morrow LB $9.36).

6323. Aliki. *Wild and Woolly Mammoths* (2–3). Illus. by author. 1977, Harper $10.89; paper $3.80. A clear, succinct text describes the woolly mammoth's structure and habits and the way in which it was hunted by early peoples.

6324. Ames, Gerald, and Wyler, Rose. *The Story of the Ice Age* (5–8). Illus. by Thomas W. Voter. 1956, Harper $8.89. An introduction to this fascinating geological period told in text and pictures.

6325. Andrews, Roy Chapman. *In the Days of the Dinosaur* (4–6). Illus. 1959, Random $3.50; LB $5.99. A description of many unusual beasts and where they lived.

6326. Asimov, Isaac. *How Did We Find Out about Dinosaurs?* (5–7). 1982, Avon paper $1.95. An introduction in a simple format to these ancient, fascinating animals.

6327. Bloch, Marie. *Dinosaurs* (4–6). Illus. 1955, Putnam $5.99. A fine introduction to these prehistoric animals and why they disappeared.

6328. Branley, Franklyn M. *Dinosaurs, Asteroids, and Superstars: Why the Dinosaurs Disappeared* (4–7). Illus. by Jean Zallinger. 1982, Harper $10.51; LB $14.89. An account of the many theories concerning the extinction of the dinosaur.

6329. Carrick, Carol. *The Crocodiles Still Wait* (2–4). Illus. by Donald Carrick. 1980, Houghton $8.95. A prehistoric giant crocodile and her life in a swamp.

6330. Cobb, Vicki. *The Monsters Who Died: A Mystery about Dinosaurs* (3–5). Illus. by Greg Wenzel. 1983, Putnam $9.95. An exploration of how we found out about dinosaurs and what we have learned.

6331. Cohen, Daniel. *Monster Dinosaur* (5–7). Illus. 1983, Harper $9.57; LB $9.89. An introduction to dinosaurs and their habits.

6332. Cohen, Daniel. *What Really Happened to the Dinosaurs?* (4–6). Illus. by Haru Wells. 1977, Dutton $8.95. Founded on solid research, this is a readable account of why the dinosaurs became extinct.

6333. Cole, Joanna. *Saber-Toothed Tiger and Other Ice Age Mammals* (2–4). Illus. 1977, Morrow LB $9.55. A description in words and pictures of the giant mammals that roamed the earth during the Ice Age.

6334. Craig, M. Jean. *Dinosaurs and More Dinosaurs* (K–3). Illus. by George Solonevich. 1968, Scholastic $9.95; paper $1.95. A factual account of 46 different kinds of dinosaurs.

6335. The Diagram Group. *A Field Guide to Dinosaurs* (6–9). Illus. 1983, Avon paper $8.95. More than 50 families of dinosaurs are described.

6336. Eastman, David. *Story of Dinosaurs* (K–2). Illus. by Joel Snyder. 1982, Troll LB $8.89; paper $1.25. Simple material presented in short sentences with many illustrations. Also use: *More about Dinosaurs* by David Cutts (1982, Troll LB $8.89; paper $1.25).

6337. Fodor, R. V. *Frozen Earth: Explaining the Ice Ages* (6–9). Illus. 1981, Enslow LB $9.95. Theories of why ice ages occurred and their history are given in text and illustrations.

6338. Freedman, Russell. *Dinosaurs and Their Young* (1–3). Illus. by Leslie Morrill. 1983, Holiday $9.95. The story of how paleontology has helped us understand how young dinosaurs were raised.

6339. Freedman, Russell. *They Lived with the Dinosaurs* (3–5). Illus. 1980, Holiday LB $8.95. Animal life, including starfish and cockroaches, that has existed since the time of the dinosaur.

6340. Granger, Judith. *Amazing World of Dinosaurs* (1–3). Illus. by Pamela Baldwin Ford. 1982, Troll LB $8.89; paper $1.95. This book describes many plant and meat-eating dinosaurs.

6341. Hall, Derek. *Prehistoric Mammals* (2–4). Illus. 1984, Watts $8.90. The development of early mammals is traced with emphasis on those that have present-day counterparts.

6342. Halstead, Beverly. *A Closer Look at Prehistoric Reptiles* (3–6). Illus. 1978, Watts $9.40. A well-designed, readable account that gives a concise introduction to the subject.

6343. Jennings, Terry. *Your Book of Prehistoric Animals* (5–7). Illus. by Mary French. 1980, Faber $8.95. A thorough, up-to-date book on paleontology.

6344. Kaufmann, John. *Flying Reptiles in the Age of Dinosaurs* (4–6). 1976, Morrow $7.63. A fascinating account of the tremendous variety of flying reptiles that lived more than 100 million years ago. Also use: *Flying Giants of Long Ago* (1984, Harper $9.57; LB $9.89).

6345. Kaufmann, John. *Little Dinosaurs and Early Birds* (K–2). Illus. by author. 1977, Harper $10.89. In simple text and accurate drawings, the author explores the evolution of the earliest birds from prehistoric reptiles. Also use: *Dinosaur Time* by Peggy Parish (1974, Harper $7.64; LB $8.89; paper $2.95).

6346. Lampton, Christopher. *Dinosaurs and the Age of Reptiles* (5–7). Illus. 1983, Watts $8.90. An introductory volume that includes a useful time chart.

6347. McGowen, Tom. *Album of Dinosaurs* (3–5). Illus. by Rod Ruth. 1972, Rand McNally $6.95. Twelve types of dinosaurs are highlighted in illustrations and text.

6348. Mannetti, William. *Dinosaurs in Your Backyard* (5–7). 1982, Atheneum LB $10.95. The latest discoveries and theories concerning dinosaurs and their history are incorporated into this account.

6349. National Geographic Society. *Giants from the Past* (3–8). Illus. 1983, National Geographic Society $6.95; LB $10.30. The Age of Mammals is introduced with the beginnings of the horse, cat, and elephant.

6350. Petty, Kate. *Dinosaurs* (K–3). Illus. by Alan Baker. 1984, Watts $8.60. When and where dinosaurs lived and an introduction to a few of the most common.

6351. Pringle, Laurence. *Dinosaurs and People: Fossils, Facts and Fantasies* (4–7). Illus. 1978, Harcourt $7.95. The work and findings of paleontologists are reviewed. Also use: *Dinosaurs and Their World* (1976, Harcourt $8.95; paper $3.95).

6352. Rhodes, Frank H. *Fossils: A Guide to Prehistoric Life* (6–9). Illus. by Raymond Perlman. 1962, Western $11.54; paper $2.95. A survey of ancient life and fossil formation, as well as information on fossil collections.

6353. Ricciuti, Edward R. *Older Than the Dinosaurs: The Origin and Rise of the Mammals* (6–8). Illus. by Edward Malsberg. 1980, Harper $10.89; LB $9.89. An account of the earlier days of mammals that draws parallels between extinction then and problems of animal survival today.

6354. Roberts, Allan. *Fossils* (1–4). Illus. 1983, Childrens Pr. $6.95. An introduction to paleontology for the very young, with fine color photographs.

6355. Rosenbloom, Joseph. *Dictionary of Dinosaurs* (4–7). Illus. by Haris Petie. 1983, Messner LB $8.29. A description of various kinds of dinosaurs; arranged alphabetically.

6356. Sattler, Helen R. *Baby Dinosaurs* (1–4). Illus. 1984, Lothrop $10.00; LB $9.55. Based on fossil findings, this is the story of how infant dinosaurs lived.

6357. Sattler, Helen R. *Dinosaurs of North America* (5–9). Illus. by Anthony Rao. 1981, Lothrop $14.50. More than 80 different dinosaurs are described in text and illustration.

6358. Sattler, Helen R. *The Illustrated Dinosaur Dictionary* (5–9). Illus. by Pamela Carroll. 1983, Lothrop $17.00. More than 300 dinosaurs are described, plus scientific terms associated with their lives and habits.

6359. Selsam, Millicent E. *Sea Monsters of Long Ago* (2–4). Illus. by John Hamberger. 1978, Scholastic paper $1.95. Many strange animals that lived during the age of dinosaurs are presented.

6360. Selsam, Millicent E., and Hunt, Joyce. *A First Look at Dinosaurs* (PS–2). Illus. by Harriett Springer. 1982, Walker $7.95; LB $8.85; Scholastic paper $1.50. An explanation of how dinosaurs are classified scientifically.

6361. Simon, Seymour. *The Smallest Dinosaurs* (2–4). Illus. by Anthony Rao. 1982, Crown $9.95. An easy-to-read book that gives basic facts and introduces 7 small species.

6362. Smith, Howard E., Jr. *Living Fossils* (5–8). Illus. by Jennifer Dewey. 1982, Dodd $8.95. Animals and plants that have not changed their forms since prehistoric times.

6363. Zallinger, Peter. *Prehistoric Animals* (1–3). Illus. by author. 1981, Random LB $4.99; paper $1.50. A brief guide to prehistoric animals—chiefly dinosaurs—and their habits. Also use: *Dinosaurs* (1977, Random $4.99; paper $1.50).

6364. Zim, Herbert S. *Dinosaurs* (4–7). Illus. by James G. Irving. 1954, Morrow $8.16. A basic introduction to these prehistoric animals.

6365. Zim, Herbert S.; Rhodes, Frank; and Schaffer, Paul. *Fossils* (5–9). 1962, Western paper $2.95. This volume contains a history of fossil formation, plus tips on identification.

Anthropology

6366. Asimov, Isaac. *How Did We Find Out about Our Human Roots?* (5–8). Illus. by David Wool. 1979, Walker $6.95; LB $6.85. An overview of human evolution in theory and fossil finds.

6367. Goode, Ruth. *People of the Ice Age* (5–7). Illus. by David Palladini. 1973, Macmillan $9.95. A discussion of the first people and their evolution into farmers.

6368.   Hart, Angela. *Prehistoric Man* (3–5). Illus. 1983, Watts $8.60. The story of early man and his tools, homes, and use of fire.

6369.   McGowen, Tom. *Album of Prehistoric Man* (4–6). Illus. 1975, Rand McNally paper $2.95. An introduction to human progress from the cave to the first civilizations.

6370.   Marcus, Rebecca B. *Survivors of the Stone Age* (5–7). Illus. 1975, Hastings $8.95. A description of 9 primitive tribes in the world today.

6371.   Reynolds, Peter John. *Life in the Iron Age* (6–9). Illus. 1979, Lerner $6.95. A re-creation of life as it was experienced during the Iron Age.

6372.   Walsh, Jill Paton. *The Island Sunrise: Prehistoric Cultures in the British Isles* (6–9). 1976, Houghton $8.95. The beginning volume in a series that will explore the entire spectrum of British history.

Archaeology

6373.   Cooke, Jean et al. *Archaeology* (5–7). Illus. 1982, Watts LB $9.90. An introduction to the science, its methods and famous finds.

6374.   Ford, Barbara, and Switzer, David C. *Underwater Dig: The Excavation of a Revolutionary War Privateer* (5–9). Illus. 1982, Morrow $10.75. The story of the exploration of a ship sunk during the Revolutionary War.

6375.   Fradin, Dennis B. *Archaeology* (1–4). Illus. 1983, Childrens Pr. $7.95. A very broad topic competently introduced for primary grades.

6376.   Gemming, Elizabeth. *Lost City in the Clouds: The Discovery of Machu Picchu* (4–6). Illus. by Mike Eagle. 1980, Putnam LB $6.99. A vivid and exciting account of this spectacular discovery and of background information on the Incan civilization.

6377.   Glubok, Shirley. *Art and Archaeology* (5–7). Illus. by Gerard Nook. 1966, Harper LB $11.89. A very brief discussion of the who and what in archaeology, with photographs of sites throughout the world.

6378.   Kirk, Ruth, and Daugherty, Richard. *Hunters of the Whale: An Adventure in Northwest Coast Archaeology* (6–9). Illus. 1974, Morrow $9.95. An account of excavating an Indian site in the Pacific Coast region, with incidental information about anthropologists and their concerns.

6379.   Morrison, Velma Ford. *Going on a Dig* (5–8). Illus. 1981, Dodd LB $9.95. An overview of archaeology with special reference to digs in the United States in which young people have participated.

6380.   Porell, Bruce. *Digging the Past: Archaeology in Your Own Backyard* (5–7). Illus. 1979, Addison $8.95. A sound introduction to the science of archaeology and the methods of investigation it employs.

6381.   Rollin, Sue. *The Illustrated Atlas of Archaeology* (5–9). Illus. 1982, Watts LB $12.90. Illustrations and text supplement the maps covering the world's ancient civilizations.

6382.   Steele, William O. *Talking Bones: Secrets of Indian Mound Builders* (4–6). Illus. 1978, Harper $8.95; LB $9.89. An introduction to the findings that archaeologists have made by studying prehistoric burial grounds.

Ancient History

General

6383.   Rowland-Entwistle, Theodore. *The Illustrated Atlas of the Bible Lands* (5–7). Illus. 1981, Watts LB $12.90. Interesting text enlivens the maps.

6384.   Unstead, R. J. *How They Lived in Cities Long Ago* (5–7). Illus. 1981, Arco $10.95. Seven cities that represent different ancient cultures are described.

6385.   Unstead, R. J. *Looking at Ancient History* (5–8). Illus. 1966, Macmillan $10.95. A well-illustrated overview of the ancient world.

Egypt and Mesopotamia

6386.   Aliki. *Mummies Made in Egypt* (3–5). Illus. by author. 1979, Harper $9.57; LB $10.89. The burial practices and beliefs of the ancient Egyptians are explored in text and handsome illustrations.

6387.   Asimov, Isaac. *The Egyptians* (6–9). Illus. 1967, Houghton $11.95. The history of ancient Egypt from its rise to greatness to its downfall.

6388.   Glubok, Shirley. *The Art of Egypt under the Pharaohs* (4–6). Illus. by Gerard Nook. 1980, Macmillan $9.95. An introduction to the art of the pharaohs and to the history and social customs of the times.

6389.   Glubok, Shirley. *Discovering Tut-Ankhamen's Tomb* (5–8). Illus. 1968, Macmillan $14.95. A fascinating account of the unearthing of the rich treasures of a pharaoh's tomb.

6390.   Glubok, Shirley, and Tamarin, Alfred. *The Mummy of Ramose: The Life and Death of an Ancient Egyptian Nobleman* (6–9). 1978, Harper $9.57; LB

$10.89. Funeral practices in ancient Egypt are highlighted in this thorough and fascinating book.

6391. Katan, Norma Jean, and Mintz, Barbara. *Hieroglyphics: The Writing of Ancient Egypt* (4–6). Illus. 1981, Atheneum $10.95. A fine introduction that includes material on the Rosetta Stone and how to draw and decipher hieroglyphics.

6392. Millard, Anne. *Ancient Egypt* (5–7). Illus. 1979, Watts LB $9.90. An overview of how people in ancient Egypt lived.

6393. Pace, Mildred. *Wrapped for Eternity: The Story of the Egyptian Mummies* (6–9). Illus. 1974, McGraw paper $1.25. Not only coverage on various aspects of mummification as practiced by the ancient Egyptians but also material on their religion, tombs, and burial practices. By the same author: *Pyramids: Tombs for Eternity* (1981, McGraw $10.95).

6394. Payne, Elizabeth. *The Pharaohs of Ancient Egypt* (6–8). 1964, Random paper $2.95. A fascinating study of this important period in Egyptian history.

6395. Purdy, Susan, and Sandak, Cass R. *Ancient Egypt* (5–6). Illus. 1982, Watts $7.90. An explanation of life in ancient Egypt, plus related craft projects.

6396. Robinson, Charles A., Jr. *Ancient Egypt* (5–7). Illus. 1984, Watts $8.90. A brief outline of the history of Egypt to its fall in 1085 B.C.

6397. Scott, Geoffrey. *Egyptian Boats* (2–4). Illus. by Nancy Carlson. 1981, Carolrhoda LB $7.95. An easily read account of the various kinds of boats used in ancient Egypt.

Greece

6398. Connolly, Peter. *The Greek Armies* (6–8). Illus. by author. 1980, Silver Burdett $12.68. Detailed information plus pictures on Greek warriors from Troy to Alexander the Great.

6399. Coolidge, Olivia. *The Golden Days of Greece* (5–8). Illus. by Enrico Arno. 1968, Harper $13.50. The culture and everyday life of Athens and Sparta. Also use: *The Trojan War* (1952, Houghton $14.95).

6400. Fagg, Christopher. *Ancient Greece* (5–7). Illus. 1979, Watts LB $9.90. A fine overview of life in ancient Greece from the government to the Olympic Games.

6401. Jones, John Ellis. *Ancient Greece* (6–8). Illus. by David Salariya and Shirley Willis. 1984, Watts $9.40. Life in ancient Greece is re-created through examining old ruins and artifacts.

6402. Purdy, Susan, and Sandak, Cass R. *Ancient Greece* (5–6). Illus. 1982, Watts $7.90. Several simple craft projects are outlined, plus an introduction to the history of ancient Greece.

6403. Robinson, Charles A., Jr. *Ancient Greece* (2–4). 1984, Watts $8.90. An introduction to the history and culture of the ancient Greeks.

6404. Rutland, Jonathan. *See Inside an Ancient Greek Town* (5–7). Ed. by R. J. Unstead. Illus. 1979, Watts $9.40. A description of city life with illustrations of principal buildings.

6405. Woodford, Susan. *The Parthenon* (6–8). Illus. 1983, Lerner $6.95. The history and structure of the Parthenon and a description of the religion of ancient Greece.

Rome

6406. Andrews, Ian. *Pompeii* (4–6). Illus. 1980, Lerner LB $6.95. A description of the city of Pompeii and of its destruction.

6407. Asimov, Isaac. *The Roman Republic* (6–8). 1966, Houghton $9.95. An interesting account of ancient Rome and its culture. Also use: *Imperial Rome* by H. E. Mellersh (1964, Harper LB $10.89).

6408. Connolly, Peter. *The Roman Army* (6–8). Illus. by author. 1980, Silver Burdett $12.68. Ancient Rome's expansion in the early days of the empire.

6409. Corbishley, Mike. *The Romans* (6–8). Illus. by David Salariya and Shirley Willis. 1984, Watts $9.40. A reconstruction of Roman history through an examination of several archaeological sites.

6410. Hamey, L. A., and Hamey, J. A. *The Roman Engineers* (6–9). Illus. 1982, Lerner LB $6.95. An account of the accomplishments of the Romans as builders.

6411. Miquel, Pierre. *Life in Ancient Rome* (5–8). Illus. by Yvon LeGall. 1981, Silver Burdett LB $12.68. A broad overview of society during Roman times.

6412. Purdy, Susan, and Sandak, Cass R. *Ancient Rome* (5–6). Illus. 1982, Watts $7.90. This book supplies basic information, plus several related craft projects.

6413. Robinson, Charles A., Jr. *Ancient Rome* (5–7). Illus. 1984, Watts $8.90. In addition to a brief history of Rome, this survey covers its culture and contributions.

Middle Ages

6414.   Aliki. *A Medieval Feast* (2–6). Illus. by author. 1983, Harper $9.57; LB $9.89. A visit from the king provides the occasion for a well-described feast.

6415.   Anno, Mitsumasa. *Anno's Medieval World* (3–6). Illus. by author. 1980, Putnam $12.95; LB $12.99. An introduction to the medieval world— history, life-style, knowledge, and beliefs.

6416.   Cosman, Madeleine Pelner. *Medieval Holidays and Festivals: A Calendar of Celebrations* (6–9). Illus. by author. 1981, Scribners $12.95. An introduction to such festivals as Twelfth Night and Michaelmas and how they were celebrated in the Middle Ages.

6417.   Lasker, Joe. *Merry Ever After: The Story of Two Medieval Weddings* (3–5). Illus. by author. 1976, Penguin paper $3.50. Intricate details of medieval life are revealed through verbal descriptions and many paintings of 2 weddings from different social classes.

6418.   Morgan, Gwyneth. *Life in a Medieval Village* (5–7). Illus. by author. 1982, Lerner LB $6.95. A story of activities in a medieval village and of the effect of the church on life in the Middle Ages.

6419.   Oleksy, Walter. *The Black Plague* (4–6). Illus. 1982, Watts LB $8.90. A case study of the bubonic plague of the Middle Ages.

6420.   Sancha, Sheila. *The Castle Story* (6–9). Illus. by author. 1982, Harper $12.45; LB $12.89; paper $8.61. A book that tells how castles were constructed and about life inside this complex.

6421.   Sancha, Sheila. *The Luttrell Village: Country Life in the Middle Ages* (5–9). Illus. 1983, Harper $12.45; LB $12.89. The reconstruction for readers of a medieval village and its year-round activities.

6422.   Vaughan, Jenny. *Castles* (2–4). Illus. 1984, Watts $8.90. A description of castles and life in the Middle Ages.

World War I

6423.   Castor, Henry. *America's First World War: General Pershing and the Yanks* (5–8). 1957, Random $5.99. The story of America's contribution in World War I and of the great U.S. general.

6424.   Colby, C. B. *Fighting Gear of World War I* (4–6). Illus. 1961, Putnam $5.99. A pictorial presentation of the equipment and weapons used in World War I.

6425.   Gurney, Gene. *Flying Aces of World War I* (5–7). Illus. 1965, Random $5.99. An action-filled account of the daring exploits of World War I pilots.

6426.   Hoobler, Dorothy. *Album of World War I* (5–7). 1976, Watts $9.60. An interesting overview of the causes, campaigns, and results of this war.

6427.   Stein, R. Conrad. *The Story of the Lafayette Escadrille* (3–6). Illus. by Len W. Meents. 1983, Childrens Pr. $5.95. An account of the famous American fliers of World War I.

World War II

6428.   Blassingame, Wyatt. *Underwater Warriors* (4–7). 1982, Random paper $2.95. Suspense stories of the operations of underwater demolition teams in World War II. Original title: *The U.S. Frogmen of World War II.*

6429.   Bliven, Bruce. *From Casablanca to Berlin: The War in North Africa and Europe, 1942–1945* (6–8). Illus. 1965, Random LB $5.99. This concise account traces Allied advances in North Africa and Europe to the conclusion of the war.

6430.   Bliven, Bruce. *From Pearl Harbor to Okinawa: The War in the Pacific, 1941–1945* (6–8). Illus. 1960, Random LB $5.99. A graphic description of the course of the Pacific War from tragedy and defeat to eventual triumph.

6431.   Bliven, Bruce. *The Story of D-Day* (5–8). 1956, Random LB $5.99; paper $2.95. The story of June 6, 1944, and its effect on the outcome of World War II.

6432.   Carter, Hodding. *The Commandos of World War II* (5–7). 1981, Random $2.95. An exciting re-creation of the activities of these hit-and-run fighters who played such an important part in the war.

6433.   Claypool, Jane. *Hiroshima and Nagasaki* (6–9). 1984, Watts $9.90. The dropping of the first atomic bomb and its relevance today. Others in this World War II series are: *Midway and Guadalcanal* by Tom McGowen and *Pearl Harbor* by William D. Shapiro (both 1984, $9.90).

6434.   Colby, C. B. *The Fighting Gear of World War II* (4–6). Illus. 1961, Putnam LB $6.99. Subtitle: *Equipment and Weapons of the American G.I.*

6435.   Dank, Milton. *D-Day* (6–9). 1984, Watts $9.90. The story of the invasion of France during World War II. Others in this series are: *The Battle of Britain* by Julia Markl and *The Invasion of Poland* by Alan Saunders (both 1984, $9.90).

6436.   Frank, Anne. *Anne Frank: The Diary of a Young Girl* (6–9). 1967, Doubleday $13.95. A moving diary of a young Jewish girl hiding from the Nazis in World War II Amsterdam.

6437.   Graff, Stewart. *The Story of World War II* (4–6). Illus. 1978, Dutton $9.25. A brief account that contains many photographs.

6438. Hautzig, Esther. *The Endless Steppe: Growing Up in Siberia* (6–9). 1968, Harper $10.95. In this warm, personal narrative, 11-year-old Esther describes the life, hardships, and undaunted spirit of her family after they are shipped from Poland to Siberia in 1941.

6439. Hoobler, Dorothy, and Hoobler, Thomas. *An Album of World War II* (5–7). Illus. 1977, Watts $9.60. An overview of the war, concentrating on the military; black-and-white photographs frequently used.

6440. Janssen, Pierre. *A Moment of Silence* (5–9). Illus. 1970, Atheneum LB $4.25. A historical overview of the involvement and courage of the Dutch during World War II as seen through many of their monuments.

6441. Kluger, Ruth, and Mann, Peggy.*The Secret Ship* (4–7). 1978, Doubleday $5.95. A true story based on an escape mission during World War II.

6442. Lawson, Don. *An Album of World War II Home Fronts* (6–9). Illus. 1980, Watts $9.60. The story of civilian activities in many countries during World War II.

6443. Lawson, Don. *The French Resistance* (5–7). 1984, Messner $8.79; Wanderer paper $4.95. A description of a spy network that existed during World War II.

6444. Lawson, Don. *The Secret World War II* (6–9). Illus. 1978, Watts $8.90. A mature account of several espionage activities during World War II.

6445. Leckie, Robert. *The Story of World War II* (5–7). Illus. 1964, Random LB $8.99. A competent general account that emphasizes the war in the Pacific.

6446. Loomis, Robert D. *Great American Fighter Pilots of World War II* (5–8). Illus. 1961, Random $5.99. A moving tribute to the gallant pilots of World War II.

6447. McKay, Ernest A. *Undersea Terror: U-Boat Wolf Packs in World War II* (6–9). Illus. 1982, Messner $9.29. The story of the German U-boats of World War II and the horror they produced.

6448. Marrin, Albert. *The Airman's War: World War II in the Sky* (5–9). Illus. 1982, Atheneum LB $12.95. A look at the air power of both the Allies and their enemies during World War II.

6449. Marrin, Albert. *Overlord: D-Day and the Invasion of Europe* (6–9). Illus. 1982, Atheneum $11.95. A book that highlights the events of June 5, 1942.

6450. Meltzer, Milton. *Never to Forget: The Jews of the Holocaust* (6–9). Illus. 1976, Harper LB $12.89.

Quoting the victims themselves, Meltzer clarifies why and how the Holocaust happened.

6451. Shirer, William L. *The Sinking of the Bismarck* (5–8). Illus. with photos. 1962, Random LB $6.99. A suspenseful, true story of World War II, involving the sinking of the great German battleship in 1941.

6452. Siegal, Aranka. *Upon the Head of the Goat: A Childhood in Hungary* (6–9). 1981, Farrar $9.95. The destruction of a family at the hands of the Nazis during World War II.

6453. Skipper, G. C. *Battle of Britain* (4–6). Illus. 1980, Childrens Pr. LB $9.25; paper $2.95. A clear, simple account of this major event in World War II.

6454. Skipper, G. C. *Battle of the Atlantic* (4–6). Illus. 1981, Childrens Pr. LB $9.95; paper $2.95. An account that portrays the horror and gallantry of this battle. Several other "battle" books are: *Battle of Midway* (1980); *Battle of Leyte Gulf* (1981); *Battle of Stalingrad* (1981); *Battle of the Coral Sea* (1981) (all LB $9.95; paper $2.95).

6455. Skipper, G. C. *Death of Hitler* (4–6). Illus. 1980, Childrens Pr. LB $9.95; paper $2.95. The story of the end of the hated dictator. Other books in this series dealing with World War II in Europe are: *Fall of the Fox: Rommel* (1980); *Goering and the Luftwaffe* (1980); *Invasion of Sicily* (1981); *Mussolini: A Dictator Dies* (1981); *Invasion of Poland* (1983) (all LB $9.95; paper $2.95).

6456. Skipper, G. C. *Pearl Harbor* (4–6). Illus. 1983, Childrens Pr. LB $9.95; paper $2.95. An overview of this day of infamy. Another in this series is: *Submarines in the Pacific* (1980, LB $9.25; paper $2.95).

6457. Snyder, Louis L. *World War II* (5–7). Illus. 1981, Watts $8.90. A brief account of the events leading to World War II and the conflict that ensued.

6458. Stein, R. Conrad. *Battle of Guadalcanal* (4–6). Illus. 1983, Childrens Pr. $6.50. A realistic account of this World War II Pacific battle. Two others in this series are: *Fall of Singapore* and *Hiroshima* (both 1982, $6.50).

6459. Stein, R. Conrad. *Dunkirk* (4–6). Illus. 1982, Childrens Pr. $6.50. The story of the dramatic evacuation of Allied troops from France. Other books about World War II in this series are: *Resistance Movements* (1982, $6.50); *Siege of Leningrad* (1983, $6.50).

6460. Stein, R. Conrad. *The Story of D-Day* (4–6). Illus. by Tom Dunnington. 1977, Childrens Pr. $8.60; paper $2.50. Events surrounding the landing in Normandy, June 6, 1944.

6461. Stein, R. Conrad. *The Story of the Battle for Iwo Jima* (4–6). Illus. by Len W. Meents. 1977, Childrens Pr. $8.60. The heartbreaking story of the battle that cost thousands of American lives.

6462. Stein, R. Conrad. *The Story of the Battle of the Bulge* (4–6). Illus. by Lou Aronson. 1977, Childrens Pr. $8.60. The story of the Germans' final attempt to stop an Allied victory.

6463. Sullivan, George. *Strange but True Stories of World War II* (6–9). Illus. 1983, Walker $10.95. Eleven fascinating vignettes on World War II.

6464. Taylor, Theodore. *Air-Raid—Pearl Harbor! The Story of December 7, 1941* (6–9). Illus. by W. T. Mars. 1971, Harper $10.95. A detailed, well-documented account of the events preceding the tragedy of Pearl Harbor.

6465. Taylor, Theodore. *Battle in the Arctic Seas: The Story of Convoy PQ 17* (6–9). Illus. by Robert Andrew Parker. 1976, Harper $10.95. An exciting account, for better readers, of a World War II naval disaster involving an ill-fated convoy.

6466. Tregaskis, Richard. *Guadalcanal Diary* (5–9). 1955, Random $5.99. An agonizing account of the battles in the Solomon Islands during World War II.

Polar Regions

6467. Asimov, Isaac. *How Did We Find Out about Antarctica?* (5–7). Illus. by David Wool. 1979, Walker $6.95; LB $6.85; Avon paper $1.95. Ideas, people, and occupations that have influenced our knowledge of Antarctica.

6468. Hagbrink, Bodil. *Children of Lapland* (3–5). Trans. by George Simpson. Illus. by author. 1979, Tundra $14.95. The day-to-day activities of 2 Lapp children are recounted in text and bold, full-color illustrations.

6469. Johnson, Sylvia A. *Animals of the Polar Regions* (4–6). Illus. by Alcuin C. Dornisch. 1976, Lerner $5.95. In addition to describing the environment, the author highlights 10 animals from these regions.

6470. Laycock, George. *Beyond the Arctic Circle* (5–7). Illus. 1978, Four Winds $8.95. The history of and contemporary conditions in the Arctic.

6471. Lye, Keith. *Take a Trip to Antarctica* (1–3). 1984, Watts $8.40. A simple introduction to the fifth largest continent.

6472. Meyer, Carolyn. *Eskimos: Growing Up in a Changing Culture* (6–8). 1977, Atheneum $8.95. An account that stresses present-day problems of the Eskimos.

6473. Pluckrose, Henry, ed. *Arctic Lands* (2–3). Illus. by Maurice Wilson. 1982, Watts LB $7.90. Geography, flora, and fauna are described simply.

6474. Purdy, Susan, and Sandak, Cass R. *Eskimos* (5–6). Illus. 1982, Watts $7.90. An introduction to Eskimo culture and several craft projects, such as making a model kayak.

6475. Schlein, Miriam. *Antarctica: The Great White Continent* (4–6). Illus. 1980, Hastings $8.95. An overview of the history, wildlife, and importance of Antarctica.

Africa

General

6476. Murphy, E. Jefferson. *Understanding Africa* (6–9). Illus. by Louise E. Jefferson. 1978, Harper LB $17.89. A survey brimming with information about the past, present, and future of Africa by an author well qualified to explode popularly held misconceptions about the Dark Continent.

6477. Musgrove, Margaret. *Ashanti to Zulu: African Traditions* (3–5). Illus. by Leo Dillon and Diane Dillon. 1976, Dial $11.95; LB $11.89; paper $2.95. A Caldecott Medal winner that describes distinctive life-styles of 26 African tribes in text and stunning pictures.

6478. Percefull, Aaron W. *The Nile* (6–8). 1984, Watts $8.90. The history and importance of this river.

6479. Pine, Tillie S., and Levine, Joseph. *The Africans Knew* (2–4). Illus. by Ann Grifalconi. 1967, McGraw $7.95. A survey of knowledge possessed by the ancient Africans that we use today.

North Africa

6480. Cross, Wilbur. *Egypt* (4–6). Illus. 1982, Childrens Pr. $9.95. An introduction to this country that briefly covers history and geography.

6481. Englebert, Victor. *Camera on Africa: The World of an Ethiopian Boy* (3–5). Illus. 1970, Harcourt $5.50. The life of a young boy is depicted through excellent photographs.

6482. Lye, Keith. *Take a Trip to Egypt* (2–3). Illus. 1983, Watts $8.90. A basic introduction highlighted by many fine illustrations.

Central and East Africa

6483. Bleeker, Sonia. *The Pygmies: Africans of the Congo Forest* (3–6). Illus. by Edith G. Singer. 1968,

Morrow LB $9.55. An intriguing picture of the life of this tribe.

6484. Foster, Blanche F. *East Central Africa: Kenya, Uganda, Tanzania, Rwanda and Burundi* (6–8). 1981, Watts LB $8.90. A description of 5 interesting countries and their troubled pasts.

6485. Jacobs, Francine. *Africa's Flamingo Lake* (4–6). Illus. 1979, Morrow $8.95; LB $8.59. An interesting description of the ecology of Lake Nakuru in Kenya.

6486. Kaula, Edna M. *The Land and People of Kenya* (6–8). Illus. 1973, Harper $9.89. This account covers the history and geography of and subjects related to the country, and its flora and fauna.

6487. Kaula, Edna M. *The Land and People of Tanzania* (4–7). Illus. 1972, Harper $9.89. Background on geography, history, and social conditions.

6488. Khalfan, Zulfm, and Amin, Mohamed. *We Live in Kenya* (4–7). Illus. 1984, Watts $9.90. In text and pictures, several residents describe their lives and their country.

6489. Lauber, Patricia. *The Congo: River into Central Africa* (4–6). Illus. by Ted Schroeder. 1964, Garrard $3.98. A simple account of the explorations of the Congo and the countries and people along this waterway.

6490. Newman, Gerald. *Zaire, Gabon and the Congo* (6–8). Illus. 1981, Watts $8.90. Basic information is given on these 3 countries.

6491. Shachtman, Tom. *Growing Up Masai* (3–6). Illus. 1981, Macmillan LB $8.95. The Masai tribal life as seen through the experiences of 2 children.

West Africa

6492. Anderson, Lydia. *Nigeria, Cameroon, and the Central African Republic* (6–8). Illus. 1981, Watts LB $8.90. A valuable overview of this area.

6493. Bernheim, Marc, and Bernheim, Evelyne. *African Success Story: The Ivory Coast* (6–9). Illus. 1970, Harcourt $6.95. A history of the Ivory Coast before and after gaining independence in 1960 and a good picture of how the inhabitants live.

6494. Clifford, Mary Louise. *The Land and People of Sierra Leone* (5–7). Illus. 1974, Harper $9.57. Geography, history, economy, and present-day conditions are covered in this survey volume.

6495. Gilfond, Henry. *Countries of the Sahara: Chad, Mali, Mauritania, Niger, Upper Volta and Western Sahara* (6–8). Illus. 1981, Watts LB $8.90. A useful country-by-country introduction to this area.

6496. Jenness, Aylette. *Along the Niger River: An African Way of Life* (5–9). Illus. by author. 1974, Harper $10.53. The author, who lived in Africa for many years, describes in this photographic documentary the history and way of life of the people who live along the banks of the Niger River.

6497. Latchem, Colin. *Looking at Nigeria* (4–6). Illus. 1976, Harper $10.53. A highly readable introduction to various aspects, chiefly geographical, of this country.

6498. Lye, Keith. *Take a Trip to Nigeria* (2–3). Illus. 1984, Watts $8.90. The land and people of this African nation are introduced simply.

South Africa

6499. Boyd, Herb. *The Former Portuguese Colonies: Angola, Mozambique, Guinea-Bissau, Cape Verde, Sao Tome and Principe* (6–8). Illus. 1981, Watts LB $8.90. A brief introduction to these South African countries and the islands in the Indian Ocean.

6500. Paton, Alan. *The Land and People of South Africa* (5–9). Illus. 1972, Harper $10.89. An excellent introduction to this land, which includes background material on racial tensions.

Asia

China

6501. Caldwell, John C. *Let's Visit China Today* (4–6). Illus. 1973, Harper LB $9.89. A heavily illustrated simple account that gives basic background material.

6502. China Features. *We Live in China* (5–8). Illus. 1984, Watts $9.90. Several residents from various strata of society describe life in China.

6503. Dunster, Jack. *China and Mao Zedong* (5–8). Illus. 1983, Lerner $6.95. Mao's rise to power and his regime are described.

6504. Filstrup, Chris, and Filstrup, Janie. *China: From Emperors to Communes* (5–6). Illus. 1983, Dillon $9.95. A handy guide to the history, geography, and culture of this country.

6505. Gray, Noel. *Looking at China* (4–6). Illus. 1974, Harper $11.06. A well-illustrated account of how people live in China. Also use: *People's Republic of China: Red Star of the East* by Jane Werner Watson (1976, Garrard $8.88).

6506. Kan, Lai Po. *The Ancient Chinese* (4–6). Illus. 1981, Silver Burdett LB $12.68. All aspects of Chinese life are covered in this account, which spans thousands of years.

6507. Knox, Robert. *Ancient China* (4–6). 1978, Watts $9.90. An account of many aspects of the history and culture of ancient China.

6508. Lawson, Don. *The Long March: Red China under Chairman Mao* (6–9). 1983, Harper $10.89. A history of the formation of modern China.

6509. McLenighan, Valjean. *China: A History to 1949* (5–8). Illus. 1983, Childrens Pr. $12.95. China from its earliest days to the founding of the People's Republic in 1949.

6510. Mason, Sally. *Take a Trip to China* (1–3). Illus. 1981, Watts LB $8.40. The geography, principal cities, and ways of life are introduced simply.

6511. Nancarrow, Peter. *Early China and the Wall* (6–9). Illus. 1980, Lerner LB $6.95. A history of China from the Stone Age to about the death of Christ.

6512. Perl, Lila. *Red Star and Green Dragon: Looking at New China* (5–8). Illus. 1983, Morrow $9.00. After a brief discussion of Chinese history, the author concentrates on contemporary Chinese life.

6513. Poole, Frederick K. *An Album of Modern China* (6–9). Illus. 1981, Watts $9.60. An introduction to modern China with some historical and geographical background.

6514. Rau, Margaret. *Holding Up the Sky: Young People in China* (6–9). 1983, Dutton $11.17. Life in China is introduced through the lives of young people.

6515. Rau, Margaret. *The Minority Peoples of China* (6–9). Illus. 1982, Messner LB $9.29. A description of some of the 56 minority groups that live in China today.

6516. Rau, Margaret. *Our World: The People's Republic of China* (5–7). Illus. 1978, Messner $7.79. The author discusses at length internal conditions and concerns in this fine survey of the history and government of China.

6517. Rau, Margaret. *The People of the New China* (4–6). Illus. 1978, Messner $8.79. A cursory view, augmented by the author's own photographs.

6518. Roberson, John R. *China: From Manchu to Mao (1699–1976)* (6–9). Illus. 1980, Atheneum $10.95. An objective account of this period in Chinese history; for better readers.

6519. Sadler, Catherine Edwards. *Two Chinese Families* (4–6). Illus. 1981, Atheneum LB $9.95. A view of contemporary life-styles in China through the eyes of two different families.

6520. Spencer, Cornelia. *The Land and People of China* (6–7). Illus. 1972, Harper $9.89. A fine, if somewhat detailed, introduction for a younger group. Also use: *The Yangtze: China's River Highway* (1963, Garrard $4.47).

6521. Willcox, Isobel. *Acrobats and Ping-Pong: Young China's Games, Sports, and Amusements* (5–8). Illus. 1981, Dodd LB $8.95. The recreational pursuits of the people of China.

6522. Yungmei, Tang. *China, Here We Come! Visiting the People's Republic of China* (4–7). Illus. 1981, Putnam $9.95. Modern China is seen through the eyes of visiting high school children.

Japan

6523. Ashby, Gwynneth. *Take a Trip to Japan* (2–4). Illus. 1981, Watts LB $8.40. A brief introduction to general facts about the country.

6524. Davidson, Judith. *Japan: Where East Meets West* (4–6). Illus. 1983, Dillon $9.95. An introduction to the country and the contributions immigrants have made to the United States.

6525. Dolan, Edward F., Jr. and Finney, Shan. *The New Japan* (6–9). Illus. 1983, Watts $9.90. Life in Japan today.

6526. Greene, Carol. *Japan* (5–6). Illus. 1983, Childrens Pr. $12.95. The history and geography of Japan, with excellent color photographs.

6527. Jacobsen, Karen. *Japan* (1–4). Illus. 1982, Childrens Pr. $6.95. A simple introduction with many illustrations and large type.

6528. Kawamata, Kazuhide. *We Live in Japan* (4–7). 1984, Watts $9.95. A cross section of people in Japan talk about their lives.

6529. Lewis, Brenda Ralph. *Growing Up in Samurai Japan* (6–9). Illus. 1981, David and Charles $14.95. Seven hundred years of feudal Japanese history are discussed.

6530. Maruki, Toshi. *Hiroshima No Pika* (3–6). Illus. by author. 1982, Lothrop $12.00. The story of a 7-year-old girl and the bombing of Hiroshima in 1945.

India

6531. Galbraith, Catherine Atwater, and Mehta, Rama. *India: Now and through Time* (6–8). Illus. 1980, Houghton $13.95. A survey of India's geography, history, and culture.

6532. Jacobsen, Peter Otto, and Preben, Sejer Kristensen. *A Family in India* (3–4). 1984, Watts $8.90. The story of a comfortably situated Indian family and how they live.

6533. Lye, Keith. *Take a Trip to India* (2–3). Illus. 1982, Watts LB $8.40. A series of photographs and captions give an introductory look at India.

6534. Sandal, Veenu. *We Live in India* (5–8). Illus. 1984, Watts $9.90. Life in India is described through several different first-person accounts.

6535. Watson, Jane Werner. *Indus: South Asia's Highway of History* (4–7). Illus. 1970, Garrard $4.47. Historical and geographical introduction to the land and people along the course of this river.

Other Asian Countries

6536. Clifford, Mary Louise. *The Land and People of Afghanistan* (5–7). Illus. 1973, Harper LB $10.89. An introduction to past life in this central Asian country.

6537. Farley, Carol. *Korea: A Land Divided* (4–6). Illus. 1984, Dillon $9.95. The history, geography, customs, and daily life of Koreans and their contributions to the United States.

6538. Goldfarb, Mace. *Fighters, Refugees, Immigrants: A Story of the Hmong* (4–6). 1982, Carolrhoda LB $9.95. The story of the refugee camp in Thailand where the Hmong survivors gathered.

6539. Lang, Robert. *The Land and People of Pakistan* (6–9). 1974, Harper $10.89. Includes material on the civil war and separation of Bangladesh.

6540. Laure, Jason, and Laure, Ettagale. *Joi Bangla! The Children of Bangladesh* (4–6). Illus. 1974, Farrar $7.95. Interviews with children from various social strata give information on their lives, customs, and problems.

6541. Lightfoot, Paul. *The Mekong* (5–8). Illus. 1981, Silver Burdett LB $12.68. A journey down this river important in world history.

6542. Lim, John. *Merchants of the Mysterious East* (3–5). Illus. by author. 1981, Tundra $14.95. Several trades as they exist in Singapore are described.

6543. Lye, Keith. *Take a Trip to Hong Kong* (2–4). Illus. 1984, Watts $8.90. This British colony is introduced in text and pictures.

6544. Smith, Datus C. *The Land and People of Indonesia* (6–9). Illus. 1983, Harper $10.10; LB $10.89. A brief history of this small country with incidental material on geography.

Australia and the Pacific Islands

6545. Ball, John. *We Live in New Zealand* (5–8). Illus. 1984, Watts $9.90. Several people from different walks of life describe life in New Zealand.

6546. Blunden, Godfrey. *The Land and People of Australia* (6–9). Illus. 1972, Harper LB $10.89. In addition to discussing the geography and native people, the author describes the government and social life of the modern nation.

6547. Burns, Geoff. *Take a Trip to New Zealand* (2–3). Illus. 1983, Watts $8.90. Fine illustrations highlight this introduction to the land of New Zealand.

6548. Ellis, Rennie. *We Live in Australia* (5–9). Illus. 1983, Watts $9.90. A variety of people talk about their country and what it means to them.

6549. Henderson, W. F. *Looking at Australia* (4–6). Illus. 1977, Harper $10.53. This work covers history, government, education, and social life.

6550. Higham, Charles. *The Maoris* (5–8). Illus. 1983, Lerner $6.95. A history of the Maoris and their history in New Zealand from A.D. 1000 on.

6551. Kaula, Edna M. *The Land and People of New Zealand* (6–8). Illus. 1972, Harper LB $10.89. After a short history, this introductory account tells about present-day New Zealand.

6552. Lepthien, Emilie U. *Australia* (5–8). Illus. 1982, Childrens Pr. $9.95. Many color photographs help introduce this country to youngsters.

6553. Lepthien, Emilie U. *The Philippines* (4–7). 1984, Childrens Pr. $12.95. These islands are introduced through a discussion of their history, geography, and culture.

6554. Nance, John. *The Land and People of the Philippines* (5–8). Illus. 1977, Harper $10.89. A description of the varied peoples and cultures that comprise these islands.

6555. Nance, John. *Lobo of the Tasaday: A Stone Age Boy Meets the Modern World* (4–6). 1982, Pantheon $9.95; LB $9.99. A true account of the Tasadays, the Stone Age people of the Philippines.

6556. Rau, Margaret. *Red Earth, Blue Sky: The Australian Outback* (6–8). Illus. 1981, Harper $8.95; LB $9.89. A description of this bleak, barren area where few live.

6557. Truby, David. *Take a Trip to Australia* (2–4). Illus. 1981, Watts LB $8.40. A brief account giving basic material on geography and the way of life in Australia.

Europe

Great Britain and Ireland

6558. Anno, Mitsumasa. *Anno's Britain* (K–3). Illus. by author. 1982, Putnam $10.95. A wanderer moves through Britain mingling with its people and visiting famous places.

6559. Barber, Richard. *A Strong Land and a Sturdy: England in the Middle Ages* (6–8). Illus. 1976, Houghton $8.95. The Norman period in British history is brilliantly re-created.

6560. Branley, Franklyn M. *The Mystery of Stonehenge* (4–6). Illus. by Victor G. Ambrus. 1969, Harper $10.89. Mysteries about this ancient spot fall under scientific scrutiny.

6561. Crossley-Holland, Kevin. *Green Blades Rising: The Anglo-Saxons* (6–9). Illus. 1976, Houghton $8.95. A comprehensive survey of the history, living habits, and religion of the Anglo-Saxons to the time of the Norman Conquest.

6562. Denny, Norman, and Filmer-Sankey, Josephine. *The Bayeux Tapestry: The Story of the Norman Conquest, 1066* (5–8). Illus. 1984, Merrimack $15.00. A picture story of the Norman Invasion of England in 1066.

6563. Drabble, Margaret. *For Queen and Country: Britain in the Victorian Age* (6–9). Illus. 1980, Houghton $8.95. A mature account of the Victorian age, its paradoxes and glories.

6564. Fairclough, Chris. *Take a Trip to England* (K–3). Illus. 1982, Watts LB $8.40. Simple text and many photos highlight this introduction to the people and common sights in England.

6565. Fairclough, Chris. *We Live in Britain* (5–8). Illus. 1984, Watts $9.90. A number of different people from the British Isles describe life there.

6566. Fradin, Dennis B. *The Republic of Ireland* (4–7). Illus. 1984, Childrens Pr. $12.95. An introduction to this country that touches briefly on many subjects.

6567. Goodall, John S. *The Story of an English Village* (2–6). Illus. 1979, Atheneum $8.95. Five hundred years in the history of an English village, in text and pictures.

6568. Greene, Carol. *England* (4–6). Illus. 1982, Childrens Pr. $9.95. A profusely illustrated volume that briefly covers history as well as contemporary topics.

6569. James, Ian. *Take a Trip to Ireland* (2–4). Illus. 1984, Watts $8.90. A brief introduction to the people and the land in both the South and the North.

6570. Magorian, Michelle. *Back Home* (6–9). 1984, Harper $13.95; LB $13.89. A young English girl returns home after spending World War II in Connecticut.

6571. Meyer, Kathleen Allan. *Ireland: Land of Mist and Magic* (4–7). Illus. 1983, Dillon $9.95. An introduction to Ireland and its people, plus a section on the Irish contribution to the United States.

6572. O'Brien, Elinor. *The Land and People of Ireland* (5–7). Illus. 1972, Harper $10.89. A basic introduction to life, history, and culture in Ireland.

6573. Sasek, M. *This Is Ireland* (3–5). Illus. by author. 1969, Macmillan $8.95. An engagingly illustrated introduction to the major sights.

6574. Snodin, David. *A Mighty Ferment* (6–9). Illus. 1978, Houghton $8.95. Subtitled: *Britain in the Age of Revolution, 1750–1850*.

Low Countries

6575. Fairclough, Chris. *Take a Trip to Holland* (K–3). Illus. 1982, Watts LB $8.40. A simple introduction to the land, people, and industries of Holland.

6576. Fradin, Dennis B. *The Netherlands* (5–7). Illus. 1983, Childrens Pr. $11.95. An introduction to the history, geography, and the people of Holland.

6577. Jacobsen, Peter Otto, and Preben, Sejer Kristensen. *A Family in Holland* (3–4). 1984, Watts $8.90. A real Dutch family is portrayed, with a description of how they live.

6578. Komroff, Manuel. *The Battle of Waterloo: The End of an Empire* (6–8). 1964, Macmillan $8.95. An account of the battle that changed the destiny of Europe.

Spain and Portugal

6579. Bristow, Richard. *We Live in Spain* (5–8). Illus. 1984, Watts $9.90. A description of life in Spain is given through several first-person accounts.

6580. Gidal, Sonia. *My Village in Portugal* (4–6). Illus. 1972, Pantheon $5.69. Carlos Verissumo tells of his life in the small fishing village of Nazare.

6581. Loder, Dorothy H. *The Land and People of Spain* (5–8). Illus. 1972, Harper $10.89. An introduction to the history and civilization of Spain, with emphasis on famous Spaniards and their contributions to world culture. For a younger group use: *Looking at Spain* by Rupert Martin (1970, Harper $11.06).

6582. Rutland, Jonathan. *Take a Trip to Spain* (2–4). Illus. 1981, Watts LB $8.40. A simple introduction to principal regions, cities, and customs.

France

6583. Balerdi, Susan. *France: The Crossroads of Europe* (5–8). Illus. 1984, Dillon $9.95. An overview of the culture and people of France with a final chapter on French migration to the United States.

6584. Hills, C. A. R. *The Seine* (5–8). Illus. 1981, Silver Burdett LB $12.68. A trip down this river, usually associated only with Paris.

6585. Holbrook, Sabra. *Growing Up in France* (6–8). Illus. 1980, Atheneum $8.95. An introduction to the life-styles of several French children from many different social levels and geographical areas.

6586. Jacobsen, Peter Otto, and Preben, Sejer Kristensen. *A Family in France* (3–4). 1984, Watts $8.90. The story of a real French family and their life-style.

6587. Rutland, Jonathan. *Take a Trip to France* (2–4). Illus. 1981, Watts LB $8.40. Plenty of color photographs enliven this brief account.

6588. Tomlins, James. *We Live in France* (5–9). Illus. 1983, Watts $9.90. A number of people from different areas and social strata describe their native land.

Germany

6589. Fairclough, Chris. *Take a Trip to West Germany* (1–3). Illus. 1981, Watts LB $8.40. A very simple introduction to the geography and way of life in this country.

6590. Gray, Ronald. *Hitler and the Germans* (6–9). Illus. 1983, Lerner $6.95. The story of Hitler's rise to power and its effect on the world.

6591. Hintz, Martin. *West Germany* (5–7). Illus. 1983, Childrens Pr. $11.95. Color photographs are used to detail the geography and history of this country.

6592. Singer, Julia. *Impressions: A Trip to the German Democratic Republic* (5–8). Illus. 1979, Atheneum $8.95. Subjective but telling impressions of a country behind the Iron Curtain.

6593. Stadtler, Christa. *We Live in West Germany* (4–7). 1984, Watts $9.90. A number of residents of West Germany talk about their country.

6594. Wohlrabe, Raymond A., and Krusch, Werner E. *The Land and People of Germany* (5–7). Illus. 1972, Harper $9.89. A basic introduction to the past and present of the 2 Germanys.

Scandinavia

6595. Anderson, Madelyn Klein. *Greenland: Island at the Top of the World* (5–8). Illus. 1983, Dodd $10.95. The story of Greenland from Arctic exploration to the present.

6596. Anderson, Ulla. *We Live in Denmark* (5–8). Illus. 1984, Watts $9.90. A collection of first-person accounts gives a cross section of life in Denmark.

6597. Atkinson, Ian. *The Viking Ships* (5–8). Illus. 1980, Cambridge Univ. Pr. $3.95; Lerner LB $6.95. A book originally published in England that concentrates on Viking activities in Europe.

6598. Berry, Erick. *The Land and People of Finland* (6–8). Illus. 1972, Harper LB $10.89. A basic introduction covering many facets of Finnish life, past and present.

6599. Berry, Erick. *The Land and People of Iceland* (5–8). Illus. 1972, Harper LB $10.89. An introduction to this island republic.

6600. Hintz, Martin. *Finland* (5–7). Illus. 1983, Childrens Pr. $11.95. This northern European country is introduced through its history, geography, and famous citizens.

6601. Hintz, Martin. *Norway* (4–6). Illus. 1982, Childrens Pr. $9.95. The land and the people of Norway are introduced in text and pictures.

6602. Hughes, Jill. *Vikings* (4–6). Illus. by Ivan Lapper. 1984, Watts $8.90. An account of how the Vikings lived and of the explorations that made them famous.

6603. Janeway, Elizabeth. *The Vikings* (4–6). 1981, Random paper $2.95. A basic introduction to the Vikings, their explorations, exploits, and contributions.

6604. Lye, Keith. *Take a Trip to Sweden* (1–4). Illus. 1983, Watts $8.90. Some text and many color photos are found in this introductory work.

6605. Olsson, Kari. *Sweden: A Good Life for All* (4–7). Illus. 1983, Dillon $9.95. The story of this country, its geography and people, and the contributions of their immigrants to the United States.

6606. Pluckrose, Henry, ed. *Vikings* (1–4). Illus. by Ivan Lapper. 1982, Watts LB $7.90. A simple account of these seafarers and their effects on history.

6607. Rudstrom, Lennart. *A Home* (2–4). Illus. by Carl Larsson. 1974, Putnam $9.95. A beautifully illustrated picture book from Sweden. Also use: *A Farm* (1976, Putnam $9.95).

Greece and Italy

6608. deZulueta, Tana. *We Live in Italy* (5–9). Illus. 1983, Watts $9.90. A series of first-person narratives introduce this country to young people.

6609. DiFranco, Anthony. *Italy: Balanced on the Edge of Time* (4–6). Illus. 1983, Dillon $9.95. An introduction to the history, culture, and geography of Italy and what Italians have contributed to the United States.

6610. Elliott, Drossoula Vassiliou, and Elliott, Sloane. *We Live in Greece* (4–7). 1984, Watts $9.90. Through the eyes of several people, the reader is introduced to life in Greece.

6611. Fairclough, Chris. *Take a Trip to Italy* (1–3). Illus. 1981, Watts LB $8.40. A simple introduction to life in this country.

6612. Gianakoulis, Theodore. *Land and People of Greece* (6–7). 1972, Harper $9.89. An introduction (somewhat dated) to the geography and history of Greece.

6613. Lye, Keith. *Take a Trip to Greece* (2–3). Illus. 1983, Watts $8.90. Impressive color photographs highlight this simple introduction to Greece.

6614. Sasek, M. *This Is Greece* (4–6). 1966, Macmillan $8.95. A colorful introduction that presents the major sights in bold drawings.

6615. Warren, Ruth. *Modern Greece* (4–6). Illus. 1979, Watts $8.90. An excellent introduction to politics and social life in present-day Greece.

6616. Winwar, Frances. *The Land and People of Italy* (6–9). 1972, Harper $10.89. A thorough account for mature readers.

Central and Eastern Europe

6617. Greene, Carol. *Poland* (5–7). Illus. 1983, Childrens Pr. $11.95. Poland is introduced through an account of its history and geography as well as famous sights and people.

6618. Greene, Carol. *Yugoslavia* (4–7). Illus. 1984, Childrens Pr. $12.95. The history and geography of Yugoslavia are introduced, plus customs and culture.

6619. Hale, Julian. *The Land and People of Romania* (6–8). 1972, Harper $9.59. A somewhat out-of-date introduction to Romania.

6620. Hall, Elvajean. *The Land and People of Czechoslovakia* (6–9). Illus. 1972, Harper LB $10.89. An account that concentrates on daily conditions.

6621. Kelly, Eric P., and Kostich, Dragos. *The Land and People of Poland* (6–9). Illus. 1972, Harper $10.50. An introductory survey of Polish history and geography. Somewhat out-of-date.

6622. Lengyel, Emil. *The Land and People of Hungary* (6–8). 1972, Harper $9.89. A somewhat dated account of the geography, history, and culture of the country.

6623. Pfeiffer, Christine. *Poland: Land of Freedom Fighters* (5–8). Illus. 1984, Dillon $9.95. An introduction to the land and people of Poland and of their migration to the United States.

6624. Wohlrabe, Raymond A., and Krusch, Werner E. *The Land and People of Austria* (6–9). 1972, Harper $9.89. The people, history, geography, and culture of Austria are treated in this now dated survey volume.

6625. Worth, Richard. *Poland: The Threat to National Renewal* (6–9). 1982, Watts LB $9.90. A history of Poland with emphasis on events since World War II.

Russia

6626. Fisher, Leonard Everett. *A Russian Farewell* (5–8). Illus. by author. 1980, Four Winds $9.95. Following the Sino-Japanese War, a Jewish family flees persecution in Russia.

6627. Hewitt, Phillip. *Looking at Russia* (4–6). Illus. 1977, Harper $8.95. A brief introduction to the land and its people. Also use: *Soviet Union: Land of Many Peoples* by Jane Werner Watson (1973, Garrard $7.95).

6628. Karlowich, Robert A. *Young Defector* (4–6). Illus. 1983, Messner $8.79. The story of 12-year-old Walter Polovchak, who defected from the Soviet Union in 1980.

6629. Lawson, Don. *The K.G.B.* (5–7). 1984, Wanderer paper $3.95. An account of the Soviet Union's secret police organization.

6630. Lye, Keith. *Take a Trip to Russia* (2–4). Illus. 1982, Watts LB $8.40. Some important aspects of Russian life are introduced through photos and captions.

6631. Nazaroff, Alexander. *The Land and People of Russia* (5–8). 1972, Harper LB $9.89. This is primarily an overview of Russian history from early times to the late 1960s.

6632. Resnick, Abraham. *Russia: A History to 1917* (5–8). Illus. 1983, Childrens Pr. $12.95. A history of Russia from about the ninth century to the end of the Russian Revolution.

Middle East

6633. Barlow, Christopher. *Islam* (6–9). Illus. 1983, David and Charles $14.95. An introduction to Islamic history and the religious beliefs of Islam.

6634. Batchelor, John, and Batchelor, Julie. *The Euphrates* (5–8). Illus. 1981, Silver Burdett LB $12.68. A journey down one of the world's most famous rivers.

6635. Berger, Gilda. *Kuwait and the Rim of Arabia* (4–6). Illus. 1978, Watts LB $8.90. A well-researched guide to the Persian Gulf states.

6636. Copeland, Paul W. *The Land and People of Syria* (6–8). 1972, Harper $9.89. Though dated, a useful background book on this country.

6637. Fichter, George S. *Iraq* (4–6). Illus. 1978, Watts $8.90. History, geography, and culture are highlighted in this basic account.

6638. Gilfond, Henry. *Afghanistan* (6–7). Illus. 1980, Watts LB $8.90. An introduction to this country with coverage of the recent Russian occupation.

6639. Jacobs, David, and Mango, Cyril. *Constantinople: City of the Golden Horn* (6–8). Illus. 1969, Harper LB $14.89. A lavishly illustrated history of Constantinople from ancient times to the 1920s.

6640. Lancaster, Fidelity. *The Bedouin* (4–6). Illus. by Maurice Wilson. 1978, Watts $9.40. An overview of the life, history, and customs of these nomads.

6641. Lengyel, Emil. *Iran* (4–6). Illus. 1981, Watts $7.90. Good background information on the land, its people, and its economy.

6642. Newman, Gerald. *Lebanon* (4–6). Illus. 1978, Watts $8.90. Current political and economic problems are well handled in this basic account.

6643. Pine, Tillie S., and Levine, Joseph. *The Arabs Knew* (3–5). 1976, McGraw $8.95. An exploration of the discoveries, inventions, and other contributions made to civilization by the Arabs.

6644. Poole, Frederick K. *Jordan* (5–7). Illus. 1978, Watts $9.60. An introductory survey that simplifies without distorting the complex history of this divided land. With an older group use: *The Land and People of Jordan* by Paul W. Copeland (1972, Harper $10.53).

6645. Spencer, William. *The Land and People of Turkey* (6–8). 1972, Harper $9.89. A somewhat dated account that emphasizes history and geography.

Egypt

6646. Jacobs, Francine. *The Red Sea* (4–6). Illus. 1978, Morrow $8.40. A thorough study that includes history and geography as well as biology.

6647. Lengyel, Emil. *Modern Egypt* (5–7). Illus. 1978, Watts $8.90. In addition to standard background material, this book includes material on Egyptian-Israeli relations.

6648. Mahmoud, Zaki N. *The Land and People of Egypt* (6–8). Illus. 1972, Harper LB $9.89. Although there is some material on ancient history, this now dated account concentrates on contemporary conditions.

Israel

6649. Adler, David A. *A Picture Book of Israel* (3–6). Illus. 1984, Holiday $10.95. Many photographs and a clear, straightforward text highlight this account.

6650. Bergman, Denise, and Williams, Lorna. *Through the Year in Israel* (6–9). Illus. 1983, David and Charles $14.95. A month-by-month introduction to the country, its history and people.

6651. Levine, Gemma. *We Live in Israel* (5–9). Illus. 1983, Watts $9.90. Several people from different walks of life describe life in Israel.

6652. Rutland, Jonathan. *Take a Trip to Israel* (1–3). Illus. 1981, Watts LB $8.40. A short, heavily illustrated introduction to the country.

Middle America

Mexico

6653. Beck, Barbara L. *The Aztecs* (4–7). 1983, Watts LB $8.90. A history of the Aztecs and their civilization.

6654. Epstein, Sam, and Epstein, Beryl. *The First Book of Mexico* (4–7). Illus. 1967, Watts $4.90. A tour of various towns and cities and highlights from Mexican civilization.

6655. Jacobsen, Karen. *Mexico* (1–4). Illus. 1983, Childrens Pr. $6.95. This country is introduced in simple language with many illustrations.

6656. Jacobsen, Peter Otto, and Preben, Sejer Kristensen. *A Family in Mexico* (3–4). 1984, Watts $8.90. The story of a Mexican family and how they live.

6657. Karen, Ruth. *Feathered Serpent: The Rise and Fall of the Aztecs* (6–9). Illus. 1979, Four Winds

$9.95. A survey of the Aztec civilization enriched by frequent quotations from primary sources.

6658. Larralde, Elsa. *The Land and People of Mexico* (3–5). 1968, Harper LB $10.89. The history and geography of Mexico are given in this now dated account.

6659. Lewis, Thomas P. *Hill of Fire* (1–3). Illus. by Joan Sandin. 1971, Harper $7.64; LB $8.89; paper $2.95. The eruption of the volcano Paricutin and its effect on the lives of the people.

6660. Lye, Keith. *Take a Trip to Mexico* (2–4). Illus. 1982, Watts LB $8.40. Pictures are used to introduce some important topics about this country.

6661. Perl, Lila. *Mexico, Crucible of the Americas* (6–8). Illus. 1978, Morrow LB $11.47. A background book that surveys both historical and present-day conditions in Mexico.

6662. Purdy, Susan, and Sandak, Cass R. *Aztecs* (5–6). Illus. 1982, Watts $7.90. The history and civilization of the Aztecs are briefly introduced, plus several craft projects.

6663. Smith, Eileen Latell. *Mexico: Giant of the South* (4–6). Illus. 1983, Dillon $9.95. Several chapters on Mexico plus a final one on Mexican immigration to the United States.

6664. Stein, R. Conrad. *Mexico* (5–7). Illus. 1984, Childrens Pr. $12.95. A realistic look at this country, its past, present, and important problems.

Central America

6665. Beck, Barbara L. *The Ancient Maya* (5–7). Illus. 1983, Watts $8.90. A discussion of Mayan culture and contributions to civilization.

6666. Karen, Ruth. *The Land and People of Central America* (5–7). 1972, Harper $10.89. A general but dated introduction to life in each of the Central American countries.

6667. Markun, Patricia Maloney. *Central America and Panama* (4–7). Illus. 1983, Watts $8.90. An account of each Central American country with good background information.

6668. Markun, Patricia Maloney. *The Panama Canal* (5–7). Illus. 1979, Watts $8.90. Includes the 1978 treaty and its implications. Also use: *The Story of the Panama Canal* by R. Conrad Stein (1982, Childrens Pr. $5.95).

6669. Perl, Lila. *Guatemala: Central America's Living Past* (6–9). Illus. 1982, Morrow $9.75. The economy, history, and contemporary problems of this Central American country are discussed.

Puerto Rico and Other Caribbean Islands

6670. Carroll, Raymond. *The Caribbean: Issues in U.S. Relations* (6–8). 1984, Watts $9.90. An overview of the various Caribbean islands and our relations with each.

6671. Haskins, James. *The New Americans: Cuban Boat People* (6–8). Illus. 1982, Enslow LB $9.95. The waves of migration from Cuba in 1965, 1971, and 1980 are described.

6672. Lindon, Edmund. *Cuba* (5–7). 1980, Watts LB $8.90. An objective account that concentrates on the island's history since Castro's takeover.

6673. Lye, Keith. *Take a Trip to the West Indies* (2–4). Illus. 1984, Watts $8.90. A brief tour of the islands and an introduction to the people and how they live.

6674. Ortiz, Victoria. *The Land and People of Cuba* (6–8). Illus. 1973, Harper $9.89. A sympathetic but now dated account that concentrates on Cuban history and Castro's regime.

6675. Radlauer, Ruth. *Virgin Islands National Park* (4–6). Illus. 1981, Childrens Pr. LB $10.60. An exploration of the flora and fauna of this park, located on St. John.

6676. Singer, Julia. *We All Come from Puerto Rico, Too* (3–5). Illus. by author. 1977, Atheneum $6.95. Life in Puerto Rico as seen through the eyes of several children of varying interests and backgrounds.

6677. Telemaque, Eleanor Wong. *Haiti through Its Holidays* (4–5). Illus. by Earl Hill. 1980, Blyden Pr. $7.50. An introduction to Haiti through its holidays and customs surrounding them.

South America

6678. Beals, Carleton. *The Incredible Incas: Yesterday and Today* (5–7). Illus. 1974, Harper $12.45. A history that concentrates on everyday life.

6679. Beck, Barbara L. *The Incas* (6–9). 1983, Watts LB $8.90. A thorough and enthralling picture of the Incas.

6680. Bleeker, Sonia. *Inca: Indians of the Andes* (3–6). Illus. by Patricia Boodell. 1960, Morrow LB $9.95. A fine introduction to Inca culture.

6681. Brown, Rose, and Warren, Leslie F. *The Land and People of Brazil* (6–8). Illus. 1972, Harper LB $9.89. A now dated picture of Brazil and the life-style of its people.

6682. Carter, William E. *South America* (4–7). Illus. 1983, Watts $8.90. History, folklore, and religion.

6683. Cheney, Glenn Alan. *The Amazon* (6–8). Illus. 1984, Watts $8.90. A fascinating look at the past and present of this important world river.

6684. Crosby, Alexander L. *The Rimac, River of Peru* (4–6). Illus. 1966, Garrard LB $4.47. The story of the river that has played a major role in the history of Peru.

6685. Dobler, Lavinia. *The Land and People of Uruguay* (6–8). Illus. 1972, Harper LB $10.89. This account includes materials on facets of life in Uruguay.

6686. Hall, Elvajean. *The Land and People of Argentina* (6–8). Illus. 1972, Harper $10.89. An introductory but dated volume on the history and the people.

6687. Huber, Alex. *We Live in Argentina* (4–7). 1984, Watts $9.90. People from various walks of life describe their country.

6688. Jenness, Aylette. *A Life of Their Own: An Indian Family in Latin America* (4–7). Illus. 1975, Harper $10.53. A documentary of the Hernandez family, told in words and many photographs.

6689. Lye, Keith. *Take a Trip to Brazil* (2–4). Illus. 1984, Watts $8.90. A brief introduction to South America's largest country.

6690. Shuttlesworth, Dorothy E. *The Wildlife of South America* (6–9). Illus. by George F. Mason. 1974, Hastings $7.95. An overview of South American wildlife, how it has been used in the past, and the need for present-day conservation.

6691. Warren, Leslie F. *The Land and People of Bolivia* (6–8). Illus. 1974, Harper $9.89. A somewhat dated overview of life in this republic.

North America

Canada

6692. Ferguson, Linda W. *Canada* (5–8). Illus. 1979, Scribners $10.95. Canadian history, geography, and current concerns are nicely traced in this account.

6693. Hanmer, Trudy J. *The St. Lawrence* (6–8). 1984, Watts $8.90. An introduction to the past and present of the river that divides Canada and the United States.

6694. Holbrook, Sabra. *Canada's Kids* (6–8). Illus. 1983, Atheneum $11.95. Stories of children in the 10 provinces and 2 territories.

6695. Lye, Keith. *Take a Trip to Canada* (2–4). Illus. 1983, Watts $8.90. The land, people, and industries of Canada are introduced in text and many photos.

6696. Ross, Frances Aileen. *The Land and People of Canada* (5–7). Illus. 1964, Harper LB $10.89. This now dated account traces the political and social history and geography of Canada.

6697. Watson, Jane Werner. *Canada: Giant Nation of the North* (4–6). Illus. 1968, Garrard LB $8.88. A summary overview of history and geography.

6698. White, Anne Terry. *The St. Lawrence: Seaway of North America* (4–7). Illus. 1961, Garrard LB $4.47. The history of the St. Lawrence River from the early explorers to the building of the seaway. Also use: *The Mackenzie: River to the Top of the World* by Beatrice R. Lambie (1967, Garrard LB $4.47).

United States

General

6699. Anno, Mitsumasa. *Anno's U.S.A.* (2–5). Illus. by author. 1983, Putnam $10.95. A wordless trek across the United States in imaginative and often humorous drawings.

6700. Arnold, Pauline, and White, Percival. *How We Named Our States* (5–7). Illus. 1966, Harper $12.95. The origins of the names of the 50 states and their capitals interestingly told.

6701. Berg, Annemarie. *Great State Seals of the United States* (4–7). Illus. 1979, Dodd $8.95. In pictures and descriptive text, the seals of all the states are covered.

6702. Brandt, Sue R. *Facts about the Fifty States* (5–7). Illus. 1970, Watts $7.90. A rundown of information and salient facts about each of the 50 states. Also use: *Stories of the States* by Frank Ross, Jr. (1969, Harper $12.95).

6703. Carpenter, Allan. *Far-Flung America* (5–7). Illus. 1979, Childrens Pr. $11.95. A brief, attractive introduction to the geography of America.

6704. Crisman, Ruth. *The Mississippi* (6–8). 1984, Watts $8.90. A history of the river and its present importance.

6705. Dowden, Anne Ophelia. *State Flowers* (5–9). Illus. by author. 1978, Harper $9.95; LB $9.89. Background information is given along with detailed drawings of each flower.

6706. Earle, Olive L. *State Trees* (4–7). Illus. by author. 1973, Morrow $8.16. Through text and detailed illustrations, information on each of the state trees is interestingly presented.

6707. Fisher, Leonard Everett. *The Newspapers* (5–8). Illus. by author. 1981, Holiday LB $7.95. The story of the growth of American newspapers and such people as Noah Webster, Horace Greeley and William R. Hearst.

6708. Fisher, Leonard Everett. *The Schools* (4–6). Illus. by author. 1983, Holiday $10.95. A history of education in nineteenth-century America.

6709. Holling, Holling C. *Paddle-to-the-Sea* (3–6). Illus. by author. 1941, Houghton $11.95; paper $5.95. From Ontario to the Atlantic in a toy canoe, in this classic juvenile tale.

6710. Loeper, John J. *By Hook and Ladder: The Story of Fire Fighting in America* (4–6). Illus. 1981, Atheneum LB $8.95. A partly fictional approach to the history of fighting fires in the United States.

6711. Loeper, John J. *The House on Spruce Street* (5–7). Illus. by author. 1982, Atheneum $9.95. The true story of a house built in 1772 in Philadelphia.

6712. Marty, Martin E. *Christianity in the New World: From 1500 to 1800* (4–7). 1984, Winston $12.95. Three hundred years of church history in the New World.

6713. National Geographic Society. *Wilderness Challenge* (6–9). 1980, National Geographic Society $6.95; LB $8.50. A variety of camping experiences in different locales by young people is included.

6714. Radlauer, Ruth. *Shenandoah National Park* (3–6). Illus. 1982, Childrens Pr. LB $11.95. An introduction to the geography of and the life forms in the Virginia park.

6715. Ronan, Margaret. *All about Our 50 States* (4–6). Illus. by William Meyerriecks. 1978, Random $6.95; LB $6.99. Useful information plus maps and photographs.

6716. Sedeen, Margaret, ed. *Picture Atlas of Our Fifty States* (4–6). 1978, National Geographic Society $14.95; LB $16.95. An atlas plus hundreds of photos, charts, and other illustrations.

6717. Simon, Hilda. *Bird and Flower Emblems of the United States* (4–8). Illus. 1978, Dodd $12.95. Alphabetically by state, the author gives details on flower and bird emblems.

6718. Swanson, June. *The Spice of America* (3–6). Illus. by Priscilla Kiedrowski. 1983, Carolrhoda $7.95. Fifteen unusual factual stories from our past, such as how the doughnut got its hole.

Northeast

6719. Carmer, Elizabeth, and Carmer, Carl. *The Susquehanna: From New York to Chesapeake* (4–6). Illus. 1964, Garrard LB $4.47. The 400-mile

course of this river is chronicled with historical information.

6720. Carpenter, Allan. *Connecticut* (4–6). Illus. 1979, Childrens Pr. $11.95. A basic introduction; part of The New Enchantment of America series, which also includes *Massachusetts* (1978); *New York* (1978); *Pennsylvania* (1978); *Maine* (1979); *New Hampshire* (1979); *New Jersey* (1979); *Rhode Island* (1979); *Vermont* (1979) (all $11.95).

6721. Fradin, Dennis B. *Connecticut in Words and Pictures* (2–5). Illus. by Richard Wall. 1980, Childrens Pr. $10.60. A brief overview of the state and its history. Also use: *Delaware in Words and Pictures* (1980); *Maine in Words and Pictures* (1980); *Massachusetts in Words and Pictures* (1981); *New Hampshire in Words and Pictures* (1981); *New Jersey in Words and Pictures* (1980); *New York in Words and Pictures* (1981); *Pennsylvania in Words and Pictures* (1980); *Rhode Island in Words and Pictures* (1981); *Vermont in Words and Pictures* (1980) (all LB $10.60).

6722. Gilfond, Henry. *The Northeast States* (5–8). Illus. 1984, Watts $8.90. An overall look at the characteristics of this region and an introduction to each state.

6723. Kraske, Robert. *Statue of Liberty Comes to America* (3–6). Illus. by Victor Mays. 1972, Garrard $6.95. A complete, fascinating history of the concept of the Statue of Liberty, its execution, and the people behind it.

6724. McNeer, May. *The Hudson: River of History* (4–7). 1962, Garrard $3.89. The history and geography of this important waterway.

6725. Miller, Natalie. *The Story of the Statue of Liberty* (4–6). Illus. by John Hawkenson and Lucy Hawkenson. 1965, Childrens Pr. $8.60. The story of Miss Liberty from France to the New World.

6726. Radlauer, Ruth. *Acadia National Park* (3–5). Illus. 1978, Childrens Pr. $10.60. An introduction and visitor's guide to this park in Maine.

6727. Schnurnberger, Lynn. *Kids Love New York!* (4–8). Illus. 1984, St. Martins paper $9.95. A group of suggestions for various activities in New York.

South

6728. Berger, Gilda. *The Southeast States* (5–8). Illus. 1984, Watts $8.90. An introduction to the region and the individual states.

6729. Carpenter, Allan. *Alabama* (4–6). Illus. 1978, Childrens Pr. $11.95. Part of The New Enchantment of America series. Also use: *Arkansas* (1978); *Georgia* (1978); *Delaware* (1979); *District of Columbia* (1979); *Florida* (1979); *Louisiana* (1979); *Maryland* (1979) (all $11.95).

6730. Carpenter, Allan. *Mississippi* (4–6). Illus. 1978, Childrens Pr. $11.95. Part of The New

Enchantment of America series. Also use: *Virginia* (1978); *North Carolina* (1979); *South Carolina* (1979); *Tennessee* (1979); *West Virginia* (1979) (all $11.95).

6731. Cohen, Peter Z. *The Great Red River Raft* (3–6). Illus. by James Watling. 1984, Whitman $9.25. The story of Henry Shreve and how he broke the massive logjam on the Red River in Texas.

6732. Epstein, Sam, and Epstein, Beryl. *Washington, D.C.: The Nation's Capital* (4–6). Illus. 1981, Watts LB $8.90. This revised edition brings coverage up to the present.

6733. Fichter, George S. *Florida in Pictures* (5–7). Illus. 1979, Sterling $6.69; paper $2.95. A useful but superficial overview, also suitable for browsing.

6734. Fradin, Dennis B. *Alabama in Words and Pictures* (2–5). Illus. by Richard Wahl. 1980, Childrens Pr. LB $10.60. A brief history, geography, and travelogue of the state. Others are: *Arkansas in Words and Pictures; Florida in Words and Pictures; Mississippi in Words and Pictures* (all 1980, LB $10.60); *Virginia in Words and Pictures* (1976, $9.25).

6735. Fradin, Dennis B. *Tennessee in Words and Pictures* (2–5). Illus. by Richard Wahl. 1980, Childrens Pr. $10.60. An introduction to the state and its history. Also use: *Georgia in Words and Pictures* (1981); *Kentucky in Words and Pictures* (1980); *Louisiana in Words and Pictures* (1981); *Maryland in Words and Pictures* (1980); *North Carolina in Words and Pictures* (1980); *South Carolina in Words and Pictures* (1980); *West Virginia in Words and Pictures* (1980) (all LB $10.60).

6736. Lumley, Kathryn Wentzel. *District of Columbia: In Words and Pictures* (2–4). Illus. by Richard Wahl. 1981, Childrens Pr. LB $10.60; paper $3.95. Historical and geographical information is given. All 50 states are now part of this set.

6737. Prolman, Marilyn. *The Story of the Capitol* (3–5). Illus. by Darrell Wiskur. 1969, Childrens Pr. $8.60. The history and architecture of the nation's capitol.

6738. Radlauer, Ruth. *Mammoth Cave National Park* (3–5). Illus. 1978, Childrens Pr. $10.60. Interesting material about this Kentucky park.

6739. Sasek, M. *This Is Washington* (2–4). Illus. 1969, Macmillan paper $3.95. An introduction to the U.S. Capitol in picture book format.

Midwest

6740. Carpenter, Allan. *Illinois* (4–6). Illus. 1979, Childrens Pr. $11.95. Part of The New Enchantment of America series. Also use: *Michigan* (1978);

Minnesota (1978); *Indiana* (1979); *Iowa* (1979); *Kansas* (1979) (all $11.95).

6741. Carpenter, Allan. *Missouri* (4–6). Illus. 1978, Childrens Pr. $11.95. Part of The New Enchantment of America series. Also use: *South Dakota* (1978); *Wisconsin* (1978); *Nebraska* (1979); *North Dakota* (1979); *Ohio* (1979) (all $11.95).

6742. Fradin, Dennis B. *Minnesota in Words and Pictures* (2–5). Illus. by Richard Wahl. 1980, Childrens Pr. LB $10.60. A simple introduction to this state and its history and geography. Also use: *Illinois in Words and Pictures* (1976); *Iowa in Words and Pictures* (1980); *Michigan in Words and Pictures* (1980); *Nebraska in Words and Pictures* (1980); *North Dakota in Words and Pictures* (1981); *South Dakota in Words and Pictures* (1981) (all LB $10.60).

6743. Fradin, Dennis B. *Wisconsin in Words and Pictures* (2–5). Illus. 1977, Childrens Pr. $10.60. Interesting background information is interspersed with essential historical and geographical facts. Also use: *Indiana in Words and Pictures; Kansas in Words and Pictures; Missouri in Words and Pictures* (all 1980); *Ohio in Words and Pictures* (1977) (all LB $10.60).

6744. Frazier, Carl, and Frazier, Rosalie. *The Lincoln Country in Pictures* (4–6). Illus. 1963, Hastings $6.95. An introduction to the land where Lincoln was born.

6745. Jacobson, Daniel. *The North Central States* (4–6). Illus. 1984, Watts $8.90. A brief history and description of the region, plus profiles of each of the states.

Mountain States

6746. Carpenter, Allan. *Colorado* (4–6). Illus. 1978, Childrens Pr. $11.95. Part of The New Enchantment of America series. Also use: *Idaho; Montana; Nevada; Utah; Wyoming* (all 1979, $11.95).

6747. Fradin, Dennis B. *Wyoming in Words and Pictures* (2–5). Illus. by Richard Wahl. 1980, Childrens Pr. LB $10.60. A brief history and geography of the state. Also use: *Colorado in Words and Pictures* (1980); *Idaho in Words and Pictures* (1980); *Montana in Words and Pictures* (1981); *Nevada in Words and Pictures* (1981); *Utah in Words and Pictures* (1980) (all LB $10.60).

6748. Radlauer, Ruth. *Bryce Canyon National Park* (3–5). Illus. 1980, Childrens Pr. $10.60. An overview of the extraordinary park in southwest Utah.

6749. Radlauer, Ruth. *Zion National Park* (3–5). Illus. 1978, Childrens Pr. $10.60. The Utah park introduced in text and many color photographs.

6750. Taylor, L. B., and Taylor, C. L. *The Rocky Mountain States* (4–6). Illus. 1984, Watts $8.90. A strong portrait of this region in text and pictures.

Southwest

6751. Carpenter, Allan. *Arizona* (4–6). Illus. 1979, Childrens Pr. $11.95. Part of The New Enchantment of America series. Also use: *New Mexico* (1978); *Oklahoma* (1979); *Texas* (1979) (all $11.95).

6752. Fardin, Dennis B. *Arizona in Words and Pictures* (2–5). Illus. by Richard Wahl. 1980, Childrens Pr. LB $10.60. A brief tour of this state and its history. Also use: *New Mexico in Words and Pictures; Oklahoma in Words and Pictures; Texas in Words and Pictures* (all 1981, LB $10.60).

6753. Johnson, Raymond. *The Rio Grande* (5–8). Illus. 1981, Silver Burdett LB $12.68. The history and geography of the land surrounding this important river.

6754. Peacock, Howard. *The Big Thicket of Texas: America's Ecological Wonder* (6–9). Illus. 1984, Little $13.45. The exploration of this amazing region in Southeast Texas.

6755. Radlauer, Ruth. *Grand Canyon National Park* (3–4). Illus. 1977, Childrens Pr. $10.60. A simple treatment of the physical characteristics and the plant and animal life of this scenic park.

6756. Radlauer, Ruth. *Grand Teton National Park* (3–5). Illus. 1980, Childrens Pr. LB $10.60. The history, geography, plants, and animals of this beautiful park in Wyoming.

6757. Woods, Harold, and Woods, Geraldine. *The South Central States* (4–6). Illus. 1984, Watts $8.90. A look at the region and at each individual state.

Pacific States

6758. Bauer, Helen. *Hawaii: The Aloha State* (4–7). Illus. by Bruce S. McCurdy. 1982, Bess Pr. $12.95; paper $10.95. A revision of a standard work on Hawaii.

6759. Carpenter, Allan. *California* (4–6). Illus. 1978, Childrens Pr. $11.95. Part of The New Enchantment of America series. Also use: *Alaska; Hawaii; Oregon; Washington* (all 1979, $11.95).

6760. Cheney, Cora. *Alaska: Indians, Eskimos, Russians, and the Rest* (6–9). Illus. 1980, Dodd $7.95. A history of Alaska that goes back to the days of the mastodon.

6761. Fradin, Dennis B. *Hawaii in Words and Pictures* (2–5). Illus. by Richard Wahl. 1980, Childrens Pr. LB $10.60. A simple introduction to this state. Also use: *Alaska in Words and Pictures* (1977); *California in Words and Pictures* (1977); *Oregon in Words and Pictures* (1980); *Washington in Words and Pictures* (1980) (all LB $10.60).

6762. Latham, Jean Lee. *The Columbia: Powerhouse of North America* (4–7). Illus. 1967, Garrard LB $4.47. History and geography are combined in this account of a great river.

6763. Lawson, Don. *The Pacific States* (4–6). Illus. 1984, Watts $8.90. An introduction to Washington, Oregon, California, Alaska, and Hawaii.

6764. Lewin, Ted. *World within a World—Baja* (5–7). Illus. by author. 1978, Dodd $7.95. An impressionistic view of the flora and fauna of Baja, California.

6765. Lewin, Ted. *World within a World: Pribilofs* (4–7). Illus. by author. 1980, Dodd $7.95. The flora and fauna of the Pribilof Islands off Alaska are examined.

6766. Pratt, Helen Jay. *The Hawaiians: An Island People* (6–8). Illus. 1963, Tuttle $9.75. An account of early Hawaii and its inhabitants, with emphasis on folk customs.

6767. Radlauer, Ruth. *Denali National Park and Preserve* (4–6). Illus. 1981, Childrens Pr. LB $11.95. A description of the park formerly known as Mount McKinley National Park.

6768. Radlauer, Ruth. *Haleakala National Park* (3–5). Illus. 1979, Childrens Pr. LB $11.95. Maui's national park in Hawaii comes alive in photographs and text.

6769. Radlauer, Ruth. *Olympic National Park* (3–5). Illus. 1978, Childrens Pr. LB $11.95. A gratifying visit to the famous Washington park.

6770. Rublowsky, John. *Born in Fire: A Geological History of Hawaii* (6–9). Illus. 1981, Harper $9.95; LB $9.89. The story of the birth of Hawaii plus a description of flora and fauna.

6771. Sasek, M. *This Is San Francisco* (3–5). Illus. by author. 1973, Macmillan paper $0.95. Colorful pictures introduce the reader to important landmarks and the way of life in the Golden Gate city.

6772. Stefansson, Evelyn Baird. *Here Is Alaska* (5–8). Illus. 1983, Scribners $12.95. All aspects of Alaskan life are explored in this well-organized, nicely illustrated guide.

History—General

6773. Asimov, Isaac. *The Shaping of North America* (6–9). Illus. 1973, Houghton $5.95. Subtitled: *From Earliest Times to 1763*.

Indians of North America

6774. Amon, Aline, adapt. *The Earth Is Sore: Native Americans on Nature* (5–9). Illus. by adapt. 1981, Atheneum LB $9.95. Songs and poetry reveal the Indians of North America and their love of nature.

6775. Ashabranner, Brent. *Morning Star, Black Sun: The Northern Cheyenne Indians and America's*

Energy Crisis (6–8). Illus. 1982, Dodd LB $10.95. How the Northern Cheyenne tribe is trying to create development projects that do not exploit the land.

6776. Baker, Betty. *Settlers and Strangers: Native Americans of the Desert Southwest and History as They Saw It* (3–6). Illus. 1977, Macmillan $9.95. A concise history of Southwest Indians, including the Pueblos and Hopi, from their arrival via the land bridge from Siberia to the present.

6777. Baldwin, Gordon C. *The Apache Indians: Raiders of the Southwest* (6–8). Illus. 1978, Four Winds $9.95. A carefully researched, accurate description of the Apache history and culture.

6778. Batherman, Muriel. *Before Columbus* (2–3). Illus. by author. 1981, Houghton $8.95. The Basket Maker Indians of the Southwest are the subjects of this account.

6779. Baylor, Byrd. *Before You Came This Way* (2–4). Illus. by Tom Bahti. 1969, Dutton $8.95. The illustrations are based on prehistoric Indian rock drawings found in the southwestern United States; an introduction to the way of life of these people.

6780. Baylor, Byrd. *The Desert Is Theirs* (2–4). Illus. by Peter Parnall. 1975, Scribners $12.95; paper $2.95. Through colorful, strong pictures and a lyric text, the life of the Papago Indians and their reverence for the desert are revealed.

6781. Bealer, Alex W. *Only the Names Remain: The Cherokees and the Trail of Tears* (4–6). Illus. by William Sauts Bock. 1972, Little $7.95. A history of the Cherokees with emphasis on their tragic exile west of the Mississippi in 1839.

6782. Behrens, June. *Powwow* (3–6). Illus. 1983, Childrens Pr. $6.95. A description of Indian powwows, their history, and the activities associated with them.

6783. Benchley, Nathaniel. *Small Wolf* (1–3). Illus. by Joan Sandin. 1972, Harper $8.89. The relationship between Indians and whites on Manhattan Island in pre-Revolutionary days.

6784. Bleeker, Sonia. *The Cherokee: Indians of the Mountains* (3–6). Illus. by Althea Karr. 1952, Morrow $8.40. An excellent account of the life of the Cherokee. Also use: *The Delaware Indians: Eastern Fishermen and Farmers* (1953, Morrow $8.40).

6785. Bleeker, Sonia. *The Chippewa Indians: Rice Gatherers of the Great Lakes* (5–6). Illus. 1955, Morrow $9.55. Life and social organization are highlighted. Also use: *The Sioux Indians: Hunters and Warriors of the Plains* (1962, Morrow $9.55).

6786. Bleeker, Sonia. *The Navajo: Herders, Weavers and Silversmiths* (4–6). Illus. by Patricia

Boodell. 1958, Morrow LB $9.55. This account includes material on history, customs, and present-day life. Other Indian tribes of the Southwest in this series (Morrow) are: *The Apache Indians: Raiders of the Southwest* (1951, $9.36); *The Pueblo Indians: Farmers of the Rio Grande* (1955, LB $9.55).

6787. Brown, Virginia Pounds, and Owens, Laurella. *The World of the Southern Indians* (6–9). Illus. by Nathan H. Glick. 1983, Beechwood $15.95. A review of the many Indian groups that live in southeastern United States.

6788. Davis, Christopher. *Plains Indians* (6–8). Illus. 1978, Watts $9.40. A well-illustrated overview of the culture of the Plains Indians.

6789. Erdoes, Richard. *The Native Americans: Navajos* (4–6). Illus. 1979, Sterling $19.99. A fully realized treatment of the history, traditions, and life-styles of the Navajos.

6790. Erdoes, Richard. *Native Americans: The Pueblos* (5–8). Illus. 1984, Sterling $16.95; LB $19.99. The history and culture of this southwest Indian tribe.

6791. Erdoes, Richard. *Native Americans: The Sioux* (6–9). Illus. 1982, Sterling $14.95; LB $13.99. The story of the Sioux—past and present; well illustrated.

6792. Fichter, George S. *How the Plains Indians Lived* (4–8). Illus. by Alexander Farquharson. 1980, McKay $8.95. Topics covered include housing, social life, customs, and recreation.

6793. Gorsline, Marie, and Gorsline, Douglas. *North American Indians* (6–8). Illus. 1978, Random $4.99; paper $1.50. Major tribes are identified and briefly described.

6794. Hodgson, Pat. *Growing Up with the North American Indians* (6–8). 1980, David and Charles $14.95. An overview of life with North American Indians before the white man.

6795. Hofsinde, Robert. *Indian Warriors and Their Weapons* (4–6). Illus. 1965, Morrow $9.36. An overview of weapons and battle tactics used by several tribes.

6796. Hofsinde, Robert. *Indians at Home* (4–7). Illus. by author. 1964, Morrow LB $9.36. A description of the homes of various Indian tribes.

6797. Hofsinde, Robert. *Indians on the Move* (4–6). Illus. by author. 1970, Morrow LB $9.36. All about Indian migration—its causes, destinations, and equipment.

6798. Hughes, Jill. *Plains Indians* (4–6). Illus. by Maurice Wilson and George Thomson. 1984, Watts $8.90. A look at the tribes that make up the Plains Indian group and an account of how they lived.

6799. Jacobson, Daniel. *Indians of North America* (5–9). Illus. 1983, Watts $8.90. A review of major tribes, customs, and personalities in dictionary format.

6800. Luling, Virginia. *Indians of the North American Plains* (5–8). Illus. 1979, Silver Burdett $12.68. A well-illustrated narrative that gives a rounded picture of the life of the Plains Indians.

6801. Lyons, Grant. *Pacific Coast Indians of North America* (4–7). Illus. 1983, Messner $8.79. The ways and culture of the many different groups of West Coast Indians before and after the white man.

6802. McGovern, Ann. *If You Lived with the Sioux Indians* (2–4). Illus. by Robert Levering. 1974, Scholastic paper $1.95. Using a question-and-answer technique, the author gives a great deal of information about the daily life of the Sioux and their relationship with white people.

6803. Martini, Teri. *Indians* (1–4). Illus. 1982, Childrens Pr. LB $10.60. A well-organized introduction, illustrated with color photos.

6804. Nabakov, Peter, ed. *Native American Testimony* (6–9). Illus. 1978, Harper LB $10.89; paper $4.95. A mature book of readings subtitled: *An Anthology of Indian and White Relations—First Encounter to Dispossession.*

6805. Payne, Elizabeth. *Meet the North American Indians* (1–3). Illus. 1965, Random $4.95. A narrative that introduces many tribes, their locations and life-styles.

6806. Purdy, Susan, and Sandak, Cass R. *North American Indians* (5–6). Illus. 1982, Watts $7.90. Craft activities are used to help introduce the culture of the North American Indians.

6807. Siegel, Beatrice. *Indians of the Woodland, Before and after the Pilgrims* (4–6). Illus. by Baptiste Shunatona. 1972, Walker LB $5.85. A look at how the Indians lived before the white settlers came and how their lives were destroyed soon after.

6808. Stein, R. Conrad. *The Story of the Little Bighorn* (4–6). Illus. by David J. Catrow III. 1983, Childrens Pr. $6.45. The battle involving Custer and Sitting Bull. This story is continued in: *The Story of Wounded Knee* (1983, $6.45).

6809. Supree, Burton, and Ross, Ann. *Bear's Heart: Scenes from the Life of a Cheyenne Artist of One Hundred Years Ago with Pictures by Himself* (5–9). Illus. 1977, Harper $12.45. The harrowing story of the flight of several Plains Indians from their reservations in 1874, their capture and later imprisonment, told through text and pictures.

6810. Tunis, Edwin. *Indians* (5–9). Illus. by author. 1979, Harper $16.95; LB $16.89. Superlative text and illustrations enliven this revision of a classic originally published in 1959.

6811. Watson, Jane Werner. *The First Americans: Tribes of North America* (2–3). Illus. by Troy Howell. 1980, Pantheon $6.95; LB $7.99. A simple introduction to North American Indian tribes before the white man came.

6812. Wheeler, M. J. *First Came the Indians* (2–4). Illus. by James Houston. 1983, Atheneum $9.95. An introduction to Native Americans and their major groups.

6813. Yue, Charlotte. *The Tipi: A Center of Native American Life* (4–7). Illus. by David Yue. 1984, Knopf $10.95; LB $10.99. The construction of the tipi and its place in the lives of the Plains Indians.

Discovery and Exploration

6814. Benchley, Nathaniel. *Snorri and the Strangers* (1–2). Illus. by Don Bolognese. 1976, Harper $8.61. Snorri was the first white child born in America, and this Viking boy's adventures make a fascinating story for beginning readers.

6815. Donovan, Frank P. *The Vikings* (6–8). Illus. 1964, Harper $12.95; LB $12.89. The life and times of the Vikings and their voyages.

6816. Foster, Genevieve. *Year of Columbus, 1492* (4–7). Illus. by author. 1959, Scribners $5.95. An account that includes material on Columbus and others who lived at that time.

6817. Holbrook, Sabra. *The French Founders of North America and Their Heritage* (6–9). Illus. 1976, Atheneum $7.95. A full account of the many contributions to North American history made by the French, with concluding chapters on the contemporary situation in Quebec.

6818. Irwin, Constance. *Strange Footprints on the Land* (6–9). 1980, Harper $11.89. An investigation of the exploits of the Vikings in America.

6819. Neal, Harry Edward. *Before Columbus: Who Discovered America?* (4–6). Illus. 1981, Messner LB $9.79. A discussion of possible visitors to America before Columbus.

6820. Stein, R. Conrad. *The Story of Marquette and Jolliet* (3–5). Illus. by Richard Wahl. 1981, Childrens Pr. LB $9.00; paper $2.95. A simple account of the exploration of the Mississippi.

Colonial Period

6821. Alderman, Clifford L. *The Story of the Thirteen Colonies* (5–7). Illus. by Leonard Everett Fisher. 1966, Random LB $5.99. How the colonies were founded and who their leaders were.

6822. Behrens, June, and Brower, Pauline. *Colonial Farm* (2–4). Illus. 1975, Childrens Pr. $9.25. A look at a colonial farm in Virginia, illustrated with color photographs.

6823. Campbell, Elizabeth A. *The Carving on the Tree* (3–6). Illus. by William Bock. 1968, Little $7.95. An account of the lost colony of Roanoke.

6824. Cook, Fred J. *The New Jersey Colony* (4–6). 1969, Macmillan $9.95. The early history of New Jersey.

6825. Daugherty, James. *The Landing of the Pilgrims* (5–7). Illus. by author. 1950, Random $2.95. Based on his own writings, this is the story of the Pilgrims from the standpoint of William Bradford.

6826. DeLage, Ida. *Pilgrim Children Come to Plymouth* (2–3). Illus. by Herman Vestal. 1981, Garrard LB $7.47. The first year in New England of the Mayflower's children.

6827. Foster, Genevieve. *The World of Captain John Smith* (5–7). Illus. by author. 1959, Scribners $20.00. A comparative history of the world during John Smith's time.

6828. Foster, Genevieve. *The World of William Penn* (4–7). Illus. by author. 1973, Scribners $17.50. Using the main events in Penn's life as a framework, the author supplies details on contemporary happenings in other areas of the world and relates U.S. history to that of other lands.

6829. Fritz, Jean. *Who's That Stepping on Plymouth Rock?* (3–5). Illus. by J. B. Handelsman. 1975, Putnam $8.95. An entertaining, lively, and accurate romp through history by this prolific author.

6830. Giffen, Daniel H. *New Hampshire Colony* (4–6). Illus. 1970, Macmillan $8.95. The colony's story told from the first exploration by a white man in the seventeenth century to the American Revolution.

6831. Jackson, Shirley. *The Witchcraft of Salem Village* (4–7). Illus. 1956, Random $6.99. An account of the witch-hunting hysteria that hit Salem Village.

6832. Knight, James E. *Blue Feather's Vision: The Dawn of Colonial America* (4–6). Illus. by George Guzzi. 1982, Troll LB $7.59; paper $1.95. The first volume of a 10-volume set on Colonial America. Followed by: *Boston Tea Party: Rebellion in the Colonies; The Farm: Life in Colonial Pennsylvania; Jamestown: New World Adventure; Journey to Monticello: Traveling in Colonial Times; Sailing to America: Colonists at Sea; Salem Days: Life in a Colonial Seaport; Seventh and Walnut: Life in Colonial Philadelphia; The Village: Life in Colonial Times; The Winter at Valley Forge: Survival and Victory* (all 1982, LB $7.59; paper $1.95).

6833. Lobel, Arnold. *On the Day Peter Stuyvesant Sailed into Town* (K–3). Illus. by author. 1971, Harper $11.89. How Peter Stuyvesant, the new governor of the Dutch Colony, put the citizens to work cleaning up their town, told in humorous verse and pictures.

6834. Loeper, John J. *Going to School in 1776* (3–6). Illus. 1973, Atheneum $9.95. An interesting account of education and childhood activities in Colonial America. Also use: Ann McGovern's *If You Lived in Colonial Times* (1966, Scholastic paper $1.50).

6835. Loeper, John J. *The Shop on High Street: The Toys and Games of Early America* (5–8). Illus. 1978, Atheneum $7.95. A history of leisure pursuits of children in America from 1750 to 1850.

6836. McGovern, Ann. *If You Sailed on the Mayflower* (3–4). Illus. by J. B. Handelsman. 1970, Scholastic paper $1.50. In a question-and-answer format, information is given on the historic voyage and the settlement in New England. For a slightly older group use: *The Story of the Mayflower Compact* by Norman Richards (1967, Childrens Pr. $8.60; paper $2.50).

6837. Payne, Elizabeth. *Meet the Pilgrim Fathers* (4–6). Illus. 1966, Random $5.99. The lives and living conditions of the Pilgrims in early New England.

6838. Raskin, Joseph, and Raskin, Edith. *Tales of Indentured Servants* (5–7). Illus. by William Sauts Bock. 1978, Lothrop $11.25; LB $11.88. Eight stories based on fact about indentured servants during the Colonial Period.

6839. Siegel, Beatrice. *Fur Trappers and Traders: The Indians, the Pilgrims and the Beaver* (4–6). Illus. by William Sauts Bock. 1981, Walker $8.50; LB $8.85. The story of the influence of the fur trade in the early history of this country.

6840. Siegel, Beatrice. *A New Look at the Pilgrims: Why They Came to America* (5–7). Illus. by Douglas Morris. 1977, Walker LB $5.85. Extensive background information on Puritans and Separatists and the true nature of those who came over on the *Mayflower.*

6841. Smith, Robert. *The Massachusetts Colony* (6–8). Illus. 1969, Macmillan $5.95. From the Plymouth Pilgrims to the Revolution.

6842. Spier, Peter. *The Legend of New Amsterdam* (2–4). Illus. by author. 1979, Doubleday $7.95. The town of New Amsterdam in paintings and text that ends with an unexpected glimpse into the future.

6843. Stevens, S. K. *The Pennsylvania Colony* (5–7). Illus. 1970, Macmillan $8.95. A well-organized, compact history.

6844. Szekeres, Cyndy. *Long Ago* (3–4). Illus. 1977, McGraw $8.95. Costumed animals re-create the social life and customs of the Colonial Period.

6845. Thane, Elswyth. *The Virginia Colony* (6–8). Illus. 1969, Macmillan $9.95. A brief history from Jamestown to the Revolution.

6846. Tunis, Edwin. *Colonial Living* (5–9). Illus. by author. 1976, Harper $16.95. A beautifully illustrated account of everyday life in Colonial America. Also use: *Colonial Craftsmen: The Beginnings of American Industry* (1976, Harper $16.95).

6847. Tunis, Edwin. *The Tavern at the Ferry* (4–7). Illus. by author. 1973, Harper $16.95. Through outstanding illustrations and accompanying text, focusing principally on a New Jersey ferry and tavern owned by Quakers, the author gives a great amount of information about the Colonial Period.

Revolutionary Period

6848. Avi. *The Fighting Ground* (5–7). Illus. by Ellen Thompson. 1984, Harper $11.06; LB $11.89. Thirteen-year-old Jonathan marches off to fight the British.

6849. Benchley, Nathaniel. *George, The Drummer Boy* (1–2). Illus. by Don Bolognese. 1977, Harper $8.61; LB $8.89. The beginning of the American Revolution from the viewpoint of a young British soldier, told simply and dramatically.

6850. Benchley, Nathaniel. *Sam the Minuteman* (2–4). Illus. by Arnold Lobel. 1969, Harper $7.64; LB $8.89. An easy-to-read book that gives information on the way of life at the beginning of the Revolution.

6851. Bliven, Bruce. *The American Revolution 1760–1783* (5–7). Illus. 1958, Random paper $2.95. The causes, principle events, and results of the war are given in this basic overview.

6852. Dalgliesh, Alice. *The Fourth of July Story* (3–5). 1956, Scribners $11.95. The history behind the writing of the Declaration of Independence, readably retold.

6853. Haley, Gail E. *Jack Jouett's Ride* (3–4). Illus. by author. 1973, Penguin paper $2.95. Based on a true incident in the Revolutionary War, the story of a 40-mile midnight ride to warn the southern revolutionaries of the coming of the British dragoons.

6854. Lomask, Milton. *The First American Revolution* (6–8). Illus. 1974, Farrar $7.95. This book covers the years 1763 to 1784 from various viewpoints—military, political, economic, and social.

6855. Lowrey, Janette Sebring. *Six Silver Spoons* (1–3). Illus. by Robert Quackenbush. 1971, Harper $8.89. Tim and Debbie ride to Lexington to bring Mother a birthday present of 6 silver spoons during the American Revolution.

6856. Miller, Natalie. *The Story of the Liberty Bell* (4–6). Illus. 1965, Childrens Pr. $8.60; paper $2.50. The story of one of our country's most famous symbols.

6857. Phelan, Mary Kay. *The Story of the Boston Massacre* (5–9). Illus. by Allan Eitzen. 1976, Harper $10.95. A present-day narrative adds immediacy to this well-presented account. Also use: *The Story of the Boston Tea Party* (1974, Harper $10.95).

6858. Stein, R. Conrad. *The Story of Lexington and Concord* (3–6). Illus. by Keith Neely. 1983, Childrens Pr. $5.95. A re-creation of 2 famous battles of the Revolution.

6859. Taylor, Theodore. *Rebellion Town: Williamsburg, 1776* (6–9). Illus. by Richard Cuffari. 1973, Harper $11.95. The surge to independence as seen through the activities of the inhabitants of Williamsburg as they band together to oppose British rule.

The Young Nation 1789–1861

6860. Baker, Betty. *The Pig War* (K–2). Illus. by Robert Lopshire. 1969, Harper LB $8.89. A humorous confrontation in 1858 between the United States and Canada over an island that each side insists belongs to them.

6861. Bowen, Gary. *My Village, Sturbridge* (4–6). Illus. by author. 1977, Farrar $6.95. A series of pictures with commentary depicting everyday life in an 1827 New England village.

6862. Cabral, Olga. *So Proudly She Sailed: Tales of Old Ironsides* (5–9). Illus. 1981, Houghton $8.95. This is the story of the *USS Constitution*, which ruled the waves for 80 years.

6863. Costabel, Eva Deutsch. *A New England Village* (3–5). Illus. by author. 1983, Atheneum $10.95. Drawings and simple text capture the atmosphere of nineteenth-century New England.

6864. Fisher, Leonard Everett. *The Factories* (5–7). Illus. by author. 1979, Holiday $9.95. Part of the series Nineteenth Century America, this account describes the origins and development of manufacturing in America.

6865. Fisher, Leonard Everett. *The Hospitals* (5–8). Illus. by author. 1980, Holiday $7.95. An account of the growth and expansion of hospitals in nineteenth-century America.

6866. Gemming, Elizabeth. *Blow Ye Winds Westerly: The Seaports and Sailing Ships of Old New England* (6–9). Illus. 1972, Harper $7.95. A fantastic compendium of information about many aspects of life in the age of sailing ships.

6867. Hilton, Suzanne. *We the People: The Way We Were* (6–9). 1981, Westminster $12.95. The story of life in America immediately after the Revolution.

6868. Macaulay, David. *Mill* (5–9). Illus. by author. 1983, Houghton $14.45. The construction of an early nineteenth-century spinning mill in Rhode Island.

6869. Mitchell, Barbara. *Cornstalks and Cannonballs* (1–3). Illus. by Karen Ritz. 1980, Carolrhoda $6.95. The town of Lewis, Delaware, defeats the British Navy during the War of 1812.

6870. Phelan, Mary Kay. *The Story of the Louisiana Purchase* (6–8). 1979, Harper $10.95; LB $10.89. An exciting, suspenseful account of this event, well illustrated from original documents.

6871. St. George, Judith. *The Amazing Voyage of the New Orleans* (3–5). Illus. by Glen Rounds. 1980, Putnam $6.95. An amazing account of the 1811 voyage of a steamboat down the Mississippi.

6872. Stein, R. Conrad. *The Story of the Barbary Pirates* (4–6). Illus. by Tom Dunnington. 1982, Childrens Pr. $5.95. The story of our involvement in the Tripolitan War of 1801 to 1805.

6873. Stein, R. Conrad. *The Story of the Underground Railroad* (3–5). Illus. by Ralph Canaday. 1981, Childrens Pr. LB $9.00; paper $2.95. A simple history of an engrossing aspect of the struggle against slavery.

6874. Tallant, Robert. *The Louisiana Purchase* (5–7). Illus. by Warren Chappell. 1952, Random $5.99. The negotiations and results of one of the most interesting and significant land sales in world history.

6875. Tunis, Edwin. *The Young United States 1783 to 1830* (4–6). Illus. 1976, Harper $16.95. A simple history of the first days of the republic.

Westward Expansion and Pioneer Life

6876. Freedman, Russell. *Children of the Wild West* (5–8). Illus. 1983, Houghton $12.95. The life of children on the frontier told in text and old photos.

6877. Gorsline, Marie. *The Pioneers* (3–5). Illus. 1982, Random $4.99; paper $1.50. A trip along the Oregon Trail is re-created.

6878. Gorsline, Marie, and Gorsline, Douglas. *Cowboys* (3–4). Illus. 1980, Random LB $4.99; paper $1.50. An amazing amount of information is included in this slim text.

6879. Hilton, Suzanne. *Getting There: Frontier Travel without Power* (6–8). Illus. 1980, Westminster $10.95. A look at such forms of nineteenth-century travel as the stagecoach and canal flatboats.

6880. Laycock, George, and Laycock, Ellen. *How the Settlers Lived* (5–8). Illus. by Alexander Farquharson. 1980, McKay $8.95. Such topics as shelter, clothing, food, and recreation are covered.

6881. Neuberger, Richard L. *The Lewis and Clark Expedition* (4–7). Illus. 1951, Random $6.99. A suspenseful retelling of the expedition that explored the Louisiana Territory.

6882. Poynter, Margaret. *Gold Rush! The Yukon Stampede of 1898* (6–9). Illus. 1979, Atheneum $7.95. An anecdotal account that stresses human values.

6883. Rounds, Glen. *The Cowboy Trade* (5–8). 1972, Holiday $10.95. The authentic life of the cowboy is introduced.

6884. Rounds, Glen. *The Prairie Schooners* (4–6). Illus. 1968, Holiday $10.95. A report of life on a wagon train in 1843 during a trip from Missouri to the Oregon Territory.

6885. Seidman, Laurence I. *The Fools of '49: The California Gold Rush 1848–1856* (6–8). Illus. by Sallie Baldwin. 1976, Knopf $7.95. This fascinating text is enlivened with such primary materials as maps, songs, and old prints.

6886. Stein, R. Conrad. *The Story of the Gold at Sutter's Mill* (3–5). Illus. by Lou Aronson. 1981, Childrens Pr. LB $9.00. The thrilling story of the discovery of gold in California.

6887. Stein, R. Conrad. *The Story of the Homestead Act* (3–6). Illus. 1978, Childrens Pr. LB $9.00; paper $2.95. The events around this important piece of legislation of 1804.

6888. Stein, R. Conrad. *The Story of the Pony Express* (3–5). Illus. by Len W. Meents. 1981, Childrens Pr. LB $9.00; paper $2.95. An introduction to this important early form of postal service.

6889. Strait, Treva Adams. *The Price of Free Land* (5–7). Illus. 1979, Harper $9.57. A true account of a family of Nebraskan homesteaders who settled there in 1914.

6890. Talbot, Charlene Joy. *The Sodbuster Venture* (6–8). 1982, Atheneum LB $10.95. Two young women eke out a livelihood on a Kansas prairie claim.

6891. Tunis, Edwin. *Frontier Living* (5–9). Illus. by author. 1976, Harper $16.95. Excellent, large illustrations and accompanying text convey the flavor of life on the frontier.

The Civil War

6892. Foster, Genevieve. *Year of Lincoln: 1861* (3–6). Illus. by author. 1970, Scribners $5.95. Coverage of the Civil War and other world events in this brief survey. For an older group use: *Abraham Lincoln's World* (1944, Scribners LB $20.00).

6893. Kantor, MacKinlay. *Gettysburg* (5–9). Illus. 1952, Random $4.99. This explains how Gettysburg became the site of the bloodiest Civil War battle; a vivid re-creation of the struggle.

6894.   Levenson, Dorothy. *The First Book of the Civil War* (5–7). Illus. by Leonard Everett Fisher. 1968, Watts $7.90. A basic introduction to the War between the States. Also use: *Album of the Civil War* by William Katz (1974, Watts LB $9.60).

6895.   Stein, R. Conrad. *The Story of the Monitor and the Merrimac* (3–6). Illus. by Keith Neely. 1983, Childrens Pr. $5.95. The story of the 2 Civil War ships and their fateful encounter.

Reconstruction to the Korean War 1865–1950

6896.   Davis, Daniel S. *Behind Barbed Wire: The Imprisonment of Japanese Americans during World War II* (6–9). 1982, Dutton $12.95. An account of the internment of Japanese-Americans during World War II and its consequences.

6897.   Fisher, Leonard Everett. *The Unions* (5–8). Illus. by author. 1982, Holiday LB $9.95. The story of labor unions in this country, particularly in the latter part of the nineteenth century.

6898.   Freedman, Russell. *Immigrant Kids* (3–7). Illus. 1980, Dutton $11.95. An account of the immigration to the United States from 1880 to 1920.

6899.   Hilton, Suzanne. *The Way It Was—1876* (6–9). Illus. 1975, Westminster $6.95. All aspects of everyday life long ago in the United States discussed in a lively, often amusing style.

6900.   Hoffman, Edwin D. *Fighting Mountaineers: The Struggle for Justice in the Appalachians* (6–9). 1979, Houghton $8.95. The struggle against oppression throughout history of the mountain people of Appalachia.

6901.   Katz, William L. *An Album of the Great Depression* (5–8). Illus. 1978, Watts $8.90. A book of photographs and running commentary that reconstructs the 1930s in the United States.

6902.   Lawson, Don. *FDR's New Deal* (6–8). Illus. 1979, Harper $10.53. A fine re-creation of the period without undue emotion or sentiment.

6903.   Loeper, John J. *Going to School in 1876* (4–8). Illus. 1984, Atheneum $10.95. A book about education in 1876—curriculum, types of schools, recreation, discipline, etc.

6904.   Sandin, Joan. *The Long Way to a New Land* (1–3). Illus. by author. 1981, Harper $8.61; LB $8.89. A simply read account of a Swedish family's journey to New York in the late 1860s.

6905.   Sandler, Martin W. *The Way We Lived: A Photographic Record of Work in Vanished America* (4–7). Illus. 1977, Little $11.45. Working conditions in this country before the twentieth century, told in text and photos.

6906.   Schwartz, Alvin, ed. *When I Grew Up Long Ago* (5–8). 1978, Harper $9.57. Oral histories that cover the United States in the years 1890–1914.

6907.   Sterling, Dorothy, ed. *The Trouble They Seen: Black People Tell the Story of Reconstruction* (6–8). Illus. 1976, Doubleday $9.95. A dramatic retelling of the post–Civil War period as seen by free blacks.

6908.   Weitzman, David. *Windmills, Bridges, and Old Machines: Discovering Our Industrial Past* (5–9). Illus. 1982, Scribners $13.95. The early industrial development of this country is covered through its machinery.

The 1950s to the Present

6909.   Ashabranner, Brent. *The New Americans: Changing Patterns in U.S. Immigration* (6–9). Illus. 1983, Dodd $13.95. The story of present-day immigrants to the United States and where they came from.

6910.   Bentley, Judith. *Busing: The Continuing Controversy* (6–9). Illus. 1982, Watts LB $9.90. A history of busing and the pros and cons of its future use.

6911.   Emmens, Carol A. *An Album of the Sixties* (5–8). Illus. 1981, Watts $9.60. An album of photographs and text that present highlights from the decade.

6912.   Fincher, E. B. *The War in Korea* (6–8). Illus. 1981, Watts LB $8.90. Background history is given as well as an account of the war and its aftermath.

6913.   Hoobler, Dorothy, and Hoobler, Thomas. *An Album of the Seventies* (6–9). Illus. 1981, Watts LB $9.60. An introduction to the decade that included the Vietnam War, Watergate, and the hostage crisis in Iran.

6914.   Hoobler, Dorothy, and Hoobler, Thomas. *U.S.-China Relations since World War II* (6–9). Illus. 1981, Watts $7.45. A straightforward account of the growing strength of our relations with China.

6915.   Lawson, Don. *The United States in the Vietnam War* (6–9). Illus. 1981, Harper $11.00; LB $10.89. A well-written account that helps young people understand this controversial war.

6916.   Lawson, Don. *The War in Vietnam* (6–9). Illus. 1981, Watts LB $8.90. From the French withdrawal to Vietnam's entry into Cambodia after the war, told for young readers.

6917.   Meltzer, Milton. *The Hispanic Americans* (6–9). Illus. 1982, Harper $11.49; LB $11.89. A look at the 12 million Hispanic Americans, their way of life and the lands they came from.

Biography

Historical and Contemporary Americans

Collective

6918. Beard, Charles A. *The Presidents in American History* (5–7). Illus. 1981, Messner $9.79. Brief but revealing sketches of the men and their times.

6919. Coy, Harold. *Presidents* (4–6). Illus. 1981, Watts $6.90. This revised edition includes a biography of Reagan.

6920. Davis, Burke. *Black Heroes of the American Revolution* (4–6). 1976, Harcourt $9.95. A look at American blacks who performed key roles in the American Revolution.

6921. Feerick, John, and Feerick, Amalie. *The Vice-Presidents of the United States* (5–7). 1977, Watts $8.90. Thumbnail sketches of the vice presidents, their elections, and terms of office.

6922. Johnston, Johanna. *A Special Bravery* (3–5). Illus. by Ann Grifalconi. 1967, Dodd $5.95. Mood-evoking illustrations and brief sketches of bravery performed by 15 black Americans from Crispus Attucks to Martin Luther King, Jr., make an excellent visual introduction to black history.

6923. Katz, William L. *Black People Who Made the Old West* (6–8). Illus. 1977, Harper $7.95. Sketches of 35 black explorers, pioneers, etc., who helped open up the West.

6924. Lawson, Robert. *They Were Strong and Good* (4–6). Illus. by author. 1940, Viking $10.95. The author has drawn word-and-pen portraits of his grandparents, typical Americans of their time. Caldecott Medal, 1941.

6925. Levinson, Nancy Smiler. *The First Women Who Spoke Out* (5–8). Illus. 1983, Dillon $8.95. A look at 6 women who early in our history fought for women's rights.

6926. Rollins, Charlemae. *They Showed the Way: Forty American Negro Leaders* (5–7). 1964, Harper $10.95. Brief stories of blacks who were pioneers in a particular field or occupation.

6927. Ross, Pat. *Young and Female* (5–8). Illus. 1972, Random LB $4.99. Personal accounts of important moments in the lives of 8 contemporary women.

6928. Ulyatt, Kenneth. *Outlaws* (6–8). Illus. 1978, Harper $9.57. A fascinating collection of tales about the Daltons, Billy the Kid, and other miscreants.

Historical Figures

Adams, Samuel

6929. Fritz, Jean. *Why Don't You Get a Horse Sam Adams?* (3–5). Illus. by Trina S. Hyman. 1974, Putnam $9.95; paper $4.95. How Sam Adams was finally persuaded to ride a horse is told in this humorous re-creation of Revolutionary times.

Arnold, Benedict

6930. Fritz, Jean. *Traitor: The Case of Benedict Arnold* (6–8). 1981, Putnam $9.95. An intimate, straightforward portrait of this fascinating military man.

Brown, John

6931. Graham, Lorenz. *John Brown: A Cry for Freedom* (6–9). Illus. 1980, Harper $10.53; LB $10.89. An interesting account of the life of the abolitionist.

Carnegie, Andrew

6932. Shippen, Katherine B. *Andrew Carnegie and the Age of Steel* (5–8). 1964, Random $5.99. Story of a poor Scottish boy who became a millionaire-philanthropist.

Farragut, David

6933. Latham, Jean Lee. *Anchor's Aweigh: The Story of David Glasgow Farragut* (5–9). Illus. by Eros Keith. 1968, Harper $9.89. The biography of the American naval officer who gained fame during the Civil War.

Franklin, Benjamin

6934. Aliki. *The Many Lives of Benjamin Franklin* (1–3). Illus. by author. 1977, Prentice LB $6.95. Franklin's life is described through captioned cartoons.

6935. Cousins, Margaret. *Ben Franklin of Old Philadelphia* (6–8). 1981, Random paper $2.95. A well-rounded portrait of this major figure in American history.

6936. D'Aulaire, Ingri, and D'Aulaire, Edgar. *Benjamin Franklin* (3–5). Illus. by author. 1950, Doubleday $9.95. A story biography enriched with full-page color lithographs.

6937. Fritz, Jean. *What's the Big Idea, Ben Franklin?* (3–5). Illus. by Margot Tomes. 1976, Putnam $9.95; paper $4.95. Franklin's life told in the clever, lively manner associated with this author.

Gallaudet, Thomas

6938. Neimark, Anne E. *A Deaf Child Listened: Thomas Gallaudet, Pioneer in American Education* (6–9). 1983, Morrow $8.00. The life story of the founder of education for the deaf in America.

Hancock, John

6939. Fritz, Jean. *Will You Sign Here, John Hancock?* (3–5). Illus. by Trina S. Hyman. 1976, Putnam $9.95; paper $4.95. Under the sprightly title is a delightful, well-researched biography of this signer of the Declaration of Independence.

Henry, Patrick

6940. Fritz, Jean. *Where Was Patrick Henry on the 29th of May?* (3–5). Illus. by Margot Tomes. 1975, Putnam $9.95; paper $4.95. A biography that is fun to read.

Jackson, Stonewall

6941. Fritz, Jean. *Stonewall* (6–9). Illus. by Stephen Gammell. 1979, Putnam $10.95. A realistic, honest portrayal of the complex Stonewall Jackson.

Jones, John Paul

6942. Brandt, Keith. *John Paul Jones: Hero of the Seas* (3–5). Illus. by Susan Swan. 1983, Troll $6.89; paper $1.95. The U.S. Naval hero is introduced in an account that does not ignore either his strengths or his weaknesses.

6943. Grant, Matthew. *John Paul Jones* (2–3). Illus. 1974, Creative Ed. LB $7.95. The U.S. naval hero is introduced in an account that does not ignore his strengths or his weaknesses.

LaGuardia, Fiorello

6944. Kamen, Gloria. *Fiorello: His Honor, the Little Flower* (3–5). Illus. by author. 1981, Atheneum $8.95. A readable account of the Little Flower and his many contributions.

Oglethorpe, James Edward

6945. Blackburn, Joyce. *James Edward Oglethorpe* (5–8). 1983, Dodd $8.95. The story of a remarkable man who helped found Georgia.

Paine, Thomas

6946. Coolidge, Olivia. *Tom Paine, Revolutionary* (6–8). 1969, Scribners $15.00. The story of the pamphleteer who influenced the leaders of the Revolution.

Pinkerton, Allan

6947. Anderson, Lavere. *Allan Pinkerton* (3–6). Illus. by Frank Vaughan. n.d., Dell paper $1.25. The exciting story of the first "private eye" and his exploits, ranging from the pioneering use of fingerprinting to pursuing Jesse James.

Revere, Paul

6948. Forbes, Esther. *America's Paul Revere* (5–9). Illus. by Lynd Ward. 1946, Houghton $8.95; paper $2.95. Includes informative background of the Revolutionary period.

Williams, Roger

6949. Eaton, Jeanette. *Lone Journey: The Life of Roger Williams* (5–6). Illus. 1944, Harcourt paper $0.75. A biography of the founder of Providence, Rhode Island.

Presidents

Jackson, Andrew

6950. Coit, Margaret. *Andrew Jackson* (6–9). Illus. by Milton Johnson. 1965, Houghton $7.99. Description and explanation of Jackson's administrations, including domestic and foreign affairs, and the men and women around the president.

6951. Remini, Robert V. *The Revolutionary Age of Andrew Jackson* (6–8). 1976, Harper $10.89. The story of the seventh president.

Jefferson, Thomas

6952. Barrett, Marvin. *Meet Thomas Jefferson* (2–4). Illus. by Angelo Torres. 1967, Random $4.95; LB $5.99. A simple, informal story of the third president.

Johnson, Lyndon Baines

6953. Lynch, Dudley M. *The President from Texas: Lyndon Baines Johnson* (4–6). Illus. 1975, Harper $11.95. A balanced account of this controversial president.

Kennedy, John F.

6954. Graves, Charles P. *John F. Kennedy* (2–5). Illus. by Paul Frame. 1966, Dell paper $1.95. The life of our thirty-fifth president.

Lincoln, Abraham

6955. Coolidge, Olivia. *The Statesmanship of Abraham Lincoln* (6–9). Illus. 1977, Scribners $1.95. Lincoln's presidency is the focus of this excellent book that continues *The Apprenticeship of Abraham Lincoln* (1974, $1.79).

6956. D'Aulaire, Ingri, and D'Aulaire, Edgar. *Abraham Lincoln* (2–5). Illus. by author. 1957, Doubleday $12.95. Lincoln's life from boyhood to a tired war-president. Caldecott Medal, 1970.

6957. Phelan, Mary Kay. *Mr. Lincoln's Inaugural Journey* (5–6). Illus. by Richard Cuffari. 1972, Harper $10.83. A detailed, factual account of Lincoln's trip from Springfield to Washington, enlivened by the discovery of a plot to assassinate the new president.

6958. Sandburg, Carl. *Abe Lincoln Grows Up* (6–9). Illus. by James Daugherty. 1975, Harcourt paper $2.95. Classic account of Lincoln's boyhood based on Volume I of *The Prairie Years*.

Reagan, Ronald

6959. Fox, Mary Virginia. *Mister President: The Story of Ronald Reagan* (6–8). Illus. 1982, Enslow LB $10.95. A slight account of our president's life.

6960. Lawson, Don. *The Picture Life of President Reagan* (4–6). Illus. 1981, Watts $7.90. A photo essay that introduces the life of Ronald Reagan.

Roosevelt, Franklin D.

6961. Feinberg, Barbara Silberdick. *Franklin D. Roosevelt, Gallant President* (5–7). Illus. 1981, Lothrop $9.75; LB $9.36. A simply written introduction to this president's life with many photographs.

6962. Peare, Catherine O. *The FDR Story* (5–8). Illus. 1962, Harper $8.95. An excellent picture of a president, which explains the many forces that helped to mold Roosevelt's life and personality.

Roosevelt, Theodore

6963. Foster, Genevieve. *Theodore Roosevelt: An Initial Biography* (6–9). Illus. by author. 1954, Scribners $5.95. An objective view of the life and times of the twenty-sixth president, profusely illustrated with photographs, paintings, drawings, and political cartoons of the time.

6964. Quackenbush, Robert. *Don't You Dare Shoot That Bear! A Story of Theodore Roosevelt* (3–6). Illus. by author. 1984, Prentice $8.95. A biography that mixes humor and fact.

Washington, George

6965. d'Aulaire, Ingri, and d'Aulaire, Edgar. *George Washington* (2–3). Illus. by author. 1936, Doubleday $12.95. A simple recounting of the life of the first president.

Black Americans

Bethune, Mary McLeod

6966. Carruth, Ella Kaiser. *She Wanted to Read: The Story of Mary McLeod Bethune* (4–7). Illus. by Herbert McClure. 1966, Abingdon $5.95. The inspiring story of the black woman who founded a school and hospital for black people in Florida.

6967. Greenfield, Eloise. *Mary McLeod Bethune* (2–4). Illus. by Jerry Pinkney. 1977, Harper $10.89. Bethune was the only one of 17 children in her family to go to school. Through courage and hard work, she became an educator of national importance.

Brown, William Wells

6968. Warner, Lucille. *From Slave to Abolitionist: The Life of William Wells Brown* (6–9). 1976, Dial $8.95. Adapted from an autobiography published in 1847, this is the story of an escaped slave who founded the Abolitionist movement.

Douglass, Frederick

6969. Patterson, Lillie. *Frederick Douglass: Freedom Fighter* (2–5). Illus. 1965, Garrard $6.69. The biography of a onetime slave who, as a free man, became a noted author and speaker.

6970. Ritchie, Barbara. *The Mind and Heart of Frederick Douglass* (6–9). 1968, Harper $11.95. Subtitle: *Excerpts from Speeches of the Great Negro Orator.*

6971. Santrey, Laurence. *Young Frederick Douglass: Fight for Freedom* (3–5). Illus. by Bert Dodson. 1983, Troll $6.89; paper $1.95. The story of the slave who became a leader of the Abolitionist Movement.

DuBois, W. E. B.

6972. Hamilton, Virginia. *W. E. B. DuBois: A Biography* (5–9). Illus. 1972, Harper $10.53. Chronicles the successes and failures of this fighter for black rights.

Fortune, Amos

6973. Yates, Elizabeth. *Amos Fortune: Free Man* (6–9). Illus. by Nora S. Unwin. 1967, Dutton $11.95. The simplicity and dignity of the human spirit and its triumph over degradation are movingly portrayed in this portrait of a slave who bought his freedom. Newbery medal winner.

Freeman, Elizabeth

6974. Felton, Harold W. *Mumbet: The Story of Elizabeth Freeman* (4–6). Illus. by Donn Albright. 1970, Dodd $6.95. A black slave who gained her freedom in 1781 by fighting her case through the Massachusetts courts.

Jackson, Jesse

6975. Halliburton, Warren J. *The Picture Life of Jesse Jackson* (2–4). Illus. 1984, Watts $9.90. A simple biography that ends with Jackson's bid for the presidential nomination.

6976. Westman, Paul. *Jesse Jackson: I Am Somebody* (3–6). Illus. by Judith Leo. 1981, Dillon LB $7.95. A simple biography of one of the most important black leaders in the United States.

Jordan, Barbara

6977. Roberts, Naurice. *Barbara Jordan: The Great Lady from Texas* (2–4). Illus. 1984, Childrens Pr. $6.95. A heavily illustrated account of the former Texas Congresswoman.

King, Martin Luther, Jr.

6978. Clayton, Edward T. *Martin Luther King: The Peaceful Warrior* (4–6). Illus. by David Hodges. 1968, Pocket paper $1.75. The life of the great civil rights leader.

6979. Harris, Jacqueline L. *Martin Luther King, Jr.* (6–9). Illus. 1983, Watts $8.90. A readable account of King's life and death. Also use: *Martin Luther King, Jr.: A Man to Remember* by Patricia McKissack (1984, Childrens Pr. $8.95).

6980. Preston, Edward. *Martin Luther King: Fighter for Freedom* (4–7). Illus. 1970, Doubleday $7.95. A short, objective portrait of the late civil rights leader and the ideals for which he stood.

Malcolm X

6981. Adoff, Arnold. *Malcolm X* (3–5). Illus. by John Wilson. 1970, Harper $10.89; paper $3.95. A realistic portrayal of this spokesman for the black cause in the United States until his assassination in 1965.

Parks, Rosa

6982. Greenfield, Eloise. *Rosa Parks* (2–4). Illus. by Eric Marlow. 1973, Harper LB $10.89. A convincing sketch of the woman whose brave stand precipitated the Montgomery bus strike and her ensuing involvement with the civil rights struggle.

Taylor, Marshall B.

6983. Scioscia, Mary. *Bicycle Rider* (2–5). Illus. by Ed Young. 1983, Harper $9.57; LB $9.89. The fictionized biography of the black man who at one time was the fastest bicyclist in the world.

Truth, Sojourner

6984. Ortiz, Victoria. *Sojourner Truth: A Self-Made Woman* (6–9). Illus. 1974, Harper $12.45. The story of the slave who fought for abolition and women's rights.

Tubman, Harriet

6985. Petry, Ann. *Harriet Tubman: Conductor on the Underground Railroad* (6–9). 1955, Harper $14.38; Pocket paper $2.25. A dramatic and stirring biography of an indomitable woman.

Wheatley, Phillis

6986. Fuller, Morris. *Phillis Wheatley: America's First Black Poetess* (4–6). Illus. by Victor Mays. 1971, Garrard $7.12. The tragic life of one of America's first black poets, a slave during the Colonial Period.

Williams, Daniel Hale

6987. Patterson, Lillie. *Sure Hands, Strong Heart: The Life of Daniel Hale Williams* (5–7). 1981, Abingdon $7.95. A simple biography of this black surgeon's life and work.

Young, Andrew

6988. Haskins, James. *Andrew Young: Man with a Mission* (5–8). 1979, Lothrop $10.95; LB $10.51. The life of the famous black American statesman is well told in this account.

6989. Roberts, Naurice. *Andrew Young: Freedom Fighter* (2–4). Illus. 1983, Childrens Pr. $6.95. A simple-to-read biography of the prominent black politician.

Indians of North America

Crazy Horse

6990. Meadowcroft, Enid. *Crazy Horse: Sioux Warrior* (4–6). Illus. 1965, Garrard LB $6.69. The life of this valiant chief of the Oglala tribe of the Sioux.

Eastman, Charles

6991. Lee, Betsy. *Charles Eastman* (6–8). Illus. 1979, Dillon LB $7.95. The story of the Santee Sioux who helped keep his people's culture alive in the early twentieth century.

Geronimo

6992. Wilson, Charles Morrow. *Geronimo* (5–7). Illus. 1973, Dillon $7.95. The story of the last great war leader of the Apaches.

Hopkins, Sarah Winnemucca

6993. Kloss, Doris. *Sarah Winnemucca* (6–8). Illus. 1981, Dillon LB $7.95. The biography of an American Indian woman and her fight for her people.

Ishi

6994. Kroeber, Theodora. *Ishi, Last of His Tribe* (5–7). Illus. by Ruth Robbins. 1964, Parnassus $7.95. A California Yahe Indian, the last of his tribe, leaves his primitive life and enters the modern world.

6995. Meyer, Kathleen Allan. *Ishi* (5–7). Illus. 1980, Dillon LB $7.95. The story of the last survivor of an Indian tribe that perished because of warring tribes and the white man.

Little Turtle

6996. Cunningham, Maggi. *Little Turtle* (6–8). Illus. 1978, Dillon $7.95. Little Turtle was a chief of the Miami Indian tribe.

Pocahontas

6997. D'Aulaire, Ingri, and D'Aulaire, Edgar. *Pocahontas* (2–4). Illus. by author. 1949, Doubleday $7.95. The story of the Indian girl who saved the life of John Smith.

6998. Fritz, Jean. *The Double Life of Pocahontas* (4–7). Illus. by Ed Young. 1983, Putnam $9.95. A biography of the Indian maiden now chiefly associated with Captain John Smith.

Ross, John

6999. Harrell, Sara Gordon. *John Ross* (5–7). Illus. 1979, Dillon $7.95. The story of a Cherokee Indian leader and his fight to save his people's land.

Sealth (Indian Chief)

7000. Boring, Mel. *Sealth: The Story of an American Indian* (5–8). Illus. 1978, Dillon LB $7.95. The story of the Indian chief for whom Seattle was named.

Sitting Bull

7001. Anderson, Lavere. *Sitting Bull: Great Sioux Chief* (3–5). Illus. by Lois F. Cary. 1970, Garrard $6.69; Dell paper $0.95. A simple account of the man and his struggle to save his people.

Squanto

7002. Bulla, Clyde Robert. *Squanto, Friend of the Pilgrims* (3–6). Illus. by Peter Burchard. 1954, Harper $11.49. The first American Indian to reach Europe.

7003. Kessel, Joyce K. *Squanto and the First Thanksgiving* (2–3). Illus. by Lisa Donze. 1983, Carolrhoda $6.95. An easily read story of an Indian sold into slavery but eventually freed close to the Plymouth Colony.

Tecumseh

7004. Fleischer, Jane. *Tecumseh: Shawnee War Chief* (3–4). Illus. by Hal Frenck. 1979, Troll $6.89; paper $1.75. A basic account of this Indian chief and his fight to prevent a territorial takeover by the white settlers.

7005. Schraff, Anne E. *Tecumseh* (5–7). Illus. 1979, Dillon $7.95. The moving story of the Shawnee Indian chief and his losing battle to save the land of his people.

Hispanic Americans

Chavez, Cesar

7006. Franchere, Ruth. *Cesar Chavez* (2–5). Illus. by Earl Thollander. 1973, Harper LB $10.89; paper $2.95. An inspiring story of the man who rose from poverty to become the union organizer of his people.

Famous American Women

Barton, Clara

7007. Boylston, Helen D. *Clara Barton, Founder of the American Red Cross* (5–8). Illus. by Paula Hutchison. 1955, Random LB $6.99. The story of a courageous woman who devoted her life to others. For a younger group use: *Clara Barton: Soldier of Mercy* by Mary Catherine Rose (1960, Garrard LB $7.47).

Benchley, Belle Jennings

7008. Poynter, Margaret. *The Zoo Lady: Belle Benchley and the San Diego Zoo* (5–7). Illus. 1980, Dillon LB $7.95. The story of the woman who operated the San Diego Zoo from 1927 to 1952.

Fremont, Jessie Benton

7009. Morrison, Dorothy Nafus. *Under a Strong Wind: The Adventures of Jessie Benton Fremont* (5–8). Illus. 1983, Atheneum $10.95. The story of John Fremont's wife and her adventures accompanying the explorer/politician.

Jemison, Mary

7010. Lenski, Lois. *Indian Captive: The Story of Mary Jemison* (6–9)). Illus. by author. 1941, Harper $12.95. True story of a 22-year-old girl as a captive of the Senecas.

Jones, Mary Harris

7011. Atkinson, Linda. *Mother Jones: The Most Dangerous Woman in America* (6–8). 1978, Crown $10.95. A graphic biography of the woman who devoted her life to secure justice for coal miners.

Keller, Helen

7012. Peare, Catherine O. *The Helen Keller Story* (5–7). 1959, Harper $9.95. A stirring tale of the blind and deaf girl who learned to communicate with others and who became an outstanding force as writer and lecturer. For younger readers use *Helen Keller: Toward the Light* by Stewart Graff and Polly Graff (1965, Garrard $7.47; Dell paper $1.95).

Kemble, Fanny

7013. Scott, John A. *Fanny Kemble's America* (6–9). Illus. 1973, Harper $10.95. An adroit biography of the woman who contributed to the antislavery crusade and the feminist movement.

La Flesche, Susan

7014. Brown, Marion Marsh. *Homeward the Arrow's Flight* (5–7). Illus. 1980, Abingdon $7.95. A fictionized biography of the first female native American doctor, Susan La Flesche.

Liliuokalani

7015. Malone, Mary. *Liliuokalani, Queen of Hawaii* (4–6). 1975, Garrard $6.69. The story of a most unusual woman and splendid queen.

O'Connor, Sandra Day

7016. Fox, Mary Virginia. *Justice Sandra Day O'Connor* (5–7). Illus. 1983, Enslow $9.95. A simple account of the first woman Supreme Court Justice. For older readers use: *Justice Sandra Day O'Connor* by Judith Bentley (1983, Messner $9.29).

Roosevelt, Eleanor

7017. Goodsell, Jane. *Eleanor Roosevelt* (2–4). Illus. by Wendell Minor. 1970, Harper $10.89. Concentrates on the transformation from ugly duckling to renowned world figure.

7018. Jacobs, William Jay. *Eleanor Roosevelt: A Life of Happiness and Tears* (5–8). Illus. 1983, Putnam $10.95. A well-rounded portrait of the first lady.

7019. Whitney, Sharon. *Eleanor Roosevelt* (6–9). Illus. 1982, Watts LB $9.90. A biography that discusses not only her accomplishments but also her strengths and weaknesses.

Ross, Betsy

7020. Mayer, Jane. *Betsy Ross and the Flag* (4–6). Illus. 1952, Random $5.99. A simple biography of the seamstress who made the first American flag that had stars and stripes.

Sampson, Deborah

7021. Clapp, Patricia. *I'm Deborah Sampson: A Soldier in the War of the Revolution* (5–8). 1977, Lothrop $10.32. A first-person retelling of the amazing woman who served in the Continental Army during the Revolution.

7022. McGovern, Ann. *The Secret Soldier: The Story of Deborah Sampson* (3–5). Illus. by Ann Grifalconi. 1975, Scholastic paper $1.75. The story of the girl who, disguised as a man, served in the Continental Army.

World Figures

Collective

7023. Meyer, Edith Patterson. *In Search of Peace: The Winners of the Nobel Peace Prize, 1901–1975* (6–9). Illus. by Billie J. Osborne. 1978, Abingdon $7.95. A useful reference work on the prize recipients, their lives and accomplishments.

Individual

Alexander the Great

7024. Krensky, Stephen. *Conqueror and Hero: The Search for Alexander* (6–9). Illus. by Alexander Farquharson. 1981, Little $8.95; paper $4.95. A readable biography that remains faithful to the facts.

7025. Lasker, Joe. *The Great Alexander the Great* (2–5). Illus. by author. 1983, Viking $13.95. A picture book biography of Alexander.

Charles, Prince of Wales

7026. Nugent, Jean. *Prince Charles: England's Future King* (3–6). Illus. 1982, Dillon LB $8.95. A biography of Britain's King-to-be.

Churchill, Winston

7027. Keller, Mollie. *Winston Churchill* (6–9). Illus. 1984, Watts $8.90. The biography of this British soldier, writer, and statesman.

Columba, Saint

7028. Fritz, Jean. *The Man Who Loved Books* (2–4). Illus. by Trina S. Hyman. 1981, Putnam $8.95. The story of the saint who banished himself from Ireland over a book.

Eleanor, Queen

7029. Brooks, Polly Schoyer. *Queen Eleanor, Independent Spirit of the Medieval World* (6–9). Illus. 1983, Harper $9.57; LB $9.89. The story of Eleanor of Acquitaine, Queen of both France and England.

Elizabeth I, Queen of England

7030. Zamoyska, Betka. *Queen Elizabeth I* (6–9). Illus. 1981, McGraw $7.95. Not only a life story but also an introduction to Elizabethan times.

Elizabeth II, Queen of Great Britain

7031. Hamilton, Alan. *Queen Elizabeth II* (4–6). Illus. by Karen Heywood. 1983, Hamish Hamilton $7.95. The long and successful reign of Great Britain's present Queen.

Francis of Assisi, Saint

7032. de Paola, Tomie. *Francis the Poor Man of Assisi* (4–7). Illus. by author. 1982, Holiday LB $14.95. A simple retelling of the life of St. Francis with fine pictures by de Paola. Also use: *St. Francis of Assisi* by Nina Bawden (1983, Lothrop $10.00; LB $10.88).

George III

7033. Fritz, Jean. *Can't You Make Them Behave, King George?* (3–5). Illus. by Tomie de Paola. 1982, Putnam $9.95; paper $4.95. A charming, amiable biography of George III, which includes an approach to the American Revolution not usually found in children's books.

Hannam, Charles

7034. Hannam, Charles. *A Boy in That Situation* (6–8). Illus. 1978, Harper $9.95. An autobiographical account of a young Jew growing up in Nazi Germany.

Hitler, Adolf

7035. Devaney, John. *Hitler, Mad Dictator of World War II* (6–8). Illus. 1978, Putnam $8.95. A clear, detailed, lucid account. Also use: *Adolf Hitler* by Joshua Rubenstein (1982, Watts $8.90).

7036. Shirer, William L. *The Rise and Fall of Adolf Hitler* (5–8). Illus. 1967, Random $5.99. A simple but accurate account of Germany's dictator.

Hsiao, Ellen

7037. Hsiao, Ellen. *A Chinese Year* (4–6). Illus. by author. 1970, Evans $3.95. An autobiographical incident from childhood when the author spent a year in a small Chinese town with her grandfather.

Joan of Arc

7038. Boutet de Monvel, Maurice. *Joan of Arc* (3–6). Illus. 1980, Viking $14.95. A facsimile of an 1896 French book about the Maid of Orleans.

John Paul II, Pope

7039. Sullivan, George. *Pope John Paul II: The People's Pope* (4–7). Illus. 1984, Walker $11.95. A brief retelling of the life of this controversial pope.

7040. Wolfe, Rinna. *The Singing Pope: The Story of Pope John Paul II* (4–7). Illus. 1980, Winston $8.95. The story of the present Pope, from his boyhood in Poland to current times. Also use: *John Paul II: The Pilgrim Pope* by Robert W. Douglas (1980, Childrens Pr. LB $9.25); *Pope John Paul II* by Mary Craig (1982, Hamish Hamilton $7.95; Penguin paper $2.50); *Pope John Paul II: Bringing Love to a Troubled World* by Anthony DiFranco (1983, Dillon $7.95).

Kherdian, David

7041. Kherdian, David. *The Road from Home: The Story of an Armenian Childhood* (6–9). 1979, Greenwillow $11.96. A memoir of a survivor of the Turkish slaughter of Armenians.

Meir, Golda

7042. Davidson, Margaret. *The Golda Meir Story* (5–7). 1976, Scribners $12.95. A heavily fictionized account of this important world leader.

7043. Keller, Mollie. *Golda Meir* (6–9). Illus. 1983, Watts $8.90. A biography of the woman who was Prime Minister of Israel from 1969 to 1974. For a younger audience use: *Our Golda: The Story of Golda Meir* by David A. Adler (1984, Viking $10.95).

Royale, Madame

7044. Powers, Elizabeth. *The Journal of Madame Royale* (5–8). Illus. 1976, Walker LB $7.39. The French Revolution as seen through the eyes of Marie Antoinette's daughter.

Sadat, Anwar

7045. Sullivan, George. *Sadat: The Man Who Changed Mid-East History* (5–8). Illus. 1981, Walker

$9.95; LB $9.85. The life story of the man who shaped modern Egypt's destiny.

Sasaki, Sadako

7046. Coerr, Eleanor. *Sadako and the Thousand Paper Cranes* (3–5). Illus. by Ronald Himler. 1977, Putnam $8.95; Dell paper $1.95. The moving biography of a young Japanese girl who dies of leukemia that developed as a result of radiation sickness from the bombing of Hiroshima.

Schweitzer, Albert

7047. Daniel, Anita. *The Story of Albert Schweitzer* (4–6). Illus. 1957, Random $5.99. The great doctor and humanitarian comes to life in this biography.

7048. Gollomb, Joseph. *Albert Schweitzer: Genius in the Jungle* (6–9). Illus. 1949, Vanguard $8.95. The story of the famous doctor and musician who founded a hospital in the African jungle.

Singer, Isaac Bashevis

7049. Singer, Isaac Bashevis. *A Day of Pleasure: Stories of a Boy Growing up in Warsaw* (6–9). 1969, Farrar paper $5.95. A Hasidic Jew's fond remembrances of the world in which he grew up.

Teresa, Mother

7050. Craig, Mary. *Mother Teresa* (5–7). Illus. by Janet Fahy. 1983, Hamish Hamilton $7.95. A biography of the nun who worked in the slums of Calcutta.

Tolstoy, Alexandra

7051. Sadler, Catherine Edwards. *Sasha: The Life of Alexandra Tolstoy* (6–9). Illus. 1982, Putnam $9.95. The story of the gallant daughter of Leo Tolstoy and her struggles for the oppressed.

Wesley, John

7052. McNeer, May, and Ward, Lynd. *John Wesley* (4–6). Illus. 1951, Abingdon $4.95; paper $3.50. The life of a great reformer in the Christian religion.

Explorers and Adventurers

Collective

7053. Lye, Keith. *Explorers* (5–7). Illus. 1984, Silver Burdett $10.50. A quick rundown of the major explorers of the world and the areas they visited.

7054. Sobol, Donald J. *True Sea Adventures* (4–7). 1975, Lodestar $7.95. Twenty-two stories of the sea retold briefly and with great gusto.

Individual

Allen, Ethan

7055. Holbrook, Stewart. *America's Ethan Allen* (5–7). Illus. by Lynd Ward. 1949, Houghton LB $8.95; paper $3.95. The story of the Green Mountain boys and of their fearless leader, the hero of Fort Ticonderoga.

Appleseed, Johnny

7056. Aliki. *The Story of Johnny Appleseed* (K–3). Illus. by author. 1963, Prentice $9.95; paper $3.95. A picture story of the man who wandered through the Midwest spreading love and apple seeds.

Armstrong, Neil

7057. Westman, Paul. *Neil Armstrong: Space Pioneer* (3–5). Illus. 1980, Lerner LB $5.95. A simple account of this astronaut's life.

Bluford, Guion

7058. Haskins, James, and Benson, Kathleen. *Space Challenger: The Story of Guion Bluford* (4–7). Illus. 1984, Carolrhoda $8.95. The story of the first black man to have ridden in space.

Boone, Daniel

7059. Brandt, Keith. *Daniel Boone: Frontier Adventures* (3–5). Illus. by John Lawn. 1983, Troll $6.89; paper $1.95. A readable account about the famous wilderness scout.

Borman, Frank

7060. Westman, Paul. *Frank Borman: To the Moon and Back* (3–5). Illus. 1981, Dillon LB $8.95. The biography of the man who commanded Apollo VIII on its moon mission.

Bowditch, Nathaniel

7061. Latham, Jean Lee. *Carry On, Mr. Bowditch* (6–9). Illus. by John O'Hara Cosgrave. 1955, Houghton $10.95; paper $4.95. This fictionalized biography of the great American navigator is enlivened by fascinating material on sailing ships and the romance of old Salem. Newbery medal winner.

Burningham, John

7062. Burningham, John. *Around the World in Eighty Days* (3–7). Illus. 1979, Merrimack $14.95.

The author describes a memorable trip he took on the same route as Phileas Fogg.

Cartier, Jacques

7063. Averill, Esther. *Cartier Sails the St. Lawrence* (3–6). Illus. by Feodor Rojankovsky. 1956, Harper $12.89. A beautifully designed book describing the Frenchman's North American exploration.

Columbus, Christopher

7064. Ceserani, Gian Paolo. *Christopher Columbus* (3–4). Illus. by Piero Ventura. 1979, Random $4.99. A familiar story told brightly and with good humor.

7065. Fritz, Jean. *Where Do You Think You're Going, Christopher Columbus?* (3–5). Illus. by Margot Tomes. 1980, Putnam $8.95; paper $3.95. A fresh, interesting account of Columbus and his voyages.

7066. Weil, Lisl. *I, Christopher Columbus* (1–3). Illus. by author. 1983, Atheneum $10.95. A simple biography. For an older audience use: *Columbus: Finder of the New World* (1952, Morrow $7.63).

Crockett, Davy

7067. Holbrook, Stewart. *Davy Crockett* (5–7). 1955, Random $5.99. All sorts of stories about Davy Crockett, one of the most interesting frontier scouts. Also use: *Davy Crockett: Young Pioneer* by Laurence Santrey (1983, Troll $6.89; paper $1.95).

Earhart, Amelia

7068. Sabin, Francene. *Amelia Earhart: Adventure in the Sky* (3–5). Illus. by Karen Milone. 1983, Troll $6.89; paper $1.95. A biography that shows this amazing woman's courage and endurance.

Ericson, Leif

7069. Jensen, Malcolm C. *Leif Ericson the Lucky* (6–8). Illus. 1979, Watts $6.90. The text is brought to life with many authentic prints and documents.

Heyerdahl, Thor

7070. Blassingame, Wyatt. *Thor Heyerdahl: Viking Scientist* (5–7). Illus. 1979, Lodestar $7.95. Both the scientist and the man of adventure are revealed in this lively biography.

7071. Heyerdahl, Thor. *Kon-Tiki: A True Adventure of Survival at Sea* (3–6). Illus. 1984, Random $4.99; paper $1.95. A fine adaptation of the adult adventure story.

7072. Westman, Paul. *Thor Heyerdahl: Across the Seas of Time* (3–5). Illus. 1982, Dillon LB $8.95. The story of the intrepid contemporary explorer and his adventure.

Lindbergh, Charles

7073. Stein, R. Conrad. *The Story of the Spirit of St. Louis* (2–4). Illus. by Len W. Meents. 1984, Childrens Pr. $6.45. The story of Charles Lindbergh and his famous flight.

Magellan, Ferdinand

7074. Syme, Ronald. *Magellan: First around the World* (4–7). Illus. by William Stobbs. 1953, Morrow $7.92. The first voyage around the world highlights this life story of the Portuguese navigator.

Polo, Marco

7075. Ceserani, Gian Paolo. *Marco Polo* (2–5). Illus. by Piero Ventura. 1982, Putnam $9.95. A lavishly illustrated biography of this fearless visitor to China.

Richthofen, Freiherr von

7076. Wright, Nicolas. *The Red Baron* (5–9). Illus. 1977, McGraw $7.95. The first biography for a young audience on Freiherr von Richthofen, the audacious German air ace of World War I.

St. Brendan

7077. Fritz, Jean. *Brendan the Navigator: A History Mystery about the Discovery of America* (3–5). Illus. 1979, Putnam $7.95. An imaginative re-creation of what could have been the discovery of America by St. Brendan.

Young, John

7078. Westman, Paul. *John Young: Space Shuttle Commander* (4–6). Illus. 1981, Dillon LB $8.95. The story of an astronaut and his several space flights culminating in the space shuttle.

Scientists and Inventors

Collective

7079. Bowman, Kathleen. *New Women in Medicine* (5–7). Illus. 1976, Creative Ed. LB $8.95. Part of the fine New Women In series, this book supplies 7 short biographies of women who have succeeded in medicine.

7080. Emberlin, Diane. *Contributions of Women: Science* (5–7). Illus. 1977, Dillon $8.95. Short biographies of women who have excelled in science.

7081. Facklam, Margery. *Wild Animals, Gentle Women* (6–9). Illus. 1978, Harcourt $5.95. Biographies of 11 women who have studied various wild animals.

7082.   Gleasner, Diana C. *Breakthrough: Women in Science* (6–9). 1983, Walker $12.95. Biographies of 6 women who have pursued successful careers in various areas of science.

7083.   Haber, Louis. *Women Pioneers of Science* (6–9). 1979, Harcourt $8.95. An introduction to some of the lesser-known women scientists and their contributions.

7084.   Quackenbush, Robert. *Watt Got You Started, Mr. Fulton: A Story of James Watt and Robert Fulton* (4–5). Illus. by author. 1982, Prentice $7.95. The story of the invention of James Watt and how it helped Robert Fulton.

7085.   Richards, Norman. *Dreamers and Doers: Inventors Who Changed Our World* (6–8). Illus. 1984, Atheneum $10.95. Four inventors—Goddard, Goodyear, Edison, and Eastman—are highlighted.

7086.   Vandivert, Rita. *To the Rescue: Seven Heroes of Conservation* (6–9). Illus. 1982, Warne $9.95. Seven biographies of men who have contributed in different ways in protecting our natural resources.

Individual

Bell, Alexander Graham

7087.   Quackenbush, Robert. *Ahoy! Ahoy! Are You There? A Story of Alexander Graham Bell* (3–5). Illus. by author. 1981, Prentice $8.95. An account that tells more about the subject than the invention of the telephone.

7088.   Shippen, Katherine B. *Alexander Graham Bell Invents the Telephone* (3–8). Illus. 1982, Random paper $2.95. The life of the inventor of the telephone interestingly told.

Blackwell, Elizabeth

7089.   Wilson, Dorothy Clarke. *I Will Be a Doctor! The Story of America's First Woman Physician* (5–8). 1983, Abingdon paper $6.95. The amazing story of the woman who faced incredible odds to become a doctor.

Burbank, Luther

7090.   Quackenbush, Robert. *Here a Plant, There a Plant, Everywhere a Plant, Plant! A Story of Luther Burbank* (2–5). Illus. by author. 1982, Prentice $8.95. A profile of the American naturalist and plant breeder, Luther Burbank.

Clark, Eugenie

7091.   McGovern, Ann. *Shark Lady: True Adventures of Eugenie Clark* (3–5). Illus. by Ruth Chew.

1979, Four Winds $8.95. An account of the work and accomplishments of this scientist and director of a marine laboratory.

Cousteau, Jacques

7092.   Iverson, Genie. *Jacques Cousteau* (3–5). Illus. by Hal Ashmead. 1976, Putnam $5.99. A simple-to-read biography of the underwater explorer and fighter for sea life.

7093.   Westman, Paul. *Jacques Cousteau: Free Flight Undersea* (4–8). Illus. by Reg Sandland. 1980, Dillon LB $7.95. An easy-to-read biography of the great underwater scientist and explorer.

Curie, Marie

7094.   Brandt, Keith. *Marie Curie: Brave Scientist* (3–5). Illus. by Karen Milone. 1983, Troll $6.89; paper $1.95. An account that emphasizes the struggle before eventual success. Also use: *Marie Curie* by Mollie Keller (1982, Watts LB $8.90); *Marie Curie: Pioneer Physicist* by Carol Greene (1984, Childrens Pr. $8.95).

Darwin, Charles

7095.   Quackenbush, Robert. *The Beagle and Mr. Flycatcher: A Story of Charles Darwin* (4–6). Illus. by author. 1983, Prentice $8.95. Old facts and routine biography are mixed to create an entertaining account.

7096.   Ward, Peter. *The Adventures of Charles Darwin: A Story of the Beagle Voyage* (5–7). Illus. by Annabel Large. 1982, Cambridge Univ. Pr. $8.95. Darwin's adventures on the *Beagle* as seen through the eyes of a cabin boy.

da Vinci, Leonardo

7097.   Cooper, Margaret. *The Inventions of Leonardo da Vinci* (6–9). Illus. 1968, Macmillan $7.95. An account of the scientific aspects of da Vinci's life.

Edison, Thomas Alva

7098.   Quackenbush, Robert. *What Has Wild Tom Done Now? A Story of Thomas Alva Edison* (3–4). Illus. by author. 1981, Prentice $7.95. A humorous biography of Edison that reveals little-known facts.

7099.   Sabin, Louis. *Thomas Alva Edison: Young Inventor* (3–5). Illus. by George Ulrich. 1983, Troll $6.89; paper $1.95. An account that concentrates on Edison's childhood. Also use: *The Story of Thomas Alva Edison* by Margaret Cousins (1981, Random paper $2.95).

Einstein, Albert

7100.   Lepscky, Ibi. *Albert Einstein* (2–4). Illus. by Paolo Cardoni. 1982, Barron's $6.50. Einstein's accomplishments as well as his personal life are covered.

Ericsson, John

7101. Burnett, Constance Buel. *Captain John Ericsson: Father of the Monitor* (6–9). 1960, Vanguard $6.95. A story of the American engineer and inventor who designed and built the *Monitor*.

Galileo

7102. Rosen, Sidney. *Galileo and the Magic Numbers* (6–9). Illus. by Harve Stein. 1958, Little $9.95. The Italian astronomer who was persecuted for his beliefs concerning the earth's relationship to the sun.

Goodall, Jane

7103. Coerr, Eleanor. *Jane Goodall* (2–4). Illus. by Kees de Kiette. 1976, Putnam $5.99. The amazing story of the young woman who went to Tanzania to study chimpanzees.

7104. Fox, Mary Virginia. *Jane Goodall: Living Chimp Style* (3–5). Illus. by Nona Hengen. 1981, Dillon $8.95. A simple account of the scientist who studied chimpanzees in Tanzania.

Goodyear, Charles

7105. Quackenbush, Robert. *Oh, What an Awful Mess! A Story of Charles Goodyear* (3–4). Illus. 1980, Prentice paper $3.95. The story of Charles Goodyear's many failures and final success.

Halley, Edmond

7106. Heckart, Barbara Hooper. *Edmond Halley: The Man and His Comet* (4–6). Illus. 1984, Childrens Pr. $8.95. The story of the accomplished scientist and the comet that bears his name.

Lavoisier, Antoine Laurent

7107. Grey, Vivian. *The Chemist Who Lost His Head: The Story of Antoine Laurent Lavoisier* (5–8). Illus. 1982, Putnam $9.95. A victim of the French Revolution, this scientist named oxygen and organized the science of chemistry.

Leakey, Louis

7108. Malatesta, Ann, and Friedland, Ronald. *The White Kikuyu* (6–8). Illus. by author. 1978, McGraw $9.95. The fascinating story of Dr. Louis Leakey, the anthropologist who discovered remains of primitive peoples in Africa.

Mayo, William and Charles

7109. Goodsell, Jane. *The Mayo Brothers* (2–4). Illus. by Louis Glanzman. 1972, Harper paper $1.45. Will and Charles Mayo learned medicine

from their father and established their famous clinic in 1914.

Mead, Margaret

7110. Epstein, Sam, and Epstein, Beryl. *She Never Looked Back: Margaret Mead in Samoa* (4–6). Illus. by Victor Juhasz. 1980, Putnam $6.99. A narrative that concentrates on Margaret Mead's study of Samoan youth in the 1920s.

Mitchell, Maria

7111. Morgan, Helen L. *Maria Mitchell: First Lady of American Astronomy* (5–8). 1977, Westminster $8.95. The story of the astronomer and her career at Vassar.

Morse, Samuel F. B.

7112. Quackenbush, Robert. *Quick, Annie, Give Me a Catchy Line! A Story of Samuel F. B. Morse* (2–5). Illus. by author. 1983, Prentice $8.95. A humorous, easily read biography of Morse.

Pasteur, Louis

7113. Sabin, Francene. *Louis Pasteur: Young Scientist* (3–5). Illus. by Susan Swan. 1983, Troll $6.89; paper $1.95. A simple biography that concentrates on the boyhood of Pasteur.

Pauling, Linus

7114. White, Florence Meiman. *Linus Pauling: Scientist and Crusader* (5–7). Illus. 1980, Walker $8.95; LB $9.85. A biography that stresses Pauling's contributions to science and humanity.

Petrofsky, Jerrold

7115. Gaffney, Timothy R. *Jerrold Petrofsky: Biomedical Pioneer* (5–8). Illus. 1984, Childrens Pr. $8.95. The story of the young medical man who used computers and electrical impulses to help paralyzed limbs.

Ramon y Cajal, Santiago

7116. Clifford, Eth. *The Wild One* (6–9). Illus. by Arvis Stewart. 1974, Houghton $5.95. A biography in the first person about the youth of Santiago Ramon y Cajal, who won the 1906 Nobel prize for medicine.

Wright, Wilbur and Orville

7117. Reynolds, Quentin. *The Wright Brothers* (4–7). 1981, Random paper $2.95. The lives of 2 mechanical geniuses.

7118. Sabin, Louis. *Wilbur and Orville Wright: The Flight to Adventure* (3–5). Illus. by John Lawn. 1983, Troll $6.89; paper $1.95. An interesting biography of these early aviators.

Artists, Writers, Composers, and Performers

Collective

7119. Goffstein, M. B. *Lives of the Artists* (3–8). Illus. 1982, Farrar $8.95. Five free-verse biographies, including Rembrandt and Nevelson.

7120. Harris, Stacy. *Comedians of Country Music* (5–8). 1978, Lerner LB $5.95. An introduction to well-known country music comics.

7121. Henry, Marguerite. *The Illustrated Marguerite Henry: With Wesley Dennis, Robert Lougheed, Lynd Ward and Rich Rudish* (5–8). Illus. 1980, Rand McNally $9.95; LB $9.97. Marguerite Henry introduces the artists who have worked with her on her books.

7122. Horwitz, Elinor. *Contemporary American Folk Artists* (6–9). Illus. 1975, Harper $8.50; paper $3.95. After a general introduction to folk art, the author devotes single chapters to such individual artists as Simon Rodie, the builder of Watts Tower.

7123. Jones, Hettie. *Big Star Fallin' Mama! Five Women in Black Music* (6–8). 1974, Viking $9.95. The lives of Ma Rainey, Bessie Smith, Mahalia Jackson, Billie Holiday, and Aretha Franklin sensitively presented.

7124. Krishef, Robert K. *More New Breed Stars* (5–9). Illus. 1980, Lerner LB $5.95. Ten short biographies of country-pop stars such as Kris Kristofferson, Linda Ronstadt, and Charley Pride.

7125. Polsky, Milton E. *Today's Young Stars of Stage and Screen* (5–8). Illus. 1979, Watts $6.90. Twelve short biographies of such stars as Gary Coleman, Melissa Gilbert, and Brooke Shields.

Artists

Bell, Bill

7126. Bell, Bill. *Saxophone Boy* (4–6). Illus. by author. 1980, Tundra $14.95. The story of Bill Bell's Philadelphia boyhood in the 1930s.

Blegvad, Erik

7127. Blegvad, Erik. *Self-Portrait: Erik Blegvad* (5–8). Illus. by author. 1979, Addison $8.95. A candid, lively autobiography of the well-known picture-book illustrator.

Bourke-White, Margaret

7128. Iverson, Genie. *Margaret Bourke-White: News Photographer* (4–6). Illus. 1980, Creative Ed. LB $7.95. A simple biography illustrated with some of her finest photography.

7129. Siegel, Beatrice. *An Eye on the World: Margaret Bourke-White, Photographer* (5–9). Illus. 1980, Warne $8.95. A biography of the famous photographer with many examples of her work.

Calder, Alexander

7130. Lipman, Jean, and Aspenwall, Margaret. *Alexander Calder and His Magical Mobiles* (5–8). Illus. 1981, Hudson Hills $15.00. An exciting biography of this controversial sculptor.

Chagall, Marc

7131. Raboff, Ernest. *Marc Chagall* (4–6). Illus. 1982, Doubleday $8.95; paper $4.95. Beautifully illustrated introduction to the contemporary artist.

Disney, Walt

7132. Montgomery, Elizabeth Rider. *Walt Disney: Master of Make-Believe* (3–5). Illus. by Victor Mays. 1971, Garrard $7.12. A simple account of the life of a master cartoonist, with emphasis on his rise to fame.

Homer, Winslow

7133. Hyman, Linda. *Winslow Homer: America's Old Master* (6–7). Illus. 1973, Doubleday $5.95. All aspects of this famous painter's life, including his work as a Civil War illustrator, are well depicted.

Hyman, Trina Schart

7134. Hyman, Trina S. *Self-Portrait: Trina Schart Hyman* (4–6). Illus. by author. 1981, Addison LB $8.95. An introduction to the life and work of this fine artist.

Kurelek, William

7135. Kurelek, William. *A Prairie Boy's Summer* (3–5). Illus. by author. 1975, Houghton $7.95. Each of this Canadian artist's paintings depicts a farm activity, which the accompanying text describes in this companion piece to the author's earlier *A Prairie Boy's Winter* (1973, $10.95; paper $4.95).

Leonardo da Vinci

7136. Sachs, Marianne. *Leonardo and His World* (5–7). Illus. 1981, Silver Burdett $13.00. The life of the Renaissance artist with examples of his paintings and inventions.

Muybridge, Eadweard

7137. Manes, Stephen. *Pictures of Motion and Pictures That Move: Eadweard Muybridge and the*

Photography of Motion (6–8). Illus. 1982, Putnam $9.95. The biography of the photographer who invented the first motion picture projector.

O'Kelley, Mattie Lou

7138. O'Kelley, Mattie Lou. *From the Hills of Georgia: An Autobiography in Paintings* (4–8). Illus. by author. 1983, Little $14.45. Twenty-eight paintings illustrate the author's childhood in rural Georgia.

Potter, Beatrix

7139. Aldis, Dorothy. *Nothing Is Impossible: The Story of Beatrix Potter* (3–6). Illus. by Richard Cuffari. 1969, Atheneum $7.95. The story of a remarkable woman whose lonely childhood in London was relieved only by her pets, her reading, and her drawings.

Van Der Zee, James

7140. Haskins, James. *James Van Der Zee: The Picture Takin' Man* (6–9). 1979, Dodd $8.95. The portrait of a man who spent his life photographing his world.

West, Benjamin

7141. Henry, Marguerite. *Benjamin West and His Cat Grimalkin* (4–6). Illus. by Wesley Dennis. 1947, Bobbs-Merrill $7.95. West's struggle to study painting against the wishes of his Quaker parents and the cat who was his friend and ally.

Zemach, Margot

7142. Zemach, Margot. *Self-Portrait: Margot Zemach* (4–7). Illus. by author. 1978, Addison LB $12.95. An autobiographical portrait in words and pictures of the famous picture book artist.

Writers

Blume, Judy

7143. Lee, Betsy. *Judy Blume's Story* (4–6). 1981, Dillon LB $8.95; Scholastic paper $1.95. A simple biography of this amazingly popular writer.

Dickinson, Emily

7144. Barth, Edna. *I'm Nobody! Who Are You? The Story of Emily Dickinson* (5–8). Illus. by Richard Cuffari. 1971, Houghton $10.95. A well-researched but informal tale that begins when Emily is 9 years old; numerous quotations from her writings, plus a selection of poems at the end of the biographical material.

Faversham, Charles

7145. Gerrard, Roy. *The Favershams* (1–4). Illus. by author. 1983, Farrar $10.95. Rhyming verses tell the story of the Favershams in Victorian England and Charles, the famous writer.

Fritz, Jean

7146. Fritz, Jean. *Homesick: My Own Story* (5–7). Illus. by Margaret Tomes. 1982, Putnam $10.95; Dell paper $2.25. Growing up in the troubled China of the 1920s.

Hughes, Langston

7147. Meltzer, Milton. *Langston Hughes: A Biography* (6–9). 1968, Harper $12.02. An excellent portrayal of the noted black poet.

7148. Walker, Alice. *Langston Hughes: American Poet* (2–4). Illus. by Don Miller. 1974, Harper LB $11.89. An easy-to-read biography that emphasizes Hughes's early life.

Sandburg, Carl

7149. Hacker, Jeffrey H. *Carl Sandburg* (6–9). Illus. 1984, Watts $8.90. A well-organized life story of Carl Sandburg and an introduction to his work.

Stowe, Harriet Beecher

7150. Scott, John A. *Woman against Slavery: The Story of Harriet Beecher Stowe* (6–9). Illus. 1978, Harper $10.95; LB $10.89. A well-documented, mature account of the life of the abolitionist and feminist.

Thoreau, Henry David

7151. Roach, Marilynne K. *Down to Earth at Walden* (6–8). Illus. by author. 1980, Houghton $7.95. Thoreau and his life at Walden are well re-created.

Twain, Mark

7152. Quackenbush, Robert. *Mark Twain? What Kind of Name Is That? A Story of Samuel Langhorne Clemens* (3–6). Illus. by author. 1984, Prentice $8.95. A simple biography of one of America's great humorists.

Wilder, Laura Ingalls

7153. Blair, Gwenda. *Laura Ingalls Wilder* (2–4). Illus. by Thomas B. Allen. 1981, Putnam LB $6.99; paper $3.95. A simple biography of the author of the Little House books.

Yates, Elizabeth

7154. Yates, Elizabeth. *My Diary—My World* (6–9). Illus. 1981, Westminster $12.95. The story of the early life of the author of *Amos Fortune, Free Man*. Also use: *My Widening World* (1983, Westminster $12.95).

Composers

Guarneri del Gesee

7155. Wibberley, Leonard. *Guarneri: Story of a Genius* (6–9). 1974, Farrar $5.95. A biography told through the eyes of a young apprentice of Guarneri del Gesee and the other master violin makers of Cremona.

Mozart, Wolfgang Amadeus

7156. Lepscky, Ibi. *Amadeus Mozart* (2–4). Illus. by Paolo Cardoni. 1982, Barron's $6.50. A simple biography that concentrates on the boyhood of Mozart.

Entertainers

Alonso, Alicia

7157. Siegel, Beatrice. *Alicia Alonso: The Story of a Ballerina* (4–6). Illus. 1979, Warne $8.95. In spite of being almost blind, Alicia Alonso has become one of the world's greatest ballerinas.

Armstrong, Louis

7158. Iverson, Genie. *Louis Armstrong* (3–5). Illus. by Kevin Brooks. 1976, Harper LB $10.89. A well-rounded account of a jazz great and a remarkable human being.

Baryshnikov, Mikhail

7159. Goodman, Saul. *Baryshnikov* (5–8). Illus. 1979, Harvey House $6.59. An introduction to the private and professional life of this ballet superstar.

Chaplin, Charlie

7160. Sacranie, Raj. *Charlie Chaplin* (4–6). Illus. by Trevn Stubley. 1981, Hamish Hamilton $7.95. The life of the comedian which includes the hardships of his childhood. Also use: *Charlie Chaplin* by Gloria Kamen (1982, Atheneum $10.95).

Cosby, Bill

7161. Woods, Harold, and Woods, Geraldine. *Bill Cosby: Making America Laugh and Learn* (4–7). Illus. 1983, Dillon $7.95. A biography of the outstanding black comedian, educator, and humanitarian.

Dunham, Katherine

7162. Haskins, James. *Katherine Dunham* (6–8). Illus. 1982, Putnam $10.95. A detailed life story of the black dancer who has also contributed to anthropology.

Duran Duran

7163. Martin, Susan. *Duran Duran* (6–9). Illus. 1984, Messner $8.29; paper $2.95. An introduction to this rock group with chapters on each member.

Gordy, Pop

7164. Gordy, Berry, Sr. *Movin' Up: Pop Gordy Tells His Story* (5–8). Illus. 1979, Harper $10.53. The autobiography of the founder of Motown Records.

Jackson, Mahalia

7165. Jackson, Jesse. *Make a Joyful Noise unto the Lord! The Life of Mahalia Jackson, Queen of Gospel Singers* (6–9). Illus. 1974, Harper $11.06. The inspiring story of a woman who overcame prejudice and poverty to pursue her art as she wished without abandoning her principles. For younger readers use: *Mahalia Jackson: Queen of Gospel Song* by Jean Gay Cornell (1974, Garrard $7.12).

Jackson, Michael

7166. Halliburton, Warren J. *The Picture Life of Michael Jackson* (2–4). Illus. 1984, Watts $8.90. A profusely illustrated, simple biography of the star.

7167. Mabery, D. L. *This Is Michael Jackson* (4–6). Illus. 1984, Lerner $8.95. A biography of the very popular entertainer.

7168. Matthews, Gordon. *Michael Jackson* (5–7). Illus. 1984, Messner $8.79; Wanderer paper $2.95. A simple retelling of the life of this pop hero.

Kain, Karen

7169. Zola, Meguido. *Karen Kain: Born to Dance* (3–5). Illus. 1983, Watts $7.90. A story of the Canadian dancer now a star with the National Ballet of Canada.

Mitchell, Arthur

7170. Tobias, Tobi. *Arthur Mitchell* (3–5). Illus. by Carole Byard. 1975, Harper LB $11.89. An affectionate portrait of the black dancer who founded the Dance Theater of Harlem.

Oakley, Annie

7171. Alderman, Clifford L. *Annie Oakley and the World of Her Time* (6–8). 1979, Macmillan $9.95. A straightforward account of Annie Oakley, her career, and her life with Frank Butler.

Ringling Brothers

7172. Cone, Molly. *The Ringling Brothers* (2–4). Illus. by James McCrea and Ruth McCrea. 1971, Harper $11.49; LB $10.89. By hard and persistent work, the 6 Ringling boys developed their show into the largest circus in the world.

Robeson, Paul

7173. Greenfield, Eloise. *Paul Robeson* (4–6). 1975, Harper $10.89. The complex life of the black entertainer, well presented.

Rodgers, Jimmie

7174. Krishef, Robert K. *Jimmie Rodgers* (4–6). Illus. 1978, Lerner $5.95. An entertaining biography of the father of country and western music. Also use: *Loretta Lynn* (1978, Lerner $5.95).

Rogers, Fred

7175. DiFranco, JoAnn, and DiFranco, Anthony. *Mister Rogers: Good Neighbor to America's Children* (3–5). Illus. 1983, Dillon $7.95. A biography of the familiar TV personality.

Spielberg, Steven

7176. Collins, Tom. *Steven Spielberg: Creator of E.T.* (4–6). Illus. 1983, Dillon $7.95. A look at the famous motion picture personality and his creations.

Springfield, Rick

7177. Gillianti, Simone. *Rick Springfield* (6–9). Illus. 1984, Messner $8.29; paper $2.95. A slim biography with many pictures of this popular music figure.

Stratton, Charles Sherwood

7178. Cross, Helen Reeder. *The Real Tom Thumb* (4–6). Illus. by Stephen Gammell. 1980, Four Winds $8.95. The life story of the midget whose career was furthered by P. T. Barnum.

White, Josh

7179. Siegel, Dorothy S. *The Glory Road: The Story of Josh White* (6–8). Illus. 1982, Harcourt $10.95. The story of the famous folksinger and musician.

Williams, Hank

7180. Krishef, Robert K. *Hank Williams* (5–9). Illus. 1978, Lerner $5.95. The tragic life of one of the great stars of western music.

Wonder, Stevie

7181. Edwards, Audrey, and Wohl, Gary. *The Picture Life of Stevie Wonder* (6–9). Illus. 1977, Avon paper $1.75. An easy-to-read text illustrated with many black-and-white photographs.

Sports Figures

Collective

7182. Aaseng, Nathan. *Baseball's Hottest Hitters* (4–6). Illus. 1983, Lerner $7.95. Biographies of 8 currently important batters. Also from the same author and publisher: *Baseball's Finest Pitchers* (1980, $7.95); *Baseball's Brilliant Managers* (1982, LB $6.95); *Baseball's Power Hitters* (1983, LB $7.95); *Baseball's Ace Relief Pitchers* (1984, LB $7.95).

7183. Aaseng, Nathan. *Basketball's Playmakers* (4–6). Illus. 1983, Lerner $7.95. A look at the often underrated guards in a basketball team. Also by the same author and publisher: *Basketball's High Flyers* (1980, LB $7.95); *Basketball's Sharpshooters* (1983, LB $7.95).

7184. Aaseng, Nathan. *Comeback Stars of Pro Sports* (4–6). Illus. 1983, Lerner LB $7.95. Biographies of stars who returned to the top. Also use: *Supersubs of Pro Sports* (1983, Lerner LB $7.95).

7185. Aaseng, Nathan. *Football's Cunning Coaches* (5–7). Illus. 1981, Lerner LB $7.95. Profiles of 8 important coaches. Four others in this series are: *Football's Fierce Defenses; Football's Sure-Handed Receivers; Football's Winning Quarterbacks* (all 1980); *Football's Steadiest Kickers* (1981) (all LB $7.95).

7186. Aaseng, Nathan. *Football's Daring Defensive Backs* (5–9). Illus. 1984, Lerner $7.95. The functions of this position are explained, and the careers of 8 players are outlined. Others in this series are: *Football's Breakaway Backs* (1980, LB $7.95); *Football's Toughest Tight Ends* (1981, LB $7.95); *Football's Crushing Blockers* (1982, $7.95); *Football's Hard-Hitting Linebackers; Football's Punishing Pass Rushers* (both 1984, LB $7.95).

7187. Aaseng, Nathan. *Football's Super Bowl Champions I–VIII* (4–6). Illus. 1982, Lerner LB $7.95. A look at the winning teams of the first Super Bowls. A companion volume is: *Football's Super Bowl Champions IX–XVI* (1982, Lerner LB $7.95).

7188. Aaseng, Nathan. *Hockey's Fearless Goalies* (4–7). Illus. 1984, Lerner LB $7.95. The goalie's position is explained, and 8 famous goalies are profiled. Also use: *Hockey's Super Scorers* (1984, Lerner LB $7.95).

7189. Aaseng, Nathan. *Track's Magnificent Milers* (5–7). Illus. 1981, Lerner LB $7.95. Biographies of famous track stars.

7190. Aaseng, Nathan. *Winners Never Quit: Athletes Who Beat the Odds* (5–8). Illus. 1980, Lerner LB $7.95. Stories of athletes who conquered amazing obstacles.

7191. Aaseng, Nathan. *Winning Women of Tennis* (4–8). Illus. 1981, Lerner LB $7.95. The story of 8 famous women tennis players.

7192. Aaseng, Nathan. *World-Class Marathoners* (4–8). Illus. 1982, Lerner LB $7.95. The story of some of the world's most famous marathon winners.

7193. Alfano, Pete. *Super Bowl Superstars: The Most Valuable Players in the NFL's Championship Game* (5–7). Illus. 1982, Random paper $1.95. Brief biographies of the greatest stars of the Super Bowl.

7194. Borstein, Larry. *After Olympic Glory: The Lives of Ten Outstanding Medalists* (6–9). Illus. 1978, Warne $8.95. The lives of 10 Olympic winners, including Dr. Benjamin Spock, who continued to achieve throughout their lives.

7195. Burchard, S. H. *The Book of Baseball Greats* (3–6). Illus. 1983, Harcourt LB $10.95; paper $4.95. Brief biographies of such greats as Babe Ruth and Sandy Koufax.

7196. Glickman, William G. *Winners on the Tennis Court* (4–7). Illus. 1978, Avon paper $1.95. Simple, short introductions to some major athletes in tennis.

7197. Hollander, Phyllis, and Hollander, Zander, eds. *Dan Fouts, Ken Anderson, Joe Theismann and Other All-Time Great Quarterbacks* (5–8). Illus. 1983, Random paper $2.50. In addition to the 3 mentioned in the title, there are several other biographies, including Unitas, Tarkenton, and Namath.

7198. Jones, Billy Millsaps. *Wonder Women of Sports* (4–7). Illus. 1981, Random LB $4.99; paper $3.95. Twelve short biographies that start at the turn of the century and end with Billie Jean King and Nadia Comaneci.

7199. Litsky, Frank. *Winners in Gymnastics* (4–7). Illus. 1978, Watts $9.90; Avon paper $1.25. Easily read, brief accounts of important athletes.

7200. Lundgren, Hal. *NFL Superstars* (4–8). Illus. 1983, Childrens Pr. $7.95. A profile of 25 of the current best in the NFL.

7201. Murray, Tom, ed. *Sport Magazine's All-Time All Stars* (6–9). 1977, NAL $2.50. Twenty-two articles that appeared in *Sport Magazine* from 1948 through 1974 on the greatest baseball players.

7202. Olney, Ross R. *Modern Speed Record Superstars* (6–9). Illus. 1982, Dodd $8.95. Profiles of 6 daredevils and the speed records they created.

7203. Olney, Ross R. *Super Champions of Auto Racing* (5–7). Illus. 1984, Houghton $11.95; paper $4.95. Profiles of 6 very different stars of the racing world.

7204. Olney, Ross R. *Super Champions of Ice Hockey* (5–8). Illus. 1982, Houghton $11.50; paper $4.95. A look at not only some star players but also the rudiments of the game.

7205. Sabin, Francene. *Women Who Win* (6–9). Illus. 1977, Dell paper $1.75. Biographies of 14 women athletes from a variety of sports.

7206. Smith, Robert. *Pioneers of Baseball* (6–9). Illus. 1978, Little $8.95. Short sketches of outstanding baseball players, many now relatively unknown.

7207. Sullivan, George. *Baseball's Wacky Players* (6–9). Illus. 1984, Dodd $10.95. A book that concentrates on the light side of baseball.

7208. Sullivan, George. *Modern Olympic Superstars* (3–6). Illus. 1979, Dodd $8.95. The story of 6 champions, such as Bruce Jenner, who won gold medals.

7209. Sullivan, George. *Superstars of Women's Track* (5–9). Illus. 1981, Dodd LB $8.95. Six brief biographies of current track stars.

7210. Van Steenwyk, Elizabeth. *Stars on Ice* (5–9). Illus. 1980, Dodd $7.95. Biographies of famous 1980 Olympic figure skaters.

Baseball

Aaron, Henry

7211. Hahn, James, and Hahn, Lynn. *Henry! The Sports Career of Henry Aaron* (5–9). Illus. 1981, Crestwood House LB $6.95; paper $3.95. The life and career of this quiet black baseball player.

Brett, George

7212. Twyman, Gib. *Born to Hit: The George Brett Story* (3–6). Illus. 1982, Random paper $1.95. A profile of the outstanding baseball hitter. For a younger group use: *Picture Story of George Brett* by George Sullivan (1981, Messner $7.95); also use: *Sports Star: George Brett* by S. H. Burchard (1982, Harcourt $6.95; paper $2.95).

Carlton, Steve

7213. Aaseng, Nathan. *Steve Carlton: Baseball's Silent Strongman* (5–8). Illus. 1984, Lerner LB $6.95. A biography of the Phillies's famous pitcher.

Carter, Gary

7214. Buck, Ray. *Gary Carter: The Kid* (3–6). Illus. 1984, Childrens Pr. $6.50. An easily read biography of the young catcher of the New York Mets.

DiMaggio, Joe

7215. Schoor, Gene. *Joe DiMaggio: A Biography* (6–9). Illus. 1980, Doubleday $8.95; LB $9.80. An introspective biography of the legendary Yankee Clipper.

Fidrych, Mark

7216. Burchard, S. H. *Sports Star: Mark "The Bird" Fidrych* (3–6). Illus. 1977, Harcourt $14.95; paper $2.95. An easily read biography of the colorful Detroit Tiger pitcher.

Foster, George

7217. Drucker, Malka, and Foster, George. *The George Foster Story* (5–9). Illus. 1979, Holiday $8.95. The life of the New York Mets' mighty hitter.

Garvey, Steve

7218. Vass, George. *Steve Garvey: The Bat Boy Who Became a Star* (5–8). Illus. 1979, Childrens Pr. $8.65; paper $2.50. An easily read, basic biography.

Hunter, Jim "Catfish"

7219. Burchard, S. H. *Sports Star: Jim "Catfish" Hunter* (3–5). Illus. by Paul Frame. 1976, Harcourt $4.95; paper $2.50. An easily read biography of the major league pitcher.

Jackson, Reggie

7220. Burchard, S. H. *Sports Star: Reggie Jackson* (3–6). Illus. 1979, Harcourt $6.95; paper $2.95. An easily read biography of the flamboyant former New York Yankee outfielder.

7221. Gutman, Bill. *The Picture Life of Reggie Jackson* (3–4). Illus. 1978, Watts $9.90; Avon paper $1.95. An acceptable biography of baseball's famous outfielder.

7222. Vass, George. *Reggie Jackson: From Superstar to Candy Bar* (5–8). Illus. 1979, Childrens Pr. $8.65; paper $2.50. Plenty of interesting biographical details in this easy-to-read biography. Also use: *The Reggie Jackson Story* by Bill Libby (1979, Lothrop $10.95).

John, Tommy

7223. Burchard, S. H. *Sports Star: Tommy John* (3–6). Illus. 1981, Harcourt paper $3.95. An easy biography of this pitching star.

LeFlore, Ron

7224. Knapp, Ron. *From Prison to the Major Leagues: The Picture Story of Ron LeFlore* (4–6). Illus. 1980, Messner LB $9.29. The story of the Detroit Tiger player who started on a prison team.

Mays, Willie

7225. Epstein, Sam. *Willie Mays: Baseball Superstar* (4–6). Illus. 1975, Garrard $7.95. The life story of the star player who made baseball history

Rizzuto, Phil

7226. Schoor, Gene. *The Scooter: The Phil Rizzuto Story* (6–9). Illus. 1982, Scribners $11.95. The story of the colorful shortstop and his later broadcasting days.

Robinson, Jackie

7227. Rudeen, Kenneth. *Jackie Robinson* (2–4). Illus. by Richard Cuffari. 1971, Harper LB $11.89; paper $2.95. The life story of the first black man to play in the major leagues.

Rose, Pete

7228. Rose, Pete. *Pete Rose: My Life in Baseball* (4–7). Illus. 1979, Doubleday $8.95; LB $7.90. A candid account of this baseball star's phenomenal career, told in conversational style. Also use: *Pete Rose: Baseball's Charlie Hustle* by Nathan Aaseng (1981, Lerner LB $6.95).

7229. Rubin, Bob. *Pete Rose* (5–7). 1975, Random $3.69. The story of "Charlie Hustle" will be especially popular with young readers. For a younger audience use: *Pete Rose: "Charlie Hustle"* by Ray Buck (1983, Childrens Pr. $5.95).

Ruth, Babe

7230. Hahn, James, and Hahn, Lynn. *Babe! The Sports Career of George Ruth* (3–5). Illus. 1981, Crestwood House LB $6.95; paper $3.95. A slight but simple introduction to the life of the baseball legend.

Schmidt, Mike

7231. Herbert, Mike. *Mike Schmidt: The Human Vacuum Cleaner* (4–8). Illus. 1983, Childrens Pr. $6.50. A very simple biography of the Phillies's third baseman. For a slightly older audience use: *Mike Schmidt: Baseball's King of Swing* by Stan Hochman (1983, Random paper $2.50).

Seaver, Tom

7232. Burchard, Marshall, and Burchard, S. H. *Sports Star: Tom Seaver* (1–5). Illus. by Paul Frame. 1976, Harcourt paper $3.95. An easy-to-read biography of one of the greatest pitchers in baseball history.

Stengel, Casey

7233. Hahn, James, and Hahn, Lynn. *Casey! The Sports Career of Charles Stengel* (5–9). Illus. 1981,

Crestwood House LB $6.95; paper $3.95. The career of the legendary Casey simply told.

7234. Verral, Charles. *Casey Stengel: Baseball's Great Manager* (4–7). Illus. 1978, Garrard $7.98. The breezy, informal writing style matches the life-style of this colorful man.

Valenzuela, Fernando

7235. Burchard, S. H. *Fernando Valenzuela* (4–6). Illus. 1982, Harcourt $8.95; paper $2.95. The biography of a young Mexican who gained early fame on the Los Angeles Dodgers.

7236. Littwin, Mike. *Fernando Valenzuela: The Screwball Artist* (3–6). Illus. 1983, Childrens Pr. $5.95. Ample black-and-white photographs highlight the story of this baseball great.

Winfield, Dave

7237. Liss, Howard. *Picture Story of Dave Winfield* (3–6). Illus. 1982, Messner LB $9.29. The story of the famous New York Yankee outfielder.

Football

Bradshaw, Terry

7238. Pierson, Don. *Terry Bradshaw—Super Bowl Quarterback* (4–8). Illus. 1981, Childrens Pr. LB $9.25; paper $2.25. An easy-to-read biography of this football great.

Brown, James

7239. Hahn, James, and Hahn, Lynn. *Brown! The Sports Career of James Brown* (3–5). Illus. 1981, Crestwood House LB $6.95; paper $3.95. A portrait of this once important football player now active in other areas.

Bryant, Paul W.

7240. Smith, E. S. *Bear Bryant: Football's Winning Coach* (6–9). Illus. 1984, Walker $10.95. The story of one of the most famous coaches in football history.

Campbell, Earl

7241. Burchard, S. H. *Sports Star: Earl Campbell* (3–6). Illus. 1980, Harcourt $6.95; paper $2.95. The life of the star running back of the Houston Oilers simply told.

Dorsett, Tony

7242. Burchard, S. H. *Sports Star: Tony Dorsett* (2–4). Illus. 1979, Harcourt paper $4.95. A simple account that traces Dorsett's career from high school football to the Dallas Cowboys.

7243. Conrad, Dick. *Tony Dorsett: From Heisman to Super Bowl in One Year* (5–8). Illus. 1979, Childrens Pr. $8.65; paper $2.50. The life of the gifted black football player told in text and pictures.

Greene, Joe

7244. Burchard, S. H. *Sports Star: "Mean" Joe Greene* (3–6). Illus. 1976, Harcourt paper $3.95. A simple biography of the Pittsburgh Steelers's great defensive tackle.

Griese, Bob

7245. Burchard, S. H. *Sports Star: Bob Griese* (3–6). Illus. 1975, Harcourt $5.25; paper $2.50. A simple biography of the Miami Dolphin quarterback who starred in the Super Bowls of 1973 and 1974.

Harris, Franco

7246. Hahn, James, and Hahn, Lynn. *Franco Harris* (4–6). 1979, EMC $6.95; paper $3.95. A biography of the Pittsburgh Steelers's star running back. Also use: *Franco Harris* by Thomas Braun (1975, Creative Ed. $6.95).

Payton, Walter

7247. Conrad, Dick. *Walter Payton: The Running Machine* (5–8). Illus. 1979, Childrens Pr. $8.65; paper $2.50. An interesting biography of the famous black football player.

Sayers, Gale

7248. Hahn, James. *Sayers! The Sports Career of Gale Sayers* (3–5). Illus. 1981, Crestwood House LB $6.95; paper $3.95. The short but brilliant career of this tragic football hero.

Tarkenton, Francis A.

7249. Hahn, James, and Hahn, Lynn. *Tark! The Sports Career of Francis Tarkenton* (5–9). Illus. 1981, Crestwood House LB $6.95; paper $3.95. The football giant's life told in simple text and many photographs.

Walker, Herschel

7250. Burchard, S. H. *Sports Star: Herschel Walker* (4–6). Illus. 1984, Harcourt $11.95; paper $5.95. The life of this fine black football player that includes material on the Heisman Trophy. Also use: *Herschel Walker: From the Georgia Backwoods and the Heisman Trophy to the Pros* by Jeff Prugh (1983, Random paper $2.50).

White, Danny

7251. Buck, Ray. *Danny White: The Kicking Quarterback* (3–6). Illus. 1983, Childrens Pr. $6.50. A glimpse at the home life of this Dallas Cowboy quarterback.

Tennis

Austin, Tracy

7252. Burchard, S. H. *Sports Star: Tracy Austin* (4–6). Illus. 1982, Harcourt $7.95; paper $2.95. A brief, straightforward biography of this tennis ace.

7253. Hahn, James, and Hahn, Lynn. *Tracy Austin: Powerhouse in Pinafore* (4–6). 1978, EMC $6.95. The career of the teenage tennis powerhouse.

King, Billie Jean

7254. Hahn, James, and Hahn, Lynn. *King! The Sports Career of Billie Jean King* (4–6). Illus. 1981, Crestwood House LB $6.95; paper $3.95. The story of this world famous tennis star.

Lloyd, Chris Evert

7255. Burchard, S. H. *Sports Star: Chris Evert Lloyd* (2–4). Illus. 1976, Harcourt $5.25; paper $3.25. This brief, simply written biography of the popular tennis player will be enjoyed by young children. Also use: *Chris! The Sports Career of Chris Evert Lloyd* by James Hahn and Lynn Hahn (1981, Crestwood House LB $6.95; paper $3.95).

McEnroe, John

7256. Burchard, S. H. *Sports Star: John McEnroe* (3–6). Illus. 1979, Harcourt $5.95. A standard biography that includes coverage through victory in the 1979 U.S. Open.

Track and Field

Decker, Mary

7257. Henkel, Cathy. *Mary Decker: America's Nike* (3–6). Illus. 1984, Childrens Pr. $6.50. The story of the American runner told in very simple language and with many pictures.

Thorpe, Jim

7258. Fall, Thomas. *Jim Thorpe* (2–5). Illus. by John Gretzer. 1970, Harper $10.89; paper $2.95. A well-rounded biography of the Indian athlete who won the Olympic decathlon in 1912. Also use: *Thorpe! The Sports Career of James Thorpe* by James Hahn and Lynn Hahn (1981, Crestwood House LB $6.95; paper $3.95); *Jim Thorpe: Young Athlete* by Laurence Santrey (1983, Troll $6.89; paper $0.95).

Basketball

Abdul-Jabbar, Kareem

7259. Haskins, James. *From Lew Alcindor to Kareem Abdul-Jabbar* (5–9). Illus. 1978, Lothrop $9.36. A newer edition of the popular biography that tells of an astounding basketball career.

Bird, Larry

7260. Corn, Frederick Lynn. *Basketball's Magnificent Bird: The Larry Bird Story* (5–9). 1982, Random paper $1.95. Highlights in the life of the Celtics's star shooter.

Chamberlain, Wilt

7261. Hahn, James, and Hahn, Lynn. *Wilt! The Sports Career of Wilton Chamberlain* (5–9). Illus. 1981, Crestwood House LB $6.95; paper $3.95. The life story of the fabulous basketball player, in simple text and with many photographs.

7262. Rudeen, Kenneth. *Wilt Chamberlain* (2–5). Illus. by Frank Mullins. 1970, Harper $11.49; LB $11.89; paper $2.95. An easily read biography of the basketball superstar.

Hayes, Elvin

7263. Burchard, S. H. *Sports Star: Elvin Hayes* (3–6). Illus. 1980, Harcourt paper $2.50. An easily read biography of the star forward of the Washington Bullits.

Johnson, Earvin "Magic"

7264. Haskins, James. *"Magic": A Biography of Earvin Johnson* (4–6). Illus. 1982, Enslow LB $10.95. The story of the star who earned the title "Magic."

McAdoo, Bob

7265. Haskins, James. *Bob McAdoo: Superstar* (5–9). Illus. 1978, Morrow $10.50. A chatty biography of this superstar of basketball, including his fight for civil rights.

Malone, Moses

7266. Lundgren, Hal. *Moses Malone: Philadelphia's Peerless Center* (3–6). Illus. 1983, Childrens Pr. $5.95. The story of the sports star twice named the N.B.A.'s most valuable player.

Thomas, Isiah

7267. Rosenthal, Bert. *Isiah Thomas: Pocket Magic* (3–8). Illus. 1984, Childrens Pr. $6.50. The story of the Detroit Pistons's star.

Walton, Bill

7268. Hahn, James, and Hahn, Lynn. *Bill Walton: Maverick Cager* (3–6). 1978, EMC $6.95. The life of the controversial basketball star, interestingly told.

Boxing

Leonard, Sugar Ray

7269. Haskins, James. *Sugar Ray Leonard* (6–9). Illus. 1982, Lothrop $10.00. The story of the boxing champion who broke new grounds in various sports. For a younger group use: *Sports Star: Sugar Ray Leonard* by S. H. Burchard (1983, Harcourt $10.95; paper $4.95).

Louis, Joe

7270. Libby, Bill. *Joe Louis: The Brown Bomber* (6–9). Illus. 1980, Lothrop $10.95; LB $10.51. A readable account of the great boxer's life.

Muhammad Ali

7271. Edwards, Audrey, and Wohl, Gary. *Muhammad Ali, the People's Champ* (6–9). Illus. 1977, Little $8.95. An absorbing record that contains much personal information, although it tends to idealize. For a younger group use: *Ali! The Sports Career of Muhammad Ali* by James Hahn and Lynn Hahn (1981, Crestwood House LB $6.95; paper $3.95).

Automobile Racing

Foyt, A. J.

7272. Olney, Ross R. *A. J. Foyt: The Only Four Time Winner* (4–6). 1978, Harvey House $6.59. The phenomenal career of a race car driver.

Guthrie, Janet

7273. Fox, Mary Virginia. *Janet Guthrie: Foot to the Floor* (3–5). Illus. 1981, Dillon LB $8.95. A simple biography about the famous automobile racing driver.

7274. Olney, Ross R. *Janet Guthrie: First Woman at Indy* (4–9). Illus. 1979, Harvey House $6.59. The incredible career of a race car driver.

Rutherford, Johnny

7275. Higdon, Hal. *Johnny Rutherford* (5–8). 1980, Putnam $6.99. A biography of the 2-time winner of the Indy 500.

Other Sports

Beckenbauer, Franz

7276. Hahn, James, and Hahn, Lynn. *Franz Beckenbauer* (4–6). 1978, EMC $6.95. The career of the German soccer superstar.

Comaneci, Nadia

7277. Braun, Thomas. *Nadia Comaneci* (4–6). Illus. 1977, Creative Ed. $6.95. The story in text and pictures of the phenomenal young star of the 1976 Olympics.

7278. Burchard, S. H. *Sports Star: Nadia Comaneci* (4–6). Illus. 1977, Harcourt $4.95; paper $2.95. A simple biography of the girl who at 14 won 4 medals at the 1976 Olympics.

Fleming, Peggy

7279. Young, Stephanie, and Curtis, Bruce. *Peggy Fleming: Portrait of an Ice Skater* (3–7). Illus. 1984, Avon paper $2.25. The story of Peggy Fleming, but chiefly an introduction to figure skating.

Gretzky, Wayne

7280. Benagh, Jim. *Picture Story of Wayne Gretzky* (3–5). Illus. 1982, Messner LB $9.29. A photograph-filled biography of the star of the Edmonton Oilers. Also use: *Wayne Gretzky: The Great Gretzky* by Bert Rosenthal (1983, Childrens Pr. $5.95).

7281. Burchard, S. H. *Sports Star: Wayne Gretzky* (4–6). Illus. 1982, Harcourt $8.95; paper $2.95. A well-illustrated biography of the hockey star. Also use: *Gretzky! Gretzky! Gretzky!* by Meguido Zola (1983, Watts $7.95).

Hamill, Dorothy

7282. Hamill, Dorothy, and Clairmont, Elva. *On and Off the Ice* (5–9). Illus. 1983, Knopf $10.95; LB $10.99. The skater's own story, from the beginning, to the Olympics, and then the Ice Capades. Also use: *Sports Star: Dorothy Hamill* by S. H. Burchard (1978, Harcourt paper $4.95).

Heiden, Eric

7283. Aaseng, Nathan. *Eric Heiden: Winner in Gold* (4–7). Illus. 1980, Lerner LB $6.95. The life story of the 1980 Olympic gold medalist speed skater.

Johnston, Carol

7284. Donovan, Pete. *Carol Johnston: The One-Armed Gymnast* (3–5). Illus. 1982, Childrens Pr. $5.95. Inspired story of a handicapped person who became a fine athlete.

Killy, Jean-Claude

7285.   Hahn, James, and Hahn, Lynn. *Killy! The Sports Career of Jean-Claude Killy* (3–5). Illus. 1981, Crestwood House LB $6.95; paper $3.95. A simple glimpse at the life and accomplishments of this skiing hero.

Lopez, Nancy

7286.   Robison, Nancy. *Nancy Lopez: Wonder Woman of Golf* (5–8). Illus. 1979, Childrens Pr. $8.65; paper $2.50. A well-illustrated basic biography about a dedicated Mexican-American athlete.

Pele

7287.   Burchard, S. H. *Sports Star: Pele* (4–6). Illus. 1976, Harcourt paper $4.95; paper $2.95. An easy-to-read life story of the world's greatest soccer player. Also use: *Pele: The Sports Career of Edson do Nascimento* by James Hahn and Lynn Hahn (1981, Crestwood House LB $6.95; paper $3.95).

Pickett, Bill

7288.   Hancock, Sibyl. *Bill Pickett: First Black Rodeo Star* (4–6). Illus. by Lorinda Bryan Cauley. 1977, Harcourt paper $1.95. An exciting story of a brave young black man's rise to fame.

Podborski, Steve

7289.   Coady, Mary Frances. *Steve Podborski: Fast—Faster—Fastest!* (3–5). Illus. 1983, Watts $7.90. The biography of a Canadian star skier.

Reynolds, Roger

7290.   Shyne, Kevin. *The Man Who Dropped from the Sky* (5–8). Illus. 1982, Messner LB $9.29. Roger Reynolds survived a terrible skydiving accident.

Russo, Leslie

7291.   Haney, Lynn. *Perfect Balance: The Story of an Elite Gymnast* (5–7). Illus. 1979, Putnam $9.95. The story of Leslie Russo and her struggle to become an Olympic-caliber gymnast.

Zaharias, Babe Didrikson

7292.   Hahn, James, and Hahn, Lynn. *Zaharias! The Sports Career of Mildred Zaharias* (5–9). Illus. 1981, Crestwood House LB $6.95; paper $3.95. A simple biography, complete with many black-and-white photographs.

The Individual and Society

Ecology and Environment

General

7293. Billington, Elizabeth. *Understanding Ecology* (5–7). Illus. by Robert Galster. 1971, Warne $6.95. Such concepts as food chains and ecosystems are introduced in this fascinating account that includes some projects.

7294. Ford, Barbara. *Alligators, Raccoons, and Other Survivors: The Wildlife of the Future* (5–7). Illus. 1981, Morrow $11.95; LB $11.47. An account of animals that are successfully surviving in the United States.

7295. Fradin, Dennis B. *Fires* (4–6). Illus. 1982, Childrens Pr. $7.50. The several characteristics of disastrous fires are discussed, as well as how to prevent them.

7296. Gates, Richard. *Conservation* (1–4). Illus. 1982, Childrens Pr. LB $10.60. A simple but informative introduction intended for the primary grades.

7297. Hirsch, S. Carl. *The Living Community: A Venture into Ecology* (6–9). Illus. by William Steinel. 1966, Viking $8.95. A study of the interrelationships among plants and animals.

7298. Hopf, Alice L. *Misplaced Animals, Plants and Other Living Creatures* (6–9). Illus. 1976, McGraw $7.95. A description of the problems caused when a stable ecology is set off balance by artificially introducing a new element.

7299. Kerrod, Robin. *The World of Tomorrow* (4–8). Illus. 1980, Watts $9.90. An account of concerns that we should be involved with in planning our future world.

7300. Miles, Betty. *Save the Earth! An Ecology Handbook for Kids* (4–6). Illus. by Claire Nivola. 1974, Knopf $6.99; paper $2.50. A concise introduction to the study of ecology.

7301. Poynter, Margaret. *Wildland Fire Fighting* (6–9). Illus. 1982, Atheneum $9.95. A history and modern-day account of firefighting in the outdoors.

7302. Pringle, Laurence. *Natural Fire: Its Ecology in Forests* (4–6). Illus. 1979, Morrow LB $8.59. How fire plays a natural and necessary part in our environment.

7303. Pringle, Laurence. *The Only Earth We Have* (5–8). Illus. 1969, Macmillan $9.95; paper $1.96. A discussion of how man has misused this planet.

7304. Pringle, Laurence. *Our Hungry Earth: The World Food Crisis* (5–7). Illus. 1976, Macmillan $9.95. A beginning discussion of the many factors, such as food production and population, that have created our world food crisis.

7305. Pringle, Laurence. *What Shall We Do with the Land: Choices for America* (6–9). Illus. 1981, Harper $10.53; LB $10.89. Questions involving land use today and in the future are explored.

Cities

7306. Muller, Jorg. *The Changing City and the Changing Countryside* (4–8). Illus. 1977, Atheneum $11.95. Two folios of loose pictures without text. The first shows the history of a city from 1953 to 1976; the second depicts the gradual destruction of a natural environment by the encroachment of industrialized society.

7307. Pringle, Laurence. *City and Suburb: Exploring an Ecosystem* (4–7). Illus. 1975, Macmillan $9.95. A study of all forms of life—human, animal, vegetable—in a metropolitan area.

Endangered Species

7308. Brown, Joseph E. *Rescue from Extinction* (6–8). Illus. 1981, Dodd LB $8.95. Causes of extinction of species and ways we can combat them.

7309. Burt, Olive W. *Rescued! America's Endangered Wildlife on the Comeback Trail* (5–7). Illus. 1980, Messner $7.79. Existing efforts to save specific species are chronicled.

7310. Burton, Robert. *Wildlife in Danger* (5–7). Illus. 1984, Silver Burdett $10.50. An account that stresses why species become endangered and how they can be protected.

7311. Hendrich, Paula. *Saving America's Birds* (6–9). Illus. 1982, Lothrop $11.25. The causes of some bird species being endangered are explored and methods used to save them.

7312. Jacobs, Francine. *Bermuda Petrel: The Bird That Would Not Die* (4–7). Illus. by Ted Lewin. 1981, Morrow $8.95; LB $8.59. The efforts to save a seabird once thought to be extinct.

7313. McClung, Robert M. *America's Endangered Birds* (6–8). Illus. by George Founds. 1979, Morrow $10.95; LB $10.51. Subtitle: *Programs and People Working to Save Them.*

7314. McClung, Robert M. *Hunted Mammals of the Sea* (6–8). Illus. by William Downey. 1978, Morrow $10.75. A discussion of various sea mammals from whales to polar bears that are objects of current conservation efforts.

7315. McClung, Robert M. *Lost Wild Worlds: The Story of Extinct and Vanishing Wildlife of the Eastern Hemisphere* (6–9). Illus. by Bob Hines. 1976, Morrow $12.50. A comprehensive survey of ecological concerns in this area.

7316. McClung, Robert M. *Vanishing Wildlife of Latin America* (5–8). Illus. by George Founds. 1981, Morrow $9.95; LB $9.55. A fascinating account divided by regions.

7317. Rice, Paul, and Mayle, Peter. *As Dead as a Dodo* (4–6). Illus. by Shawn Rice. 1981, Godine $10.95. An examination of many animals that are extinct and why they disappeared.

7318. Stone, Lynn M. *Endangered Animals* (1–3). Illus. 1984, Childrens Pr. $7.95. The reasons why some species become endangered are explored and what can be done about it.

7319. Stuart, Gene S. *Wildlife Alert: The Struggle to Survive* (3–6). Illus. 1980, National Geographic Society $6.95; LB $8.50. This book outlines the steps being taken to help endangered animals around the world.

7320. Wegen, Ron. *Where Can the Animals Go?* (4–7). Illus. 1978, Greenwillow $11.25; LB $11.88. An account of the effect people have had on African wildlife.

Garbage

7321. Black, Hallie. *Dirt Cheap: The Evolution of Renewable Resource Management* (6–8). Illus. 1979, Morrow $11.50; LB $11.04. This account stresses methods by which we can conserve our natural resources.

7322. Lauber, Patricia. *Too Much Garbage* (5–7). 1974, Garrard $7.22. A discussion of the problems of disposing of solid waste.

7323. Shanks, Ann Zane. *About Garbage and Stuff* (K–2). Illus. by author. 1973, Viking $11.50. An introduction to recycling waste materials, told in terms young children can readily understand, and what they can do to help.

7324. Showers, Paul. *Where Does the Garbage Go?* (2–3). Illus. by Loretta Lustig. 1974, Harper LB $10.89. A discussion of the problems of sanitation, conservation, and recycling of garbage as seen from a child's point of view.

7325. Weiss, Malcolm E. *Toxic Waste: Clean Up or Cover Up* (6–9). Illus. 1984, Watts $8.90. A controversial topic objectively handled.

Pollution

7326. Bartlett, Margaret F. *The Clean Brook* (1–3). Illus. by Aldren A. Watson. 1960, Harper LB $10.89. The process of dirtying and purifying a brook is told through the activities of plants and animals.

7327. Breiter, Herta S. *Pollution* (2–4). Illus. 1978, Raintree LB $14.25. A clear overview of this topical subject.

7328. Brown, Joseph E. *Oil Spills: Danger in the Sea* (6–9). Illus. 1978, Dodd $6.95. The sources and effects of a growing pollution problem.

7329. Kalina, Sigmund. *Three Drops of Water* (3–5). Illus. by Charles Robinson. 1974, Lothrop $9.36. The water cycle from melting snow to streams and rivers, with material on pollution and the animal food chain.

7330. Kiefer, Irene. *Poisoned Land: The Problem of Hazardous Waste* (6–9). Illus. 1981, Atheneum LB $10.95. Toxic waste and disposal problems are discussed in this timely work.

7331. McCoy, Joseph J. *A Sea of Troubles* (6–8). Illus. by Richard Cuffari. 1975, Houghton $7.95. Upsetting material on the many human-caused problems, such as pollution, that have been inflicted on the oceans.

Population

7332. Lowenherz, Robert J. *Population* (4–7). Illus. 1970, Creative Ed. $8.95. An introduction to the science of population study.

7333. Stwertka, Eve, and Stwertka, Albert. *Population, Growth, Change and Impact* (6–8). Illus. 1981, Watts LB $9.90. A study of population, its growth, decline, and the problem of overpopulation.

Economics and Business

General

7334. Adler, David A. *Prices Go Up, Prices Go Down: The Laws of Supply and Demand* (1–3). Illus. by Tom Huffman. 1984, Watts $8.90. A simple economics lesson that uses common examples.

7335. Brown, Fern. *The Great Money Machine: How Your Bank Works* (5–7). Illus. 1981, Messner LB $9.29. An introduction to banks and banking—their history and present uses.

7336. Claypool, Jane. *Manufacturing* (6–8). Illus. 1984, Watts $8.90. A history of manufacturing and the status of mass production today.

7337. Claypool, Jane. *Unemployment* (6–9). Illus. 1983, Watts $8.90. The cause and effect of unemployment, plus a history through President Reagan's supply-side economics.

7338. Elkin, Benjamin. *Money* (1–4). Illus. 1983, Childrens Pr. $7.95. A well-organized introduction to the history and function of money.

7339. Fodor, R. V. *Nickels, Dimes and Dollars: How Currency Works* (4–6). Illus. 1980, Morrow $9.95; LB $9.55. A discussion of the U.S. money system and such topics as inflation, international exchange, and money management.

7340. Molloy, Anne. *Wampum* (6–8). Illus. 1977, Hastings $7.95. A richly historical account of the origins and meanings behind the beads used by North American Indians for currency.

7341. Scott, Elaine. *The Banking Book* (6–8). Illus. by Kathie Abrams. 1981, Warne $8.95. A readable introduction to the banking business.

7342. Wallace, G. David. *Money Basics* (5–8). Illus. by Janet D'Amato. 1984, Prentice $9.95. A history of the monetary system is given, plus material on banking, inflation, and other related topics.

Consumerism

7343. Berger, Melvin. *Consumer Protection Labs* (6–8). Illus. 1975, Harper LB $10.89. How various governmental and private testing labs work to protect the consumer.

7344. Sullivan, George. *How Do They Package It?* (5–7). 1976, Westminster $7.50. The history and contemporary use of packaging, which also touches on allied facets of conservation and pollution.

Retail Stores

7345. Schwartz, Alvin. *Stores* (3–5). Illus. 1977, Macmillan $9.95. Different stores and their workers are described in the town of Princeton, New Jersey.

Money-making Ideas

7346. Belliston, Larry, and Hanks, Kurt. *Extra Cash for Kids* (4–8). Illus. 1982, Writer's Digest paper $6.95. A number of profit-making projects for youngsters are described.

7347. Byers, Patricia, and Preston, Julia. *The Kids Money Book* (6–9). 1983, Liberty paper $4.95. A number of ways kids can make money.

7348. Horn, Yvonne Michie. *Dozens of Ways to Make Money* (6–9). 1977, Harcourt paper $2.95. Thirty-five projects for young entrepreneurs.

7349. James, Elizabeth, and Barkin, Carol. *How to Grow a Hundred Dollars* (5–7). Illus. by Joel Schick. 1979, Lothrop $10.00; LB $10.88. Simple budgetry and financial concepts are explained through a story of a girl who sets out to earn some money.

7350. Kyte, Kathy S. *The Kid's Complete Guide to Money* (5–8). 1984, Knopf paper $8.99. A guide to the wise use of money.

7351. Lewis, Shari. *How Kids Can Really Make Money* (4–6). Illus. 1979, Holt $4.95; paper $1.95. Information on various ways to make money.

7352. Sattler, Helen R. *Dollars from Dandelions: 101 Ways to Earn Money* (6–9). Illus. by Rita Floden. 1979, Lothrop $11.50; LB $11.04. All kinds of ways for young people to earn money, from farm work to helping in the kitchen.

7353. Shanaman, Fred, and Malnig, Anita. *The First Official Money-Making Book for Kids* (5–8). Illus. by Durell Godfrey. 1983, Bantam paper $2.50. An interesting collection of money-making ideas.

7354. Stine, Jane, and Stine, Jovial Bob. *Everything You Need to Survive: Money Problems* (5–9). Illus. by Sal Murdocca. 1983, Random paper $1.95. An amusing and fact-filled guide to managing money.

Politics and Government

United Nations

7355. Greene, Carol. *United Nations* (1–4). Illus. 1983, Childrens Pr. $7.95. A brief history of the United Nations is given, plus its organization and responsibilities.

Courts and the Law

7356. Beaudry, Jo, and Ketchum, Lynne. *Carla Goes to Court* (3–6). Illus. 1983, Human Sciences $9.95. The court process is explored through Carla's experience after she witnesses a burglary.

7357. Coy, Harold. *The Supreme Court* (4–6). Illus. 1981, Watts LB $8.90. The composition and functions of the Supreme Court are explained.

7358. Levy, Elizabeth. *Lawyers for the People: A New Breed of Defenders and Their Work* (6–9). 1974, Dell paper $1.25. Biographical sketches and material on their cases are given for 9 dedicated lawyers who have worked to provide justice for the defenseless.

7359. McKown, Robin. *Seven Famous Trials in History* (6–8). 1963, Vanguard $9.95. Aspects of our legal system are explored through famous cases.

7360. Stevens, Leonard. *Death Penalty: The Case of Life vs. Death in the United States* (6–9). 1978, Putnam $8.99. An in-depth look at the 1972 *Furman* v. *Georgia* court case and its consequences.

United States Government

Constitution

7361. Lawson, Don. *The Changing Face of the Constitution: Prohibition, Universal Suffrage and Women's Civil Rights and Religious Freedom* (6–9). 1979, Watts LB $8.40. A useful look at prohibition, women's rights, and other constitutional matters.

7362. Peterson, Helen Stone. *The Making of the United States Constitution* (4–7). 1974, Garrard $7.12. A useful survey of the U.S. Constitution and how it came into being.

7363. Stein, R. Conrad. *The Story of the Nineteenth Amendment* (4–6). Illus. by Keith Neely. 1982, Childrens Pr. $5.95. The story of the beginnings of the women's suffrage movement.

7364. Weiss, Ann E. *God and Government: The Separation of Church and State* (6–9). 1982, Houghton $8.95. A discussion of the First Amendment and what it means today.

Federal Government

7365. Blassingame, Wyatt. *The Look-It-Up Book of Presidents* (3–6). Illus. 1984, Random $8.95; LB $9.99. There is good coverage on each of our presidents and on their terms of office.

7366. Bruse, Preston et al. *From the Door of the White House* (6–9). Illus. 1984, Lothrop $11.00. A doorman at the White House for almost 20 years shares his experiences.

7367. Burt, Olive W. *I Am an American* (4–6). Illus. 1968, Harper $9.89. An explanation of what good citizenship means.

7368. Coy, Harold. *Congress* (4–6). Illus. 1981, Watts LB $8.90. A revision of a standard account that is a useful introduction to Congress.

7369. Gilfond, Henry. *The Executive Branch of the United States Government* (6–8). Illus. 1981, Watts LB $8.90. An examination of the president, the Cabinet, and other components.

7370. Hoopes, Roy. *The Changing Vice-Presidency* (6–9). Illus. 1981, Harper $11.49; LB $11.89. A history of the office and thumbnail sketch of each vice president.

7371. Hoopes, Roy. *What a United States Senator Does* (5–8). 1975, Harper $10.89. A basic guide to the Senate and the activities of its members.

7372. Johnson, Gerald W. *The Cabinet* (5–7). Illus. by Leonard Everett Fisher. 1966, Morrow $9.52. In addition to a description of the history and role of the U.S. cabinet, this survey highlights important past cabinets.

7373. McElroy, Richard L. *American Presidents: Fascinating Facts, Stories and Questions of Our Chief Executives and Their Families* (5–9). Illus. by Walt Neal. 1984, Daring paper $3.95. A collection of trivia about our presidents.

7374. Roth, Harold. *First Class! The Postal System in Action* (4–6). Illus. 1983, Pantheon $10.95; LB $10.99. A book that introduces the postal system and how it works.

7375. Seuling, Barbara. *The Last Cow on the White House Lawn* (4–7). Illus. by author. 1978, Doubleday LB $6.95. A collection of little-known, often amusing facts about the presidency.

7376. Stevens, Leonard. *How a Law Is Made: The Story of a Bill against Pollution* (6–9). Illus. by Robert Galster. 1970, Harper $10.95. An explanation of the process by which the average citizen helps to make the laws that affect our lives.

Elections and Political Parties

7377. Kronenwetter, Michael. *Are You a Liberal? Are You a Conservative?* (6–9). 1984, Watts $8.90. A history of liberalism, its role in human development, and its counterpart, conservatism.

Municipal Government

7378. Eichner, James A. *The First Book of Local Government* (4–7). Illus. by Bruce Bacon. 1983, Watts LB $8.90. Forms of organization, main functions, and the complex problems of local political units.

Civil Rights

7379. Bullard, Pamela, and Stoia, Judith. *The Hardest Lesson: Personal Accounts of a Desegregation Crisis* (6–9). 1980, Little $8.95. Fourteen narratives that explore the Boston 1974 school desegregation crisis.

7380. Burns, Marilyn. *I Am Not a Short Adult: Getting Good at Being a Kid* (5–7). Illus. by Martha Weston. 1977, Little $8.95; paper $5.95. Many facets of childhood are discussed, including children's legal status and institutions that affect them.

7381. Carlson, Dale B. *Girls Are Equal Too: The Women's Movement for Teenagers* (6–9). Illus. by Carol Nicklaus. 1973, Atheneum $9.95; paper $2.95. A discussion with many examples of sexism as it exists in society. Also use: *Boys Have Feelings Too: Growing Up Male for Boys* (1980, Atheneum $9.95).

7382. Chute, Marchette. *The Green Tree of Democracy* (6–9). 1971, Dutton $9.95. A history of suffrage in the United States from its limited application during colonial days to the extension of voting privileges to 18-year-olds in 1970.

7383. Englebardt, Leland S. *You Have a Right* (6–8). 1979, Lothrop $9.75; LB $9.36. The legal rights of young people and sources of help are discussed.

7384. Fincher, E. B. *The Bill of Rights* (6–9). Illus. 1978, Watts $8.90. An examination of our basic civil rights and how they are protected.

7385. Kohn, Bernice. *The Spirit and the Letter: The Struggle for Rights in America* (5–8). Illus. 1974, Viking $9.95. The story of the Civil Rights movement in the United States.

7386. Snyder, Gerald S. *Human Rights* (5–8). Illus. 1980, Watts LB $8.90. The concepts of freedom and rights are introduced with examples of how they are violated.

Crime and Criminals

7387. Healey, Tim. *Spies* (6–8). Illus. 1979, Silver Burdett $12.68. A fascinating glimpse at spying through the ages.

7388. Kosof, Anna. *Prison Life in America* (6–10). Illus. 1984, Watts $9.95. An appraisal of what life is like in prison from interviews with prisoners.

7389. Madison, Arnold. *Arson!* (5–8). Illus. 1978, Watts LB $7.90. An introduction to the causes and results of this crime.

Ethnic Groups

7390. Avakian, Arra S. *The Armenians in America* (4–6). 1977, Lerner $6.95. A history of the Arme-

nian immigration to America and of the contributions of these people.

7391. Buckmaster, Henrietta. *Flight to Freedom: The Story of the Underground Railroad* (5–7). 1958, Harper $8.95. In addition to the history of the railroad, the author traces the growth of the abolition movement and its leaders.

7392. Engle, Eloise. *The Finns in America* (5–7). 1977, Lerner $6.95. An account of Finnish migration, their settlement in and contribution to America.

7393. Greenfield, Eloise, and Little, Lessie Jones. *Childtimes: A Three-Generation Memoir* (5–8). Illus. 1979, Harper LB $9.57. The childhood of 3 generations of black women.

7394. Hartmann, Edward George. *American Immigration* (5–8). Illus. 1979, Lerner $6.95. The people who came to America and why, from the Colonial Period to the present.

7395. Jones, Jayne Clark. *The Greeks in America* (5–7). Illus. 1969, Lerner LB $6.95. One of the many interesting titles in the In America series. Others are: *The French in America* by Virginia B. Kunz (1966); *The Norwegians in America* by Percie V. Hillbrand (1967); *The Russians in America* by Nancy Eubank (1973) (all Lerner LB $6.95).

7396. Lester, Julius. *To Be a Slave* (5–8). Illus. by Tom Feelings. 1968, Dial $8.95. Through the words of the victims themselves, the reader is helped to realize what it was like to be a slave in America.

7397. Meltzer, Milton. *All Times, All Peoples: A World History of Slavery* (5–9). Illus. by Leonard Everett Fisher. 1980, Harper $10.10; LB $10.89. A poignant and revealing history of slavery, from 10,000 years ago to today.

7398. Meltzer, Milton. *The Chinese Americans* (6–9). Illus. 1980, Harper $9.57; LB $9.89. A fine overview of the Chinese immigrants to the United States, why they came, their problems, and accomplishments.

7399. Meltzer, Milton, ed. *In Their Own Words: A History of the American Negro, Volume I, 1619–1865* (6–9). Illus. 1964, Harper $10.53; paper $3.95. The first of 3 volumes, a social history of black Americans dramatically told in their own words and illustrated with many reproductions. Followed by: *Volume II, 1865–1916* (1965, $8.95; paper $1.65); *Volume III, 1916–1966* (1967, $10.53; paper $1.65).

7400. Meltzer, Milton, ed. *The Jewish Americans: A History in Their Own Words* (6–9). Illus. 1982, Harper $10.53; LB $10.89. The Jewish experience in America, from Colonial times to 1950.

7401. Meltzer, Milton. *World of Our Fathers* (6–9). 1974, Farrar $7.95. Subtitle: *The Jews of Eastern Europe.*

7402. Thum, Marcella. *Exploring Black America: A History and Guide* (6–9). Illus. 1975, Atheneum $10.95. Each chapter is devoted to a single important topic in black history, such as slavery and the Underground Railway. In addition to an informational overview, material is given on such sources as museums and historic sites.

7403. Wolf, Bernard. *In This Proud Land: The Story of a Mexican American Family* (6–9). Illus. 1978, Harper $8.95. An inspiring, affectionate picture of the Hermandez family in Texas.

Youth Groups

7404. Blassingame, Wyatt. *Story of the Boy Scouts* (4–7). Illus. by David Hodges. 1968, Garrard $7.12. An interesting account of the history and worldwide activities of the scouting movement.

7405. Boy Scouts of America. *Boy Scout Handbook* (5–7). 1972, Boy Scouts of America $3.50. The standard handbook. Other BSA handbooks are: *Field Book* (1967, $3.95); *Bear Cub Scoutbook* (1973, $2.25); *Webelos Scoutbook* (1973, $2.25); *Wolf Cub Scout Book* (1973, $2.25).

7406. Boy Scouts of America. *Official Boy Scout Handbook* (5–9). Illus. 1979, Simon & Schuster $9.95; paper $3.00. The ninth edition of this standard handbook has some illustrations by Norman Rockwell.

7407. Girl Scouts of the U.S.A. *Junior Girl Scout Handbook* (4–7). 1963, Girl Scouts of the United States of America $3.50. A handbook for 9-to-11-year-olds on the activities of Girl Scouts. For a younger group, this organization also publishes: *The Brownie Girl Scout Handbook* (1963, $3.50).

7408. James, Laurie. *Adventure* (4–6). Illus. by Beth Charney. 1973, Camp Fire Girls $1.35. The basic handbook of the Camp Fire Girls, which outlines the aims and activities of the organization. Also use: *The Blue Bird Wish* (1970, $1.25); *Discovery* (1971, $1.35).

7409. Walz, Lila Phillips. *Camp Fire Blue Bird Series* (1–3). Illus. by Margaret A. Hartelius. 1973, Camp Fire Girls $1.00 per volume. Three booklets that describe activities and projects for younger Camp Fire Girls.

Personal Development

Behavior

General

7410. Ancona, George. *Team Work: A Picture Essay about Crews and Teams at Work* (4–5). Illus. 1983, Harper $10.53; LB $10.89. A series of pictures and commentaries of situations, such as mountain climbing and gas drilling, where teamwork is important.

7411. Anders, Rebecca. *Look at Prejudice and Understanding* (4–6). Illus. by Maria Forrai. 1976, Lerner $4.95. A discussion of the origins and effects of prejudice and what to do when one encounters it.

7412. Bell, Neill. *Only Human* (4–6). Illus. by Sandy Clifford. 1983, Little $13.45; paper $7.70. Subtitle: *Why We Are the Way We Are.*

7413. Berger, Terry. *I Have Feelings* (K–5). Illus. by I. Howard Spivack. 1971, Human Sciences $10.95. Text and photos show children that their feelings and emotions—good and bad—are natural.

7414. Gilbert, Sara. *By Yourself* (4–6). Illus. by Heidi Johanna Selig. 1983, Lothrop $9.55; paper $7.00. A survival guide for latchkey children.

7415. Gilfond, Henry. *How to Give a Speech* (6–9). 1980, Watts LB $8.90. A clear, step-by-step approach from choosing a topic to the delivery.

7416. Hall, Elizabeth. *From Pigeons to People: A Look at Behavior Shaping* (6–9). 1975, Houghton $6.95. Opinion and facts concerning reinforcement theory and behavior modification are well explored.

7417. Haskins, James. *Gambling: Who Really Wins?* (6–9). Illus. 1979, Watts $8.90. A description of types of gambling plus a discussion of the causes and treatment of compulsive gambling.

7418. Kalb, Jonah. *What Every Kid Should Know* (4–6). Illus. 1976, Houghton $5.95. An introduction to the study of how people behave toward each other.

7419. Kyte, Kathy S. *In Charge: A Complete Handbook for Kids with Working Parents* (6–10). Illus. by Susan Detrich. 1983, Knopf $8.99; paper $5.95. A manual for youngsters who must cope alone while parents are at work.

7420. Laiken, Deidre S., and Schneider, Alan J. *Listen to Me, I'm Angry* (6–9). Illus. by Bernice Myers. 1980, Lothrop $10.00; LB $10.88. A narrative on causes and types of anger and how young people can cope with it.

7421. Long, Lynette. *On My Own: The Kids' Self-Care Book* (4–6). Illus. by Joann Hall. Acropolis paper $6.95. A self-help survival guide for latchkey children.

7422. Meyer, Linda D. *Safety Zone: A Book Teaching Children Abduction Prevention Skills* (PS–5). 1984, Chas. Franklin Pr. $8.00; paper $3.00. This book for parents and children deals with abduction and sexual abuse.

7423. Naylor, Phyllis Reynolds. *Getting Along with Your Friends* (4–6). Illus. by Rick Cooley. 1980, Abingdon $7.95. A commonsense manual on how to make and keep friends.

7424. Naylor, Phyllis Reynolds. *Getting Along with Your Teachers* (4–6). Illus. by Rick Cooley. 1981, Abingdon $7.90. A useful guide on how to get along in the classroom.

7425. Stine, Jane, and Stine, Jovial Bob. *Everything You Need to Survive: Homework* (5–9). Illus. by Sal Murdocca. 1983, Random paper $1.95. A survival kit on study skills, including test-taking.

7426. Weiss, Ann E. *Polls and Surveys* (4–6). 1979, Watts $8.90. The history and present-day uses of public opinion research.

Etiquette

7427. Leaf, Munro. *Manners Can Be Fun* (3–4). Illus. by author. 1955, Harper $10.89. Includes material on television manners.

7428. Parish, Peggy. *Mind Your Manners* (6–9). Illus. 1979, Greenwillow $7.92. A useful guide to basic etiquette.

7429. Post, Elizabeth L. *The Emily Post Book of Etiquette for Young People* (5–7). Illus. 1967, Putnam

$15.00. A basic etiquette book that stresses unselfishness and consideration for others.

7430.　Slobodkin, Louis. *Thank You—You're Welcome* (PS–2). Illus. by author. 1957, Vanguard $8.95. Simple, clever verse and artistic illustrations teach good manners in a humorous manner. Also use: *Excuse Me! Certainly* (1959, Vanguard $8.95).

7431.　Stewart, Marjabelle Young, and Buchwald, Ann. *What to Do When and Why* (4–7). 1975, McKay $9.95. An easily read introduction to the basics of good manners and behavior.

7432.　Stine, Jane, and Stine, Jovial Bob. *Everything You Need to Survive: First Dates* (5–9). Illus. by Sal Murdocca. 1983, Random paper $1.95. A breezy guide to dating including a chapter on what not to say on a date.

Family Relationships

7433.　Berger, Terry. *How Does It Feel When Your Parents Get Divorced?* (3–4). Illus. 1977, Messner $7.59. Guidance, help, and understanding are given to young people experiencing the effects of divorce.

7434.　Berman, Claire. *"What Am I Doing in a Stepfamily?"* (3–6). Illus. by Dick Wilson. 1982, Lyle Stuart $12.00. A somewhat superficial view of stepfamilies and the adjustments necessary in these situations.

7435.　Boeckman, Charles. *Surviving Your Parents' Divorce* (6–9). 1980, Watts $8.90. A straightforward self-help book to help youngsters through the conflicts of a divorce.

7436.　Bradley, Buff. *Where Do I Belong? A Kid's Guide to Stepfamilies* (4–7). Illus. by Maryann Cocca. 1982, Addison $10.95; paper $5.95. A book on various kinds of stepfamilies and how to fit in.

7437.　Drescher, Joan. *Your Family, My Family* (K–3). Illus. by author. 1980, Walker $7.95; LB $8.85. All kinds of family arrangements, for example, single parents, working mothers, are described.

7438.　Gardner, Richard. *Boys and Girls Book about Divorce* (5–9). Illus. 1971, Aronson $15.00; Bantam paper $2.95. A self-help book written for adolescents trying to cope with parental marriage problems.

7439.　Glass, Stuart M. *A Divorce Dictionary: A Book for You and Your Children* (4–7). Illus. by Bari Weissman. 1980, Little $7.95. Information about divorce is given in brief definitions of such terms as "alimony" and "custody."

7440.　Goff, Beth. *Where Is Daddy? The Story of a Divorce* (3–5). Illus. by Susan Perl. 1969, Beacon $7.64. The reasons for divorce are discussed, as well as adjustments children must make.

7441.　Haskins, James, and Connolly, Pat. *The Child Abuse Help Book* (6–9). 1982, Addison $9.95. A description of the various types of child abuse and where help can be obtained.

7442.　Holz, Loretta. *Foster Child* (4–6). Illus. 1984, Messner $9.29. The story of Peter, an 11-year-old boy, who enters a foster home.

7443.　Hyde, Margaret O. *Foster Care and Adoption* (6–9). 1982, Watts LB $8.90. A thorough discussion of what happens to children who are not part of their biological families.

7444.　Krementz, Jill. *How It Feels to Be Adopted* (5–9). Illus. 1982, Knopf $11.95. Interviews with 19 young people, ages 8 to 16, on how it feels to be adopted.

7445.　Krementz, Jill. *How It Feels When a Parent Dies* (4–7). Illus. 1981, Knopf $11.95. Eighteen experiences of parental death are recounted.

7446.　LeShan, Eda. *Grandparents: A Special Kind of Love* (5–8). Illus. by Tricia Taggart. 1984, Macmillan $9.95. An explanation of the differences in generations that often separate children from their grandparents.

7447.　LeShan, Eda. *Learning to Say Good-by: When a Parent Dies* (5–7). Illus. by Paul Giovanopoulos. 1976, Macmillan $8.95; Avon paper $3.95. A sympathetic explanation of the many reactions children have to death.

7448.　LeShan, Eda. *What's Going to Happen to Me? When Parents Separate or Divorce* (4–7). Illus. by Richard Cuffari. 1978, Four Winds $8.95. The various steps involved in getting a divorce and adjusting to it are examined as they affect a young person.

7449.　Perry, Patricia, and Lynch, Marietta. *Mommy and Daddy Are Divorced* (PS–2). Illus. 1978, Dial $6.95; LB $6.46. A first-person account in fictional terms, but with realistic photographs.

7450.　Powledge, Fred. *So You're Adopted* (6–9). 1982, Scribners $9.95. A guide that answers many questions asked by children who are adopted.

7451.　Rofes, Eric E., and Fayerweather Street School. *The Kids' Book about Parents* (5–7). Illus. 1984, Houghton $12.45. Youngsters talk about their problems with parents.

7452.　Rofes, Eric E., and Fayerweather Street School. *The Kids' Book of Divorce: By, for and about Kids* (6–9). Illus. 1981, Greene $9.95; Random paper $3.95. Youngsters of various ages tell how their parents' divorce affected them.

7453.　Rosenberg, Maxine B. *Being Adopted* (3–5). Illus. 1984, Lothrop $9.50; LB $9.12. The subject of interracial adoption is explored through 3 stories of adoption.

7454. Rossel, Seymour. *Family* (6–8). Illus. 1980, Watts LB $8.90. A survey of the various forms of family life through the ages.

7455. Seixas, Judith S. *Living with a Parent That Drinks Too Much* (4–7). 1979, Greenwillow $10.50; LB $10.08. Common behavior patterns of alcoholics are cited and ways to cope with them are suggested.

7456. Showers, Paul. *Me and My Family Tree* (2–3). Illus. by Don Madden. 1978, Harper LB $10.89. An elementary lesson in genealogy, taught by a master.

7457. Simon, Norma. *All Kinds of Families* (4–6). Illus. by Joe Lasker. 1976, Whitman $9.75. Explores various kinds of families and their problems.

7458. Sinberg, Janet. *Divorce Is a Grown Up Problem: A Book about Divorce for Young Children and Their Parents* (PS–2). Illus. 1978, Avon paper $3.95. A book to be shared by parent and child.

7459. Sobol, Harriet Langsam. *We Don't Look Like Our Mom and Dad* (3–5). Illus. by Patricia Agre. 1984, Putnam $9.95. The story of an interracial adoption as seen through the eyes of 2 Korean boys.

7460. Stein, Sara Bonnett. *On Divorce* (2–4). Illus. 1979, Walker $8.95. Photographs and text cover this subject in an elementary fashion.

7461. Stein, Sara Bonnett. *That New Baby* (1–3). Illus. 1974, Walker $8.95; paper $4.95. A very helpful book in getting youngsters to accept a new member in the family.

7462. Stine, Jane, and Stine, Jovial Bob. *Everything You Need to Survive: Brothers and Sisters* (5–9). Illus. by Sal Murdocca. 1983, Random paper $1.95. The care and handling of siblings are discussed in this witty guide.

7463. Wasson, Valentina P. *The Chosen Baby* (PS–K). Illus. by Glo Coalson. 1977, Harper $7.64. A later edition of an excellent book on adoption.

7464. Worth, Richard. *The American Family* (6–9). Illus. 1984, Watts $9.90. The story of the family and its various formations through history.

Careers

General

7465. Alexander, Sue. *Finding Your First Job* (6–9). Illus. 1980, Dutton $8.95; paper $2.50. Simple tips for the junior job hunter.

7466. Ancona, George. *And What Do You Do? A Book about People and Their Work* (2–5). Illus. 1975, Dutton $12.00. A description of more than 20 careers that do not require a college degree.

7467. Anders, Rebecca. *Careers in a Library* (2–4). Illus. 1978, Lerner $5.95. An introductory look at many types of jobs involving libraries.

7468. Compton, Grant. *What Does a Meteorologist Do?* (4–7). Illus. 1981, Dodd LB $6.95. An introduction to the science of weather prediction. Also use: *A Day in the Life of a Meteorologist* by Margot Witty and Ken Witty (1981, Troll LB $8.79; paper $2.50).

7469. Criner, Beatrice, and Criner, Calvin. *Jobs in Personal Services* (3–5). Illus. 1974, Lothrop $10.25. Such jobs as plumber, travel agent, and veterinarian are described, along with qualifications. Also use: *Jobs in Public Service* (1974, $10.25).

7470. Fodor, R. V. *What Does a Geologist Do?* (5–7). Illus. 1978, Dodd $6.95. Such usual topics as necessary educational background are covered along with a fine breakdown of the fields of specialization.

7471. Foote, Patricia. *Girls Can Be Anything They Want* (4–8). Illus. 1980, Messner LB $9.29. An interesting array of careers for women.

7472. Giblin, James. *Chimney Sweeps: Yesterday and Today* (4–8). Illus. by Margot Tomes. 1982, Harper $10.53; LB $10.89. A look at chimney sweeps today and yesterday as well as the lore surrounding them.

7473. Goldreich, Gloria, and Goldreich, Esther. *What Can She Be? A Legislator* (4–6). 1978, Lothrop $10.50; LB $10.08. An account that centers around the career of Carol Bellamy, state senator and president of the New York City Council. Also use: *What Can She Be? A Lawyer* (1974, $10.08).

7474. Gutman, Bill. *Women Who Work with Animals* (4–6). Illus. 1982, Dodd LB $8.95. Six profiles of women who have careers—from veterinarian to show dog trainer—that involve animals.

7475. Houlehen, Robert J. *Jobs in Agribusiness* (4–6). Illus. 1974, Lothrop $10.95. An introduction to the various and varied career opportunities in agriculture and allied industries.

7476. Jaspersohn, William. *A Day in the Life of a Marine Biologist* (5–8). Illus. 1982, Little $10.95. A career portrait of the director of a marine biology program at Woods Hole, Massachusetts.

7477. Jaspersohn, William. *A Day in the Life of a Television News Reporter* (4–6). Illus. 1981, Little $9.95. An eventful day for Boston's WBZ-TV reporter Dan Rea.

7478. Kurelek, William. *Lumberjack* (5–9). Illus. by author. 1974, Houghton $8.95. Using his own experience as a basis, a Canadian painter describes, through text and pictures, life and work in a lumber camp.

7479. Lerner, Mark. *Careers in Toy Making* (3–6). Illus. 1980, Lerner LB $5.95. A variety of jobs, from designer to parts inspector, are described.

7480. Martini, Teri. *Cowboys* (1–3). Illus. 1981, Childrens Pr. LB $10.60. Color photographs and large type are used in this simple account.

7481. O'Connor, Karen. *Maybe You Belong in a Zoo! Zoo and Aquarium Careers* (6–9). Illus. 1982, Dodd $12.95. All sorts of zoo careers are introduced and explained.

7482. O'Connor, Karen. *Working with Horses: A Roundup of Careers* (6–9). Illus. 1980, Dodd $7.95. A description of many horse-oriented careers and some of the people who work in this field.

7483. Palladian, Arthur. *Careers in the Air Force* (2–4). Illus. 1978, Lerner $5.95. A brief overview of jobs in the air force, from navigator to recruiter.

7484. Palladian, Arthur. *Careers in the Army* (2–4). Illus. 1978, Lerner $5.95. A simple guide to a variety of jobs in the army.

7485. Ricciuti, Edward R. *They Work with Wildlife: Jobs for People Who Want to Work with Animals* (6–9). Illus. 1983, Harper $10.95; LB $10.89. An overview of several wildlife-related careers.

7486. Ross, Frank, Jr. *Jobs in Marine Science* (5–7). Illus. 1974, Lothrop $10.25. Describes the work of oceanographers and fishermen, as well as those involved in marine salvage and construction.

7487. Saul, Wendy. *Butcher, Baker, Cabinetmaker: Photographs of Women at Work* (K–2). Illus. 1978, Harper LB $10.89. The lives of women in a variety of jobs, told in text and photographs.

7488. Skurzynski, Gloria. *Safeguarding the Land: Women at Work in Parks, Forests, and Rangelands* (6–9). Illus. 1981, Harcourt $9.95; paper $3.95. The careers of 3 women working in a male-dominated area.

7489. Sobol, Harriet Langsam. *Cosmo's Restaurant* (2–4). Illus. 1978, Macmillan $8.95. A young boy learns about restaurants when he helps out in the one owned by his parents.

7490. Weiss, Harvey. *How to Be an Inventor* (5–8). Illus. by author. 1980, Harper $8.95; LB $10.89. A book that explores the process of inventing and gives ideas for future developments.

7491. Witty, Ken. *A Day in the Life of an Illustrator* (4–6). Illus. 1981, Troll LB $8.79; paper $2.50. A nicely illustrated introduction to this fascinating career. Two others in this series are: *A Day in the Life of a Marine Biologist* by David Paige (1981, Troll LB $8.79; paper $2.50); *A Day in the Life of a School Basketball Coach* by David Paige (1981, Troll LB $8.79; paper $2.50).

Business

7492. Storms, Laura. *Careers with an Advertising Agency* (4–6). Illus. 1984, Lerner $5.95. How an advertising agency works and a description of the jobs involved.

Engineering and Technology

7493. DiCerto, Joseph J. *Looking into TV* (4–6). Illus. 1983, Messner $8.79. A rundown on many of the careers in the television industry.

7494. Kessel, Joyce K. *Careers with an Electric Company* (3–6). Illus. 1984, Lerner $5.95. Fifteen positions, including engineer and plant operator, are discussed.

7495. Liebers, Arthur. *You Can Be a Welder* (6–8). Illus. 1977, Lothrop $10.25; LB $9.84. An introduction to the trade, types of jobs, and future occupational prospects. By the same author and publisher: *You Can Be a Machinist* (1975); *You Can Be a Mechanic* (1975) (both $10.25).

7496. Zim, Herbert S., and Skelly, James R. *Telephone Systems* (4–6). Illus. by Lee J. Ames. 1974, Morrow paper $1.25. A description of various jobs in the telephone field.

Fine Arts

7497. Berger, Melvin. *Jobs in Fine Arts and Humanities* (5–8). Illus. 1974, Lothrop $10.25. Career opportunities in music, theater, literature, and allied fields.

7498. Blumenfeld, Milton J. *Careers in Photography* (3–4). Illus. by author. 1979, Lerner $5.95. An easy career book that introduces various jobs in this field.

7499. Goldreich, Gloria, and Goldreich, Esther. *What Can She Be? An Architect* (2–4). 1974, Lothrop $11.08. An introduction to architects and the jobs they do, from a woman's point of view.

7500. Klever, Anita. *Women in Television* (6–8). Illus. 1975, Westminster $5.95. An overview of various careers for women in television.

7501. Liebers, Arthur. *You Can Be a Professional Photographer* (6–8). Illus. 1979, Lothrop $10.25; LB $9.84. An overview of the various occupations and fields of specialization open to the professional photographer.

7502. Meyer, Charles Robert. *How to Be a Juggler* (5–8). Illus. 1977, McKay $6.95. Useful tips on how to juggle.

7503. Paige, David. *A Day in the Life of a Rock Musician* (3–4). Illus. 1979, Troll $8.79; paper $2.50. A somewhat idealized account of a typical day in a songwriter-musician's life.

7504. Trainer, David. *A Day in the Life of a TV News Reporter* (3–4). Illus. 1979, Troll $8.79; paper $2.50. An exciting career explained through a "typical-day" technique. Also use: *What Can She Be? A Newscaster* by Gloria Goldreich and Esther Goldreich (1973, Lothrop $10.08).

7505. Van Wormer, Joe. *How to Be a Wildlife Photographer* (5–7). Illus. 1982, Lodestar $10.95. Equipment, its use, and camera techniques are 3 of the topics covered.

Medicine and Health

7506. Englebardt, Stanley L. *Jobs in Health Care* (5–7). Illus. 1973, Lothrop $10.25. Sixty-six careers in health care are described, such as lab technician, nurse's aide, and medical secretary.

7507. Fricke, Pam. *Careers in Dental Care* (3–6). Illus. 1984, Lerner $5.95. An examination of the work of different kinds of dentists and their techniques.

7508. Greene, Carla. *Doctors and Nurses: What Do They Do?* (1–3). 1963, Harper LB $8.89. A very simple introduction to these professions.

7509. Kane, Betty. *Looking Forward to a Career: Dentistry* (4–6). Illus. by Dick Sutphen. 1972, Dillon LB $6.95. A description of dental careers and how to prepare for them.

7510. Oleksy, Walter. *Paramedics* (5–7). Illus. 1983, Messner $8.79. A review of the types of paramedics, their duties, and their working conditions.

7511. Ranahan, Demerris C. *Contributions of Women: Medicine* (6–8). Illus. 1981, Dillon LB $8.95. Biographies and career descriptions of 5 women involved in medicine are detailed.

7512. Witty, Margot. *A Day in the Life of an Emergency Room Nurse* (3–4). Illus. 1979, Troll $8.79; paper $2.50. A realistic account of a day's experience in this exciting profession.

Police and Firefighters

7513. Beame, Rona. *Ladder Company 108* (3–5). Illus. 1973, Messner $6.64. The activities of a firefighting unit serving a section of Brooklyn, New York, with emphasis on what happens when a fire alarm is answered.

7514. Broekel, Ray. *Fire Fighters* (2–3). Illus. 1981, Childrens Pr. LB $10.60; paper $3.95. An easy reader with many color photographs.

7515. Broekel, Ray. *Police* (2–3). Illus. 1981, Childrens Pr. LB $10.60; paper $3.95. Large, clear type is featured in this easy reader.

7516. Bundt, Nancy. *The Fire Station Book* (PS–3). Illus. 1981, Carolrhoda LB $7.95. Clear photographs and lively text highlight this account.

7517. Goldreich, Gloria, and Goldreich, Esther. *What Can She Be? A Police Officer* (4–6). Illus. by Robert Ipcar. 1975, Lothrop LB $11.88. A rundown on various careers in law enforcement.

7518. Nau, Patrick. *State Patrol* (4–5). Illus. 1984, Carolrhoda $7.95. A photo essay that explains what state troopers do.

7519. Paige, David. *A Day in the Life of a Police Detective* (4–6). Illus. 1981, Troll LB $8.79; paper $2.50. A typical police detective's day, richly illustrated.

7520. Scotti, Paul C. *Police Divers* (4–5). Illus. 1982, Messner LB $8.79. The roles that divers play in the police force in New York City and Dade County, Florida.

7521. Smith, Betsy. *A Day in the Life of a Firefighter* (4–6). Illus. 1981, Troll LB $8.79; paper $2.50. A typical day of a firefighter told in text and pictures.

7522. Torbert, Floyd James. *Fire Fighters, the World Over* (2–4). Illus. by author. 1967, Hastings LB $6.95. How 17 countries face different problems in fire fighting and how they have tried to solve them.

7523. Wolf, Bernard. *Firehouse* (5–7). 1983, Morrow $9.50; LB $8.59. A behind-the-scenes look at a big-city firehouse.

Transportation

7524. Dean, Jennifer Brooks. *Careers with an Airline* (3–5). Illus. 1973, Lerner $5.95. Discusses 18 careers involving a variety of talents and qualifications.

7525. Gray, Genevieve. *Jobs in Transportation* (4–7). Illus. 1973, Lothrop $10.25. Qualifications, working conditions, and job opportunities are described for several occupations involving vehicles.

7526. Greene, Carla. *Truck Drivers: What Do They Do?* (1–3). Illus. by Leonard Kessler. 1967, Harper $8.89. An introduction to various kinds of truck drivers and how they help the community.

7527. Hodgman, Ann, and Djabbaroff, Rudy. *Skystars: The History of Women in Aviation* (6–9). Illus. 1981, Atheneum $12.95. A variety of flying exploits are chronicled, as well as women's struggle to find a place in aviation.

7528. Lerner, Mark. *Careers in Auto Racing* (3–6). Illus. 1980, Lerner $5.95. A description of jobs directly (e.g., pit crew) or indirectly (e.g., cashier) connected with car racing.

7529. Lerner, Mark. *Careers in Trucking* (3–4). Illus. by Milton J. Blumenfeld. 1976, Lerner $5.95. A simple account that supplies only basic information.

7530. Meade, Chris. *Careers with a Railroad* (4–6). Illus. 1975, Lerner $5.95. Fifteen different jobs on railroads are discussed. For an older group use: *Your Future in Railroading* by Thomas M. Goodfellow (1970, Rosen $7.97).

7531. Pelta, Kathy. *What Does an Airplane Pilot Do?* (5–6). Illus. 1981, Dodd LB $6.95. An explanation of various kinds of pilots and their jobs.

7532. Schleier, Curt. *The Team behind Your Airline Flight* (4–6). Illus. 1981, Westminster $9.95. An explanation of the people who are behind a safe flight.

Veterinarians

7533. Bellville, Rod, and Walsh, Cheryl. *Large Animal Veterinarians* (2–3). Illus. 1983, Carolrhoda $7.95. The story of the animal doctors that care for cattle, horses, sheep, and pigs.

7534. Berger, Melvin. *Animal Hospital* (4–7). Illus. 1973, Harper $10.89. The roles of veterinarians and their assistants.

7535. Gillum, Helen L. *Looking Forward to a Career: Veterinary Medicine* (5–7). Illus. 1976, Dillon $6.95. A discussion of obvious and lesser-known careers in working with animals.

7536. Jaspersohn, William. *A Day in the Life of a Veterinarian* (3–6). Illus. by author. 1978, Little $8.95. A description of one day's activities of a vet in rural Vermont.

The Human Body and Health

The Human Body

7537. Aliki. *My Hands* (1–3). Illus. by author. 1962, Harper $10.89. The structure and uses of our hands are presented.

7538. Asimov, Isaac. *The Human Body: Its Structure and Operation* (6–9). Illus. 1963, Houghton $11.95. A mature introduction to the systems and parts of the human body.

7539. Berger, Gilda, and Berger, Melvin. *The Whole World of Hands* (3–7). Illus. by True Kelley. 1982, Houghton $8.95. A discussion of the hand, its structure, uses, and care.

7540. Berger, Melvin. *Why I Cough, Sneeze, Shiver, Hiccup, and Yawn* (PS–3). Illus. by Holly Keller. 1983, Harper $10.52; LB $10.89. A clear, interesting introduction and explanation of some basic body functions.

7541. Berry, James R. *Why You Feel Hot, Why You Feel Cold: Your Body's Temperature* (2–4). Illus. by Bill Ogden. 1973, Little $6.95. This book tells how body temperature is maintained and why abnormal cold and heat can be a sign of illness.

7542. Branley, Franklyn M. *Shivers and Goose Bumps: How We Keep Warm* (4–6). Illus. by True Kelley. 1984, Harper $11.06; LB $10.89. The ways by which humans and animals keep warm.

7543. Brenner, Barbara. *Bodies* (K–3). Illus. by George Ancona. 1973, Dutton $9.95. The qualities that make the animal world different from plants and inanimate objects are pointed out, and the uniqueness of each individual is stressed.

7544. Bruun, Ruth Dowling, and Bruun, Bertel. *The Human Body* (4–7). Illus. by Patricia J. Wynne. 1982, Random $7.99; paper $6.95. A simple account that concentrates on parts of the body and its systems.

7545. Buxbaum, Susan Kovacs, and Gelman, Rita Golden. *Body Noises* (2–4). Illus. by Angie Lloyd. 1983, Knopf $8.95; LB $8.99. Hiccups and snores are only 2 of the many phenomena discussed.

7546. Gilbert, Sara. *Feeling Good: A Book about You and Your Body* (6–9). 1978, Four Winds $8.95. A book about the body changes that occur during adolescence.

7547. Goldsmith, Ilse. *Anatomy for Children* (4–6). Illus. 1974, Sterling $8.95; LB $10.99. A good basic introduction to the various parts of the human body.

7548. Goode, Ruth. *Hands Up!* (5–8). Illus. by Anthony Kramer. 1984, Macmillan $8.95. The physiology and fun of hands.

7549. Kettelkamp, Larry. *A Partnership of Mind and Body: Biofeedback* (5–9). Illus. 1976, Morrow LB $8.59. A direct and clear explanation of theories, experiments, conclusions, and the present status of this topical but often controversial subject.

7550. Klein, Aaron E. *You and Your Body* (3–6). Illus. by John Love. 1977, Doubleday $7.95; Pocket paper $1.50. A manual that emphasizes activities that can help the young reader to learn about his or her body. Also use: *Your Body and How It Works* by Patricia Lauber (1962, Random LB $6.99).

7551.   Lerner, Marguerite Rush. *Lefty: The Story of Left-Handedness* (4–6). Illus. by Rov Andre. 1960, Lerner LB $3.95. The life of this "oppressed minority" is described, as well as how left-handedness occurs.

7552.   Miller, Jonathan. *The Human Body* (5–8). Illus. by Harry Willcock. 1983, Viking $16.95. A pop-up book that explains the systems of the human body.

7553.   Rothman, Joel, and Palacios, Argentina. *This Can Lick a Lollipop: Body Riddles for Kids/Esto Goza Chupando un Caramelo: Las Partes del Cuerpo en Adivinanzas Infantiles* (4–6). Illus. 1979, Doubleday $7.95. Pictures and short poems illustrate the parts of the body in this bilingual book.

7554.   Showers, Paul. *How You Talk* (1–3). Illus. by Robert Galster. 1966, Harper $10.89; paper $2.95. Simple introductory explanation about how numerous speech sounds are produced; includes experiments.

7555.   Simon, Seymour. *Body Sense, Body Nonsense* (3–6). Illus. by Dennis Kendrick. 1981, Harper $10.10; LB $9.89. Twenty-one familiar sayings about the body are analyzed for fact or fiction.

7556.   Ward, Brian R. *Body Maintenance* (5–8). Illus. 1983, Watts $8.90. A description of glands, hormones, and related body organs and functions are described.

7557.   Wilson, Ron. *How the Body Works* (4–7). Illus. 1979, Larousse $8.95. Parts of the body and its systems are covered from the standpoint of how they function.

7558.   Zim, Herbert S. *What's Inside Me?* (2–5). Illus. by Herschel Wartik. 1952, Morrow $8.59. An explanation of the functions of the human body—a book for parents and children to read together. Also use: *Blood and Guts: A Working Guide to Your Own Little Insides* by Linda Allison (1976, Little $11.45; paper $6.70).

Circulatory System

7559.   Baldwin, Dorothy, and Lister, Claire. *Your Heart and Lungs* (4–6). Illus. 1984, Watts $8.90. The structure of the heart and lungs is explained and the composition of blood is shown.

7560.   Limburg, Peter R. *The Story of Your Heart* (4–6). Illus. by Ellen G. Jacobs. 1979, Putnam $6.99. The human heart with its functions and possible malfunctions is discussed in this basic account.

7561.   Schneider, Leo. *Lifeline* (6–9). Illus. 1958, Harcourt $6.95. Subtitle: *The Story of Your Circulatory System*. Also use: *Circulatory Systems: The Rivers Within* by Alvin Silverstein (1970, Prentice $9.95).

7562.   Showers, Paul. *Hear Your Heart* (1–3). Illus. by Joseph Low. 1968, Harper $10.89; paper $3.95. A simple introduction to the heart and how it works. Also use: *Drop of Blood* (1967, Harper $10.89; paper $3.95).

7563.   Silverstein, Alvin, and Silverstein, Virginia B. *Heartbeats: Your Body, Your Heart* (3–6). Illus. 1983, Harper $9.57; LB $9.89. A description of the heart and how it works, plus sections on various forms of heart malfunction.

7564.   Tully, Mary-Alice, and Tully, Marianne. *Heart Disease* (5–9). Illus. 1980, Watts LB $8.90. Common types of heart disease are introduced, plus an explanation of the heart and its function.

7565.   Ward, Brian R. *The Heart and Blood* (4–7). Illus. 1982, Watts LB $8.90. An easily read account with fine diagrams and pictures.

7566.   Weart, Edith L. *The Story of Your Blood* (4–6). Illus. by Z. Onyshkewych. 1960, Putnam $6.99. An elementary introduction to the composition and uses of blood.

7567.   Zim, Herbert S. *Your Heart and How It Works* (4–6). Illus. by Gustav Schrotter. 1959, Morrow $8.16. A description of the structure and function of the heart and its role in the circulatory system.

Digestive and Excretory Systems

7568.   Baldwin, Dorothy, and Lister, Claire. *Your Body Fuel* (4–6). Illus. 1984, Watts $8.90. A simple introduction to the digestive system.

7569.   Berger, Melvin. *Enzymes in Action* (6–9). 1971, Harper $10.53. An interesting view of the uses and functions of enzymes, including a history of research in the area and an explanation of their production through synthetic means.

7570.   Eagles, Douglas A. *Your Weight* (4–7). Illus. 1982, Watts LB $8.90. A book about body weight, how it can be regulated, and what a balanced diet involves.

7571.   Showers, Paul. *What Happens to a Hamburger* (1–3). Illus. by Anne Rockwell. 1970, Harper $10.89; paper $3.95. A beginning, easily read introduction to the digestive system.

7572.   Silverstein, Alvin, and Silverstein, Virginia B. *The Digestive System: How Living Creatures Use Food* (4–6). Illus. 1970, Prentice $9.95. A clear text with simple, informative illustrations.

7573.   Silverstein, Alvin, and Silverstein, Virginia B. *The Story of Your Mouth* (5–8). Illus. by Greg

Wenzel. 1984, Putnam LB $7.99. The mouth's structure and its many functions are discussed.

7574. Thompson, Paul. *Nutrition* (5–8). Illus. 1981, Watts LB $8.90. An explanation of food groups, the digestive system, and the importance of good nutrition.

7575. Ward, Brian R. *Food and Digestion* (4–7). Illus. 1982, Watts LB $8.90. An explanation of the digestive system with special emphasis on the organs involved.

7576. Zim, Herbert S. *Your Stomach and Digestive Tract* (4–6). Illus. by Rene Martin. 1973, Morrow LB $8.16. A tour through the digestive tract.

Nervous System

7577. Abrams, Lawrence F. *Mysterious Powers of the Mind* (6–9). Illus. 1982, Messner $9.29. An account of strange psychic phenomena, including ESP.

7578. Baldwin, Dorothy, and Lister, Claire. *Your Brain and Nervous System* (4–6). Illus. 1984, Watts $8.90. The structure and function of the brain and spinal cord are highlighted in this account.

7579. Berger, Melvin. *Exploring the Mind and Brain* (5–7). Illus. 1983, Harper $10.53; LB $10.89. An account that stresses recent findings on how the brain works.

7580. Facklam, Margery, and Facklam, Howard. *The Brain: Magnificent Mind Machine* (6–9). Illus. by Paul Facklam. 1982, Harcourt $12.95. A book that reviews what we have learned about the brain.

7581. Freedman, Russell. *The Brains of Animals and Man* (5–9). Illus. 1972, Holiday $8.95. The similarities and differences in brain composition are explored.

7582. Gallant, Roy A. *Memory: How It Works and How to Improve It* (6–9). Illus. 1980, Four Winds $9.95. An account that includes material on the brain, types of memory, and techniques of memorization.

7583. Gilbert, Sara. *Using Your Head: The Many Ways of Being Smart* (6–8). 1984, Macmillan $9.95. A discussion of the many forms of intelligence and how to find one's strong areas.

7584. Kettelkamp, Larry. *Your Marvelous Mind* (4–6). Illus. by author. 1980, Westminster $9.95. An introduction to the brain, with concentration on memory and how to train it.

7585. Sharp, Pat. *Brain Power! Secrets of a Winning Team* (4–7). Illus. by Martha Weston. 1984, Lothrop $10.00; LB $9.55. How the brain works and its composition and function are described.

7586. Showers, Paul. *Use Your Brain* (2–3). Illus. by Rosalind Fry. 1971, Harper $10.53; paper $2.95. The structure and function of the brain and some information on the other parts of the nervous system are included in this simple text.

7587. Ward, Brian R. *The Brain and Nervous System* (5–7). Illus. 1981, Watts LB $8.90. An overview of the system and a description of each component.

7588. Weart, Edith L. *The Story of Your Brain and Nerves* (5–7). Illus. by Alan Tompkins. 1961, Putnam $6.99. Simple introduction to the human nervous system and its functions.

7589. Zim, Herbert S. *Your Brain and How It Works* (4–6). Illus. by Rene Martin. 1972, Morrow $8.16. The growth and development of the human brain, its parts and functions, and a comparison with the brains of other animals are covered in this fascinating treatment.

Respiratory System

7590. Branley, Franklyn M. *Oxygen Keeps You Alive* (2–3). Illus. by Don Madden. 1971, Harper $11.49; LB $10.89. A description of how oxygen is carried throughout the body, how plants and fish use it, and how people who can't get enough oxygen must carry a supply with them.

7591. Gaskin, John. *Breathing* (3–5). Illus. 1984, Watts LB $8.90. The composition of air and how its intake affects the body.

7592. Silverstein, Alvin, and Silverstein, Virginia B. *The Respiratory System: How Living Creatures Breathe* (4–6). Illus. by George Bakacs. 1969, Prentice $8.95. The breathing of several kinds of animals and plants is outlined, with emphasis on humans. Also use: *Breath of Air and a Breath of Smoke* by John S. Marr (1971, Evans $4.95).

7593. Ward, Brian R. *The Lungs and Breathing* (4–7). Illus. 1982, Watts LB $8.90. A look at the respiratory system in simple text and many pictures.

7594. Weart, Edith L. *The Story of Your Respiratory System* (4–7). Illus. 1964, Putnam $6.99. The anatomy and physiology of the human lung and the respiratory system.

Skeletal-Muscular System

7595. Baldwin, Dorothy, and Lister, Claire. *The Structure of Your Body* (4–6). Illus. 1984, Watts LB $8.90. An introduction to the skeleton and the muscles of the body.

7596. Balestrino, Philip. *The Skeleton inside You* (2–4). Illus. by Don Bolognese. 1971, Harper $10.89; paper $2.95. This matter-of-fact, informal discussion of bones of the body describes their shape, structure, and function.

7597. Cosgrove, Margaret. *Your Muscles and Ways to Exercise Them* (4–6). Illus. by author. 1980, Dodd LB $6.95. A description of the composition and uses of muscles, as well as how to keep them in shape.

7598. Showers, Paul. *You Can't Make a Move without Your Muscles* (K–3). Illus. 1982, Harper LB $9.89. An introduction to the muscular system in simple text and fine illustrations.

7599. Silverstein, Alvin, and Silverstein, Virginia B. *The Skeletal System: Frameworks for Life* (4–6). Illus. by Lee J. Ames. 1972, Prentice $9.95. The skeletal structures of several animals are pictured and discussed, with concentration on the human body.

7600. Ward, Brian R. *The Skeleton and Movement* (5–7). Illus. 1981, Watts LB $8.90. The entire skeletal system is introduced through text and 4-color illustrations.

7601. Zim, Herbert S. *Bones* (3–6). Illus. by Rene Martin. 1969, Morrow $8.16. Parts and functions of the human skeleton with an explanation of the composition and formation of bones. Also use: *The Story of Your Bones* by Edith L. Weart (1966, Putnam $6.99).

Senses

7602. Adler, Irving, and Adler, Ruth. *Your Eyes* (3–5). Illus. 1962, Harper $8.79. This account treats the structure of the eye and the nature of sight.

7603. Aliki. *My Five Senses* (1–3). Illus. 1962, Harper $10.89; paper $2.95. A very basic introduction to human senses and how they work.

7604. Baldwin, Dorothy, and Lister, Claire. *Your Senses* (4–6). Illus. 1984, Watts LB $8.90. The various sensory organs are explored and their functions explained.

7605. Berger, Gilda. *Speech and Language Disorders* (6–9). Illus. 1981, Watts LB $8.90. The organs of speech are examined, as well as such disorders as stuttering and lisping.

7606. Cobb, Vicki. *How to Really Fool Yourself: Illusions for All Your Senses* (5–8). Illus. by Leslie Morrill. 1981, Harper $10.53; LB $10.89; paper $4.95. Experiments that prove that the senses can't be relied upon.

7607. Finney, Shan. *Noise Pollution* (6–9). Illus. 1984, Watts $9.90. A book about noise and its effect on people.

7608. Hyman, June. *Deafness* (5–7). Illus. 1980, Watts $8.90. A discussion of various kinds of hearing loss, their causes, and treatment.

7609. Kelley, Alberta. *Lenses, Spectacles, Eyeglasses, and Contacts: The Story of Vision Aids* (6–9). 1979, Lodestar $8.95. A precise, detailed account of past, present, and possible future aids to human vision.

7610. Litchfield, Ada B. *A Button in Her Ear* (1–3). Illus. by Eleanor Mill. 1976, Whitman $8.75. A simple introduction to hearing problems and correctional devices such as the hearing aid.

7611. Robinson, Marlene M. *Who Knows This Nose?* (2–4). Illus. 1983, Dodd $10.95. Animal noses are used to introduce the sense of smell.

7612. Showers, Paul. *Follow Your Nose* (1–3). Illus. by Paul Galdone. 1963, Harper $10.89; paper $2.95. An elementary account of the sense of smell and how we use our noses.

7613. Showers, Paul. *Look at Your Eyes* (1–3). Illus. by Paul Galdone. 1962, Harper $10.89; paper $3.95. Such topics as eye color and the uses of eyelids and eyebrows are discussed in this elementary book.

7614. Silverstein, Alvin, and Silverstein, Virginia B. *The Story of Your Ear* (5–8). Illus. by Susan Gaber. 1981, Putnam LB $6.99. The parts of the ear and common ailments are discussed.

7615. Simon, Hilda. *Sight and Seeing: A World of Light and Color* (6–9). Illus. by author. 1983, Putnam $12.95. A description of the sense of sight and the organs that produce this in man and other animals.

7616. Simon, Seymour. *Mirror Magic* (2–4). Illus. by Lisa Campbell Ernst. 1980, Lothrop $10.95; LB $10.51. A simple book about mirrors, with a few experiments.

7617. Ward, Brian R. *The Ear and Hearing* (5–7). Illus. 1981, Watts LB $8.90. A description of the ear and the process of hearing highlight this account.

7618. Ward, Brian R. *The Eye and Seeing* (5–7). Illus. 1981, Watts LB $8.90. A description of the sense of sight and the components that make sight possible.

7619. Ward, Brian R. *Touch, Taste and Smell* (4–7). Illus. 1982, Watts LB $8.90. An introduction to 3 important senses and the organs involved.

7620. White, Anne Terry, and Lietz, Gerald S. *Windows on the World* (4–6). Illus. 1965, Garrard $7.12. A review of the functions of the 5 senses.

Skin and Hair

7621. Goldin, Augusta. *Straight Hair, Curly Hair* (1–3). Illus. by Ed Emberley. 1966, Harper $10.89; paper $3.95. A very simple explanation of the composition and characteristics of human hair.

7622. Showers, Paul. *Your Skin and Mine* (1–3). Illus. by Paul Galdone. 1965, Harper $10.89; paper $3.95. An explanation of the many functions of our skin and other related information.

7623. Zim, Herbert S. *Your Skin* (4–6). Illus. by Jean Zallinger. 1979, Morrow $8.75; LB $8.40. The composition, uses, and layers of the body's covering and problems in dysfunction.

Teeth

7624. Betancourt, Jeanne. *Smile! How to Cope with Braces* (4–8). Illus. by Mimi Harrison. 1982, Knopf LB $8.99; paper $5.95. The types of braces and their many uses are discussed.

7625. Gaskin, John. *Teeth* (3–5). Illus. 1984, Watts LB $8.90. The different kinds of teeth we have and their parts are discussed.

7626. Rockwell, Harlow. *My Dentist* (1–2). Illus. 1975, Greenwillow $11.25; LB $11.88. A matter-of-fact, informative book about dentists and the instruments they use.

7627. Showers, Paul. *How Many Teeth?* (1–3). Illus. by Paul Galdone. 1962, Harper LB $10.89; paper $2.95. An explanation of the types of teeth and their numbers.

7628. Silverstein, Alvin, and Silverstein, Virginia B. *So You're Getting Braces: A Guide to Orthodontics* (6–9). Illus. 1978, Harper $8.89; paper $3.95. An excellent introduction to the subject, which should lessen fears and frustrations.

Sleep and Dreams

7629. Showers, Paul. *Sleep Is for Everyone* (1–3). Illus. by Wendy Watson. 1974, Harper $10.89. A clear explanation of what happens to our bodies and brains during sleep, and the effects of lack of sleep.

7630. Silverstein, Alvin, and Silverstein, Virginia B. *Sleep and Dreams* (6–8). 1974, Harper $9.89. A study of the sleeping habits of animals, including humans, and of the importance of dreams.

Genetics

7631. Cohen, Robert. *The Color of Man* (5–8). Illus. by Ken Heyman. 1968, Random LB $6.99; paper $1.95. An objective study of the biological and sociological aspects of color differences in humans, which does much to dispel the myths of color prejudice.

7632. Dunbar, Robert E. *Heredity* (4–9). Illus. 1978, Watts $8.90. An insightful introduction to the subject, which includes interesting historical information.

7633. Engdahl, Sylvia Louise, and Roberson, Rick. *Tool for Tomorrow* (5–8). 1979, Atheneum $6.95. An account of recent studies and knowledge in the field of genetics.

Bionics and Transplants

7634. Silverstein, Alvin, and Silverstein, Virginia B. *The World of Bionics* (5–7). Illus. 1979, Methuen $8.95. An overview of the use of artificial organs using television's "Six Million Dollar Man" as a starting place.

7635. Skurzynski, Gloria. *Bionic Parts for People* (6–8). Illus. 1978, Four Winds $9.95. Subtitle: *The Real Story of Artificial Organs and Replacements*.

Hygiene and Physical Fitness

7636. Antonacci, Robert J. *Physical Fitness for Young Champions* (4–6). Illus. 1975, McGraw $9.95. An introduction for those who wish to start a physical fitness program.

7637. Arnold, Caroline. *Too Fat? Too Thin? Do You Have a Choice?* (6–9). Illus. 1984, Morrow $8.59; paper $4.75. A guide to weight watching that explains the roles of genetics, exercise, and nutrition.

7638. Carr, Rachel. *Be a Frog, a Bird or a Tree* (1–3). 1973, Doubleday $8.95. A simple introduction to yoga for young children. For an older group use: *Wheel, Camel, Fish and Plow: Yoga for You* (1981, Prentice $9.95).

7639. Goodbody, Slim. *The Force inside You* (4–6). Illus. 1983, Putnam $9.95; paper $4.95. A television personality shows how simple exercises can produce a healthy body.

7640. Herzig, Alison C., and Mali, Jane L. *Oh, Boy! Babies!* (4–6). Illus. 1980, Little $9.95; paper $6.95. The story of an infant-care class where boys cared for real babies.

7641. Kozuszek, Jane Everly. *Hygiene* (3–5). Illus. 1978, Watts LB $8.90. A straightforward guide to cleanliness and its importance.

7642. Lyttle, Richard B. *The New Physical Fitness: Something for Everyone* (6–8). Illus. 1981, Watts LB

$6.90. An introduction to exercises, particularly aerobics, their value, and programs.

7643. McGrath, Judith. *Pretty Girl: A Guide to Looking Good, Naturally* (5–9). Illus. by Frederic Marvin. 1981, Lothrop LB $12.88; paper $6.95. A guide to personal beauty and good grooming.

7644. Paul, Aileen. *The Kids' Diet Cookbook* (5–8). Illus. by John Delulio. 1980, Doubleday $8.95. A manual for young dieters.

7645. Petersen, W. P. *Meditation Made Easy* (5–9). Illus. by Terry Fehr. 1979, Watts $8.90. A history of meditation and a step-by-step guide to its practice are included in this overview.

7646. Phillips, Betty Lou. *Brush Up on Hair Care* (6–8). Illus. by Lois Johnson. 1982, Messner $9.29. An easily read guide to healthy and attractive hair.

7647. Sullivan, George. *Better Weight Training for Boys* (6–9). Illus. 1983, Dodd $8.95; paper $2.95. The principles of keeping the body fit through weight training (not weight lifting) are explained.

7648. Terkel, Susan Neiburg. *Yoga Is for Me* (3–5). Illus. 1982, Lerner LB $7.95. Basic positions and exercises are given in text and photographs.

7649. Trier, Carola S. *Exercise: What It Is, What It Does* (K–3). Illus. by Tom Hoffman. 1982, Greenwillow $8.50; LB $8.88. An easy-to-read introduction to the subject, plus a few simple exercises.

Diseases and Other Illnesses

7650. Berger, Melvin. *Disease Detectives* (5–9). Illus. 1978, Harper $9.57; LB $10.89. A discussion of the work of the Centers for Disease Control that uses Legionnaires disease as a focal point.

7651. Blanzaco, Andre. *VD: Facts You Should Know* (5–9). Illus. 1970, Lothrop $10.50; LB $10.08. In a direct, honest treatment, the author describes the types of VD, symptoms, prevention, and treatment, and the alarming growth of this disease.

7652. Burns, Sheila L. *Allergies and You* (4–7). Illus. 1980, Messner LB $7.59. A simple introduction to the causes and cures of allergies.

7653. Burns, Sheila L. *Cancer: Understanding It* (4–6). Illus. 1982, Messner $7.79. An introduction to this disease, its characteristics, and methods of prevention and treatment.

7654. Burstein, John. *Slim Goodbody: What Can Go Wrong and How to Be Strong* (2–5). Illus. 1978, McGraw $8.95; paper $4.95. An introduction to common illnesses and injuries and how to combat them.

7655. Claypool, Jane, and Nelson, Cheryl Diane. *Food Trips and Traps: Coping with Eating Disorders* (6–9). Illus. 1983, Watts $8.90. A survey of such eating disorders as compulsive eating and anorexia nervosa.

7656. Connelly, John P., and Berlow, Leonard. *You're Too Sweet: A Guide for the Young Diabetic* (4–6). Illus. 1969, Astor-Honor $5.95. The cause and treatment of diabetes from the standpoint of a 9-year-old boy.

7657. Haines, Gail Kay. *Cancer* (4–7). 1980, Watts LB $8.90. This disease is explored through examining the case histories of 5 patients.

7658. Kipnis, Lynne, and Adler, Susan. *You Can't Catch Diabetes from a Friend* (3–5). Illus. 1979, Triad Scientific $9.95. The facts of the disease are revealed through the lives of 4 diabetic children.

7659. Knight, David C. *Viruses: Life's Smallest Enemies* (6–9). Illus. by Christine Kettner. 1981, Morrow $9.25; LB $8.88. An in-depth description of the nature of viruses and their effects on human life.

7660. Nourse, Alan E. *Fractures, Dislocations and Sprains* (4–8). Illus. 1978, Watts $8.90. The nature of these injuries is explained along with some first aid tips.

7661. Nourse, Alan E. *Viruses* (5–7). Illus. 1983, Watts LB $8.90. An account that begins with the work of Jenner and Pasteur and traces the research on viruses to the present day.

7662. Nourse, Alan E. *Your Immune System* (4–6). Illus. 1982, Watts LB $8.90. A discussion of our defenses against disease and what happens when they break down.

7663. Patent, Dorothy. *Germs!* (4–6). Illus. 1983, Holiday $9.95. Enlarged photos help explain what germs are and what they do.

7664. Pringle, Laurence. *Radiation: Waves and Particles/Benefits and Risks* (6–9). 1983, Enslow LB $9.95. An overview of radiation and how it can help and harm us.

7665. Riedman, Sarah R. *Allergies* (4–6). Illus. 1978, Watts $8.90. All kinds of allergies are discussed together with their causes and treatments.

7666. Riedman, Sarah R. *Diabetes* (5–9). Illus. 1980, Watts LB $8.90. An explanation of the causes and effects of this common ailment. For a younger audience use: *Runaway Sugar: All about Diabetes* by Alvin Silverstein and Virginia B. Silverstein (1981, Harper $10.53; LB $10.89).

7667. Showers, Paul. *No Measles, No Mumps for Me* (1–3). Illus. by Harriett Barton. 1980, Harper $10.53; LB $10.89; paper $3.95. In story form, an introduction to germs and viruses and to the practice of vaccination.

7668. Silverstein, Alvin, and Silverstein, Virginia B. *Cancer* (5–7). Illus. by Andrew Antal. 1977, Harper $9.89. An excellent introduction to types of cancerous cells and how they function, and the current status of cancer prevention and treatment.

7669. Silverstein, Alvin, and Silverstein, Virginia B. *Diabetes: The Sugar Disease* (6–8). Illus. 1979, Harper $9.57. A well-organized, straightforward treatment aimed chiefly at nondiabetics.

7670. Silverstein, Alvin, and Silverstein, Virginia B. *Epilepsy* (6–8). 1975, Harper $9.95. The causes, types, and treatment of epilepsy.

7671. Silverstein, Alvin, and Silverstein, Virginia B. *Itch, Sniffle and Sneeze* (3–5). Illus. by Roy Doty. 1978, Four Winds $7.95. Subtitle: *All about Asthma, Hay Fever and Other Allergies.*

Drugs, Alcohol, and Smoking

7672. Curtis, Robert H. *Questions and Answers about Alcoholism* (5–7). Illus. 1976, Prentice $7.95. In question-and-answer form, many facets of alcohol are explained. Also use: *Alcoholism* by Alvin Silverstein and Virginia B. Silverstein (1975, Harper LB $9.89; paper $3.50).

7673. Englebardt, Stanley L. *Kids and Alcohol, the Deadliest Drug* (5–8). 1975, Lothrop $10.00; LB $10.88. An explanation of what alcohol is and how it affects the human body.

7674. Hyde, Margaret O. *Know about Alcohol* (5–8). Illus. 1978, McGraw $8.95. Objective presentations on the effects of alcohol on the body.

7675. Hyde, Margaret O. *Know about Smoking* (5–7). Illus. by Dennis Kendrick. 1983, McGraw $8.95. The effects of smoking and how to say "no" when offered a cigarette.

7676. Hyde, Margaret O., and Hyde, Bruce G. *Know about Drugs* (4–6). Illus. by Bill Morrison. 1979, McGraw $10.95. Drug use and abuse are covered succinctly in this account.

7677. Madison, Arnold. *Drugs and You* (4–7). Illus. 1982, Messner LB $9.79. The various forms of drugs, their uses and effects, and the legalities involved are discussed in a nonpedantic yet realistic fashion. Also use: *Mind Drugs* by Margaret O. Hyde (1981, McGraw $9.95).

7678. Marr, John S. *The Good Drug and the Bad Drug* (3–4). Illus. by Lynn Sweat. 1970, Evans $4.95. The courses in the body of a beneficial and a harmful drug and their effects.

7679. Seixas, Judith S. *Alcohol: What It Is, What It Does* (2–4). Illus. by Tom Huffman. 1977, Green-

willow $8.25; LB $7.92; paper $2.95. A very simple account of the physical and social effects of alcohol.

7680. Seixas, Judith S. *Tobacco: What It Is, What It Does* (1–4). Illus. by Tom Huffman. 1981, Greenwillow $8.50; LB $8.88. A history of tobacco and the consequences of using it.

7681. Sonnett, Sherry. *First Book of Smoking* (4–6). Illus. 1977, Watts $8.90. After a brief history of tobacco and its use, the author concentrates on the harmful effects of smoking as revealed by modern research. Also use: *Smoking and You* by Arnold Madison (1975, Messner $6.97).

7682. Stwertka, Eve, and Stwertka, Albert. *Marijuana* (5–8). Illus. 1979, Watts $8.90. The history, production, uses, and effects of marijuana are well presented in this basic account.

7683. Tobias, Ann. *Pot* (3–4). Illus. by Tom Huffman. 1979, Greenwillow $7.92; paper $2.95. The basic facts about marijuana, its uses and dangers.

7684. Woods, Geraldine. *Drug Use and Drug Abuse* (5–8). Illus. 1979, Watts $8.90. From caffeine to narcotics, the entire drug spectrum is covered, with emphasis on the effects for users.

Safety and Accidents

7685. Gore, Harriet M. *What to Do When There's No One but You* (2–5). Illus. by David Lindroth. 1974, Prentice $4.95. The causes and treatment of 26 common household accidents. Also use: *Try It Again, Sam: Safety When You Walk* by Judith Viorst (1970, Lothrop LB $11.88).

7686. Kessler, Leonard. *Who Tossed That Bat?* (4–6). Illus. 1973, Lothrop $9.84. A guide to sports safety.

7687. Kyte, Kathy S. *Play It Safe: The Kids' Guide to Personal Safety and Crime Prevention* (5–9). Illus. by Richard Brown. 1983, Knopf paper $5.95. There are chapters on safety at home, school, on public transportation, and a section on rape prevention.

7688. Leaf, Munro. *Safety Can Be Fun* (1–3). Illus. 1961, Harper $10.89. A first look at safety and accident prevention.

7689. Vandenburg, Mary Lou. *Help! Emergencies That Could Happen to You and How to Handle Them* (2–5). Illus. by R. L. Markham. 1975, Lerner LB $3.95. Emergencies such as fire, lightning, and common accidents are discussed with helpful hints for treatment of injuries.

Doctors and Medicine

7690. Ardley, Neil. *Health and Medicine* (4–6). Illus. 1982, Watts LB $8.90. A review of possible strides in medical science during the coming century.

7691. Berger, Melvin. *Sports Medicine: Scientists at Work* (6–8). Illus. 1982, Harper $10.10; LB $10.89. A look at all of the types of people involved in sports medicine, the centers of research, and this area of science in general.

7692. Eberle, Irmengarde. *Modern Medical Discoveries* (5–8). 1968, Harper $10.95. A glimpse at some important medical breakthroughs.

7693. Graham, Ada, and Graham, Frank. *Three Million Mice: A Story of Modern Medical Research* (6–8). Illus. by Robert Shetterly. 1981, Scribners $9.95. The story of the germ-free Jax mice and their role in research.

7694. Kavaler, Lucy. *Cold against Disease: The Wonders of Cold* (6–9). Illus. 1971, Harper $10.95. A matter-of-fact presentation of the ways in which cold helps in medicine, from space applications to organ transplants.

7695. Kettelkamp, Larry. *The Healing Arts* (6–8). Illus. 1978, Morrow $8.40. Healing techniques— conventional and unconventional (like spiritual healing)—are covered.

7696. Rockwell, Harlow. *My Doctor* (2–4). Illus. by author. 1973, Macmillan $7.95. A first look at doctors and what they do.

7697. Silverstein, Alvin, and Silverstein, Virginia B. *Futurelife: The Biotechnology Revolution* (6–9). Illus. by Marjorie Thier. 1982, Prentice $9.95. Such topics in biotechnology as CAT scanners, DNA experiments, and test-tube babies are discussed.

7698. Weiss, Ann E. *Biofeedback: Fact or Fad?* (6–9). Illus. 1984, Watts $9.90. A discussion of this controversial topic involving the autonomic nervous system.

7699. Zim, Herbert S. *Medicine* (4–6). Illus. by Judith Hoffman Corwin. 1974, Morrow $7.20; LB $8.16. The many uses of medicine and precautions concerning dosage.

Hospitals

7700. Holmes, Burnham. *Early Morning Rounds: A Portrait of a Hospital* (5–8). Illus. 1981, Four Winds $9.95. A tour of various medical areas of a hospital from obstetrics to surgery.

7701. Howe, James. *The Hospital Book* (4–6). Illus. 1981, Crown $10.95; paper $4.95. A straightforward account of what a child can expect when sent to a hospital.

7702. Stein, Sara Bonnett. *A Hospital Story* (1–3). Illus. 1974, Walker $8.95; paper $4.95. A fine

introduction to hospitals and what a hospital stay involves.

7703. Wolfe, Bob, and Wolfe, Diane. *Emergency Room* (4–6). Illus. 1983, Carolrhoda $7.95. A behind-the-scenes view of the emergency room in a hospital.

Aging and Death

7704. Ancona, George. *Growing Older* (3–5). Illus. 1978, Dutton $8.95. Interviews with 13 elderly people explore the process of getting old.

7705. Anderson, Lydia. *Death* (4–6). Illus. 1980, Watts LB $8.90. A straightforward account that explores such topics as life expectancy and euthanasia.

7706. Burnstein, Joanne E., and Gullo, Stephen V. *When People Die* (K–3). Illus. by Rosemarie Hausher. 1977, Dutton $9.95. Written by a psychologist, this is a sensible, fairly comprehensive, and tender discussion of death, neither somber nor mawkish.

7707. Pringle, Laurence. *Death Is Natural* (4–5). Illus. 1977, Four Winds $7.95. An explanation of death as interpreted through the balance-of-nature concept.

7708. Silverstein, Alvin, and Silverstein, Virginia B. *Aging* (6–9). 1979, Watts $7.90. An account of the aging process, its changes, causes, and problems.

Physical and Mental Handicaps

7709. Adams, Barbara. *Like It Is: Facts and Feelings about Handicaps from Kids Who Know* (5–8). Illus. 1979, Walker LB $8.85. A group of handicapped kids talk about their problems and adjustments.

7710. Berger, Gilda. *Physical Disabilities* (6–8). Illus. 1979, Watts $8.90. The characteristics, causes, and consequences of common physical handicaps are discovered.

7711. Curtis, Patricia. *Cindy: A Hearing Ear Dog* (3–5). Illus. 1981, Dutton $10.25. The story of a dog trained to help the deaf.

7712. Curtis, Patricia. *Greff: The Story of a Guide Dog* (3–7). Illus. 1982, Lodestar $9.95. The training of a guide dog up to its life with its first owner.

7713. Dunbar, Robert E. *Mental Retardation* (4–7). Illus. 1978, Watts $8.90. A basic, honest account of the causes of mental retardation and its effects.

7714. Greenfield, Eloise, and Revis, Alesia. *Alesia* (5–8). Illus. by George Ford. 1981, Putnam $9.95.

The true story of a girl who has gallantly fought severe physical handicaps.

7715. Hyde, Margaret O. *Is This Kid "Crazy"?* (6–9). 1983, Westminster $9.50. A description of various mental disorders and their treatments.

7716. Kamien, Janet. *What If You Couldn't? A Book about Special Needs* (5–7). Illus. by Signe Hanson. 1979, Scribners $9.95. A discussion of various physical handicaps and how they are treated.

7717. Killilea, M. *Karen* (5–9). 1983, Dell paper $2.50. The inspirational story of Karen, who, though born with cerebral palsy, conquers this handicap. The sequel is: *With Love from Karen* (1983, $2.50).

7718. Marcus, Rebecca B. *Being Blind* (6–8). Illus. 1981, Hastings $9.95. A book that explores the causes of blindness and adjustments made by blind people.

7719. Peter, Diana. *Claire and Emma* (2–4). Illus. 1977, Harper LB $10.89. Two sisters, though deaf, fit into the family's activities.

7720. Redpath, Ann. *Jim Boen: A Man of Opposites* (4–6). Illus. 1980, Creative Ed. LB $8.95. The inspiring story of a quadriplegic who is now a university professor.

7721. Rosenberg, Maxine B. *My Friend Leslie: The Story of a Handicapped Child* (K–3). Illus. 1983, Lothrop $8.00; LB $7.63. A handicapped child in a regular school, told through text and pictures.

7722. Stein, Sara Bonnett. *About Handicaps* (2–3). Illus. 1974, Walker paper $3.95. A book about learning to accept people who have physical handicaps.

7723. Sullivan, Mary Beth. *Feeling Free* (4–8). 1979, Addison LB $10.95; paper $5.95. Physical disabilities are explored through the perceptions of young people.

7724. Sullivan, Mary Beth, and Bourke, Linda. *A Show of Hands: Say It in Sign Language* (4–7). Illus. by Linda Bourke. 1980, Addison LB $6.95. An introduction to signing, the language of the deaf.

7725. Weiss, Malcolm E. *Blindness* (5–9). Illus. 1980, Watts LB $8.90. This account is told through the story of Sarah, a young blind girl.

7726. Wolf, Bernard. *Anna's Silent World* (2–4). Photos by author. 1977, Harper $12.45. Six-year-old Anna was born deaf. How she learns to talk and is able to attend classes with children who have normal hearing is shown through text and excellent photographs.

7727. Wolf, Bernard. *Don't Feel Sorry for Paul* (3–6). Illus. by author. 1974, Harper $12.45. A true story dramatically illustrated with photographs about 7-year-old Paul Jockimo and his adjustment to severe birth defects.

Sex Education and Reproduction

Sex Education

7728. Baldwin, Dorothy, and Lister, Claire. *How You Grow and Change* (4–6). Illus. 1984, Watts $8.90. Puberty, fertilization, and childbearing are 3 topics discussed in this brief sex education manual.

7729. Elgin, Kathleen, and Osterritter, John F. *Twenty-Eight Days* (5–7). Illus. 1973, McKay $6.95. A book about the menstrual cycle that includes information on the reproductive organs.

7730. Goldner, Kathryn Allen, and Vogel, Carole Garbuny. *The Dangers of Strangers* (K–3). Illus. by Lynette Schmidt. 1983, Dillon $10.95. A cautionary volume about the dangers of strangers who make advances.

7731. Hyde, Margaret O. *Sexual Abuse: Let's Talk about It* (6–9). 1984, Westminster $8.95. Case studies are used to explore this delicate topic.

7732. Johnson, Eric W. *Love and Sex in Plain Language* (6–9). Illus. by Edward C. Smith. 1977, Harper $9.95; Bantam paper $2.25. A discussion of the physical, emotional, and moral aspects of love and sex.

7733. Mintz, Thomas, and Mintz, Lorelie. *Threshold: Straightforward Answers to Teenagers' Questions about Sex* (5–8). Illus. 1978, Walker LB $7.85. Answers to a series of direct questions in brief, straightforward terms.

7734. Pomeroy, Wardell B. *Boys and Sex* (6–8). 1981, Delacorte $10.95; Dell paper $2.50. Straightforward advice addressed to young teenage boys. The companion book by the author: *Girls and Sex* (1981, $10.95; paper $2.25).

7735. Wachter, Oralee. *No More Secrets for Me* (3–5). Illus. by Jane Aaron. 1983, Little $12.95; paper $4.70. Four stories about sexual abuse of young people.

Human Reproduction

7736. Arnold, Caroline. *Sex Hormones: Why Males and Females Are Different* (6–9). Illus. by Jean Zallinger. 1981, Morrow $10.25; LB $9.84. An easily understood introduction to this area of science.

7737. Cole, Joanna. *How You Were Born* (PS–2). Illus. 1984, Morrow $10.25; LB $9.55. The story of pregnancy from fertilization to birth in outstanding text and explicit photographs.

7738.   Dragonwagon, Crescent. *Wind Rose* (K–3). Illus. by Ronald Himler. 1976, Harper $9.57. An authentic and dignified treatment of birth as a mother tells her daughter what her parents did, felt, and planned before she was born.

7739.   Girard, Linda Walvoord. *You Were Born on Your Very First Birthday* (PS). Illus. by Christa Kieffer. 1983, Whitman $8.25. A simple introduction to pregnancy and birth.

7740.   Holland, Viki. *We Are Having a Baby* (1–3). Illus. 1972, Scribners $8.95; paper $5.95. Photographs show 4-year-old Dana and her family as they look forward to the birth of a baby—and then Dana's adjustment to having a new little brother at home. Also use: *Did the Sun Shine before You Were Born?* by Sol Gordon and Judith Cohen (1974, Okpaku $6.95).

7741.   Jessel, Camilla. *The Joy of Birth: A Book for Parents and Children* (4–6). Illus. 1983, Dutton $12.95. A straightforward account of pregnancy, childbirth, and child care.

7742.   Miller, Jonathan, and Pelham, David. *The Facts of Life* (3–9). Illus. 1984, Viking $18.95. A pop-up book on the human reproductive system.

7743.   Nilsson, Lennart. *How Was I Born?* (3–6). Illus. 1975, Delacorte $10.95. An excellent book described as "a photographic story of reproduction and birth for children."

7744.   Nourse, Alan E. *Menstruation: Just Plain Talk* (5–7). Illus. 1980, Watts LB $8.90. An account for girls who are reaching sexual maturity.

7745.   Sheffield, Margaret. *Before You Were Born* (PS). Illus. by Sheila Bewley. 1984, Knopf $10.95. The story of the human fetus.

7746.   Ward, Brian R. *Birth and Growth* (4–6). Illus. 1983, Watts LB $8.90. Fertilization, pregnancy, and birth are carefully introduced in this volume.

Babies

7747.   Ancona, George. *It's a Baby* (1–4). Illus. 1979, Dutton $10.95. The first 12 months of a baby's life in simple text and many photographs.

7748.   Harris, Robbie H., and Levy, Elizabeth. *Before You Were Three: How You Began to Walk, Talk, Explore and Have Feelings* (5–8). Illus. 1977, Delacorte paper $7.95. The first 3 years of life and the accompanying developmental processes as experienced by a boy and a girl.

7749.   Showers, Paul. *Baby Starts to Grow* (K–3). Illus. by Rosalind Fry. 1969, Harper LB $10.89; paper $3.95. The first months of a baby's life told in text and drawings.

The Sciences

General

7750. Ardley, Neil et al. *Why Things Are* (3–6). Illus. by Bob Bampton. 1984, Messner $9.79. Questions and answers on a wide variety of science topics.

7751. Asimov, Isaac. *Great Ideas of Science* (6–9). Illus. by Lee J. Ames. 1969, Houghton $6.95. A description of the major theories in science and how each has contributed to our body of knowledge.

7752. Asimov, Isaac. *Words of Science and the History behind Them* (5–9). Illus. by William Barss. 1959, Houghton $10.95. Both the reader interested in science and the reader interested in language will find this a fascinating book.

7753. Cobb, Vicki. *Gobs of Goo* (3–5). Illus. by Brian Schatell. 1983, Harper $9.57; LB $9.89. All kinds of gooey substances are examined, even "goo from you."

7754. Cutchins, Judy, and Johnston, Ginny. *Are Those Animals Real? How Museums Prepare Wildlife Exhibits* (3–6). Illus. 1984, Morrow $11.25. Taxidermy and other methods of preservation in museums are explained.

7755. Gutnik, Martin J. *The Science of Classification: Finding Order among Living and Nonliving Objects* (4–7). Illus. 1980, Watts LB $8.90. An explanation of the methods of classifying used to bring order to both living and nonliving objects.

7756. Haines, Gail Kay. *Test-Tube Mysteries* (6–9). Illus. 1982, Dodd $11.95. Fourteen mysteries that were solved in the laboratory.

7757. Hiller, Ilo. *Young Naturalist* (5–7). Illus. 1983, Texas A & M Univ. Pr. $15.95. A collection of articles written for young people in the magazine *Texas Parks and Wildlife*.

7758. Hutchins, Ross E. *Nature Invented It First* (4–6). Illus. 1980, Dodd $6.95. An explanation of how many inventions such as sonar first occurred in nature.

7759. Knight, David C. *Bees Can't Fly, but They Do: Things That Are Still a Mystery to Science* (3–5). Illus. by Barbara Wolff. 1976, Macmillan $8.95. Some of the several mysteries that are inexplicable to scientists, such as fire walkers, the 6-sided snowflake, and divining rods.

7760. Simon, Seymour. *The Dinosaur Is the Biggest Animal That Ever Lived: And Other Wrong Ideas You Thought Were True* (3–5). Illus. by Giulio Maestro. 1984, Harper $10.95; LB $10.89. Twenty-nine popularly believed science myths are exposed.

7761. Simon, Seymour. *Hidden Worlds: Pictures of the Invisible* (5–8). Illus. 1983, Morrow $10.00; LB $9.55. A variety of different photographs show the many ways we can see the invisible.

7762. Stein, Sara B. *The Science Book* (4–8). Illus. by author. 1980, Workman paper $6.95. A whole-earth approach to strange and fascinating science facts.

7763. Stone, Lynn M. *Microscopes and Telescopes* (1–4). Illus. 1983, Childrens Pr. $7.95. A simple, well-organized introduction to the history and functions of microscopes and telescopes.

Experiments

7764. Allison, Linda, and Katz, David. *Gee Wiz! How to Mix Art and Science, the Art of Thinking Scientifically* (5–7). Illus. by Linda Allison. 1983, Little LB $13.45; paper $7.70. A group of science projects and experiments arranged by subject.

7765. Ardley, Neil. *Working with Water* (4–6). Illus. 1983, Watts LB $8.90. Twenty-three experiments that explore the properties of water.

7766. Arnold, Caroline. *Sun Fun* (1–4). Illus. 1981, Watts LB $8.90. A book of easy projects involving the sun.

7767. Arnov, Boris. *Water: Experiments to Understand It* (4–7). Illus. by Giulio Maestro. 1980, Lothrop $10.00; LB $10.88. Thirteen properties are revealed through experiments.

7768. Broekel, Ray. *Sound Experiments* (1–4). Illus. 1983, Childrens Pr. $6.95. Simple experiments that introduce the principles of sound to primary school children.

7769. Cherrier, Francois. *Fascinating Experiments in Physics* (6–9). 1979, Sterling $14.95; LB $17.79.

A project book for the better reader and more mature student.

7770. Cobb, Vicki. *Lots of Rot* (K–3). Illus. by Brian Schatell. 1981, Harper LB $9.89; paper $4.95. Decay is explored in a series of interesting experiments.

7771. Cobb, Vicki. *Science Experiments You Can Eat* (5–7). Illus. by Peter Lippman. 1972, Harper LB $9.89; paper $4.95. Experiments illustrating principles of chemistry and physics utilize edible ingredients. Also use: *More Science Experiments You Can Eat* (1979, Harper LB $9.57; paper $4.95).

7772. Cobb, Vicki, and Darling, Kathy. *Bet You Can't! Science Impossibilities to Fool You* (5–8). Illus. by Martha Weston. 1980, Lothrop $9.75; LB $9.55; paper $1.95. Sixty different tricks and experiments involving such scientific subjects as fluids and energy. Also use: *Bet You Can! Science Possibilities to Fool You* (1983, Avon paper $1.95).

7773. Cooper, Elizabeth K. *Science in Your Own Back Yard* (5–8). Illus. 1958, Harcourt $6.95. An invitation to firsthand experimentation for the young naturalist.

7774. Gardner, Robert. *Kitchen Chemistry: Science Experiments to Do at Home* (4–8). Illus. by Jeff Brown. 1982, Messner $9.29. Simple experiments that can be performed in the kitchen with everyday equipment and supplies.

7775. Herbert, Don. *Mr. Wizard's Experiments for Young Scientists* (5–9). Illus. by Don Noonan. 1966, Doubleday $9.95. Directions for 13 science experiments that can be done easily with equipment found in the home.

7776. Herbert, Don. *Mr. Wizard's Supermarket Science* (4–7). Illus. by Roy McKie. 1980, Random LB $6.99; paper $3.95. More than 100 projects using supermarket items.

7777. Moorman, Thomas. *How to Make Your Science Project Scientific* (5–9). Illus. 1974, Atheneum $9.95. A highly readable introduction to the scientific method of research and the various forms (experiments, surveys) of its methodology.

7778. Nestor, William P. *Into Winter: Discovering a Season* (4–6). Illus. by Susan Banta. 1982, Houghton $9.95. A handbook describing nature in winter, plus activities for the young experimenter.

7779. Rosenfeld, Sam. *Science Experiments for the Space Age* (5–7). Illus. 1972, Harvey House $7.29. Clear directions are supplied for experiments dealing with space technology using inexpensive materials.

7780. Schneider, Herman, and Schneider, Nina. *Science Fun for You in a Minute or Two: Quick Science Experiments You Can Do* (2–5). Illus. by Leonard Kessler. 1975, McGraw $7.95. Simple, speedy science experiments with little equipment are related to important scientific principles.

7781. Selsam, Millicent E. *Is This a Baby Dinosaur? And Other Science Puzzles* (K–3). Illus. with photographs. 1972, Harper LB $9.89; paper $3.25. Magnified black-and-white photographs on one page that show part of an animal or plant; on the following page the picture shows the whole life form.

7782. Simon, Seymour. *Exploring Fields and Lots: Easy Science Projects* (3–5). Illus. 1978, Garrard $7.22. Simple activities involving sunlight, common insects, everyday plant life, and the like, are well introduced.

7783. Simon, Seymour. *How to Be a Space Scientist in Your Own Home* (6–8). Illus. by Bill Morrison. 1982, Harper $10.10; LB $9.89; paper $4.75. Simple projects involving common household items demonstrate space exploration principles.

7784. Simon, Seymour. *Science in a Vacant Lot* (2–5). Illus. by Kizo Domoda. 1970, Viking $8.95. A book of projects involving nature study in a typical empty city lot.

7785. Smith, Henry. *Amazing Air* (5–7). Illus. by Barbara Firth et al. 1983, Lothrop $8.16; paper $5.25. A well-illustrated book of experiments on air.

7786. Stanley, Leon R. *Easy to Make Electric Gadgets* (4–6). Illus. by author. 1981, Harvey House LB $6.79. Sample projects include a buzzer, metal engraving tool, and a magnetic compass.

7787. Stone, George K. *Science Projects You Can Do* (4–6). Illus. by Stephen R. Peck. 1963, Prentice $4.95. Some fine ideas for the amateur scientist.

7788. Supraner, Robyn. *Science Secrets* (1–3). Illus. by Renzo Barto. 1981, Troll LB $8.11; paper $1.95. Science principles like magnetism and gravity are simply explained.

7789. UNESCO. *700 Science Experiments for Everyone* (6–8). 1958, Doubleday $10.95. An excellent collection of experiments, noted for its number of entries and breadth of coverage.

7790. Webster, Vera. *Plant Experiments* (1–4). Illus. 1982, Childrens Pr. LB $10.60. A manual of simple experiments with plants. Also use: *Science Experiments* (1982, Childrens Pr. LB $10.60).

7791. Webster, Vera. *Weather Experiments* (1–4). Illus. 1982, Childrens Pr. LB $10.60. A simple explanation of how weather evolves is presented through some activities.

7792. Zubrowski, Bernie. *Messing Around with Baking Chemistry* (4–6). Illus. by Signe Hanson.

1981, Little $9.95; paper $4.95. Cake ingredients and their function are examined.

7793. Zubrowski, Bernie. *Messing Around with Drinking Straw Construction* (4–6). Illus. by Stephanie Fleischer. 1981, Little $9.95; paper $4.95. Projects illustrate the principles of construction.

7794. Zubrowski, Bernie. *Messing Around with Water Pumps and Siphons* (4–6). Illus. by Steven Lindblom. 1982, Little $9.95; paper $4.95. Simple experiments show how water can be moved.

Mathematics

General

7795. Bendick, Jeanne, and Levin, Marcia. *Mathematics Illustrated Dictionary: Facts, Figures and People Including the New Math* (4–7). Illus. 1965, McGraw $10.95. About 2,000 entries trace the history and present status of terms and famous people involved in the world of mathematics.

7796. Gersting, Judith L., and Kuczkowski, Joseph. *Yes-No; Stop-Go; Some Patterns in Mathematical Logic* (3–5). Illus. by Don Madden. 1977, Harper $10.89. In solving a king's problems, the reader is introduced to mathematical logic.

Numbers and Number Systems

7797. Adler, David A. *Base 5* (3–5). Illus. by Larry Ross. 1975, Harper $10.53; LB $9.89. Through the use of everyday objects, the author explains number systems with bases of 5 and 10.

7798. Adler, David A. *3D, 2D, 1D* (1–3). Illus. by Harvey Weiss. 1975, Harper $10.53; LB $10.89. The concept of dimension is introduced and explored in simple text and fine illustrations.

7799. Anno, Mitsumasa. *Anno's Mysterious Multiplying Jar* (4–6). Illus. by author. 1983, Putnam $10.95. Everyday objects are used to explain factorials.

7800. Carona, Philip. *Numbers* (1–4). Illus. 1982, Childrens Pr. $6.95. The origins of numbers and various numerical systems.

7801. Charosh, Mannis. *Number Ideas through Pictures* (2–4). Illus. by Giulio Maestro. 1974, Harper $10.89. The concept of odd and even numbers, square and triangular numbers, and how they can be combined and used is clearly explained through simple text and excellent pictures.

7802. Dennis, J. Richard. *Fractions Are Parts of Things* (2–4). Illus. by Donald Crews. 1971, Harper LB $10.89; paper $1.45. An introduction to simple fractions, beginning with one-half, through thirds and fourths.

7803. Fisher, Leonard Everett. *Number Art: Thirteen 123's from Around the World* (5–7). Illus. by author. 1982, Four Winds $10.95. The development of numbers in various cultures.

7804. Froman, Robert. *The Greatest Guessing Game: A Book about Dividing* (2–4). Illus. by Gioia Fiammenghi. 1978, Harper $10.89. Through real-life situations, the principles of division are introduced and explained.

7805. Froman, Robert. *Less Than Nothing Is Really Something* (2–4). Illus. by Don Madden. 1973, Harper $10.53. A clear presentation of positive and negative numbers and how they may be added and subtracted.

7806. Froman, Robert. *Venn Diagrams* (1–3). Illus. by Jan Pyk. 1972, Harper LB $10.89. In a simple text, Venn diagrams are introduced and used to solve various mathematical problems.

7807. Sitomer, Harry, and Sitomer, Mindel. *Zero Is Not Nothing* (2–4). Illus. 1978, Harper $10.89. A beginning math book on the value of negative numbers.

7808. Sitomer, Mindel. *How Did Numbers Begin?* (3–5). Illus. 1972, Harper $10.89. An account of the history of various numerical systems.

7809. Srivastava, Jane Jonas. *Number Families* (1–3). Illus. 1979, Harper $10.89. Such concepts as odd, even, triangle, and square are explained in this picture book.

7810. Watson, Clyde. *Binary Numbers* (2–4). Illus. by Wendy Watson. 1977, Harper $10.89. One of the simplest descriptions of the binary system published for children, this has a lucid text and helpful illustrations.

Metric System

7811. Ardley, Neil. *Making Metric Measurements* (4–5). Illus. 1984, Watts LB $8.90. A series of experiments demonstrate various metric measurements.

7812. Deming, Richard. *Metric Power: Why and How We Are Going Metric* (6–9). 1974, Lodestar $8.95. The advantages of the metric system, as well as the history of its development and the resistance to its adoption in the United States. Also use: *The Metric System: Measures for All Mankind* by Frank Ross, Jr. (1974, Phillips $12.95).

7813. Lamm, Joyce. *Let's Talk about the Metric System* (4–6). Illus. 1974, Jonathan David $5.95. A simple introduction to the meaning and use of the metric system.

7814. Leaf, Munro. *Metric Can Be Fun* (4–6). 1976, Harper $10.89; paper $1.95. A clear and informative introduction to the metric system.

7815. Rahn, Joan Elma. *Metric System* (6–9). 1976, Atheneum $6.95. A discussion of the metric system, particularly as related to the United States.

7816. Shimek, William J. *The Metric System* (K–2). Illus. by George Overlie. 1975, Lerner $4.95. A general introduction to this system of measurement. Others in the series: *The Gram; The Liter; The Meter* (all 1975, $4.95).

Weights and Measures

7817. Asimov, Isaac. *The Realm of Measure* (6–8). Illus. by Robert Belmore. 1960, Houghton $8.95. This work contains an explanation of measurement concepts and tools.

7818. Shimek, William J. *Celsius Thermometer* (4–6). Illus. 1975, Lerner $4.95. An introduction to the thermometer and its measuring value in the metric system.

7819. Srivastava, Jane Jonas. *Spaces, Shapes and Sizes* (1–3). Illus. by Loretta Lustig. 1980, Harper $10.53; LB $10.89. The concepts of volume, plus weights and measures, are introduced interestingly.

7820. Srivastava, Jane Jonas. *Weighing and Balancing* (1–3). Illus. 1970, Harper paper $1.45. An introduction to how weight is calculated.

Geometry

7821. Barr, Stephen. *Experiments in Topology* (6–9). Illus. by Ava Morgan. 1964, Harper $10.95. An explanation of sets through various activities geared to advanced science.

7822. Charosh, Mannis. *Straight Lines, Parallel Lines, Perpendicular Lines* (3–4). Illus. by Enrico Arno. 1970, Harper $10.89. A basic mathematics book that explores the interrelationships of various kinds of lines and cites examples from everyday objects. Also use: *The Ellipse* (1971, Harper $9.89).

7823. Diggins, Julia E. *String, Straightedge and Shadow: The Story of Geometry* (6–8). Illus. by Corydon Bell. 1965, Viking $9.95. The history of geometry told through the simple tools used by early scientists.

7824. Ellison, Elsie C. *Fun with Lines and Curves* (3–6). Illus. by Susan Stan. 1972, Lothrop LB $11.88. Geometric design is explored with string art.

7825. Froman, Robert. *Angles Are Easy as Pie* (3–5). Illus. by Byron Barton. 1976, Harper $10.89. Activities of several hungry alligators are used to point out characteristics of angles.

7826. Phillips, Jo. *Exploring Triangles: Paper Folding Geometry* (2–4). Illus. by Jim Rolling. 1975, Harper $10.89. The properties of triangles are explored through paper-folding exercises.

7827. Sitomer, Mindel, and Sitomer, Harry. *Circles* (2–4). Illus. by George Giusti. 1971, Harper $10.89; paper $1.45. The concepts of radius and circumference are explained in this introduction to the mathematical principles involved in circles.

Statistics

7828. James, Elizabeth, and Barkin, Carol. *What Do You Mean by "Average"?* (5–7). Illus. by Joel Schick. 1978, Lothrop $9.95; LB $6.67. Simple statistical concepts are explained using a classroom situation as a setting. For younger groups use: *Averages* by Jane Jonas Srivastava (1975, Harper $10.89).

7829. Linn, Charles F. *Probability* (2–4). Illus. by Wendy Watson. 1972, Harper $10.89. An introduction to such concepts as data gathering, ratios, and other laws of probability, lucidly explained and illustrated with cartoon-style pictures.

7830. Riedel, Manfred G. *Winning with Numbers: A Kid's Guide to Statistics* (5–8). Illus. by Paul Coker, Jr. 1978, Prentice $7.95. How to lie with statistics is shown in this lively guide.

7831. Srivastava, Jane Jonas. *Statistics* (2–4). Illus. by John J. Reiss. 1973, Harper $10.89. What statistics are, how they are gathered, and their uses, as well as methods of presentation. Also use: *Sports-Math* by Lee Arthur (1975, Lothrop $9.84).

Mathematical Puzzles

7832. Adler, Peggy, and Adler, Irving. *Math Puzzles* (4–6). Illus. by Peggy Adler. 1978, Watts $7.90. Forty-four story problems involving humans and hedgehogs.

7833. Burns, Marilyn. *The I Hate Mathematics! Book* (5–8). Illus. by Martha Hairston. 1975, Little $9.70; paper $6.70. A lively collection of puzzles and other mind stretchers that illustrates mathematical concepts. Also use: *Math for Smarty Pants: Or Who Says Mathematicians Have Little Pig Eyes* (1982, Little $10.95; paper $6.95).

7834. Gardner, Martin. *Mathematical Puzzles* (6–9). Illus. by Anthony Ravielli. 1961, Putnam $9.95. Many different kinds of puzzles provide "stimulating glimpses into the fascinating endless patterns of mathematics." Also use: *A Miscellany of*

Puzzles: Mathematical and Otherwise by Stephen Barr (1965, Harper $10.95).

7835. Gardner, Martin. *Perplexing Puzzles and Tantalizing Teasers* (4–7). Illus. by Laszlo Kubinyi. 1969, Pocket paper $1.50. An assortment of math problems, visual teasers, and tricky questions to challenge young, alert minds; perky drawings.

7836. Kadesch, Robert M. *Math Menagerie* (6–9). Illus. by Mark A. Binn. 1970, Harper $6.79. Twenty-five ingenious mathematical puzzles, clearly described and illustrated.

7837. Weiss, Malcolm E. *Solomon Grundy, Born on Oneday: A Finite Arithmetic Puzzle* (K–3). Illus. by Tomie de Paola. 1977, Harper $10.89. Solving the problem of Solomon Grundy is used to introduce an arithmetic system.

Time and Clocks

7838. Breiter, Herta S. *Time and Clocks* (2–4). Illus. 1978, Raintree LB $14.25. A carefully planned, well-organized beginner's book.

7839. Brindze, Ruth. *The Story of Our Calendar* (4–7). Illus. by Helene Carter. 1949, Vanguard $9.95. From Babylonian sky gazers to the present.

7840. Burns, Marilyn. *This Book Is about Time* (5–7). Illus. 1978, Little $8.95; paper $5.95. This work explores many facets of the concept of time, including a history of the calendar.

7841. Gibbons, Gail. *Clocks and How They Go* (2–4). Illus. by author. 1979, Harper $9.57; LB $9.89. An introductory account that explains how clocks work.

7842. Ziner, Feenie, and Thompson, Elizabeth. *Time* (1–4). Illus. 1982, Childrens Pr. LB $10.60; paper $3.95. The concept of time is introduced in simple text and color photographs.

Physics

General

7843. Anderson, Norman D. *Investigating Science in the Swimming Pool and Ocean* (5–8). Illus. 1978, McGraw $8.95. Such concepts as buoyancy and water displacement are explored.

7844. Apfel, Necia H. *It's All Relative: Einstein's Theory of Relativity* (6–9). Illus. 1981, Lothrop $12.25; LB $11.76. The basic principles of relativity illustrated with many examples.

7845. Branley, Franklyn M. *Floating and Sinking* (1–3). Illus. by Robert Galster. 1967, Harper $10.89. A discussion of why things float and sink, with simple text and interesting activities. For an older group use: *What Makes a Boat Float?* by Scott Corbett (1970, Little $6.95).

7846. Branley, Franklyn M. *Gravity Is a Mystery* (1–3). Illus. by Don Madden. 1970, Harper $10.53; LB $10.89. With the use of color illustrations, the concept of gravity is explained in a lighthearted, amusing fashion.

7847. Branley, Franklyn M. *Weight and Weightlessness* (1–3). Illus. by Graham Booth. 1972, Harper $10.89. Gravity, spaceships, and weightlessness are introduced in this elementary explanation.

7848. Brewer, Mary. *What Floats?* (1–3). Illus. by Nancy Inderieden. 1976, Childrens Pr. $6.50; paper $2.75. The idea of floating and sinking is explained in relation to a variety of objects.

7849. Fisher, David E. *The Ideas of Einstein* (3–5). Illus. by Gwen Brodkin. 1980, Holt $8.95. A basic explanation of the concept of relativity.

7850. Smith, Howard E., Jr. *Balance It!* (4–6). Illus. 1982, Four Winds $10.95. Objects and activities are used to define balance and symmetry.

Energy and Motion

7851. Adkins, Jan. *Moving Heavy Things* (5–8). Illus. by author. 1980, Houghton $6.95. The art and science of moving heavy objects.

7852. Ardley, Neil. *Making Things Move* (3–5). Illus. 1984, Watts LB $8.90. The properties of friction, inertia, and gravity are explored.

7853. Gardner, Robert, and Webster, David. *Moving Right Along: A Book of Science Experiments and Puzzlers about Motion* (6–9). Illus. 1978, Doubleday $8.95. A useful book about science experiments.

7854. Hellman, Hal. *Energy and Inertia* (4–7). 1970, Evans $3.95. Energy and its different forms and uses are discussed.

7855. Rutland, Jonathan. *Exploring the World of Speed* (3–6). Illus. 1979, Watts LB $7.90. The concept of speed is explored in nature, transportation, sports, and even photography.

7856. Watson, Philip. *Super Motion* (4–6). Illus. 1983, Lothrop LB $10.88; paper $5.25. Spinning, vibrations, and balance are 3 elements of motion explored in this book of experiments.

Heat

7857. Adler, Irving. *Fire in Your Life* (6–9). Illus. by Ruth Adler. 1955, Harper $9.87. The concept of combustion, the chemical changes it produces, and its uses.

7858. Daub, Edward E. *Fire* (2–4). Illus. 1978, Raintree $14.25. Attractive color illustrations accompany this text on characteristics and precautions involving fire.

7859. Fichter, George S. *Disastrous Fires* (5–8). Illus. 1981, Watts LB $8.90. Famous historical fires are discussed, plus the use of fire in war.

7860. Satchwell, John. *Fire* (2–4). Illus. by Tom Stimpson. 1983, Dial $9.95. The cause and effect of fire are explained in this picture book.

Magnetism and Electricity

7861. Ardley, Neil. *Discovering Electricity* (3–5). Illus. 1984, Watts LB $8.90. The basic properties of electricity are explored through simple experiments.

7862. Ardley, Neil. *Exploring Magnetism* (4–7). Illus. 1984, Watts LB $8.90. A book of simple experiments that illustrates properties of magnets.

7863. Bailey, Mark W. *Electricity* (2–4). Illus. 1978, Raintree $13.30. A well-organized introduction.

7864. Bains, Rae. *Discovering Electricity* (1–3). Illus. by Joel Snyder. 1982, Troll LB $8.89; paper $1.95. A simple explanation of what makes electricity work.

7865. Branley, Franklyn M. *Mickey's Magnet* (K–3). Illus. by Crockett Johnson. n.d., Scholastic paper $1.50. A simple account of the properties and uses of magnets.

7866. Cosner, Sharon. *The Light Bulb* (4–6). Illus. 1984, Walker $10.85. A history of various forms of lighting, the light bulb, and the electrical industry.

7867. Epstein, Sam, and Epstein, Beryl. *The First Book of Electricity* (5–7). Illus. by Rod Stater. 1978, Watts $7.90. A slim volume that reveals the basics on electricity, from the theoretical to practical.

7868. Kirkpatrick, Rena K. *Look at Magnets* (K–2). Illus. 1978, Raintree $14.25. A basic introduction, suitable for browsing.

7869. Leon, George. *The Electricity Story: 2500 Years of Experiments and Discoveries* (4–6). Illus. 1983, Arco LB $12.95; paper $6.95. The history of the discovery of the properties of electricity is given, plus some simple experiments.

7870. Math, Irwin. *Wires and Watts: Understanding and Using Electricity* (6–8). 1981, Scribners $12.95. Several projects for readers with some experience in this area.

Light and Color

7871. Anderson, L. W. *Light and Color* (2–4). Illus. 1978, Raintree $14.25. Color illustrations enliven this easily read introduction.

7872. Beeler, Nelson F., and Branley, Franklyn M. *Experiments with Light* (4–6). Illus. by Anne Marie Jauss. 1958, Harper $9.57. A simple experiment book involving light and shadow.

7873. Branley, Franklyn M. *Color: From Rainbows to Lasers* (6–9). Illus. 1978, Harper $10.89. The relationships between color and light waves are clearly explained.

7874. Branley, Franklyn M. *Light and Darkness* (1–3). Illus. 1975, Harper $10.89. A simply read explanation of what light is, its importance, and how it travels.

7875. Kettelkamp, Larry. *Lasers, the Miracle Light* (6–9). Illus. 1979, Morrow $8.75; LB $8.40. The laser—its origin and uses—is described in text and photographs.

7876. Lewis, Bruce. *What Is a Laser?* (4–5). Illus. 1979, Dodd $7.95. This and other related questions are answered in simple terms and through accompanying cartoonlike illustrations.

7877. Schneider, Herman. *Laser Light* (6–9). Illus. by Radu Vero. 1978, McGraw $9.95. A mature account of this amazing beam of light and its uses.

7878. Simon, Hilda. *The Magic of Color* (4–6). Illus. 1981, Lothrop $11.25; LB $11.88. An explanation of what color is, optical illusions, and color mixtures.

7879. Watson, Philip. *Light Fantastic* (4–6). Illus. 1983, Lothrop LB $10.88; paper $5.25. Simple experiments that demonstrate the properties of light.

Optical Illusions

7880. Beeler, Nelson F., and Branley, Franklyn M. *Experiments in Optical Illusion* (5–7). Illus. by Fred H. Lyon. 1951, Harper $9.89. After explaining the composition of the eye, the authors describe many fascinating experiments to prove its fallibility.

7881. Paraquin, Charles H. *Eye Teasers: Optical Illusion Puzzles* (4–6). 1976, Sterling $7.95; LB $9.99; paper $3.50. Fun with optical illusions and explanations that are also entertaining.

7882. Simon, Seymour. *The Optical Illusion Book* (4–6). Illus. by Constance Flera. 1976, Morrow $8.95; paper $5.25. In addition to illustrations that show several optical illusions, there are explanations for each illusion and a chapter on illusion in art. Also use: *Tricks of Eye and Mind: The Story of Optical Illusion* by Larry Kettelkamp (1974, Morrow $8.59).

7883. Supraner, Robyn. *Stop and Look! Illusions* (1–3). Illus. by Renzo Barto. 1981, Troll LB $8.11; paper $1.95. Optical illusions with colors, shapes, and sizes are shown.

Sound

7884. Branley, Franklyn M. *High Sounds, Low Sounds* (1–2). Illus. by Paul Galdone. 1967, Harper $10.89. How sounds are produced and received in the ear is described simply with related activities.

7885. Kettelkamp, Larry. *The Magic of Sound* (4–7). Illus. by Anthony Kramer. 1982, Morrow $7.00; LB $6.67. The nature of sound and its manifestations in such areas as movie sound tracks and ultrasound are discussed.

7886. Kohn, Bernice. *Echoes* (2–4). Illus. by Dan Connor. 1979, Dandelion $3.50; paper $1.50. Sound and sound waves are carefully explained for a young audience.

Simple Machines

7887. Hellman, Hal. *The Lever and the Pulley* (3–5). Illus. by Lynn Sweat. 1971, Evans $4.95. Through clear, uncluttered diagrams and a simple text, the principles and functions of these machines are explored.

7888. Pine, Tillie S., and Levine, Joseph. *Simple Machines and How We Use Them* (3–5). Illus. 1965, McGraw $8.95. A basic introduction to such simple machines as the pulley and lever.

7889. Rockwell, Anne, and Rockwell, Harlow. *Machines* (PS–2). Illus. by author. 1972, Macmillan $9.95. Simple machines such as levers and wheels are described with a minimum of words and watercolor pictures.

7890. Weiss, Harvey. *Machines and How They Work* (4–7). Illus. by author. 1983, Harper $10.53; LB $10.89. An explanation of such simple machines as the pulley and the axle.

Chemistry

7891. Freeman, Mae, and Freeman, Ira. *The Story of Chemistry* (4–6). 1962, Random $5.99. An introduction to the world of chemistry.

7892. Gleasner, Diana C. *Dynamite* (4–7). Illus. 1982, Walker $7.95; LB $8.85. The story of Nobel's discovery and its effects on the world.

7893. Morgan, Alfred P. *First Chemistry Book for Boys and Girls* (5–7). Illus. 1977, Scribners paper $2.95. An introduction to this science, with accompanying interesting projects and activities.

7894. Watson, Philip. *Liquid Magic* (4–6). Illus. by Elizabeth Wood and Ronald Fenton. 1983, Lothrop LB $10.88; paper $5.25. Through clear, simple experiments, the properties of liquids are introduced.

Astronomy

General

7895. Adler, David A. *Hyperspace! Facts and Fun from All Over the Universe* (4–6). Illus. by Fred Winkowski. 1981, Viking $10.95; paper $4.59. Chapters on the sun, moon, planets, etc., plus related puzzles and riddles.

7896. Asimov, Isaac. *How Did We Find Out about Black Holes?* (5–7). Illus. by David Wool. 1978, Walker $7.95; LB $7.85. A well-researched and logically organized account.

7897. Asimov, Isaac. *How Did We Find Out about Outer Space?* (5–8). Illus. 1977, Walker LB $6.85; Avon paper $1.95. An account in simple format that traces space traveling, from air balloons to moon exploration.

7898. Asimov, Isaac. *How Did We Find Out about the Universe?* (5–8). Illus. 1982, Walker $7.95; LB $8.85. The discoveries of both ancient and modern astronomers are introduced.

7899. Asimov, Isaac. *To the Ends of the Universe* (6–9). 1967, Walker LB $7.85. A stimulating history of astronomy.

7900. Berger, Melvin. *Comets, Meteors and Asteroids* (5–7). Illus. 1981, Putnam LB $6.99. A look at each of these astral bodies and the possibility of collision.

7901. Berger, Melvin. *Planets, Stars and Galaxies* (4–6). Illus. 1978, Putnam $6.99. A well balanced, up-to-date introduction to astronomy.

7902. Berger, Melvin. *Quasars, Pulsars, and Black Holes in Space* (4–6). Illus. 1977, Putnam LB $6.99. Three phenomena about outer space are discussed.

7903. Branley, Franklyn M. *Comets* (K–3). Illus. by Giulio Maestro. 1984, Harper $11.05; LB $11.06. A discussion of comets, including Halley's, the most famous of all.

7904. Ciupik, Larry A. *The Universe* (2–4). Illus. 1978, Raintree $14.25. Difficult-to-understand concepts are well handled in this simple account.

7905. Couper, Heather, and Henbest, Nigel. *Astronomy* (4–6). Illus. 1983, Watts LB $9.90. Our solar system and beyond are described and the methods used to find out about them.

7906. D'Ignazio, Fred. *The New Astronomy: Probing the Secrets of Space* (4–6). Illus. 1982, Watts LB $8.90. The latest discoveries and theories related to the universe are discussed.

7907. Fradin, Dennis B. *Astronomy* (1–4). Illus. 1983, Childrens Pr. $6.95. The science is introduced in a simple text, many photographs, and a glossary of terms.

7908. Fradin, Dennis B. *Comets, Asteroids, and Meteors* (1–3). Illus. 1984, Childrens Pr. $7.95. A definition of these heavenly bodies, some of the most famous of them, and a description of their paths and properties.

7909. Freeman, Mae, and Freeman, Ira. *The Sun, the Moon and the Stars* (2–4). Illus. 1979, Random $3.95; LB $5.99. The easy first look at astronomy in a revised edition.

7910. Gallant, Roy A. *101 Questions and Answers about the Universe* (4–6). 1984, Macmillan $10.95. A question-and-answer approach to the study of astronomy.

7911. Hamer, Martyn. *The Night Sky* (2–3). Illus. 1983, Watts LB $8.90. A review of the planets and the constellations.

7912. Herbst, Judith. *Sky Above and Worlds Beyond* (5–9). Illus. 1983, Atheneum $13.95. A reader's trip through the world of astronomy.

7913. Jacobs, Francine. *Cosmic Countdown: What Astronomers Have Learned about the Life of the Universe* (6–9). Illus. 1983, Evans $9.95. An update on theories concerning the past, present, and the future of the universe.

7914. Kraske, Robert. *Is There Life in Outer Space?* (5–8). Illus. 1976, Harcourt $7.95. A fascinating account that discusses many topics such as UFOs, radio telescopes, and the new science of exobiology.

7915. Lewellen, John. *Moon, Sun and Stars* (2–3). Illus. 1981, Childrens Pr. LB $10.60; paper $3.95. Large type and color photographs are featured in this simple account.

7916. McFall, Christie. *Wonders of Dust* (5–7). Illus. by author. 1980, Dodd $9.95. Dust's role in causing disease and in both natural and man-made disasters is explored.

7917. McGowen, Tom. *Album of Astronomy* (4–6). Illus. by Rod Ruth. 1979, Rand McNally $8.95. A basic introduction to the various entities found in space, from stars to black holes.

7918. Mayall, R. Newton et al. *The Sky Observer's Guide: A Handbook for Amateur Astronomers* (6–8). Illus. by John Polgreen. 1965, Western $2.95. A guide to stars and their placement in each of the seasons.

7919. Maynard, Christopher. *The Young Scientist Book of Stars and Planets* (4–7). Illus. 1978, EMC $7.95. Attractive illustrations and plentiful experiments and projects add to this book's appeal.

7920. Moche, Dinah L. *Astronomy Today* (6–8). Illus. by Harry McNaught. 1982, Random $7.99; paper $6.95. A survey of astronomy and space exploration.

7921. Muirden, James. *Our Universe* (6–8). Illus. 1981, Watts LB $11.90. An oversized book that introduces astronomy, the stars, and the planets.

7922. Poynter, Margaret, and Klein, Michael J. *Cosmic Quest: Searching for Intelligent Life among the Stars* (6–8). Illus. 1984, Atheneum $10.95. A fascinating look at the possibility of life outside our earth.

7923. Rey, H. A. *Find the Constellations* (5–7). Illus. 1976, Houghton $10.95; paper $7.95. Through clear text and illustrations, the reader is helped to recognize stars and constellations in the northern United States. Also use: *The Stars: A New Way to See Them* (1967, Houghton $11.95).

7924. Richards, Gregory B. *Satellites* (1–4). Illus. 1983, Childrens Pr. $7.95. A well-illustrated introductory volume for the primary grades.

7925. Ridpath, Ian. *Space* (5–7). Illus. 1984, Silver Burdett $10.50. An introduction to the bodies like stars and planets found in space.

7926. Ridpath, Ian. *The Young Astronomer's Handbook* (7–9). Illus. 1984, Arco $9.95. A history of astronomy and techniques of sky watching.

7927. Seevers, James A. *Space* (2–4). Illus. 1978, Raintree $14.25. Clear descriptions and color illustrations help this simply read introduction.

7928. Simon, Seymour. *The Long Journey from Space* (3–5). Illus. 1982, Crown LB $9.95. A description of the life of comets and meteors.

7929. Simon, Seymour. *The Long View into Space* (3–5). Illus. 1979, Crown $7.95. A well-organized introduction to the universe, nicely illustrated with photographs.

7930. Simon, Seymour. *Look to the Night Sky* (5–7). 1977, Viking $11.50; Penguin paper $3.95. Subtitle: *An Introduction to Star Watching*.

7931. Vaughan, Jenny, ed. *On the Moon* (PS–2). Illus. by Tessa Barwick and Elsa Godfrey. 1983, Watts LB $8.60. For young readers, the story of the first moon landing.

7932. Weiss, Malcolm E. *Sky Watchers of Ages Past* (5–8). Illus. by Eliza McFadden. 1982, Houghton $7.95. The story of astronomy as practiced in ancient civilizations like the Mayan and Pueblo.

7933. Yount, Lisa. *The Telescope* (4–8). Illus. 1983, Walker $8.95; LB $9.85. The story of the telescope through the ages and how it functions.

7934. Zim, Herbert S. *The Universe* (4–6). Illus. 1973, Morrow $7.20; paper $1.25. Interesting historical information is supplied in this account that also gives concepts about the universe.

Stars

7935. Apfel, Necia H. *Stars and Galaxies* (4–6). Illus. 1982, Watts LB $8.90. A discussion of the formation and composition of stars, plus recent theories concerning them.

7936. Berger, Melvin. *Bright Stars, Red Giants and White Dwarfs* (5–9). Illus. 1983, Putnam $6.99. How stars come into existence and how they die.

7937. Branley, Franklyn M. *The Big Dipper* (K–2). Illus. by Ed Emberley. 1962, Harper $10.89. An introduction to the composition, mythology, and location of the Big and Little Dippers.

7938. Branley, Franklyn M. *The Sky Is Full of Stars* (2–4). Illus. by Felicia Bond. 1981, Harper $11.49; LB $10.53; paper $3.80. A simple introduction to constellations and star watching.

7939. Branley, Franklyn M. *Sun Dogs and Shooting Stars: A Skywatcher's Calendar* (4–6). Illus. by True Kelley. 1980, Houghton $6.95. A month-by-month guide for sky watchers.

7940. Gallant, Roy A. *The Constellations: How They Came to Be* (5–8). Illus. 1979, Four Winds $12.95. Mythology and fact are combined in this guide to 44 northern hemisphere constellations.

7941. Gallant, Roy A. *Once Around the Galaxy* (6–9). Illus. 1983, Watts LB $9.90. An explanation and history of the study of our galaxy, the Milky Way.

7942. Jobb, Jamie. *The Night Sky Book* (5–8). Illus. by Linda Bennett. 1977, Little $9.95; paper $6.70. A primer for novice stargazers.

7943. Knight, David C. *Galaxies, Islands in Space* (5–7). Illus. 1979, Morrow $7.92. Good information on the formation and functions of galaxies.

7944. Polgreen, John, and Polgreen, Cathleen. *The Stars Tonight* (5–9). 1967, Harper $9.89. Instructions for locating constellations and legends to aid in remembering them, plus detailed star charts.

7945. Santrey, Laurence. *Discovering the Stars* (1–3). Illus. by James Watling. 1982, Troll $8.89;

paper $1.95. A simple book that tells about galaxies, constellations, and other astral bodies.

7946. Simon, Seymour. *Look to the Night Sky: An Introduction to Star Watching* (4–6). Illus. 1977, Viking $11.50; paper $3.95. Directions on how to identify constellations with the naked eye, as well as material on binoculars and simple telescopes.

7947. Zim, Herbert S., and Baker, Robert H. *Stars* (5–8). Illus. by James G. Irving. 1956, Western $11.54; paper $2.95. Subtitle: *A Guide to the Constellations, Sun, Moon, Planets and Other Features of the Heavens.*

Solar System

7948. Anderson, Norman D., and Brown, Walter R. *Halley's Comet* (6–8). Illus. 1981, Dodd $8.95. A history of the most famous of comets.

7949. Asimov, Isaac. *How Did We Find Out about Comets?* (5–7). Illus. 1975, Walker LB $8.95; Avon paper $1.95. The history of comets, their nature, and their effects on people are covered in this overview.

7950. Branley, Franklyn M. *Halley: Comet 1986* (5–7). Illus. 1983, Lodestar $10.95. The story of this comet and what to expect when it returns in 1986.

7951. Couper, Heather, and Murtagh, Terence. *Heavens Above!* (6–8). Illus. 1981, Watts LB $9.90. An introduction to our solar system.

7952. Fichter, George S. *Comets and Meteors* (4–6). Illus. 1982, Watts LB $8.90. A readable informative account with hints on meteor watching.

7953. Fodor, R. V. *Meteorites: Stones from the Sky* (4–6). Illus. 1976, Dodd $7.95. The types, sizes, and shapes of meteorites are discussed, as well as the effects of their fall to earth.

7954. Ford, Adam. *Spaceship Earth* (4–6). Illus. 1981, Lothrop LB $14.88; paper $7.95. A nontechnical account that introduces the solar system.

7955. Zim, Herbert S. *Comets* (4–6). Illus. by Gustav Schrotter. 1957, Morrow $8.16. Comets—their size, composition, and orbits—are explored in simple text and illustrations.

Sun

7956. Allison, Linda. *The Reasons for Seasons* (5–7). Illus. 1975, Little $11.45; paper $6.70. A project-experiment book that also contains fascinating information about the 4 seasons.

7957. Asimov, Isaac. *What Makes the Sun Shine?* (4–6). Illus. by Marc Brown. 1971, Little $5.95. In addition to an explanation of the sun and the nature of its energy, this book outlines simple experiments to explore the solar system. Also use: *The Sun* by Herbert S. Zim (1975, Morrow LB $9.36).

7958. Borland, Hal. *The Golden Circle: A Book of Months* (4–6). Illus. by Ann O. Dowden. 1977, Harper $12.45. An explanation of the origin of the months and their relationships to the sun.

7959. Branley, Franklyn M. *Eclipse: Darkness in Daytime* (2–4). Illus. by Donald Crews. 1973, Harper $10.89. A clear explanation of the total solar eclipse phenomenon, as well as the effects of the eclipse on animals and people in ancient times.

7960. Branley, Franklyn M. *The Sun: Our Nearest Star* (1–3). Illus. by Helen Borten. 1962, Harper $10.89. An easily read book about the sun and its importance in our lives.

7961. Branley, Franklyn M. *Sunshine Makes the Seasons* (3–4). Illus. by Shelley Freshman. 1974, Harper $10.89. A very simple account that explains the seasons by exploring the relationship of the sun to the earth and its orbit.

7962. Gibbons, Gail. *Sun Up, Sun Down* (1–3). Illus. by author. 1983, Harcourt $12.95. An introductory account of the sun and its effects on earth.

7963. Lampton, Christopher. *The Sun* (4–6). Illus. 1982, Watts LB $8.90. A usable account that has material on the formation, composition, and future of the sun.

7964. Markle, Sandra. *Exploring Winter* (3–6). Illus. by author. 1984, Atheneum $11.95. Science and recreation are mixed in this book about winter and activities that are associated with it.

Planets

7965. Asimov, Isaac. *Jupiter: The Largest Planet* (6–8). Illus. 1976, Lothrop $10.51. A well-organized account that gives a capsule report on what was once believed, and is now known, about this planet and its satellites.

7966. Asimov, Isaac. *Mars: The Red Planet* (6–9). Illus. 1977, Lothrop $12.25; LB $11.76. A well-researched account for the better reader.

7967. Asimov, Isaac. *Saturn and Beyond* (6–9). Illus. 1979, Lothrop $11.04. A general discussion of the planets and their moons.

7968. Asimov, Isaac. *Venus, Near Neighbor of the Sun* (6–8). Illus. by Yukio Kondo. 1981, Lothrop LB $10.80. An introduction to this planet and what we know about it.

7969. Branley, Franklyn M. *A Book of Mars for You* (3–6). Illus. 1968, Harper LB $10.89. Mars, in fact

and fiction, including the Mariner flights. Also use: *Mars and the Inner Planets* by Gregory Vogt (1982, Watts LB $8.90).

7970. Branley, Franklyn M. *Jupiter: King of the Gods, Giant of the Planets* (6–8). Illus. 1981, Lodestar $10.95. The information from Pioneer and Voyager space probes is integrated into this account.

7971. Branley, Franklyn M. *The Nine Planets* (6–8). Illus. by Helmut K. Wimmer. 1978, Harper $9.89; LB $10.89. A clearly written and well-organized description of the planets in our solar system and the mythology that surrounds them.

7972. Branley, Franklyn M. *The Planets in Our Solar System* (1–3). Illus. by Don Madden. 1981, Harper $11.49; LB $10.89; paper $3.80. A clear introduction to our solar system and the individual planets, plus comets and asteroids.

7973. Branley, Franklyn M. *Saturn: The Spectacular Planet* (4–6). Illus. by Leonard Kessler. 1983, Harper $11.95; LB $11.89. An up-to-date view that uses material from the Pioneer and Voyager probes.

7974. Gallant, Roy A. *The Planets: Exploring the Solar System* (6–9). Illus. 1982, Four Winds $14.95. A tour of the solar system with associated text.

7975. Knight, David C. *The Moons of Our Solar System* (5–9). Illus. 1980, Morrow LB $9.55. A work that covers all the planets except Pluto.

7976. Lauber, Patricia. *Journey to the Planets* (5–7). Illus. 1982, Crown $11.95. A tour of the planets that incorporates the findings of recent probes.

7977. Nourse, Alan E. *The Giant Planets* (5–7). Illus. 1982, Watts LB $8.90. Information on the large planets, plus their formation and composition is given.

7978. Petty, Kate. *The Planets* (K–3). Illus. by Mike Sanders. 1984, Watts LB $8.90. A very simple introduction to the planets in our solar system.

Earth

7979. Branley, Franklyn M. *A Book of Planet Earth for You* (3–5). Illus. by Leonard Kessler. 1975, Harper $10.89. A description of the size, composition, and motion of the earth as it might be observed from another planet.

7980. Branley, Franklyn M. *The End of the World* (5–9). Illus. by David Palladini. 1974, Harper $10.89. A revealing account of the causes and the eventual death of our planet billions of years from now.

7981. Branley, Franklyn M. *North, South, East, West* (1–3). Illus. by Robert Galster. 1966, Harper

$10.89. The author gives a basic introduction to directions, the position of the sun, and the compass.

7982. Branley, Franklyn M. *What Makes Day and Night* (K–3). Illus. by Helen Borten. 1961, Harper $10.89. A book for beginning readers that explains how the earth's rotation causes day and night.

7983. Lampton, Christopher. *Planet Earth* (5–7). Illus. 1982, Watts LB $8.90. The story of the earth's formation and its geological composition are examined.

7984. Lye, Keith. *The Earth* (5–7). Illus. 1984, Silver Burdett $10.50. A book that describes how the earth was formed and the forces, like earthquakes, that are still changing it.

7985. Scarry, Huck. *Our Earth* (4–7). Illus. 1984, Wanderer $12.95; Messner $11.97. A look at the earth—its composition, place in the solar system, and the life on it.

7986. Schwartz, Julius. *Earthwatch: Space-Time Investigations with a Globe* (6–8). Illus. by Radu Vero. 1977, McGraw $8.95. A group of experiments about the earth that can be accomplished by examination of common phenomenon.

7987. Simon, Seymour. *Earth: Our Planet in Space* (3–6). Illus. 1984, Four Winds $10.95. A simple well-illustrated account of the earth and its position in space.

Moon

7988. Apfel, Necia H. *The Moon and Its Exploration* (4–6). Illus. 1982, Watts LB $8.90. A readable, informative book that supplies a fine introduction.

7989. Blumberg, Rhoda. *The First Travel Guide to the Moon: What to Pack, How to Go, and What to See When You Get There* (5–8). Illus. by Roy Doty. 1980, Four Winds $7.95. An amusing guidebook to the moon and its wonders.

7990. Branley, Franklyn M. *A Book of Moon Rockets for You* (1–3). Illus. 1970, Harper $9.89. Simple explanation of what moon rockets are and how they were used to help us understand the moon.

7991. Branley, Franklyn M. *Pieces of Another World: The Story of Moon Rocks* (5–8). Illus. by Herbert Danska. 1972, Harper $10.89. A description of how the crew of Apollo 11 gathered soil and rock specimens from the moon and a discussion of their composition and significance.

7992. Branley, Franklyn M. *What the Moon Is Like* (1–3). Illus. by Bobri. 1963, Harper $10.89; paper $2.95. A simple introduction to the composition of the moon.

7993. Jay, Michael, and Hewish, Mark. *The Moon* (2–4). Illus. by Christopher Forsey et al. 1982, Watts LB $8.60. An easily read introduction to the moon that incorporates recent findings.

7994. Simon, Seymour. *The Moon* (3–6). Illus. 1984, Four Winds $10.95. A simple description of the moon and its effect on earth.

7995. Taylor, G. Jeffrey. *A Close Look at the Moon* (4–7). Illus. 1980, Dodd $10.95. A book about lunar exploration and what we have learned from it.

7996. Zim, Herbert S. *The New Moon* (4–6). Illus. 1980, Morrow $8.25; LB $7.92. A discussion of the moon and its phases.

Earth and Geology

7997. Asimov, Isaac. *How Did We Find Out the Earth Is Round?* (4–6). Illus. by Matthew Kalmenoff. 1972, Walker $5.85. Early theories about the shape and structure of the earth are discussed, ending with the proof supplied by the explorations of Columbus and Magellan.

7998. Berger, Melvin. *The New Earth Book: Our Changing Planet* (5–7). Illus. by George DeGrazio. 1980, Harper $9.57; LB $9.89. Descriptions and experiments involving the earth—its crust, continents, atmosphere, etc.

7999. Branley, Franklyn M. *The Beginning of the Earth* (2–4). Illus. by Giulio Maestro. 1972, Harper $10.89. The evolution of the earth told succinctly and directly.

8000. Branley, Franklyn M. *Shakes, Quakes and Shifts: Earth Tectonics* (5–9). Illus. by Daniel Maffia. 1974, Harper $10.89. An informative, clear explanation of the theory of plate tectonics, of how earth movements occur, and the theory's status today.

8001. Burton, Virginia L. *Life Story* (3–5). Illus. by author. 1962, Houghton paper $4.50. A work about the changes that have taken place on the earth and in its flora and fauna, from the beginning of time until the present.

8002. Dixon, Dougal. *Geology* (5–7). Illus. by Christopher Forsey. 1983, Watts LB $8.90. A number of topics like volcanoes and continental drifts are introduced.

8003. Fodor, R. V. *Earth in Motion: The Concept of Plate Tectonics* (5–8). Illus. 1978, Morrow $8.75; LB $8.40. A difficult subject introduced with clarity and accuracy.

8004. Gans, Roma. *Rock Collecting* (1–3). Illus. 1984, Harper $11.06; LB $10.89. A book that introduces geology and the formation of the rocks.

8005. Kerbo, Ronal. *Caves* (3–5). Illus. 1981, Childrens Pr. LB $11.95; paper $3.95. An introduction to caves that shows how they were formed, what lives in them, and how to explore them.

8006. Kiefer, Irene. *Global Jigsaw Puzzle: The Story of Continental Drift* (6–8). Illus. by Barbara Levine. 1978, Atheneum $8.95. A basic knowledge of the subject is presupposed in this account that concentrates on theoretical aspects.

8007. Lauber, Patricia. *Tapping Earth's Heat* (3–5). Illus. 1978, Garrard $7.22. Present and possible uses for the earth's tremendous internal heat.

8008. Leutscher, Alfred. *Earth* (K–2). Illus. by John Butler. 1983, Dial $9.66. A basic introduction to types of soil and the life they support.

8009. McNulty, Faith. *How to Dig a Hole to the Other Side of the World* (2–4). Illus. by Marc Simont. 1979, Harper LB $10.89. A journey to the center of the earth.

8010. Matthews, William H. *The Story of the Earth* (6–9). 1968, Harvey House $7.29. An introduction to the history of our earth.

8011. Rhodes, Frank H. *Geology* (4–9). Illus. 1971, Western paper $2.95. A book on the composition, structure, and development of the earth.

8012. Updegraff, Imelda, and Updegraff, Robert. *Continents and Climates* (3–5). Illus. 1983, Penguin paper $3.50. An introduction to our earth which includes suggested experiments.

Space Exploration

8013. Ardley, Neil. *Out into Space* (4–6). Illus. by author. 1981, Watts LB $8.90. Life in future space colonies is explored.

8014. Asimov, Isaac. *Environments Out There* (5–7). Illus. 1967, Harper $12.45. A discussion of known facts about planets and the possibility of life on them.

8015. Becklake, John. *Man and the Moon* (5–7). 1981, Silver Burdett LB $13.80. An account of the history of our Apollo series moon probe.

8016. Bendick, Jeanne. *Artificial Satellites* (5–7). Illus. 1982, Watts LB $8.90. A look at how satellites are placed in orbit and the function they fulfill.

8017. Bendick, Jeanne. *Space Travel* (3–4). Illus. 1982, Watts $8.90. An introduction that answers basic questions.

8018. Berger, Melvin. *Space Shots, Shuttles and Satellites* (4–6). Illus. 1984, Putnam $7.99. A history of the U.S. space program and NASA—the first 25 years.

8019. Branley, Franklyn M. *Is There Life in Outer Space?* (PS–3). Illus. by Don Madden. 1984, Harper $10.89. A discussion of the ideas and misconceptions about life in outer space.

8020. Branley, Franklyn M. *Space Colony: Frontier of the 21st Century* (7–9). Illus. by Leonard D. Dank. 1982, Lodestar $10.95. Life in a space colony via letters from colonists.

8021. Ciupik, Larry A., and Seevers, James A. *Space Machines* (2–4). Illus. 1979, Raintree $14.65. A simple introduction to all kinds of space vehicles.

8022. Collins, Michael. *Flying to the Moon and Other Strange Places* (6–7). Illus. 1976, Farrar $10.95. A first-person account of taking part in a manned space flight.

8023. Coombs, Charles. *Passage to Space: The Shuttle Transportation* (4–6). Illus. 1979, Morrow $9.25; LB $8.88. A glimpse of tomorrow's network for space exploration and use.

8024. Cromie, William J. *Skylab: The Story of Man's First Station in Space* (6–9). Illus. 1977, McKay $10.95. An authoritative, direct account of the 3 space missions that involved teams of astronauts living in an orbiting laboratory. Also use: *Workshops in Space* by Ben Bova (1974, Dutton $8.50).

8025. DiCerto, Joseph J. *Star Voyage* (6–8). Illus. by author. 1981, Messner LB $7.79. An account that graphically tells what it is like to travel in space.

8026. Elting, Mary. *Spacecraft at Work* (3–5). Illus. by Ursula Koering. 1966, Harvey House $5.99. Project Apollo, the American and Russian satellites, space probes, and plans for future space stations and moon bases.

8027. Fichter, George S. *The Space Shuttle* (6–8). Illus. 1981, Watts LB $8.90. A nontechnical introduction that deals with both the history and future of the shuttle program.

8028. Fields, Alice. *Satellites* (3–5). Illus. 1981, Watts LB $8.60. An explanation of the types of satellites and their uses.

8029. Fradin, Dennis B. *Skylab* (1–3). Illus. 1984, Childrens Pr. $7.95. An account of the sky laboratory—how it came into being and what we have learned from it.

8030. Friskey, Margaret. *Space Shuttles* (1–4). Illus. 1982, Childrens Pr. LB $10.60; paper $3.95. Though simple enough for primary grades, this is informative and lucid.

8031. Gatland, Kenneth. *The Young Scientist Book of Spacecraft* (4–7). Illus. 1978, EMC $7.95. A nicely illustrated introduction with several interesting projects.

8032. Greene, Carol. *Astronauts* (1–3). Illus. 1984, Childrens Pr. $7.95. An account of the men and women in our space program.

8033. Hawkes, Nigel. *Space Shuttle* (3–6). Illus. by Denis Bishop et al. 1983, Watts LB $9.90. The design and multiple uses of space shuttles are described. Two other books on this subject are: *The Space Shuttle Action Book* by Patrick Moore (1983, Random $11.95); *Space Shuttle* by Michael Jay (1984, Watts LB $8.60).

8034. Kerrod, Robin. *See Inside a Space Station* (6–8). Illus. 1979, Watts $9.40. A slim overview with emphasis on cutaway illustrations.

8035. Moche, Dinah L. *The Astronauts* (1–3). Illus. 1979, Random $4.99; paper $1.50. A description of various spacecraft and how astronauts are trained to use them.

8036. O'Connor, Karen. *Sally Ride and the New Astronauts: Scientists in Space* (5–8). Illus. 1983, Watts LB $8.90. The story of the first American woman in space and her colleagues.

8037. Petty, Kate. *Space Shuttle* (K–3). Illus. by Tessa Barwick. 1984, Watts LB $8.60. An introduction to the space shuttle, for very young readers.

8038. Podendorf, Illa. *Space* (1–4). Illus. 1982, Childrens Pr. $6.95. The story of space and our attempts to explore it.

8039. Poynter, Margaret, and Lane, Arthur L. *Voyager: The Story of a Space Mission* (6–9). Illus. 1981, Atheneum LB $9.95. A step-by-step account of the space mission to Jupiter and Saturn.

8040. Ross, Frank, Jr. *The Space Shuttle: Its Story and How to Make Flying Paper Models* (6–9). Illus. 1979, Lothrop $9.95; LB $9.55. A mature account that is quite technical in approach.

8041. Sasek, M. *This Is Cape Kennedy* (2–5). Illus. by author. 1964, Macmillan $8.95. Pictorial treatment of the space center, its rockets, and equipment.

8042. Taylor, L. B. *Space Shuttle* (5–9). Illus. 1979, Harper $10.95. An account that stresses the construction of space shuttles and the many benefits we will derive from them.

8043. Vogt, Gregory. *Model Rockets* (5–9). Illus. 1982, Watts LB $8.90. The project book for the outer space enthusiasts.

8044. Vogt, Gregory. *A Twenty-Fifth Anniversary Album of NASA* (5–9). Illus. 1983, Watts $9.60; paper $4.95. A history of NASA and our space program.

8045. Weiss, Malcolm E. *Far Out Factories: Manufacturing in Space* (6–9). Illus. 1984, Dutton $9.95. A look at what will happen when we begin manufacturing in space.

Physical Geography

8046. Amos, William Hopkins. *Life in Ponds and Streams* (PS–3). Illus. 1981, National Geographic Society $12.20. Simple descriptions of pond life, plus outstanding photographs.

8047. Bain, Iain. *Water on the Land* (4–5). Illus. 1984, Watts $9.40. A discussion of the earth's bodies of water with a concentration on rivers.

8048. Bains, Rae. *Wonders of Rivers* (1–3). Illus. by Yoshi Miyake. 1982, Troll LB $8.89; paper $1.95. An explanation of what rivers are and their role in our world. Other titles in this series are: *Wonders of the Seasons* by Keith Brandt; *Wonders of the Forest* and *Wonders of the Pond* by Francene Sabin; *Wonders of the Desert* by Louis Sabin (all 1981 LB $8.89; paper $1.95).

8049. Batten, Mary. *The Tropical Forest* (5–7). Illus. 1973, Harper $11.95. The author describes the characteristics of tropical forests and the relationship between the animals and plants that grow there.

8050. Berger, Gilda. *Mountain Worlds: What Lives There* (2–4). Illus. by Stefen Bernath. 1978, Putnam $5.99. An interesting description of the flora and fauna in mountainous regions.

8051. Browne, Tom. *Rivers and People* (6–8). Illus. 1982, Silver Burdett $14.96. An account that explains the importance of rivers in human existence.

8052. Carlisle, Norman, and Carlisle, Madelyn. *Rivers* (1–4). Illus. 1982, Childrens Pr. LB $10.60. A lucid and very simple introduction to the subject.

8053. Catchpole, Clive. *Deserts (The Living World)* (2–4). Illus. by Brian McIntyre. 1984, Dial $10.63. The story of deserts and their flora and fauna. Three other titles in this series are: *Grasslands (The Living World)* (1984, $10.95); *Jungles (The Living World); Mountains (The Living World)* (both 1984, $10.63).

8054. Cowing, Sheila. *Our Wild Wetlands* (4–6). Illus. by Deborah Cowing. 1980, Messner LB $7.79. An explanation of the formation of and life in swamps, marshes, and boglands.

8055. Fodor, R. V. *Chiseling the Earth: How Erosion Shapes the Land* (6–9). Illus. 1983, Enslow $10.95. The ways in which the face of the earth changes through sudden phenomena or gradual erosion.

8056. Freschet, Berniece. *A Year on Muskrat Marsh* (3–5). Illus. by Peter Parnall. 1974, Scribners $6.95. A year in the animal and plant life found in a Minnesota marshland.

8057. Gans, Roma. *Caves* (2–4). Illus. by Giulio Maestro. 1977, Harper $10.89. How caves are formed, their varying sizes, some of their peculiar features, and the lure of cave exploration are simply and directly explained in this book for the young reader.

8058. George, Jean Craighead. *One Day in the Alpine Tundra* (4–7). Illus. by Walter Gaffney-Kessell. 1984, Harper $9.57; LB $9.89. An introduction to the geology and ecology of the Alpine Tundra and an exciting story are woven together.

8059. George, Jean Craighead. *One Day in the Desert* (3–6). Illus. by Fred Brenner. 1983, Harper $9.57; LB $9.89. A day in the desert with both record heat and torrential rain.

8060. Goetz, Delia. *Deserts* (3–7). Illus. by Louis Darling. 1956, Morrow $8.16. A simple introduction that discusses the origin of deserts and the life-styles of those who live there.

8061. Goetz, Delia. *Valleys* (3–5). Illus. 1976, Morrow $7.95; LB $7.63. Concepts about the formation and importance of valleys are explored through examples in the United States.

8062. Graham, Ada, and Graham, Frank. *The Changing Desert* (4–8). Illus. by Robert Shetterly. 1981, Scribners $11.95. An account that concentrates on the current threats to desert life.

8063. Jaspersohn, William. *How the Forest Grew* (1–3). Illus. by Chuck Eckart. 1980, Greenwillow $8.25; LB $7.92. A simple account of how a farm field is changed into a dense forest.

8064. Kirkpatrick, Rena K. *Look at Pond Life* (K–2). Illus. 1978, Raintree $14.25. An introduction to the subject through brief text and many illustrations. Also use: *Pond Life* by George K. Reid (1967, Western $11.45; paper $2.95).

8065. Lambert, David. *The Active Earth* (4–6). Illus. 1982, Lothrop LB $10.00. An introduction to various earth formations like lakes and mountains.

8066. Laycock, George. *Caves* (5–7). Illus. 1976, Four Winds $8.95. How caves are formed and what life one can expect to find when exploring them are well presented.

8067. Lerner, Carol. *On the Forest Edge* (2–3). Illus. 1978, Morrow $8.40. An exploration of both plant and animal life found where forest and field meet.

8068. List, Albert, and List, Ilka. *A Walk in the Forest: The Woodlands of North America* (5–9). Illus. by author. 1977, Harper $12.95. A survey of life in forests, complete with activities and many pictures in question-and-answer format.

8069. Newton, James R. *Forest Log* (4–6). Illus. by Irene Brady. 1980, Harper $8.61; LB $8.89. A narrative that explains how a dead Douglas fir continues to support life.

8070. Norden, Carroll R. *Deserts* (2–4). Illus. 1978, Raintree $14.25. An introduction to the climate, plants, and animals involved with desert life.

8071. Norden, Carroll R. *The Jungle* (2–4). Illus. 1978, Raintree $14.25. Tropical rain forests and their inhabitants are presented clearly with good illustrations.

8072. Padget, Sheila. *Coastlines* (4–5). Illus. 1984, Watts LB $9.40. An introduction to types of coastlines and the forces that shape them.

8073. Podendorf, Illa. *Jungles* (1–4). Illus. 1982, Childrens Pr. $6.95. The flora and fauna in jungles described simply in this introductory volume.

8074. Pope, Joyce. *A Closer Look at Jungles* (4–7). Illus. 1978, Watts $8.90. A brief narrative that explores jungle life, from forest floor to the skies.

8075. Posell, Elsa. *Deserts* (1–4). Illus. 1982, Childrens Pr. LB $10.60. Straightforward, simple text and fine color photographs are highlights of this book.

8076. Pringle, Laurence. *Frost Hollows and Other Microclimates* (4–7). Illus. 1981, Morrow $9.75; LB $8.88. A discussion of microclimates and the significance of this pocket area.

8077. Pringle, Laurence. *The Gentle Desert* (4–6). Illus. 1977, Macmillan $9.95. The flora and fauna in the desert and their adjustments to a hostile environment are introduced in this survey volume.

8078. Rowan, James P. *Prairies and Grasslands* (1–4). Illus. 1983, Childrens Pr. $7.95. The flora and fauna in this geographical area are discussed simply.

8079. Selsam, Millicent E. *See through the Forest* (3–6). Illus. 1956, Harper $10.89. An introduction to the forest and the life in it.

8080. Sigford, Ann E. *Eight Words for Thirsty (Story of Environmental Action)* (6–8). Illus. 1979, Dillon LB $9.95. An explanation of the water problems faced in deserts.

8081. Sigford, Ann E. *Tall Grass and Trouble: A Story of Environmental Action* (5–9). Illus. 1978, Dillon $9.95. An introduction to prairies and the need to preserve them.

8082. Stewart, Anne. *What's a Wilderness Worth? A Story of Environmental Action* (6–8). Illus. 1979, Dillon LB $9.95. The value of a wilderness area and a description of the flora and fauna.

8083. Stone, Lynn M. *Marshes and Swamps* (1–4). Illus. 1983, Childrens Pr. $6.95. The characteristics of these wetlands and their flora and fauna are introduced to the young reader.

8084. Stone, Lynn M. *Mountains* (1–4). Illus. 1983, Childrens Pr. $7.95. Mountain ecology is introduced in basic terms with excellent photographs.

8085. Stone, Lynn M. *Pond Life* (1–4). Illus. 1983, Childrens Pr. $7.95. Striking photographs and a sparse but well-organized text are used to introduce life in ponds.

8086. Tresselt, Alvin. *The Beaver Pond* (1–3). Illus. by Roger Duvoisin. 1970, Lothrop LB $8.59. The tremendous variety of life in a pond is presented in very simple text and lovely pictures.

8087. Updegraff, Imelda, and Updegraff, Robert. *Mountains and Valleys* (3–5). Illus. by author. 1981, Childrens Pr. $8.95. A simple introduction to topographical geography.

8088. Updegraff, Imelda, and Updegraff, Robert. *Rivers and Lakes* (3–5). Illus. by author. 1981, Childrens Pr. $8.95; Penguin paper $3.50. An introduction to the roles that lakes and rivers play in our lives.

8089. Watson, Jane Werner. *Deserts of the World: Future Threat or Promise?* (6–9). Illus. 1981, Putnam $13.95. An account that concentrates on what causes deserts and what happens when land becomes a desert.

8090. Welch, Martha McKeen. *Close Looks in a Spring Woods* (2–5). Illus. 1982, Dodd LB $7.95. A description of the growth cycle that begins in the spring.

8091. White, Anne Terry. *All about Great Rivers of the World* (4–6). 1957, Random $5.39. An introduction to the most important rivers in the world and the life they sustain.

Rocks, Minerals, and Soil

8092. Fenton, Carroll Lane, and Adams, Mildred. *Rocks and Their Stories* (4–6). Illus. 1951, Doubleday $5.95. A brief but expert account that, among other information, discusses 40 different minerals.

8093. Fichter, George S. *Rocks and Minerals* (4–6). Illus. by Patricia J. Wynne. 1982, Random paper $2.95. In a small format, this book from the Audubon Society introduces rocks and minerals.

8094. Gallob, Edward. *City Rocks, City Blocks, and the Moon* (3–5). Photos by author. 1973, Scribners $6.95. Excellent photographs and a clear text show how city blocks can make an inviting treasure hunt for a beginning geologist.

8095. Kehoe, Michael. *The Rock Quarry Book* (2–3). Illus. 1981, Carolrhoda LB $7.95. An explanation of how rocks are mined and finished.

8096. McGowen, Tom. *Album of Rocks and Minerals* (5–8). Illus. by Rod Ruth. 1981, Rand McNally $7.95; LB $7.97. A well-illustrated introduction to the most common rocks and minerals.

8097. Podendorf, Illa. *Rocks and Minerals* (1–4). Illus. 1982, Childrens Pr. LB $10.60; paper $3.95. A straightforward, well-organized account for the young reader.

8098. Russell, Helen Ross. *Soil, a Field Trip Guide* (4–6). Illus. 1972, Little $4.95. Various kinds of soil are introduced and many projects outlined.

8099. Selsam, Millicent E., and Hunt, Joyce. *A First Look at Rocks* (K–3). Illus. by Harriett Springer. 1984, Walker LB $9.85. An introduction to rocks, how they were formed, and where they are found.

8100. Zim, Herbert S. *Quartz* (3–5). Illus. 1981, Morrow $11.25; LB $10.80. The nature and uses of this important mineral.

8101. Zim, Herbert S., and Schaffer, Paul. *Rocks and Minerals* (5–9). Illus. 1957, Western paper $2.95. A handbook on the properties, origin, and structure of rocks and minerals.

Earthquakes and Volcanoes

8102. Asimov, Isaac. *How Did We Find Out about Earthquakes?* (4–5). Illus. 1978, Walker LB $8.85; Avon paper $1.95. An introductory survey that begins with the Lisbon quake of 1755 and ends at the present.

8103. Asimov, Isaac. *How Did We Find Out about Volcanoes?* (5–9). Illus. by David Wool. 1981, Walker $7.95; LB $8.85; Avon paper $1.95. An overview of volcanoes, from Pompeii to Mount St. Helens.

8104. Aylesworth, Thomas G. *Geological Disasters: Earthquakes and Volcanoes* (6–8). Illus. 1979, Watts $8.90. Major quakes and volcanoes are discussed, plus plate techniques and prediction methods.

8105. Aylesworth, Thomas G., and Aylesworth, Virginia L. *The Mount St. Helens Disaster: What We've Learned* (6–9). 1983, Watts LB $8.90. A recounting of the Mount St. Helens eruption of 1980 and what it has added to our knowledge of volcanoes.

8106. Berger, Melvin. *Disastrous Volcanoes* (4–7). Illus. 1981, Watts LB $8.90. The causes and types of volcanoes are discussed, plus a list of the most famous ones.

8107. Carson, James. *Volcanoes* (4–6). Illus. 1984, Watts LB $9.40. A simple introduction with many photos, mostly in color.

8108. Challand, Helen J. *Earthquakes* (1–4). Illus. 1982, Childrens Pr. $6.95. The causes and effects of earthquakes, simply told.

8109. Challand, Helen J. *Volcanoes* (1–4). Illus. 1983, Childrens Pr. $6.95. A simple, straightforward text enhanced by color photographs.

8110. Fodor, R. V. *Earth Afire! Volcanoes and Their Activity* (5–8). Illus. 1981, Morrow $10.25; LB $9.84. Beginning with Mount St. Helens, this is a fine overview of the causes and effects of volcanoes.

8111. Gilfond, Henry. *Disastrous Earthquakes* (4–7). Illus. 1981, Watts LB $8.90. An overview of the causes and frequency of earthquakes, plus a listing of some of the earth's major ones.

8112. Goldner, Kathryn Allen. *Why Mount St. Helens Blew Its Top* (4–7). Illus. by Roberta Aggarwal. 1981, Dillon LB $9.95. The causes and types of volcanoes are explored.

8113. Harris, Susan. *Volcanoes* (2–4). Illus. 1979, Watts $8.60. A complex subject nicely simplified by accompanying fine color photographs.

8114. Lauber, Patricia. *Earthquakes* (4–6). Illus. 1974, Random $5.39. Causes, prediction, and possible effects are covered in this basic volume.

8115. Nixon, Hershell H., and Nixon, Joan Lowery. *Earthquakes: Nature in Motion* (3–6). Illus. 1982, Dodd LB $7.95. Why and how earthquakes take place are explored in this account.

8116. Nixon, Hershell H., and Nixon, Joan Lowery. *Volcanoes: Nature's Fireworks* (3–5). Illus. 1978, Dodd $7.95. The history and causes of this destructive force, plus a description of the world's major volcanoes.

8117. Place, Marian T. *Mount St. Helens: A Sleeping Volcano Awakes* (6–9). Illus. 1981, Dodd LB $9.95. A detailed account based on eyewitness accounts.

8118. Poynter, Margaret. *Volcanoes: The Fiery Mountains* (4–7). Illus. by Igor E. Sedor. 1980, Messner LB $8.79. Popular beliefs and legends as well as facts are presented in this readable account.

8119. Radlauer, Ruth. *Volcanoes* (3–6). Illus. 1981, Childrens Pr. LB $9.65; paper $2.95. Beginning with 1981 and Mount St. Helens, this book gives valuable information on volcanoes.

8120. Simon, Seymour. *Danger from Below: Earthquakes—Past, Present, and Future* (5–7). Illus. by author. 1979, Four Winds $8.95. A history of important earthquakes is included in this account, which concentrates on causes and effects.

8121. Stein, R. Conrad. *The Story of the San Francisco Earthquake* (4–6). Illus. by Nathan Greene. 1983, Childrens Pr. $6.45. A colorful account of the earthquake that destroyed a city.

8122. Taylor, G. Jeffrey. *Volcanoes in Our Solar System* (6–8). Illus. 1983, Dodd $10.95. Volcanoes as they exist on the earth and other bodies of the solar system.

8123. Updegraff, Imelda, and Updegraff, Robert. *Earthquakes and Volcanoes* (3–5). Illus. 1981, Childrens Pr. $8.95; Penguin paper $3.50. Two of the mightiest forces in nature are simply explained.

Icebergs and Glaciers

8124. Anderson, Madelyn Klein. *Iceberg Alley* (6–8). 1976, Messner LB $7.97. An overview of what scientists know about icebergs, with references to such events as the sinking of the *Titanic*.

8125. Gans, Roma. *Icebergs* (1–3). Illus. by Bobri. 1964, Harper LB $10.89. The formation of icebergs, how they reach the ocean, and how they are useful as well as dangerous.

8126. Nixon, Hershell H., and Nixon, Joan Lowery. *Glaciers: Nature's Frozen Rivers* (3–5). Illus. 1980, Dodd $7.95. A brief account that gives information on the causes and effects of glaciers.

Energy

General

8127. Ardley, Neil. *Our Future Needs* (4–6). Illus. 1982, Watts LB $8.90. A discussion primarily of our energy needs in the twenty-first century.

8128. Boyle, Desmond. *Energy* (6–8). Illus. 1982, Silver Burdett LB $13.00. A good introduction to various forms of energy.

8129. Branley, Franklyn M. *Energy for the Twenty-First Century* (6–9). Illus. by Henry Roth. 1975, Harper $11.49. An introduction to future energy sources. A companion volume is: *Feast or Famine? The Energy Future* (1980, Harper $9.57; LB $9.89).

8130. Breiter, Herta S. *Fuel and Energy* (2–4). Illus. 1978, Raintree $14.25. A complex subject treated in a simple but accurate manner.

8131. Carey, Helen H. *Producing Energy* (6–8). 1984, Watts LB $8.90. A look at the many sources of energy today.

8132. Kiefer, Irene. *Energy for America* (6–8). Illus. 1979, Atheneum $11.95. An advanced discussion of the forms and uses of energy.

8133. McDonald, Lucile. *Windmills: An Old-New Energy Source* (6–9). Illus. by Helen Hawkes Battey. 1981, Lodestar $10.95. The power of the wind, explored as an energy source.

8134. Podendorf, Illa. *Energy* (1–4). Illus. 1982, Childrens Pr. LB $10.60. A remarkably clear introduction that explains simply principles and application.

8135. Satchwell, John. *Energy at Work* (4–6). Illus. 1981, Lothrop LB $14.88; paper $7.95. A description of all kinds of energy is given, as well as several energy projects.

8136. Satchwell, John. *Future Sources* (4–6). Illus. by Denis Bishop et al. 1981, Watts LB $8.90. An exploration with many photographs of possible energy sources and how to conserve what we have.

8137. Shuttlesworth, Dorothy E., and Williams, Lee Ann. *Disappearing Energy: Can We End the Crisis?* (5–7). 1974, Doubleday $8.95. The use and misuse of various kinds of energy are described in this well-organized account.

8138. Watson, Jane Werner. *Alternate Energy Sources* (5–8). Illus. 1979, Watts $8.90. A discussion of capturing energy from water, wind, and sun.

Coal, Gas, and Oil

8139. Anderson, Madelyn Klein. *Oil in Troubled Waters* (6–9). Illus. 1983, Vanguard $9.95. The story of oil spills—their causes and effects.

8140. Asimov, Isaac. *How Did We Find Out about Coal?* (5–7). Illus. by David Wool. 1980, Walker LB $7.85. A history of this natural resource and its future role in energy use.

8141. Asimov, Isaac. *How Did We Find Out about Oil?* (4–7). Illus. by David Wool. 1980, Walker $6.95; LB $8.85. This book explores the formation of oil deposits and the many uses made from petroleum.

8142. Chaffin, Lillie D. *Coal: Energy and Crisis* (3–5). Illus. by Ray Abel. 1974, Harvey House $5.49. This book not only gives generous background information on coal but also presents material on the energy crisis and pollution.

8143. Coombs, Charles. *Coal in the Energy Crisis* (5–7). Illus. 1980, Morrow $8.75; LB $8.40. An extensive treatment that includes history, mining methods, and environmental concerns.

8144. Coombs, Charles. *Pipeline across Alaska* (4–6). Illus. 1978, Morrow $8.25; LB $7.92. The history, present status, and potential of the world's most expensive construction project.

8145. Cross, Wilbur. *Petroleum* (6–8). Illus. 1983, Childrens Pr. $9.95. The history and uses of oil are discussed, as well as the present and future of the petroleum industry.

8146. Gans, Roma. *Oil: The Buried Treasure* (2–3). Illus. by Giulio Maestro. 1975, Harper LB $10.89. An explanation of oil deposits, methods of drilling for oil, and how it is used in many manufactured products.

8147. Harter, Walter L. *Coal: The Rock That Burns* (6–8). Illus. 1979, Lodestar $8.95. An account of the origins and uses of coal, as well as material on mining techniques.

8148. Koenig, Teresa, and Bell, Rivian. *Careers with a Petroleum Company* (4–6). Illus. 1983, Lerner $5.95. Through career descriptions, material is presented on finding and processing oil.

8149. Kraft, Betsy H. *Coal* (4–6). Illus. 1982, Watts LB $8.90. The story of how coal is formed, mined, and used.

8150. Kraft, Betsy H. *Oil and Natural Gas* (4–6). Illus. 1982, Watts LB $8.90. The story of how these energy sources are located, mined, and transported.

8151. Olney, Ross R. *Offshore! Oil and Gas Platforms in the Ocean* (5–8). Illus. 1982, Dutton $11.50. An explanation of offshore energy drilling told in many photographs with captions.

8152. Potter, Neil. *Oil* (4–6). Illus. 1980, Silver Burdett LB $11.96. What oil is and where it can be found are 2 questions answered in this clear text.

8153. Scott, Elaine. *Doodlebugging: The Treasure Hunt for Oil* (6–9). Illus. 1982, Warne $8.95. An introduction to the work and accomplishments of those who look for oil.

Nuclear Energy

8154. Adler, Irving. *Atomic Energy* (5–7). Illus. by Ellen Viereck. 1971, Harper LB $10.89. The structure of the atom, radiation, and atomic energy are 3 of the topics discussed in this work.

8155. Ardley, Neil. *Atoms and Energy* (5–7). Illus. by Ron Jobson et al. 1982, Watts LB $9.90. Concise, simple information is given in this introductory account.

8156. Asimov, Isaac. *How Did We Find Out about Atoms?* (5–7). Illus. by David Wool. 1976, Walker $8.85; Avon paper $1.95. This simple account covers the earliest theories on atom structure through the status of our present knowledge. Also use: *How Did We Find Out about Nuclear Power?* (1976, Walker $8.95).

8157. Bronowski, J., and Selsam, Millicent E. *Biography of an Atom* (4–7). Illus. by Weimer Pursell.

1965, Harper $10.89. The evolutionary journey of the carbon atom and the ever-changing roles it may have played upon the earth.

8158. Chester, Michael. *Particles: An Introduction to Particle Physics* (6–8). Illus. by Erick Ingraham. 1978, Macmillan $10.95. A fresh look at the atom and the gaps in our knowledge about it.

8159. Hawkes, Nigel. *Nuclear Power* (4–6). Illus. by Denis Bishop et al. 1981, Watts LB $9.90. A description of the present and future of nuclear energy and how a nuclear power station operates.

8160. Pringle, Laurence. *Nuclear Power* (6–9). 1979, Macmillan $9.95. A pronuclear power account that, nevertheless, stresses caution.

Solar Energy

8161. Adams, Florence. *Catch a Sunbeam: A Book of Solar Study and Experiments* (4–6). Illus. 1978, Harcourt $11.95. A good source of projects involving solar energy.

8162. Asimov, Isaac. *How Did We Find Out about Solar Power?* (5–7). Illus. by David Wool. 1981, Walker $7.95; LB $8.85; Avon paper $1.95. An account that explains what solar power is and how we use it.

8163. Berger, Melvin. *Energy from the Sun* (1–3). Illus. by Giulio Maestro. 1976, Harper $9.89. A simple explanation of how important the sun is in our lives.

8164. Knight, David C. *Harnessing the Sun: The Story of Solar Energy* (5–7). Illus. 1976, Morrow $8.59. The history, theory, and present status of solar energy and its uses.

8165. Metos, Thomas H., and Bitter, Gary G. *Exploring with Solar Energy* (5–8). Illus. 1978, Messner LB $8.97. An overview of the subject that also includes several projects.

8166. Spooner, Maggie. *Sunpower Experiments: Solar Energy Explained* (4–9). Illus. 1980, Sterling $9.95; LB $12.49. A number of interesting projects illustrate the principles of solar energy.

Weather and Atmosphere

Weather

8167. Ford, Adam. *Weather Watch* (4–6). Illus. 1982, Lothrop $10.00. A simple introduction to such weather phenomena as snow, rain, and clouds.

8168. Fradin, Dennis B. *Blizzards and Winter Weather* (4–8). Illus. 1983, Childrens Pr. $7.50. An account of the causes and effects of blizzards, plus a history of the most important ones.

8169. Fradin, Dennis B. *Droughts* (4–8). Illus. 1983, Childrens Pr. $7.50. The causes of droughts and the problems they produce are explored.

8170. Heuer, Kenneth. *Rainbows, Halos and Other Wonders* (5–8). Illus. 1978, Dodd $8.95. Various forms of atmospheric optics are described and explained.

8171. Heuer, Kenneth. *Thunder, Singing Sands and Other Wonders: Sound in the Atmosphere* (5–9). Illus. 1981, Dodd LB $8.95. An exploration of sounds that weather makes, like thunder and wave sounds.

8172. Lambert, David. *Weather* (3–5). Illus. 1983, Watts LB $8.90. An explanation of various kinds of weather and their causes.

8173. Purvis, George, and Purvis, Anne. *Weather and Climate* (4–5). Illus. 1984, Watts LB $9.40. Many illustrations and some maps help introduce weather to young readers.

8174. Sattler, Helen R. *Nature's Weather Forecasters* (5–7). 1978, Lodestar $8.95. How to foretell weather using nature's indicators.

8175. Updegraff, Imelda, and Updegraff, Robert. *Weather* (3–5). Illus. 1981, Childrens Pr. $8.95; Penguin paper $3.50. A science book that shows the effects of various kinds of weather.

8176. Williams, Terry Tempest, and Major, Ted. *The Secret Language of Snow* (4–8). Illus. by Jennifer Dewey. 1984, Pantheon $10.95; LB $10.99. Different words for snow in the Eskimo language are used to explore this phenomenon.

Air

8177. Branley, Franklyn M. *Air Is All around You* (1–3). Illus. by Robert Galster. 1962, Harper $10.59. An introduction to our atmosphere and its importance.

8178. Brewer, Mary. *The Wind Is Air* (1–3). Illus. 1975, Childrens Pr. $6.95; paper $2.75. A very simple introduction to the wind, its force, and usefulness.

8179. Lloyd, David. *Air* (2–4). Illus. by Peter Visscher. 1983, Dial $9.95. A simple picture book that explains what air is and how it is necessary for life.

8180. Santrey, Laurence. *What Makes the Wind?* (1–3). Illus. by Bert Dodson. 1982, Troll $8.89; paper $1.95. A simple, straightforward account on aspects of weather and the atmosphere.

Water

8181. Brandt, Keith. *What Makes It Rain? The Story of a Raindrop* (1–3). Illus. by Yoshi Miyake. 1982, Troll LB $8.89; paper $1.95. A simple book about the water cycle.

8182. Branley, Franklyn M. *Water for the World* (5–8). Illus. by True Kelley. 1982, Harper $10.53; LB $10.89. The water cycle and water conservation are 2 topics discussed in this account.

8183. Gunston, Bill. *Water* (6–8). Illus. 1982, Silver Burdett LB $13.00. An overview of the various states of water and their properties.

8184. Leutscher, Alfred. *Water* (K–2). Illus. by Nick Hardcastle. 1983, Dial $9.66. The various forms of water and their importance to life support are discussed.

8185. Newton, James R. *Rain Shadow* (1–4). Illus. by Susan Bonners. 1983, Harper $10.53; LB $10.89. The land that lies on the leeward side of the western Cascade mountains.

8186. Pringle, Laurence. *Water: The Next Great Resource Battle* (6–9). Illus. 1982, Macmillan $10.95. The author concentrates on problems of water supply and pollution.

Storms

8187. Alth, Max, and Alth, Charlotte. *Disastrous Hurricanes and Tornadoes* (4–7). Illus. 1981, Watts LB $8.90. A book that explains the origins of these storms, plus a chronicle of famous hurricanes and tornadoes.

8188. Branley, Franklyn M. *Flash, Crash, Rumble and Roll* (1–3). 1965, Harper $10.89. A simple explanation of the causes and effects of thunderstorms. Also use: *Rain and Hail* (1983, Harper LB $9.89).

8189. Brindze, Ruth. *Hurricanes: Monster Storms from the Sea* (4–6). Illus. 1973, Atheneum $7.95. The origins and characteristics of these storms are discussed.

8190. Broekel, Ray. *Storms* (1–4). Illus. 1982, Childrens Pr. LB $10.60. In only 40 pages the causes and effects of storms are revealed.

8191. Busch, Phyllis S. *A Walk in the Snow* (2–4). Photos by Mary M. Thacher. 1971, Harper $9.57. Beautiful photographs show winter scenes and enable children to find out many answers to their questions about snow. Also use: *Snow Is Falling* by Franklyn M. Branley (1963, Harper $10.89).

8192. Fodor, R. V. *Angry Waters: Floods and Their Control* (4–7). Illus. 1980, Dodd $7.95. The major causes of floods and some outstanding examples are explored.

8193. Fradin, Dennis B. *Floods* (4–6). Illus. 1982, Childrens Pr. $7.50. Starting with the terrible 1976 floods in Colorado, this account discusses floods— causes, effects, and possible precautions. Also use: *Hurricanes* (1982, Childrens Pr. $7.50).

8194. Jennings, Gary. *The Killer Storms: Hurricanes, Typhoons, and Tornadoes* (5–7). Illus. 1970, Harper $9.89. An account of how these storms are created and forecast, along with their effects on people and land.

Botany

Seeds

8195. Jordan, Helene J. *How a Seed Grows* (2–4). Illus. by Joseph Low. 1960, Harper $10.89; paper $3.95. This book describes how seeds germinate and become plants and supplies useful experiments.

8196. Jordan, Helene J. *Seeds by Wind and Water* (1–3). Illus. by Nils Hogner. 1962, Harper LB $10.89. A very simple account of how seeds travel.

8197. Kuchalla, Susan. *All about Seeds* (K–3). Illus. by Jane McBee. 1982, Troll LB $8.89; paper $1.25. A simple account that explains how and where seeds grow.

8198. Lauber, Patricia. *Seeds: Pop, Stick, Glide* (2–5). Illus. by Jerome Wexler. 1981, Crown $10.95. An exploration of the many ways seeds travel.

8199. Overbeck, Cynthia. *How Seeds Travel* (4–6). Illus. 1982, Lerner LB $9.95. An explanation of the various ways seeds are dispersed.

8200. Steffeud, Alfred. *The Wonders of Seeds* (4–6). 1956, Harcourt $4.95. The great variations among seeds, how they germinate, and travel.

Plants

8201. Barnard, Philip. *Don't Tickle the Elephant Tree: Sensitive Plants* (3–5). Illus. by author. 1982, Messner LB $8.97. The effects of such elements as temperature, noise, and moisture on plants.

8202. Branley, Franklyn M. *Roots Are Food Finders* (2–4). Illus. 1975, Harper LB $10.89. An explanation of the function and importance of a plant's root system.

8203. Busch, Phyllis S. *Cactus in the Desert* (2–3). Illus. by Harriett Barton. 1979, Harper $10.89. How cacti grow in the desert and their various uses are highlighted in this easily read account.

8204. Cole, Joanna. *Plants in Winter* (1–3). Illus. by Kuzue Mizumura. 1973, Harper $10.89. An account of how certain plants survive the winter.

8205. Cross, Diana Harding. *Some Plants Have Funny Names* (K–3). Illus. by Jan Brett. 1983, Crown $8.95. The stories behind the strange names of 12 North American plants, like Indian paintbrush.

8206. Dowden, Anne Ophelia. *From Flower to Fruit* (6–9). Illus. 1984, Harper $12.98; LB $12.89. The reproductive cycle of flowering plants.

8207. Hogan, Paula Z. *The Dandelion* (1–3). Illus. by Yoshi Miyake. 1979, Raintree $14.25. Simple text and large bold illustrations highlight this elementary introduction.

8208. Holmes, Anita. *Cactus: The All-American Plant* (6–9). Illus. by Joyce Ann Powzyk. 1982, Four Winds $14.95. A thorough introduction to all sorts of cacti, as well as where and how they live. Also use: *Cacti* by Frank Venning (1974, Western $11.54; paper $1.95).

8209. Holmes, Anita. *The 100-Year-Old Cactus* (1–3). Illus. by Carol Lerner. 1983, Four Winds $10.95. The story of the long-lived saguaro cactus.

8210. Janulewicz, Mike. *Plants* (5–7). Illus. 1984, Gloucester $9.95. The parts of plants are described, plus the kinds of plants found in various regions.

8211. Lerner, Carol. *Pitcher Plants: The Elegant Insect Traps* (5–7). Illus. by author. 1983, Morrow $11.00; LB $10.08. A good introduction to these carnivorous plants.

8212. Lerner, Carol. *Seasons of the Tall-Grass Prairie* (4–6). Illus. by author. 1980, Morrow $9.75; LB $9.36. A well-illustrated book about prairie plants.

8213. Martin, Alexander C. *Weeds* (7–9). Illus. by Jean Zallinger. 1973, Western paper $2.95. A discussion of identification and the effects—both beneficial and detrimental—of weeds.

8214. Overbeck, Cynthia. *Cactus* (3–6). Illus. 1982, Lerner $8.95. A description of the cactus and how it lives.

8215. Overbeck, Cynthia. *Carnivorous Plants* (4–9). Illus. 1982, Lerner LB $9.95. How these plants exist is discussed, plus a mention of several types.

8216. Patterson, Geoffrey. *The Story of Hay* (3–5). Illus. 1983, Andre Deutsch $9.95. An account of what hay is, how it is harvested, and what its uses are.

8217. Pringle, Laurence. *Being a Plant* (6–8). Illus. by Robin Erickman. 1983, Harper $10.95. A description of the mechanisms at work that keep a plant alive.

8218. Pringle, Laurence. *Water Plants* (2–3). Illus. 1975, Harper $10.89. Several plants are pictured and discussed, along with facts about parts and reproductive processes.

8219. Rahn, Joan Elma. *How Plants Are Pollinated* (5–7). Illus. 1975, Atheneum $8.95. An explanation of the reproduction process in plants.

8220. Rahn, Joan Elma. *Plants Up Close* (5–8). Illus. 1981, Houghton $8.95. Close-up, black-and-white photographs of the parts of 5 different plants.

8221. Rahn, Joan Elma. *Watch It Grow, Watch It Change* (6–8). Illus. 1978, Atheneum $7.95. Growth patterns of plants are explained through use of a variety of prototypes.

8222. Ricciuti, Edward R. *Plants in Danger* (6–9). Illus. by Ann Zwinger. 1979, Harper $9.57; LB $9.89. A well-researched, advanced treatment of our endangered plant life and how it can be saved.

8223. Selsam, Millicent E. *The Amazing Dandelion* (2–4). Illus. by Jerome Wexler. 1977, Morrow LB $8.59. The life cycle, structure, and reproduction methods of this tenacious weed are fascinatingly described.

8224. Selsam, Millicent E. *Catnip* (3–6). Illus. 1983, Morrow $9.00; LB $8.59. An interesting introduction to this interesting herb.

8225. Selsam, Millicent E., and Hunt, Joyce. *A First Look at the World of Plants* (3–6). Illus. by Harriett Springer. 1978, Walker $8.75. A simple description of the various groups of plants, with proper terminology.

8226. Selsam, Millicent E., and Wexler, Jerome. *Mimosa, the Sensitive Plant* (2–5). Illus. 1978, Morrow $9.36. A useful introduction to this unusual plant, plus a number of experiments that can be performed on it.

8227. Tarsky, Sue. *The Potted Plant Book* (5–6). Illus. by Will Giles et al. 1981, Little $6.95. A fine introduction to the care of potted plants in various environments. One other in this series is: *The Prickly Plant Book* (1981, $6.95).

8228. Weiner, Michael. *Man's Useful Plants* (4–7). Illus. 1976, Macmillan $9.95. A variety of plants that benefit humans are introduced, from supplying food to providing paper.

8229. Wexler, Jerome. *Secrets of the Venus's Fly Trap* (3–6). Illus. 1981, Dodd LB $8.95. The inner workings of a Venus's fly trap in text and amazing photos.

8230. Wilson, Ron. *How Plants Grow* (6–9). Illus. 1980, Larousse $8.95. For better readers, an oversize volume notable for its fine illustrations.

Trees and Leaves

8231. Adler, David A. *Redwoods Are the Tallest Trees in the World* (2–3). Illus. by Kuzue Mizumura. 1978, Harper $11.89. A young boy tells about the giant redwoods he has seen in a California national park.

8232. Brandt, Keith. *Discovering Trees* (1–3). Illus. by Christine Willis Nigoghossian. 1982, Troll LB $8.89; paper $1.95. How a tree is born and how it grows.

8233. Brockman, Frank C. *Trees of North America* (6–9). Illus. by Rebecca Merrilees. 1968, Western $10.95; paper $7.95. More than 730 species are introduced.

8234. Bulla, Clyde Robert. *A Tree Is a Plant* (K–2). Illus. by Lois Ligrell. 1960, Harper $9.89; paper $2.95. Several types of trees and their life cycles are introduced and nicely illustrated.

8235. Dowden, Anne Ophelia. *The Blossom on the Bough: A Book of Trees* (6–9). Illus. by author. 1975, Harper $10.95. In this beautifully illustrated volume, the well-known botanical artist describes trees, their flowers and fruits, and the importance of forests.

8236. Hamer, Martyn. *Trees* (3–5). Illus. 1983, Watts LB $8.60. The structure and life cycle of trees are introduced.

8237. Hogan, Paula Z. *The Oak Tree* (1–3). Illus. by Kinuko Craft. 1979, Raintree $14.25. An informative, although elementary, introduction to trees—their function and annual changes.

8238. Kirkpatrick, Rena K. *Look at Leaves* (K–2). Illus. 1978, Raintree $14.25. Brief text and many illustrations provide a basic introduction to the subject.

8239. Kirkpatrick, Rena K. *Look at Trees* (K–2). Illus. 1978, Raintree $14.25. A simple introduction to the subject with a few projects.

8240. Lerner, Sharon. *I Found a Leaf* (2–4). Illus. 1967, Lerner $4.95. The life story of leaves, from spring to fall.

8241. Mabey, Richard. *Oak and Company* (2–5). Illus. by Clare Roberts. 1983, Greenwillow $9.50. The story of an oak that lived 300 years.

8242. Nagel, Shirley. *Tree Boy* (5–7). Illus. 1978, Scribners $6.95. A boy's personal crusade to plant thousands of trees.

8243. Podendorf, Illa. *Trees* (1–4). Illus. 1982, Childrens Pr. LB $10.60; paper $3.95. Excellent photographs and a clear writing style make this simple account suitable for the primary grades.

8244. Selsam, Millicent E. *Tree Flowers* (4–6). Illus. by Carol Lerner. 1984, Morrow $10.50; LB $10.08. A dozen flowering trees like the apple and magnolia are featured.

8245. Zim, Herbert S. *Trees* (5–8). Illus. 1952, Western $11.54; paper $2.95. A small, handy volume packed with information and color illustrations that helps identify our most important trees.

Flowers

8246. Busch, Phyllis S. *Wildflowers and the Stories behind Their Names* (4–6). Illus. by Anne Ophelia Dowden. 1977, Scribners $9.95. Common wild flowers are featured in text and paintings.

8247. Crowell, Robert L. *The Lore and Legends of Flowers* (4–7). Illus. by Anne Ophelia Dowden. 1982, Harper $13.95; LB $13.89. The history and characteristics of 10 familiar flowers.

8248. Dowden, Anne Ophelia. *Look at a Flower* (6–8). Illus. by author. 1963, Harper $10.95. Guide to the study of botany, with many drawings of flower parts.

8249. Fichter, George S. *Wildflowers of North America* (4–6). Illus. by Dorothea Barlowe. 1982, Random paper $2.95. A beginner's field guide from the Audubon Society arranged by flower color.

8250. Lerner, Carol. *Flowers of a Woodland Spring* (3–5). Illus. by author. 1979, Morrow LB $9.36. An exquisite book in which text and drawings combine to give an accurate picture of spring foliage.

8251. Milne, Lorus J., and Milne, Margery. *Because of a Flower* (4–6). Illus. by Kenneth Gosner. 1975, Atheneum $6.95. Unusual facts about a variety of plants.

8252. Munari, Bruno. *A Flower with Love* (3–6). Illus. 1974, Harper $9.89. A well-illustrated book on the art of Japanese flower arrangement using simple household items and common flora.

8253. Overbeck, Cynthia. *Sunflowers* (4–7). Illus. 1981, Lerner LB $9.95. An excellently illustrated introduction to the beautiful and useful plant.

8254. Podendorf, Illa. *Weeds and Wildflowers* (2–3). Illus. 1981, Childrens Pr. LB $10.50. Simple, clear type and color photographs are used in this account.

8255. Selsam, Millicent E., and Hunt, Joyce. *A First Look at Flowers* (K–3). Illus. by Harriett

Springer. 1977, Walker $6.85. A succinct, direct introduction to flowers and flower parts, describing differences in shape, number of stamens and pistils, number of petals, and so on.

8256. Welch, Martha McKenn. *Sunflower!* (2–4). Illus. 1980, Dodd LB $7.95. An introduction to this plant and its uses.

8257. Zim, Herbert S. *Flowers: A Guide to Familiar American Wildflowers* (5–8). 1950, Western $10.38; paper $2.95. An identification guide that describes many species in words and pictures.

Fungi

8258. Froman, Robert. *Mushrooms and Molds* (1–3). Illus. by Grambs Miller. 1972, Harper $10.89. A simple account that defines its subjects and supplies activities to identify their characteristics.

8259. Johnson, Sylvia A. *Mosses* (5–8). Illus. 1983, Lerner $8.95. An introduction to mosses and their complex reproductive system.

8260. Johnson, Sylvia A. *Mushrooms* (4–6). Illus. 1982, Lerner LB $9.95. The structure and growth patterns of this fungus.

8261. Shuttleworth, Floyd S. *Non-Flowering Plants* (4–8). Illus. 1967, Western LB $11.54. A useful well-illustrated guide to these unusual plants.

Foods, Farming, and Fishing

Foods

8262. Adler, Irving. *Food* (3–5). Illus. by Peggy Adler. 1977, Harper $9.89. An interesting overview that introduces a variety of subjects—from the uses of food to data and problems on cultivation.

8263. de Paola, Tomie. *The Popcorn Book* (1–3). Illus. n.d, Holiday $10.95; paper $1.95. While Tony makes a plate of popcorn, Tiny tells interesting facts about this delicious food.

8264. Earle, Olive L., and Kantor, Michael. *Nuts* (3–5). Illus. 1975, Morrow $8.50. Various kinds of nuts are described.

8265. Fenton, Carroll Lane, and Kitchen, Hermine B. *Plants We Live On* (4–7). Illus. 1971, Harper LB $10.89. Subtitle: *The Story of Grains and Vegetables*. Also use: *The Plants We Eat* by Millicent E. Selsam (1981, Morrow $11.25; LB $10.80).

8266. Fischer, Robert. *Hot Dog!* (4–6). Illus. by Steve Gregg. 1980, Messner LB $6.97. The origin, history, and composition of the lowly hot dog.

8267. Hearn, Michael Patrick, sel. *The Chocolate Book: A Sampler for Boys and Girls* (3–5). Illus. by Anthony Chen et al. 1983, Caedmon $12.95; LB $13.45. Lore, poetry, stories, and recipes—all about chocolate.

8268. Horwitz, Joshua. *Night Markets: Bringing Food to a City* (3–6). Illus. 1984, Harper $11.49; LB $11.89. How a large city gets a daily food supply and the operation of these huge markets.

8269. Lasky, Kathryn. *Sugaring Time* (4–7). Illus. 1963, Macmillan $10.95. Through photos and text, the process of maple sugar production in New England is described.

8270. Loeper, John J. *Mr. Marley's Main Street Confectionery* (5–8). Illus. 1979, Atheneum $6.95. The history of candy, ice cream, and other sweets and how they came into being in America.

8271. Mitgutsch, Ali. *From Cacao Bean to Chocolate* (1–3). Illus. by author. 1981, Carolrhoda $5.95. A simple introduction to this process.

8272. Mitgutsch, Ali. *From Grain to Bread* (1–3). Illus. by author. 1981, Carolrhoda LB $5.95. This is one of the 21 start-to-finish books that explain such processes as glass making, wool weaving, furniture making, etc.

8273. Penner, Lucille Recht. *The Honey Book* (5–7). Illus. 1980, Hastings $9.95. This natural sweetener is introduced, plus several excellent recipes.

8274. Pizer, Vernon. *Eat the Grapes Downward: An Uninhibited Romp through the Surprising World of Food* (6–9). 1983, Dodd $9.95. A collection of myths and beliefs about food.

8275. Pringle, Laurence. *Wild Foods* (4–6). Illus. 1978, Four Winds $10.95. Subtitle: *A Beginner's Guide to Identifying, Harvesting and Cooking Safe and Tasty Plants from the Outdoors*.

8276. Rahn, Joan Elma. *Plants That Changed History* (6–9). Illus. by author. 1982, Atheneum $10.95. Five episodes—like the potato famine—where plants changed history are covered.

8277. Rice, Karen. *Does Candy Grow on Trees?* (3–5). Illus. by Sharon Cohen. 1984, Walker $9.95; LB $10.85. A discussion of the ingredients found in candy.

8278. Selsam, Millicent E. *Popcorn* (2–5). Illus. by Jerome Wexler. 1976, Morrow LB $8.59. Excellent photographs and a clear text explain the difference between popcorn and other corn varieties.

8279. Woodside, Dave. *What Makes Popcorn Pop?* (3–6). Illus. by Kay Woon. 1980, Atheneum $9.95. The lore, myths, and legend of the world of popcorn.

Fruit

8280. Ancona, George. *Bananas: From Manolo to Margie* (4–7). Illus. 1982, Houghton $11.50. The story of bananas, from the standpoint of those involved with them.

8281. Cuyler, Margery. *The All-Around Pumpkin Book* (3–6). Illus. by Corbett Jones. 1980, Holt $8.95; paper $3.95. A book about growing and using pumpkins, as well as the lore surrounding this fruit.

8282. Gemming, Elizabeth. *The Cranberry Book* (4–8). Illus. 1983, Putnam $9.95. The story of cranberries—where and how they are grown and ways to use them.

8283. Johnson, Hannah Lyons. *From Apple Seed to Applesauce* (3–5). Illus. 1977, Lothrop $11.25; LB $10.80. Apples, from growing them to their uses.

8284. Johnson, Sylvia A. *Apple Trees* (5–8). Illus. 1983, Lerner $8.95. The story of the apple tree and seed and fruit formation.

8285. McMillan, Bruce. *Apples, How They Grow* (2–7). Illus. 1979, Houghton LB $6.95. A well-presented work on the life cycle and uses of the apple, as revealed in a series of captioned photographs.

8286. Selsam, Millicent E. *Eat the Fruit, Plant the Seed* (2–5). Illus. 1980, Morrow $9.75; LB $9.36. An introduction to various kinds of fruit and their cultivation.

Vegetables

8287. Aliki. *Corn Is Maize: The Gift of the Indians* (2–4). Illus. by author. 1976, Harper $10.89; paper $3.95. A simply written, comprehensive treatment of corn, its origins, how it is husbanded and harvested, and its many uses.

8288. Brown, Elizabeth Burton. *Vegetables: An Illustrated History with Recipes* (6–9). Illus. by Marisabina Russo. 1981, Prentice $9.95. A history of the growing and eating of vegetables.

8289. Johnson, Sylvia A. *Potatoes* (4–7). Illus. 1984, Lerner $9.95. A description of this vegetable and how and where it grows.

8290. Perl, Lila. *Eating the Vegetarian Way: Good Food from the Earth* (5–9). Illus. 1980, Morrow $9.75; LB $9.36. The history of vegetarianism and of the diets followed.

8291. Selsam, Millicent E. *More Potatoes!* (1–3). Illus. by Ben Shecter. 1972, Harper LB $8.89. Sue's class visits the farm and the market to learn more about this popular vegetable and how it is grown and sold.

8292. Sobol, Harriet Langsam. *A Book of Vegetables* (3–5). Illus. 1984, Dodd $10.95. A book that shows how 14 different vegetables grow.

Farms and Ranches

8293. Bellville, Cheryl Walsh. *Farming Today—Yesterday's Way* (3–5). Illus. 1984, Carolrhoda LB $8.95. The examination of a farm that uses old-fashioned methods (mainly work horses) to farm today.

8294. Bellville, Cheryl Walsh. *Round-up* (2–3). Illus. 1982, Carolrhoda LB $8.95. A number of photographs depict this exciting time.

8295. Bellville, Rod, and Bellville, Cheryl Walsh. *Stockyards* (3–6). Illus. 1984, Carolrhoda LB $8.95. An introduction to the buying and selling of animals in stockyards.

8296. Demuth, Patricia. *Joel: Growing Up a Farm Man* (4–7). Illus. 1982, Dodd LB $12.95. Joel is an enterprising young farmer who works hard for his money.

8297. Fradin, Dennis B. *Farming* (1–4). Illus. 1983, Childrens Pr. $7.95. Fine photos and a well-organized introduction to this topic.

8298. Freedman, Russell. *Farm Babies* (2–4). Illus. 1981, Holiday LB $9.95. An array of farm babies is shown in photographs and an informative text.

8299. Hawkes, Nigel. *Food and Farming* (4–7). Illus. 1982, Watts LB $8.90. How energy is used in food production in this country.

8300. Helfman, Elizabeth S. *Wheels, Scoops, and Buckets: How People Lift Water for Their Fields* (3–6). Illus. 1968, Lothrop $9.75. An introduction to irrigation.

8301. Jacobsen, Karen. *Farm Animals* (4–6). Illus. by author. 1981, Childrens Pr. LB $10.60. Large typeface is used in this simple introduction with many color photographs.

8302. Kushner, Jill Menkes. *The Farming Industry* (6–8). Illus. 1984, Watts LB $8.90. A look at modern farming and the technology it uses.

8303. Lavine, Sigmund A., and Casey, Brigid. *Wonders of Draft Horses* (4–7). Illus. 1983, Dodd $9.95. A look at the most popular types of draft horses.

8304. Marston, Hope Irvin. *Machines on the Farm* (3–5). Illus. 1982, Dodd $8.95. A photo album of farm machines with text that explains their uses.

8305. Miller, Jane. *Lambing Time* (1–3). Illus. 1978, Methuen $7.95. The first 2 weeks in the lives of twin lambs.

8306. Patent, Dorothy. *Farm Animals* (4–6). Illus. 1984, Holiday $11.95. All sorts of farm animals and pets are introduced.

8307. Patent, Dorothy. *A Picture Book of Cows* (2–4). Illus. 1982, Holiday $9.95. A very well-illustrated volume that explores the world of cattle.

8308. Scott, Jack Denton. *The Book of the Pig* (3–5). Illus. 1981, Putnam $8.95. A book that explores the pig—its habits, intelligence, and breeds. For an older group use: *Wonders of Pigs* by Sigmund A. Lavine and Vincent Scuro (1981, Dodd LB $9.95).

8309. Scuro, Vincent. *Wonders of Cattle* (4–8). Illus. 1980, Dodd LB $9.95. A review of cattle breeds, their history, and an account of the cattle industry.

8310. Smith, E. Boyd. *The Farm Book* (2–5). Illus. by author. 1982, Houghton $12.45. A picture book that details many activities associated with farm life.

8311. Williams, Garth. *Baby Farm Animals* (1–3). Illus. by author. 1959, Western LB $10.93. A charmingly illustrated book on the young of several domesticated animals.

8312. Wykeham, Nicholas. *Farm Machines* (2–4). Illus. 1979, Raintree LB $14.65. Combines, harvesters, and other farm machines are pictured and described in simple text.

Nutrition

8313. Berger, Melvin, and Berger, Gilda. *The New Food Book: Nutrition, Diet, Consumer Tips, and Foods of the Future* (6–8). Illus. by Byron Barton. 1978, Harper $9.57. An up-to-date account of present food sources, the nature of today's food, and future developments.

8314. Bershad, Carol, and Bernick, Deborah. *Bodyworks: The Kids' Guide to Food and Physical Fitness* (5–8). Illus. by Heidi Johanna Selig. 1981, Random LB $8.99; paper $5.95. An enjoyable book on health and nutrition.

8315. Burns, Marilyn. *Good for Me: All about Food in 32 Bites* (6–8). Illus. by Sandy Clifford. 1978, Little $9.95; paper $6.95. Nutrition and digestion are the major topics discussed in this book.

8316. Gilbert, Sara. *Fat Free: Common Sense for Young Weight Worriers* (6–9). 1975, Macmillan $8.95. A solid, fact-filled book about fat and fat storage in the body, food intake, and types of diets, with wholesome cautionary advice.

8317. Gilbert, Sara. *You Are What You Eat: A Commonsense Guide to the Modern American Diet* (5–8). 1977, Macmillan $10.95. An introduction to food, nutrition, and the world food crisis.

8318. Newton, Lesley. *Meatballs and Molecules: The Science behind Food* (4–7). 1984, Black $7.95. An exploration of various kinds of food and how they effect the human body.

8319. Nourse, Alan E. *Vitamins* (6–9). Illus. 1977, Watts $8.90. The history of vitamin research, as well as the nature, effects, and sources of vitamins, is interestingly treated.

8320. Perl, Lila. *Junk Food, Fast Food, Health Food: What America Eats and Why* (6–9). 1980, Houghton $10.95; paper $4.95. A book about America's eating habits.

8321. Riedman, Sarah R. *Food for People* (4–6). 1976, Harper $9.95. An account of how the world is fed.

8322. Seixas, Judith S. *Junk Food—What It Is, What It Does* (2–5). Illus. by Tom Huffman. 1984, Greenwillow $8.25; LB $7.95. A simply read account of food that contains many calories but not much nutrition.

8323. Simon, Seymour. *About the Foods You Eat* (4–7). Illus. by Dennis Kendrick. 1979, McGraw $8.95. A breezy account that introduces digestion and nutrition and gives simple experiments.

8324. Watson, Tom, and Watson, Jenny. *Breakfast* (4–6). Illus. 1983, Childrens Pr. $8.45. Starting with England, the authors describe breakfast in many lands. Two others in this series are: *Evening Meal; Midday Meal* (both 1983, $8.45).

8325. Weiner, Michael. *Bugs in the Peanut Butter: Dangers in Everyday Food* (5–8). 1976, Little $6.95. A discussion of the natural and artificial poisons found in the food we eat.

Commercial Fishing

8326. Ferrell, Nancy Warren. *The Fishing Industry* (6–8). Illus. 1984, Watts $8.90. A look at commercial fishing, the fish that are caught, and the methods used.

8327. Zim, Herbert S., and Krantz, Lucretia. *Commercial Fishing* (3–5). Illus. by Lee J. Ames. 1973, Morrow $9.75; LB $8.16. An overview of commercial fishing that stresses modern methods of fish detection and catching.

Textiles and Clothing

8328. Eiseman, Alberta, and Eiseman, Nicole. *Gift from a Sheep: The Story of How Wool Is Made* (3–5). 1979, Atheneum $9.95. Jenny raises a lamb, has it sheared, and makes a poncho.

8329. Lasky, Kathryn. *The Weaver's Gift* (4–8). Illus. by Christopher G. Knight. 1981, Warne $8.95; paper $5.95. Wool making, from the lamb to weaving.

8330. LeTord, Bijou. *Picking and Weaving* (K–3). Illus. by author. 1980, Four Winds $8.95. The story of cotton, from plant to product.

8331. Selsam, Millicent E. *Cotton* (3–5). Illus. 1982, Morrow $10.75; LB $9.84. A history of this fabric, how the plant is grown, and how the fabric is woven.

8332. Shepherd, Walter. *Textiles* (6–8). Illus. 1971, Harper $7.89. A generous introduction to the manufacture of textiles, with a special section on synthetics.

Biology

8333. Asimov, Isaac. *How Did We Find Out about Genes?* (5–9). Illus. by David Wool. 1983, Walker $7.95; LB $8.85. The key discoveries in this field are outlined.

8334. Asimov, Isaac. *How Did We Find Out about the Beginning of Life?* (5–8). Illus. by David Wool. 1982, Walker $7.95; LB $8.85. The theories about the origin of life are explained and the possibility of life on other planets.

8335. Billout, Guy. *Squid and Spider: A Look at the Animal Kingdom* (4–7). Illus. by author. 1982, Prentice $10.95. Thirteen animals are treated in color illustrations and brief text.

8336. Black, Hallie. *Animal Cooperation: A Look at Sociobiology* (6–8). Illus. 1981, Morrow $10.25; LB $9.84. A look at social behavior in animals and whether it is learned or innate.

8337. Boorer, Michael. *Animals* (5–7). Illus. 1984, Silver Burdett $10.50. A simple introduction to the main animal grouping—insects, birds, mammals, etc.

8338. Graham-Barber, Lynda. *Round Fish, Flatfish and Other Animal Changes* (2–4). Illus. by Pamela Carroll. 1983, Crown $8.95. The concept of life cycles or a metamorphosis is explained through various animal changes.

8339. Hirschmann, Linda. *In a Lick of a Flick of a Tongue* (K–2). Illus. by Jeni Bassett. 1980, Dodd LB $7.95. The uses of tongues and how they vary from one species to another are introduced through pictures and short rhymes.

8340. Hughey, Pat. *Scavengers and Decomposers: The Cleanup Crew* (5–8). Illus. by Bruce Hiscock. 1984, Atheneum $11.95. Vultures, sharks, beatles, and roaches are only a few of the creatures described as nature's scavengers.

8341. Hutchins, Ross E. *Nature Invented It First* (5–8). Illus. by author. 1980, Dodd $6.95. This wildlife study points out that such phenomena as air-conditioning and chemical warfare originated in nature.

8342. Jacobs, Francine. *Nature's Light: The Story of Bioluminescence* (4–6). 1974, Morrow $8.95; LB $8.59. A fascinating introduction to the phenomenon of self-luminescence in present-day animal forms.

8343. Patent, Dorothy. *Animal and Plant Mimicry* (6–9). Illus. 1978, Holiday $6.95. An extensive account that gives many examples of how plants and animals fool each other.

8344. Patent, Dorothy. *Plants and Insects Together* (5–7). Illus. by Matthew Kalmenoff. 1976, Holiday $8.95. Both beneficial and harmful relationships between plants and insects are described in this well-organized text.

8345. Pringle, Laurence. *Chains, Webs and Pyramids: The Flow of Energy in Nature* (4–7). Illus. by Joan Adkins. 1975, Harper LB $10.89. Food chains and allied systems are explored, as well as how the world food crisis may be lessened.

8346. Pringle, Laurence. *The Hidden World, Life under a Rock* (3–6). Illus. 1977, Macmillan $9.95. Life in cool, dark places is explored, and creatures that live under objects on land and in water are described.

8347. Rahn, Joan Elma. *Traps and Lures in the Living World* (6–9). Illus. 1980, Atheneum $8.95. A description of animals and plants that lure or trap their food.

8348. *Reader's Digest ABC's of Nature: A Family Answer Book* (4–8). Illus. 1984 Random $21.50. A question-and-answer format is used on topics about flora and fauna.

8349. Riedman, Sarah R. *Biological Clocks* (6–8). Illus. by Leslie Morrill. 1982, Harper $10.53; LB $10.89. Several examples from plants, insects, and animals show how living things are time-regulated.

8350. Rights, Mollie. *Beastly Neighbors: All about Wild Things in the City, or Why Earwigs Make Good Mothers* (4–7). Illus. by Kim Solga. 1981, Little $11.45; paper $5.95. A nature history of the plants and animals that live in cities, plus projects involving them.

8351. Roberts, Allan. *Underground Life* (1–4). Illus. 1983, Childrens Pr. $6.95. The underground life of plants, animals, and insects is introduced.

8352. Selsam, Millicent E. *Benny's Animals and How He Put Them in Order* (1–3). Illus. by Arnold Lobel. 1966, Harper $6.89. A small boy with a penchant for tidiness and order decides he wants to arrange his sea shells and animal pictures. With help from a museum zoologist, he learns how to classify.

8353. Selsam, Millicent E. *How to Be a Nature Detective* (2–4). Illus. by Ezra Jack Keats. 1966, Harper LB $10.89. Very simple information on identifying the tracks of 2 birds, 6 small animals, and 3 amphibians.

8354. Silverstein, Alvin, and Silverstein, Virginia B. *Nature's Champions: The Biggest, the Fastest, the Best* (1–5). Illus. by Jean Zallinger. 1980, Random $5.95; LB $5.99. Twenty-nine plants and animals that are nature's record holders.

8355. Simon, Hilda. *The Racers: Speed in the Animal World* (4–6). Illus. by author. 1980, Lothrop $10.95; LB $10.51. A presentation of the method of locomotion used by 14 different creatures.

8356. Simon, Seymour. *Little Giants* (3–6). Illus. by Pamela Carroll. 1983, Morrow $10.00; LB $9.55. Oversize oddities like giant earthworms are explored.

8357. Simon, Seymour. *The Secret Clocks: Time Senses of Living Things* (4–6). Illus. 1979, Penguin paper $3.50. The time sense of living things presented in a well-organized way.

8358. Simon, Seymour. *Strange Creatures* (4–7). Illus. by Pamela Carroll. 1981, Four Winds $8.95. A collection of science's oddities including the vampire bat and stonefish.

8359. Wilkins, Marne. *The Long Ago Lake: A Child's Book of Nature Lore and Crafts* (5–7). Illus. by Martha Weston. 1978, Scribners paper $5.95. A poem to nature, as expressed by the author in northern Wisconsin during the 1930s.

8360. Yount, Lisa. *Too Hot, Too Cold, or Just Right: How Animals Control Their Temperatures* (3–6). Illus. by Harriett Springer. 1982, Walker $9.95; LB $9.85. Temperature control is discussed in terms of over 30 animals and insects.

Microbiology

8361. Anderson, Lucia. *The Smallest Life Around Us* (4–6). Illus. 1978, Crown LB $7.95. An overview of the life and structure of one-celled animals and plants.

8362. Grillone, Lisa, and Gennaro, Joseph. *Small Worlds Close Up* (6–9). Illus. 1978, Crown $8.45. Everyday objects as seen through the microscope.

8363. Kavaler, Lucy. *Green Magic: Algae Rediscovered* (6–9). Illus. by Jean Helmer. 1983, Harper $10.53; LB $10.89. The story of the one-celled plants, algae, their growth cycle and uses.

8364. Schneider, Leo. *Microbes in Your Life* (3–6). 1966, Harcourt $6.50. The place of microbes in everyday life.

8365. Selsam, Millicent E. *Greg's Microscope* (K–3). Illus. by Arnold Lobel. 1963, Harper $8.89. Greg and his parents observe small household items through a microscope.

Land Invertebrates

8366. Hess, Lilo. *The Amazing Earthworm* (3–5). Illus. 1979, Scribners $8.95. The life, structure, and behavior of earthworms are revealed in text and excellent photographs.

8367. Hess, Lilo. *A Snail's Pace* (3–5). Illus. 1974, Scribners $5.95. A survey of snails—habits, food, and life cycles.

8368. Holling, Holling C. *Pagoo* (4–6). Illus. 1957, Houghton LB $10.95. Life cycle of the hermit crab.

8369. Jacobson, Morris K., and Franz, David R. *Wonders of Snails and Slugs* (6–9). Illus. 1980, Dodd $9.95. An interesting account on the similarities and differences of these 2 species.

8370. Johnson, Sylvia A. *Snails* (4–6). Illus. 1982, Lerner $8.95. The structure, habits, and life cycle of a snail.

8371. O'Hagan, Caroline, ed. *It's Easy to Have a Snail Visit You* (1–3). Illus. by Judith Allan. 1980, Lothrop $7.95; LB $7.63. How to gather and take care of this live specimen.

8372. O'Hagan, Caroline, ed. *It's Easy to Have a Worm Visit You* (1–3). Illus. by Judith Allan. 1980, Lothrop $7.95; LB $7.63. Young naturalists are given instructions for collecting, caring for, and observing worms.

8373. Patent, Dorothy. *The World of Worms* (5–8). Illus. 1978, Holiday $7.95. A description of the life and habits of various types of worms.

8374. Simon, Hilda. *Snails of Land and Sea* (6–9). Illus. by author. 1976, Vanguard $8.95. A multi-faceted account of the varieties, uses, and growth patterns of snails and other gastropods.

Insects

General

8375. Causey, Don. *Killer Insects* (6–9). Illus. 1979, Watts $7.90. A full description of insects that bite, sting, and cause death in other ways.

8376. Cole, Joanna. *An Insect's Body* (3–6). Illus. 1984, Morrow $9.00; LB $8.59. The anatomy of the cricket in text and excellent photographs.

8377. Cole, Joanna, and Wexler, Jerome. *Find the Hidden Insect* (2–3). Illus. 1979, Morrow $8.75; LB $8.40. Animal mimicry for camouflage is covered in photos and text.

8378. Conklin, Gladys. *How Insects Grow* (3–6). Illus. 1969, Holiday $7.95. A description of the life cycle of insects, from egg to adult.

8379. Conklin, Gladys. *When Insects Are Babies* (K–3). Illus. by Arthur Marokvia. 1969, Holiday $7.95. Children will be drawn to these easy-to-read descriptions of the growth cycles of 16 insects.

8380. dos Santos, Joyce Audy. *Giants of Smaller Worlds Drawn in Their Natural Sizes* (3–6). Illus. by author. 1983, Dodd $12.95. An introduction to insects with illustrations drawn in proper scale.

8381. Graham, Ada, and Graham, Frank. *Busy Bugs* (3–6). Illus. by D. D. Tyler. 1983, Dodd $9.95. Fourteen insects are introduced, plus the busiest periods in their life cycles.

8382. Griffen, Elizabeth. *A Dog's Book of Bugs* (1–2). Illus. by Peter Parnall. 1967, Atheneum paper $2.95. A dog with more curiosity than itch undertakes an elementary study of bugs, including ants, stinging bugs, friendly bugs, beetles, and fleas.

8383. Hogner, Dorothy Childs. *Good Bugs and Bad Bugs in Your Garden* (5–8). Illus. by Grambs Miller. 1974, Harper $7.50. A survey of the insects we call bugs and their effects on people.

8384. Hornblow, Leonora. *Insects Do the Strangest Things* (2–9). Illus. by Michael K. Frith. 1968, Random $4.95; LB $4.99. A glimpse at the fascinating world of insects.

8385. Horton, Casey. *Insects* (5–7). Illus. 1984, Gloucester $9.90. A general introduction to the anatomy and behavior of insects and some of the most common species.

8386. Patent, Dorothy. *How Insects Communicate* (4–7). 1975, Holiday $8.95. Many examples are cited and explained on how insects use various senses to communicate, with emphasis on the role of hormones called pheromones.

8387. Petie, Haris. *A Book of Big Bugs* (K–3). Illus. by author. 1977, Prentice paper $2.95. Informative, accurate, handsome pictures demonstrate many insects. The entries are arranged in order of increasing size, making this a useful book for identification.

8388. Podendorf, Illa. *Insects* (2–3). Illus. 1981, Childrens Pr. LB $10.60. An easy reader that introduces common insects.

8389. Ritchie, Carson I. *Insects, the Creeping Conquerors and Human History* (6–9). 1979, Lodestar $8.95. A mature account of the effects of insects on the course of human history.

8390. Selsam, Millicent E. *Where Do They Go? Insects in Winter* (2–4). Illus. by Arabelle Wheatley. 1982, Four Winds $8.95. How 12 species of insects cope with the harsh weather of winter.

8391. Selsam, Millicent E., and Goor, Ron. *Backyard Insects* (K–3). Illus. 1983, Four Winds $9.95; Scholastic paper $1.95. How backyard insects camouflage themselves for protection.

8392. Simon, Hilda. *Exploring the World of Social Insects* (4–6). Illus. by author. 1963, Vanguard $8.95. The activities of honeybees, ants, termites, and wasps.

8393. Stevens, Carla. *Insect Pets: Catching and Caring for Them* (3–5). Illus. 1978, Greenwillow $8.50; LB $8.88. A fascinating how-to approach that reveals important insect lore, including some learning experiments.

8394. Zim, Herbert S., and Cotton, Clarence. *Insects* (4–7). Illus. 1961, Western $11.54; paper $2.95. Subtitle: *A Guide to Familiar American Insects.*

Ants

8395. Hutchins, Ross E. *A Look at Ants* (3–6). Illus. 1978, Dodd $7.95. An informative, straightforward account supplemented by excellent photographs.

8396. Myrick, Mildred. *Ants Are Fun* (1–3). Illus. by Arnold Lobel. 1968, Harper LB $8.89. Three boys try to rebuild an ant colony and in the process learn about the inhabitants.

8397. Overbeck, Cynthia. *Ants* (3–5). Illus. 1982, Lerner LB $9.95. A description of the parts of an ant's body, plus an introduction to their complex society.

8398. Sabin, Francene. *Amazing World of Ants* (1–3). Illus. by Eulala Conner. 1982, Troll LB $8.89; paper $1.95. An examination of an ant colony, its inhabitants, and construction.

8399. Simon, Seymour. *Deadly Ants* (4–6). Illus. by William Downey. 1979, Four Winds $8.95. A vivid account of army ants.

Bees and Wasps

8400. Hawes, Judy. *Bees and Beelines* (K–2). Illus. by Aliki. 1964, Harper $10.89. Simple description about beehive activity and why bees always find their way home.

8401. Hoban, Brom. *Jason and the Bees* (1–3). Illus. by author. 1980, Harper $7.64; LB $8.89. A local beekeeper answers Jason's questions about bees in this easily read account.

8402. Hogan, Paula Z. *The Honeybee* (1–3). Illus. by Geri K. Strigenz. 1979, Raintree $14.25. A simple treatment of the life cycle of the bee.

8403. Johnson, Sylvia A. *Wasps* (4–6). Illus. 1984, Lerner $8.95. A year in the life of a wasp is presented in a clear text and fascinating illustrations.

8404. Tarrant, Graham. *Honeybees* (PS–3). Illus. by Tony King. 1984, Putnam $6.95. A toy book that shows how bees live and the interior of a hive.

Beetles

8405. Johnson, Sylvia A. *Beetles* (4–7). Illus. 1982, Lerner LB $9.95. Color photography highlights this account that concentrates on the scarab beetle.

8406. Milne, Lorus J., and Milne, Margery. *Nature's Clean-Up Crew: The Burying Beetles* (4–6). Illus. 1982, Dodd LB $7.95. The story of nature's garbage collectors and undertakers, the burying beetles.

8407. Patent, Dorothy, and Schroeder, Paul C. *Beetles and How They Live* (6–9). Illus. 1978, Holiday $7.95. A well-organized, thorough account of various types of beetles and their living habits.

Butterflies and Moths

8408. Cutts, David. *Look . . . A Butterfly* (K–3). Illus. by Eulala Conner. 1982, Troll LB $8.89; paper $1.25. A very simple introduction to butterflies for the primary grades.

8409. Dallinger, Jane, and Overbeck, Cynthia. *Swallowtail Butterflies* (4–7). Illus. 1982, Lerner LB $9.95. Parts of the body and the life cycle of these glamorous butterflies are 2 topics explored.

8410. Hogan, Paula Z. *The Butterfly* (1–3). Illus. by Geri K. Strigenz. 1979, Raintree $14.25. Large, bright illustrations highlight this introductory account.

8411. Johnson, Sylvia A. *Silkworms* (4–7). Illus. 1982, Lerner LB $9.95. The life cycle of the silkworm, told in text and striking color pictures.

8412. Jourdan, Eveline. *Butterflies and Moths Around the World* (4–9). Illus. 1981, Lerner LB $8.95. The life cycles and traits of more than 50 species are introduced.

8413. McClung, Robert M. *Sphinx: The Story of a Caterpillar* (2–5). Illus. by Carol Lerner. 1981, Morrow $9.25; LB $8.88. The story format includes information on the life cycle of the caterpillar.

8414. O'Hagan, Caroline, ed. *It's Easy to Have a Caterpillar Visit You* (1–3). Illus. by Judith Allan. 1980, Lothrop $7.95; LB $7.63. Children are told where to find caterpillars and how to care for them.

8415. Overbeck, Cynthia. *The Butterfly Book* (2–4). Illus. 1978, Lerner $4.95. A colorful introduction to the life of butterflies and to 10 of the most popular varieties.

8416. Rowan, James P. *Butterflies and Moths* (1–4). Illus. 1983, Childrens Pr. $7.95. A nicely organized and well-illustrated introduction for young readers.

8417. Sabin, Louis. *Amazing World of Butterflies and Moths* (1–3). Illus. by Jean Helmer. 1982, Troll LB $8.89; paper $1.95. A simple account for young readers with brief text and many illustrations.

8418. Selsam, Millicent E. *Terry and the Caterpillars* (K–3). Illus. by Arnold Lobel. 1962, Harper $8.89. The life cycle of a caterpillar is simply told with charming pictures.

8419. Zim, Herbert S., and Mitchell, Robert T. *Butterflies and Moths* (5–9). Illus. 1964, Western paper $2.95. Hundreds of varieties are identified and discussed.

Spiders

8420. Billings, Charlene W. *Scorpions* (3–5). Illus. 1983, Dodd $7.95. Many kinds of scorpions are described, their life-styles, and where they are found.

8421. Cloudsley-Thompson, J. L. *Spiders and Scorpions* (5–8). Illus. 1973, McGraw $6.95. A nicely illustrated introductory volume.

8422. Conklin, Gladys. *Black Widow Spider— Danger!* (2–4). Illus. 1979, Holiday $6.95. An interesting account that includes material on living habits, including food, of the black widow.

8423. Conklin, Gladys. *Tarantula: The Giant Spider* (1–3). Illus. by Glen Rounds. 1972, Holiday $6.95. The life cycle of male and female California tarantulas.

8424. Dallinger, Jane. *Spiders* (4–7). Illus. 1981, Lerner LB $9.95. Excellent color photographs complement the text.

8425. Freschet, Berniece. *The Web in the Grass* (1–2). Illus. by Roger Duvoisin. 1972, Scribners $8.95. Clear, bright, colorful illustrations and a poetic text describe the life cycle of a spider.

8426. Goldin, Augusta. *Spider Silk* (1–3). Illus. by Joseph Low. 1964, Harper LB $10.89. The complete story of spiders and the various kinds of webs they weave.

8427. Hawes, Judy. *My Daddy Longlegs* (1–3). Illus. by Walter Lorraine. 1972, Harper $11.06; LB $9.89. In a simple text, the reader is given directions on how to study this spider.

8428. Lane, Margaret. *The Spider* (1–2). Illus. by Barbara Firth. 1982, Dial $9.95. Information is given on kinds of spiders and how they live.

8429. Levi, Herbert, and Levi, Lorna R. *Spiders and Their Kin* (7–9). Illus. by Nicholas Strekalovsky. 1969, Western paper $2.95. This handbook helps you identify types of spiders and gives you collecting tips.

8430. Lexau, Joan M. *The Spider Makes a Web* (2–4). Illus. by Arabelle Wheatley. 1979, Scholastic paper $1.95. A simple introductory account of the life cycle of a spider.

8431. Patent, Dorothy. *The Lives of Spiders* (5–8). Illus. 1980, Holiday $9.95. The social and antisocial habits of spiders.

8432. Patent, Dorothy. *Spider Magic* (2–5). Illus. 1982, Holiday LB $9.95. A simple introduction with amazing black-and-white photographs.

8433. Podendorf, Illa. *Spiders* (1–4). Illus. 1982, Childrens Pr. LB $10.60. Color photographs and a well-organized text are highlights of this simple introduction.

8434. Selsam, Millicent E., and Hunt, Joyce. *A First Look at Spiders* (2–4). Illus. by Harriett Springer. 1983, Walker $7.95; LB $8.85. An introduction to spiders to emphasize their anatomy.

8435. Victor, Joan Berg. *Tarantulas* (3–5). Illus. by author. 1979, Dodd $7.95. The facts about this spider are much less frightening than the incorrect stories often believed.

8436. Walther, Tom. *A Spider Might* (3–5). Illus. 1978, Scribners paper $4.95. All sorts of things you could do, if you were a spider.

Other Insects

8437. Conklin, Gladys. *I Watch Flies* (1–3). Illus. by Jean Zallinger. 1977, Holiday LB $6.95. There are 27 species of flies, and the reader learns about each.

8438. Conklin, Gladys. *Praying Mantis: The Garden Dinosaur* (2–3). Illus. by Glen Rounds. 1978, Holiday LB $6.95. Simple text and forceful drawings are used to tell about the life and habits of a praying mantis.

8439. Dallinger, Jane. *Grasshoppers* (4–7). Illus. 1981, Lerner LB $9.95. The life cycle of grasshoppers, well illustrated.

8440. Hawes, Judy. *Ladybug, Ladybug Fly Away Home* (2–4). Illus. 1967, Harper $10.89; paper $2.95. A lively account of the life cycle of this familiar beetle.

8441. Johnson, Sylvia A. *Ladybugs* (5–8). Illus. 1983, Lerner $8.95. A description of the ladybug, its habits, behavior, and uses.

8442. Johnson, Sylvia A. *Mantises* (4–6). Illus. 1984, Lerner $8.95. The life cycle and habits of this praying insect.

8443. McClung, Robert M. *Green Darner* (2–3). Illus. by Carol Lerner. 1980, Morrow $8.75; LB $8.40. The classic account of the life and habits of a dragonfly, originally published in 1956.

8444. Overbeck, Cynthia. *Dragonflies* (3–6). Illus. 1982, Lerner $8.95. The structure and life cycle of the dragonfly.

8445. Oxford Scientific Films. *Dragonflies* (3–5). Illus. by George Bernard. 1980, Putnam $8.95. The life cycle of the dragonfly with remarkable color photography.

8446. Ryder, Joanne. *Fireflies* (1–3). Illus. by Don Bolognese. 1977, Harper $8.61; LB $8.89. An easily read introduction to the life history of a firefly. Also use: *Fireflies in the Night* by Judy Hawes (1963, Harper paper $1.45).

Reptiles and Amphibians

General

8447. Ballard, Lois. *Reptiles* (1–4). Illus. 1982, Childrens Pr. LB $10.89. A straightforward, logically arranged introduction.

8448. Billings, Charlene W. *Salamanders* (3–6). Illus. 1981, Dodd $7.95. Several representative species and their habits are introduced.

8449. Fichter, George S. *Reptiles and Amphibians of North America* (4–6). Illus. by Sy Barlowe. 1982, 1982, Random paper $2.95. In small format, a beginner's guide from the Audubon Society.

8450. Harris, Susan. *Reptiles* (1–4). Illus. 1978, Watts $7.40. An easily read science book that supplies basic information.

8451. Hornblow, Leonora. *Reptiles Do the Strangest Things* (2–4). Illus. by Michael K. Frith. 1970, Random $4.95; LB $4.99. A description of the major reptiles and their living habits.

8452. Lambert, David. *Reptiles* (5–7). Illus. 1983, Gloucester $9.40. The 4 main reptile groups are introduced in text and many pictures.

8453. Patent, Dorothy. *Reptiles and How They Reproduce* (6–9). Illus. by Matthew Kalmenoff. 1977, Holiday $8.95. Introductory material on reptiles, followed by a detailed account of reproduction in various species.

8454. Smith, Hobart M. *Amphibians of North America* (5–9). Illus. by Sy Barlowe. 1978, Western $10.95; paper $7.95. A volume that supplies detailed color illustrations and material on identification and habitats.

8455. Stonehouse, Bernard. *A Closer Look at Reptiles* (3–5). Illus. by Gary Hincks, Alan Male and Phil Weare. 1979, Watts $8.90. A discussion of 4 groups of reptiles—snakes, lizards, crocodiles, and tortoises.

Crocodiles and Alligators

8456. Gross, Ruth Belov. *Alligators and Other Crocodilians* (3–5). Illus. 1978, Four Winds $8.95. The characteristics and behavior of 4 members of the crocodilian family.

8457. Lauber, Patricia. *Who Needs Alligators?* (2–4). Illus. 1974, Garrard $7.22. A very useful book on alligators—their habits, homes in ponds and streams, reproductive cycle, and animals that prey on them.

8458. Shaw, Evelyn. *Alligator* (1–2). Illus. by Frances Zweifel. 1972, Harper $7.64; LB $8.89. An accurate description of the alligator's life cycle told in simple narrative form.

Frogs and Toads

8459. Blassingame, Wyatt. *Wonders of Frogs and Toads* (3–7). Illus. 1975, Dodd $9.95. A well-illustrated account that introduces these amphibians.

8460. Cole, Joanna. *A Frog's Body* (3–5). Illus. 1980, Morrow $9.95; LB $9.55. An excellent introduction to the anatomy of a young bullfrog.

8461. Dallinger, Jane, and Johnson, Sylvia A. *Frogs and Toads* (2–5). Illus. 1982, Lerner LB $9.95. The life cycle and different species of these amphibians are described.

8462. Hawes, Judy. *Spring Peepers* (2–3). Illus. by Graham Booth. 1975, Harper LB $10.06. A simply written description of a tree frog's life, with advice on how to observe these common spring peepers.

8463. Hawes, Judy. *What I Like about Toads* (K–3). Illus. by James McCrea and Ruth McCrea. 1969, Harper LB $10.89; paper $2.95. A beginner's book that describes a toad's life, from egg to adult.

8464. Hawes, Judy. *Why Frogs Are Wet* (1–3). Illus. by Don Madden. 1968, Harper paper $2.95. The life of frogs and their history back to prehistoric times.

8465. Hogan, Paula Z. *The Frog* (2–3). Illus. by Geri K. Strigenz. 1979, Raintree $14.25. The growth and development of the frog in a well-illustrated account.

8466. Lane, Margaret. *The Frog* (K–4). Illus. by Grahame Corbett. 1981, Dial $7.95; paper $3.50. A description of a frog's life, from tadpole to maturity.

8467. McClung, Robert M. *Peeper, First Voice of Spring* (2–4). Illus. by Carol Lerner. 1977, Morrow

$8.59. This simple, direct account follows one tiny frog through its life cycle. Also use: *Hyla (Peep) Crucifer* by Carol Cornelius (1978, Child's World LB $6.95).

8468. Patent, Dorothy. *Frogs, Toads, Salamanders and How They Reproduce* (4–7). Illus. by Matthew Kalmenoff. 1975, Holiday $9.95. Fascinating facts about amphibians, with excellent material on their many adaptations.

Lizards

8469. Chace, G. Earl. *The World of Lizards* (6–8). Illus. 1982, Dodd LB $10.95. First a history of lizards, then a detailed description of many kinds.

8470. Conklin, Gladys. *I Caught a Lizard* (K–3). 1967, Holiday $6.95. A close-up look at a small lizard.

8471. Freschet, Berniece. *Lizard Lying in the Sun* (1–3). Illus. by Glen Rounds. 1975, Scribners LB $5.95. An easily read account of a lizard's adventure and escape.

8472. Hopf, Alice L. *Biography of a Komodo Dragon* (4–5). Illus. by Jean Zallinger. 1981, Putnam LB $6.99. An account of a young female Komodo dragon.

Snakes

8473. Brenner, Barbara. *A Snake-Lover's Diary* (5–9). Illus. 1970, Childrens Pr. $6.95. How to catch and care for reptiles, with many details on habits, appearance, and behavior.

8474. Broekel, Ray. *Snakes* (1–4). Illus. 1982, Childrens Pr. LB $10.60; paper $3.95. An introduction to snakes for the primary grades.

8475. Chace, G. Earl. *Rattlesnakes* (3–6). Illus. 1984, Dodd $7.95. A clear, well-organized text introduces the life and behavior of rattlesnakes. A well-illustrated companion volume is: *Rattlesnakes* by Russell Freedman (1984, Holiday $11.95).

8476. Cole, Joanna. *A Snake's Body* (2–5). Illus. 1981, Morrow $10.25; LB $9.84. An exploration of the body and living habits of the 6-foot python.

8477. Fichter, George S. *Poisonous Snakes* (4–6). Illus. 1982, Watts LB $8.90. Poisonous snakes are described by species, plus a section on treatment of snake bites.

8478. Freedman, Russell. *Killer Snakes* (4–6). Illus. 1982, Holiday $9.95. A look at the various groups of snakes that are dangerous to man.

8479. Green, Carl R., and Sanford, William R. *The Rattlesnake* (4–6). Illus. 1984, Crestwood $8.95. The structure, behavior, and habitat of the reptile are introduced.

8480. Gross, Ruth Belov. *Snakes* (3–5). Illus. 1975, Four Winds $7.95. An easy-to-read introduction, well illustrated with black-and-white and color photographs.

8481. Leen, Nina. *Snakes* (4–8). Illus. 1978, Holt $7.95. A brief text on the various life functions of snakes, expertly illustrated with fine photographs.

8482. Leetz, Thomas. *The T.F.H. Book of Snakes* (5–8). Illus. 1983, TFH Pubns. $6.95. An introduction to snakes and how to keep them as pets.

8483. McClung, Robert M. *Snakes: Their Place in the Sun* (3–5). Illus. 1979, Garrard $7.22. The structure and life cycle of the snake are covered in this introductory account.

8484. Roever, Joan M. *Snake Secrets* (6–9). Illus. 1979, Walker $11.85. This volume entertainingly explores the habits and behavior of snakes and how to raise one as a pet.

8485. Simon, Seymour. *Meet the Giant Snakes* (3–5). Illus. by Harriett Springer. 1979, Walker LB $10.85. A straightforward account of the habits and life cycle of such reptiles as pythons and boas.

8486. Simon, Seymour. *Poisonous Snakes* (3–6). Illus. by William Downey. 1981, Four Winds $11.95. The 4 main venomous groups of snakes are introduced.

8487. Zim, Herbert S. *Snakes* (3–5). Illus. 1949, Morrow $8.16. The snake, its structure, and anatomy are simply introduced.

Turtles and Tortoises

8488. Bare, Colleen Stanley. *The Durable Desert Tortoise* (3–5). Illus. by author. 1979, Dodd $7.95. The life cycle of the desert tortoise, including mating and egg-laying habits.

8489. Freschet, Berniece. *Turtle Pond* (K–3). Illus. by Donald Carrick. 1971, Scribners LB $6.95. Many facets of pond life, centering on a turtle and her eggs.

8490. Goode, John. *Turtles, Tortoises and Terrapins* (4–6). Illus. by Alec Bailey. 1974, Scribners paper $1.29. Many species from around the world are introduced, along with material on their history, characteristics, and life cycles.

8491. Holling, Holling C. *Minn of the Mississippi* (4–6). Illus. by author. 1951, Houghton $15.95; paper $3.95. A snapping turtle's trip down the Mississippi.

Birds

General

8492. Austin, Oliver L., Jr. *Families of Birds* (4–7). Illus. by Arthur Singer. 1971, Western paper $2.95. A simple guide to the classification of birds.

8493. Brenner, Barbara. *Have You Ever Heard of a Kangaroo Bird?* (4–6). Illus. by Irene Brady. 1980, Putnam $7.95. Twenty unusual birds are introduced.

8494. Cole, Joanna. *A Bird's Body* (3–5). Illus. 1982, Morrow $9.75; LB $8.88. A description of a bird's body and how this enables flight.

8495. Fichter, George S. *Birds of North America* (4–6). Illus. by Arthur Singer. 1982, Random paper $2.95. A tiny volume that introduces the major birds of North America.

8496. Friskey, Margaret. *Birds We Know* (K–4). Illus. by author. 1981, Childrens Pr. LB $10.60. Many color photographs are featured in this simple reader.

8497. Hornblow, Leonora. *Birds Do the Strangest Things* (1–3). Illus. by Michael K. Frith. 1965, Random $4.95. Simply presented material on many interesting birds such as the hummingbird and the ostrich.

8498. Kuchalla, Susan. *Birds* (K–3). Illus. by Gary Britt. 1982, Troll LB $8.89; paper $1.25. A simple introduction with a few short sentences and many illustrations.

8499. Lavine, Sigmund A. *Wonders of Flightless Birds* (5–8). Illus. 1982, Dodd LB $9.95. A description and history of the many species of birds, like penguins and ostriches, that don't fly.

8500. McGowen, Tom. *Album of Birds* (4–8). Illus. by Rod Ruth. 1982, Rand McNally $8.95; LB $8.97. A description of birds, their history, and habits, plus some common species.

8501. Pluckrose, Henry. *Small World of Birds* (2–4). Illus. by John Rignall and Maurice Wilson. 1979, Watts $2.95. The habits, behavior, and varieties of birds are briefly introduced in this simple account.

8502. Robbins, Chandler. *Birds of North America: A Guide to Field Identification* (6–9). Illus. by Arthur Singer. 1965, Western $10.95; paper $7.95. Describes hundreds of birds on the continent.

8503. Scott, Jack Denton. *Orphans from the Sea* (4–6). Illus. 1982, Putnam $10.95. An account of how injured and ailing seabirds are helped at the Suncoast Seabird Sanctuary in Florida.

8504. Selsam, Millicent E., and Hunt, Joyce. *A First Look at Birds* (2–4). Illus. by Harriett Springer. 1973, Walker $8.95. Through questions and simple text, the authors introduce the salient characteristics of birds and their various environmental adaptations.

8505. Shachtman, Tom. *The Birdman of St. Petersburg* (5–7). Illus. 1981, Macmillan $8.95. The story of a bird sanctuary in Florida and how orphaned and injured birds can be treated.

8506. Stone, Lynn M. *Birds of Prey* (1–4). Illus. 1983, Childrens Pr. $6.95. Excellent color photographs highlight this volume for the young reader.

8507. Storms, Laura. *The Bird Book* (K–3). Illus. by Sharon Lerner. 1982, Lerner LB $4.95. Twelve common North American birds are introduced with paintings and simple text.

8508. Wildsmith, Brian. *Birds by Brian Wildsmith* (K–4). Illus. by author. 1967, Oxford paper $7.95. Excellent illustrations of common birds.

8509. Zim, Herbert S. *Birds: A Guide to the Most Familiar American Birds* (6–9). Illus. 1956, Western $11.54; paper $2.95. A guide to the most commonly seen birds, with accompanying illustrations and basic materials.

Habits and Behavior

8510. Conklin, Gladys. *If I Were a Bird* (1–3). Illus. by Arthur Marokvia. 1965, Holiday $6.95. Songs, calls, and characteristics of 27 common birds. Musical notations for easily recognized calls.

8511. Flanagan, Geraldine, and Morris, Sean. *Window into a Nest* (5–9). Illus. 1976, Houghton $10.95. Through an ingenious device, the authors were able to see and record the behavior of a family of chickadees.

8512. Freedman, Russell. *How Birds Fly* (4–6). Illus. by Lorence Bjorklund. 1977, Holiday $8.95. A logical, lucid explanation of the elements in a bird's structure that contribute to its ability to fly.

8513. Gans, Roma. *Bird Talk* (1–3). Illus. by Jo Polseno. 1971, Harper LB $11.06. An explanation of how birds make different sounds on different occasions.

8514. Gans, Roma. *When Birds Change Their Feathers* (1–3). Illus. by Felicia Bond. 1980, Harper LB $9.89. An easily read account of the molting habits of birds.

8515. Graham, Ada. *Six Little Chickadees: A Scientist and Her Work with Birds* (4–5). Illus. 1982, Four Winds $8.95. A book on observing the life-styles of birds.

8516. Gustafson, Anita. *Burrowing Birds* (4–6). Illus. by Joel Schick. 1981, Lothrop $11.25; LB $11.88. An unusual group of birds in an interesting presentation.

8517. Henry, Marguerite. *Birds at Home* (2–5). Illus. by Jacob B. Abbott. 1972, Rand McNally $7.95. A description of over 20 common birds and how they care for their young.

8518. Kaufmann, John. *Birds Are Flying* (2–4). Illus. by author. 1979, Harper $10.53; LB $10.89. Information on how birds fly is given along with various ways of flying.

8519. Weber, William J. *Attracting Birds and Other Wildlife to Your Yard* (6–9). Illus. 1982, Holt $10.25. A guide to helping birds and animals survive during periods when food is scarce.

Reproduction

8520. Arnold, Caroline. *Five Nests* (1–3). Illus. by Ruth Sanderson. 1980, Dutton $7.95. An easy-to-read introduction to 5 bird species and how they care for their young.

8521. Flanagan, Geraldine. *Window into an Egg* (3–6). Illus. 1969, Addison $8.95. A valuable introduction to embryology for young readers.

8522. Henley, Karyn. *Hatch!* (2–4). Illus. by Susan Kennedy. 1980, Carolrhoda $6.95. A variety of nestmaking, egg-laying, and hatching methods are described.

8523. Johnson, Sylvia A. *Inside an Egg* (5–8). Illus. 1982, Lerner LB $9.95. The chicken egg, from fertilization to hatching.

8524. Lauber, Patricia. *What's Hatching Out of That Egg?* (2–4). Illus. 1979, Crown $9.95. Photographs enliven this question-and-answer approach to the birth of various animals.

8525. McCauley, Jane R. *Baby Birds and How They Grow* (1–4). Illus. 1984, National Geographic Society $6.95; LB $8.50. Pictures of 16 young birds and how they are cared for.

8526. McClung, Robert M. *The Amazing Egg* (5–7). Illus. by author. 1980, Dutton $12.95. An overview of the role of eggs in reproduction.

8527. May, Julian. *Millions of Years of Eggs* (3–5). Illus. by Tom Dolan. 1970, Creative Ed. $7.95. How eggs have been a method of reproduction throughout world history is presented with eye-catching illustrations.

8528. Selsam, Millicent E. *All about Eggs and How They Change into Animals* (K–3). Illus. by Helen Ludwig. 1952, Addison paper $6.95. A concise guide to how an egg develops. Also use: *Egg to Chick* (1970, Harper LB $8.89).

Ducks and Geese

8529. Ahlstrom, Mark E. *The Canada Goose* (4–6). Illus. 1984, Crestwood $8.95. This book introduces this bird and its migratory habits in color photographs and text.

8530. Fegely, Thomas D. *Wonders of Geese and Swans* (4–6). Illus. 1976, Dodd $9.95. The swans and geese of North America are introduced through interesting text, photographs, and line drawings.

8531. Fegely, Thomas D. *Wonders of Wild Ducks* (5–9). Illus. 1975, Dodd $9.95. A manual about ducks—habits, enemies, flight patterns—with emphasis on conservation.

8532. Ferguson, Dorothy. *Black Duck* (2–4). Illus. by Douglas Morris. 1978, Walker $6.95. Salt marsh life as seen from the viewpoint of a black duck and her 7 ducklings.

8533. Goldin, Augusta. *Ducks Don't Get Wet* (K–2). Illus. by Leonard Kessler. 1965, Harper LB $10.89. An easy experiment that enables children to clarify why ducks can shed water. Pictures of various ducks in migration.

8534. Isenbart, Hans-Heinrich. *A Duckling Is Born* (K–3). Illus. by Othmar Baumli. 1981, Putnam $9.95. From the mating of 2 ducks to the duckling's first swim.

8535. Nentl, Jerolyn Ann. *The Mallard* (3–5). Illus. 1983, Crestwood $8.95. This member of the duck family is introduced in text and many fine color photographs.

8536. Shaw, Evelyn. *A Nest of Wood Ducks* (1–2). Illus. by Cherryl Pape. 1976, Harper $7.64; LB $8.89. The yearly cycle of a wood duck, with a description of the mating, nesting, and brooding of one pair and the hatching of their young.

Eagles and Hawks

8537. Kaufmann, John, and Meng, Heinz. *Falcons Return* (5–9). Illus. 1975, Morrow $9.55. An introduction to how falcons live and the current methods used to try to save this endangered species.

8538. McConoughey, Jana. *The Bald Eagle* (3–5). Illus. 1983, Crestwood $8.95. In addition to introducing our national bird in text and pictures, efforts for preservation are detailed.

8539. Patent, Dorothy. *Where the Bald Eagles Gather* (4–7). Illus. 1984, Ticknor & Fields $11.95. A description of our national bird, its habits, and behavior.

Gulls

8540. Holling, Holling C. *Seabird* (4–6). 1978, Houghton LB $15.95; paper $5.95. A gull accompanies a whaling expedition.

Owls

8541. Catchpole, Olive. *Owls* (3–6). Illus. 1978, McKay $7.95. An attractive addition to the literature on one of the most interesting bird families.

8542. Flower, Phyllis. *Barn Owl* (1–3). Illus. by Cherryl Pape. 1978, Harper $7.64. An easily read science book about the first year in an owl's life.

8543. Frewer, Glyn. *Tyto: The Odyssey of an Owl* (6–8). Illus. by Dick Kramer. 1977, Lothrop $11.25. Five years in the life of a barn owl, carefully but dramatically told.

8544. Hunt, Patricia. *Snowy Owls* (4–6). Illus. 1982, Dodd LB $7.95. The nature, habits, and habitats of this Arctic bird are described.

8545. Hurd, Edith Thacher. *The Mother Owl* (2–5). Illus. by Clement Hurd. 1974, Little $4.95. An introduction to owls and their habits and habitats.

8546. Sadoway, Margaret W. *Owls: Hunters of the Night* (4–6). Illus. 1981, Lerner $7.95. Over a dozen varieties are described in text and color photographs.

8547. Storms, Laura. *The Owl Book* (2–4). Illus. by Jack Sadoway. 1983, Lerner $4.95. A basic introduction to 12 kinds of owls found in this country.

Penguins

8548. Bonners, Susan. *A Penguin Year* (K–4). Illus. by author. 1981, Delacorte $9.95; LB $9.89. An introduction to the life-style of penguins of the South Pole.

8549. Coldrey, Jennifer. *Penguins* (2–4). Illus. 1984, Andre Deutsch $9.95. Following a factual introduction, there is a delightful album of color photos.

8550. Hogan, Paula Z. *The Penguin* (1–3). Illus. by Geri K. Strigenz. 1979, Raintree $14.25. For very young readers, an account that has marvelous illustrations.

8551. Johnson, Sylvia A. *Penguins* (4–7). Illus. 1981, Lerner LB $9.95. Handsome photographs enliven the text of this introduction to penguins and their habitats.

8552. Lepthien, Emilie U. *Penguins* (1–4). Illus. 1983, Childrens Pr. $6.95. This account is distinguished by a simple text and fine color photographs.

8553. Stonehouse, Bernard. *Penguins* (5–8). Illus. by Trevor Boyer. 1980, McGraw $8.95. A simple introduction to the habits and characteristics of these birds.

8554. Strange, Ian J. *Penguin World* (6–9). Illus. by author. 1981, Dodd LB $8.95. The life and habits of penguins that live on an island of the Falklands.

8555. Todd, Frank S. *The Sea World Book of Penguins* (4–6). Illus. 1984, Harcourt $12.95; paper $6.95. A book of fascinating details and color photographs.

Other Birds

8556. Blassingame, Wyatt. *Wonders of Crows* (6–8). Illus. 1979, Dodd $9.95. Scientific facts are presented entertainingly, plus the inclusion of several humorous pet crow stories.

8557. Blassingame, Wyatt. *Wonders of Egrets, Bitterns, and Herons* (5–9). Illus. 1982, Dodd LB $9.95. A look at the kinds of these long-legged birds and their habits.

8558. Brenner, Barbara. *Baltimore Orioles* (1–2). Illus. by J. Winslow Higginbottom. 1974, Harper LB $8.89. The yearly life cycle of one oriole family, accurately and simply described for the beginning reader.

8559. Dunham, Terry. *The T.F.H. Book of Finches* (5–8). Illus. 1984, TFH Pubns. $6.95. A book on finches and how to keep them as pets.

8560. Gans, Roma. *Hummingbirds in the Garden* (2–4). Illus. 1969, Harper LB $10.89. An excellently illustrated introduction to this amazing bird.

8561. Heilman, Joan Rattner. *Bluebird Rescue* (4–6). Illus. 1982, Lothrop $11.25; LB $11.88. An introduction to the bluebird and the methods used to protect it from extinction.

8562. Hogan, Paula Z. *The Black Swan* (1–3). Illus. by Kinuko Craft. 1979, Raintree $14.25. An introductory account about this exotic bird.

8563. Holmgren, Virginia C. *The Pheasant* (3–6). Illus. 1983, Crestwood $8.95. The life cycle of this bird is presented in text and many color photos.

8564. Hopf, Alice L. *Chickens and Their Wild Relatives* (6–8). Illus. 1982, Dodd $9.95. Grouse, pheasant, and quail, as well as chickens, are introduced.

8565. Kaufmann, John. *Robins Fly North, Robins Fly South* (3–5). Illus. by author. 1970, Harper $10.89. An introduction to the life and habits of robins, with particular emphasis on annual migrations.

8566. Lavine, Sigmund A. *Wonders of Peacocks* (4–6). Illus. 1982, Dodd LB $9.95. This unusual bird is introduced in text and black-and-white photographs.

8567. Lavine, Sigmund A., and Scuro, Vincent. *Wonders of Turkeys* (4–6). Illus. 1984, Dodd $9.95. The story of turkeys in fact, fiction, and tradition.

8568. Martin, Lynne. *Puffin: Bird of the Open Seas* (4–6). Illus. by Ted Lewin. 1976, Morrow LB $8.59. A description of the life cycle, habits, and habitats of these interesting sea birds.

8569. Nolan, Dennis. *The Joy of Chickens* (4–7). Illus. by author. 1981, Prentice $12.95. An introduction to the world of chickens.

8570. Pasca, Sue-Rhee. *The T.F.H. Book of Canaries* (6–9). Illus. 1982, TFH Pubns. $6.95. A mature introduction to canaries through text and excellent color photographs.

8571. Pringle, Laurence. *Listen to the Crows* (4–6). Illus. by Ted Lewin. 1976, Harper $10.89. Twenty-three different sounds made by crows and their possible meanings.

8572. Scott, Jack Denton. *Discovering the American Stork* (5–9). Illus. 1976, Harcourt $6.50. A satisfying and thorough description of the life-style and habits of the American stork, complemented by excellent photographs.

8573. Scott, Jack Denton. *Discovering the Mysterious Egret* (5–7). Illus. 1978, Harcourt $7.95. A photo essay about a mysterious and fascinating bird.

8574. Stemple, David. *High Ridge Gobbler: A Story of the American Wild Turkey* (5–7). Illus. by Ted Lewin. 1979, Putnam $8.95. A brood of turkeys are examined, from hatching to their first mating.

Land Animals

General

8575. Berger, Gilda. *All in the Family: Animal Species Around the World* (2–4). Illus. by Tom Huffman. 1981, Putnam LB $6.99. A book that explores the subject of species and families of animals.

8576. Brady, Irene. *Wild Babies: A Canyon Sketchbook* (4–5). Illus. by author. 1979, Houghton LB $8.95. A sketchbook on such common wildlife as young deer, bobcats, and squirrels.

8577. Clemens, Virginia Phelps. *Super Animals and Their Unusual Careers* (4–6). 1979, Westminster $9.95. Animals that perform unusual tasks are highlighted.

8578. Cober, Alan E. *Cober's Choice* (3–7). Illus. by author. 1979, Dutton $10.95. A series of animal studies drawn by a master.

8579. Cooper, Gale. *Inside Animals* (3–5). Illus. by author. 1978, Little $7.95. The innards of 14 animals, from the simple amoeba to the guinea pig.

8580. Freedman, Russell. *Animal Superstars: Biggest, Strongest, Fastest, Smartest* (5–8). Illus. 1982, Morrow paper $5.95. The "Guinness" book of animal records.

8581. Goor, Ron, and Goor, Nancy. *All Kinds of Feet* (K–3). Illus. 1984, Harper $10.53; LB $10.89. In an easily read format, this is an account of all kinds of animal feet and their uses.

8582. Gustafson, Anita. *Some Feet Have Noses* (4–7). Illus. by April Pete Flory. 1983, Lothrop $12.00; LB $11.47. An introduction to feet in the animal world—from human to salamanders.

8583. Hartman, Jane E. *Armadillos, Anteaters, and Sloths: How They Live* (5–9). Illus. 1980, Holiday $7.95. A fine introduction to these interesting species.

8584. Hopf, Alice L. *Misplaced Animals, Plants and Other Living Creatures* (6–9). 1975, McGraw LB $7.95. An account that highlights some of nature's oddities.

8585. Johnson, Sylvia A. *Animals of the Deserts* (5–7). Illus. by Alcuin C. Dornisch. 1976, Lerner $5.95. One of a 6-volume set that describes and samples animal life in various climatic regions. Another volume is: *Animals of the Mountains* (1976, $5.95).

8586. Johnson, Sylvia A. *Animals of the Grasslands* (3–5). Illus. by Alcuin C. Dornisch. 1976, Lerner $5.95. One title in a fine series. Others are: *Animals of the Temperate Forests; Animals of the Tropical Forests* (both 1976, $5.95).

8587. Johnson, Sylvia A. *The Wildlife Atlas* (5–7). Illus. by Alcuin C. Dornisch. 1977, Lerner $14.95. Sixty animals of various species are presented in relation to the 6 major geographical areas of the world.

8588. Leen, Nina. *Rare and Unusual Animals* (4–6). Illus. by author. 1981, Holt $8.95. Forty lesser known animals are introduced, each with a photograph.

8589. Lumley, Kathryn Wentzel. *Work Animals* (1–4). Illus. 1983, Childrens Pr. $7.95. A brief survey of animals that help by performing chores.

8590. McClung, Robert M. *Mammals and How They Live* (4–6). Illus. 1963, Random $5.99. The life and structure of a number of mammals.

8591. Palazzo, Tony. *Animals of the Night* (4–6). Illus. by author. 1970, Lion LB $5.98. Interesting information about nocturnal denizens from all around the world.

8592. Palazzo, Tony. *Biggest and Littlest Animals* (4–7). Illus. by author. 1970, Lion LB $7.21. Many ways of comparing animals, including size and mobility, are explored.

8593. Patent, Dorothy. *Sizes and Shapes in Nature: What They Mean* (6–9). Illus. 1979, Holiday $7.95. An explanation of how environmental needs have affected structural changes in various animals.

8594. Pringle, Laurence. *Feral: Tame Animals Gone Wild* (6–9). Illus. 1983, Macmillan $9.95. The story of what happens when domestic animals run wild.

8595. Purcell, John Wallace. *African Animals* (1–4). Illus. 1982, Childrens Pr. $6.95. A brief introduction to the most common animals associated with Africa.

8596. Rosenthal, Mark. *Predators* (1–4). Illus. 1983, Childrens Pr. $7.95. Animals that prey on others are briefly introduced in text and fine photos.

8597. Selsam, Millicent E. *When an Animal Grows* (1–3). Illus. by John Kaufmann. 1966, Harper $7.64. A simple introduction to growth patterns among different species.

8598. Shuttlesworth, Dorothy E. *Animals That Frighten People: Fact Versus Myths* (4–6). 1973, Dutton $8.95. The truth behind the reputations of many animals.

8599. Simon, Seymour. *Animal Fact/Animal Fable* (2–3). Illus. by Diane de Groat. 1978, Crown $8.95. Facts and fallacies about animals, entertainingly presented.

8600. Tee-Van, Helen D. *Small Mammals Are Where You Find Them* (5–7). Illus. by author. 1966, Knopf $5.99. Seven small species of mammals from the United States are introduced with maps and identifying data.

8601. Torgersen, Don Arthur. *Elephant Herds and Rhino Horns* (4–6). Illus. 1982, Childrens Pr. LB $11.25; paper $3.95. Two animal species are carefully introduced in text and color photos. Also use: *Giraffe Hooves and Antelope Horns* (1982, Childrens Pr. LB $11.25; paper $3.95).

8602. Venino, Suzanne. *Amazing Animal Groups* (PS–3). Illus. 1981, National Geographic Society LB $12.95. A well-illustrated introduction to such groups as elephants and gorillas.

8603. Zim, Herbert S. *Mammals* (4–6). Illus. 1955, Western paper $2.95. Subtitle: *A Guide to Familiar Species.*

8604. Zim, Herbert S. *Mice, Men and Elephants: A Book about Mammals* (4–6). 1942, Harcourt $5.95. An introduction to the characteristics and habits of mammals.

8605. Zim, Herbert S. *What's Inside of Animals?* (3–6). Illus. by Herschel Wartik. 1953, Morrow $8.59. This well-organized account introduces the comparative anatomy of various animals.

Habits and Behavior

8606. Arnold, Caroline. *Animals That Migrate* (7–9). Illus. by Michele Zylman. 1982, Carolrhoda $7.95. A simple introduction to the "whys" and "wheres" of animal migration.

8607. Arnosky, Jim. *Secrets of a Wildlife Watcher* (3–6). Illus. by author. 1983, Lothrop $9.50; LB $9.12. Tips on how to examine animal behavior in the wild.

8608. Branley, Franklyn M. *Big Tracks, Little Tracks* (1–3). 1960, Harper $10.89. A simple guide to types of animal tracks.

8609. Ford, Barbara. *Why Does a Turtle Dove Live Longer Than a Dog?* (5–7). 1980, Morrow $8.75; LB $8.40. Subtitle: *A Report on Animal Longevity.*

8610. Freedman, Russell. *Animal Games* (K–4). Illus. by St. Tamara. 1976, Holiday $5.95. Sixteen common animals and the games they play.

8611. Freedman, Russell. *Can Bears Predict Earthquakes? Unsolved Mysteries of Animal Behavior* (5–7). Illus. 1982, Prentice $8.95. Mysteries of animal behavior are explored.

8612. Hornblow, Leonora, and Hornblow, Arthur. *Animals Do the Strangest Things* (1–3). Illus. by Michael K. Frith. 1964, Random $4.95; LB $4.99. Interesting facts and habits of such animals as the camel, lion, and polar bear.

8613. Kohl, Judith, and Kohl, Herbert. *Pack, Band and Colony: The World of Social Animals* (6–8). Illus. by Margaret La Farge. 1983, Farrar $11.95. How animals live together in various social arrangements.

8614. Kohl, Judith, and Kohl, Herbert. *The View from the Oak: The Private Worlds of Other Creatures* (6–8). Illus. by Roger Bayless. 1977, Scribners $12.95. An exciting exploration of the animal world as animals experience it.

8615. McCauley, Jane R. *The Way Animals Sleep* (PS–3). Illus. 1983, National Geographic Society $10.50; LB $12.95. The sleep habits and locations of 25 animals are discussed.

8616. McClung, Robert M. *Mysteries of Migration* (4–6). Illus. 1983, Garrard $7.22. The mystery of animal migration is explored in illustrations and text.

8617. National Geographic Society. *Secrets of Animal Survival* (4–8). Illus. 1983, National Geographic Society $8.75; LB $10.30. The survival tactics of animals in 5 geographical environments are discussed.

8618. Patent, Dorothy. *Hunters and the Hunted: Surviving in the Animal World* (4–6). Illus. 1981, Holiday LB $7.95. A well-illustrated account of predators and their prey.

8619. Peck, Robert Newton. *Path of Hunters: Animal Struggle in a Meadow* (4–6). Illus. by Betty Fraser. 1973, Knopf LB $5.99. Life-styles of several forms of wildlife—from brown beetle to skunk—are described.

8620. Rahn, Joan Elma. *Keeping Warm, Keeping Cool* (6–9). 1983, Atheneum $10.95. The heating and cooling systems of various animals.

8621. Sattler, Helen R. *Fish Facts and Bird Brains: Animal Intelligence* (4–6). Illus. by Giulio Maestro. 1984, Lodestar $10.95. A study of animal intelligence, from worms to primates.

8622. Selsam, Millicent E. *How Animals Live Together* (4–6). Illus. 1979, Morrow $8.40. A fascinating study of how various animals share their food and homes.

8623. Selsam, Millicent E. *How Animals Tell Time* (4–6). Illus. 1967, Morrow $9.55. A simple discussion of the built-in biological clocks that enable animals to regulate their activities.

8624. Walter, Eugene J., Jr. *Why Animals Behave the Way They Do* (6–8). Illus. 1981, Scribners $10.95. An introduction to animal behavior through a question-and-answer approach.

Babies

8625. Freedman, Russell. *Hanging On* (2–4). Illus. 1977, Holiday LB $5.95. The carrying and nurturing of 22 different animal babies, described with photographs and text.

8626. Hartman, Jane E. *How Animals Care for Their Young* (5–7). Illus. 1980, Holiday $7.95. How various insects, birds, and animals care for their young.

8627. Weber, William J. *Wild Orphan Babies* (6–9). Illus. 1978, Holt $9.75; paper $4.95. Subtitle: *Mammals and Birds: Caring for Them and Setting Them Free.*

8628. Weber, William J. *Wild Orphan Friends* (6–9). Illus. by author. 1980, Holt paper $3.50. A sequel to the author's *Wild Orphan Babies.*

8629. Zweifel, Frances. *Animal Baby-Sitters* (PS–4). Illus. by Irene Brady. 1981, Morrow $10.25; LB $9.84. How various social animals protect their young.

Camouflage

8630. Selsam, Millicent E. *Hidden Animals* (1–3). Illus. 1969, Harper $8.61; LB $8.89. The concept of animal camouflage is introduced and developed.

Communication

8631. Jacobs, Francine. *Secret Languages of Animals* (5–8). Illus. 1976, Morrow LB $6.73. An examination of the variety of ways in which animals send signals. For a younger group use: *What Is That Alligator Saying?* by Ruth Belov Gross (1972, Hastings $6.95).

8632. Ricciuti, Edward R. *Sounds of Animals at Night* (4–7). Illus. 1977, Harper $10.89; LB $8.79. How frogs, birds, and other animals make noises at night and what these sounds mean.

8633. Van Woerkom, Dorothy O. *Hidden Messages* (2–4). Illus. by Lynne Cherry. 1979, Crown LB $6.95. A book on animal communication in the animal kingdom, particularly as practiced by ants.

8634. Winter, Ruth. *Scent Talk among Animals* (4–6). Illus. by Richard Cuffari. 1977, Harper $9.57. Communication by scent and its implications for mating and survival are explored in this unusual nature book.

Defenses

8635. Schlein, Miriam. *Snake Fights, Rabbit Fights and More* (2–4). Illus. by Sue Thompson. 1979, Scholastic paper $1.95. An explanation of how and why animals fight each other.

Hibernation

8636. Barker, Will. *Winter-Sleeping Wildlife* (5–7). Illus. by Carl Burger. 1958, Harper $10.89. An exploration of animals that hibernate.

8637. Cosgrove, Margaret. *Wintertime for Animals* (3–5). Illus. by author. 1975, Dodd $6.95. How all kinds of life, including insects and reptiles, adjust to winter.

8638. Yabuuchi, Masayuki. *Animals Sleeping* (PS–K). Illus. 1983, Putnam $8.95. A picture book that shows the many ways animals settle down to sleep.

Homes

8639. Batherman, Muriel. *Animals Live Here* (1–3). Illus. 1979, Greenwillow $8.50; LB $8.99. An examination of animals arranged by where they live.

8640. Cohen, Daniel. *Animal Territories* (5–8). Illus. 1975, Hastings $7.95. How animals stake out and defend their territories, as well as implications for humans.

8641. Hopf, Alice L. *Whose House Is It?* (2–4). Illus. by Leigh Grant. 1980, Dodd $6.95. How and where animals live in the prairies.

8642. Leon, Dorothy. *The Secret World of Underground Creatures* (4–6). Illus. 1982, Messner $8.29.

An introduction to the animal life that spends most or all of its life underground.

8643.   Nussbaum, Hedda. *Animals Build Amazing Homes* (2–5). Illus. by Christopher Santore. 1979, Random LB $4.99. Fifteen examples are presented in easy-to-read text.

8644.   Podendorf, Illa. *Animal Homes* (1–4). Illus. 1982, Childrens Pr. $6.95. A general description of the types of homes animals use.

Ape Family

8645.   Alston, Eugenia. *Growing Up Chimpanzee* (2–3). Illus. by Haru Wells. 1975, Harper LB $11.49. A direct text that describes many aspects of a chimpanzee's life.

8646.   Amon, Aline. *Orangutan: Endangered Ape* (5–9). Illus. 1977, Atheneum $7.95. The story of this endangered species as seen through the lives of a mother and child.

8647.   Anderson, Norman D., and Brown, Walter R. *Lemurs* (4–6). Illus. 1984, Dodd $9.95. An appealing look at these endangered animals and their home in Madagascar.

8648.   Harding, Diana, and Manzolillo, Deborah. *Baboon Orphan* (4–6). Illus. by Nina Bohlen. 1981, Dutton $10.25. Baboon behavior is explored through the activities of 3 members of a troupe. Also use: *Chimps and Baboons* by Emily d'Aulaire (1974, National Wildlife $2.00).

8649.   Hunt, Patricia. *Gibbons* (4–6). 1983, Dodd $7.95. The life and habits of these small Asian apes.

8650.   Hurd, Edith Thacher. *The Mother Chimpanzee* (PS–3). Illus. by Clement Hurd. 1978, Little $6.95. The daily life in the growing up of a baby chimp under the watchful eyes of her mother.

8651.   Kevles, Bettyann. *Watching the Wild Apes: The Primate Studies of Goodall, Fossey and Galdikos* (6–9). 1976, Dutton $9.95. A thorough, fascinating survey of the people, methodology, and findings involved in 3 important studies of primates.

8652.   Koebner, Linda. *From Cage to Freedom: A New Beginning for Laboratory Chimpanzees* (5–9). Illus. 1981, Lodestar $10.75. The description of a project to save chimpanzees after they have been used in the laboratory. Also use: *Forgotten Animals: The Rehabilitation of Laboratory Primates* (1984, Lodestar $12.95).

8653.   Lumley, Kathryn Wentzel. *Monkeys and Apes* (1–4). Illus. 1982, Childrens Pr. $6.95. An introduction in simple language with many color illustrations.

8654.   McDearmon, Kay. *Gorillas* (4–6). Illus. 1979, Dodd $7.95. The life, habits, and society of the gorilla in text and photographs.

8655.   McDearmon, Kay. *Orangutans: The Red Apes* (4–6). Illus. 1983, Dodd $7.95. The life cycle, habits, and homes of orangutans are described.

8656.   Meyers, Susan. *The Truth about Gorillas* (K–3). Illus. by John Hamberger. 1980, Dutton $7.95. An easily read account that presents the true nature and habits of the gorilla.

8657.   Michel, Anna. *The Story of Nim* (3–6). Illus. 1980, Knopf $6.95; LB $6.99. A narrative about a chimpanzee who learned language.

8658.   Overbeck, Cynthia. *Monkeys: The Japanese Macaques* (4–7). Illus. 1981, Lerner LB $9.95. An account that focuses on the life cycle, homes, and enemies of the Macaque.

8659.   Selsam, Millicent E., and Hunt, Joyce. *A First Look at Monkeys and Apes* (1–3). Illus. by Harriett Springer. 1979, Walker LB $7.85. An introductory account that emphasizes principles of classification.

Bats

8660.   Kaufmann, John. *Bats in the Dark* (2–3). Illus. 1972, Harper LB $9.89. A succinct discussion of a variety of bats, their nocturnal habits, and food-gathering techniques.

8661.   Lauber, Patricia. *Bats: Wings in the Night* (4–6). 1968, Random LB $5.99. Based on scientific studies, lucid descriptions of the habits and distinctive features of the more than 800 varieties of this flying mammal.

8662.   Laycock, George. *Bats in the Night* (4–6). Illus. 1981, Four Winds $9.95. A thorough introduction to the structure and living habits of this misunderstood mammal.

8663.   Leen, Nina. *The Bat* (4–7). Illus. 1976, Holt $7.50. Annotated photographs that explore the life-style and usefulness of the bat.

8664.   Schlein, Miriam. *Billions of Bats* (4–6). Illus. by Walter Kessell. 1982, Harper $10.10; LB $9.89. A general description of the bat family and the various species found around the world.

Bears

8665.   Bailey, Bernadine. *Wonders of the World of Bears* (4–6). Illus. 1975, Dodd $9.95. An explanation of the various kinds of bears and how they live.

8666. Ford, Barbara. *Black Bear: The Spirit of the Wilderness* (6–8). Illus. 1981, Houghton $8.95. A full account of the black bear, its habitat, and nature.

8667. Freschet, Berniece. *Black Bear Baby* (1–3). Illus. by Jim Arnosky. 1981, Putnam LB $6.99. An easily read account of the first months of a black bear's life.

8668. Graham, Ada, and Graham, Frank. *Bears in the Wild* (3–6). Illus. by D. D. Tyler. 1981, Delacorte $8.95; LB $8.44; Dell paper $2.25. A thorough history of the black and grizzly bear in America.

8669. Kuchalla, Susan. *Bears* (K–3). Illus. by Kathie Kelleher. 1982, Troll LB $8.89; paper $1.25. Colorful illustrations and easy vocabulary are present in this brief introduction.

8670. McClung, Robert M. *Samson: Last of the California Grizzlies* (4–6). Illus. by Bob Hines. 1973, Morrow LB $8.16. The life story of a member of a now extinct species—the golden bear that is depicted on the California state flag.

8671. McDearmon, Kay. *Polar Bear* (3–5). Illus. 1976, Dodd $7.95. The life cycle of the polar bear, including material on defense mechanisms, mating habits, and how they are studied by humans.

8672. Moore, Tara. *Polar Bears* (2–5). Illus. 1982, Garrard $8.95. A look through drawings and text at this Arctic endangered species.

8673. Nentl, Jerolyn Ann. *The Grizzly* (4–6). Illus. 1984, Crestwood $8.95. The structure and behavioral patterns of this endangered species are given in pictures and text.

8674. Patent, Dorothy. *Bears of the World* (5–7). Illus. 1980, Holiday $9.95. A thorough and interesting account of 7 present-day species of bears.

8675. Rosenthal, Mark. *Bears* (1–4). Illus. 1983, Childrens Pr. $6.95. Various bears and their habits are introduced, mainly through color photographs.

8676. Schwartz, Alvin. *Fat Man in a Fur Coat: And Other Bear Stories* (5–8). Illus. 1984, Farrar $10.95. A collection of factual and fictional material on bears.

8677. Weaver, John L. *Grizzly Bears* (3–5). Illus. 1982, Dodd LB $7.95. A discussion of this fearsome animal that has become an endangered species.

Big Cats

8678. Adamson, Joy. *Born Free* (6–9). Illus. 1960, Pantheon $7.95; paper $3.95. A lioness is raised among people and then retrained to return to the wilds of Kenya. A sequel is: *Living Free: The Story of Elsa and Her Cubs* (1961, Harcourt $15.95).

8679. Bronson, Wilfrid S. *Cats* (4–6). Illus. by author. 1950, Harcourt $7.80. All about cats, from stray tomcats to the cats of the jungle. Also use: *The Big Cats* by Herbert S. Zim (1976, Morrow $7.20).

8680. Eaton, Randall L. *The Cheetah: Nature's Fastest Racer* (5–9). Illus. 1981, Dodd LB $9.95. The life and behavior of the cheetah and an appeal to help prevent their extinction.

8681. Hunt, Patricia. *Tigers* (4–8). Illus. 1981, Dodd LB $7.95. Many aspects of these large cats, including appearance and habits, are explored.

8682. McClung, Robert M. *Rajpur, Last of the Bengal Tigers* (4–6). Illus. by Irene Brady. 1982, Morrow $10.25. The life story of a Bengal tiger in Nepal.

8683. McDearmon, Kay. *Cougar* (3–5). Illus. 1977, Dodd $5.95. Two years in the lives of 2 cougar cubs are described graphically in text and photographs.

8684. Michel, Anna. *Little Wild Lion Cub* (1–3). Illus. by Tony Chen. 1980, Pantheon $6.95; LB $7.99. An introductory account of the habits of lions.

8685. Nentl, Jerolyn Ann. *The Wild Cats* (4–6). Illus. 1984, Crestwood $8.95. A description of the habits, appearance, and behavior of wild cats and of the various kinds.

8686. Overbeck, Cynthia. *Lions* (4–7). Illus. 1981, Lerner LB $9.95. The life of a lion is traced, plus information on its life-style and habits.

8687. Ryden, Hope. *Bobcat* (4–6). Illus. 1983, Putnam $10.95. A first look at the bobcat and its history, present habits, and behavior.

8688. Schaller, George B., and Selsam, Millicent E. *The Tiger: Its Life in the Wild* (5–8). Illus. by Richard Keanes and S. Schauer. 1969, Harper $8.79. Fascinating observations of the world's largest cat, which the authors studied and photographed in India's Kanha Park.

8689. Schick, Alice. *Serengeti Cats* (6–8). Illus. by Joel Schick. 1977, Harper $10.53. The hunting, mating, and rearing habits of types of cats that live in the Serengeti National Park in Tanzania.

8690. Torgersen, Don Arthur. *Lion Prides and Tiger Tracks* (4–6). Illus. 1982, Childrens Pr. LB $11.25; paper $3.95. A discussion of appearance and characteristics of these 2 branches of the cat family.

8691. Winston, Peggy D. *Wild Cats* (PS–3). Illus. 1981, National Geographic Society $12.20; LB $10.95. The photographs are the outstanding element in this introductory volume.

8692. Zim, Herbert S. *Little Cats* (2–4). Illus. 1978, Morrow $8.40. Included in this simple account is information on such cats as the lynx and the bobcat.

Elephants

8693. Hintz, Martin. *Tons of Fun: Training Elephants* (3–6). Illus. 1983, Messner LB $9.29. A look at the training of elephants and the tricks they can perform.

8694. Jurmain, Suzanne. *From Trunk to Tail: Elephants Legendary and Real* (6–8). Illus. 1978, Harcourt $6.95. The elephant in fact, fiction, and legend.

8695. Lavine, Sigmund A., and Scuro, Vincent. *Wonders of Elephants* (5–8). Illus. 1980, Dodd $9.95. The structure and living habits of both African and Indian elephants are presented in a lively way.

8696. Michel, Anna. *Little Wild Elephant* (PS–1). Illus. by Peter Parnall and Virginia Parnall. 1979, Pantheon $6.95; LB $7.99; Scholastic paper $1.50. The first 4 years of an elephant's life told in simple text.

8697. Overbeck, Cynthia. *Elephants* (4–7). Illus. 1981, Lerner LB $9.95. Elephants and their life cycle and habitats are discussed in this well-illustrated volume.

8698. Posell, Elsa. *Elephants* (1–4). Illus. 1982, Childrens Pr. LB $10.60. An introductory volume that combines a good text with fine illustrations.

8699. Stewart, John. *Elephant School* (4–7). Illus. 1982, Pantheon $10.95; LB $10.99. The story of how a 15-year-old Cambodian boy becomes an elephant trainer.

8700. Van Wormer, Joe. *Elephants* (5–8). Illus. 1976, Dutton $8.95. Excellent photographs highlight this book, which contains only short passages of text.

Giraffes

8701. Brown, Louise C. *Giraffes* (3–5). Illus. by Audrey Ross. 1980, Dodd $5.95. A clear and straightforward account about the world's tallest animal.

8702. MacClintock, Dorcas. *Natural History of Giraffes* (3–6). Illus. 1973, Scribners $7.95. The habits, behavior, and appearance of giraffes.

Deer Family

8703. Ahlstrom, Mark E. *The Whitetail* (3–6). Illus. 1983, Crestwood $8.95. The habits and behavior of this member of the deer family are introduced in text and color photos.

8704. Bare, Colleen Stanley. *Mule Deer* (4–6). Illus. 1981, Dodd $7.95. A life story of a mule deer buck, told through pictures and text.

8705. Nentl, Jerolyn Ann. *The Caribou* (4–6). Illus. 1984, Crestwood $8.95. The physical appearance, activities, and habits of the caribou are explained, plus details on where one can be found.

8706. Rue, Leonard Lee. *The World of the White-Tailed Deer* (4–6). Illus. 1966, Harper $12.45. A year in the life of a white-tailed deer, beautifully illustrated with photographs.

8707. Scott, Jack Denton. *Moose* (4–6). Illus. 1982, Putnam $9.95. An attractive, informative introduction to the moose family.

Marsupials

8708. Eugene, Toni. *Koalas and Kangaroos: Strange Animals of Australia* (PS–3). Illus. 1982, National Geographic Society $12.20. Beautiful pictures of Australian animals highlight this volume.

8709. Hunt, Patricia. *Koalas* (3–5). Illus. 1980, Dodd LB $7.95. A brief survey of this famous Australian animal.

8710. Lavine, Sigmund A. *Wonders of Marsupials* (5–8). Illus. 1979, Dodd $9.95. The physical appearance and living habits of several of the most important species are covered.

8711. Noguere, Suzanne et al. *Little Koala* (1–3). Illus. by Tony Chen. 1979, Holt $6.95. The early months in the life of this Australian marsupial.

8712. Sherman, Geraldine. *Animals with Pouches—The Marsupials* (2–4). Illus. by Lorence Bjorklund. 1978, Holiday $7.95. Seventeen marsupials, including kangaroos, koalas, and opossums, are described.

Pandas

8713. Bonners, Susan. *Panda* (3–5). Illus. 1978, Delacorte $6.95; LB $6.89. The birth and life of a giant panda in text and pictures.

8714. Gross, Ruth Belov. *A Book about Pandas* (2–4). Illus. 1973, Dial $4.95; LB $4.58; Scholastic paper $1.50. This excellent introduction to the panda's habits and way of life contains many photographs.

8715. Rau, Margaret. *The Giant Panda at Home* (4–6). Illus. by Eva Hulsmann. 1977, Knopf LB $6.99. Beautiful full-page drawings illustrate this account of physical characteristics and habits of the panda.

8716. Schlein, Miriam. *Project Panda Watch* (3–6). Illus. by Robert Shetterly. 1984, Atheneum $11.95. An account of the work of Chinese and American scientists studying pandas in China.

Rodents

8717. Bare, Colleen Stanley. *Ground Squirrel* (4–6). Illus. 1980, Dodd $7.95. An introduction to the life and habits of these squirrels. Followed by: *Tree Squirrels* (1983, Dodd $8.95).

8718. Bare, Colleen Stanley. *Rabbits and Hares* (4–7). Illus. 1983, Dodd $8.95. A well-organized text that introduces all types of rabbits and their relatives.

8719. Brady, Irene. *Beaver Year* (3–5). Illus. by author. 1976, Houghton $8.99. The story of 2 young beavers, from birth to founding their own colony, told convincingly and with authenticity.

8720. Brady, Irene. *Wild Mouse* (2–4). Illus. by author. 1976, Scribners $6.95. Told in diary form, this is the story of the first 16 days of 3 white-footed mice.

8721. Feder, Jan. *The Life of a Rabbit* (3–4). Illus. by Tilman Michalski. 1982, Childrens Pr. $6.95. Through the story of a single rabbit named Buck, information is given about the habits and behavior of rabbits.

8722. Hess, Lilo. *Diary of a Rabbit* (3–6). Illus. 1982, Scribners $10.95. Photographs and text are used to describe the life of a rabbit named Daisy.

8723. Hogan, Paula Z. *The Beaver* (K–3). Illus. by Yoshi Miyake. 1979, Raintree $14.75. The life cycle and habits of the beaver in a simple narrative.

8724. Lane, Margaret. *The Beaver* (2–4). Illus. by David Nockels. 1982, Dial $8.95. A handsome book filled with lush illustrations and basic information about these unusual creatures.

8725. Lane, Margaret. *The Squirrel* (K–4). Illus. by Kenneth Lilly. 1981, Dial $7.95; paper $3.95. A discussion of the habits and habitats of both red and grey squirrels.

8726. Lavine, Sigmund A. *Wonders of Woodchucks* (4–6). Illus. 1984, Dodd $9.95. Photographs and drawings help introduce this rodent and its ways.

8727. McConoughey, Jana. *The Squirrels* (3–5). Illus. 1983, Crestwood $8.95. Squirrels and their characteristics and habits are described in color photographs and text.

8728. McNulty, Faith. *Woodchuck* (1–3). Illus. 1974, Harper $7.64; LB $8.89. The life cycle of the woodchuck told in text and pictures.

8729. Miles, Miska. *Beaver Moon* (2–5). Illus. by John Schoenherr. 1978, Little $6.95. An old beaver survives many dangers to build a new home.

8730. Nentl, Jerolyn Ann. *The Beaver* (3–5). Illus. 1983, Crestwood $8.95. This hardworking animal is introduced in clear text and many color photographs.

8731. Oxford Scientific Films. *Harvest Mouse* (3–5). Illus. by George Bernard. 1982, Putnam $8.95. Superb photographs highlight this introductory account.

8732. Oxford Scientific Films. *The Wild Rabbit* (3–5). Illus. by George Bernard. 1980, Putnam $8.95. Vivid color photographs highlight this account of a wild rabbit's life and habitat.

8733. Pringle, Laurence. *Vampire Bats* (5–7). Illus. 1982, Morrow $8.75; LB $7.92. A much-feared and misunderstood rodent is explored in text with some photographs.

8734. Rounds, Glen. *The Beaver: How He Works* (2–4). Illus. by author. 1976, Holiday $6.95. Highlights the construction feats of the beaver.

8735. St. Tamara. *Chickaree: A Red Squirrel* (1–3). Illus. by author. 1980, Harcourt $7.95. An introduction to the habits and life cycle of the red squirrel.

8736. Silverstein, Alvin, and Silverstein, Virginia B. *Mice: All about Them* (3–6). Illus. 1980, Harper $9.95; LB $9.79. An introduction to mice, their habits, and to raising them as pets. Also use: *Wonders of Mice* by Sigmund A. Lavine (1980, Dodd LB $9.95).

Sheep and Goats

8737. Ahlstrom, Mark E. *The Sheep* (4–6). Illus. 1984, Crestwood $8.95. The physical appearance, behavior, and usefulness of this farm animal are explained.

8738. Chiefari, Janet. *Kids Are Baby Goats* (2–4). Illus. 1984, Dodd $9.95. The life of baby goats on a New York dairy farm.

8739. Jenkins, Marie M. *Goats, Sheep and How They Live* (5–7). Illus. by Matthew Kalmenoff. 1978, Holiday $7.95. The characteristics, habitat, and various species are among the topics treated.

8740. Lavine, Sigmund A., and Scuro, Vincent. *Wonders of Goats* (5–8). Illus. 1980, Dodd $9.95. The characteristics, history, lore, and uses of goats are explained.

8741. Lavine, Sigmund A., and Scuro, Vincent. *Wonders of Sheep* (5–8). Illus. 1983, Dodd $9.95. Both domesticated and wild sheep are introduced, plus material on their habits and life-styles.

8742. McDearmon, Kay. *Rocky Mountain Bighorns* (3–5). Illus. 1980, Dodd $7.95. The life and habits of these sturdy acrobatic mountain animals are detailed.

Wolves, Foxes, and Coyotes

8743. Ahlstrom, Mark E. *The Foxes* (3–6). Illus. 1983, Crestwood $8.95. A brief account that covers anatomy, habits, and the life cycles.

8744. Barry, Scott. *The Kingdom of the Wolves* (4–6). Illus. 1979, Putnam $9.95. A sympathetic view of the life and habits of the wolf enhanced by the author's photographs.

8745. Dixon, Paige. *Silver Wolf* (3–6). Illus. 1973, Atheneum paper $1.95. A sympathetic portrayal of an often misunderstood animal.

8746. Hansen, Rosanna. *Wolves and Coyotes* (4–5). Illus. by Pamela Baldwin Ford. 1981, Grosset $6.95. The habits and behavior of wolves and coyotes are explored.

8747. Lane, Margaret. *The Fox* (1–4). Illus. by Kenneth Lilly. 1982, Dial $9.95; paper $3.50. This book explores the life of a fox, from birth to maturity.

8748. McConoughey, Jana. *The Wolves* (3–5). Illus. 1983, Crestwood $8.95. A description of wolves is given, plus information on how they live.

8749. McDearmon, Kay. *Foxes* (3–5). Illus. 1981, Dodd LB $7.95. A survey of North American foxes and where and how they live.

8750. Pringle, Laurence. *The Controversial Coyote* (6–8). Illus. 1977, Harcourt $5.95. The "pros" and "cons" of the coyote in the ecological cycle are explored.

8751. Pringle, Laurence. *Wolfman: Exploring the World of Wolves* (6–9). Illus. 1983, Scribners $12.95. The story of David Meek, a wildlife biologist, and what he has found out about wolves.

Other Animals

8752. Arundel, Jocelyn. *Land of the Zebra* (1–6). Illus. by Angeline Culfogienis. 1974, National Wildlife $2.00. The story of the life and habits of the zebra.

8753. Blassingame, Wyatt. *Porcupines* (4–6). Illus. 1982, Dodd LB $7.95. An introduction to these animals, their defense mechanisms, and their behavior.

8754. Blassingame, Wyatt. *Skunks* (4–6). Illus. 1981, Dodd LB $6.95. Striped, spotted, and hog-nosed skunks are discussed.

8755. Blassingame, Wyatt. *The Strange Armadillo* (4–6). Illus. 1983, Dodd $7.95. A look at the life and habits of this amazing animal.

8756. Blassingame, Wyatt. *Wonders of Raccoons* (5–7). Illus. 1977, Dodd $9.95. An affectionate but not coy description of the life-style and habits of this mischievous creature.

8757. Dinneen, Betty. *The Family Howl* (4–7). Illus. by Stefen Bernath. 1981, Macmillan $8.95. A year in the life of a family of jackals.

8758. Dinneen, Betty. *Striped Horses: The Story of a Zebra Family* (5–7). Illus. by Stefen Bernath. 1982, Macmillan $9.95. An informational book told in story form about a family of zebras in the Nairobi National Park.

8759. Earle, Olive L. *Camels and Llamas* (4–6). Illus. 1961, Morrow $9.36. The history and characteristics of these animals.

8760. Goodall, Daphne Machin. *Zebras* (2–4). Illus. 1978, Raintree $14.65. Good introductory material on this frequently misunderstood animal.

8761. Hopf, Alice L. *Hyenas* (4–6). Illus. 1983, Dodd $7.95. The life and habits of this much maligned animal.

8762. Hopf, Alice L. *Pigs Wild and Tame* (6–8). Illus. 1979, Holiday $7.95. Domestic breeds are discussed, as well as such wild varieties as the warthog and peccary.

8763. Lavine, Sigmund A. *Wonders of Hippos* (4–7). Illus. 1983, Dodd $9.95. The habits, behavior, and lore of the mammoth beast are described.

8764. Lavine, Sigmund A. *Wonders of Rhinos* (4–7). Illus. 1982, Dodd $8.95. The types and habits of rhinos, plus material on them as endangered species.

8765. Lavine, Sigmund A., and Scuro, Vincent. *Wonders of Donkeys* (5–8). Illus. 1979, Dodd $9.95. The history and habits of this much misunderstood animal.

8766. Lavine, Sigmund A., and Scuro, Vincent. *Wonders of Mules* (5–7). Illus. 1982, Dodd LB $9.95. The story of mules, how they came to be, and the many uses they serve.

8767. MacClintock, Dorcas. *A Raccoon's First Year* (4–6). Illus. 1982, Scribners $10.95. A photographic study of an orphaned raccoon cub, from infancy to parenthood.

8768. Nentl, Jerolyn Ann. *The Raccoon* (4–6). Illus. 1984, Crestwood $8.95. This nocturnal animal is introduced in full color pictures and a straightforward text.

8769. Patent, Dorothy. *Raccoons, Coatimundis and Their Family* (4–7). Illus. 1979, Holiday $8.95. An authoritative account of this mammal family, including pandas.

8770. Patent, Dorothy. *Weasels, Otters, Skunks and Their Families* (4–6). Illus. 1973, Holiday $8.95. These animals and their life-styles are interestingly introduced.

8771. Rau, Margaret. *Musk Oxen: Bearded Ones of the Arctic* (3–7). Illus. by Patricia Collins. 1976, Harper $9.89. A fine introduction to the habits and living problems of these huge arctic beasts.

8772. Rue, Leonard Lee, III, and Owen, William. *Meet the Opossum* (5–8). Illus. 1983, Dodd LB $7.95. Excellent photographs highlight this introduction to this unusual animal.

8773. Schlein, Miriam. *Lucky Porcupine!* (PS). Illus. by Martha Weston. 1980, Four Winds $8.95. A simple text and expressive drawings are used to introduce the porcupine.

8774. Scuro, Vincent. *Wonders of Zebras* (4–7). Illus. 1983, Dodd $9.95. The "whys" and "wherefores" of this animal's appearance are explained, plus material on its behavior.

8775. Waters, John F. *Camels: Ships of the Desert* (1–3). Illus. by Reynold Ruffins. 1974, Harper LB $10.89. A simple text that concentrates on how the camel can withstand harsh desert life.

Oceanography, Marine, and Freshwater Life

Oceanography

8776. Asimov, Isaac. *How Did We Find Out about Life in the Deep Sea?* (4–6). Illus. by David Wool. 1982, Walker $7.95; LB $8.85; Avon paper $1.95. What is under the sea and how we found out about it.

8777. Berger, Melvin. *Oceanography Lab* (4–6). Illus. 1973, Harper $10.89. The work of oceanographers and their laboratories are described in simple, clear language.

8778. Blumberg, Rhoda. *The First Travel Guide to the Bottom of the Sea* (5–8). Illus. 1983, Lothrop $10.00. An imaginary research submarine tours the ocean's bottom.

8779. Boyer, Robert E. *The Story of Oceanography* (6–8). 1975, Harvey House $7.29. An introduction to various forms of plant and animal life in the sea.

8780. Carson, Rachel. *The Sea Around Us* (6–8). Illus. 1958, Oxford $19.95. A special, well-illustrated edition of the adult title.

8781. Carter, Katharine Jones. *Oceans* (1–4). Illus. 1982, Childrens Pr. LB $10.60. A well-organized, simple account for the primary grades.

8782. Cook, Jan Leslie. *The Mysterious Undersea World* (3–6). Illus. 1980, National Geographic Society LB $8.50. A richly illustrated book on the sea and its inhabitants.

8783. Davies, Eryl. *Ocean Frontiers* (4–8). Illus. 1980, Viking $11.50. All kinds of equipment, such as diving suits, are described and pictured in this book.

8784. Elting, Mary. *Mysterious Seas* (3–6). Illus. by Fiona Reid. 1983, Putnam $7.95. Some unusual characteristics of sea creatures are explored.

8785. Goldin, Augusta. *The Bottom of the Sea* (1–3). Illus. by Ed Emberley. 1966, Harper $10.53. A description of the plants and animals that live on the bottom of the ocean. Also use: *The Sunlit Sea* (1968, Harper $11.06).

8786. Hargreaves, Pat, ed. *The Antarctic* (4–8). Illus. 1981, Silver Burdett $13.00. The first of 8 volumes on seas and oceans that explore not only their history and ecology but also the countries that border them. Others in this series are: *The Arctic; The Atlantic; The Caribbean and Gulf of Mexico; The Indian Ocean; The Mediterranean; The Pacific; The Red Sea and Persian Gulf* (all 1981, $13.00).

8787. Lambert, David. *The Oceans* (4–7). Illus. 1984, Watts $9.40. An English book that explores the nature of oceans and gives a rundown on what we know of them.

8788. Miller, Susanne Santoro. *Whales and Sharks and Other Creatures of the Deep* (3–6). Illus. by Lisa Bonforte. 1982, Little $6.95. A wide range of sea creatures is briefly introduced.

8789. Myers, Arthur. *Sea Creatures Do Amazing Things* (2–4). Illus. by Jean Zallinger. 1981, Random LB $5.99. Such sea creatures as jellyfish and giant clams are described in this easily read book.

8790. Oleksy, Walter. *Treasures of the Deep: Adventures of Undersea Exploration* (5–8). Illus. 1984, Messner $9.79. A fine collection of accounts involving all sorts of underwater adventures.

8791. Pick, Christopher C. *The Young Scientist Book of the Undersea* (4–7). Illus. 1978, EMC $7.95. Essential information is covered interestingly in this British import.

8792. Podendorf, Illa. *Animals of Sea and Shore* (1–4). Illus. 1982, Childrens Pr. LB $10.60. A fine introduction to marine life for primary grades.

8793. Polking, Kirk. *Oceans of the World: Our Essential Resource* (5–8). Illus. 1983, Putnam $14.95. The many resources of the oceans are explored and the issues and problems involved with them.

8794. Poynter, Margaret, and Collins, Donald. *Under the High Seas: New Frontiers in Oceanography* (5–7). Illus. 1983, Atheneum $10.95. The science of oceanography, its concerns, and accomplishments are discussed.

8795. Russell, Solveig Paulson. *What's Under the Sea?* (3–5). Illus. by Nancy Gugelman Johnstone. 1982, Abingdon $8.95. An introduction to the various layers of the ocean and how we find out about them.

8796. Rutland, Jonathan. *The Sea* (5–7). Illus. 1984, Silver Burdett $10.50. The nature of oceans and how we find out about them.

8797. Sabin, Louis. *Wonders of the Sea* (1–3). Illus. by Bert Dodson. 1982, Troll LB $8.89; paper $1.95. An easy-to-read account for primary grades that covers basic topics.

8798. Settle, Mary Lee. *Water World* (5–8). Illus. 1984, Dutton $10.63. A history of what we have learned about the ocean, starting with myths and ending with the present.

8799. Updegraff, Imelda, and Updegraff, Robert. *Seas and Oceans* (3–5). Illus. 1981, Childrens Pr. $8.95; paper $3.50. A simple book that explains such phenomena as tidal waves.

8800. Weiss, Malcolm E. *One Sea, One Law: The Fight for a Law of the Sea* (6–9). Illus. 1982, Harcourt $10.95. A book that describes the riches of the sea and how these riches have been abused as well as used.

8801. Wright, Thomas. *The Undersea World* (5–7). Illus. 1981, Silver Burdett LB $13.80. An account of the life and riches of the sea world.

Waves, Tides, and Currents

8802. Berger, Melvin. *Disastrous Floods and Tidal Waves* (4–7). Illus. 1981, Watts LB $8.90. The reasons for various kinds of floods and sources of prevention when possible.

8803. Brendze, Ruth. *The Gulf Stream* (5–7). Illus. by Helene Carter. 1945, Vanguard $9.95. An examination of water currents, plus the Gulf Stream and its importance.

Sea Mammals

8804. Brown, Joseph E. *Wonders of Seals and Sea Lions* (5–7). Illus. 1976, Dodd $9.95. An excellent introduction to the various types of these sea animals and how they live.

8805. Brown, Louise C. *Elephant Seals* (3–4). Illus. 1979, Dodd $5.99. A simple introduction to the habits and life-style of elephant seals.

8806. Fields, Alice. *Seals* (2–5). Illus. by David Astin. 1980, Watts LB $8.60. An easily read, brief introduction to seals.

8807. May, Julian. *Sea Otter* (3–5). Illus. by William Barss. 1972, Creative Ed. $8.95. The habits of sea otters, plus a discussion of the way in which they are threatened with extinction and are now a protected species.

8808. Meyers, Susan. *Pearson: A Harbor Seal Pup* (3–5). Illus. 1981, Dutton $9.95. Five months in the life of an orphaned harbor seal pup.

8809. Rabinowich, Ellen. *Seals, Sea Lions, and Walruses* (5–7). Illus. by author. 1980, Watts LB $8.90. The life and habits of these 3 marine mammals are discussed.

8810. Scheffer, Victor B. *A Natural History of Marine Mammals* (6–9). Illus. by Peter Parnall. 1976, Scribners paper $5.95. Six marine mammals, including sea otters and 2 types of seals, are thoroughly described.

8811. Scott, Jack Denton. *The Fur Seals of Pribilof* (4–8). Illus. 1983, Putnam $10.95. The story of the Alaskan fur seals and their yearly meeting on the Pribilof Islands.

8812. Shaw, Evelyn. *Elephant Seal Island* (1–2). Illus. by Cherryl Pape. 1978, Harper $7.64; LB $8.89. A simple account of seal life told in story form.

8813. Shaw, Evelyn. *Sea Otters* (1–3). Illus. by Cherryl Pape. 1980, Harper $7.64; LB $8.89. An easily read account of a mother sea otter and how she cares for her son.

8814. Torgersen, Don Arthur. *Killer Whales and Dolphin Play* (4–6). Illus. 1982, Childrens Pr. LB $11.25. Two deep-sea animals described in text and outstanding color pictures.

Dolphins

8815. Fox, Michael W. *The Way of the Dolphin* (5–7). Illus. by Betty J. Lewis. 1981, Acropolis $8.95. The ways of dolphins are recounted in this story of Nick-Nick, a dolphin, and his family.

8816. Lauber, Patricia. *The Friendly Dolphins* (3–4). Illus. by Jean Simpson. 1963, Random LB $5.99. Scientific facts and deductions, drawings, diagrams, and photographs are explained. Also use: *Dolphins* by Mickie Compere (1970, Scholastic paper $1.50).

8817. Morris, Robert A. *Dolphin* (K–3). Illus. by Mamoru Funai. 1975, Harper LB $8.89; paper $2.95. A simple account of the first 5 months of this lovable sea mammal.

Whales

8818. Bunting, Eve. *The Sea World Book of Whales* (5–7). Illus. 1980, Harcourt $9.95. An account of the evolution, habits, and dangers involving whales.

8819. Gardner, Robert. *The Whale Watchers' Guide* (6–8). Illus. by Don Sineti. 1984, Messner $10.79; paper $5.95. Not only a guide to this spectator sport but also a fine introduction to whales and their behavior.

8820. Graham, Ada, and Graham, Frank. *Whale Watch* (6–8). Illus. 1978, Delacorte $7.95; LB $7.89; Dell paper $2.25. A history of the whale, with emphasis on its present precarious position.

8821. Harris, Susan. *Whales* (2–4). Illus. by Jim Channell. 1980, Watts $8.60. A well-organized introductory narrative that covers basic material thoroughly.

8822. Hoke, Helen, and Pitt, Valerie. *Whales* (4–7). Illus. by Thomas R. Funderburk. 1981, Watts $8.90. An introduction to the types, characteristics, and habits of whales, porpoises, and dolphins.

8823. Hurd, Edith Thacher. *The Mother Whale* (2–3). Illus. by Clement Hurd. 1973, Little $5.95. This simple informative description of the life cycle of the sperm whale begins with the birth of a calf and its gradual growth to independence; attractively illustrated with block prints.

8824. Jacobs, Francine. *Sounds in the Sea* (4–6). Illus. by Jean Zallinger. 1977, Morrow LB $7.63. The noisy sea is examined, with special attention to the language of the whale and porpoise.

8825. McGovern, Ann. *Little Whale* (2–4). Illus. by John Hamberger. 1979, Four Winds $8.95; Scholastic paper $1.95. The life of a humpback whale from birth to adulthood.

8826. McGowen, Tom. *Album of Whales* (4–6). Illus. by Rod Ruth. 1980, Rand McNally $8.95. An introduction to the history of whales, their habits, and species.

8827. McNulty, Faith. *Whales, Their Life in the Sea* (4–6). Illus. by John Schoenherr. 1975, Harper $10.89. A variety of interesting information is given about these large sea animals.

8828. Mizumura, Kazue. *The Blue Whale* (2–3). Illus. 1971, Harper $10.89. An easy-to-read book about the blue whale, its habits, and how it is threatened by humans. Also use: *Catch a Whale by the Tail* by Edward R. Ricciuti (1969, Harper LB $8.89).

8829. Patent, Dorothy. *Whales: Giants of the Deep* (5–8). Illus. 1984, Holiday $12.95. A fine introduction to various kinds of whales and where and how they live.

8830. Posell, Elsa. *Whales and Other Sea Mammals* (1–4). Illus. 1982, Childrens Pr. $6.95. A description of these sea animals in large type and many color illustrations.

8831. Selsam, Millicent E., and Hunt, Joyce. *A First Look at Whales* (2–3). Illus. by Harriett Springer. 1980, Walker LB $8.85. Descriptions of whales are included that show the various species and how they differ from fish.

Fish

8832. Arnold, Caroline. *Electric Fish* (3–5). Illus. by George Gershinowitz. 1980, Morrow $8.75; LB $8.40. Many fish—not just eels, but even sharks—use electric signals.

8833. Broekel, Ray. *Dangerous Fish* (1–4). Illus. 1982, Childrens Pr. $6.95. An introduction to some of the less friendly members of the fish family.

8834. Brown, Anne Ensign. *Wonders of Sea Horses* (5–7). Illus. 1979, Dodd $9.95. A well-organized account that includes a section on the care and raising of sea horses.

8835. Cole, Joanna, and Wexler, Jerome. *A Fish Hatches* (3–5). Illus. 1978, Morrow $9.75; LB $9.36. The story of a trout, from egg to fully grown fish, in text and photographs.

8836. Eastman, David. *What Is a Fish?* (K–3). Illus. by Lynn Sweat. 1982, Troll LB $8.89; paper $1.25. A simple account that shows various kinds of fish.

8837. Fegely, Thomas D. *The World of Freshwater Fish* (6–9). Illus. 1978, Dodd $7.95. A general overview of the structure and environment of the many freshwater species of fish.

8838. Fletcher, Alan M. *Fishes Dangerous to Man* (4–6). Illus. 1969, Addison LB $6.95. About 25 fish—including the stingray, shark, and piranha—are described.

8839. Freedman, Russell. *Killer Fish* (3–5). Illus. 1982, Holiday LB $9.95. An account of such fish as the stingray that attack humans.

8840. Friedman, Judi. *The Eels' Strange Journey* (2–3). Illus. by Gail Owens. 1976, Harper $10.89. An account of the puzzling migrations of Atlantic Coast eels.

8841. Hogan, Paula Z. *The Salmon* (1–3). Illus. by Yoshi Miyake. 1979, Raintree $14.25. The life cycle of the salmon in very simple text and pictures.

8842. Horton, Casey. *Fish* (5–7). Illus. 1983, Watts $9.40. A well-illustrated volume that introduces fish by type and characteristics.

8843. Jacobs, Francine. *Barracuda: Tiger of the Sea* (2–4). Illus. by Harriett Springer. 1981, Walker

$8.95; LB $9.85. The life cycle of the barracuda, plus its hunting habits.

8844. Lane, Margaret. *The Fish: The Story of the Stickleback* (2–4). Illus. by John Butler. 1982, Dial $8.95; paper $3.50. A superior nature work with clear text and meticulous illustrations.

8845. Morris, Robert A. *Sea Horse* (1–3). Illus. by Arnold Lobel. 1972, Harper LB $8.89. A simply written explanation of the habits of the Atlantic sea horse.

8846. Overbeck, Cynthia. *The Fish Book* (3–5). Illus. by Sharon Lerner. 1978, Lerner $4.95. An introduction to 12 varieties of tropical fish found in aquariums.

8847. Patent, Dorothy. *Fish and How They Reproduce* (6–9). Illus. by Matthew Kalmenoff. 1976, Holiday $9.95. After introductory chapters on the types of fish and their adaptations, there is a detailed account of mating habits, spawning, and other related topics.

8848. Phleger, Fred. *Red Tag Comes Back* (1–3). Illus. by Arnold Lobel. 1961, Harper $8.89. The life cycle of a salmon in an easily read, charmingly illustrated account.

8849. Pringle, Laurence. *The Minnow Family: Chubs, Dace, Minnows and Shiners* (3–5). Illus. by Dot Barlowe and Sy Barlowe. 1976, Morrow $7.95; LB $7.63. The whys and wherefores of the world's largest fish family.

8850. Selsam, Millicent E., and Hunt, Joyce. *First Look at Fish* (1–3). Illus. by Harriett Springer. 1972, Scholastic paper $1.50. The anatomy of fish and an introduction to the most important species are 2 of the topics discussed in this elementary treatment.

8851. Zim, Herbert S., and Shoemaker, Hurst H. *Fishes* (5–8). Illus. by James G. Irving. 1957, Western $10.38; paper $2.95. Subtitle: *A Guide to Fresh and Saltwater Species.*

Sharks

8852. Blumberg, Rhoda. *Sharks* (4–6). 1976, Watts $8.90; Avon paper $2.25. An excellent introduction to sharks—their food, habits, and enemies.

8853. Bunting, Eve. *The Great White Shark* (5–6). Illus. 1982, Messner LB $9.29; paper $4.95. An easy-to-read account that introduces its fearsome subject well.

8854. Bunting, Eve. *The Sea World Book of Sharks* (4–9). Illus. 1979, Harcourt $12.95; paper $6.95. A profile of the structure, life, and habits of sharks.

8855. Carrick, Carol. *Sand Tiger Shark* (2–4). Illus. by Donald Carrick. 1977, Houghton $9.95. An informative and dramatic account of tiger sharks and other marine creatures—hungry, hostile, predatory, and solitary. Also use: *Hungry Sharks* by John F. Waters (1973, Harper $10.89).

8856. McGovern, Ann. *Sharks* (K–3). Illus. by Murray Tinkelman. 1976, Four Winds $7.95; Scholastic paper $1.50. In question-and-answer format, the author gives introductory information about sharks, including their habitat and eating habits.

8857. McGowen, Tom. *Album of Sharks* (4–6). Illus. by Rod Ruth. 1977, Rand McNally LB $8.95. Eleven types of sharks, with material on structure, habits, size, and stories surrounding each. Also use: *Sharks* by Herbert S. Zim (1966, Morrow LB $7.63).

8858. Selsam, Millicent E., and Hunt, Joyce. *A First Look at Sharks* (1–3). Illus. by Harriett Springer. 1979, Scholastic paper $1.50. The physical characteristics and behavior of the shark are covered in this beginning account.

Crustaceans

8859. Johnson, Sylvia A. *Crabs* (4–6). Illus. 1982, Lerner LB $9.95. A look at the structure and life cycle of various crabs.

Oysters, Sponges, Starfish

8860. Hurd, Edith Thacher. *Starfish* (2–4). Illus. 1962, Harper $10.89. The structure of the starfish, its eating habits, and its reproductive pattern are simply explained.

8861. Jacobson, Morris K., and Pong, Rosemary. *Wonders of Sponges* (5–8). Illus. 1976, Dodd $9.95. An explanation of the life and habits of sponges, well illustrated with photographs.

8862. Zim, Herbert S. *Sea Stars and Their Kin* (5–7). Illus. 1976, Morrow $7.63. The types of starfish are discussed, their feeding habits, and the growth and reproduction cycles.

Octopus

8863. Bunting, Eve. *The Giant Squid* (5–9). Illus. 1981, Messner $9.29. An easily read account of these mysterious monsters of the deep.

8864. Carrick, Carol. *Octopus* (2–4). Illus. by Donald Carrick. 1978, Houghton $7.95. The day-to-day life of a female octopus that ends with the egg-laying process.

Corals and Jellyfish

8865.   Berger, Gilda. *The Coral Reef: What Lives There* (2–4). Illus. by Murray Tinkelman. 1977, Putnam $5.99. How coral reefs are formed and their wildlife are 2 of the topics in this book.

8866.   Jacobson, Morris K., and Franz, David R. *Wonders of Corals and Coral Reefs* (6–9). Illus. 1979, Dodd $9.95. A well-researched and thorough account of coral reefs and their inhabitants.

8867.   Johnson, Sylvia A. *Coral Reefs* (4–7). Illus. 1984, Lerner $9.95. The creation and composition of coral reefs and the life they support.

8868.   Oxford Scientific Films. *Jellyfish and Other Sea Creatures* (2–6). Illus. 1982, Putnam $8.95. Extraordinary photographs are featured in this beginner's book.

8869.   Radlauer, Ruth, and Anderson, Henry M. *Reefs* (4–6). Illus. 1983, Childrens Pr. LB $11.95; paper $3.95. The story of coral reefs, where they are, and what life they support.

8870.   Ronai, Lili. *Corals* (2–3). Illus. by Arabelle Wheatley. 1976, Harper $10.89. An excellent first book on corals, describing how reefs are formed, how corals eat and regenerate, and the different kinds of coral.

8871.   Waters, John F. *A Jellyfish Is Not a Fish* (2–3). Illus. by Kazue Mizumura. 1979, Harper $10.53; LB $9.89. A simple introduction to the life and habits of jellyfish.

Shells

8872.   Abbott, R. Tucker. *Sea Shells of the World* (3–6). Illus. 1962, Western paper $2.95. A basic guide, well illustrated. Also use: *Seashells of North America* (1969, Western paper $7.95).

8873.   Goudey, Alice E. *Houses from the Sea* (K–3). Illus. by Adrienne Adams. 1959, Scribners LB $8.95. A picture storybook about shells.

8874.   Selsam, Millicent E., and Hunt, Joyce. *A First Look at Seashells* (1–3). Illus. by Harriett Springer. 1983, Walker $7.95; LB $9.85. A simple explanation of how seashells are classified.

Seashores

8875.   Cooper, Elizabeth K. *Science on the Shores and Banks* (6–9). 1960, Harcourt paper $1.50. Animal and plant life in or near water.

8876.   Kirkpatrick, Rena K. *Look at Shore Life* (K–2). Illus. 1978, Raintree $14.25. A very superficial introduction that is suitable for browsing purposes.

8877.   Kohn, Bernice. *Beachcomber's Book* (4–6). Illus. by Arabelle Wheatley. 1970, Penguin paper $3.95. An interesting guide to seashore life.

8878.   Zim, Herbert S., and Ingle, Lester. *Seashores* (5–8). Illus. 1955, Western $11.54; paper $2.95. Subtitle: *A Guide to Animals and Plants along the Beaches.*

Zoos and Marine Aquariums

8879. Buchenholz, Bruce. *Doctor in the Zoo* (6–9). 1976, Viking $16.95. Although written for adults, this account of a zoo veterinarian's typical week will intrigue a younger audience.

8880. Hewett, Joan. *Watching Them Grow: Inside a Zoo Nursery* (4–6). Illus. 1979, Little $9.95. The care and feeding of baby zoo animals during a period from November to March.

8881. Hoffmeister, Donald. *Zoo Animals* (5–7). Illus. 1967, Western $11.54. A discussion of zoo animals and how captivity affects their welfare.

8882. Jacobsen, Karen. *Zoos* (1–4). Illus. 1982, Childrens Pr. $6.95. A very general introduction to zoos with simple language and large color photographs.

8883. Paige, David. *Behind the Scenes at the Aquarium* (4–6). Illus. 1979, Whitman $9.95. An absorbing view of the administration and management of an aquarium such as the Shedd Aquarium in Chicago.

8884. Paige, David. *Behind the Scenes at the Zoo* (5–7). Illus. 1978, Whitman $9.95. How zoos initiate and carry out the best care possible for their charges.

8885. Shuttlesworth, Dorothy E. *Zoos in the Making* (5–7). Illus. 1977, Dutton $8.50. Important zoos and animal parks are identified and described, plus a discussion of how zoos are designed; well illustrated with photographs. Also use: *Zoos without Cages* by Judith E. Rinard (1981, National Geographic Society $6.95; LB $8.50).

Pets

General

8886. Arnold, Caroline. *Pets without Homes* (2–5). Illus. 1983, Houghton $10.95. Through the story of a lost puppy, a city's animal control department is studied.

8887. Case, Marshall T. *Look What I Found!* (4–6). Illus. 1971, Devin $8.95. A description of how to catch, house, and care for small wildlife.

8888. Chrystie, Frances. *Pets: A Complete Handbook on the Care, Understanding and Appreciation of All Kinds of Animal Pets* (5–9). Illus. by Gillett Good Griffin. 1974, Little $8.95. A perennial favorite, particularly comprehensive in the great variety of pets discussed.

8889. Curtis, Patricia. *Animal Partners: Training Animals to Help People* (6–9). Illus. 1982, Lodestar $10.63. Five situations (other than Hearing Ear or Seeing Eye dogs) where animals are trained to help humans.

8890. Curtis, Patricia. *The Animal Shelter* (6–8). Illus. 1983, Dutton $11.60. The problem of animals that end up in public shelters is explored.

8891. Hill, Rose. *Small Pets* (2–4). Illus. by Ian Jackson et al. 1982, Usborne $5.95; paper $2.95. Includes information on such pets as parakeets, gerbils, rats, and other rodents.

8892. Podendorf, Illa. *Pets* (2–3). Illus. 1981, Childrens Pr. LB $10.60; paper $3.95. A very simple account that features many color photographs.

8893. Poynter, Margaret. *Too Few Happy Endings: The Dilemma of the Humane Societies* (6–9). Illus. 1981, Atheneum LB $9.95. What happens to unwanted animals when they are sent to a humane society.

8894. Reynolds, Michelle. *Critters's Kitchen* (4–6). 1979, Atheneum $6.95; paper $2.95. A seventh-grade student gives recipes for 32 foods that her pets and other animals like.

8895. Sabin, Francene, and Sabin, Louis. *Perfect Pets* (5–7). Illus. 1978, Putnam $8.95. All kinds of pets—from insects to hamsters—are introduced.

8896. Simon, Seymour. *Pets in a Jar: Collecting and Caring for Small Wild Animals* (4–6). Illus. by Betty Fraser. 1975, Viking $11.50; Penguin paper $3.95. How to catch and care for such small wild creatures as snails, toads, and ants. Also use: *Shelf Pets: How to Take Care of Small Wild Animals* by Edward R. Ricciuti (1971, Harper LB $10.89).

8897. Vandivert, Rita. *Understanding Animals as Pets* (4–6). Illus. by William Vandivert. 1976, Warne $6.95. A comprehensive text for country and city children on how to care for a variety of pets, from dogs and gerbils to snakes and horses.

8898. Weber, William J. *Care of Uncommon Pets* (4–8). Illus. 1979, Holt $8.95. Chickens, lizards, rabbits, canaries, tortoises, and 15 other animals are presented.

Cats

8899. Cole, Joanna. *A Cat's Body* (PS–6). Illus. 1982, Morrow $9.75; LB $8.88. A description of the cat's anatomy in text and photographs.

8900. Fischer-Nagel, Heiderose, and Fischer-Nagel, Andreas. *A Kitten Is Born* (PS–6). Illus. 1983, Putnam $9.95. The birth of a litter to a cat named Tabitha.

8901. Hess, Lilo. *A Cat's Nine Lives* (2–4). Illus. 1984, Scribners LB $11.95. The story of a Persian cat and her several owners.

8902. Hess, Lilo. *Listen to Your Kitten Purr* (4–6). Illus. 1980, Scribners $9.95. The life story of a tabby cat, from kitten to mother.

8903. Hill, Rose. *Cats and Kittens* (2–4). Illus. by David Wright et al. 1982, Educational Development Corp. $6.95; LB $11.95; paper $2.95. Simple information on how to keep a cat as a pet.

8904. Leen, Nina. *Cats* (3–6). Illus. 1980, Holt $7.95. A fine introduction to cats.

8905. Overbeck, Cynthia. *Cats* (4–6). Illus. 1983, Lerner $8.95. This work concentrates on domestic cats and their habits and appearance.

8906. Posell, Elsa. *Cats* (1–4). Illus. 1983, Childrens Pr. $6.95. Some wild cats are introduced, but the concentration is on the cat as a pet.

8907. Schilling, Betty. *Two Kittens Are Born: From Birth to Two Months* (K–3). Illus. by author. 1980,

Holt LB $6.95; Scholastic paper $1.95. The birth and growth of 2 kittens, told in text and photos.

8908. Selsam, Millicent E. *How Kittens Grow* (1–2). Illus. by Esther Bubley. 1975, Scholastic paper $1.95. Photographs and simply written text describe the stages in a kitten's growth.

8909. Selsam, Millicent E., and Hunt, Joyce. *A First Look at Cats* (1–4). Illus. by Harriett Springer. 1981, Walker $7.95; LB $8.85. A primer for identifying both wild and domestic cats.

8910. Silverstein, Alvin, and Silverstein, Virginia B. *Cats: All about Them* (3–5). Illus. 1978, Lothrop $10.95; LB $10.51. A compendium of information about cats, such as their history and domestication.

8911. Steinberg, Phil. *You and Your Pet: Cats* (4–6). Illus. by Judith Leo. 1978, Lerner LB $5.95. An easily understood manual on the care of cats.

8912. Stevens, Carla. *The Birth of Sunset's Kittens* (K–3). Illus. by Leonard Stevens. 1969, Childrens Pr. $7.95. Appealing photographs show the birth process of a litter of kittens.

8913. Zaum, Marjorie. *All about Cats As Pets* (3–6). Illus. 1981, Messner LB $9.29. A book that covers all aspects, from history to health problems.

Dogs

8914. Bethell, Jean. *How to Care for Your Dog* (2–4). Illus. by Norman Birdwell. 1967, Four Winds $6.95. A simple guide that includes sections on illnesses, housebreaking, and grooming. Also use: *A Puppy for You* by Lilo Hess (1975, Scribners paper $2.95).

8915. Casey, Brigid, and Haugh, Wendy. *Sled Dogs* (5–8). Illus. 1983, Dodd $9.95. An introduction to breeds of sled dogs and their life.

8916. Fichter, George S. *Working Dogs* (5–7). Illus. 1979, Watts $8.90. An overview of the work that dogs do, from herding sheep to aiding the blind.

8917. Foster, Sally. *A Pup Grows Up* (2–4). Illus. 1984, Dodd $10.45. A description of 15 breeds of dogs.

8918. Hess, Lilo. *A Dog by Your Side* (3–6). Illus. 1977, Scribners $9.95. A basic introduction to the various breeds of dogs, as well as material on how to care for a trained dog.

8919. Hess, Lilo. *Life Begins for Puppies* (2–5). Illus. 1978, Scribners LB $1.79. The birth and first 4 weeks of life of sheepdog puppies. Also use: *My Puppy Is Born* by Joanna Cole (1973, Morrow LB $8.16).

8920. Jessel, Camilla. *The Puppy Book* (PS–3). Illus. 1980, Methuen $8.95. An account that focuses on one dog and her litter.

8921. Kuklin, Susan. *Mine for a Year* (4–6). Illus. 1984, Putnam $10.95. A puppy spends a year with George before entering the Seeing Eye dog program.

8922. McCloy, James. *Dogs at Work* (4–6). Illus. by Sheila Beatty. 1979, Crown LB $2.98. In brief sections, the author describes various breeds of working dogs and their uses.

8923. Pfloog, Jan. *Puppies* (PS). Illus. by author. 1979, Random $3.50. The behavior and needs of puppies and how to care for them are briefly covered. A companion to: *Kittens* (1977, Random $3.50).

8924. Pinkwater, Jill, and Pinkwater, D. Manus. *Superpuppy* (4–6). Illus. 1977, Houghton $4.95. All one needs to know about choosing and rearing the "best possible" dog.

8925. Posell, Elsa. *Dogs* (2–3). Illus. 1981, Childrens Pr. LB $10.60. A well-illustrated (with color photographs) easy reader that introduces dogs and their ways.

8926. Sabin, Francene. *Dogs of America* (6–8). Illus. by William P. Gilbert. 1967, Putnam $6.99. A guide to the major breeds in text and illustrations.

8927. Sabin, Louis. *All about Dogs As Pets* (3–6). Illus. 1983, Messner $8.79. This is a comprehensive guide, from selection of the breed you want to caring for an old dog.

8928. Selsam, Millicent E. *How Puppies Grow* (1–2). Illus. by Esther Bubley. 1972, Scholastic paper $1.95. The stages in a puppy's life—from birth through walking, seeing, eating, and playing—described in excellent photographs and simple text.

8929. Selsam, Millicent E., and Hunt, Joyce. *A First Look at Dogs* (1–3). Illus. by Harriett Springer. 1981, Walker $7.95; LB $8.85. A history of dogs and an introduction to present breeds.

8930. Sendak, Maurice, and Margolis, Matthew. *Some Swell Pup: Or Are You Sure You Want a Dog?* (K–4). Illus. by author. 1976, Penguin paper $3.95. Cartoon-style illustrations introduce children to the responsibility of having and caring for a pet.

8931. Wolf, Bernard. *Connie's New Eyes* (5–8). Illus. 1976, Harper $12.45. The training of a Seeing Eye dog, from birth to use with a blind owner.

8932. Wolters, Richard A. *Kid's Dog: A Training Book* (3–5). Illus. 1978, Doubleday $7.95. How to select and train a dog, illustrated with fine photographs.

Horses

8933. Brady, Irene. *America's Horses and Ponies* (5–7). Illus. by author. 1969, Houghton $12.95. Background information on all sorts of equines in a lucid, well-organized account.

8934. Brown, Fern G. *Behind the Scenes at the Horse Hospital* (5–6). Illus. 1981, Whitman LB $11.25. The story of the Illinois Equine Hospital and Clinic in Napersville, Illinois.

8935. Callahan, Dorothy M. *Thoroughbreds* (4–6). Illus. 1983, Crestwood $8.95. An introduction to this breed that dominates the racing world of today. Others in this series are: *Ruffian* by Dorothy M. Callahan; *Draft Horses* by Jerolyn Ann Nentl; *Hunters and Jumpers* by Nancy Robison; *Pleasure Horses* by Jerolyn Ann Nentl; *The Ponies* by Nancy Robison; *Rodeo Horses* by Candice Tillis Philp (all 1983, $8.95).

8936. Cole, Joanna. *A Horse's Body* (3–6). Illus. 1981, Morrow $7.95; LB $7.63. The evolution of the horse and its present structure.

8937. Darling, Lois, and Darling, Louis. *Sixty Million Years of Horses* (4–7). Illus. 1960, Morrow $8.16. The horses, its relatives and usefulness in the past and present.

8938. Demuth, Jack, and Demuth, Patricia. *City Horse* (4–6). Illus. 1979, Dodd $7.95. Various aspects of the life of a New York City police officer's horse are described.

8939. Farley, Walter. *Man O' War* (4–6). Illus. 1983, Random paper $2.95. The story of the famous racehorse.

8940. Ford, Barbara. *The Island Ponies: An Environmental Study of Their Life on Assateague* (6–8). 1979, Morrow $8.88. An introduction to these famous wild horses.

8941. Freedman, Russell. *Getting Born* (3–4). Illus. 1978, Holiday $8.95. Photographs and text describe the birth of a pony.

8942. Hall, Lynn. *A Horse Called Dragon* (5–7). Illus. by Joseph Cellini. 1971, Modern Curriculum $5.95; LB $4.98. A nonfiction account of the Mexican mustang that was eventually brought to Texas to help establish the "Pony of the Americas" breed.

8943. Henry, Marguerite. *All about Horses* (5–8). Illus. by Wesley Dennis. 1963, Random $6.95. From prehistoric beginnings to present-day breeds, including the horse's place in history. Also use: *Album of Horses* (1951, Rand McNally LB $8.95).

8944. Hess, Lilo. *A Pony to Love* (4–6). Illus. by author. 1974, Scribners $8.95. The purchase, care, and handling of a pony, described in clear, direct prose and illustrated with photographs.

8945. Lavine, Sigmund A., and Casey, Brigid. *Wonders of Ponies* (5–8). Illus. 1980, Dodd $9.95. The care and handling of a pony are described.

8946. MacClintock, Dorcas. *Horses As I See Them* (6–9). Illus. by Ugo Mochi. 1980, Scribners $9.95. A history of horses with detailed illustrations.

8947. Miller, Jane. *Birth of a Foal* (1–4). Illus. by author. 1977, Harper $10.53. Pictures illustrate this sensitive account of birth and maternal love. Also use: *A Foal Is Born* by Hans-Heinrich Isenbart (1976, Putnam $7.95).

8948. Patent, Dorothy. *Arabian Horses* (4–8). Illus. 1982, Holiday $11.95. A description of Arabian horses and how they have influenced other breeds.

8949. Patent, Dorothy. *Horses and Their Wild Relatives* (5–8). Illus. 1981, Holiday $8.95. The evolution of the horse and its herd habits, plus its relatives like the zebra.

8950. Patent, Dorothy. *Horses of America* (4–8). Illus. 1981, Holiday LB $11.95. A study of American horse breeds in brief text and black-and-white photographs.

8951. Patent, Dorothy. *A Picture Book of Ponies* (3–5). Illus. 1983, Holiday $9.95. What ponies are and the most important breeds are explained.

8952. Posell, Elsa. *Horses* (2–3). Illus. 1981, Childrens Pr. LB $10.60. Color photographs and simple text are used in this introductory volume. Also use: *The Book of Horses* by Glenn Balch (1967, Four Winds $8.95).

8953. Robertson, Alden. *The Wild Horse Gatherers* (6–9). Illus. 1978, Scribners paper $6.95. A vivid description of a wild horse roundup on government rangelands.

8954. Rounds, Glen. *Wild Horses on the Red Desert* (2–4). Illus. by author. 1969, Holiday $7.95. An account of how wild horses live in the Badlands of South Dakota.

8955. Thompson, Neil. *A Closer Look at Horses* (5–8). Illus. 1978, Watts LB $9.40. A basic introduction is given to the structure, behavior, and evolution of the horse.

8956. Ventura, Piero. *Man and the Horse* (3–5). Illus. by author. 1982, Putnam $11.95. A history of the horse, from prehistoric times to the present.

8957. Weeks, Morris. *Last Wild Horse* (6–8). Illus. 1977, Houghton $6.95. The story of Przhevalski's horse that now only survives in zoos.

Fish

8958. Axelrod, Herbert R. *Tropical Fish in Your Home* (5–7). Illus. 1960, Sterling $9.95; LB $12.49. A guide to selection and care.

8959. Broekel, Ray. *Tropical Fish* (1–4). Illus. 1983, Childrens Pr. $6.96. An introduction to tropical fish and their care in aquariums. Also use: *Aquariums and Terrariums* (1982, Childrens Pr. $6.95).

8960. Halstead, Bruce, and Landa, Bonnie L. *Tropical Fish* (4–8). Illus. 1975, Western paper $2.95. A handbook on types and characteristics of specific species, plus tips on their care.

8961. Henrie, Fiona. *Fish* (3–5). Illus. 1981, Watts LB $7.90. An easily understood guide to care and keeping fish.

8962. Paysan, Klaus. *Aquarium Fish from Around the World* (3–6). Illus. 1971, Lerner LB $9.95. Over 100 fish species are introduced in color photographs and text.

8963. Sarnoff, Jane, and Ruffins, Reynold. *A Great Aquarium Book: The Putting-It-Together Guide for Beginners* (4–8). Illus. 1977, Scribners $8.95. Straightforward explanations presented with verve in a readable manual.

8964. Wong, Herbert H., and Vessel, Matthew F. *My Goldfish* (1–3). Illus. by Arvis Stewart. 1969, Addison $6.95. With fictional overtones, this account describes the habits of a goldfish.

8965. Zim, Herbert S. *Goldfish* (2–5). Illus. by Jay Buba. 1947, Morrow $8.16. An interesting account of the types of goldfish, their needs, and how to care for them.

Other Pets

8966. Bielfeld, Horst. *Guinea Pigs: Everything about Purchase, Care, Nutrition and Diseases* (4–6). Illus. 1983, Barron's paper $3.95. Drawings, photographs, and text introduce this pet.

8967. Broekel, Ray. *Gerbil Pets and Other Small Rodents* (1–4). Illus. 1983, Childrens Pr. $6.95. A simple introduction to these pets and their needs.

8968. Fichter, George S. *Keeping Amphibians and Reptiles as Pets* (4–6). 1979, Watts $8.90. Practical tips on how to care for such animals as frogs, snakes, and turtles.

8969. Hahn, James, and Hahn, Lynn. *Hamsters, Gerbils, Guinea Pigs, Pet Mice and Pet Rats* (4–6). Illus. 1977, Watts LB $8.90; Avon paper $1.95. Here is all one needs to know to give these pets good homes.

8970. Henrie, Fiona. *Guinea Pigs* (K–4). Illus. 1981, Watts LB $7.90. Simple, basic instructions are given. Another in this series is: *Mice and Rats* (1981, LB $7.90).

8971. Hess, Lilo. *Bird Companions* (3–6). Illus. 1981, Scribners $10.94. Birds as pets is the main topic in this simple introduction.

8972. Hess, Lilo. *Making Friends with Guinea Pigs* (4–6). Illus. 1983, Scribners $11.95. The story of 3 guinea pigs—2 pets and one lab animal—plus material on how to care for them.

8973. Overbeck, Cynthia. *Curly the Piglet* (2–4). Illus. 1976, Carolrhoda $4.95. Two children on a farm observe the growth of a small pig.

8974. Roy, Ron. *What Has Ten Legs and Eats Corn Flakes? A Pet Book* (2–4). Illus. by Lynne Cherry. 1982, Putnam $9.25. A pet book about hermit crabs, gerbils, and chameleons.

8975. Rubins, Harriett. *Guinea Pigs: An Owner's Guide to Choosing, Raising, Breeding and Showing* (4–8). Illus. by Pamela Carroll. 1982, Lothrop $11.25. A compendium of information for the serious guinea pig owner.

8976. Shuttlesworth, Dorothy E. *Gerbils and Other Small Pets* (3–6). Illus. 1970, Dutton $8.95. An interesting account of how to care for these popular pets.

8977. Silverstein, Alvin, and Silverstein, Virginia B. *Gerbils: All about Them* (5–8). 1976, Harper $10.95; paper $3.95. The most extensive work for young readers on the subject.

8978. Silverstein, Alvin, and Silverstein, Virginia B. *Hamsters: All about Them* (4–7). Illus. 1974, Lothrop $9.84. A basic manual for the hamster owner, full of excellent photographs. Also use: *Golden Hamsters* by Herbert S. Zim (1951, Morrow $8.16).

8979. Silverstein, Alvin, and Silverstein, Virginia B. *Rabbits* (3–6). Illus. 1973, Lothrop $10.32. A well-organized account that explores many facets about rabbit life, with a section on legends and lore. Also use: *Rabbits* by Herbert S. Zim (1948, Morrow $8.16).

8980. Stein, Sara Bonnett. *How to Raise Mice, Rats, Hamsters, and Gerbils* (3–5). Illus. 1976, Random $5.99; paper $3.95. A handbook on how to keep these rodents as pets.

8981. Zappler, George, and Zappler, Lisbeth. *Amphibians as Pets* (6–8). Illus. 1973, Doubleday $7.95. The structure and living habits of amphibians, as well as information on the care and raising of them.

8982. Zim, Herbert S. *Homing Pigeons* (6–9). Illus. by James G. Irving. 1949, Morrow $8.16. A guide to the raising and flying of homing pigeons.

8983. Zim, Herbert S. *Parakeets* (4–6). Illus. by Larry Kettelkamp. 1953, Morrow $7.63. Everything a young person needs to know about caring for these pets.

Technology and Engineering

General

8984. Abrams, Kathleen, and Abrams, Lawrence. *Logging and Lumbering* (4–7). Illus. 1980, Messner $7.79. An account of the history and methods of the logging industry.

8985. Ardley, Neil et al. *How Things Work* (3–6). Illus. by Bob Bampton et al. 1984, Messner $9.79; Wanderer paper $8.95. A question-and-answer book on technology.

8986. Cosner, Sharon. *Paper through the Ages* (1–4). Illus. by Priscilla Kiedrowski. 1984, Carolrhoda $7.95. A very simple, brightly illustrated primer about paper and other writing surfaces.

8987. Gibbons, Gail. *Locks and Keys* (3–6). Illus. by author. 1980, Harper $8.61; LB $8.89. A history of locks and keys, from the caveman to the present.

8988. Gottlieb, Leonard. *Factory Made: How Things Are Manufactured* (5–8). Illus. 1978, Houghton $7.95. The stories behind the manufacture of 13 commonplace objects.

8989. Hehnergarth, John, illus. *Small Inventions That Make a Big Difference* (4–8). 1984, National Geographic Society $6.95; LB $8.50. A description of all kinds of inventions.

8990. National Geographic Society. *How Things Work* (5–7). Illus. 1983, National Geographic Society $8.75; LB $10.30. A handsome volume that explains how a variety of objects, from toasters to space shuttles, work.

8991. Sherwood, Martin. *Industry* (4–7). Illus. 1982, Watts LB $8.90. How industry uses energy, from raw materials to finished product.

8992. Weiss, Harvey. *What Holds It Together* (5–8). Illus. by author. 1977, Little $7.95. Clamps, glue, cement, and thread are only a few of the ways by which we hold objects together.

Computers and Automation

8993. Ardley, Neil. *Computers* (4–8). Illus. 1983, Watts $9.90. An introduction distinguished by both text and pictures.

8994. Asimov, Isaac. *How Did We Find Out about Computers?* (4–7). Illus. by David Wool. 1984, Walker $8.95. A brief history of the computer, from abacus to the present.

8995. Ault, Roz. *BASIC Programming for Kids* (5–8). Illus. 1983, Houghton $10.45; paper $7.70. BASIC programming is outlined in relation to 6 commercial computers.

8996. Baldwin, Margaret, and Pack, Gary. *Computer Graphics* (5–9). Illus. 1984, Watts $8.90. A fine introduction to the history and present status of computer-generated graphics and their place in the art world.

8997. Baldwin, Margaret, and Pack, Gary. *Robots and Robotics* (5–8). Illus. 1984, Watts $8.90. The kinds of jobs that robots can perform are explored, plus career opportunities in the field.

8998. Berger, Melvin. *Computer Talk* (3–6). Illus. by Geri Greinke. 1984, Messner $9.29. A dictionary of about 200 computer terms.

8999. Berger, Melvin. *Computers in Your Life* (5–7). Illus. 1981, Harper $10.10; LB $9.89; paper $4.95. An explanation of where computers are used today.

9000. Berger, Melvin. *Data Processing* (5–8). Illus. 1983, Watts LB $8.90. A basic volume in the Computer Awareness First Book series. Others in the series are: *Careers in the Computer Industry* by Laura Greene; *Computer Languages* by Christopher Lampton; *Computers in Our World Today and Tomorrow* by Sandy Hintz and Martin Hintz; *Invent Your Own Computer Games* by Fred D'Ignazio; *Programming in BASIC* by Christopher Lampton (all 1983, LB $8.90).

9001. Berger, Melvin. *Word Processing* (5–7). Illus. 1984, Watts LB $8.90. A survey of the functions that can be performed by word processing.

9002. Billard, Mary. *All about Robots* (3–6). Illus. by Walter Wright. 1982, Platt and Munk $6.95. What are robots and how are they used are 2 topics covered.

9003. Bitter, Gary G. *Exploring with Computers* (4–7). Illus. 1983, Messner LB $9.29; paper $4.95.

An account that emphasizes the inner workings of the computer.

9004. Bolognese, Don, and Thornton, Robert. *Drawing and Painting with the Computer* (4–6). Illus. 1983, Watts $8.90; paper $4.95. An introduction to computer graphics.

9005. Chester, Michael. *Robots: Facts behind the Fiction* (5–9). Illus. 1983, Macmillan $9.95. The development, uses, and the future of robots are discussed. Also use: *The Robots Are Here* by Alvin Silverstein and Virginia B. Silverstein (1983, Prentice $10.95).

9006. Christian, Mary Blount. *Microcomputers* (5–7). Illus. 1983, Crestwood $8.95. An account of how microcomputers are made.

9007. Cohen, Daniel, and Cohen, Susan. *The Kids' Guide to Home Computers* (5–8). Illus. 1983, Archway paper $1.95. A guide that uses brand name evaluations.

9008. Corbett, Scott. *Home Computers: A Simple and Informative Guide* (6–8). Illus. 1980, Little $11.45; paper $6.70. An overview of the many present and future uses of computers.

9009. Davies, Helen, and Wharton, Mike. *Inside the Chip* (4–8). Illus. by Graham Round et al. 1984, Usborne $8.95; LB $12.95; paper $5.95. The history, operation, and uses of the silicon chip.

9010. D'Ignazio, Fred. *Messner's Introduction to the Computer* (6–10). Illus. 1984, Messner LB $10.29. A history of the computer and an explanation of its parts.

9011. D'Ignazio, Fred. *Working Robots* (7–9). Illus. 1981, Lodestar $11.50. An introduction to the various kinds of robots and what they can and, in the future, will be able to do.

9012. D'Ignazio, Fred, and Wold, Allen L. *The Science of Artificial Intelligence* (5–8). Illus. 1984, Watts LB $8.90. An explanation of artificial intelligence, recent developments in the field, and possible ethical considerations.

9013. Dilson, Jesse. *The Abacus: A Pocket Computer* (5–7). Illus. by Angela Pozzi. 1968, St. Martins paper $5.95. A history of the abacus, with directions on how to construct and use it.

9014. Gallagher, Sharon. *Inside the Personal Computer: An Illustrated Introduction in 3 Dimensions* (5–8). 1984, Abbeville $19.95. A pop-up guide to the inner workings of the personal computer.

9015. Graham, Ian. *Computer* (4–6). Illus. by Denis Bishop et al. 1983, Watts LB $9.90. A discussion of the many uses of computers, plus general introductory material.

9016. Greene, Carol. *Robots* (K–3). Illus. 1983, Childrens Pr. $6.95. A broad, simple introduction for young readers.

9017. Hardy, Jack B. *Adventures with the Atari* (6–9). Illus. 1983, Prentice paper $14.95. The planning and execution of a computer adventure program are presented, plus some actual programs.

9018. Hargrove, Jim. *Microcomputers at Work* (1–3). Illus. 1984, Childrens Pr. $7.95. A review of the components of computers and their main uses.

9019. Harris, Dwight, and Harris, Patricia. *Computer Programming 1, 2, 3!* (5–9). Illus. by John Nez. 1983, Putnam paper $4.95. Many often used commands in BASIC are reviewed and 7 programs, some not for the beginner, are given.

9020. Hawkes, Nigel. *Computers: How They Work* (4–6). Illus. 1983, Watts LB $9.40. A simple introduction to the parts and innards of a computer. Also use: *Computers in the Home* (1984, Watts $9.40).

9021. Hawkes, Nigel. *Computers in Action* (4–5). Illus. 1984, Watts LB $9.40. The uses of computers in such fields as business, medicine, and space exploration.

9022. Hellman, Hal. *Computer Basics* (4–6). Illus. 1983, Prentice $8.95. A history of computers, plus glimpses at programming, the binary system, and components.

9023. Henson, Hilary. *Robots* (4–7). Illus. 1982, Watts LB $9.90. The author discusses the place of robots in today's world with many full-page illustrations.

9024. Herda, D. J. *Microcomputers* (5–8). Illus. 1984, Watts LB $8.90. An introduction to microcomputers, plus a description of 23 currently available models and guidelines for purchasing one.

9025. Hyde, Margaret O. *Computers That Think: The Search for Artificial Intelligence* (6–8). Illus. 1982, Enslow LB $10.95; paper $4.95. "How intelligent should computers become?" is one question asked in this book.

9026. Jacobsen, Karen. *Computers* (1–4). Illus. 1982, Childrens Pr. LB $10.60; paper $3.95. A well-organized, lucid beginner's book on computers.

9027. Jespersen, James, and Fitz-Randolph, Jane. *Rams, Roms and Robots: The Inside Story of Computers* (6–9). Illus. by Bruce Hiscock. 1984, Atheneum $13.95. An excellent introduction to the world of robotics.

9028. Kleiner, Art. *Robots* (4–6). Illus. by Jerry Scott. 1981, Raintree LB $15.52. Robot mechanisms and their possible uses are explored.

9029. Knight, David C. *Robotics: Past, Present, and Future* (5–7). Illus. 1983, Morrow $8.50. A book that concentrates on the past and future of robots.

9030. Lambert, Mark. *Fifty Facts about Robots* (4–6). Illus. 1983, Watts LB $8.90. A question-and-answer book that gives good background information.

9031. Lampton, Christopher. *BASIC for Beginners* (5–8). Illus. 1984, Watts LB $8.90. An introduction to this computer language. Three other companion volumes are: *COBOL for Beginners; FORTRAN for Beginners; PASCAL for Beginners* (all 1984, Watts LB $8.90).

9032. Lampton, Christopher. *The Micro Dictionary* (6–9). 1984, Watts LB $10.90. A reference work that explains basic computer terms.

9033. Leder, Jane Mersky. *Video Games* (5–7). Illus. 1983, Crestwood $8.95. A description of how these games are made in a brief commentary and many photos.

9034. Lewis, Bruce. *Meet the Computer* (3–5). Illus. by Leonard Kessler. 1977, Dodd $7.95. An introductory glimpse at these machines with an emphasis on their usefulness.

9035. Lipscomb, Susan Drake, and Zuanich, Margaret Ann. *BASIC Fun with Adventure Games* (4–7). 1984, Avon paper $2.95. A game, CIA, that can be run on certain Apple and IBM computers. Also use: *BASIC Beginnings* (1983, Avon paper $2.25).

9036. Lipson, Shelley. *It's BASIC: The ABC's of Computer Programming* (3–6). Illus. by Janice Stapleton. 1982, Holt $8.70. A very simple introduction to this language and some simple commands. A more advanced account is: *BASIC Fun: Computer Games, Puzzles and Problems Children Can Write* by Susan Drake Lipscomb and Margaret Ann Zuanich (1982, Avon paper $2.25).

9037. Litterick, Ian. *Computers and You* (5–7). Illus. 1984, Watts LB $9.40. A discussion of the positive and negative impact of computers on our lives.

9038. Litterick, Ian. *Computers in Everyday Life* (5–9). 1984, Watts LB $9.40. A description of what computers do for us at present and how this is changing our life-styles. Also use: *How Computers Work; The Story of Computers* (both 1984, Watts LB $9.40).

9039. Litterick, Ian. *Programming Computers* (5–7). Illus. 1984, Watts LB $9.40. An introduction to program language and the principles of good programming.

9040. Litterick, Ian. *Robots and Intelligent Machines* (5–7). Illus. 1984, Watts LB $9.40. What robots are and what they can do.

9041. Madison, Arnold, and Drotar, David L. *Pocket Calculators: How to Use and Enjoy Them* (5–8). Illus. 1978, Lodestar $8.95. Four kinds of calculators are featured, with possible uses.

9042. Manes, Stephen, and Somerson, Paul. *Computer Olympics* (4–9). 1984, Scholastic paper $4.95. A collection of 39 BASIC programs related to the Olympics.

9043. Marsh, Peter. *Robots* (4–6). Illus. 1984, Watts LB $9.40. A slim overview with a section on artificial intelligence.

9044. Metos, Thomas H. *Robots A Two Z* (4–6). Illus. 1980, Messner $7.79. A history of robots, their place in today's world, and their possible future.

9045. Milton, Joyce. *Here Come the Robots* (5–7). Illus. by Peter Stern. 1981, Hastings $9.95. A history of robots, how they function today, and a possible list of uses in the future.

9046. Richard, Ian. *Computers* (2–5). Illus. 1983, Watts LB $8.90. A simple introduction to computers and what they can do to help us.

9047. Rothfeder, Jeffrey. *Home Computer Basics* (4–6). Illus. by Michael Petronella. 1983, Prentice $8.95. A description of the components and a guide to purchasing a home computer.

9048. Ruane, Pat, and Hyman, Jane. *Logo Activities for the Computer: A Beginner's Guide* (4–7). Illus. by Leslie Morrill. 1984, Messner $9.79; paper $4.94. A step-by-step guide to Logo computer language.

9049. Simon, Seymour. *Computer Sense, Computer Nonsense* (3–5). Illus. by Steven Lindblom. 1984, Harper $10.10; LB $9.89. A smattering of information about computers.

9050. Srivastava, Jane Jonas. *Computers* (2–4). Illus. by James McCrea and Ruth McCrea. 1972, Harper $10.89. Introduction to the computer as a counting machine, explained simply and accompanied by graphic illustrations.

9051. Stevens, Lawrence. *Computer Programming Basics* (4–5). Illus. 1984, Prentice $9.95. An introduction to programming through 10 fundamental BASIC commands.

9052. Sturridge, Helena. *Microcomputers* (4–6). Illus. 1984, Watts LB $9.40. A rundown on components, software, and programming.

9053. Sullivan, George. *Computer Kids* (4–7). Illus. 1984, Dodd $10.95. Eight youngsters are interviewed on the way they use computers.

9054. Sullivan, George. *Screen Play: The Story of Video Games* (6–9). Illus. 1983, Warne $9.95; paper $4.95. An explanation of how video games work and a rundown on some of the most popular.

9055. Thornburg, David D. *Picture This! PILOT Turtle Geometry: An Introduction to Computer Graphics for Kids of All Ages* (5–9). Illus. 1982, Addison paper $14.95. Computer graphics on an Atari 400 or 800 with a PILOT language cartridge.

9056. Thornburg, David D. *Picture This Too!* (5–9). 1984, Creative Publications $15.95. Subtitle: *An Introduction to Computer Graphics for Kids of All Ages.*

9057. Wall, Elizabeth S. *Computer Alphabet Book* (3–4). Illus. by Julia E. Cousins. 1979, Bayshore $9.95. The letters of the alphabet are used to introduce computer terms.

9058. Zuanich, Margaret Ann, and Lipscomb, Susan Drake. *BASIC Fun with Graphics: The Apple Computer Way* (4–7). Illus. 1983, Avon paper $3.95. Several programs capable of revisions are given for computer graphics. Companion volumes are: *BASIC Fun with Graphics: The Atari Computer Way; BASIC Fun with Graphics: The IBM/PC Computer Way* (both 1983, Avon paper $3.95).

Transportation

9059. Ancona, George. *Monsters on Wheels* (4–6). Illus. by author. 1974, Dutton $9.95. A description in text and photos of 17 huge machines.

9060. Ardley, Neil. *Transport on Earth* (6–8). Illus. 1981, Watts LB $8.90. A look at transportation in the future.

9061. Ault, Phil. *Whistles Round the Bend: Travel on America's Waterways* (6–8). Illus. 1982, Dodd $10.95. The story of inland water transportation, from canoes to steamers.

9062. Barton, Byron. *Wheels* (PS–K). Illus. by author. 1979, Harper $9.57; LB $10.89. A history of wheels and their importance through the ages.

9063. Billout, Guy. *By Camel or by Car* (2–3). 1979, Prentice $8.95; paper $5.95. A simple discussion of how various vehicles can move across different surfaces.

9064. Carlisle, Norman, and Carlisle, Madelyn. *Bridges* (1–4). Illus. 1983, Childrens Pr. $6.95. Types of bridges and their construction are introduced.

9065. Corbett, Scott. *Bridges* (5–7). Illus. 1978, Four Winds $9.95. Beginning with the ancient Romans, this account traces the history of bridges and their architectural characteristics.

9066. Gibbons, Gail. *Tunnels* (1–4). Illus. by author. 1984, Holiday $12.95. Different kinds of tunnels are pictured and described.

9067. Goor, Ron, and Goor, Nancy. *In the Driver's Seat* (2–4). Illus. 1982, Harper $10.53; LB $10.89. How it feels to operate such vehicles as a tank and a Concorde.

9068. Hamer, Mick. *Transport* (4–7). Illus. 1982, Watts LB $8.90. A look at how energy effects transportation.

9069. Hellman, Hal. *Transportation in the World of the Future* (5–7). Illus. 1974, Evans $6.95. A fascinating glimpse of possible future modes of transportation.

9070. Kehoe, Michael. *Road Closed* (2–5). Illus. 1982, Carolrhoda LB $7.95. What happens when a road and its underground communication are rebuilt.

9071. Moolman, Valerie. *The Future World of Transportation* (5–9). Illus. 1984, Watts $11.90. A look at land, air, and water transportation in the year 2050.

9072. St. George, Judith. *The Brooklyn Bridge: They Said It Couldn't Be Built* (6–9). Illus. 1982, Putnam $10.95. The history of this miracle construction now over 100 years old.

9073. Sandak, Cass R. *Bridges* (4–6). Illus. by Jane Kendall. 1983, Watts LB $8.90. A look at various bridge types and how they are constructed. Also use: *Canals; Dams* (both 1983, Watts LB $8.90).

9074. Sandak, Cass R. *Roads* (4–6). Illus. 1984, Watts LB $8.90. A history of roads, the many types there are, and how they are constructed.

9075. Sandak, Cass R. *Tunnels* (3–6). Illus. 1984, Watts LB $8.90. A look at tunnel building and the differences between land and underwater construction.

9076. Sullivan, George. *How Does It Get There?* (5–8). 1973, Westminster $5.95. A description of the various ways goods and materials are shipped, from supertankers to zoo transports.

9077. Tunis, Edwin. *Wheels: A Pictorial History* (6–8). 1977, Harper $16.95. Through carefully executed drawings, a history of transportation is presented.

9078. Wolfe, Louis. *Disaster Detectives* (6–9). Illus. 1981, Messner LB $6.90. The work of the National Transportation Safety Board.

Aeronautics

9079. Bendick, Jeanne. *Airplanes* (3–5). Illus. by author. 1982, Watts $7.90. In simple text and illustrations, why planes fly and a brief history of flight.

9080. Berliner, Don. *Aerobatics* (5–8). Illus. 1980, Lerner LB $7.95. The thrills of stunt flying are conveyed in brief text and many photos. Also use: *Yesterday's Airplanes* (1980, Lerner LB $7.95).

9081. Berliner, Don. *Helicopters* (4–6). Illus. 1983, Lerner $7.95. A history of helicopters and their uses, plus a description of the major types now in existence.

9082. Berliner, Don. *Personal Airplanes* (4–7). Illus. 1982, Lerner LB $7.95. The story of small airplanes and how they are made.

9083. Chant, Chris. *Jetliner: From Takeoff to Touchdown* (4–8). Illus. 1982, Watts LB $9.90. The inside story of what goes on during a transcontinental jet flight.

9084. Coombs, Charles. *Ultralights: The Flying Featherweights* (6–10). Illus. 1984, Morrow $10.50. A description of these aircraft, used mainly for recreation, and tips on how to fly one.

9085. Corbett, Scott. *What Makes a Plane Fly?* (3–6). Illus. by Len Darwin. 1967, Little $5.95. The principles of flight clearly described with suggested experiments for added clarification.

9086. Dahnsen, Alan. *Aircraft* (2–4). Illus. 1978, Watts $8.60. In simple terms, the characteristics and uses of major modern aircraft are explained.

9087. Dean, Anabel. *Up, Up, and Away!* (5–8). Illus. 1980, Westminster $11.95. The history of ballooning from a sport to today's practical uses.

9088. Delear, Frank J. *Airplanes and Helicopters of the U.S. Navy* (5–9). Illus. 1982, Dodd LB $10.95. Forty aircraft are covered, plus a history of naval aircraft.

9089. Delear, Frank J. *Famous First Flights across the Atlantic* (6–9). Illus. 1979, Dodd $8.95. Ten early transatlantic flights are highlighted in this account.

9090. Delear, Frank J. *Helicopters and Airplanes of the U.S. Army* (4–9). Illus. 1977, Dodd $7.95. A statistical rundown with photographs of the present and past aircraft used by the U.S. Army.

9091. Doss, Helen Grigsby. *The U.S. Air Force: From Balloons to Spaceships* (4–6). Illus. 1981, Messner LB $9.29. An account that covers our military aircraft, from the Civil War to the present.

9092. Dwiggins, Don. *Flying the Frontiers of Space* (6–9). Illus. 1982, Dodd LB $10.95. An introduction to all the aircraft that preceded the space shuttle.

9093. Freeman, Tony. *Blimps* (3–6). Illus. 1979, Childrens Pr. $10.00; paper $2.95. Background information is given through a visit to the airship *Columbia.*

9094. Harris, Susan. *Helicopters* (2–4). Illus. by E. Smart. 1979, Watts $8.60. The history of heli-

copters, their many varieties, and how they operate are covered in this simple account.

9095. Hewish, Mark. *The Young Scientist Book of Jets* (4–7). Illus. 1978, EMC $7.95. An attractive semicomic book format is used to cover basic material.

9096. Kanetzke, Howard. *Airplanes and Balloons* (2–4). Illus. 1978, Raintree $14.25. Principles of flight are explained simply with many concrete examples.

9097. Maynard, Christopher, and Paton, John. *The History of Aircraft* (5–7). Illus. 1982, Watts LB $8.90. From nineteenth-century gliders to the Concorde, in pictures and text.

9098. Messenger, Charles. *Combat Aircraft* (5–7). Illus. 1984, Watts LB $9.90. A book that explores the types and uses of combat aircraft.

9099. Mohn, Peter B. *The Thunderbirds* (4–6). Illus. 1980, Childrens Pr. $10.60. The story of the Air Force's crack flying team. Also use: *Blue Angels* (1977, Childrens Pr. $10.60).

9100. Navarra, John Gabriel. *Superplanes* (7–9). Illus. 1979, Doubleday $8.95. A narrative on high-speed planes and their many uses.

9101. Percefull, Aaron W. *Balloons, Zeppelins, and Dirigibles* (5–7). Illus. 1983, Watts LB $8.90. A history of balloons and their related airships ending with today's sport of hot-air ballooning.

9102. Petersen, David. *Helicopters* (1–4). Illus. 1983, Childrens Pr. $6.95. Color photographs, simple text, and a glossary are used to introduce the helicopter.

9103. Provensen, Alice, and Provensen, Martin. *The Glorious Flight across the Channel with Louis Bleriot* (1–5). Illus. by author. 1983, Viking $13.45. The story of an historic flight by a French aviation pioneer.

9104. Rosenblum, Richard. *The Golden Age of Aviation* (3–6). Illus. by author. 1984, Atheneum $10.95. The story of aviation between the 2 World Wars.

9105. Rosenblum, Richard. *Wings: The Early Years of Aviation* (3–5). Illus. by author. 1980, Four Winds $8.95. The history of aviation, from the Wright brothers to Lindbergh.

9106. Stein, R. Conrad. *The Story of the Flight at Kitty Hawk* (3–5). Illus. by Len W. Meents. 1981, Childrens Pr. LB $9.00; paper $2.95. The landmark flight of the Wright brothers.

9107. Wilson, Mike, and Scagell, Robin. *Jet Journey* (2–7). Illus. 1978, Viking $8.95. Many illustrations and easily read text in this account of a trip by jet aircraft.

9108. Zisfein, Melvin B. *Flight: A Panorama of Aviation* (5–9). Illus. by Robert Andrew Parker. 1981, Pantheon $11.95; LB $17.99; paper $11.95. The history of aviation is given in watercolors and very readable text.

Automobiles and Trucks

9109. Ancona, George. *Monster Movers* (3–6). Illus. 1983, Dutton $11.95. A book on how 16 large haulers work.

9110. Bendick, Jeanne. *Automobiles* (3–5). Illus. by author. 1984, Watts $8.95. Different types of cars are presented, with special material on traffic problems and pollution.

9111. Broekel, Ray. *Trucks* (1–4). Illus. 1983, Childrens Pr. $6.95. An overview of types of trucks with many color photographs.

9112. Clark, James. *Cars* (4–6). Illus. by John Bailey and John Dyess. 1981, Raintree LB $15.52. The basic systems in an automobile, like the transmission, are explained simply.

9113. Colby, C. B. *Trucks on the Highway* (4–6). Illus. 1964, Putnam $5.99. Simple text and many photographs introduce several kinds of trucks.

9114. Cole, Joanna. *Cars and How They Go* (2–4). Illus. by Gail Gibbons. 1983, Harper $9.89. In picture book format, here is a simple description of cars and how they operate.

9115. Dexler, Paul R. *Yesterday's Cars* (6–9). Illus. 1979, Lerner $7.95. A fine browsing book on some of this world's most elegant old automobiles.

9116. Dorin, Patrick C. *Yesterday's Trucks* (4–7). Illus. 1982, Lerner LB $7.95. A history of trucks, from 1900 to 1940.

9117. Foster, Genevieve. *The Year of the Horseless Carriage* (5–6). Illus. by author. 1975, Scribners $1.79. The work of Trevithick Fulton and Stephenson on developing steam-driven vehicles is described within the context of the world in which they lived.

9118. Hatmon, Paul W. *Yesterday's Fire Engines* (5–8). Illus. 1980, Lerner LB $7.95. An account of the history and development of these engines and how they are restored.

9119. Kanetzke, Howard. *The Story of Cars* (2–4). Illus. 1978, Raintree $14.25. A brief history of cars, plus material on their parts and construction.

9120. Knudson, Richard L. *Classic Sports Cars* (5–9). Illus. 1979, Lerner $7.95. A collection of sports cars such as MG, Jaguar, and Mercedes-Benz.

9121. Knudson, Richard L. *Fabulous Cars of the 1920's and 1930's* (5–9). Illus. 1981, Lerner LB $7.95. Stunning old models of cars are displayed in text and photographs.

9122. Lord, Harvey G. *Car Care: For Kids and Former Kids* (6–8). Illus. 1983, Atheneum $14.95; paper $9.95. Basic car maintenance is introduced.

9123. Marston, Hope Irvin. *Big Rigs* (6–9). Illus. 1960, Dodd $9.95. A description of the kinds and uses of tractor-trailers, the largest trucks on the highway.

9124. Marston, Hope Irvin. *Fire Trucks* (2–3). Illus. 1984, Dodd $10.95. Various kinds of fire trucks are introduced and their uses explained.

9125. Murphy, Jim. *Tractors: From Yesterday's Steam Wagons to Today's Turbocharged Giants* (5–7). Illus. 1984, Harper $10.53; LB $10.89. A history of tractors and their many uses.

9126. Navarra, John Gabriel. *Supercars* (5–9). Illus. 1975, Doubleday $8.95. A series of brief chapters on a number of new or experimental cars that represent advances from standard models.

9127. Nentl, Jerolyn Ann. *Big Rigs* (4–7). Illus. 1983, Crestwood $8.95. The story of how tractor-trailers are made.

9128. Olney, Ross R. *The Internal Combustion Engine* (4–8). Illus. by Steven Lindblom. 1982, Harper $9.13; LB $9.89. A simple explanation of the parts of the engine, how they work, and how they power the car.

9129. Parker, Nancy W. *The President's Car* (3–5). Illus. by author. 1981, Harper $10.53; LB $10.89. A look at what each president's limousine was like.

9130. Ready, Kirk L. *Custom Cars* (6–8). Illus. 1982, Lerner LB $7.95. An introduction to car customizing with many examples.

9131. Rich, Mark. *Diesel Trucks* (3–6). Illus. 1978, Childrens Pr. $10.00; paper $2.95. A simple introduction to various kinds of diesel trucks and the work they do.

9132. Richards, Norman, and Richards, Pat. *Trucks and Supertrucks* (4–5). Illus. 1980, Doubleday $9.95. This picture album examines a wide variety of vehicles.

9133. Robbins, Ken. *Trucks of Every Sort* (3–5). Illus. 1981, Crown LB $9.95. A description in photos and text of many kinds of trucks and their uses.

9134. Sheffer, H. R. *Tractors* (4–6). Illus. 1983, Crestwood $7.95. A survey of the kinds of tractors in existence today and their uses.

9135. Tessendorf, K. C. *Look Out! Here Comes the Stanley Steamer* (4–6). Illus. by Gloria Kamen. 1984,

Atheneum $11.95. A history of the Stanley brothers and their fantastic machine.

9136. Timms, Arthur W. *Finding Out about Trucks* (4–6). Illus. 1981, Enslow LB $9.95. A variety of large trucks and their parts are introduced.

9137. Wilkinson, Sylvia. *Automobiles* (1–4). Illus. 1982, Childrens Pr. $6.95. A history of the automobile, plus a brief description of how it operates.

9138. Wolfe, Robert L. *The Truck Book* (PS–2). Illus. 1981, Carolrhoda LB $7.95. Thirteen kinds of trucks are examined in photographs and text.

9139. Wolverton, Ruth, and Wolverton, Mike. *Trucks and Trucking* (4–6). Illus. 1982, Watts LB $8.90. Two truckers and their jobs are examined.

9140. Young, Frank. *Automobile: From Prototype to Scrapyard* (4–8). Illus. by Denis Bishop. 1982, Watts LB $9.90. All the steps that are involved in the design and production of an automobile.

9141. Zim, Herbert S., and Skelly, James R. *Trucks* (4–6). Illus. by Stan Riernacki. 1970, Morrow $8.16; paper $1.25. All kinds of trucks are described, as well as their specific uses. Also use: *Tractors* (1972, Morrow $8.16; paper $1.25).

Railroads

9142. Ault, Philip H. *All Aboard! The Story of Passenger Trains in America* (5–7). Illus. 1976, Dodd $7.95. A history of American passenger trains that concentrates on the unusual and bizarre.

9143. Crews, Donald. *Freight Trains* (PS–K). Illus. by author. 1978, Greenwillow $10.95; LB $10.51. A description in text and pictures of the various cars included in a freight train, from engine to caboose.

9144. Fisher, Leonard Everett. *The Railroads* (4–6). Illus. 1979, Holiday $9.95. The history of our railroads in a well-illustrated volume.

9145. Kanetzke, Howard. *Trains and Railroads* (2–4). Illus. 1978, Raintree $14.25. A good overview of the subject, with simple explanations.

9146. Pierce, Jack. *The Freight Train Book* (1–3). Illus. 1980, Carolrhoda LB $7.95. A photographic essay with brief captions on freight carriers.

9147. Smith, E. Boyd. *The Railroad Book* (2–4). Illus. by author. 1984, Houghton $12.95. An introduction to railroads via a book originally published in 1913.

9148. Stein, R. Conrad. *The Story of the Golden Spike* (3–6). Illus. 1978, Childrens Pr. $8.60; paper $2.50. The building and completion in 1869 of the transcontinental railroad.

9149. Yepsen, Roger. *Train Talk: An Illustrated Guide to Lights, Hand Signals, Whistles, and Other Languages of Railroading* (5–8). Illus. 1983, Pantheon $9.95; LB $9.99. An introduction to nonverbal communication used in railroading.

Ships and Boats

9150. Adkins, Jan. *Wooden Ship* (4–6). Illus. 1978, Houghton $6.96. An explanation in text and pictures of how a ship was built in the 1870s.

9151. Brown, Walter R., and Anderson, Norman D. *Sea Disasters* (5–8). Illus. 1981, Addison LB $7.95. Eight disasters, including the *Lusitania*, *Titanic*, and *Andrea Doria*, are recounted.

9152. Bushey, Jerry. *The Barge Book* (3–5). Illus. 1984, Carolrhoda $7.95. A trip by barge down the Mississippi to New Orleans.

9153. Carter, Katharine. *Ships and Seaports* (1–4). Illus. 1982, Childrens Pr. $6.95. Various kinds of ships are introduced and the ports they consider home.

9154. Coombs, Charles. *Tankers: Giants of the Sea* (5–7). Illus. 1979, Morrow $8.75; LB $8.40. The history, design, and functions of oil-carrying vessels are covered.

9155. Hancock, Ralph. *Supermachines* (2–7). 1978, Viking $11.50. A heavily illustrated account of such machines as the hydrofoil, supertanker, and bathyscaphe.

9156. Harris, Susan. *Boats and Ships* (3–4). 1979, Watts $8.60. A survey of boats, from canoes to large passenger liners and oil tankers.

9157. Lasky, Kathryn. *Tall Ships* (5–9). Illus. 1978, Scribners LB $9.95. A re-creation of the era of sailing ships and the accompanying seafaring life.

9158. Lewis, Thomas P. *Clipper Ship* (1–3). Illus. 1978, Harper $7.64; LB $8.89. An easily read account of our sailing ships.

9159. Petersen, David. *Submarines* (1–3). Illus. 1984, Childrens Pr. $7.95. A history of submarines and their uses chiefly in warfare and ocean exploration.

9160. Plowden, David. *Tugboat* (5–8). Illus. by author. 1976, Macmillan $9.95. Life aboard the *Julia C. Moran*, a New York City harbor tugboat, as explored in text and photographs.

9161. Rutland, Jonathan. *Ships* (5–7). Illus. 1982, Watts LB $9.90. A well-illustrated account of various kinds of ships and their history.

9162.   Scarry, Huck. *Life on a Barge: A Sketchbook* (3–6). Illus. by author. 1982, Prentice $10.95. The story of the author's trip on a barge in Holland.

9163.   Scarry, Huck. *Life on a Fishing Boat: A Sketchbook* (3–6). Illus. by author. 1983, Prentice $10.95. Another interesting trip, this time on a fishing boat.

9164.   Sullivan, George. *Supertanker: The Story of the World's Biggest Ships* (6–9). Illus. 1978, Dodd $8.95. A thorough account that also sheds light on the world's oil situation. A companion volume is: *The Supercarriers* (1980, Dodd LB $8.95).

9165.   Tunis, Edwin. *Oars, Sails and Steam: A Picture Book of Ships* (2–4). 1977, Harper $16.95. A beautifully illustrated account of the development of water transportation.

9166.   Van Orden, M. D. *The Book of United States Navy Ships* (5–8). Illus. 1979, Dodd $8.95. A rundown on ships of the navy, plus a special section on ships of the future.

9167.   Zeck, Pam, and Zeck, Gerry. *Mississippi Sternwheelers* (3–5). Illus. by George Overlie. 1982, Carolrhoda LB $7.95. A history of these paddle steamers that were once so numerous on the Mississippi.

9168.   Zim, Herbert S., and Skelly, James R. *Cargo Ships* (3–6). Illus. by Richard Cuffari. 1970, Morrow $7.44. An account of the design, construction, and uses of today's cargo ships.

Building and Construction

General

9169.   Ceserani, Gian Paolo. *Grand Constructions* (6–8). Illus. by Piero Ventura. 1983, Putnam $12.95. An album of photographs that illustrate various types of buildings and styles.

9170.   Cherry, Mike. *Steel Beams and Iron Men* (6–9). Illus. 1980, Four Winds $9.95. Personal stories of men involved in building superstructures.

9171.   Fagg, Christopher, and Sington, Adrian. *How They Built Long Ago* (5–8). Illus. 1981, Watts LB $9.90. A history of building, from prehistoric times to the Renaissance.

9172.   Ford, Barbara. *The Elevator* (4–7). Illus. 1982, Walker $7.95; LB $8.85. The innovation of the elevator and its effects on construction are discussed.

9173.   Haldane, Suzanne. *Faces on Places: About Gargoyles and Other Stone Creatures* (5–7). Illus. 1980, Viking $11.50. A photo essay on architectural carvings.

9174.   Horwitz, Elinor. *How to Wreck a Building* (4–6). Illus. 1982, Pantheon $9.95; LB $9.99. A description of how an old school building is demolished.

9175.   Lewis, Alan. *Super Structures* (6–9). Illus. 1980, Viking $11.50. An explanation of construction techniques and an examination of such buildings as the Empire State and Sydney Opera House.

9176.   Macaulay, David. *Unbuilding* (5–9). Illus. 1980, Houghton $12.95. A book that explores the concept of tearing down the Empire State Building.

9177.   Macaulay, David. *Underground* (5–8). Illus. by author. 1976, Houghton $10.95; paper $5.95. An exploration in text and detailed drawings of the intricate network of systems under city streets.

9178.   MacGregor, Anne. *Domes: A Project Book* (5–7). Illus. by Anne MacGregor and Scott MacGregor. 1982, Lothrop LB $11.88; paper $6.00. A discussion of domes and their history, plus projects to do and make.

9179.   MacGregor, Anne, and MacGregor, Scott. *Skyscrapers: A Project Book* (4–7). Illus. by author. 1981, Lothrop LB $12.88; paper $5.95. A history of skyscrapers and a discussion of their components, plus a model to assemble. For an older group use: *The Skyscraper* by James Giblin (1981, Harper $10.53; LB $9.89).

9180.   Olney, Ross R. *They Said It Couldn't Be Done* (5–7). Illus. 1979, Dutton $10.95. Ten enterprises—from the building of the Brooklyn Bridge to the moon landing—that seemed impossible at the time.

9181.   Salvadori, Mario. *Building: The Fight against Gravity* (6–8). Illus. by Saralinda Hooker and Christopher Ragus. 1979, Atheneum $10.95. The principles of building and architecture are explained in simple terms.

9182.   Sandak, Cass R. *Skyscrapers* (4–6). Illus. 1984, Watts LB $8.90. Why and how skyscrapers are built, plus a look at their insides.

9183.   Younker, Richard. *On Site: The Construction of a High-Rise* (4–7). Illus. 1980, Harper $7.95; LB $7.89. The construction of a high-rise building is told in text and photographs.

9184.   Zim, Herbert S., and Skelly, James R. *Pipes and Plumbing Systems* (3–6). Illus. 1974, Morrow $8.50; LB $8.16. The history of plumbing and contemporary methods and manufacture and use of pipes, pumps, etc., are discussed in this basic account.

Houses

9185. Adler, Irving. *Houses* (2–4). Illus. by Ruth Adler. 1964, Harper LB $10.89. A description of the ways houses are built and of their parts.

9186. Ardley, Neil. *Tomorrow's Home* (4–6). Illus. 1982, Watts LB $8.90. What homes will be like in the twenty-first century.

9187. Carter, Katharine. *Houses* (K–3). Illus. 1982, Childrens Pr. $6.95. Types of houses and how they are constructed.

9188. Cohen, Daniel. *The Last Hundred Years: Household Technology* (6–9). Illus. 1983, Dutton $9.95. The development of houses in the last 100 years.

9189. Myller, Rolf. *From Idea into House* (5–9). Illus. by Henry K. Szwarce. 1974, Atheneum $7.95. A detailed, fascinating account of an architect's steps in planning a house according to a particular family's specifications.

9190. Robbins, Ken. *Building a House* (3–6). Illus. 1984, Four Winds $11.95. From architect to move-in day, in clear photographs and text.

9191. Sobol, Harriet Langsam. *Pete's House* (2–4). Illus. 1978, Macmillan $8.95. Through detailed photographs, the process of house building is explored from blueprints to finished product.

Machinery

9192. Adkins, Jan. *Heavy Equipment* (2–5). Illus. by author. 1980, Scribners $8.95. An introduction to heavy moving equipment, illustrated with pen sketches.

9193. Aylesworth, Thomas G. *It Works Like This* (4–6). Illus. 1968, Natural History $5.50. This simple account gives an explanation of the workings of 33 common machines, such as the sewing machine.

9194. Gardner, Robert. *This Is the Way It Works: A Collection of Machines* (6–9). Illus. 1980, Doubleday $9.95. An explanation of how several different machines work.

9195. Hahn, Christine. *Amusement Park Machines* (2–4). Illus. 1979, Raintree $14.65. Very simple text and many photographs on such machines as the roller coaster.

9196. Olney, Ross R. *Construction Giants* (1–4). 1984, Atheneum $9.95. A description of such machines as cranes and bulldozers.

9197. Pick, Christopher C. *Oil Machines* (2–4). Illus. 1979, Raintree $14.65. Drilling rigs are included in this well-illustrated account.

9198. Pick, Christopher C. *Undersea Machines* (2–4). Illus. 1979, Raintree $14.65. All kinds of devices used to explore the ocean and the sea bottom are described.

9199. Renner, Al G. *How to Make and Use Electric Motors* (5–7). Illus. 1974, Putnam $6.69. Clear, detailed instructions are given for the construction of 3 different battery-powered engines.

9200. Rutland, Jonathan. *See Inside an Oil Rig and Tanker* (5–7). Illus. 1979, Watts LB $9.40. How the world gets its oil is revealed in text and pictures.

9201. Siegel, Beatrice. *The Sewing Machine* (3–6). Illus. 1984, Walker $10.85. The story of the sewing machine, its inventors Howe and Singer, and its effects on the world.

9202. Stone, William. *Earth Moving Machines* (2–4). Illus. 1979, Raintree $14.65. All sorts of tractors and various other machines are featured in text and pictures.

9203. Weiss, Harvey. *Motors and Engines and How They Work* (5–8). Illus. by author. 1969, Harper $12.45. A lucid demonstration of the basic technology of water, wind, steam, electricity, and jet rocket engines.

9204. Zim, Herbert S., and Skelly, James R. *Hoists, Cranes and Derricks* (3–6). Illus. by Gary Ruse. 1969, Morrow $8.16; paper $1.25. An introduction to the 3 basic types of lifting machines.

9205. Zim, Herbert S., and Skelly, James R. *Machine Tools* (3–6). Illus. by Gary Ruse. 1969, Morrow paper $1.25. Descriptions, explanations, and diagrammatic illustrations of the mechanisms common to the machinist's trade.

Electronics

9206. Branley, Franklyn M. *The Electromagnetic Spectrum* (5–8). Illus. by Leonard D. Dank. 1979, Harper LB $10.89. How we are able to investigate our universe and communicate over long distances.

9207. Englebardt, Stanley L. *Miracle Chip: The Microelectronic Revolution* (5–8). Illus. 1979, Lothrop $10.25; LB $9.84. The story of silicon chips and their many uses, primarily in information storage and retrieval.

9208. Laron, Carl. *Electronics Basics* (5–8). Illus. 1984, Prentice $9.95. A discussion of such electronic marvels as transistors, the telegraph, and the computer.

9209. McKie, Robin. *Lasers* (3–6). Illus. 1983, Watts $9.40. An introduction to lasers, what they do, and how they are used.

9210. White, Jack R. *The Invisible World of the Infrared* (5–8). Illus. 1984, Dodd $9.95. The discovery of infrared radiation, its composition, and many uses.

Telephone and Telegraph

9211. Jespersen, James, and Fritz-Randolph, Jane. *Mercury's Web: The Story of Telecommunications* (6–9). Illus. by Judith Fast. 1981, Atheneum $10.95. A book about communications, particularly today and in the future.

Television, Radio, and Recording

9212. Aldous, Donald. *Sound Systems* (4–6). Illus. 1984, Watts $9.40. A view of turntables, receivers, speakers, cassette decks, and the new compact disk technology.

9213. Berger, Melvin. *The Stereo-Hi Fi Handbook* (6–8). Illus. 1979, Lothrop $10.25. Valuable basic information about sound systems and pieces of equipment.

9214. Gilmore, Susan. *What Goes On at a Radio Station?*. Illus. 1984, Carolrhoda $7.95. An account of what goes on at a radio station through several job descriptions.

9215. Griffin-Beale, Christopher, and Gee, Robyn. *TV and Video* (6–8). Illus. by Ian Stephen et al. 1983, Educational Development Corp. $7.95; LB $12.95; paper $4.95. A history of television, how television works, and a peek into future developments.

9216. Hawkins, John, and Meredith, Susan. *Audio and Radio* (6–8). Illus. by Jeremy Banks et al. 1982, Educational Development Corp. $7.95; LB $12.95; paper $4.95. The scientific principles of broadcasting are explained, plus information on the radio and recording industries.

9217. Hawkins, Robert. *On the Air: Radio Broadcasting* (5–9). 1984, Messner $9.29. A description of many facets of radio broadcasting.

9218. Irvine, Mat. *TV and Video* (4–7). Illus. 1984, Watts $9.40. A simple explanation of how TV and VCRs work.

9219. Jacobsen, Karen. *Television* (1–4). Illus. 1982, Childrens Pr. $6.95. Historical information is given, plus simple material on how a set works.

9220. Leder, Jane Mersky. *Cassettes and Records* (5–7). Illus. 1983, Crestwood $8.95. A simple account of how cassettes and records are made, in text and photographs.

9221. Maie, Sondra. *The Top Forty: Making a Hit Record* (6–8). 1984, Messner $9.79. All of the steps in making a hit record are outlined.

9222. Mintern, Helen. *Television and Video* (4–6). Illus. 1984, Watts $9.40. Topics like how TV sets work, transmission, and video recordings are discussed.

9223. Morgan, Alfred P. *The First Book of Radio and Electronics for Boys and Girls* (4–6). Illus. 1977, Scribners paper $1.25. A fine introduction that concentrates on basics.

9224. Renowden, Gareth. *Video* (4–6). Illus. 1983, Watts $9.90. The technology of video is described.

9225. Yurko, J. T. *Video Basics* (5–8). Illus. by Janet D'Amato. 1983, Prentice $8.95. An overview of television and how it works.

Metals

9226. Coombs, Charles. *Gold and Other Precious Metals* (4–6). Illus. 1981, Morrow $10.25; LB $9.84. The discovery in this country, mining techniques, and uses of this precious metal are discussed.

9227. Fisher, Douglas Alan. *Steel: From the Iron Age to the Space Age* (6–8). Illus. 1967, Harper $10.89. A history of steel with emphasis on present-day uses and manufacturing techniques.

9228. Gay, Kathlyn. *Junkyards* (4–6). Illus. 1982, Enslow $8.95. The story of scrap metal, its handling, and uses.

9229. Kerrod, Robin. *Metals* (5–8). Illus. 1982, Silver Burdett LB $13.00. A good overview of metals, their properties, and uses.

Weapons and the Armed Forces

9230. Ardley, Neil. *Future War and Weapons* (4–6). Illus. 1982, Watts LB $8.90. An overview of weapons in the twenty-first century.

9231. Colby, C. B. *Two Centuries of Weapons: 1776–1976* (4–6). Illus. 1976, Putnam LB $6.99. Typical weapons of 1776, 1876, and 1976 are pictured and briefly discussed.

9232. Hogg, Ian. *Tanks and Armored Vehicles* (5–7). Illus. 1984, Watts $9.90. A history of tanks and pictures of those presently in use.

9233. Morrison, Sean. *Armor* (6–9). Illus. by author. 1963, Harper $12.95. Thorough, detailed description of arms and armor from 4000 B.C. to the Renaissance, with a brief chapter on modern armor.

9234. Peterson, Harold L. *Forts in America* (5–8). Illus. by Daniel D. Feaser. 1964, Scribners $5.95. Illustrated history that traces the development of forts and identifies models or actual sites that can be visited.

9235. Rossiter, Mike. *Nuclear Submarine* (4–6). Illus. 1983, Watts $9.90. A straightforward account that is easily understood.

9236. Sullivan, George. *Inside Nuclear Submarines* (6–9). Illus. 1982, Dodd $10.95. The history and development of nuclear subs and the role they play in our defense network.

9237. Sullivan, George. *Return of the Battleship* (5–9). Illus. 1983, Dodd $10.95. A history of the battleship until its retirement in the Vietnam War.

9238. Weiss, Ann E. *The Nuclear Arms Race: Can We Survive It?* (5–9). 1983, Houghton $10.95. A complicated subject is well introduced but with a somewhat antinuclear bias.

Author/Illustrator Index

Authors and illustrators are arranged alphabetically by last name. Authors' names are followed by book title and the text entry number; illustrators' names are followed only by the entry number. Joint authors are identified as (jt. auth.) with the entry number immediately following.

Hail Columbia, 4202; Wait for Me, Watch for Me, Eula Bee, 4203; Turn Homeward Hannalee, 4226; Lacy Makes a Match, 4238

Beatty, Sheila, 8922

Beaudry, Jo. Carla Goes to Court, 7356

Beck, Barbara L. The Aztecs, 6653; The Ancient Maya, 6665; The Incas, 6679

Becker, John. Seven Little Rabbits, 64

Becker, Joyce. Hanukkah Crafts, 4789; Jewish Holiday Crafts, 4790

Becklake, John. Man and the Moon, 8015

Beckman, Delores. My Own Private Sky, 2411

Beckman, Thea. Crusade in Jeans, 3160

Beekman, Dan. Forest, Village, Town, City, 1668

Beeler, Nelson F. Experiments with Light, 7872; Experiments in Optical Illusion, 7880

Behn, Harry. The Faraway Lurs, 4062; Cricket Songs: Japanese Haiku, 5772; Crickets and Bullfrogs and Whispers of Thunder: Poems, 5832

Behr, Joyce, 1619; 4845; 4884; 4885; 5546

Behrens, June. Fiesta!, 1109; Gung Hay Fat Choy: Happy New Year, 4473; Feast of Thanksgiving, 4748; Hanukkah: Festivals and Holidays, 4791; Powwow, 6782; Colonial Farm, 6822

Behrman, Carol H. The Remarkable Writing Machine, 5469

Beim, Jerrold. (jt. auth.) 2412

Beim, Lorraine. Two Is a Team, 2412

Beisner, Monika, 4392; Book of Riddles, 4829

Bell, Anthea. The Great Menagerie, 994; Stories of the Arabian Nights, 6211

Bell, Bill. Saxophone Boy, 7126

Bell, Corydon, 7823

Bell, Neill. The Book of Where, or How to Be Naturally Geographic, 6301; Only Human, 7412

Bell, Rivian. (jt. auth.) 8148

Bell, William Bruce. A Little Dab of Color, 2226

Bellairs, John. The Treasure of Alpheus Winterborn, 2632; The Curse of the Blue Figurine, 3161; The Mummy, the Will, and the Crypt, 3161; The Spell of the Sorcerer's Skull, 3161; The Dark Secret of Weatherend, 3162; The Figure in the Shadows, 3163; The House with a Clock in Its Walls, 3163; The Letter, the Witch and the Ring, 3163

Beller, Janet. A-B-Cing: An Action Alphabet, 10

Belli, Frederick Henry, 5845

Belliston, Larry. Extra Cash for Kids, 7346

Belloc, Hilaire. The Bad Child's Book of Beasts, 5778; Cautionary Tales, 5779

Bellville, Cheryl Walsh. Farming Today—Yesterday's Way, 8293; Round-up, 8294; (jt. auth.) 8295

Bellville, Rod. Large Animal Veterinarians, 7533; Stockyards, 8295

Belmore, Robert, 7817

Belpre, Pura. Dance of the Animals, 6222; Once in Puerto Rico, 6222; Perez and Martina, 6223; The Rainbow-Colored Horse, 6224

Belton, John. Solitaire Games, 5296; Card Games, 5302

Bemelmans, Ludwig, 578; Madeline, 1489; Madeline and the Bad Hat, 1489; Madeline and the Gypsies, 1489; Madeline in London, 1489; Madeline's Rescue, 1489

Benagh, Jim. Picture Story of Wayne Gretzky, 7280

Benary-Isbert, Margot. Blue Mystery, 2633

Benchley, Nathaniel. Walter, the Homing Pigeon, 401; Feldman Fieldmouse: A Fable, 1842; A Ghost Named Fred, 1843; Oscar Otter, 1844; Red Fox and His Canoe, 1845; The Strange Disappearance of Arthur Cluck, 1846; Kilroy and the Gull, 2072; Demo and the Dolphin, 3164; Beyond the Mists, 4063; Small Wolf, 6783; Snorri and the Strangers, 6814; George, The Drummer Boy, 6849; Sam the Minuteman, 6850

Bendick, Jeanne. Scare a Ghost, Tame a Monster, 4309; Mathematics Illustrated Dictionary: Facts, Figures and People Including the New Math, 7795; Artificial Satellites, 8016; Space Travel, 8017; Airplanes, 9079; Automobiles, 9110

Benjamin, Alan. A Change of Plans, 805

Benjamin, Carol Lea. Nobody's Baby Now, 3632; The Wicked Stepdog, 3745; Cartooning for Kids, 5084

Bennett, Anna Elizabeth. Little Witch, 3165

Bennett, Jill. Jack and the Robbers, 806; 3011; 3209; 3434; 4543; 4544; Days Are Where We Live and Other Poems, 5640; Roger Was a Razor Fish and Other Poems, 5641; Tiny Tim: Verses for Children, 5642; 5648

Bennett, Linda, 7942

Bennett, R., 733; 2041

Bennett, Richard, 4982

Benson, Kathleen. Joseph on the Subway Trains, 1338; (jt. auth.) 7058

Benson, Patrick, 915

Benson, Rolf. Skydiving, 5146

Benson, Sally. Stories of the Gods and Heroes, 4376

Bentley, Judith. Busing: The Continuing Controversy, 6910; Justice Sandra Day O'Connor, 7016

Berends, Polly. The Case of the Elevator Duck, 2073

Berenstain, Janice. (jt. auth.) 402; (jt. auth.) 1847

Berenstain, Stanley. Inside, Outside, Upside Down, 114; The Berenstain Bears in the Dark, 402; The Bear's Almanac, 1847; Bears in the Night, 1847; Bears on Wheels, 1847

Berg, Annemarie. Great State Seals of the United States, 6701

Berg, Joan, 4064

Berger, Fredericka. Nuisance, 3746

Berger, Gilda. Religion, 4408; Easter and Other Spring Holidays, 4658; Kuwait and the Rim of Arabia, 6635; The Southeast States, 6728; The Whole World of Hands, 7539; Speech and Language Disorders, 7605; Physical Disabilities, 7710; Mountain Worlds: What Lives There, 8050; (jt. auth.) 8313; All in the Family: Animal Species Around the World, 8575; The Coral Reef: What Lives There, 8865

Berger, Melvin. The Supernatural: From ESP to UFO's, 4310; The Funny Side of Science, 4830; The Photo Dictionary of Football, 5258; The Story of Folk Music, 5496; The Trumpet Book, 5516; The World of Dance, 5570; Consumer Protection Labs, 7343; Jobs in Fine Arts and Humanities, 7497; Animal Hospital, 7534; (jt. auth.) 7539; Why I Cough, Sneeze, Shiver, Hiccup, and Yawn, 7540; Enzymes in Action, 7569; Exploring the Mind and Brain, 7579; Disease Detectives, 7650; Sports Medicine: Scientists at Work, 7691; Comets, Meteors and Asteroids, 7900; Planets, Stars and Galaxies, 7901; Quasars, Pulsars, and Black Holes in Space, 7902; Bright Stars, Red Giants and White Dwarfs, 7936; The New Earth Book: Our Changing Planet, 7998; Space Shots, Shuttles and Satellites, 8018; Disastrous Volcanoes, 8106; Energy from the Sun, 8163; The New Food Book: Nutrition, Diet, Consumer Tips, and Foods of the Future, 8313; Oceanography Lab, 8777; Disastrous Floods and Tidal Waves, 8802; Computer Talk, 8998; Computers in Your Life, 8999; Data Processing, 9000; Word Processing, 9001; The Stereo-Hi Fi Handbook, 9213

Berger, Terry. Ben's ABC Day, 11; Special Friends, 2413; Black Fairy Tales, 5940; I Have Feelings, 7413; How Does It Feel When Your Parents Get Divorced?, 7433

Bergman, David. (jt. auth.) 6078

Bergman, Denise. Through the Year in Israel, 6650

Berliner, Don. Flying-Model Airplanes, 4993; Scale-Model Airplanes, 4994; Aerobatics, 9080; Yesterday's Airplanes, 9080; Helicopters, 9081; Personal Airplanes, 9082

Berlow, Leonard. (jt. auth.) 7656

bit Rip-Off, 2758; Manhattan Is Missing, 2758; The Top-Flight Fully-Automated Junior High School Girl Detective, 2758; The Ghost Squad Breaks Through, 3289

Hilgerdt, Erik, 4046

Hill, Barbara W. Cooking the English Way, 4929

Hill, Donna. Eerie Animals: Seven Stories, 3290

Hill, Earl, 6677

Hill, Elizabeth Starr. Evan's Corner, 1153

Hill, Eric. Spot Goes to School, 1907; Spot's Birthday Party, 1907; Spot's First Walk, 1907

Hill, Helen. Straight on Till Morning: Poems of the Imaginary World, 5669; Dusk to Dawn: Poems of Night, 5837

Hill, Rose. Small Pets, 8891; Cats and Kittens, 8903

Hillbrand, Percie V. The Norwegians in America, 7395

Hiller, Ilo. Young Naturalist, 7757

Hillerman, Tony. The Boy Who Made Dragonfly: A Zuni Myth, 6256

Hills, C. A. R. The Seine, 6584

Hilton, Suzanne. We the People: The Way We Were, 6867; Getting There: Frontier Travel without Power, 6879; The Way It Was—1876, 6899

Himler, Ronald, 839; 1080; 1309; 1431; 1458; Wake Up, Jeremiah, 1778; 2180; 2740; 2794; 3325; 3327; 3766; 3820; 4150; 4222; 5498; 5849; 7046; 7738

Himmelman, John. Talester the Lizard, 533

Hincks, Gary, 8455

Hinds, Bill, 4340; 5164

Hines, Anna Grossnickle. Taste the Raindrops, 1154; Maybe a Band-Aid Will Help, 1688; Come to the Meadow, 1779

Hines, Bob, 7315; 8670

Hinton, Nigel. Collision Course, 3835

Hintz, Martin. Circus Workin's, 5560; West Germany, 6591; Finland, 6600; Norway, 6601; Tons of Fun: Training Elephants, 8693; (jt. auth.) 9000

Hintz, Sandy. Computers in Our World Today and To-morrow, 9000

Hirsch, Karen. My Sister, 1155

Hirsch, Linda. You're Going Out There a Kid, but You're Coming Back a Star!, 2300

Hirsch, S. Carl. The Living Community: A Venture into Ecology, 7297

Hirschmann, Linda. In a Lick of a Flick of a Tongue, 8339

Hirsh, Marilyn. Hannibal and His 37 Elephants, 1515; The Tower of Babel, 4439; The Hanukkah Story, 4811; I Love Hanukkah, 4812; Potato Pancakes All Around: A Hanukkah Tale, 4822; Could Anything Be Worse? A Yiddish Tale, 6198; The Rabbi and the Twenty-Nine Witches: A Talmudic Legend, 6199

Hiscock, Bruce, 8340; 9027

Hitchcock, Alfred. Alfred Hitchcock's Daring Detectives, 2759; Alfred Hitchcock's Supernatural Tales, 2759

Hoban, Brom, 4801; 4802; 4804; 4805; Jason and the Bees, 8401

Hoban, Lillian. Harry's Song, 534; No, No Sammy Grow, 535; 537; 543; 1091; 1156; 1294; 1319; 1320; 1332; 1345; 1349; 1460; 1546; 1877; 1888; Arthur's Honey Bear, 1908; Arthur's Pen Pal, 1908; Arthur's Prize Reader, 1908; Mr. Pig and Family, 1909; Mr. Pig and Sonny Too, 1909; The Laziest Robot in Zone One, 1910; Ready, Set, Robot!, 1910; Stick-in-the-Mud Turtle, 1911; Arthur's Funny Money, 1912; 1914; 2008; 2009; 2015; 2029; 2307; I Met a Traveller, 2461; 3291; Arthur's Christmas Cookies, 4565; It's Really Christmas, 4566; 4567; 4568; The Sugar Snow Spring, 4672; Arthur's Halloween Costume, · 4718; 4780

Hoban, Russell. Dinner at Alberta's, 536; The Little Brute Family, 537; Ace Dragon Ltd., 874; The Great

Gum Drop Robbery, 875; The Sorely Trying Day, 1156; The Flight of Bembel Rudzuk, 1359; How Tom Beat Captain Najork and His Hired Sportsmen, 1577; A Near Thing for Captain Najork, 1577; Arthur's New Power, 1912; Bargain for Frances, 1913; Bedtime for Frances, 1913; Bread and Jam for Frances, 1913; A Baby Sister for Frances, 1914; Best Friends for Frances, 1914; Tom and the Two Handles, 1915; The Twenty-Elephant Restaurant, 3048; The Mouse and His Child, 3291; Emmet Otter's Jug-Band Christmas, 4567; The Mole Family's Christmas, 4568

Hoban, Tana. A, B, See!, 32; Count and See, 78; More Than One, 125; Push, Pull, Empty, Full: A Book of Opposites, 126; Is It Red? Is It Yellow? Is It Blue? An Adventure in Color, 154; I Read Signs, 172; I Read Symbols, 172; I Walk and Read, 173; Is It Rough? Is It Smooth? Is It Shiny?, 174; Look Again!, 175; Take Another Look, 176; Circles, Triangles, and Squares, 194; Over, Under and Through and Other Spacial Concepts, 195; Round and Round and Round, 196; Shapes and Things, 197; Big Ones, Little Ones, 331; Where Is It?, 332; One Little Kitten, 1041

Hoberman, Mary Ann. A House Is a House for Me, 127; The Cozy Book, 275; Yellow Butter, Purple Jelly, Red Jam, Black Bread: Poems, 5670

Hobson, Burton. Coin Collecting as a Hobby, 5024; Getting Started in Stamp Collecting, 5025; (jt. auth.) 5027

Hochman, Stan. Mike Schmidt: Baseball's King of Swing, 7231

Hodges, C. Walter, 3121; 4298; Shakespeare's Theatre, 5619; 5645

Hodges, David, 6978; 7404

Hodges, Margaret. Persephone and the Springtime: Myths of the World, 4389; St. George and the Dragon: A Golden Legend, 6043; The Fire Bringer: A Paiute Indian Legend, 6257

Hodgman, Ann. Skystars: The History of Women in Aviation, 7527

Hodgson, James, 109

Hodgson, Mary Anne. Fast and Easy Needlepoint, 5120

Hodgson, Pat. Growing Up with the North American Indians, 6794

Hoff, Syd. Slugger Sal's Slump, 1360; Albert the Albatross, 1916; Barkley, 1917; Danny and the Dinosaur, 1918; Oliver, 1918; Sammy the Seal, 1918; Grizzwold, 1919; Happy Birthday, Henrietta!, 1920; The Man Who Loved Animals, 1921; Soft Skull Sam, 1922; Stanley, 1923; 1952; Santa's Moose, 4569; Syd Hoff's Joke Book, 4852; 5200

Hoffman, E. T. A. The Nutcracker, 6114; The Nutcracker, 6115; The Nutcracker and the Mouse King, 6116; The Strange Child, 6117

Hoffman, Edwin D. Fighting Mountaineers: The Struggle for Justice in the Appalachians, 6900

Hoffman, Phyllis. Steffie and Me, 1280

Hoffman, Rosekrans, 1468; 1527; 1748

Hoffman, Sanford, 4887; 4906

Hoffman, Tom, 7649

Hoffmeister, Donald. Zoo Animals, 8881

Hofmann, Charles. American Indians Sing, 5492

Hofsinde, Robert. Indian Picture Writing, 5416; Indian Sign Language, 5416; Indian Warriors and Their Weapons, 6795; Indians at Home, 6796; Indians on the Move, 6797

Hofstrand, Mary. Albion Pig, 538

Hogan, Paula Z. The Compass, 6304; The Dandelion, 8207; The Oak Tree, 8237; The Honeybee, 8402; The Butterfly, 8410; The Frog, 8465; The Penguin, 8550; The Black Swan, 8562; The Beaver, 8723; The Salmon, 8841

Hogg, Ian. Tanks and Armored Vehicles, 9232

Title Index

All titles in the text appear here in alphabetical sequence. The number(s) following each title refer to the entry number in the text, not the page number.

Biographical Subjects

NOTE: References are to entry number, not page number.

Aaron, Henry, 7211
Abdul-Jabbar, Kareem, 7259
Adams, Samuel, 6929
Alexander the Great, 7024, 7025
Allen, Ethan, 7055
Alonso, Alicia, 7157
Appleseed, Johnny, 7056
Armstrong, Louis, 7158
Armstrong, Neil, 7057
Arnold, Benedict, 6930
Austin, Tracy, 7252, 7253

Barton, Clara, 7007
Baryshnikov, Mikhail, 7159
Beckenbauer, Franz, 7276
Bell, Alexander Graham, 7087, 7088
Bell, Bill, 7126
Benchley, Belle Jennings, 7008
Bethune, Mary McLeod, 6966, 6967
Bird, Larry, 7260
Blackwell, Elizabeth, 7089
Blegvad, Erik, 7127
Bluford, Guion, 7058
Blume, Judy, 7143
Boone, Daniel, 7059
Borman, Frank, 7060
Bourke-White, Margaret, 7128, 7129
Bowditch, Nathaniel, 7061
Bradshaw, Terry, 7238
Brett, George, 7212
Brown, James, 7239
Brown, John, 6931
Brown, William Wells, 6968
Bryant, Paul W., 7240
Burbank, Luther, 7090
Burningham, John, 7062

Calder, Alexander, 7130
Campbell, Earl, 7241
Carlton, Steve, 7213
Carnegie, Andrew, 6932
Carter, Gary, 7214

Cartier, Jacques, 7063
Chagall, Marc, 7131
Chamberlain, Wilt, 7261, 7262
Chaplin, Charlie, 7160
Charles, Prince of Wales, 7026
Chavez, Cesar, 7006
Churchill, Winston, 7027
Clark, Eugenie, 7091
Columba, Saint, 7028
Columbus, Christopher, 7064, 7065, 7066
Comaneci, Nadia, 7277, 7278
Cosby, Bill, 7161
Cousteau, Jacques, 7092, 7093
Crazy Horse, 6990
Crockett, Davy, 7067
Curie, Marie, 7094

da Vinci, Leonardo, 7097, 7136
Darwin, Charles, 7095, 7096
Decker, Mary, 7257
Dickinson, Emily, 7144
DiMaggio, Joe, 7215
Disney, Walt, 7132
Dorsett, Tony, 7242, 7243
Douglass, Frederick, 6969, 6970, 6971
DuBois, W. E. B., 6972
Dunham, Katherine, 7162
Duran Duran, 7163

Earhart, Amelia, 7068
Eastman, Charles, 6991
Edison, Thomas Alva, 7098, 7099
Einstein, Albert, 7100
Eleanor, Queen, 7029
Elizabeth I, 7030
Elizabeth II, 7031
Ericson, Leif, 7069
Ericsson, John, 7101

Farragut, David, 6933
Faversham, Charles, 7145

Fidrych, Mark, 7216
Fleming, Peggy, 7279
Fortune, Amos, 6973
Foster, George, 7217
Foyt, A. J., 7272
Francis of Assisi, Saint, 7032
Franklin, Benjamin, 6934, 6935, 6936, 6937
Freeman, Elizabeth, 6974
Fremont, Jessie Benton, 7009
Fritz, Jean, 7146

Galileo, 7102
Gallaudet, Thomas, 6938
Garvey, Steve, 7218
George III, 7033
Geronimo, 6992
Goodall, Jane, 7103, 7104
Goodyear, Charles, 7105
Gordy, Pop, 7164
Greene, Joe, 7244
Gretzky, Wayne, 7280, 7281
Griese, Bob, 7245
Guarneri del Gesee, 7155
Guthrie, Janet, 7273, 7274

Halley, Edmond, 7106
Hamill, Dorothy, 7282
Hancock, John, 6939
Hannam, Charles, 7034
Harris, Franco, 7246
Hayes, Elvin, 7263
Heiden, Eric, 7283
Henry, Patrick, 6940
Heyerdahl, Thor, 7070, 7071, 7072
Hitler, Adolf, 7035, 7036
Homer, Winslow, 7133
Hopkins, Sarah Winnemucca, 6993
Hsiao, Ellen, 7037
Hughes, Langston, 7147, 7148
Hunter, Jim "Catfish," 7219
Hyman, Trina Schart, 7134

Ishi, 6994, 6995

585

Subject Index

The numbers following alphabetically arranged subjects refer to entry numbers in the text, not page numbers.